MW01014616

Business Transformation Strategies

Property of
Baker College
of Allen Park

Business Transformation Strategies

The Strategic Leader as Innovation Manager

Oswald A. J. Mascarenhas

$SAGE | Response Business Books

www.sagepublications.com

Los Angeles • London • New Delhi • Singapore • Washington DC

Copyright © Oswald A. J. Mascarenhas, 2011

All rights reserved. No part of this book may be reproduced or utilized in any form or by any means, electronic or mechanical, including photocopying, recording or by any information storage or retrieval system, without permission in writing from the publisher.

First published in 2011 by

SAGE Response
B1/I-1 Mohan Cooperative Industrial Area
Mathura Road, New Delhi 110 044, India

SAGE Publications Inc
2455 Teller Road
Thousand Oaks, California 91320, USA

SAGE Publications Ltd
1 Oliver's Yard, 55 City Road
London EC1Y 1SP, United Kingdom

SAGE Publications Asia-Pacific Pte Ltd
33 Pekin Street
#02-01 Far East Square
Singapore 048763

Published by Vivek Mehra for SAGE Publications India Pvt Ltd, typeset in 10/12pt Times New Roman by Star Compugraphics Private Limited, Delhi and printed at Chaman Enterprises, New Delhi.

Library of Congress Cataloging-in-Publication Data
Mascarenhas, Oswald A. J.
  Business transformation strategies : the strategic leader as innovation manager/Oswald A.J. Mascarenhas.
    p. cm.
  Includes bibliographical references and index.
  1. Organizational change—Management. 2. Strategic planning—Management. 3. Technological innovations—Management. 4. Leadership. I. Title.

HD58.8.M288	658.4'063—dc22	2010	2010048553

ISBN: 978-81-321-0501-5 (PB)

The SAGE Team: Rekha Natarajan, Sonalika Rellan and Deepti Saxena

To

Mary Victoria Basile, Havertown, Pennsylvania.

A lifelong companion in my academic journey since Wharton years.

Thank you for choosing a SAGE product! If you have any comment, observation or feedback, I would like to personally hear from you. Please write to contactceo@sagepub.in

—Vivek Mehra, Managing Director and CEO,
SAGE Publications India Pvt Ltd, New Delhi

Bulk Sales

SAGE India offers special discounts for purchase of books in bulk. We also make available special imprints and excerpts from our books on demand.

For orders and enquiries, write to us at

Marketing Department
SAGE Publications India Pvt Ltd
B1/I-1, Mohan Cooperative Industrial Area
Mathura Road, Post Bag 7
New Delhi 110044, India
E-mail us at marketing@sagepub.in

Get to know more about SAGE, be invited to SAGE events, get on our mailing list. Write today to marketing@sagepub.in

This book is also available as an e-book.

Contents

Part I Strategy in General

Part II The CEO as a Strategic Leader and Critical Thinker

Part III The CEO as a Strategic Leader of Innovation Management

List of Tables

List of Figures

Prologue

In his book, *Who Says Elephants Cannot Dance?* Lou Gerstner, who had just taken over as CEO of IBM in 1993, describes a press conference where he made a strategy statement that reverberated throughout the world of journalism: "There has been a lot of speculation as to when I am going to deliver a vision of IBM. But what I would like to say to all of you is that the last thing IBM needs right now is a vision."

The journalists lampooned Gerstner and so did academicians and politicians. In retrospect, Lou was dead right. IBM survived a close demise in 1993, as Lou helped it to reorganize and find its niche in mainframes, middleware, and software—in short, in defining and offering business information technology (IT) solutions. Gerstner did not feel compelled to pronounce a vision; he needed to *create* a vision with a *distinctive, competitive strategy* (Hamel 2000). This book is all about corporate visions and strategies.

Struggling with growing competition and globalization, more and more companies are trying to make a fundamental change in the way they operate either by introducing innovative improvements or at least by improvement programs in every business function and process. With the increasing and accelerating competitive pressure, however, radically innovative strategies of yester years quickly fade into incremental ones. Hence, companies must constantly devise new transformation strategies in order to remain on the top. This ongoing improvement and innovative process is called *revitalization or transformation* (Pascale, Millemann, and Gioja 1999). This book is about business transformation strategies with a decided focus, however, on the CEO as a strategic leader of innovation and growth management.[1]

Currently, the main problem in corporations is not lack of revitalization programs, but that the whole burden of change falls on so few people. The number of executive leaders at every level who make committed, imaginative, and innovative contributions to organizational transformation is simply too small. As a result, in the modern knowledge-based economy, any transformation strategy should not only include ongoing innovative and imaginative changes, but should also incorporate skilled, dedicated, and committed people from the bottom rank who take a greater interest, care deeply about organizational success, and have a more active role in the business. When every person in the corporation is able and eager to rise to every competitive and governmental challenge, there is revitalization and transformation in the company and the business is geared to superior performance (Collis and Rukstad 2008). Revitalization implies a permanent rekindling of individual and group activity, creativity, and responsibility—a lasting transformation of the company's internal and external relationships (Pascale, Millemann, and Gioja 1999: 57). This book also focuses on business transformation as corporate leadership strategies.

---

[1] A blind peer reviewer of this book appointed by the publisher made an insightful point in this regard: the focus on CEO as the primary strategic leader is a Harvard Business School model for U.S. corporations that may not be accepted or implemented univocally elsewhere in the world. Strategic leadership may be more diffused throughout the corporation in the oriental world than in the occident.

Older definitions of corporate strategy include elements such as differentiation from the competitor, barriers to new market entry, zero-sum games, and building scarce, non-imitable, non-transferable, and market-convertible strategic resources within the company (e.g., Barney 1991, 2001a, 2001b). This approach has not taken us very far other than to price wars, cut-throat competition, predatory pricing, price gouging, and other destructive strategies. Current corporate strategies are more "dynamic" than static (Govindarajan and Trimble 2005; Porter 1991, 1996, 2008; Porter et al. 2004), more "collaborative" than competitive (Ernst and Bamford 2005; Evans and Wolf 2005; Hamel 2006; Hamel, Doz, and Prahalad 1989; Huston and Sakkab 2006), and create new uncontested market spaces or "blue oceans" than combat with competitive markets (Kim and Mauborgne 1999, 2003, 2004). Current business transformation occurs with corporate strategic alliances or joint ventures, even with direct corporate rivals, and amidst great witness of corporate social responsibility (Porter and Kramer 2006; Yaziji 2004). The book focuses on these newer approaches to corporate strategy.

We investigate major concepts and paradigms, theories and models, contexts and structures of business transformation strategies, systems and processes. Most corporate strategies were inept in transforming troubled companies or even at maintaining the vitality of the healthy ones because they never identified the external and internal factors that produce sustainable revitalization. Our focus is on the main internal and external factors that can stimulate and sustain corporate transformation.

STRATEGY AS SEEKING ADDED VALUE

Cynthia A. Montgomery is the Timken Professor of Business Administration and Head of the Strategy Unit at the Harvard Business School (HBS), Boston, USA. She runs the strategy portion of the Owner/President Management executive program at HBS. Montgomery (2008: 57) insists that the notion of added value is core to everything they teach, experiment, and do about corporate strategy. Early in the module, executives respond to the following questions:

- If your company were shuttered, to whom would it matter and why?
- Which of your customers would miss you the most and why?
- How long would it take for another firm to step into that void?

Most executives struggle answering these questions, even though they are basic. Executives long accustomed to describing their companies by the industries they belong to and by the products/services they offer, find themselves disabled to pinpoint what is truly distinctive about their firms. In this book, we explore this trend of thinking on strategy as value augmentation.

STRATEGY CANNOT BE TAUGHT, BUT ONLY LEARNT

In their latest book, *Turning Learning Right Side Up: Putting Education Back on Track*, Russell Ackoff and Daniel Greenberg (2008) warn us that real education is not teaching but learning. Traditional education focuses on teaching, not learning. It incorrectly assumes that for every ounce of teaching there is an ounce of learning by those who are taught. On the contrary, most of what we learn before, during, and after attending schools is learned without it being taught to us. A child learns such fundamental things as how to walk, talk, eat, dress, and so on, without being taught these things. Adults learn most of what they use at work or at leisure while at work or leisure. Most of what is taught in classroom settings is forgotten, and much of what is remembered is irrelevant.

In most schools, memorization is mistaken for learning. Most of what is memorized is remembered only for a short time, but then quickly forgotten. Computers, computer software, recording machines, cameras, blogs, and the like can do better in teaching the stuff that we normally teach in our classrooms. Most often, teachers are poor surrogates for such machines, equipment and instruments. Why should students, children or adults, do something in classrooms that computers and related equipment can do much better than teachers can? What education should focus, therefore, must be on what humans can do better than the machines and instruments they create.

When we ask those whom we taught, "Who in the class learned most?" virtually all of them say, "The teacher." It is apparent to those who have taught, that teaching is a better way to learn than being taught. Teaching enables the teacher to discover what one thinks about the subject being taught. The method adopted in schools should be reversed: students should be teaching, and the faculty should be learning.

If knowledge is the capacity for effective action (Senge 1990), then knowledge is temporary, since an action is effective only in its given context. However, learning is continuous, and we should be able to identify key attributes of strategy management and leadership that manage knowledge with the following:

a. Fostering continuous learning as part of our professional work;
b. Providing continuous opportunities for educators to continuously expand their repertoire;
c. Communicating expectations for participation and contributions among educators;
d. Establishing knowledge leadership groups to inform and refine the system by identifying priorities, needs, and resources;
e. Using technology to inform professional learning, and
f. Facilitating the transformation of data and information into knowledge that can be applied to practice.

The knowledge leader who manages the integration of people, content, and technology is a key element of a knowledge and learning system (Dietz et al. 2005). Hence, in this book we will all learn by teaching each other and learning from each other. In essence, this is the philosophy behind the BTM Lab[2]—it is not a course, it does not have a fixed syllabus or a textbook; it is not discipline oriented; it is not even a classroom. It is a learning module. The focus is student–teacher learning, and not teacher-focused teaching. It is a work in progress, a process where all of us learn together and from each other. This is where teachers and students learn via teaching each other, and challenged entrepreneurs and executives learn from us and we learn from them.

---

[2] The Business Turnaround Management (BTM) Lab is a pioneering concept and learning module experimented in the required post-core, comprehensive concluding course in the BTM programs in the College of Business Administration, University of Detroit Mercy, Detroit, Michigan. The author was the prime designer and mover of the BTM masters and certificate programs, a first of its kind in the academic world of 2003–07.

There are many ways of learning, and teaching is just one of them. We learn by doing, by experimenting, by interacting with others, by listening, by reading, by reflecting, by critical thinking, by analyzing and synthesizing, by tearing things down and then building them up, and especially, by unlearning. Most of us learn from our mistakes. Good learning is risk-taking, being prepared to make "smart" mistakes as long as we learn quickly from our mistakes. Most corporate strategies were learnt and formulated after a series of costly but rich mistakes (Schoemaker and Gunther 2006).

ORGANIZING THE LAYOUT OF THE BOOK

This book explores the concepts, theory, paradigms, models, strategies, and cases of organizational transformation management from the viewpoint of the CEO as a strategic leader. Specifically, we discuss the challenges and opportunities that revitalize companies from recovery to exuberance, from normal to supernormal performance, from solvency to "built to last" (Collins and Porras 1997), from legal and social to ethical and moral corporations, and in one word, from "good to great" companies (Collins 2001). Majority of companies just remain as they are or are satisfied being "good" but aren't great. In this sense, "good is the enemy of great" (Collins 2001: 1). "Great" companies are those that make the leap from "good" results to "great" results (e.g., average cumulative total stock returns (TSR) for a decade and more are around five to seven times the general market average, indicated by S&P or Dow Jones) and sustain those results for at least 15 years (Collins 2001: 3).

Our ambition in this book is to explore, review, and analyze great transformation strategies that transform and empower companies from being just "good" to being "great" and lasting (Collins 2001; Collis and Rukstad 2008). Our primary focus throughout the book is on the CEO as the strategic leader of transformation that takes place through creativity, innovation, and corporate growth. Accordingly, our treatment of Business Transformation Strategies has two parts: the first six chapters' deal with the general aspects of a strategic leader of business transformation strategies. The following six chapters deal with specific aspects of the strategic leader that brings change and corporate growth through creativity and innovation.

Thus, as a background for understanding corporate recovery as long-term transformation strategies, the Prologue sketches a preface for business transformation strategies and a general plan of this book. The first two chapters relate to strategy in general—Chapter 1 provides the fundamental concepts, constructs, and contexts of business transformation strategies, and Chapter 2 attempts a general philosophy of corporate strategy. The next four chapters focus on the role of the Chief Executive Officer (CEO) in corporate transformations. Chapter 3 analyzes the role of the CEO as a strategic leader. Chapter 4 proposes the CEO as a systems thinker. Chapter 5 features the CEO as a critical thinker and solver of simple strategic problems, and Chapter 6 presents the CEO as a critical thinker and "tamer" of "wicked" strategic problems.

Part 2 focuses on the CEO as a strategic leader of innovation, growth, and sustainable competitive advantage. Accordingly, Chapter 7 deals with the CEO as a strategic leader of creativity and innovation management, Chapter 8 proposes the CEO as a leader of corporate-wide innovation management, Chapter 9 focuses on the CEO as a strategic leader of innovative sustainable competitive advantage, and Chapter 10 presents the CEO as an innovative manager of corporate growth. The last two chapters shift the spotlight back on the CEO as a spiritual leader: Chapter 11 features the CEO as a person of self-mastery won through executive spiritual development, and lastly, Chapter 12 models the CEO as a leader of shared personal and corporate vision.

Organized thus, this book is uniquely designed for high-potential business students, intermediate business leaders, business scholars and business practitioners alike, and especially, young business entrepreneurs who enjoy innovative management. In a typical MBA program, this book could be useful for the capstone courses in business strategy, particularly at the graduate level. As its title suggests, this book is primarily meant for all corporate executives and institutional leaders that are engaged in transforming their organizations from being good to great.

This book is also positioned for consultants concentrating on business turnaround and transformation management (BTTM), particularly for those pursuing Certificate and/or Masters in BTTM, for managers preparing for Certified Turnaround Professionals (CTP), Certified Insolvency and Restructuring Advisor (CIRA), Risk Management Association (RMA), and for Turnaround Management Association (TMA) members requiring professional updates, and the like. Business transformation executives and experts could profit from any chapter, especially the second part of this book.

As in my other recent book (Mascarenhas 2008), I safeguard five critical features of modern integrated business management.

1. Each chapter updates and blends recent concepts, theories, paradigms, models, cases, and strategies in that field of corporate strategy.
2. Each chapter integrates the traditionally compartmentalized silos of management education such as economics, accounting, finance, marketing, personnel (HRD), business law, production, and operations management.
3. Each chapter is built from ground zero and is based on recent journal articles from top tier journals such as the *Harvard Business Review*, *Sloan Management Review*, *California Management Review*, *Journal of Accounting*, *Journal of Finance*, and the *Journal of Marketing*. Thus, the material covered represents the mind and works of the best scholars in the field.
4. Each chapter is appended with executive Business Transformation Exercises (BTE) where the more challenging concepts, theories, paradigms, models, and strategies of corporate strategy are translated to ready review, application, and implementation.
5. Each chapter provides critical thinking and ethical principles that can enable and empower readers to address current ethical and moral challenges of a given corporate strategy.

The content of each chapter is best learnt and internalized against real-time, "live" cases of current market problems, episodes, "disruptive changes" (Christensen and Overdorf 2000; Christensen et al. 2002; Collins 1999) and "market busting" strategies (Gunther and MacMillan 2005) as they unfold during the academic semester of learning. This is best done by challenging students with take-home, structured and unstructured, linear and circular, problem-centered exams that invite team learning of three to four weeks in problem identification, formulation, specification, alternatives exploration, and the final choice assessment.

There is no closure to this book. The content of each chapter is continuously evolving and emerging. Hence, a book that captures the real-time process of forming strategic leaders of corporate transformation experience and accomplishment must be a "work in progress" that needs constant updates, upgrades, revisions, and restatements. In other words, this book is not about immutable and frozen conceptualizations and theories, paradigms, models, and strategies. It feeds and expands on the real, day-to-day corporate world of transformation management. The real world of corporate strategy problems is rarely simple, structured, and linear in their content and solutions. They are complex, unstructured, non-linear (i.e., often circular and spiral) and "wicked" (Rittel and Webber 1973) problems that need creative, innovative, resilient (Hamel and Välikangas 2003), analogical (Gavetti and Rivkin 2005), experimental, and entrepreneurial resolutions. We hope this book will challenge students and readers, teachers and executives to this great world of strategic leadership and organizational learning (Senge 1990, 2006) of business transformation management (Hammer 2004).

Acknowledgments

My academic background is philosophy, theology, marketing, e-business and Internet marketing, and currently, business turnaround and transformation management, with over 30 years of teaching and research experience. Several professors have molded me during my management studies. I am especially indebted to Russell Ackoff, Paul Green, Len Lodish, and Howard Perlmutter of the Wharton School of Business, Philadelphia, Pennsylvania, where I obtained my MBA and Ph.D.

This book represents my latest research and thinking in the critical domain of business transformation management, especially with a focus on revitalization strategies. This work has taken over five years from conception to execution. The origin of this book is linked with the business turnaround management (BTM) program that we designed in 2002, with the active collaboration of several business turnaround executives who were members of the BTM Steering Committee and MBA Advisory Board of the College of Business Administration, University of Detroit Mercy, Michigan. From its early beginnings, the BTM program was uniquely conceived, developed, and delivered in continuous partnership with the turnaround industry. The BTM Steering Committee of over 24 senior executives of turnaround companies formed the industrial backbone for the formulation and implementation of the Certificate and Masters level BTM programs.

In its early stages, I designed a course (BTM 500) that covered both business rescue and transformation strategies. Within a few years, the course rapidly grew in content depth and breadth, so that it gave birth to a Certificate, and then to a full Masters level program in BTM, a pioneering program, the first of its kind in the business academic world in 2007. As a part of this BTM program, this book focuses only on business transformation. A successor or sequel to this book will focus on business turnaround (rescue) strategies. The plan and contents of this book were discussed with the BTM Steering Committee members at different stages. I am grateful for their incisive comments.

When this book was nearing completion, I wanted to test its contents by teaching it. Meanwhile, Rev. Abraham Enthemkuzhy SJ, Director of Xavier Labour Relations Institute (XLRI), a premier business school in Jamshedpur, India invited me to give a keynote address for the annual Association of International Jesuit Business Schools (AIJBS) Conference hosted by XLRI in June 2009, and I readily accepted the invitation on the condition that I could teach this course after the conference. Professor Pingali Venugopal, Dean (Academics) of XLRI was enthused with the idea, and the rest is history. I had over 30 brilliant Business Management and Personnel Management students, all engineers with over three years of work experience in big multinational companies. who took this elective course titled, Global Business Transformation Strategies. They read all the chapters, discussed them in class, dialogued on their direction and prospects, and provided other considered comments. I am grateful for their passionate participation in class and for their great pre-reviews.

While at XLRI, Fr. Abraham encouraged me to get the book published, and enabled me to contact various publishers. SAGE Publications undertook a peer blind review of the book, based on which the book was accepted for publication. I am very grateful to the reviewers, and to the management of SAGE Publications for their expeditious and professional production of this book.

Several of my graduate research assistants at the University of Detroit Mercy have helped me in the work in progress: Sundaresan Balasubramaniam, Preethi Venkataraman, and Raoul Pinto provided technical assistance in formatting the entire text, in developing the table of contents 'in brief' and 'in detail', and in constructing the author, company, and subject indices. Several of my current junior and senior MBA students at Aloysius Institute of Management and Information Technology (AIMIT), Beeri Campus, Mangalore, India have generously devoted their time and talent for proof reading the entire text, and for organizing the subject, author and company indices, and I greatefully acknowledge their assistance. The chapters of this book were used for teaching "Creativity and Innovation Management" to both junior and senior MBA students at AIMIT this year, and their comments have been useful and encouraging. I am deeply grateful for their dedicated assistance.

This book is lovingly dedicated to Mary Victoria Basile of Havertown, Pennsylvania. Mary and the Basile Family were my emotional, intellectual, and financial support all through my Wharton Business School Years and thereafter. Mary Basile, in particular, by her simple but persistent ways, was a strategic leader and innovation manager of my academic years since the early 1970s.

PART I

Strategy in General

Chapter 1

An Introduction to
Business Transformation Strategies:
Concepts, Constructs, and Contexts

A brilliant strategy, a breakthrough technology, a radical innovation, a blockbuster product, and a superbly matched service can put you on the competitive map, but only solid execution can keep you there. That is, all of the above factors must quickly translate into market-ready actions. Strategic execution is the result of thousands of decisions made every day by field and line employees, senior and junior executives along all the strategic points of the company's value chain. Any organizational transformation needs effective information flows, clearly spelt decision rights, aligning motivators, and often, realigning organizational structure. Everyone should have a good idea of the decisions and actions for which they are responsible and understand the bottom-line impact of these choices and decisions; important information about the competitive environment should freely and quickly flow along all the rungs of the management ladder and organizational boundaries; line managers who make operating decisions should have access to the metrics that measure the key drivers of their business; and once decisions are made, they should be rarely second-guessed (Neilson et al. 2008).

"Strategic" is the most overused word in the vocabulary of business and executives. Frequently, it is just another way of saying, "This is important." The reality is that there are only a few situations in which a company's strategy affects positive outcomes. The aim of any true strategy is to master a market environment by understanding and anticipating the actions of other economic agents, especially competitors. However, this will happen only if there are a limited number of competitors or if there are strong barriers to competitive entry. Hence, firms operating in markets without barriers have no choice but to forget about strategy and run their businesses as efficiently as possible (Greenwald and Kahn 2005: 95).

Most often, bankruptcy is a failed corporate strategy. Between 1981 and 2006, argue Carroll and Mui (2008), 423 major companies with combined assets of more than $1.5 trillion filed for bankruptcy. Hundreds more took huge write-offs, discontinued major operations, or were acquired during financial duress. Again and again, company executives follow the same wrong-headed strategies. The number one cause of failure was not sloppy execution, poor leadership, bad luck, or any other circumstantial factor; the number one cause was a misguided strategy that was poorly defined, formulated, and communicated, or a strategic error of entering the wrong markets or industries, at the wrong time—errors that could have been avoided. Hence, there is need for a deeper understanding of what a strategy is what it can do for a company, for society, and for the world. Corporate America has been spending billions of dollars producing educational failures in recent decades.

HISTORY OF THE CONCEPT OF CORPORATE STRATEGY

The concept, domain, and formulation of strategy have largely been shaped around a framework first suggested by Kenneth R. Andrews in his classical book, *The Concept of Corporate Strategy* (Andrews 1971). He defined strategy as the match between what a company can do (organizational strengths and weaknesses) within the universe of what it might do (environmental opportunities and threats). Although simple by definition, most managers did not know how to assess either side of the equation systematically. The first important breakthrough to this impasse came from Michael Porter's book, *Competitive Strategy: Techniques for Analyzing Industries and Competitors*. Porter built on the *structure-conduct-performance* paradigm of the then famous industrial-organizational economics. Porter believed that the structure of an industry determines the state of competition within that industry and sets the context for the conduct or strategy of the company. Porter identified five drivers or forces that shape industry structure and competition—threat of new entrants, threat of substitute products or services, bargaining power of suppliers, bargaining power of buyers, and rivalry among existing competitors (Porter 1979). These five structural forces determine the average profitability of the industry, and hence, of the firm within it. Therefore, a firm's major strategy should be to choose the right type of industry.

Given the correct choice of industry, the next emphasis in strategy was on developing core skills, core competencies, core brands, and core market niches. Hence, the attention of scholars and business practitioners swung dramatically in the other direction, from the outside (industry and competition) to the inside (core tangibles and intangibles) of the company. The new approach focused on developing skills and collective organizational learning. Hence, the growing belief was that the roots and source of sustained competitive advantage was within the firm. Accordingly, the adoption of new strategies was all about developing one's scarce assets and resources. The external environment received little attention. The resource-based view (RBV) acknowledges the importance of company-specific resources and competencies, in the context of the competitive environment (Amit and Schoemaker 1993; Barney 1986a; Peteraf 1993; Wernerfelt 1984).

The RBV shares another view with the industrial economists—it invokes economic reasoning. It views capabilities and resources as the heart of a company's competitive position, subject to the interplay of three fundamental market forces:

1. Customer Demand (i.e., do the scarce resources respond to customer needs and differentiate from the competitor?)
2. Resource Scarcity (i.e., are resources slow to depreciate, non-imitable, and non-substitutable?)
3. Profits Appropriability (i.e., do they generate sufficient profits for the investors?)

The dynamic interplay of these fundamental market forces determines the strategic value of a resource or a capability. If these three forces are drawn as three intersecting circles in a Venn diagram, the common intersection of the three market forces is the *value creation zone* (Collis and Montgomery 1995). I will discuss this in more details in a separate chapter on sustainable competitive advantage.

In 1996, Adam Brandenburger and Barry Nalebuff published a celebrated book titled *Co-opetition,* which proposed the theory that in order to claim value, firms must create value. This requires bringing something new to the world, something customers want that is different from or better than what others are providing. The authors urged managers to consider the world with their firm versus the world without it. The difference, if there is one, is the firm's unique added value—what would be lost to the world if the firm ceased to exist (see the Prologue to this book). The unique added value is the *raison d'être* for the firm, its specific purpose in existing. Companies have started valuing themselves not necessarily in terms of the industry they belong to and the products/services they offer, but by the value they add to the world.

BASIC TERMS IN FORMULATING A CORPORATE STRATEGY

- A corporation, as opposed to proprietorship or partnership, is a legal entity that is separate and distinct from its owners. Corporations enjoy most of the rights and responsibilities that an individual possesses; that is, a corporation has the right to enter into contracts, loan and borrow money, sue and be sued, hire employees, own assets, and pay taxes.
- **Limited Liability**: The most important aspect of a corporation is limited liability. That is, shareholders have the right to participate in the profits, through dividends and/or the appreciation of stock, but are not held personally liable for the company's debts. A corporation is created (incorporated) by a group of shareholders who have ownership of the corporation, represented by their holding of common stock. Shareholders elect a board of directors (generally receiving one vote per share) who appoint and oversee management of the corporation. Although a corporation does not necessarily have to be for profit, the vast majority of corporations are set up with the goal of providing a return for its shareholders. When you purchase stock of a corporation, you become a part owner of that corporation.
- **Enterprise**: An enterprise is a nexus of customer-oriented contracts between itself and its stakeholders (Jones 1995). An enterprise may be engaged with customers at every possible level and is characterized by relationships with many groups and individual stakeholders, each with the power to affect the enterprise's performance and/or a stake in the firm's performance (Freeman 1984). In many cases, both conditions apply. Stakeholders are included, but are not limited to, shareholders.
- **Structure**: A structure is not necessarily a set of external constraints on the individual or the organization. As in complex living systems (e.g., the cardiovascular or neuromuscular structures), structure means "the basic interrelationships that control behavior" (Senge 1990: 40). In human systems, structure includes how people make decisions—the operating principles whereby we translate perceptions, goals, rules, and norms into actions. In this sense, *structure influences behavior.* A system causes its own behavior. Different people in the same structure tend to produce qualitatively different results. Conversely, when placed in the same system, people, however different, tend to produce similar results (Senge 1990: 40–42).
- **Corporate Mission**: What the corporation or organization exists for. It spells out the underlying motivation for being in business in the first place—the specific contribution to society (consumption) that the firm aspires to make. Hence, many firms in the same business could have the same mission. Nevertheless, each firm's mission may be distinguished by its vision, specific goals and objectives. For instance, the mission of all insurance firms is to provide financial security and freedom from anxiety to its customers; but each firm may choose to deliver that service differently.
- **Corporate Vision**: How does the firm view and understand the market, environment, and competitive atmosphere in the industry it wants to function, and accordingly, why does it want to be in that environment? A vision is an indeterminate future goal such as being the recognized leader

in the industry, in the specific market, in the country, in the region, or in the global market. For instance, GE's vision is to be the first in electric and electronic appliances; P&G's vision is to be the leader in the consumer goods industry; Sony poses as the pioneer and leader of electronic computer-based or palm-held games; and Microsoft wants to be the leader in computer software engineering. Obviously, two or more competitors may have the same vision given the industry or any of its major markets. Thus, both Lever Brothers (U.K.) and P&G want to be leaders in the consumer goods industry; both Dell and HP want to dominate the personal computer (PC) market, and so on.

- **Corporate Values**: What and why does the firm believe in its vision, and how and why will it behave in accomplishing its vision? That is, what values, opportunities, benefits, reasons, and motivations does the firm perceive in the industry or market so as to be involved in it, immersed in it, and be passionate about its mission and vision? Specifically, what are the ethical and moral goals of the firm in being in this business or industry? How does it vision and value its corporate social responsibility? Here again, two or more firms may have similar or comparable values operating in the same industry or market, but it is highly unlikely that they will have the same objectives.

- **Corporate Objectives**: Objectives are long-term ideals or ends, and short-term goals. Ends or ideals, by definition, may not be achievable, but they provide the direction, vision, and mission. On the contrary, short-term goals are achievable within a horizon. Thus, what is the single precise goal or objective that will drive a firm for the next five years or so in a given business, industry, or market? It is very unlikely that two or more competitor firms have the same goals and objectives. If they do, to that extent they are either ineffective, or result in head-on collision. For instance, maximizing shareholder value or maximizing customer satisfaction are not real corporate objectives, as all firms aspire to do the same. Objectives are more specific to the organization, its structure and culture, its organizational learning and skills, its unique position and positioning. Hence, a related strategic and actionable question is what objective is most likely to help the firm to maximize its sales revenues, maximize customer satisfaction, become a market leader, or maximize shareholder wealth? Such a strategic objective is specific and unique, measurable, time-bound, growth- or profit-oriented, customer- or competitor-focused. That is, the ultimate objective that will drive the firm and its operations over the next several years should always be very clear and precise. The more people in a given firm are clear about this, the more effective is the business organization.

- **Corporate Scope**: A firm's scope encompasses at least three dimensions: (*a*) customer or offering, (*b*) geographic location, and (*c*) vertical integration. Clearly defined boundaries under each dimension should empower managers to determine what activities to pursue and what not to in realizing corporate objectives. To ensure that the borders are clear to all employees, the corporate scope should specify where the firm will go and where it will not. The firm's scope, however, does not prescribe all activities, given the boundaries. It encourages entrepreneurship, experimentation, and initiative. For instance, should the firm go after many customers or concentrate on a few big profitable clients is a question of customer scope. Should a company enter new markets, new countries, new trading regions, or trade online are questions dealing with geographic location. Should the company seek vertical integration by buying suppliers or brokers or distributors or retailers, or via mergers or acquisitions, via strategic alliances or joint ventures, and the like. These questions deal with vertical integration.

- **Corporate Advantage**: This is the result of clear corporate mission, vision, values, objectives, and scope. Sustainable competitive advantage (SCA) is the essence of any corporate strategy.

SCA follows one's *customer value proposition*—what precisely do you offer your customers that your competitors do not, or why your customers prefer you to your competitors. For instance, Wal-Mart's customer value proposition is low price or everyday low price (EDLP), great selection across a variety of product categories, rural convenience, reliable prices, and in-stock merchandise. It may yield, however, to its competitors (KMart, Sears, Target) on other values such as store ambience, sales help, suburban convenience, selection within categories, and store designer fashions.

Hindsight is rarely profitable. Today's best run businesses are more clearly focusing on the present to help them secure their place in the future. Starting a journey is more important than regressing in the past. Learning quickly from the mistakes of the past, a company must forge ahead to do well in a challenging new world.

The choice of the objective must have a profound impact on the firm. When Boeing shifted its objective from being the largest player in the aircraft industry to being the most profitable, it stopped from competing with Airbus, restructured the entire organization, from sales to manufacturing, and abandoned its goal of maintaining a manufacturing capacity that could serve more than half a peak year's demand for air planes (Collis and Rukstad 2008: 86).

Similarly, Starbucks wanted to surpass McDonald's in the number of outlets or franchises in less than half the years McDonald's took to build its empire. By the end of 2008, it boasted 16,875 locations worldwide with 11,537 in the U.S. alone. Meanwhile, Starbucks forgot its original core product and objective of being a great coffee bar experience. Starbucks is failing since 2008; its market share and stock price have decreased significantly. Currently, Dunkin' Donuts and McDonald's are vigorously competing in the coffee experience market. In recent market tests, Dunkin' Donuts is #1, McDonald's is #2, and Starbucks is #3 in the coffee experience business. A misguided corporate objective could spell one's demise.

WHAT IS A STRATEGY?

The word "strategy" has military origins. Webster's *New World Dictionary* defines strategy as "the science of planning and directing large-scale military operations. Of maneuvering forces into the most advantageous position prior to actual engagement with the enemy." In order to ascertain the "most advantageous position," however, one must study, understand, and maneuver around the battleground. The domain and scope of business strategy has remained the same. But in this context, the battleground is the "mind" of your customers and prospects.

Given one's corporate mission, vision, values, objectives, and scope, a strategy is the creation of a unique and valuable position involving a different set of activities. The quintessence of strategy is *differentiation* that counts with the customer and the competition. The focus of a strategy is to leverage the core strengths of the organization in order to achieve acceptable risk-adjusted returns in an existing market (Kim and Mauborgne 2009: 74). Competitive strategy is about being different. It means deliberately choosing a different set of activities to deliver a unique mix of value. The essence of a strategy is in the activities—choosing to perform activities differently or to perform different activities than rivals. Otherwise, a strategy is nothing more than a marketing slogan that will not withstand competition (Porter 1996: 64–68). Strategy is "what makes you unique and what is the best way to put that difference into the minds of your customers and prospects" (Trout 2004: xiv). Strategy is all about being different. In the land of positioning, a successful strategy is based on finding a way to be different from your sea of competitors (Trout 2004: 35). Strategy, however, looks beyond the day-to-day grind of operational improvement—the latter is *tactics*. Strategy is beyond incremental tactical planning punctuated by strategic investments (Hamel and Prahalad 1994: 280–83).

Most executives cannot articulate the vision, mission, values, objectives, scope, and advantage of their business in a single statement. If they cannot, neither will the employees. One way of testing is to see if the company has a well-defined statement—whether all its thousands of employees can summarize the company strategy in 35 words or less. A well-understood statement of strategy aligns behavior within the business. It allows everyone in the organization to make individual choices that reinforce one another, rending all the thousands of employees exponentially more effective (Collis and Rukstad 2008: 84). To achieve excellence in strategy is to be clear about what the strategy is and to communicate it constantly to customers, employees, and stockholders. It is a simple, focused value proposition (Trout 2004: 11).

Strategy embodies clear priorities, based on understanding the strengths we need to preserve and weaknesses that threaten our prosperity the most. Strategy addresses what to do, as also, what not to do. In dealing with a crisis, such as the current financial market debacle, experience teaches us that steps to address the immediate problem must support a long-term strategy. Yet it is far from clear that we are taking the steps most important to America's long-term economic prosperity (Porter 2008: 39).

Based on our discussions thus far, Table 1.1 presents a hierarchy of corporate strategic statements. Crafting a strategic statement requires a clear understanding of corporate mission, vision, value, objectives, scope, and corporate advantage in that order. A first critical step in creating a great strategy is a careful analysis of the industry landscape you want to enter, that is, understanding customer needs, wants and desires, segmenting customers based on their needs, wants, and desires, and then identifying

TABLE 1.1 A Hierarchy of Corporate Strategic Statements

Corporate strategic statements on	What this statement stands for in the company	Further specification of these statements
Mission	Why the company exists. Several competing companies may have the same mission, but they differ in values, vision, and strategy.	What is the precise mission of the company in a given product/service, industry, market, state, country, trade region? How does it intend to serve its target customers?
Vision	What the company wants to be. This is an indeterminate future goal. Here again, several companies may share a common vision, but they will differ in the way the vision is specified, framed, and realized.	Typical vision statements are: to be the best or second best in the industry (GE); to set the standard in office management software (Microsoft); to be the recognized world leader in beauty care products (Revlon).
Values	What the company believes in and how it will behave. These may include ethical, moral, and spiritual principles and values. These values guide general behavior of company and employee (e.g., to do things rightly) but not specific behavior (e.g., to do right things).	Ends: Long-term ultimate purpose and ideals and objectives may not always be achievable, but they give the direction to the company; e.g., maximizing employee fulfillment, optimizing consumer delight, maximizing shareholder wealth.

(Continued)

TABLE 1.1 *(Continued)*

Corporate strategic statements on	What this statement stands for in the company	Further specification of these statements
		Objectives: These are subordinate, middle-term, and achievable objectives, but within the mission and scope of the company (e.g., 20% better motivation and skills-training for employees within the next 2 years; ROI of more than 12% each year for the next 5 years).
		Means: What the company decides and does to achieve the objectives (e.g., additional and top class skills-trainers for the employees; divest unused assets for augmenting ROI).
Strategy	What is the company's competitive game plan? The strategic objective should be specific, measurable, and time bound. It should include the basic elements of a strategy statement. While several companies may share common mission, values, and vision, it is very rare that they share common strategic objectives. If they do, the strategy may not be effective.	This is an actionable strategic statement that tells how the company is going to achieve its mission, vision, and values. For instance, will the company maximize shareholder wealth via growth in size, or increasing market share, or becoming a market leader, or radical cost-containment, or innovative revenue generation, or by penetrating new markets, or by proactive compliance with government regulation?
Trade-Offs	In achieving its strategic objective what are the available trade-offs the company should choose from? If the choice domain is too vast, the company must narrow down its specific choices.	Every strategy implies some trade-offs. Hence, should the company focus on: • Cost-containment or revenue generation? • Standardization or customization? • Centralization or decentralization? • Specialization or diversification? • Growth in size or profits? • Scale, scope, time, or new market space economies? • Competition-driven or seek blue ocean strategies? • Market share and leadership or market expansion? • EDLP or upscale fashion and designer products?
Balanced Scorecard	How will the company monitor and implement the competitive game plan? What are the metrics by which you monitor progress?	How will the company monitor and implement the competitive game plan specifics? What are the specific metrics by industries, cross-industries, product categories, production departments, product brands, retail stores, market segments, and preferred customers by which you monitor progress and financial success?

Source: Author's own.

Note: See also Collis and Rukstad (2008: 85–90).

unique ways of creating and delivering values to your target customers, given your unique resources and competitor strategies, is the essence of every strategic statement (Collis and Rukstad 2008: 89).

Figure 1.1 captures the dynamic inputs, process, and outputs of a corporate strategy. Given corporate mission, vision, values, goals, and objectives, the corporation studies its industry landscape, filtering it through its understanding of its competitive landscape. Corporate process includes corporate structures, corporate focus, and organizational learning, each influencing the other. Figure 1.1 depicts several loops and iterative processes—thus indicating the "wicked" problem that every corporate

FIGURE 1.1 The Dynamic Inputs, Process, and Outputs of a Corporate Strategy

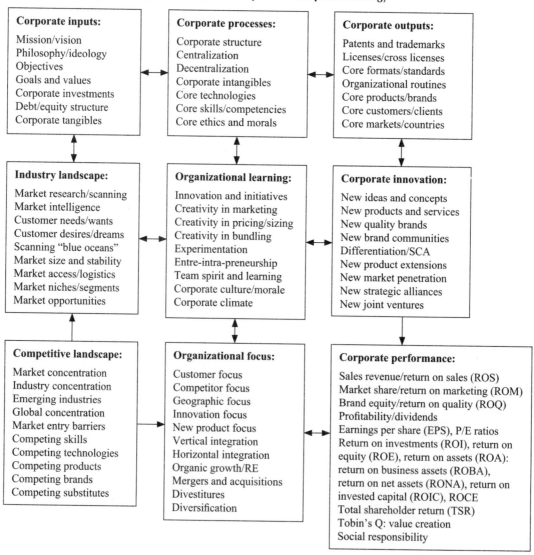

strategy implies (Camillus 2008). Corporate outputs include corporate patents, licenses, products and brands, corporate innovation and differentiation, and corporate financial and social performance. As noticed in Figure 1.1, there is constant interaction between all nine components of a corporate strategy, which makes it dynamic, unpredictable, risk-prone, but controllable with careful research and strategic planning. The measure of a successful corporate strategy is the measure of its corporate performance and social impact.

STRATEGY VERSUS TACTICS

In a military context, *Webster's New World Dictionary* (2002; 4th edition) defines tactics as the "science of arranging and maneuvering military and naval forces in action or before the enemy, especially (as distinguished from strategy) with reference to short-range objectives." Tactics, accordingly, deal with matters of arrangement. They are skillful methods and procedures used to gain an end. Normally, tactics follow and fulfill a concrete strategic plan. They represent the implementation and execution of a strategy in an operations-oriented, make-things-happen activity aimed at performing core business activities in a strategy-supportive manner (Thompson et al. 2008: 42).

As a strategy-execution process, tactics include:

- Recruiting, developing, and retaining leadership skills and operational expertise for supporting strategy and for combating competition.
- Allocating ample resources to those activities critical to strategic success.
- Enforcing and ensuring policies and procedures that facilitate strategy execution.
- Accumulating best practices and organizational routines that enable, assess, and improve strategy-execution on a continual basis.
- Installing information and operating systems that enable company personnel to fulfill their strategy-execution roles and responsibilities.
- Motivating, training, and empowering key strategy-execution people by proper training, rewards, and incentives.
- Creating and sustaining a company culture and work climate conducive to successful strategy execution.

Some of these tactics are included in Figure 1.1 in one or other of the three blocks in the middle column of "corporate process." In fact, any activity included in the "process" block must be differentiating the company from its rivals. If strategy is essentially differentiation, then tactics must also involve differentiating activities and procedures. Each tactic must have an element of differentiation. It could be in being smaller, bigger, lighter, heavier, cheaper, or more expensive, or it could be having a different distribution system. A tactic must have a competitive angle; it must be competitive in the total marketing arena, and not just competitive in relation to one or two products or services. In this sense, a tactic is a competitive advantage. A strategy is designed to maintain that competitive advantage.

A tactic is communications- and action-oriented, while a strategy is innovation-, product-, service-,or company-oriented. A tactic is specialization, while a strategy tends to be general. A tactic is one thing in which you are very skilled as compared to your competitors.

In World War II, General George S. Patton was very skilled in tank warfare—that was his tactic. Herb Kelleher of Southwest Airlines was very skilled in short-haul air travel—that was a specialization tactic (Trout 2004: 70–75). Gatorade is a very powerful specialist in sports drinks—the highest level in brand success—and a generic name in sports drinks. Gillette, before its merger with P&G, was a multi-billion company that specialized in razor blades, with a worldwide market share of more than 60 percent. Subaru, a Japanese carmaker, specializes in all-wheel drive technologies. When George Muller became its president in 1993, he defined Subaru as an all-wheel drive company thus differentiating it from Toyota and Honda. The company survived bankruptcy because it used a specialty to differentiate itself. It is better to be exceptional at one thing than be good at many things (Trout 2004: 76–89).

Great and successful companies are known for their specialized focus word or slogan. Federal Express specializes in *overnight* package delivery only. Prego combated leader Ragu in the spaghetti sauce market and captured a 16 percent market share with an idea borrowed from Heinz—"thicker." Papa John's Pizza uses two words: *better ingredients*. Today, most consumers associate Crest with cavities, Mercedes with engineering, BMW with driving, Volvo with safety, Dell with PCs, Xerox with copiers, Sony with play-stations, Nordstrom with retail service, Sachs Fifth Avenue with elegance, Domino's with home delivery, Pepsi-Cola with youth drinks, Gatorade with sports drinks, Gillette with razor blades, and Toyota with hybrids. It is specialization that differentiates. Big strategic ideas almost always come in small words (Trout 2004: 102–11). [See *Business Transformation Exercise 1.4.*]

ESSENTIAL COMPONENTS OF A GOOD STRATEGY

There are three components to a good strategy statement—objective, scope, and advantage. A company's top executive should be crystal clear about all three components. These elements are a simple yet sufficient list for any strategy (whether business or military) that addresses competitive interaction over unbounded terrain (Collis and Rukstad 2008: 84):

- **The End Objective**: Any strategy statement should begin with the definition of the ends that the strategy is designed to achieve. This definition must also include a time frame and a method for reaching it.
- **The Scope**: Since most firms compete in a more or less unbounded landscape, it is also crucial to define the scope or domain of the business—that is, the part of the landscape the firm will operate. It must state the boundaries beyond which it will not venture presently. For instance, if you are in a restaurant business, your boundaries will be sit-down or quick service, bar or without bar, fixed or open menu, casual or upscale atmosphere, French, American, Indian, or Mexican food, what geographic area will you serve, what days and hours, and the like.
- **The Advantage**: How are you going to reach the scope and the objective? What and how will you do differently from others? What is your competitive advantage vis-á-vis your competitors—this is the essence of your strategy. What are your core competencies and skills that make you deliver your product better than others do? How will you align your internal business activities so that only your firm can deliver your value proposition? In short, why would your target customer patronize your business more than your competitors or other alternatives?

Defining the objective, scope, and advantage require trade-offs, which Porter (1996) identifies as fundamental to strategy. Strategy "is making trade-offs in competing" (Porter 1996: 70). The essence of a strategy is choosing what *not* to do. Without trade-offs there would be no need for choice and thus no need for strategy. It is through proper and timely trade-offs that one can improve upon operational effectiveness. (See the cases of Southwest Airlines versus Continental Lite described in the following.)

If the firm prefers growth in size, then the capital investments may erode profits. If the firm prefers to serve institutional clients, then it may have to ignore retail customers. If the firm agrees on EDLP or every-day-low-price, then fashion, fame, and fit may have to be compromised. Finally, if the firm wants to capitalize scale economies that lead to standardized products, then it may not be able to exploit scope, space, and time economies that accommodate personalized and individualized customer needs. Such trade-offs strategically distinguish competing companies (Collis and Rukstad 2008: 85).

Table 1.2 sketches major types of corporate strategies based on strategic environment, strategic choices or activities, strategic trade-offs, and strategic desired outcomes. The listing of strategies in Table 1.2 is not mutually exclusive or collectively exhaustive (MECE). Each strategy has the necessary and sufficient contents as described by Porter (1996), Prahalad and Hamel (1990), Collis and Rukstad (2008), and others. Given one's corporate mission, vision, and objectives, each corporate executive must determine what strategy is best for the company, whether it should be competition-driven, customer-driven, technology-driven, organizational learning driven, or combinations thereof.

TABLE 1.2 Major Corporate Strategies Defined by Strategic Environment

Strategic environment	Strategic activities	Strategic trade-offs	Strategic advantage
Competition Driven	*Design, quality, form, functionality*: Differentiating features, attributes, and benefits from the rivals	Competitor versus customer focus Competitor versus newer technology focus Competitor versus new product development focus	Competitive advantage Market dominance Product uniqueness Service uniqueness
	Bundling and marketing: Differentiating from the rivals in pricing, packaging, product bundling, price-product bundling, placing, financing; delivery logistics, retail service, consumer redress	Red ocean versus blue ocean strategies Pure pricing versus price-product bundling Downscale versus upscale retailing Easy versus restricted consumer credit	Combating competition Market barriers Category dominance Brand market share
Customer-Driven	Differentiation with respect to customer needs, wants, and desires fulfillment	Customization versus standardization Personalization versus individualization Localization versus globalization Premium versus marginal pricing High volume versus high margins High time, cost, energy, anxiety, and effort intensive versus low Customer satisfaction versus customer excitement/delight	Brand equity and Renown Brand image and Draw Company flagship brands Name/designer brands National brands Convenience brands User-friendly brands Customer delight brands

(Continued)

TABLE 1.2 *(Continued)*

Strategic environment	Strategic activities	Strategic trade-offs	Strategic advantage
	Differentiation with respect to customer segments, market niches, emerging markets, industry, cross-industry, and emerging industries	Market segmentation versus generalization Direct versus cross-selling Industry concentration versus multi-industry diversification Old versus new markets Domestic versus foreign markets Divergent versus emergent industries Divergent versus emergent markets	Target market niche Target market success Brand community Brand loyalty Domestic loyalty International loyalty Inter-industry synergies Inter-market dynamics
Technology-Driven	Differentiation by new technologies, new patents, mergers, acquisitions, alliances, joint ventures, radical innovation, and new product/service development	Radical versus incremental innovations Technology versus market breakthroughs Cost containment versus revenue generation technologies High versus medium growth Organic growth versus Mergers & Acquisitions (M&A)	New products New product revenues New product patents New product growth Financial performance Company growth
	Differentiation via greening, reducing carbon emissions, Environmental Protection Agency (EPA)compliance, new safety products, new national security products	Ecology versus non-ecology conscious Proactive versus reactive EPA compliance National security versus personal privacy Organic versus inorganic foods	Social responsibility Green trade advantage Cause marketing Corporate citizenship
Organization-Culture-Driven	Differentiation in organizational learning, scale economies, efficiencies, culture	Centralization versus decentralization Fat versus lean management	Scale economies Scope, space, and time economies
	Differentiation in organizational bonding, camaraderie, morale, worker commitment, and culture	Discipline versus bonding Control versus worker freedom Rigidity versus flexibility Assembly versus team learning	Employee bonding Worker morale Skills retention Worker productivity

Source: Author's own.

Note: See *Business Transformation Exercises 1.5 and 1.6.*

STRATEGIC PROPOSITIONS AS COMPONENTS OF A STRATEGY

According to Kim and Mauborgne (2009), a strategy should have at least three propositions or components:

a. A value proposition that attracts buyers.
b. A profit proposition that enables the company and its shareholders to make money from the value proposition (a).
c. An execution or people proposition that motivates other stakeholders (e.g., employees, bankers, suppliers) to execute the strategy.

The value and profit propositions define the content of the strategy, while the execution proposition defines the quality of its execution. Given these three propositions, a "strategy is the development and alignment of the three propositions to either exploit or reconstruct the industrial and economic environment in which an organization operates" (Kim and Mauborgne 2009: 75). Focusing on the alignment and development of all three propositions is crucial for any successful strategy. Focusing on one or two propositions to the exclusion of the others results in failure. Table 1.3 illustrates this and proposes taxonomy of corporate strategies based on the three propositions.

For example, if the value and profit propositions are strong, but the execution proposition does not really motivate the employees and suppliers, then this is the classic case of execution failure, and the company may experience temporary but unsustainable success—the case of most domestic auto companies. In the case of Napster, the value and profit propositions were strong but execution was a failure. Founded in 1999, Napster.com, an online music provider, had registered 80 million users because of its unique and great value (simple, easy-to-use software that allowed music files to be indexed, searched, downloaded, stored, and freely shared across computers throughout the world). Yet within a year, its market-creating innovation failed to deliver commercial success as Napster was shut down under a barrage of copyright infringement suits from the Record labels and music industry.

In contrast, Apple launched its iTunes Music Store in 2003 with carefully copyrighted or leased tens of thousands of music labels and became the number one music seller in America by 2008. Apple's iTunes enabled buyers to browse freely more than 200,000 songs, including exclusive tracks, listen to 30-second samples, and download an individual song for 99 cents or an entire album for $9.99. Moreover, iTunes guaranteed high sound quality resolution along with intuitive navigation, search, and browsing functions (Kim and Mauborgne 2009: 79).

Additionally, a strategy may not be successful if the value and profit propositions are aligned around differentiation while the execution proposition focuses on low cost or containment. When high differentiation combines with low cost, then you break new target markets or create new market spaces—as was the case with Southwest Airlines, the New York Police Department (NYPD), Cirque du Soleil, and the like. In the latter case, *strategy shapes market structure*. While alignment of one or two strategy propositions may be imitated by the competitor, imitating alignment of all three strategic propositions is difficult—thus leading to sustainable competitive advantage.

Kim and Mauborgne (2009: 76–79) cite the city-state of Dubai as an excellent example of a perfect blend of all three strategy propositions with unprecedented corporate and profit growth. Dubai's unforgiving deserts, relentless heat, politically turbulent regions, and other structural disadvantages made the city-state nothing more than a dead oil base about 30 years ago. Today, Dubai is arguably the only Arab economy that has achieved substantial integration into the world economy and has emerged as premier tourist and business destination across the globe. Now, only five percent of its revenues come from oil and natural gas.

Dubai's value proposition, among other things, includes a dozen world-class free zones with unbeatable incentives for investors. They are: 100 percent foreign ownership, freedom to repatriate 100 percent of capital and profits, transparency of regulations and a legal system based on British law, no import or re-export duties, zero corporate tax rate for the first 15 to 50 years of operations, easy business registration process, all documentation in English, logistics efficiency with world-class airports and shipping services, and transparent internationally acceptable judicial system in free zones. Clearly, this great value proposition provides high differentiation with low cost compared to other investment opportunities or countries.

TABLE 1.3   A Taxonomy of Strategies

Focusing on	Strategic implications	Market outcomes	Industry examples
No proposition (e.g., no focus on value, execution, and profits)	No strategy No direction No mission No vision Chaotic strategy No patent No product	Strategy formulation failure Total company failure Organizational failure Cash crisis, insolvency	Most start-ups that fail within a year Erratic and despotic leaders Chapter 7/11 bankruptcies
Profit proposition only (e.g., profit and/or shareholder value dominance)	Profiteering strategy Fly-by-night strategy Price gouging Creative accounting	Market failure Employees demoralized Merchant greed Corporate fraud	Dot.com bubbles that burst Fly-by-night companies Oil & gas companies Enron, Tyco, World.com
Execution proposition only (e.g., low cost or cost containment or great innovations)	Exaggerated execution Over perfectionist strategy Cutting-edge tech with no value to customers Goal-less strategy Ruthless cost-cutting	Market failure Corporate failure Customer failure Morale failure Purposeless driven company Plant closing & mass labor layoffs	Companies that focus only on ideas and inventions without taking them to the market All concept cars that never reached the market Domestic auto companies
Value proposition only (e.g., unique added value; differentiation)	Exaggerated customer focus Exaggerated marketing focus Exaggerated quality focus Exaggerated function focus Exaggerated form focus	ROI, ROA, ROE, ... down ROS, ROM, ... down Return on quality (ROQ) down Great functionality; no profits Great form; no returns	Toyota Prius, Amazon.com Hefty rebates, subsidies Ford Focus, Hybrids Saturn, Edsel, EV1 Big mansions that lost value
Value + Profits	No organization focus Labor as production-factor Supplier goals disregarded Bank covenants violated Trademark infringement	Execution failure Employee dissatisfaction Supplier disloyalty or loss Creditor displeasure Supplier resentment	Home mortgage companies Sweatshops, child labor Auto supplier bankruptcies All bank workouts that failed Napster.com
Execution + Profits	Exaggerated execution Exorbitant profit strategy Employee union domination No customer focus	Market failure Brand equity loss Customer/client/consumer loss Employee benefits legacy Customer dissatisfaction	Patents that failed markets Customers priced out Unjust labor boycotts Health insurance companies
Execution + Value	High differentiation High quality focus Unique customer-value but no steady profits	Differentiation without profits Low ROQ, ROIC, and ROBA Corporate shareholder loss Financial performance failure	Auto hybrids, concept cars Some hospitals, hotels, diners Highly competing companies Cut-throat competition
Values + Execution + Profits	Great strategic planning Well balanced strategy All stakeholder strategy Comprehensive strategy All-inclusive strategy High performance strategy Ecology-driven strategy Sustainable strategy Responsible strategy Social innovation strategy	Strategy formulation success Sustainable competitive advantage All stakeholders satisfied Max efficiency + effectiveness Nobody left out or left behind All systems at high performance Water, air, land conservation Global sustainability Corporate social responsibility (CSR) Corporate social entrepreneurship	All "built-to-last" companies Dell, HP, GE, Toyota, Sony Singapore, Luxemburg Audi, Toyota, Nokia Switzerland, Germany, Dubai All "good to great" companies All green companies Companies with great legacy All CSR-driven companies Companies that also serve the bottom of the pyramid (BOP)

Source: Author's own.

Dubai's profit proposition is low-cost and high differentiation. The emirate of Dubai reaps abundant profits (not from corporate and personal taxes) from investing heavily in the infrastructure. It owns and operates its world-class airports, aviation (Emirate Airlines), shipping and port services, tourism, real-estate development, export commerce, and telecommunications—all these are run on high differentiation and low cost, as it does with its value proposition. For instance, the government-owned DP World operates the Jebel Ali port and complex in Dubai, where more than 6,000 companies are based. DP World now operates over 50 ports in 31 countries. The emirate also owns Nakheel, now one of the world's biggest real-estate developers, that has slated to develop half of all residential construction projects (e.g., for foreigner housing) in the emirate over the next 10 years. Moreover, by deciding to become a part of the United Arab Emirates (UAE), Dubai does not need its own military, diplomatic corps, or monetary agency. Abu Dhabi, the UAE capital and possessor of the vast oil reserves, bears most of the cost of maintaining the federal government.

Finally, Dubai's execution proposition is unique. With no citizenship, social rights, and benefits offered to foreigners, Dubai still has more than a million foreigners from over 100 countries living prosperously with high religious and social tolerance. Qualified foreign workers, however, have access to a generous social security system and are virtually guaranteed a government job. They benefit from an extensive state assistance that includes medical care, sickness and maternity benefits, childcare, free or subsidized education, pensions and unemployment benefits, and in some cases, housing and disability benefits. All foreigners are considered expatriates with zero income tax, easy housing with 100 percent ownership, and all invested capital and profits can be 100 percent expatriated. All cultures find home here with their own cuisines, pubs, wines, and restaurants. Dubai has the world's largest indoor ski facility. Cultural and religious heritage is well maintained by its Arab citizens who receive free plots of land from the government along with interest-free loans or grants to build homes; their children attend nearby Arabic schools that provide Islamic religious teachings along with modern education.

Dubai today is a cosmopolitan state with a compelling low-cost and differentiated value proposition that is excellently executed and reaping abundant profits for all its stakeholders. Dubai has superbly aligned the three strategy propositions with tremendous reinforcing synergies.

Thus, it is the responsibility of the top management that each strategy proposition is fully developed and all the three propositions are aligned. Only top executive leaders who view the whole company can develop and align all its propositions. Functional executives (e.g., VP of marketing, VP of finance, VP of HR, VP of accounting, and VP of IT) are biased, and normally tend to develop their respective proposition turfs to the neglect of others. [See *Business Transformation Exercise 1.7.*]

STRATEGIC THINKING AND STRATEGIC PLANNING

Clay Christensen (1997b) argued more than a decade ago that competent strategic thinking was atrophying in the executive suites because it occurs so infrequently relative to other regular activities. The problem has worsened since (Olson, Van Beer, and Verry 2008: 61).

A strategic plan includes a strategic vision, clear strategic goals and objectives, and a well-honed corporate strategy to implement the strategic goals and objectives. Developing a strategic vision and mission, setting goals and objectives, and crafting a strategy are basic elements of direction-setting or strategic planning. A strategic plan lays out the company's future direction, performance targets, and strategy to achieve those performance targets. A strategic plan copes with industry and competitive conditions, the expected actions of the industry's key players, and the challenges and issues that stand as obstacles to the company's success (Thompson, Strickland, and Gamble 2008: 41). On a periodic basis, strategic planning is reviewing your corporate mission, vision, goals, and objectives against previous measures and budgets, and planning the future. Strategic planning sets the competitive direction, dictates product/service planning, tells how to communicate internally and externally, and tells you what to focus on. Market success is not about having the right people, the right attitude, the right tools, the right role models, or the right organization. They all help, but they do not put you over the top. Strategy and strategic planning does.

Strategy is about "next-generation" planning in technology, of customer needs, wants and desires, market dynamics, competitor development, government regulation, supplier and creditor markets, and globalization factors. Given this, strategic thinking involves minimally the following critical issues:

- **Who are we?** What business, market, industry are we in? Who is our competitor? Who are our customers? What are their needs that we can serve? These questions relate to vision, mission and identity, strategic thinking, and strategic planning.
- **What are we?** What are our tangible resources? What are our intangible resources? What are our strengths? What are our weaknesses? What is our competition? What is our sustainable competitive advantage? These questions relate to strategic inputs, strategic resources, inputs mapping, and inputs sourcing.
- **Where are we?** What is our position in innovation, patents, new products, new markets, new product sales, market share, profits, growth, Wall Street assessment, shareholder satisfaction, employee commitment, creditor approval, supplier trust, and customer delight? These questions relate to assessment, evaluation, strategic mapping, and process mapping.
- **What is our future?** Where do we want to go? Why do we want to go there? How do we reach there (strategic architecture)? When do we reach there? How would we know that we have reached there? Who do we want to be three, five, seven, or ten years from now? These questions relate to the future, industry foresight, direction, destiny, outcomes-mapping, and strategic architecture.
- **Hence what shall we do?** How do we reinvent the future? How shall we identify new horizons and new opportunities in them? How do we reshape the industry to our advantage? What new resources shall we build? What new core competencies should we generate? What new core products should we develop? What new functionalities should our products and services create for our customers? How do we deliver old functionalities in new ways? How do we rewrite industry rules and create new competitive spaces? These questions relate to strategy, strategy making, strategy process, and strategy mapping.

Thinking strategically starts with the reflection of the deepest nature of an undertaking and on the central challenges it poses. It develops with understanding of focus and timing.

- **Focus** means where to place one's attention, to know what is truly essential, what is secondary, and what cannot be ignored without risking the success of the enterprise.
- **Timing** means having a sense of an unfolding dynamic. Some changes are intrinsically long-term; they cannot be achieved quickly. Others can be started relatively quickly, but only assume lasting importance in concert with long-term, slowly occurring changes. We can achieve some changes directly whereas others occur as by-products of efforts focused elsewhere.

Understanding such issues is the essence of strategic thinking. Strategic thinking also addresses core organizational dilemmas such as centralization versus decentralization, command and control versus distributed power and authority, mission and identity versus diversification, productivity versus creativity, revenue generation versus cost containment, and the like. Good strategic thinking brings such dilemmas to the surface, and uses them to catalyze imagination and innovation (Senge et al. 1994: 16–17). Systems thinking can empower good strategic thinking.

Risk is inherent in every decision and strategy. Effective managers know how to assess risk in every major decision they take.[1] Any decision or strategy in general is a strategy for risk management. Thus, a divestiture strategy seeks to get rid of one's very risky, low-use, and low-profit assets; a merger and acquisition strategy, on the other hand, seeks to avoid the risk of low market control by buying companies that will provide better competitive market advantage. An outsourcing strategy looks for reducing risks of prohibitive production costs and cost overruns. In general, all vertical or horizontal, backward or forward, integration strategies aim at reducing risk of supplier, distributor, creditor, and customer markets. Many fundamental operational, financial, marketing, and strategic choices seek to quantify and minimize risk that plague financial and consumer markets. Further, most strategies transfer risks from the company owner to other stakeholder parties. If firms can value and transfer risks, they can focus on managing and acquiring risks for which they have a competitive advantage. Engineering and managing a company's evolving risk portfolio has become an organizing principle for strategic choice, and companies that succeed in doing this generate far higher returns on their equity than those that optimize their traditional portfolios (Buehler et al. 2008: 104). [See *Business Transformation Exercise 1.8.*]

STRATEGIC POSITIONING AND STRATEGIC DIFFERENTIATION

"Strategic positioning" is choosing activities that are different from competitors (Porter 1996: 68). Strategic positioning is how you differentiate yourself in the mind of your customers and prospects; it is how you survive in a world of killer competition. In a military context, positioning is finding the most advantageous position against the enemy.

The sheer proliferations of competing brands contribute to the "tyranny of choice" (Trout 2004: 1). Table 1.4 illustrates the tyranny of choice situation in the U.S. Simple products have multiple choices. For instance, in the early 1970s, we had 160 breakfast cereals; we now have over 360. During the same period, airports have increased from 11,260 to 18,500, Frito-Lay chip varieties have gone from 10 to 78, soft drink brands from 20 to 90, bottled water brands 16 to 80, mouthwashes 15 to 70, dental flosses 12 to 64, amusements parks from 362 to 1,200, magazine titles 340 to 825, over-the-counter pain relievers 17 to 145, TV channels 5 to 185, radio stations 7,038 to 12, 460, women's hosiery styles 5 to 90, McDonald's menu items 13 to 55, PC models 0 to 400, websites 0 to 5 million, and software titles 0 to 250,000 (Trout 2004). Consumer choice can be tyrannical, that is, absolute, harsh, confusing, and cruel.

---

[1] Behavioral scientists claim there are five forms of perceived risk in relation to purchasing a product: (*a*) monetary risk (possibly, I will lose money by investing on this product), (*b*) functional risk (may be, it will not work or do what it is supposed to do), (*c*) physical risk (it looks dangerous; it could hurt), (*d*) social risk (my friends will be shocked if I buy this), and (*e*) psychological risk (I might feel guilty or irresponsible for buying this).

It can get only worse, for choice begets choice, competition begets competition. With so many choices, consumers are bound to pay dearly for their mistakes. With enormous competition, markets today are driven by consumer choice than ever before. Strategic positioning is driven by choice and competitive choices. Superior performance in this competitive world is not Customer Relationship Management (CRM), Total Quality Management (TQM), Statistical Process Control (SPC), Council of Quality and Leadership (CQL), Supply Chain Management (SCM), Six Sigma, Just in Time (inventory management) (JIT), and other tools and fads, but mastering business basics of good blocking and tackling. How do you get your customers and prospects to remember and cherish your brand in the oceanic multiplicity of brands? If learning is how humans acquire new information, and if memory is to retain that information over time, then strategic positioning is how you empower your customers to learn, remember, recall, and use your market offerings?

A landmark study published in *Harvard Business Review* (HBR) argued that companies could improve profits by at least 25 percent by reducing customer defections by 5 percent. A successful strategy is to hang on to your customers and never lose them. Mere customer satisfaction is not a differentiator. Creating unique customer experience or customer delight is a potent but challenging differentiator in retaining customers.

Strategic positions arise from three different sources that are not mutually exclusive and often overlap—customers' needs, customers' accessibility, and the variety of a company's products and services. Hence, there are three different types of strategic positioning (Porter 1996: 65–67):

1. **Variety-based Positioning**: If you can offer unique variety of products or services using distinctive set of activities, then you must pursue variety-based strategic positioning. For instance, Jiffy Lube International specializes in automotive lubricants and does not offer other car repair or maintenance services. Its value chain produces faster service at a lower cost than broader line repair shops. Many customers partition their shopping for auto services: they go to Jiffy Lube for oil changes, and to others, for other services.

2. **Needs-based Positioning**: This strategy targets a segment of customers that has differing needs that can be served with a unique set of activities. Differences in needs will not translate into strategic positions unless the company that launches the set of activities to serve those needs *also differs* (Porter 1996: 66). For instance, Ikea, the global furniture retailer based in Sweden, targets young furniture buyers who want style at low cost but are ready to trade off service for cost. Ikea seeks to meet all the home-furnishing needs of its target customers, not just a subset of them. It has a tailored set of activities to serve them uniquely. Ikea designs its own, low-cost, modular, ready-to-assemble furniture to fit its target market positioning. In huge stores, Ikea displays every product it sells in room-like settings that customers can leisurely look, examine, and choose without any salesperson trailing them. Adjacent to the furnished showrooms is a warehouse section with the products in boxes on pallets. Customers are expected to do their own pickup and delivery, and Ikea will even sell you a roof rack for your car that you can return for a refund on your next visit. Ikea is open for extended hours and on weekends, and has in-store child care, so that young families with children can comfortably shop.

3. **Access-based Positioning**: This strategy targets segments of customers who are accessible in different ways. Access can be a function of customer geography or customer scale—or of anything that requires a different set of activities to reach customers in the best way. For instance, Carmike Cinemas operates movie theaters exclusively in cities and towns with a population under 200,000. Its unique set of activities include a lean cost structure that serves its target

TABLE 1.4 The Tyranny of Choice: Proliferation of Competing Models and Brands in the U.S. Market

Product categories	Basic choices in the 1950s	Choices in the 21st century
Autos	GM, Ford, Chrysler, American Motors	GM, Ford, Daimler-Chrysler, Toyota, Honda, Volkswagen, Fiat, Nissan, Mitsubishi, Renault, Suzuki, Daihatsu, BMW, Hyundai, Daiwa, Mazda, Isuzu, Kia, Tata, Hindustan, and Volvo
Luxury Car	Cadillac, Ferrari	Lamborghini, Bentley sports car, Aston Martin, Jaguar, Porsche, Mercedes Vision SLR, Cadillac, and Ferraris
Car Models	140	Over 270
Vehicle Styles	Large, medium, small, and compact passenger cars	Sport utility vehicles (SUVs), roadsters, hatchbacks, coupes, minivans, wagons, jeeps, pickups, crossovers—some of these in large, medium, and small sizes
Tires	Goodyear, Firestone, General, and Sears	Armstrong, Goodyear, Firestone, Bridgestone, Cordovan, Michelin, Cooper, Dayton, Dunlap, General, Multi-Mile, Pirelli, Sears, Sentry, Uniroyal, and 25 other brands
Auto Parts	GM, Ford, Chrysler, American Motors	GM, Ford, Delphi, Visteon, Mopar, Johnson Controls, American Axle, Arvinmeritor, Autoliv, Borgwarner, Carlisle, Cooper-Standard Holdings, Dana, Denton, Dura Automotive Systems, Exide Technologies, Federal Mogul, Fleetwood Enterprises, Hayes-Lemmerz, Lear, Modine Manufacturing, Oshkosh Truck, Paccar, Tenneco, Thor Industries, Tower Automotive, TRW Automotive Holdings
Health Care	Local doctor, local hospital, Blue Cross, Medicare or Medicaid	Aetna/U.S. Healthcare, Americare, Cigna, Columbia, Kaiser, Multiplan, Oxford, Quorum, Wellpoint, BCBS, Medicare, Medicaid, Disability, and concepts like health maintenance organizations (HMOs), health alliance plan (HAP), peer review organizations (PROs), physician hospital organizations (PHOs), and preferred provider organizations (PPOs). Currently, U.S. has over 1,000 health care insurance companies!
Pharmaceuticals	Johnson & Johnson, Pfizer, Ciba	Abbot Laboratories, Allergan, Amgen, Biogen Idec, Bristol-Myers, Cephalon, Ciba-Geigy, Elililly, Forest Laboratories, Genzyme, Gilead Sciences, Hospira, Johnson & Johnson, King Pharmaceuticals, Merck, NBTY, Pfizer, Schering-Plough, Watson Pharmaceuticals, Wyeth
Household and Personal Products	Proctor & Gamble (P&G), Colgate	Alberto Culver, Avon Products, Church & Dwight, Clorox, Colgate-Palmolive, Energizer Holdings, Estee Lauder, Kimberly-Clark, P&G, Solo-Cup, Spectrum Brands, Stanley Works, Tupperware Brands, Unilever
Commercial Banks	Chase-Manhattan, Lehman Brothers, Bank of America,	City-Group, Bank of America, JP Morgan Chase, Wells Fargo, Wachovia, U.S. Bancorp, Capital One Financial, SunTrust Banks, National City, Bank of New York, PNC Financials, State Street Corp., BB&T Corp., Fifth Third Bancorp, Regional Financial, Keycorp, Mellon Financial, Marshal & Ilsley, Comerica, Northern Trust Corp., M&T Bancorp, Synovus Financial, Zions Bancorp, Commerce Bancorp, Popular, First Horizon National Corp., Compass Bancshares, Huntington Bancshares, Colonial Bancgroup, Associated Banc

Source: Author's own.

Note: See also Trout (2004: 1–12).

customers by a standardized, low-cost theater complex requiring fewer screens, less sophisticated projection technology, less maintenance and with a single theater manager. Through its centralized purchasing it pays lower movie rents; its rural locations command less payroll costs, less land or lease costs, and rock-bottom corporate overhead (of two percent compared to industry average of five percent). Operating in small town communities enables Carmike Cinemas to personalize its marketing via known sponsors and patrons, schools and institutions. Carmike is now the largest theater chain in the U.S.—it owes its rapid growth to its disciplined concentration on small markets (Porter 1996: 77). The company quickly sells any big-city theaters that comes to it as part of an acquisition.

Jiffy Lube International represents focused differentiation—national and international lubricants. Its highly focused brand of auto service is one that stands for a certain type of service idea (oil change), in the arena of unfocused service called auto repair. If you extended the service line by other product lines or service variations, the customer mind would lose focus. [See *Business Transformation Exercise 1.9*]

As a contrast, a brand like Chevrolet means so many things that it means nothing to a given customer. Scott, the leading brand of toilet tissues, extended its name into Scotties, Scotkins, ScotTowels, and soon, the customers lost focus. Brand extensions and product line extensions, while good in themselves, pay a heavy price of losing customer focus and loyalty. Just at this time, the likes of Mr. Whipple and his squeezable Charmin tissue arrived on the scene. It did not take too long for Charmin to become the number one tissue. The more you lose focus, the more vulnerable you become. Similarly, for years P&G's Crisco was the leading shortening. Then the world turned to vegetable oil, and, of course, P&G came with Crisco Oil. Nevertheless, the big winner in the corn-oil melee was Mazola. Later, when no-cholesterol corn oil margarine arrived, Mazola introduced Mazola Corn Oil Margarine. However, the real winner in the corn-oil margarine category was Fleischman's. In each case, the specialist or the well-focused competitor wins. That is, specialization or highly differentiated focus wins (Trout 2004: 31–32).

Pioneering, or being the first to enter a given market, is differentiation. It is much easier to get into the mind of your customer first than to convince them you have a better product or brand than that of the pioneer. If you are first, when your competitors try to copy you, they will be just reinforcing your original idea. The fact that you pioneered the idea, product category or brand, makes you different from your followers and competitors. There are several pioneers that are still first as market leaders: Johnny Black Label since 1820, Chivas Regal since 1825, Glenfidich single malt scotch since 1850, Singer sewing machine since 1851, Anheuser-Busch beer since 1852, Manhattan shirts since 1857, Sherwin Williams paints since 1870, Ivory soap since 1879, and Coca-Cola since 1886, to name a few (Golder and Tellis 1993: 64–65; Stremersch and Tellis 2002).

Being first, however, does not guarantee perpetual differentiation. Your product or brand needs constant innovation and updates. Otherwise, the competitor may erode your market share. For instance, Ampex pioneered VCR in 1956, but today RCA and Matsushita are leading since 1977; Raytheon pioneered microwave ovens in 1946, but today GE, Samsung, and China hold the leading market share. Crescent pioneered dishwashers in early 1900s, but today GE leads the market since 1935. Canton introduced laundry dryers in 1925, but today Whirlpool holds the lead since 1950. Wisk pioneered liquid laundry detergents in 1956, but Liquid Tide (P&G) has been the leader since 1984 (see Golder and Tellis 1993: 64–65). Market leadership is the most powerful way to differentiate a brand. Brand leadership is the most direct way to establish your credentials, and brand credentials are the collateral you put up to guarantee the performance of your brand (Trout 2004: 41).

Attribute ownership is probably the number-one way to differentiate a product or service. A product has several benefits, costs, features, and attributes associated with it, but what makes it stand distinctly superior to others is its specific attribute. Thus, Crest toothpaste is known for its attribute of cavity prevention more than other features such as plaque prevention, teeth whitening, breath freshening, and taste. Intel's Pentium technology still dominates the semiconductor and microprocessor markets. Microsoft's word platform and its willingness to cannibalize its own products by introducing constant updates (e.g., WP 1995, WP 1998, XP 2000, WP 2002, WP 2004, WP 2006, WP 2008) has made it highly differentiated and undefeatable in the office software industry.

Gillette (before its buyout by P&G in 2005) used to quickly replace its existing blade with a new idea—it had two-bladed razors (Atra), shock-absorbent razors (Sensor), and three-bladed razors (Mach 3). A rolling company gathers few competitors. When Bic introduced the disposable razor, Gillette quickly countered it with its twin-blade disposable (Good News), and soon dominated that category. An aggressive leader always blocks competitive moves. By 2004, Gillette owned over 60 percent of the blade market. That was a differentiation leadership. Unfortunately, however, Gillette stopped rolling after 2002, developed no new innovative products after Mach 3, and quickly began to fail, its stock plummeted, and P&G bought it in 2005. Attribute ownership has to be maintained vigorously.

Category ownership is another differentiation strategy. Thus, we associate computers with IBM, PCs with Dell, iPods with Apple, copiers with Xerox, telephones with AT&T, colas with Coke, chocolates with Hershey's, ketchup with Heinz, coffee house with Starbucks, stock brokers with Merrill Lynch, office software with Microsoft, French fries with McDonald's, fried chicken with KFC, cereals with Kellogg, Aron Streit with matzo breads, laundry detergents with P&G's Tide, sewing machines with Singer, tires with Goodyear, cameras with Kodak, shampoos with P&G's Head & Shoulders, safety razors with Gillette, and flashing batteries with Eveready. These category ownerships have continued to differentiate specific companies and dominate the world markets for over decades. Consumers will believe whatever you say about your product, if they perceive you as a leader in that product category.

Sales leadership also differentiates. For instance, Toyota Camry is still the best-selling car in America. Other sales leaderships may be restricted—for instance, Chrysler's Dodge Caravan is the top-selling minivan; Ford Explorer is the top-selling SUV; Cadillac is the best-selling luxury car, and so on. Sales leadership differentiates because people tend to buy what a great number of people buy.

Technology leadership can also differentiate. Thus, the Austrian rayon fiber manufacturer, Lenzing, is a world leader in viscose fiber technology; New York's Corning leads the world in silicon glass technologies; Intel leads in Pentium technologies; IBM in supercomputer technologies; Canon in copier technologies; Silicon Graphics in visual workstation and high performance computing technologies; GM in power-train technologies; Ford in assembly line technologies; and Toyota in hybrid technologies. These companies differentiate themselves because they pioneered many of the industry's technological and market breakthroughs related to their dominant technology. [See *Business Transformation Exercise 1.10.*]

Whatever the basis of strategic positioning and strategic differentiation, variety, need or access, or a combination of the three, it is the unique set of activities on the supply side that makes the difference that must respond to a unique set of customers on the demand side. However, strategic positioning is not enough for SCA; though it is enough for competitive advantage (CA) for a short while. The reason is that the competitor could imitate the company's unique set of activities in at least two ways:

1. **Repositioning to Match the Superior Performer**: For instance, J. C. Penney has been repositioning itself following Sears to a more upscale, fashion-oriented, soft-goods retailer. This is a repositioning strategy. K-Mart tried to reposition itself matching Wal-Mart but failed. Most gas stations reposition themselves against their immediate neighbor competitors.
2. **Straddling the Superior Performer**: The imitator matches the benefits and offerings of the superior performer while maintaining its existing position. For instance, Continental Airlines while remaining a full-service airline was desperately trying to match Southwest Airlines, a limited-service airline, by offering a similar limited airline service, and called it Continental Lite.

However, how can you fight repositioning and straddling among your competitors? By trade-offs, says Porter (1996: 68–69). A trade-off implies more of one thing that necessitates less of another. Trade-offs occur when activities of a company become incompatible. An airline cannot be full-service and point-to-point semi-service on the same routes. Consider Neutrogena soap: its variety-based product positioning strategy is based on a "kind to skin", residue-free soap formulated for pH balance. Its target markets are dermatologists and drug stores. Neutrogena avoids price promotions, advertises in medical journals, sends direct mail to doctors, attends medical conferences, and performs research at its own Skincare Institute. In choosing this specialist position, Neutrogena had to stay away from the popular market of the deodorants and skin softeners that many customers like in their soap and also sacrifice large volume potential of selling through supermarkets. Neutrogena uses a slow, more expensive manufacturing process to mold its fragile soap, unlike those of Ivory or Dove soap brands. It is by such costly trade-offs that Neutrogena protected itself from its straddling or repositioning competitors.

A host of improper trade-offs grounded Continental Lite. While straddling with Southwest Airlines, it hung to its main hubs operating in major cities and with its primary airports. It ticketed using travel agents. It also did inter-airline baggage transfer—all these things that Southwest carefully and consistently avoided. Lite's planes were delayed leaving congested hub cities or slowed at the gate by baggage transfers. Late flights and cancellations generated over thousand complaints a day. Travel agent commissions, multiple types of aircraft and their expensive maintenance, and the additional costs of baggage transfers hiked the prices of its tickets. Lite lost hundreds of millions of dollars, and the CEO lost his job. These are straddling penalties. *Quality is not always free.* You cannot offer quality service of full-service airlines with prices of point-to-point airline services. [See *Business Transformation Exercise 1.11.*]

CHOOSING THE RIGHT STRATEGIC APPROACH

Typical corporate strategy discussions start with an analysis of the business environment of markets and competition to judge their attractiveness and growing opportunities. Against this analysis, companies next assess their own strengths and weaknesses, technologies and capabilities, and accordingly, carve out a strategic position where they can outperform their rivals by building a SCA. To obtain such a SCA, a company adopts a competing mindset that generally chooses either to differentiate itself from the competition for a premium price or to pursue low costs. Alternately, better companies choose an innovative mindset of creating technological and market breakthroughs, creating new market spaces, offering new products, and the like. The organization aligns its value-chain accordingly, and streamlines its procurement, designing, production, distribution, and marketing strategies in the process. Based on these strategies, corporate executives propose financial targets and make budget allocations. Table 1.5 sketches an eightfold strategy path that arises from high versus low market attractiveness, high versus low corporate resources and capabilities, and innovating versus competing mindsets. Highly diversified companies could represent a combination of many cells and strategic approaches.

Organizational or corporate strategic planning, therefore, has several constituent component stages:

a. Assess the attractiveness of your target markets.
b. Assess your firm's corresponding resources, human skills, and technological capabilities.
c. Assess your predominant corporate mindset, whether it is mere competing (combating red oceans) or radically innovating (exploring blue oceans).
d. Given (a) to (c), align your talents and resources to respond to the market opportunity and growth that you analyzed under (a) and (b).

Table 1.5 illustrates this approach. Given this four-stage analysis, we can easily understand, assess, and classify major corporate strategies of the last decade. This approach is illustrated in Table 1.2 (last column).

The underlying logic in Table 1.5 is that the company's strategic options are bounded by the environment. In other words, *industry or market structure shapes strategy*. This logic or the structure-response-performance paradigm of industrial organization economics has dominated the practice of corporate and organizational strategy for the past 30 years (see Sherer 1970). In this deterministic view, strategy and causality flow from external conditions down to corporate decisions that seek to capitalize on these conditions.

Instead, let strategy define the structure. That is, instead of letting the environment define your strategy, design and formulate a strategy that defines your market and its environment—this is *blue ocean strategy* (Kim and Mauborgne 2004, 2009). Typical examples when strategy defined the industry structure are Ford's Model T car of 1908, Internet in 1992, Amazon.com and eBay in 1994, Nintendo's Wii in 1998, Sony's Play-Stations I and II in 1999 and 2001, Nokia's cell phone in 2002, and Apple's iPod, iTunes and iPhones in 2003–05.

The fundamental logic of blue ocean strategies is from the emerging school of economics called "endogenous growth" (see Romer 1994). This paradigm suggests that the ideas and actions of individual players can shape the economic and industrial landscape. That is, strategy can shape external structure. Kim and Mauborgne (2009) call this the "reconstructionist" approach. The reconstructionist approach is particularly appropriate when the markets are saturated, when industries are stagnant, and consumers are disenchanted with existing products and services (see Table 1.5). In the current recessionary environment and depressing market conditions, reconstructionist strategies of creating new products, new markets, new job opportunities, and new consumer lifestyles are critically important. [See *Business Transformation Exercise 1.12.*]

STRATEGIC CORPORATE CONTEXT

Experienced executives know that all strategic decisions and tactics depend heavily on context, and the main context is the customer. As early as August 1960, Theodore Levitt wrote in his most cited (HBR) article "Marketing Myopia" that businesses should stop defining themselves by what they produce and

TABLE 1.5   Choosing the Right Strategic Approach: Structuralist versus Reconstructionist Strategies

Industry/ market attractiveness	Firm's resources and capabilities	Firm's strategic mindset	Strategic approach	Strategic outcomes	Industry examples
High (growth, profitability, opportunity; size, stability, infrastructure)	High	Innovating	Reconstructionist	Radical innovation Technological breakthroughs Creating new industries and market spaces	Apple, GE, Sony, Audi, Amazon.com, eBay, Intel, Microsoft
		Competing	Structuralist	High differentiation Market breakthroughs Medium tech breakthroughs	Toyota, Honda, J&J, P&G, IBM, HP, Dell, Boeing, Airbus, Wal-Mart, Ikea
	Low	Innovating	Reconstructionist	Marketing breakthroughs Incremental innovations Medium differentiation	All big Casinos, Southwest, Cirque du Soleil
		Competing	Structuralist	Cost containment Medium differentiation Aggressive marketing Targeting new markets	GMC, Ford, Chrysler/Fiat, Las Vegas, K Mart, TJ Max, Ann Hauser Busch
Low (BOP; cut-throat competition, low profit margins, volatile markets)	High	Innovating	Reconstructionist	Market breakthroughs Creating new spaces Catalytic innovations Social entrepreneurship Global sustainability	Grameen Bank, Ashoka, World eye-glass, World life-saving drug companies
		Competing	Structuralist	High differentiation New market spaces Low-cost-high-quality market offerings Creative rebates	Dubai, Bangalore, Mumbai, Emerging nations
	Low	Innovating	Reconstructionist	Catalytic innovations Social entrepreneurship Social courage Social innovations Humanization Philanthropy	Mahatma Gandhi, Martin L. King, Habitat for humanity, Mother Teresa, Nelson Mandela
		Competing	Structuralist	City revitalization City rezoning Tax havens FDI incentives Government subsidies Good law and order Patent and copyrights Good infrastructure	Cleveland, Raleigh, Pittsburgh, Atlanta, Atlantic City, Grand Rapids, Detroit

Source: Author's own.

Note: See also Kim and Mauborgne (2009).

instead reorient themselves toward customer needs, toward what consumers really seek. Accordingly, Levitt advises corporate and organizational executives to make their industry customer-oriented, and not product-oriented. In order to create, develop, and retain one's customers, the entire corporation must be viewed as customer-value creating and customer-satisfying organism. That is, the management must think of itself not as producing just a product or service but as providing customer-creating value satisfaction and delight. Customer orientation should continuously inform and transform every part and division of the company. Otherwise, the company will be a series of pigeonholed parts, with no consolidating sense of purpose or direction.

For instance, the railroad industry in North America failed because it was railroad-product oriented and not transportation (customer-need) oriented. At the same time, the auto industry flourished, especially under Henry Ford, because it fashioned its production system (e.g., assembly line) to respond to market needs and conditions. Ford responded to customer needs with an affordable car at US$500 in 1907, all the way to 1912—and the Model T car was a perfect response. He standardized the car and mass-produced it, precisely because of his low-pricing strategy. That is, he did not mass-produce the car so that he could achieve economies of scale and, thus, afford the low US$500 price tag. He focused on the less affordable customer, and there were millions of them in 1907 in the U.S., and accordingly, designed the Model T car, which, in turn, needed the mass assembly line to achieve the required scale economies.

STRATEGIC FIT

In highly competitive situations, it is misleading to explain SCA or even success by specifying individual strengths (Barney 1991, 2001a), core competencies (Prahalad and Hamel 1990), or critical resources (Priem and Butler 2001a, 2001b). That is, the competitive values of individual activities, individual skills and specializations are not enough. These company competencies and resources must fit with the main corporate mission, vision, scope, and strategy; we cannot decouple them from the entire system or the strategy. The strategic fit constitutes a company's SCA: It is harder for a rival to match an array of tightly interlocked activities whose combined synergy systems generate the unique strength in which the company thrives.

In this connection, it is more useful to think in terms of "themes" that pervade many activities, such as low cost, specific type of customer service, or a special value delivered to the customer. Such themes are embodied in nests of tightly linked, first-order, second-order, and third-order activities (Porter 1996: 73). For instance, Southwest's activities complemented one another in ways that created real economic value. The better the strategic fit among its activities, the better its SCA.

There are three types of fit:

1. **Consistency**: A first-order fit or *consistency* occurs between each activity and the overall strategy. Consistency spells single-mindedness in the corporation and assures that the SCA of each activity accumulates and does not cancel out. It did so in the case of Southwest but eroded in the case of Continental Lite. A consistent strategy is easy to communicate to customers, employees, and other stakeholders.
2. **Reinforcement**: A second-order fit occurs when activities are *reinforcing*. Neutrogena, for instance, markets to upscale hotels where its products are packaged with its other soaps. Once guests try Neutrogena products in a luxury hotel, they are more likely to purchase them at the drug store

or ask their doctor about it. Thus, Neutrogena's luxury hotel and medical marketing activities reinforce each other.

3. **Optimization**: A third-order fit *optimizes* the marketing effort. Coordination and information exchanges across activities eliminate redundancy and minimize waste. For instance, Gap, a retailer of casual clothes, considers product availability in its stores a critical element of its strategy. It either holds store inventory or restocks almost daily from its three major warehouses in the U.S. depending upon the demand. The emphasis is on daily restocking, so that in-store inventory levels are low but always available on demand. True to its name "Gap," it carries inventory that supermarkets do not carry: casual wear *basic items* in all available colors, shapes, and sizes that fit all, and representing almost all national brands. The correct fit that Gap strives for minimizes alteration costs for the customers. Gap has an inventory turnover ratio of 7.5 per year, while comparable retailers have 3.5. Rapid stocking can also cover the latest fads and fashions in casual wear.

Under all three types of fit, there is a systems effect. The whole matters more than its individual parts. "Competitive advantage grows out of the entire system of activities" (Porter 1996: 73). The fit among activities substantially reduces costs or increases differentiation, and makes imitation difficult. [See *Business Transformation Exercise 1.13.*]

Often, rivals tend to match or replicate an activity or two of their leading competitor. Amazon.com did this in relation to eBay's competitive bidding, but did not totally succeed as did eBay. Barnes & Noble tried to imitate Amazon.com in Internet marketing of books and CDs, and is barely catching up to match Amazon.com's strengths. K mart tried to replicate or even buy the cross-docking inventory management system of Wal-Mart but did not succeed.

The big three U.S. automakers tried to replicate for a decade and more the TQM techniques of the Japanese automakers but did not yet realize either zero defects or zero recalls. Continental Lite tried to imitate Southwest Airline's point-to-point low-cost airline service but failed and was grounded. Child World and Lionel Leisure tried to imitate the best-fit activity system of Toys R Us and did not succeed.

It is difficult to match the entire system of synergies of several-order fit activities of the successful competitor. Most of the imitating companies "homogenized competition" (Porter 1996: 75) and tried to replicate this homogenized version to fall flat in their face. Companies imitate one another in "a type of herd behavior," each assuming rivals know something they do not.

CONCLUDING SYNTHESIS

Given one's corporate mission, vision, values, objectives, and scope, various scholars emphasize different aspects of strategies as follows:

- A strategy is the creation of a unique and valuable position involving a different set of activities.
- The quintessence of strategy is *differentiation* that counts with the customer and the competition. Competitive strategy is about being different. It means deliberately choosing a different set of activities to deliver a unique mix of value.
- The essence of a strategy is in the activities—choosing to perform activities differently or to perform different activities than rivals. Otherwise, a strategy is nothing more than a marketing slogan that will not withstand competition (Porter 1996: 64–68).

- Strategy is "what makes you unique and what is the best way to put that difference into the minds of your customers and prospects" (Trout 2004: xiv).
- Strategy is all about being different. In the land of positioning, a successful strategy is based on finding a way to be different from your sea of competitors (Trout 2004: 35).
- A well-understood statement of strategy aligns behavior within the business. It allows everyone in the organization to make individual choices that reinforce one another, rendering all the thousands of employees exponentially more effective (Collis and Rukstad 2008: 84).
- Strategy embodies clear priorities, based on understanding the strengths we need to preserve and the weaknesses that threaten our prosperity the most.
- Strategy implies a strategic fit between various activities of the firm. The first-order fit or consistency, for instance, between product designing and promotional marketing activities is essential; a second-order fit or reinforcement between various marketing activities (e.g., pricing, sizing, labeling, packaging, distributing, advertising, promoting, and sales service) is critical; and a third-order fit or optimizing all the activities of the firm along the entire value-chain (upstream, midstream, and downstream) generates long-term strategic strength (Porter 1996).
- Strategy addresses what to do, as also, what not to do. That is, defining the objective, scope, and advantage requires trade-offs that are fundamental to strategy. In this connection, *the essence of a strategy is choosing what not to do.*
- Without trade-offs there would be no need for choice and thus no need for strategy. It is through proper and timely trade-offs that one can improve upon operational effectiveness.

In highly competitive situations, however, it is misleading to explain success by specifying individual strengths, core competencies or critical resources. That is, the competitive values of individual activities, individual skills, and specializations are not enough; company competencies and resources must fit with the main corporate mission, vision, scope, and strategy; we cannot decouple them from the entire system or the strategy. The strategic fit constitutes a company's SCA: it is harder for a rival to match an array of tightly interlocked activities whose combined synergy systems generate the unique strength in which the company thrives (Porter 1996).

BUSINESS TRANSFORMATION EXERCISES

1.1 Given one's corporate mission, vision, values, objectives, and scope, various scholars emphasize different aspects of strategies as follows:

- A strategy is the creation of a unique and valuable position involving a different set of activities.
- The quintessence of strategy is *differentiation* that counts with the customer and the competition.
- Competitive strategy is about being different.
- It means deliberately choosing a different set of activities to deliver a unique mix of value.
- The essence of a strategy is in the activities—choosing to perform activities differently or to perform different activities than rivals. Otherwise, a strategy is nothing more than a marketing slogan that will not withstand competition (Porter 1996: 64–68).
- Strategy is "what makes you unique and what is the best way to put that difference into the minds of your customers and prospects" (Trout 2004: xiv).
- Strategy is all about being different. In the land of positioning, a successful strategy is based on finding a way to be different from your sea of competitors (Trout 2004: 35).

- A well-understood statement of strategy aligns behavior within the business. It allows everyone in the organization to make individual choices that reinforce one another, rendering all the thousands of employees exponentially more effective (Collis and Rukstad 2008: 84).
- Strategy embodies clear priorities, based on understanding the strengths we need to preserve and weaknesses that threaten our prosperity the most.
- Strategy addresses what to do, as also, what not to do.

Given these strategy propositions or definitions, do the following executive exercises:

a. What is the one common underlying business model that all these propositions presume?
b. Is this presumption valid and universal?
c. What is the function of these strategy models in a monopolistic or monopsonistic market, and why?
d. To what extent can you ignore or bypass competition and still meaningfully craft your effective strategy (see Kim and Mauborgne 2004, 2005)?
e. What are the basic assumptions, presuppositions, and generalizations that each strategy proposition makes and to what effect? [For useful definitions of these terms, see Chapters 3–4.]
f. What do you consider is the most critical and important definitional proposition among these for your company and why?
g. What unique and valuable proposition does your company offer, and how successful?
h. What is the unique and non-imitable differentiation of that value proposition and why?
i. Which among these propositions is the most critical in implementing your company strategy effectively, and why?
j. Which among these propositions is the least critical in implementing your company strategy effectively, and why?

[Hints: Regarding (a): Some of the common underlying business models presumed are: There is a market that is large, stable, accessible, and profitable where strategy works; there is market opportunity to exploit via differentiation; that differentiation works, is needed, and can be exploited, and so on.]

1.2 Table 1.1 presents a hierarchy of corporate strategic statements. Crafting a strategic statement requires a clear understanding and communication of corporate mission, vision, value, objectives, scope, and corporate advantage, and in that order. A first critical step in creating a great strategy is a careful analysis of the industry landscape you want to enter, given your competitive landscape.

a. Rewrite Table 1.1 in all its 6 x 3 matrix details to describe your company as it was 5 to 10 years ago. Explain your entries.
b. Rewrite Table 1.1 in all its 6 x 3 matrix details to describe your company as it is now. Explain and defend your entries.
c. Get two of your top executive colleagues to do the same as in (b), and then compare notes. What do you learn and why?
d. Rewrite Table 1.1 in all its 6 x 3 matrix details to describe your company you want it to be in 3 to 5 years. Explain and defend your entries.
e. Get two of your top executive colleagues to do the same as in (d), and then compare notes. What do you learn and why?
f. How will you convince the Board of Directors about it? What are your fears and premonitions in this regard and why?
g. What are the greatest strengths of your Strategy Template?
h. What are the greatest weaknesses of your Strategy Template?
i. Thus, finalize your version of Table 1.1 for your company as a strategy formulation template for the next 3–5 years.

1.3 Figure 1.1 captures the dynamic inputs, process, and outputs of a corporate strategy. Given corporate mission, vision, values, goals, and objectives, the corporation studies its industry landscape, filtering it through its understanding of its competitive landscape. Corporate process includes corporate structures, corporate focus, and organizational learning, each influencing the other. Figure 1.1 depicts several loops and iterative processes—thus indicating the "wicked" problem that every corporate strategy implies (Camillus 2008). That is, there are constant interactions between all nine components of a corporate strategy, which make it dynamic, unpredictable, risk-prone, but controllable with careful research and strategic planning. The measure of a successful corporate strategy, however, is the measure of its corporate performance and social impact.

   a. Redesign Figure 1.1 in all its nine interdependent boxes to describe your company as it was 5 to 10 years ago. Explain your entries and interdependencies.
   b. Redesign Figure 1.1 in all its nine interdependent boxes to describe your company as it is now. Explain and defend your entries and interdependencies.
   c. Get two of your top executive colleagues to do the same as in (b), and then compare notes. What do you learn and why?
   d. Redesign Figure 1.1 in all its nine interdependent boxes to describe your company you want it to be in 3 to 5 years. Explain and defend your entries and interdependencies.
   e. Get two of your top executive colleagues to do the same as in (d), and then compare notes. What do you learn and why?
   f. How will you convince the Board of Directors about it? What are your fears and premonitions in this regard and why?
   g. What are the greatest strengths of your Strategy Design Template?
   h. What are the greatest weaknesses of your Strategy Design Template?
   i. Thus, finalize your version of Figure 1.1 for your company as a strategy formulation design template for the next 3–5 years.

1.4 Tactics deal with matters of arrangement; they are skillful methods and procedures used to gain an end—that is, they follow and fulfill a concrete strategic plan. They represent the implementation and execution of strategy in an operations-oriented, make-things-happen activity aimed at performing core business activities in a strategy-supportive manner (Thomson, Strickland, and Gamble 2008: 42). A strategy-execution process implies tactics that include:

   • Recruiting, developing, and retaining leadership skills and operational expertise for supporting strategy and for combating competition.
   • Allocating ample resources to those activities critical to strategic success.
   • Enforcing and ensuring policies and procedures that facilitate strategy execution.
   • Accumulating best practices and organizational routines that enable, assess and improve strategy-execution on a continual basis.
   • Installing information and operating systems that enable company personnel to fulfill their strategy-executions roles and responsibilities.
   • Motivating, training, and empowering key strategy-execution people by proper training, rewards, and incentives.
   • Creating and sustaining a company culture and work climate conducive to successful strategy execution.

Some of these tactics are included in Figure 1.1 in one or other of the three blocks in the middle column of "corporate process." Using the above list of tactics, and others of your coinage, do the following executive exercises.

a. Each tactic must have an element of differentiation. How would you ensure that any activity you choose to include in the "process" block is differentiating the company from its rivals? For instance, a tactic could be to redesign your product smaller, bigger, lighter, heavier, cheaper or more expensive, high functionality but low form, or vice versa (as in P&G), or it could be a different distribution-transportation-logistics system (e.g., Wal-Mart).

b. If strategy is essentially differentiation, then so must tactics be differentiating activities and procedures. For instance, a tactic must have a competitive angle, it must be competitive in the total marketing arena, and not just competitive in relation to one or two products or services. How would you ensure that any tactic procedure you choose to adopt in the "process" block is differentiating the company from its rivals?

c. A tactic is a competitive advantage; it must be designed to maintain that competitive advantage. How would you ensure that your tactics in the "process" block are providing that sustained competitive advantage (SCA)?

d. A tactic is communications and action oriented, while a strategy is innovation, product, service, or company oriented. How would you ensure that any tactic you include in the "process" block is clearly communicated, doable, and action-driven, thus additionally differentiating the company from its rivals?

e. A tactic is specialization, while a strategy tends to be general. A tactic is one thing in which you are very skilled as compared to your competitors. Hence, how would you ensure that any skill-activity you include in the "process" block is differentiating the company from its rivals in terms of specialization?

1.5 There are three components to a good strategy statement—*objective, scope,* and *advantage.* A company's top executive should be crystal clear about all three components. These elements are a simple yet sufficient to address competitive interaction over unbounded terrain (Collis and Rukstad 2008: 84):

- **The End Objective**: Any strategy statement should begin with the definition of the ends that the strategy is designed to achieve, with a time frame and a method for reaching it.
- **The Scope**: Most firms compete in an unbounded landscape, and hence need to define the scope or domain of the business, the part of the landscape the firm will operate, and state its boundaries beyond which it will not venture presently.
- **The Advantage**: How is your differentiation advantage to reach the scope and the objective? What are your core competencies and skills that make you deliver your product better than others do? Why would your target customer patronize your business more than the competing alternatives?

Further, defining the objective, scope, and advantage requires trade-offs that are fundamental to strategy. In this connection, the essence of a strategy is choosing what *not* to do. Without trade-offs there would be no need for choice and thus no need for strategy. It is through proper and timely trade-offs that one can improve upon operational effectiveness.

Using this paradigm, undertake these executive business transformation exercises:

a. Define the end objective of your company as clearly, succinctly, and persuasively as possible.

b. Define the scope in geography, time, pace, space, and economies of your company as clearly, succinctly, and measurably as possible.

c. Given (a) and (b), define the sustainable competitive advantage of your company as clearly, persuasively, and measurably as possible.

d. Get two of your top executive colleagues to do the same as in (a), (b), and (c).

e. Compare colleague-notes on the end objective, the scope, and the advantage. What do you learn? Are you different, and why?

f. Next, specify your strategy "trade-offs" under each, the end objective, the scope, and the advantage.

    g. Get two of your top executive colleagues to do the same as in (f).

    h. Compare colleague-stated trade-offs on the end objective, the scope, and the advantage. What do you learn? Are you different, and why?

    i. Hence, what does your stated strategy choose what to do, and what not to do, and why?

1.6   Table 1.2 sketches major types of corporate strategies based on strategic environment, strategic choices or activities, strategic trade-offs, and strategic desired outcomes. The listing of strategies in Table 1.2 is not MECE. Given corporate mission, vision, and objectives, as a corporate executive to be you must determine what strategy is best for the company, by undertaking the following executive exercises:

    a. What are your competition-driven strategic activities, and why?

    b. What are your competition-driven strategic trade-offs, and why?

    c. What are your competition-driven strategic advantages, and why?

    d. What are your customer-driven strategic activities, and why?

    e. What are your customer-driven strategic trade-offs, and why?

    f. What are your customer-driven strategic advantages, and why?

    g. What are your technology-driven strategic activities, and why?

    h. What are your technology-driven strategic trade-offs, and why?

    i. What are your technology-driven strategic advantages, and why?

    j. What are your organization-learning-driven strategic activities, and why?

    k. What are your organization-learning-driven strategic trade-offs, and why?

    l. What are your organization-learning-driven strategic advantages, and why?

1.7   Table 1.3 presents taxonomy of corporate strategies based on the development and alignment of three strategic propositions that relate to customer value, organizational execution, and corporate profits. Based on this paradigm as proposed by Kim and Mauborgne (2009), the listing of strategies in Table 1.3 is mutually exclusive and collectively exhaustive (MECE). Given your corporate analysis and experience, do the following executive exercises:

    a. What current companies do you identify as following no strategic propositions at all, and why? What was their subsequent fate?

    b. What current companies do you identify as following only the profit proposition, and why? What was their subsequent fate?

    c. What current companies do you identify as following only the execution proposition, and why? What was their subsequent fate?

    d. What current companies do you identify as following only the customer value proposition, and why? What was their subsequent fate?

    e. What current companies do you identify as following only execution and value propositions without regard to profits, and why? What was their subsequent fate?

    f. What current companies do you identify as following only execution and profit propositions without regard to customer value, and why? What was their subsequent fate?

    g. What current companies do you identify as following only value and profit propositions without regard to organizational execution, and why? What was their subsequent fate?

    h. Finally, what past and current companies do you identify as developing and aligning all three strategic propositions of value, execution, and profits, and why? What was their subsequent success?

1.8   *Strategic planning* sets the competitive direction, dictates market-offering planning, tells how to communicate internally and externally, and tells you what to focus on. Market success is not about having the right people, the right attitude, the right tools, the right role models, or the right organization. They all help, but they do not put you over the top. Strategy and strategic planning does. Strategic is about "next-generation" planning in technology, planning of products that satisfy next generation of customer needs, wants and desires, given market dynamics, competitor development, government regulation, supplier and creditor markets, and globalization factors. Thinking strategically starts with the reflection of the deepest nature of an undertaking and on the central challenges it poses. It develops with understanding of focus and timing. Given this, define your *strategic thinking and planning* that involves minimally the following critical issues:

a. **Who are you?** What business, market, industry are you in? Who is your competitor? Who are your customers? What are their needs that you can serve? These questions relate to vision, mission and identity, strategic thinking, and strategic planning.

b. **What are you?** What are your tangible resources? What are your intangible resources? What are your strengths? What are your weaknesses? What is your sustainable competitive advantage? These questions relate to strategic inputs, strategic resources, inputs mapping, and inputs sourcing.

c. **Where are you?** What is your position in innovation, patents, new products, new markets, new product sales, market share, profits, growth, Wall Street assessment, shareholder satisfaction, employee commitment, creditor approval, supplier trust, and customer delight? These questions relate to assessment, evaluation, strategic mapping, and process mapping.

d. **What is your future?** Where do you want to go? Why do you want to go there? How do you reach there (strategic architecture)? When do you reach there? How would you know that you have reached there? Who do you want to be 3, 5, 7, or 10 years from now? These questions relate to the future, industry foresight, direction, destiny, outcomes-mapping, and strategic architecture.

e. **Hence what shall you do?** How do you reinvent the future? How shall you identify new horizons and new opportunities in them? How do you reshape the industry to your advantage? What new resources shall you build? What new core competencies should you generate? What new core products should you develop? What new functionalities should your products and services create for your customers? How do you deliver old functionalities in new ways? How do you rewrite industry rules and create new competitive spaces? These questions relate to strategy, strategy making, strategy process, and strategy mapping.

1.9 Strategic positions arise from three different sources that are not mutually exclusive and often overlap: customers' needs, customers' accessibility, or the variety of a company's products and services. Hence, there are three different types of strategic positioning (Porter 1996: 65–67):

- **Variety-based Positioning**: If you can offer unique variety of products or services using distinctive set of activities, then you must pursue variety-based strategic positioning.
- **Needs-based Positioning**: This strategy targets a segment of customers that has differing needs that can be served with a unique set of activities. Differences in needs will not translate into strategic positions unless the company launches the set of activities to serve those needs *also differ*.
- **Access-based Positioning**: This strategy targets segments of customers who are accessible in different ways. Access can be a function of customer geography or customer scale—or of anything that requires a different set of activities to reach customers in the best way.

Analyze the strategic positioning of your market offerings, using the following exercises:

a. Is it variety-based positioning? Why or why not? Explain and illustrate your view using company products and services.

b. Is it needs-based positioning? Why or why not? Explain and illustrate your view using company products and services.

c. Is it access-based positioning? Why or why not? Explain and illustrate your view using company products and services.

d. Is it a combination of variety- and needs-based positioning? If so, explain your view using specific company products and services that illustrate this two-way combination.

e. Is it a combination of variety- and access-based positioning? If so, explain your view using specific company products and services that illustrate this two-way combination.

f. Is it a combination of needs- and access-based positioning? If so, explain your view using specific company products and services that illustrate this twofold combination.

g. Is it a combination of variety-, needs-, and access-based positioning? If so, explain your view using specific company products and services that illustrate this three-way combination.

h. Lastly, is it a combination of neither variety-, needs-, nor access-based positioning? If so, explain your view using specific company products and services that illustrate this null combination.

i. Thus, is Porter's (1996) threefold list of strategic positioning *mutually exhaustive*, if not mutually exclusive?

1.10 There are other established strategies for strategic differentiation. Some of these described by Porter (1996) are:

- *Pioneering*, or being the first to enter a given market, is differentiation. It is much easier to get into the mind of your customer first than to convince them you have a better product or brand than that of the pioneer. Pioneering, however, does not guarantee perpetual differentiation. Your product or brand needs constant innovation and updates.
- *Attribute ownership* is probably the number-one way to differentiate a product or service. A product has several benefits, costs, features, and attributes associated with it, but what makes it stand distinctly superior to others is its specific attribute.
- *Category ownership* is another differentiation strategy. Thus, we associate computers with IBM, PCs with Dell, iPods with Apple, and copiers with Xerox; category ownerships have continued to differentiate specific companies and dominated the world markets for over decades. Consumers tend to believe whatever you say about your product if they perceive you as a leader in that product category.
- *Sales leadership* differentiates. For instance, Toyota Camry is still the best selling car in America.
- *Technology leadership* can also differentiate. Thus, Lenzing is a world leader in viscose fiber technology; Corning leads the world in silicon glass technologies; Intel leads in Pentium technologies and IBM in supercomputer technologies.

Given these differentiating activities, undertake the following executive exercises:

a. What is the level of *pioneering differentiation* in your company in terms of patents, trademarks, licenses, brands, products, and services, and how do you assess it in terms of SCA?

b. What is the level of *attribute-ownership-based differentiation* in your company in terms of patents, trademarks, licenses, brands, products, and services, and how do you assess it in terms SCA?

c. What is the level of *category-ownership-based differentiation* in your company in terms of patents, trademarks, licenses, brands, products, and services, and how do you assess it in terms of SCA?

d. What is the level of *sales-leadership-based differentiation* in your company in terms of patents, trademarks, licenses, brands, products and services, landline and online outlets, and how do you assess it in terms of SCA?

e. What is the level of *technology-leadership-based differentiation* in your company in terms of patents, trademarks, licenses, cross-licenses, brands, products, and services, and how do you assess it in terms of SCA?

1.11   Whatever the basis of strategic positioning and strategic differentiation, variety, need, or access, or a combination of the three, it is the unique set of activities on the supply side that makes the difference that must respond to a unique set of customers on the demand side. However, strategic positioning is not enough for SCA; it may be enough for a competitive advantage (CA) for a short while. The reason is that the competitor could imitate the company's unique set of activities in at least two ways:

- **Repositioning to match the superior performer**: For instance, J. C. Penney has been repositioning itself following Sears to a more upscale, fashion-oriented, soft-goods retailer.
- **Straddling the superior performer**: The imitator matches the benefits and offerings of the superior performer while maintaining its existing position. For instance, Continental Airlines while remaining a full-service airline was desperately trying to match Southwest Airlines, a limited-service airline, is offering, and called it the *Continental Lite*.

How can you fight repositioning and straddling among your competitors? By trade-offs that imply more of one thing that necessitates less of another (Porter 1996: 68–69). Trade-offs occur when activities of a company become incompatible. An airline cannot be a full-service and point-to-point semi-service on the same routes. Given these differentiating considerations, undertake the following executive exercises:

a.   What is the unique set of activities on the supply side that makes the difference that your unique set of customers on the demand side cannot resist?

b.   How will this unique set of activities resist *repositioning to match* on the part of your competitor, and to what lasting effect?

c.   What trade-offs would you offer in this regard, why, and to what effect?

d.   How will this unique set of activities stall *straddling* by your competitor, and to what lasting effect?

e.   What trade-offs would you offer in this regard, why, and to what effect?

f.   To what extent was Neutrogena successful in doing all the above five defense strategies and why?

g.   To what extent was Continental Lite unsuccessful in doing all the above five defense strategies and why?

1.12   Table 1.5 sketches an eightfold strategy path that arises from high versus low market attractiveness, high versus low corporate resources and capabilities, and innovating versus competing mindsets. Highly diversified companies could represent a combination of many cells and strategic approaches.

a.   Identify companies that are in highly attractive markets, with high corporate resources and capabilities, and with highly innovating mindsets? Describe their strategic success.

b.   Identify companies that are in highly attractive markets, with high corporate resources and capabilities, but with highly competing mindsets? Describe their strategic success. How does it compare with those in (a)?

c.   Identify companies that are in highly attractive markets, but with low corporate resources and capabilities, and still with highly innovating mindsets? Describe their strategic success, and compare it to that of companies under (a) and (b).

d.   Identify companies that are in highly attractive markets, but with low corporate resources and capabilities, and with highly competing mindsets? Describe their strategic success and compare it to that of companies under (a) to (c).

e.   Identify companies that are in low attractive markets, but with high corporate resources and capabilities, and with highly innovating mindsets? Describe and explain their strategic success and compare it to that of companies under (a) to (d).

f.   Identify companies that are in low attractive markets, but with high corporate resources and capabilities, and with highly competing mindsets? Describe and explain their strategic success and compare it to that of companies under (a) to (e).

g. Identify companies that are in low attractive markets, with low corporate resources and capabilities, but with highly innovating mindsets? Describe and explain their strategic success and compare it to that of companies under (a) to (f).

h. Finally, identify companies that are in low attractive markets, are with low corporate resources and capabilities, but with highly competing mindsets? Describe and explain their strategic success and compare it that of companies under (a) to (g).

i. Which among these companies do you consider great and globally sustaining, and why?

1.13 In highly competitive situations, however, it is misleading to explain success by specifying individual strengths, core competencies, or critical resources. That is, the competitive values of individual activities, individual skills, and specializations are not enough; company competencies and resources must fit with the main corporate mission, vision, scope, and strategy; we cannot decouple them from the entire system or the strategy. The strategic fit constitutes a company's SCA: It is harder for a rival to match an array of tightly interlocked activities whose combined synergy systems generate the unique strength in which the company thrives. Accordingly, Michael Porter (1996) describes three levels of strategic fit:

- A first-order fit or *consistency* between each activity and the overall strategy. Consistency spells single-mindedness in the corporation and assures that the SCA of each activity accumulates and does not cancel out.
- A second-order fit occurs when activities are *reinforcing*. Neutrogena, for instance, markets to upscale hotels where its products are packaged with its other soaps. Once guests try Neutrogena in a luxury hotel, they are more likely to purchase it at the drug store or ask their doctor about it. Thus, Neutrogena's luxury hotel and medical marketing activities reinforce each other.
- A third-order fit *optimizes* the marketing effort. Coordination and information exchanges across activities eliminate redundancy and minimize waste. For instance, Gap, a retailer of casual clothes, considers product availability in its stores a critical element of its strategy. It either holds store inventory or restocks almost daily from its three major warehouses in the U.S. depending upon demand. The emphasis is on daily restocking so that in-store inventory levels are low but always available on demand.

Under all three types of fit, there is a *systems effect*: The whole matters more than its individual parts. *Competitive advantage grows out of the entire system of activities* (Porter 1996: 73). Mindful of this three-level framework of strategic fit, do the following business transforming exercises:

a. In your company, how well do company competencies and resources fit with the main corporate mission, vision, scope, and strategy? How do you demonstrate and measure this fit?

b. Specify the first-order fit of this strategic fit of *consistency* between each activity and the overall strategy.

c. Analyze, next, the second-order fit that occurs when various activities are *reinforcing* each other.

d. Thirdly, investigate the third-order fit that *optimizes* the marketing effort. Do coordination and information exchanges across activities eliminate redundancy and minimize waste?

e. Explore the interactive effects of first-order and second-order strategic fits.

f. Explore the interactive effects of first-order and third-order strategic fits.

g. Explore the interactive effects of second-order and third-order strategic fits.

h. Finally, examine the three-way interactive effects of first-order, second-order, and third-order strategic fits.

i. Is this the "systems fit" that Porter (1996: 73) describes?

Chapter 2

Toward a Philosophy of Corporate Transformation Strategies

Adam Smith (1776/1961: 338) pointed out that "Consumption is the sole end and purpose of all production; and the interest of the producer ought to be attended to, only so far as it may be necessary for promoting that of the consumer. The maxim is so perfectly self-evident that it would be absurd to attempt to prove it." In this regard, the aggregate marketing system is involved directly in delivering consumption to society, and this makes the marketing system—both at the aggregate and firm levels—a social institution. Vigorous and growing consumption is the chief indicator of a prosperous and self-confident society, and vigorous consumption requires that consumers are confident of their future earnings and that they enjoy the purchase of consumer goods (Borgmann 2000). In the final analysis, it is consumer confidence and spending that have contributed to the astounding economic boom of the 20th century in the U.S., and in this sense, it is the spending economy or the consuming society that fuels the aggregate marketing system—the latter is as much a social enterprise, as it is corporate genius.

CONSUMER AND CONSUMPTION FOCUSED CORPORATE STRATEGY

If consumption is the sole purpose of a firm, then consumers are the primary purpose or stakeholders of a company. Thus,

- Webster (1988) asserts that everyone in the firm must be charged with responsibility for understanding customers and contributing to developing and delivering value for them.
- The common focus on customer value and relationship management may result in much stronger coordination of the procurement, sales, and marketing functions (Webster 1992).
- The true mission of the firm is to create value for three key constituencies: customers, employees, and investors; but the customers should be treated as "first among equals" because their loyalty is most fluid (Reichheld 1994).

Properly guided and stimulated consumption boosts the economy positively, and hence, promotes economic development and prosperity. Properly guided consumption assumes innovation. The following innovations have upgraded our consumption and prosperity exponentially, thus improving our quality of life:

- Mass agriculture (inorganic foods, organic goods, health foods).
- Speedy transportation (greyhounds, bullet trains, aircraft, air cargo, FedEx).
- Storage (refrigeration, freezing, canning preservatives).
- Financing (credit, revolving credit, debit and credit cards, General Motors Auto-Financing Corporation [GMAC], Ford, GE-Fin).
- Convenience (blenders, dishwasher, microwave, washers and dryers).
- Communication and information (phone, car phones, cello-phones, iPods, iPhones, iTunes, e-mail, Internet, facebook, twitter, blogs).
- Entertainment (radio shows, TV shows, podcasts, webcasts, sportscasts, newscasts, TiVo, iPods, Wii, play-stations, Nintendos, Nickelodeon).

That is why Adam Smith proclaimed consumption as the sole purpose of production. Prosperity implies a higher standard of living and a higher quality of life. Thus, the basic philosophy of any corporate strategy is to support, stimulate, and enhance industrial consumption, and derivatively, consumer consumption.

It is not to brands that consumers are loyal to, but to images and symbols that they produce while they are consumed. Sign value replaces exchange value as the basis of consumption. Consumers are active producers of symbols and signs of consumption, while manufacturers are active producers of products as values. Products as values are not consumed unless and until consumers see relevant meanings, signs, and symbols of their socio-cultural life in them. Modern marketing culture, through its dominance of promotion and advertising over everyday life, prompts, suggests, and sells packaged symbols and meanings (Levy 1959) to help consumers in their signification process. Marketing culture is the transformation of the product from a natural thing into a linguistic and cultural sign. Thus, production and consumption are not ends in themselves—they are means to celebrate and aestheticize life; they are opportunities that invite higher levels of marketing executive responsibility. That is, marketing executive responsibility is expanded with the expanding role of culture today. Even though commodities may have symbolic meanings that go far beyond the intended producer (Barthes 1972), yet responsible marketing executives will carefully design, market, and monitor their products and services; such that they generate culturally uplifting meanings and wholesome consumer behavior (Mascarenhas 2008).

CORPORATE STRATEGY AND CORPORATE LEGITIMACY

Based on the foundational work of Weber (1978) and Parsons (1960), management scholars have considered organizational legitimacy as an anchor point that constructs, constrains, and empowers organizational actors. In general, "legitimacy" relative to businesses refers to socially accepted and expected structures and behaviors. However, the concept of organizational legitimacy is more often invoked than described, and more often described than defined (Suchman 1995). Here are some definitions of legitimacy:

- Legitimization is the process whereby an organization justifies to peers or society (in general) its right to exist (Maurer 1971: 361).

- "Society grants legitimacy and power to business. In the long run, those who do not use power in a manner which society considers responsible will tend to lose it" (Davis 1973: 314).
- Legitimacy also connotes "congruence between the social values associated with or implied by organizational activities and the norms of acceptable behavior in a larger social system" (Dowling and Pfeffer 1975: 122).
- Legitimacy is congruence between the organization and its cultural environment (Meyer and Scott 1983).
- "Legitimacy is a generalized perception or assumption that the actions of an entity are desirable, proper, or appropriate within some socially constructed system of norms, values, beliefs, and definitions" (Suchman 1995: 574).

These definitions of legitimacy stress the evaluative side—organizations are legitimate or legitimized when they are understandable and comparable to existing norms or social expectations, rather than when they are desirable.

Legitimacy is the currency of institutions. For an aspiring institution such as the corporation, the halo of social legitimacy is a difficult achievement often requiring effort and commitment and the steady observance of exacting standards over an extended period of time. Corporations need to put forth legitimate reasons as to why they should exist, why they should be given access to scarce resources, and what distinct benefits they will bring to society that are not already provided by existing institutions. Like trust, legitimacy, however, can vanish very quickly and, once lost, is difficult to regain. When an institution loses legitimacy, external critics call even everyday activities into question, and perfectly sincere actions may be interpreted as disingenuous or masking a hidden agenda. Thus, for organizations and corporations, legitimacy is an important aspect of the social fitness that enables them to secure advantages in economic and political markets and improve their chances of survival. Thus, legitimacy is both a goal and a resource, and corporations compete with another to establish their claims of legitimacy (Khurana 2007: 14, 401).

Thus, the principle of corporate legitimacy assumes that social legitimacy is desirable for firms, and states that society legitimizes businesses as long as they serve and secure the well-being of society as a whole. This principle reflects more a prohibition (of corporate power abuse) than an affirmation of corporate duty (Wood 1991). It states that corporations as social institutions may legitimize their existence by avoiding abuse of their power by regularly engaging in self-criticism and by recognizing that ones self interests are best served by an other-directed behavior. Thus, a corporate strategy is best when it is sustained by corporate legitimacy.

THE CURRENT CONTEXT OF CORPORATE STRATEGY

No strategy functions in a vacuum. All strategy is ultimately customer-focused, whether industrial client or household customer. The specific context of the customer determines the specific strategy designed, planned, and implemented. Thus, to be concrete, we examine the context of (*a*) the broadened role of the customer today, (*b*) the broadened role of societal culture today, and (*c*) the broadened role of corporate environment today.

The Broadened Role of Customers Today

[See Mascarenhas (2008: 109–11)]

In today's economy, the customer defines the nature of the business.

> The business will be defined by its customers, not its products, factories or offices. This is a critical point-in network organizations, it is the ongoing relationship with a set of customers that represents the most important business asset. Marketing as a distinct management function will be responsible for being expert on the customer and keeping the rest of the network organization informed about the customer. (Webster 1992: 14)

This expanded definition of a customer includes within its domain not only the traditional group of end-product consumers, but also distributors, channel members, employees, suppliers, creditors, governments, and even competitors and producers themselves. According to Webster (2000), a consumer is a person who uses or consumes the product, whereas, a customer is an individual or business entity that buys the product, and may include major classes of customers such as intermediaries or channel members (e.g., wholesalers, brokers, agents, retailers) who buy for resale to their customers. Parasuraman and Zinkham (2002) also extend the domain of "customers" to include all members in the various levels of a supply chain (e.g., suppliers, creditors, and business-to-business partners), since all of them basically "buy" business and customer service from the company they supply to or are supplied from. In other words, the major stakeholders of an enterprise are its customers. Customers are individuals, groups, or institutions an enterprise depends upon and serves or intends to serve (prospects) (Freeman 1984; Webster 1994).

In opposition to the classical or modernist view that defines consumers in opposition to producers (i.e., producers as creating value and consumers as destroying and devouring value), the neoclassical or *postmodernist* view considers customers, consumption, and production as part of the value-adding productivity chain (Firat and Venkatesh 1995). A firm survives, grows, and increases its wealth by creating value for its customers (Falkenberg 1996). Products and services are better designed and experienced when they involve customer participation (Lengnick-Hall 1966), customer co-option (Prahalad and Ramaswamy 2000), and customer co-creation (Mascarenhas, Kesavan, and Bernacchi 2004).

Following this new and expanded definition of customers, we may distinguish at least three levels of customers: primary, secondary, and tertiary, in terms of the degree of corporate dependence or interdependence in relation to customers:

1. **Primary customers** are individuals, groups, or institutions (domestic, international, or global target markets) that an enterprise chooses to serve formally and directly. These are hard-core consumers variedly designated as customers, clients, buyers, purchasers, users, or stockholders.
2. **Secondary customers** are individuals, groups, or institutions from target markets (domestic, international, or global) that an enterprise chooses to serve formally and directly, and hence, indirectly and reciprocally, would also choose to serve. The enterprise has (or will have) contracts (with varying degrees of formality and specificity) with these target markets (Lusch and Brown 1996). Examples of secondary customers are creditors, suppliers, employees, labor unions,

business-to-business partners, distributors, agents and brokers, intermediaries, retailers, and local and federal governments.

3. **Tertiary customers** are individuals, communities, or institutions around target markets (domestic, international, or global) that an enterprise chooses to serve informally or indirectly. The enterprise has no formal or direct contracts with these customer groups other than implicit and "relational contracts" (Macneil 1980; Williamson 1985). Tertiary customer orientation is one form of corporate social responsibility. For example, the local communities, especially the needy, poor, handicapped and elderly, local charitable institutions, local community involvement groups, local sports groups, local or global ecology project groups—all of these could be a firm's tertiary customers.

All three layers or levels of customers and the various constituencies they represent are *stakeholders,* as Ansoff (1965) or Freeman (1984) define them. They affect the corporation and/or the corporation affects them. While the concept of stakeholders relates to their relevance to the corporation, the concept of customers specifies the contractual or fiduciary duty the corporation has toward them. As cited earlier, the true mission of the firm is to create value for three key constituencies: customers, employees, and investors; but the customers should be treated as "first among equals" because their loyalty is most fluid (Reichheld 1994). An enterprise engages with customers at every possible level and is characterized by relationships with many groups and individual stakeholders, each with the power to affect the enterprise's performance and/or has a stake in the firm's performance (Freeman 1984). In many cases, both conditions apply. Stakeholders include, but are not limited to, shareholders. In fact, the enterprise is a nexus of customer-oriented contracts between itself and its stakeholders (Jones 1995).

Achrol, Reve, and Stern (1983) provide a similar analysis—the denotation is the same, but not the connotation. They analyze the marketing environment of channel dyads, and distinguish between primary task environment, a secondary task environment, and a macro-environment. The *primary task environment* is composed of a focal dyad's immediate suppliers and customers, in which any impact can be traced back to specific firms and their direct exchange network with the marketing firm. The primary task environment, in turn, is assumed to be affected by the *secondary task environment*, which comprises actors that are indirectly connected to the focal dyad through exchange relations with actors in the primary task environment. Finally, the *macro-environment* is an amorphous entity bearing amorphous effects on the primary and secondary task environments.

Webster (1992, 1994, 2000, 2002a, 2002b) would consider *primary customers* as consumers, and a significant part of *secondary customers* as customers. Parasuraman and Grewal (2000) include our *secondary customers* as "customers." From a moral responsibility viewpoint, we place special emphasis on *tertiary customers*. They too are customers in the Websterian (2000) sense, since they are the (often forced) buyers of company impact because of their proximity or connection with the corporation. They are "passive consumers" of the "social externalities" of manufacturers, distributors, and retailers (Mascarenhas, Kesavan, and Bernacchi 2005a, 2005b, 2005c). Also, given the new view of the firm, its environment, the business network, and the emerging phenomena of globalization and inter-competitor strategic alliances, there is an expanded customer-focus—to see and serve customers everywhere (Webster 1997). Webster (1988) asserts that everyone in the firm must be charged with responsibility for understanding customers and contributing to developing and delivering value for them. The common focus on customer value and relationship management may result in much stronger coordination of the procurement, sales and marketing functions (Webster 1992).

Obviously, the degree of producer–distributor dependence is highest in relation to primary customers, but is less in relation to the secondary, and presumably, the least in terms of the tertiary customers. That is, the corporation depends most upon the end-product-buyer-user customers for their purchase-patronage, sales revenues, continued loyalty, and market feedback. The second level of dependence is upon employees, channel members, major suppliers and creditors, local and federal governments for their infrastructure and legal systems of production, distribution, quality supplies, law and order, respectively. The third level of dependence is on local, national, and international communities the corporation operates in—because they provide continued legitimacy (Mascarenhas, Kesavan, and Bernacchi 2005a, 2005b). In general, the longer and deeper the dependency upon a customer group, the higher are marketing executive responsibilities, both managerial and moral, to that group. Serving tertiary customers implies more moral, voluntary, and relational responsibilities (Mascarenhas 2008).

Table 2.1 records some transactional and relational corporate responsibilities to primary, secondary, and tertiary customers. While transactional responsibilities to primary customers deal with profit maximization, legal justice, shareholder justice, distributive justice, cost reduction, and liability reduction strategies, relational responsibilities toward the same primary customers invoke broader justice theories, such as procedural justice, commutative justice, compensatory justice, and mutual risk-reduction strategies. Transactional responsibilities toward secondary customers relate to justice of wages, salaries, prices, costs, contracts, and payment—all these are relative to employees; suppliers, creditors, channels, governments, and other intermediaries. Relational responsibilities toward secondary customers relate to fiduciary justice, egalitarian justice, preventive justice, protective justice, and ecological justice toward employees, suppliers, creditors, channels, and governments. Thirdly, transactional responsibilities toward tertiary customers are based on social justice, ecological justice to local air, land, and water environment, promotional justice toward local communities, and the like. Finally, relational responsibilities toward tertiary customers invoke very challenging theories of justice such as beneficent justice, humanitarian justice, libertarian justice, egalitarian justice, global justice, and even cosmic justice. [See *Business Transformation Exercises 2.1 and 2.2.*]

The Broadened Role of Culture and Consumption Today

[See Mascarenhas (2008: 111–13)]

The broadened domain and role of today's customer is reinforced by the broadened role of culture today, and vice versa. "Culture is an historically transmitted pattern of meanings embodied in symbols, a system of inherited conceptions expressed in symbolic forms by means of which men communicate, perpetuate and develop their knowledge about and attitudes toward life" (Geertz 1973: 80). Culture is

> [...] the set of meanings, values and patterns which underlie the perceptible phenomena of a concrete society, whether they are recognizable on the level of social practice (e.g., acts, customs, tools, techniques, habits, forms, traditions) or whether they are the carriers of signs, symbols, meanings and representations, conceptions and feelings that consciously or unconsciously pass from generation to generation and are kept as they are or transformed by people as expression of their human reality. (Azevedo 1982: 10)

There is a dual aspect to consumption—it fulfills a consumer's material need and a socio-cultural need. Consumption is embedded within the social, cultural, and symbolic structures (e.g., Belk 1985, 1988;

TABLE 2.1 Corporate Transactional and Relational Responsibilities as a Function of Primary, Secondary, and Tertiary Customers

Customer types	Definition	Customer groups	Transactional responsibilities	Relational responsibilities
Primary	Individuals, groups, or institutions an enterprise chooses *to serve formally and directly.*	Domestic, international, or global buyers, users, customers, clients, and consumers	Quality products and services, brand equity, sufficient variety of products/services, fair prices, prompt delivery, adequate post-purchase service, consumer feedback, handling consumer complaints and redress	Products and services upholding healthy, safe, ethical, moral, family-oriented, and family values No targeting of vulnerable groups such as children, teens, and the elderly No artificial shortages in inner cities and ghetto areas No redlining No deceptive advertising No advertising stereotypes No exorbitant pricing Adequate compensation to consumers when harmed
Secondary	Individuals, groups, or institutions from target markets an enterprise chooses *to be served formally and directly.*	Domestic, international, or global employees, creditors, suppliers, distributors, agents and brokers, intermediaries, retailers, competitors, labor unions, local and federal governments	Fair wages, perks, compensation, and promotion of employees No child labor Fair treatment of suppliers, creditors, shareholders, brokers, intermediaries, and distributors, with no kick-backs No bribery Proper interpretation and implementation of local, state, country, and international laws that apply No antitrust violations No price gouging. No dumping No violation of contracts. Objective accounts-auditing No illegal insider trading No monopolies and monopsonies No illegal market entry barriers No tax evasions No ecological degradation of land, water, and air	Proper and timely development and retraining of workers Equal treatment to all channels, brokers, distributors, and suppliers, with some preferential treatment for minority and disadvantaged workers and suppliers Promotion of Third World country products and services Fair treatment of competitors, especially small entrepreneurs No predatory pricing No overstatement of financial positions for boosting stock prices Social auditing Corporate social responsibility for all social externalities
Tertiary	Individuals, communities, or institutions around target markets an enterprise chooses *to serve informally or indirectly.*	Domestic, international, or global communities, especially the needy, poor, handicapped, elderly, charity or cause-related institutions, and ecology project groups	Cause-related production, advertising, promotion, employment, and purchasing among local communities Promotion of local schools and community events, sports, parks, children's programs, and senior citizen welfare Promotion and hiring of local employees, skills, youth, and the elderly Promotion of local suppliers, entrepreneurs, banks, credit unions, and markets	Special concern for the local poor, handicapped, minorities, and other disadvantaged groups Tithing for worthy causes, especially those that relate to disadvantaged children, adults, and the elderly Special projects for combating global poverty, hunger, disease, unemployment, malnutrition, injustice, terrorism, political despotism, violation of human rights and dignity

Source: Author's own.

Fox and Lears 1983; Sherry 1983). Commodities have symbolic meaning or "signification" that extends far beyond what the producer intended (Barthes 1972). Consumer tastes are determined not privately but socially, that is, within social groups; consumption takes place within social structures, or the social structure is the site of consumption (Bourdieu 1984).

Thus, consumption is best understood within a socio-cultural context. Consumption is an active appropriation of signs and symbols and not just the simple destruction of the product or object. At every moment of consumption, something is created and produced—consumption is not a private act of value-destruction but a social act wherein symbolic meanings, social codes, political ideologies, and relationships are produced and reproduced (Breen 1993).

Further, production and consumption are both simultaneous phases of each other rather than opposite poles. "There is no natural distinction between production and consumption; they are one and the same, occurring simultaneously. Each act of production is also an act of consumption, and vice versa; that is, there is a cycle of production and consumption" (Firat and Venkatesh 1995: 254). Production and promotion can stimulate a culture of consumption (Fox and Lears 1983). In this sense, productivity is the function of social structure (Mascarenhas 1980). Thus, commerce and culture are complementary terms.

Economics and aesthetics, however, interact dialectically to produce the aesthetics of commodity form and the "commodification" of the aesthetic subject (Fox and Lears 1983; Sherry 1983). The market is replete with meanings and cultural images. The market is a vibrant clash of culturally-mediated sensibilities and historical images that render the market a theater rather than a timeless, context-free site of economic exchanges (Agnew 1986). Markets may produce goods like food, clothing, and transportation, but when these are consumed, the goods become highly symbolic activities invested with meanings derived from cultural frameworks. Goods become means of conveying messages among individuals and groups of individuals (Douglas and Isherwood 1979). [See *Business Transformation Exercise 2.3*]

The Broadened Role of the Environment of the Firm Today

[See Mascarenhas (2008: 89–93)]

The old notion of the environment was that it was something external to the firm, something imposed and faceless. Environment was defined as "anything not part of the organization itself" (Miles and Snow 1980: 195). Firms were viewed as "solitary units confronted by faceless environment" (Astley 1984: 526). "A firm's relationship with its environment is one of adapting to constraints imposed by an intractable externality" (Astley and Fombrun 1983).

In contrast, the emerging new view of the environment is that it is primarily "socially constructed" wherein "the boundary between organizations and their environments begins to dissolve" (Astley 1984: 533; Johnson, Sohi, and Grewal 2004; Marinova 2004). The firm is embedded within a context of business networks that is itself enveloped by an involved environment (Anderson, Håkansson, and Johansson 1994).

Further, in contrast to the older notion of the environment, *a business network* perspective better captures the notion that the boundary between the firm and its environment is much more diffused. "A business network can be defined as a set of two or more connected business relationships, in which each exchange relation is between business firms that are conceptualized as collective actors"

(Emerson 1981).[1] They are connected in the sense that exchange in one relation is contingent upon exchange (non-exchange) in another relation (Cook and Emerson 1978).

Traditionally, the firm and the market have been the unit of analysis. The industrial organization economists (e.g., Scherer and Ross 1990) explained the firm's performance as a function of the structure of the industry and the firm's environment. The focus on an individual firm, however, is insufficient for an understanding of how the firm creates wealth for itself. It is necessary to look at the network of companies that surround it and participate in the value-creation process (Falkenberg 1996). Alderson (1964) described this process as the marketing systems approach. In the Scandinavian tradition, the firm is analyzed as a part of a cross-industry network (Norman and Ramirez 1993) wherein inter-organizational relationships "domesticate markets" (Arndt 1979, 1981) to generate long-term trustworthy relationships (Ganesan 1994; Morgan and Hunt 1994; Kalwani and Narayandas 1995). Customer value and wealth for the firm is created by the coordinated interaction of multiple firms in the industry (Falkenberg 1996; Mizik and Jacobson 2003).

Hence, the unit of analysis is not an individual autonomous firm, but a system of interconnected firms in the industry or across industries. That is, the business environment of a firm is essentially its functional relationships. The identity of a firm is embedded in its network of connected relationships. The uniqueness of a firm lies in how and with whom it is connected (Håkansson and Snehota 1989). In this new view, the "business environment"[2] is a set of dyadic business relationships between a focal firm and its stakeholders (e.g., suppliers' customers, suppliers' suppliers, customers' customers and ancillary firms) (Anderson and Narus 1990; Anderson, Håkansson, and Johansson 1994).

Firms do not treat the environment in a generalized or standardized or faceless way but interact with specific "faces" (Håkansson and Snehota 1989). Hence, there are no fixed but fluid boundaries between a firm and its environment; each dyadic relationship gives one firm a certain influence over the other, and vice versa (Anderson and Narus 1990). In gaining control over a part of its environment, the firm gives up some of its internal control.[3] The network approach does not merely suggest that it

---

[1] Two or more businesses are "connected" when "exchange in one relation is contingent upon exchange (non-exchange) in the other relation" (Cook and Emerson 1978: 725). Two connected business relationships can themselves be both directly and indirectly connected with other relationships that have some bearing on them, as part of a larger business network. Thus, the "environment is not completely given by external forces but can be influenced and manipulated by the firm, and there will also exist external, known factors that are influencing some of the firm's internal functions" (Anderson, Håkansson, and Johansson 1994: 4).

[2] Hence, a firm is essentially its functional relationships. Some functions are primary such as dyadic relationships between two focal firms (producer versus supplier); other functions are secondary network relationships connected with the focal dyadic relationship, such as between supplier firm's suppliers and producer firm's customers, or between their ancillary firms and supplementary suppliers (Anderson, Håkansson, Johansson 1994).

[3] A *business environment* is supposed to have three network elements (Anderson, Håkansson, and Johansson 1994): (*a*) A *network context* involving *actors* involved, *activities* performed, and *resources* used in the business network and the patterns of adaptation between them. (*b*) A *network identity* which is the perceived attractiveness (or repulsiveness) of a firm as an exchange partner based on its unique set of connected relations, activities, and resources with other firms. Two or more firms may share a network context. (*c*) A *network horizon*: the network context and identity can theoretically extend farther and farther away from the focal actors and hence dyadic relationships may become invisible and diffuse; a network horizon denotes what a focal actor's view of the network context and the identity is. The network horizon clearly demonstrates that any business network context boundary is arbitrary and depends upon the network identity.

is not meaningful to draw a clear boundary between the firm and its environment, but that much of the uniqueness of a firm lies in how and with whom it is connected and bounded (Håkansson and Snehota 1989; Jong, Ruyter, and Lemmnik 2004).

The new concept of business environment as the "business network" generates newer business executive responsibilities. Some of these are included in Table 2.2. New relational executive responsibilities are derived from three perspectives: (*a*) the nature of the firm under the new environment concept; (*b*) the nature of the new environment; and (*c*) the nature of the response of the firm to the environmental challenge. For instance, firms must establish a congruent understanding of each other's network identity for a relationship between them to prosper (Ring and Van de Ven 1994). This is a firm's *strategic network identity*: a reference point against which the firm perceives and judges its own and other firms' actions (Ring and Van de Ven 1994).[4] A firm's strategic orientations, competencies, and

TABLE 2.2 **The Impact of the New Concept of Environment on Corporate Strategy and Executive Responsibility**

Dimensions	Features under the old environment concept	Highlights under the new environment concept	New global executive strategic responsibilities
Nature of the Firm	Independent solitary units.	Interdependent connected and collector units.	Every strategy must be responsible to interdependent units and collector actors.
Nature of the Environment	Environment is intractably external, not part of the firm.	The environment is a network of dyadic relationships and business identities.	Every corporate strategy must take into account dyadic responsibilities to business networks.
	It is something imposed and faceless, confronting the firm.	It is socially constructed networks interacting with the firm.	Every strategy is a responsibility to socially constructed networks.
	There are clear boundaries between the firm and its environment.	The firm is embedded in the environment; the boundaries of the firm are diffuse and fluid.	Every strategy should imply fiduciary responsibility of the firm to fluid boundary environments.
Response to the Environment	Adapt to the environment, or fight its constraints.	Construct your environment; interact it with specific faces.	Responsibility to create socially beneficial environments.
	Cut-throat competition to raise entry barriers.	Collaborate to compete; entry barriers are not needed.	Responsibility to collaborating units.
	Sustain competitiveness of your resources.	Create leveraging of mutual resource heterogeneity via enhanced interactions.	Mutual responsibility to enhance efficiency of combined resources.
	Innovate to fight constraints.	Collaborate to innovate; sustain innovative relationships.	Combined responsibility to innovate better products and sustain relationships.

Source: Author's own.

Note: See Mascarenhas (2008: 92).

---

[4] Applied to health care, Shortell and Zajac (1990: 168) describe the business network environment of the health care industry: "We prefer to demystify the discussion of organizational environments by viewing the environment of a health care organization as simply the collection of other specific organizations that are interconnected to or interdependent with it .... In other words, when a health care organization 'looks out' with concern at its turbulent environment, what it sees are other organizations 'looking out' at it."

resources are actualized through exchange interactions of connected interrelationships. In fact, one's interrelationships with the business environment give actual meaning to one's strategic orientations, competencies, and resources.

> This is a critical point: in network organizations, it is the ongoing relationship with a set of customers that represents the most important business asset. Marketing as a distinct management function will be responsible for being expert on the customer and keeping the rest of the network organization informed about the customer (Webster 1992: 14). [See *Business Transformation Exercises 2.4 and 2.5.*]

POSTMODERNIST VIEW OF PRODUCTION AND CONSUMPTION STRATEGIES

Following Althusser (1970) and Althusser and Balibar (1970), one could define any social system as characterized by "practices." That is, any process of transformation of a determinate input to a determinate output passes through a process called the determinate transformation. Thus, determinate raw materials (e.g., minerals, parts, money, labor, or technology) as inputs are churned into determinate products (produce, goods, commodities, products, services) as outputs through a determinate transformation process called fabrication, design, and production.

There are basically three structured aggregates of practices called "instances" that produce three kinds of products:

1. Economic processes that produce economic goods (e.g., produce, commodities, products, services, patents, trademarks, and investments).
2. Political processes that produce political goods (e.g., law and order, governance, bureaucracy, hierarchies, legislatures, courts, and prisons).
3. Ideological processes that produce ideological goods (e.g., oral or written texts, scripts, ideologies, constitutions, scriptures, creeds, religions, meanings, symbols, language, books, literature, theories, paradigms, visions, missions, ideals, slogans, cultures, and civilizations).

Within each instance we can distinguish three functions or "transformation modes": production, circulation, and consumption.

1. **Production**: Transformation of production-means (raw materials, money, labor, technology) to products and services. Parenting and reproduction is an important instance of production. Production can be economic, political, or ideological. It involves work, and work implies postponement of consumption.
2. **Circulation**: Transformation by transferring economic, political, and ideological products and services from the sphere of production to the sphere of consumption. Circulation implies storage, inventories, warehousing, brokerage, transportation, delivery, logistics, information, promotion, advertising, and retailing (breaking bulk).
3. **Consumption**: This is transformation of purchased economic, political, and ideological products by use, disuse, abuse, and disposal. Production and circulation achieve their purpose: namely, customer satisfaction in the short run, and in the long run, customer loyalty that incorporates these

products and services into family values and lifestyles, which in turn create cultures, subcultures, social classes, and social formations.

All three are functions or modes of structured aggregate *social transformation* or wealth formation.[5] A social formation is a complex aggregate, forming a structured whole, of the various distinct and relatively autonomous instances, the latter being interpreted according to specific modes of determination that are established in the last analysis by the economic instance (Althusser and Balibar 1970: 104–05).

Table 2.3 is a broad canvas of a social formation comprising of the three instances of production, circulation, and consumption that are conditioned by economic, political, or ideological value-expression modes. Table 2.3 lists various economic, political, and ideological goods under the three transformation modes of production, circulation, and consumption. Every entry in Table 2.3 is a form of wealth formation, whether it is production, circulation, or consumption. We assume that every form of product, economic, political, or ideological, goes through three transformation processes: production, circulation, and consumption. Every cell in Table 2.3 involves corporate strategy.

Thus, human skills are produced and developed at home, at school, and at work place; they are circulated in the hiring–firing process, which implies the concept of division of labor, and they are consumed as self-training, specialization, and self-development. Fixed labor hours in the production phase enable the circulation of labor in shifts, moonlighting, the resultant consumption in terms of rest from labor, and additional earnings and comforts that moonlighting implies. Similarly, labor as production produces wages and income. Wages, income, and profits are circulated by various reward–punishment processes of salary determination and promotions, and the resultant consumption is in terms of cash income, wealth, and credit. The reader can interpret other entries in Table 2.3 under "economic goods" in a similar manner.

A special case of social formation is among humans. If human beings could be understood as "factors of production" or "economic" products (at least, as producers, generators of income, distributors, and consumers), then their parenting and reproduction (adoption) is the production phase, their living together at home as siblings and their multiplication as grand and great grand children is the circulation phase,[6] and the actual family, children, nurturing, growing, bonding, and belonging constitute the consumption phase.

Modern alternate methods of parenting, such as single parenting, artificial donor insemination, surrogate motherhood, and legal and/or open adoption will be reproduction–circulation modes. Analogously,

---

[5] In the beginning, especially in tribal or agrarian economies, there was not much of a difference and distance between production, circulation, and consumption. The three were intimately linked as a self-subsistence or group-subsistence communal social formation mode. What was produced by the producers was consumed by the same producers as soon it was produced, with no middle people or without much of hoarding. But with industrial revolution and industrial civilization, labor began to be specialized and separated from both production and consumption, and so did production in general, and circulation of products become necessary. Industrial work forces the postponement of consumption. In fact, cities are the result of a greater specialization in work and of increased exchanges; they are the place where a new class of artisans called merchants come into existence alongside of, and in dependence of, the class of producers (Belo 1981: 17).

[6] Here, the production–circulation–consumption phases are closest to each other, as in self-sufficient agricultural home-production. This is a case of self-subsistence or "zero degree circulation" (Terray 1972: 152–56).

TABLE 2.3   Social Formation as Structured Aggregation of Wealth Formation

Structured modes of value-expression	*Structured modes of wealth formation*		
	Production as:	*Circulation as:*	*Consumption as:*
Economic Goods	Courting, reproduction	Siblings live and multiply	Children, family, bonding
	Developing and using skills	Division of labor, hiring	Specialization, training
	Distributing labor hours	Shifts, moonlighting	Rest, additional earnings
	Earning wages, income	Salaries and promotions	Cash, wealth, credit
	Creating and inventing	Patenting, licensing	Technology diffusion
	Discovering land, mines, ...	Exploring, mining,	New lands and discoveries
	Developing land, water, ...	Business zoning, housing	Businesses, homes, parks
	Farming, herding, fishing	Meat and produce markets	Groceries, dairies, meats
	Manufacturing products, energy	Distributing, retailing	Shopping goods, purchase, use
		Retailing services	Using services, dining
	Clerking, servicing, cooking	Branding, packaging	Designer, national brands use
	Differentiating products	Media, TV, radio, ads	News, sports, music, ...
	Communicating, entertaining	Phones, Cables, Internet	Networking, conferencing
	Network hardware, software	Banking, loans, bonds	Credit, interest, safety
	Debt financing, equity financing	Stocks, NYSE, NASDAQ	Shares, dividends, wealth
	Financial products (derivatives)	Marketing, promoting	Sales, market share, profit
	Corporate planning, strategizing		
Political Goods	Legislating, de-legislating	Promulgation, enforcement	Law, order, peace, harmony
	Governing, planning, budgeting	Bureaucracies, hierarchies	Representation, access, voice
	Defending, weapons production	Armies, air force, marines	Defense, wars, superpowers
	Adjudicating, prosecuting	Federal, state, county courts	Due process, justice, appeal
	Sentencing, punishing	Detentions, prisons,	Crime-prevention, safety
	Taxing for development	IRS and state fiscal systems	Tax money used: infrastructure
	Political contesting	Campaigning, caucusing	Franchising, voting
	Controlling business and markets	Lobbying, liaising, PR	Manipulation, market power
	Privatization, denationalizing	Auctioning public companies	Bid rigging, exclusive bids
	Nationalizing, de-privatizing	National buyback or recall	Public access to privatized firms
Ideological Goods	Educating, counseling	Universities, colleges, schools	Learning, thinking, maturing
	Writing, scripting, composing	Publishing, media, libraries	Texts, literature, languages
	Painting, sculpting, music	Museums, reprints, albums	Entertainment, fine arts
	Ideating, creating, theorizing	Diffusing ideas, creations	Influence, power, theories
	Visioning—dreaming	Sharing visions—dreams	Influence, revolution, control
	Founding religions, cults, ...	Evangelizing, churches	Faith, religious affiliation
	Revealing—inspiring by God	Scribing, diffusing, tradition	Bible, scriptures, word of God
	Crafting policies, programs, ...	Lobbying, advocacy, ...	Boycotts, strikes, hold-ups...
	Ethno-centering (e.g., Nazism)	Racial (ethnic) discrimination	Racism, social classes
	Dictatorship, demagogy	Totalitarianism, communism	Command economy, bondage
	Market capitalism, production	Democracy, egalitarianism	Liberty, pursuit of happiness

Source: Author's own.

modern methods of de-parenting such as artificial birth control and abortion become reproduction–de-circulation modes. This is also an instance when higher technology tends to differentiate and distance production from consumption via complex circulation mechanisms.

In the domain of political goods, a basic production process is legislation (de-legislation) in terms of laws, ordinances, policies, standards, and codes; they are circulated when officially promulgated and their enforcement mechanisms are determined, and both production and circulation result in law, order, peace, harmony which we all enjoy as civic consumption. Government executives produce in terms of governance, planning, budgeting, and implementing laws and growth plans. These are circulated through extensive wings of bureaucracies, hierarchies, delegations, states, counties, cities, townships, and villages. A major consumption phase here is that all citizens can access the democratically elected government officials, represent matters, voice opinions, and be heard—the political consumption privileges of the governed. A major political production is domestic and foreign defense, and the creation of defense systems and weaponry. Defense is circulated through the armed forces, the air forces, the marines, and the National Guard. The citizens enjoy protection through defense-protection, wars won, and being super-powers. One can interpret other entries under "political products" in Table 2.3 in a similar manner.

In regard to ideological products, a basic production process is *writing* (as Derrida (1976) understands it) in the form of oral and written texts, literature, arts, ideographs, pictographs, philosophies, ideologies, family codes, school codes, work-ethic codes, business conduct codes, slogans, emblems, signs, music compositions, painting, sculpting, crafting policies and programs, ideating, conceptualizing, theorizing, empirical research and verification. Much of this writing is ideological, normatively and descriptively moral, historical, or bound by one's tribe, ethnic group, nationality, class, research-tradition, paradigm, policy or program, lifestyle, life-circumstances, and philosophy of life. All writings (textual as well as oral) are circulated through established dissemination processes such as printing, publications, albums, landline and online media, libraries, universities, schools, colleges, museums, theaters, concert halls, churches, temples, missionaries and rabbis, lobbies, and advocacy groups, and currently, through iPods, iTunes, and iPhones. Writings are consumed by "readers" to enjoy learning, competence, thinking skills, analytical skills, self-development, entertainment, information, influence, religious affiliation, faith, freedom or bondage.

Consumption is a function of consumer demand, and the latter is the function of the totality of the needs, wants, and desires (economic, political, and ideological) of the social formation. Need fulfillment is a function of the use-value of the product. Consumption of economic products relates to their utility or "use-value" (Marx 1967); consumption of political products relates to their "order-value" (Althusser 1970), and consumption of ideological products relates to their "significance-value" (especially, semantic) as found in the texts (Derrida 1976). Consumption activity of each society is also a function of its utopia (defined by its sets of wants, desires, dreams, and visions). Some of these utopias are induced by producers (e.g., brand and fashion designers), circulators (e.g., celebrity endorsers, persuasive advertisements), and other consumers (e.g., innovators in the sense of pioneer users of new products or opinion leaders).

Thus, postmodernism views culture not merely as a superstructure but as a foundational constituent of society. Firat and Venkatesh (1995) argue that postmodernism provides a broadened outlook on culture and consumption. It is concerned with the celebration and *aestheticization* of life, while its precursor, modernism, with its logic of production (order, coherence, scientific thinking, and laws), views life as determined by the forces of economic production (Mascarenhas 1980, 1981). Postmodernist writings of Althusser, Barthes, Bourdieu, Douglas, and others lead to an important conclusion: culture and economics are closely linked; material production and cultural configurations go solidly hand-in-hand (Firat and Venkatesh 1995). No product or object has any inherent function or value independent of the symbolic and cultural framework in which it is inserted. Derivatively, no corporate strategy has any inherent function or value independent of the symbolic and cultural framework of the company in which it is inserted. [See *Business Transformation Exercises 2.6 to 2.8.*]

Production never ceases; it is a continual process. At every moment of production, circulation, and consumption, something is produced—an object, a person, or in general, the signifier, the image and the symbol. Sign value replaces exchange value as the basis of consumption.[7] Consumers are active producers of symbols and signs of consumption, while manufacturers are active producers of products as values. Products as values are not consumed unless and until consumers see in them the relevant meanings, signs, and symbols of their socio-cultural life in them. Modern marketing culture, through its dominance of promotion and advertising of everyday life, bundles, prompts, suggests, and sells packaged symbols and meanings to help consumers in their signification process. Marketing culture is the transformation of the product from a natural thing into a linguistic, social, and cultural sign. Marketing creates, diffuses, and institutionalizes symbols in individual, family, and social lives (e.g., the trademarks, logos, slogans, and punch lines used in advertising spews symbols of "good life," "conspicuous consumption," "celebrities," and the like). In as much as marketing can and does wantonly create moods, fads, fashions, lifestyles, and cultures, it bears the responsibility of its destructive, dehumanizing, and addictive after effects.

Production and consumption, however, are not ends in themselves—they are means to humanize, celebrate, and aestheticize life. These are opportunities that invite higher levels of corporate and marketing executive responsibility—producers, distributors, and marketers affect consumption, society and culture by the products and services they introduce in the markets. They may either choose to humanize, aestheticize, and enhance consumers, societies, and cultures, or to dehumanize, commodify, and degrade them. Given the broadened role of the customer and culture today, every major product or service produces a chain reaction: purchasing, consumption, symbolization, socialization, and culturization. Each stage in the social, value-added chain implies an added corporate and marketing executive responsibility. Even though commodities may have symbolic meanings that go far beyond what the producer intended (Barthes 1972), yet responsible corporate and marketing executives will carefully design, anticipate, market, and monitor their products and services—so that they generate culturally uplifting meanings and motivate wholesome consumer and social behavior. [See *Business Transformation Exercise 2.9 and 2.10.*]

---

[7] A symbol is some finite piece of this world, something, person, event, idea, or proposition through which something else, other than itself, is known or encountered. A symbol, then, mediates something else and makes it present. Often the other thing that is known, can only be known through its symbol; as a dream mediates the subconscious, or a religious symbol represents God. Thus, a symbol introduces human beings into spheres inside themselves and levels of reality outside that would not be known without this mediation. Symbol, then, is not a weak but a strong concept indicating a depth perception of reality. Symbols, by their very nature, are dialectical: While retaining their finite identity, they may mediate or make present what is transcendent (e.g., God in religious symbols), or what is beyond themselves. Symbols may be conceptual (as in words, parables, or the text of sacred scriptures), theoretical (as in paradigms and doctrines), persons or things (as in art objects, celebrities). The symbolic mediation is usually imagined, since there is a distinct role of the imagination in all knowing. In this sense, any culture is a cluster of symbols mediating values and psycho-social meanings beyond the symbols.

THE SOCIAL MARKETING CONCEPT OF CORPORATE STRATEGY

With the roles of the customer and cultures broadening, the marketing concept has also correspondingly broadened from the "production concept" of the 1850s, to the "product concept" of the 1900s, to the "selling concept" of post World War II, and the "marketing concept" of the 1960s (Kotler 2002). We foresee and advocate a "social marketing concept" that can best respond to the latest technological and cultural advances of the 21st century. Briefly the five concepts may be defined as follows:

1. Production Concept (1850s): Demand exceeds supply; hence, consumers prefer products that are widely available and inexpensive; they are interested in obtaining the product and not necessarily its attribute and features.
2. Product Concept (1900s): Supply exceeds demand; products and their information are easily available; hence, consumers can easily appraise quality and performance. No consumer input is necessary for new product development. Manufacturers and marketers, however, must offer superior products and services via continuous improvement and innovation.
3. Selling Concept (1945s): Supply far exceeds demand. Products do not sell unless they are aggressively promoted and sold. Consumers suffer from inertia or laziness; they have too many choices for the same product (see Table 1.4: The Tyranny of Choice); hence, consumers need coaxing. Producers and sellers must have aggressive selling skills.
4. Marketing Concept (1960s): Supply can match or create demand. Customers know and have specific needs. Consumers are perceptive and selective; they can appreciate quality, variety, and information. Products do not sell unless you create, communicate, and deliver better value to the target customer than the competitor. There are target markets that can be accessed.[8]
5. Social Marketing Concept (2000s): Supply to create socially responsible demand. Products and services should not be sold unless they uphold or create good individual and family experiences and culturally uplifting values to all target customers. The broadened role of customers and cultures mandate an equally broadened role of socially responsible production and marketing.

Concern for public and social good has regularly featured under the rubric of *social marketing* (e.g., Andreasen 1997, 2002; Kotler and Levy 1969; Kotler and Zaltman 1971). Social marketing seeks to resolve social problems directly, and not via commercial marketing (Brenkert 2002: 15). Andreasen (1997: 7) defines social marketing as "the application of commercial marketing technologies to the analysis, planning, execution, and evaluation of programs designed to influence the voluntary behavior of target audiences in order to improve their personal welfare and that of their society." Marketing as

---

[8] More recently, another trend called the "experience concept" is coming into vogue, even though not yet internalized by mainstream marketing (see Berry, Carbone, and Haeckel 2002; Calhoun 2001; Carbone and Haeckel 1994; Gilmore and Pine 2002; Pine and Gilmore 1998). *Experience Concept* mandates that producers and marketers must create value for their customers in the form of new experiences (Pine and Gilmore 1998). Customers are relatively immune to mere marketing messages; they need memorable and engaging experiences of products and services (Gilmore and Pine 2002). Customers need and desire *total customer experience* (TCE) in all market offerings. Offering TCE provides sustainable competitive advantage to firms (Berry, Carbone, and Haeckel 2002). A firm will be successful when TCE is its focus (Calhoun 2001). [For more details on TCE, see Chapter 13].

viewed by its founding fathers was primarily a social process and they emphasized the "transcendent importance of this social institution" (Vaile, Grether, and Cox 1952: v). Breyer (1934: 192) linked marketing as "intermediate sorting" to social processes: "Marketing is not primarily a means for garnering profits for individuals. It is in the larger, more vital sense, an economic instrument used to accomplish indispensable social ends." Alderson (1957) insisted on developing a holistic look for marketing: The provisioning technology that marketing provides should be assessed by its impact on the whole system of trade, political, and social processes. Following Alderson, Fisk (1974) studied the relationship between marketing and the larger natural environment. The concept of social marketing somehow died thereafter.

It is gratifying to note, however, that recent marketing thought is re-emphasizing the role of social and public good in various types of marketing decisions. Rothschild (1999) considers public health and social issue behaviors within the field of social marketing. Brenkert (2002) and Andreasen (1995) believe that social problems arise because the well-being or the "good" of a substantial number or groups of people has not been realized. Social marketing is a virtue-ethics based approach to marketing—that is, to define, develop, and sustain the social and public good of all stakeholders (Mascarenhas 2002). In fact, marketers must assume responsibility not only for the exchange-consequences but for the common good that the function and evolution of markets generate (Day and Montgomery 1999).

Table 2.4 summarizes this discussion, contrasts the five marketing orientations, and spells out the marketing executive social responsibilities of the social marketing concept.

The social concept is a sequel to relational marketing responsibilities in relation to primary, secondary, and especially, tertiary, customers discussed in earlier sections and Table 2.1. The social concept does not discourage innovation; it invites products and services that save time, energy, and cost for consumers such that the saved resources of time, talent, and money can be better spent on promoting family and cultural values. The social concept does not believe that markets should only respond to consumer needs. Some 20 years ago, customers did not know or need microwave ovens, walkmans, CDs, VCRs, ATMs, cell phones, personal computers (PCs), iPods, Blackberry, Internet shopping, and digital cameras. All these products were primarily innovation-driven or manufacturer-driven, and have been very well-received and if well-used, can promote healthy family and cultural values. Given the broadened role of customer and sellers today, the social marketing concept invites a buyer–seller collaborative venture to humanize society and culture through genuine family and socially benefiting value-products and services. [See *Business Transformation Exercise 2.11 and 2.12.*]

ECONOMIC GROUNDING OF TRANSFORMATION STRATEGIES

Every strategy belongs to a certain economic era or stage of industry evolution. Richard L. Sandour is the founder of the world's first and North America's only voluntary, legally binding integrated greenhouse gas emissions reduction, registry, and trading system. He is the father of carbon trading, and currently, Chairman and CEO of the *Chicago Climate Exchange*, a financial institution that administers the "cap and trade" program. Sandour (2008) distinguishes the following eras of wealth and value creation since 1945. Table 2.5 summarizes his analysis.

During the post-World War II era of 1945–70, manufacturing dominated the U.S. economic scene, with nearly 70 percent of employment and wealth generated by this sector. The primary strategy was to create new structures for maximizing manufacturing productivity such as refineries, factories, coal-fired

TABLE 2.4   Contrasting Executive Responsibilities of Social Marketing with Those of Other Marketing Concepts

Dimensions	Production concept: 1850s	Product concept: early 1900s	Selling concept: 1945s	Marketing concept: 1960s	Social marketing concept: 2000s
Main Definitional Assumptions	Consumers prefer products that are widely available and inexpensive. Demand exceeds supply.	Consumers favor products that offer most quality, performance, or innovative features. Demand exceeds supply.	Products do not sell unless aggressively promoted and sold. Supply exceeds demand.	Products do not sell unless you create, communicate, and deliver better value to the target customer than the competitor. Supply far exceeds demand.	Products should not be sold unless they uphold or create good cultural values to all target customers. Supply should promote social and public good; i.e., humanize society and culture.
Product Strategy	Achieve high production efficiency and low cost.	Produce superior products. Improve or innovate continuously.	Factory-focus: clear inventories Product-focus: make products and services attractive	Consumer-needs focus; dovetail product to specific needs. Anticipate customer needs.	Consumer-culture focus dovetails products and services to foster new cultural values and meanings.
Pricing Strategy	Beat the competitor.	Price should signal and uphold quality.	Price wars: aggressive pricing, predatory pricing	Integrated pricing: discounts, payment, and financing	Surcharge products that perpetuate or create negative cultures: e.g., tobacco, drugs, alcohol, pornography, waste, and extravagance.
Distribution Strategy	Mass distribution	Distribution should signal quality.	Mass 24/7 distribution Mass-customized selling	Distribution should satisfy customer needs and convenience.	Distribute products that enhance, revamp, and perpetuate good family values and responsible living.
Promotional Strategy	None: impersonal and poor-quality service	Promotion to signal quality. Hard selling is needed.	Hard and aggressive selling to beat competition. Personalized selling.	Integrated marketing: All departments and functions should focus on the customer.	Promotions should indicate quality, value, and responsibility of new products and services. Promotional information should aestheticize products.
Major Problems	Wrong assumptions: no market glut (Say's Law: Everything produced is sold.)	Marketing myopia: Look out through window, and not into the mirror.	Quality neglected. Product/service flaws concealed. No post-purchase satisfaction. Coaxed products dissatisfy.	Customer myopia: Customer needs do not always stimulate innovation or markets.	This concept will provoke resistance. However, marketing vision needs to be expanded.

Source: Author's own.

TABLE 2.5   Economic Stages of Wealth and Value Creation in the U.S. and in the Post-World War II World

Time period	Source of wealth and value creation	Initial structural changes	Subsequent value creation structures	Examples of wealth and value creation
1945–70	Manufacturing businesses, about 70% of wealth and value came from the manufacturing sector	Industrial revolution, post-World War II economic revival plan, the Marshall Plan	Coal-fired facilities; refineries; factories; assembly lines; blue-collar worker dominance; labor unions; Occupational Safety and Health Administration (OSHA)	GMC, Ford, Chrysler, American Motors, GE, Exxon, … U.S. produced two-thirds of world GDP.
1970–80	Commodity trading Oil crisis Corn and soybean prices hit $10 Metal trading	Oil embargoes of 1973 and 1979, Organization of Petroleum Exporting Countries (OPEC) crisis	Commodity trading centers; oil cartels; world commodity markets; GATT; bond houses	Trading companies like Solomon Brothers Grain companies like Cargills, Continentals, Bungees, and Dreyfusses
1980–90	Commoditization of money, media, and new financial instruments such as equity bonds, mortgages, interest rates, stock indices, bank debt, or junk bonds	Awareness of social costs in the form of risk and debt, securitization of risk, greed for money and quick wealth	Commercial banks; investment banks; mortgage companies; financial trading centers Media giants	Banks, Savings and Loans Institutions (S&Ls), Federal Housing Administration FHA loans packed by companies such as Ginnie Maes, Ted Turner, CNN, Terry McGaw—all were financed by junk bonds.
1990–2000	Commoditization of information, news, sports, entertainment, movies, and videogames: infomediaries, horizontal and vertical portals, software languages, business software, cell phones	Information explosion and proliferation of PCs and laptops, the creation of the WWW and the commercialization of the Internet	Semiconductors, mainframe computers, computers, PCs, laptops, notebooks, Internet, WWW, ITP/CP, e-mails, videogames, PDAs, National Information Infrastructure (NII), Global Information Infrastructure (GII); cell phone infrastructure	IBM, Unisys, Intel, Microsoft, Netscape, HP, Dell, Gateway, Sony, Acer, Amazon.com, eBay, Yahoo, Google, Expedia, AltaVista, Travelocity.com, SAP, Oracle, Nokia, Nextel, Verizon, Singular, AT&T
2000–10	Commoditization of clean air and drinking water: greenhouse emissions trading, "cap and trade" emissions standards, measure, monitor, and trade carbon emissions, energy alternatives (ethanol, wind mills, solar)	General awareness of global climate change, trade markets for emission reductions	1997 Kyoto Treaty for enabling "cap and Trade"; EPA, EPA compliance trade, incentives for higher carbon emission controls, buy carbon reductions from those doing better	9/11; dot.com bubble burst; Afghan War; Iraq War; U.S. opts out of Kyoto Treaty; global climate change movements like the Chicago Climate Exchange
2010–20	Commoditization of greed, winning odds, wealth, power, and popularity? Commoditization of global financial, mortgage, insurance, and health care markets	The collapse of the domestic financial markets, proliferation and glorification of corporate fraud and greed, progressive impoverishment of the taxpayers and the low-income groups	The survival of the fittest financial institutions—the emergence of financial, mortgage, insurance, and health care giants. Industrial and financial concentration. The rise of China, India, Poland, and Brazil.	The 2008–09 Rescue and Economic Recovery Plans by the U.S. President with the Federal Reserve Board and the U.S. Treasury. Income inequality worsened; global poverty and disease on the rise provoking global terrorism and revolution.

Source: Author's own.

Note: See also Sandour (2008).

energy, assembly lines, labor unions, transportation logistics, and railroads and highway network. We commanded close to two-thirds of world GDP.

During the next decade, 1970–80, wealth creation occurred in the commodity markets of metals, oil, corn, soybeans, and wheat, and the enabling structures were trading centers, General Agreement on Tariffs and Trade (GATT), oil cartels (that resulted in two Arab oil embargoes of 1973 and 1979). The grain companies (e.g., Cargills, Continentals, Bungees, and Dreyfusses) symbolized accumulated wealth. The basic strategy was maximization of grain production and wealth creation through commodity price trading.

During the 1980–90, we witness the avid "commoditization of financial instruments" and equity markets such as treasury bills, bonds, international currencies, real estate, home mortgages, preferred and common stock, stock indices, derivatives, hedge funds, bad debt or junk bonds, asset and liability management. The basic underlying theory of social cost was proposed by Ronald Coase: you could issue property rights to scarce resources. We could create a secondary market for products that could not be divided (e.g., mortgages, bonds, debt, risk) but could actually be exchanged. The wealth creating and accumulating institutions were secondary markets such as gigantic commercial banks (e.g., Bank of America, Chase Manhattan, Bank One, JP Morgan), investments banks (e.g., Merrill Lynch, Lehman Brothers, Morgan Stanley, Goldman Sachs), debt securitization banks (e.g., Washington Mutual, American International Group (AIG), Bear Stearns), and mortgage companies (e.g., Fannie May, Freddie Mac, Countrywide). This decade experienced the highest interest rate volatility, and thousands of banks closed and a few giants survived. This was the decade of junk bonds that financed Ted Turner, McGaw, CNN, and the cellular phone companies.

During 1990–2000, we witness the "commoditization of information" via World Wide Web (WWW) and the Internet with information packaging and marketing giants such as Yahoo, Google, AOL, Travelocity.com, Alta Vista, Expedia, Amazon.com, eBay, Microsoft, and Netscape. The proliferation of microprocessors, computers, laptops, PDAs, cellular phones, information storage and retrieval devices (e.g., tapes, drums, cassettes, CDs, word files, PDF and Adobe files, and flash drives) facilitated the rapid commoditization of information markets.

ECOLOGICAL GROUNDING OF CURRENT TRANSFORMATION STRATEGIES

Finally, in the current decade 2000–10, we are experiencing the "commoditization of clean air and drinking water" via new instruments such as emissions trading, and the "cap and trade" carbon reductions. The structural change was the warming of the planet.

- The Clean Air Act Amendments of 1990 created a property right, the right to emit sulfur dioxide.
- In 1992, at the UN Earth Summit in Rio, they said there are six greenhouse gases. They soon commoditized and traded them.
- In 1997, the Kyoto Treaty enabled "cap and trade." The Chicago Climate Futures Exchange traded a future contract on the EPA compliance instrument. For instance, the exchange securitized a rainforest in Costa Rica.
- The Chicago Climate Exchange that followed created credits for capturing methane from landfills in Chicago and Tucson, and sold them to Ontario Power. The 400 or so global Fortune

500 companies that belong to the Chicago Climate Exchange have made legally binding pledges of reducing the emissions by 6 percent by 2010 (using 2000 as a baseline year). In fact, they achieved 12 percent reduction during the first four years (2001–04). Cumulatively, they reduced 180 million tons of carbon—over the total emissions of France and Belgium combined.

- The Chicago Climate Futures Exchange, a sister concern of Chicago Climate Exchange, trades sulfur dioxide contracts under the U.S. Clean Air Act Amendments of 1990. Since 1990, this CCF Exchange has cut sulfur dioxide emissions from 17.5 million tons to 9 million tons.

Every ton of emission reduction is a millions of dollar win-win situation. For instance, in the 1990s, each year the crop of sulfur dioxide was roughly 18 million tons but the social cost of the crop was about 9 billion, a price of $500 a ton. Reducing sulfur dioxide emissions by 12 percent of 18 million tons during 2001–04 has a compounded value of over 10 million tons, and thus, a saving of over $5 billion. Similarly, garbage dumps produce methane that is 21 times more potent than carbon. If you tap and prevent it from leaking into the atmosphere, you have that much clean air. Companies that do this could earn greenhouse emission reduction offset credits that are tradable.

Sandour (2008: 25) cites the case of a Minnesota dairy farmer who had a lagoon of animal waste that annoyed all, family members and workers alike, because of the stink and its potential to contaminate water. The farmer threw a tarp over the lagoon and siphoned off the methane. He used the methane to power a Caterpillar generator that turned it into electricity that, in turn, powered his 11 buildings and his milking machines. It was a sustainable loop. He came to the Chicago Climate Exchange (CCX) and sold offset credits that he earned by preventing the release of methane into the air. He made US $10,000 that year, a sizable extra income given that an average farmer that year in Minnesota made just about US $35,000. Moreover, his electricity bills came down significantly.

Dick Lugar is a member of the CCX. At the Lugar Stock Farms, he has taken 200 of his 600 acres and planted walnut trees that are sequestering carbon dioxide. Thus, he collects carbon credits on a regular basis from CCX.

Sandour (2008: 27) has another interesting example. Teaming up with a local NGO, CCX started a project in a very poor village of Kerala, India. Typically, every morning the young women would go out for several hours hunting for firewood and would burn it for their cooking in the evening. The women could not go to school, and moreover, burning wood indoors exposed them to severe health problems. CCX financed a little project. Each was given a micro-digestor made up of concrete or plastic in which all animal (cow, goats) waste was collected and sealed; the methane extracted was piped into the homes for cooking. Women did not have to collect firewood anymore; instead, they went to school and got educated. Meanwhile, the village got cleaner from less methane emissions. CCX started with about a thousand families; it has now reached over hundred thousand. CCX links financial incentives to social and environmental objectives and accomplishments. We need to change the mindsets from environmental apathy to ecology—this is our planet's future.

According to Sandour (2008), under each era or decade, what created the corresponding market was a seven-stage process:

1. There is a big structural change in what is commoditized.
2. The structural change creates the demand for capital.
3. Some professionals develop commodity standards.
4. The commodity standards create legal evidences of ownership which are traded.
5. The informal markets spring and trade evidence of ownership (and not commodities or securities).

6. The informal markets are controlled by centralized exchanges.
7. Lastly, the next evolution emerges—mostly, derivatives resulting in complex over-the-counter transactions.

CONCLUDING REMARKS

If Sandour's historical analysis is valid, then we must face further critical questions such as the following:

- To what extent do we currently commoditize great values such as quality of life, happiness, peace, harmony, and common well-being?
- What is the big structural change under-grounding the commoditized product?
- What are the commoditization standards?
- To what extent are we trading or eroding such standards?
- What are the centralized industry or market exchanges that determine such standards?
- How do we de-commoditize such value products and services in order to humanize it for the greater good of society and the *greater glory of God*?

For instance, to the extent that we tend to commoditize or standardize MBA programs into a fixed generalized or finished product, we are expendable, our students are expendable, and we are doing a disservice to the students of tomorrow. The MBA skills of solving "simple problems" with straight-forward linear and analytical solutions can be easily outsourced. The *differentiating MBA skill and curriculum* that we desperately need today is the capacity to understand and address "wicked" problems of business. This requires integration of diverse disciplines and divergent perspectives. Our current MBA program with its management silos is useful only to solve simple and routine problems—it is a 150-year old dated product that is struggling to survive (Khurana 2007).

It is for such reasons that we need a philosophy of corporate strategy. In a world of dynamic and volatile change, our business assumptions and presuppositions begin to change and so do our academic generalizations about business. Even our philosophy of corporate transformation strategies must evolve because we ground it on the role of consumers today, on the role of culture today, and the role of environment today. With all the three domains changing constantly, our philosophy of corporate strategy must change, but change for the better to make it more refined and principled, more directing and illuminating.

BUSINESS TRANSFORMATION EXERCISES

2.1 Table 2.1, last column, lists relationship responsibilities by transaction types from pure discrete transactions to global strategic alliances to online exchanges. Based on this listing, now specify corporate strategic responsibilities to both industrial and household consumers against each of the following exchanges: [Note: Responsibilities increase as one is involved with exchanges from (a) to (j)].

    a. Pure one-time discrete transaction on eBay.
    b. Many disconnected transactions on Amazon.com.
    c. Transfers of outdated technologies to developing countries.
    d. Centralized purchasing in GM to augment GM's bargaining power.

    e. Mutually contracted transactions between K-Mart and its stakeholders, both before and after seeking bankruptcy protection in 2002.

    f. Mutual purchase agreements between Ford and its suppliers.

    g. Domestic foreign collaborations between GM and Daewoo, Ford and Honda, and Chrysler and Mitsubishi.

    h. Multinational equity and technology collaborations between Enron and its foreign subsidiaries both before and after Chapter 11 reorganization in 1999.

    i. Co-marketing alliances between Wal-Mart and its major suppliers.

    j. Global strategic alliances between GE and its competitors.

2.2 Following the definition of primary, secondary, and tertiary customers provided in this chapter, do the following:

    a. Identify the primary customers of tobacco companies like R.J. Reynolds or Philip Morris.

    b. Specify and justify the marketing executive responsibilities of these companies to their primary customers.

    c. Next, identify the secondary customers of R.J. Reynolds or Philip Morris.

    d. Specify and justify the executive responsibilities of these companies to their secondary customers.

    e. Identify and justify the tertiary customers of R.J. Reynolds or Philip Morris.

    f. Specify and justify the executive responsibilities of these companies to their tertiary customer groups.

2.3 Following the definition of primary, secondary, and tertiary customers discussed in this chapter, how would you characterize the following "customer" groups and why? Also, specify and justify the corporate responsibilities of tobacco companies to the six customer groups identified below.

    a. Secondary smokers in one's home

    b. Secondary smokers in the workplace

    c. Secondary smokers in bars and restaurants

    d. Lung-cancer patients who were past smokers

    e. Families of lung-cancer patients

    f. Medical insurees who pay high premiums owing to high incidence of lung-cancer victims

2.4 According to business network theory, a firm is essentially its functional relationships. Some functions are primary such as dyadic relationships between two focal firms (producer versus supplier); other functions are secondary network relationships connected with the focal dyadic relationship, such as between supplier firm's suppliers and producer firm's customers, or between their ancillary firms and supplementary suppliers (Anderson, Håkansson, and Johansson 1994; Corsten and Kumar 2005; Wathne and Heide 2004). Identify the following in relation to the company you work for, and specify corresponding exchange responsibilities:

    a. Producer and supplier relationships

    b. Producer and supplier's supplier relationships

    c. Producer and employee relationships

    d. Producer and employee's supplier relationships

    e. Producer and customer relationships

    f. Producer and customer's supplier relationships

2.5 Consider the following emerging relational principles: (*a*) The environment of a firm is primarily "socially constructed" and hence, the boundaries between organizations and their environments are dissolving (Astley 1984). (*b*) Since there are no fixed but fluid boundaries between a firm and its environment, each dyadic relationship between the firm and the stakeholder in the environment gives one firm a certain influence over the other, or vice versa (Anderson and Narus 1990). (*c*) Thus, in this new competitive world, rivalries are redefined: Two legally separate and competing firms may collaborate more strongly in product design and development today than any divisions within a conglomerate (Prahalad 1995). (*d*) Thus, competing companies collaborate to compete better (Bleeke and Ernst 1991a; Prahalad 1995). Apply these principles to the Dow Corning Case (see Mascarenhas (2008), *Responsible Marketing*, Chapter 11 for details) to do the following:

a. Identify and specify the socially constructed environment of Dow Corning in relation to its production and marketing of silicon-gel-filled breast implants.
b. Specify some of the major dyadic relationships between Dow Corning and its stakeholders.
c. Redefine Dow Corning's rivalries: How could it collaborate with its competitors in manufacturing safer and more natural products for breast implants?
d. Identify new marketing executive responsibilities implied under (a) to (c). How would they differ if Dow Corning had not followed steps (a) through (c)?
e. Do (a) to (d) in relation to GMC's C/K pickup trucks with more efficient and collision-proof tank placements (see Mascarenhas (2008), Chapter 12 for details).

2.6 Applying the new global executive responsibilities that have emerged from the new concept of the environment (see Table 2.5), redefine some of the global marketing executive responsibilities implied in the following strategies:

a. Dow Corning's strategy to manufacture and globally market safer breast implants for breast reconstruction or cosmetic surgery.
b. Philip Morris' and R.J. Reynolds's collaborative strategy to globally produce and market non-nicotine based tobacco products for rest and relaxation.
c. Global production and marketing of products (other than guns) for better customer safety and security of women (see Blair and Hyatt 1995).
d. Intercontinental collaboration to globally control and monitor pornography diffusion via satellites, TV and radio networks, Internet and other WWW sites.
e. Targeting vulnerable customers with non-alcoholic products for celebration and relaxation (see Smith and Cooper-Martin 1997).

2.7 A major tenet of postmodernism is that culture, economics, production, circulation, and consumption are closely linked. Thus, commerce and culture are complementary projects; that is, material production and cultural configurations go hand-in-hand. Thus, it is not brands that consumers are loyal to, but to images, meanings, and symbols that they produce while they consume. Hence, corporate strategic responsibility is expanded with the expanded role of culture today. Thus, how would you redefine products: (*a*) casino-gambling products, (*b*) liqor and wine products, and (*c*) tobacco products, such that:

a. They promote and safeguard consumer safety.
b. They fulfill a genuine consumer need or want.
c. They generate humanizing images and symbols of life.
d. They adopt safe, healthy, and human production modes.
e. They safeguard healthy circulation and consumption modes.
f. They generate healthy cultural and aesthetic meanings.
g. They guarantee responsible consumer-user behavior.
h. They ensure equitable distribution of jobs, profits, and opportunities.

2.8   Study Table 2.3: Social Formation as Structured Aggregation of Wealth Formation. Each of the nine cells in the table is a source of wealth formation. Each of the entries in the nine cells is a specific mode of wealth formation. As corporate executives, how would you ensure that each cell and each item therein:

    a. Safeguards basic human rights of dignity, freedom, privacy, and self-respect.
    b. Protects worker rights of safety, social wages, social security, and self-development.
    c. Protects consumer rights of adequate information, non-deception, non-coercion, safety, variety, consumer education, and consumer redress.
    d. Prevents harm, liability, and damage to every stakeholder.
    e. Protects the environment of water, air, and land from waste and degradation.
    f. Protects the resources, opportunities, rights, and interests of future generations.
    g. Reduces global inequalities of income, health, education, wealth, and opportunity.

2.9   Advertising, promotion, and product symbols, by their very nature, are dialectical: that is, while retaining their finite identity, they may mediate or make present what is transcendent (e.g., "heaven" in symbols of "good life") or what is beyond themselves. Symbols may be conceptual (as in words, scripts, narratives of promotional campaigns), theoretical (as in marketing theories and paradigms), or persons or things (as in art objects, heroes, celebrities). The symbolic mediation is usually imagined, since there is a distinct role of the imagination in all knowing. In this sense, any culture is a cluster of symbols mediating values and psycho-social meanings beyond the symbols. Marketing promotions create and play on symbols, diffuse symbols and thereby create symbols-based short-lived cultures such as moods, fads, fashions, and lifestyles. With this discussion in view,

    a. What are the major symbols of "good life," "immortality," and "conspicuous consumption" of this decade engendered by marketing promotions?
    b. Study their dialectical nature: that is, what do they symbolize beyond themselves?
    c. Study their symbolic mediations: How do they play upon consumer imagination?
    d. Study their psychosocial meanings that go beyond the symbols.
    e. What positive, uplifting, ethical, and moral images and paradigms do they project on consumer cultures?
    f. What negative, destructive, unethical, and immoral images and paradigms do they impose on consumer and social cultures?
    g. How should marketing executive take responsibility for the damages under (f)?

2.10   Product as values is not consumed unless and until consumers see in them relevant meanings, signs, and symbols of their socio-cultural life and lifestyle in them. Modern marketing culture, through its dominance of promotion and advertising of everyday life, can prompt, suggest, and enforce prepackaged symbols and meanings that condition consumers in their signification process. Hence, marketing executive's responsibility is expanded with the expanded role of customers and cultures today. Thus, how would you redefine your role in producing and marketing products like alcohol or tobacco products, violence and sex movies or other pornographic products, such that you:

    a. Offer better alternatives for consumer rest and relaxation?
    b. Do not over-target them to vulnerable populations?
    c. Shield children from their deleterious and demoralizing influence?
    d. Desist from projecting them as signs and symbols of "American good life"?
    e. Protect and prevent consumers from compulsions and addictions they may create?
    f. Assume responsibility when they do create wasteful addictive dependencies?

2.11 Given the broadened definition and role of culture today, both producers and marketers assume larger executive responsibilities to humanize, aestheticize, and celebrate genuinely human cultures by the products and services they offer in the markets. How would you apply this proposition and the moral responsibilities it implies to the following?

 a. Exorbitant pricing of lifesaving drugs like those that treat AIDS/HIV positive patients
 b. Peddling pornography via TV, radio, movies, Internet, and other media
 c. Forcing accelerated product obsolescence to outdate lifestyles
 d. Commoditizing religion, values, family, marriage, and parenting
 e. Over-commercializing religious and civic holidays and celebrations
 f. Secularizing virtue, sacralizing vice, and glorifying sin in casino gambling
 g. Stereotyping African-American Images in tobacco or liquor advertising

2.12 The customer is now considered in a broader context of society and social processes. The older marketing concept failed to consider the broader social and economic functions associated with marketing (e.g., Kotler and Levy 1969). No product or object has any inherent function or value independent of the symbolic and cultural framework in which it is inserted (Firat and Venkatesh 1995). Keeping these new developments in mind, and assuming that your company is involved in producing and/or marketing alcohol or tobacco products, how would you fulfill the following added corporate and marketing executive responsibilities?

 a. Brainstorm target customers to suggest better and healthy alternatives or substitutes.
 b. Involve target customers in their production process: that is, empower them to suggest more safe and healthy alcohol and/or tobacco products.
 c. Involve prospective customers in their signification process: that is, empower them to suggest culturally and morally uplifting symbols and activities for alcohol or tobacco products promotion campaign.
 d. Involve prospective customers in their de-marketing process: that is, enable them to voluntarily reduce consumption and seek better alternatives for rest and relaxation.

2.13 The employee as a customer should also be considered in a broader context of society and social processes rather than as a factor of production subjected to a routine production process. Productivity can be dovetailed to generate a healthy and moral social structure (Mascarenhas 1982). Assuming that your company is involved in producing and/or marketing alcohol and tobacco products, how would you fulfill the following employee-related corporate and marketing executive responsibilities?

 a. Brainstorm your production and marketing crew to suggest better and healthy alternatives or substitutes to tobacco and liquor products.
 b. Involve your employees in the entire production process, enabling and empowering them to suggest more safe, non-addictive and healthy alcohol and/or tobacco products.
 c. Involve employees, especially sales representatives, in their signification process: that is, empower them to suggest culturally and morally uplifting symbols and activities for their promotion campaign.
 d. Reward and recognize your employees for significant contributions under (a) to (c).

2.14 The rise of the industrial North during the early 20th century also opened opportunities to individuals from the South and Appalachia who were then trapped in a dead (mostly, plantation and slave trade) economy. The Great Migration of 1910–30 brought droves of African-Americans to the Great Lakes. In 1910, before the migration, 89 percent of the nation's African-Americans lived in the predominantly rural South. By 1960, 40 percent of the nation's African-Americans lived outside the South and 75 percent lived in the nation's cities. For instance, during 1910–30 alone, Chicago's African-American population grew from 44,000 to 235,000 and that of Detroit from 6,000 to 120,000 (Johnson 2006). While the industrial North represented a great melting pot of different backgrounds, races, and religions, the different populations did not coexist harmoniously. While the nation's African-Americans and Hispanics migrated to the Great Lake cities for jobs and better livelihood, anti-immigrant, anti-Catholic, and racial conflicts proliferated. Tensions culminated in riots (e.g., the 1908 riot in Springfield, IL, the 1916 Alderman's riot, the 1919 race riot in Chicago, the 12th Street (now named Rosa Parks Boulevard) riot in 1967 in Detroit, and the 2005 riot in Toledo, OH). Racial tensions accelerated the rise of the nation's most segregated metropolitan communities. Given this racial divide in several U.S. cities, how can you transform them into harmonious (if not homogeneous) groups living and growing together? For instance,

a. The labor movement (that reached its zenith in the successful fight for better wages and working conditions, time-off, and generous health, education, and retirement benefits in the big industry sectors) also indirectly served to unite whites and African-American workers together, spearheading important struggles for civil rights (Goldfield 2005). As a transformation expert, how would you deploy the labor unions to bring about a race fusion?
b. The production floor (especially, the assembly line production floor) created an increasingly integrated industrial workplace. The most integrated institution in America was the shop floor (cited in Austin 2004: 11). How would you empower the shop floor to bring about racial harmony in Detroit?
c. The public school system has been an efficient (if not always effective) learning center for students of all races. How would you energize the public school system in Southeast Michigan to accept, plan, and strategize racial harmony among students and their families?

PART II

The CEO as a Strategic Leader and Critical Thinker

Chapter 3

The CEO as a Strategic Leader

Transformations often begin when an organization has a new head who is a good leader and who sees the need for a major change. If the entire company needs to be changed, the CEO is the key player. If a divisions needs change, the divisional general manager is the key. If any of these key players are not great leaders or change champions, transformation is difficult. If these leaders honestly believe and are convinced that the status quo is unacceptable, and must do something about it, then the transformation process is on. The number one error in a transformation process is not establishing a great enough sense of urgency (Kotter 2007: 97–98).

Most successful transformation change efforts begin when some passionate individuals or some groups within an organization start to look hard at a company's competitive situation, market position, the emergence of a new industry or market, technology trends, and financial performance. They constantly monitor expiring patents, declining margins in a core business, potential cash crises, and great opportunities that are very current, and communicate this information timely and effectively throughout the firm. Just getting a transformation program started requires the aggressive cooperation of many individuals. Without motivation and a sense of urgency, a corporation goes nowhere. A paralyzed senior management comes from having too many managers and not enough leaders. Change, by definition, is creating a new system, which in turn always demands new and real leadership (Kotter 2007: 97). [See *Business Transformation Exercise 3.1.*]

Unfortunately, in the past 50 years or so, strategy has been presented as an analytical problem to be solved, a kind of left-brain exercise. Hence, there has been much infusion of economics into the study of strategy. This perception and trend, combined with strategy's high stakes, has led to an era of strategy specialists—legions of MBAs and strategy consultants—armed with frameworks and techniques, skills, and algorithms, eager to help managers analyze their industries, their market position, and forge the firms to competitive advantage. Strategy spawned into an industry by itself. Corporate planning departments emerged and introduced formal systems and standards for strategic analysis. Each consulting firm developed its own framework—most celebrated among them, the BCG growth-share matrix and McKinsey's 7-S framework. In the process that has outlasted over 50 years, however, strategy has been narrowed to a competitive game plan, divorcing it from a firm's larger sense of purpose; the CEO's unique role as arbiter and steward of strategy has been progressively eclipsed. While strategy gained depth in terms of analytical precision of tool kits and techniques, it lost its organizational breadth and stature. This chapter focuses on strategy from the CEO's role of strategic effective leadership.

The leader is a conduit for change, but the leader gets the people in the organization to make actual change happen. A leader should derive great satisfaction seeing his subjects succeed. Every CEO as a leader must ask:

- Are our markets changing?
- Is our competition changing?
- Is our world changing?
- Am I changing?
- How am I changing?
- Is our organization changing?
- How am I changing it?

THE STRATEGIC LEADERSHIP ROLE OF A CEO

A few days before he died in November 2005, the management guru, Peter Drucker, wrote about the role of the CEO. The CEO is the link between the Inside (i.e., the organization) and the Outside (i.e., the society, economy, technology, markets, and customers). Inside is mostly costs; the outside is results. Without the outside, there is no inside. The sustainable competitive advantage and growth of a company is the CEO's responsibility and legacy, and inward focus is the enemy of growth. Salespeople as frontline ambassadors of a company's brands and services are outwardly focused, whereas, everyone else is inwardly focused.

The CEO alone experiences the meaningful outside at the enterprise level and is responsible for understanding it, interpreting it, advocating for it, and presenting it so that the company can respond in a way that enables sustainable sales, profit, and total shareholder return (TSR) growth. It is the job only a CEO can and should do because everybody else in the organization is focused on a narrower part of the inside or the outside of the firm. The CEO must integrate the inside and the outside—a very difficult task. Without a deep understanding of the external stakeholders and their competing interests, and how these interests correspond with the capabilities and limitations of the organization, a CEO cannot function optimally or succeed. The CEO is the only one held responsible and accountable for the performance and the results of the entire company, judged not only by his standards, but by those of his stakeholders.

A. G. Lafley, the 2009 CEO of Proctor & Gamble (P&G), prescribes his own version of the role of CEO. In linking the outside with the inside, the role of the CEO, says Lafley, comes down to four fundamentals (Lafley 2009: 56–59):

- **Define and interpret the meaningful outside**: Of all your external stakeholders (e.g., customers, suppliers, investors, distributors, retailers, governments, and local communities) which are the ones that matter the most? What results are the most meaningful?
- **Constantly clarify what business the company is in, and in what it is not**: Where should you play it in, and where you not at all? These questions are difficult and require thorough evaluation, discussion, and dialogue. Only the CEO can claim enterprise-wide perspective to answer these questions.
- **Balance sufficient yield in the present with necessary investment in the future**: This implies learning to strike the right balance between the short-term and the long-term goals, as also determining what goals are "good enough" for the short term and what goals could be critical for the future; this also implies how to prepare high-potential leaders for the future.
- **Shape the values and the standards of the organization**: Values establish a company's identity; they define company behavior. If the company must win, these values must be connected to the

meaningful outside, and be relevant for the present and the future. Standards are about expectations; they define what winning on the outside looks like. Standards are best defined by two questions: Are we winning with those who matter most? Are we winning against the very best?

The simplicity and clarity of these fundamentals is their strength. A CEO's challenge is to resist being drawn into other works that is not the unique responsibility of the CEO (micromanagement). The CEO must define and interpret the relevant outside—where the results are most meaningful, which external constituency mattered most, and which results were the most important. Of all the stakeholders, both inside and outside, the primary one is the consumer. The consumer is indeed the king.

Peter Drucker also said that the purpose of a business is to create a customer. If we are not in constant touch with our customer, we are wasting ourselves and our resources, working on initiatives consumers do not want and incurring costs that consumers are forced to pay for. To keep in constant touch with the customers, for instance, P&G employees include in-home and in-store visiting consumers, and virtually every P&G office and innovation center has consumers working inside with employees. A CEO must enable the company to win the consumer value equation every day at two critical moments of truth: (*a*) the consumer chooses the company's products over all the others in the store; (*b*) the consumers derive a delightful and memorable experience from the company's products. [See *Business Transformation Exercise 3.2.*]

EXECUTIVE TRANSFORMATIONAL LEADERSHIP

Doris Kearns Goodwin, a Pulitzer Prize winner, in her best-selling account of President Abraham Lincoln that she wrote in 2005 and titled, *Team of Rivals* [incidentally, the one book (apart from the Bible) that President Obama opted to take to the White House in January 2009], delineates essential features of a great leader, mostly patterned after those of President Lincoln. Some of these are (Goodwin 2009: 43–47):

- A great leader surrounds oneself with people who can argue with him and question his assumptions. It particularly helps if you can bring in people whose temperaments differ from yours.
- A great leader should figure out how to share credit for your success with your inner team so that they feel part of the mission. Basically, you want to create a reservoir of positive feelings, and that implies that you not only acknowledge your errors but even shoulder the blame for the failures of some of your subordinates.
- A great leader should know how to relax and possess a sense of humor so that she can replenish her energies for the struggles she has to face tomorrow. Lincoln went to the theater about a hundred times while he was in Washington. Although he suffered from a certain melancholy, he had a tremendous sense of humor, and would entertain people long into the night with his stories. And hence, was widely admired as a great storyteller. The ability to recharge your batteries in the midst of great stress and crisis is crucial for successful leadership.
- A great leader should have an extraordinary amount of emotional intelligence, the ability to feel with and motivate people. He must be able to put past hurts behind him and never allow wounds to fester. He should be able to acknowledge his errors and learn from his mistakes to a remarkable degree.

- Every great leader has flaws. Lincoln's greatest flaw came out of his strength—he generally liked people and did not want to hurt them. He always wanted to give somebody a second or even a third chance. For example, because of his inability to hurt people, Lincoln just could not fire George McClellan, head of the Union Army for months near the beginning of the Civil War, but who was very narcissistic and insubordinate. As a result, battles were lost, and thousands of soldiers died who might have lived had Lincoln fired McClellan much earlier. When Lincoln brought Edwin Stanton into the cabinet in 1862 as Secretary of War, Stanton was much tougher and very secretive. Their opposite temperaments balanced each other.
- A leader never quits no matter how terrible the problem or crisis. Lincoln faced the crisis of the Civil War. Roosevelt weathered a banking crisis, an economic crisis, and the war by his fireside chats. The current economic crisis is no different than any other by scale and magnitude, even when it does surpass the Great Depression in some areas. The U.S. will weather this storm as it has weathered worse crises before. Moreover, in the times of crisis, things become possible that would not be possible at other times. It almost takes a deep crisis to move forward. Lincoln did during the Civil War; Franklin D. Roosevelt had his opportunity in the Depression; Obama has the great opportunity now—he can pull the country together in new ways to get out of this hole, and work across party lines. [See *Business Transformation Exercise 3.3.*]

Here are other great traits of a leader, according to David McCullough, another great American historian, a two-time Pulitzer Prize winner and well-known public television host (McCullough 2008: 45–49):

(a) A leader is a visionary who is able to generate a great sense of mission; her enthusiasm is infectious; she is willing to take risks. She personifies the old adage: nothing ventured, nothing gained.

(b) A good leader does not rule by an organization chart; people are more important than paper positions. He makes other people's success, his success.

(c) A great leader has his door always open so that anyone can talk to him about anything.

(d) A good leader takes full responsibility for his actions, and never points fingers towards others to shoulder the blame.

(e) Being a leader means a person of integrity, courage, resilience and strength of character. A leader is somebody we can count on when the chips are down.

(f) A leader is never afraid to have people around him, who are more accomplished than he is. President Harry Truman was not afraid to have brilliant people surround him; he had the best cabinet any president had since George Washington.

(g) A true leader never asks any of his people to do anything he would not do himself.

(h) A true leader has the power of persuasion—the ability to get people to do, what they ought to know to do, without being told.

(i) A true leader listens—listening means asking good questions and taking in what people have to say. It also means hearing what people are not saying—what is bothering them about the job, their company, or country.

(j) A true leader never feathers one's own interests or popularity at the expense of corporate results; he never puts his own status before that of the corporation he works for.

(k) A good leader has very high standards and lives up to them; he has a sense that his work matters, that his efforts contribute to something bigger than him and his salary.

- A good leader may be a short-term pessimist, but a long-term optimist. America certainly experienced a time of great stress, danger, and concern during the recent recession and economic crisis. However, there has never been a time when America did not have serious problems. The current financial, political, and corporate crisis is by no means the darkest or the most dangerous time America has been through. America has risen from the dumps in the past; so will it now. I remain optimistic about America because I believe it still has the most productive, most innovative, and most dedicated workers in the world. The current crisis offers opportunities that America has never had before. A great leader mines opportunities from the darkest of chaos.

Leaders must lead. Managers must manage. Both do, but this does not mean, however, that creative and innovative ideas have to come from the top. Good leaders and managers know how to generate new ideas from the ranks and files. They enable and empower their employees to think big, to think far into the future, to redesign the company, and to reinvent and help in coming up with innovative ideas for the company. Richard Teerlink attributed his remarkable success of turning around Harley-Davidson to just this: "You get power by releasing power." Sheryl Sandberg asked her people to give frank feedback on whatever they see is or is not working. She learnt this lesson early at Google before moving into the company's Facebook unit as its Chief Operating Officer (COO): "I thank every person who ever raised a problem publicly" (Neumeier 2009). In this sense, a leader becomes a steward of organizational energy.

A leader cares for and is committed to his workforce. Honoring your commitment and responsibility to your workers is an important part of executive leadership. A great deal of Fiat's recent success has come about from a committed workforce. However, to earn that level of commitment, the company had to give ordinary folks, not just its leaders, a sense of connection. Sergio Marchionne, the CEO of Fiat, did not indiscriminately close plants and lay off workers. Instead, he worked around them. He opened kindergartens and grocery stores near plants to make it easier for his workers to balance work and domestic obligations. He redecorated their dressing rooms, bathrooms, and other facilities. Nobody asked him to do these changes. Fiat recognized that the commitment it makes as leaders to its workforce goes beyond what is negotiated in the labor contracts. [See *Business Transformation Exercise 3.4.*]

TRANSFORMATIONAL LEADERSHIP AND ACTION LOGIC

[See Rooke and Torbert (2005)]

After over 25 years of extensive survey-based consulting on leadership at large corporations, Rooke and Torbert (2005) conclude that what differentiated leaders is not so much their philosophy of leadership, their personality, or their style of management, but their internal "action logic" by which they interpret their environment and react to it when their power or safety is challenged. Based on sentence-completion surveys administered across hundreds of American and European company executives over the last 25 years, the authors found that the levels of corporate and individual performance vary according to action logic. They categorize their findings into seven action logics described in Table 3.1.

- **The Opportunists**: They react to the world in terms of controlling and exploiting it for directing intended outcomes. Their style is self-aggrandizement and they engage in constantly firefighting

TABLE 3.1   Seven Action Logics of Organizational Leadership

Action logic	Characteristics	Strengths	Weaknesses	Percentage in the research sample
Opportunist	Focus on personal wins and see the world and people as opportunities to be exploited.	Good in emergencies and in exploiting markets and sales opportunities.	Mistrustful, ego-centric, and manipulative. Might makes right. Treat people as objects.	5%
Diplomat	Please higher-status colleagues while avoiding conflict. They may not initiate change.	They help bring people together and create bonding.	They ignore conflict. They are so polite and diplomatic that they cannot provide challenging feedback to others.	12%
Expert	Experts in data, facts, logic, and knowledge of their chosen field, they do not seek consensus or collaboration.	See continuous improvement, efficiency, and perfection, but the yardstick is one's expertise.	Watertight thinking: my way or the high-way. Tend to view collaboration as a waste of time. Low on empathy and emotional intelligence.	38%
Achievers	Meet strategic goals via team work and delegation.	Well-suited to managerial roles; they are action and goal oriented.	They rarely think and act out of the box. May not encourage creativity and innovation.	30%
Individualists	They may interweave personal and company logic to create unique structures to resolve gaps between strategy and performance.	Good as entrepreneurs, venture leaders, and for consulting assignments.	Very individualistic; they disdain customs, conventions, and rules.	10%
Strategists	They are good at building personal, organizational, and international relationships. They consider ethical investing as a viable business.	Highly effective change agents; very comfortable in conflict resolution. They are socially responsible. Effective as transformation leaders.	They may tend to frustrate the opportunists, diplomats, experts, achievers, and the individualists.	4%
Alchemists	They renew and reinvent themselves and their organizations. They speak in symbols and metaphors that speak directly to hearts and minds.	They are charismatic leaders trying to develop the best in people. Extremely truthful and moral, they infuse such spirit in others.	There are too few of these in the world.	1%

Source: Author's own.

Note: See Rooke and Torbert (2005: 66–76).

their environment. They write their own rules, feel they could do anything, and pull-off everything. They treat people as objects or as factors of production. They legitimize and rationalize their evil behavior, reject feedback, externalize blame, and retaliate harshly. They do not last long. Some leaders in Enron, Tyco, and Halliburton seemed to fit this style.

- **The Diplomats**: They make sense of the world around them more benignly than the opportunists. This action logic is focused on gaining control of one's own behavior than on controlling the external environment and people. The goal, thereby, is to gain acceptance of people and influence them by cooperating with them and abiding by group norms. These leaders primarily work at junior executive levels such as frontline supervisors.
- **The Experts**: These formed the largest group (38 percent) of the research sample. They control the world around them by perfecting their knowledge of the profession. They rarely seek consensus nor ask for collaboration.
- **The Achievers**: They create a positive work environment and focus on deliverables. Unfortunately, they do not think outside the box. They are open to feedback but interpret it within their box or framework of thinking, and hence may clash with experts. They also delegate responsibility.
- **The Individualists**: They exhibit unique, unconventional ways of thinking and operating. They believe all actions and logics are constructed and abstract ideas. They ignore customs and conventions, traditions, and rules as irrelevant. They fail to acknowledge organizational processes and routines. These are effective as entrepreneurs, ventures, and consulting roles.
- **The Strategists**: They focus on organizational constraints and perceptions in order to transform themselves. They are adept at creating shared visions across different action logics such that they achieve personal and organizational transformation. They deal comfortably with conflict, and are good in handling people's resistance to change. Consequently, they are highly effective change agents. Michael Dell, Bill Gates, Jack Welch are examples of the strategists.
- **The Alchemists**: They have great ability to renew and reinvent themselves and their organizations in historically significant ways. They can deal with kings and commoners. They have an extraordinary capacity to deal with many situations at multiple levels. They can deal with immediate priorities while never losing sight of long-term goals. They are typically charismatic, live by high moral standards, and are extremely self-aware individuals who focus intensely on truth. They can pick up historic moments of their organizations and create strong symbols and metaphors out of them to speak to people's hearts and minds. Good examples of this leadership are Nelson Mandela, Mother Teresa, and Pope John Paul II.

Leaders are made, not born, and how they develop is critical to organizational change. Hence, leaders can transform from one action logic to another, all the way from opportunists and diplomats to strategists and alchemists. Critical personal changes (e.g., training, counsel, coaching, feedback, work-ethic, new forms of spiritual practice, new forms of centering and self-expression) and external events (e.g., promotions, high-caliber organizational climate and culture, top management support, executive training, and leadership teams) can also trigger and support such transformations. "Those who are willing to work at developing themselves and becoming more self-aware can almost certainly evolve over time into truly transformational leaders" (Rooke and Torbert 2005: 76). [See *Business Transformation Exercises 3.5 and 3.6.*]

STRATEGIC LEADERSHIP: DO NOT OVERDO YOUR STRENGTHS

Conventional wisdom in leadership development is that as leaders you should discover and capitalize on your strengths, assuming they are aligned with organizational needs. In addition, no matter how hard you work on certain weaknesses, you will make only marginal success, and hence, do not waste too much time overcoming flaws; thus, better focus on what you do best and surround yourself with people who have complementary strengths. This approach is reasonable as an antidote to unhealthy fixation on weaknesses. Nevertheless, it can also lead to overdoing your strengths.

More is not always better. Often, executives lose their jobs when their one-time strengths become weaknesses through overuse. Based on extensive research on senior, middle, and junior level leaders for over 25 years, Robert E. Kaplan and Robert B. Kaiser (2009) suggest strategies and tools to help managers recognize when they overuse their strengths and how they can correct this counter-productive tendency.

Taking your strength to an extreme is always detrimental to performance measured by vitality (e.g., morale, engagement, and cohesion) and productivity (e.g., quantity, cost, and quality of output). Costs of overdoing strengths are many:

a. **Forceful Leadership**: This type of leadership exercises influence on the basis of one's own intellect and energy. It takes charge, starts all initiatives, and gives directions to all others. It takes a position, defends it, announces it, and enforces it. In the process, it pushes people to their limits, sets high expectations, and holds people accountable. It is just as harmful to overdo one's forceful leadership as it is to under-do it. If you are over-forceful, output may increase but vitality may decrease. Overall effectiveness (say, measured by coworker ratings of leader's managerial effectiveness) is very low at both ends, that is, at the very low and very high levels of leadership forcefulness, but maximizes at the median or right amount of forcefulness (i.e., an inverted U parabola).

b. **Enabling Leadership**: This type of leadership creates conditions for other people to contribute. It empowers subjects and gives them latitude to do their jobs. It includes everybody, listens to them, seeks inputs from them, and is open to their influence. It supports people, shows appreciation and sensitivity to subjects. It is just as harmful to overdo one's enabling leadership as it is to under-do it. If you are too enabling, vitality may flourish but productivity may also take a hit. Overall effectiveness is very low at both very low and very high levels of enabling leadership, but peaks at the median or right amount of enabling-ness (i.e., the interrelationship between enabling leadership and overall effectiveness is an inverted U parabola).

c. **Strategic Leadership**: This type of leadership positions the organization for the future. This leadership plans ahead and takes the long view over a big corporate canvas. It pursues growth and seeks ways to grow the business and expand its markets and capabilities. It promotes innovation, questions the status quo, and encourages new thinking. Once again, it is just as harmful to overdo one's strategic leadership as it is to under-do it. Overall managerial and performance effectiveness is very low at both ends, that is, at very low and very high strategic leadership levels, but reaches a maximum at the median or right amount of strategic leadership (i.e., the correlation between the two variables is an inverted U parabola).

d. **Operational Leadership**: This type of leadership focuses the organization on short-term ends and goals. It manages the day-to-day details of implementation, and concentrates on results. It maximizes efficiency, conserves resources by cutting costs, and is selective about priorities.

It maintains order, and gets things done using the discipline of procedures and processes. Once again, it is just as harmful to overdo one's operational leadership as it is to under-do it. Overall effectiveness is very low at both ends, that is, at very low and very high levels of operational leadership, but aces at the median or right amount of operational leadership (i.e., the relation is an inverted U parabola).

Leadership types (c) and (d) describe the "what" of leadership, while (a) and (b) define the "how" of executive leadership. All four types of leadership perform best at their golden mean or balance between aggressiveness and inaction. The golden mean is characterized with great respect for people involved, much listening, being transparent, being passionate without losing compassion, being right without being righteous, being decisive without being rigid—a balance between overdoing and under-doing. [See *Business Transformation Exercise 3.7*]

EXECUTIVE LEADERSHIP AS BUILDING YOUR STRENGTHS

Guided by the belief that good is the opposite of bad, we have unduly focused on our faults and failings in building our strengths. For instance, doctors study diseases and its symptoms in order to learn about health; psychologists investigate sadness in exploring joy; marriage therapists study causes of divorce in identifying characteristics of a happy marriage; in schools and workplaces we are advised to look into our faults and weaknesses assuming that we can build strengths by eliminating weaknesses. Buckingham and Clifton (2001) disagree with this approach. According to them, faults and failings deserve investigation, but they reveal little about strengths. Strengths have their own patterns. To excel in your chosen field and to find lasting satisfaction in doing so, you will need to understand your strengths and their unique patterns.

Executive leaders and HR managers must not only accommodate the fact that each employee is different, they must capitalize on these differences. They must watch for clues to each employee's natural talents and then position and develop each employee so that his or her talents transform into bona fide strengths. By changing the way you select, measure, develop, and channel the careers of your people, your organization can be revolutionary and could build your entire enterprise around the strengths of each person. To spur high-margin growth and thereby increase their value, great organizations need only focus inward to find the wealth of unrealized capacity that resides in every single employee (Buckingham and Clifton 2001: 6).

Most organizations are built on two flawed assumptions about people:
Each person can learn to be competent in almost anything;
Each person's greatest room for growth is in his or her areas of greatest weakness.

Thus, if everyone can learn to be competent in almost anything, those who have learnt the most must be most valuable, and hence, by design, the organization gives the most prestige, respect, and promotions based on the skills or experiences they have acquired in the company. Hence, organizations spend more money in training people once they hire them than on selecting them properly in the first place. They spend most of their training, time and money on trying to plug the gaps in the employee's skills or competencies, calling the latter weaknesses as "areas of opportunity." In training the incompetent, organizations legislate work styles by emphasizing on work rules, policies, procedures, and behavioral competencies. Most organizations take their employees' strengths for granted and focus on minimizing their weaknesses. Most HRD learning-experiments focus on fixing each employee's weaknesses than building on their strengths. Most often, however, this is not human development, but just damage control. Damage control is a poor strategy for elevating either the employee or the organization to world-class performance.

Buckingham and Clifton (2001: 8) offer alternative counter-assumptions:

Each person's talents are enduring and unique;
Each person's greatest room for growth is in the areas of his or her greatest strength.

These two assumptions should guide HR managers to select, develop, measure, and channel the strengths and careers of their people. These assumptions should explain why great managers are careful to look for talent in every role, why they focus performance on outcomes than on work styles, why they treat each person differently, and, finally, why they spend most time with their best people.

Hence, in this context, a critical thinking exercise should start with you:

- What are your strengths?
- How can you capitalize on them?
- How can you combine them?
- What are your most powerful combinations?
- Where do they take you?

The real tragedy of life is not that each of us does not have enough strengths, but that we fail to use the ones we have. Benjamin Franklin called wasted strengths "sundials in the shade." Hence, identify your sundials wasting in the shade. Look inside yourself and identify your strongest strengths, reinforce them by practice, learning and training, and then carve out a role that draws on these strengths every-day. When you do this, you will be more productive, more fulfilled, and more successful (Buckingham and Clifton 2001: 21).

Warren Buffett once said to the students at the University of Nebraska: "If there is any difference between you and me, it may be simply that I get up every day and have a chance to do what I love to do, every day. If you want to learn anything from me, this is best advice I can give you" (Buckingham and Clifton 2001). Buffett was a patient man; his mind was more practical than conceptual. Like many people who are both fulfilled and successful, he found a way to cultivate his strengths and put them to work. His investor strength was his now famous "twenty-year perspective" that led him to invest only in those companies whose products and services he could intuitively understand and the trajectory he could forecast with some level of confidence for the next 20 years. Some such companies were Dairy Queen, The Coco-Cola Company, and the Washington Post Company. He started his first investment partnership with US $100 in 1956. He has honed this patient investor talent, perfected it, and stuck to it despite the quick high-margins in the other high-tech companies.

Tiger Woods had a different strength—his length with his woods and his irons, and tremendous accuracy in putting. His ability to chip out of a bunker was no good; he did not need it either; and much less did he cultivate it. Instead, he deliberately played to his strengths. He loved what he did because he deliberately played to his strengths.

Bill Gate's strength was at taking innovations and transforming them into user-friendly applications and marketing them effectively. His inability to maintain and build an enterprise in the face of legal and commercial assault was his weakness—he let Steve Ballmer handle that.

Buckingham and Clifton (2001: 25–61) offer some useful definitions and rules in this regard:

- **Strength**: near consistent or perfect performance in an activity. Talents, knowledge, and skills combine to create your strengths.
- **Talents**: are your natural recurring patterns of thought, feeling, or behavior that can be productively applied. Most talents, like intelligence, leadership, and team-building, are value-neutral. Talents are innate, and are not the same as *values*. You can learn values; you can change values; but your innate talents grow with you. We accept our talents, become aware of them, and build and refocus our lives around them.
- **Knowledge**: consists of the facts and lessons you learn. Knowledge is factual, experiential, also conceptual and theoretical, logical and rational.
- **Skills**: are steps to an activity. Skills bring structure to experiential knowledge. That is, you can sit back and formalize your accumulated knowledge into a sequence of steps that lead to a trained activity. Think of a concert pianist, a great preacher or public speaker, a creative writer, a trained diplomat, and a patient mother—they all have accumulated knowledge at their fingertips. Skills enable you to avoid trial and error, and empower you to immerse directly into performance. However, skills without underlying innate talents may lead you somewhere, but not to glory.

Talents, knowledge, and skills are raw materials to building strengths; but most important among these are talents. Talents are innate, while knowledge and skills can be learned and cultivated. You can never possess a strength (e.g., salesmanship, closing a sale) without requisite talent (e.g., gift of persuasion, talent for negotiation). The key to building your strengths is to identify your dominant talents and then refine them with knowledge and skills. Skills determine if you can do something, whereas talents reveal how well and how often you do it. Buckingham and Clifton (2001: 26–27) state three principles in this regard:

1. For an activity to be a strength, you must be able to do it consistently, and you must derive some intrinsic satisfaction from that activity. This implies that it is a predictable part of your performance.
2. You do not have to have strength in every aspect of your role in order to excel. Tiger Woods and Bill Gates had their limitations; they got around them. Excellent performers do not have to be well-rounded; they are sharp.
3. You will excel only by maximizing your strengths, never by fixing your weaknesses. Of course, you do not ignore your weaknesses, but manage around them. Find people whose strengths are your weaknesses. That would free you up to hone your strengths to a sharper point.

Buckingham and Clifton (2001: 28–35) suggest three "revolutionary" tools to build strengths:

1. **Distinguish your natural talents from things you can learn (e.g., knowledge, skills, experience, and self-awareness)**: Your natural talents are innate; they directly build your strengths.
2. **Identify your dominant talents**: Step back and watch yourself for a while—try any activity and see how quickly you pick it up; how quickly you skip steps in the learning and add twists

and kinks to make that activity your own. See, next, if that activity absorbs you, that you have a passion for it, and time spent on that activity satisfies and fulfills you. This is your talent zone.

3. **Use a common language to explain or share your talents and accept those of others**: Our language to describe, explains, and treats weaknesses such as diseases, neurosis, psychosis, depression, mania, hysteria, panic-attack, and schizophrenia is well-developed. However, our language to describe, shares, and accepts natural talents are sparse. The terms that we use such as, she is people-skilled, he is self-motivated, she is a born leader, she is a team-builder, and the like, are still vague, undefined, unmeasured, and hence, underdeveloped. HR people are rarely on the same page when they discuss these talents.

What are talents? If you are instinctively inquisitive, then it is a talent. If you are competitive, it is a talent. If you are persistent, persuasive, and compelling, then this is a talent. If you are ethical, moral, responsible, sensitive to others, then this is a good talent. If you can readily pick up on the feelings of others, then you have the talent of empathy. Some negative talents (e.g., obstinacy, pride) and frailties (e.g., stammering, dyslexia, and autism) can be developed into positive talents and strengths. Most of these recurring patterns of behavior we call talents are woven in our brain as a network of our strongest synaptic connections. "Your talents, your strongest synaptic connections, are the most important raw material for strength building. Identify your most powerful talents, hone them with skills and knowledge, and you will be well on your way to living the strong life" (Buckingham and Clifton 2001: 61). [See *Business Transformation Exercises 3.8 and 3.9.*]

FORMULATING STRATEGY IN RELATION TO CORPORATE VALUES

Sam Palmisano, when he succeeded the legendary Lou Gerstner in 2002, had a clear mandate when he was appointed CEO of IBM: to continue IBM's transformation that Lou Gerstner started in 1993. His strategic response was a bottom-up reinvention of IBM's venerable values. Palmisano believed that a company is an organic system that needs to adapt. In the process of adaptation, values, principles, beliefs, and even DNA come alive.

The last time IBM examined its values was in 1914, when its founder, Thomas Watson, Sr., laid out three principles he called *basic beliefs*:

1. Respect for the individual
2. The best customer service
3. The pursuit of excellence

These were top-down values, but given the culture of the times (with much emphasis on manual-skills based manufacturing), they played a significant role in driving IBM's success during 1914–93, that is, the most of the 20th century. The rule of thumb those days was, "Employees do not do what you expect; they do what you inspect." Hence, management was basically supervisory. Workers were skilled in limited number of job routines in assembly lines and were often paid piece-meal wages. The prevailing employee-motivation philosophy was that money was a motivator, and workers did not care for freedom on their jobs but just dictation. Frederick Taylor (1856–1917) pioneered this philosophy, and Henry Ford (1863–1947) gladly implemented it in his auto assembly lines of Dearborn, Michigan.

However, with IBM's highly skilled employees, Watson's values got distorted and metamorphosed into entitlement and arrogance within the organization. IBM became inward-looking, complacent, and ego-driven, and hence, blind to market changes in the early 1990s. This attitude almost led to its demise in 1992, when Lou Gerstner took over. He quickly changed the IBM business model to respond to the market challenges. IBM then was 60 percent computer hardware and around 40 percent computer software and services. He more than reversed this trend. IBM became almost 70 percent software and services, a knowledge-based skill and profession. In fact, IBM redefined its mission as a business IT problem-solutions-service company. With this massive change, IBM was no more product- and brand-oriented, but totally, employee-focused and client-customer-driven.

A strong bottoms-up (and not top-down) value system is crucial to bringing together and motivating a highly skilled IBM workforce as large and diverse and spread around 170 countries. More than 200,000 of IBM employees have college degrees working on more than 60 to 70 major product lines, and serving more than a dozen different, sophisticated, industrial customer segments. A top-down values imposition would create a smothering bureaucracy at IBM, a bureaucracy that could kill speed, flexibility, creativity, and innovation. You have to create a management system that empowers people and provides a sure basis for decision-making that is consistent with who we are at IBM, said Palmisano (2004: 65). Any way that would optimize IBM's enormous and complex organizational structure which must assure that all its 320,000 workforce is empowered and enabled to make the right calls the right way and at the right time.

In 2003, when Sam Palmisano took over, his major thrust was to rediscover a set of values that could empower employees and enrich customers. Additionally, with the drastic change in the computer hardware–software industry and a sprawling and diverse enterprise that IBM became in 2000s, Palmisano needed a new beginning. He announced four values, three of them from Watson's basic beliefs, and one to reflect the change in the industry:

- Respect
- Customer
- Excellence
- Innovation

He test-marketed these four concepts through surveys and focus groups with more than 1,000 IBM employees. The test market rejected the notion of "respect" as it connoted condescension and arrogance of the IBM past. Instead of four concepts, three equivalent statements were proposed:

1. Commitment to the customer
2. Excellence through innovation
3. Integrity that earns trust

To this effect, Palmisano started with a company-wide value-discovery exercise in 2003. He hosted a 72-hour online ValuesJam via the corporate intranet in which he asked IBM's nearly 320,000 employees to weigh in on the following questions:

- If our company disappeared tonight, how different would the world be tomorrow?
- Is there something about our company that makes a unique contribution to the world?

All these questions relate to core added-value that strategy should bring to the organization (Montgomery 2008). Over the three-day ValuesJam session, an estimated 50,000 employees, including Sam Palmisano, checked out the discussion, posting nearly 10,000 comments about the proposed values. The first day was typically marked by negative and cynical critics who unleashed lot of anger and steam. The second day, the counter critics began to weigh in with values such as integrity, excellence, and quality. The question of what was worth preserving and what needed to be changed in IBM was at the heart of the ValuesJam. When the jam session was over, a specially tailored "jamalyzer tool" (based on IBM's e-classifier software but turbocharged with additional capabilities designed to process the constantly changing content of the ValuesJam) mined the over-a-million words text. Later, Palmisano summarized IBM's future values in November 2003 (Palmisano 2004) as follows:

1. Dedication to every client's success.
2. Innovation that matters—for our company and for the world.
3. Trust and personal responsibility in all relationships.

The only thing that bond, bound, and bind such a great institution like IBM is not management top-down dictates, but genuine, sincere, and fundamental values that all IBM employees accept, own, and get energized by. These values would be the basis of what IBM employees dream and do, and feel passionate about their mission and identity as a company. These values would be the touchstone for decentralizing decision-making. Especially since IBM changed its business model from a hardware company to an integrated IT business solutions services company, its brands are not its products and services, but its very people. They are its frontline ambassadors to the customer world and the environment. In this context, one thing that can inform, transform, and bond such ambassadors and make their behavior globally consistent and persistent is a set of dynamic values they choose, own, operationalize, and live. That is the reason why a right set of values is critically important for an ongoing corporate strategy, a set of values that is enduring, a credo of beliefs that would guide the company through economic cycles and geopolitical shifts, through recessions and depressions, through booms and busts, a set of values that would transcend changes in products, technologies, employees and leaders, and even business models. Instead of galvanizing employees through fear of failure, you have to galvanize them through hope and aspiration. [See *Business Transformation Exercise 3.10.*]

At IBM in 2003, during and after the ValuesJam, there was remarkable unanimity regarding the values. The debate, however, was whether IBM today is able and willing to live them. The employees understood the need to reintegrate IBM so that inter-country, inter-departmental, and inter-functional silos could network and participate better. A typical IBM complaint would be, "I am in Tokyo, prototyping software for a client, and I need a software engineer based in Austin, TX right now to help in a blade server configuration. However, I cannot just say, 'please come to Tokyo and help'. I need to get a charge code first so I can pay his department for his time." Employees found several blocks in the way of serving clients—the financial control processes that required several levels of management approval. Often the money would come, but too late. In such cases, the first value, "dedication to every client's success," will bring together all of IBM's capability, in the laboratory, in the field, and in the back office to help solve difficult client problems. For instance, to make financial transactions effective and quick, each of the 700 major client-facing salespersons had access to a discretionary fund of $5,000 for such inter-country skill transactions. When this strategy worked well, it was extended to well-over 22,000 IBM first-line employees. The salespeople were reminded of the third value of taking full responsibility in using the Managers' Value fund (that easily exceeded $100 million) responsibly (Palmisano 2004: 69).

Similarly, the second value, "innovation that matters," meant more than innovating and building great products, it talked about how innovation can touch people and society (e.g., through cutting-edge biotechnology with Mayo Clinic or by helping governments to fight terrorism with its data technology). These kinds of innovations enable IBM to attract great scientists to its workforce anywhere in the world. Innovation was also needed in pricing client-problem solutions. For instance, with 60–70 product lines serving over 12 different customer segments across 170 countries, each brand or product or component unit having its own autonomous profit and loss (P&L) department, and all the people who determine prices organized by brand—pricing a complex multi-component, multi-skill, multi-technology integrated IT solution could be an administrative nightmare. Hence, IBM found a method of setting a single price for each integrated offering, keeping "client success" in mind. IBM had to come up with similar innovations in purchasing, especially in relation to cross-IBM bids.

Inspired by this set of values, IBM employees never stop questioning old assumptions, trying out different models, testing the limits, pushing the envelope—whether in technology, business, or in progressive workforce policies. The third value, "trust and personal responsibility in all relationships," helps to focus on relationships among people at IBM, with suppliers, investors, governments, and with communities.

STRATEGIC LEADERSHIP AS ONGOING STEWARDSHIP

A CEO's job is not done once a carefully formulated strategy has been made ready for implementation or is implemented. The job of a CEO as a strategist never ends. For one thing, no strategy, howsoever comprehensive, defined and compelling, can be a sufficient guide for a firm that aspires to a long and prosperous life. Just as complete contracts are difficult to write with your trading partners, so are complete strategies specifying all the particulars. There will be some choices or alternatives that are not obvious at the time of strategy formulation. There could be numerous contingencies that could not be foreseen or factored into the strategic framework. There will always be limits to communicating the strategy so that all will understand it unequivocally. At the heart, most strategies, like most people, involve some mystery. Interpreting that mystery is an abiding responsibility of the CEO, the chief strategist in a company (Montgomery 2008: 59).

Articulating and tending to a purpose-driven strategy is no easy task. It is a human endeavor in the deepest sense of the term, keeping all the parts of a company in proper balance while moving the enterprise forward in a highly competitive and turbulent world. A CEO must constantly confront the challenges that competition and environment generate and the opportunities they spawn. Some CEOs get it right, others do not. British Petroleum Inc.(BP) failed on several counts—in investments, operating practices, compromised worker safety, threatened environment, and CEO Browne had to resign. On the other hand, Michael O'Leary, CEO of Ryanair since 1994 got everything right. During its early years, the Irish airline entered the Dublin–London market with full service priced at less than half the fares of incumbents like British Airways and Air Lingus. This stimulated a fierce fare war that brought Ryanair almost to its knees. The CEO revamped the fare strategy and transformed the company into a no-frills player with a true low-cost business model. The latter involved changing the airline's fleet, cost, fare, and route structures. Ryanair went on to become a major airline and one of the world's most profitable. The case of Southwest Airlines in the U.S. is similar.

While faithfully translating purpose into practice, the CEO must also remain open that the purpose itself may need to change. The judgments made at these moments of transition can make or break a leader or a firm. Lou Gerstner, the legendary CEO of IBM, faced such a moment in 1993. To redeem and resurrect the troubled company, Lou concluded that a radical shift in its mindset was necessary. This task required taking a fearless moral inventory of the business, realistically evaluating the core capabilities of the firm, and divesting everything else. He announced that IBM would no longer concern itself with the invention of technology but instead would focus on application. IBM would now move beyond its long history of creating a computer hardware, but provide instead integrated IT solutions and services. During tough times, the CEO must choose a company's identity, decline certain opportunities, and pursue others. In this sense, the CEO serves as the guardian or steward of organizational mission, identity, and purpose, steering its course through troubled waters, but always bringing it back on track. Hence, the job of the CEO cannot be outsourced to strategy consultants; it is a job never done (Montgomery 2008). [See *Business Transformation Exercise 3.11.*]

STRATEGIC DECISION-MAKING: WHY GOOD LEADERS MAKE BAD DECISIONS

The daunting reality is that intelligent and responsible people with the best information and intentions make enormous decisions that are badly flawed. Here are some examples:

- Jürgen Schrempp, CEO of Daimler-Benz, spearheaded the merger of Chrysler and Daimler against much internal opposition. Nine years later, Daimler abandoned the deal and let Chrysler be bought by Cerberus, a private equity firm.
- Steve Russell, CEO of Boots, the U.K. drugstore chain, launched a health care strategy designed to differentiate the stores from competitors and grow through new health care services such as dentistry. It turned out that the managers at Boots did not have the skills needed to succeed in health care services. Moreover, many of these health care markets in the U.K. offered little profit potential. The strategy flopped, and Russell had to resign.
- Brigadier General Matthew Broderick, Chief of the Homeland Security Operations Center, was responsible for alerting President Bush and other senior government officials if Hurricane Katrina breached the levees in New Orleans. He went home on August 25, 2005 reporting all was well, even though he received multiple reports of breaches.
- William Smithburg, former chairman of Quaker Oats, acquired Snapple because of his vivid memories of Gatorade, a very successful deal of Quaker Oats. He thought that Snapple, like Gatorade, appeared to be a new drinks company that could be improved with the marketing and distribution expertise of Quaker Oats. Unfortunately, the similarities between Snapple and Gatorade proved to be very superficial, and the acquisition of Snapple quickly destroyed the value of Quaker Oats. Snapple was Smithburg's worst deal. Later, Quaker Oats was acquired by Pepsi.

All these executives were highly intelligent and much qualified for their jobs, and yet they made important decisions that soon proved to be clearly wrong. Researching such and other flawed decisions, Campbell, Whitehead, and Finkelstein (2009) argue that all flawed decisions start with errors of judgment made by influential individuals. Why and how did these errors of judgment occur? These authors explain the origin of such errors of judgment using some fundamentals of neuroscience.

Neuroscience holds that we depend primarily on two hardwired processes for decision-making:

- **Pattern Recognition**: This is a complex process that integrates information from as many as 30 different parts of the brain. When we face a new situation, we make assumptions based on prior experiences and judgments and accordingly recognize a pattern in the new situation. However, pattern recognition can also mislead us, especially if we think we understand the new situation when, in reality, we do not. For instance, General Broderick had much experience in operations centers in Vietnam and in other military engagements, and had even successfully led the Homeland Security Operations Center through previous hurricanes in the U.S.A. These experiences also taught him that early reports surrounding a major event are often false. Hence, he believed that it is better to wait until "ground truth" arrives from reliable first-hand reporters. Unfortunately, Broderick had no experience with a hurricane hitting a city built below sea level. Late August 29, 2005, some 12 hours after Katrina hit New Orleans, Broderick received 17 reports of major flooding and levee breaches. But there was conflicting information: for instance, the Army Corps of Engineers reported that it had no evidence of levee breaches; a late afternoon CNN report from Bourbon Street in the French Quarter of New Orleans showed city dwellers partying and claiming they had dodged the hurricane. Broderick considered the latter two pieces of information as the "ground truth" he was waiting for, and issued a statement that night before heading home that there were no levee breaches (but that he would make fresh assessment the next day).
- **Emotional Tagging**: This is a process whereby emotional information attaches to the thoughts and experiences stored in our memories. Emotional information tells us whether to pay attention to some data/fact/event or not, and what should be our appropriate immediate response (e.g., fight or flight; act now or act later). When the parts of the human brain controlling emotions are impaired, we could become slow and incompetent decision makers, even though we can retain the capacity of objective analysis (e.g., via pattern recognition).

When pattern recognition and emotional tagging function well, our decisions tend to be more sensible. However, both could mislead us. Consider Wang Laboratories, the top company in the word-processing industry in the early 1980s. Aware that his company's future was much dependent upon the personal computer (PC) industry, An Wang, the founder and CEO, built a machine based on a proprietary operating system that was incompatible to IBM PC, which was then the industry standard. This decision was ruled by unconscious emotional tagging: Wang felt he was cheated by IBM over a new technology he had invented earlier in his career. These emotional links made Wang reject the industry software platform linked to IBM even though the platform was provided by a third party, Microsoft. This bad decision led to the demise of Wang Laboratories a few years later. Similarly, Broderick was unconsciously ruled by his emotional attachment to "ground truth" rules in the case of Katrina, an error he quickly realized after the disaster had progressed beyond immediate intervention. [See *Business Transformation Exercise 3.12.*]

How can pattern recognition and emotional tagging fail us? Campbell, Whitehead, and Finkelstein (2009) believe that much of the mental work we do is unconscious, which makes it hard for us to check the logic and data we use when we make a decision. The conscious logic of our pattern recognitions gets confounded by our unconscious emotional tagging. The two processes happen almost instantaneously. Our brains leap to conclusions and are reluctant to consider alternatives. Moreover, we are particularly inept in revisiting our initial frame of assessment of a given situation.

That said, Campbell, Whitehead, and Finkelstein (2009) propose three "red flag conditions" that our emotional tag can conspire to distort our pattern recognition:

1. **The Presence of Inappropriate Self-interest**: This can bias the emotional importance we place on information, which in turn positions us to see the pattern we want to see. Research shows that even well-intentioned professionals, such as doctors and auditors, are disabled from preventing self-interest from biasing their professional judgments.
2. **The Presence of Distorting Attachments**: We can become attached to people, places, and things, and these bonds can affect the judgments about a new situation we face and subsequent decisions and actions. Thus, executives find it very difficult to abandon their pet projects or ego-products despite their long history of market failure.
3. **The Presence of Misleading Memories**: These are memories and experiences that we deem relevant to invoke when we face a new situation, and which unfortunately lead to wrong conclusions and decisions. They cause us to overlook or undervalue some important differentiating factors. This is even truer if in the past we have attached undue emotional tag to our past mental models, frames, or experiences. This is what happened when Smithburg, chairman of Quaker Oats, attached too much emotional importance to Gatorade in planning the acquisition deal with Snapple.

When it comes to strategy and strategic decisions we must remember that the greater part of our decision-making could be unconscious and biased with emotional tags. Before we finalize our strategic decisions, it is therefore imperative that we involve some independent but expert third parties (e.g., bank consultants, strategy consultants) to sift our pattern recognitions and emotional tags, or to examine our "red flag conditions." They may discover other critical information that our emotional tags failed to use, and hence, empower us to consider other options based on new information. The third party may help us to confront our biases, assumptions, and presuppositions, all of which condition our pattern recognition. [See *Business Transformation Exercise 3.13.*]

STRATEGIC DECISION AND SUSTAINABLE COMPETITIVE ADVANTAGE

Conventional wisdom would say that what a strategist should achieve is sustainable competitive advantage (SCA). Cynthia A. Montgomery (2008: 59–60), professor of strategy at HBS, challenges this view. Although critically important, SCA is not the ultimate goal. SCA is a means to an end and not an end in itself. Strategizing only in terms of SCA mistakes the means for the end and puts mission managers on an unachievable quest. SCA is essential to strategy, argues Montgomery, but it is only a part of a bigger story, one frame in a motion picture. Strategic advantage changes from time to time, even as the world, both inside and outside the firm, changes not only in big, discontinuous leaps but in frequent, smaller ones. Corporate identities are changed not only by cataclysmic restructurings and grand pronouncements but also by strategic decision after strategic decision, year after year, CEO after CEO. An "organic" conception of strategy, therefore, recognizes that whatever constitutes strategic advantage will eventually change. Thus, the very notion that there is a strategic holy grail, that is, a strategy brilliantly conceived, carefully implemented, and valiantly defended through time—is dangerous. Because:

- The role of the CEO, the chief strategist, should not be limited to maintaining just SCA, but an overall and continuous leadership of the firm.

- The role of a CEO as a chief strategist is to steer the entire organization from point A to point B, from now to then, from here to there.
- The role of a CEO as a chief strategist is to capitalize on the organizational learning it accumulates along the way.
- The role of a CEO as a chief strategist is to recognize the difference between defending a firm's added value as established at a given moment and ensuring that the firm is adding value over time.

Holding too strongly to one SCA or one purpose locks the CEO and the organization by a perception of value long after that value has diminished in significance.

STRATEGIC THINKING AND MIND-TRAPS

Being welded to one SCA may be tantamount to the anchoring trap, the status quo trap, the sunk cost trap, the confirming-evidence trap, the framing trap, and even the prudence trap that Hammond, Keeney, and Raiffa (2006) are talking about. That is, executives could wrongly assess strategy alternatives owing to several hidden traps such as:

The Anchoring Trap: When considering a decision, the mind gives disproportionate weight to the first information it receives. That is, initial impressions, estimates, or data anchor subsequent thoughts and judgments. Anchors are often guises or stereotypes we draw from a person's color, looks, accent, nationality, age, or even dress. In business, past sales and forecasts become our anchor when predicting the future. In negotiations, the initial proposal by one party with all its terms and conditions can anchor counter bargaining and paralyze creative counter-proposals.

You can fight the anchoring trap by:

- Reviewing a problem from different perspectives, alternative starting points and approaches rather than getting stuck by the first line of thought that occurs to you.
- Thinking about the problem on your own before consulting others lest you should be anchored by their biases.
- Being open-minded, transparent, and seeking information and opinions from a variety of people to widen your frame of reference and suggest fresh directions.

The Status Quo Trap: Decision makers display a strong bias toward alternatives that perpetuate the status quo. The source of the status quo trap lies deep within our psyche, in our unconscious desire to protect our egos from damage. Status quo puts us on less psychological risk and focuses on the tried and tested, rather than waste resources on untested ideas. The first automobiles called "horseless carriages" looked very much like the buggies they replaced. The first "electronic newspapers" on the World Wide Web looked very much like their print precursors. People who inherit stocks rarely sell them to make new investments. In general, "the more choices you have, more the influence of the status quo." This is because additional alternatives imply additional processing efforts and risk, and we instinctually tend to the status quo. In organizations where sins of commission get punished more severely than sins of omission, status quo holds sway. Most mergers flounder because both firms seek individual status quo.

Managers can disarm status quo mind trap by:

- Changing it especially if it fails to achieve your current goals and objectives.
- Identifying other alternatives as counterbalances with all their positives and negatives.
- Avoid exaggerating the effort or cost of switching from the status quo.
- Daring to rock the boat if need be.

The Sunk-Cost Trap: Sunk costs represent old investments of time and money that are currently irrecoverable. While we rationally believe that sunk costs are irrelevant to the present decision, they nevertheless prey on our minds, leading us to make inappropriate decisions. We use the sunk-cost bias to defend our previous decisions even though they currently reveal to be errors or mistakes, and admitting mistakes is painful. Often, we continue to invest into wrong choices hoping to be lucky or recover, but thereby we throw good money into bad, and drag failing projects endlessly.

You can combat the sunk-cost bias by:

- Seeking out and listening carefully to the views of the people who were uninvolved with the earlier bad decisions.
- Examining why admitting past mistakes distresses you and by encountering the distress (e.g., sunk-self-esteem, losing face).
- Remembering Warren Buffet's advice: "[W]hen you find yourself in a hole, the best thing you can do is to stop digging."
- Reassess past decisions not only by the quality of the outcomes but also by the decision-making process (taking into account what information and alternatives you had then).

The Confirming-Evidence Trap: This bias leads us to seek out information that supports our existing instinct or point of view while avoiding information that contradicts it. This bias affects us not only where and when we go to collect information but also in interpreting the evidence. We automatically accept the supporting information and dismiss the conflicting information. Two fundamental psychological forces entrap us here: (*a*) our tendency to subconsciously decide *what* we want to do before we figure out *why* we want to do it; (*b*) we are inclined to be more engaged by things we like than by things we dislike.

You can undermine the confirming-evidence bias by:

- Examining all the evidence with equal vigor, and by avoiding to accept confirming evidence without question.
- Building counter-arguments for yourself or by a devil's advocate; that is, identify the strongest reasons for doing something else.
- Being honest with yourself about your motives; look for smarter choices and stop collecting evidence to perpetuate old choices.
- Do not surround yourself with yes-people as consultants; if there are too many that support your point of view, change your consultants.

The Framing Trap: The first step in making a decision is to frame your problem or question. However, framing can also be very dangerous: the way you frame a problem can profoundly influence the choices you make. A frame is often closely related to other psychological traps. For instance, your frame can establish a status quo or introduce an anchor; it can highlight sunk costs or lead you toward confirming evidence. Our frames are often affected by possible gains or losses. People are *risk-averse* when a problem is posed in terms of *gains*, but are *risk-prone* when a problem is posed in terms of *losses*. Losing triggers a conservative response in many people's minds. Frames are also affected by different reference points: for instance, the same problem impacts you differently whether you have a $2,000 balance in your checking account versus zero.

You can reduce the framing bias by:

- Reframing the problem in various ways (i.e., do not automatically accept your initial frame or those of others).
- Re-position the problem with different trade-offs of gains and losses or different reference points.
- Checking your frame and framing strategy; ask yourself how your thinking might change if the framing changed.
- When others offer solutions, check and challenge their frame.

The Prudence Trap: Some managers are just overcautious or over-prudent in their forecasts, estimates, and budgets. Policy makers often go by "worst case scenario analysis" and get overcautious. When faced with high-stake decisions, managers tend to adjust their estimates and forecasts "just to be on the safer side." For instance, the Big Three Auto Companies have periodically produced more millions of cars just to be on the safer side, despite less anticipated sales, higher dealer inventories, and more aggressive competitive action. Large accumulated stocks cost billions of dollars to the domestic auto companies.

You can circumvent the prudence trap:

- Avoid overcautious or overconfident forecasting traps by considering the extremes, the low and the high ends of the possible range of values.
- Challenge your estimates of both extremes.
- Avoid the prudence trap by honestly stating your estimates to third parties who will be using them unadjusted.
- Examine your assumptions and impressions of the past, and get statistics to back them.

Table 3.2 summarizes the discussion on organizational underperformance as related to the various psychological and economic traps already discussed.

Even the highest performers cannot and do not avoid mishaps, mistakes, and missteps. But according to a groundbreaking study by Accenture of over 500 world's most successful companies, high performers are adept and resilient at recovering from setbacks as they are at avoiding them in the first place (Cheese et al. 2008). [See *Business Transformation Exercise 3.14.*]

THE FIVE TRAPS OF PERFORMANCE MEASUREMENT

Andrew Likierman, Dean of London School of Business, warns CEOs and senior executives of five most common traps in measuring performance (Likierman 2009: 96–101):

TABLE 3.2 · Organizational Underperformance as a Function of Psychological and Economic Traps in Decision-making

Trap type	Trap type definition	Trap type symptoms	Combating trap type symptoms	Organization examples
Anchoring Trap	When considering a decision, the mind gives disproportionate weight to the first information it receives.	Initial impressions, estimates, or data anchor subsequent thoughts and judgments.	(a) Review a problem from different perspectives, alternative starting points, and approaches; (b) think about the problem on your own before consulting others lest you should be anchored by their biases; and (c) be open-minded, transparent, seeking information and opinions from a variety of people to widen your frame of reference and fresh directions.	Stereotypes draw from a customer's color, looks, accent, nationality, age, or even dress. Past sales and forecasts become our anchor when predicting the future.
Status Quo Trap	Decision makers display a strong bias toward alternatives that perpetuate the status quo. Status quo implies less psychological risk.	Our unconscious desire to protect our egos from damage; the more choices we have, the more the influence of the status quo.	(a) Change status quo especially if it fails to achieve your current goals and objectives; (b) identify other alternatives as counterbalances with all their positives and negatives; (c) avoid exaggerating the effort or cost of switching from the status quo; and (d) dare to "rock the boat" if need be.	The first automobiles called "horseless carriages" looked very much like the buggies they replaced. The first "electronic newspapers" on the World Wide Web looked very much like their print precursors. Most mergers flounder because both firms seek individual status quo.
Sunk-Cost Trap	We are inordinately attached to sunk-costs that represent old investments of time and money and which are currently irrecoverable. Admitting past mistakes is painful.	While we rationally believe that sunk-costs are irrelevant to the present decision, they, nevertheless, prey on our minds, leading us to make inappropriate decisions.	(a) Listen carefully to the views of the people who were uninvolved with the earlier bad decisions; (b) examine why admitting past mistakes distresses you and encounter the distress (e.g., sunk-self-esteem, losing face); (c) remember Warren Buffet's advice: "when you find yourself in a hole, the best thing you can do is to stop digging"; and (d) reassess past decisions not only by the quality of the outcomes but also by the decision-making process.	Firms use the sunk-cost bias to defend previous decisions even though they currently reveal to be errors or mistakes. Often, we continue to invest into wrong choices hoping to be lucky to recover; thereby we throw good money into bad, and drag failing projects endlessly.
Confirming Evidence Trap	This bias leads us to seek out information that supports our existing instinct or point of view while avoiding data that contradicts it.	This bias affects our information collection and its interpretation. We accept supporting information and dismiss conflicting information.	(a) Examine all the evidence with equal vigor and avoid confirming evidence without question; (b) build counter-arguments for yourself or use a devil's advocate; that is, identify the strongest reasons for doing something else; and (c) be honest with yourself about your motives; look for smarter choices and stop collecting evidence to perpetuate old choices.	Surrounding yourself with yes-people as consultants; if there are too many that support your point of view, change your consultants. Two fundamental psychological forces entrap us: (a) we subconsciously decide what we want to do before we figure out why we want to do it; (b) we are inclined to be more engaged by things we like than by things we dislike.
Framing Trap	We often frame a problem or question. However, framing can also be very dangerous.	The way we frame a problem can profoundly influence the choices we make. Our frames are affected by possible gains or losses.	(a) Reframe the problem in various ways (i.e., do not automatically accept your initial frame or those of others); (b) re-position the problem with different trade-offs of gains and losses or different reference points; and (c) check your framing strategy; ask yourself how your thinking might change if the framing changed.	People are risk-averse when a problem is framed in terms of gains and risk-prone when a problem is posed in terms of losses. Losing triggers a conservative response in many people's minds.

Source: Author's own.

Note: See Hammond, Keeney, and Raiffa (2006).

1. **Measuring against Yourself**: When assessing the performance of your company, do not evaluate it only by your plans or budgets. Look at your major competition. You may look good against your proposed plans and budgets, but your competitor could have done far better against more aggressive plans and demanding budgets. Benchmarking against competition or the industry champion will help you set your competitive priorities, and connect executive compensation to relative rather than absolute performance numbers. That is, reward your executives for doing better than everyone in the industry. If you do not have the competitor's performance data in time for your performance appraisal, or if the competition is following a different fiscal cycle, then get the ongoing data (product perceptions, ratings) from your key customers, repeat buyers, switchers, and those patronizing your main competition. Additionally, obtain comparative information from professional consultants.

2. **Looking Backward**: This trap focuses on your past performance statistics. Beating last year's numbers is not enough; look if your current assessment decisions help you in the coming months. Look for numbers that lead rather than lag the profits in your business. Seek preventive strategies that can save losses and minimize risk. Look also at what you are *not* doing—your omission errors. Thus, assess yourself by the outcomes of deals you have turned down (Type I or alpha errors) and by the outcomes of deals others have won and succeeded. Good management is about making choices—a decision not to do something should be assessed against the decision of doing the next best alternative.

3. **Putting Your Faith in Numbers**: Most performance metrics are numeric, quantitative, and large-volume-data-driven. But watch for low-quality data based on responses that come from biased questions or "leading" or misleading probes. Best data and real stories come from qualitative responses of customers whose anonymity is well protected. Be sure your reports do not doctor the data or omit bad assessments. Performance data is best when it is collected by independent agencies and from all customers (randomly selected) whose anonymity is well protected. Do not overdo some measures such as return on investments (ROI), return on assets (ROA), or return on invested capital (ROIC), unless you are very sure that the returns are causally linked to your investment, assets, or invested capital.

4. **Gaming Your Metrics**: Avoid the trap of overstating your income, understating your debt and other liabilities, or indulging in other creative accounting shenanigans. Enron did that for five years before it bankrupted in 2001. Since 2004 Royal Dutch Shell has paid U.S.$470 million to settle lawsuits relating to its overstatement of reserves. You cannot prevent people from gaming numbers, especially when you rely so much on number metrics. Several Fortune 500 companies are tempted to game their numbers in order to obtain better Wall Street ratings. Metrics are only proxies for performance. In reducing the risk of gaming numbers, adopt several metrics, and diversify them. For instance, do not reward employees by billable hours alone, but also consider respect and mentoring, quality of work, excellence in client service, integrity, contribution to the community, and contribution to the firm as an institution. Metrics should have varying sources (customers, colleagues, line managers, finance managers, and bosses). Additionally, you can vary the boundaries of your measurement—by defining responsibility more narrowly or by broadening it. For instance, in reducing delays in gate-closing, Southwest Airlines applied the metric not only to gate agents, but included all members of the ground crew (ticketing staff, gate staff, and loaders) so that everyone had an incentive to participate. You should set metrics by ranges rather

than by single numbers. Loosen the links between meeting budgets and performance—too many subjects know how to pad or pare their budgets for pleasing bosses, and thus, destroying value.

5. **Sticking to Your Numbers too Long**: Numbers do not mean everything and every time. In the early stages of your company, performance may be all about survival, cash flows, and growth; and assessment could be every week, month, or quarter. But as the business matures, measurement could focus on profits and comparisons with competitors. Evaluate your measures before they fail you; know precisely what you want to assess, why, how, and that everyone is clear about it. As the saying goes, *you manage what you measure*. The moment you choose to manage by a metric, you invite your managers to manipulate it. Customize your measures—one size does not fit all! Attracting, developing, and retaining few, big but profitable accounts is not the same as doing the same with many, small and less profitable accounts. The credit rating agencies have come under attack because they gave AAA ratings to so many borrowers who turned out to be bad risks (Likierman 2009: 101).

A really good measurement system should bring finance managers and line managers into some kind of meaningful dialogue such that you safeguard the relative independence of the former and the expertise of the latter. Finance managers are good at tracking expenses, monitoring risks, and raising capital. Line managers know how operating realities connect with performance, but they could be biased.

For instance, Stephen P. Kaufman, a former CEO of Arrow Electronics for 14 years, a director of six public and four private companies, and currently a senior lecturer at HBS, tells us how he evaluated his executive team: "I collected input from many sources and assessed performance on multiple dimensions. I worked with my reports to identify flaws in their management styles, and I tried to help them adjust before problems arose or their careers got stalled" (Kaufman 2008: 53).

EVALUATING THE CEO

[See Kaufman (2008)]

All of us need to be assessed and evaluated periodically, and much more so, a CEO. Any assessment of a top executive, particularly, that of the CEO, begins with certain financial metrics and progress against strategy. Financial metrics do not illuminate key management attributes, and progress on strategy is often a manufactured set of data carefully orchestrated in order to put the company in the best possible light. Both areas of assessment do not uncover what the CEO is doing that might help or hurt the company in the long term. Moreover, much of CEO assessment takes place in structured settings (board meetings and diners) where the CEOs tend to be on their best behavior (Kaufman 2008: 54).

Thus, when CEOs stumble or fall, they pull their company down with them. The feedback that most CEOs receive from the board is based solely on the company's financial performance. Often, in assessing the total worth of a CEO, the board of directors may consider just three or four financial measures (e.g., market share, profits, dividends, and ROI) based on which the board decides the executive compensation. On the other hand, senior executives on their way up the corporate ladder are subjected to extensive and comprehensive performance reviews.

But all the incentives in the world will not transform CEOs into better decision makers. The boards have an obligation to shareholders to ensure that CEOs lead companies well; if not, they should be able to detect problems with the CEOs, much before the damage has already been done. Failing which, by the time the board recognizes that the CEO is not functioning as he/she should, it may be too late, and the damage might have already been done. Further, the board may take almost a full year to replace the CEO and develop the next CEO. That amounts to two years of costly stasis.

Instead, the board could observe the CEO on a daily basis without being an intrusive micro-management, and obtain inputs from multiple levels of management. As a result, the board could be more aware of how the CEO performs throughout the year and detect and give advice on how to fix problems the CEO may have missed, and apply correctives in a timely manner. This is how CEO Stephen P. Kaufman was evaluated at Arrow Electronics. This is what Jack Welsh did at GE—he encouraged his board of directors to visit major business units and meet with the senior operating executives on their own each year. This is also common practice with the board of directors of Home Depot—independent directors visit a store once every quarter and draw their own conclusions about its operations, and give the feedback to the CEO during quarterly board meetings.

Some areas in which you can assess CEO's leadership effectiveness on a regular basis are:

- How does the CEO perform on corporate strategic planning, corporate culture, competitive positions, and major operations?
- How well does the CEO motivate and energize the organization, and is the company's culture reinforcing its mission and values?
- Is the corporate strategy working, is the company aligned behind it, and is it being effectively implemented?
- Is the CEO placing the right people in the right job, and understudy a stream of high-potentials to succeed his key executives?
- Are sales, profits, productivity, asset utilization, quality, and customer satisfaction heading in the right direction?
- How well does the CEO engage with the company's external constituencies such as customers, suppliers, creditors, and local communities?
- How does a CEO observe how a senior manager interacts with peers and subordinates?
- Does the CEO ride his senior executives too hard? Is the CEO often stressed and hot-tempered? Does the CEO over-compensate his people to make up for abusing them?
- Does a CEO hoard resources and not invest them wisely? Does the CEO support key growth initiatives coming from the senior executives?
- How does the CEO assess procurement and supply chain management initiatives?
- How does the CEO manage HR and talent management in the company in the long run?
- Does the CEO cross-check to see if the company hits the numbers because of performance or aggressive accounting?

In order to do the assessment of a CEO's effective leadership on a regular basis in any or all of the foregoing areas, each independent director from the board must regularly meet with two or three senior executives that report to the CEO, pool these observations, and provide a composite feedback to the CEO at quarterly board meetings. Executive compensation should be aligned to the positive feedback that the CEO gets from almost all the independent board members every quarter. Such a feedback could expose the CEO's blind spots much before they could spell trouble. Such an assessment process can render CEOs more effective and companies more progressive. The board could make such an assessment process a condition of the job for its next CEO. When CEOs think they no longer need real, credible feedback, they can get into trouble.

LEADERSHIP AT FIAT

[See Marchionne (2008: 45–48)]

During 2001–04, Fiat had ploughed through four CEOs, and Sergio was put at the helm as the fifth guy to resuscitate the Fiat cadaver. When Sergio took over, Fiat was a laughing stock everywhere, and especially in Italy. Fiat had lost tons of money, its new car had flopped, and a labor strike was on somewhere. Sergio was almost a foreigner (born in Italy, he had left Italy in 1966 for U.S.), was new to the auto industry, and was getting into an incredibly tough business.

Sergio Marchionne, CEO Fiat Group in 2004, a global automotive manufacturer based in Turin, Italy, tells us the story of how he saved Fiat by carefully identifying, grooming, and empowering leadership from within. He turned around Fiat that was sinking for years to triumph during 2004–08. "The key to his success was his leadership strategy. He got his employees energized around clear and ambitious targets." This is a crucial job of the top management. The leader is a conduit for change, but the leader gets the people in the organization to make actual change happen. "A leader should derive great satisfaction seeing his subjects succeed."

In late July 2004 Sergio announced that Fiat would make euro 2 billion profits in 2007. He arrived at that figure after discussing for three days with 20 of his senior executives. When they did not agree with him, he imposed this target on them, and argued how they could achieve it. If you set what people think is an unrealistic target, you have to help them reach it. That is another crucial part of a leader's job. Helping them is not the same as doing the job for them. "Sergio immersed himself in the business not so that he could make all the decisions but that he could delegate decisions"—guide the folks on the ground to make the right decisions and be accountable for them (Marchionne 2008: 46).

The prevalent belief then was that chemical companies set the benchmark for value destruction; but the auto industry (possibly with the exception of Porsche in Germany and Toyota in Japan) was a close runner-up, and had destroyed value over decades. Fiat was one of the worst offenders. But Sergio turned around and transformed Fiat by 2008, with its bottom line solidly in the black. Its latest car, Cinquecento, one of the smallest compacts in the world, is the pride of the industry.

Fiat's culture was traditionally dominated by engineers. While it provided some advantage to Fiat (e.g., in diesel engines), it also made the company inward looking. "Part of a leader's job is to get the organization looking outward at the markets, the competition, and outside the box." Instead of battling with problems within the company and in the process wasting time and resources, it is good to look outside for ready-made solutions. Fiat looked at the Apple leadership in its branding. Sergio considers the Cinquecento as the Fiat iPod. There was much wastage and worker malaise within the company. Sergio looked at the best factory practices of Toyota for quicker solutions.

The job of the top management is to challenge the assumptions under-grounding objectives and targets of his subjects. For instance, he questioned why it took more than 48 months to roll out a new car model. The production crew explained that some parts and components got delayed. Then let us get at the suppliers for speedier delivery of critical parts, Sergio argued. It worked. That is how Sergio managed to cut the time for new product arrivals from four years to less than 18 months, which was then an industry standard. The Fiat compact model Cinquecento was out in 18 months, a talk of the industry now. Fiat had to ramp production by 60 percent from 120,000 units in its first year. It takes euro 600 million to get a car to the market; but shrinking the production time can get you more bang for those bucks (Marchionne 2008: 47).

In bringing about this dramatic turnaround in Fiat, Sergio had to abandon the Great Man top-down vertical model of leadership that long characterized Fiat, in favor of the horizontal platform of leadership where everyone is expected to lead. The former leadership model was possibly appropriate for the 1950s when businesses were small enough for the top executive to manage, and when most of the rank-and-file workers were much less educated and experienced. Such top-down models, however, cannot be sustained currently when corporations have grown too big for one executive to lead, and when workers are more educated and informed. Sergio had to train lower level executives to take responsibility for major decisions. Those who resisted such changes were let go.

Sergio found that the more he got from the center, the more autonomous the management was, and he soon realized that Fiat had plenty of leadership potential in Latin America, India, China, and Australia. He also discovered that lot of young talent was locked up in marketing and other functions that historically were not considered high-potential career paths. Sergio discovered such talent in his periodical walkabouts through the plants of Brazil and Argentina. He also hired a smart outsider to head the Fiat HR department, who also advised Sergio whom to take a closer look at during his plant visits.

Once Sergio identified high-potentials, he invested a lot of time engaging with them—spent four to five months conducting performance reviews for the top 700 people. Sergio went beyond mere performance review numbers to how well the leaders led people and lead change. He based his assessment overwhelmingly on this engagement. The engagement was informal; Sergio always text-messaged his high potentials or called them at all odd hours to talk about the business and their careers. They knew that Sergio cared about what happens to them. If an organization can feel that kind of connection with its leadership, Sergio argues, you can get a very sound culture aligned around strongly held common values. As Sergio gave them more responsibility, he also expected higher accountability from them. "If you want to grow leaders, then you cannot let explanations and excuses become a way of life" (Marchionne 2008: 46).

CONCLUDING REMARKS

A CEO must be the steward of a living strategy that defines what the firm is and what it will become. Strategy is not just a plan, not just an idea, but a way of executive life for a company. Strategy does not just position or differentiate a firm in its external competitive landscape, it defines what a firm will be. Strategy is the CEO's greatest opportunity not only to outwit the competition but also to shape the firm itself. Strategy is about creating unique value, about the specific mission and purpose the company exists for. As private equity firms and hedge funds proliferate and supply chains open up around the world, there is nothing more important for multinational businesses than to have a clear sense of purpose, a clear sense of who they are, a clear sense of direction, what makes them distinctive, and why they matter to the world. Purpose should be at the heart of strategy. It should give direction to every part of the firm, from the corporate office to the loading dock. Sitting at the hub of the strategy wheel, purpose should align all the functional pieces and draw the company into a logically consistent whole (Montgomery 2008).

Exaggerated attention on sustainable competitive advantage has diverted attention from the fact that strategy must be a dynamic tool for guiding the development of the company over time. To redress these issues, we need to rethink strategy as a stewardship of leadership—one that recognizes the essential fluid and volatile nature of competition and the consequent need for continuous leadership and not periodic problem-solving executive exercise (Montgomery 2008: 54–56). In the chapters that follow, we propose to rethink strategy as strategic leadership, a sacred trust, and responsible stewardship of the organization one is commissioned to serve.

BUSINESS TRANSFORMATION EXERCISES

3.1 According to Kotter (2007), an executive leadership guru:

- Business transformations often begin when an organization has a new head who is a good leader and who sees the need for a major change.
- The leader is a conduit for change, but the leader gets the people in the organization to make actual change happen.
- Change, by definition, is creating a new system, which in turn always demands new and real leadership.
- The number one error in a transformation process is not establishing a great enough sense of urgency.
- Without motivation and a sense of urgency, a corporation goes nowhere. A paralyzed senior management comes from having too many managers and not enough leaders.
- Most successful transformation change efforts begin when some passionate individuals or some groups within an organization start to look hard at a company's competitive situation, market position, the emergence of a new industry or market, technology trends, and financial performance.

  a. As a potential executive leader, how do you understand and accept each of these six statements?
  b. What are the assumptions and generalizations behind each statement?
  c. Are these assumptions valid? Note, the validity of a model, is the validity of its assumptions.
  d. Are these generalizations applicable along all demographics of gender, race, age, color, and nationality? Why?
  e. What are the presuppositions under each statement? What if these are not verified?
  f. Why does Kotter emphasize on motivation, passion, and a sense of urgency as paramount for transformative leadership?
  g. Are these three traits one and the same version of one underlying trait? What is it?
  h. What is your version of the sine qua non of transformative leadership, and why?

3.2 According to A. G. Lafley, CEO of P&G, Cincinnati, OH, the largest consumer goods company in the U.S. (world competitor is Lever Brothers):

- The CEO is the link between the inside (i.e., the organization) and the outside (i.e., the society, economy, technology, markets, and customers).
- Inside is mostly costs; the outside is results. Without the outside, there is no inside.
- The CEO alone experiences the meaningful outside at the enterprise level and is responsible for understanding it, interpreting it, advocating for it, and presenting it so that the company can respond in a way that enables sustainable sales, market share, and profitability.
- It is the job only a CEO can and should do because everybody else in the organization is focused on a narrower part of the inside or the outside of the firm.
- The CEO must integrate the inside and the outside—a very difficult task.

- Without a deep understanding of the external stakeholders and their competing interests, and how these interests correspond with the capabilities and limitations of the organization, a CEO cannot function optimally or succeed.
- The CEO is the only one held responsible and accountable for the performance and the results of the entire company, judged not only by his standards, but by those of his stakeholders.

a. As a potential executive leader, how do you understand and accept each of these seven statements of CEO leadership?
b. What are the assumptions and generalizations behind each statement?
c. Are these assumptions valid? Note, the validity of a leadership model, is the validity of its assumptions.
d. Are these generalizations applicable across all demographics of gender, race, age, color, and nationality? Why?
e. What are the presuppositions under each statement? What if these are not verified?
f. Why does A. G. Lafley emphasize on the outside–inside paradigm of executive transformative leadership?
g. Does this paradigm conflict with the resource-based view (RBV) of sustainable competitive advantage (SCA) as proposed by Barney (1991, 2001a) and others? Why? [See Chapter 6 for details.]
h. Does this paradigm conflict with the market-based view (MBV) of sustainable competitive advantage (SCA) as proposed by industrial organization (IO) theory of Michael Porter (1980, 1986a, 1986b 1991, 1996) and others? Why? [See Chapter 6 for details.]
i. What does Lafley (2009) say that is different from Kotter (2007), and why?

3.3 Doris Kearns Goodwin, in her best-selling account of President Abraham Lincoln, *Team of Rivals*, delineates essential features of a great leader such as President Lincoln as follows (Goodwin 2009: 43–47): A great leader:

- Surrounds oneself with people who can argue with him and question his assumptions. It particularly helps if you can bring in people whose temperaments differ from yours.
- Should figure out how to share credit for your success with your inner team so that they feel part of the mission.
- Should know how to relax and possess a sense of humor so that she can replenish her energies for the struggles she has to face tomorrow. The ability to recharge your batteries in the midst of great stress and crisis is crucial for successful leadership.
- Should have extraordinary amount of emotional intelligence, the ability to feel with and motivate people. He must be able to put past hurts behind him and never allow wounds to fester.
- Should be able acknowledge his errors and learn from his mistakes to a remarkable degree.
- Has flaws—Lincoln's greatest flaw was that he generally liked people and did not want to hurt them. He always wanted to give somebody a second or even a third chance.
- Never quits no matter how terrible the problem or crisis. Lincoln faced the crisis of the Civil War. Roosevelt weathered a banking crisis, an economic crisis, and the war by his fireside chats.

a. As a potential executive leader, how do you understand and accept each of these statements on executive leadership?
b. What are the assumptions and generalizations behind each statement?
c. Are these assumptions valid? Note, the validity of a model, is the validity of its assumptions.
d. Are these generalizations applicable along all demographics of gender, race, age, color, and nationality? Why?
e. What are the presuppositions under each statement? What if these are not verified?
f. What one feature does Goodwin emphasize as absolutely necessary for transformative leadership?

g. Based on Goodwin (2009), what is your version of the sine qua non of transformative leadership, and why?

h. What does Goodwin (2009) say that is different from Kotter (2007), and why?

i. What does Goodwin (2009) say that is different from Lafley (2008), and why?

3.4 According to David McCullough (2008: 45–49), a good leader has the following traits:

- Is a visionary who is able to generate a great sense of mission; her enthusiasm is infectious; she is willing to take risks.
- Does not rule by an organizational chart; people are more important than paper positions. She makes other people's success, her success.
- Has her door always open and that anyone can talk to her about anything.
- Takes full responsibility for her actions, and never finger points to others for blame.
- Is a person of integrity, courage, resilience, and strength of character. A leader is somebody we can count on when the chips are down.
- Is never afraid to have people around her who are more accomplished than she is.
- Never asks any of her people to do anything she would not do herself.
- Has the power of persuasion—the ability to get people to do what they ought to know to do without being told.
- Listens—listening means asking good questions and taking in what people have to say.
- It also means hearing what people are not saying—what is bothering them about the job, their company, or country.
- Never feathers one's own interests or popularity at the expense of corporate results; she never puts her own status before that of the corporations she works for.
- Has very high standards and lives up to them; she has a sense that her work matters, that her efforts contribute to something bigger than her and her salary.
- A great leader may be a short-term pessimist, but a long-term optimist.
- A great leader mines opportunities from the darkest of chaos.
- Leaders must lead. Managers must manage. Both do, but this does not mean, however, that creative and innovative ideas have to come from the top.
- Good leaders and managers know how to generate new ideas from the ranks and files. They enable and empower their employees to think big, to think far into the future, to redesign the company, and to reinvent and innovate the company.
- A leader becomes a steward of organizational energy. A leader cares for and is committed to his workforce. Honoring your commitment and responsibility to your workers is an important part of executive leadership.

a. As a potential executive leader, how do you understand and accept each of these statements on executive leadership?

b. What are the assumptions and generalizations behind each statement?

c. Are these assumptions valid?

d. What is the model of executive leadership, according to McCullough (2008)? Note, the validity of a model, is the validity of its assumptions.

e. Are these generalizations applicable along all demographics of gender, race, age, color, and nationality? Why?

f. What are the presuppositions under each statement? What if these are not verified?

g. What one feature does McCullough (2008) emphasize as absolutely necessary for transformative leadership?

h. Based on McCullough (2008), what is your version of the sine qua non of transformative leadership, and why?

    i.   What does McCullough (2008) say that is different from Kotter (2007), and why?

    j.   What does McCullough (2008) say that is different from Lafley (2008), and why?

    k.   What does McCullough (2008) say that is different from Goodwin (2009), and why?

3.5   After extensive survey-based consulting on leadership at large corporations, Rooke and Torbert (2005) conclude that what differentiated leaders is not so much their philosophy of leadership, their personality, or their style of management, but their internal "action logic" by which they interpret their environment and react to it when their power or safety is challenged. Do the following self-reflective executive leadership exercises: [See Table 3.1]

1. **The Opportunists**: They react to the world in terms of controlling and exploiting it for directing intended outcomes. Their style is self-aggrandizement and they engage in constant firefighting their environment. They write their own rules, feel they could do anything, and pull-off everything. They treat people as objects or as factors of production. They legitimize and rationalize their evil behavior, reject feedback, externalize blame, and retaliate harshly. They do not last long. How do you plan to forestall and spare yourself from this opportunist trap?

2. **The Diplomats**: They make sense of the world around them more benignly than the opportunist. This action logic is focused on gaining control of one's own behavior than on controlling the external environment and people. The goal, thereby, is to gain acceptance of people and influence them by cooperating with them and abiding by group norms. These leaders primarily work at junior executive levels such as frontline supervisors. Would you settle to be diplomat at the next job opportunity? Why or why not?

3. **The Experts**: They control the world around them by perfecting their knowledge of the profession. They rarely seek consensus nor ask for collaboration. Would you foresee your leadership role in the next 5 years to be that of an "expert?"

4. **The Achievers**: They create a positive work environment and focus on deliverables. Unfortunately, they do not think outside the box. They are open to feedback but interpret it within their box or framework of thinking, and hence may clash with experts. They delegate responsibility. Are you an "achiever" in this sense? Would you like to be? Why?

5. **The Individualists**: They exhibit unique, unconventional ways of thinking and operating. They believe all actions logics are constructed and abstract ideas. They ignore customs, conventions, traditions, and rules as irrelevant. They fail to acknowledge organizational processes and routines. These are effective as entrepreneurs, ventures, and consulting roles. Are you an individualist of this mold? Does this role bring out the best in you for others?

6. **The Strategists**: They focus on organizational constraints and perceptions in order to transform them. They are adept at creating shared visions across different action logics such that they achieve personal and organizational transformation. They deal comfortably with conflict, and are good in handling people's resistance to change. Consequently, they are highly effective change agents like Jack Welch, Bill Gates, and Michael Dell. Are you planning to be a strategist in the next 5 to 10 years? What are your tools and strategies?

7. **The Alchemists**: They have great ability to renew and reinvent themselves and their organizations in historically significant ways. They can deal with kings and commoners. They have an extraordinary capacity to deal with many situations at multiple levels. They can deal with immediate priorities while never losing sight of long-term goals. They are typically charismatic, live by high moral standards, and are extremely aware individuals who focus intensely on truth. They can pick up historic moments of their organizations and create strong symbols and metaphors out of them to speak to people's hearts and minds. Good examples of this leadership are Mahatma Gandhi, Martin Luther King, Jr., Nelson Mandela, Mother Teresa, and Pope John Paul II. Do you vision yourself as an alchemist somewhere down your executive career? If so, what are your strengths and weaknesses?

3.6   Compare and contrast the foregoing five leadership profiles by undertaking the following:

- What do Rooke and Torbert (2005) say that is different from Kotter (2007), and why?
- What do Rooke and Torbert (2005) say that is different from Lafley (2008), and why?
- What do Rooke and Torbert (2005) say that is different from Goodwin (2009), and why?
- What do Rooke and Torbert (2005) say that is different from McCullough (2008), and why?
- What do Rooke and Torbert (2005) say that is similar to Kotter (2007), and why?
- What do Rooke and Torbert (2005) say that is similar to Lafley (2008), and why?
- What do Rooke and Torbert (2005) say that is similar to Goodwin (2009), and why?
- What do Rooke and Torbert (2005) say that is similar to McCullough (2008), and why?
- What is common across all five leadership profiles, and why?

3.7   Based on extensive research on senior, middle, and junior level leaders for over 25 years, Robert E. Kaplan and Robert B. Kaiser (2009) suggest strategies and tools to help managers recognize when they overuse their strengths and how they can correct this counterproductive tendency. Taking your strength to an extreme is always detrimental to performance measured by *vitality* (e.g., morale, engagement, and cohesion) and *productivity* (e.g., quantity, cost, and quality of output). Leadership types (c) and (d) describe the "what" of leadership, while (a) and (b) define the "how" of executive leadership. Costs of overdoing strengths are many:

- **Forceful Leadership**: Exercises influence on the basis of one's own intellect and energy. It takes charge, starts all initiatives, and gives directions to all others. It takes a position, defends it, announces it, and enforces it. In the process, it pushes people to their limits, sets high expectations, and holds people accountable. It is just as harmful to overdo one's forceful leadership as it is to under-do it.
- **Enabling Leadership**: Creates conditions for other people to contribute. It empowers subjects and gives them latitude to do their jobs. It includes everybody, listens to them, seeks inputs from them, and is open to their influence. It supports people, shows appreciation and sensitivity to subjects. It is just as harmful to overdo one's enabling leadership as it is to under-do it.
- **Strategic Leadership**: Positions the organization for the future. This leadership plans ahead and takes the long view over a big corporate canvas. It pursues growth and seeks ways to grow the business and expand its markets and capabilities. It promotes innovation, questions the status quo, and encourages new thinking. Once again, it is just as harmful to overdo one's strategic leadership as it is to under-do it.
- **Operational Leadership**: Focuses the organization on short-term ends and goals. It manages the day-to-day details of implementation, and concentrates on results. It maximizes efficiency, conserves resources by cutting costs, and is selective about priorities. It maintains order, and gets things done using the discipline of procedures and processes. Once again, it is just as harmful to overdo one's operational leadership as it is to under-do it.

1. Which leadership category best describes you, and why?
2. What are native and cultivated leadership styles that match this category?
3. All four types of leadership perform best at their golden mean or balance between aggressiveness and inaction. What is your golden mean in relation to each leadership type, and why?
4. The golden mean is characterized with great respect for people involved, much listening, being transparent, being passionate without losing compassion, being right without being righteous, being decisive without being rigid—a balance between overdoing and under-doing. Do you verify such traits in you?
5. Could you cultivate them? What tools and tactics will you adopt?

3.8 Strengths have their specific patterns. To excel in your chosen field and to find lasting satisfaction in doing so, you will need to understand your strengths and their unique patterns. Buckingham and Clifton (2001: 25–61) offer some useful definitions and rules in this regard:

- **Strength**: consistent near perfect performance in an activity. Talents, knowledge, and skills combine to create your strengths.
- **Talents**: are your natural recurring patterns of thought, feeling, or behavior that can be productively applied. Most talents, like intelligence, leadership, and team-building, are value-neutral. Talents are innate, and are not the same as *values*. You can learn values; you can change values; but your innate talents grow with you. We accept our talents, become aware of them, and build and refocus our lives around them.
- **Knowledge**: consists of the facts and lessons you learn. Knowledge is factual, experiential, also conceptual and theoretical, logical, and rational.
- **Skills**: are steps to an activity. Skills bring structure to experiential knowledge. That is, you can sit back and formalize your accumulated knowledge into a sequence of steps that lead to a trained activity. Skills enable you to avoid trial and error, and empower you to immerse directly into performance. However, skills without underlying innate talents may lead you somewhere, but not to glory.

Keeping this schema in mind, do the following executive exercises:

a. Talents, knowledge, and skills are raw materials for building strengths; but most important among these are talents. Talents are innate, while knowledge and skills can be learned and cultivated. Assess your talents, especially executive leadership talents.
b. The key to building your strengths is to identify your dominant talents and then refine them with knowledge and skills. Skills determine if you can do something, whereas talents reveal how well and how often you do it. What are your dominant talents? Since they are innate, where do you trace them, to genetics, to personality, to siblings?
c. For an activity or talent to be a strength, you must be able to do it consistently, and you must derive some intrinsic satisfaction from that activity. This implies that it is a predictable part of your performance. Given this rule, what are your consistent strengths that give you much satisfaction? And why?
d. You do not have to have strength in every aspect of your role in order to excel. Tiger Woods and Bill Gates had their limitations; they got around them. Excellent performers do not have to be well-rounded; they are sharp. In this regard, what are your limitations? How do you plan to cope with them?
e. You will excel only by maximizing your strengths, never by fixing your weaknesses. Of course, you do not ignore your weaknesses, but manage around them. Find people whose strengths are your weaknesses. That would free you up to hone your strengths to a sharper point.
f. **Distinguish your natural talents from things you can learn** (e.g., knowledge, skills, experience, and self-awareness). Your natural talents are innate; they directly build your strengths.

3.9 Review BTE 3.7 and BTE 3.8. Kaplan and Kaiser (2009) suggest strategies and tools to help managers recognize when they overuse their strengths and how they can correct this counterproductive tendency. On the other hand, Buckingham and Clifton (2001) insist on building on your strengths while ignoring your weaknesses. Strengths have their specific patterns. To excel in your chosen field and to find lasting satisfaction in doing so, you will need to understand your strengths and their unique patterns.

a. Do you see apparent contradictions in their approaches to talent development? Explain.
b. What are the basic differences between their approaches to executive talent development? Explain.
c. What are the basic similarities in their respective approaches? Explain.
d. What do Kaplan and Kaiser (2009) understand by "strengths," and how do they differ from "strengths," "talents," "knowledge," and "skills" of Buckingham and Clifton (2001)? Explain.

    e. Study the four types of leadership styles of Kaplan and Kaiser (2009), namely, forceful, enabling, strategic, and operational leaderships. Which of the four areas that Buckingham and Clifton (2001) suggest, namely, strengths, talents, knowledge, and skills, best fit each leadership style of Kaplan and Kaiser (2009), and why?

    f. How can you combine both approaches to maximize your talent development, while coping with your weaknesses? Explain.

3.10 Palmisano summarized IBM's future values in November 2003 (Palmisano 2004) as follows:

- Dedication to every client's success.
- Innovation that matters—for our company and for the world.
- Trust and personal responsibility in all relationships.

    The only thing that bond and bind such a great institution like IBM is not management top-down dictates, but genuine, sincere, and fundamental values that all IBM employees accept, own, and get energized by. These values would be the basis of what IBM employees dream and do, and feel passionate about their mission and identity as a company. Given the background of the IBM/Palmisano story, do the following exercises:

1. Undertake a similar "value-jam" session across all the employees of your company, and derive a three to four phrase statement-slogan describing the mission/vision statement for your company.
2. How would you ensure that these values become the touchstone for decentralizing decision-making in your company? Explain.
3. Your flagship brands are not so much your products, but your people; they are your frontline ambassadors to the customer world and the environment. How would you ensure that these values become the defining watchword of your frontline ambassadors? Explain.
4. Additionally, how would you ensure that the one thing that can inform, transform, and bond such ambassadors and make their behavior globally consistent and persistent is this set of dynamic values they choose, own, operationalize, and live? Explain.
5. That is the reason why a right set of values is critically important for an ongoing corporate strategy, a set of values or a credo of beliefs that would guide the company through economic cycles and geo-political shifts, through recessions and depressions, through booms and busts, a set of values that would transcend changes in products, technologies, employees, and leaders, and even business models. Instead of galvanizing employees through fear of failure, how would you galvanize them through hope and aspiration? Explain.

3.11 According to Montgomery (2008):

- A CEO's job is not done once a carefully formulated strategy has been made ready for implementation or is implemented. The job of a CEO as a strategist never ends, as no strategy, howsoever comprehensive, defined and compelling, can be a sufficient guide for a firm that aspires to a long and prosperous life.
- Articulating and tending to a purpose-driven strategy is no easy task. It is a human endeavor in the deepest sense of the term, keeping all the parts of a company in proper balance while moving the enterprise forward in a highly competitive and turbulent world.
- While faithfully translating purpose into practice, the CEO must also remain open that the purpose itself may need to change. The judgments made at these moments of transition can make or break a leader or a firm.
- During tough times, the CEO must choose a company's identity, decline certain opportunities, and pursue others. In this sense, the CEO serves as the guardian or steward of organizational mission, identity, and purpose, steering its course through troubled waters, but always bringing it back on track.

1. Verify these principles in the executive leadership of Lou Gerstner at IBM during 1993–2003.
2. Verify these principles in the executive leadership of Sam Palmisano at IBM during 2003–09.
3. Verify these principles in the executive leadership of Sergio Marchionne at Fiat during 2004–09.
4. Verify these principles in the executive leadership of Mr. Ratan Tata at the Tata House ever since he took the reign.
5. Verify these principles in the executive leadership of Mr. B. Muthuraman of Tata Steel Ltd ever since he assumed the position of Managing Director.
6. Verify these principles in the executive leadership of any other CEO or managing director that you worked for.

3.12 Campbell, Whitehead, and Finkelstein (2009) argue that all flawed executive decisions start with errors of judgment made by influential individuals. These authors explain the origin of such errors of judgment using some fundamentals of neuroscience. Neuroscience holds that we depend primarily on two hardwired processes for decision-making:

- **Pattern Recognition**: This is a complex process that integrates information from as many as 30 different parts of the brain. When we face a new situation, we make assumptions based on prior experiences and judgments and, accordingly, recognize a pattern in the new situation. However, pattern recognition can also mislead us, especially if we think we understand the new situation when, in reality, we do not.
- **Emotional Tagging**: This is a process whereby emotional information attaches to the thoughts and experiences stored in our memories. Emotional information tells us whether to pay attention to some data/fact/event or not, and what should be our appropriate immediate response (e.g., fight or flight, act now or act later). When the parts of the human brain controlling emotions are impaired, we could become slow and incompetent decision makers, even though we can retain the capacity of objective analysis (e.g., via pattern recognition).

When pattern recognition and emotional tagging function well, our decisions tend to be more sensible. However, both could mislead us.

a. Recall and review major executive decisions in the Steel Authority of India Ltd (SAIL) that were flawed during the last decade. See if you can trace these errors to problems of pattern recognition, emotional tagging, or a combination thereof.
b. As a contrast, study the unflawed decisions of successful companies in this industry in India.
c. Recall and review major executive decisions in the Air India and the Indian Airlines companies that were flawed ever since both companies are progressively failing. See if you trace these errors to problems of pattern recognition, emotional tagging, or a combination thereof.
d. As a contrast, study the unflawed decisions of successful companies in this industry in India.
e. Recall and review major executive decisions in the North American auto industry that were flawed. Investigate to trace the errors of General Motors, Ford, and Chrysler to problems of pattern recognition, emotional tagging, or a combination thereof.
f. As a contrast, study the unflawed decisions of successful companies in the auto industry of the world, including India.
g. Recall and review major executive decisions in the North American airline industry that were flawed. Investigate to trace the errors of American Airlines, Continental Airlines, and Northwest Airlines to problems of pattern recognition, emotional tagging, or a combination thereof.
h. As a contrast, study the unflawed decisions of successful companies in the airline industry of the world, with specific references to those of India.

3.13 Campbell, Whitehead, and Finkelstein (2009) propose three "red flag conditions" that our emotional tag can conspire to distort our pattern recognition:

- **The presence of inappropriate self-interest**: This can bias the emotional importance we place on information, which in turn positions us to see the pattern we want to see. Research shows that even well-intentioned professionals, such as doctors and auditors, are disabled from preventing their self-interest from biasing their professional judgments.
- **The presence of distorting attachments**: We can become attached to people, places, and things, and these bonds can affect the judgments about a new situation we face and subsequent decisions and actions. Thus, executives find it very difficult to abandon their pet projects or ego-products despite their long history of market failure.
- **The presence of misleading memories**: These are memories and experiences we deem relevant to invoke when we face a new situation, and which unfortunately lead to wrong conclusions and decisions. They cause us to overlook or undervalue some important differentiating factors. This is even truer if in the past we have attached undue emotional tag to our past mental models, frames, or experiences.

1. Recall and review major executive decisions in the Steel Authority of India Ltd (SAIL) that were flawed during the last decade. See if you can also trace these errors to the presence of inappropriate self-interest, distorting attachment, and misleading memories, or any combination thereof.
2. As a contrast, study the unflawed decisions of successful companies in this industry in India if they reveal no such baggage.
3. Recall and review major executive decisions in the Air India and the Indian Airlines companies that were flawed ever since both companies are progressively failing. See if you can also trace these errors to the presence of inappropriate self-interest, distorting attachment, and misleading memories, or any combination thereof.
4. As a contrast, study the unflawed decisions of successful companies in this industry in India if they reveal no such baggage.
5. Recall and review major executive decisions in the North American auto industry that were flawed. Investigate to trace the errors of General Motors, Ford, and Chrysler to the presence of inappropriate self-interest, distorting attachment, and misleading memories, or any combination thereof.
6. As a contrast, study the unflawed decisions of successful companies in the auto industry of the world, including India, if they reveal no such baggage.
7. Recall and review major executive decisions in the North American airline industry that were flawed. Investigate to trace the errors of American Airlines, Continental Airlines, and Northwest Airlines to trace these errors to the presence of inappropriate self-interest, distorting attachment, and misleading memories, or any combination thereof.
8. As a contrast, study the unflawed decisions of successful companies in the airline industry of the world, with specific references to those of India.

3.14 Hammond, Keeney, and Raiffa (2006) identify several hidden traps of bad decision-making that generally lead to organizational underperformance. Study these traps in relation to the loser companies discussed under BTE 3.13. Specifically,

a. Define, illustrate, and explain how the *Anchoring Trap* plagued the losers.
b. Define, illustrate, and explain how the *Status Quo Trap* constrained the losers.
c. Define, illustrate, and explain how the *Sunk-Cost Trap* vexed the losers.
d. Define, illustrate, and explain how the *Confirming-Evidence Trap* stalled the losers.
e. Define, illustrate, and explain how the *Framing Trap* restricted the losers.
f. Define, illustrate, and explain how the *Forecasting Trap* miscued the losers.
g. Define, illustrate, and explain how the *Prudence Trap* stymied the losers.

Chapter 4

The CEO as a Systems Thinker

Systems thinking is one form of holistic organizational learning. It is thinking for people who want to make their organization more effective, while realizing their personal visions. It seeks to blend the individual development of every person in the organization with superior economic performance. It is for managers who are facing an array of problems that resist current ways of thinking. It helps to deal with the problems and opportunities of today, and invest in our capacity to embrace tomorrow, because people who do systems thinking are continually focused on enhancing and expanding their collective awareness and capabilities.

Systems thinking creates an organization that learns. Change and learning may not be synonymous, but they are inextricably linked. If there is one single thing that a learning organization does well, it is helping people to embrace change. People in learning organizations react more quickly when their environment changes because they know how to anticipate changes that are going to occur (which is different from trying to forecast or predict the future), and how to create the kinds of changes they want.

SYSTEMS THINKING AS THE FIFTH DISCIPLINE

Senge (1990: 6–13) speaks of five disciplines as "component technologies" that convergently help us to innovate a learning organization: *self-mastery, mental models, building shared vision, team-learning, and systems thinking.* Though developed separately, Senge (1990: 6) hopes that the five disciplines will prove critical to the success of each other, and that each would provide a vital discipline in building an organization that can truly learn, enhance and empower its capacity to realize the highest aspirations of its stakeholders. It is vital that the five disciplines develop as an ensemble; this is challenging because it is much harder to integrate new independently developed tools into one learning organization than apply them separately. This is why "systems thinking" is the "fifth discipline"—a discipline that integrates the disciplines, fusing them into a coherent body of theory and practice (Senge 1990: 12).

Lofty corporate vision is not enough to turn around a firm's fortunes. Without systems thinking, the seed of vision falls on harsh soil. Without systemic thinking, the first condition for nurturing a vision is not met—because systems thinking will make our vision real in the future. However, systems' thinking also needs the disciplines of building shared vision, mental models, team learning, and self-mastery to realize its potential. Building shared vision fosters a commitment in the long-term. Mental models focus on the openness and transparency needed to unearth shortcomings in our present myopic ways of seeing the world. Team learning develops the skills of groups of people to look for the larger picture beyond individual perspectives. In addition, personal mastery fosters the personal motivation to learn continually how our actions affect our world.

At the heart of a learning organization is a shift of mind—from seeing ourselves as separate from the world to being connected to the world, from seeing problems as created by someone else "out there" to seeing how our own actions create the problems we experience. In a learning organization, people should continually discover how they create their reality and change it, and empower themselves or perhaps impoverish as a result of it. Archimedes said, "Give me a lever long enough ... and single-handed I can move the world" (see Senge 1990, 2006: 12–13).

THE IMPORTANCE OF SYSTEMS THINKING

Systems thinking is more than a powerful problem-solving tool; it is a powerful language, augmenting and changing the ordinary ways we think and talk about complex issues and problems. It is a dynamic language for describing how to achieve fruitful change in organizations. Jay Forrester and his colleagues at the Massachusetts Institute of Technology (MIT) have developed this language as "systems dynamics" over the last 50 years. It has its own terms, tools and methods, links and loops, archetypes, stock-and-flow modeling, all of which help us to understand how complex feedback processes can generate problematic patterns of behavior within organizations and large-scale human systems (Senge et al. 1994: 89–90).

You cannot practice systems thinking as an individual—you need many perspectives from different cross-functional disciplines to bear upon complex problems and issues. Hence, systems thinking by its very nature points out and thrives on interdependencies and the need for collaboration—it is a collective and collaborative team discipline.

Without learning about the industry, the business, its specific vision and mission, as well as their own tasks, employees cannot make the contributions of which they are capable. This requires dramatic learning efforts, both for the employees who must learn to act in the interest of the whole enterprise, and for the senior managers who must learn how to extend mastery and self-determination throughout the organization (Senge et al. 1994: 11). It is the process of systems thinking can enable this process. [See *Business Transformation Exercise 4.1.*]

There are many paradoxes in organizational life. For instance, the time of your greatest growth is the best moment to plan for harder times. The policies that gain the most for your current dominant market position may ultimately drain your resources most quickly. The harder you strive for what you want, the more you may undermine your own chances of achieving it. Systems principles like these are meaningful not so much in themselves, but because they represent a more effective way of thinking and acting. Incorporating them into your corporate strategic behavior requires "peripheral vision"— the ability to pay attention to the world as if through a wide-angle lens, so you can see how your actions interrelate with other areas of activity (Senge et al. 1994: 87–88). [See *Business Transformation Exercise 4.2.*]

In this chapter, we explore the concepts, domain, principles, rules, archetypes, and laws of systems thinking. In Chapters 11 and 12, we will investigate the confines of self-mastery, mental models, building shared vision, and team-learning.

Chapter 4 explores the following systems thinking topics:

- What is a System?
- What is Systems Thinking?

- Major Features of Systems Thinking.
- The Concept of Feedback.
- The Reinforcing and Balancing Feedback Processes.
- The Concept of Delays in Systems Thinking.
- Laws of Systems Thinking.
- Archetypes of Systems Thinking: Nature's Templates that Control Human Events.
- Synthesizing Archetypes.
- The Concept and Principle of Leverage.
- Case Applications of the Laws and Archetypes of Systems Thinking.

WHAT IS A SYSTEM?

A system is a perceived whole whose elements hang together because they continually affect each other over time and operate toward a common purpose. The word "system" originates from a Greek verb *sunisthánai*, which originally meant, "to cause to stand together." Etymologically, therefore, a system implies a structure that holds the parts together in a functional whole. In this sense, the human body, the heart and its organs, the home and the factory, the ecology and the atmosphere, diseases and epidemics, are systems or structures that hang together via forces of interrelationships and inter-actions (Senge et al. 1994: 90).

In this sense, a system is any thing (subject, object, property, or event) that is made up of two or more parts. In this context, everything in the universe has two or more parts, and is therefore, a system. The universe with all its constellations, galaxies, stars, and planets is a system. Our mother earth is a unique planetary system comprising of the geo-sphere, hydrosphere, thermosphere, and atmosphere that make plant, animal, and human life possible.

In systems thinking, the "structure" (from the Latin *struere* = to build) is the pattern of interrelation-ships among key components of the system. The interrelationships are not only organizational such as strategic decision-making processes, hierarchies and process flows, product quality and control, but also include human components such as attitudes, perceptions and emotions, beliefs and meanings, social relations and cultures. Not all structures are visible or conscious; they are built from choices people and organizations make over time, consciously or unconsciously.

Every system has an environment, either internal (elements within the system that you cannot control) or external. A system without an environment does not exist in our universe. An environment of a system is itself "a system whose contents, properties, and events impact a given system, but the latter cannot impact or control the system that impacts it." If a system can control its environment, then the environment becomes a part of the system. For instance, if competitors, new government regulations, new globalization challenges, or new technologies impact and control your company, and your com-pany, in turn, cannot control them, they form your environment.

A problem is a "system at unrest" (Ackoff and Emery 1972). The "unrest" is caused by the internal or external environment beyond your control, but still controlling you or your organization.

There are various ways or levels of thinking in complex situations. Some are disabled to think; their thinking is "inactive" or "passive"—the object of their inactive thinking are everyday events—they either ignore them or leave them unexplained. The next most common level of thinking is "reactive," whereby, most people "react" to everyday events. This is an "event explanation" that addresses questions such as who did, what, when, and to whom? Some anticipate events in "proactive" thinking and offer futuristic explanation. Some think together—their thinking is "interactive" or team thinking, and the outcome of such thinking is "consensual explanation" of events. The next higher level of thinking is "responsive" whereby you search for "patterns of behavior" among everyday events, and thus derive pattern explanation. Presumably, the highest level of thinking is "generative" whereby we search, research, analyze, and explain underlying causes of patterns of behavior (Senge 2006: 52). Table 4.1 summarizes various ways of hierarchical thinking in complex situations and environments.

WHAT IS SYSTEMS THINKING?

At its broadest level, systems thinking or systemic thinking encompasses a large and fairly amorphous body of methods, tools, and principles, all oriented towards looking at the interrelatedness of forces, and seeing them as part of a common process.[1] From our infancy and our kindergarten days, we are taught to break things apart in order to understand them. A destructive child breaks its new Christmas toy and may fail to put it together, while a constructive kid may not only put the pieces together but may even mold the toy, in order to make it his own reconstruction and discovery. When we get older, we are taught to fragment the complex world in order to understand it. This apparently, suggests Senge (1990, 2006: 3), makes complex tasks and subjects more manageable. If we just admire the broken pieces, our vision remains fragmented, each of us mistaking the piece for the whole (as did the blind men trying to define the elephant). We may even give up trying to see the whole together and be happy with our reductionistic picture of the world.

If we reassemble and reorganize the pieces, however, we see connections, interactions, and inter-relationships between parts and components we have never seen and registered before and eventually see a larger whole, and understand reality around us better. This is systems thinking. Systems thinking helps us to destroy our illusion that the world is created of separate and unrelated forces. When we do this, our homes, our schools, our universities, our organizations, our institutions, and we are truly learning organizations.

Systems thinking is a conceptual framework, a body of knowledge and tools that has developed over the past 50 years, to identify and explore patterns in reality around, to make the full patterns clear, and to help us see how to change them effectively (Senge 2006: 7). Like any other discipline, one needs to practice systems thinking as a lifelong process for honing and developing this talent. It is not simply a "subject of study," but a body of technique, based on some underlying theory or understanding of the world. As we develop this proficiency, our perceptual capacity develops, and we gradually surrender to new ways of looking at our world (Senge et al. 1994: 6–7).

---

[1] The field of systems thinking includes cybernetics and chaos theory; gestalt therapy; the work of Gregory Bateson, Russell Ackoff, Eric Trist, Ludwig von Bertallanfy, and the Santa Fe Institute; "systems dynamics" as developed by Jay Forrester at MIT over the past several decades; and dozens of other techniques for "process mapping" flows of activity at work. All of these diverse approaches have one guiding idea in common, that is, the behavior of all systems follows certain common principles, the nature of which are being discovered and articulated (Senge et al. 1994: 89).

TABLE 4.1 Alternative Ways of Thinking in Complex Environments

Hierarchical level of thinking	Object of thinking	Frequently asked questions	Type of explanation	Outcomes of explanation
Inactive	Everyday events	None	Passive explanation	Inaction Ignorance Status quo
Reactive	Everyday events	Who did, what, to whom, and when?	Event explanation	Description Narrative
Proactive	Past events Current events Future events	Who will do? What? When? To whom? With what results?	Prospective explanation Futuristic explanation	Anticipation Speculation Forecasting Foreseeing
Interactive	Past events Current events Future events	Who did, what, to whom, and when?	Consensual explanation Discursive explanation	Dialogue–discussion Team learning Shared meaning
Interpretive	Language of events Meaning of events History of events	Who are these people? How do they think? How and why and with whom do they communicate?	Linguistic explanation Hermeneutic explanation Archetypal explanation	Linguistic analysis Interpretation Human archetypes Social archetypes
Responsive	Patterns of behavior Long-term trends	What happened? How did it happen? How long did it happen? With whom did it happen? Why did it happen? With what consequences?	Trend explanation Pattern explanation Significance explanation Causal explanation	Analysis–synthesis Patterns, trends History; social fabric Meaning waves Shared meaning Culture Civilization
Creative	All or none of the above	What are market trends? What are market needs? What are market wants? What are market desires? What are market gaps? What are market niches?	Creative explanation Inventive explanation Discovery explanation Innovative explanation Adventurous explanation	Market opportunities Undertaking risk Entrepreneurship Incremental innovation Radical innovations Market breakthroughs Tech breakthroughs Institution building Venture creation Founding corporations
Generative	Structures and processes of behavior and events; your mental models	What are the underlying structures, determinants, antecedents, and causes of current and past events? What causes patterns of human or social, national, or global behavior? What are your mental models that underlie your current explanations of events and patterns of behavior?	Structural explanation Mental model explanation Inductive explanation Deductive explanation Causal explanation Metaphysical explanation	Hypotheses Theory Knowledge Structures Mental models Change and growth Truth and wisdom Philosophy Theology

Source: Author's own.

MAJOR FEATURES OF SYSTEMS THINKING

Systems thinking is a discipline for seeing wholes. It is a framework for seeing interrelationships rather than linear cause–effect chains and things, for seeing processes and patterns of change rather than static snapshots. Systems thinking is a sensibility for the subtle interconnectedness that gives living systems their unique character. It is a discipline for seeing the "structures" that underlie complex situations, and for discerning high from low leverage change. It is a shift of mind from seeing parts to seeing wholes, from reacting to the present to creating the future, from seeing ourselves as helpless reactors to changing reality and to seeing ourselves as active participants in shaping that reality. "The unhealthiness of our world today is in direct proportion to our inability to see it as a whole" (Senge 2006: 68).

More specifically, systems thinking is a way of thinking about, and a language for describing and understanding, the forces and interrelationships that shape the behavior of systems. The discipline helps us to see how we change systems more effectively, and to act more in tune with the larger processes of the natural and economic world.

Systems thinking is a fundamental shift from linear thinking to circular thinking, from seeing things as static structures or objects to viewing them as dynamic processes. A tree is not an object, but an expression of process, such as photosynthesis, which connect the sun and the earth. A human being is not just an object/subject, but also a dynamic process of inhaling and exhaling, metabolism and anabolism, thinking and reasoning, deciding and choosing, growth and renewal. The same is true of our bodies, our jobs, our families, our organizations, and neighborhoods—they all are dynamic processes. Often order emerges from chaos, stability from turbulent environments, meaning from confusion, and unity from diversity (Senge et al. 1994: 96–97).

Reality is made up of circles of interdependencies and structures of systems, but we see reality linearly in straight lines. One of the reasons for fragmentation in our thinking stems from our language. "Language shapes perception." What we see (i.e., our perception) depends on what we are prepared or trained to see. Western languages with their subject–verb–object structure are biased towards a linear view of reality. By contrast, many Eastern languages (e.g., Sanskrit, Japanese and Chinese) do not build up from subject–verb–object sequences. If we want to see system-wide interrelationships, we need a language made up of circles, that is, a language of interrelationships. "A language of interrelationships is critical in facing and understanding dynamically complex problems, issues and strategic choices in business." Individuals, teams, and organizations must see beyond events and observe forces that shape events and change.

The art of systems thinking lies in seeing through complexities, to the underlying structures which are generating change. Systems thinking does not ignore complexity; on the contrary, it organizes complexity into a coherent story that empowers us to detect and distinguish between causes and effects of problems, their separation in space and time, and how we can remedy them in enduring ways. The greatest benefit of systems thinking is to distinguish between high-leverage from low-leverage changes in highly complex situations.

The increasing complexity of today's world leads many managers to assume that they lack information to act effectively. The problem is not lack of information, but too much information. "Information overload adds unnecessary complexity" (Senge 1990: 128). Systems thinking enables us to sift through what is important and what is not important, in the world of information explosion that we confront everyday. By using the systems "archetypes", we can learn how to structure mountains of information and relevant variables into a coherent picture of the forces that play.

The essence of the discipline of systems thinking lies in the shift of mind along two dimensions (Senge 2006: 73):

- Seeing interrelationships rather than linear cause–effect chains in reality.
- Seeing processes and patterns of change rather than static snapshots of reality.

The practice of systems thinking starts with understanding a simple concept called "feedback'" that shows how actions can reinforce or counteract (balance) each other. Systems thinking recognizes "structures" or patterns of change that recur again and again. It enables us to simplify life by helping us to see the deeper patterns lying behind the events and the details of ordinary life and reality. [See *Business Transformation Exercise 4.3.*]

THE CONCEPT OF FEEDBACK

An important concept in systems thinking is "feedback." The term means a much broader concept than the positive or negative feedback we receive from our customers, colleagues, or bosses. In systems thinking, feedback means "any reciprocal flow of influence." Feedback, in this sense, is the foundation of reality. The key to seeing reality systemically is seeing circles of influence rather than straight lines. Every circle tells a story. By tracing the flows of influence, we can see patterns that repeat themselves, time after time, making situations better or worse.

In systems thinking, feedback is an axiom that states, "every influence is both cause and effect. Nothing is ever influenced in just one direction. Reality exists in structures, and structures cause behavior." Figure 4.1B captures this phenomenon. Seeing only individual actions and missing the structure underlying our actions, is the root of our linear thinking and powerlessness in understanding complex systems. In contrast, Figure 4.1A represents the traditional linear sequence of cause and effect influence.

Local and domestic problems have international and global antecedents, concomitants, determinants, and consequences.

FIGURE 4.1A   The Traditional Linear Influence of Cause and Effect in Non-systemic Thinking

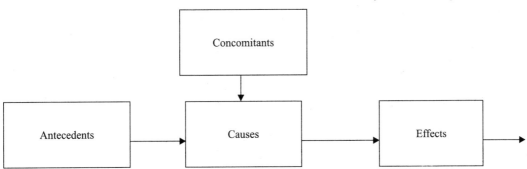

Source: Author's own.

FIGURE 4.1B   The Reciprocal or Circular Influence of Cause and Effect in Systems Analysis

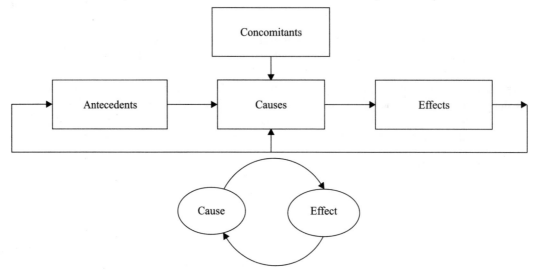

Source: Author's own.

- Antecedents are factors and events that precede but influence the problem at hand.
- Concomitants are factors and events that accompany and influence the problem at hand. In statistics, these are called moderator variables or situational contingencies.
- Determinants are factors and events that cause (and are necessary or sufficient conditions to) the problem.[2]
- Consequences are effects and outcomes that are causally connected to the problem or its selected solution.

A problem correctly identified and well formulated is half solved (Dewey 1910:10). To solve a problem, you have to get ahead of it and change the determinants for its occurrence. Formulating a

---

[2] A condition A is said to be *necessary* for a condition B, if and only if the falsity (or non-existence/non-occurrence) of A guarantees the falsity (or non-existence/non-occurrence) of B. That is, if there is no A, then there is no B. Example: without air, we cannot breathe; air is necessary condition for life. A condition A is said to be *sufficient* for a condition B, if and only if the truth (or existence/occurrence) of A guarantees the truth (or existence/occurrence) of B. That is, if A occurs, then B occurs. Example: Coke is sufficient for quenching thirst. Often, several conditions are "individually or jointly necessary" or "individually or jointly sufficient" in bringing about outcomes. Also, note that if x is a necessary condition for y, then y is a sufficient condition for x, and vice versa. Example: Air is necessary for life; life guarantees existence of air. Being a father is a sufficient condition for being male, and being male is a necessary condition for being a father. But being a father is not a necessary condition for being a male, and being a male is not a sufficient condition for being a father. For instance, John could be male but not a father, but John must be a male before being a father (see Shwartz 1997).

problem carefully can help you identify the reasons (why) it is occurring. A linear solution is good enough for simple and unstructured problems. We need circular (or non-linear) systems solutions to understand and resolve "wicked problems."

A cloud masses, the sky darkens, leaves twist upwards, and we know that it will rain, and it rains. The storm runoff feeds into groundwater miles away and the sky clears by tomorrow. All these events may be distant in time and space, and yet they are connected within the same pattern. Each has an influence on the rest, even though invisible to us. We can understand the system of a rainstorm by contemplating the whole, and not just any individual part of the pattern (Senge 1990, 2006: 6).

Everything there is, is a system. As human beings we are systems, our homes and workplaces are systems, our schools and universities are systems, our corporations and governments are also systems, and our planet and the universe are mega systems. Our businesses and markets, our work and human endeavors are systems bound by an inevitable fabric of interrelated forces and actions that often take years to fully play out their effects on each other. Since we are part of the lacework, it is doubly difficult for us to see the whole pattern of change. Instead, we often focus on snapshots of isolated parts of the system, and wonder why our complex problems never get solved. [See *Business Transformation Exercise 4.4.*]

A poignant example of destructive linear thinking was the U.S.–U.S.S.R. arms race. Each one perceived the other as a threat for some 40 years, and accordingly, piled up nuclear arms. The long-term result of each party's effort to be more secure was a heightened insecurity for all and an escalation dynamic—a combined nuclear stockpile 10,000 times the total firepower of World War II (Senge 1990: 71–72). The current U.S.-Al Qaeda confrontation is a replication of the U.S.–U.S.S.R. arms race. The only difference is vengeance and violence—each one attacks the other in defense and offense. The 9/11 attacks of 2000 and the current anti-terrorist U.S.-led wars on Iraq, Afghanistan, and Pakistan are instances of violence and counter-violence. Figures 4.2A and 4.2B typify this linear thinking of short-term goals and solutions. Both sides respond to perceived threats, and their actions create more threats, and hence, escalate offensive response that results in heightened danger and insecurity for everyone. A linear view of defense and offense will not enable us to escape the illogic and tragic of reciprocal war.

The arms race is, most fundamentally, a problem of dynamic complexity. Dynamic complexity implies many complex effects (Senge 2006: 71):

- The same action has dramatically different effects in the short run and the long run.
- The same action has one set of consequences locally and a very different set of consequences in another part of the system.
- Obvious interventions produce non-obvious consequences.

Conventional linear methods such as forecasting, planning, and analysis are ill-equipped to deal with dynamic complexity. Insights into causes and possible cures require seeing interrelationships between various actors and variables and at various times and contexts. For instance, in the U.S. and U.S.S.R. arms race, each party independently estimated each one's arms build up, assessed the additional threat, and built arms further to neutralize the threat. The process became circular—each one's reactive strategy causing counter-acting strategy. Figure 4.2C characterizes this circular thinking. Linear thinking has no hope of a solution; each one keeps blaming the other and builds up defenses against the other. A real solution is to seek collective blame and guilt, and initiate negotiations and abide by agreed upon reductions in nuclear arsenal; that is, run the vicious cycle of arms race and escalation in reverse. [See *Business Transformation Exercise 4.5.*]

FIGURE 4.2   A Linear versus Circular Cause–Effect Systems Analysis of the U.S.–U.S.S.R. and the Current U.S.–Al Qaeda Crisis

4.2A   U.S.'s Linear Offensive View

4.2B   The Enemy's Linear Offensive View

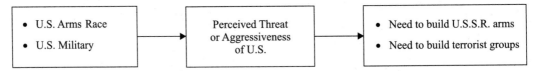

4.2C   The U.S./Enemy's Circular Offensive View

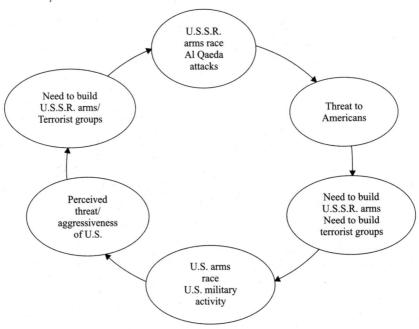

The current mess of financial market collapse and crisis are effects of previous causes. Nothing happens randomly. We identify the following factors that led to the current financial crisis:

- Ingenious *financial instruments* (e.g., derivatives, bond options, hedge funds, and the Ponzi scheme) created by human ingenuity.

- Various *financial by-products* that were created to sell debt or spread risk (e.g., risk insurance, debt securitization, collateralized debt organization (CDO), default credit swaps (DCS), and the like), and thus, presumably, to offer better credit conditions.
- Various lending rates that we have devised for example, constant tampering with the Federal Reserve Bank rates, almost zero or even less than zero percent federal treasury bill rates, lowering prime interest rates, subprime mortgage rates, zero collateral easy home mortgage credit, and adjustable rate mortgage (ARMs)), are all "causes" that conspire together to create various effects.
- Various "effects"—the blasting mortgage homeowner markets, the real estate and housing price boom, seeking large dream homes that one could not afford, credit payment default, mortgage payment defaults, housing price collapse, home foreclosure, personal bankruptcies, and commercial and investment bank bankruptcies—led to a mega financial mess.

Our state, federal, and global level bailout plans are only quick-fix temporary solutions in this regard. The root causes of the financial crisis are still left unexplored, unexamined, unregulated, and unaccountable. The effects are just the tip of the iceberg of an array of unintended consequences. Using the cause–effect circular thinking represented in Figure 4.1B, Figure 4.3 illustrates a systems-analysis of the current financial market crisis.[3]

FIGURE 4.3   **A Circular Cause–Effect Systems Analysis of the Current Financial Market Crisis**

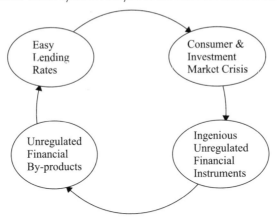

---

[3] Any discussion about the financial crisis and risk management involves some theorizing about derivatives. One of the architects of modern risk management was Robert Merton (a HBS professor and Nobel Prize winner in economics in 1997). His Nobel was awarded in recognition of his role in developing a new method for valuing derivatives in 1973. Since 1973, the markets in derivatives have exploded, and today in October 2009, the notional value of outstanding contracts is estimated to exceed $500 trillion! When asked if derivatives caused the global financial crisis, Merton replied: "NO. Derivatives are ubiquitous in the financial system, and thus will be part of any crisis, but the instruments themselves cannot be its cause. They are simply tools that can be used either, functionally to reduce risk, or dysfunctionally, in ways that increase risk without offsetting benefits. That said, innovation is structurally linked to an increased likelihood of a crisis: Successful innovation by its very nature initially outstrips our ability to regulate it, since existing infrastructural supports will be insufficient to apply safely its full potential" (Merton 2009: 84).

We also anthropomorphize actions, making us humans, as the center of all actions. From the systems perspective, the human actor is part of the feedback process, not standing apart from it. We are part of nature, not separate from nature or standing apart from it. This represents a profound shift in awareness. It enables us to see how we are continually both influenced by and influencing our reality. This shift of awareness is fundamental to ecology and global climate change—unless we see ourselves as part of the nature that surrounds us, not separate from it, we will not feel responsible to the harm that we do to nature by our wasteful habits (Senge 1990: 78).

THE REINFORCING AND BALANCING FEEDBACK PROCESSES

There are two distinct types of feedback processes or building blocks of systems language:

- Reinforcing Feedback Loop: These are "amplifying processes" that constitute the engine of growth. In any growth or decline situation, reinforcing feedback is at work.
- Balancing Feedback Loop: These are "stabilizing processes" whenever there is goal-oriented behavior. The goal can be any desired target such as higher market share, plant shutdown, cost-containment, or massive layoffs. Nature loves balance, and has built-in balancing mechanisms.

Reinforcing loops generate exponential growth or collapse, in which the growth or collapse continues at an ever-increasing rate. For instance, if you add US$100 a year to your piggy bank, it grows linearly and steadily to US$4,000 at the end of 40 years. Whereas, if you invested each year US$100 in a seven percent interest yielding the Certificate of Deposit (CD) without withdrawing the interest, it could exponentially grow to more than US$40,000 in 40 years. In all reinforcing processes, as in a bank account, a small change builds on itself. High birth rates lead to higher birth rates; industrial growth begets more industrial growth; high deficits lead to higher deficits; high crime generates higher crime. Reinforcing loops can be positive or negative, constructive or destructive, exponentially rising or collapsing, a virtuous or vicious cycle.

There can be a number of elements in a reinforcing loop—all in a circle, all propelling each other's growth. More could be added or deleted. By definition, a reinforcing loop is incomplete. Often it may have balancing elements built within the loop. For instance, start at the top right of the circle and proceed clockwise with each of the following connected reinforcing elements:

- Your team's agenda is full.
- The fuller the agenda, lesser the time people have to explore issues in depth.
- This scatters the team's level of focus.
- The more scattered the focus, the lower the level of shared understanding, and the more superficial the treatment of problem at hand.
- Thus, decisions made are not momentous and do not stick.
- Therefore, problems arise adding to the team's agenda.
- Over time, as the team moves around the cycle, more and more problems pile up.
- And your team's agenda is overfull again.

In an organizational context, a common reinforcing feedback is when managers influence their subordinates by their prior expectations about them. For instance, if a manager sees high potential in Jack, a subordinate, and accordingly gives him much attention to develop that potential, Jack may actually fulfill the manager's expectation and turn out to be a great leader, and the manager may feel reinforced in his original appraisal of Jack. Conversely, if a manager labels Jane as a low-potential subject, and consequently, pays less attention to her, she may actually turn out to be ineffective, and the manager may feel reinforced in his belief. The psychologist Robert Merton (1968) called this phenomenon as the "self-fulfilling prophecy." It is also known as the Pygmalion effect. [Pygmalion is a character in Greek and Roman mythology, who believed so strongly in the beauty of the statue he had carved that it came to life. George Bernard Shaw wrote a play, *The Pygmalion Effect* (which later became *My Fair Lady*) to describe a similar phenomenon.]

Pygmalion effect often occurs in schools when teachers pre-label students as first-track or second-track, or third-track candidates, and treat them accordingly. The students are victimized by such pre-classifications and labeling, and often, and possibly, because of this negative tag, persist in their learning disabilities. In reinforcing feedback processes such as the Pygmalion effect, a small change builds on itself, amplifies itself, and produces more movement in the same direction. These are vicious cycles. There are virtuous cycles, however, reinforcing feedback processes that reinforce in desired directions. For instance, physical exercise can lead to a reinforcing spiral—you exercise more, you feel better, you eat better, you work better, and all these, in turn, spur you to keep exercising regularly. The growth of any new product involves positive reinforcing spirals—a word-of-mouth by satisfied customers can snowball and produce a positive spiral chain effect among potential customers. Conversely, a defective product can generate the chain in the opposite direction. Similarly, the extinction of corporations or certain rare species, ecological damage, gas crisis, financial crisis, and the like are vicious cycles of negative, reinforcing feedback processes, unless counteracted in time by balancing feedback. [See *Business Transformation Exercise 4.6.*]

The human body has thousands of balancing mechanisms whereby it maintains *homeostasis*, an ability to maintain conditions for survival in a changing environment. Mechanisms such as eating when hungry, drinking when thirsty, resting when tired, keeping warm in cold temperatures, keeping cool in warmer climates—are all balancing self-correcting processes. Besides these externally fed mechanisms, our human body has thousands of internal mechanisms by which it maintains desired levels of body temperature, oxygen level, blood sugar, and cardiovascular rhythm to maintain blood pressure and heartbeat, and neuromuscular mechanisms to maintain neural balance, and the like.

The balancing mechanisms often maintain the status quo, and hence, go unnoticed. In general, balancing loops are more difficult to see than reinforcing loops because it often seems that nothing is happening. The balancing processes, however, can generate surprising and problematic behavior if they go long undetected. Most human sicknesses and diseases, and eventually death, are problems of undetected strained balancing loops.

THE CONCEPT OF DELAYS IN SYSTEMS THINKING

Delays occur often in both reinforcing and balancing loops. Delays are points where the chain of influence takes particularly long time to play out. Delays have enormous influence in a system, frequently accentuating the impact of other forces. Typical delays in relation to customers are: delays in customer satisfaction, delays in product acceptance, delays in customer dissatisfaction, delays in customer loyalty, delays in a customer's decisions to quit, and longer delays in customer return, if ever. In reinforcing loops, delays can shake our confidence, because growth does not come quickly as expected. In balancing loops, delays can dramatically change the behavior of the system (Senge et al. 1994: 119).

Delays occur when the effect of one variable on another takes time. Delays between actions and consequences are everywhere in human systems. Virtually all feedback processes have some form of delay. We invest now in projects to reap harvest in the future; we hire people today, but it may be months before they are trained and skilled to produce desired results. We often do not recognize or understand such delays, and hence, we become unstable, and tend to "overshoot," going further than needed to produce a desired result. We overbuild inventory, we overbuild bridges, we overbuild houses and real estate markets, and invariably, there is an eventual shakeout. The mortgage-lending crisis is an overbuilding of real estate markets; we overbuilt houses, we overpriced houses, and we overextended home mortgage credit. The first shakeout was subprime lending; the second shakeout was payment defaults; the third shakeout was declining real estate prices; the fourth shakeout was home foreclosure; the fifth shakeout was the collapse of Fannie May and Freddie Mac until the federal government came to their rescue. Currently, even Countrywide is in trouble. Unrecognized delays can lead to instability and breakdowns, especially when the delays are long. The more aggressive we are in our overshooting behavior, the worse the shakeout crises. [See *Business Transformation Exercise 4.7.*]

In corporations, we introduce certain balancing processes (e.g., innovating to sustain competitive advantage, lowering price to fight sluggish demand or tough competition, firing labor to cut costs, ordering materials to replenish depleting inventory, and short-term borrowing for maintaining desired levels of cash flow balances). Planning creates long-term balancing processes. Strategic planning sets long-term goals of sales, market share, profits and shareholder returns, and designs and implements several balancing loops to achieve those goals. Leaders who attempt organizational change often find themselves unwittingly caught in balancing processes. They often confront resistance to change, and whenever there is strong resistance to change, there are strong hidden balancing processes. Resistance to change almost always arises from threats to traditional ways of doing things or norms or status quo. Often these norms are woven into the fabric of established power relationships. That is, the norm is entrenched because the distribution of authority and control is entrenched. Good leaders do not strive to overcome resistance to change but discern the source of resistance to change. They focus directly on the implicit norms and power relationships within which the norms are embedded.

Government regulation can be a balancing process if formulated and executed well. Given the current financial crisis we clearly need regulatory changes, both in the rules, instruments, structure, and in their execution. But, Robert Merton argues, as we expand the regulatory scope, we place greater demands on the regulators to exercise judgment on technically complex financial instruments and financial issues. If regulators must function effectively, they need properly trained staffs. There is always a danger that we will regulate too quickly and what we do will have bad financial consequences, as happened with Sarbanes-Oxley (Merton 2009: 85).

LAWS OF SYSTEMS THINKING

Peter Senge (1990, 2006: 57–67) enunciates some laws of the "fifth discipline" that can help us in understanding the origins of problems and its systemic solutions. A first law, in this regard is:

Law 1: Today's Problems Come from Yesterday's Solutions

The causes of our problems are immediate—we merely need to look at our own solutions to other problems in the past. For instance:

- A well-established firm finds its current quarter's sales are off sharply—a problem. The cause: the highly successful rebate program last quarter allured many customers to buy last quarter than this quarter.
- A new manager cuts down high inventory levels to solve the high carrying cost problem. Salespeople now, however, are spending more time responding to angry customers who are still either waiting for shipments or for the brands they want.
- Police cracking down on drugs in downtown New York arrested narcotics on Thirtieth Street. The addicts have now transferred the crime center to the Fortieth Street.
- Federal officials intercepted a large shipment of narcotics. This, in turn, reduced the drug supply, drove up the price, and generated more crime by addicts desperate to maintain their habit.

In each case, solutions merely shift problems from one part of the system to another. They often go undetected because those who "solved" the first problem are different from those who inherit the new problem.

No forecasting model predicted the impact of the current economic crisis, and its consequences continue to surprise businesses, economists, and academics. The crisis was compounded by the risk-management models of the banks, which increased their exposure to risk instead of limiting it and rendered the global economic system more fragile than ever. Low probability but high impact events, called Black Swan events, are increasingly dominating the business environment. Because of the Internet and globalization, the world has become a complex system, composed of a tangled web of relationships and other interdependent factors. Complexity not only increases the incidence of Black Swan events but also makes forecasting (even) ordinary events impossible. Companies that ignore Black Swan events will likely go under. Instead of perpetuating the illusion that we can anticipate or predict the future, risk management should try to reduce the impact of the threats we do not understand (Taleb, Goldstein, and Spitznagel 2009: 78–79).

Jay Forrester called systems thinking the "new dismal science," because it points out the vulnerabilities, limited understandings, and fallibilities of the past, and the assurance that today's thinking will be the source of tomorrow's problems (cited in Senge et al. 1994: 93). But finally, things do get better. People bring formerly "undiscussable" problems to the surface; they also realize that their old ways of thinking have anchored and trapped them with current problems.

Law 2: Harder you Push, Harder the System Pushes Back

This is the second law. Consider another source-pattern of problems (Senge 1990, 2006: 58–59):

- In the 1960s, there were massive federal programs to build low-income housing and improve job skills in decrepit inner cities in the U.S. Despite this great welfare program, these cities were worse off in the 1970s. Why? One reason was that low-income people from other cities and rural areas migrated to these high-welfare cities, thus overcrowding them and the job training programs were swamped with applicants. The city's tax base began to erode, being overcrowded with welfare recipients.

- The developed countries have great programs that subsidize or assist food and agricultural programs of the developing countries. More food, however, reduces deaths due to malnutrition, that, in turn, causes higher net population growth, and eventually more malnutrition.
- In the mid-1980s, in order to correct the U.S. trade imbalance the federal government let the dollar depreciate. Foreign guerilla competitors, however, let the prices of their goods fall in parallel, thus "compensating" or neutralizing the value of the depreciated dollar.
- A marketing manager finds that one of his products suddenly starts to lose its market-attractiveness. He compensates by aggressive marketing—lowers the price, spends more on advertising, offers rebates—that temporarily bring back the customers. But the costs of aggressive marketing reduce resources for improving quality inspection, speeding delivery, and honoring product warranties and guarantees. In the long run, the more fervently the company markets, the more customers it loses!
- We often act in ways to reduce the impact of Black Swan (low probability-high-impact) events in our life (e.g., house fire, earthquake, fatal accident). It is impossible to predict Black Swan events; hence, we readily buy insurance for houses, health care, cars, and other catastrophic events), only to find that the insurance premiums accumulate quickly to make us broke. We buy insurances to hedge our risk; but hereby we increase our vulnerability to cash flow crisis, if not insolvency. This is what happened with the recent house-mortgage crisis (Taleb, Goldstein, and Spitznagel 2009).

Under each case, there is a well-intentioned intervention that calls forth responses from the system that, in turn, offsets the benefits of the intervention. In systems thinking, this phenomenon is called the "compensating feedback." Compensating feedback is not confined only to "larger systems" but occurs in smaller or personal systems. Consider the following (Senge 1990, 2006: 59):

- Jack quits smoking only to find he is gaining weight, and suffers so much loss in self-image that he takes up to smoking again to relieve the stress. He is back to square one, but possibly in worse condition than before.
- A protective mother who wants so much for her young son to get along with his schoolmates that she repeatedly steps in to resolve problems, ending up with a child that never learns to settle differences by himself.
- Jane is an enthusiastic newcomer so eager to be liked that she never responds to subtle criticisms of her work and ends up embittered and labeled "a difficult person to work with."

Senge (1990: 59) concludes: "Pushing harder, whether through an increasingly aggressive intervention or through increasingly stressful withholding of natural instincts, is exhausting. Yet, as individuals and organizations, we not only get drawn into compensating feedback, we often glorify the suffering that ensues. When our initial efforts fail to produce lasting improvements, we 'push harder'. We hope that hard work will overcome all obstacles, all the while blinding ourselves to how we are contributing to the obstacles ourselves."

Law 3: Behavior Grows Better before it Grows Worse

This is the third law in systems thinking. Low-leverage investments and solutions actually work, but mostly in the short term. Consider the following problems:

- New housing developments mushroom: New houses are built. But lo and behold, the connecting roads get congested, water supply is overstrained, sewerage buckles up, electricity runs in short supply, trash collection gets delayed, children need to be bussed to far away schools, groceries and gas stations are too far, police stations are over-tasked, and emergency hospitals are tens of miles away! The new housing subdivisions and developments were great additions to the township, but soon they cause unintended consequences that become "wicked" problems.
- More homework supplements reinforce classroom work and study: Hence, teachers load children with homework—25 math problems to learn a procedure, 50 multiple-choice questions to learn a concept, reading 50 pages of the textbook and answering 10 questions in preparation for the next class, and so on. The class is structured, the teacher is satisfied, the school principal is positive, and the parents feel they are getting their money's worth. Everybody thinks that if the student does not have enough homework every night, the student is not learning and the teacher is not doing a good job. More is better. Everybody believes that more homework means better mastery of the subject. Soon the child is bored, the overseeing parent is overtaxed, and the teacher that must grade all these repetitive homework assignments is overworked. The children cannot use home time for creative reading, writing, and designing; the over-demanding homework keeps them from learning new stuff. The kids get bad grades on their homework that eventually piles up to pull the semester grade down. The parents are disappointed. The child is frustrated with the final low grade. The back-to-basics homework overload strategy has busted (see Senge et al. 2000: 181–84).

Law 4: The Easy Way Out usually Leads Back In

This fourth law of systems thinking is very much connected with all three previous laws. We all find comfort applying familiar solutions to complex problems, sticking to what we know best. If solutions were easy to find to these problems, they would already have been found. In complex human systems, there are always many short-term strategies to make things look better. Only eventually the compensating feedback comes back to haunt you. A typical short-term solution feels wonderful when it first cures the symptoms. You feel the improvement; you think the problem has gone away. It may be a year or two later, however, when the problem recurs with vengeance. The initial cure can be worse than the disease. We all find comfort applying familiar solutions to unfamiliar problems, sticking to what we know best. "Pushing harder and harder on familiar solutions, while fundamental problems persist or worsen, is a reliable indicator of non-systemic thinking" (Senge 1990, 2006: 61).

Consider the following easy way out sequences and their corresponding backfiring sequences:

- Global financial crisis entered a potentially new phase when many credit markets stopped working normally during September–October of 2008, and as investors around the world moved their money into the ultra safe investments, like treasury bills (Bajaj 2008). This in turn, sent the yield on one-month treasury bills from 1.507 a week earlier to 0.259 percent, down by almost 53 percent within the space of three business days. That is, during September 15–17, 2008, the yield on short-term treasury bills plummeted from 1.507 percent to 0.259 percent as nervous investors scrambled for financial safety. During the same three-day period, borrowing costs for banks and companies escalated from 2.50 percent to 3.03 percent, fueling the credit crisis. The NYSE was down on Monday (September 15, 2008) by 4.4 percent, rebounded a little (+1.3 percent) on the news that the Fed agreed to help American International Group (AIG), and tumbled again on the following Wednesday by 4.1 percent as the federal bailout failed to stem runaway fears (*New York Times*, Thursday, September 18, 2008, A1).

• Meanwhile, the Secretary of the Treasury, Henry Paulson, in conjunction with the Fed Chairman, is desperately trying to bail out the financial market in crisis. A former CEO of Goldman Sachs, Paulson accepted this job in 2006 with trepidation. With a lame-duck President and a Democrat-dominated Congress that is reluctant to take risks during these election months, Paulson has seized the initiative. Earlier in 2008, he had brokered the compromise between Congress and the White House producing a $168 billion economic stimulus package. He was a point man for the rescue of Bear Stearns in March 2008. He has laid out a blue print to modernize regulation of the financial markets. Early September 2008, he bailed out Fannie May and Freddie Mac, each one with $100 billion.

In all these tragic and frightful sequences, all four laws of the "fifth discipline" were playing out: Today's problems come from yesterday's solutions; the harder you push, the harder the system pushes back; behavior gets better before it gets worse; and the easy way out usually leads back in.

We overestimate our abilities and underestimate what can go wrong. The biggest risk lies within us—it is our hubris or arrogance. The ancients considered hubris the greatest defect, and the gods punished it mercilessly. Thus, Achilles and Agamemnon died as a price of their arrogance; Xerxes failed because of his conceit when he attacked Greece; many generals have died throughout history for not recognizing their limits. Any corporation that does not recognize its Achilles' heel is fated to die because of it (Taleb, Goldstein, and Spitznagel 2009: 81).

Psychologists distinguish between acts of commission and those of omission. Although their economic impact is the same in economic terms (e.g., a dollar not lost is a dollar earned), yet risk managers do not treat them equally. They place a greater emphasis on earning profits than they do on avoiding losses. Risk managers do not like not to invest and thereby conserve value. However, a company can be also successful by preventing losses while its rivals fail, and it can then grab market share from them. In chess, grand masters focus on avoiding errors and rookies try to win. Suppose you had not invested in stocks during the last two years but kept your money in low-interest paying banks, when everyone else investing in stocks lost capital by 40 percent. Not losing half your retirement is undoubtedly a victory (Taleb, Goldstein, and Spitznagel 2009: 80). Good hindsight can be a good foresight.

Law 5: The Cure Can be Worse than the Disease

Senge's fifth law of "fifth discipline" states that "Often, the easy, familiar and short-term solution is not only ineffective, it could be addictive and dangerous." Consider the following cases:

- Social drinking starts often as a solution to the problem of low-self esteem or work-related stress. Gradually, the cure becomes worse than the disease; among its other problems it makes self-esteem and stress even worse than before.
- Government welfare, subsidy, unemployment, and disability programs are great, but they foster increasing addictive dependencies on public resources and lessen abilities of local people to solve their own problems.
- In business, we shift the burden of internal problems to "consultants" who make the company dependent upon them instead of training the client managers to solve problems on their own.
- In cities, we shift the burden from diverse local communities to low-income uniform mono-ethnic housing projects.
- We take away extended families, and shift the burden for care of the aged to nursing homes.
- We shift the burden of doing simple math from our knowledge of arithmetic to a dependency on pocket calculators.
- We shift the art and challenge of writing, composing, spelling, grammar, and research-based writing to computer-based search engines, spell-checks, and grammar checks.
- The Cold War shifted responsibility for peace from negotiation to armaments, thereby strengthening the military and related industries, nuclear proliferation, biochemical weapons, and, now, the problem of nuclear disarmament.

In each of these cases, the phenomenon of short-term improvements leads to long-term dependency. Systems thinking calls this malady, "Shifting the burden to the intervener." The intervener may be federal assistance to cities, the elderly, the unemployed, the disabled, food relief agencies, public schools, and other welfare programs. All help a host system on a short-term basis, only to leave the system fundamentally weaker than before and more in need of help. Long-term solutions, on the other hand, strengthen the ability of the system to be self-sufficient and shoulder its own burdens.

Next, consider the dreadful consequences of the financial markets crisis and the quick-solutions—the cure was worse than the disease!

- The cost of borrowing soared for many companies, and global financial investment companies, like Goldman Sachs and Morgan Stanley, that declared themselves relatively strong a week ago, came under assault by waves of selling. Less than a week thereafter, both Morgan Stanley and Goldman Sachs who almost faced bankruptcy requested the federal government for a change of status from investment banks (that served as securities brokers and under the Securities Exchange Commission (SEC) vigilance) to mainline commercial banks (that can do loans and deposits like any other commercial bank but come under more federal regulatory control).
- The financial services industry has posted losses close to US$800 billion since July 2007. Giant financial companies are experiencing deep trouble. Table 6.1 (see Chapter 6) presents market-capitalization performance statistics of 17 mega U.S. financial firms. Together, they had a market-capitalization total of over $1.6 trillion on October 9, 2007. It quickly eroded within a year, however, to a total of $865.6 billion by September 12, 2008, a total loss of $791.72 billion (47.8 percent), or an average of $46.6 billion per company.
- Ripple effects of the collapse of these financial giants have been felt all over Europe, Japan, and the Asian financial markets. While Congress initially turned down a US$700 billion bailout deal hurriedly packaged by the Treasury Secretary and the Reserve Bank Chairman, a follow-up

deal was crafted by the Senate House and soon voted in. The bailout plan bailed out some of the largest surviving financial companies of the world (e.g., CitiGroup, Bank of America and Goldman Sachs). The trickle down effects of this bailout, however, are highly dubious and questionable. In short, the entire financial world was experiencing a distress situation and needed a massive global turnaround.

Another current illustration of Law 5: While most of the economy suffered during the current recession, candy sales were up. Kraft's recent US$16.7 billion offer to buy Cadbury, the British chocolate maker, is another sign of the appeal of candy and comfort foods during these hard times. Mars bought the gum maker Wrigley for US$23 billion—this was another bright spot in a market shy of deals during the recession. Cadbury's share jumped by 40 percent since Kraft's offer. Candy sales were up by 3.5 percent in the past year. During hard times people eat more candy. Hershey thrived during the Great Depression, and the 1930s gave us an array of new sweets, including Tootsie Pops, Snickers, and Mars bars (see *Fortune*, October 26, 2009, p. 14). Consumption of sweets during recession causes obesity and elevated cholesterol levels. The cure to recession could be worse than the disease.

Law 6: Faster is Slower

For most Americans, in general, and business technocrats, in particular, the best rate of growth is fast, faster, and fastest. Together with this illusion are other parallel illusions: "bigger is better; taller the better; more is desirable; sooner the better; the more pleasurable the more awesome; the less risky the better; and the more I get the better it is." Hence, we love gigantic corporations, massive cities, sky-reaching massive structures, larger GDPs and annual incomes, instant and immediate gratification, sensuous and sensational products, theaters, restaurants, and sports arenas, high-protection comprehensive insurances on life and limb and everything we do and possess, and massive accumulation of wealth. Unfortunately, in the long run, all these illusions slow us down:

- Gigantic corporations are soon weighed down by massive bureaucratic hierarchies.
- Massive cities are congested in traffic, dwelling places, transportation, recreation parks, and other public spaces.
- Sky-topping massive structures have killed migratory birds, slowed down elevators, and experienced storm and wind shakes.
- Larger and faster growing GDPs and household incomes have caused meltdown and slowing mechanisms such as overheated economies, wage-inflation, price-inflation, higher interest rates, dollar devaluation and foreign currency appreciation, and increasing trade deficit, federal deficit, and foreign debt.
- Instant and immediate gratification have slowed us down via obesity and disease, and slowed progress via degraded ecology and ecosystems.
- Sensuous and sensational media, products, theaters, restaurants, and sports arenas have killed simplicity of life and frugality, and eventually slowed us down by our exotic, extravagant, and conspicuous lifestyles.
- High-protection comprehensive insurances on almost everything we do and possess have slowed us down by overshot premiums, decreased disposable incomes, and the current financial market crisis.

- Lastly, our massive accumulation of wealth, personal, national, and global, has, unwittingly, increased consumer, merchant, and corporate fraud and tax evasions, and considerably slowed us down by our increased preoccupation for deregulation, privacy, safety, and security.

Yet, virtually all natural systems (e.g., animals, ecosystems, forests) have intrinsic optimal rates of growth that are neither fast nor slow. When growth becomes excessive, as in cancer, the system itself will seek to compensate by slowing down. The current stories of shaky gigantic corporations (e.g., GM, Ford, Chrysler, Toyota, Wal-Mart, Northwest-KLM-Delta, Bear Stearns, AIG, Washington Mutual, Fannie May, Freddie Mac, Merrill Lynch, CitiGroup, Goldman Sachs, and Morgan Stanley) are basically problems of overgrowth and faster growth. They are all slowing down, seeking government bailouts, or Chapter 11 protection, or just bankrupt. With such complex systems, you cannot drum up easy quick-solutions (such as the current federal bailout or economic stimulus plans) with long-term positive outcomes. This realization is one of the sore discouragements of our century. Systems thinking is both more challenging and more promising than our natural ways of dealing with these problems (Senge 2006: 62–63).

Law 7: Cause and Effect are not Closely Related in Time or Space

Delays between cause and effects are normal since cause and effect are not closely related in time and space—this is the fundamental characteristic of complex systems, human or organizational. "Effects" are the obvious symptoms (e.g., declining sales, eroding profits, worker malaise, absenteeism, or under-productivity) that indicate there are problems. "Causes" on the other hand, are the interaction of the underlying system that is most responsible for generating the symptoms (Senge 1990: 63). If you recognize the symptoms in time and do something about it, you can bring about appropriate change to stop the symptoms. Here lies the difficulty—symptoms do not appear soon after the causes. Cause and effect are not closed in time and space.

We look for immediate effects from causes. Hence, if there is a problem on the manufacturing line, we look for a cause in manufacturing. When salespeople cannot meet targets, we think the problem is with the sales force and devise new incentives. If there is inadequate housing, we build more houses. If there is poverty, we increase welfare.

In systems thinking, we "do not look for leverage near the symptoms of the problem"—we need to go upstream and back-stream in time and space to ferret out the root cause. Often, the most effective action is the subtlest. Sometimes it is best to do nothing, letting the system make its own correction or guide the action. Other times, the highest leverage is found in a completely unexpected source. For instance, Cray Supercomputer Company found its highest leverage for supercomputer applications not within the supercomputer industry, but in aeronautical engineering and movie animation (Disney World)—projects that need supercomputers (Senge et al. 1994: 92).

There is a fundamental mismatch between the nature of reality in complex systems and our predominant ways of thinking about that reality. The root of our difficulties is neither recalcitrant problems nor evil adversaries, but ourselves. The first step in correcting that mismatch is to let go the notion that cause and effect are close in time (Senge 1990: 63).

For instance, in relation to Figure 4.2B:

- The ingenious unexamined and unregulated "financial instruments" (e.g., derivatives, bond options, hedge funds, and the Ponzi scheme) were introduced 20 years ago and more.
- Various "financial by-products" that sell debt or spread risk [e.g., risk insurance, debt securitization, collateralized debt organization (CDO)] were created synchronously with the financial instruments, and some of them (especially, debt securitization) belong to the early 1970s; the credit default swaps (CDS) are a major concoction of the last decade or so.
- Various unconventional lending rates (e.g., constant tampering with the Federal Funds rates) were primarily during Alan Greenspan's tenure as chairman of the Federal Reserve from August 11, 1987 to January 31, 2006, during which decade there were two bubbles, in stocks and then in real estate, with almost zero percent treasury bills, lowering prime interest rates, subprime mortgage rates, and zero collateral easy home mortgage credit (Fleckenstein 2008).
- The easy credit conditions encouraged middle- and low-income classes to buy homes that they could not normally afford, and mortgage companies like Countrywide, Fannie May, and Freddie, who controlled close to 67 percent of the mortgage market in the U.S., harvested great profits. Most of the investment banks that provided the money (e.g., Merrill Lynch, Lehman Brothers, Morgan Stanley, and Goldman Sachs) experienced their best years in 2006. The housing market skyrocketed, and massive dream homes mushroomed all along the map of contiguous U.S.
- The effects: the mortgage bubble burst in the beginning of 2008. The overpriced and overheated housing market began to decline, mortgage homeowners began paying premiums of houses that had lost 20 to 40 percent of their original value, and hence, millions of them chose to foreclose. Credit payment defaults, mortgage payment defaults, accompanied by recession and loss of jobs, went beyond home foreclosures to mounting debts and personal bankruptcies. More than 10 million homes went under foreclosure by the end of 2008. Most major investment banks on Wall Street either faced or opted bankruptcies—a mega financial mess that primarily happened during 2008.

Law 8: Small Changes Can Produce Big Results—but the Areas of Higher Leverage are often the Less Obvious

Small well-focused actions that take place at the right place and the right time can sometimes produce significant, enduring improvements—in systems thinking; we call this principle as "leverage." Tackling a difficult problem is often a matter of seeing where the high leverage lies—a small strategic change that produces lasting and significant improvements.

High-leverage changes, however, are usually not obvious, as effects are separated from causes in time and space (Law 7). There are no simple rules to find high-leverage changes. Learning to see underlying structures and processes (rather than events) is a good starting point. In the section that follows we will examine systems archetypes that may enable us to identify and capitalize on high and low leverage points.

Law 9: You Can Have your Cake and Eat it Too—but Not at Once

Most of our so-called problematic "dilemmas" are not real dilemmas; they are products of static thinking; they are effects of "snapshot thinking" rather than process thinking. The classical dilemmas such as cost-containment versus revenue generation, low-costs versus high-quality products, earning gains versus avoiding losses, centralization versus decentralization, global versus local control, happy committed employees versus competitive labor costs, individualization versus standardization, individual one-on-one training versus team training, and the like, are by-products of static thinking. These dilemmas imply "either–or" choices only at a static, fixed point snapshot view of reality. But when we view reality dynamically as a continuous flow, and study the processes involved, then the either–or choices become "both" choices, but at different times.

For instance, for over a century American manufacturing engineers believed that they had to choose low cost or high quality, but not both. The basic argument was that higher quality implies higher technology, better materials, more time to assemble, more start-up costs, more expensive parts and components, and more expensive and continuous quality controls. Systems or process thinking that looks at the whole system enables us to have both low cost and high quality—that is, have one's cake and eat it too—though in different times, ways, and sequences. High-quality basic improvements in materials and work processes eventually should eliminate re-work, recall, reduce quality inspectors, reduce customer complaints, lower warranty and guarantee costs, lower promotions costs such as rebates and free samples, and increase customer loyalty—each of which more than makes up for the higher costs of higher quality processes. This is precisely what Toyota has been doing for the last 50 years in its famous TPS–Toyota Production System.

Investing time and money to develop new skills and methods of assembly, including new methods for involving everyone on the assembly line for improving quality may involve short-term high up-front costs. Nevertheless, they produce immense cost-saving dividends in the long run.

Law 10: Dividing an Elephant in Half Does not Produce Two Elephants

Most of our institutions and organizations suffer from man-made boundaries that impede organizational learning and effectiveness. For instance, businesses comfortably divide business functions into manufacturing or production, accounting and financing, marketing, and human resources management. Correspondingly, most MBA programs teach these business functions as separate disciplines. Each one may see a business problem clearly from the narrow perspective of one's discipline, but not see how the policies and strategies of their solutions impact and interact with other departments or disciplines. This is like several blind men examining different parts of the elephants independently and arriving at different definitions or descriptions of the elephant. Consequently, because of these parochial boundaries, businesses fail to see the whole picture of systems and processes, and the century-old MBA program is still struggling to study and teach integrated business management. Systems thinking does not imply that no business functions or business discipline should be studied in isolation; occasionally, it may be advantageous to do so. But by and large, we must examine, explore, and analyze the entire business system and the entire discipline of business management, emphasizing on the interactive effects of various functions and disciplines.

Living systems and organisms have integrity, and their character and quality depend upon the whole. Organizations and institutions such as schools and homes, should be viewed as living organisms with different parts constantly interacting to produce whole effects. If we systematically do so, then we should be better poised to resolve some age-old social problems such as school crime and violence, increasing high school dropout rates, family dysfunctions and divorce, street gangs and crime, crowded prisons, entrenched poverty, structured injustices, and income inequality, obesity and health care problems.

Ghetto areas today such as Harlem in New York and Roxbury in Boston were originally upper-class suburbs. Corporations buy businesses to harvest them rather than reinvest in them to strengthen them. This is what Cerberus did with Chrysler, and the latter is experiencing financial crisis again. This is boundary thinking; and this is, often, exploitative thinking.

Law 11: There is no Blame

This law follows from most of the previous 10 laws. We tend to finger point at others for the problems we face such as the competition, regulation, taxes, erratic marketplace, labor unions, legacy issues, and, now, outsourcing and globalization. At a deep level, there is no difference between the inside and the outside of the business, the inner sanctum and the outer forum—as most of these are created by artificial boundaries we impose upon ourselves, our thinking, disciplines and departments, our corporations and institutions.

Boundaries are symptoms of linear thinking. Hence, we ask linear questions such as: Who was responsible for the arms race? Who perpetrated 9/11? Who was the terrorist group behind the Bali massacre? Who master-minded the November 26, 2008 attack on Mumbai? Who caused the 2008 Wall Street meltdown? Who propelled the 2007–09 global recessions? We ask linear, one-way causation questions, and we expect linear, one-way causation answers.

If we think in feedback circles, however, then we must remember the axiom, "every influence is both cause and effect." Every incident mentioned earlier, from this perspective, is a chain of causes and effects. We ignore some, and over-emphasize others; that is, we search for scapegoats, and this generates problems in thinking and problems in understanding solutions.

Thus, the feedback issue complicates the ethical issue of responsibility. In the U.S.S.R.–U.S. arms race, we asked, who was responsible? In the U.S. and global war on terrorism, we continue to ask, who is responsible? In our linear analysis of current events we ask, who is responsible for the current financial market crisis? Who is responsible for the current health care distribution crisis in the U.S.? Who caused the Southeast Michigan domestic auto crisis? Who is responsible for the current home mortgage crisis? From a linear view point (see Figures 4.1A, 4.2A, and 4.2B), we place responsibility flatly on the "other" side or "out" side. That is, we search for scapegoats. These are problems and limitations of our linear thinking, linear analysis and assessment, and linear judgments. At a deep level, however, there is no difference between blame and guilt, as both arise from linear perceptions. From the linear view, we are always looking for someone or something that must be responsible.

For instance, most recently we have been blaming the Chinese money markets for our current financial market and housing crisis (Lindler 2008; see Appendix 4.1). China, the world's third largest economy, did get herself beaten up in the recent downturn, but has recovered faster than any other country. Its GDP was growing 7.9 percent in the third quarter of 2009. Moreover, given the leadership in Beijing, there is a very conscious transformation of the Chinese economy. Besides investing in America, Australia, and Europe, China is also changing its focus of its investments from raw materials to finished goods. Its buying power and shopping spree are increasing exponentially (*Fortune*, October 26, 2009, p. 12). Far from blaming China for our recession, we should be grateful for its reverse foreign direct investments in U.S.A.

Systems thinking shows that there is no outside; that we and the causes of our problems are part of a single system. The cure or solution lies in the relationship we build with the outside or the enemy.

Hence, a corollary: "Everyone shares responsibility for problems generated by a system." This axiom does not imply that everyone involved exerts equal leverage in changing the system. Some may share responsibility (i.e., blame or guilt) more, some less (Senge 1990, 2006: 78). [See *Business Transformation Exercise 4.8.*]

ARCHETYPES OF SYSTEMS THINKING: NATURE'S TEMPLATES THAT CONTROL HUMAN EVENTS

Systems seem to have a mind of their own. Nowhere is this more evident than in delays—delay between cause and effect, interruptions between our actions and their consequences. One of the highest leverage points for improving system performance is the minimization of system delays. For instance, American manufacturers typically reduce delay by controlling inventory, while Japanese counterparts reduce delays by reducing the entire new product development cycle—a much better competitive advantage.

Americans hate redundancy. Hence, we focus on Just in Time (Inventory Repletion) (JIT), the lowest bank reserves possible, the thinnest staff necessary, and the like. Mother Nature is the best risk manager of all. That is partly because she loves redundancy. Evolution has given us spare parts—we have two lungs, two kidneys, two eyes, two ears, two hands, two feet, two brain hemispheres—that allow us to survive. "Biological systems cope with change because of redundancy. We're all born with two eyes, two ears, two hands, and two brain hemispheres. Two eyes give us perspective. Two ears give us sound location. Two hands give us the ability to use tools. And the two sides of our brain give us the ability to grasp problems in the pincer grip of logic and intuition" (Neumeier 2009: 45).

Most executive do not realize that optimizations makes companies vulnerable to changes in the environment. In companies, redundancies consist of apparent inefficiencies such as idle capacities, unused parts, large inventories, and monies that are not put to work. The opposite is leverage, which we think is good, but its not so always. Too much debt leverage, for instance, can make the company and the economy fragile. If you are highly leveraged, you could go under if your company misses a sales forecast, interest rate change, or when other risks crop up. When you do not carry too much debt on your books, you can cope better with changes in the environment (Taleb, Goldstein, and Spitznagel 2009: 81).

"Structures of which we are unaware hold us prisoners." Conversely, learning to see structures within which we operate begins a process of freeing ourselves from previously unforeseen forces. Certain patterns of structures recur again and again. These "systems archetypes" or "generic structures" empower us to see structures in our personal and organizational lives. In Greek, *archetypes* mean "the first of its kind." Archetypes are accessible tools with which managers can quickly construct credible and consistent hypotheses about the governing forces of their systems. They are also a natural vehicle for clarifying and testing mental models about those systems. They are powerful tools for coping with the astonishing number of details that frequently overwhelm novices in systems thinking (Senge et al. 1994: 121). Systems archetypes are reinforcing (amplifying) processes that are set in motion to produce a desired result. They can either create a spiral of success or a spiral of failure.

Archetype 1: Limits to Growth
Management Principle: *Do not push growth; remove the factors limiting growth.*
Archetypes are limits to growth structures. Individuals and organizations grow for a while, and then slow down or stop growing. Many well-intentioned efforts to improve can meet with bumps or limits

to growth. Often growth suddenly comes to a halt, and even reverses itself. Limits to growth structures operate in organizations at many levels. For example:

- A high-tech organization grows rapidly because of its innovative products. As new products grow, revenues grow, the R&D budget grows, and the technical staff grows. Eventually, the burgeoning staff becomes increasingly complex and difficult to manage; bureaucracy sets in; and gradually internal competition for promotions, positions, and power slows down innovation and the introduction of new products. Senior management is divided or just cannot handle this complexity. Your quality suffers and perhaps unknowingly or inadvertently you lower the standards. These, in turn, after a delay, reduce revenues and the R&D budget, and eventually, the growth mysteriously levels off.
- Consider a services firm such as a law firm, a consultancy firm, or an investment bank. Initially, each firm draws the best talent, brings in good clients, grows rapidly, and the profits are fed into the business to grow further. Morale grows, with the young talent highly motivated, and hoping to become partners within ten years. However, as the firm grows larger, complexity sets in, and the growth slows down. Tough competition or market saturation could also be reasons for growth slowing down. Possibly, the founding partners are no longer interested in sustaining rapid growth. Occasionally, some sort of in-fighting may also disaffect the company morale. The slowing down of the growth rate, means less promotion opportunities, less hiring, even firing, and the limits to growth also set in.

In both cases, limits to growth become powerful. Often, the high-tech company, the law firm, the consultancy firm, or the investment bank may never recapture their capabilities for developing new breakthrough products and services or generating rapid growth. The more aggressively you try to change the process, the more your subordinates perceive risk, and the more they resist. Eventually, relationships sour, mutual trust breaks down, adversarial attitudes develop, and rumor and suspicion dank the organization climate. The reinforcing spiral turns around and runs in reverse.

This is how some of the giant energy companies (e.g., Enron, Tyco, World.com, and Dynergy) ended. This is, presumably, where the domestic automakers (e.g., GM, Ford, and Chrysler) are now. This is where the big investments banks (e.g., AIG, Bear Sterns, CitiGroup, Goldman Sachs, Lehman Brothers, Morgan Stanley, and Wachovia) are. This is where giant mortgage companies are (e.g., Country-wide, Fannie Mae, and Freddie Mac).

Typically, most managers react to limits to growth by trying to push hard. When the rate of growth or improvement slows down, managers compensate by striving even harder. Unfortunately, the more vigorously you push the familiar levers (e.g., R&D, innovation, promotions, strategic alliances, recruitment of new and young talent, borrowing, new debt-equity structures, venture capital, mergers and acquisitions, or new joint ventures), the more strongly the balancing process resists, and the more futile your efforts become.

Nevertheless, there is a way out of this loop. In each case, the leverage lies in the balancing loop, not the reinforcing loop. To change the behavior of the system, you must identify and change the limiting factor. This may require actions or choices you have never noticed or considered, or difficult changes in norms or rewards. The easiest way to recognize limits to growth structures is through the pattern of behavior. That is, see if you can identify the appropriate elements of your reinforcing and balancing loops.

First, "identify the reinforcing loop or process"—what is getting better and what is the action or strategy that leads to improvement? For instance, in dieting, you not only cut down on fatty foods but also exercise. In recruiting, you not only get the best talent, but also insist on equal opportunity hiring program. In maintaining morale and productivity in your professional firm, you not only introduce a new set of norms and rewards, but distribute them equitably regardless of gender, color, age, or nationality. In maintaining new steady breakthrough products, you not only step up R&D, but also continuously foster creativity and innovation among all people concerned. In maintaining optimal inventory, you not only need JIT, but also trusting relationships with your critical suppliers. Once you have identified the reinforcing factors, you should look for leverage by deploying them effectively.

The second step "is to identify the limiting factors and the balancing process it creates." What is the "slowing mechanism" or resisting force that stalls your process of continuous improvement? For instance, sustaining loving relationships requires giving up the ideal of the "perfect partner"— the implicit goal that limits the continued improvement of any relationship. Some managers work on an ideal number of men and women on the job; this unspoken number is a limiting factor; as soon as that threshold approaches, you may abandon the equal opportunity hiring law, or may look for ways of getting rid of some on the pretext of maintaining gender balance. Once you have identified the limiting factors, look for leverage by removing them effectively.

Archetype 2: Shifting the Burden
Management Principle: *Beware of the symptomatic solution.*
Symptomatic solutions address only the symptoms of a problem, and not the fundamental causes, and tend to have short-term benefits at best. There is always an underlying problem that generates the symptoms; it may be obscure and difficult to notice, or too costly to confront. Thus, you "shift the burden" of the problem to well-intentioned easy fixes that may work well in the short-term. Unfortunately, easier solutions only worsen the symptoms; they leave the underlying problem unaltered or even worse. In the long-term, the problem resurfaces and there is an increased pressure for a symptomatic response. Meanwhile, the system loses whatever abilities it had, to solve the underlying problem; the capability for fundamental solutions can atrophy (Senge 2006: 103).

Typical symptomatic solutions are:

- Managers believe in delegating work to subordinates but still rely on their own ability to step in and handle things at the first sign of difficulty—this is the quick fix of micro-management. The subordinate never gets the necessary experience to do the job.
- Busy HR managers bring in external HR consultants to sort out personnel problems, and the HR managers are unwilling to change the status quo or improve their ability to resolve the problems by themselves. Soon, the HR managers become addicted to outside experts.
- Indulging in incrementalism (e.g., incremental innovations and products) rather than targeting breakthrough and radical innovations for winning larger market share.
- Excessive advertising of products for shoring up sales and not working on improving their quality.
- Businesses losing market share to foreign competitors seek a quick fix in tariff protection or press legislature to ban foreign products, and find themselves disabled to operate without such short-term solutions.
- Countries that experience trade deficits go for the quick fix of devaluating their currency.
- Countries with gaping federal deficits seek printing more money thus fueling inflation.

- Controlling world grain prices by providing domestic farmer subsidies not to grow.
- Prescribing drugs to fight the problems originated by unhealthy lifestyles (e.g., smoking, drinking, over-eating, lack of exercise) rather than change the lifestyle itself.

All symptomatic interventions shift burdens and are quick fixes; they may solve the symptoms of the problem quickly, but only temporarily. These are low-leverage changes and solutions. We focus on symptoms where the stress is greatest. We repair or ameliorate the symptoms. We think thereby that we have solved the real problem, thereby diverting our attentions from the fundamental problem. Seeking symptomatic solutions progressively reduces our capacity to find fundamental solutions, and increases our addictive dependence on symptomatic solutions. The problem resurfaces to haunt you with added complexities. Most quick-fix symptomatic solutions make matters worse over the long term.

Some 95 percent or more of U.S. businesses are family-owned, or family-controlled (i.e., in which the family can control the succession to CEO). Relationships and consensus-building are very critical in family-owned businesses. The company cannot improve unless the relationships among the family members improve simultaneously. When such relationships are ignored there is a large likelihood the family business may begin to flounder (e.g., Campbell's Soup family; Binghams of St. Louis). Family members fight for control, and in the process ignore the needs of the company and its customers. When situations get out of control, family business patriarchs seek "symptomatic solutions" through lawyers, consultants, outside experts or professionals for arranging inheritance, wills, and settlements—for revamping business, and the like. The outside experts may do the job but in "shifting the burden" to the experts, the more fundamental issues of family dynamics get side-tracked and even worsened. Instead, one should get all the family members to understand the family dynamics and the dynamics of the firm, dialogue about it, discuss the main problems, and arrive at a consensus. Perhaps, all could get special training so that all family members have equitable opportunities to participate in shared governance (Senge et al. 1994: 472–73).

Often, in shifting the burden structures, there is also an additional reinforcing (amplifying) process created by "side effects" of the symptomatic solution. For instance, take the side effects of drugs administered to correct a health problem. If the original health problem was caused by an unhealthy lifestyle (e.g., overeating, drinking, smoking, or lack of exercise), the only fundamental solution lies in a change in lifestyle. The drugs may make the symptom better—shift the burden of changing lifestyle to medication—but in the end, the side effects accumulate leading to even worse health problems. An alcoholic who admits to his drinking problem and to the fact, that he will be an addict all his life—knows very well that drinking on the sly is a symptomatic solution, and that he should seek support and power from Alcoholic Anonymous. Consider the problem of stress when we need to juggle work, family, and community responsibilities. Quick symptomatic solutions to such stress are often smoking, drinking, eating, or overworking, each of which has its own side effects. Nevertheless, good long-term solutions do exist. If the workload increases beyond our capacity, the only fundamental solution is to limit the workload. It may mean passing up a promotion that entails more travel and being away from the family, or declining a position on the local school board. But it also means prioritizing and making the right choices.

The character of an organization is in its ability to resolve fundamental problems and lessen its interventions of symptomatic solutions. That is, the character of an organization is in its ability (or inability) to face shifting-the-burden structures. Strengthening fundamental responses almost always requires a long-term orientation and a sense of shared vision. Weakening the symptomatic response requires willingness to distinguish between quick-fix palliatives and long-term solutions. Sometimes symptomatic solutions are needed as palliatives but they must be acknowledged as such, and must be combined with strategies for rehabilitating one's capacity for fundamental solutions. In fact, fundamental solutions and symptomatic solutions are relative terms. What is most valuable is that you can recognize multiple ways of addressing the problem from the most fundamental to the most superficial (Senge 1990: 110–13).

Archetype 3: Fixes that Backfire
Management Principle: *A continuing series of fixes to a stubborn problem improves only momentarily.*
The familiar expression, "The squeaky wheel gets the oil," or "Whoever makes the greatest noise, grabs the attention," are indicative of "fixes that backfire." Suppose you are annoyed with a squeaky wheel in your car, and instead of lubricating it with proper oil, you hastily throw a can of water on the wheel. The noise stops momentarily, but to return louder. The air and water have joined forces to rust the joint. Suppose, not knowing the problem you splash water again onto the wheel, thinking it worked last time and keep on doing this the whole day or for a whole week. At the end, the wheel has stopped squeaking altogether because by now it is encased with rust. A solution is quickly implemented (the fix) which alleviates the symptoms (in the balancing loop). But the unintended consequences of the fix (the vicious cycle of the reinforcing loop) actually worsen the performance that we are attempting to correct (Senge et al. 1994: 125–26).

A squeaky wheel could be a dissatisfied customer screaming for a product that is two weeks late. How do I treat this customer—by splashing with a water palliative or treating the disease with proper oil? The central theme of this archetype is that "almost any decision carries long-term and short-term consequences, and the two are often diametrically opposed." A problem's symptom improves (the quick fix enables the problem variable to go down) and deteriorates alternately (the unintended consequences set in, problem escalates, worse than before). If the problem's symptoms keep gyrating in your company with small triumphs and long troughs, then you are in a "fixes that backfire" archetype.

Examples of business symptoms that attract quick fixes that backfire are:

- Your (de-seasonalized) sales are up and down, either steadily increasing or flat.
- Your salesperson productivity (measured by salesperson-time per sale or dollar profits per employee) is vacillating.
- Your manufacturing productivity (judged by scale, scope, and time) is undulating badly.
- Your net cash flows (cash inflows minus cash outflows) are precipitously ebbing downward.
- Your debt/equity ratio is over-leveraged.
- Your work-in-progress (WIP) inventories are mounting.
- You are plagued with delayed deliveries.
- Your finished product (FP) inventories are overstocked and eat your cash flows.
- Your receivables are exponentially increasing, but some are ending in bad debts.
- Your employee apathy (judged by non-punctuality, unenthused work, absenteeism, and high turnover) is unpredictably destroying productivity.
- Your product quality (judged by recalls, returns, and warranty-failure) is badly fluctuating downwards.
- Your company is vexed with cost-overruns forcing you to downsize.

- Your profitability judged by return on sales (ROS), return on investments (ROI), return on equity (ROE), and retun on invested capital (ROIC) is spiraling downward.

Each of these problem symptoms has its traditional quick-fix solutions, most of which do not work in the long run. After all, a quick fix only alleviates a symptom, but does not eradicate it. Hence, are you trying to splash water or apply lubricating oil to the problem? Are you trying the same quick-fix solution a little more, and then a little more—until you catch yourself resisting the idea of trying something else. Soon, you will be overwhelmed with a sense of powerlessness when confronting too many unintended consequences of your quick fixes.

For avoiding quick fixes that backfire, Senge et al. (1994: 129) suggest the following:

- Make a commitment to address the real problem now.
- Engage in shared vision: What do others think of your quick fixes?
- Increase awareness of the unintended consequences by opening up people's mental models.
- Do you need to fix the problem right now? Will the system take care of itself in the long run?
- Reduce quick fixes by both number and repetition.
- Can you manage or minimize the undesirable consequences of your fixes?
- Select interventions that produce the least harmful or most manageable consequences.
- Reframe and address the root problem. Every fix that backfires is driven by an implicit target in the balancing loop. So make it explicit.

Archetype 4: Tragedy of the Commons
Management Principle: *A continuing increase of use of a common resource will eventually overstrain the resource until it crashes.*
Any new resource (e.g., a new expressway, a new airport, a new mall, a new charter school, a children's park, a new credit union) always opens with people benefiting individually by sharing a common resource (e.g., the city or state budget). Soon, at some point, the amount of traffic grows too large for the "commons" to support; congestion, overcrowding, and overuse lessen the benefits of the common resource for everyone—hence, the tragedy of the commons!

If the new resource cannot be expanded or replenished with additional space, it becomes a constraint or a problem, and you cannot solve the problem on your own and in isolation from your fellow drivers or pedestrians or competing users. The total activity on this new resource keeps increasing, and so does individual activity; but both begin to fall after a peak, the latter faster than the former. Eventually, if the dynamic of common use and overuse continues too long, the total activity will also hit a peak and crash. What makes the "tragedy of commons" tragic is the crash dynamic—the destruction or degeneration of the common resource's ability to regenerate itself. The tragedy of the commons, thus, is a corollary of the "limits to growth" archetype.

Some examples of the "tragedy of the commons":

- Putting increasing number of cattle on a rangeland eventually undermines the ability of the soil to grow grass.
- Draining the financial resources of an enterprise, past a certain point, threatens the life of the enterprise.

- In Ford's 1994 Lincoln Continental project, the number of electricity-draining components designed for the car overloaded the battery power available. None of the component designers would back down and reduce their power consumption, because it was in their interest to design electrical components with high functionality.
- Divisional heads making tremendous demands from one centralized sales force or technical support. The central sales staff grows increasingly burdened by all the field requests, and the net gains for each division are greatly diminished.
- A common reservoir that feeds many cities and villages runs easily dry owing to increasing number of users and increasing intensity of use. The reservoir needs to be shut down periodically in order to replenish itself to full capacity.
- A common district school budget may fund public elementary, middle, and high schools, some charter schools, cornerstone schools, and several day-care centers. All have good reasons to exist but all draw from the same common source. If the budget is finite and difficult to replenish, then each group will feel pressure to get its share, and the more ingenuous win while the remaining less ingenuous lose. If the archetype "success to the successful" dominates (see Archetype 6), then only the winners win (see Senge et al. 2000: 507–10).
- A common forest has been progressively deforested by timber and lumber merchants such that the forest cannot regenerate itself anymore—it is forced to remain fallow.
- The Sahel region in sub-Saharan Africa was once a fertile pastureland. In the 1950s, it supported over 100,000 herdsmen and over a million head of grazing cattle called Zebu. Today, it is a barren desert, yielding a small fraction of the vegetation it produced before. Each herdsman expanded his Zebu cattle for a better share of the pie, and overgrazing tended to consume more foliage than the Sahel ranges could generate. The desertification reinforced itself as decreases in plant cover allowed wind and rain to erode the soil. A series of droughts in the 1960s and 1970s worsened the vicious spiral. By the early 1970s, 50 to 80 percent of livestock was dead and much of the Sahel population was destitute (Senge 1990: 294).
- Overused police or law enforcement force—when poverty and/or high school dropouts increase, crime also normally increases, and overstrains a limited police department. The criminals may increase crime knowing that the police officers are overburdened.

In most of these tragic cases, individual users cannot do much, even if they stop using the common resource. A tragedy of the commons often involves a catastrophic crash—the destruction or degeneration of the common resource to replenish itself. When resources are depleted beyond a certain point, they cannot be replaced. Yet despite the dwindling resources, every one pushes harder to get one's share of the shrinking pie. Doing so stresses the overall system capacity even more, making a crash more likely and more dangerous (Senge et al. 2000: 508).

There are three potential forms of leverage to counteract the tragedy of the commons (Senge et al. 1994: 144):

- Bring to individual attention the collective costs of their actions; the more clearly they see the structure, the more likely they may stop overusing.
- Close the common resource for replenishment or delayed maintenance—this is the best leverage in the case of ecological resources.
- If it is a technology, then innovate technology with doubled capacity.

Archetype 5: Accidental Adversaries
Management Principle: *Understand your partner's needs, see if you are unintentionally undermining them, and look for ways that support each other.*

Jennifer Kemeny developed this archetype (Senge et al. 1994: 145–48). It explains how groups or people who ought to be or want to be in partnership with each other, end up bitterly opposed. They get locked up in fierce combat and resentment. The archetype of accidental adversaries applies to teams working across functions or disciplines, strategic alliances among overspecialized engineers, joint ventures between organizations, aggressive marketing among highly imaginative and innovative promotional artists, union-management battles, civil wars, family disputes, and teenager rivalry. Is there a structural reason for this adversarial stance?

For instance, Proctor & Gamble (P&G) and Wal-Mart, two of the most capable corporations of the world, had long been aware of the advantages of cooperating as suppliers and distributors. Nevertheless, their relations have long since strained. In the mid-1980s, P&G believed in aggressive marketing of their products via deep discounts, and other price promotions. Wal-Mart did not believe in heavy marketing, hoping to pass on the saved costs to the consumers. Moreover, Wal-Mart does "forward buying" or stocking up—that is, buying large quantities of the product during the discount period, selling it at a regular price when the promotion ends, and using the extra income to improve their margins. This strategy is part of Wal-Mart's balancing loop but it undermined P&G's productivity and profitability, creating great swings in manufacturing volume. This strategy would be adding to the costs of P&G, as distributors (who have already stockpiled) would not order more products for months. An impasse resulted; a reinforcing loop had formed in the middle, causing a death spiral of mutually detrimental actions. Each partner's symptomatic solution turned out to be unintentionally counterproductive and obstructive to the partner's success. They became accidental adversaries or good-willed enemies.

One way to get out of this social mess is for both sides to seek ways to strengthen one's understanding of the partner's fundamental needs, and how one can unintentionally undermine them. Its important to dialogue and discuss how you can support each other. This may include helping to remove or weaken the constraints in your partner's system that resists your own solution. Both P&G and Wal-Mart started a dialogue, met in the same room, and gradually understood the structure they had built up. Their individual strategy made sense locally for their own corporation, but not collectively. Hence, having recognized this they had to craft a new joint strategy. Their new resolution: If you help me realize my goals, I can help you realize yours. P&G offered, for the first time, to stop promotions at Wal-Mart, and instead, provide for an "everyday low price" (EDLP) strategy. Wal-Mart would order from P&G in such a way as to strengthen P&G's productivity. From accidental adversaries, P&G and Wal-Mart became purposeful and strategic allies.

Archetype 6: Success to the Successful
Management Principle: *Should the success of the successful spell failure of the failed? Break this vicious zero-sum game cycle.*
[See Senge et al. (2000: 355–59)]

In the "success to the successful" archetype, two reinforcing cycles come into conflict: one is a virtuous spiral where things get better and better for some; the other is a vicious spiral where things get worse and worse for others. At the beginning of the spirals, both groups may be equally competent or promising. The virtuous group, however, shows its promise more quickly and visibly.

Every year the administrators of a school resolve that all the students will be given equal opportunity to succeed. Nevertheless, every year, some students get caught in a vicious spiral of defeat (e.g., they come to school less prepared, the teachers see them as sullen, they do not seem to fit in with the prevailing school culture of clothes, diction, and language). Despite the educators' best of efforts to help all children learn, the school system seems to separate the goods kids from the bad kids or the Track One students from Track Two or Three. Eventually, there is so much strain on the school's resources of time, effort, and energy, that some "poor" kids get left behind and automatically written off! It is natural for the teachers to focus their interest and attention on the "good" kids—which is symbolic of a virtuous cycle of success and approval.

This happens also at the level of schools. No matter how much money and talent is invested on some schools, they continue to do worse, at least so the perception goes, and eventually, they get written off! Resources are taken from such "bad schools" and allocated to "good schools." There is an overwhelming temptation to stick with the winners!

In this context one must ask: What causes a child or school to be assigned an intangible status of a "winner" or a "loser?" In other words, what determines success to the successful, and failure to the failed? That is, what determines from the beginning when every child and school are equally and competitively placed, that the successful school or child gets into the virtuous cycle of improvement, while the failed school or child is trapped into the vicious cycle of doom and decline? This is the archetype of the "success to the successful"!

This dynamic also illustrates the subtle but pervasive influence of "cultural capital" in education. In many schools and school districts, the prevailing curriculum and the processes by which it is taught is geared to an upper-middle class, white, male, Anglo-Saxon, verbal/analytical, and facile pattern of thinking and learning. Studies show, for example, that concise, direct, and linear speech—so called "masculine" speech—is considered to evoke higher status, whether among male or female children. Nevertheless, many children do not speak that way, especially if they hail from poor and non-white backgrounds, having learning disabilities, or are female. Thus, the latter feel invisible, and the less they feel invisible, the less they attract the attention, approval, opportunities of the school authorities, unless as "problem" children. Thus, is it true that our "cultural capital" pre-selects and pre-labels children or schools to success or failure?

Senge et al. (2000: 357–59) suggest some corrective strategies in this regard:

- Reconsider or redesign the curriculum so as to minimize its "cultural capital" baggage effects on children, schools, and school districts.
- Decouple the two reinforcing loops of virtuous and vicious cycles. Right now, they are competitive, one working at the expense of the other in a zero-sum contest. Make them complementary, one supporting the other.
- If possible, and in reversing the cycle, devote more time and resources to those falling behind or for whatever reasons have been dubbed as a "low achievement" group. Frame new policies that compensate the vicious spiral effects.
- Entertain a shared vision and work out an overarching goal that will include the success of both groups. The intrinsic goal of any school is compromised when one group is favored against another.
- Look into the mental models that underground this archetype. For instance, study the values, attitudes, and characteristics of the students, teachers, and principals of the "high-achiever" schools

versus "low-achiever" schools. What attitudes and values reflect the "self-serving prophecy," thus keeping people from being considered successful or unsuccessful?

- How broad is your attitude of success? What stops the school from celebrating and fostering the potential of a much larger group of successful people?
- Reconsider the ways you measure success. "Do you believe what you measure, or do you measure what you believe?" What measures contribute your favoring one group over the other? How could you change those measures without compromising your vision of academic excellence?

Archetype 7: Balancing Process with Delay
Management Principle: *In a sluggish system, aggressiveness produces instability. Either be patient or make the system more responsive.*
[See Senge (1996: 378–79)]

A person, a group, or an organization, acting toward a goal, adjusts its behavior in response to delayed feedback. If they are not conscious of the delay, they may end up taking more corrective action than needed or (sometimes) just giving up because they cannot see any progress is being made.

Examples:

- Real estate developers keep building new properties until the market has gone soft; but by then, there are already enough additional properties still under construction to guarantee a glut.
- Home mortgage lenders keep lending to build or buy very large homes with or without due process into borrowers' collateral or affordability until the market explodes. By then, however, before any corrective is applied, the overpriced housing market collapses. Soon, home mortgage premiums far exceed the value of the homes, and distressed homeowners are forced to opt for home foreclosure.
- Each year, domestic auto manufacturers pre-set their annual goals for X millions of vehicles to be sold in order to maintain their target market share. Meanwhile, they overbuild inventories, while in reality the auto demand has slackened. Overstocked inventories start piling up and sucking up too much cash, and the domestic automakers soon experience cash-flow crisis.
- In the glorious 1980s of the domestic auto industry, the top HR managers struck unusual labor contracts with United Auto Workers (UAW) union leaders, resulting in the current heavy and constraining "legacy" costs of overextended health care coverage, job assurance (e.g., job banks), generous vacations, and comfortable working conditions. Today, the domestic automakers pay more than $23 additional dollars per hour in wages compared to the foreign automakers in the U.S.
- The U.S. health care industry is the most advanced and the best in the world. Its costs, however, have been growing with double-digit inflationary pressure for the last 15 years. With an aging U.S. population, the distribution of health care costs have been very uneven, with more than 33 percent of the health care dollar spent on last-minute emergency life-saving medical equipment and procedures for the very elderly. As a consequence, neo-natal and child health care is deeply neglected, infantile mortality has been increasing, and, by and large, more than 40 million people remain uninsured and another 60 million people are underinsured in terms of basic health care coverage.

- Cycles in production rates and in process inventory enlarge due to long manufacturing cycle times.
- The Tiananmen Square massacre—the Chinese government delayed its reaction to the protest, and then cracked down unexpectedly hard slaughtering over 3,000 students.
- The New York Stock Exchange (NYSE) market (especially as judged by Dow Jones Industrial Average, and the more broad Standard & Poor Index) was overheated and (soaring) peaking at 12,500 DJ industrial average points in the mid-2007, and in late October 2008 crashed well below 8,000 points in a delayed reaction to the current financial market crisis. In 2008 alone, most of the NYSE indices lost over 40 percent of their market capitalization, losing almost all the capital gains since 2003.

In most of the foregoing cases, people thought they were in balance, while overshooting the mark. Later they keep overshooting in other directions. Hence, most cases end up in a high level of crisis and the resulting ramifications. Hence, as a corrective:

- Watch for the early symptoms of imbalance, and seek immediate correction. Costs of delayed maintenance or adjustment could be soon insurmountable.
- A stitch in time saves nine. Prevention is better than the cure. Procrastination is the thief of time. Correcting effectively today is better than doing it tomorrow.
- "Preemptive" strategies are proactive, and are better than "protective" (i.e., protecting people from harm) and "non-malfeasance" (i.e., doing no harm to people) strategies.
- Other things being equal, "corrective" justice is better and more effective than long-term "distributive" justice and "utilitarian" justice strategies (Mascarenhas, Kesavan, and Bernacchi 2008).

Archetype 8: Growth and Underinvestment
Management Principle: *If there is a genuine potential for growth, build capacity in advance of demand, as a strategy for creating demand.*
[See Senge (1990: 122–25, 389–90)]

This is another archetype of systems thinking—growth and under-investment—much more subtle than other archetypes such as the "limits to growth" and "shifting the burden." Growth approaches a limit that either can be eliminated or pushed into the future if the firm or the individual invests in additional capacity. The additional investment, however, must be aggressive and sufficiently rapid to forestall reduced growth and produce tangible results. Meanwhile, you must hold the vision, especially in relation to key goals and performance standards, and accordingly, evaluate whether the additional capacity can meet potential demand.

Often, firms fail to understand the potential for higher demand, and hence adopt flat or under-investment. Some corporations prefer to grow profits more slowly via cutting costs or incrementally increasing prices. These slow growth strategies may backfire, as competition may outpace you, and consequentially the morale of your employee may deteriorate, your service quality may fall, and your loyal customers may abandon you. Constant market vigilance is needed to assess market demand. If the demand is sluggish, aggressive firms create demand by attractive promotions or by introducing market breakthrough and radical innovations. For instance, People Express Airlines (see later in this chapter) found it unable to build service capacity to keep pace with exploding demand.

This archetype operates whenever a company limits its own growth through under-investment. Under-investment means building less capacity than is really needed to serve rising customer demands. Our thinking goes this way: "Well, we used to be the best, and we will be the best again, but right now we have to conserve our resources and not over-invest." We also lower our goals and performance standards to justify under-investment. When this happens, there is a self-fulfilling prophecy—lower goals lead to lower expectations, and lower expectations lead to lower performance.

Often, financial stress makes aggressive investment difficult. The underlying problem of financial distress, however, is that it is the cause and effect of under-investment of the past. It is a vicious circle. This structure underlies the "boiled frog" syndrome. The frog's standards for water temperature steadily erode, and its capacity to respond to the threat of boiling atrophies goes down.

Typical examples that suffer from this archetype include:

- See the case of WonderTech that follows later in this chapter.
- People Express Airlines (see later in this chapter) found it unable to build service capacity to keep pace with exploding demand.
- Toyota Prius, the first successful hybrid commercial vehicle, launched around 2000, is still not catching up with the backlog of demand.
- The U.S. Immigration System has slowed down considerably since 9/11, mostly worried about inland security systems. Meanwhile, people from various countries who were expecting to get their paper processed and called for an immigration interview are backlogged by at least four years!
- The U.S. trade deficit has been widening irretrievably since 1972, and was over a trillion dollars in 2008. The accumulated trade deficit since 1972 has clearly exceeded $20 trillion. The U.S. governments and corporations have progressively under-invested in competitive technologies that would fight the trade deficit.
- Starting in 1997, low-skilled jobs like call-centers were the first to migrate to the developing countries. Lately, however, during 2001–02, high skilled jobs have also been moving abroad. Specifically, financial companies are expected to farm out more than half a million jobs overseas in the next five years, India being the top destination (Palvia 2003). While most Americans hate to see their jobs being exported, yet both the U.S. governments and corporations have not done anything to reverse this trend.
- Currently, more sophisticated jobs such as software development, manufacturing design, litigation support, yields analysis, market analysis, and pharmaceutical research are being migrated to low-wage countries (Farrell 2004). Unemployment in the U.S. is reaching two digits, for the first time since the Depression of 1929. A few stimulus packages lobbied thus far are merely "symptomatic quick-fix solutions" whose even short-term effects are questionable.
- Ford has widespread operations in Western Europe. It is also superbly positioned to compete with unified Europe. Its first overseas plants were built in France in 1908, and its first assembly plant outside North America was in U.K. in 1911. Ford International invested $10 billion between 1989 and 1993. Currently, Ford has a major presence in India and in other Southeast Asian countries; while it is languishing domestically.
- So are global tech giants like GM, GE, IBM, EDS, Dell, Microsoft, EMC, HP, Intel, Motorola, NCR, Unisys, and even financial giants like Lehman Brothers and Merrill Lynch. The recession period saw these companies rushing to hire tech workers offshore while liquidating thousands of jobs in America (Baker and Kripalani 2004). They were ready to face a major recession in the

country than do anything about the migration of our jobs to China, India, Indonesia, and the East European countries.

- After failing to meet its annual growth target for 2003, DuPont announced its plans to move its "center of gravity" to emerging markets such as Asia and Eastern Europe by accelerating the shift of facilities and staff to these countries. DuPont is an offshore pioneer company and was the first to break through international boundaries in the chemical industry. Its plants started in China in the 1980s and are currently posting a 30 percent improvement in revenues, compared to the general stagnancy of the chemical industry. It plans to source less expensive raw materials in Shanghai, which could save the company $200 million. Until about 1999, DuPont performed all its engineering work domestically. Today, it conducts 50 percent of its production and design engineering offshore. Its contractors use low-cost centers in countries such as India, the Philippines, and China for their production and engineering work.

Under-investment in the past along with critical factors of growth (e.g., product quality, design and manufacture, delivery service, warranty and guarantee service, and dealer network service) is what is ailing our American industries today, especially, railroad, steel, autos, machine tools, and consumer electronics. The steady decline in market share and profitability since the late 1980s, the increasing vulnerability of foreign competitors with better and higher standards since the early 1990s, have both happened so slowly and gone long unnoticed, that these domestic industries, like the boiling frog, are unable to respond anymore. Meanwhile, we have shifted the burden by several symptomatic solutions such as aggressive marketing, promotional advertising, rebates, consumer credit, easy financing, discounts, lobbying for tariff protection, restructuring—all masking palliatives that make us insensitive to the underlying eroding standards. The problem of growth and under-investment also plagues several services industries in the U.S., especially, schools, hospitals, radio and television stations (Senge 1990: 124–26).

Archetype 9: Escalation
Management Principle: *Look for a way for both sides to win, or to achieve their objectives.*
[See Senge (1990: 122–25, 384–85)]

Two groups or organizations, each see their welfare as dependent on a relative advantage over the other. Whenever one side gets ahead, the other feels threatened, and acts more aggressively to re-establish its advantage. This situation, in turn, disturbs the other and makes it more aggressive, and so on. Often, each organization sees its own aggressive behavior as a "defensive" response to the other organization's aggression. Obviously, each side acting in "defense" keeps building-up aggressive defenses that escalate far beyond the desires of each side.

Typical examples of escalation include:

- In the U.S.–U.S.S.R. arms race, each one perceived the other as a threat for some 40 years, and accordingly, piled up nuclear arms. The long-term result of each party's effort to be more secure was a heightened insecurity for all and a dynamic escalation—a combined nuclear stockpile 10,000 times the total firepower of World War II (Senge 1990: 71–72).
- The current U.S.–Al Qaeda confrontation is a replication of the U.S.–U.S.S.R. arms race. The only difference is vengeance and violence—each one attacks the other in defense and offense.

- The 9/11 attacks of Al Qaeda in 2000 and the recent anti-terrorist U.S.-led wars on Iraq, Afghanistan, and Pakistan are instances of violence and counter-violence, and resulting escalation.
- The current escalation of tension, revenge, and violence between Israel and the Gaza Strip is a critical case in point. Both sides are mounting missives and rockets in order to vanquish the other's defense or offense. Meanwhile, civilian casualties are mounting on both sides. No peaceful solution is still in the horizon despite timely interventions by great nations such as U.S.A., U.K., France, Egypt, and the UN Security Council.
- Aggressive price wars between airlines, gas stations, car rentals, car leases, motels and hotels, especially during high-demand holidays seasons, are business examples of price escalation or price gouging.
- Aggressive advertising wars between competing casinos in a given city, each one outdoing the other's offer or odds of winning.
- Political campaigning when each side raises more millions to outshine the rival candidate. The recent 2007–08 Republican versus Democratic political campaign battle raised over a billion dollars on each side, the highest in the history of the U.S.
- Most of the recent aggressive accounting frauds of Enron, Qwest, Tyco, Dynergy, Duke Energy, El Paso, and Global Crossing in the form of round-trip swap sales, and creative accounting mostly to please Wall Street Analysts, escalated far beyond the control of each of these companies, and most of them kept on restating their earnings and write-downs until most declared bankruptcy.
- In particular, Bristol-Myers Squibb inflated its 2001 revenue by $1.5 billion by "channel stuffing" (i.e., forcing wholesalers to accept more inventory than they can sell to get it off manufacturer's books). Efforts to get inventory back to acceptable size was expected to reduce Squibb's earnings by 61 cents per share through 2003 (*Forbes*, July 2002). The scandal was disclosed in July 2002.
- Kmart (January 2002): Allegedly, its securities practices were intended to mislead investors about its financial health. The company, then in a bankruptcy situation, was undertaking a "stewardship" review to be completed by the end of 2002. On February 26, 2003, two Kmart executives were indicted by a Detroit grand jury on federal charges of fraud, conspiracy, and making false statements over their recording of a $42 million payment that resulted in an over-statement of Kmart's results (Hays 2003).
- Expanding consumption is presumed essential to an expanding economy. It involves more people spending more money for more goods and services to satisfy more wants. This leads to escalation, an overheated economy, an inflationary market, and all their ramifications. Thus, big is not always better than small—"small is beautiful" (Shoemaker 1964).

In such situations, each side wishes its opponent would slow down, in which case we could stop fighting this battle, and divert our attention and resources to more productive and peaceful purposes. In many instances, one side could unilaterally reverse the vicious spiral by taking overtly aggressive "peaceful" actions that would neutralize the threat the other sides perceives.

Civilization, in the real sense of the term, consists not in the multiplication but in the deliberate and voluntary restriction of wants. This alone promotes real happiness and contentment, and increases the capacity for service. (M. K. Gandhi: Yaravada Mandir 1935)

Archetype 10: Eroding Goals
Management Principle: *Hold the vision; do not compromise established standards for short-term gains.*
[See Senge (1990: 122–25, 383–84)]

This is a subset of Archetype 2: Shifting the Burden. The organization shifts the burden by adopting a short-term solution that essentially compromises its long-term goals and performance standards.

Whenever there is a gap between our goals and our current situation, there are two sets of pressures: (*a*) to improve the situation or (*b*) lower the goals or standards. Most of the typical symptomatic solutions (see under Archetype 2) either try a prophylactic improvement of the situation or lower the standards. In 1992, President Clinton inherited the largest budget deficit in U.S. history. However, with the help of Budget Omnibus Act in 1993, he converted the deficit into a record budget surplus of $200 billion by the end of the 1990s. In 2005, the Bush administration lowered the standards and ended with a budget deficit of $318 billion. Similar eroding goals dynamics affect R&D targets, personnel management growth projects, organizational improvement objectives in most organizations today.

Some examples of "eroding goals":

- Lowering standards of full employment from four percent unemployment in the 1960s to six to seven percent in the early 1980s was a symptomatic U.S. government solution. This means we are willing to tolerate 50 to 75 percent more unemployment as "natural." Likewise, three to four percent inflation was considered severe in the 1960s, but a "victory" for anti-inflation policies in the 1980s.
- Eroding standards is a failure to invest in time, rightly, and in the right place. WonderTech under-invested in capacity expansion (see the story that follows).
- People Express failed to build the composite of people, skills, and organizational infrastructure that it needed to serve customer demand at high levels of quality. Failing to maintain service quality (despite no frills) made price its only competitive advantage, which in turn made it vulnerable. People would not mind paying a little extra fare, as long as they got basic quality of service via higher service standards. Sustained high service standards create a commitment to service quality as a competitive advantage. (For details, see the full story of People Express that follows.) [See *Business Transformation Exercise 4.9.*]

SYNTHESIZING ARCHETYPES

Most of the archetypes are strategically related to each other. Table 4.2 presents a family tree of archetypes that can help as a diagnostic tool in working through relationships. One should start systems thinking about the nature of the phenomenon you want to understand. Is it related to growth? Then you are primarily in the zone of reinforcing loops. Or, is it related to fixing problems? Then you are primarily in the zone of balancing loops.

Table 4.3 links the 11 "laws" of systems thinking to their corollaries, primary feedback process, and source archetypes. [See *Business Transformation Exercise 4.10.*]

TABLE 4.2 Synthesizing the Archetypes or Templates of Systems Thinking

Archetypes: reinforcing loop	Major focus of systems thinking		Archetypes: balancing loop
	Seeking growth	Fixing problems	
Limits to Growth	Nothing grows forever	My short-term fixes come back to haunt me	Fixes that Backfire
Success to the Successful	My growth seems to lead to your decline	My problem-fix is your nightmare	Escalation
Accidental Adversaries	My partnership for growth with you ends up adversarial	Delayed fixes often erode or drift standards and goals	Eroding/drifting Goals
Tragedy of the Commons	Our collective effort to grow may hit the same limit or resource	I am not really attacking the underlying cause	Shifting the Burden
Attractiveness Principle	I have more than one limit to growth, and I cannot handle them equally	I have more than one problem to fix, and I cannot handle them equally	Attractiveness Principle
Growth and Underinvestment	My capacity is my limit	I am tempted to let slip my values	Growth and Underinvestment

Source: Author's own.

Note: See also Senge et al. (1994: 149–50).

A relatively small number of system archetypes are common to a large variety of management situations. In many ways, the greatest promise of the systems perspective is the unification of knowledge across all fields—for these same archetypes recur in biology, psychology, economics, ecology, political science, and in business management. Experienced managers may recognize them but are not able to explain them. Systems archetypes recondition our perceptions so that we can see better the structures at play, and see the leverage in those structures. Once we identify systems archetypes, they will always suggest areas of high- and low-leverage change (Senge 1990: 95). The purpose of investigating systems archetypes (such as limits to growth and shifting the burden) is to help us see those structures, and thus find leverage, especially amid the pressures and cross-currents of real-life business situations (Senge 1990: 114). Both archetypes were "translations" of generic structures—mechanisms that Jay Forrester and other pioneers in systems thinking had described in the 1960s and 1970s (Senge et al. 1994: 121).

Thinking strategically starts with the reflection of the deepest nature of an undertaking and on the central challenges it poses. It develops with understanding of focus and timing. "Focus" means where to place one's attention, to know what is truly essential, what is secondary, and what cannot be ignored without risking the success of the enterprise. "Timing" means having a sense of an unfolding dynamic. Some changes are intrinsically long-term; they cannot be achieved quickly. Others can be started relatively quickly, but only assume lasting importance in concert with long-term slowly occurring changes. We can achieve some changes directly; others occur as by-products of efforts focused elsewhere. Understanding such issues is the essence of strategic thinking.

TABLE 4.3 Linking Laws of Systems Thinking to Source Archetypes

Laws	Statement	Corollary	Primary feedback process	Source archetype
1	Today's problems come from yesterday's solutions.	Symptomatic solutions merely shift problems from one part of the system to another.	Balancing loop	Archetype 2: Shifting the burden Archetype 3: Fixes that backfire
2	Harder you push, harder the system pushes back.	Pushing harder via aggressive interventions or stressful withholding is exhausting.	Balancing loop; compensating feedback	Archetype 3: Fixes that backfire Archetype 10: Eroding goals
3	Behavior grows better before it grows worse.	Compensating feedback usually involves a "delay" between the short-term benefit and long-term disbenefit.	Balancing loop; compensating feedback	Archetype 7: Balancing process with delay
4	The easy way out usually leads back in.	We stick with what we know best; we push harder and harder on familiar solutions, while fundamental problems persist or worsen.	Reinforcing loop Balancing loop	Archetype 3: Fixes that backfire Archetype 6: Success to the successful
5	The cure can be worse than the disease.	The easy symptomatic solution is not only ineffective, but can be addictive and dangerous.	Reinforcing loop Balancing loop	Archetype 3: Fixes that backfire Archetype 2: Shifting the burden Archetype 9: Escalation
6	Faster is slower.	The natural optimal rate of growth is far less than the fastest possible growth.	Balancing loop; the system compensates by slowing down	Archetype 1: Limits to growth Archetype 8: Growth and underinvestment
7	Cause and effect are not closely related in time or space.	Cause and effect are not close in time and space; effects may have causes outside industry and present time.	Balancing loop; one system compensates the other as causes and effects	Archetype 7: Balancing process with delay
8	Small changes can produce big results—but the areas of higher leverage are often the least obvious.	Corollary of Law 7; the area and effects of high leverage may not be close in time and space.	Balancing loop; one high leverage compensates another in time and space	Archetype 7: Balancing process with delay
9	You can have your cake and eat it too—but not at once.	Most dyadic dilemmas are by-products of non-systemic thinking; e.g., you cannot have low cost and high quality products.	Balancing loop; focus on one component of the dilemma each time	Archetype 7: Balancing process with delay
10	Dividing an elephant in half does not produce two elephants.	The principle of the system boundary: regardless of parochial organizational boundaries, interactions between parts of the organization (elephant) may be the most important issues at hand.	Balancing loop; your high leverage may be in the interactions of your sub-systems	Archetype 2: Shifting the burden Archetype 7: Balancing process with delay
11	There is no blame.	There is no "out" side; you and the cause of your problems are part of a single system; everyone shares responsibility for problems generated by a system.	Reinforcing loop: shared responsibility is shared guilt	Archetype 4: Tragedy of the commons Archetype 5: Accidental adversaries Archetype 6: Success to the successful

Source: Author's own.

In any balancing or stabilizing process there is self-correction (via pushing for stability, resistance, and limits) to maintain some goal or target. Balancing feedback processes occur everywhere. We use different expressions to describe balancing loops: "we are on a roller coaster," "we are being flung up and down like a yo-yo," "we are running into walls," "we cannot break through this barrier," or "no matter how much we try, we cannot change the system." Despite the frustration they often engender, balancing loops are not intrinsically bad; they often ensure there is some way to stop a runaway vicious spiral. Our survival and revival depend upon the many balancing loops or processes that regulate our bodies and our earth. They underlie all goal-oriented behavior.

Balancing loops are always tied to a goal or target, which is often implicitly set by the forces of the system. Whenever current reality does not match the balancing loop's target, the resulting gap (between the target and the system's actual performance) generates a kind of pressure that the system cannot ignore. The greater the gap, the greater the pressure. Until you recognize the gap, and identify the goal or constraint that drives it, you will not understand the behavior of the balancing loop. Often, the target moves or changes, because it too is subject to the forces within the system. In fact, discovering or creating new targets is often the key to overcoming the resistance that confronts you (Senge et al. 1994: 117–18).

THE CONCEPT AND PRINCIPLE OF LEVERAGE

The bottom line of systems thinking is the concept of leverage—the capacity to see where actions and changes in structures can bring about significant and enduring improvements. Remember Law 8: "Small changes can produce big results—but the areas of higher leverage are often the least obvious."

"Leverage lies in the balancing loop, not the reinforcing loop. To change the behavior of the system, you must identify and change the limiting factor (Senge 1990: 101, 2006: 100)." This may require analysis, decisions, and strategies you have not yet considered, choices you never identified, or difficult changes in rewards or norms. For instance, targeting to reach your desired weight by dieting alone need not be the only action; you may also need to speed up your body's metabolic rate via aerobic exercise. Boosting the morale and productivity in your firm may require more than rewards and promotions, bonuses and commissions; you may need to improve your personal attitude, relationship, and bonding with your employees.

However, high-leverage changes as observed before, are usually not obvious, as effects are separated from causes in time and space (Law 7). There are no simple rules to find high-leverage changes. Learning to see underlying structures and processes (rather than events) is a good starting point.

Of every ten start-up companies, five fail within the first five years, the next four survive another five years, and only three may celebrate their 15th year. Whenever a company fails, people single out specific events as causes of failure, such as product problems, mismanagement, loss of key people, aggressive competition, business downturn, and the like. Yet, the real causes that could be underlying the symptoms go unnoticed and not understood. Systems archetypes help us to unearth these causes and treat them with timely policies. This is the principle of leverage.

Leverage looks for underlying structures such as limits to growth (Archetype 1) and shifting the burden (Archetype 2); that is, it looks for reinforcing and balancing processes that underlie symptomatic changes. In case of a business failure, a good systems thinker first looks for symptomatic solutions or shifting the burden's events or policies. In shifting the burden structure, the first thing a systems thinker looks for is what might be weakening the fundamental response. Senge (1990: 115–26) illustrates the principle of leverage by several examples of companies in the manufacturing (e.g., WonderTech) and the services (e.g., People Express) industries.

Systems thinking does not always advocate long-term solutions. It also believes in short-term and well-focused solutions that can produce significant and enduring improvements. Only as long as, they are in the right place, at the right time, and in the right hands. Systems thinking refers to this principle as "leverage." The only problem is that high-leverage points and changes are usually non-obvious to most participants in the system, unless one understands the forces at play in those systems that offer leverage. Most often the leverage lies in the interactions between people and variables that form the system. The real leverage in most management situations lies in understanding dynamic complexity and detail complexity (Senge 1990: 72).

If small well-focused strategies and actions take place through the right people, at the right place and the right time, they can produce significant, enduring improvements—that is, the basic principle of "leverage" is already at work. Tackling a difficult or wicked problem is often a matter of seeing where the high leverage lies—a small strategic change that produces lasting and significant improvements.

For instance, brand equity does not come from aggressive marketing alone, or from brand quality alone, or from upscale retailing, or from long-standing customer loyalty alone. It comes from the inter- actions between these factors and events. Problems of falling sales are not necessarily in the marketing department, but in the design and manufacturing, packaging and sizing, distribution and logistics, human resources, accounting, trade credit and consumer credit departments. Looking at the problem holistically as an interaction of all business systems in the company may indicate the right leverage to resolve the declining sales problem. "Organizations break down despite individual brilliance and innovative products, because they are unable to pull their diverse functions and talents into a productive whole" (Senge 1990: 69).

Similarly, balancing market growth and capacity expansion is a dynamic problem. Developing a profitable mix of price, product, quality, design, availability, and service that together make a strong market position is a dynamic problem. Improving quality, lowering total costs, and satisfying cus- tomers in a sustainable manner are dynamic problems. All these dynamic problems have more dynamic complexity than detail complexity. [See *Business Transformation Exercise 4.11.*]

CASE APPLICATIONS OF THE LAWS AND ARCHETYPES OF SYSTEMS THINKING

Senge (1990, 2006) and Senge et al. (1994, 1999, 2000) provide some interesting case applications of systems thinking which we now review.

WonderTech and its Premature Failure

WonderTech, a new electronics company, was a highly successful company when it started in the mid-1960s. With its engineering know-how, it had a virtual lock on its market niche. It enjoyed an enormous demand for its products, and its sales revenues doubled annually. There were enough investors to guarantee financing requirements. Yet WonderTech began to fail by the end of its third year, and eventually went bankrupt. What do you think happened? Sales were so good that backlog of orders began to pile up midway through their second year. We number sequential symptomatic solutions for tracking and analyzing as follows:

a. Even with steadily increasing capacity (e.g., more factories, more shifts, more advanced technology), WonderTech could not meet its exploding demand.
b. It doubled its sales force during the third year. Despite this, sales dropped to crisis levels by the middle of the fourth year.
c. To reduce backlog, the company heavily invested in additional factories, additional skilled labor, and additional sales force.
d. But the demand was too low, and soon, there was over-capacity and under-utilization.
e. The new marketing VP held high-powered sales meetings, with one message to all: sell, sell, sell!
f. He fired the low performers.
g. He increased sales incentives, added special discounts, and ran new advertising promotions.
h. The company revived for a while but sales slumped again.
i. The company pushed hard on marketing.
j. The company rebounded for a while again.
k. Eventually, WonderTech was bankrupt and dead in less than 10 years.

Was the "limits to growth" structure, a balancing process at work? In a limits-to-growth structure, the worse thing you can do is to push against the reinforcing process. But that is exactly what WonderTech managers did. Strategies (a), (c), (e), (f), (g), and (i) were typical symptomatic solutions—pushing against the reinforcing processes, none of which had any leverage. The real leverage would lie in the balancing process. Strategies (a), (c), (e), (f), (g), and (i) were also a classic form of shifting the burden structure—they put the correction elsewhere along with the symptoms or effects rather than with the causes.

They did not address the underlying problem that caused sales to decline. The managers could not see the reasons for the decline. This was not for lack of information—they had all the facts—but they could not see the structures or archetypes implicit in those facts. The managers did see a pattern of behavior: great demand and growth in the beginning, amplifying it to grow stronger and stronger. It stopped growing, however, and eventually stopped altogether.

Sales slow down, however, when a market saturates and when competition grows suddenly, or when customers grow disenchanted. The first two reasons were not true. There was one factor that turned off customers—long delivery times—the balancing process. As backlogs rise relative to production capacity, delivery times and lines increase. WonderTech's financially oriented top management did not pay much attention to their delivery service. They mainly tracked sales, assessed market share, profits, and return on investment. Delivery times were their least concern. The managers got even complacent and arrogant: "[O]ur computers are so good that some customers are willing to wait fourteen weeks for them," they said. "We know it is a problem, we are working to fix it, but nonetheless, our customers are still glad to get the machines when they get them!"(Senge 2006) Since WonderTech's managers did not solve the real fundamental problem of waiting lines fast enough, disgruntled would-be customers "solved" the problem by walking away.

They did act, but it was six months after they detected the long delivery backlogs. They decided to borrow money to build a new factory. Meanwhile, to make sure the demand kept up, the managers invested heavily into marketing and promotions. Since the company sold its computers only through its direct sales force, it hired and trained more salespeople. Both were symptomatic solutions. By the time the new factory produced enough computers, it was too late. In general, if you wait until demand falls off, and then get concerned about delivery times, it is much too late.

At WonderTech, delivery times grew worse during the third year, the last year of rapid growth. Customers were dissatisfied, and the negative word-of-mouth spread like wildfire. Nevertheless, owing to the great number of potential customers, there was a delay between the cause (customer dissatisfaction due to delivery lags) and the effect (falling sales). WonderTech's managers were prey to the classic learning disability of being unable to detect cause and effect that were separated in time.

The tragic dynamics of WonderTech confirm an intuition of many senior managers—"it is vital to hold critical performance standards, and to do whatever it takes to do that." The most important standards, obviously are those that matter most to the customer. They usually include product quality (design and manufacture), delivery service, service reliability and quality, and friendly and concerned salespeople. Eroding standards and sluggish capacity expansion undermined the growth of WonterTech. The underlying structure of destruction was a combination of "limits to growth" (eroding standards of delivery times, disgruntled customers, customer exit—balancing processes) and "shifting the burden" (over-investing in marketing promotions, sales incentives, salespeople recruitment and training—reinforcing processes).

Eroding standards is a failure to invest in time at the right place. WonderTech underinvested in capacity expansion.

People Express Airlines and its Premature Disappearance

People Express Airlines, founded by Don Burr in 1980, was a low-cost, high-quality airline service to travelers in the Eastern United States. It was the first airline founded after the 1978 U.S. airline deregulation. People Express was an innovative concept—a combination of deeply discounted airfares and friendly, no-frills services (meals and baggage handling were extra charges). People Express's success was reflected in several of the following events:

- On many of its East Coast routes, it offered fares cheaper than taking a bus or a train.
- Passenger seat miles more than doubled in 1982, and again in 1983.
- By third quarter of 1982, People Express became the largest carrier in terms of departures, at any New York airport.
- By 1983, People Express was one of the most profitable carriers in the industry.
- Its stock traded at $22, up from $8.50 Initial Public Offering (IPO) price.
- Despite overwork, People Express employees were growing happy, contended, and wealthy.
- Revenues doubled again in 1984, although profits did not rise proportionately.
- By 1985, People Express grew in five years to be the nation's fifth largest carrier.
- In 1985, the company bought Denver-based Frontier Airlines together with its 4,000 employees.

Yet, despite its meteoric success, People Express reported a loss of $133 million in the first six months of 1986 alone. By September 1986, Texas Air Corporation bought People Express in a distress bid. What happened? Some factors that could partially explain include:

- In 1957, American Airlines and IBM teamed up to form the Semi-Automatic Business Research Environment (Sabre), the first major system to use interactive and real-time computing (which IBM helped develop for the military). In 1960, the first Sabre reservation system was installed in Briarcliff Manor, NY (on two IBM 7090 computers); it processes 84,000 telephone calls per day. In 1976, the Sabre system was installed in a travel agency for the first time, triggering a wave of travel automation. In 1984, Sabre introduced BargainFinder, the industry's first automated low-fare search capability. The same year, American Airlines introduced its Sabre seat-reservation computer system, ushering in a new era of "load management"—that is, airlines could offer a limited number of seats at much-reduced prices, while still booking business and other regular passengers at higher costs. This was a dramatic change in the airline business, bringing People Express up against significant price competition for the first time.
- Given its early pioneering reputation and low prices in the airlines industry, People Express faced overwhelming demand by mid-1982, outstripping its ability to serve. The company had inadequate staff. By November 1982, one-third of the staff was made of hired temporaries with 400 temporary staff in all.
- Customers began to complain about service problems: There were more and more ticketing and reservation delays, and cancelled or overbooked flights.
- On board, flight attendants became less friendly and less efficient.
- The stock price began to fall. This diminished the morale of the workers who owned company stock, and service suffered yet further.
- Customers nicknamed People Express to *People Distress*! Loyal customers soon switched to other competitive carriers.

Customers overlooked all these inconveniences, and kept loyal to People Express. The company did not yet pay any penalties for its poor service. The customers, however, began to drift away during 1984 and 1985, as they were price-conscious and not so much quality-conscious. That is, growth began to be driven entirely by price.

In WonderTech, a manufacturing company, the critical capacity variable was "production capacity," being a service business, whereas, the critical capacity variable at People Express was "service capacity," the composite of personnel, experience, and morale. While WonderTech drove growth through aggressive additions to its sales force, People Express drove growth through aggressive additions to its fleet and flight schedule. While WonderTech floundered because of worsening delivery times and eroding delivery standards, People Express began to fail because of declining customer service quality and eroding standards of service. Its service quality failed to keep pace with passenger growth.

Despite all these differences, however, what explains the failure in both companies is the archetype "growth and under-investment," one of the most common ways that organizations inadvertently limit their growth. The critical under-investment was not in "fleet" and "service capacity" (both grew proportionately to demand; they also bought Frontier Airlines), but in its "service quality" that was virtually flat. People Express failed to build the composite of people, skills, and organizational infrastructure that it needed to serve customer demand at high levels of quality. Failing to maintain service quality (despite no frills) made price its only competitive advantage, which in turn made it vulnerable. People would not mind paying a little extra fare, as long as they got the basic quality of service via higher service standards. Sustained high service standards create a commitment to service quality as a competitive advantage.

People Express grew too fast, but the leverage lay in pricing somewhat higher, both to slow down growth (temporarily, of course, as it could lower prices any time to fight competition) and to increase profits to invest in building high service quality. People Express could afford to slow down growth but not its service quality—it is the right combination of growth and investment that responds to the challenge of complexity and change. [See *Business Transformation Exercises 4.12 and 4.13.*]

The Acme Story

[See Senge et al. (1994: 97–112)]

Michael Goodman, Jennifer Kemeny, and Rick Karash are systems thinking consultants at Innovation Associates. All three studied at MIT's Sloan School of Management where they did systems thinking and developed a comprehensive guide to non-technical systems thinking practice. Goodman, Kemeny, and Karash suggest that as good systems thinkers in an organizational setting, one should see four levels operating simultaneously: events, patterns of behavior, systems, and mental models. This is a summary of their Acme Story as told in Senge et al. (1994: 97–112).

First Level: Events at Acme

The Acme Company sold high-quality industrial equipment, known both for its innovative design and its durability to customers representing purchasing departments of *Fortune 1000* companies. Many of them were repeat customers for over 30 to 40 years. In late 1992, the senior management team met to consider the following events that recently plagued the company:

a. Sales were steady all through the 1980s.
b. Late deliveries noticeably increased in 1989 and accelerated thereafter.
c. Time per sale (i.e., time each salesperson had to spend to make a sale) increased 16 percent in 1990.
d. Billing errors noticeably increased in 1991 and accelerated thereafter.
e. Sales took a dramatic downturn in 1991.
f. Time per sale continued to increase, climbing to 21 percent in 1992.
g. Customer service staff complained of overwork and stress in 1992.

Considering each event linearly and independently, each department roared its solution:

- Senior VP of marketing: "We are way off our sales targets. We better remind the salespeople that they must be accountable to meet targets if they should receive bonuses."
- Senior VP of sales: "We need new promotions and lower prices; otherwise we will have hard time replacing our lost customers. I would like to see us start delivering outside our service area."

- Senior VP of manufacturing: "I understand the need to sell at low cost, but we are getting real behind. We must invest more to reduce both production times and technical problems with the equipment."
- General Manager: "No way; our finances are too tight right now. You will have to make do with what you have got."
- Asked the CEO: "Can we be proactive about this? We could ask for more investment if it would pay off and solve these problems." (Senge et al. 1994: 97–112)

Nobody addressed the real problem nor tried to solve it. Each department went about doing what it had to do: for example, speeding deliveries, cutting billing errors, improving customer service, new pricing promotions, establishing better sales incentives, and the like. Result: Sales and profits dropped even more precipitously during the next three quarters!

Second Level: Investigating Patterns of Behavior

Six months later, they met again. Instead of trying the same routine of finger-pointing and independent solutions, the General Manager assigned a task force to research the "patterns of behavior" of the system over time. Instead of listing isolated events, the task force would select key variables and track their behavior back three or four years. The findings: Most of these are service problems spread over time and sequenced as follows: B → D → G → C → F → E. Hence,

- To cut the billing errors, rewrite the billing manual and redesign the training program.
- To speed up deliveries, institute a new delivery system.
- To improve customer service, install more training and documentation; if customer service problems continue, plan a system redesign.
- To reduce time per sale and boost sales, install new promotions (special pricing, non-stocked products, delivery outside the normal delivery area).

There were no tangible improvements. The trends did not explain why some product lines were falling while others were rising. No new action, other than improvements on the previous. All these quick policy reforms are quick-fix solutions that do not last.

Third Level: Unraveling Systemic Structure

What is the root of the problem? Are not these trends influencing each other in ways we have not explored yet? Every time our sales go down, we redouble our efforts to get new customers. The harder we try to sell our products, the more sales we lose! It is a vicious spiral (see Laws 2–5). But why do our sales go down in the first place? Obviously, our customers perceive service problems that have been escalating lately. Thus, the management team started looking for new inter-relationships between all major variables or factors involved in Acme.

Fourth Level: Sharing Mental Models

At this level, each senior manager examined one's own mental model of assumptions and beliefs. Examples of mental models:

- When sales go down, we must make up the difference with new accounts.
- Salespeople tacitly assumed that their job was primarily to "do whatever it takes to get a new customer," which kept up the pressure on customer service.
- If salespeople, instead, focused on retaining old customers they would concentrate on service problems that drive existing customers away.
- Salespeople need incentives and bonuses to drive up sales to reach sales targets.
- We have to make our sales targets. Acme annually sets sales targets as part of its planning process. As each year unfolds, managers would monitor their targets. If sales fell below targets, then pressure on incentives and bonuses to drive sales would increase, and so on.

One should revise or question mental models and discover the root of the problem—such as, why are you losing old customers? What are your high-leverage points in boosting sales? Should you not redistribute salespeople along points of high leverage? Thus, what can best reduce billing errors, speed up deliveries, and retain old customers? The problem was that Acme could not increase its sales, and all its special promotions just produced temporary "blips" of improvement. Another problem was that Acme's district marketing offices should have been able to handle all their own technical support needs, while they have been seeking more and more of the same from the corporate tech group. Acme started looking hard into these problems with its linked loops and high-leverage points.

Goodman, Kemeny, and Karash, accordingly, give us a few hints in identifying and specifying problems [Senge et al. (1994: 103–12)]:

1. The issue should be important to you and your organization, and something you genuinely care about, and want to understand; it should not be a mere academic exercise.
2. Choose a chronic problem, something that troubles your organization repeatedly, rather than focus on a one-time event.
3. Choose a problem of limited scope, which you can expand later. Choosing a problem with unlimited scope can overwhelm you with abstractions such as "everything is connected to everything."
4. Choose a problem whose history is known and which you can describe. Getting consensus on some key aspects of the history can be insightful.
5. If possible, choose a problem that has been tackled before, with little or no success. This ensures that a systemic dynamic is at play.
6. Be accurate in your problem description, its history, and its major features. Like a good detective, stick to the facts and evidence. Do not sanitize the problem for political reasons or bias it toward a particular solution.
7. In stating your problem, do not jump to conclusions by inducing a suggested solution. You are inquiring into the problem just because the solution is not intuitively clear; or else, you would have implemented it.
8. Be non-judgmental. Avoid blaming anybody, any policy, or any situation. Do not assume the motives of any other participant, particularly if she or he is not present in the discussion.

Given some form of problem identification and formulation using the foregoing eight steps, the next steps are to:

9. Bring as many participants to come forth with their versions of the problem and its specific-ation. Compare notes. You can view a series of events from many vantage points. Identify key themes and recurring patterns. A diverse set of problem versions enriches subsequent discus-sion and dialogue.

10. Narrate stories that really underlie your version of the problem, and bring them to the surface. This process is also known as "model-building," and can be a powerful learning process, especially for teams.

11. During this phase, you may also develop a theory or state a hypothesis that is logically consistent and may help to explain the genesis of the problem. But you should also question, whether the theory explains the observations, facts, and evidence? If not, then you should change or revise the theory.

12. Ask yourselves as a team: How did our internal thinking, processes, practices, and procedures contribute to or create the circumstances (good and bad) we now face? You may need sustained deliberation to respond to this central question.

13. Identify key factors that seem to capture the problem (e.g., sluggish sales, billing errors, delayed deliveries, poor technical support, unskilled customer service, increasing salesperson time per sale, and the like), and study them from various viewpoints (e.g., the frontline service people, the service technicians, the accounting/financing managers, the customers, the exiting customers, the senior VP of marketing, the senior VP of manufacturing, the General Manager, and the CEO). What key factors become extra visible from that viewpoint?

14. Draw charts and pictures: Using time as X-axis, study the trends and patterns of all key factors identified under (13) along the Y-axis, either by single factor or by groups of related factors.

15. Analyze the charts and pictures: Which chart tells the most critical story, the defining trend or the real heart of the problem? When did the real problem start and along which key factor variable? How did the key associate or moderator factors behave during the same period?

16. Combine graphs and look for links, loops, archetypes, systems structures, feedback processes, and circles of influence. The purpose is not to produce a diagram that everyone can agree on, but to provoke a mutual sense of the story in the minds of team members. If a common picture or common problem is emerging, then see how it differs from any of the problems each indi-vidual introduced at stages 1–9.

17. Identify gaps: gaps between what customers need (e.g., technical support, price breaks, customized products) and what we can deliver.

18. Finally, identify high-leverage points for short-term and long-term solutions.

In systems thinking, every picture tells a story. From any major event (e.g., sluggish sales) you can connect a series of influencing events, till you reach the root cause. For instance, in the Acme story:

- The level of service influences sales.
- The level of service is influenced, in turn, by delayed deliveries and lack of technical support.
- Delayed deliveries are a manufacturing problem.
- Lack of technical support comes from poorly trained service technicians and cumbersome manuals.
- Lack of technical support and delayed deliveries prompt billing errors.
- Billing errors infuriate customers, some of whom then quit.

- Salespeople double efforts to create new customers.
- This drives the time per sale and cost per sale rocket upward.
- This in turn affects profitability.
- Lack of profitability erodes finances for improving manufacturing and technical support.
- These, in turn, drive sales downwards—we are back to the original problem again.

All key factors are connected. Links never exist in isolation; they always comprise a circle of causality, a feedback loop, in which every element is both a cause and an effect, influencing some, or influenced by others. [See *Business Transformation Exercise 4.14.*]

Eroding Goals in Detroit Public and Private School Systems

What vitalizes a city in the long run is primarily its schools and the learning-system it designs, nurtures, and inculcates into its student body. Downtown Detroit is currently experiencing a very challenging phase with the nation's highest high school drop out rate. "The devastating news is that three-quarters of students who enter freshmen classes in Detroit Public Schools aren't around on graduation day" (*The Detroit News*, Editorial, April 2, 2008). This tragic result is eventually a case of "eroding goals" in the Detroit Public School (DPS) system.

- Seventeen of the nation's 50 largest cities had high school graduation rates lower than 50 percent, with the lowest graduation rates reported in Detroit, Indianapolis, and Cleveland, according to a report released Tuesday (Associated Press, Washington, April 1, 2008). The report was issued by America's Promise Alliance. It found that about half of the students served by public school systems in the nation's largest cities receive diplomas. Students in suburban and rural public high schools were more likely to graduate than their counterparts in urban public high schools, the researchers said.
- Nationally, about 70 percent of U.S. students graduate on time with a regular diploma and about 1.2 million students drop out annually. "When more than 1 million students a year drop out of high school, it's more than a problem, it's a catastrophe," said former Secretary of State Colin Powell, founding chair of the Promise Alliance.
- Moreover, according to the Organization for Economic Co-operation and Development (OECD) surveys, U.S. spends an average of $7,560 per student per year—both at the primary and the secondary level (only two nations spend more: Denmark with $7,562 and Luxembourg at $7,871) but has less to show for it. Our public elementary and high schools are simply not making the grade in cultivating high-caliber domestic talent (Kao 2007: 96). What can we do about it?

There is something wrong with our school systems. There is a steady erosion of standards and goals—both among students and their schools. Opinion polls document that U.S. high school students would rather take out the trash, clean up their bedrooms, or wash dishes than study math or science. They seem increasingly indifferent to education. California high school statistics for 2007 reported that 33 percent of high school students failed to graduate, and that was after costly modifications to education—smaller class sizes, higher education standards, and additional teacher-training. American students' low scores on standardized tests are also consistent with these declining trends.

We should not measure the progress of a school just by Scholastic Aptitude Test (SAT) scores of high school students, but by how our school curriculum helps students to qualify for good colleges and jobs. Much of the school curriculum is to prepare students for testing and teachers "teach for testing." This process ruins creativity and innovation in school curricula. Robert Stenberg, dean of the School of Arts and Sciences and professor of psychology at Tufts University writes: "The increasingly massive and far-reaching use of standardized testing is one of the most effective, if unintentional, ways we have created for suppressing creativity" (cited in Kao 2007: 99).

Unless the school curriculum takes math and science seriously very early in the K-12 equation, the future of our schools is bleak. In China, a rotating group of science specialists starts working with students as early as the third grade. Once in high school, Chinese students must successfully complete mandatory courses in biology, chemistry, physics, algebra, and geometry before they graduate. By contrast, 40 percent of U.S. high school students take no science subject beyond introductory biology. Moreover, the vast majority of Chinese math and science teachers have advanced degrees, whereas, less than 60 percent of U.S. eight-grade teachers have completed a major in a science-related discipline, and only 48 percent of math teachers have completed a math major. Throughout East Asia, about 90 percent of eighth-grade science teachers have science degrees as well as science education training (Kao 2007: 69).

The Program for International Student Assessment (PISA) that measures the academic performance of 15-year-olds in 41 countries, placed U.S. students 24th in math literacy and 26th in problem-solving; they were below the international average in every component of math literacy. While our competing nations (e.g., India, China, Australia) focus on educating and training engineers and inventors, U.S. schools are turning youngsters into better consumers than creators. In schools serving low-income students, just about 30 percent of junior high math teachers majored in math in college (Kao 2007: 34).

Good schools challenge their students to sign on to the International Baccalaureate (IB) curricula. [The IB was originated in 1968 by the International Baccalaureate Organization (IBO) headquartered in Geneva, Switzerland, to provide a private school, universally recognized, portable education for youngsters whose parents are diplomats or foreign multinational executives. Currently, IBO offers a full schedule of academic courses at three age levels—3–12, 11–16, and 16–19—with a large menu of courses. IB courses are generally more rigorous, more comprehensive (e.g., including the British and French view of the American Revolution), and more diverse (e.g., courses in Mandarin and Japanese) than the usual public school fare with a greater focus on testing students' mastery of the material.] For instance, the Jefferson County IB School, near Birmingham, Alabama, has just 325 students most of whom take IB courses and excel in them. Newsweek named Jefferson the best high school in the U.S. in 2005. Currently, more than 700 schools have signed on to IB, offering courses at all three age levels, but most of them being offered in the 16–19 category. However, the 700 schools offering IB level courses are just a very small fraction (less than 1 percent) of the total number of U.S. high schools.

If the high school dropouts are uncared for, they could easily breed poverty, crime, and addictive behaviors—all of which are detrimental to revitalizing Southeast Michigan (SEM), in general, and Detroit, in particular. High school dropouts consume a great deal of the state's resources. 40 percent of those receiving welfare are dropouts, as are 70 percent of Michigan prison inmates. Welfare and Corrections are the most rapidly growing segments of Michigan's budget. Aggressively tackling this problem benefits not just Detroit and other urban areas, but also taxpayers across states that pay the bills when the dropouts end up on welfare or in prison. The Detroit Public School (DPS) Superintendent, Connie Calloway, got out in front of the report from America's Promise Alliance with a surprise announcement that the district will dismantle five of the city's worst performing schools and replace them with smaller, innovative programs. Calloway was not talking cosmetic changes. The district will remove all of the principals and teachers, change the names of the schools and start all over with a reform-minded strategy targeted at overcoming the challenges faced by many urban students (*The Detroit News*, Editorial, April 2, 2008).

Simply extending the school year, assigning more homework, hiring more trained teachers, providing more bandwidth in schools, and the like are mere incremental strategies. These are the too familiar kinds of incremental initiatives we should have been doing on a routine basis and long ago. Such incremental moves will make things better, but they are not the game-changing innovations that will alter the fundamentals of education and lead us to a more desired future (Kao 2007: 81).

We must make the most of our human resources and enhance our human capital. Following Singapore, the country with a brand identity in education, "Thinking Schools, Learning Nation," Detroit schools must generate quality curricula with bio-technologies, life sciences, and environmental technologies. They should train and reward high-performing teachers, showcase and celebrate bright kids' talents, experiment with new learning technologies, and think outside the confines of traditional disciplines and bureaucratic silos. They should cultivate a relentless focus on education, develop creative reading and writing habits with power tools freely available in futuristic (frontier of interactive and digital media) city libraries. In short, anything and everything to stoke a dynamic, talent-driven innovation machine (Kao 2007: 88).

We need a disciplined commitment to innovative leadership in Detroit public schools. In Singapore, two-thirds of government officials have advanced degrees. Their doctoral programs in premier universities match Harvard, MIT, or Oxford. Detroit public schools must invest in good education that creates creative, imaginative, agile, and innovative minds and mindsets. Inculcating a sense of respect for knowledge and ethics should be as important as improving cognitive skills and abilities. Educators and education must establish an ongoing link between learning and purpose. We must first articulate national priorities based on a vision of our desired role in the world, and that, in turn, should drive our educational agenda and academic excellence standards.

One of the largest post-World War II investments in the human capital was the GI Bill of Rights of 1944. Shortly before the Normandy invasion and the National Defense Education Act (NDEA) of 1958, President Roosevelt signed the GI Bill and backed it by a multi-billion education and housing commitment to returning veterans. More than eight million veterans took advantage of the opportunity of the GI Bill to become scientists and engineers, doctors and teachers, thus paving the way for the boom years that followed. President Eisenhower continued the education revolution when he signed the NDEA in 1958. The Act provided low-cost student loans and fellowships aimed at increasing the number of students in graduate programs.

CONCLUDING REMARKS

We restate some important principles in synthetic systems thinking: What we assert about a public system renewal such as Detroit and SEM, can, *mutatis mutandis*, be applied to a corporation, with the CEO as the principal and cardinal (pivotal) systems thinker.

- In systems thinking, feedback is an axiom that states, "every influence is both cause and effect." Nothing is ever influenced in just one direction. Reality exists in structures, and structures cause behavior.

- The bottom-line of systems thinking is "the concept of leverage—the capacity to see where actions and changes in structures can bring about the most significant and most enduring improvements."
- Leverage looks for underlying structures such as limits to growth (Archetype 1) and shifting the burden (Archetype 2), that is, looks for reinforcing and balancing processes that underlie symptomatic changes.
- In case of a business failure, a good systems thinker first unravels symptomatic solutions for shifting the burden events or policies. In shifting the burden structure, the first thing a systems thinker looks for is what might be weakening the fundamental response.
- Leverage lies in the balancing loop, not the reinforcing loop. "To change the behavior of the system, you must identify and change the limiting factor" (Senge 1990: 101, 2006: 100). This may require analysis, decisions, and strategies you have not yet considered, choices you never noticed, or difficult changes in rewards or norms.
- Strategic thinking also addresses core organizational dilemmas such as centralization versus decentralization, command and control versus distributed power and authority, mission and identity versus diversification, productivity versus creativity, revenue generation versus cost containment, and the like. Good strategic thinking brings such dilemmas to the surface, and uses them to catalyze imagination and innovation (Senge et al. 1994: 16–17). Systems thinking can empower good strategic thinking.

In conclusion, one could apply systems thinking to revitalizing Detroit and SEM. Most of us agree that SEM in general, and Detroit in particular, need revitalization and growth. Our basic question then is, what can revitalize SEM, and Detroit in particular? What are the best points of greatest leverage? That is, how can we systematically stimulate growth, expansion, and prosperity in SEM despite national recessionary threats?

A. Positively and externally, some basic questions in this regard are:

- How can we attract both domestic and foreign investment into SEM in the near future? Alternatively, how can we effectively attract venture capitalists, private equity firms, and domestic and foreign investors to invest into the SEM revitalization project? That is, what is the differentiating strategy of SEM/Detroit for attracting investments into it? A nation's talent pool is not only the ones it trains, but what talents it can attract, develop, and retain from domestic and foreign sources.
- What tax havens, subsidies, and other stimulants can the federal, state, and city governments introduce in the SEM for rapid and sustained growth in the coming decades?
- Further, what is the quality of inter-organizational trust (e.g., between state/local governments of SEM/Detroit and investor corporations) that will make such investments into SEM/Detroit safe and secured for the future?
- How can key influential groups such as major school networks, community colleges and universities, labor unions, consumer advocacy groups, non-governmental organizations (NGOs), EPA and environmental watchdogs, main line churches, synagogues, mosques, and temples collaborate to attract, retain, and develop human and non-human investments into SEM/Detroit?

B. Conversely, that is negatively and externally, some basic questions are:

- What can stop SEM from its present malaise of apathy, stagnancy, and stalling?
- How can we stop the drain of talent, energy, and investment from SEM?
- How can we stop and hold back, objectively and effectively, corporations, establishments, and venture capital institutions from abandoning SEM and migrating into other more lucrative neighboring states?

C. Positively and internally, some basic questions are:

- What creativity, innovation, and innovativeness programs and projects does SEM need to revitalize SEM from within? What we need are not default strategies and incremental innovations but radical innovations that change our mindset of complacency to game-changing innovations that will alter the fundamentals or lead us toward a more desired future.
- What entrepreneurial and intrapreneurial talent can be identified, developed, and retained for catapulting SEM into an exponential and rapid growth path?
- What corporate, organizational, and cultural change agents must we cultivate in transforming SEM as a sustainable and competitively strong corporate community?

D. Negatively but internally, some basic questions are:

- What is failing SEM and its defining corporations and government institutions?
- What are the major symptoms of corporate and institutional stalling, stagnancy, sickness, downturn, decline, distress, and insolvency crises that are gripping and choking SEM, in general, and Detroit, in particular?
- How can we diagnose and control these symptoms so that we can turnaround SEM and get it on the track of renaissance and vitality?

Systematic research into D and C should indicate at least partial answers to the basic questions raised under B and A. That is, research in D should lead us to C—that is, SEM turnaround management should spur SEM transformation management.

For instance, Table 4.4 explores the three objectives under C in relation to the "laws" of systems thinking, and Table 4.5 does the same in relation to the "Archetypes" of systems thinking. Both tables provide an initial canvas and framework for SEM revitalization based on systems thinking.

TABLE 4.4 Corporate Strategies to Revitalize Southeast Michigan (SEM) as Derived from the Laws of Systems Thinking

Systems thinking laws	Statement	Corporate strategies that transform SEM		
		Radical innovations and game-changing breakthroughs that will transform SEM	Entrepreneurial talent that can be identified, developed, and retained for catapulting SEM into an exponential growth path	Organizational and cultural change agents that transform SEM into a sustainable and competitively strong corporate community
1	Today's problems come from yesterday's solutions.	Yesterday's product solutions should not create problems for SEM's today or hereafter.	Yesterday's entrepreneurial talent should not create problems for SEM's present and future.	Yesterday's organizational routines and best practices should not create problems for SEM of tomorrow.
2	Harder you push, harder the system pushes back.	Desist from pushing your past innovations into SEM's future lest they backfire.	Desist from pushing your entrepreneurial mental models into SEM's future without re-examining them.	Desist from pushing your organizational routines and best practices into SEM's future lest they backfire.
3	Behavior grows better before it grows worse.	Radical innovations should sustain SEM as a viable community in the long term.	Entrepreneurial talent should sustain SEM as a viable community in the long term.	Radical innovations should sustain SEM as a viable community in the long term.
4	The easy way out usually leads back in.	Avoid easy innovations that backfire to endanger SEM's future.	Avoid easy entrepreneurial solutions that backfire to endanger SEM's future.	Give up old organizational routines that backfire to endanger SEM's future.
5	The cure can be worse than the disease.	Avoid easy product innovations that lead to addictive and dangerous behaviors in SEM.	Avoid entrepreneurial solutions that lead to addictive and dangerous consequences for SEM.	Avoid old organizational routines and practices that lead to addictive and dangerous SEM behaviors.
6	Faster is slower.	Do not promote faster and heavier consumption of your innovative products.	Do not always measure entrepreneurial success by faster and larger productivity rates.	Do not foster organizational changes that cause speedier and heavier consumption of your local resources.
7	Cause and effect are not closely related in time or space.	Prevent "effects" of your innovations on SEM that you cannot control in time and space.	Prevent "effects" of your entrepreneurship on SEM that you cannot control in time and space.	Prevent "effects" of your organizational changes on SEM that you cannot control in time and space.
8	Small changes can produce big results.	Innovate products that generate high leverage to all SEM stakeholders.	Entrepreneurs should innovate products that generate high leverage to all SEM stakeholders.	All organizational changes should generate high leverage to all SEM stakeholders.
9	You can have your cake and eat it too—but not at once.	Offer low-cost but high-quality innovative products that stimulate the SEM economy.	Entrepreneurship should generate low-cost but high-quality innovative products that stimulate the SEM economy.	Organizational changes should generate low-cost/high-quality innovations that stimulate the SEM economy.
10	Dividing an elephant in half does not produce two elephants.	Offer holistic innovative product solutions that keep SEM united despite diverse cultures.	Entrepreneurship should generate holistic innovative product solutions that keep SEM united despite diverse cultures.	Organizational changes should stimulate holistic innovations that keep SEM united despite diverse cultures.
11	There is no blame.	Given innovation responsibilities 1–10, share praise/blame with all SEM people.	Given entrepreneurship responsibilities 1–10, share praise/blame with all SEM people.	Given organizational change responsibilities 1–10, share praise/blame with all SEM people.

Source: Author's own.

TABLE 4.5 Corporate Strategies to Revitalize SEM as Derived from the Archetypes of Systems Thinking

Systems thinking archetypes	Management principle	Corporate strategies that transform SEM		
		Radical innovations and game-changing breakthroughs that will transform SEM	Entrepreneurial talent that can be identified, developed, and retained for catapulting SEM into an exponential growth path	Organizational and cultural change agents that transform SEM into a sustainable and competitively strong corporate community
1. Limits to Growth	Do not push growth; remove the factors limiting growth.	Let your radical innovations enable healthy growth among all SEM constituencies.	Let your entrepreneurial innovations enable healthy growth among all SEM constituencies.	Let your organizational changes enable healthy growth among all SEM constituencies.
2. Shifting the Burden	Beware the symptomatic solution.	Resist using easy and symptomatic product innovations solutions to current SEM needs and wants.	Resist using easy and symptomatic entrepreneurial solutions to current SEM needs and wants.	Resist using easy and symptomatic organizational changes to address current SEM needs and wants.
3. Fixes that Backfire	A continuing series of fixes to a stubborn problem improves only momentarily.	Avoid quick and easy innovation fixes to your current SEM problems.	Avoid quick and easy entrepreneurial fixes to your current SEM problems.	Avoid quick and easy organizational changes to quick fix your current SEM problems.
4. Tragedy of the Commons	A continuing increase of use of a common resource will eventually overstrain the resource until it crashes.	Resist from over-straining the limited money resources of your SEM constituents.	Resist your entrepreneurial strategies from over-straining the limited money resources of your SEM constituents.	Resist your organizational changes from over-straining the limited money resources of your SEM constituents.
5. Accidental Adversaries	Understand your partner's needs; see if you are unintentionally undermining them, and look for ways that support each other.	Innovate product solutions that address (and not undermine) the needs and wants of your SEM customers.	Let your entrepreneurial solutions address (and not undermine) the needs and wants of your SEM customers.	Let your organizational changes address (and not undermine) the needs and wants of your SEM customers.
6. Success to the Unsuccessful	Should the success of the successful spell failure of the failed? Break this vicious zero-sum game cycle.	Do not build your innovation fortunes at the expense of your primary SEM customers.	Do not build your entrepreneurial fortunes at the expense of your primary SEM customers.	Do not foster your organizational changes at the expense of your primary SEM customers.
7. Balancing Process with Delay	In a sluggish system, aggressiveness produces instability. Either be patient or make the system more responsive.	Avoid aggressive innovations and marketing that destabilize your SEM customers.	Avoid aggressive entrepreneurial innovations and marketing that destabilize your SEM customers.	Avoid aggressive organizational changes that destabilize your SEM customers.
8. Growth and Underinvestment	If there is a genuine potential for growth, build capacity in advance of demand, as a strategy for creating demand.	Foster growth of SEM by investing in innovative resources.	Foster growth of SEM by investing in entrepreneurial resources.	Foster growth of SEM by investing in innovative organizational changes.
9. Escalation	Look for a way for both sides to win, or to achieve their objectives.	Avoid undue escalation of wants, needs, and desires among SEM customers via your innovations.	Do not let your entrepreneurship foster undue escalation of wants, needs, and desires among the SEM customers.	Do not let your organizational changes stimulate undue escalation of wants, needs, and desires among SEM customers.
10. Eroding Goals	Hold the vision; do not compromise established standards for short-term gains.	Do not let your innovations erode goals and standards of your SEM customers.	Do not let your entrepreneurial products erode goals and standards of your SEM customers.	Do not let your organizational changes erode goals and standards of your SEM customers.

Source: Author's own.

APPENDIX 4.1: DID CHINA PRECIPITATE THE CURRENT U.S. FINANCIAL AND MORTGAGE CRISIS?*

In March 2005, a Princeton economist who had become a Federal Reserve governor, Ben S. Bernanke, suggested a novel theory to explain the growing tendency of Americans to borrow from foreigners, particularly the Chinese, to finance their heavy spending. Bernanke argued that the problem was not that Americans spend too much, but that foreigners save too much. The Chinese have so much accumulated excess savings that they lend money to the U.S. at low rates, thus underwriting American industrial, commercial, and residential consumption. There is a savings glut in China, Bernanke argued; but unlike in the U.S., the Chinese save money to pay for hospital visits, housing, and retirement.

Today, apparently, this phenomenon is haunting us. Our dependence on Chinese money looks less benign. These cross-border transfers of funds and money flows are reaching stratospheric levels. During 1998–2008, China has invested more than $1 trillion, mostly earnings from manufacturing exports, into American bonds and government-backed mortgage debt. This investment has allegedly lowered interest rates and "helped fuel a historic consumption binge and housing bubble in the United States" (Lindler 2008: A1). Most economists now agree, in hindsight, that the U.S. should have recognized that borrowing from abroad for consumption and deficit spending at home was not a formula for economic success. Despite this recognition, however, U.S. is showing growing addictive dependence on Chinese creditors to finance record government spending to revive the broken economy. Both were addicted, however, and were disinclined to break the addiction—it helped China and its manufacturing economy, and it helped the U.S. to secure cheap imports and low-cost foreign loans. Further, cheap Chinese imports in the form of toys, shoes, flat-screen televisions, and auto parts have definitely helped the American consumers, possibly exerting downward pressure on inflation rates.

Some critics argue that the U.S. could have pushed Beijing harder not to control and lower the value of its currency—a policy that made its exports cheaper, imports costlier, and in turn, made it into a leading manufacturing power. If China had allowed its currency value to be determined by the open market during the last decade, critics argue, China's manufacturing power and foreign-investment dollars would not have exploded. Other critics counter-argue, however, that the Chinese lending was a giant stimulus to the American economy (unlike interest rates cuts by the Fed). These critics blame the Fed under Alan Greenspan to have contributed to the creation of the housing bubble by leaving interest rates too low for too long, even as Chinese investment further stoked an easy-money economy. The Fed should have cut interest rates less in the middle of the past decade, and started raising them sooner, to help reduce speculation in real estate (Fleckenstein 2008).

Some panic: What if Chinese lenders decided to withdraw money from the U.S. at a moment's notice, creating a devastating run on the U.S. dollar? Others think this is an abstract threat. Both Greenspan and President Bush treated the record American trade deficit, federal deficit, and foreign debt as an abstract threat, not an urgent problem. When Mr. Bernanke took over the Fed in August 2006, he warned that the imbalances between China and the U.S. were growing more serious, but agreed it was too late to do much about them. The White House still regarded imbalances as an arcane subject best left to economists.

True, in classical economics, a gaping trade deficit could not have persisted for long without bankrupting the American economy. Except that China ploughed back its trade profits into the U.S. in terms of reverse foreign direct investments (RFDI) in manufacturing. Chinese dollar reserves are increasing, however, rapidly. In 2000, China's dollar reserves were just $200 billion; today at the end of 2008, they are about $2.00 trillion! Chinese leaders chose to park the bulk of those reserves in safe securities backed by the American government, including Treasury bonds

---

*This is one of the series of articles by NYT called the "Reckoning Series." For details, see Lindler, Mark (2008), "Dollar Shift: Chinese Pockets filled as Americans Emptied theirs," *New York Times*, Friday, December 26, 2008, A1 and A14.

and the debts of Fannie May and Freddie Mac, which had implicit government backing. Total foreign holdings of Treasury securities rose from $1 trillion in 2000 to $3 trillion in 2008, and China owns close to $0.65 trillion of such holdings. The Treasury conducts nearly daily auctions of billions of dollars' worth of government bonds, and China, for the past 5 years, has been one of the most prolific bidders. It holds $652 billion in Treasury debt, up from $459 billion a year ago in 2007. If you add Chinese investments in Fannie May and Freddie Mac bonds, currently, China owns $1 of every $10 of America's public debt.

By itself, money from China is not a bad thing—it speaks of the attractiveness of the U.S. as a destination for foreign investment. In the 19th century, the U.S. built its railroads with capital borrowed from the British. The difference is, however, while the railroads helped the American public largely, the excessive debt that we owe China today has fueled the Iraq and other terrorist wars, and the consumers used the low-interest rate loans to buy sport utility vehicles and larger homes. Moreover, banks and investors seeking higher interest rates in this easy-money environment, created risky new securities like collateralized debt obligations (CDOs).

Moreover, the U.S. has been here before. In the 1980s, it ran heavy trade deficit with Japan, which recycled some of its trading profits into American government bonds. Then, such threats were considered more serious than now. Several developed nations took action called the Plaza Accord of 1985, whereby the world's major economies intervened in currency markets to drive down the value of the dollar and drive up the Japanese yen—an arrangement that did slow the growth of the trade deficit for a time. To avert this crisis, China in 1995, devalued its currency and set a firm exchange rate of 8.3 to the dollar, a level that has remained fixed for more than a decade. It was only in 2005, under heavy pressure from Congress and the White House, that China acted to amend its currency policy, but moved cautiously. The renminbi was allowed to climb only 2 percent. Little changed as China's exports kept soaring and investment poured into steel mills and garment factories. In 2006, when Henry Paulson, ex-CEO of Goldman Sachs, became the Treasury Secretary, he undertook several trips to China negotiating with them to let the renminbi be market-determined. He conceded—he did not get what he wanted.

Meanwhile, America needs more foreign money—to finance its $700 billion bailout of the banks, and still more, for the stimulus package of the incoming Obama administration. U.S. economists agree that America will have to depend upon China to buy that debt, perpetuating the American habit.

QUESTIONS FOR REFLECTION FROM SYSTEMS THINKING

a. Apply each of the 11 laws of systems thinking to the basic argument of this article. What do you read?
b. Apply each of the 10 archetypes of systems thinking to the basic argument of this article. What do you find and why? [Particularly, look at "Shifting the Burden" and "Fixes that Backfire."]
c. Combine both the laws and the archetypes of systems thinking and analyze the "causes" and the "effects" of the financial market crisis in the U.S. in relation to China's role in it.
d. Combine both the laws and the archetypes of systems thinking and analyze the "causes" and the "effects" of the home mortgage crisis in the U.S. in relation to China's role in it.
e. From a systems perspective, is U.S.'s addictive dependence upon Chinese money markets a positive long-term growth policy for the U.S.?

BUSINESS TRANSFORMATION EXERCISES

4.1 In discussing the importance of systems thinking, how will your organization internalize and implement the following fundamental principles of systems thinking?

a. Systems thinking is more than a powerful problem-solving tool; it is a powerful language, augmenting and changing the ordinary ways we think and talk about complex issues and problems. It is a dynamic language for describing how to achieve fruitful change in organizations.

b. You cannot practice systems thinking as an individual—you need many perspectives from different cross-functional disciplines to bear upon complex problems and issues.

c. Systems thinking by its very nature points out and thrives on interdependencies and the need for collaboration—it is a collective and collaborative team discipline.

d. Without learning about the industry, the business, its specific vision and mission, as well as their own tasks, employees cannot make the contributions of which they are capable. This requires dramatic learning efforts, both for the employees who must learn to act in the interest of the whole enterprise, and for the senior managers who must learn how to extend mastery and self-determination throughout the organization (Senge et al. 1994: 11). Systems thinking can enable this process.

e. We fragment the complex world in order to understand it. This makes complex tasks and subjects more manageable. If we just admire the broken pieces, however, our vision remains fragmented, each of us mistaking the piece for the whole (as did the blind men trying to define the elephant). If we reassemble and reorganize the pieces, however, we see connections, interactions, and interrelationships between parts and components we have never seen before nor registered, and eventually see a larger whole, and understand reality around us better. This is systems thinking.

f. Systems thinking helps us to destroy our illusion that the world is created of separate and unrelated forces. When we do this, our homes, our schools, our universities, our organizations, our institutions, and we ourselves truly become learning organizations.

4.2 There are many paradoxes in organizational life. Systems principles like these are meaningful not so much in themselves, but because they represent a more effective way of thinking and acting. Incorporating them into your corporate strategic behavior requires "peripheral vision"—the ability to pay attention to the world as if through a wide-angle lens, so you can see how your actions interrelate with other areas of activity (Senge et al. 1994: 87–88). Explain the following paradoxes in relation to your firm:

a. The time of your greatest growth is the best moment to plan for harder times.

b. The policies that gain the most for your current dominant market position may ultimately drain your resources most quickly.

c. The harder you strive for what you want, the more you may undermine your own chances of achieving it.

4.3 In understanding the distinctive features and benefits of systems thinking, how will you internalize, organize, and implement the following in your corporation?

a. Systems thinking is a discipline for seeing wholes. It is a framework for seeing interrelationships rather than linear cause–effect chains and things, for seeing processes and patterns of change rather than static snapshots.

b. Systems thinking is a sensibility for the subtle interconnectedness that gives living systems their unique character.

c. It is a discipline for seeing the "structures" that underlie complex situations, and for discerning high from low leverage change.

d. It is a shift of mind from seeing parts to seeing wholes, from reacting to the present to creating the future, from seeing ourselves as helpless reactors to changing reality to seeing ourselves as active participants in shaping that reality.

e. More specifically, systems thinking is a way of thinking about, and a language for describing and understanding, the forces and interrelationships that shape the behavior of systems. The discipline helps us to see how to change systems more effectively, and to act more in tune with the larger processes of the natural and economic world.

f. Systems thinking is a fundamental shift from linear thinking to circular thinking, from seeing things as static structures or objects to viewing them as processes. A tree is not an object, but an expression of process, such as photosynthesis, which connect the sun and the earth. A human being is not just a subject, but also a dynamic process of inhaling and exhaling, metabolism and anabolism, growth and renewal.

g. The art of systems thinking lies in seeing through complexity to the underlying structures generating change. Systems thinking does not ignore complexity; on the contrary, it organizes complexity into a coherent story that empowers us to detect and distinguish between causes and effects of problems, their separation in space and time, and how we can remedy them in enduring ways.

h. The greatest benefit of systems thinking is to distinguish between high-leverage from low-leverage changes in highly complex situations.

4.4 Review the following principles of feedback in systems thinking, and explore how you will internalize, organize, and implement an objective "feedback process" in your corporation so as to monitor, control, and improve its organizational learning and effectiveness:

a. In systems thinking, feedback means *any reciprocal flow of influence*. Feedback, in this sense, is the foundation of reality.

b. In systems thinking, feedback is an axiom that states, *every influence is both cause and effect*. Nothing is ever influenced in just one direction.

c. Reality exists in structures, and structures cause behavior. Seeing only individual actions and missing the structure underlying our actions, is the root of our linear thinking and powerlessness in understanding complex systems.

d. Our businesses and markets, our work and human endeavors are systems bound by inevitable fabrics of interrelated forces and actions that often take years to play out fully their effects on each other.

e. Since we are part of the lacework, it is doubly difficult for us to see the whole pattern of change. Instead, we often focus on snapshots of isolated parts of the system, and wonder why our complex problems never get solved.

4.5 In systems thinking, *dynamic complexity* implies many complex effects (Senge 2006: 71):

- The same action has dramatically different effects in the short run and the long run.
- The same action has one set of consequences locally and a very different set of consequences in another part of the system.
- Obvious interventions produce non-obvious consequences.

Conventional linear methods such as forecasting, planning, and analysis are ill-equipped to deal with dynamic complexity. Insights into causes and possible cures require seeing interrelationships between various actors and variables and at various times and contexts.

Given the properties of dynamic complexity as stated, examine the nature and control of:

a. Dynamic complexity in GM currently.
b. Dynamic complexity in Delphi currently.
c. Dynamic complexity in Ford currently.
d. Dynamic complexity in Visteon currently.
e. Dynamic complexity in Chrysler currently.
f. Dynamic complexity in Tata Motors currently.
g. Dynamic complexity in Mahindra & Mahindra currently.

    h. Dynamic complexity in Toyota currently.

    i. Dynamic complexity in Honda currently.

    j. Dynamic complexity in Nissan currently.

    k. Dynamic complexity in Hyundai currently.

    l. Dynamic complexity in Mopar currently.

4.6   An important concept in understanding systems dynamics is the reinforcing and balancing loops. There are two distinct types of feedback processes or building blocks of systems language:

- **Reinforcing feedback loop**: These are *amplifying processes* that constitute the engine of growth. In any growth or decline situation, reinforcing feedback is at work.
- **Balancing feedback loop**: These are *stabilizing processes* whenever there is goal-oriented behavior. The goal can be any desired target such as higher market share, plant shutdown, cost-containment, massive layoffs. Nature loves balance, and has built-in balancing mechanisms.

Identify, analyze, and enhance the reinforcing and balancing loops in the following turnaround situations (see Barbaro 2008; Wilson 2008):

    a. Last quarter 2008 sales are significantly down (compared to the same quarter in 2007) among all domestic auto companies in the U.S.

    b. Last quarter 2008 sales are significantly down (compared to the same quarter in 2007) among almost all non-domestic auto companies in the U.S.

    c. During fall of 2007 until early spring of 2008, eight mid-sized chains have filed for bankruptcy (e.g., furniture store Levitz, the electronics seller Sharper Image, the furniture chain Wickes, Fortunoff, the jewelry and home furnishing chain in the Northeast, the catalog retailer Lillian Vernon, and Harvey Electronics) as they staggered under mounting debt and declining sales.

    d. Linens 'n Things, the bedding and furniture retailer with 500 stores in 47 states, which is owned and operated by Apollo Management, a private equity firm, is considering bankruptcy after years of poor performance and mounting debt.

    e. Foot Locker threatens to close 140 stores over the next year, Ann Taylor will start to shutter 117 stores, and the jeweler Zales will close 100 stores.

    f. Charming Shoppes, which owns the women's clothing retailers Lane Bryant and Fashion Bug, is closing at least 150 stores in 2008. Wilsons the Leather Experts will close 158.

    g. Pacific Sunwear is shutting its 153-store chain called Demo.

    h. Most of the ailing retailing companies have filed for Chapter 11 reorganization, but not Chapter 7 liquidation. Such liquidity crises could set, in turn, recessionary chain reactions in the retailing industry. Because retailers rely on a broad network of suppliers, the cash-short retailers have to postpone payables to the tune of millions of dollars, which in turn is hurting the supplier. For instance, when they filed for bankruptcy, Sharper Image owed $6.6 million to United Parcel Service, and Levitz owed Searly $1.4 million. The big suppliers are cutting down on advertising, thus spreading the economic pain.

4.7   An important force in understanding systems dynamics is the concept of *delays*. *Delays* occur often in both reinforcing and balancing loops. Delays are points where the chain of influence takes particularly long time to play out. Delays have enormous influence in a system, frequently accentuating the impact of other forces. Typical delays in relation to customers are delays in customer satisfaction, delays in product acceptance, delays in customer dissatisfaction, delays in customer loyalty, delays in a customer's decisions to quit, and longer delays in customer return, if ever. In reinforcing loops, delays can shake our confidence, because growth does not come quickly as expected. In balancing loops, delays can dramatically change the behavior of the system.

Identify, analyze, and explain the "delays" that affect the reinforcing and balancing loops in all the turnaround situations listed in BTE 4.6 (see also Barbaro 2008; Wilson 2008):

4.8 Recall and review the 11 "laws" of systems thinking:

Law 1: "Today's problems come from yesterday's solutions."
Law 2: "Harder you push, harder the system pushes back."
Law 3: "Behavior grows better before it grows worse."
Law 4: "The easy way out usually leads back in."
Law 5: "The cure can be worse than the disease."
Law 6: "Faster is slower."
Law 7: "Cause and effect are not closely related in time or space."
Law 8: "Small changes can produce big results."
Law 9: "You can have your cake and eat it too—but not at once."
Law 10: "Dividing an elephant in half does not produce two elephants."
Law 11: "There is no blame."

a. What theme, if ever, seems to unify them, and why?
b. How does the unifying theme explain them better?
c. How does it make the laws complementary to each other?
d. What theme, if ever, seems to make each law distinct from another, and why?
e. How does it explain the uniqueness of the law better?
f. Which is the most important law among these, and why?
g. Which "laws" are corollaries to another, and why?
h. How are these "laws" different from the "paradoxes" mentioned under BTE 4.2, and why?
i. Are these laws mutually exclusive and collectively exhaustive (MECE), and why?
j. If so, what fundamental human behavior do they explain?
k. If so, what fundamental organizational behavior do they explain?

4.9 Recall and analyze the archetypes or templates of systems thinking that seem to control human events and their corresponding "management principle" (MP):

- Archetype 1: Limits to Growth: MP: Do not push growth; remove the factors limiting growth.
- Archetype 2: Shifting the Burden: MP: Beware the symptomatic solution.
- Archetype 3: "Fixes that Backfire": MP: A continuing series of fixes to a stubborn problem improves only momentarily.
- Archetype 4: "Tragedy of the Commons": MP: A continuing increase of use of a common resource will eventually overstrain the resource until it crashes.
- Archetype 5: "Accidental Adversaries": MP: Understand your partner's needs, see if you are unintentionally undermining them, and look for ways that support each other.
- Archetype 6: "Success to the Successful": MP: Should the success of the successful spell failure of the failed? Break this vicious zero-sum game cycle.
- Archetype 7: "Balancing Process with Delay": MP: In a sluggish system, aggressiveness produces instability. Either be patient or make the system more responsive.
- Archetype 8: "Growth and Underinvestment": MP: If there is a genuine potential for growth, build capacity in advance of demand, as a strategy for creating demand.
- Archetype 9: "Escalation": MP: Look for a way for both sides to win, or to achieve their objectives.
- Archetype 10: "Eroding Goals": MP: Hold the vision; do not compromise established standards for short-term gains.

   a. What theme, if ever, seems to unify all these archetypes, and why?
   b. How does the unifying theme explain their relevance better?
   c. How does this common theme make the archetypes complementary to each other?
   d. What theme, if ever, seems to make each archetype distinct from another, and why?
   e. How does it explain the uniqueness of each archetype better?
   f. Which is the most important archetype, and why?
   g. Which "archetypes" are corollaries to another archetype, and why?
   h. Are these archetypes mutually exclusive and collectively exhaustive (MECE), and why?
   i. If so, what fundamental human behavior do they explain?
   j. If so, what fundamental organizational behavior do they explain?
   k. If so, what fundamental collective or cultural behavior do they explain?

4.10 Study, synthesize, compare, and contrast the "laws" (BTE 4.8) and "archetypes" (BTE 4.9) of systems thinking, and do the following (see Tables 4.2 and 4.3 for a sample):

   a. Explore each "law" in relation to each "archetype" and analyze the interconnection, if any.
   b. Which "law" explains which "archetype" best, and why?
   c. Which "law" is a direct corollary to which "archetype," and why?
   d. Which is the most fundamental "law" or "archetype," and why?
   e. What can explain all other laws or archetypes, and why?
   f. Are the archetypes strategically related to one another, and why?
   g. Are the laws strategically related to one another, and why?
   h. Are each "law" and each "archetype" strategically related to one another, and why?

4.11 An important concept in understanding the dynamics of systems thinking is "leverage"—the capacity to see where actions and changes in structures can bring about significant and enduring improvements. Explore and apply high- versus low-leverage points in the turning around situations listed under BTE 4.6 using the following leverage principles:

   a. *Leverage lies in the balancing loop, not the reinforcing loop. To change the behavior of the system, you must identify and change the limiting factor.* This may require analysis, decisions, and strategies you have not yet considered, choices you never identified, or difficult changes in rewards or norms.
   b. However, high-leverage changes are usually not obvious, as effects are separated from causes in time and space (Law 7). There are no simple rules to find high-leverage changes. Learning to see underlying structures and processes (rather than events) is a good starting point.
   c. Whenever a company fails, people single out specific events as causes of failure, such as product problems, mismanagement, loss of key people, aggressive competition, business downturn, and the like. Yet, the real causes could be underlying the symptoms that go unnoticed and not understood. Systems archetypes help us to unearth these causes or underlying structures and treat them with timely policies. This is the principle of leverage.
   d. Leverage looks for underlying structures such as limits to growth (Archetype 1) and shifting the burden (Archetype 2); that is, leverage looks for reinforcing and balancing processes that underlie symptomatic changes. In case of a business failure, a good systems thinker looks beyond symptomatic solutions or shifting the burden events or policies. In the shifting the burden structure, the first thing a systems thinker looks for is what might be the underlying structure that is weakening the fundamental response of the failing company.
   e. Systems thinking does not always advocate long-term solutions. It also believes in short-term well-focused solutions that can produce significant and enduring improvements, but as long as they are in the right place, at the right time, and in the right hands. Systems thinking refers to this principle as "leverage." Tackling a difficult problem is often a matter of seeing where the high leverage is.

4.12 For almost 100 years, Clifford Security Trucks (CST), a highly committed and dedicated armored truck car in communities throughout North America, has served primarily banks, in both large centers as well as outlying rural regions. With increasing competition recently, CST's relationships with customers have come under pressure. The banking industry has successfully played security firms against each other. As a result, some armored car companies bid for contracts at prices well below the cost of doing business. If CST bid and accepted contracts at such low prices, it could not provide service at desired levels, could not adequately train its employees, nor could it cover the remote rural regions. If it failed to bid, then CST would lose market share and visibility, as also lose its large bank clients (see Senge et al. 1994: 151–53 for details).

    a. Identify the key variables in this case (e.g., contract price, cost per fulfilling each contract, revenue per contract).
    b. Study their projected trends under bidding versus not bidding.
    c. Which strategy would you adopt, and why?
    d. What systems archetypes would you use to understand better the ramifications of your decisions?
    e. Would bidding at low prices be tantamount to "shifting the burden"?
    f. Is competition a sign of "limits to growth" or "accidental adversaries" that CST must accept?
    g. Would undue cost-cutting disable CST from serving the underserved rural banks, where the risk of theft is high?
    h. Should CST hold on to its vision of committed dedication, and ignore price issues?

4.13 Early July 2008, Starbucks announced it would shutter 600 of its underperforming stores and lay off some 14,000 employees in the process. It has significantly scaled back plans to open new outlets. The current recession in the U.S. is hurting countless retailers and restaurant chains. From a few dozens of stores in 1992 when Starbucks went public, the coffee bar giant has grown exponentially to 16,875 stores in 2008, 11,537 stores in the U.S. and the remaining 5,000 being abroad. The company was long renowned for its expertise at selecting prime locations for its ubiquitous stores. For much of the last 15 years, the commercial real estate executives at Starbucks were known for their rigor in selecting locations for their stores. Besides studying demographics, Starbucks evaluated its potential locations by other specific factors such as the education level in various neighborhoods, the traffic flow on both sides of a given street, the ease with which drivers could make a right turn for their java fix on their way to the office. Nevertheless, currently, the company has been straying from the exacting real estate science that it had perfected and which guided it through its first expansion wave of 1992–2008. Though a flagging recessionary economy and soaring gas prices could account for at least some of Starbuck's woes, there seem to be other major in-company problems triggering this sudden decline (Bradstone 2008). Analyze and resolve some of the following internal inherent "wicked" problems of Starbucks in the light of the "laws" and "archetypes" of systems thinking:

    a. Starbucks was so determined to meet its growth promises to Wall Street that it relaxed its standards for selecting new store locations. The potential rewards of rapid growth led Starbucks astray.
    b. Its recent overexpansion in some regions and putting stores too close together in others has backfired. Starbucks misjudged the risks of planting stores close to each other, leading to decline in store sales. The company agreed that 70 percent of the stores marked for closing in July 2008 were opened after 2006.
    c. It also overextended itself in certain regions (e.g., Florida and the South and in Southern California which are among the hardest hit by the housing crisis) where the older demographics and hot weather are not generally conducive to creating long lines of customers eager to cough up $4 for foam-top lattes.
    d. In 2004, Starbucks announced it would double its pace of expansion with a goal of reaching 15,000 stores in the U.S. by 2010. That ambitious target led to a frenzy of getting locations opened disregarding cannibalization and location demographics, psychographics, and ergographics (work-related demographic shifts).

e. Many of the newer stores were located in areas of potential but unrealized population growth. The housing crisis and real estate chaos derailed much of that planned potential for development—the projected traffic patterns never materialized. Some of these areas did not pan out as expected.

f. Starbucks has too many licensed stores in bookstores and supermarkets which can siphon traffic from more profitable company-owned stores. Some stores were licensed to locate within hundred yards from an existing licensed or company-owned store.

4.14 Goodman, Kemeny, and Karash (Peter Senge's students at MIT, MA) suggest that as good systems thinkers in an organizational setting, one should see four levels operating simultaneously: events, patterns of behavior, systems, and mental models. They illustrate this process in relation to their Acme Story as told in Senge et al. (1994: 97–112). Use the following four steps in re-analyzing and transforming the companies involved in BTE 4.6, Clifford Security Trucks (BTE 4.12), and Starbucks (BTE 4.13). (See also Table 4.1.)

a. **Step One: Explore Key Events**: First identify key events, negative and positive, happening in your company in the recent critical months. Consider each event linearly and independently. Also, list and evaluate the solutions independently suggested by each of the top management (e.g., VP: Marketing, VP: Finance, VP: HR, VP: Accounting, General Manager, COO, CFO, and CEO).

b. **Step Two: Investigate Patterns of Behavior among Key Events**: Next, set up a task force with members from each key department of your company, and reanalyze select key variables identified in Step One in order to track trends and patterns in their behavior during recent years. Determine which key event or trend causes another or a series of other key events or trends.

c. **Step Three: Unravel Systemic Structures underlying Key Events and Trends**: What is the root of the problem? Are not key events and trends influencing each other in ways you have not explored before? For instance, every time your sales go down, you double up efforts to get new customers. However, the harder you try to sell, the more sales you lose! It is a vicious spiral. See if Laws 1–11 and Archetypes 1–10 help to unravel underlying structures. Hence, start looking for new inter-relationships between all major variables or trends involved in your firm.

d. **Step Four: Share your Mental Models**: Expose and unravel your mental models of presumptions, assumptions, and beliefs regarding the market, your customers, your corporation, your competition, coming from your major departments or from your major top management in relation to the key events and trends identified under steps one and two. Revise or question mental models. Discover the root of the problem—why are you losing old customers? What are your high-leverage points in boosting sales? Should you not redistribute salespeople along points of high leverage?

Chapter 5

The CEO as a Critical Thinker of Simple Strategic Problems

Real life in the offline and online world challenges us with many business and e-business problems. Each problem may be a threat but it is also an opportunity. Each problem is both a turnaround and transformation challenge to the business executive. In this context, identifying, defining, formulating, specifying, and resolving business problems, in general, and turnaround transformation problems, in particular, becomes urgent. This chapter proposes a "systems approach" to a simple problem definition, identification, formulation, specification, alternatives solution generation, evaluation, and the final resolution of the problem.

No problem can be resolved until you recognize it and failure to identify a problem correctly, may lead to disastrous consequences. When problems arise with a particular course of action or turnaround or transformation strategy, the problem relates to the gap between the actual state and some desired state of knowledge and outcomes. When the gap is difficult to bridge, and you perceive it to be important enough for your organization or the course of action, problem recognition occurs (Smith 1987).

WHAT IS A PROBLEM?

A problem is a "system at unrest" (Ackoff and Emerey 1972). A system is any thing (subject, object, property, or event) that is made up of two or more parts. In this sense, everything in the universe has two or more parts, and, therefore, is a system. The universe with all its constellations, galaxies, stars, and planets is a system. Our mother earth is a unique planetary system of geo-, hydro-, thermo-, and atmosphere that makes plant, animal, and human life possible.

Every system has an environment, either internal (elements within the system that you cannot control) or external. The "unrest" is caused by the internal or external environment beyond your control, but still controlling you or your organization.

A system without an environment does not exist in our universe. An environment is a system by itself. A business environment is defined as a system whose contents, properties, and events impact your business organization, but the latter cannot impact or control the system that impacts it. If a system can control its environment, then the environment becomes a part of the system. For instance, if competitors, new government regulations, new globalization challenges, or new technologies impact and control your corporation, and you, in turn, cannot control them, then they form your environment.

An economy is a market system with an environment. All products and services offered in that market economy are systems. A business corporation or organization that offers such products and services is a system. A market that absorbs these products and services is a social or economic system.

Any of these systems could be at unrest at a given time. That is, there are economic, market, business, and environmental problems. Governments, politics, laws and legislatures, economy, culture, religion, civilization, historical eras and epochs are systems in the world. When they are at unrest, there are problems. When any of these environments control you, there is a problem.

For instance, a business problem that is a "system at unrest" implies that any or all of the following parts are dysfunctional and non-coordinating:

- Subjects (e.g., people, employees, executives, and suppliers).
- Objects (products, services, machinery and equipment, patents, cash and inventory).
- Properties (e.g., skills, talents, quality, R&D, technology, logistics, promotions, service, market research, and complaints feedback).
- Events (e.g., new product development, new product announcements, press release, progress, peak market share, peak profits, peak losses, peak stock prices, and peak market evaluation).

A business system at unrest, accordingly, may be unclear in its vision and mission, its goals and objectives, its policies and procedures, in its strategies and tactics, and, hence, fail to realize expected goals and objectives. This is a business problem. In this chapter we focus on simple, linear, structured, and resolvable strategic problems. In the next chapter we will deal with complex, non-linear, circular, unstructured, and un-resolvable problems, in short, "wicked" strategic problems.

STEP ONE: PROBLEM DEFINITION AND IDENTIFICATION

Herbert Simon in his *The New Science of Management* (1960) proposes one of the most widely used framework's for problem-solving. He uses a three-stage approach: intelligence, design, and choice.

- Intelligence involves recognizing the problem and analyzing problem-related information to develop a useful problem definition.
- Design involves generating solution alternatives.
- Choice involves the selection and implementation of a solution.

The Simon model is generic. Several others have suggested models for problem-solving, but one can map them all into the Simon model. Table 5.1 maps the thinking of five other models into the Simon model. The activities within each stage are rarely mutually exclusive, sequential, or linear. They could be interdependent, non-linear, and recursive and activities in one phase will affect the others (VanGundy 1988). One often moves to and from the various phases in a typical problem-solving or opportunity-identification situation (Couger 1995: 121). In a problem where we do not have access to all the data we need, such as projecting future conditions in which the turnaround-transformation company will operate, we can use the simulation technique to enable us to identify a large number of scenarios. We may not be able to define a problem until after the "intelligence" phase, that is, after reviewing all the data. Often we may need more data to fully understand the problem, threat, or opportunity. We can often turn a problem into an opportunity.

Guilford (1957, 1967) identified five layers of mental operations after extensive testing on large numbers of people. According to his *Structure of the Intellect*, our mental process (of which problem-solving is a subset) operates in many layers:

TABLE 5.1 **Mapping Alternative Approaches to Problem-solving to Herbert Simon's Model: Intelligence, Design, and Choice**

Problem-solving model	Stages of problem-solving	Simon's model
Kingsley and Garry (1957): *The Nature and Conditions of Learning*	1. A difficulty is felt 2. The problem is clarified and defined 3. A search for clues is made	Intelligence
	4. Various suggestions appear and are evaluated	Design
	5. A suggested solution is accepted or the thinker gives up in defeat 6. The solution is tested	Choice
Von Fange: *G. E. Creative Engineering Program*	1. Investigate direction 2. Establish measures 3. Develop methods	Intelligence
	4. Optimize a structure 5. Accomplish this structure	Design
	6. Convince others	Choice
Gregory: *The Scientific Problem-Solving Method*	1. Deciding on objective 2. Analyzing problems 3. Gathering data 4. Organizing data	Intelligence
	5. Inducting 6. Planning 7. Pre-checking	Design
	8. Activating plans 9. Evaluating	Choice
Bailey: *Disciplined Creativity*	1. Problem inquiry 2. Specifying goals 3. Determining means	Intelligence
	4. Solution optimization	Design
	5. Construction and verification 6. Convince others	Choice
Isaksen and Treffinger (1985): *Creative Problem Solving*	1. Mess finding 2. Data finding 3. Problem finding 4. Idea finding	Intelligence
	5. Solution finding	Design
	6. Acceptance finding	Choice
Couger (1995): *Creative Problem Solving and Opportunity Finding*	1. Opportunity delineation; problem definition 2. Compiling relevant information: fact finding 3. Generating ideas	Intelligence
	4. Evaluating and prioritizing ideas	Design
	5. Developing implementation plan	Choice

Source: Author's own.

Note: See also Couger (1995: 111–14).

1. **Cognition**: Discovery, rediscovery, or recognition.
2. **Memory**: Retention of what is cognized and recognized.
3. **Convergent Thinking**: Thinking that results in the right or wrong answer to a question that can have only one right answer. [e.g., what is swine (H1N1) flu? What is the cure?]
4. **Divergent Thinking**: Thinking in different directions, or searching for a variety of answers to questions that may have many right answers. [Example: What is global climate change and what is the cause?]
5. **Evaluation**: Reaching decisions about the accuracy, goodness, or suitability of information gathered under layers 1–4.

All five layers may be in use in problem-solving or creative thinking. While divergent thinking is essential to generate a wide range of ideas, and is related to "wicked" problems (see Chapter 6), convergent thinking identifies the most useful or appropriate of the possible solutions that convergent thinking generates.

Simple problems can be real or perceived. In either case, we would need many facts, figures, and findings to prove or dismiss the problem. Many problems are "fuzzy" and poorly defined. That is, many problems involve a "mess" of problems. According to Russell Ackoff (1974, 1981), a mess is a "system of external conditions that produces dissatisfaction; alternatively, a mess can be conceptualized as a system of problems." Problems often interact and are interconnected, and that makes them "messy" and complicated. Problems that deal with human beings and human response concerns are much more messy than technical or scientific problems.

Brightman (1988) classifies problem into two categories: disturbance problems and entrepreneurial problems. Both problems involve "gaps" in knowledge or required information. In disturbance problems, the gap is the difference between the normal state of affairs and the state resulting from the disturbance; eliminating this gap is the goal of disturbance problem-solving. In entrepreneurial problems, the goal is to close the gap between the present level of performance and a desired higher level. The performance gap can result from a variety of causes, such as cost over-runs, competition, poor quality, tougher Environmental Protection Agency (EPA) or Occupational Safety and Health Administration (OSHA) standards, or globalization. Changing consumer lifestyles and demand profiles can cause a performance gap—for instance, people may not accept quality levels in products and services that they accepted two or three years ago.

Fabian (1990: 86) distinguishes between people who are analytical and those who are intuitive in their approach to problem-solving. "Analytical people" have a practical, sensing, quick-closure tendency; they often like to have the constraints upfront; they want detailed criteria and boundaries before they come up with ideas. They do not like to generate options that might be wasted or not meet the requirements. "Intuitive people," on the other hand, dislike criteria and boundaries at the initial stages of problem-solving. They believe that setting the criteria before searching for ideas is putting a noose around one's thinking. They like to generate ideas that can get around or obliterate what seems to them unreasonable or unrealistic constraints. Elements of both approaches may be necessary for creative problem definition and solving. We need to push back or expand the boundaries in order to understand the problem or opportunity thoroughly. At the same time, to be practical, we must stay within the time and resource constraints available to us.

According to Hogarth (1987), selective perception can seriously impair problem identification and definition. Selective perception entails four stages: (*a*) people structure problems on the basis of their own experience; (*b*) one's expectations or anticipations based on what one does see; (*c*) people seek information consistent with their own view/bias/hypothesis; and (*d*) people downplay or disregard conflicting evidence. Managers tend to perceive information selectively according to their functional background; that is, individuals develop knowledge structures based on their functional expertise (e.g., engineering, legal, marketing, finance, or accounting). Problem identification should avoid biases of selective perception.

Given this discussion, and using Table 5.1, we identify the transformation problem along any one or more of the following areas. That is, basically, we look for subjects, objects, properties, and events along any of these areas that impact us negatively. All four problem zones can generate both disturbance and entrepreneurial problems. Problems recur. As long as Wal-Mart was trailing KMart, the problem was how to surpass KMart. Once Wal-Mart did excel KMart in 1991, the recurrent problem was how to reduce the gap between actual global sales of Wal-Mart and its global sales potential.

In identifying and assessing the problem, the following questions may help to classify or characterize it, as long as it is a simple, linear, and structured problem:

- **Is the problem market related?** Is it a customer unmet need, want, or desire? An under-served market in the inner city, urban, or rural areas? An over-served market dense with competition and market entry barriers? Is it a new market? An unexplored market? A distribution problem? A logistics problem? A delivery problem? A retailing problem? An advertising or promotional problem? A redlining problem? A monopoly? A monopsony? A dominant supplier? A minority supplier suppressed and harassed by dominant suppliers? Converging industries? Converging markets? Converging trade zones? Converging continents? Converging countries (e.g., E.U.)? Converging consumer lifestyles? Converging consumer values? Converging consumer expectations?

- **Is the problem product related?** Is it cost related (e.g., cost overruns, high wage, high salary, organizational slack, or outdated technology)? Is it overpriced via gouging? Is there predatory pricing? Is there dumping? Is it quality related? Is it technology related? Is it revenue related (low sales, market share erosion, low profits, low Return on Sales (ROS), Return on Marketing (ROM), Return on Quality (ROQ), Return on Investment (ROI), Return on Assets (ROA), Return on Equity ROE)? Is it an outdated or obsolesced product? Does the product involve long product cycles? Does the product involve very short life cycles via planned product or service obsolescence? Is it a much needed, wanted, or desired product and service? A new product that is new to the firm, or new to the industry, or new to the country, or new to the world? Lack of product or service instructions and information? A defective product? A harmful product? A confusing label or package? Confusing product or service instructions? Are there any confusing product warranties and guarantees? Lack of adequate financing programs? A confusing brand? A confusing product bundle? A confusing price bundle? Poor quality? Confusing quality-surrogates via pricing, branding, bundling, advertising, promoting, and retailing? Converging technologies? Converging competencies? Converging core products? Converging core processes? Converging products? Converging services?

- **Is it a legal problem?** Does the product or service violate any written or unwritten law, ordinance, or contract (e.g., antitrust, OSHA, equal access)? Does it violate any tort law such as deception, under-disclosure, over-disclosure, or information overload, buyer–seller information asymmetry? Is it misleading? Is there misrepresentation, negligence, or lack of due care? Does it violate patent law? Is there any trademark infringement? Does it violate any law on ecological systems (e.g., EPA, CAFÉ, carbon emissions)? Any trade law (General Agreement on Tariffs and Trade (GATT), World Trade Organization (WTO), North American Free Trade Agreement (NAFTA), and E.U.) violation? Does the product or service violate consumer rights such as right to information, right to choice or variety, right to safety, right to consumer education, right to complain, or right to redress? Does it violate individual, consumer, and social privacy? Does it violate basic safety and security laws?

- **Is it an environment-related problem?** Does the product harm land, water, sea, or air? Does it protect local and social landscape? Does it prevent ecological harm? Does it benefit ecology and ecosystems? Does the product or service offend any social, national, cultural, religious, political, racial, and ethnic sensitivities, customs and mores? Does it undermine local communities, local businesses, local institutions, and markets? Does the product or service promote global inequalities of income, opportunity, and entrepreneurship? Does the product or service meet global lifesaving needs (e.g., drinking water, HIV-positive drugs) through social entrepreneurship? Does the product or service eliminate or progressively eradicate global poverty, hunger, health-hazards, homelessness, joblessness, illiteracy, crime, and disease? [See *Business Transformation Exercise 5.1.*]

STEP TWO: PROBLEM FORMULATION

Albert Einstein wrote, "The formulation of a problem is often more essential than its solution which may be merely a matter of mathematical or experimental skill. To raise new questions from a new angle, requires creative imagination and marks a real advance in science" (cited in Getzels and Csikszentmihalyi (1975)). Careful problem definition and formulation ensures that we are working on the right problem. Tukey coined the term "Type III Error" for representing errors of solving the wrong problem in order to emphasize the importance of avoiding it. Solving the wrong problem could be more detrimental than ignoring the problem altogether.

The process of formulating the problem and of conceiving a solution for it are identical, since "every specification of the problem is a specification of the direction in which a treatment is considered" (Rittel and Webber 1973).

Peter Senge (1990) in his *The Fifth Discipline* speaks about the excitement of defining a problem. He characterizes it as a mystery to be solved. He regrets that "the way knowledge is organized and structured in contemporary society destroys this sense of mystery." The compartmentalization of knowledge (e.g., economics, accounting, marketing, psychology) creates a false sense of confidence in identifying and assessing a problem, since the boundaries that make the compartments are fundamentally arbitrary. "Life comes to us whole. It is only the analytic lens we impose that makes it seem as if problems can be isolated and solved. When we forget that it is only a lens, we lose the spirit of mystery" (Senge 1990: 283).

Hence, a useful technique of problem formulation is "boundary examination." Boundaries determine how information is gathered, organized, and processed. Boundary examination is based on the assumption that the boundaries of a problem are either correct or incorrect. The goal is to restructure assumptions (boundaries to our thinking) and provide new ways of looking at the problem. That is, another way of thinking about a problem is to identify and suspend assumptions. "Suspending assumptions is lot like seeing leaps of abstraction and inquiring into the reasoning behind the abstraction" (Senge 1990: 244–45).

THE PROCESS OF PROBLEM FORMULATION

Mintzberg, Raisinghari, and Theoret (1976) were among the first to propose a formal process of problem formulation and resolution. They distinguish two phases in the problem definition phase: recognition and diagnosis.

* **Recognition**: The problem is sensed as provoked by the accumulation of relevant stimuli (e.g., falling sales, customer dissatisfaction, overstocked inventory, overextended receivables, worker apathy, or retailer complaints). As stimuli build up beyond an "action threshold" (a point beyond which the problem cannot be ignored), action is necessary. One becomes aware of the problem for a while, until accumulated stimuli "trigger" and force action.
* **Diagnosis**: It is the next step where the management tries to understand the stimuli and establish cause–effect relationships in the problem situation. This involves a process of information gathering in order to clarify and define the issues such that the problem is clearly identified and defined. Managers individually or in teams discuss the information gathered, confront it, and seek solutions to resolve it. At this problem definition stage, some managers may choose to ignore the problem, stall it, postpone diagnosing it or give it a top priority until a solution is arrived on. Ignoring the problem or stalling it may imply several lost opportunities and the development of a crisis-situation.

Different individuals understand and interpret information differently. Carl Jung (1971) in describing psychological personality types also tells us how people handle information and data. According to Jung, people take in data in two ways, sensation and intuition, and evaluate information in two ways, thinking and feeling. Combinations of these four types produce different types of individuals. Thus, people with sensing as primary style rely on senses, hard facts and details; whereas intuition dominant types tend to view the whole situation, the relationship between various facts and figures, and focus on hypothetical possibilities of the situation rather than facts and details. When evaluating information, the thinking dominant types approach problems with impersonal, formal, and structured methods, looking for similarities among different situations, thus looking for generalizations. The feeling dominant types use their value judgments to evaluate information, tend to look for differences (or dissimilarities) since their orientation is toward particularizing. They focus on judgments of good or bad, right or wrong.

A dominant descriptive view on human problem-solving is the "Information Processing Model" of Newell and Simon (1972). According to this model, when encountering a problem, the problem solvers perceive the raw data and process these perceptions until they recognize the "task environment" (i.e., the components of the problem or the terms in which it is presented). Next, they transform this perceived problem into their "problem space" (i.e., mental representation of the task environment, the interpretation of where the goal is, and what kinds of actions they must perform to obtain the goal). While mapping current problems into past problem spaces, problem solvers use various kinds of information drawn from memory and a variety of related past experiences. Thus, how the data is taken in, understood, and interpreted can vary across individuals depending upon how they are "hard-wired" to their innate and acquired capabilities and experiences. Hence, in a problem formulation process, not every individual in a team will view the problem the same way, even if all other factors, situations, and motives are held the same. [See *Business Transformation Exercise 5.2.*]

Past experiences can have a negative effect on problem solvers if the former cause "functional fixation" (Duncker 1945: 270) or "mental over-preparedness" such that the information processing is prematurely truncated to fit past models of the one's problem space (Luchins 1946). If past experience, however, has been a genuine learning experience, it can have a positive effect on subsequent problem formulation (Wertheimer 1982).

Problem solvers often use "heuristics" that may prove to be biases in problem formulation. In this connection, Tversky and Kahneman (1982) and Kahneman and Tversky (2000) studied many such heuristics, especially the "anchoring framework." They found that people tend to anchor their judgments on initially presented information, and adjust subsequently arriving information in relation to the initial anchoring information. In this information processing model, the first information has more influence and weight on final judgments and evaluations. Another heuristic commonly used in problem definition is "analogy" (drawing inferences based on similar situations in other fields or industries), which, while a very valuable creative thinking technique, can generate confusion if not properly used (Mascarenhas, Kesavan, and Bernacchi 2005d).

Janis and Mann (1977) discuss two types of irrational attitudes when processing information under stress and anxiety. "Defensive avoidance" is an attempt simply to avoid the problem by ignoring information about it, or the feeling of low confidence with regard to taking effective action, or relying on others for decision. "Hyper-vigilance" is a typical panic behavior where the problem-solver acts hastily and makes decision based on insufficient information. Both attitudes will always lead to ineffective problem formulation and solving.

Table 5.2 summarizes our discussions thus far and characterizes the problem-resolving process in six sequential stages. These six stages are not necessarily sequential, mutually exclusive or collectively exhaustive (MECE). The problem-solving process is too human, social, institutional, and complex for these neat MECE distinctions. The actual problem-solving process could involve several stages simultaneously, recursively and interactively. Nevertheless, we may recognize and document some hierarchical, logical, and sequential stages in the process of problem-resolving.

For instance, at stage one you identify the problem. Your input sources are your own immediate environment (external) and your own somatic dispositions and gut feelings (internal). These inputs are primarily sense-related audio-visuals (things you hear, converse, read, and see in terms of facts, figures, numbers, graphs, and charts). Your input filters at this stage are very basic, such as: attention, analysis of trends, graphs and charts; you categorize data and identify "disturbance" and "entrepreneurial" problems. Either your evaluation at this stage is to deny the existence of the problem, and quickly dismiss it and exit, or you recognize the problem, stay with it, and transit to stage two—"problem specification."

At stage two, you expand your environment and your boundaries in order to search for other relevant sets of data such as law and regulatory ordinances, competition, and globalization constraints and challenges. From "audio-visual inputs" of the first stage, you may delve into "symbolic data" such as brands and brand communities, patents and trademarks, company reputation and brand equity, in relation to both your company and your major competitors. Your input filters are more sophisticated such as boundary examination, boundary expansion, lateral thinking, analogical thinking, competition scanning, market vigilance, suspending assumptions, examining your presuppositions, and questioning your mental models and paradigms. Given all this inquiry, you still judge the problem either as trivial

TABLE 5.2 Creative Problem-solving Stages

Stage	Input sources	Input types	Input filters	Evaluation/reaction
One: Problem Identification	One's own environment (E) and one's inner dispositions (somatic inputs); company annual reports and other financial statements	Mostly audio-visual in terms of conversations, facts, figures, numbers, charts, and graphs	Attention; facts categorization Graphs–charts analysis Identify disturbance problems Identify entrepreneurial problems	Deny the problem. Dismiss the problem. Exit 1 Recognize the problem: go to stage two
Two: Problem Specification	Larger environmental data; competitive data; legal data; expand boundaries.	Symbolic data: patents, trademarks, brands, company logos, brand equity, company reputation	Competition scanning Market scanning Boundary examination Lateral thinking Suspending assumptions Examining presuppositions Analogical thinking	The problem is trivial and not worth delving into. Exit 2 Recognize the importance of the problem: go to stage three
Three: Problem Formulation	Cash flow statements; 10K and 10Q statements Company covenants and contracts Company white papers Company archives	Semantic data: verbal data, contracts data, scripts/journal data, time-series data, 401K and 8Q data, archival data, company history and journals	Discussion and dialogue Analysis, intuition, synthesis Drawing meaningful conclusions Information gap analysis Disturbance analysis Performance analysis	The problem is too complex; beyond our time and capital resources. Exit 3 The problem is vital for the company's survival and growth: go to stage four.
Four: Alternatives Generation	Behavioral data; interviews; survey research; e-surveys Quality research Production search Supplier analysis New information search; hostile takeover scanning Divestiture search	Behavioral data Organizational data such as culture, climate, morale, and ethics data Customer feedback Supplier feedback Divestiture data	Divergent thinking Simulation; interaction Team analysis Productivity analysis Responsibility analysis Social and ethical auditing Alternative scenarios Information-gap bridging	The problem is too diverging with divergent solutions. Hence, quit. Exit 4 The problem is critical and can be managed with additional talent and resources. Various solution alternatives can be evaluated— go to stage five.
Five: Alternatives Evaluation	Consultant search Turnaround expert search New talent-skills search New leadership search Collaborative search Joint ventures search Strategic alliance search Acquisitions scanning Mergers and due diligence	Team-building data Talent registry data Collaborative data Joint ventures data Strategic alliance data Acquisitions data Merger data Hostile takeover data Due diligence data	Interactive thinking Convergent thinking Team-building and team-thinking Applying real boundaries Thinking within constraints Expert consulting Incremental innovations? Radical innovation? Market breakthroughs? Prioritization Problem reversal/review	The solutions are too expensive; possible legal complications; possible cash crises or insolvency. Hence, quit. Exit 5 The best solution can be identified, tested, and financed—go to stage six.
Six: Optimal Solution Choice	Environment reevaluation Competition reassessment Legal reevaluation Sustainable competitive advantage assessment Alternative solutions evaluation	Updated information Reexamining joint venture or other collaborative data solutions Mergers and acquisitions portfolio data	Testing alternative solutions for feasibility and viability Convergent solution thinking and design analysis Final decision-making Execute divestitures, if any Execute strategic alliances and/or mergers and acquisitions	Pre-announce solution choice Implement solution Project sales outcomes Project financial outcomes Project growth outcomes Monitor continuous improvement Scan new problems—go to stage one.

Source: Author's own.

or too complicated to delve into, and hence quit, or you recognize the importance of the problem and go to stage three—"problem formulation."

At stage three, you further expand your data search to cash flow statements, company contracts with employees, and covenants with banks, company archives, company white papers, and other company journal entries. Your data domain is primarily semantic and hermeneutic. You analyze all your data, interpret it carefully via discussion and dialogue, undertake information and performance gap analysis by some disturbance and performance analysis, and draw meaningful conclusions from the data. At this stage you may decide the problem is too complex and beyond your skills and financial resources and choose to exit, or you judge the problem vital to the company's future growth and opt to go to stage four—"alternatives generation."

At stage four, you are further expanding your input sources to interview and survey data, qualitative and quantitative searches, behavioral data, market data in relation to possible divestitures, mergers, and acquisitions, and you scan hostile takeovers. From the organizational and behavioral data you are looking for "patterns" of customs and conventions, climate and morale symbols, values and priorities, moral and ethical codes, if any. Typical types of filters at this stage could be divergent thinking (seeking multidimensional data and multidimensional solutions), simulations, experimentations, team analysis and group thinking, social and ethical auditing, productivity and responsibility analysis. At this stage, you may be overwhelmed by the divergence and multidimensionality of the problem and choose to exit, or may accept the challenge of the problem, understand its critical importance and urgency, and transit to stage five—"alternatives evaluation."

At stage five, you are further expanding your input resources by bringing in turnaround experts and consultants, hiring new technical and administrative skills. Simultaneously, you could be researching other alternatives such as technical collaboration, strategic alliances, joint ventures, acquisitions, mergers, and other innovative forms of partnerships. Each alternative may require due diligence in terms of objective assessment of skills, resources, liabilities, and constraints on either side of the exchange equation and your input filters at this stage must be advanced. One of these is "convergent thinking" (you are selectively reducing the dimensionality and diversity of the problem in hand to derive one solution alternative). You also undertake group expert interactive thinking. In the process, you could introduce new meaningful boundaries to replace those abandoned at earlier stages. In addition, given your expanded resource base, you could research new alternatives such as incremental or radical innovations, and market and technological breakthroughs for generating new products and market offerings. Given your current constraints, you evaluate all these solution alternatives. You may choose to exit at this stage if the solution choice is beyond your skills and resources, or you may proceed to identify the best alternative, assess it, and choose to implement it at stage six—"optimal solution choice and implementation."

Lastly, at stage six, given your analysis from stage one to stage five, you re-evaluate your environment, customers, suppliers, distributors, competition, all new alternatives and their legal implications, assess the incremental sustainable competitive advantage that you expect from the final choice alternative, and decide to implement it. After pre-announcing your final choice to the target market public, you undertake the serious business of monitoring the final solution for its expected performance outcomes. By this time, new problems would have emerged, and you may have to go to stage one—"problem identification."

A STRUCTURE FOR PROBLEM FORMULATION

All problems are embedded in a system of variables some of which are controllable by the firm and some of which are uncontrollable by the firm. Succinctly, the problem P is a function of x and y:

$$P = f(x, y),$$

where **x** is a vector of your controllable variables, and **y** represents the vector of your uncontrollable variables or the environment. Identification of the controllable and uncontrollable variables is problem formulation.

In general, any system has some set of controllable variables and some set of uncontrollable variables. [That is, **x** and **y** can never be null sets. Theoretically, however, if **y** is null, there is no problem.] The set of uncontrollable variables causes the system to be at "unrest," and causes the problems. For instance, if you can control your product, its brand name, its quality, its distribution and promotion, but your competitor controls the price, market share, and profitability, then you have a problem. KMart had a problem in this sense in relation to Wal-Mart. Similarly, General Motors, Ford, and Chrysler have had problems with the quality of certain passenger car models in relation to Toyota, Honda, and Nissan. In general, all business organizations have problems as long as there is competition. Monopolistic (i.e., the firm is a sole supplier) and monopsonistic (i.e., the firm is sole buyer) firms have problems with anti-trust or related government regulations.

Given, then, your main problem that you have identified under step one, do the following:

a. Identify almost all the *relevant* variables that cause the problem.
b. Categorize these variables into "controllable" and "uncontrollable" from the company's viewpoint.

Then question the following:

c. To what extent are the uncontrollable variables associated with your customers?
d. To what extent are the uncontrollable variables associated with their changing lifestyles?
e. To what extent are the uncontrollable variables associated with cost?
f. To what extent are the uncontrollable variables associated with pricing?
g. To what extent are the uncontrollable variables associated with quality?
h. To what extent are the uncontrollable variables associated with technology?
i. To what extent are the uncontrollable variables associated with employees?
j. To what extent are the uncontrollable variables associated with supplies and materials?
k. To what extent are the uncontrollable variables associated with exports or imports?
l. To what extent are the uncontrollable variables associated with suppliers?
m. To what extent are the uncontrollable variables associated with creditors, banks, and shareholders?
n. To what extent are the uncontrollable variables associated with competition?
o. To what extent are the uncontrollable variables associated with market demand or glut?
p. To what extent are the uncontrollable variables associated with governments, laws and ordinances?

q. To what extent are the uncontrollable variables associated with globalization, outsourcing, and global competition?

Categorize variables into "controllable" and "uncontrollable" from the consumer's viewpoint.

a. To what extent are the uncontrollable variables associated with pricing as perceived by the consumers?
b. To what extent are the uncontrollable variables associated with quality as perceived by the consumers?
c. To what extent are the uncontrollable variables associated with technology as perceived by consumers?
d. To what extent are the uncontrollable variables associated with the convenience of saving time?
e. To what extent are the uncontrollable variables associated with the convenience of saving energy?
f. To what extent are the uncontrollable variables associated with saving anxiety and worries?
g. To what extent are the uncontrollable variables associated with changing fads, fashions, and lifestyles?
h. To what extent are the uncontrollable variables associated with shifting demographics, sociographics, psychographics, ergographics, ethnographics, or chirographics?
i. Correctly identify and formulate the main problem together with subsidiary or embedded sub-problems. That is:

   • Identify the various contexts the problem is nested or embedded in (e.g., economic, political, global, technological, social, and cultural).
   • Understand the connections and ramifications (e.g., antecedents, determinants, concomitants, consequences) of the problem on these contextual environments.
   • Recognize the good or bad consequences of the selected alternative (i.e., best solution) on these contextual environments. [See *Business Transformation Exercises 5.3* and *5.4*.]

The "contextual environment" goes beyond the domain of internal and external stakeholders. In a highly globalized and networked world, the contextual domain is ever expanding. It is a borderless world. We should also think globally about business turnaround problems. Local and domestic problems have international and global antecedents, concomitants, determinants, and consequences.

• **Antecedents** are factors and events that precede but influence the problem at hand.
• **Concomitants** are factors and events that accompany and influence the problem at hand.
• **Determinants** are factors and events that cause the problem (i.e., they are necessary and sufficient conditions to the occurrence of the problem).
• **Consequences** are effects and outcomes that are causally connected to the problem or its selected solution.

A problem correctly identified and well-formulated is half solved (John Dewey). To solve a problem, you have to get ahead of it and change the reasons it is occurring. Formulating a problem carefully can help you identify the reasons by which it is occurring.

STEP THREE: PROBLEM SPECIFICATION

Next, understand the relationships between the controllable and the uncontrollable variables of the problem identified and formulated under stages one and two. The uncontrollable variables are salient factors that define and specify your problem. At this stage, you need to relate the controllable variables to the uncontrollable variables. This is "problem specification." You may also need to specify each variable in your list of controllable and uncontrollable variables. For example, if price is an uncontrollable variable, then, specify how price should be defined: for example, unit price, bulk price, discount price, deep discount price, rebate price, everyday low price (EDLP), premium price (the price you charge for your first customers), penetration price (i.e., the price at which you can penetrate the competitive market), clearance price, liquidation price, and so on.

Relations between variables may be just sequences, associations, or correlations. They may be necessary or sufficient conditions for one another. Finally, they may be causally connected with one another. For instance, how are factors of price, quality, advertising, promotions, brand name, brand equity, and brand community related to those of your major competitor? Hence, in understanding relations between your controllable and uncontrollable variables, you must ask these questions:

a. Are these relationships just sequences?
b. Are these relationships mere associations?
c. Are these relationships weak or strong correlations?
d. Are these relationships necessary conditions? [Note: If Y is false, non-existing, or non-verifying when X is false, non-existing, or non-verifying, then X is a necessary condition for Y] (Mascarenhas 2008).
e. Are these relationships sufficient conditions? [Note: If Y is true, exists, or verifies when X is true, exists, or verifies, then X is a sufficient condition for Y] (Mascarenhas 2008).
f. Are these relationships necessary and sufficient conditions or causal connections?
g. If two or more factors are causally related, are these causal relationships straight-line linear or curved non-linear?
h. Are these relationships unidirectional or multidirectional?
i. What is the magnitude of such relationships?
j. What are the dependent variables in your problem–solution equation?
k. What are the independent variables in your problem–solution equation?
l. What are the residual (unaccountable) variables in your problem–solution equation?
m. Are the relationships between dependent and independent variables linear or non-linear?
n. How can you establish or verify these relationships?
o. Do you have representative and random samples of relevant data or responses to empirically verify these relationships?
p. Have others tested such relationships that you can follow?
q. Are there any theories that you can use to hypothesize these relationships?
r. Are there research streams to enable you to verify these relationships?
s. Are there any strong trends or managerial hunches to support these relationships?
t. Do past data, practices, relations, and trends support the present projected relationships?
u. Do past data, practices, relations, and trends condition the present or future relationships?

v. Are market, cost, scale, price, technology, and innovation discontinuities so strong as to totally force you to reinvent the present and the future relationships between your dependent and independent variables in the problem–solution equation?

In general, real life relations between variables may not be linear, even though the business world assumes them as linear and, conveniently uses linear regression models to predict linear outcomes. One should also check the direction of the relationship and its magnitude. Most real life relationships could be multi-directional and non-linear. For instance, the relationships between pricing, distribution channels, level of sales service and profitability may not always be linear and unidirectional (Martin 2007). [See *Business Transformation Exercises 5.5* and *5.6*.]

KNOWLEDGE, CERTAINTY, RISK, UNCERTAINTY, AND AMBIGUITY

Most of the foregoing questions relate to the domain of a company's "knowledge" regarding the problem and what the company knows and does not know. That is, knowledge is always associated with certainty, uncertainty, risk, and ambiguity. Some systems definitions of these terms are necessary at this juncture of problem specification.

Business problems imply at least three knowledge sets: technological, market-, and business-related. All three are necessary for a successful product/service venture: the first, in producing it, the second, in marketing it, and the third, for both producing and marketing it.

1. **Technological knowledge** is the knowledge of materials, components, parts, and linkages between components, parts, methods, processes, and techniques of production (e.g., designing, casting, fabricating, sizing, packaging, bundling, labeling, and customizing).
2. **Market knowledge** is knowledge of competition and substitution, distribution, logistics, pricing, promotion, channel selection and management, product use and applications, customer expectations, and customer preferences, needs, wants, and desires.
3. **Business knowledge** relates to general economic climate that is largely influenced by macroeconomic indicators such as domestic and international trade, WTO, labor laws, interest rates and money supply, unemployment and wage inflation rates, government policies, and international supply and demand conditions.

Hence, a business problem is associated with three kinds of uncertainty:[1]

1. **Technological Uncertainty**: This is an information gap between what one has and needs regarding materials, components, their relationships, methods, techniques, and processes of production.

---

[1] Uncertainty associated with innovation is primarily *information related*. Uncertainty is the difference between the information you have and the information you need (Galbraith 1974). Uncertainty is " (1) the lack of information regarding environmental factors associated with a given decision-making situation, (2) not knowing the outcome of a specific decision in terms of how much the organization would lose if the decision were incorrect, and (3) the inability to assign probabilities with any degree of confidence with regard to how environmental factors are going to affect the success or failure of the decision …" (Duncan 1972). In this sense, information is merely the negative of uncertainty, or vice versa (Arrow 1974). See also Hart (1986).

2. **Market Uncertainty**: This is an information gap between what one has and needs regarding customers, their needs, wants, expectations, and desires, their price-quality sensitivity, and their satisfaction; regarding distributional channel members, sales force, and retailers.
3. **Business Uncertainty**: This is an information gap between what one has and needs regarding business economy, interest and inflation rates, unemployment and consumer buying power, government policies and new laws.

Each level of uncertainty and ambiguity implies an equivalent level of risk. For instance, technological uncertainty on the production floor entails plant security, product recall, supply chain delays, workers compensation costs, greening, and carbon caps. Market uncertainty in the consumer markets includes demographic shifts, eroding discretionary incomes, changing lifestyles, volatile fads and fashions, brand switching, changing loyalties, and increasingly sophisticated buyer perceptions. Business uncertainty involves emerging markets of China and India, dollar depreciation and other currency fluctuations, gaping trade deficits, merger and acquisition challenges, data and identity theft, liability, and property loss.

Hart (1986) offers a "state of knowledge" spectrum ranging from certainty–risk–uncertainty–ambiguity. One has certainty if one knows all the relevant variables and the relationships between them. One has risk if one knows the variables, but their relationships can only be estimated. One has uncertainty if all the variables are known, but some cannot be measured, and the relationships among others are unknown. Lastly, one has ambiguity if all the relevant variables are not yet identified. For an illustration of these four states of knowledge, see Table 5.3.

Each of these areas of uncertainty implies specific zones of risk. For instance, workers compensation implies rising costs, mounting claims, and workplace challenges, and one must combat risk by finding

TABLE 5.3   Hart's (1986) Four States of Knowledge Illustrated: Certainty, Risk, Uncertainty, and Ambiguity

Can you identify most of the relevant variables?	*Do you have adequate knowledge of relationships among identified variables?*	
	Yes	*No*
Yes	**Certainty:**	**Risk:**
	Exploit certainty by creation, invention, causality, explanation, and control	*Diminish risk by empirical research, hypotheses, theory, experimentation, prediction, estimation, extrapolation, and verification*
	Mostly in some parts of hard sciences like mathematics, physics, chemistry, biology, botany, and zoology	Mostly in economics, business, bio-medics, athletics, social sciences, some parts of physics and chemistry, and all of behavioral sciences
No	**Uncertainty:**	**Ambiguity:**
	Combat uncertainty by discovery, innovation, venture, faith, and hope	*Manage ambiguity by hermeneutics, interpretation, aesthetics, linguistics, and philosophy*
	Mostly in political, religious, theological, organizational, and environmental sciences	Mostly in arts, fine arts, cultural, philosophical, ethical, and moral sciences

Source: Author's own.

ways to develop safer and more productive workplaces. Similarly, supply chain uncertainty includes logistic interruptions, design delays, transportation bottlenecks, tarmac delays, and manufacturing risks, and one can minimize risk by building more reliable and resilient supply chains. Emerging markets currently imply problems of talent-retention, offshore outsourcing, mergers and acquisitions, due diligence, and intellectual property protection, and one must find ways of reducing uncertainty from one's global strategies. [See *Business Transformation Exercise 5.7*]

RAPID LEARNING FROM DELIBERATE MISTAKES

In general, innovation strategies, experimentation, trial and error, site testing, prototype testing, test marketing, market research and feedback, and buying information can reduce some of these uncertainties, risk, and ambiguities. Experimentation, venturing and risk-taking, navigating unchartered seas, exploring "blue oceans" (Kim and Mauborgne 2005) where no competitor has entered, even though all these alternatives may be fraught with risks, errors, and mistakes, can be high roads to reducing uncertainty and improve organizational performance. This is especially true, if our fundamental assumptions whereby we avoid mistakes are wrong. Philosophers of science have long advocated falsification (i.e., disproving a hypothesis and testing new ones) as a legitimate search and fastest way for truth. That is, making mistakes can be the quickest way to discover solutions to a problem. "Sometimes, committing error is not the just the fastest way to the correct answer, it's the only way" (Schoemaker and Gunther 2006: 113).

Companies need to carefully analyze the trade-off between the costs (e.g., expenses incurred) of a mistake and potential benefits of learning from that mistake. Schoemaker and Gunther (2006) encourage executives to make potentially "smart" mistakes when the following conditions are prevalent:

a. The potential gain from learning greatly outweighs the cost of the mistake.
b. Decisions are made repeatedly (e.g., routine decisions of hiring, running ads, assessing credit risks). The idea is that the benefits will be multiplied over a large number of future decisions.
c. The environment has dramatically changed and cannot justify the prevailing assumptions. The environment can change the problem, the context, the assumptions, and the presuppositions.
d. The problem is complex and solutions are numerous. The more complex the problem and the environment, the more difficult it is to define, formulate, and specify the relations between the controllable and uncontrollable variables of the problem, and hence, possibly, would necessitate searching for more alternative solutions.
e. Your organization's experience with the problem is limited. Your unfamiliarity (e.g., because of new products, new markets, new regulations, new competition) with the problem should make you open-minded about it. Making deliberate mistakes at the outset can expedite learning.

A mistake that is deliberately undertaken is an experiment and not a mistake. A decision or an act can be viewed as a mistake from one viewpoint and as an experiment from another. Daniel Kahneman, the Nobel Laureate in economics, identified two levels of thinking, known as System 1 and System 2, to which Schoemaker and Gunther (2006) add System 3 as follows:

- **System 1: Instinctive and intuitive**: Thoughts and actions come to mind spontaneously; these are mostly reflex, internalized, or routine actions that we just do (e.g., driving a car, speaking one's native language, cooking an ethnic meal, running a mom and pop business). This stage could be emotional and loaded with feelings.

- **System 2: Linear, logical, and objective reasoning**: This stage requires conscious effort and attention, analysis and evaluation. An action might be considered a mistake in System 1 but sensible in System 2, and vice versa.
- **System 3: Thinking about thinking**: Challenging conclusions of Systems 1 and 2. Systems 1 and 2 do not guarantee right answers or solutions if they are based on erroneous assumptions. System 3 allows for a deliberate mistake or a unique alternative consideration that may yield better solution to the problem in hand.

Research attests that those who test their assumptions by deliberately making mistakes or undertaking experimentation are faster in finding the better solution to the problem than otherwise. In bringing Craig Mundie, who had founded a supercomputer company that ultimately failed, to Microsoft, Bill Gates noted that, "every company needs people who have made mistakes—and then made most of them" [cited in Schoemaker and Gunther (2006: 115)].

As Otto von Bismarck once remarked, "A fool learns from his experience. A wise person learns from the experience of others."(Schoemaker et al. 2006) In business, especially in the volatile world of e-business and e-commerce, it is a big mistake not to learn everything you can from the mistakes, especially the fatal mistakes, others have made in your business. If you do not learn from their mistakes, you might just repeat them. [See *Business Transformation Exercise 5.8.*]

INTEGRATIVE THINKING

Most of us avoid complexity and ambiguity in decided preference for simplicity and clarity. We simplify where we can because we crave the certainty of choosing between well-defined alternatives and the closure that comes when a decision has been made. We love to adopt the "right" alternative and eliminate the "wrong" ones. We may even defend the chosen model as a better choice. In the process of rejecting "wrong" models, however, we lose the opportunities that the "wrong" models could offer despite their complexity and ambiguity. "By forcing a choice between the two, we disengage the opposing mind before it can seek a creative solution" (Martin 2007: 64). Integrative thinking is a remedy to this dilemma.

After decades of management consultancy, including deanship at the School of Business, University of Toronto, and having interviewed over 50 prominent CEOs and observed and analyzed their decision processes, Roger Martin (2007) proposes his theory of what he calls "Integrative Thinking." The latter is an efficient way of problem-solving. Most of us espouse one solution model that is consistent and profitable. Integrative thinkers, however, feel comfortable considering two or more opposing ideas, opposing models, and opposing solutions. Instead of choosing one "right" model and eliminate the "wrong" ones, integrative thinkers resolve tension between multiple opposing models and ultimately choose a model that is a combination of the features of several models and is superior to all of them. Martin (2007) calls this process of considering and synthesizing several opposing models integrative thinking. It is this discipline—not mere superior strategy or faultless execution—that defines decision-making of exceptional businesses and the people who run them (Martin 2007: 62).

Jack Welch is an integrative thinker. In his early career at General Electric, Welch insisted that each of GE's businesses should be either first or second in its industry. Later, he held an opposing idea that each of these businesses should define their markets so that GE's share was no greater than 10 percent, thereby forcing managers to look for opportunities beyond the confines of a narrowly conceived market.

Bob Young, CEO of Red Hat that sells packaged versions of Linux open-source software, was an integrative thinker. The computer software runs on two models: (*a*) the classic proprietary software model of big players (e.g., Microsoft, Oracle, SAP) that sells customer operating software but not the source code at high prices and fat margins, thus locking customers into purchasing regular upgrades; (*b*) the free software model by which suppliers sell both the software and the source code with modest prices and margins (e.g., most small companies such as Red Hat). Bob Young did not like either of these models.

Buying proprietary software, argued Young, is like buying a car with the hood-welded shut. If anything goes wrong, you cannot fix it. On the other hand, the free-software model operated in a fringe market scraping slim profits with no big potential for market growth. Bob Young repackaged his new product by synthesizing two seemingly irreconcilable business models. He combined the free-software model's low product price with the proprietary model's profitable service component, in the process creating something new—the Linux operating system. Young gave the software free but as something the customer could download from the Internet rather than from the cumbersome CD-ROM. This strategy placed Red Hat firmly on the software market by acquiring scale and market leadership. Red Hat soon generated trust and faith among its customers. What Red Hat sold now was not software but a service. In 1999, Red Hat went public with its first IPO skyrocketing in price. By 2000, Red Hat captured 25 percent of the server operating market and more than 50 percent of the global market for Linux systems (Martin 2007: 63).

Table 5.4 summarizes our discussion on integrative thinking. Integrative thinking works through four related but distinct stages. The first step is determining "salience." We must figure out which factors to take into account. The conventional strategy is to discard as many factors as possible in the first place. Within the company, each functional unit will use its narrow view to decide on what merits consideration. Typically, organizational behavior departments avoid metrics; financial department disregard emotional factors; marketing units will disregard costing, inventories, and receivables.

Integrative thinking considers factors that are significant to those outside the immediate reach and domain of your specializations. The integrative thinker actively seeks the less obvious but potentially relevant factors. The more salient factors we consider the more complexity we may have to face. Integrative thinkers love complexity because it can generate some best solutions. It was by incorporating the day-to-day concerns of corporate Chief Information Officer (CIOs) and their systems administrators that Red Hat defined and captured the entirely new corporate Linux-based market of products and services.

The second step is analyzing "causality." Here we analyze how the numerous salient factors relate to one another. As stated before, we consider all relationships between two or more relevant variables: sequential, association, correlation, necessary conditions, sufficient conditions, joint necessary and sufficient conditions, linear and non-linear relationships, unidirectional and multidirectional relationships, and stable and unstable relationships.

The third step is envisioning the "decision architecture." Having understood the multiplicity of relationships between multiple salient factors, the integrative thinker now focuses on the decision itself. However, decisions could be many. For instance, going for a movie involves many decisions: which movie, which show, which theater, which day, and with whom? Each of these five questions may have many options or restrictions that may affect the order in which you make these decisions. For instance,

TABLE 5.4   Conventional versus Integrative Thinking for Problem-solving

Type of thinkers	Step one: determining salience	Step two: analyzing causality	Step three: envisioning the decision-architecture	Step four: achieving resolution
Conventional Thinkers	Focus only on relevant features. Eliminate non-salient features.	Consider one-way, linear, obvious relationships between two or more relevant variables.	Break a given problem into parts and components, and consider each separately and sequentially.	Make either/or choice; settle for the best available option.
Integrative Thinkers	Seek less obvious but potentially relevant features.	Consider almost all possible relationships between all salient variables: sequence, association, correlation, necessary conditions, sufficient conditions, joint necessary and sufficient conditions, linear and non-linear relationships, single and multiple directions, stable and unstable relationships.	See all related problems with all their salient factors and their inter-relationships holistically and simultaneously, examining how the parts fit together and how decisions affect one another.	Creatively resolve tensions between opposing ideas, solutions, and business models, and thus generate creative combinations with innovative outcomes, and choose the best combination.

Source: Author's own.
Note: See Martin (2007: 60–67).

if you must be back home by 9:00 pm for a business conference call, then this restriction may affect the choice of the show, movie, day, theater, and the companions. Similarly, business models involve many critical decision-making variables. View all of them together, identify the overriding issues, and do not breakdown a problem into independent pieces and work on them separately. See the entire architecture of the problem—how its various parts fit together and how one decision will affect another.

For example, a new product design affects costs, manufacturing, tooling, quality, size, packaging, bundling, market, market share, service, and profitability. Product design depends upon the original idea, concept, and prototype testing and experimenting. Hence, where should you start the decisions-making process, with what variable and why? Much would depend upon the role of a given variable (e.g., design), on variables that precede and succeed it. Much would also depend upon what is most important for your company, say, dominant market share or profitability, and this could determine your decisions-sequence (Martin 2007: 66–67).

The fourth step is "achieving resolution." Decision-making involves many competing choices, such as, should the company be a high-cost and high-quality producer, offer the high-price, high-quality brand or the high-quality but low-cost generic brand, or be a low-quality, low-cost manufacturer. Normal executive training entails weighing the pros and cons of each alternative and then making one choice. One should really think in terms of combination of several choices. Integrative thinking generates more options and new solutions by meaningful combinations of alternatives, all of which minimize unattractive trade-offs. We need "multiple working hypotheses" than the most commonly applied scientific method of testing the validity of a single hypothesis through trial and error. Instead of entertaining several hypotheses in a linear fashion considering one at a time, we need to consider several connected hypotheses, non-linearly, holistically, and simultaneously. This cultivates and generates a simultaneous integrative vision from different standpoints.

The previous three stages, determining what is controllable and what is not, analyzing causal relationships between significant controllable and uncontrollable variables, and examining the holistic architecture of the problem, lead to an outcome, the problem resolution. At this stage, we identify all alternatives to the problem, and assess and choose the best alternative as our solution to the problem. Too often, given our desire for simplicity and our time constraints, we quickly converge on the "best" alternative with all its unpleasant trade-offs. Meanwhile, we ignore opportunities for minimizing trade-offs and for rethinking in interesting and novel ways in the previous three stages. Do not go for "either–or" solutions, advises Roger Martin (2007), but "either and more options" combined to weed painful trade-offs. To take advantage of our opposing minds, we must resist our natural inclination for simplicity and certainty. Best models can emerge from the tensions between opposing models.

An integrative thinker embraces holistic rather than segmented thinking and can creatively resolve the tensions that launched the decision-making process. Such a leader accepts creative delays, sends new teams back to examine things more deeply and differently, and generates new options even at the 11th hour, until most costly trade-offs are eliminated and even unconventional options are considered (Martin 2007: 67). Thus, integrative thinking improves people's odds.

STEP FOUR: PROBLEM RESOLUTION

Given your findings under steps one, two, and three, now do the following:

a. Identify almost all the feasible and viable alternatives to resolve the identified problem.

   - **Feasibility** of an alternative relates to the objective possibility and capability of it being done or used.
   - **Viability** reflects whether the company has resources to implement this alternative.

b. Identify almost all efficient and effective alternatives to resolve the identified problem.

   - **Efficiency** of an alternative to resolve the problem relates to outcomes—for example, generating revenues, reducing costs, meeting obligations, and improving labor relations.
   - Efficiency concerns doing things rightly; but one could do wrong things rightly too.
   - Efficiency supposes thinking that maximizes benefits and minimizes costs.
   - **Effectiveness** of an alternative to resolve the problem relates to selecting good means for realizing good outcomes that are beneficial to all relevant stakeholders.
   - Effectiveness, thus, concerns doing right things rightly.
   - Effectiveness supposes critical thinking that maximizes benefits and minimizes costs to all stakeholders.
   - **Stakeholders within the company** are employees, unions, suppliers, retail partners, other divisions and departments.
   - **Stakeholders outside the company** are customers, creditors, brokers, media, shareholders, and local communities.

c. Present a good comparative analysis of all the identified alternatives in terms of:

- Feasibility and viability.
- Efficiency to resolve the main problem.
- Least net costs to internal stakeholders.
- Least net costs to external stakeholders.
  [See *Business Transformation Exercise 5.9.*]

The foregoing comparative analysis should be objective with no biases or prejudices to any solution. Clearly distinguish between facts, opinions, and value judgments in the selection of the best alternative. Identify your basic assumptions, presumptions, suppositions, and presuppositions underlying the best-selected alternative.

- A "prejudice" implies a judgment or opinion formed before the facts are known. It is a preconceived idea, favorable, or usually, unfavorable, marked by a suspicion, intolerance, or irrational hatred for other races, creeds, and occupations (e.g., anti-Semitism, xenophobia, cultural hegemony).
- An "assumption" is a more basic act of assuming a fact, property, or event for granted without critically assessing its accuracy and veracity, reliability and validity.
- A "presumption" is a subset of assumption and implies taking something for granted or unjustifiably accepting it as true, usually on the basis of improper evidence.
- A "supposition" is the act of assuming something to be true for the sake of an argument or to illustrate a proof. It is regarding something as true without actual knowledge, hence, often tantamount to conjecture, guessing, or mere imagination. In this sense, a supposition is a subset of assumption.
- A "presupposition" is an act or statement of supposing or assuming beforehand. It also means to require or imply as a preceding condition for something. It is a subset of supposition, and hence, of assumption.

The root cause of nearly every business crisis, says Drucker (2006), is not that things are done poorly; it is not even that wrong things are being done. Indeed in most business crises the right things were being done, but fruitlessly. The reasons for this paradox are many. Chief among them, are the assumptions on which the organization was or has been built and is being currently run no longer fit reality. These assumptions shape the organization's behavior, dictate its decisions about what to do and what not to do, and define what the organization considers meaningful results. These assumptions are about markets, about identifying customers and competitors, their values and behavior. They are about technology and its dynamics, about a company's strengths and weaknesses. They are about what a company gets paid for. They are what Drucker calls, a company's "theory of the business." [See *Business Transformation Exercise 5.10.*]

For over 70 years General Motors did well, and its theory of the business worked. In the late 1970s, however, its assumptions about markets and production became invalid. The market was fragmenting into highly volatile lifestyles. Income was just one factor among many in buying decisions. At the same time, lean manufacturing created an economics of small scale. It made short runs and variations in models less costly and more profitable than long runs of uniform products. GM knew all this but could not believe it. It maintained the existing divisions based on income segmentation, with each division "offering a car for every purse." It tried to compete with lean manufacturing by automating the large-scale, long-run mass production system (losing some $30 billion in the process). Meanwhile, GM neglected its real growth market, where it had leadership and was unassailable: light trucks and minivans. GM has never quite recovered from this loss in sales and market share.

Merck's CEO, on the contrary, successfully changed its theory of the business. It ceased from focusing solely on the research and development of patented, high-margin breakthrough drugs, to radically changing its theory by acquiring a large distributor of generic and non-prescription drugs. He did this without causing an internal crisis in Merck. Merck is the world's largest and most successful pharmaceutical business till this day.

Similarly, Sony, the world's best-known manufacturer of consumer electronic hardware, changed the company's theory of the business. The new CEO of Sony acquired a Hollywood movie production company around the early 1990s . With this acquisition, Sony changed its core business from being a hardware manufacturer in search of software to being a "software producer that creates a market demand for hardware."

The validity of your assumptions underlying your business model is the validity of your business model. Hence, check your:

- Assumptions about your core business.
- Assumptions about your core mission and objectives.
- Assumptions about your core business vision.
- Assumptions about your target customers.
- Assumptions about your major competitors.
- Assumptions about your core markets.
- Assumptions about your technologies.
- Assumptions about your core competencies.
- Assumptions about your core product lines.
- Assumptions about your flagship brands.
- Assumptions about your environment and the laws that govern them.
- Assumptions about your employees and their concerns.
- Assumptions about your creditors and bankers.
- Assumptions about your suppliers.
- Assumptions about your distributors.
- Assumptions about your retail outlets.
- Assumptions about your warranties and guarantees.
- Assumptions about your customer service and redress.

Are any of these assumptions affected by your biases and prejudices? Are your assumptions affected by your suppositions and presuppositions? Hence, select the best solution alternative given all your earlier analysis and provide convincing evidence and data to support the selected best solution alternative. [See *Business Transformation Exercise 5.11.*]

Selecting the best solution needs some critical thinking. Critical thinking asks: The best solution is best for whom? To the corporation, its customers, its employees, its suppliers, its creditors, its supporting local communities, or its shareholders? Whose priorities should define the "best" solution? Hence, at this point, we digress to discuss the theory and tenets of critical thinking.

CRITICAL THINKING AND PROBLEM FORMULATION AND RESOLUTION

Recently, there is a surge in understanding and implementing critical thinking in business schools and their curricula. Specifically, critical thinking is invoked in connection with problem definition, identification, specification, formulation, and resolution. We summarize this thinking here.

What is Critical Thinking?

- Critical thinking (CT) is questioning and challenging what you learn.
- CT is letting students question and challenge what you teach.
- The best students are those who never quite believe their professors.
- CT does not reject the data merely because one does not like what the data implies. CT confronts the implications.
- CT does not reject the data merely because it rejects the theory one espouses. CT questions one's espoused theory.
- CT does not reject the data merely because it rejects one's assumptions and presuppositions.
- It questions and challenges one's assumptions and presuppositions.
- It does not reject the theory merely because the data does not confirm it.
- It sifts the data and questions its reliability, validity, and objectivity or veracity.
- It is prepared to revise the theory if the data justifies it.
- It offers everything for the thoughtful consideration of one's students or customers, but not for their blind acceptance.
- CT is independence in reasoning, especially, in one's moral reasoning. You must be able to think for yourself, and then, benchmark your thinking against the consensus of the majority in your society (MacIntyre 1981).

Positive science is a body of systematized knowledge concerning "what is." A normative science is a body of systematized knowledge discussing criteria of "what ought to be." Critical thinking-based business education should be a balanced mixture of both of what is and what ought to be. That is, the is/ought, fact/value, descriptive/prescriptive, and positive/normative dichotomies should be part of the business education vocabulary and the teaching–learning-assessment process.

Each area of risk and uncertainty has its more valuable and more rewarding side, if you can properly manage the advantage of risk using critical thinking and trade-offs balancing. Critical thinking fortifies you with insights to see the advantage in risk that others do not, and accordingly, unlock the opportunities of risk others cannot. In every risk, there is an upside, if you know how to look for it. Critical thinking empowers you with confidence, up and down the organization, allowing you to do things you simply could not do before.

Various Approaches to Critical Thinking

The concept of "critical thinking" is variedly defined in the relevant literature. We select a few thematic views of CT, especially as they relate to turnaround and transformation business problems and resolutions and business education.

Critical Thinking as Making Better Sense of the World around Us

Chaffee (1988) views CT as an active and organized effort to make a better sense of the world around us. Thinking is "our active, purposeful, organized efforts to make sense of the world" (Chaffee 1988: 26). Thinking critically is "our active, purposeful, organized efforts to make sense of the world by carefully examining our thinking and the thinking of others in order to clarify and improve our understanding" (Chaffee 1988: 27).

Thinking is the way we make sense of the world; thinking critically is thinking about our thinking so that we can clarify and improve it. Critical thinking is not simply one way of thinking. It is a total holistic approach to understanding how we make sense of the world and the universe. When we think critically, we are actively using our intelligence, knowledge, and skills to effectively deal with our life's situations and ourselves (Chaffee 1988: 30). Critical thinking involves taking an active attitude toward the situations encountered in life. Thinking critically does not mean simply having thoughts and waiting for things to happen. This would be passive thinking—we would be letting events, others and their thinking control and define us. Watching too much television, for instance, is passive thinking; we allow ourselves to be influenced by the thinking and acting of others. Critical thinking[2] is an active, proactive, and interactive encounter with our world of people, properties, and events.

Critical Thinking as Thinking Critically

According to Paul and Elder (2002), CT is reflective thinking or thinking critically. Thinking critically is reflection—to think back on what we are thinking or feeling. It is thinking *back* on thinking. To think critically is to think carefully about our thinking and the thinking of others. It is a serious study of thinking. It is serious thinking *about* thinking. You become the "critic" of your own thinking.[3] Critical thinking is to improve your thinking. "Critical thinking is the disciplined art of ensuring that you use the best thinking you are capable of in any set of circumstances" (Paul and Elder 2002: 7). Our thinking influences everything we do, want or feel. Critical thinking refuses biases, prejudices or stereotypes, false beliefs, myths or illusions to influence our thinking.

There is what we might call a "first-order thinking" that is our everyday thinking, spontaneous and non-reflective thinking. It contains insight, prejudice, truth and error, good and bad reasoning, misconceptions and ideological rigidities. Critical thinking is "second-order thinking": it reflects on, reconstructs, analyzes, and assesses the first-order thinking (Paul and Elder 2002: 14). Critical thinking is

---

[2] The word "critical" is closely associated with the concept of a threshold or a *critical point*. For instance, in physics the critical point is the point above or below which certain physical changes will not occur. In thermodynamics the properties of the substance at this point are called its *critical constants*. There are numerous other instances of this application of the word critical as "limiting." Applied to business knowledge, critical point would mean a critical threshold beyond which we want the students to emerge free from their "critical constants" of management apathy and malaise, value-hybernation, self-centeredness and individuality to thinking for others, for the 5 billion that are poor in the world and for the masses that our business education or capitalist system does not benefit.

[3] Critical thinking must be distinguished from *literary criticism* that has come down from ancient philosophers such as Plato and Aristotle to modern thinkers such as Francis Bacon, S. T. Coleridge, and T. S. Eliot. As understood by these scholars, literary criticism is a reasoned and systematic discussion of the arts (especially poetry, drama, rhetoric, and oratory) in terms of explaining or evaluating their genres, techniques, and products.

"self-directed, self-disciplined, self-monitored, and self-corrective thinking. It presupposes assent to rigorous standards of excellence and mindful command of their use. It entails effective communication and problem-solving abilities" (Paul and Elder 2002: 15).

Second-order thinking has several traits of a disciplined mind: intellectual integrity, intellectual humility, and intellectual sense of justice, intellectual perseverance, intellectual fair-mindedness, and intellectual confidence in reason, intellectual courage, intellectual empathy, and intellectual autonomy. In contrast, the traits of an undisciplined mind are: intellectual hypocrisy, intellectual arrogance, intellectual unfairness, intellectual laziness, intellectual disregard for justice, intellectual distrust of reason, intellectual cowardice, intellectual self-centeredness, and intellectual conformity (Paul and Elder 2002: 19–20). See Table 5.5 for definitions and applications of these opposite traits. [See *Business Transformation Exercise 5.12*]

Critical Thinking as Thinking that Challenges

According to Collins (2001), CT is questioning and challenging what you learn. Critical thinking is letting students question and challenge what you teach. The best students are those who never quite believe their professors (Collins 2001: 16).

Critical thinking does not reject the data merely because one does not like what the data implies. CT confronts the implications. CT does not reject the data merely because it rejects the theory one espouses. CT questions one's espoused theory. CT does not reject the data merely because it rejects one's assumptions and presuppositions. CT questions and challenges one's assumptions and presuppositions about oneself, the society, and the world.

Critical thinking does not reject the theory merely because the data does not confirm it. CT sifts the data and questions its reliability, validity, and objectivity or veracity. CT prepares us to revise the theory if the data justifies it and does not generalize when there is no evidence to back the generalization.

Critical thinking offers everything for the thoughtful consideration of one's students, not for their blind acceptance. In CT, the teacher is the lawyer that presents and argues from the facts, figures, and events objectively. It lets the students be the jury or the judge; that is, CT lets the evidence speak.

Critical Thinking as Independence in Moral Reasoning

According to MacIntyre (1981), CT is independent reasoning. He argues as follows: Every art and every inquiry, every action and choice, seems to aim at some good; hence, the good has rightly been defined as that which all things aim (Aristotle 1985). There are different goods corresponding to different arts and sciences. For the doctor's art, it is health, for the economy, it is wealth, and for business turnarounds, it is, presumably, the "happiness or fulfillment of all stakeholders." However, this happiness is multi-dimensional and longitudinal, and thus, should include both the present and the future stakeholders. In fact, Aristotle's concept of eudemonia that results from virtue includes "human flourishing" (Cooper 1986: 89) that lasts throughout one's adult life (Sherman 1989).

"The exercise of independent practical reasoning is one essential constituent to full human flourishing" (MacIntyre 1999: 105). Not to be able to reason soundly at the level of practice is a grave disability; it is also a defect not to be independent in one's reasoning. By "independence" MacIntyre (1999: 105) means, "both the ability and the willingness to evaluate the reasons for action advanced to one by other,

TABLE 5.5 **Traits of Disciplined Critical Thinking versus those of Undisciplined, Uncritical, and Blind Thinking**

Critical thinking as disciplined unbiased thinking		*Uncritical thinking as undisciplined, biased, or blind thinking*	
Intellectual Virtue	Operational Definition and Applications	Intellectual Vice	Operational Definition and Applications
Intellectual Integrity	Holding us to the same standards of evidence and proof to which we hold our opponents. Practice what you preach. Acknowledging and being sensitive to inconsistencies and contradictions in our own thinking.	Intellectual Hypocrisy	Egocentric thinking that imposes standards on others that we do not live by or accept. We preach values and excellence without practicing either. Insensitive to inconsistencies and contradictions in our own thinking but sensitive to those of others.
Intellectual Humility	Being aware of our own ignorance, biases and prejudices, and limitations. Claim to know what we know.	Intellectual Arrogance	Refusing to be aware of our own ignorance, biases and prejudices, and limitations. Claim to know more than we know.
Intellectual Perseverance	Not giving up but working one's way through intellectual complexities despite the frustration involved in the task. Struggling with confusion and unsettled questions till one reaches some insight.	Intellectual Laziness	Intellectual indolence. Giving up quickly when confronted by intellectual confusion and complexity. Low tolerance for intellectual pain and frustration that is called for in understanding others.
Intellectual Fair-mindedness	Intellectual sense of justice and fairness. Objective and unbiased understanding and assessment of others' viewpoints. Giving credit to each one's ideas and insights.	Intellectual Disregard for Justice	Intellectual injustice and unfairness. Unjust assessment of others and their ideas and work; i.e., using different criteria and standards for others than those used to assess one's own ideas and work.
Intellectual Confidence in Reason	Recognizing that good reasoning has proven its worth. Faith in the unbiased reasoning capacity of oneself and others in arriving at truth and certainty.	Intellectual Distrust of Reason	Cognitive nihilism. Belief in the basic irrationality and incapacity of the human mind in relation to obtaining truth and certain principles, connections, and causalities.
Intellectual Courage	Willingness to challenge pet ideas, beliefs, or viewpoints. Willingness to challenge the set ideas, beliefs, or viewpoints of society. Courage to unlearn in order to learn.	Intellectual Cowardice	Fear of ideas, beliefs, or viewpoints that do not conform to our own. Hence, refusal to be challenged. Irrational defense of one's own "sacred" identity rooted in absurd and dangerous doctrines.
Intellectual Empathy	Understanding opposite views. Putting oneself in the place of others in order to understand them, their ideas and values, premises, presuppositions, and assumptions.	Intellectual Self-centeredness	Thinking and attention centered on self. Refusal to understand thoughts, feelings, and emotions of others. Inability to consider issues, problems, and questions from the viewpoint of others.
Intellectual Autonomy	Being an independent thinker; self-authorship of one's beliefs, values, and behavior.	Intellectual Conformity	Being very dependent upon others for one's thinking, ideas, beliefs, and motivations.

Source: Author's own.

Note: Based on Paul and Elder (2002: 17–36).

so that one makes oneself accountable for one's endorsements of the practical conclusions of others as well as for one's own conclusions." One cannot be an independent practical reasoning person without being able to give others an intelligible account of one's reasoning.

At the same time, MacIntyre (1999: 107) insists that practical reasoning is, by its nature, reasoning together with others and generally within some determinate set of social relationships. Some of these relationships may be results of our independent practical reasoning. But to participate in this network of relationships of giving and receiving as the virtues require, we must understand that we may be called upon to give disproportionately more than what we have received, to care for others unconditionally, since the measure of what is required of us is determined in key part by their needs (MacIntyre 1999: 108). This does not necessarily mean that the individual good must be subordinated to the good of the community or vice versa. The common good is not a summation of individual goods, it transcends individual goods; it is a social good, a good of the entire community, which at times may take primacy over one's individual good. An independent practical reasoning should perceive this readily. There are certain social goods that are good for their own sake and not for what they will do to us individually. Thus, acts of generosity, justice, and compassion are done for the sake of others and are worth doing for themselves. It is only through the acquisition and exercise of these virtues that individuals and communities can flourish in a specifically human mode (MacIntyre 1999: 112).

Some ends are subordinate to other and more ultimate ends. The end of prescribing a certain medicine may be to induce sleep, but this immediate end is subordinate to the wider and more comprehensive end of health. But if there is an end which we desire for its own sake and for the sake of which we desire all other subordinate ends or goods, then this ultimate good will be the best good, in fact, *the good*. According to Aristotle (1985), this ultimate good for human beings is the subject matter of ethics and as such cannot be deductively derived from any first principles with some mathematical exactitude but inductively derived from the conclusions of actual moral judgments of good people. Ethical inquiry should start from the actual moral judgments of good people; and by comparing, contrasting, and sifting it can help formulate general principles. This view presupposes that human beings have some natural tendencies for good, and Aristotle founded his ethic on the universal characteristics of human nature. Hence, Aristotle's ethics "presupposes his metaphysical biology"; his account of the good is "at once local and particular—located in and partially defined by the characteristics of the *polis*—and yet also cosmic and universal; the tension between the poles is felt throughout the argument of the Ethics" (MacIntyre 1984: 148).

Critical Thinking as Positive and Normative Science

According to Hunt (2002), positive science is a body of systematized knowledge concerning what is. A normative science is a body of systematized knowledge discussing criteria of what ought to be. Critical thinking, then, should be a balanced mixture of both of what is and what ought to be. That is, the is/ought, fact/value, knowledge/wisdom, relative/absolute, temporal/eternal, descriptive/prescriptive, and positive/normative dichotomies should be part of:

- The business transformation management (BTM) education inputs (e.g., vocabulary, books, articles).
- The BTM teaching–learning process (e.g., inquiry, search, analysis, synthesis, assessment).

- The BTM learnt/internalized outputs (e.g., values, service learning, voluntary hours, meaning and quality of life, ethical and moral behavior, social justice, spirituality, and eternity).

Applied to business turnaround education, CT should deal with three dichotomies: the micro versus macro aspects of turnaround institutions, organizations and markets, their profit versus non-profit orientations, and positive versus normative evaluations. Any institution, organization, or a corporate entity could be analyzed from these three dichotomies. Table 5.6 presents a schema of such an analysis. [See *Business Transformation Exercise 5.13.*]

Critical Thinking as Spiritual Intelligence

According to Stephen Covey (2004), the four magnificent parts of our nature consist of the body, mind, heart, and the spirit that have corresponding four capacities or intelligences: physical or body intelligence (PQ), mental intelligence (IQ), emotional intelligence (EQ), and spiritual intelligence (SQ).

Mental intelligence or IQ is our ability to analyze reason, think abstractly, use language, visualize, conceptualize, and comprehend. PQ is something that happens within our body controlling the respiratory, circulatory, metabolic, nervous, and other vital systems. PQ constantly scans our environment, adjusts to it, destroys diseased cells, and fights for survival. PQ controls and coordinates the function of roughly seven trillion cells of our body with a mind-boggling level of biochemical and biophysical coordination that controls our reflexes, instincts, drives, passions, habits, manual skills, and body routines. PQ manages the entire system, much of it unconscious. EQ is one's self-knowledge, self-awareness, social sensitivity, empathy, and ability to communicate successfully with others. It is a sense of timing and social appropriateness, and having the courage to acknowledge weaknesses and express and respect differences. Abilities such as leadership, successful communications, and relationships are primarily a function of EQ than IQ (Covey 2004: 50–51).

Spiritual intelligence is today becoming more mainstream in scientific inquiry and philosophical and psychological discussions. SQ is the central and the most fundamental of all four intelligences because it becomes the source of guidance of the other three. SQ represents our drive for meaning and connection with the infinite. SQ is "thinking with your soul" (Wolman 2001: 26) and represents the ancient and abiding human quest for connectedness with something larger and trust-worthier than our world and us. Unlike IQ that computers have, and EQ that higher mammals possess, SQ is uniquely human and most fundamental. It stands for our quest for our longing for meaning, vision, and value; it allows us to dream and to strive; it underlies the things we believe in and hope for; it makes us human.

Spiritual intelligence relates to the whole reality and dimension that is bigger, more creative, more loving, more powerful, more visionary, wiser, and more mysterious—than the materialistic daily human existence. While IQ relates to becoming more knowledgeable, PQ to becoming more healthy and strong, EQ relates to becoming more relational and sensitive, SQ relates to becoming a person (Rogers 1961).

High IQ is not enough: brilliance is not necessarily humanizing. High PQ is not enough: athletes, boxers, and heavy weight fighters have it and it does not necessarily humanize them. High EQ is good but not sufficient: it provides passion but not humanity. High IQ may provide vision, high PQ may imply discipline, and high EQ may mean passion. Adolph Hitler had all three but produced shockingly different results (Collins 2001: 69). High IQ, EQ, and SQ is a great combination: Nelson Mandela, Martin Luther King, Jr., Mohandas Gandhi, and a few others had them. High IQ, PQ, EQ, and SQ is a perfect combination. The prophets and patriarchs of the Old and News Testaments are good examples. A contemporary example is Mother Teresa.

TABLE 5.6 The Domain of Transformation Business Executive's Critical Thinking: The Three Dichotomies Model

General business phenomena	General business orientation	General business analysis	Problems, issues, and imperatives for critical thinking
Micro	Profit	Positive	Business transformation mission, goals, and objectives. Business suppliers, creditors, shareholders, and employees. Individual business producer–distributor behavior. New products and services development. Old products/services maintenance and phase out. Packaging, labeling, pricing, and distribution policies. Communication and promotion policies. Product liability and customer redress policies. Trade payables and customer receivables policies.
		Normative	What should a transformation company produce? (Product-mix) What should a transformation company market? (Marketing-mix) To whom should the transformation company market? (Customer-mix) What is an equitable wage or salary? What is a fair executive compensation? What is an equitable price for products and services? What is non-deceptive honest advertising? What is non-deceptive securities-trading? What is a fair trade payables and customer receivables policy?
	Non-profit	Positive	Transformation institutional mission, goals, and objectives. Transformation institutional stakeholders. Transformation institutional offerings and services. Transformation institutional communications and promotions. Transformation institutional dues, pricing, and distribution.
		Normative	What should be transformation institutional mission, goals, and objectives? Who should be transformation institutional stakeholders? What should be transformation institutional offerings and services? What should be transformation institutional communications and promotions? What should be transformation institutional dues, pricing, and distribution?
Macro	Profit	Positive	Transformation industry markets, suppliers, brokers, and distributors. Domestic, international, and global transformation markets, trades and tariffs. Domestic, international, and global transformation labor markets, wages and benefits. Domestic, international, and global transformation media and communications.
		Normative	Laws regarding transformation industry suppliers, brokers, and distributors. Laws on domestic, international, and global transformation trades and tariffs. Laws on domestic, international, and global transformation labor wages and benefits. Laws on domestic, international, and global transformation communications.
	Non-profit	Positive	Federal and state transformation business mission, goals, and objectives. Federal and state transportation and communication transformation infrastructure. National and international transformation sources of scarce resources. International and global transformation communication and transportation networks.
		Normative	What should be federal and state mission, goals, and objectives for transformation? What is an equitable interstate transportation and communication transformation infrastructure? What is an equitable distribution of national, international, and global non-renewable transformation sources of scarce resources? What is an ethical and educative international and global transformation media and communication network?

Source: Author's own.

Note: See also Hunt (1991: 10–11).

Table 5.7 compares various views of CT of representative thinkers discussed thus far. While creative thinking is generative thinking and divergent thinking, CT is evaluative thinking and convergent thinking (Couger 1995: 154–56). Creative thinking is not logical thinking.

According to de Bono (1970, 1976), logical thinking impedes creative thinking because the former follows the most obvious line of thought. Often, logical thinking represents our past experiences of tried and true methods, but most new problems demand new and fresh creative thinking.

Ruggiero (1990) lists several behaviors/attitudes that can impair one's CT:

- **Mine is Better**: Undue preference of one's own idea.
- **Resistance to Change**: Preferring old (status quo) and familiar to new and unfamiliar ideas.
- **Conformity**: Thinking the way others do. Conversely, thinking the way others do not, simply because they do not.
- **Face Saving**: Attempting to preserve your self-image or the image you project to others via pretenses and excuses.
- **Stereotyping**: Making fixed and unflattering generalizations about people, places, and things.
- **Oversimplification**: Distorting reality to oversimplify it. This is different from scaling down complex problems to manageable proportions.
- **Hasty Conclusions**: Judgments made before sufficient evidence and deliberation.
- **Unwarranted Assumptions**: Ideas and facts you take for granted without questioning them. They unduly influence your thinking.
- **Logical Fallacies**: Specific logical errors that contaminate your reasoning (e.g., false generalization from inadequate sampling; sequence, hence, cause; strong correlation, hence, causation; necessary, therefore sufficient condition).

Parnes (1981) offers the following guidelines for divergent thinking (see also Couger 1995: 124–25):

- **Defer Judgment**: Deferring judgmental evaluations encourages thinking up, sharing ideas, and building ideas. Avoid criticism in brainstorming.
- **Quantity Breeds Quality**: The higher the number of productive ideas, the higher is the probability that some good ideas will reach the innovation and market stages. The best way to have a good idea is to have lots of ideas. Generate many new ideas via spontaneous "associative thinking."
- **Hitchhiking is Good**: Piggybacking on another person's idea generates additional ideas.
- **Combine and Modify Ideas**: Combine ideas of others; make new connections; build on previous ideas.
- **Think in Pictures**: Use all five senses in thinking; smell, feel, taste, hear, and see your ideas. Use imagination (comes from the word "image" making) to fertilize ideas.
- **Stretch for Ideas**: Surprise by extending brainstorming time for generating more ideas, especially if the going is good.

Hierarchy in Critical Thinking

Edward de Bono (1976: 84) argues that the best form of thinking is problem-solving, the attempted achievement of some end. He believes that thinking must be viewed within the "educational trinity of

TABLE 5.7 Synthesizing Various Definitions of Critical Thinking

Definition of critical thinking	Inputs to critical thinking	Process to critical thinking	Outputs to critical thinking	Remarks
Making sense of the world (Chaffee 1988)	Our own thinking and the thinking of others about this world.	Active, purposeful, and organized effort to make sense of the world by examining thinking patterns and thoughts.	Clarify and improve our understanding of the world. Active and independent thinking. Receptive to new ideas and evidence.	Epistemological approach to thought and truth about the world. Restrictive to this world—a cosmological inquiry.
Thinking critically (Paul and Elder 2002)	Our thinking and the thinking of others. First-order thinking.	Reflection—to think back on what we are thinking or feeling. Second-order thinking.	Serious study of thinking. To be a critic of our own thinking. Unbiased thinking. A disciplined mind.	A cognitive approach to thinking that focuses on the mechanics of good and sound thinking. An ethical treatise on intellectual "virtues."
Thinking that challenges thinking (Collins 2001; Collins and Porras 1989)	What you learn at home, from your peers and teachers, the media and the books.	Questioning and challenging what you learn, its premises and principles, assumptions and prejudices. No blind acceptance. Let evidence speak.	Updated and revised facts, events data and information, and hence, revised theory and knowledge, laws and generalizations.	A verification–falsification based methodological approach to findings and theory.
Independent moral reasoning (MacIntyre 1981)	Good childhood, good upbringing, good education, good sense of values and being good.	Training in logical and moral reasoning, training in the concept of good and values, and benchmarking our thinking with moral consensus of elders.	Intellectual and moral virtues; thinking for oneself; confidence in moral reasoning. Common good may occasionally take primacy over private good.	A moral and virtue-ethics approach to critical thinking. Could be a good starting point for ethical thinking.
Positive–normative thinking (Hunt 1991, 2002)	Organizational practices that are micro or macro, profit or non-profit in nature and content.	Analyzing their positive versus normative content in relation to is/ought, relative/absolute, or descriptive/prescriptive values.	Positive versus normative benefits and values of all human institutions, especially business organizations.	An axiological (value-based) analysis of institutional phenomena and practices.
Spiritual intelligence (SQ) (Covey 1989, 2004)	Physical intelligence (PQ), intellectual intelligence (IQ), and emotional intelligence (EQ) as lived and experienced by individuals and organizations.	An abiding human quest for connectedness with something larger and more trustworthy than ourselves and our world.	SQ as meaning vision, value, and motivations for humanization of our doing, becoming, and being.	A theological and eschatological assessment of human and institutional routines, practices, and orientations. SQ is the source of all critical thinking, including IQ, PQ, and EQ.
Hierarchical thinking	Facts, figures, data, and statistics about our world of subjects, objects, properties, and events.	The hierarchical process of deriving information from data, theory from information, knowledge from theory, values from knowledge, and wisdom from values	Information, theory, knowledge, values and wisdom, in that order of sequence and subservience.	A hierarchy of resources for critical thinking, research methodologies, and building critical thought and wisdom. Real education is a journey of critical inquiry from data to information to theory to knowledge to values and ultimately to wisdom.

Source: Author's own.

knowledge, intelligence, and thinking." Intelligence is an innate quality that may depend upon one's genes, early environment, or a mixture of the two. According to de Bono, thinking is the operating skill through which innate intelligence acts upon experience and is put into action. At one extreme, thinking is impossible without some information on the subject. At the other extreme, perfect information would make thinking unnecessary. In between these two extremes, both thinking and information are required.

Critical thinking distinguishes between:

- **Data**: Facts, figures, events, information, narration, grand narratives, descriptions, and statistics.
- **Analysis**: Interpretation of "data" in terms of looking for connections between data, deriving inferences or conclusions from data, and thus seeking meaning and significance of data.
- **Knowledge**: Based on one's "analysis" of data from various fields, disciplines, and domains one derives intelligent (or empirically verifiable) propositions, hypotheses, and conclusions, and accordingly, frames axioms, propositions, hypotheses, theories, models, and paradigms. Knowledge can grow from theory that is verified by data (deductive: theory to data) or from data that grounds theory (inductive: data to theory), and based on both theory and data to forecasting the future (*inductive–deductive* or *predictive*: from the past to the future).
- **Values**: What are the lasting, enhancing, and humanizing values in data, analysis, and knowledge that will make life better for all? What are also the temporal, degrading, and dehumanizing values that could make life worse for all? What are the permanent, eternal, and transforming values that will transfigure humankind?
- **Wisdom**: Based on data, experience, analysis, knowledge, and values, one finally stores and derives wisdom that discerns what is truth from error and falsehood, right from wrong, good from evil, just from unjust, ethical from the unethical, moral from the immoral, virtue from vice, grace from sin, life from death, lasting values from the ephemeral, and from earth to heaven, time to eternity.

In this connection, De George (1995: 347–49) distinguishes between facts, data, information, knowledge, and understanding.

- **Fact** is defined as "a statement of the way the world is" (p. 347), the way of the world being independent of our knowledge. Any individual may appropriate these facts without depriving anyone else from them. In this sense, facts, information, and knowledge are infinitely shareable. However, the discovery of some facts, collecting and sorting them, often involves time and expense, and this provides a basis for claims to some "facts" as proprietary, at least for a short period of time.
- **Knowledge** can be of facts, known or at times unknown but speculated.
- **Understanding** consists of knowledge that is integrated in some unified way and evaluated.
- **Information** is sometimes used to include data, facts, and knowledge, as when we speak of information systems.
- This information is entered or fed into the (computer) information system by way of codes as numbers, words, letters, and symbols; these are called *data*.

Critical thinking-based turnaround or transformation business education should lead executives and students from data to analysis, from analysis to knowledge, from knowledge to value, from value to wisdom.

Thus, CT should guide and direct the turnaround and transformation executive:

- From data to information via data mining and analysis.
- From information to inferences or knowledge via empirical research, falsification, experimentation, and interpretation.
- From knowledge to values via experience, internalization, and application.
- From values to wisdom via lived experiences and shared values.

Resolving Problems: Choose the Right Means for the Right Ends

Wisdom should be distinguished from cleverness, shrewdness, cunningness, and one's manipulative capacities. All these so-called skills imply taking right steps but to wrong ends. Real wisdom or prudence takes right steps to right ends, especially, those that serve common good. There may be a strategic virtue in doing things rightly; but there is a moral virtue in doing right things rightly. Table 5.8 presents

TABLE 5.8   A Fourfold Typology of Critical Thinking and its Outcomes

	To achieve	
Employing	*Right transformation ends or outcomes*	*Wrong transformation ends or outcomes*
Right Transformation Means	*Critical Thinking to Achieve:* *Knowledge, value, and excellence* *Virtue of wisdom and prudence* *Spiritual intelligence and morality*	*Critical Thinking to Avoid:* *Trickery, chicanery, skullduggery* *Shrewdness, cunningness, street smarts* *Worldliness, vanity, conspicuous consumption*
	Examples: Transformation fortitude and courage Compassion and kindness to stakeholders Fairness, justice to all stakeholders Respecting dignity of all customers Truth and rectitude in all transformations Honesty and integrity in BTM Balance and maturity in BTM	Examples: Collateral damage to stakeholders Corporate bankruptcy to renege labor contracts Transformation service to dominate suppliers Transformation service to manipulate customers Divestitures to cheat the buyers Mergers to kill competition Acquisition to kill competition
Wrong Transformation Means	*Critical Thinking to Avoid:* *Under-informing, misinforming* *Misrepresentation, deception* *Manipulation, Machiavellianism*	*Critical Thinking to Avoid:* *Wickedness, malice, blackmail* *Vice, crime, felony, misdemeanor* *Evil intent, evil scheming, evil doing*
	Examples: Transformation villain's courage Transformation murderer's fortitude Preemptive war against competition Unjust massive labor layoffs Lie to save one's life or the corporation Fraud for better bond ratings Overstating revenues for bank approval	Examples: Avarice and greed resulting in bankruptcy Verbal or physical violence in BTM Counterfeiting competitor goods and patents Indiscriminate plant closings Conspiracy against and murder of opposition Exploitation and oppression of labor Exploitation and suppression of suppliers

Source: Author's own.

a fourfold typology based on choice of good versus evil means to achieve good versus evil ends. Critical thinking should empower all turnaround executives to deploy the right means to right ends.

Using this fourfold CT paradigm, one could easily classify the following behaviors: jobs outsourcing to reduce costs, child labor, sweatshops, employing illegal immigrants, transferring outmoded technologies, forced obsolescence, planned obsolescence, artificial shortages, market gluts, downsizing to improve efficiency but creating ghost towns, bait and switch, deceptive ads, deceptive contracts, dumping, price war, predatory pricing, insider trading, round trip sales, under-disclosure in ads, information overload or over-disclosure in media, hostile takeover, mergers, divestitures, acquisitions, plant closing, declaring insolvency or bankruptcy, executive compensation, greenmail, golden parachutes, and bribing.

One hardly admires "courage" in a villain or "charity" in a thief who donates stolen goods, or "fortitude" in a murderer. In a similar sense, vices such as vanity, avarice, and worldliness are contrary to wisdom, since they pursue wrong values. Vanity sees admiration as the highest value; worldliness pursues good life primarily in terms of wealth and power; avarice seeks money and other money equivalents (such as land, investments, and businesses) as supreme values. [See *Business Transformation Exercise 5.14*]

While facts are common property and cannot be owned, data representing facts may be owned to the extent that a person can collect facts and enter them into the computer as classified and organized data. Data are not owned as tangible objects are owned; but print out of data can be owned to the extent one has collected, organized, and classified them and made available in a package form usable for a given target market. Facts cannot be falsified, but data can be. Data may represent falsehood as well as facts. Such distinctions have legal implications: to what extent can data as mailing lists be (collection of names, addresses, social security numbers, credit card numbers), stored and sorted in computers by an information broker, be owned, and hence, sold as a commodity?

Scientific theories must be both general in scope and formally manageable. Such theories will involve simplifications, abstractions, and idealizations. Hence, CT notes the following:

- The distinctive aim of any scientific theory is to provide systematic and reasonably supported explanations of phenomena.
- The purpose of a theory is to increase scientific understanding through a systematized structure capable of both explaining and predicting phenomena" (Hunt 1983: 10).
- A theory, therefore, is a system of hypotheses, most of which are law-like formulas deductively connected with each other (Suppe 1977).
- A theory is "set of propositions which are consistent among themselves and are relevant to some aspect of the factual world" (Alderson 1957: 5).
- Some of these propositions are "non-observational, from which other propositions that are at least testable in principle can be deducted" (Zaltman, Pinson, and Angelmar 1973: 78–79).
- Theories are systematically related sets of statements, including some law-like generalizations that are empirically testable.
- An extra dimension of a good theory is that its theoretical domain should be large enough to include, explain, and unify as many phenomena as possible (Hunt 1983).

Not all terms or constructs in a scientific theory need to be observable or testable—this is "logical positivism" that is untenable. A modified version of logical positivism is "logical empiricism" that maintains that all abstract or theoretical terms in a theory should be linked to directly observable terms via devices known as "correspondence rules." Even this requirement may be too stringent, and hence, some require just "testability" (i.e., find in some way if they are true or false) rather than "observability" of all terms in statements. However, "while a decent regard for empirical findings is essential in a positive science, empiricism must not be pushed so far as to make attainment of generality in scope and formal manageability impossible" (Cyert and Pottinger 1979: 207). Thus, Zaltman, LeMasters, and Heffring (1982: 107) propose: "Once a general theoretical statement has been made, the next step is to make a deduction and translate it into an empirical statement so that observations can be made and the 'truth' of the statement tested. This testability of a statement is of extreme importance to logical deductive analysis."

According to Godel's theorem (Hofstadler 1979), as a formal system, no theory can be both complete and consistent. Hence, CT turnaround executives will note the following:

- Consistency is the condition under which symbols acquire meanings; consistency seeks to derive true statements.
- Completeness, on the other hand, is the confirmation of these meanings; completeness seeks all true statements.
- Formal theory systems have to balance inconsistency and incompleteness.
- No theory is intended to answer all questions.
- Theories that seek too much comprehensiveness can become so over-extended as to become ambiguous and complicated.
- As a social science, BTM theory can best develop through layered assertions into an integral theory.
- Just as a collection of sentences does not necessarily make a story, nor can a collection of assertions, even when verified, necessarily becomes a theory (Sutton and Staw 1995).

STEP FIVE: PROBLEM RESOLUTION ASSESSMENT

Given all four stages described earlier and the CT that accompanies, one must be now ready to derive the final resolution to the problem and evaluate it. For instance, given various approaches to CT, you must frame and respond to problem-resolution-assessment questions such as:

Will the final solution-alternative selected for implementation:

a. Make a better sense of the world around us? (Chaffee 1988).
b. Minimize biases, prejudices, stereotypes, false beliefs, myths, or illusions that influence our choices? (Paul and Elder 2002).
c. Reject real data because one does not like it or it ill-fits one's pet theory? (Collins 2001).
d. Adequately respond to is/ought and positive/normative dichotomies? (Hunt 2002).
e. Develop the body intelligence (PQ), mental intelligence (IQ), emotional intelligence (EQ), and spiritual intelligence (SQ) of its target customers? (Covey 2004).
f. Represent the choice of right means to a right end?
g. Indicate an advance from data, information, and knowledge to wisdom?

Table 5.9 presents the Boston Consultancy Group (BCG) product portfolio matrix as an alternative way of evaluating the business solution. The solution could be evaluated further by using the grid of strengths and weaknesses vis-à-vis the competitor, as outlined in Table 5.10. That is, given your best solution, do you strengths reinforce and weaknesses diminish in relation to your competitor or your business environment?

TABLE 5.9 Boston Consultancy Group Product Portfolio Matrix

Market demand growth rate for your product or business solution	Relative market share of your product or business solution	
	High	Low
High	Stars: These require substantial cash or energy to sustain high growth and high Relative Market Share (RMS).	Problem Children: These drain your cash or energy; hence either give them up or gain strength via RMS.
Low	Cash Cows: These require low investment to retain RMS; hence cash them quickly.	Dogs: These do not generate cash; hence liquidate or phase out.

Source: Author's own.

TABLE 5.10 Your Business Solution's Strengths/Weaknesses Grid

Assess your business solution or service in terms of its:	Assess your competing solution in terms of its:	
	Strengths	Weaknesses
Strengths	Competition; price war	Opportunities; capitalize them
Weaknesses	Improve yourself or quit	Eliminate your weaknesses

Source: Author's own.

Objectively, one should assess the net costs to internal or external stakeholders in terms of loss of revenues, increased expenses, loss of morale and goodwill, non-compliance with laws and ordinances, ecological hazards, and loss to local communities. The following considerations should help in this regard:

- Correctly assess the efficiency of these alternatives to resolve the main identified problem.
- Correctly assess the ramifications of these alternatives on various stakeholders within the company.
- Correctly assess the ramifications of these alternatives on various stakeholders outside the company.

You should also assess the solution in terms of the goals and objectives that the problem failed to realize. Thus, does the problem resolution:

a. Generate adequate and increasing sales revenues?
b. Generate adequate and increasing market shares?
c. Generate adequate and increasing profitability?
d. Generate adequate and decreasing costs of capital and labor?
e. Generate adequate and increasing return on sales (ROS)?

f. Generate adequate and increasing return on quality (ROQ)?
g. Generate adequate and increasing return on marketing (ROM)?
h. Generate adequate and increasing return on assets (ROA)?
i. Generate adequate and increasing return on equity (ROE)?
j. Generate adequate and increasing return on investments (ROI)?
k. Generate adequate and increasing earnings per share (EPS)?
l. Generate adequate and increasing price/earnings ratio on stock (P/E)?
m. Generate adequate and increasing market evaluation of the firm (MV)?
n. Generate adequate and increasing Tobin's Q ratio (= MV/replacement value of the total assets)?

It is important to assess the problem solution in terms of the consumer and social goals and objectives that the solution failed to realize. Thus, does the problem resolution:

a. Generate adequate and increasing consumer satisfaction?
b. Generate adequate and increasing consumer total experience?
c. Generate adequate and increasing consumer loyalty?
d. Generate adequate and increasing consumer lifetime loyalty and value?

Identify the legal { (e.g., OSHA, EPA, Food and Drug Adminstration (FDA), Federal Communications Commission (FEC), Consumer Product Safety Commission (CPSC), and Department of Justice (DOJ) } ramifications of the best alternative. Legality relates to compliance or non-compliance to existing laws that apply to the selected alternative.
Thus, does the problem resolution:

a. Generate increasingly decreasing consumer complaints?
b. Generate increasingly decreasing producer deceptions?
c. Generate increasingly decreasing producer negligence?
d. Generate increasingly decreasing consumer product liability?
e. Generate adequate and increasing consumer redress when harmed?
f. Generate adequate and increasing consumer safety?
g. Generate adequate and increasing consumer privacy?
h. Generate adequate and increasing consumer quality of life?
i. Generate increasingly decreasing consumer theft and crime?

Identify the relevant ethical issues (e.g., privacy, consumer rights, justice, fairness, equity, wage inequalities, unjust structures) with respect to the selected alternative. Ethicality goes beyond law to mores, customs, ethical codes, international agreements, and imperatives.
Thus, does the problem resolution:

a. Generate increasingly decreasing consumer oppression and injustice?
b. Generate adequate and increasing social ecology?
c. Generate adequate and increasing environmental development?
d. Generate adequate and increasing consumer ethics and morals?
e. Generate adequate and increasing corporate social responsibility?

f. Generate adequate and increasing consumer social responsibility?
g. Generate adequate and increasing consumer justice?
h. Generate adequate and increasing social justice?
i. Generate adequate and increasing consumer distributive justice?
j. Generate adequate and increasing social distributive justice?

Study the moral (e.g., conscience, compassion, human rights and dignity, natural rights and duties, respect for life, religious freedom) dimensions of the chosen alternative. Morality relates to natural and positive rights and duties of all internal and external stakeholders.

Examine the spiritual (e.g., inner harmony and peace, worldview and path, faith in humanity, hope, love, trust, personhood, sacred parenthood, self-sacrifice and generosity) dimensions of the selected alternative on all stakeholders.

Spirituality relates to uplifting and empowerment of the human spirit (personal and social) within and without the organization. [See Steven Covey's "Eighth Habit" or "Spiritual Intelligence" (SQ). SQ represents our drive for meaning and connection with the infinite. SQ is "thinking with your soul." SQ relates to the whole reality and dimension that is bigger, more creative, more loving, more powerful, more visionary, and mysterious—than the materialistic daily human existence.]

CONCLUDING REMARKS: THE BASIC TENETS OF CRITICAL THINKING

Be a critic of your own thinking and what you learn from other sources (e.g., home, classes, courses, books) by asking:

a. Does this thinking and my "best solution" make a better sense of the world? (Chaffee 1988).
b. Does the best solution help me to be unbiased and unprejudiced in my thinking? (Paul and Elder 2002).
c. Does it help me to understand the assumptions and presuppositions behind this thinking? (Collins 2001; Collins and Porras 1989).
d. Does it help me to appreciate the positive and normative content in this thinking? (Hunt 1991; 2002).
e. Does it inspire me with spiritual meaning, vision, value, and motivation to reach out to others? (Covey 1989).
f. Does it help me to rise beyond data, information, and knowledge to lasting values and wisdom? Does it empower me to be a servant leader for others? (Kahl 2004).

Be a risk-taker. Some people are more willing to take risks than others do. Risk-taking should be an attribute of creative managers if they are to encourage creativity and creative problem-solving among their colleagues and charges. The creative-innovative person deliberately and systematically dreams, envisions, and then uses creative problem-solving to turn these images into reality. Creative problem solvers engage in divergent thinking (and not convergent thinking in which they were trained in schools and universities). Most education emphasizes early convergence on one right answer, instead of divergent thinking.

APPENDIX 5.1: THE COLLAPSING SUBPRIME LENDING MARKET

A subprime mortgage is a type of loan granted to individuals with poor credit histories (i.e., poor credit rating with credit scores often below 600–620; inability to prove income), and hence, would not qualify for conventional mortgages. The subprime market judges loan qualification on a number of factors including income, assets, and credit rating. Because subprime borrowers present a higher risk for lenders, subprime mortgages charge interest rates above the prime lending rate. One may obtain a loan from the home mortgage banks for home purchase, home refinance, car purchase, debt consolidation, home equity or improvement.

In addition to having higher interest rates than prime-rate loans, subprime loans often come with higher fees. Unlike prime-rate loans, which are quite similar from lender to lender, subprime loans vary greatly. A process known as risk-based pricing is used to calculate mortgage rates and terms—that is, the worse your credit is, the more expensive is the loan. Other fees include: prepayment penalties that do not allow borrowers to pay off the loan early, making it difficult and expensive to refinance or retire the loan prior to the end of its term. Some of these loans also come with balloon maturities, which require a large final payment. Still others come with artificially low introductory rates that ratchet upward substantially, increasing the monthly payment by as much as 50 percent. Moreover, borrowers often do not realize that a loan is subprime because lenders rarely use that terminology. From a marketing perspective, "subprime" is not an attractive term.

THE STRUCTURE OF THE SUBPRIME MARKET

There are several different kinds of subprime mortgage structures available. The most common is the adjustable rate mortgage (ARM), which initially charges a fixed interest rate, and then converts to a floating rate based on an index such as London Interbank Offering Rate (LIBOR), plus a margin. The better-known types of ARMs include 3/27 and 2/28 ARMs.

ARMs are somewhat misleading to subprime borrowers in that the borrowers initially pay a lower interest rate. When their mortgages reset to the higher variable rate, mortgage payments increase significantly. This is one of the factors that lead to the sharp increase in the number of subprime mortgage foreclosures in August of 2006, and the subprime mortgage meltdown that ensued.

Homeowners may borrow against the equity they have built up in their house using a home-equity loan. That is, the homeowner is taking a loan out against the value of his or her home. A good method of determining the amount of home equity available for a loan would be to take the difference between the home's market value and the amount still owed on the mortgage. The interest rates on home-equity loans are very reasonable—the terms of these loans typically range from 15 to 20 years, making them particularly attractive for those looking to borrow large amounts of money. Perhaps the most attractive feature of the home-equity loan, however, is that the interest is usually tax deductible.

The downside to these loans is that consumers can easily over-borrow by mortgaging their homes to the hilt. Furthermore, home-equity loans are particularly dangerous in situations where only one family member is the breadwinner and the family's ability to repay the loan might be hindered by that person's death or disability or unemployment. Even a 1 percent increase in interest rates could mean the difference between losing and keeping your home if you rely too heavily on this style of loan.

The Demand Side: On the one hand, subprime loans have increased the opportunities for homeownership, adding 9 million households to the ranks of homeowners in less than a decade and catapulting the U.S. into the top tier of developed countries on homeownership rates, on par with the U.K. and slightly behind Spain, Finland, Ireland, and Australia, according to the Federal Reserve. More than half of those added to the ranks of new homeowners are minorities. Because home equity is the primary savings vehicle for a significant percentage of the population, home ownership is a good way to build wealth.

On the other hand, subprime loans are expensive. They have higher interest rates and are often accompanied by prepayment and other penalties. Adjustable-rate loans are of particular concern, as the payments can jump dramatically when interest rates rise. All too often, subprime loans are made to people who have no other way to access funds and little understanding of the mechanics of the loan.

The Supply Side: The Community Reinvestment Act of 1977 and later liberalization of regulations gave lenders strong incentive to loan money to low-income borrowers. In 1978, the Supreme Court decided *Marquette National Bank of Minneapolis v. First of Omaha Services Corp.*, which effectively released consumer credit providers from usury limits, and thereby encouraged the creation of a national, rather than purely local, market for consumer credit. The Deregulation and Monetary Control Act of 1980 enabled lenders to charge higher interest rates to borrowers with low credit scores. That is, innovations in point-of-purchase technology and risk-based credit scoring models permitted lenders to discriminate between high- and low-risk borrowers, and impose fees and finance charges on high-risk borrowers that would have been viewed as usurious in a pre-Marquette world. The Alternative Mortgage Transaction Parity Act, passed in 1982, enabled the use of variable-rate loans and balloon payments. Finally, the Tax Reform Act of 1986 eliminated the interest deduction for consumer loans, but kept the mortgage interest deduction. These acts set the destruction of subprime lending in motion.

Over time, businesses adapted to this changing environment, and subprime lending expansion began in earnest. While subprime loans are available for a variety of purchases, mortgages are the big-ticket items for most consumers, so an increase in subprime lending naturally gravitated toward the mortgage market. According to statistics released by the Federal Reserve Board in 2004, from 1994 to 2003, subprime lending increased at a rate of 25 percent per year, making it the fastest growing segment of the U.S. mortgage industry. Furthermore, the Federal Reserve Board cites the growth as a "nearly ten-fold increase in just nine years."

THE CURRENT CRISIS IN THE SUBPRIME MARKET

Where and what exactly is the current subprime lending crisis? The current crisis in the subprime market stems from several factors. Two major reasons: (*a*) excess liquidity that created a disassociation between perceived and actual risks involved; (*b*) lack of clarity and accuracy of information transmitted through the supply chain. The financial engineering of the deals did help to an extent in spreading the total risk. Unfortunately, however, the reduced transparency significantly increased the information asymmetries in the lender–borrower transactions. In the recent past with high liquidity in the U.S. housing market, mortgage companies extended 95 percent loans on appraiser inflated home prices only to see the prices come crashing down. While, at the same time the monthly payments began skyrocketing for those who got in at low teaser rates. Not being able to afford the unexpected high revised mortgage payments, millions of homes had to be foreclosed, making many hardworking Americans "homeless." The other causes of the crisis include declining home prices, corporate layoffs, increasing mortgage rates, and increases in personal bankruptcies.

Other factors exasperating the subprime crisis include:

- Many lenders were more than liberal in granting loans from 2004 to 2006 because of lower interest rates and high capital liquidity.
- Lenders sought additional profits through these higher risk loans, and they charged interest rates above prime in order to compensate for the additional risk they assumed.
- Consequently, once the rate of subprime mortgage foreclosures skyrocketed, many lenders experienced extreme financial difficulties, and even bankruptcy.
- Recently, the risk/reward relationship has become much skewed in the market, especially in the subprime mortgage sector. Companies originating loans began to decrease lending standards, which made it easier for people with poor credit histories to borrow.

- This is now coming back to haunt the lenders, as rising defaults on these mortgages are severely damaging some businesses, and even causing some to close up shop.
- The U.S. economy is slipping. The latest survey of economists by Blue Chip indicators projects a 1.5 percent growth annually from the fourth quarter of 2007 to the second quarter of 2008. That is, the economy is expected to grow well below the 2.5 percent mark needed to create jobs for all the people looking for work. This downward pressure of wage growth means less purchasing power, less pricing power to businesses, and less paying power to home mortgage owners (Cooper 2008).
- Most mortgage loan companies are embroiled in a complicated loaning process from loan origination to ultimate payback by the borrowers. For instance, the loan originating company may sell the loan papers to another bank that, in turn, may either securitize them or sell them to another bank. This process may pass several hands, each transaction causing the loan to increase in value (owing to commissions that jack the variable rate) and the ultimate borrower may both fail to understand the process and be disabled to get out owing to prepayment penalties. In this connection, the Illinois Attorney General has subpoenaed Countrywide's documents related to origination practices (Hochstein 2007). The entire process augments buyer–seller information asymmetry (Stiglitz 2000).

The combined result of all these multiple factors was utter lending industry chaos and housing market turmoil. Several mortgage lenders (including the giant Countrywide Inc.) declared bankruptcy. The real estate market plummeted. Home foreclosure rates doubled. There is a huge inventory of homes currently for sale on the market, and there is nearly universal decline in home prices.

The subprime-storm is still gathering momentum. At the end of January 2008, the U.S. government announced that the annual economic growth slowed to just 0.6 percent in the fourth quarter of 2007 (indicating a possible recession ahead) as home construction plunged at a 24 percent annual rate. The Standard & Poor's home price index fell 7.7 percent in November from the year before, the biggest decline since the index was created in 2000 (http://www.huffingtonpost.com/tag/subprime-mortgage-crisis).

HOME MORTGAGE STOCK PRICES ARE DOWN

Some of the biggest names in the subprime and related industries are encountering serious problems such as Countrywide Financial (NYSE: CFC), American Home Mortgage (OTC: AHMIQ), Accredited Home Lenders (NASDAQ: LEND), and Thornburg Mortgage (NYSE: TMA). By mid-July 2007, the subprime crisis had already escalated. From July 16 through August 27, 2007, the following stock shares plummeted:

- Countrywide stock went from $34.84 to $19.68, a 46 percent drop by August 2007, to $5 by early January 2008, a drop of over 85 percent from $34.84. They fell 28.4 percent Tuesday, January 8, 2008.
- Accredited Home Lenders plummeted from $13.90 to $5.87, a 58 percent drop.
- Thornburg Mortgage sunk $26.20 to $12.39, a 54 percent drop (down 70 percent at one point).

For perspective, over the same period, the S&P 500 and Dow Jones Industrials Average dropped 5.26 percent and 4.16 percent respectively. Some mortgage companies have even had to shut their doors, the biggest being American Home Mortgage. The company filed for bankruptcy on August 8 citing the recent impact on its liquidity, and problems in the secondary mortgage markets. The share price has dropped 99 percent over July and August 2007.

Countrywide Financial Corporation, a holding company, engages in mortgage lending and other finance-related operations. The company operates in five segments: Mortgage Banking, Banking, Capital Markets, Insurance, and Global Operations. The company, founded in 1969, is based in Calabasas, California. Countrywide has nine million loans in its servicing portfolio. It has 25 percent share of the loan origination market. It has 1,000 offices and 15,000 sales officers in the U.S. Around March 2007, its CEO Angelo Mozilo protested that the massive mortgage company would not be affected by the then growing subprime fears. By January 2008, it was overwhelmed by such fears.

In fact, Countrywide has been at the center of the subprime storm. Because of seven percent of all its borrowers are in default mainly due to the subprime crisis, it reported a loss of 1.2 billion dollars in 2007. The company's market value has dropped from 24 billion to just four billion as of December 2007—a drop of 85 percent in value. There was even a rumor of bankruptcy as an option for Countrywide that the company is fighting (Terris 2008). However, it found a "white knight" in Bank of America. The latter had bought a 16 percent share of Countrywide in Summer 2007 for US$2 billion; it announced in January 2008 it will acquire the rest of Countrywide for US$4 billion (i.e., at only 16.7 percent of last year's value). In the first nine months of 2007, Bank of America originated US$145 billion of mortgages, making it the fifth largest player in the business. With a servicing portfolio of nearly US$500 billion, it ranked sixth in mortgage servicing. This deal with Countrywide would make Bank of America the nation's largest mortgage lender, with a 25 percent share of the origination market and a 17 percent share of the servicing market.

Toll Brothers (NYSE-TOL) announced in a press release on November 8, 2007 that homebuilding revenue in its fiscal fourth quarter declined a hefty 36 percent from last year to US$1.17 billion. It also announced that its backlog slipped 36 percent from the comparable period last year to US$2.85 billion. This is a big setback. It demonstrates that Toll's new home deliveries will most likely be weak for the next several quarters. In addition, Toll Brothers said that gross signed contracts for the period totaled approximately US$693.7 million from 1,073 homes. That is markedly slower than the comparable period last year when it had US$1.12 billion in gross signed contracts for 1,595 homes. This may indicate that Toll Brothers may not be near a bottom as some in the industry have suggested. Finally, management indicated that the average price per unit of the gross contracts signed during the period was $646,000 versus $667,000 in the third quarter of last year. Toll's stock is currently traded right near its 52-week low. That is a big sequential decline and indicates that its core demographic, upscale consumers that have substantial income, are growing more and more reluctant to spend the big bucks on real estate. The only positive is that CEO Robert Toll seems to have accepted reality. His comments associated with the preliminary earnings show that he is now finally aware that the company faces very difficult times ahead.

Apparently, the worst is not yet. It will be awhile before we can fully tell where all the problems are. Accredited Home Lenders seems to be on thin ice. After Lone Star Funds backed out of buying Accredited, the company had to stop issuing home loans, and said it will shut down many of its retail and wholesale operations. Soon after, an announcement came from the CEO, John Buchanan, that he was also resigning. The company is in turmoil, and will have a hard time achieving any stability in its business.

Meanwhile, the other giants are being hit as well. Lehman Brothers (NYSE: LEH), Capital One (NYSE: COF) and HSBC Holdings (NYSE: HBC) have discontinued mortgage operations. We could add Citigroup (NYSE: C), American International Group (NYSE: AIG), Goldman Sachs (NYSE: GS), Morgan Stanley (NYSE: MS), and Merrill Lynch (NYSE: MER) to the list of strong undervalued financials. It is still uncertain whether this will have much broader effects on the economy, but the subprime problems are clearly not as contained as once hoped. When there are bad problems, however, opportunities can also arise. Warren Buffet said the frenzy in the markets is exciting because "dislocations" can occur in pricing.

BUSINESS TRANSFORMATION EXERCISES

5.1 Read Appendix 5.1, update relevant information, and do the following:

    a. Define the problem in the current subprime market. Why is the "system at unrest"?
    b. Is it a market-related problem and why?
    c. Is it a product-related problem and why?
    d. Is it a legal-related problem and why?

e. Is it an environment-related problem and why?

f. Is it a combination of all four (market, product, law, and environment) problem and why?

5.2 Read Appendix 5.1, update relevant information, and do the following:

a. How will you formulate the problem of the subprime market?

b. Using the two-stage problem formulation model of Mintzberg, Raisinghari, and Theoret (1976), reformulate the problem.

c. According to the "anchoring framework" of Kahneman and Tversky (2000) and Tversky and Kahneman (1982), people tend to anchor their judgments on initially presented information, and adjust subsequently arriving information in relation to the initial anchoring information. To what extent does this anchoring trap create buyer–seller information asymmetry in the subprime market?

d. Janis and Mann (1977) discuss two types of irrational attitudes when processing information under stress and anxiety. *Defensive avoidance* is an attempt simply to avoid the problem by ignoring information about it, or the feeling of low confidence with regard to taking effective action, or relying on others for decision. *Hyper-vigilance* is a typical panic behavior where the problem solver acts hastily and makes decision based on insufficient information. How do defensive avoidance and hyper-vigilance explain buyer–seller information asymmetry in the subprime market?

e. Using the Information Processing Model of Newell and Simon (1972), reformulate the problem of the subprime market. How does your reformulation differ from (b), (c), and (d), and why?

5.3 Read Appendix 5.1, update relevant information, and do the following:

a. Identify almost all the relevant variables that cause the problem in the subprime market.

b. Categorize these variables into "controllable" and "uncontrollable" from the company's viewpoint?

c. To what extent are the uncontrollable variables associated with your customers?

d. To what extent are the uncontrollable variables associated with their changing lifestyles?

e. To what extent are the uncontrollable variables associated with cost?

f. To what extent are the uncontrollable variables associated with pricing?

g. To what extent are the uncontrollable variables associated with quality?

h. To what extent are the uncontrollable variables associated with technology?

i. To what extent are the uncontrollable variables associated with the mortgage loan companies?

j. To what extent are the uncontrollable variables associated with the intermediaries?

k. To what extent are the uncontrollable variables associated with competition?

l. To what extent are the uncontrollable variables associated with market demand or glut?

m. To what extent are the uncontrollable variables associated with governments, laws, and ordinances?

5.4 Read Appendix 5.1, update relevant information, and do the following: Categorize variables into "controllable" and "uncontrollable" from the consumer's viewpoint.

a. To what extent are the uncontrollable variables associated with pricing as perceived by the consumers?

b. To what extent are the uncontrollable variables associated with quality as perceived by the consumers?

c. To what extent are the uncontrollable variables associated with technology as perceived by consumers?

d. To what extent are the uncontrollable variables associated with convenience of saving time?

e. To what extent are the uncontrollable variables associated with convenience of saving energy?

f. To what extent are the uncontrollable variables associated with saving anxiety and worries?

g. To what extent are the uncontrollable variables associated with changing fads, fashions, and lifestyles?

h. Hence, correctly identify and formulate the main problem together with subsidiary or embedded sub-problems. That is:

- Identify the various contexts the problem is nested or embedded in (e.g., economic, political, global, technological, social, and cultural).
- Understand the connections and ramifications (e.g., antecedents, determinants, concomitants, consequences) of the problem on these contextual environments.

5.5 Next, understand the relationships between the controllable and the uncontrollable variables of the subprime problem identified and formulated under Business Transformation Exercise (BTE) 5.1 through BTE 5.4. Relations between variables may be just sequences, associations, correlations, necessary or sufficient conditions, and causations. Hence, in understanding relations between your controllable and uncontrollable variables, respond to these questions:

a. Are these relationships just sequences and why?
b. Are these relationships mere associations and why?
c. Are these relationships weak or strong correlations and why?
d. Are these relationships necessary conditions and why?
e. Are these relationships sufficient conditions and why?
f. Are these relationships necessary and sufficient conditions or causal connections and why?
g. If two or more factors are causally related, are these causal relationships linear or non-linear?
h. Are these relationships unidirectional or multidirectional and why?
i. What is the magnitude of such relationships?

5.6 If you were to test the relationships between the controllable and the uncontrollable variables of the subprime problem identified and formulated under BTE 5.1 through BTE 5.5. How will you go about doing the following:

a. What will be the dependent variables in your problem–solution equation and why?
b. What will be the independent variables in your problem–solution equation and why?
c. What will be the residual (unaccountable) variables in your problem–solution equation and why?
d. Are the relationships between dependent and independent variables linear or non-linear, and why?
e. How can you establish or verify these relationships?
f. Have others tested such relationships that you can follow?
g. Are there any theories that you can use to hypothesize these relationships?
h. Are there research streams to enable you to verify these relationships?
i. Are there any strong trends or managerial hunches to support these relationships?
j. Do past data, practices, relations, and trends support the present projected relationships?
k. Do past data, practices, relations, and trends condition the present or future relationships?

5.7 Hart (1986) offers a "state of knowledge" spectrum ranging from *certainty–risk–uncertainty–ambiguity*. One has certainty if one knows all the relevant variables and the relationships between them. One has risk if one knows the variables, but their relationships can only be estimated. One has uncertainty if all the variables are known, but some cannot be measured, and the relationships among others are unknown. Lastly, one has ambiguity if all the relevant variables are not yet identified. Using the illustration of these four states of knowledge in Table 5.3, answer the following questions:

a. What variables and their relations in the subprime market are you certain about?
b. How can you capitalize these certain variables and relations to resolve the subprime problem?
c. What variables and their relations in the subprime market are risky and why?
d. What can you do about these risky variables and relations?

   e. What variables and their relations in the subprime market are you uncertain about and why?
   f. What can you do about these uncertain variables and relations?
   g. What variables and their relations in the subprime market are you ambiguous about and why?
   h. What can you do about these ambiguous variables and relations?

5.8 A mistake that is deliberately undertaken is an experiment and not a mistake. A decision or an act can be viewed as a mistake from one viewpoint and as an experiment from another. Daniel Kahneman, the Nobel Laureate in economics, identified two levels of thinking, known as System 1 and System 2, to which Schoemaker and Gunther (2006) add System 3. In avoiding the present crisis of the subprime market how could the market have learned from these systems?

   - *System 1: Instinctive and intuitive*: Thoughts and actions come to mind spontaneously; these are mostly reflex, internalized, or routine actions that we just do. This stage could be emotional and loaded with feelings.
   - *System 2: Linear, logical, and objective reasoning*: This stage requires conscious effort and attention, analysis and evaluation. An action might be considered a mistake in System 1 but sensible in System 2, and vice versa.
   - *System 3: Thinking about thinking:* Challenging conclusions of Systems 1 and 2. Systems 1 and 2 do not guarantee right answers or solutions if they are based on erroneous assumptions. System 3 allows for a deliberate mistake or a unique alternative consideration that may yield better solution to the problem in hand.
      a. Research attests that those who test their assumptions by deliberately making mistakes or undertaking experimentation are faster in finding the better solution to the problem than otherwise. How could, for example, Countrywide undertake experimentation to avoid the chaos it is in currently?
      b. "A fool learns from his experience. A wise person learns from the experience of others" (von Bismarck). In business, especially in the volatile world of subprime markets, it is a big mistake not to learn everything you can from the mistakes others have made in your business. How could, for example, Countrywide have learnt from the mistakes of others?

5.9 In relation to the subprime problem, identify all efficient and effective alternatives to the present cumbersome and corrupted mortgage loan system, by examining the following parameters:

   a. *Feasibility* relates to possibility and capability of being done or used.
   b. *Viability* reflects whether the company has resources to implement this alternative.
   c. *Efficiency* of an alternative to resolve the problem relates to outcomes—for example, generating revenues, reducing costs, meeting obligations, improving labor relations.
   d. Efficiency concerns doing things rightly; but one could do wrong things rightly too.
   e. Efficiency supposes thinking that maximizes benefits and minimizes costs.
   f. *Effectiveness* of an alternative to resolve the problem relates to good means for realizing good outcomes that are beneficial to all relevant stakeholders.
   g. Effectiveness, on the other hand, concerns doing right things rightly.
   h. Effectiveness supposes critical thinking that maximizes benefits and minimizes costs to all stakeholders.

5.10 An objective resolution of the subprime crisis should be one with no biases or prejudices to any solution. Hence, clearly distinguish between facts, opinions, and value judgments in the selection of the best alternative. Identify your basic assumptions, presumptions, suppositions, and presuppositions underlying the best-selected alternative.

a. A *prejudice* implies a judgment or opinion formed before the facts are known. It is a preconceived idea, favorable, or usually, unfavorable, marked by a suspicion, intolerance, or irrational hatred for other races, creeds, and occupations. What are the basic prejudices in the subprime transactions?

b. An *assumption* is a more basic act of assuming a fact, property, or event for granted without critically assessing its accuracy and veracity, reliability and validity. What are the basic assumptions in the subprime transactions?

c. A *presumption* is a subset of assumption and implies taking something for granted or unjustifiably accepting it as true, usually on the basis of improper evidence. What are the basic presumptions in the subprime transactions?

d. A *supposition* is the act of assuming something to be true for the sake of an argument or to illustrate a proof. It is regarding something as true without actual knowledge, hence, often tantamount to conjecture, guessing, or mere imagination. In this sense, it is a subset of assumption. What are the basic suppositions in the subprime transactions?

e. A *presupposition* is an act or statement of supposing or assuming beforehand. It also means to require or imply as a preceding condition for something. What are the basic presuppositions in the subprime transactions?

5.11 The validity of your assumptions underlying your subprime business model is the validity of your subprime business model. Hence, check your:

a. Assumptions about your core subprime business.
b. Assumptions about your core subprime mission and objectives.
c. Assumptions about your core subprime business vision.
d. Assumptions about your target subprime customers.
e. Assumptions about your major subprime competitors.
f. Assumptions about your core subprime markets.
g. Assumptions about your subprime information sharing technologies.
h. Assumptions about your core loan processing competencies.
i. Assumptions about your core subprime product lines.
j. Assumptions about your flagship subprime brands.
k. Assumptions about your subprime environment and the laws that govern them.
l. Assumptions about your subprime salespeople and their concerns.
m. Assumptions about your creditors and bankers.
n. Assumptions about your suppliers.
o. Assumptions about your distributors.
p. Assumptions about your customer service and redress.

5.12 Uncritical thinking is undisciplined, biased, or blind thinking. The collapse of the subprime market may also be attributed to some corporate vices of its major decision makers. In this connection, examine the following corporate vices and how they might have triggered the current subprime crisis in the U.S.

a. **Intellectual Hypocrisy**: Egocentric thinking that imposes standards on others that we do not live by or accept. We preach values and excellence without practicing either. Insensitive to inconsistencies and contradictions in our own thinking but sensitive to those of others.

b. **Intellectual Arrogance**: Refusing to be aware of our own ignorance, biases and prejudices, and limitations. Claim to know more than we know.

c. **Intellectual Laziness**: Intellectual indolence. Giving up quickly when confronted by intellectual confusion and complexity. Low tolerance for intellectual pain and frustration that is called for in understanding others.

    d. **Intellectual Disregard for Justice**: Intellectual injustice and unfairness. Unjust assessment of others and their ideas and work; that is, using different criteria and standards than those used to assess one's own ideas and work.

    e. **Intellectual Distrust of Reason**: Cognitive nihilism. Belief in the basic irrationality and incapacity of the human mind in relation to obtaining truth and certain principles, connections, and causalities.

    f. *Intellectual Cowardice*: Fear of ideas, beliefs, or viewpoints that do not conform to our own. Hence, refusal to be challenged. Irrational defense of one's own "sacred" identity rooted in absurd and dangerous doctrines.

    g. **Intellectual Self-centeredness**: Thinking and attention centered on self. Refusal to understand thoughts, feelings, and emotions of others. Inability to consider issues, problems, and questions from the viewpoint of others.

5.13 Following the Three Dichotomies Model of Hunt (1991), redesign the subprime market by examining the following ethical imperatives:

    a. What should a subprime mortgage loan company produce? (Product-mix)

    b. What should a subprime mortgage loan company market? (Marketing-mix)

    c. To whom should the subprime mortgage loan company market? (Customer-mix)

    d. What is an equitable mortgage rate in a subprime mortgage loan?

    e. What is a fair executive compensation in a subprime mortgage loan company?

    f. What is an equitable price (e.g., fees, penalties) for products and services in a subprime mortgage loan company?

    g. What is non-deceptive honest advertising in a subprime mortgage loan company?

    h. What is a fair customer receivables policy in a subprime mortgage loan company?

    i. What are equitable laws for controlling subprime mortgage loan industry suppliers, brokers, and distributors?

    j. What should be fair laws for domestic, international, and global subprime mortgage loan trading and securitization?

    k. What should be just laws on domestic and international subprime mortgage loan education and communications to customers so that buyer–seller information asymmetry may be minimum?

    l. What should be federal and state mission, goals, and objectives for subprime mortgage loans?

5.14 Table 5.8 presents a Fourfold Typology of Critical Thinking and its Outcomes based on choice of good versus evil means to achieve good versus evil ends. Critical thinking should empower all subprime market executives to deploy the right means to right ends. Specifically, examine the current subprime market crisis and the role of each of the four following types of executive behavior:

    a. **Wisdom and excellence**: Employing right means rightly toward right ends.

    b. **Shrewdness, cunningness**: *Wisdom*: Employing right means toward wrong ends.

    c. **Misrepresentation and deception**: Employing wrong means toward right ends.

    d. **Wickedness and malice**: Employing wrong means toward wrong ends.

Chapter 6

The CEO as a Critical Thinker of "Wicked" Strategic Problems

The industrial age has delivered some dazzling capabilities, including the power to churn out high quality products at affordable prices. It has also trapped us, however, in a tangle of what social planner Horst Rittel called "wicked" problems—problems so persistent, pervasive or slippery that they seem insoluble. Unlike the relatively "tame" problems we find in math, chess, bridge or cost accounting, wicked problems tend to morph and shift disconcertingly when we attempt to solve them. Their solutions are never right or wrong, just better or worse. The world's wicked problems crowd us like piranha: pollution, over-population, dwindling of natural resources, global warming, global poverty, global crime, global disease, technological warfare, and a lopsided distribution of power that has failed to address massive ignorance or Third World hunger (Neumeier 2009: 1).

Increasingly, today's CEOs as strategists face wicked problems for which they are ill-equipped (Camillus 2008). Too often even economic or financial scholars succumb to problem complexity by offering simplistic solutions to incorrectly defined problems (Christensen, Grossman, and Hwang 2009: iv). Wicked problems arise amidst market uncertainty and turbulence, excessive shareholder pressure, undue Securities Exchange Commission (SEC) vigilance and pressure, constant changes in consumer lifestyles, uncontrolled money greed, inordinate attachment to power, unfair labor demands and strikes, credit crunch, and other unprecedented challenges. Most wicked problems imply discontent, discord, confusion, lack of progress, and angst amongst its stakeholders. They involve many stakeholders with different values and priorities and include issues that are complex and tangled. The problem keeps on changing the more you address it; its challenge may not have a precedent, and there may not be a right answer or resolution to the wicked problem. Convergence of industries can also create wicked problems. For instance, the computer industry and the Internet have brought about a radical change in the postal mail, music, sports entertainment, film, TV, radio, telephone, and intellectual property industries. Similarly, computers and Internet have profoundly affected the bio-medic, bio-informatics, and bio-metric industries.

In a 2008 survey sponsored by Neutron and Stanford University, 1,500 top executives were asked to identify the wickedest problems plaguing their companies today. The following list of top ten wicked problems emerged:

1. Balancing long-term goals with short-term demands.
2. Predicting the returns on innovative concepts.
3. Innovating at the increasing speed of change—organizational agility.
4. Winning the war by world-class talent.

5. Combining profitability with social responsibility.
6. Protecting margins in a commoditizing industry.
7. Multiplying success by collaborating across silos.
8. Finding unclaimed yet profitable market space.
9. Addressing the challenge of eco-sustainability.
10. Aligning strategy with customer experience.

In the list, items 5, 7, 9, and 10 reveal concerns that had not shown up on the corporate radar screen until now. They were not the concerns of 20th century managers. The management obsession of the 20th century was Six Sigma, and Dr. Edwards Deming's doctrine of total quality management. That is, most 20th century management concerns dealt with quality. Six Sigma has been so successful that quality has virtually become a commodity. Customers now expect every product and service to be reliable, affording no single company a competitive advantage. Unfortunately, the more progressive elements of Deming's philosophy were all but ignored by a business mindset that preferred the measurable over the meaningful (Neumeier 2009: 2–3).

THE WICKED PROBLEM OF THE GLOBAL FINANCIAL CRISIS OF 2008

Very recently, the Wall Street experienced a horrendous meltdown of one-time stalwart financial companies such as Bear Stearns, Lehman Brothers, American International Group (AIG), Wachovia, Merrill Lynch, Fannie Mae, Freddie Mac, Washington Mutual, and others. Here is a sample chronicle of events that took place during just three days of September 2008 (*New York Times*, Thursday, September 18, 2008, A1):

- Monday, September 15, 2008, a bankruptcy: Lehman Brothers collapses, and Merrill Lynch is sold to Bank of America.
- Tuesday, September 16, 2008, a bailout: The Federal Reserve provides $85 billion to keep AIG out of trouble.
- Wednesday, September 17, 2008, a credit squeeze: Washington Mutual, the largest thrift in the nation, puts itself for sale, and Morgan Stanley and Wachovia engage in merger talks.
- During September 15–17, 2008, the yield on short-term treasury bills plummeted from 1.507 percent to 0.259 percent as nervous investors scrambled for financial safety.
- During the same three-day period, borrowing costs for banks and companies escalated from 2.50 percent to 3.03 percent, fueling the credit crisis.
- The New York Stock Exchange (NYSE) was down on Monday by 4.4 percent, rebounded a little (+1.3 percent) on the news that the Fed agreed to help AIG, and tumbled again on Wednesday by 4.1 percent as the federal bailout failed to stem runaway fears.

Global financial crisis entered a potentially new phase when many credit markets stopped working normally, as investors around the world moved their money into ultra safe investments such as treasury bills (Bajaj 2008). This, in turn, sent the yield on one-month treasury bills from 1.507 percent a week earlier to 0.259 percent, down by almost 53 percent within the space of three business days. Consequently, the cost of borrowing soared for many companies and global financial investment companies like Goldman Sachs and Morgan Stanley, that declared themselves relatively strong a week ago, but came under assault by waves of selling. Less than a week thereafter, both Morgan Stanley and Goldman Sachs who almost faced bankruptcy, requested the federal government for a change of status from investment banks (that served as securities brokers, and under SEC vigilance) to mainline commercial banks (that can do loans and deposits like any other commercial bank, but come under more federal regulatory control).

Meanwhile, the then Secretary of the Treasury, Henry Paulson, in conjunction with the Fed Chairman, was desperately trying to bail out the financial market in crisis. A former CEO of Goldman Sachs, Paulson, accepted this job in 2006 with trepidation. With a lame-duck President and a Democrat-dominated Congress that is reluctant to take risks during the election months, Paulson seized the initiative. Earlier in 2008, he had brokered the compromise between Congress and the White House producing a $168 billion economic stimulus package. He was a point man for the rescue of Bear Stearns in March 2008. Thereafter, he laid out a blueprint to modernize regulation of the financial markets. Early September 2008, he bailed out Fannie Mae and Freddie Mac, each one by $100 billion.

Ripple effects of the collapse of these financial giants have been felt all over Europe, Japan, and the Asian financial markets. While Congress initially turned down a $700 billion bailout deal hurriedly packaged by the Treasury Secretary and the Reserve Bank Chairman, a follow-up deal was crafted by the Senate House and soon voted in. The bailout plan bailed out some of the largest surviving financial companies of the world (e.g., CitiGroup, Bank of America, Goldman Sachs), the trickle-down effects of this bailout, however, are highly dubious and questionable. In short, the entire financial word is experiencing a wicked problem, a distress situation that needs a massive global turnaround.

The financial services industry has posted losses close to $800 billion since July 2007. Giant financial companies are experiencing deep trouble. Table 6.1 presents market-capitalization performance statistics of 17 mega U.S. financial firms. Together, they had a market-capitalization total of over $ 1.6 trillion on October 9, 2007. It quickly eroded within a year, however, to a total of $865.6 billion by September 12, 2008, a total loss of $791.72 billion (47.8 percent), or an average of $46.6 billion per company.

We believe the foregoing problems of crisis in financial markets are not simple but complex, unstructured, involved, circular, iterative, recursive, and often not solvable. In the past two decades, as global markets have grown increasingly competitive and as global connectivity through the Internet has rapidly advanced, the world has seen record numbers of corporations dramatically restructure their assets, operations, and capital resources. In Europe, with the establishment of the monetary union and the adoption of the Euro, high-cost companies can no more hide behind devaluations of their home currencies or pass these costs along to consumers. Furthermore, significant reduction of import tariffs and other export barriers have exposed inefficient high-cost firms to the discipline of the global marketplace (Gilson 2001).

This chapter studies these problems with a new lens or rubric called "wicked problems"—it helps us to redefine, re-characterize, and reframe the new emerging problems of the past two decades for understanding and resolving them more effectively.

PART I: THE THEORY OF WICKED PROBLEMS

In a landmark article in 1973, Horst Rittel and Melvin Webber, both of them urban planners at the University of Berkley in California, defined the notion and domain of what they called "wicked" problems

TABLE 6.1 Shrinking U.S. Financial Giants

Financial firm	Market capitalization in $ billions (October 9, 2007)	Market capitalization in $ billions (September 12, 2008)	Absolute loss in $ billions	Percentage change	Rank in percentage loss of capitalization	Rank in capitalization loss in absolute mumbers
1. Citigroup	236.7	97.76	139.10	−58.7	8	2
2. Bank of America	236.5	150.18	86.32	−36.5	13	3
3. AIG[1]	179.8	32.36	147.44	−82.0	5	1
4. JP Morgan Chase	161.0	142.16	18.84	−11.7	15	13
5. Wells Fargo	124.1	113.18	10.92	−8.8	16	15
6. Wachovia	98.3	30.87	67.43	−68.6	6	4
7. Goldman Sachs	97.7	61.36	36.34	−37.2	12	8
8. American Express	74.8	45.03	29.77	−39.8	11	11
9. Morgan Stanley	73.1	41.08	32.02	−43.8	9	9
10. Fannie May[2]	64.8	0.713	64.09	−98.9	2	5
11. Merrill Lynch[3]	63.9	24.22	39.68	−62.1	7	7
12. U.S. Bancorp	57.8	58.44	+0.64	+1.1	17	17
13. Bank of NY Melon	51.8	45.43	6.37	−12.3	14	16
14. Freddie Mac	41.5	0.291	41.21	−99.3	1	6
15. Lehman Brothers	34.4	2.546	31.85	−92.6	3	10
16. Washington Mutual[4]	31.1	2.892	28.21	−90.7	4	12
17. Capital One	29.9	17.13	12.77	−42.7	10	14
Total	1,657.20	865.64	791.72	−		
Mean	97.48	50.92	46.57	−52.04		
Std. Deviation	65.66	46.59	41.53	32.13		
Range	206.60	149.89	148.08	100.4		
18. Bear Stearns[5]	14.8	−	−	−	Bought by JP Morgan Chase under Federal Insurance	

Source: Author's own.

Notes: Columns 2 and 5 are compiled from *New York Times*, September 17, 2008, C8.

---

[1] Tuesday, September 16, 2008, the Federal Reserve agreed to lend to AIG $85 billion in return for a 79.9 percent stake in the company.

[2] On September 8, 2008, the treasury commits to provide Fannie May and Freddie Mac, each as much as $100 billion to backstop any shortfalls in capital.

[3] Merrill Lynch is forced to find a buyer in Bank of America for $50 billion on Monday, September 15, 2008; the day after, stocks of Merrill Lynch rose by 30 percent and that of Bank of America by 11.3 percent.

[4] Washington Mutual is up for sale, Wednesday, September 17, 2008; TPG Capital refuses to help; meanwhile, Morgan Stanley and Wachovia engage in merger talks.

[5] On March 16, 2008, under much government pressure, JP Morgan Chase agrees to buy Bear Stearns for $29 billion with a federal (FDIC) guarantee.

as opposed to ordinary tame problems. They recognized a new class of problems arising from extreme degrees of uncertainty, risk, and social complexity. They were dealing with social issues such as crime, poverty, and social segregation that were the outcomes of the planned housing projects of the 1950s and 1960s (Senge 1990: 58–59). They recognized that such problems not only do not have clear solutions, they do not have a clear understanding or formulation of the problems they were trying to resolve. They observed that such problems couldn't be resolved with traditional analytical approaches. They labeled them "wicked problems." Wicked problems are inherently social in nature. Rittel and Webber (1973) were the first to introduce the notion of "wicked" in relation to social problems as opposed to "ordinary" problems. A year later, Ackoff (1974) called such problems a "mess," and years later, Horn (2001) called them a "social mess."

Ackoff (1974) distinguishes between puzzles, problems, and messes by stating the following:

- **Puzzles** are well-defined and well-structured problems with a specific solution that can be worked out.
- **Problems** are well-formulated or defined issues but with no single solution—and where different solutions are possible.
- **Messes** are complex issues that are not well formulated or defined.

Complexity comes from the multiplicity of variables involved in a problem (this is "detail complexity"), and from the multiplicity of the interactions that occur between the variables over time (this is "dynamic complexity").

Dynamic complexity arises from many factors such as:

- Causes and effects are subtle, separated in time and space, and the effects of interventions are not obvious.
- When the same cause or action has dramatically different effects in the short run and the long run.
- When an action or strategy has one set of consequences locally and a very different set of consequences in another part of the system or the world.
- When obvious interventions or resolution strategies produce non-obvious consequences.

The current public high school dropout crisis in the U.S.A., teenage suicide escalation, the current credit squeeze, the Wall Street meltdown, the national health care crisis, the home mortgage and foreclosure crisis, and the national domestic unemployment—are all typical examples of dynamic complexity. Conventional forecasting, planning, and linear analytic methods are not equipped to deal with dynamic complexity (Senge 1990: 71).

A Simple Classification of Problems

In general, literature on problems (e.g., Ackoff and Emery 1972; King 1993; Rittel and Webber 1973) distinguishes several basic types of problems:

- **Simple Problems**: Both the problem and the solution are known. This is a problem with a clear goal and one can easily map it onto a feedback loop of method/action and measure/test. These are "tame" problems that are manageable with known algorithms for arriving at correct solutions. The solution presupposes clear user-goals, a bounded solution space, and there is a stopping condition with a right answer. Tame problems allow us to work "inside the box." Problem–solution is a user-centered design. For example: you have a leak under your kitchen sink. The problem is known, and two plumbers will likely agree on what the solution is. Simple problems can be solved in relative isolation from other problems. These problems are "puzzles" (Ackoff 1974). Simple problems lend themselves to a scientific solution and reductionistic thinking (Senge et al. 1994: 14).

- **Complex Problems**: The problem is known but the solution is not. Alternatively, there could be multiple solutions. The goal is not yet clear but it is possible to agree on it, and agreeing transforms it into a simple problem. The major task is to do some planning such that your major stakeholders buy-in into its goals. Resolution presupposes several agreed-on goals. Problem–solution is a multiple user-centered design of planning, agreement, and deliberation. Example: you need to define a higher-capacity disc drive. The problem is clear if you can agree on what is "higher capacity" but understanding how to solve the problem is far from clear. Partial solutions can be derived if we organize ourselves to solve complex problems as tame problems, such as through specialization, departmentalization, compartmentalization, and division of specialized labor, cross-disciplinary approaches, and the like. That is, deriving solutions to complex problems often requires "organizational learning" (Senge 1990).

- **Pseudo Problems**: The problem is not known or formulated, but the solutions are freely generated and marketed. For instance, you "carve out" a piece of a problem, and find a solution to that piece disregarding other pieces of the problem. Such an approach could lead to deception: you deceive the innocent public that such a solution "solves" or "tames" the problem. Deception raises issues of morality—the morality of deceiving people into thinking that something (e.g., a solution) is true, when it is not. This can be a serious moral issue when one deceives the public that something is safe (e.g., a new drug, a new procedure, preventive war) when it is highly dangerous (Churchman 1974). For instance, currently nobody does or wants to formulate the problem of the current financial market precipitous crisis but several bailout solutions are spun and heavily marketed. Similarly, we still fail to formulate the American health care problem that leaves over 100 million citizens either uninsured or underinsured. Nevertheless, different interested groups are offering solutions ranging from a totally privatized health care plan to a totally nationalized health care solution model. More specifically, we have no definite formulation of the cancer problem but we have a multiplicity of beneficial and unproven solutions. In the auto world, we have no clear definitions of the driver or passenger safety problem but have numerous partial solutions (e.g., seatbelts, airbags, or heavier metal doors). Similarly, we have not yet defined the problem of increasing teenager crime and violence in the U.S., but have offered many inefficient solutions (e.g., gun control, more police, metal detectors in schools, juvenile courts, stricter sentencing, and increasing prisons). This procedure is tantamount to what Tukey (1972) described as the Type III error: solving the wrong problem. Therefore, the solutions proposed create further problems or exacerbate the original problem. Successful problem-solving requires finding the right solution to the right problem. We fail in solving problems more often because we solve the wrong problem than because we get the wrong solution to the right problem (Ackoff 1974). Proposed solutions often turn out to be worse than the symptoms. In our turbulent world, it is strategic necessity that we solve the right problems (King 1993) at the right time and in the right place.

- **Wicked Problems**: Both the problem and the solutions are not known. Here, the problem is so complex that there is no definitive statement to it; in fact, there is a broad disagreement of what the problem is. That is, there may not be any agreement on the problem, its nature, its goals, and its consequences among its multiple stakeholders. Obviously, without a definitive statement of the problem there is no definitive solution either. Since the people involved in the problem cannot agree on goals, a wicked problem cannot be converted into a complex problem, unless you reframe the problem and innovate its goals-realization. Stakeholders have multiple viewpoints about the wicked problems, their goals, and their consequences. All may be equally expert or ignorant—which implies a "symmetry of ignorance." The only way to understand the problem is by devising solutions and seeing how they further our knowledge about the problem. This procedure reverses the normal flow of our traditional analytical thinking; with wicked problems, the solution should come before the problem! Any potential problem resolution presupposes consensual sympathy about the different sets of goals. The problem-resolution design implies much teamwork, conversation, dialogue, argument, rhetoric, and deliberation. Team members leverage information and knowledge to create value and consensus. The whole process may be political and ideological. Wicked problems force us to work "outside the box." Problem definition and identification may require much dialogue between the relevant stakeholder teams. We do not really "solve" wicked problems; rather we "design" more or less effective solutions based on how we define the problem.

Table 6.2 characterizes these four problem types. The "wicked problems" that belong to Quadrant IV are presumably unsolvable. Are these objectively unsolvable problems or do they reflect our present incapacity to resolve them, given our current level of scientific, sociological, and technological research advances? If the latter is true, then the problems are wicked in the sense they are malignant or vicious.

Problems, however, rarely fall neatly into nice and clean categories. Rittel and Webber's (1973) classification describes a continuous spectrum, one end of which are simple tame problems, and the other end of each are non-tamable wicked problems. We should not recast wicked problems into tame categories in order to solve them. Treating wicked problems as tame misdirects energy and resources resulting in ineffective solutions, and often, such solutions create more difficulty.

Tame Problems: According to Rittel and Webber (1973), the opposite of wicked problems is a "tame" problem. Tame problems, however, may be quite complex, but they lend themselves to analysis and solutions by known techniques. Traditional linear processes are sufficient to produce a solution to a tame problem in an acceptable period of time, and it is clear when a solution emerges. But this is not true of wicked problems.

In wicked problems the problem statement changes, its constraints keep changing, its stakeholders keep increasing and their goals and targets are constantly moving (i.e., its requirements are volatile), and accordingly, stakeholder resistance to the problem resolutions keeps mounting. Such is the case with current wicked problems such as eradicating global poverty, controlling violence and crime in schools and university campuses, making cars more safe, locating new freeways, prisons and homeless shelters, controlling corporate fraud, saving sub-prime mortgage markets, and bailing out financial markets.

TABLE 6.2   Characterizing Problems

Is there a definite problem formulation?	Is there is a definitive problem solution?	
	Yes	*No*
Yes	**Simple Problems**	**Complex Problems**
	Simple scientific (e.g., mathematical, chemistry, physics, economics, or engineering) problems that have potentially clear problem formulations and equally clear solutions.	Complex or unstructured scientific problems (e.g., bio-social, biochemical, bioengineering, ecological) problems that have potentially clear problem formulations but no definitive solutions.
	Examples: Most trivial problems, puzzles, mazes, and conundrums; most academic undergrad homework problems; most home economics problems; simple business production and growth, and marketing and promotions problems; all game problems such as in chess, bridge, and gambling.	Examples: Stem cell research, abortion, euthanasia, physician-assisted suicide, carbon emissions, water–air–land pollution, same sex marriage, gay rights, personal bankruptcy, corporate bankruptcy, government bankruptcy, widening trade deficit, increasing federal deficit, trade inequities, trade embargoes, international law, international courts, international patent law, and labor law.
No	**Pseudo Solutions**	**Wicked Problems**
	Socially complex or unstructured economic and political problems (e.g., cancer, auto safety, teenage violence) problems that are not formulated clearly but politicians and social activists offer and market several potentially "feasible" solutions.	Socially complex or unstructured economic and political problems (e.g., terrorism, corporate fraud, corporate greed, consumer overspending) problems that have no known clear problem formulations and no known, clearly "viable" and "feasible" solutions.
	Examples: Cancer, HIV positive, autism, Down syndrome, impulse buying, exotic buying, exorbitant executive compensation, price gouging, extravagance, preventive wars, collateral damage, regime change, nuclear détente, nationalization, privatization, balkanization, and command economies.	Examples: Global climate change, tsunami, persistent hurricanes, global peace, global racial harmony, ethnic cleansing, genocide, global poverty, global income inequalities, pandemic disease, global terrorism, Internet pornography, cyber fraud, executive fraud, merchant fraud, consumer fraud, compulsive buying, pathological addictions, avarice and greed.

Source: Author's own.

Given that the problems are wicked (i.e., problem formulation and problem resolution are unknown), and given our current state of knowledge and technology, we may distinguish four situations in relation to the causes and effects of wicked problems:

- **Causes known, effects known**: For example, obesity, HIV positive, aging, home mortgage crisis in the U.S., consumer over-spending, and bad debts;
- **Causes known, effects unknown**: For example, global poverty, global inequality, global diseases, global pollution, global recession, and global inflation;
- **Causes unknown, but effects known**: For example, corporate fraud, cancer, multiple sclerosis, Alzheimer's disease, chronic asthma, teenage suicide in the U.S.; campus violence, gangster

violence, increasing high school dropouts in the U.S., most compulsive addictions, and most natural disasters; and;

- **Causes unknown and effects unknown**: For example, current global financial crisis, global climate change, global terrorism, racial animosity, racial genocide, religious bigotry, and global drug trade.

Typical examples of extended and entrenched socio-political wicked problems are urban planning, degraded city revitalization, entrenched poverty, inner city ghettos, crime prevention and control, wealth creation and equitable distribution, building new expressways connecting populous cities, applying the doctrine of eminent domain, fair trial, fair elections, reforming public education and the health care industry in U.S., creating and maintaining environmentally sustainable communities, reducing drug trade, abuse, teenage pregnancy, abortions, and teenage suicides.

General Nature of Wicked Problems

Most of these problems are linked with horizontal and vertical cross-cutting dimensions, multiple stakeholders, trade-offs between values, and quality of family life. Wicked problems are linked and have ramifications on larger constituencies. Thus, one could link the wicked problem of terrorism to some nations seeking superpower over others. Possibly, we could connect the current wicked problem of health care in U.S. to the inordinate profit-seeking goals of health care systems such as the pharmaceutical companies, health insurance companies, hospital companies, and the medical professions. Most public issues in the world today (e.g., poverty, income inequality, genocide, and global climate change) stem from and create wicked problems of avarice, greed, and exploitation.

Wicked problems, as opposed to simple mechanical problems, are voluble and volatile, stubborn and obstinate, subtle and mysterious, complex and dissensual. Wicked problems are ill defined, ambiguous, and associated with strong moral, political, and professional issues. Since they are strongly stakeholder dependent, there is often little consensus about what the problem is and its solution (Ritchey 2005). Most major public projects today (e.g., constructing freeways, subways, bridges, and industrial parks; offshore oil or natural gas mining; controlling and containing crime and violence in our schools) have a significant wicked component.

In general, and as discussed in Chapter 5, any problem solving process involves six major steps:

- **Step 1: Problem identification**: Solving the wrong problem is Type III error (Tukey).
- **Step 2: Problem formulation**: Identify and specify the critical variables underlying the problem identified under Step 1.
- **Step 3: Problem specification**: Understand the critical relationships between major critical variables identified under Step 2 that generate the problem under Step 1.
- **Step 4: Problem-resolution alternatives identification**: Identify various alternatives that can begin to resolve the problem formulated and specified under Steps 2 and 3.
- **Step 5: Problem-resolution alternatives assessment**: Assess, rank, compare, and contrast the problem-resolution alternatives identified under Step 4 in relation to their efficiency, effectiveness, and comprehensiveness in resolving the problem identified under Step 1.

- **Step 6: Best problem-resolution alternative selection and implementation**: Assuming the resolution alternatives under Step 4 are mutually exclusive and collectively exhaustive (MECE), select the best alternative as judged under Step 5, and set up procedures for implementing it and monitoring the results.

In relation to wicked problems, detail complexity, dynamic complexity, uncertainty, risk, and ambiguity—all arise along all the six steps stated above. The process, far from linear, is highly iterative, and forces going back and forth between all the six steps before the leverage value of any information becomes known. The value of any piece of information along each step remains unknown until the desired outcome is achieved. Wicked problems often deal with complex emerging social market issues such as uncertainty and turbulence, information explosion, cultural pluralism and diversity, social and ethnic anarchy, and multi-racial discrimination. They are also often triggered by structures of social injustice, inequity, and violence. They are indeed "wicked."

Rittel and Webber's Characterizing of Wicked Problems

Rittel and Webber (1973: 161–69) believe that wicked problems have ten characteristics:

1. Wicked problems are not easily definable. One cannot easily formulate wicked problems with a well-defined statement. The problem is hard to define, often including interlocking issues. The information needed to understand the problem depends upon one's idea of solving it. That is, in order to describe a wicked problem in sufficient detail, one must develop an exhaustive inventory for all the conceivable solutions, which could be almost impossible. The process of formulating the problem and of conceiving a solution is identical; that is, the problem cannot be defined until the solution has been found. You do not understand the problem until you have developed a solution. Every solution investigated exposes new aspects of the problem, requiring further adjustments of the potential solution. Proposed solutions may lead to a reformulation of the problem as the latter keeps changing.

2. Wicked problems have no stopping rules. This follows from Proposition 1: If a problem cannot be defined exhaustively, neither can you stop searching for solutions. The search for problem formulation and resolution never stops. This is also because the wicked problem is continually evolving and mutating. The problem-solving process ends when you run out of resources, such as time, budget, funds, grants, and energy, and not when an optimal solution emerges. The focus of the wicked problem changes from one of scientific research, intellectual capital (judged by the articles and books it generates), to social capital (amount of social resources, issues, rights, patents, and royalties it involves) and financial capital (amount of money, stock price increases, and speculative bonds it generates). There are no optimal solutions for wicked problems. There are only "satisfying" solutions—you stop when you have a solution that is "good enough" (Simon 1969), given your resources and that you have done all that can be done. While physical and mathematical problems can be solved, and solved permanently, social problems can only be resolved, and each resolution itself causes further problems. For instance, when does a car become "safe" enough as to stop engineers and physicists researching on car safety? When does an auto become enough pollution-free and optimal in gas-mileage that auto engineers and

ecologists can stop worrying about these wicked problems? When does a nuclear power plant become "safe" enough such that a Chernobyl disaster or a Bhopal spill will never occur in the future? These are not merely design or engineering problems, but they can also become highly political, PR, and social problems. Is it politically correct to stop research on car safety, economy, and pollution? Would stopping to research on these problems make consumers uncomfortable and force them to buy foreign cars? Similarly, when and how can we make our public schools crime and violent free? Because the process of solving a wicked problem is identical with the process of understanding its nature because there are no criteria's for a sufficient understanding of the problem and there are no ends to the causal chains that link interactive open systems, and no finished stage to the formulation and solution of the problem—it is an on-going process.

3. Solutions to wicked problems are not objectively true or false, right or wrong, but only judgmentally better or worse, good enough or bad (not good enough). With no absolute criteria for resolving a wicked problem, a solution agreement may be that it is just good enough. That is, we cannot objectively assess the solutions without considering the social context in which the problems arose. The social context is most often that of multiple stakeholders who create the problem and are equipped, interested, and entitled to resolve the problem. The criteria for judging the validity of a "solution" to a wicked problem is strongly stakeholder-dependent. Different stakeholders judge different solutions as simply better or worse from their viewpoints. Their judgments often vary and so do their goals and objectives for the problem resolution. Formulating and resolving wicked problems is part of a social planning process where the personal interests, value-sets, and ideological predilections of participants play a major role and no one individual has the power to set formal decision rules to determine the correctness of the solution.

4. There is no immediate and no ultimate test of a solution to a wicked problem. With numerous variables involved, no two wicked problems are identical and solutions are not customized. Solutions to wicked problems generate "unexpected consequences" over time, making it difficult to measure their effectiveness. That is, there is no immediate or ultimate closure solution since any solution chosen can generate waves of consequences over extended and unbounded periods of time. "The full consequences cannot be appraised until the waves of repercussions have completely run out, and we have no way of tracing *all* the waves through *all* the affected lives ahead of time or within a limited time span" (Rittel and Webber 1973: 163). Hence, each wicked problem demands a customized solution that addresses its unique, personal, social, cultural, ethical, moral, legal, and political issues.

5. Every solution to a wicked problem is a "one shot operation" as solutions to wicked problems are not learnt by trial and error. Every implemented solution is a "one shot operation" that is, it is consequential and causes ripples of serious intended, unknown and unintended consequences that cannot be undone. Every attempt to reverse a decision or correct the undesired consequences of a previous solution poses yet another set of wicked problems. One cannot build a subway or a freeway to see how it works. This is the Catch 22 about wicked problems—you cannot learn about the problem without trying solutions, but every solution you try is expensive, often irreversible, and has lasting unintended consequences that may spawn new wicked problems. With wicked problems, every resolution is consequential; it leaves ramifications that cannot be easily undone. Most public policies, projects, programs, and works that are large (e.g., building freeways, nationalizing health care, deregulating health care, or deregulating

advertising) have irreversible consequences and the lives of many people are irreversibly influenced by them. These cannot be learnt by trial and error, since every trial counts and has untold ramifications. For instance, the drive in embryonic stem cell research is to cure hitherto incurables diseases. However, the costs may be enormous in terms of personal freedom, privacy, genetic rights, property rights, and human rights of just-conceived human embryos and infants. Consequences cannot take a back seat to the apparent superior value of therapeutic potential of identifying cures.

6. Wicked problems do not have a well-described set of potential solutions. While ordinary problems have a limited number of potential solutions, wicked problems do not have an exhaustively describable set of potential solutions with a well-defined set of permissible operations. We do not have criteria to prove if all resolutions to wicked problems have been identified and assessed. For instance, nobody has identified all possible solutions to crime, terrorism, voter apathy, human mistrust, and merchant or corporate fraud. Often, such problems are ill-defined and hence, generate ill-definable solutions. Nor is there a well-described set of permissible operations that may be incorporated into the implementation plan.

7. Every wicked problem is essentially unique and novel, while ordinary problems belong to a class of problems that one can solve in the same way. No two wicked problems are alike because of the unique social and political context in which they are embedded. A wicked problem may not have a precedent, and experience may not help you to address it. They are unique in their occurrence, context, causes, resolutions, and consequences. Hence, they are not classifiable for the most part. "Part of the art of dealing with wicked problems is the art of not knowing too early which type of solution to apply" (Rittel and Webber 1973: 164). Hence, their solutions are also unique, custom designed and fitted. Wicked problems being unique, their solutions are also unique, and not easily transferable. Wicked problems have only seeming similarities; often, some particulars of the problem override their commonalities. For instance, the problem of constructing a subway in one state or city of the U.S. is not identical everywhere; much would depend upon the differences in residential patterns, business logistics, commuter habits, population densities, labor legacies, geographical conditions, river patterns, subterranean conditions, and the like. Similarly, the problems of health care in England, Germany, France, Spain, Italy, Canada, and U.S. are not the same, nor are the solutions and the contexts in which they occur. Particulars like aging populations, infant mortality, obesity, and levels of addictions in each country may override any commonality of solutions.

8. Every wicked problem is a symptom of another wicked problem with which it is entwined; these problems do not have one cause. Wicked problems are not spawned in isolation; their genesis is often complex social issues or challenges that merge into a new problem. By contrast, ordinary problems are self-contained with traceable causes. For instance, street crime may be a symptom of high school dropouts, peer pressure, gangster groups, boredom in schools, dysfunctional homes, poverty or wealth, general moral decay, permissiveness, lack of police vigilance and action, inadequate laws, too many criminals, too many guns, phrenologic aberrations, cultural deprivation, spatial dislocation, degraded neighborhoods, or their combinations thereof. Each of these symptoms offers a direction for attacking street crime. There is nothing like a natural level of a wicked problem. The higher the level of problem formulation in terms of its symptoms, the more complicated and demanding is its resolution. In addition, many internal aspects of a wicked problem (e.g., crime and violence in schools) can be considered to be symptoms

of other internal aspects (e.g., boredom in schools, non-cooperative parents, dysfunctional homes, peer pressure) of the same problem. Some wicked problems, accordingly, involve a good deal of mutual and circular causality, and the problem must be considered at many causal levels (Ritchey 2005).

9. The cause of a wicked problem can be explained in numerous ways. The choice of explanation determines the nature of the problem's solution. That is, a wicked problem involves many stakeholders who have different ideas about defining the problems and tracing its causes. That is, there is a wide discrepancy in defining a wicked problem. For instance, each symptom of street crime and its degree of perceived severity may alert a different set of stakeholders who champion to attack that symptom. However, multiplicity of stakeholders and multiplicity of explanations reflect the long and difficult process of problem-resolution, but by themselves, such explanations do not imply that the wicked problem cannot be solved. Moreover, the nature of the problem and its solution should determine the choice of explanation. The reverse process is a flawed process that creates wicked problems but not constitute them (Bahm 1975: 105).

10. Executives confronted with a wicked problem have no right to be wrong; they are liable to the consequences of the actions they take to resolve the wicked problems. While scientists may play around with different hypotheses in proving or disproving a theory, social and city planners resolving wicked social problems for governments have no such theoretical luxury. They are expected to get things right at the first shot, as people and businesses rely on their resolution framework. That is, the resolution (e.g., freeways, dams, water reservoirs, airports, or sewerage) must work; the decisions and consequences are irreversible or prohibitively expensive. Unlike a scientist, the planner has no right to be wrong. The aim in wicked problem resolution is not to find the truth (as this may be a long process riddled with controversy), but to improve some characteristics of the world where people live. City and urban planners are liable for the consequences of the actions they take. Thus, depending upon how you state the problem and symptoms of street crime, so is your possible resolution, but you must take responsibility for that resolution. You are not free or immune in formulating and resolving wicked social problems—the social consequences are too serious and irreversible in most cases. For instance, a turnaround executive who elects to shutdown plants and consequent massive layoffs must accept accountability and responsibility for the consequences of his choice.

Much has been written about wicked problems since Rittel and Webber (1973). Table 6.3 summarizes multiple viewpoints in conjunction with Rittel and Webber (1973) characterizing wicked problems.

ASSESSING THE WICKEDNESS OF THE STRATEGIC PROBLEM

Note that even if a problem does not meet all the criteria of a wicked problem, we can still classify it as an "ill-structured" problem (Simon 1969) that is often characterized by a lack of agreement on problem statement, solution paths, and solutions that are plagued with high degree of uncertainty. If it verifies too few of the listed criteria, then it can be categorized differently (e.g., simple or complex). The key characteristic of all wicked problems is that they have a social domain; they involve people, multiple stakeholders, personal goals and objectives that may be mutually conflicting, and involve improving some aspect of the environment in which people live and work (Becker 2007).

TABLE 6.3   Characterizing Wicked Problems: Multiple Viewpoints

Rittel and Webber (1973); Ritchey (2005)	Robert Horn (2001): Social mess	Jeff Conklin (2000)	Roberts (1997, 2000, 2002)
1. Not easily definable; there is no definitive statement of the problem. The problem definition seems vague or keeps changing.	No unique correct view of the problem. Data are often uncertain or missing Considerable uncertainty and ambiguity.	The problem is not understood until after formulation of a solution.	The wicked problems are unstructured; that is, causes and effects are extremely difficult to identify and model, thus adding complexity, dissensus, and uncertainty.
2. No stopping rule because there is no definitive statement of the problem. You do not know when the solution is reached. The proposed solution creates a new, related problem (unveiling boundaries). Problem formulation is not independent of its solution.		The problem is never solved.	Wicked problems are relentless. The number of stakeholders keeps increasing. There are multiple solutions, but no consensus or convergence. Each attempt at creating a solution changes the understanding of the problem.
3. Solutions are not objectively true or false, right or wrong, merely better or worse, good enough or not good enough.	Different views of the problem may lead to contradictory solutions.	Stakeholders have radically different worldviews and different frames for understanding the problem.	There are competing solutions that activate a great deal of discord among stakeholders.
4. No immediate or ultimate test of a solution.			Problems are not solved once and for all. The constraints on the solution keep changing constantly.
5. Solutions are "one-shot" operations as there are no opportunities for trial and error.			
6. The solution set to a wicked problem could be inexhaustible; wicked problems do not have a well-described set of potential solutions.	There are numerous possible intervention points. There are ideological and cultural constraints. There are political constraints. There are economic constraints.	Constraints and resources to solve the problem change over time.	The social and political complexity associated with the problems can be overwhelming. There are many political and organizational issues.
7. Every wicked problem is essentially unique and non-classifiable.			There are no "classes" of solutions that can be applied to a specific wicked business transformation (BT) problem.
8. Every wicked problem is a symptom of another wicked problem.	Most wicked problems are connected to other problems.		The wicked problem space comprises multiple, overlapping, and interconnected subsets of problems.
9. The existence of a discrepancy representing a wicked problem can be explained in many ways; but the choice of explanation determines the nature of the problem.	Wicked problem involve many stakeholders each with multiple value conflicts. Often there is a logical or illogical or multi-valued thinking. Great resistance to change. Problem solvers are out of contact with the problems and potential solutions.		Participants or stakeholders are numerous, with a variety of worldviews, political agendas, cultural traditions, educational and professional backgrounds, and programmatic responsibilities.
10. Problem solvers of wicked problems have no right to be wrong: because each solution has unexpected and irreversible consequences.	Consequences are difficult to imagine; it is impossible to consider all possible consequences beforehand. We cannot know how all the consequences will eventually play out.		Solutions to wicked problems generate waves of consequences. Efforts to solve the problems will have consequences for other policy arenas.

Source: Author's own.

As a quick illustration, Table 6.4 applies the 10 criteria's of Rittel and Webber (1973) to some of the major financial institutions that have experienced crisis recently—this template can initially establish the degree of the wickedness of the problems these companies are facing. As is clear from Table 6.4, each financial firm displays its own intensity of wickedness and hence, the corresponding complexity of an effective solution. Thus, the wicked problem in each failing financial institution is unique and calls for unique analysis, and careful resolutions. A universal bailout solution via the Federal Reserve or the U.S. Treasury may not work as it may generate unintended consequences in the days, months or years to come.

Wicked Problems as Social Messes

We are increasingly facing problems of "organized complexity," that is, clusters of inter-related or inter-dependent problems or systems of problems that Ackoff (1974: 21) called a "mess." Messes are problems that we cannot solve in relative isolation from one another. According to Senge (1990, 2006: 67), a mess is a "complicated problem where there is no leverage to be found because the leverage lies in inter-actions that cannot be seen from looking only at the piece you are holding."

Current examples of messes are: detecting and preventing corporate fraud and organized white collar crime, treating HIV positive and AIDS, manufacturing affordable life-saving drugs, reducing carbon emissions, minimizing traffic congestion in major cities, eradicating entrenched poverty, inner-city ghettos, and structured injustices, eliminating water pollution in lakes and rivers, controlling forest fires, containing hurricane disasters, and the like. We sort these messy problems through "systems" methods, focusing on "processes," cross-functional groups, and interdisciplinary approaches. Rather than break things down into components and fix components as we do with simple or complex problems, in messes we examine the patterns of interactions among parts such as clusters, deviation-amplifying feedback loops, causal loops, vicious circles, virtuous circles, and self-fulfilling or self-defeating prophecies. In understanding and resolving messes, we need a commitment to search for meanings, patterns, inter-actions, and interdependencies between hosts of variables and stakeholders that make messes.

Messes offend our sense of linear logic, the linear syntax of our language, and our continuing belief in prediction, explanation, and control (King 1993: 107). For instance, the problem of safety in nuclear power plants is a mess and not a complex problem. We need new methods of risk assessment and risk management if we are to achieve any significant improvements in the safety of complex, well-defined, socio-technical systems (Reason 1990). Otherwise, we easily seem to overlook things that matter.

When messes enter the socio-political-cultural domain of conflicting interests and multiple stake-holders with different goals, they become "social messes" (Horn 2001). The concept of social messes is relative. For instance, the problem of AIDS is messier than that of smallpox; cancer is messier than Alzheimer's disease; dealing with water pollution is messier than building sewage systems, and building bridges over water is messier than building underwater tunnels, and the like (King 1993). Managers, executives, and administrators must know how to identify and think in terms of messes; they must learn how to sort social messes through complex socio-technical systems. The way we think about social messes matters, and the way we talk about social messes also matters. In tackling social messes, we cannot think linearly looking for unilateral causation, independent and dependent variables, origins and terminations (Weick 1979: 86). We must learn to think non-linearly, in circles, looking for circular causations, interdependent variables and systems, with no defined origins or terminations.

TABLE 6.4   Establishing Wickedness of Current Financial Market Problems

Characteristic of wicked problems	Fannie may	Freddie mac	Lehman brothers	AIG	Washington mutual	Financial markets in general
Not easily definable	x	x	?	x	x	x
No stopping rule	x	x	x	x	x	x
Solutions are not objectively true or false	x	x	x	x	x	x
Solutions have unexpected consequences over time	x	x	x	x	x	x
Solutions are not learnt by trial and error	?	?	?	x	x	x
Solution set could be inexhaustible	?	?	?	x	x	x
Problem is essentially unique and non-classifiable	x	x	?	x	x	x
Symptom of other wicked problems	x	x	x	x	x	x
Involve many stakeholders	x	x	x	x	x	x
Executives resolving wicked problems have no right to be wrong	x	x	x	x	x	x
X totals	8	8	6	10	10	10

Source: Author's own.

On Type I, Type II, Type III, and Type IV Errors

Traditionally, error literature discusses two errors: Type I and Type II. Type I errors (also called Alpha errors) relate to the rejection of statements, hypotheses, solutions, and facts as "false," when they are actually "true." There is loss of market or producer opportunity due to these errors—for example, good ideas are squashed, good business concepts are killed, good inventions are rejected, good innovations are discontinued, good products and services are not brought to the market—typically, a producer error and a "producer risk." Type II errors (also called Beta errors) relate to the acceptance of statements, hypotheses, solutions, and facts as true, when they are actually false. This error implies actual losses—for example, consumers are offered defective products and services; patients are mis-diagnosed, and accordingly, incorrectly treated; markets are overestimated and hence flooded with overstocked products—typically, a "consumer risk."

According to Tukey (1972), a Type III error (we call it Gamma error) takes place when we answer the wrong question or solve the wrong problem. For instance, we avoid answering the question, "What causes this disease?" by answering related narrow questions such as "Why do some people in this population have the disease and not others?" or "Why is the rate higher in group A than in group B?" or "Why is the rate of disease increasing in country A?" It is not that we deliberately avoid the original question on causes of the disease, but that we avoid the question because current advances in epidemiology do not enable us to understand the causal question but only the related narrow questions. Since all statistical methods require variation, research questions are best addressed with data that include substantial variation in the variables of interest. Because variation is often maximal at the individual level as opposed to the population level, factors most frequently examined in epidemiology tend to be individual (Schwartz and Carpenter 1999: 1177).

That is, the problem of Type III errors can arise when methodologies designed to address the latter narrow questions are used to address the first question of causes. That is, we solve the wrong problem owing to the limitations of our current statistical methodologies. Nevertheless, the causes for differences in disease occurrence or disease intensity in different populations are not exactly the cause of the disease itself. Similarly, examining causes of inter-individual differences in risk for homelessness, infant mortality, obesity, and other social problems is not useful for understanding the cause of these problems, because the causes of inter-individual variation in risk for homelessness, infant mortality, or obesity do not appreciably contribute to the current incidence of such problems. Specifically, individual differences between who are homeless and who are not at any point in time may pertain to the question of who "becomes homeless" but not to the cause of the rise of homelessness in the U.S. since the 1980s. Structural factors such as the amount of affordable housing largely determines the "rate of homelessness," and not the cause. Moreover, the causes of between-group and inter-individual variations in homelessness, obesity, or infant morality in ethnic groups may interact, thus confounding the cause of the social disease itself. One could reduce Type III errors, however, by the examination of multiple groups and/or multiple time periods (Schwartz and Carpenter 1999: 1179). While the Type I error leads to producers' risk, Type II error is vexed with consumers' risk, Type III error combines both risks, and leads to "market risk."

Moreover, epidemiology causes work in conjunction to produce diseases. For any particular disease, there may be different combinations of complementary component causes leading to many different "sufficient" causes. For instance, one sufficient cause combination for "stroke" could be chronic stress + diabetes + genetic vulnerability, while a second sufficient cause could be job stress + poverty + high blood pressure, and so on. This is Rothman's (1986) model for understanding causal inferences in epidemiology. Under each sufficient cause combination, the effect size of one factor (e.g., diabetes) would depend upon the prevalence and joint distribution of other two factors (e.g., chronic stress and genetic susceptibility).

We may distinguish a Type IV error—when you solve the wrong problem with a wrong (or right) solution, we call it Delta error. Doing the right thing for the wrong reason can be the worst treason, said T. S. Eliot. The problem identification, formulation, and specification are wrong, and the problem resolution in terms of exploring alternative solutions and choosing the final solution alternative are consequently wrong. Often these errors occur in the context of wicked problems where both the problem formulation and the problem solution are unknown. One needs critical thinking to recognize that these problems are challenging in their identification, formulation, specification, alternative solutions explorations, and the final solution assessment. Table 6.5 distinguishes between Type I, Type II, Type III, and Type IV errors more formally.

Perrow's Characterization of Problems

According to Charles Perrow (1984), there are four types of problems:

- **Type I**: Problems with known outcomes and fixed sequences that make them "deterministic" systems;
- **Type II**: Problems with known outcomes and known probabilities associated with sequences that make them "stochastic" systems;
- **Type III**: Problems with known outcomes and unknown probabilities associated with sequences that make them "uncertain" systems; and

TABLE 6.5 Characterizing Type I, Type II, Type III, and Type IV Error Problems

Dimension	Type I error (alpha error)	Type II error (beta error)	Type III error (gamma error)	Type IV error (delta error)
Definition	Rejection of statements, hypotheses, solutions, and facts as *false*, when they are actually *true*.	Acceptance of statements, hypotheses, solutions, and facts as *true*, when they are actually *false*.	Right answer to the wrong question, or solve the wrong problem with a right solution; hence combination of Type I and Type II errors.	Resolve the wrong problem with a wrong solution. Double jeopardy! The real problem is ignored or postponed.
Normal Source of Error	You do not define the problem clearly; you do not do the right thing.	You do not define the solutions clearly; you do the wrong thing;	You do not define the problem or solutions owing to the limitations of our current statistical methodologies; hence, you do not do the right or the wrong thing.	You do not define or identify the problem correctly; you do the right thing for the wrong reason.
Nature of Errors	Errors of omission	Errors of commission	Errors of omission and commission with the wrong problem; you tackle the symptom of problems and not their causes.	Errors of omission and commission with ignoring or postponing the problem
Systems Thinking Laws that Operate	Law 1: Today's problems come from yesterday's solutions.	Law 4: The easy way out usually leads back in. Law 5: The cure can be worse than the disease. Law 6: Faster is slower.	Law 2: Harder you push, the harder the system pushes back. Law 8: Small changes can produce big results. Law 10: Dividing an elephant in half does not produce two elephants.	Law 3: Behavior gets better before it gets worse. Law 7: Cause and effect are not closely related in time and space. Law 9: You can have your cake and eat it too; but not at once. Law 11: There is no blame.
Psychology of the Errant	You avoid things you dislike. You avoid things you are worse at.	You embrace things you like. You do things you are best at.	You are bound by your likes and dislikes, biases and prejudices	With ignoring the problem, you have no likes or dislikes relative to the problem.
Predominant Type of Mind Traps	Prudence trap Status quo trap Confirming evidence trap	Sunk cost trap Anchoring trap	Anchoring trap Framing trap	Framing trap Anchoring trap Avoidance trap
Domain of Risk	Producers' risk: loss of market or producer opportunity due to these errors	Consumers' risk: actual losses of consumers via producers' wrong choices by way of defective products and services	Market risk: combination of producers' and consumers' risk	Industry and economy risk: serious problems are ignored or not identified or postponed when identified.
Financial Risk	Potential losses from lost opportunities	Actual losses from wrong choices	Actual and potential losses from symptomatic solutions to a wrong problem	Actual and potential losses from ignoring, postponing, masking, or destroying problems
Solution Methodology	Falsification based on variance unexplained	Verification based on variance explained	You explore structures that explain the *intensity* but not the *causes* of the problem; hence, wrong verification and wrong falsification with no causal variance captured.	No verification No falsification Back to square one
Corporate Strategy	Minimize or avoid financial risk or losses	Maximize or embrace financial gains	Act quickly to avoid losses and maximize gains; hence, high chance of solving the wrong problem.	Do not act to avoid risk, uncertainty. And ambiguity.
Long-term Outcomes	Persistent Type I errors · breed inaction, status quo, complacency, and lack of growth.	Persistent Type II errors breed overreaction, sunk costs, product recalls, and consumer disloyalty.	Persistent Type I errors breed inaction, status quo, complacency, and lack of growth	Persistent Type I errors breed inaction, status quo, complacency, and lack of growth.

Source: Author's own.

- **Type IV**: problems with unknown, unanticipated, or unimagined outcomes with unknown probabilities—these are "emergent" systems that are on the horizon.

Conventional methods of risk assessment and risk management apply to Type I and Type II problems. We may understand auto-, home-, and life-liability insurances as Type I and Type II systems with known outcomes and known fixed or probabilistic sequences. On the other hand, safety of high-speed vehicles, carbon emissions, and modern nuclear plants are Type III problems wherein our current level or degree of ignorance is high owing to what Perrow (1984) calls "interactive complexity" and "coupling." Interactive complexity is a measure of the degree to which we cannot foresee all the ways things go wrong—this is because there are too many interactions that we cannot foresee, understand, and manage. "Coupling" is a measure of the degree to which we cannot stop an impending disaster once it starts—this is because we do not have enough of resources, time, knowledge, or technologies to do so.

Other things being equal, the greater the degree of interactive complexity, the less is our capacity to prevent surprises; the greater the degree of coupling, the less is our capacity to cure surprises. The greater the degree of interactive complexity and coupling, the greater the likelihood that a system is a time bomb, or an accident waiting to happen. In the latter case, "operator errors" merely serve as triggers—putting the blame on them for such major accidents such the Chernobyl spill, the Bhopal spill, or any nuclear power plant disaster is a "fundamental attribution error" (King 1993: 108). Such disasters are best described as "systems breakdown" rather than any deliberate "human interventions" (Mitroff and Alpaslan 2003). Increasing our capacity to *prevent* unanticipated interactions among system components entails simplifying systems; increasing our capacity to *cure* unanticipated interactions entails de-coupling major components (e.g., built-in longer times-to-respond).

Type IV problems with unknown, unanticipated, or unimagined outcomes accompanied with unknown probabilities are "emergent" systems that are future challenges. These problems are riddled with unknown sequences with unknown probabilities leading to an unknown sequence of failures or disasters that we cannot control by known methods and technologies. Typical Type IV examples are global climate change, global Arctic drift, global tsunami, continental hurricanes, global terrorism such as 9/11, global financial market crisis such as the current Wall Street meltdown, global hacking, global cyber fraud, global invasion of privacy, and global holocausts or genocide.

A Synthesis of Problems

Table 6.6 maps errors Types I, II, III, and IV to Perrow's classification of fourfold problem types. We assume that all problems, deterministic, probabilistic, uncertain, and emergent, have causes. Some of these causes are known, and hence the problems or effects that arise from these causes are basically tamable. Some of these causes are not known, and hence, the problems/effects that arise from these unknown causes are not easily tamable. The complexity of unknown causes and stochastic or uncertain outcome sequences in any problem arise from several sources: demanding customers, volatile consumer behavior, demographic shifts, strong domestic competition, increasing global competition, supplier constraints, creditor covenant shifts, retailer behavior, employee disenchantment, EPA non-compliance, consumer advocacy, tough government regulation, SEC vigilance, social and political policies, and the like.

All causes have outcomes or effects. Some of these effects are known and some are not known. All outcomes or effects occur in sequences that are known or unknown. Known outcome sequences are either

TABLE 6.6   Toward a Comprehensive Characterization of Problems

Nature of the problem	Problem resolution			
	Outcomes known	Outcomes known	Outcomes unknown	Outcomes unknown
	Outcome sequences are fixed and known	Outcome sequences are probabilistic with known probabilities	Outcome sequences are known with unknown probabilities	Outcome sequences are unknown with unknown probabilities
Outcomes— Knowledge	Deterministic	Stochastic	Uncertain	Divergent/ Emergent
Formulation Known	Simple Problems Type I Problem (Perrow 1984)	Complex Problems Type II Problem (Perrow 1984)	Messes (Ackoff 1974) Type III Problem (Perrow 1984)	Social Messes (Horn 2001) Type IV Problem (Perrow 1984)
Examples	Classroom puzzles Science lab exercises	Most business problems Most medical problems with known diseases and known outcomes	Most socio-political problems with known causes but unknown outcomes (e.g., poverty)	Most medical problems with known diseases but unknown outcomes
Formulation Unknown	Created Problems Type I Error: Rejecting a true problem or solution	Pseudo Problems Type II Error: Accepting a wrong problem or solution	Wicked Problems Type III Error: Resolving a wrong problem; answering a wrong question	Wicked Problems Type IV Error: Resolving a wrong problem with a wrong solution
Examples	Created needs in marketing; products of affluence or extravagance	Treating a wrong disease in medicine, student boredom, employee malaise	Resolving a wrong problem in health care, traffic congestion, teenage violence, or terrorism; most medical problems with known diseases but unknown outcomes	Overkill of a wrong problem that happens in preventive wars, combating terrorism, or global climate change; most medical problems with unknown diseases and unknown outcomes

Source: Author's own.

fixed or deterministic or not fixed with known probabilities, and hence stochastic. Unknown outcome sequences are either uncertain but estimable, or uncertain and not estimable.

Hence,

- given that causes of problems are known or unknown,
- outcomes or effects of problems are known or unknown, and
- given that under each outcome situation, the outcome sequences are known or unknown.

We have a $2 \times 2 \times 2 = 8$ cell situation that provides a more complete taxonomy of problematic situations in terms of puzzles, problems, messes and social messes, and complex puzzles, complex problems, complex messes and complex social messes (or wicked problems). Table 6.7 presents this taxonomy with several examples under each of the eight cells. Table 6.7 assumes that "complexity" primarily occurs when the causes of problems are not known, that is, when the unknown causes of problems make them severely less tamable.

We can map Perrow's (1974) typology of Type I, Type II, Type III, and Type IV problems into Table 6.7 as indicated.

- Cell 1 includes Type I problems that have known causes.
- Cell 2 characterizes Type I problems that have unknown causes.
- Cell 3 best represents Type II problems when causes of problems are known but the outcome sequences are stochastic.
- Cell 4 best describes Type III problems, the assumption being the researcher can trace the uncertain nature of outcome sequences to their unknown causes.

Table 6.7 differentiates four classes of Type IV problems. All Type IV problems are "wicked" (Rittel and Webber 1973), but the degree of wickedness differs depending upon whether the cause of the problems is known (Cells 5 and 7) or not known (Cells 6 and 8), and whether the unknown outcome sequences are estimable (Cells 5 and 6) or not estimable (Cells 7 and 8). Thus:

- Cell 5 represents Type IV "wicked" problems when we know the cause of the problem and we can estimate its outcome sequences.
- Cell 6 represents Type IV "wicked" problems when we do not know the cause of the problem but we can estimate its outcome sequences.
- Cell 7 represents Type IV "wicked" problems when we know the cause of the problem but we cannot estimate its outcome sequences.
- Cell 8 represents Type IV "wicked" problems when we do not know the cause of the problem nor can we estimate its outcome sequences.

Problems in all eight cells imply risk from small to enormous proportions. Risk could be human and personal, economic and political, financial and ecological, social and cultural. The source, nature, size, scalability, and outcomes of risk in each cell are different. For instance, the risk is greater when the causes of problems are unknown (i.e., Cells 2, 4, 6, and 8) than when the causes are known (Cells 1, 3, 5, and 7). Similarly, problem complexity increases as we move from deterministic to stochastic to uncertain to divergent outcomes when the causes of the problem are known (i.e., from Cell 1 to Cell 3 to Cell 5 to Cell 7) and not known (i.e., from Cell 2 to Cell 4 to Cell 6 to Cell 8). In complex puzzles, complex problems, complex messes, and complex social messes, the generic risk primarily arises from unknown causes, but the risk gets differentiated by the specific nature (deterministic, stochastic, uncertainty, and divergence/emergence) of the outcomes. Thus, handling the problem situation in each cell in Table 6.7 requires special critical thinking skills; it implies unique situational dynamics and a future scenario that requires a different strategy with its unique sets of knowledge, skills, and tools.

Given the discussions thus far, we can best anatomize and understand the current financial market crisis as representing problems under each of the eight cells of Table 6.7. We will explore this anatomy in Part II.

TABLE 6.7 A Taxonomy of Problems by Causes and Effects

Causes of the problem	Outcomes (effects) of the problem			
	Known		Unknown	
	Outcome sequences known and fixed, and hence *deterministic*	Outcome sequences known, not fixed, but with known probabilities; hence *stochastic*	Outcome sequences unknown but estimable; hence, domain of *uncertainty*	Outcome sequences unknown and not estimable; hence, domain of *divergence/ emergence*
Known (hence, tamable)	Cell 1: Puzzles (Type I)+	Cell 3: Problems (Type II)	Cell 5: Messes (Type IV)	Cell 7: Social Messes (Type IV)
Examples	Simple treatable diseases Simple cash-flow problems Simple PR problems Simple HRD problems Consumer satisfaction Inventory management Advertising management Promotions management Accounting management Financial management	Plant shut downs Massive layoffs Offshore outsourcing Employee motivation Union management Costing management Pricing management Cost containment Revenue management Growth management	Forest fires Deforestation Tsunami Flooding Hurricanes Earthquakes Landslides and erosion Energy crisis Alternative fuels Drinking water crisis	Religious bigotry Fundamentalism Ethnic cleansing Corporate greed Corporate fraud Corporate bankruptcy Home mortgage crisis Monetary crisis Financial market crisis Wall Street meltdown
Unknown (hence, not easily tamable)	Cell 2: Complex* Puzzles (Type I)	Cell 4: Complex* Problems (Type III)	Cell 6: Complex* Messes (Type IV)	Cell 8: Complex* Social Messes (Type IV)
Examples	Seasonal flu and colds Seasonal allergies Consumer dissatisfaction Consumer brand switching Consumer lifestyle changes Employee malaise Supplier/creditor anxiety Market rejection Recession, stagflation Economic depression	High school dropouts High school violence Consumer obesity Consumer bankruptcy Consumer fraud Computer hacking Cyber fraud Merchant fraud Volatile interest rates Currency fluctuations	Global carbon emissions Global climate change Polar Arctic drift Nuclear disasters Chronic/incurable disease Trade embargoes Global hunger and disease Global price collusions Global trade inequities Global financial risk	Global terrorism Global inequality Global poverty Global injustices Global turbulence Global nuclear threats Global wars Global ecological damage Global instability Global revolution

Source: Author's own.

Note: * We assume complexity (especially, dynamic complexity) arises primarily from unknown causes of the problem erupting over time.

+ Type I, II, III, and IV problems refer to the categories suggested by Perrow (1984); the term "Mess" is attributed to Ackoff (1974) and "Social Messes" to Horn (2001).

PART II: MANAGERIAL CHALLENGES AND IMPLICATIONS OF WICKED PROBLEMS

We enrich the theoretical discussions of Part I by considering some practical applications and implications of wicked problems.

There is a tendency in most of us to see financial crisis problems as tame and a tendency to avoid wicked problems. Instinctively, we resist or deny that these problems are wicked and unsolvable.

Managers easily collude in systematic denial of the complex and ill-structured dynamics of wicked problems, a phenomenon that Chris Argyris (1996) called "skilled incompetence."

The first step, therefore, in coping with a wicked problem is to recognize its nature, its complexity, and its degree of wickedness (Conklin 2006: 10). That is, we must first recognize that the financial crisis problem is wicked, and not just simple or complex or even ill structured.

Second, we must realize that the wicked financial problem is real and that problem resolutions are necessary. Knowing that the problem is wicked is of no use if that does not help us to address it.

Third, we must free ourselves from being bound to any one financial model, or class of financial problems or solutions in resolving it. Flexibility is the key in the solution of a wicked financial problem, a flexibility that is needed to cope with the capricious nature of wicked problems (Becker 2007).

Problem wickedness is a force of fragmentation. The giant world of financial markets is fragmentized with almost conflicting goals, ideologies, and solution spaces. When working on wicked financial problems in the socially complex and globalized environment we live in, we need to foster and develop a "collective intelligence" through socially shared cognitions and meanings, models and methods, goals and objectives, assumptions and presuppositions. Collective intelligence is a natural enabler of collaboration.

Table 6.8 presents a sequence of problem-resolution process strategies that could be useful in tackling each of the eight problems types of Table 6.7. Each strategy may imply formulating a range of one or more futures with selection of past or present similar futures as a reference future. Here, drawing analogies from similar industries or time-periods may prove useful (Gavetti and Rivkin 2005). The higher the complexity of the problems, higher is the risk, and the higher the risk, higher is the risk of failure in controlling the outcomes of the problems. Taking higher risks takes extra courage, but the rewards are also greater. The more complex the problem, the more complex is the resolution, and accordingly, the problem-resolution process benefits larger groups of humankind and in more significant ways.

When the causes of the problems are unknown and the outcomes are unknown (that is, Cells 5, 6, 7, and 8), the problem-resolution strategy would require qualitative approaches based on the opinions, values, and expectations of major stakeholders or industry experts in the problem so that common ground for discussion and dialogue may be found and consensual resolutions may be derived. If no consensus emerges, then the whole problem-resolution process may be iterated until a working agreement among major stakeholders arises. The problem-resolution process in such cases is very collective, collaborative, and consensus-seeking (Camillus 2008). At every step of the collective process, human relationships are of paramount importance together with a high level of mutual trust (Navarro, Hayward, and Voros 2007: 19). The process should build collective trust—trust in the way the problem is defined, its known and unknown causes explored its known and unknown outcome sequences investigated, and lastly, in the final problem-resolution stage, selected, implemented, and assessed. The end-users or implementers of the solution should trust in the level of knowledge, expertise, research commitment, data and dialogue transparency, and the professionalism of the entire collective search process that the problem-resolution team brought to bear. The entire resolution process should be coherent and credible enough to explain the complexity of the mess or wicked problem in hand.

The problem-resolution process is also "iterative" as complexity increases. The entire process of problem-resolution may be an output by itself. The mess or wicked problem becomes more clearly defined after several iterations of examining the variables, the known and unknown causes, the known and unknown outcome sequences, and analyzing their inter-relationships (Navarro, Hayward, and Voros 2007: 22).

TABLE 6.8 A Taxonomy of Managerial Strategies based on Different Problem Types

Causes of the problem	Outcomes (effects) of the problem			
	Known		*Unknown*	
	Outcome sequences known and fixed, and hence *deterministic*	Outcome sequences known, not fixed, but with known probabilities; hence *stochastic*	Outcome sequences unknown but estimable; hence, domain of *uncertainty*	Outcome sequences unknown and not estimable; hence, domain of *divergence/emergence*
Known (hence, tamable)	Puzzles	Problems	Messes	Social Messes
Problem-Resolution Process	Define the problem	Define the problem	Define the problem	Define the problem
	Identify its causes	Identify its causes	Identify its causes	Identify its causes
	Collect relevant data	Collect relevant data	Collect relevant data	Collect relevant data
	Classify the data	Classify the data	Classify the data	Classify the data
	Study the fixed outcomes	*Study the probable outcomes*	*Study the uncertain outcomes*	*Study the divergent outcomes*
	Examine outcome sequences	Examine outcome sequences	Examine outcome sequences	Examine outcome sequences
	Study deterministic patterns	*Study stochastic patterns*	*Study uncertain patterns*	*Study emergent patterns*
	Hypothesize cause–effect links	Hypothesize cause–effect links	Hypothesize cause–effect links	Agree on cause–effect links
	Verify hypotheses	Verify hypotheses	*Verify alternative hypotheses*	*Verify consensual hypotheses*
	Draw critical inferences	Draw critical inferences	Draw critical inferences	Draw critical inferences
	Formulate strategies	Formulate final strategies	*Reiterate previous steps*	*Reiterate previous steps*
	Implement strategies	Implement final strategies	*Look for convergence*	*Look for convergence*
	Assess implementation	Assess implementation	Formulate final strategies	Formulate tentative strategies
			Implement final strategies	Implement some strategies
			Assess implementation	Assess implementation
Unknown (hence, not easily tamable)	Complex Puzzles	Complex Problems	Complex Messes	Complex Social Messes or "Wicked" Problems
Problem-Resolution Process	Define the problem domain	Define the problem domain	Define the problem domain	Define the problem domain
	Identify its probable causes	Identify its probable causes	Explore unknown causes	Explore unknown causes
	Collect relevant data	Collect relevant data	Collect relevant data	Collect relevant data
	Classify the data	Classify the data	Classify the data	Classify the data
	Study any fixed outcomes	Study any fixed outcomes	Study uncertain outcomes	Study uncertain outcomes
	Examine outcome sequences	Examine outcome sequences	Examine outcome sequences	Examine outcome sequences
	Study deterministic patterns	*Study stochastic patterns*	*Study uncertainty patterns*	*Study divergent patterns*
	Study probable cause–effect links	Study probable cause–effects	*Study uncertain cause–effects*	*Study divergent cause–effects*
	Hypothesize probable cause–effects	Hypothesize probable Cause–effects	Hypothesize cause–effects	Hypothesize cause–effects
	Verify hypotheses	Verify hypotheses	*Verify consensual hypotheses*	*Verify divergent hypotheses*
	Draw critical inferences	Draw critical inferences	Draw critical inferences	Draw critical inferences
	Reiterate previous steps	Reiterate previous steps	Reiterate previous steps	Reiterate previous steps
	Look for convergence	Look for convergence	*Look for common ground*	*Look for emergence*
	Formulate convergent strategies	Formulate convergent strategies	*Formulate agreed-on strategies*	*Formulate emergent strategies*
	Implement convergent strategies	Implement convergent strategies	Implement agreed-on strategies	Implement emergent strategies
	Assess implementation	Assess implementation	Assess implementation	Assess implementation
			Reiterate previous steps	*Reiterate previous steps*

Source: Author's own.

What Makes a Problem Wicked?

Many factors generate wicked problems, but the point is not to determine if a problem is wicked or not, but to have a sense of what contributes to the wickedness of a problem. The sources of problem wickedness are many (Conklin 2006):

- The problem is complex, socially, economically, technologically, and politically, and dynamic in nature.
- The causes of the problem are many, unknown, uncertain, and ambiguous.
- The consequences of the problem are hidden, social, complex, political, and universal.
- The problem is socially complex, involving multiple and diverse stakeholders (e.g., several companies, several government agencies, several advocacy groups) each with different sets of goals.
- Some of these conflicting goals could undermine or even sabotage the project if some stakeholder needs and goals are not considered (this is exactly what is happening with the U.S.A. efforts of health care reform).
- Information and knowledge on the problem are chaotic; perspectives, intentions, understanding, interpretation, knowledge, and experience of individuals involved with the wicked problem are fragmented.
- Each individual or stakeholder of the problem is convinced that his/her version of the problem is correct and complete.
- Each person makes incompatible tacit assumptions about the problem.
- The fragmenting force of social complexity makes effective communications very difficult.

More specifically, the sources of problem wickedness are:

- Most natural disasters (e.g., tsunami, Katrina, Gustav, earthquakes) are wicked problems at the geo-physical level.
- Some wicked problems are human-made such as labor strikes, sabotage, vandalism, gangsterism, terrorism, 9/11, Mumbai attack, consumer boycotts, and corporate fraud.
- Some socioeconomic problems are also wicked in nature (e.g., recession, depression, inflation, stagflation, unemployment, underemployment, organizational decline, massive layoffs, plant shutdowns, and personal or corporate bankruptcy).
- Some wicked problems arise because of hyper growth (e.g., Wal-Mart still wants to grow bigger and faster despite saturated retail markets in the U.S.; Ford, GMC, Toyota and the other automakers still want to sell more millions of vehicles when the current North American markets are saturated and recessionary).
- Some wicked problems arise because of greed, avarice, and envy (e.g., corporate fraud, ethnic cleansing, genocide, most wars, preventive wars, "holy" wars, unjust aggression, and developing and building weapons of mass destruction).
- Some wicked problems arise because of recklessness, hatred, and retaliation (e.g., crime and violence in schools, street crime, vandalism, serial murders, terrorism, cyber-hacking, and organized crime (mafia)).
- Other wicked problems arise owing to reckless corporate cost-containment methods (e.g., downsizing, plant shut downs, plant relocations, massive layoffs, offshore outsourcing, sweatshops, child labor, forcing suppliers to lower prices beyond their breakeven point, and the like).

In the panoply of problems facing corporate leaders today, the common thread is the either–or nature of trade-offs. This is what makes wicked problems so wicked. Designful leaders do not accept the hand-me-down notion that cost-cutting and innovation are mutually exclusive, or that short-term and long-term goals are irreconcilable. They reject the tyranny of "or" in favor of the genius of "and." Designful leaders are adrenalized by the ambiguity and uncertainty that come with constant change. They are driven to create wealth instead of merely unlocking it via ingenious financial instruments. They are willing to trade the false security of best practices for the insecurity of new creative design practices. A creative designer makes new laws rather than follow previous man-made laws. Those who insist on tidy phases inevitably produce mediocre results, because a too-orderly process rules out random inspiration (Neumeier 2009: 48).

Designers do not actually solve problems; they "work through" them. They use non-logical processes that are difficult to express in words but easier to express in action. They use models, mock-ups, sketches, and stories as their vocabulary. They operate in the space between knowing and doing (e.g., making), prototyping new solutions that arise from their four strengths of empathy, intuition, imagination, and idealism (Neumeier 2009: 50–52).

How to Recognize a Wicked Problem?

A wicked problem does not have to verify all the ten characteristics described by Rittel and Webber (1973). Moreover, a wicked problem can have several tame elements. Space research and placing a man on the moon were certainly wicked problems, but they could be defined, the solution was realized when we landed the first man on the moon and brought him home safely, and the solution could be assessed as right or wrong. Technically, we could even stop space research, but we may not want to do it, as it betters our understanding of meteorology, communications via satellites, zero gravity research, and the like. This proves that, "most wicked problems have degrees of wickedness" (Conklin 2006).

As you grapple with a problem, you come to know it is wicked if you encounter one or more of the following operational constraints:

- The problem definition seems vague or keeps changing.
- The proposed solution creates a new, related problem unveiling new boundaries.
- There are many meetings on the project but not much progress.
- The number of stakeholders keeps increasing.
- You cannot see easily the solution at the outset.
- There are multiple solutions, but no consensus and no convergence between them.
- The constraints on the solution keep changing.
- There are many organizational and political issues involved.
- The decision has been made, but not followed (i.e., it is not a real solution).

All nine operational constraints characterize the recent health care reform crisis and the financial market crisis in U.S.A and the bailout solutions proposed. Wicked projects arise when we organize to tackle a wicked problem, as if it were a tame problem.

For instance, a "mission-critical" project with less than half the time and resources necessary to do the job is a wicked problem and called a "death March Project" by DeGrace and Stahl (1990). Death March

Projects happen when volatile requirements, changing constraints, and stakeholder disagreements meet up against immovable deadlines. Such wicked problems have often occurred in the software development world as reported by a 1994 Standish Group Report. This report documented that about a third of software development projects are cancelled and a half do not meet their original cost projections.

Recently, several challenging projects have been organized as wicked problems, such as designing effective workplaces (Gustafsson 2002), closing the achievement gap (Dietz, Barker, and Giberson 2005), classroom instructional design (Becker 2007), canal dredging projects (Blythe, Grabill, and Riley 2008), urban street car parking (Kerley 2007), and Cat's Cradling project (Hubbard and Paquet 2007).

Are Wicked Problems Really Unsolvable?

No problem, howsoever wicked, is objectively and indefinitely unsolvable. Rittel and Weber (1973) maintain that wicked problems cannot be resolved with known traditional, analytical, and linear approaches. They do not assert that wicked problems are intrinsically unsolvable. Taming is a common way of trying to cope with a wicked problem. Instead of dealing with the full wickedness of the problem, one could simplify and break it in various (modular) ways to make it more manageable, and thereby, more resolvable; even though taming a problem thus could exacerbate the problem (Conklin 2003: 21–23).

By definition, wicked problems cannot be solved, but can be "managed" or "resolved" to a certain extent. The whole process of managing wicked problems is dynamic. For instance, the understanding of the problem comes from creating possible solutions and considering how they might work. Often, a wicked problem can be best described in terms of its solution elements. Problem understanding continues to evolve until the very end of experimentation and resolution implementation; that is, even late in the experimentation, the designer subjects may return to re-understanding the problem. This iterative or non-linear process of problem formulation is not a defect even though chaotic and experimental by nature; it is the mark of an intelligent and creative learning process that underlines the chaotic surface. The jagged non-linear process of addressing wicked problems is an opportunity-driven process of organizational and team learning. "In the current business environment, problem solving and learning, and the flow of the learning process is opportunity driven" (Conklin 2006: 6).

Simple problems, on the other hand, have a well-defined and stable problem statement; they have a limited solution space within which one can explore and find a definite final solution, and therefore, a stopping point when the solution is reached, and they have a solution that can be objectively assessed as right or wrong, good or bad. Simple problems belong to a class of similar problems that can be solved in the same way; they have a solution that can be easily tried and abandoned without serious unintended consequences.

Wickedness in wicked problems occurs when people confer immutability on value assumptions and ideological considerations. In such cases, wicked problems can easily degenerate into tyranny or chaos (King 1993: 113). Type IV problems are "wicked" problems that cannot be resolved by analytical or scientific methods, but, as Rittel and Webber (1973: 162) point out, only by logical argumentation and consensus. It is a second-generation systems approach based on a model of planning "as an argumentative process in the course of which an image of the problem and of the solution emerges gradually among participants, as a product of incessant judgment, subject to critical argument." The process of resolving Type IV wicked problems is elaborate and argumentative. In terms of participants, we need to incorporate diversity, cross-functionality, and interdisciplinary expertise. We need to build on diversity, adaptability, resilience, rapid respond times, flexibility, reversibility, and even "redundance" such that when confronted by undesirable and unanticipated outcomes we have fallback positions. We must learn how to learn and unlearn, think about how we think, and we need to build learning organizations (Senge 1990).

Above all, we need common sense—that is, common ground. Establishing common ground is a strategic necessity in our turbulent times (Bellah et al. 1991; Hunter 1991). Common ground essentially means that we realize that our differences are less significant and profound than what we share in common, and that this common sense represents the beginnings of wisdom (King 1993: 114).

Next, given these multi-specialization stakeholders, in taming such wicked problems, we need to carefully draw boundaries so that we can sort out different "images" of the problem, tame different pieces of the original wicked problem, generate hypotheses specific to this piece of the problem, and converge toward emergent resolutions. Perhaps, following one of the fundamental tenets of Edwards Deming, "we should shift from strategies that focus on results, outcomes, or objectives, to strategies that focus on continuously improving processes. This strategic shift needs a profound change in mindset for managers and executives." We also need real listening, and engaging in what David Bohm called "dialogue." We need both dialogue and listening to what Edward de Bono called "mapmaking." Listening, dialogue, and mapmaking are needed for mapping the boundaries and learning to recognize patterns of interaction—this is the crux in sorting out messes.

Real listening is also essential in establishing trust, and trust is absolutely necessary when working together. "Mistrust is the dark heart of wicked problems" (King 1993: 114). "Trust is a fundamental strategy for collectively coping with wicked problems" (King 1993: 112).

Wicked problems are what E. F. Schumacher called "divergent" as opposed to "convergent" problems. A tame problem is convergent by definition, and a convergent problem promises a solution. The more we study a convergent problem, the more its various answers eventually converge. A divergent problem, on the other hand, diverges in scope, scale, content, domain, and formulation. Hence, a divergent problem does not promise a solution. The more we study the problem, the more we come up with different solutions.

The wicked problem, however, keeps "morphing" as science develops, attitudes evolve, and economic interests shift (Lewis 2008: 194). For instance, wicked problems of the past could be tamed in the decades to come with advances in technology. The complex or wicked problems of the past, such as discovering a vaccine for smallpox, analyzing chemical components of air pollution, and estimating the effects of lowering the prime interest rate, are now tame or simple problems.

The myth about the un-solvability of our social problems, in particular, may stem from a lack of an underlying system of philosophical presuppositions that we can believe in and that can form the ultimate basis for truth and falsity, rightness and wrongness of the solutions to our social problems (Bahm 1975: 103).

Understanding the Origins of Wicked Problems

There are many reasons why we confront so many Type IV wicked problems:

- Presently, our world is becoming more turbulent with things happening faster, bigger, and beyond our control (e.g., health care crisis, preventive wars, global terrorism, genocide, political power crisis, global energy crisis, financial market turbulence, and the Wall Street meltdown).

- We do not know what we want. Should we build an economic and political infrastructure predicated on the belief that we will need more energy or more conservation? Which policy will provide us with more flexibility and adaptability, more simplicity and well-being, more health and global peace? Such policy decisions will surely determine significant aspects of our future.
- Consequently, we cannot easily predict our energy needs, our political needs, our ecology needs, our health care needs, and our consumptive lifestyles.
- We cannot predict our possible futures other than a few aspects of these futures.
- That is, most of these problems are characterized by human ignorance—what we do not know we do not know, and many do not know that they do not know.
- We just cannot foresee all the ways things can go wrong—this is the "chaos theory."
- Moreover, while we cannot easily predict our future, what we choose to do now certainly affects our future. Our current choices may have some unanticipated consequences that we do not know now.
- A "loss of orientation" can most directly give rise to divergent ideological activity, generating an inability, or a lack of usable models, to comprehend the universe of civic rights and responsibilities in which one finds oneself located (Geertz 1973).
- Different stakeholders in wicked problems hold diverse values—that what satisfies one may be abhorrent to another, that what comprises problem-solution for one is problem-generation for another. Under such circumstances, and in the absence of an overarching social theory or an overarching special ethic, there is no determining which group is right and which is wrong, and which needs to serve and which needs to be served (Rittel and Webber 1973).
- "All we have are endless fragments of theory that account for bits and pieces of individual, organizational and economic behavior. But we have no overarching or truly interconnecting theories, especially none that accounts for human behavior in turbulent times" (Michael 1985: 95).
- The new mathematics of complexity raises an even more disturbing question: Can there be an economic policy at all? Alternatively, is the attempt to control the "weather" of the economy, such as recessions and other cyclical fluctuations, foredoomed to failure (Drucker 1989: 167)?
- Moreover, there are no grounds to suspect things could be better in principle. There are no sound reasons to claim that the technological, social, and political sciences are going to mature or evolve to the point that we can more accurately predict and control our future (King 1993: 111).

A Systems Understanding of the Origins of Problems

Peter Senge (1990: 57–58), in his *Fifth Discipline*, states some laws of the "fifth discipline" that can help us in understanding the origins of problems. A first law, in this regard, is "Today's problems come from yesterday's solutions." That is, the causes of our problems are immediate—we merely need to look at our own solutions to other problems in the past. For instance (see Chapter 4):

- A well-established firm finds its current quarter's sales are off sharply—a problem. The cause: The highly successful rebate program last quarter allured many customers to buy last quarter than this.
- A new manager cuts down high inventory levels to solve the high carrying cost problem. Salespeople now, however, are spending more time responding to angry customers who are still either waiting for shipments or for the brands they want.

- Police cracking down on drugs in downtown New York arrested narcotics on Thirtieth Street. The addicts have now transferred the crime center to the Fortieth Street.
- Federal officials intercepted a large shipment of narcotics. This, in turn, reduced the drug supply, drove up the price, and generated more crime by addicts desperate to maintain their habit.

In each case, solutions merely shift problems from one part of the system to another. They often go undetected because those who "solved" the first problem are different from those who inherit the new problem.

A second law is "harder you push, harder the system pushes back." Consider another source-pattern of problems (Senge 1990: 58–59):

- In the 1960s, there were massive federal programs to build low-income housing and improve job skills in decrepit inner cities in U.S.A Despite this great welfare program, these cities were worse off in the 1970s. Why? One reason was that low-income people from other cities and rural areas migrated to these high-welfare cities, thus overcrowding them, and the job training programs were swamped with applicants. The city's tax base began to erode, being overcrowded with welfare recipients.
- The developed countries have great programs that subsidize or assist food and agricultural programs of the developing countries. More food, however, reduces deaths due to malnutrition, that, in turn, causes higher net population growth, and eventually more malnutrition.
- In the mid-1980s, in order to correct the U.S. trade imbalance the federal government let the dollar depreciate. Foreign guerilla competitors, however, let the prices of their goods fall in parallel, thus "compensating" or neutralizing the value of the depreciated dollar.
- A marketing manager finds that one of his products suddenly starts to lose its market attractiveness. He compensates by aggressive marketing—lowers the price, spends more on advertising, and offers rebates that temporarily bring back the customers. However, the costs of aggressive marketing reduce resources for improving quality inspection, speedy delivery, and honoring product warranties and guarantees. In the long run, the more fervently the company markets, the more customers it loses!

Under each case, there is a well-intentioned intervention that calls forth responses from the system that, in turn, offsets the benefits of the intervention. In systems thinking, this phenomenon is called the "compensating feedback." Compensating feedback is not confined to "larger systems" but occurs in smaller or personal systems. Consider the following (Senge 1990: 59):

- Jane quits smoking only to find she is gaining weight, and suffers so much loss in self-image that she takes up to smoking again to relieve the stress. She is back to square one, but possibly in worse condition that before.
- A protective mother who wants so much for her young son to get along with his schoolmates that she repeatedly steps in to resolve problems, ending up with a child that never learns to settle differences by himself.
- Jack is an enthusiastic newcomer so eager to be liked that he never responds to subtle criticisms of his work and ends up embittered and labeled, "a difficult person to work with."

Senge (1990: 59) concludes: "Pushing harder, whether through an increasingly aggressive intervention or through increasingly stressful withholding of natural instincts, is exhausting. Yet, as individuals and organizations, we not only get drawn into compensating feedback, we often glorify the suffering that ensues. When our initial efforts fail to produce lasting improvements, we "push harder." We hope that hard work will overcome all obstacles, all the while blinding ourselves to how we are contributing to the obstacles ourselves."

Senge's third law is "behavior grows better before it grows worse." In complex human systems, there are always many short-term strategies to make things look better. Only eventually the compensating feedback comes back to haunt you. A typical short-term solution feels wonderful when it first cures the symptoms. You feel the improvement and think the problem has gone away. It may be a year or two later, when the problem recurs with vengeance. The initial cure can be worse than the disease. We all find comfort applying familiar solutions to unfamiliar problems, sticking to what we know best. "Pushing harder and harder on familiar solutions, while fundamental problems persist or worsen, is a reliable indicator of non-systemic thinking" (Senge 1990: 61).

Senge's fourth law of "fifth discipline" states, "the cure can be worse than the disease." Often, the easy, familiar, and short-term solution is not only ineffective, it could be addictive and dangerous. Consider the following cases:

- Social drinking starts often as a solution to the problem of low-self esteem or work-related stress. Gradually, the cure becomes worse than the disease; among its other problems it makes self-esteem and stress even worse than before.
- Government welfare, subsidy, unemployment, and disability programs are great but they foster increasing addictive dependencies on public resources and diminish, if not destroy, abilities of local people to solve their own problems.
- In business, we shift the burden of internal problems to "consultants" who make the company dependent upon them instead of training the client managers to solve problems on their own.
- In cities, we shift the burden from diverse local communities to low-income uniform mono-ethnic housing projects.
- We take away extended families, and shift the burden for care of the aged to nursing homes.
- We shift the burden of doing simple math from our knowledge of arithmetic to a dependency on pocket calculators.
- We shift the art and challenge of writing, composing, spelling, grammar, and research-based writing to computer-based search engines, spell-checks, and grammar checks.
- The Cold War shifted responsibility for peace from negotiation to armaments, thereby strengthening the military and related industries, nuclear proliferation, biochemical weapons, and, now, the problem of nuclear disarmament.

In each of these cases, the phenomenon of short-term improvements leads to long-term dependency. Systems thinking calls this malady, "Shifting the burden to the intervener." The intervener may be federal assistance to cities, the elderly, the unemployed, the disabled, food relief agencies, public schools, and other welfare programs. All help a host system on a short-term basis, only to leave the system fundamentally weaker than before and more in need of help. Long-term solutions, on the other hand, strengthen the ability of the system to be self-sufficient and shoulder its own burdens.

Systems Thinking to Resolve Some Wicked Problems

We summarize relevant points from Chapter 4. Systems thinking is a discipline for seeing wholes. It is a framework for seeing interrelationships rather than linear cause–effect chains and things, and for seeing processes and patterns of change rather than static snapshots. It is a discipline for seeing the "structures" that underlie complex situations, and for discerning high from low leverage change. It is a shift of mind from seeing parts to seeing wholes, from reacting to the present to creating the future, from seeing ourselves as helpless reactors to changing reality to seeing ourselves as active participants in shaping that reality.

Systems thinking does not always advocate long-term solutions. It also believes in short-term well-focused solutions that can produce significant and enduring improvements, but as long as they are in the right place, at the right time, and in the right hands. Systems thinking refers to this principle as "leverage." Tackling a difficult problem is often a matter of seeing where the high leverage is. The only problem is that high-leverage points and changes are usually non-obvious to most participants in the system, unless one understands the forces at play in those systems that offer leverage. Most often the leverage lies in the interactions between people and variables that form the system. The real leverage in most management situations lies in understanding dynamic complexity and detail complexity (Senge 1990: 72).

For instance, brand equity does not come from aggressive marketing alone, or from brand quality alone, or from upscale retailing, or from long-standing customer loyalty alone, but in the interactions between these factors and events. Problems of falling sales are not necessarily in the marketing department, but in the design and manufacturing, packaging and sizing, distribution and logistics, human resources, accounting, trade credit and consumer credit departments. Looking at the problem holistically as an interaction of all business systems in the company may indicate the right leverage to resolve the declining sales problem. "Organizations break down despite individual brilliance and innovative products, because they are unable to pull their diverse functions and talents into a productive whole" (Senge 1990: 69).

Similarly, balancing market growth and capacity expansion is a dynamic problem. Developing a profitable mix of price, product, quality, design, availability, and service that together make a strong market position is a dynamic problem. Improving quality, lowering total costs, and satisfying customers in a sustainable manner are dynamic problems. All these dynamic problems have dynamic complexity more than detail complexity.

The arms race is, most fundamentally, a problem of dynamic complexity. Insights into causes and possible cures require seeing interrelationships between various actors and variables and at various times and contexts. For instance, in the U.S. and U.S.S.R. arms race, each party independently estimated each one's arms build up, assessed the additional threat, and built further arms to neutralize the threat. The process became circular—each one's reactive strategy causing counter-acting strategy. The long-term result of each party's effort to be more secure was a heightened insecurity for all and an escalation dynamic—a combined nuclear stockpile 10,000 times the total firepower of World War II (Senge 1990: 71–72). A real solution was in negotiations and agreed upon reductions in nuclear arsenal; that is, it runs the vicious cycle of arms race and escalation in reverse gear.

The essence of the discipline of systems thinking lies in the shift of mind along two dimensions:

- seeing interrelationships rather than linear cause–effect chains in reality;
- seeing processes and patterns of change rather than static snapshots of reality.

The practice of systems thinking starts with understanding a simple concept called "feedback'" that shows how actions can reinforce or counteract (balance) each other. Systems thinking recognizes "structures" or patterns of change that recur again and again. It enables us to simplify life by helping us to see the deeper patterns lying behind the events and the details of ordinary life and reality.

Design Thinking to Resolve Wicked Problems

Most of the wickedness of current business problems arises from two prevailing winds: the extreme clutter of the marketplace, and the relentless speed of change. The antidote to clutter is a radically differentiated product or brand. The antidote to change is organizational agility. Organizational agility was not a major issue in the 20th century when business moved at a leisurely pace. In the 21st century it is; hence, it showed up number three in the list of ten top wicked problems (see introduction to this chapter). Companies now need to be as fast and adaptable as they are innovative. A designful mind confers the ability to invent the widest range of solutions for the wicked problems now facing your company (Neumeier 2009: 19–20).

Necessity may well be the mother of invention. However, if we continue to manufacture mountains of carbon emissions and toxic stuff, invention may soon become the mother of necessity. Our natural resources will be depleted and our planet made uninhabitable. Eco-sustainability becomes a wicked problem. The answers to pollution and vanishing resources must come not from politicians but from fertile minds of scientists, researchers, engineers, architects, social planners, and entrepreneurs. Waste reduction can alter our commercial landscape beyond recognition—creating more wicked problems as well as more opportunities (Neumeier 2009: 23). In Germany, Volkswagen is demonstrating that corporate responsibility does not stop at the loading dock. The company is already selling cars that are 85 percent recyclable and 95 percent reusable, and building a zero emissions car that operates on a fuel cell, 12 batteries, and a solar panel instead of fossil fuels. There is a gradual transition from traditional technology to green technology.

One way of resolving wicked problems is by designing and redesigning everything from the factory floor to the family living floor. Engineers and entrepreneurs will have to think like designers, feel like designers, and work like designers. The narrow-gauge mindset of the past is insufficient for today's wicked problems. We can no longer play the music as written. Instead, we have to invent a whole new scale (Neumeier 2009: 27).

According to Roger Martin (Dean of the Rotman School of Management) in his *Opposable Mind* (analogous to the "opposable thumb"—Harvard Business School Press, 2007), design reasoning is different from current business reasoning. Business reasoning is inductive (i.e., observing that something works), algorithmic (known tasks with known formulae) and deductive (proving that something is). Designing reasoning, on the contrary, is "abductive" (imagining that something could be) and "integrative" (grasping and resolving the tensions inherent in wicked problems). Roger Martin believes that mastery without originality is rote, and originality without mastery is flaky, if not entirely random. Design thinking is heuristic, it creates its own rules to solve mysteries of the marketplace and the production factory. Heuristic tasks, such as motivating disgruntled employees, negotiating with unhappy bankers, forging supplier relationships, and understanding customer delight, needs creative design thinking and not inductive or deductive algorithms. Business leaders should be masters of heuristics and not masters of algorithms. Computers and robots can do the latter and far better than business managers. We need abductive, heuristic, and integrative business thinking to resolve wicked problems.

In business reasoning, you *decide* the way forward; in creative reasoning, you *design* the way forward. The deciding mode assumes that alternatives already exist on a "solution shelf" (e.g., via case studies), but deciding will be difficult. The designing mode assumes that new options must be imagined (using the design process) but once imagined, deciding will be easy. The truth is, success in the 21st century will depend upon finding the right mixture of both these modes (Neumeier 2009: 41).

After extensive study of the design process of architect Frank Gehry, Richard Boland (Weatherhead School of Management, Case Western University, OH) says, "The problems with managers today is that they do the first damn thing that pops into their heads." "There's a whole level of reflectiveness absent in traditional management that we can find in design." There is a difference between decision attitude and design attitude. Decision attitude is myopic and condemns the company to a future of limited choices. Decisions are more powerful when they are designed (Boland and Collopy 2004).

The traditional management model is a veritable thrift store of hand-me-down concepts, all perfectly tailored for a previous need and a previous era. The old business model was innovated so long ago that those who once saw business management as a cause for revolution (e.g., Frederick Taylor, Henry Ford, Alfred Sloan, and others) are long gone. We need a new band of revolutionaries to enlarge the scope of possibilities. The breakdown of the old management model is obvious; it is so bereft of ideas that it is now resorting to "unlocking wealth" through ingenious financial instruments and financial market manipulation rather than "creating" wealth through designful innovation. Boland and Collopy argue that Enron's failure was not only a failure of ethics but a failure of imagination. Its managers engaged in hiding debt with convoluted transactions because they simply did not have better ideas (Boland and Collopy 2004; Neumeier 2009).

> The key to finding solutions to wicked problems, such as Enron's, is the designer's ability to embrace paradox—a willingness to stay in the dragon gap as long as it takes, to brave the discomfort of creative tension until the conflicting issues are resolved. This ability is conferred on all human beings, not just designers, through the evolutionary principle of bilateralism. We're all born with two eyes, two ears, two hands, and two brain hemispheres. Two eyes give us perspective. Two ears give us sound location. Two hands give us the ability to use tools. And the two sides of our brain give us the ability to grasp problems in the pincer grip of logic and intuition. (Neumeier 2009: 45)

The Partners, a leading design firm in London, U.K. has coined the theory of the "third brain"— a phenomenon that emerges when the right brain and the left brain work together. The third brain can do what neither brain can do. The third brain is a metaphor for holistic or systems thinking. It is the perfect model for the "design mind" in the innovative culture of a corporation. Third-brain thinkers do not settle for easy options—they work as a team until they find the win-win ground among seemingly opposing sets of needs or constraints. They zoom in and zoom out on a wicked problem—zoom out to see where the problem fits in the larger scheme of things, then zoom back in to concentrate on the details. Zooming out facilitates strategic differentiation, while zooming in facilitates quality. To the third-brain thinkers, business solutions that fail to combine differentiation and quality are of little or questionable value.

In the many problems facing corporate leaders today, a common thread is the "either–or" nature of trade-offs. This is what makes wicked problems so wicked. Innovative designful leaders do not accept the hand-me-down notion that cost-cutting and innovation are mutually exclusive, that short-term and long-term goals are irreconcilable, and they reject the tyranny of the "or" in favor of the genius of "and." Innovative leaders are adrenalized by the ambiguity and uncertainty that come with constant change; they are driven to create wealth instead of merely unlocking or distributing it. They are willing to trade the false security of past best practices to the insecurity of new practices; they are prepared to make laws rather than just follow old ones (Neumeier 2009: 47).

Most business managers want to control creativity. They want neatly sequenced discovery, ideation, refinement, and production, so that they could manage, track, compare, and measure like manufacturing. The creative act, however, is much wilder. Those who insist on tidy phases inevitably produce mediocre results, because the too-orderly process rules out random inspiration. Rule-busting creativity and innovation require a sense of play, a sense of delight, and a refusal to be corralled into a strict method (Neumeier 2009: 48).

Contentious or wicked problems are best resolved not by imposing a single point of view at the expense of all others, but by striving for a higher-order solution that integrates the diverse perspectives of all relevant constituents. "Adversarial, win-lose decision-making is debilitating for all concerned" (Neumaier 2009). Unfortunately, win–lose decision-making was and still is the dominant mode of business. This is not a habit we invented but inherited from the Greeks (e.g., Socrates, Plato, Aristotle) who believed that sound thinking came from discussion rather than dialogue, from finding flaws in the other's arguments rather than advancing a concept together. Edward de Bono, a creativity expert, in his *Six Thinking Hats* proves how we can think through problems constructively via "parallel thinking." Parallel thinking gets everyone in the group to think in the same direction at the same time, thereby neutralizing the Socratic method of shooting down ideas before they can fly. The "hats" are simply metaphors for different ways of getting at problems.

- **The White Hat**: represents information and is factual and informative. What do we know about this issue? What are the facts, figures, and other data that can guide our work?
- **The Red Hat**: represents hot emotion and is emotional and intuitive. Normally, there is no room in meetings to display emotion, so it ends up coloring our logical conclusions. What are we feeling about this issue (Excited? Afraid? Curious?)—get it on table.
- **The Black Hat**: Here thinking is dark and cautious. This hat is contrary and cautious. This is where most of us excel—devil's advocate. Why is it likely that this new idea will fail? What are its numerous weaknesses?
- **The Yellow Hat**: This hat is sunny and positive. This is the reverse of devil's advocacy. What greatness could come from this concept? Where can we see optimism and hope?
- **The Green Hat**: Represents growth and creativity. This hat is fresh and creative. What could we do that has not been done? How could some of our black hat fears be turned into opportunities?
- **The Blue Hat**: This hat is cool and controlled. It is worn by the facilitator who acts as referee and directs the use of the other hats.

By switching from hat to hat as the conversation requires, the group can quickly work through a huge number of ideas, unencumbered by flow-stopping arguments and emotion-laden attacks. The natural consequences of parallel thinking is large-scale buy-in, since the process is designed to be transparent and inclusive (Neumeier 2009: 112–15).

A Practical Illustration: The Wicked Problem of Human Tissue Markets

[See Lewis (2008: 193–215)]

Consider, for instance, the human tissue problem and "bio-banks" that currently control it. Human tissue is a by-product of life. People give blood, donate bone marrow, have operations, and some donate organs when they die. In previous decades, tissue was primarily stored and freely shared for academic and scientific purposes. The tissue problem was either a simple or an unstructured collection and storage problem. Presently, however, human tissues are collected, maintained, commoditized, commercialized, and marketed. The value of human tissue has increased exponentially given the fact that human tissue is used for generating lucrative products for biotechnology, diagnostics, and pharmaceuticals. Some tissues have great value. A human egg can be tens of thousands of dollars. A single cadaver can be richly mined; its tendons cost $21,000, its skin can cost over $35,000, its bones almost $80,000, and so on. There is a tissue market, a tissue bank, and bio-banks have sprung all over the world, and they control the supply and price of human tissues.

The market for human tissues exploded when the human genome project was undertaken, completed, and sensationalized by the media. The value of a particularly interesting human gene, or even snippets of human genetic material can be worth billions of dollars (Andrews 2005). In the U.S. alone, over 300 million human biological materials are stored in private and public labs, tissue repositories, and health care institutions, including over 160 million human pathology specimens, with 8 million new cases added per year. Blood banks maintain over 12 million blood specimens, with about that much collected annually (Eiseman and Haga 1999). DNA Science claims that between 10,000 and 13,000 individuals in the U.S. donated their blood in 2000–01 to DNA Science's Gene Trust to build a biobank with the hope of preventing or curing diseases (Press Release, DNA Sciences, Inc., July 19, 2001).

Meanwhile, the problem of human tissue now involves ownership rights. In general, U.S. courts maintain that an individual does not have a property right on body parts that are extracted during medical procedures. With globalization emerged the convergence of different cultures and social mores. What one part of the world views as a national resource has become a stock of investment opportunity in another. What used to be pure science is now a potential profit center. What used to be donated is now negotiated.

A customer transits from being a "patient" (under medical care or treatment),

- to a "subject" or participant (involved in a formal research project or protocol, who may or may not be a patient simultaneously),
- to a "donor" (someone who intends to gift tissue for research purposes),
- and to an "owner" (with rights of privacy, ownership, confidentiality, and royalty rights attached to what is donated).

A corresponding mutation takes place on the supplier side: from a "doctor" in a hospital or clinic to a "scientific researcher" in a bio-lab to a "patent holder" charging a royalty fee to a "corporation" of medical diagnostics with a biobank that could hold billions of dollars worth of tissue property.

Obviously, in the process a new bio-bank industry has emerged. Currently, human genes are patented, and their use is restricted and linked with huge royalty fees. What was a simple problem grew to be wicked, and now is continually morphed with scientific, economic, legal, cultural, and political issues, rights, and controversies. The problem of simple human tissue has become an issue with protection of personal identity, privacy of health information, patient autonomy, confidentiality, ownership, and private property, tissue bio-banks, and court litigations. The human tissue problem has grown increasingly "wicked" with too many interlocking issues. When the donated human tissue from a mere "gift" (which it is in most of the world) became a personal gain (primarily, in the U.S.), personal, economic, social, legal, political, ethical, and moral issues erupted. The identity, formulation, and resolution of the human tissue problem became extremely difficult with the complex interlocking of all these issues.

Moreover, with the number of commercial bio-banks mushrooming as new start-ups, it is not surprising that some would fail. For instance, after running into financial trouble, the DNA Science Inc. sold its bio-banks in bankruptcy. Genaissance Pharmaceuticals bought the inventories of former rival DNA Sciences Inc. at a "fire-sale" price. The original depositors may have the chance to exercise their rights to withdraw (Brinkley 2003a, 2003b). The tissue donors did not anticipate this. Soon the new emerging bio-bank industry was riddled with problems of privacy and confidentiality issues, genetic privacy issues, ethical and moral issues, financial and property issues, legal and legislative issues. Bankruptcy laws were written to resolve insolvency issues and not privacy and confidentiality issues. The circumstance where confidential genetic material could be sold and potentially corrupted generated a new wicked problem.

If a tissue donor's consent is deemed a part of a contract, then a bankruptcy trustee could breach or break the contract via the sale of tissue, an asset (Janger 2005; Maschke 2005). On the other hand, if tissue is deemed to be neither personal property nor intellectual property (genetics is essentially a code, even though a valuable information), the transfer problem becomes even more confounding. The tissue problem, consequently, may not have true or false, right or wrong, legal or illegal, ethical or unethical, fair or unfair solutions; it could just have true, right, legal, ethical, and fair "enough" solutions as Rittel and Webber (1973) foresaw it.

The real problem is over-commodification of the body or its parts—which is a marketing problem. There is an intrusion on human dignity with the emergence of biobanks, human gene patents, and other controversial technologies. This is a consumer problem. If the tissue-donor must be compensated for the unusual lucrative gains associated with the tissues, then the problem turns to an appropriate and reasonable compensation price, royalty fee, and access fee—once again, a marketing problem. Then, again, will the payment be considered undue inducement to donate? This is a supplier-marketing problem (Bear 2004; Greely 2001). Compensation price to the tune of $50,000 for commercial access to individual DNA if used for developing pharmaceutical products has been argued (Bear 2004: 276–77). Then, will such exorbitant payments have a chilling effect on science, and more crucially, shift emphasis from donation to monetization, from bioscience to bio-commerce? This is marketing and a macro-marketing problem.

Managing Non-profits as a Wicked Problem

[See Bradach, Tierney, and Stone (2008: 88–97)]

U.S. non-profits must take on an increasing share of society's most important and difficult work. Managing violence in inner-city communities, educating disadvantaged children, stemming the loss of rain forest or marine wildlife, and the like are typical. Their boards, public and private donors, and other stakeholders are putting increasing pressure on them to demonstrate the effectiveness of their programs by expecting from the staff members of non-profits far better results than what they deliver. These are practical wicked problems. While the goals of these non-profits as stated earlier are themselves wicked problems, the problems get exacerbated by the expectations and constraints imposed on them by their stakeholder boards and donors. Typically, non-profits never have enough of money to cover everything they are already doing, let alone surplus funds to experiment and support new activities and investments. How do you tame this problem? Consider the following non-profit.example.

Rheedlen Centers for Children and Families, a New York, NY based non-profit with an annual budget of $7 million in 2001, had a Herculean mission (wicked problem)—to improve the lives of poor children in America's most devastated communities. Rheedlen provided New Yorkers with family-support networks, a homelessness-prevention program, a senior center, and a host of programs to meet the needs of troubled and impoverished children and teenagers. Rheedlen included the Harlem Children's Zone (HCZ), a fledgling 24-block neighborhood initiative in south-central Harlem. Despite Rheedlen's many good programs, however, the prospects for Harlem's children got worse. Geoffrey Canada, Rheedlen's longtime CEO, had a clear imperative: to help the greatest possible number of kids lead healthy lives, stay in school, and grow up to become independent, productive adults—a laudable goal but riddled with wicked problems.

In order to achieve this daunting goal, in 2002, the CEO changed its name and sharpened its focus. Rheedlen was too broad a focus; it became just Harlem Children's Zone (HCZ). Canada linked Rheedlen's original comprehensive mission to a very concrete statement of the impact HCZ should have—3,000 children, ages 0 to 18, living in the zone should have demographic and achievement profiles consistent with those of average middle-class American communities. With the blessings of the board, Canada and his team discontinued certain Rheedlen activities that were not the major goals of HCZ (e.g., homelessness-prevention programs outside the HCZ zone) and initiated new ones (e.g., Head Start programs and a charter elementary school). They also diversified HCZ's funding, shook up and expanded its management ranks, and invested much in evaluating results. Currently, HCZ receives almost 100 percent private funding or individual contributions. Cultivating private grants/donors require very different capabilities than those required for tapping government grants. Non-profits should be careful to note that whatever fund-raising strategy (private or public) they adopt, the goals of the non-profits are not donor-driven or public-driven, but are organizational goals focused.

By 2004, HCZ had more than doubled in scope, covering 60 square blocks that housed over 6,500 children. In 2007, HCZ added another 37 square blocks housing 4,000 kids to HCZ. During 2002–07, its budget grew from $11.6 million to $50 million. Major foundations offered to help or expand help (such as the Edna McConnell Clark Foundation). HCZ is a success in terms of its maximum social impact on children—a wicked problem was tamed by focusing scope and making stakeholders responsible. Civic and non-profit leaders in other cities are interested in replicating HCZ's approach.

Bradach, Tierney, and Stone (2008), who have studied 150 non-profits during the past eight years, analyze the secret of HCZ success. Even though there is no one "best way" to manage a non-profit, as every such organization faces unique challenges and opportunities in making decisions, the authors suggest some rigorous questions that non-profit executives must address:

- For which results will we hold ourselves accountable?
- How will we achieve them?

- What will results really cost, and how do we fund them?
- How do we build the organization we need to deliver the results?

The questions look easy and generic, but addressing them is a wicked problem. There are basic differences in responding to these questions between profits and non-profits. Table 6.9 explores some of these critical dimensions. The questions create a framework of conversation between non-profit executive directors and stakeholders in developing pragmatic and specific plans for making a tangible difference with concrete measurable results.

The most fundamental and most difficult decision a non-profit can make is addressing the first question—to define the results it needs to be accountable for and in order to be successful. The process entails translating non-profit vision and mission into goals that are simultaneously compelling enough to attract ongoing support from stakeholders and specific enough to inform resource allocations. The non-profit leaders should come up with a strong "intended impact" statement that identifies both the beneficiaries of its activities and the benefits it will provide. Such specificity gives decision makers a powerful lens for prioritizing goals, objectives, and funds. A good illustration of this approach is given by the following non-profit example.

Larkin Street Youth Services (LSYS), a San Francisco-based non-profit, is nationally recognized for its work with homeless and runaway youths. Since its founding in 1984, LSYS has become a model of innovative and effective service provision for homeless and runaway youths. Its mission is to create a continuum of services that inspires youth to move beyond the street. LSYS nurtures potential, promotes dignity, and supports bold steps by all. LSYS relies extensively (almost two-thirds) on government funding. Its "intended impact" statement is to help homeless youth, ages 12 to 24, in the San Francisco Bay area, in developing self-sufficiency and skills to live independently. The impact statement has four clear target values: target population (youth ages 12 to 24), target outcomes (self-sufficiency), geography (San Francisco Bay area), and approach (continuum of care). All stakeholders must agree on these target values.

Some of these goals need to be revised with more data. Statistics revealed that there were nearly four times as many homeless youths in San Francisco, as there were providers to help them. Should, therefore, LSYS expand its boundaries beyond the Bay area despite its historical roots in the Bay area? When limited time and money have to be allocated among various programs and activities, such expansionary decisions are difficult. Nor is the logic supporting these decisions likely to be transparent. Bradach, Tierney, and Stone (2008) contend that a strong "theory of change"—explaining how LSYS could do this—is critical. In 2007, LSYS refined its theory of change, articulating its belief how it can achieve its intended impact of "continuum of care" by:

- Making homeless youths aware of services through outreach.
- Meeting youths where they are and addressing their immediate needs.
- Providing a stable living situation and supportive environment.
- Increasing life skills and connecting youths with jobs and education.

The continuum of care is continually refined through collaboration across programs and access to evaluation data. LSYS disseminates best practices and informs thought leaders through presentations, publications, and advocacy activities. By nature, theory of change discussions must be iterative, given that several options are plausible for achieving a given set of results. For example, teacher training,

TABLE 6.9 Basic Differences in Goals and Problems among Profits and Non-profits

Critical dimensions	Business world of profits	Business world of non-profits
Missions and Ideals	Corporate vision and mission for profits and growth	Social vision and mission for enhancement of society
Goals and Objectives	Superior market and financial performance	Superior social and humanizing performance within targeted zones
Sources of Funds	Revenues, investments, debt–equity structures. Happy customers will support the profits. *The market has spoken.*	Donors, volunteers, and employees who accept modest paychecks for work they are passionate about. Major donors and volunteers donate resources influenced by personal relationships and by the emotional appeal of the non-profit mission. *The heart has spoken*
Internal Feedback Mechanisms	Up-to-the-minute operating data, cash flow, inventory, receivables, payables, performance reviews, and the like	Operating systems, technology, data bases and structures, and performance review systems are often rudimentary
External Feedback Mechanisms	Market forces of demand and customer reactions and complaints	Social and political approval which, given multiplicity of vague objectives, could be delayed and ambiguous
Reward Structures	Customers, customer loyalties, investors, and other stakeholders	Donors, well-wishers, experts who volunteer time, money, and talent
Penalizing Mechanisms	Underperformers are penalized by existing customers and investors	Lack of patronizing; donors withdraw support; volunteers may quit. If non-profits are doing very well, past donors may transfer funds to other fledgling non-profits. Thus, management may be under-compensated and overstretched
Performance Measures	Quantitative in terms of sales revenue increases, market shares, quarterly earnings, return on investments (ROI), return on assets (ROA), earnings per share (EPS), P/E, customer loyalty scores	Mostly qualitative; there is no single quantitative metric that overrides other metrics
Benchmark Measures	The quantitative measures can be calibrated and compared across industry firms, such that firms performing best will attract more capital and talent	Since many non-profits aim at the same goals (e.g., reducing high school dropouts and crime), the absence of standards offers no benchmarks
Stakeholder Expectations	Shareholders expect corporate growth, bottom line profits and dividends	Donors and volunteers expect achievement of social and humanizing results and lasting impact that the non-profits intended
Corporate Planning	Forecast, budget, and investment on people, infrastructure systems, and growth	Forging new relationships with external stakeholders for fund-raising and board-tending
Nature of major Operational Problems	Simple, structured, and solvable problems	Complex, unstructured, social messes and wicked problems

Source: Author's own.

Note: See also Bradach, Tierney, and Stone (2008).

curriculum reform, an extended school day, and personalized instruction might leverage graduation rates among disadvantaged youths in urban high schools. The "right" approach will depend upon several factors such as resources, an organization's capabilities and economics, where similar programs exist and with what proven positive outcomes, costs, and political constraints. Constraining overhead inhibits the very system and staff the non-profit needs to achieve its intended impact.

Expeditionary Learning Schools (ELS) in another non-profit that trains teachers to educate students through real work projects. To achieve results in a low-performing school, ELS staff members must work on-site 30 days a year for at least three years. When ELS assessed its existing network, it found that few schools were in non-compliance with ELS requirements of on-site work, and disqualified these schools from the ELS network. With this attrition, the ELS were reduced to almost a fourth of its schools network. However, those ELS schools that complied have shown remarkably improved student learning and performance. In 2004, ELS received a significant grant from the Bill and Melinda Gates Foundation to extend its work to new and small high schools in needy areas. Within a few years, ELS regained the schools it had lost during the previous non-compliance attrition.

Non-profits can be fragile financially. The choices of funding agencies and donors are usually influenced by personal relationships or the emotional appeal of the mission rather than by organizational performance of the non-profits. Alumni and alumnae who give millions of dollars to their alma maters do not always require clear evidence of performance. Yet they may stop funding their alma maters delivering demonstrable results when their personal interests shift, a phenomenon called "donor fatigue." In such cases, how can non-profit leaders develop a reliable funding base? There may not be a simple answer. Non-profit leaders, however, should bring their funding and their strategies into better alignment. That is, financial clarity should allow decision makers to assess the impact of their programs on both the organization's programs and its margins.

In this regard, Bradach, Tierney, and Stone (2008) suggest a 2×2 matrix of financial clarity strategies as depicted in Table 6.10. When it comes to delivering and sustaining results, having the right people in the right positions, trumps having the right strategy. Most non-profit leaders are passionate, entrepreneurial, and hard working. They are motivated more by the opportunity to help others than by personal economic benefits. Philanthropy exists in a world without marketplace pressures. Donors, however, can influence the behavior of the non-profits they fund, but when they impose their own priorities, they risk compromising the non-profit's ability to deliver intended results. Achieving impact through non-profits thus demands a shared understanding of priorities between donors and the recipients.

How Can CEOs Resolve Wicked Problems?

The first step is to recognize that a given problem is wicked and not just simple or complex or even ill-structured. Second, we must realize that the wicked problem is real and that solutions are necessary. Knowing that the problem is wicked is of no use, if that does not help us to address it. Third, we must free ourselves from being bound to any one model or class of problems or solutions in resolving it. Flexibility is the key in the solution of a wicked problem, a flexibility that is needed to cope with the capricious nature of wicked problems (Becker 2007).

Problem wickedness is a force of fragmentation. When working on wicked problems in a socially complex environment we need to foster and develop a "collective intelligence" through socially shared

TABLE 6.10 Strategic Financial Clarity in Resolving Non-profit Wicked Problems

Alignment with intended impact strategy	*Financial contribution (revenues minus costs)*	
	Negative	*Positive*
Low	These programs are *potential distractions*. Find ways to improve them or just shut them down. The donor market has spoken.	These programs *generate income*. Pursue them unless they become a management distraction. Because of their low intended impact, "donor fatigue" may set in either because their personal interests are not met or have been shifted.
High	These programs make sense or have sentimental value (e.g., alma mater projects) and *require funding* for sustenance. Pursue opportunities for additional funding and/or cost improvements.	These programs are *self-sustaining*. Invest in them and enable them to grow. Track demographic and economic shifts in target values so that the non-profits remain relevant to the publics they intend to serve.

Source: Author's own.

Note: See also Bradach, Tierney, and Stone (2008: 95).

cognitions and meanings, goals and objectives, assumptions and presuppositions. Collective intelligence is a natural enabler of collaboration.

There is a tendency in most of us to see problems as tame and a tendency to avoid wicked problems. Instinctively, we resist or deny problems that are wicked as unsolvable. CEOs and managers easily collude in systematic denial of the complex and ill-structured dynamics of wicked problems, a phenomenon that Chris Argyris (1996) called "skilled incompetence." The first step, therefore, in coping with a wicked problem is to recognize its nature, its complexity, and its degree of wickedness (Conklin 2006: 10).

We can know very little about a wicked problem, however, by solution methods of simple or complex problems. For instance, problem definition, hypotheses formulation, objective data collection and analysis, hypotheses verification/falsification, and drawing inferences will reveal almost nothing about the subtle and stubborn nature of wicked problems. This approach may lead to "analysis paralysis," a Catch 22 situation where we cannot take action until we have more information, and we cannot get more information until someone takes action.

Wicked problems, in contrast, demand an opportunity-driven approach; that is, opportunities define the way we resolve a wicked problem. For instance, if we define the recent health care problem in the U.S. as one of mal-distribution whereby close to 100 million of its people are either uninsured or are underinsured, then a solution that insures health care coverage for all Americans is opportunity-driven. Similarly, defining the present problems of advertising cigarettes or pornography as one that is targeted to vulnerable groups such as children and teenagers, then a solution that seeks to un-target these groups is opportunity-driven.

Takeuchi and Nonaka (1986) use the rugby term "Scrum" for adaptive processes that world-class companies use to resolve wicked problems of developing and marketing new products. An essential feature of Scrum is that it forces incremental action that creates basis for stakeholder dialog and project feedback. For instance, a Scrum project collects stakeholder input in a feature list called the "Backlog."

Each month, the new product development team starts at the top of the backlog and selects as many of the top priority features they can develop in a month. The new product team then works on these features for a month, when the results are presented to the stakeholders. This adaptive process provides a basis for incremental thinking and rethinking the backlog features and priorities. The stakeholders are allowed to modify and re-prioritize the backlog. The development team recesses for another month, and so on. Scrum provides a way for the development team to make regular progress even if the problem is not well understood. Scrum enables the stakeholders' regular opportunity to discuss the problem and reach consensus incrementally. The resolution of the wicked problem also emerges incrementally. Scrum facilitates control, predictability if the project is converging or diverging, and flexibility for the stakeholders to add consensual inputs. Software developers regularly use Scrum in resolving wicked problems of software development (Schwaber and Beedle 2001).

Taming wicked problems is important—it can offer good market opportunities. Giant companies like Wal-Mart, GE, Exxon, GMC, Dell, Ford, and Chrysler are constantly facing wicked problems as they are also encountering good market opportunities from them.

What CEOs Should Avoid in Resolving Wicked Problems

Corresponding to Rittel and Webber's (1973) 10 criteria's of characterizing wicked problems, Conklin (2006: 10–11) suggests six ways we should avoid in taming wicked problems:

1. **Do not lock down the problem definition**: There is a tendency in us is to "lock down" a wicked problem. That is, we restrict its domain, definition, solution space, and doable solutions. For instance, locking down a problem could be defining the issue as local or private, and not national or global. Thereby, one seeks a micro solution to a macro problem. Similarly, in reducing crime and violence in public schools, a locked down solution will be to install metal detectors in all school entrances or of increasing juvenile prison spaces. We freeze the domain and requirements of the crime problem as a way of locking it down. Federal bailing out major financial companies (e.g., Chrysler, Bear Stearns, Fannie May and Freddie Mac, or AIG) locks down their problem, does not resolve it.

2. **Do not assert the problem is solved**: Since it is almost impossible to define a wicked problem, we deny there either is a problem or assert it is solved without defining it. Autocratic politicians often adopt this process. Such an attitude can deny the existence of wicked problems such as health care, pornography, recession, terrorism in Afghanistan, and tensions in other war-torn countries.

3. **Do not objectify parameters of a wicked problem in order to measure the success of its solution**: This amounts to locking down the problem. Obviously, this is a measurement issue. That is, whatever is measured, officially and by definition, becomes the problem. For instance, we measure the problem and solution to crime in schools by reducing deaths and injuries in school premises to zero. What if such a solution should increase crime outside the school property? The wicked problem reasserts itself in a different guise. The tame solution exacerbates the problem.

4. **Do not identify current problems to previous related problems**: We cast the current wicked problem as "just like" a previous problem, and resolve it accordingly. For instance, we quickly define the Mid-eastern countries as the "axis of evil" and resolve the problems of Iraq, Afghanistan, Pakistan, and Iran the same way. We often mistake the enemy will repeat 9/11 the same way as in 2001!

In military circles, there is a saying: "we always fight the last war," a tendency to assume the enemy will behave as in the last war!

5. **Do not give up trying to search for a good solution to the problem**: We deny or postpone resolving the problem, hoping it will resolve or disappear by itself. For example, this is how we treat the wicked problems of health care, social security, inflation, recession, unemployment, underemployment, outsourcing, racial discrimination, gender discrimination, crime, and poverty in the U.S. We do not solve wicked problems; we just try not to make things worse.

6. **Do not declare a limited solution space to the wicked problem**: We tend to conclude there are just a few solutions to the problem, and focus on selecting from among these options. For instance, we combat terrorism by retaliation, change of regime, or by destroying countries. We refuse to negotiate. Framing wicked problems with "either/or" terms is another way of limiting the solution space. For instance, a politician may ask: Should we attack Iraq or let the terrorists take over the world?

Following the work of Rittel and Webber (1973) and Ackoff (1974), Jonathan Rosenhead (1996) of the London School of Economics suggests the following methodological criteria for dealing with wicked problems:

- Accommodate multiple alternative perspectives rather than prescribe single solutions.
- Function through group interaction and iteration rather than back office calculations.
- Generate ownership of the problem formulation through transparency.
- Facilitate a graphic (visual, sound, color, imaging) representation of the problem for a systematic and group exploration of the solution space.
- Focus on relationships between discrete alternatives rather than continuous variables.
- Concentrate on possibility rather than probability.

Incorporating Rittel and Webber's (1973) 10 criteria's for characterizing wicked problems, Ritchey (2002, 2005, 2006) describes a group-facilitated, computer-aided General Morphological Analysis (GMA) to handle wicked problems. Rittel and Webber (1973) suggested that "in order to describe a wicked problem in sufficient detail, one has to develop an exhaustive inventory for all the conceivable solutions ahead of time." As a process, GMA goes through a number of iterative steps or phases representing cycles of analysis and synthesis in order to develop a fairly exhaustive inventory for all the conceivable solutions to a given wicked problem. The GMA starts by identifying and defining the most important dimensions of the wicked problem. Each of these dimensions is then given a range of relevant (discrete) values or conditions. Together, these make up the variables or parameters of the complex problem. A morphological field is constructed by setting the parameters against each other in parallel columns, representing an n-dimensional configuration space. A particular constructed "field configuration" is designated by selecting a single value from each of the variables. This marks out a particular state or (formal) solution within the problem complex (Ritchey 2005: 4).

The morphological field represents the total "problem space" that can contain thousands of possible solutions. A feasible "solution space" is derived by a process of internal cross-consistency assessment (CCA). All of the parameter values in the morphological field are compared with one another, pair-wise, in the manner of cross-impact matrix. GMA next analyses each pair of conditions and judges whether the pair can co-exist, that is, represent a consistent relationship. Mutual consistency is not assessed based on causality or probability, but only by possibility. Using this technique, a typical morphological field can be reduced significantly, depending upon the nature of the problem.

Rittel and Webber's (1973) seventh criterion states: "Part of the art of dealing with wicked problems is the art of not knowing too early which type of solution to apply." GMA calls this phenomenon "remaining in the mess," that is, keeping one's options open long enough to explore as many relationships in the problem space as possible, before starting to formulate solutions. As many stakeholders as possible should be engaged in the work, in order to create a common terminology, common problem concept, and common modeling framework. Principal stakeholders should be involved in: (*a*) structuring much of the problem space, (*b*) synthesizing solution spaces, (*c*) exploring multiple solutions on the basis of different drivers and interests, and (*d*) analyzing stakeholder structures. The different stakeholders do not have to agree on a single, common solution but must be encouraged to understand each other's positions and contexts.

The results of GMA would depend much upon the quality of inputs provided in terms of the specificity of the total problem space and the total solution space, definitions of the parameters and the ranges of conditions, and the cross-consistency assessment. GMA enables "garbage detection" since poorly defined parameters and incomplete ranges of conditions surface quickly when CCA is applied.

Camillus (2008) suggests some tried and proven ways to resolve wicked problems:

1. Involve key stakeholders (e.g., customers, employees, creditors, suppliers, and shareholders) in managing the wicked problem. Brainstorm and document their ideas, approaches, and hidden assumptions. Go beyond obtaining facts and figures in order to understand their biases and opinions. Establish ongoing interactive communication between the CEOs and the key stakeholders, and among the stakeholders' via intranets, blogs, and e-bulletins.. Build up a collective intelligence to counteract individual cognitive biases and prejudices. The tacit knowledge of your key stakeholders may help you better tame the wicked problem.
2. Define the corporate identity and stay true to your corporate purpose and goals. Define your values: What is fundamentally important to your company? Assess your competencies: What does your company do better than your competitors do? Describe your aspirations: How does the company envision and measure success?
3. Focus on action. In a world of Newtonian order, it is easy to identify causes and effects and strategize accordingly. In a world of complex and chaotic wicked problems, it is tough to gauge and link causes and effects, and hence, formulate one strategy. Do some scenario-analysis: set up 2×2 blocks based on meaningful vectors. For example, suppose your *x*-axis measures two levels "weak and slow" and "strong and fast" in relation to the *x* variable "opportunities for differentiation and growth in emerging markets," and your *y*-axis assesses two states, "high and volatile" and "moderate and stable" in relation to the *y* variable "costs of energy." This frame provides four possible scenarios: analyze all four, and see which best fits your values, goals, competencies, and aspirations. Conduct several scenario analyses. Frame your strategy to tame the wicked problem based on the convergence of your scenario analyses and resulting strategies.
4. Adopt a "feed-forward" orientation. Under ordinary problems, an effective way of learning and refining strategies is via feedback. Feedback reflects learning from the past. Feedback is ineffective with wicked problems that do not have a clear past. The latter require executives to feed-forward with insights from unfamiliar time and place, with unanticipated, uncertain, and unclear futures. With wicked problems, CEOs must envision the futures. Under this version of

scenario-planning, executives must describe the set of external and internal circumstances that they would like to see in the next 10, 20, or 50 years.

Wicked problems require imagination and experimentation, innovation and entrepreneurship, launching pilot programs, testing prototypes, and seeking "good enough" solutions with the least unintended consequences. The main feature of a wicked problem is that you do not understand the problem until you have a solution. Often, social complexity (e.g., multiple stakeholders, their diversity and individuality, their organizational mission and goals) clouds the solution. Social complexity often makes the problem definition/solution method a social process with fragmented polarizations. Hence, you need much cooperation and collaboration, coherence and compassion in defining wicked problems and identifying possible solutions. We need to develop a shared understanding of the problem and a shared commitment to its solution. Shared understand of the problem requires that we recognize the individual and diverse viewpoints of the stakeholders to the problem, that we dialogue about the different interpretations of the problem, and to develop and exercise a coherence and collective intelligence about it.

Team effort is critical in addressing wicked problems. A good and effective team brings two benefits together: (*a*) a team with diverse backgrounds—the greater the diversity of experience, perspectives, and knowledge the team members bring to bear on the problems, the better their capacity to assimilate and process multiple information inputs, convert them into knowledge and accordingly strategize resolutions; (*b*) the capacity of teams, over time, to be self-directed and capable of managing significant cross-disciplinary business concerns. We must abandon the traditional hierarchical and pyramidal model that puts strategy on the top, tactics in the middle, and implementation at the bottom. This top-down model slows information sharing and processing and knowledge generation. Instead, we should place all three, strategy, tactics, and implementation, within the same rung as virtually indivisible activities that every team must manage. Top management may provide the overall vision, but everybody else works from the trenches. The top management should ensure that everybody brings commitment, empowerment, and innovation. The team culture should focus on a structure that rewards risk-taking, expects personal responsibility, and promotes high levels of trust and collaboration. Besides promoting a spirit of inquiry and creating shared displays for design, the team should create the "surround"—the whole context of learning and knowledge generation and exchange between team members (Pacanowski 1993).

Analysis versus Synthesis in Taming Wicked Problems

Taming wicked problems need analysis and synthesis. According to Ackoff (1972, 1974a), "analysis" implies: (*a*) take the thing apart you want to understand; (*b*) explain the behavior of each part taken separately; and (*c*) aggregate your explanations of the parts into an understanding of the whole. On the other hand, "synthesis" implies: (*a*) take the thing you want to understand as part of a larger whole; (*b*) explain the behavior of the containing whole; and (*c*) disaggregate the understanding of the containing whole into the role or function of the parts.

Since we are comfortable with analysis, as this has been our dominant method of inquiry, research, managing, and teaching, we are not too comfortable with synthesis. Systems thinking or systemic thinking is a method of synthesis. While the strategy of analysis is reactive, non-systemic, and its appeal is secular, the strategy of synthesis is creative, its focus is systemic, and its appeal is both artistic as well as scientific. According to Russell Ackoff, the deterministic machine-age thinking overemphasizes analysis, while the modern stochastic systems-age thinking fosters synthesis. Our empirical sciences that seek explanation, prediction, and control thrive on analysis; modern meta-empirical sciences that seek meaning, dialogue, and consensus emphasize synthesis.

Obviously, we need both in resolving wicked problems—analysis that results in explanation, prediction, and control, and synthesis that generates meaning, dialogue, collaboration, and consensus. In combining analysis with synthesis, we absorb all states of reality, deterministic, stochastic, uncertain, and chaotic; we welcome all sub-certainties and rival interpretations not necessarily as right or wrong, true or false, but as "contributory" (King 1993). As Richard Bernstein (1983) argues, we need in modern times to transcend the dilemma of "objectivism versus relativism" to the dialogue of contribution and collaboration.

The three basic modes or methods of synthesis are "metaphor," "irony," and "synecdoche"—all imply that the whole is greater than the sum of the parts.

Metaphor is a paradigm, gestalt, analogy, parable, mental model, schema, or representation. As the *Webster's College Dictionary* defines it, a metaphor is a figure of speech containing an implied comparison, in which a word or phrase ordinarily and primarily used for one thing is applied to another (e.g., Spartan courage; the curtain of night; the light of Heaven; all the world is a stage). It generates insights and confers meanings by framing unfamiliar things in familiar ways (e.g., electric current is a fluid; the U.S. is a Land of Promise; a nuclear plant is a time-bomb; what we see is the tip of the iceberg) and by reframing familiar things in other familiar ways (e.g., our ideas are half-baked; our inventions come from the back-burner). Metaphor transforms reality by reframing it. The subtle reality comes to life through metaphors. It plays a fundamental role in both hard and soft sciences. The metaphor as a type of mental model provides context for our thoughts and actions (Senge 1990: 185). Choosing a proper representation, frame or paradigm for a problem can improve significantly the solution-finding process—it is a creative act (King and Acklin 1995). For instance, the metaphor of teamwork in management is drawn from soccer, football, basketball, hockey, bridge, and other team sports. If applied properly, creative team building can shape and transform management.

For instance, mathematical theorizing in economics, and hence, in marketing, is metaphorical (McCloskey 1983: 505). The search for quantitative formulations to formalize social processes is dominant in empirical social science. For instance, in advocating deregulation, we humanize the relatively untamable market as a free enterprise, a self-correcting mechanism that will take care of itself without governmental intervention—this is all metaphorical language. Much of language is metaphorical in the sense we freely use metaphors to express our deepest thoughts. Treating a corporation as a moral person with rights and responsibilities is also a metaphor. We even represent individual careers, social movements, and organizations as "wholes," specifically as narratives or stories (Abbott 1990: 141). This is because, according to MacIntyre (1981: 211), "we dream in narrative, day-dream in narrative, remember, anticipate, hope, despair, believe, doubt, plan, revise, criticize, construct, gossip, learn, hate and love by narrative." Most narratives, stories, fictions, biographies, and autobiographies are deeply metaphorical and synthetic. They are analogies or analogues of reality as we know it. The meaningful whole of the narrative is greater than the sum of the parts. The vital information is in the connections. The road maps can lead you astray if you ignore their legends (Lakoff and Johnson 1980). At the same time, we should note that no literal paraphrase provides the insight of a metaphor, since the "insight" of a metaphor is often spelled out in psychological terms.

The opposite is also true. That is, some metaphors are not reducible to cognitively equivalent literal expressions (e.g., men are from Mars, and women from Venus). In some case, metaphors may more nearly create similarities between things, rather than merely express preexisting ones (Black 1981: 19–20, 36). The notion of "creating similarities" rather than discovering them is a good warning for all scientists that engage in modeling, prediction, and control.

Irony is a form of humor. It is a dissembler in speech, a clever juxtaposition of two things, each of which makes sense on its own, but whose forced combination creates the surprise. It is a juxtaposition of parts in a containing whole, the crucial difference is that the parts are in opposition (King 1995). Laughter is the best medicine—and humor is the best substitute for antacids. It is a method of humorous expression in which the intended meaning of the words is the direct opposite of their usual sense (e.g., that stupid plan is clever; your stupid mistake is brilliant; studied ignorance; inefficiency of the over-skilled). In this sense, an irony is dialectic logic. The dialectic logic of irony is synthetic as opposed to analytic. According to Gregory Bateson, it is "abductive" logic as opposed to "inductive" or "deductive" logic. According to Edward de Bono, it is "lateral" as opposed to "vertical" thinking. For instance, a hard line republican mingling, speaking, and agreeing with liberal democrats is ironical—yet this happened in the legalizing of the rescue package to our modern financial market crisis. The result is a tension of opposite parts in a containing whole (e.g., marriage of strange bedfellows; marriage is the union of two in one flesh yet of two separate individuals). Irony can be good or bad, bitter or sweet. Even bitter irony (e.g., an idiot savant, laughing sickness) can generate insights and confer meanings, where the interaction of opposites creates a synthesis. A good irony reframes reality and unifies reality to transform it (e.g., ghost town, blissful hell, crowded heaven).

Synecdoche is a figure of speech in which a part is used for a whole, an individual for a class, or reverse of any of these (e.g., bread for food, copper for a penny, an army for a soldier). Synecdoche is analogous to a hologram, where the parts reflect a whole and the whole is reflected in the parts. It generates insights and meanings through its layered logic. It can transform lives and reality especially when synecdoche reminds us that we individuals are part of the whole society, that we must truly represent the larger reality of society and posterity. It would be very effective in a corporation if most members understood the big picture of the organization. For example, in a customer-focused organization, dedication to customer service implies enhanced products and services that in turn reframes the meaning of work and commitment to the production-floor employees and galvanizes the supply to supply the best materials. This is a holographic picture of the firm—one part or department of the firm leading to a comprehensive networked picture of the entire corporation. In a corporation, each needs the other, and this is the whole point of synecdoche and the source of its power (King and Acklin 1995).

The hero has a thousand faces. The hero is a mythic archetype common to all cultures. Knowing one hero, you get a good idea of all heroes. This is the power of synecdoche. Ironic stories of heroes in all shapes and sizes crowd our libraries. Identifying one hero with another through synecdoche, we essentially join the hero's journey. A hero is almost always known for compassion—kindness toward all. A second acid test of a hero is integrity. Covey's (1989) *The 7 Habits of Highly Effective People* focuses the first three habits on integrity, while the second three habits essentially focus on compassion. Both integrity and compassion are master virtues and spiritual modes of synthesis. Integrity deals with the inner world of value, mind, soul, and spirit; compassion deals with the outer world of fellow human beings. Connecting and living the union of two is corporate virtue in its best form. Integrity and compassion represent the best of humanistic yearnings, far and beyond the bottom line of profits and growth of corporations. However, integrity and compassion assure both the bottom line of profits and high growth.

They are the habits of great and highly effective corporate executives (Covey 1989). Learning how to scale them up to group and organizational levels is increasingly the hallmark of effective firms (King and Acklin 1995).

Traditional business ethics is analytical with its judgments based on rule-like generalizations and infatuation with dichotomous ethical dilemma. Traditional business ethics case studies are also analytical. Orthodox business ethics has almost nothing to say about the great virtues of integrity and compassion that emphasize synthesis. It is time for a smooth transition from analysis to synthesis, from case studies to grand narratives of ethical heroes (King and Acklin 1995). Most business operations are systemic processes and lived narratives that need synthetic thinking in terms of the cardinal virtues of responsibility, trust, and the relationships of integrity and compassion. The grand corporate narratives of virtue are best understood in terms of metaphors, ironies, and synecdoche.

CONCLUDING REMARKS

Dealing with wicked problems is challenging. Ultimately, dealing with wicked problems requires tremendous trust between stakeholders who have vested interest in the problem. It requires an act of faith of all participants trying to find a better method or process or cooperative state (De Grace and Stahl 1990).

There are compelling reasons for learning to solve the right problems (King 1993: 105). By solving the wrong problem (Type III error), we unwittingly undermine our capacity to solve the right problems. Rittel and Webber (1973) claim that wicked problems do not have a definitive formulation because "in order to describe a wicked problem in sufficient detail, one has to develop an exhaustive set of all conceivable solutions ahead of time." This may not be necessarily true. In practice, scientists or city planners consider a limited set of feasible solutions that have a larger likelihood of resolving the social or political problem. Limiting the domain of investigation is an important aspect of problem formulation–resolution methodology. Often, the constraints on research grant resources enforce such problem-slicing and domain-boundaries.

Further, strategies for solving simple and tame problems differ qualitatively from strategies appropriate for solving social messes and wicked problems. Messes are puzzles. Rather than solving them, we should properly frame these problems such that we can sort out their complexities and uncertainties and dissolve the barriers to consensus implicit in wicked problems. Our present inabilities of sorting and dissolving problems may be paradigmatic of things to come—more advanced technologies will empower to dissolve or resolve problems that we cannot do now.

Epistemologically and axiologically speaking, the "good" and the "bad," the "true" and the "false" are not necessarily incompatible (Bahm 1975). A solution can be both true and good at the same time; it can even be false but good at the same time. A solution can be true and good from one perspective and false and bad from another perspective. For instance, stem cell research is good when it is based on adult cells but bad when it is solely based on embryonic cells, especially when human embryos have to be killed for saving victims of presently incurable diseases.

There is much fear about the destructive potential of the complex financial instruments, like credit default swaps, that brought AIG to its knees. The market for such dubious instruments has exploded in recent years, and it is almost entirely unregulated. While bailing out AIG would always stir controversy, the government should crack down regulation on the use of credit default swaps. The swaps are not securities and are not regulated by the SEC. While they perform the same function as an insurance policy they are not insurance in the conventional sense, and so insurance regulators do not monitor them either. AIG's crisis grew primarily out of its financial products unit, which dealt in complex debt securities and credit default swaps. AIG's complex debt securities had already lost billions of dollars in value in the months before the AIG crisis began, primarily because their value depends upon home values. However, in two days, September 11–12, 2008, the swaps AIG's financial products unit had sold began eating up billions of dollars of AIG's cash and liquid assets. This ultimately paralyzed AIG, as it could not find a way to keep up with increasing cash requirements under the terms of its swap contracts (Andrews 2008: A 18).

BUSINESS TRANSFORMATION EXERCISES

6.1 According to Perrow (1984), designing safe nuclear power plants is a Type III and/or Type IV problem. The problem is loaded with known outcomes with unknown probabilities of sequences (Type III problem) and unknown outcomes with unanticipated and unimagined consequences with unknown probabilities (Type IV problem).

   a. Re-conceptualize the nuclear power plant problem in terms of messes. What are its essential components, interactive processes, and boundaries?
   b. Isolate your current organizational learning dysfunctions that bias or oversimplify your understanding of this problem or that cause latent failures?
   c. How do you "frame" the problem in terms of our energy needs since framing the problem determines what you can know about the problem?
   d. Given your frame, how do you "image" the problem and its solution such that all participants can argue about it and converge to a consensual understanding of the problem?
   e. Next, how can you "tame" this problem by "drawing boundaries" that sort out linked pieces or components of the imaged problem? Do these boundaries reflect affordable current and future energy needs, safety needs, and EPA compliance?
   f. How do you next control the degree of "interactive complexity" between components of this problem such that you can prevent harmful surprises?
   g. How can you control the degree of "coupling" of various parts of the problem so that you can increase your capacity to cure harmful surprises?
   h. How do (a) to (g) avoid a Chernobyl disaster with high certainty?
   i. How do (a) to (h) resolve problems of nuclear waste disposal and the proliferation of weapons-grade materials?
   j. How do (a) to (i), and given risks associated with each major source of energy, help build a balanced "energy portfolio" that could spread and minimize risks of coal, natural gas, bio-methane, ethanol, oil, windmills, hydroelectric, solar, and nuclear power?
   k. Is this energy portfolio or conservation approach economically less risky than phasing out nuclear plants?
   l. Alternatively, will the conservation approach be economically more risky if it mandates significant government interventions that, in turn, lead to concentration of state power?
   m. On the other hand, will a non-conservation approach lead to concentration of private power and to a market system that is notoriously shortsighted and ignores all manners of externalities?
   n. Given (a) to (m), how can you minimize energy consumption from the industrial energy-intensive manufacturing economy of the last century to our current information-driven energy-light service economy?

6.2 The subject of compensating donors, patients, or participants for access to their human tissue (e.g., blood, bone marrow, skin, hair, vital organs) is itself a wicked problem. U.S. laws today provide a limited framework for balancing and resolving conflicts of tissue ownership and control. How would you equitably and universally resolve this issue given that:

a. The human tissue may be neither personal property nor intellectual property, per se.

b. The human tissue may be both personal property and intellectual property, per se.

c. Genetically modified microorganisms can be patented [*Diamond v. Chakrabarti*, 447 U. S. 303, 310 (1980)].

d. The corporeal (tangible, genetic) element in the tissue contains valuable information (e.g., genetic code) that could convert into lucrative products for biotechnology, diagnostics, and pharmaceutical companies.

e. The individual donor or donor families should know, in advance, for what purposes the tissue will be used.

f. The individual donor or donor families should be able to participate in any subsequent commercialization of the tissue.

g. The individual donor or donor families should be able to determine the appropriate and acceptable use of the donated tissue.

h. The individual donor or donor families express deep concern over the commodification of the body parts, despite shared proceeds.

i. The individual donor or donor families express deep concern over privacy, confidentiality, accountability, monitoring, transparency, ethics, and morality issues linked with human tissue commercialization.

j. The individual donor or donor families feel that human biobanks, human gene patents, and other commercialization of the human tissue are an intrusion on human dignity.

k. The United Nations Educational, Scientific, and Cultural Organization (UNESCO) and the European Convention on Human Rights and Biomedicine deemed it ethical to provide benefits to individuals and groups for commercial access to their DNA and found it in consonance with respect to human dignity and human rights [see footnote 63 in Lewis (2008)].

l. One of the three objectives of the Convention on Biological Diversity is the "fair and equitable sharing of the benefits arising out of the utilization of genetic resources." It includes appropriate access to genetic resources, appropriate transfer of relevant technologies, taking into account all rights over those resources and technologies, and appropriate funding [see footnote 64 in Lewis (2008)].

m. A compensation of $50,000 has been suggested for commercial access to individual DNA if used for developing a product for the clinical management of a common disorder (Bear 2004: 276–77).

n. Additional compensation (e.g., royalties) may be appropriate if the product's profitability exceeds the initial estimates used to set the access fee (Bear 2004: 282–83).

o. Benefit sharing may not be an appropriate answer to the compensation question given that it will have a chilling effect on biosciences reducing them to commerce.

p. Moving away from privatization of tissue samples and from persons as owners of "property" to citizens participating in public health for the public good may be an honorable "compensation" plan.

PART III

The CEO as a Strategic Leader of Innovation Management

Chapter 7

The CEO as a Strategic Leader of Creativity and Innovation Management

Creativity in its various forms has become the number one engine of economic growth. The "creative class" now comprises 38 million members, or more than 30 percent of the American workforce. Creative professionals in financial services, health care, high tech, pharmaceuticals, media, and entertainment, act as agents of change, producers of intangible assets, and creators of new value for their companies. Creative and innovative designs are not only associated with an iPhone, a Toyota Prius, and a Nintendo Wii, but are rapidly moving from "posters to toasters" to include processes, systems, and organizations (Neumeier 2009: 13).

A creative economy or market is different from the agricultural and industrial economies, in that the former relies on a resource called creativity. In general, every human being has creativity. The question is whether our institutions (e.g., homes, schools, universities, corporations, and governments) and their leaders can provide processes and techniques, incentives and resources to support the individuals in exercising their creativity productively. Hence, the critical role of the CEO and the top management crew in providing the required corporate resources, energy, incentives, and atmosphere for corporate creativity and innovation. For instance, Toyota Corporation reports a long-standing practice of listening to workers on the shop floor in generating new ideas and solving problems. The creative and profitable results of the corporate culture are obvious.

The greatness of America, or for that matter, any country, and its economy lies in its unbeaten capacity for innovation and venture. The average innovation ability of companies in America and in the developed world is rising, and in certain industries it is almost equalizing (e.g., autos, cell phones, information technology). A very successful company targets and achieves over 40 percent of its annual sales revenues from its new products (e.g., Microsoft, Dell Computers, Proctor & Gamble [P&G], and Sony)—that is, the company renovates every three years. Moderately successful companies target 50 percent of their annual sales from internally developed new products during the last five years—the company renovates every 10 years. Hence, new products are the best answers to most problems of all institutions.

Countries are seeking their own sources of comparative advantage in the innovation landscape. In China, the key innovation model today is the kind of brute force that comes from increasingly sophisticated massed minds working together. For India, it is building on the booming outsourcing industry and software markets. For Singapore, it is competitive socialization in bio-tech, digital media, and environmental technology. For oil-rich nations, it is the limited and fast eroding opportunity of oil mines.

THE DYNAMIC OF CREATIVITY AND INNOVATION

Creativity and innovation go together. Traditional companies view innovation narrowly and wrongly. Without creative people in top positions, they typically focus on innovations that can be divided and conquered, rather than integrate and harmonize them. They break innovations into smaller and smaller components, compartmentalize them from function to function, and then optimize each function in sequence. The underlying logic is flawed: segregating and improving the most important pieces of the most important processes will create the best results (Rigby, Gruver, and Allen 2009: 80–81). This logic often dominates in all-star major league games—you may have the best of players for all the most important positions, but without a creative coach to blend and integrate them together, you often produce boring and chaotic results. Imagine Hollywood or Bollywood hired the best of actors, scriptwriters, animated background scene designers, choreographers, and cinematographers, but neglected to engage a creative and dynamic visionary director—the results could be disastrous.

Breakthrough innovation does not function that way. Companies may have excellent patent and technology portfolios and yet grow disillusioned with the innovations' efforts and outcomes. For instance, the individual manufacturers of hundreds of portable music players may tout technical specifications that are apparently superior to that of Apple's iPod, yet the latter offers an overall total customer experience, including shopping, training, downloading, listening, and servicing, that competitors have not yet matched.

Creativity and innovation, however, are not enough. There is a big difference between being a creative firm and an innovative enterprise: the former generates much ideas; the latter generates much cash (Levitt 1963). A failing company needs innovations that turn into good markets and good markets that turn into good cash and financial returns—this is the innovation-to-cash chain (Andrew and Sirkin 2003: 78). Creating innovations are not in short supply today, but the executive intelligence to monetize them is.

There could be many creative ideas, but creative ideas by themselves are inert, and for all practical purposes, worthless—a good idea is nothing more than a tool in the hands of an entrepreneur (Timmons 1999). Venture capitalists do not invest on creative ideas, but on teams that execute them. Executive and entrepreneurial intelligence is rare but we find it in people. A firm could have a ton of interesting ideas, but they do not necessarily have a good creative idea as to how to filter them for best business or market impact. Apple in the 1990s had a load of creative ideas but they could not get them to the market; they began to do so only during the last five to eight years (i.e., 2001–08), thanks to their customer-focused strategy. P&G had over 30,000 patents to their name, but they only use less than 10 percent of them in their product lines. Creative or interesting ideas may be bad or good, great and plenty, but nothing much if they cannot solve a real industrial or consumer problem.

WHAT IS CREATIVITY?

Creativity may be defined in terms of "meaningful novelty" of some output (e.g., a painting, a chemical compound) relative to conventional practice in the domain to which it belongs (e.g., abstract art, adhesives). Thus, a creative product is that which differentiates, that is, it evokes a "meaningful difference" from other competing products in the product category. A creative marketing program (e.g., advertising, promotional campaigns) represents a meaningful difference from marketing practices (e.g., media advertising) in a given product category.

Creativity is a distinct personality trait. Not all people are creative, accomplished though they may be in other areas, and they will not usually learn it from corporate creativity programs. Others are passionately creative, both by nature and long training, and are right-brain dominant. To innately creative people, innovation comes as naturally to them as music did to Mozart, and like Mozart, they have cultivated the skills over the years. Creative people typically imagine a whole new picture and see every innovation as a part that must fit the whole. They are less concerned with perfecting any one component than with creating a holistic brand statement that enhances the entire target customer experience. At the Gucci Group, for instance, creative directors focus on anything that affects the customer—the design of new products and brands, the look, ambience, and feel of retail stores, the slogans and typography of ads, the style and quality of post-sale service, and not every facet of the brand has to meet the narrow profit-and-loss test (Rigby, Gruver, and Allen 2009: 80–81).

The French physiologist Claude Bernard once remarked, "It is what we think we know already that often prevents us from learning." Creativity looks beyond one's old learning; it is unlearning. It looks beyond the conventional. Creativity can be dampened when we become prisoners of our old ideas and conventions, dogmas, and orthodoxies (Hamel and Getz 2004: 81).

The truly creative person knows that all creating is achieved through working with constraints. Without constraints there is no creating (Fritz 1989).

Most business managers want to control creativity. That is, they want neatly sequenced discovery, ideation, refinement, and production, such that they could manage, track, compare, and measure like manufacturing. The creative act, however, is much wilder. Those who insist on tidy phases inevitably produce mediocre results, because the too-orderly process rules out random inspiration. Rule-busting creativity and innovation require a sense of play, a sense of eureka and delight, and a refusal to be corralled into a strict method (Neumeier 2009: 48).

WHO ARE CREATIVE PEOPLE?

Some 40 years ago, Herbert Simon (Nobel Laureate) wrote in *In the Sciences of the Artificial*, "Everyone designs who devises courses of action aimed at changing existing situations into preferred ones." Design is change. Designing is a powerful tool for change, not just a tool for styling products and communications. Creative designers devise tools, methods, and actions that aim at "changing existing situations into preferred ones." Creative people reduce the gap between "what is" and "what could be," between reality and vision. If you just focus on the "what is," then we focus on the status quo, and "nothing could be ventured and nothing could be gained." According to Herbert Simon, anyone who tries to improve the current or past situation into a preferred future one is a designer. A designer needs to find a situation worth improving and then work through the creative process. In this sense, all architects, artists, composers, movie directors, engineers, medical doctors, scientists, psychologists, professors, police detectives, military strategists, entrepreneurs, supply chain managers, and advertising managers are creative designers as long as they change existing situations worth improving into universally preferred ones.

- **Creative people are "empathetic"**: In the customer-centric business of today, empathy means to understand the motivations, preferences, and expectations of customers, employees, partners, and suppliers, and forge stronger emotional bonds with them in fulfilling such motivations. All stakeholders (e.g., buyers, consumers, clients, employees, creditors, suppliers, distributors, governments, local communities, including your competitors) are your customers. Salespeople today do not sell products; they design solutions to customer problems. Managers do not just supervise subordinates; they design high-functioning teams. Innovators and new product developers do not just produce products, they design engaging customer experiences.

- **Creative people are "intuitive"**: Intuition is opposite of being logical. A logical mind is linear and works in an A–B–C–D fashion. An intuitive mind skips around in a circular C–D–B–A fashion. Intuition is a short cut to understanding situations. While a logical mind is good for grounding and proving ideas, intuitive thinking is good for seeing the whole picture. Creative intuitive thinking sees how the parts of a problem fit together. Creative copywriters design a combination of words that will explode with meaning in the minds of readers.

- **Creative people are "imaginative"**: They are creative scatterbrains. New ideas come from divergent thinking, not convergent thinking. Creative R&D engineers use imagination to design disruptive product platforms and creative web designers use imagination to design surprising and satisfying connections between ideas, activities, and resources. Creative retailers use imagination to build store ambience and attract customer patronage.

- **Creative people are "idealistic"**: Creative personalities are described as histrionic, headstrong, and dreamy. Idealistic people are notorious for focusing on what is wrong, what is missing, or what they believe needs to change. Creative idealists can transform existing situations into vastly improved ones. For instance, idealistic industrial engineers are able to design better relationships between people and machines (for instance, making the latter user-friendly and very functional). Idealistic finance and accounting managers are able to design more transparent reporting frameworks (e.g., net cash flow statements). Idealistic entrepreneurs are able to design eco-driven business models and products that save on carbon emissions (e.g., hybrid cars, alternative energy sources).

- **Creative people are "reflective"**: Real designers never know what the outcome will be, nor are they interested. Instead, they prefer to learn what they are doing while they are doing it. Systems thinker Donald Schön called this phenomenon as "reflection in action"—a dynamic process based on a repertoire of skilled responses rather than a body of knowledge. Reflection in action combines thinking and doing, always in the moment, often under stress. The most innovative designers and thinkers consciously reject the standard option box of off-the-rack solutions and cultivate an appetite for "thinking wrong." At Apple Computer, star designer Jonathan Ive says, "one of the hallmarks of the team is this sense of looking to be wrong—because then you have discovered something new." Physicist Freeman Dyson believed that the appearance of wrongness was proof of true creativity (Neumeier 2009: 53).

As cited in previous chapters, according to Roger Martin (Dean of the Rotman School of Management) in his *Opposable Mind* (analogous to the *opposable thumb*: Harvard Business School Press, 2007), design reasoning is different from current business reasoning.

- Business reasoning is "inductive" (i.e., observing that something works), *algorithmic* (known tasks with known formulae), and "deductive" (proving that something is).
- Design reasoning, on the contrary, is "abductive" (imagining that something could be) and "integrative" (grasping and resolving the tensions inherent in wicked problems).

Design thinking is heuristic; it creates its own rules to solve mysteries of the marketplace and the production factory. Heuristic tasks, such as motivating disgruntled employees, negotiating with unhappy bankers, forging supplier relationships, and understanding customer delight, need creative design thinking; these are not inductive or deductive algorithms but "abductive" imaginations. The CEO and one's top business leaders should be masters of heuristics and not masters of algorithms. Computers and robots can do the latter and far better than business managers.

In business reasoning, the deciding mode assumes that alternatives already exist on a "solution shelf" (e.g., via case studies), but deciding will be difficult. Whereas, the designing mode assumes that new options must be imagined (using the design process), but once imagined, deciding will be easy. The truth is that success in the 21st century will depend upon finding the right mixture of both these modes. Off-the-rack solutions are insufficient in an age of perpetual change (Neumeier 2009: 41–42).

Creativity in an organization can be both individual creativity and team creativity. The key is finding a collaborative rhythm that incorporates and empowers both. A good rhythm should alternate between expression (where individuals or small teams work separately) and impression (where all members work together). Expression can bring deep personal experiences to bear, and impression can expose these experiences to a wider view of discussion and dialog. By working back and forth from expression to impression, the result is not compromise but addition. The sum of each session is a measurable leap in shared thinking. The primary tool for creative collaboration is the "design brief." A well-conceived design brief should have a common vision and goal, reduce the costs of orientation, allocate roles and responsibilities, and provide a framework for metrics (Neumeier 2009: 110–11). A CEO's strategic leadership is critical in crafting corporate design briefs. No issue is too big and no issue is too small for the executive designful mind.[1]

WHAT IS INNOVATION?

Innovation is a "new way of doing things" (termed *invention* by others) that is commercialized. The process of innovation cannot be separated from a firm's strategic and competitive context (Porter 1990: 780), or from the firm's strategic orientation (Gatignon and Xuereb 1997).

Innovation is the use of new technological and market knowledge to offer a new product or service that customers want (Afuah 1998: 4, 13). New knowledge here means knowledge that has not been used before to offer the product or service in question—it may include breakthrough knowledge (radical innovation) or better knowledge (incremental innovation) of technology and markets.

Hence, innovation is anything that creates new resources, new processes, or new values, or improves a company's existing resources, processes, or values. Obvious innovations include new or improved processes, business models, products, and services, and new delivery mechanisms such as new product bundles, new product guarantees or warranties, new product credit or financing services, new customer support services, and new retailing offline and online outlets.

---

[1] After extensive study of the design process of architect Frank Gehry, Richard Boland (Weatherhead School of Management, Case Western University, OH) says, "The problems with managers today is that they do the first damn thing that pops into their heads." "There's a whole level of reflectiveness absent in traditional management that we can find in design." There is difference between decision attitude and design attitude. Decisions are more powerful when they are designed (Boland and Collopy 2004). No issue is too big and no issue is too small for the designful mind.

One can innovate methodically. Success is a game of probabilities. By focusing on the key elements required to innovate successfully, one can hopefully increase one's chances. One cannot force innovation. There is a process one can follow to improve both the number and the quality of ideas one can generate, develop these ideas, and take to the market (O'Connor et al. 2003). That is, one can institutionalize innovation in one's company (Mowery and Rosenberg 1998).

Rogers (1983) identifies six characteristics of innovations from the viewpoint of their diffusion or adoption by consumers:

1. Relative advantage
2. Compatibility
3. Trialability
4. Observability
5. Complexity
6. Perceived risk

The first four characteristics are positively related, while the latter two are negatively related, to innovation-adoption (Gatignon and Robertson 1985). However, these characteristics are not independent of one another (Parker and Sarvary 1994). Of these six, relative advantage appears as a consistently important product characteristic in explaining new product adoption (Parker and Sarvary 1994) and new product success (Montoya-Weiss and Calantone 1994).

Innovation is "the ability of individuals, companies, and entire nations to create continuously their desired future" (Kao 2007: 19). Innovation is dynamic; it is always in a state of evolution with the nature of its practice evolving along with our ideas about the desired future. Innovation is to get the whole country to experience a groundswell of public interest in every form of culture—from architecture to music to the theater to the factory to the laboratory—and for everyone to be part of it. We require a thorough rethinking of our approach to national innovation (Kao 2007: 81).

Innovation means different things at different periods of a nation's history. For Benjamin Franklin and his kite, it was the artisan model of innovation. Later, geniuses in their workshops and garages, Thomas Edison and Henry Ford, came up with inventions (e.g., assembly lines) that created large-scale enterprises. Innovation is bringing new ideas and concepts to the marketplace in the form of useful products and services. Innovation is where the rubber meets the road, where you have got a market-ready solution to a problem (need, want, or dream) people experience; and its when a creative idea becomes a design concept versus an abstract one.

Fear of future, aversion to unpredictability, preoccupation with status—these are the prime assassins of innovation. The ruthless elimination of mistakes is the dogma of the 20th century management. Yet mistakes could be embraced as a necessary component of the messy, iterative, and creative process of resolving wicked problems. As Tom Kelley of design firm IDEO says, "It's okay to stumble as long as you fall forward." That is, it is okay to make mistakes, as long you learn from them (Neumeier 2009: 40). A company that automatically jumps from knowing to doing (without going through the intermediate creative and experimental step of "making") will find that innovation is unavailable to it. To be innovative, a company needs not only the head (knowing) and legs (doing), but the intuitive hands of making (Neumeier 2009: 53).

Innovations in general provide unique and meaningful benefits to products and services. Creativity or innovation is defined in terms of "meaningful novelty" of some output (e.g., a painting, a chemical compound) relative to conventional practice in the domain to which it belongs (e.g., abstract art, adhesives). Thus, a creative product is that which evokes a "meaningful difference" from other competing products in the product category. A creative marketing program (e.g., advertising) represents a meaningful difference from marketing practices (e.g., media advertising) in a given product category.

Thus, basically, innovation is anything new in the industry, market, country, or the world in terms of materials and supplies, their use and processes, production and inventory management, packaging and labeling of finished products/services, their distribution and delivery, advertising and promotions, retailing and shelving, pricing and financing of products and services, post-sales services, and consumer redress.

Neumeier (2009: 6–7) believes that, thanks to unprecedented market clutter, differentiation is becoming the most powerful strategy in business and the primary beneficiary of innovation. So, if innovation drives differentiation, what drives innovation? The answer is: design. Design contains the skills to identify possible futures, invent exciting products, build bridges to customers, crack wicked problems, and more. The fact is if you want to innovate, you have to design. The management innovation that is destined to kick Six Sigma off its throne is "design thinking." Design thinking must take over your marketing department, your R&D labs, transform your manufacturing processes, and ignite your corporate culture. It should bring finance into alignment with creativity, and reach deep into Wall Street to change the rules of investing. Design drives innovation; innovation powers brands; brands builds loyalty; and loyalty sustains profits. If you want long-term profits, do not start with technology, but start with design (Neumeier 2009: 14). That is what Google does: uses design to create differential products and services that delight customers.

IMPORTANCE OF CREATIVE INNOVATIONS AS BUSINESS GROWTH OPPORTUNITIES

Innovation, and especially radical innovation, is the engine of economic growth and source of better products. Radical innovation changes the entire shape of industries and makes the difference between life and death of many firms (Schumpeter 1942). The history of business is littered with the graveyards of entire industries that were destroyed by radical innovations: steel, communications, telegraphy, gas lighting, photography, and typewriter industries are cases in point (Utterback 1994). In each industry, some firms did not adopt a radical technology and failed to survive in the marketplace, whereas, other firms leaped from one generation of technology to the next and accordingly strategized their business operations to success (Srinivasan et al. 2002). Thus, managers in general, and new product managers in particular, need to know how to initiate and manage radical product innovation.

Understanding technological innovation is vital for marketers. Technological change is perhaps the most powerful engine of growth. It triggers the growth of new brands (e.g., Gillette's Mach I, II, III; Sony's PlayStations 1 and 2, PlayStation Plus; Intel's Pentium I, II, and III; Apple's Mackintosh, iPod, iTune, and iPhone; Microsoft's Windows 95, Windows 98, Windows NT, Windows 2000, Windows 2005, and Windows 2008). It creates new growth markets (e.g., digital video recorders, mobile phones, and Apple's iPod) and transforms small companies into market leaders (e.g., Acer, Apple, Dell, Intel, Samsung, Toyota). New product development and major investments in R&D depend upon a correct understanding of technological change and evolution (Sood and Tellis 2005).

Typewriters, telegraphs, and glass-plate cameras were all once dominant products manufactured by giant companies. They are virtually extinct now, swept away by radical innovations in the form of word processors, telephones, and celluloid-cameras brought about by relatively small new entrants into the marketplace (Utterback 1994). Hard-won customers quickly desert an incumbent firm when a radical innovation provides better performance per dollar than the incumbent's current products (Chandy and Tellis 1998).

Radical innovations have the capacity to destroy the fortunes of firms (Foster 1986; Tushman and Anderson 1986). At the same time, radical product innovation can be the source of competitive advantage to the innovator firm (Wind and Mahajan 1997), and can reap large and long-lasting profits (Geroski, Machin, and Van Reenen 1993). Both new and established firms can benefit from radical product innovation.

Only a small percentage of all new products are new-to-the-world products or market breakthroughs or radical innovations; this percentage is as low as 10 percent (see Booz, and Allen Hamilton 1983). *Fortune* also reports similar results using a study of new products from 1989 to 1993 (Martin 1995). Considering the relatively small number of breakthrough products and the disproportionate profit contributions they make, the challenge is how to increase an organization's ability to adopt radical innovations that build market breakthrough products (Wind and Mahajan 1997).

While radical innovation is an important driver of growth, success, and wealth of firms, industries, and economies, and while radical innovation merges some markets, creates new ones, and destroys old ones, what drives innovation? Various current answers are:

- Corporate culture (Tellis, Prabhu, and Chandy 2009).
- National culture and regulation (Florida 2004; Kao 2007).
- Culture of creativity and innovation (Neumeier 2009).
- Organizational learning and change (Senge 1990, 2006).
- Avoiding stall points (Olson and Van Bever 2008).
- Driving co-created value through global networks (Prahalad and Krishnan 2008).
- Disruptive solutions (Christensen 2009).
- Executive spirituality (Covey 2004, 1989; Senge 2006).

Several factors within a country or an industry or a firm spur radical innovation. Table 7.1 summarizes such factors at the firm level and the national level. These factors could be either within the organization (e.g., intrapreneurs, idea innovators, concept developers, prototype designers) or outside the organization (e.g., new idea scouts, innovation intermediaries, patent markets), or from a combination of in and out of an organization (e.g., cross-licensing, corporate strategic alliances, joint ventures, mergers and acquisitions).

INVENTION VERSUS INNOVATION

Creative ideas and patents are better termed as "inventions" or "seeds of inventions" rather than innovations. That is, creative ideas are not innovations, but seeds to innovations. Inventions are not enough; they require effective and successful implementation to be truly innovative and market-ready.

TABLE 7.1   Factors that Spur Radical Innovation within a Nation or a Firm

Factor of innovation	*Level*	*Measures*	*Data source*
Skills	National	Availability of scientists and engineers	World Economic Forum
		Quality of scientific research institutions	
		Total public expenditure on education as a percentage of GDP	World Competitiveness Report
		R&D personnel nationwide per capita	IMD World Competitiveness Report
			OECD Science and Technology Indicators
	Firm	R&D employees as a percentage of total employees	Global Innovation Survey
Capital	National	Financial market sophistication	World Economic Forum
		Soundness of banks	World Competitiveness Report
		Ease of access to loans	
		Venture capital availability	
		R&D expenditure per capita	OECD Science and Technology Indicators
	Firm	Sales revenues	Global Innovation Survey
		R&D spending as a percentage of sales	
		Firm's market-to-book ratio	Worldscope, OSIRIS
Government	National	Intellectual property protection	World Economic Forum
		University/industry research collaboration	World Competitiveness Report
		Government subsidies and tax credits for firm R&D	
		Government procurement of advance technology products	
Culture	National	Geographic location: latitude (degrees) of country's capital city	Worldatlas.com
		Basic cultural values: Hofstede's measures of power distance, uncertainty avoidance, individualism, masculinity, and long-term orientation	Hofstede website
		Religion: Percentage of population belonging to a major world religion (e.g., Catholic, Protestant, Buddhist, Muslim, Hindu-Sikh, non-affiliated, and other)	*CIA World Fact Book*
	Firm	Willingness to cannibalize	Global Innovation Survey
		Future market orientation	
		Risk tolerance	
		Product champions	
		Incentives	
		Internal markets	
Country	National	GDP	World Economic Forum
		Population	World Competitiveness Report
		Inflation	
		National credit rating	
	Firm	Citation-weighted patents	Delphion
		Primary industry	OSIRIS, Worldscope

Source: Author's own.

Note: See also Tellis, Prabhu, and Chandy (2009: 10).

In December 1903, at Kitty Hawk, NC, Wilbur and Orville Wright proved that powered flight was possible. Thus, the plane was invented. It took more than 30 years, however, before commercial aviation (e.g., McDonnell Douglas DC-3 introduced in 1935) ushered the new era of fast travel. An idea is "invented" when it is proven to work in a laboratory. The idea becomes an "innovation" only when someone replicates it reliably on a meaningful scale and cost, so that it can be commercialized. The idea is a "basic invention" if it is economically and technologically important, such as the commercial aircraft, telegraph, telephone, computer, personal computer (PC), mobile phones, and the like that resulted in radically new industries or transformed existing industries (Senge 1990: 5–6).

In engineering, when an idea moves from invention to innovation, diverse "component technologies" are often independently generated, but they come together to form an ensemble that is critical for the invention to progress and transform to innovation. In the case of the DC-3, it brought together for the first time five different component technologies: (*a*) the variable-pitch propeller, (*b*) retractable landing gear, (*c*) radial air-cooled engine, (*d*) wing flaps, and (*e*) a type of lightweight molded body construction called "monocque." To succeed, DC-3 needed all five component technologies; four were not enough. In 1934, the Boeing 247 was launched with all of them except wing flaps, which made the plane unstable on take-off and landing, and the engineers had to downsize the engine (Senge 1990: 6).

CREATION, INVENTION, DISCOVERY, INNOVATION, AND VENTURE

We may distinguish between creation, invention, discovery, innovation, and venture based on several dimensions: (*a*) starting point or inputs, (*b*) input skills needed, (*c*) input processes involved, and (*d*) terminal point or outputs. Appendix 7.1 provides one method of making such distinctions conceptually. In general:

- **Creation**: It has minimal inputs and starts from nothing. For example, a brilliant new idea (e.g., relativity, digitization), new opera or concerts (Beethoven, Mozart, or Rachmaninoff), new music form (Country, Beatles), new literary genre (Shakespeare's Drama), new language (Java), new technology (Internet, Ethernet, Broadband, digital communications), and so on.
- **Discovery**: It is usually associated with already existing but unknown lands (along the North and South Arctic poles), mines (new gold mines in Russia), elements and metals (the last added to the Mendeleyev Table with Atomic Weight exceeding 200—that of Mercury), fossils (older human skulls in Africa), archives (old manuscripts of Marx, Freud, Hopkins), scrolls (Dead Sea Scrolls of Qumran Valley), new planets (new moons of Jupiter), and so on.
- **Inventions**: They show much dependence upon creative ideas and theories of others as well as more recent discoveries, mostly related to new alloys, new chemical formulae, new production processes, new cost-reductive models, new mathematical theorems, new algorithms, new theories in physics and chemistry, new paradigms, new methods of learning and teaching, new modes of music, and new forms of literature.
- **Innovations**: These are based on older creations, discoveries, and inventions that have some market or economic value, in the form of new products, new services, new distribution methods, new packaging, new pricing methods, new financing models, new retailing procedures, new lifestyles, new political campaigns, new religious services, new managerial techniques, and new markets.
- **Ventures**: Creations of new business and organization by entrepreneurs, intrapreneurs, scientists, executives, and other risk-prone adventurers, primarily leading to new products and services, new

expansions and alliances, new subsidiaries and joint ventures, new markets and trade regions, and new communication efficiencies.

THE SOCIO-TECHNOLOGICAL PROCESS OF INNOVATION, CULTURE, AND CIVILIZATION

"Culture is an historically transmitted pattern of meanings embodied in symbols, a system of inherited conceptions expressed in symbolic forms by means of which men communicate, perpetuate and develop their knowledge about and attitudes toward life" (Geertz 1973: 80). Culture is:

[T]he set of meanings, values and patterns which underlie the perceptible phenomena of a concrete society, whether they are recognizable on the level of social practice (e.g., acts, customs, tools, techniques, habits, forms, traditions) or whether they are the carriers of signs, symbols, meanings and representations, conceptions and feelings that consciously or unconsciously pass from generation to generation and are kept as they are or transformed by people as expression of their human reality. (Azevedo 1982: 10)

Figure 7.1 characterizes the interconnected factor, technology, communication, and operations flows between creation, discovery, inventions, innovation, and venture. They all start with an idea or form, and end with culture and civilization using different routes such as science, technology, art, innovation, and venture.

FIGURE 7.1 The Socio-technological Process of Innovation, Culture, and Civilization

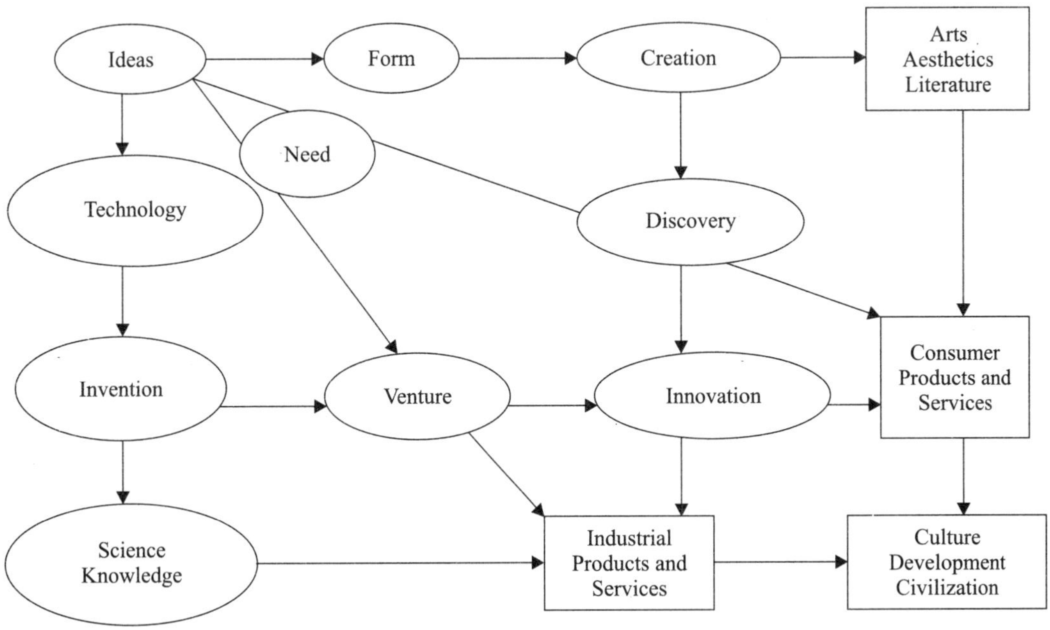

Source: Author's own.

FUNCTION- VERSUS DESIGN-DRIVEN INNOVATIONS

Some innovations are need and want driven, and hence, function and functionality driven. Most basic needs, wants, and conveniences are satisfied by function-driven innovations. Figure 7.2A characterizes the function-driven innovation process. Fancy, luxury, exotic, extravagant, and indulgent products are form- or design-driven innovations. Figure 7.2B characterizes the form- or design-driven innovation process. For instance, the whimsical, knockoff, cone-shaped kettle with the little plastic birdie affixed

FIGURE 7.2   Design-versus Function-driven Innovation Processes

7.2A   Function-driven Innovation: Form Follows Function

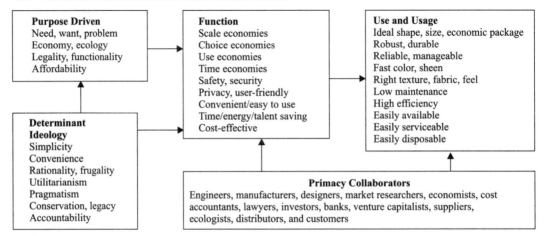

7.2B   Form (Design)-driven Innovation: Function Follows Form

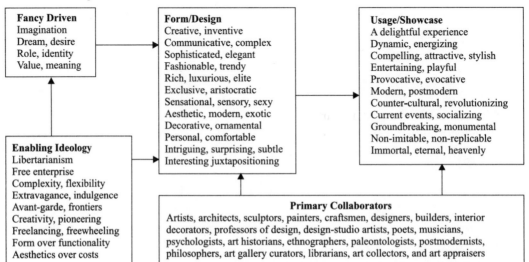

TABLE 7.2   Successful Home Furnishing Design Companies

Designer	Basic product line	Ten-year (1994–2003) growth in sales	Revenues in 2003 (million U.S. $)
Kartell	Furniture	211%	70
Cappellini	Furniture	117%	29
Flos	Lighting	106%	75
Alessi	Home furnishings	81%	104
Cassina	Furniture	60%	163
Artemide	Lighting	59%	110
B&B Italia	Furniture	54%	165
All Lombardy Collection	Home furniture	76%	716
E.U.	Furniture	11%	78,000
Italy	Furniture	28%	21,000

Source: Verganti 2006: 119).

to its spout (designed by the architect Michael Graves) is a modern typical form-driven innovative product. Since its introduction in 1985 by Alessi, the northern Italian home-furnishings manufacturer, more than 1.5 million units have been sold, even though exorbitantly priced (for details see Verganti (2006: 114–22).

Design-driven innovations are not tech-push (functionality-driven) or market-pull (need- or want-driven) innovations. Nor are they open innovations (e.g., techniques started by IBM, Microsoft, P&G, Eli Lilly). These innovations come from an amorphous free-floating and freelancing group of architects, suppliers, photographers, curators, art-critics, publishers, and craftsmen, immersed in innovation discourse and noted for originality. Their innovations are dramatic breaks from their predecessors. The Lombardy Design Cluster of northern Italy is one such group. About a quarter of all Italian furniture firms are based in Lombardy. It is Europe's largest furniture manufacturer, with 45 percent of its output exported. The factors that make Lombardy enviable are imagination and motivation.

Italy's Lombardy Design Cluster represents some of the finest and most successful examples of design-driven innovations. Table 7.2 is illustrative of this.

CONSUMERS, CONSUMPTION, AND INNOVATION

Good innovations, as long as they embody a genuine pattern of meanings, can generate wholesome humanizing cultures. Civilization reflects cultures that are transmitted, diffused, lived, and institutionalized from generation to generation. Good innovations are needed to transmit, diffuse, live, and institutionalize new patterns of human values and meanings.

There is a dual aspect to consumption: it fulfills a consumer material need and a socio-cultural need. Consumption is embedded within the social, cultural, and symbolic structures of humankind (Belk 1985, 1988; Fox and Lears 1983; Sherry 1983). Commodities have a symbolic meaning or "signification" that extends far beyond what the producer intended (Barthes 1972). Consumer tastes are determined not privately but socially, that is, within social groups; consumption takes place within social structures, or the social structure becomes the site of consumption (Bourdieu 1984).

Thus, consumption is best understood within a socio-cultural context. Consumption is an active appropriation of signs and symbols and not the simple destruction of the product or object. At every moment of consumption, something is created and produced: consumption is not a private act of value-destruction, but a social act wherein symbolic meanings, social codes, political ideologies, and relationships are produced and reproduced (Breen 1993). Figure 7.3 characterizes the role of the consumer in the innovation-production process. Figure 7.3 sketches the process of consumer–producer interdependent creativity and innovation.

FIGURE 7.3   The Market Process of Creativity and Innovation

Industry Push From engineers, technicians, employees, and suppliers	New Product/Service Ideas	Market Push From customers, clients, and consumers
Industry Response 1 Concepts, pre-models, prototypes	New Product/Service Concepts	Market Acceptance Co-partners
Industry Response 2 Design: Materials, technology, modeling	New Product/Service Prototypes	Market Testing Prototype and design testing
Industry Response 3 Style, form, size, shape, color, sheen, safety, security, quality, efficiency, and convenience	New Product/Service Packaging and Bundling	Market Co-production Package testing, quality perception, safety testing, convenience testing, bundle testing
Industry Forecast Given pricing, placing, warranty, rebates, promoting, and financing strategies	New Product/Service Promoting Pricing Placing	Pre-test Marketing Of product mix and marketing mix
Market Assessment ROS, ROM, ROQ, ROA, ROI, ROE	National Launch Sales, market share, and profitability	Market Experience Satisfaction, delight, fairness, consumer feedback

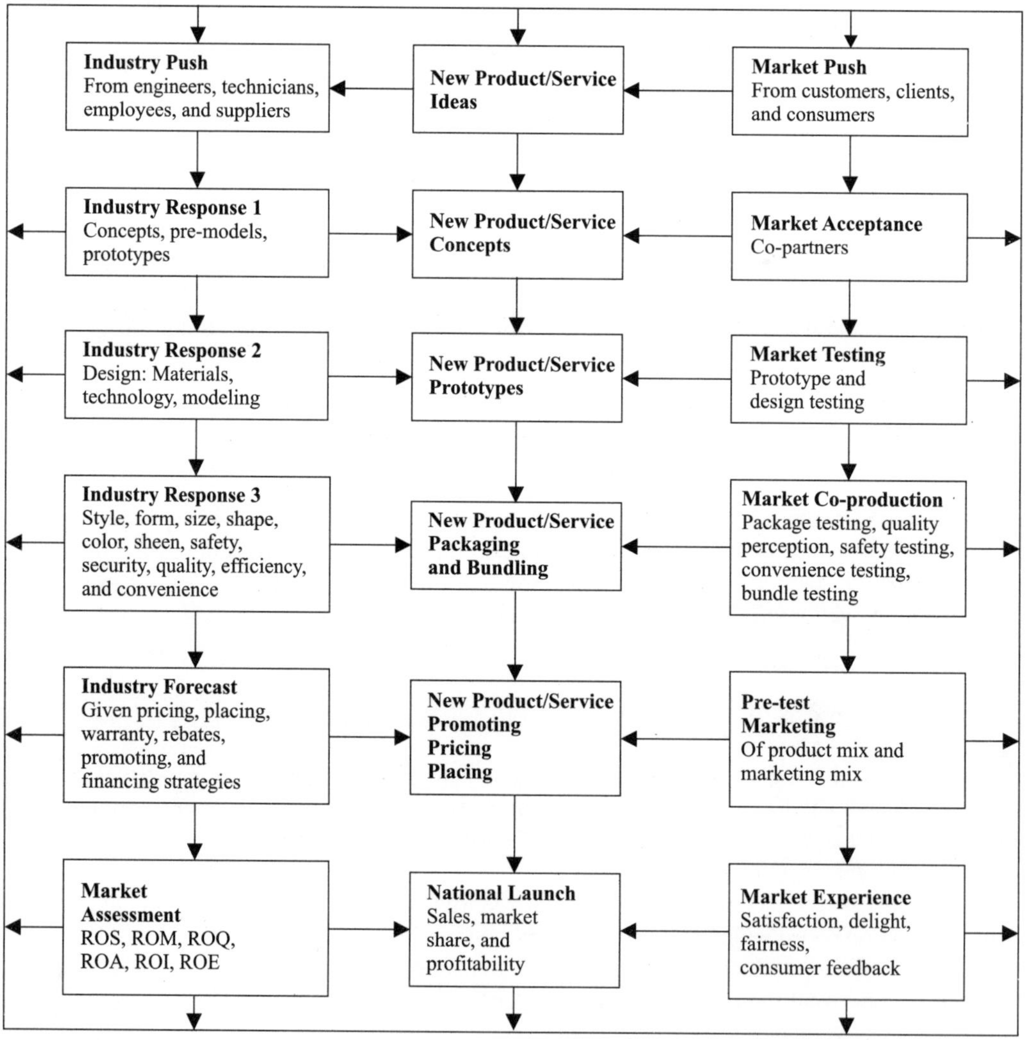

Source: Author's own.

WAVES OF INNOVATIONS

When you survey the greatest innovations of all times, you cannot help but notice that very few are products and communications. They are breakthroughs like navigation, iron plows, locomotives, cybernetics, mathematics, bio-engineering, bio-medicine, telecommunications, and the Internet (Neumeier 2009: 65). Kanter (2006) distinguishes four waves of innovation in recent decades.

- **1970–85**: The dawn of the global information age in the early 1970s and early 1980s. This era opened new industries (e.g., polyester, software, electronic hardware, and telecommunications) and toppled old ones (e.g., iron, steel, rubber, paper), generated new products (e.g., microwave ovens, polyester products, synthetic fibers, videotapes, videogames, and VCRs) and obsolesced old products (e.g., carbon paper, electric typewriters, and long-playing records). Silicon Valley became the new base for product innovation in the U.S.A and Total Quality Management (TQM) became a passion.
- **1985–95**: The dawn of buyouts, mergers, acquisitions, corporate restructuring, and strategic alliances. Seeking to unlock the value of underutilized assets, "shareholder value" became a rallying cry. In Europe, restructuring was associated with the privatization of state-owned enterprises now exposed to the pressure of capital markets. The major innovation product of this era was software and other major IT products related to process innovation (e.g., Sabre, airline reservations, and travel package reservations). Financial innovations such as derivatives, index funds, hedge funds, and other forms of financial engineering, financial supermarkets combining banks, leveraged buyouts, and some global products (e.g., Sensor Excel of Gillette, Microsoft software) emerged.
- **1995–2001**: The digital mania of the 1990s. The proliferation of PCs and global wired networks made Internet, extranet, intranet, and World Wide Web (WWW) ventures flourish. The promise (or threat) of the WWW and the Internet, forced established brick-and-mortar companies to seek Internet marketing and other stand-alone Web ventures. Eyes were on the capital markets rather than on customers, and companies (especially, the dotcoms) got instantly rich without patented products, profits, and revenues. AOL Warner was a venture that destroyed value for its customers rather than create innovation. Some e-companies emerged successfully such as eBay, Amazon.com, and MSN.com.
- **2001–Present**: The current wave of innovation started with a more sober mood with the dotcom collapse and belt-tightening of the global recession. Having recognized the limits of acquisitions and mergers and become skeptical about technology hype, companies refocused on organic growth. Survivor giants such as GE and IBM have adopted innovation as a corporate theme. Customers and consumers have returned to center stage with the emergence of videogames (e.g., Sony's Play-Stations 1 and 2, Play Station Plus), DVDs, Hi-Fi, cell phones, organizers, Blackberry, and other palm-held devices. Signature innovations of this era include Apple's iPod, iTune, and iPhone and P&G's Swifter. Creative accounting shenanigans and insider trader financial irregularities belong to this era, and corporate fraud has hit all time highs in several industries (e.g., Enron, CMS Energy, Dynergy, Duke Energy, Tyco, World.com, Global Crossing, Quest Communications, i2 Technologies, Adelphia Communications, Peregrine Systems, and Halliburton).

Each wave brought new concepts. For example, the rise of bio-technology, bio-informatics, and bio-genetics has revolutionized health care and medicine. IT and Internet have made outsourcing easy and profitable. Globalization of factor markets (money, capital, labor, technology) has globalized innovations, joint ventures, and strategic alliances. Geopolitical events (e.g., 9/11, terrorism, Afghanistan, Iraq War, Taliban, and regime changes) have spawned safety and national security products.

NEGATIVE CHAIN EFFECTS OF LACK OF INNOVATION

Lack of innovation and new products in a company creates several chained or connected problems:

1. Declining product differentiation, quality, competitive edge, state-of-the-art, variety, and assortment.
2. Declining distribution efficiency, logistics economies, and inventory management optimization.
3. Increasing company product category, brand, and store under-performance.
4. Increasing company subsidiary, affiliate, branch, division, product, brand, and store distress.
5. Declining consumer, customer, client, and shareholder enthusiasm.
6. Declining sales and repeat buyer–consumer patronage.
7. Declining customer long-term relationships, loyalty, and commitment.
8. Declining employee morale and loyalty, and increasing employee unrest and turnover.
9. Steady outward migration of better skills (managerial, technical, and professional) due to competition.
10. Lack of sustained cutting-edge competitive advantage in core supplies, competencies, and products.
11. Competitors' increasing strengths and decreasing weaknesses.
12. Easy market entry for new competitive entrants and decreasing efficiency of entry deterrent strategies.
13. Declining price-advantage and increasing (profit-eroding) price wars.
14. Declining cost-advantage and decreasing gross, operations, and net profit margins.
15. Depreciating stock price equity ratios or shareholder value.
16. Declining market evaluations and Tobin's Q.
17. Declining investor and venture capitalist confidence, trust, and patronage.
18. Increasing illegal, unethical, and unconventional accounting practices to boost sales and equity.
19. Increasing insider illegal and unethical trading.
20. Declining company product, category brand, and service extensions and expansions.
21. Declining profits, net-worth, and market capitalization.
22. Declining retained earnings for further innovation (chain reaction).
23. Increasing signs of receivership, insolvency, and corporate decline.
24. Increasing likelihood of financial buyout, hostile takeover, or merger.
25. Increasing likelihood of seeking corporate bankruptcy provisions (as in this chapter and chapter 11).

INNOVATION, CREATIVITY, AND BEAUTY

Great ideas are not enough. An idea is only a concept or an intention until it has been perfected, polished, and produced. An idea needs to be beautiful. According to Thomas Aquinas, beauty implies three things:

integrity (it stands out clearly from the background), harmony (how the parts relate seamlessly to the whole), and radiance (the ecstasy and joy the beholder experiences when viewing the beautiful art). Aristotle included all this under one name: aesthetics. Ideation, creation, and innovation should generate the beautiful (aesthetic, artistic, harmonious, pleasing, and soothing piece of art, music, dance, theater, show, entertainment, or any product or service).

Aesthetics gives a powerful toolbox for beautiful business execution.

- When you increase differentiation, you are working on the principle of integrity.
- When you optimize synergy, you are working on the principle of harmony.
- When you enhance and engage customer experience, you are working on the principle of radiance.

A well-run business is beautiful in this sense. Beauty is essential to the art of management. The more our culture becomes technology and information driven, the more do we need the emotional and metaphorical power of beauty (Neumeier 2009: 69–70). Buckminster Fuller once said, "When I am working on a problem, I never think about beauty. But when I have finished, if the solution is not beautiful, I know it is wrong" (cited in Neumeier 2009: 73).

In mathematics, Poincaré could judge the quality of a solution solely based on its aesthetic significance. Software developers can spot a great algorithm by the shape and efficiency of its coding lines. There is ample evidence of mathematical beauty in nature, including the breathtaking complexity of fractals, the ancient sacred ratios of geometry, and the surprising concordance and harmony of theories across disciplines. Take the Fibonacci sequence wherein each number in the sequence is the sum of the previous two. A Fibonacci sequence looks like 1, 1, 2, 3, 5, 8, 13, 21, 34, 55, and so on. In nature, this progression is best seen in the patterns of pine cones and palm trees, in artichoke leaves and broccoli florets, in the shapes of nautilus shells (whose walls spiral outward according to the same laws). In business, the Pax Group, a home-and-office appliance design company, borrowed Fibonacci geometry to reshape its fan blades, and produced products that are 15–35 percent more energy efficient and 50–75 percent quieter.

Bio-mimcry is another avenue for design beauty and efficiency. The tiny hairs on gecko footpads led to the design of reusable super adhesives. Klipsch Audio Technologies designs horn-loaded loudspeakers designed in the shape of the human ear—an approach that has led to speakers that accurately produce both soft and loud sounds, produce a highly directional sound pattern, deliver unaccented bass, mid-range and treble ranges, and are highly efficient. Founder Paul Klipsch often said, "Quality is directly proportional to efficiency." Simplicity and efficiency are twin threads that run through the discipline of aesthetics. All living things have an instinct to economize. The efficient use of energy, materials, and food are the best defense against entropy, the tendency for all systems to lose energy. Since aesthetics is reinforced by simplicity and efficiency, it offers a powerful tool for thriving in an era of diminishing natural resources (Neumeier 2009: 77).

In nature, beauty is the by-product of function (observes Moshe Safdie, a renowned architect). The gorgeous blue sky is beautiful because it promises sunshine and clean air. The color and shape of a flower are so because it wants to attract insects. The color and structure of insects and some animals are so because of their need to camouflage against the background to protect from the enemy. The color, masculinity, and shape of the male species are such, so that it may attract females. Leonardo da Vinci wrote in his notebook, "We will never discover an invention more beautiful, easier, or more economical that that of nature. In her inventions nothing is wanting and nothing is superfluous"(Neumeier 2009).

In nature, quality is directly proportional to efficiency. According to the bio-mimicry expert, Janine Benyus, nature designs its products using very few materials. Instead, it uses shape to create function. Any natural material that looks like plastic is one of five simple polymers. Organisms are hungry for these polymers, so they go back into the ground cycle easily. In the manufacturing world, by contrast, we produce and use 350 complex polymers that are not bio-degradable!

In the world of art and artifacts, beauty is the by-product of form. The timbre, sound, and smoothness of a tone of music are from the form of the music instrument and the form of the artist that plays it. The grandeur, majesty, and splendor of the Taj Mahal, the Eiffel Tower, St. Peter's Basilica, and the Taipei 101, are the form and art of these great structures. The glory and attraction of a David, the Pieta, the Mono Lisa, and the Sistine Chapel are their form, balance, and proportions over function. The ecstatic joy we derive from Beethoven, Mozart, Elvis Presley, The Beatles, and the country jazz is the form of the music and the form of the artists that render it. The beauty of an Aston Martin, the Bentley, the Cadillac, or the Porsche is derived from the aerodynamic form and vibrancy of the model.

While science is an inquiry into generalizable similarities amidst dissimilarities, art is the opposite: it is a quest for dissimilarity or differentiation among similarities (Ackoff and Emery 1972). Design as art is differentiation, and strategy is differentiation; hence, design is strategy. An effective strategy is a masterful design. Beauty is differentiation; aesthetics is differentiation; simplicity is differentiation. Hence, a good design is beautiful if it is simple, aesthetic, and differentiating. Hence also, a corporate strategy (and so is a CEO) is beautiful if it is simple, aesthetic, and deeply differentiating.

As the old adage says, beauty lies in the eyes of the beholder. However, this is too subjective. We need to define a beautiful design by some objective features such as simplicity, differentiation, harmony, radiance, and integrity. According to Neumeier (2009: 78), a good design exhibits aesthetics and virtues. Besides being beautiful, a good design should suggest clarity, diligence, honesty, courage, generosity, curiosity, thriftiness, and wit. By contrast, bad designs exhibit confusion, laziness, deceit, fear, selfishness, greed, avarice, apathy, wastefulness, and stupidity. We should want the same virtues from humans as well as from design. When we combine aesthetic values with ethical virtues, we have a good design. The ancient Greeks framed this ideal in the context of knowing, making, and doing: To know truth, to make beauty, and to do good.

THE DESIGN INCUBATION FACTORY

Innovation is also a numbers game. Out of 100 innovative ideas, only 15 may be worth prototyping and testing. Out of these 15, only five may be worth serious investment. Out of these five, one or two may produce game-changing or market-breakthrough results. That amounts to just about two percent success. Hence, in general, we need a large pool or "collection box" of innovations or a design incubation factory. Some companies (e.g., Royal Dutch Shell, W. L. Gore, Whirlpool) are pushing their employees to spend up to 10 percent of their time, or one day every two weeks, on the development of new ideas. Capital One, the credit card company, prototypes over 200 new products a year but it is successful with at least 10 percent of them (Neumeier 2009: 124).

Leaders must lead. Managers must manage. Both assertions do not mean, however, that creative and innovative ideas have to come from the top. Good leaders and managers know how to generate new ideas from the ranks and files. They enable and empower their employees to think big, to think far into the future, to redesign the company, and to reinvent and innovate the company. Richard Teerlink attributed his remarkable success of turning around Harley-Davidson to just this: "You get power by releasing power."

Google has a huge innovation surplus and its "design factory" keeps expanding, and hence, Google can very cannily expand into new areas with a wide array of innovations, all of which fit into the great mosaic of its master business plan. Sheryl Sandberg asked her people to give frank feedback on whatever they see is or is not working. She learnt this lesson early at Google before moving into the company's Facebook unit as its COO: "I thank every person who ever raised a problem publicly." In this sense, a leader becomes a steward of organizational energy.

Google has a lofty vision and soul-stirring goal—it asks its employees to help "organize the world's information and make it universally accessible and useful." Google uses an "idea management system" that allows employees to e-mail innovative ideas for products, processes, and even businesses to a company-wide suggestion box. Once ideas are collected, all employees can comment on them, and rate their chances of success. This type of open organizational brainstorming is an inexpensive yet a very effective tool to stimulate and build a culture of creativity and innovation. Hence, there is little wonder, that *Fortune*'s "100 Best Companies to Work For" recently named Google number one.

Innovation is currently the holy grail of many companies, but too often, we treat it as an end and not as a means. Innovation is just a tool, and as with any tool, we can use it effectively and ineffectively. Just having innovations in your company does not give you a competitive advantage. According to Howard Reinersten, each company seems to have a "design factory" in which product concepts are incubating like inventory in a company's books until released into the market where they can start earning back the investment From this perspective, there may be an innovation surplus or an overstocked inventory of inventions in the U.S. corporations, especially the Fortune 500 companies. So many thousands of inventions, patents, and innovations are lying in the back burner of corporations, mostly held there to prevent the competitors from exploiting them. At the same time, it is too risky to have "just in time" inventory of innovations—you need a sufficiently large supply of inventions to transform them to the next level of market-ready innovations.

Alternately, if you do not have in-house generated innovations, you can buy them from outside sources, as P&G currently does. The challenge now is less in generating new inventions and innovations, but identifying which of the available inventions and innovations best support new business opportunities, and best challenge our execution abilities, and see how those opportunities support our customers as well as corporate goals. In feeding frenzy over innovation, the quantity of innovation has been ramped up without being matched by an ability to identify the best/most appropriate innovations early, and bring only those to market-readiness. P&G until recently was not a particularly innovative company (they had many very good brands), but they executed better than anyone in the consumer products industry. Now they are ramping up their internal innovation capabilities, which when combined with their proven execution abilities, should make the company very effectively innovative.

Often, new products turn out to be "cash traps." Bruce Henderson, the founder of the Boston Consulting Group, warned managers over three decades ago: "The majority of products in most companies are cash traps. They will absorb more money forever than they will generate" (Andrew and Sirkin 2003). Most new products (almost five to nine out of 10 products) do not generate enough cash or enough financial returns despite massive investments in them. For instance, Apple Computer stopped making the striking G4 Cube less than a year after its launch in July 2000 as the company was losing too much cash on the investment. In 2002 P&G made half of its sales and even a bigger share in profits from just 12 of its new 250-odd products of that year (Andrew and Sirkin 2003: 77).

DESIGN THINKING AND INNOVATION

Thomas Edison did not just invent the light bulb, his signature invention; he created an entire industry around it by inventing a system of electric power and transmission. Edison's genius was his ability not only to create discrete devices such as the bulb or the phonograph, but also to conceive and create a fully developed marketplace around it. He was able to envision how people would want to use what he made. He paid great attention to user needs and preferences, and he engineered his creativity and genius toward that insight. Innovation is hard work. Edison made it a profession that blended art, craft, science, business savvy, and an astute understanding of customers and markets.

Edison's approach was an early example of what is now called "design thinking"—a methodology that imbues a full spectrum of innovation activities with a human-centered design ethos (Brown 2008: 86). Design thinking is a lineal descendant of the Edison tradition and is a discipline that uses the designer's sensibility and methods to better match and meet consumers' needs, wants, and desires. Design engineers take a feasible technology and a viable business strategy and convert them into customer value and market opportunity. During the last centuries, design thinking was a mere tactical strategy and a downstream development process where designers were brought in to make an already developed idea more attractive to consumers. Now design thinkers, however, play an active strategic role in the entire value-creation process—upstream, midstream, and downstream—and create ideas, generate concepts, fabricate prototypes, invent processes, and innovate products and services that lead to dramatic new forms of value to consumers and corporations (Brown 2008: 85–86).

For instance, using "design thinking" how will you design creative, engaging, and retentive learning for high school dropouts 18 years and older? Disqualified to sit in regular high schools because of over-age and unable to find jobs, given that the jobs they normally qualify for are outsourced, they could be potentially vulnerable to poverty, drugs, drinks, sex, and other crimes that could lead them to prisons. In fact, prisons in U.S.A. are teeming with high school dropouts. A design learning studio that would make education attractive, compelling, and valuable to them should be a team project that includes an engineer or technology expert, a creative teacher, an architectural designer, a linguist, a poet, a historian, a mathematician, a biologist, a chemist, a nurse, a lawyer, a doctor, a business analyst, a turnaround specialist, and a transformation expert. The creative and engaging learning curriculum and environment that this team designs should match and meet dropout needs, wants, and desires, fears and anxieties, constraints, and ethnic boundaries. The group will brainstorm some dropouts to unearth the fears and anxieties, difficulties and bottlenecks of learning that they experienced, how they could be transformed into challenges of engaging learning. These prototypes of creative learning modules should be experimental, exploratory, and flexible. We should be able to quickly assess their strengths and weaknesses and accordingly, identify new directions for designing more formal prototypes. The entire process should be a human-centered design methodology of learning, and not necessarily, curriculum-centered. It is a discovery process that should follow iterative cycles of ideation, inspiration, prototyping, testing, implementation, and refinement. The learning project as a holistic concept should loop back and forth through these "design spaces," especially the first two.

The learning methodology should reconnect dropouts to their learning experience as children while also dealing with the root causes of their present frustration and intimidation of high school learning. The learning experience should be fun and freedom, creativity and innovation, discovering stable humanizing values and virtues. The learning project should seek complete solutions of creative reading and writing, creative learning of math and sciences, creative engagement in social and civic sciences.

The learning project should be characterized by a deep understanding of the lives of high school dropouts and their environment, and then use the principles of design thinking to innovate and build value. That is, innovative learning must account for the vast differences in cultural and socioeconomic conditions of the target market students. The ultimate goal of learning should go far beyond the General Education Development (GED)—it should be a transformative experience that leads to college-exploration and conversion, and eventually, graduation in one's field of love and innate genius. The mission of the team should be to pursue innovation that enhances the student dropout's experience, learning, and resilience to challenges.

ON INCREMENTAL INNOVATIONS

One should distinguish between innovation that simply improves "what is" (incremental innovations) from innovations that define "what could be" (radical innovations) (Christensen 1997a).

There is nothing wrong with incremental innovations. Semi-conductors get faster every year; storage devices store more every quarter; music file sharing products have access to thousands of more songs; digital cameras store more pictures with better resolutions and more retrievable albums; you can sell more stuff online on eBay; medications become more effective; cars become more stylish and, presumably, more fuel efficient. Oreo sandwich cookies beget Oreo minis that beget mint-flavored Oreos that beget limited-edition white-fudge-covered Oreos, Easter Oreos, Halloween Oreos, and so on—today there are over 40 Oreo brand extensions in the market, including Oreo piecrust and ice-cream cones.

Innovation is about new ways of doing and seeing things, as much as it is about the breakthrough idea. Innovation flows from shifts in mindset that can generate new business models, recognize new opportunities, and weave innovations throughout the fabric of society. Innovation depends on harvesting knowledge from a range of disciplines besides science and technology—among them design, social science, and the arts. It is exemplified by more than just products; services, processes, experiences can be innovative as well. The work of entrepreneurs, scientists, and software geeks alike contributes to innovation (Kao 2007: 19).

One should integrate as many disciplines and practical systems of knowledge as possible. We have to reinvent new learning methods and modules. The traditional and the current teaching methods have not produced great results. It is still textbook, memory-retrieval, multiple choice-based test-directed learning. It is disconnected to what students care for and should care about in schools and colleges, and to what they will be doing in the real outside world. Textbooks and classroom drills are boring for many children, and the homework assignments may lack immediate relevance to their lives. Hence, high school dropout rates are increasing nationally. Table 7.3 suggests some futuristic and yet-to-be-discovered learning global curricula, content, methods, and modules. We need new creative and innovative modes of learning, that help in retaining, and enriching student life and values.

TWENTIETH VERSUS TWENTY-FIRST CENTURY BUSINESS DESIGNS

Twentieth century business lacked good design, and hence, beauty and aesthetics. It overvalued short-term goals and profits and undervalued long-term broad aesthetics and humanity. Sumantra Goshal, a global business leader and author, argued that corporate business is "under-socialized and

TABLE 7.3 Redesigning High School Curricula: An Innovation Template

Historical categories	Inputs	Process	Outputs	Remarks
Traditional	Some screening of students for qualification; Textbooks controlled by publishers; National curricula; State curricula; Syllabi-bound learning	Teaching primarily from textbooks; no-brainer challenges; Teaching for "testing"; Closed book in class; multiple choice tests; Mandatory testing; No Child Left Behind Act; Emphasis on athletics	Standardized test scores (SAT, ICT); Academic performance solely based on tests	Personalized one-on-one learning neglected; Success judged by big school enrollments; Textbook learning emphasized; Creative learning neglected
Modern and current	Better screening of students for qualification; Textbooks designed by domestic teachers and publishers; National revised and updated curricula; State updated curricula; Some schools with International Board (IB) curricula; Syllabi-bound learning; Specialized learning for impaired students	Teaching primarily from new and updated textbooks; Incremental innovations in non-textbooks learning; Reactive reaction to current national problems and events; Teaching for "testing"; Closed book in class; multiple choice tests supplemented by oral tests and experiments; Mandatory testing for state or national conformity and ranks; Specialized learning for various types and levels of impairment; No Child Left Behind Act; Interschool competition; Overemphasis on athletics; Math and science not mandatory for all	Standardized test scores (SAT, ICT); Academic performance solely based on tests; Incremental innovations in learning assessment; Percentage of high school graduates; Percentage of conversion to colleges; Percentage admitted to elite schools; Percentage gaining college scholarships in elite schools; Athletic standing of graduates	Occasional individualized and personalized one-on-one learning; Success judged by big school enrollments; Textbook learning emphasized; Creative learning encouraged but not tested; Over-emphasis on athletic neglects academics; Math and science performance still far from desired levels
Futuristic and yet to be discovered	Globalized textbooks that cover global facts, events, curricula, history, markets, and emerging cultures; New globalized core and non-core curricula; Small schools and small classrooms; fewer but longer instruction periods; Rewrite history books to include non-American studies and scholars; New faculty development approaches for producing creative/innovative teachers; New ways of recruiting, training, rewarding, and retaining domestic and foreign teachers; Primary emphasis on highly qualified math and science teachers; Encourage ethics learning, international geography, trade, and economics; Establish global pilot schools and junior colleges for benchmark learning and standards	Individualized, personalized, customized learning with high student–teacher interaction; Teaching from global authors and continuously updated textbooks; Encourage creative, innovative, and entrepreneurial learning by connecting it to real life contexts; Develop creative writing and reading, critical and ethical thinking, and forensic debates; Develop moral thinking and habits (virtues); Radical and disruptive innovations in non-textbook learning; Proactive reaction to current national and global problems and events, ethics and morals; Foster global student exchanges; Math and science mandatory thresholds for all; honors or IB programs for gifted math and science majors; Deemphasize commercialized athletics and standing; Continuously reinvent learning modules for the handicapped and the impaired	Develop and test new global or international metrics for benchmarking academic and non-academic student performance; Special rewards for math and science skills, creative reading, and writing skills; Test and reward creativity, innovation, and entrepreneurial skills of graduates; Test students' college preparation for the best national and global colleges and universities; Test for world language skills and world history skills; Test ethical and moral development skills and values; Test for student responsibility and stewardship	Non-math and non-science majors should learn world languages (e.g., Spanish, Arabic, Japanese, and Mandarin); Encourage a pool of national and international retirees (teachers, executives, military) for supplementing training schools; Rethink the role of teachers and elders in education and society; Initiate No gifted child left behind in the world Act!; Depoliticize learning in U.S.A.; Reduce education bureaucracy; encourage creative learning around creative learners and learning processes rather than around bureaucrats

Source: Author's own.

one-dimensional," and hence, it has only led to resentful customers, disgruntled and dispirited employees, and a divided society. We need a much larger focus than the bottom line. A selfish focus on the bottom line of profits is a bad design. Good design, in contrast, is a new management model that deliberately includes a moral dimension. A successful business will be a designful business.

Table 7.4 contrasts the features of 20th century business of expediency and efficiency with the hopeful 21st century business of effective and aesthetically designed strategies. A good design is a new management model that is a designful business that deliberately includes a moral dimension. It is a model that not only seeks the good of the shareholders, but the good of all other stakeholders as well such as customers, employees, suppliers, creditors, distributors, governments, and local communities. In short, its "design is depth." A deep design business model does not work on "either–or" philosophy of share-holders or stakeholders, but on the more challenging "and" philosophy of including all stakeholders, shareholders included among them.

The 20th century business model was all about manufacturing, risk management, administration, production, operations, products, services, R&D, legal compliance, marketing, advertising, sales, IT, HR, distribution, finance, accounting, and strategy associated with the foregoing functions. The 21st century business model goes beyond functions to form creative designs and innovations in terms of vision, iden-tity, culture, culture of creativity and innovation, vision design, identity design, research design, ethno-graphy design, experience design, process design, product design, service design, package design, price design, price-product bundling designs, brand design, brand community design, graphic design, web design, PR design, marketing design, promotional campaign design, events planning design, financial reporting designs, relationships design, intellectual property designs, and local community involvement designs (Neumeier 2009: 105).

William Shakespeare designed all his major plays (tragedies and comedies) with a deep design. By designing his entertainment products on multiple levels, he was able to reach out to larger and more satisfied audiences. That is, Shakespeare built on an "and" philosophy; his plays addressed every seg-ment of the audience, from the royals sitting in the top-tier boxes to the groundlings standing along ale-soaked dusty sidelines. His dialog shifted rhythmically from high philosophy to low humor; his scenes alternated from highly intellectual soliloquies to downright physical sword fights; his characters represented the full range of society, kings, queens, the nobility, the lords, the commoners, the servants, and the slaves. Shakespeare's designful and depth-design products produced profits. By the end of his career, he had the most successful acting company in London.

Another unique aspect of the 21st century business model is team learning and collaboration. The 20th century business model recognized and awarded individual specialization, contributions, and patents. Companies routinely rewarded individual employees, departments, and external firms for independent achievement. Schools, colleges, and universities have done the same. In fact, most universities have culti-vated knowledge silos, specialization enclaves, even to the extent of discouraging and disdaining inter-faculty, inter-departmental, inter-disciplinary, and inter-collegiate research and collaboration. Col-laborative research, publications, and other intellectual achievements were held suspect, and sometimes, regarded as downright cheating. This culture bred the "lone ranger" model of creativity.

By contrast, the 21st century business model should focus on team learning, team specialization, group patents, and team achievement. For instance, P&G has recently redefined its R&D as "C&D" (connect and develop) so as to benefit from a wider pool of interdependent inventors. The 21st century business slogans are shared vision, shared research, shared inventions, shared design, shared creativity, shared innovation, and hence shared patents, shared intellectual property, and shared profitability. However,

TABLE 7.4 Planning Design, Creativity, and Innovation in the Twenty-first Century World

Domain of change	The 20th century business model	The 21st century hopeful new business model
Production Philosophy	Employees: factors of production Customers as consumption markets Body of accumulated knowledge/learning Specialization Job routinization Developing better tools/procedures/ processes Solution of simple and structure problems Standardization of products and services Increase patents, trademarks, licenses Thinking and doing Thinking safe, right, and within-box Looking for what is right and reasonable Control, predict, and manage outcomes Proof of discovery: appearance of right Want certainty, clarity Reduce risk, loss Stability, routines, robustness Productivity: economies of scale Exploiting chartered markets and industries Convergent and static industries Discovery, invention, functionality Incremental innovations for differentiation Incremental breakthroughs Culture of trimming, cost-cutting, and control Competitive advantage by firefighting Building barriers to competition Customer satisfaction and retention	Employees: partners in production and innovation Customers as relationships and brand communities Spontaneous skilled responses/unlearning/experimentation Improvisation, retraining, experimentation, venturing to unleash organizational creativity, learning, and talent Resolution of unstructured, complex, and wicked problems Customization and personalization of all offerings Increase transparency, open-solutions, open-standards Thinking (know truth), making (make beauty), doing (do good) Thinking wrong and dangerous, and outside the box Looking for what is wrong, what is missing; what is unjust Learn/design outcomes as you are thinking, making, and doing Proof of creativity: appearance of wrong and crazy Love uncertainty and ambiguity to be creative Face risk, creep to leap, lose to win in the long run Organizational agility, resilience, learning, unlearning Creativity: economies of form, shape, scope, variety, and freedom Exploring un-chartered markets for creating new industries Divergent and expanding industries Form, creativity, innovation, venture Radical innovation for strategic differentiation Radical market and technological breakthroughs Culture of creativity, fun, joy, innovation, and experimentation Sustainable competitive advantage (SCA) through design and innovation Building an enduring company via untapped market spaces Loyalty via customer delight and engaging experiences
Growth Philosophy	Growth externally by mergers/acquisitions Growth by spin-offs and equity carve outs Growth and control by stock-buy-backs Heavy metrics of tangibles Massive ad campaigns Impose market entry barriers Growth via profitability Integrity via legal compliance	Grow organically by redesigning core processes/products/markets Growth by strategic alliances and joint ventures Growth by leveraging high debt/equity leverage ratios High reliance on intangibles (e.g., worker morale, strong brands) Invest on vision, creativity, innovation, and culture Ignore competition or seek blue oceans Growth and profitability via corporate social responsibility Integrity via ethics, morals, and executive spirituality
Communication Philosophy	Heavy PR to make up for poor quality Political lobbying to legalize greed Lawyers/litigations to cover product defects Mass advertising as surrogates for quality Power points, charts, tables, spreadsheets Doctoring financial reports to court Wall Street Annual reports and shareholder conventions	Great quality that generates great customer experiences Build brand equity via strong brands and brand communities Open negotiations and fairness in transactions "Social e-media"—e-mails, blogging, twitter, webinar, YouTube Narratives, stories, drawings, logos, rations, prototypes Honest and verifiable financial statements Continuous online reports and stakeholder involvement
Corporate Culture	Culture of discovery, mining, invention Investing in productivity, stability, safety Thinking, doing with low reflection Closed and myopic thinking Involution, evolution, and convolution Mining land, air, water, and resources Win–lose, zero-sum games Cost containment and ruthless downsizing	Culture of creativity, reinvention, and innovation Investing in creativity, vision, innovation, and culture Thinking, making (intuition, ideation, experimentation), doing Design thinking, visual prototyping, network advertising Revolution, renewal, resilience, renaissance Responsibility for regenerating ecosystems Win-win, mutual growth, and expansion systems Cost containment for revenue and employment generation
Corporate Performance	Sales in dollars and units; return on sales (ROS) Market share in units and dollars Growth in profitability Unlocking wealth by mergers/acquisitions Return on assets (ROA), return on investments (ROI), return on equity (ROE), earnings per share (EPS), P/E, total shareholder return (TSR) High shareholder value	

Source: Author's own.

we need both individual expression and collaborative impression to bear on our market offerings. The neglect of one at the expense of the other can be disastrous.

THE CULTURE OF CREATIVITY, DESIGN, AND INNOVATION

A culture of innovation is not empty corporate mission slogans like, "Our number one goal is innovation," "Our vision is to develop innovative solutions," or "Innovation is our only business," or "We think, live and do innovation 24/7." If a company wants to innovate, it must first build a culture of innovation. A culture of innovation must clarify, include, and incorporate the following corporate components (Neumeier 2009: 81):

- **Vision**: The core elements of the business including its purpose, mission, values, and strategies.
- **Identity**: The symbols that express the company's vision, including its brands, trademarks, logos, slogans, voice, visual presentation, personality, and character.
- **Culture**: The way the company works together, including its processes, organizational routines, organizational learning and structure, and organizational relationships and language.
- **Offerings**: These are the products, services, and experiences that the company offers and that give the company its strategic differentiation and sustainable competitive advantage.
- **Brands**: These are behaviors and communications that convert vision, identity, culture, and market offerings into customer value.

This is the supply side. All these five constituents of a company are meaningless and ineffective unless and until they are supported and reinforced by the following demand-side responses:

- **Perception**: The surface of our experience, including what we see, hear, touch, smell, and taste in relation to company's products, services, and experiences.
- **Reason**: The logical processes we use to make sense of products, services, companies, and their market offerings.
- **Emotion**: The feelings that drive many of our decisions, including those that are hidden beneath our reason.
- **Resonance**: The intuition that relationship with a given company, its products, services, and other market offerings are just "right" for us.
- **Ideology**: The tribal connection we feel with a brand—the deep knowledge that we belong to the brand community.

A culture of design, creativity, and innovation should emanate from a clear and compelling vision and identity that arises not necessarily from the top but from the top and bottom, vertically and horizontally. That creates a new culture of organizational togetherness and cooperation that, in turn, can generate the best of market offerings that stimulate great brand loyalties and communities. In a company, human energy is the most important resource, more than money, time, and other tangibles. Individuals and organizations can create, synergize, and expand their energy (we cannot expand our time). A good leader is a steward of human energy; he or she rivets the attention and passion of everyone in the company.

One way of doing this is to identify the wicked problems the company faces (that it has not tackled before) and confront them together. Tackling simple and structured everyday problems is not everything in business, and these problems can be resolved by linear thinking, spreadsheet computing, and simple algorithms. The real future of the larger companies is to tackle the wicked problems they create or they must face. Ignoring wicked problems is under-visioning your company. For instance, for GM tackling hybrid cars was a wicked problem of the 1990s that it ignored with an easy "can't do" culture.

By contrast, Toyota faced it, and broke the market with Toyota Prius in 1998, that still dominates the world auto hybrid market. Bob Lutz later commented, "It cost us our reputation for technology and innovation." GM's top management literally devalued its brand to protect their jobs. This was not a culture of innovation, but a culture of fear and turf protection, where talent stayed latent. The leaders who can articulate a compelling vision give the employees the courage to create.

Visioning the future is a design–creativity–innovation problem. When you infuse your vision with design thinking, you use "making" skills to discover and illustrate a wider set of options. You begin to design your way forward rather than decide your way forward. That is, decisions should not guide your design, but designs should inform and transform your decisions. Most companies fail not because they chose the wrong course, but because they cannot imagine a better one. Unimaginative leaders reach for a vision from the ready-made rack, and then wonder why the leadership does not have follow-ship. Few people are inspired by the safe and easy plans from the ready-made shelf. If the vision includes outperforming the competition, then we need to think big, and dream large from day one.

Vision may also be woven into an interesting story or a gripping narrative. Particularly, if the vision formulation starts from the bottom as well, then:

- The low ranks can tell the story of their involvement in the vision fabric, in the exciting work they do, and the ecstatic satisfaction they derive from working for the company.
- The customers can also tell their engaging and memorable experiences of the products and services they buy from the company.
- The creditors, banks, and shareholders can tell their stories as how proud and rewarding they feel in investing in the company or establishing a credit with the company.
- Add to these the exciting stories of the suppliers, distributors, retailers, and the local communities.

Thus, you have a complete continuous picture, a living blog, a dynamic YouTube, a Twitter, a Facebook, or website of company's shared vision—that should be the best advertisements and brilliant social media productions (Postman 2009). Such stories should be simple, unexpected, concrete, credible, and emotional. Several companies tell their story this way (e.g., JetBlue, Mini Cooper, Made to Stick—for details see Neumeier 2009: 88–95).

Such stories could be powerful building blocks for a culture of design, creativity, and innovation. They can lead to brand guidelines, tools, case studies, process manuals, design elements, design standards, branded training, service design, graphics, slides, training modules, music video, training videos, photo libraries, talent directories, performance metrics, collaborative spaces, innovative blogs, and many other intangible shared assets.

In order to derive the best brand leverage or design leverage from these stories, they must be properly organized, edited, and packaged, and posted on the company intranet in the form of an innovation center, an incubator, or an independent design studio. When all these shared assets are organized, designed, and linked stories, they have the power to transform the company into a dynamic creative center. The ability to multiply talent by working in teams is at the core of continuous innovation, a great competitive weapon (Neumeier 2009: 96–97).

THE SIX-COMPONENT WHEEL OF INNOVATING CONSUMER PRODUCTS/SERVICES

In general, all innovations generate value by saving on cost and time and by improving quality.

Naumann (1995) posits customer value as a function of three components: price-value, goods-value, and service-value, placed along the three vertices of a triangle. Goods-value and service-value are placed along the base of the triangle, indicating that they support price-value. Customer-value is created when customer expectations in each of the three areas are met or exceeded.

Since the expectations paradigm of consumer satisfaction has serious problems, and that the recent customer-satisfaction paradigms need to be much more comprehensive, we propose a six-component wheel of customer value sketched in Figure 7.4.

FIGURE 7.4   The Six-component Innovation Wheel of Perceived Quality and Customer Satisfaction

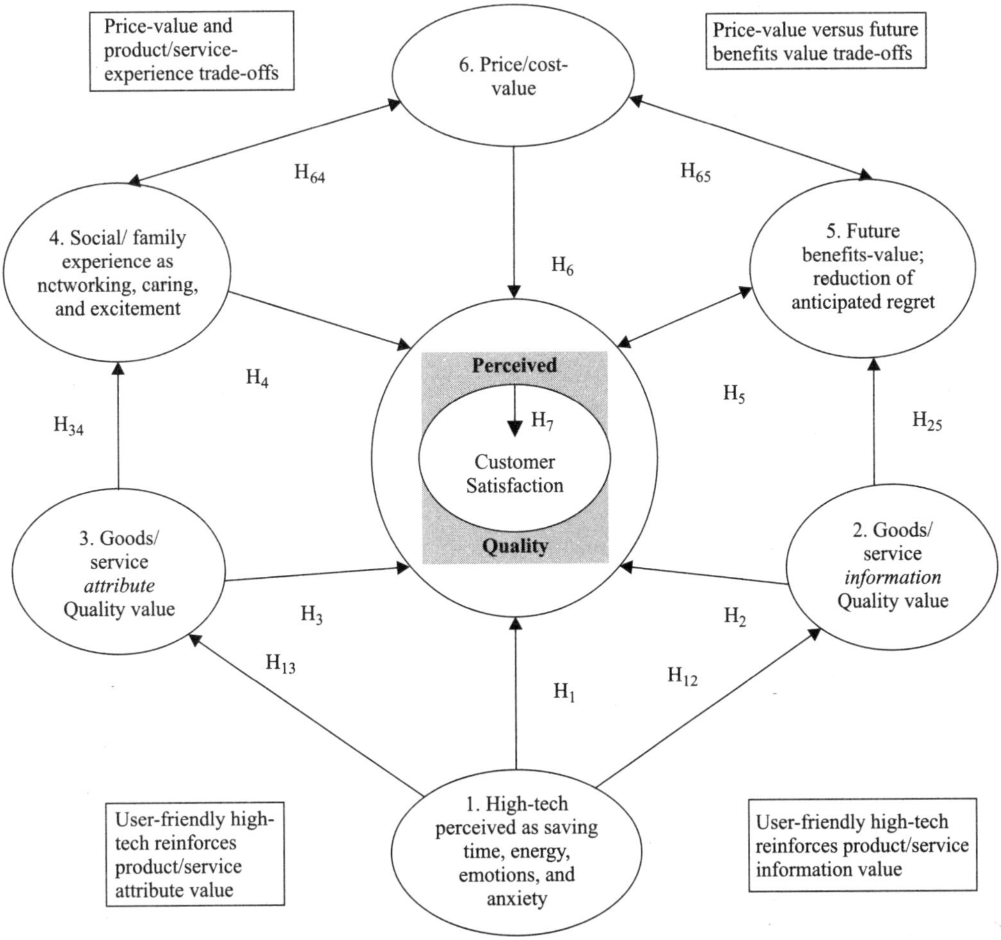

Source: Author's own.

The following hypotheses can be tested for their main effects:

- H_1: The higher the perceived high-tech or state-of-the-art value of the product/service the higher is its perceived quality.
- H_2: The higher the perceived information value of the product/service the higher is its perceived quality.
- H_3: The higher the perceived attribute value of the product/service the higher is its perceived quality.
- H_4: The higher the perceived customer, whether personal or social, experience-value of the product/service, the higher is its perceived quality.
- H_5: The higher the perceived future benefits value of the product/service the higher is its perceived quality.
- H_6: The higher the perceived (per customer dollar) cost value of the product/service the lower is its perceived quality.
- H_7: The higher the perceived quality of the product/service the higher is its customer satisfaction.

The following hypotheses could be tested for their moderating or interactive effects:

- H_{12}: The higher the perceived high-tech and state-of-the-art value of the product/service the higher is its information value satisfaction.
- H_{13}: The higher the perceived high-tech and state-of-the-art value of the product/service the higher is its attribute value satisfaction.
- H_{25}: The higher the perceived information value of the product/service the higher is its future benefits value.
- H_{34}: The higher the perceived attribute value of the product/service the higher is its social experience value.
- H_{64}: The higher the perceived (per customer dollar) cost value of the product/service the lower is its social experience value.
- H_{65}: The higher the perceived (per customer dollar) cost value of the product/service the lower is its future benefits value satisfaction.

TYPES OF CREATIVITY AND INNOVATIONS

Innovations in general provide unique and meaningful benefits to products and services. Innovation does not always mean a new technology; for instance, it can imply market innovation. Market innovation is one's ability to meet changing market conditions by using innovation to drive the market intangibles (e.g., a new niche, market void, new fad, new need) to become your weapon to conquer the market chaos, find your niche and succeed (Morris 2001). This is what Wal Mart did in outrunning KMart, and what Michael Dell did in becoming number one in PCs, outpacing IBM, Apple, HP, Compaq, and Gateway. Most of their innovations did not imply radical new technologies: they excelled in inventory management, distribution, logistics, customization, and service.

Incremental versus Radical Innovation

A useful classification of innovations has been that of radical versus incremental innovations (Anderson and Tushman 1990; Henderson and Clark 1990).

- Incremental innovations provide marginally improved performance along an established performance trajectory (e.g., a new toothpaste flavor, a new ice cream flavor, a new cereal mix, a new salad mix or dressing, a new paint color, a new shade for car color, and the like).
- Radical innovations provide dramatically improved performance along an established performance trajectory (e.g., microwave ovens from convection ovens, magnetic resonance imaging [MRI] from ultrasounds and X-ray, arthroscopic surgery from old invasive surgeries, plastic cosmetic surgery from older forms of facelift, cable radio from ordinary transistor radios, computers from ordinary calculators, PCs from macro and micro processors, CD ROMs from old LP records, mobile phones from landline phones, Internet from Electronic Data Interchange [EDI], HDTVs from ordinary color TVs, CDs from tape decks, videophones from ordinary phones, broadband data transmissions from telegraphs, bluetooth wireless technology from wired communications, and space walk from moon walk).

Radical innovations are technological discontinuities that "advance by an order of magnitude the technological state-of-the-art that characterizes an industry" (Anderson and Tushman 1990: 27). This concept is related to that of relative advantage proposed by Rogers (1983) because an innovation that is similar to existing products cannot be highly differentiated, and therefore, cannot yield a major advantage over existing products or competitors (Gatignon and Xuereb 1997).

For instance, the much lauded Swifter of P&G; for years, we had disposable diapers, disposable razors, disposable pens, and even disposable cameras. Swifter was a disposable mop. But it is hardly a radical innovation; it is hardly innovative but rather a formulaic or extension of the disposable industry. The big innovation may be in the fabric's unique ability to attract dust and particles. Taking a common item and making it disposable does not strike as being innovative. Swifter arose from a technology patented by P&G that involved picking up dust particles by static electricity. Developing that into a product that a consumer can use resulted in Swifter. It may be a novel means to clean the floor, the disposable cloth may be novel, and most importantly, it has fascinated the end-user. Perhaps the innovation lies in Swifter's market success—it was a market breakthrough. There is a vital connection between an innovation and the problem it solves for the end-user. The Swifter solved the problem of the consumer who wanted a tidier floor and when the ordinary broom did not do a good job and the mop was too much trouble. The problem of a tidier floor gets exacerbated by the increasing popularity of hardwood, bamboo, and polished concrete floors.

Old and new products can also be distinguished depending upon, on the one hand, whether they respond to an old, improved or radically new technology, or on the other, whether they serve an old, augmented or new market. The resulting 3x3 technology–market newness grid helps to better understand and position products and their strategies. Tables 7.5 and 7.6 illustrate innovations in the technology–market newness grid. Augmented markets are expanded markets for the same product by extending the product category (e.g., public telephones in the rural areas in the early 1950s, diapers for the elderly, jeans for kids and the elderly, cereals-based night snacks for kids and the elderly).

TABLE 7.5 The Technology–Market Newness Grid for Classifying New Products

Product objectives	Product-market technology		
	No change	Improved technology	New technology
No Change: Old Markets	Penetration Merger strategy	Reformulation Re-packaging	Replacement Innovation
	Corner store Typewriter Carbon copy Old phone	Supermarkets Electronic typewriter Xeroxing Digital dialing	Electronic markets Word processors Laser printing Video phones
Augmented Markets	Re-merchandizing Re-launching	Product expansion Differentiation	Diffusion Mass merchandizing
	Factory outlets Full-service gas stations Rural phones	Shopping malls Self-service gas stations Phone booths	Internet markets Pay at the pump technology gas stations Cordless car phones
New Markets	First entry New country	Extensive Differentiation	Diversification Diffusion
	Developing markets PC for home Plastic toys Overseas phones Express delivery	Electronic kiosks PC for entertainment Plastic surgery Phones and modems Federal Express	Global electronic malls PCs for businesses Cosmetic surgery Video conferencing WWW networks

Source: Author's own.

From an organizational view innovations can also be classified as incremental versus radical innovations; that is, corporate "knowledge" underpins the firm's ability to generate innovations.

Most innovations are incremental. They build on existing knowledge of technology or markets to innovate new processes (process innovations), new products (product innovation) or new marketing strategies (marketing innovations or commercializations). They enhance existing corporate competence (Tushman and Anderson 1986). For example, a "shrink" of Intel's Pentium chip to make it run at 200 MHz is an incremental innovation since the knowledge required for doing so was built on Intel's previous knowledge of microprocessor development.

A radical technology innovation contains a high degree of new knowledge compared with current technology and represents a clear departure from existing practices (Dewar and Dutton 1986). Some use technology and innovation interchangeably (e.g., Srinivasan, Lilien, and Rangaswamy 2002).

From a marketing viewpoint, incremental innovations are me-too-products, line extensions, brand extensions, and category building. Almost 90 percent of the new products belong to this class. From a marketing viewpoint, radical innovations are new-to-the-world products, market breakthroughs, technological breakthroughs, brand new creations, inventions, and discoveries. Only 10 percent of all new products belong to this category (Booze, Allen, and Hamilton 1982; Martin 1995).

A radical product innovation is a new product that incorporates a substantially different core technology and provides substantially higher customer benefits relative to previous products in the industry (Chandy and Tellis 1998). Technological knowledge implied in these innovations is very different from

TABLE 7.6 The Technology–Market Newness Grid for Classifying Some Integrated Circuit Electronic Products

Product objectives	Product-market technology		
	No change	*Improved technology*	*New technology*
No Change: Old Markets	Electromechanical cash registers in banks Electronic cash registers using small scale integrated (SSI) circuits in 1969 8.5 inch disks Computers with vacuum tubes (e.g., ENIAC 1946) Intel 4004, 8080 in 1975	Electronic cash registers using medium scale integrated (MSI) circuits in 1970 5.25- and 3.5-inch disks Computers with transistors in 1963 Intel 8086 in 1980	Electronic cash registers using LSI, printers, and inventory management in big banks 3.5 inch zip disk Computers with SSI circuits in 1967 Intel 80-286 and 80-386 in 1985 for businesses
Augmented Markets	Electromechanical cash registers in retail outlets Electromechanical watches Intel 80-286 and 80-386 in 1985 for PCs at work places	Electronic cash registers using large scale integrated (LSI) circuits in 1973 Electronic liquid crystal display (LCD) watches in 1973 Intel 80-486 and 80-586 in 1985 for PCs at work places Memory Jump Drives	Electronic cash registers using VLSI, printers, and inventory management in big department stores in 1975 Electronic watches with SSI in 1973 Computers with VLSI such as minicomputers in 1974 Intel 80-686, Pentium V, and Micro 2000 in 1998–99 Internet call centers
New Markets	Electromechanical cash registers in the world Intel 80-286 and 80-386 in 1985 for PCs at home Mobile phones	Electronic cash registers using very large scale integrated (VLSI) circuits in 1975 for regular retail outlets Intel 80-486 or 80-586 for laptops, notebooks Electronic organizers Mobile phones with text messaging	Electronic cash registers using VLSI, printers, and inventory management in regular retail outlets PCs with VLSI for businesses, homes Palm pilots and PDA iPods and Blackberry mobiles phones with security markets

Source: Author's own.

existing knowledge, rendering the latter obsolete, and "destroying" existing competence (Tushman and Anderson 1986). For example, refrigerators at one time were radical innovations based on the new knowledge integrating thermodynamics, coolants, and electric motors, which was radically different from knowledge of harvesting and hauling ice.

From an economic or competitive viewpoint, innovations can also be viewed as incremental or radical. Since innovations result in superior products (lower costs, better quality, better features), they may render older products totally obsolete and non-competitive (radical innovations) or less useful and partially competitive (incremental innovations). From this viewpoint, electronic point-of-sale (EPOS) checking systems were radically different from mechanical cash registers, while diet and caffeine-free sodas were incremental innovations over regular sodas, since the latter still remain competitive.

Sustaining, Low-end Disruptive and New Market Disruptive Innovations

In his *The Innovator's Dilemma*, Christensen (1997a) popularizes the concept of a "disruptive" innovation. A typical disruptive innovation is not attractive to mainstream customers at the time of introduction because it offers inferior performance on the attribute that these consumers value most (e.g., Southwest Airlines and its multiple no-frill trips to off-main airports in large cities). At the same time, there is an emerging market that places little or no value on this particular attribute. That is, these customers value a different attribute delivered by the disruptive innovation. Over time, the new product's performance on the attribute valued by the mainstream customers rises to a level that satisfies them. Thus, incumbents (e.g., large national airlines) may first ignore the new technology or product and the emerging market that responds to it; it is irrelevant to their customers. But eventually, it satisfies their mainstream customers, thereby disrupting their core business.

Christensen (1997a) proposes three types of innovations: sustaining innovations, low-end disruptive innovations, and new-market disruptive innovations. Certain innovations disrupt the normal trajectory of life and organizations, and hence, they are also called disruptive innovations. Disruptive innovations introduce a new value proposition either by creating new markets or reshaping existing markets. (Christensen and Raynor 2003).

- **Sustaining Innovations**: Most new product and service innovations are sustainable. They provide better quality or additional functionality for a firm's most demanding customers. These innovations move companies along established improvement categories. These are basically incremental innovations along an established product or brand, on dimensions historically valued by customers (e.g., incremental innovations by changing brand's size, speed, shelf-life, color, texture, flavor, package, bundle, financing, delivery, after-sales service, usage). Typical examples are new flavors of ice cream, new family sizes and flavors for toothpaste, rental cars with added conveniences, airplanes that fly farther, computers that process faster, cellular phone batteries that last longer, and televisions with incrementally clearer images and resolutions.
- **Low-end Disruptive Innovations**: Low-end disruptive innovations occur when existing products or services are so transformed that they become "too good" that they can be sold at premium prices. Typical automotive examples are GM's Geoprism and Saturn, Ford's Escort and Focus, Chrysler's PT Cruiser, and Toyota's Toyota Corolla. Non-automotive examples include Nucor's steel minimill, Vanguard's index mutual funds, Dell's direct-to-customer business model, and Wal Mart's everyday low price (EDLP) discount store. They all began by offering existing customers a low-priced, relatively straightforward product or service.
- **New-market Disruptive Innovations**: Disruptive innovations, by traditional measures, do not meet existing customer needs nor do they characterize existing products and services. They are typically simpler, more convenient, less expensive, and so they appeal to less demanding customers. Typical examples are Southwest Airlines, PCs, cellular phones—all these are low-cost, no-frill, less-sophisticated products that serve a large underserved market for their affordability, even though limited capabilities. These occur when characteristics of existing products limit the number of potential consumers (e.g., Harley-Davidson and PT Cruiser's limited editions, Sony's Walkman radio, Xerox photocopier) or force consumption to take place in inconvenient, centralized settings (e.g., Home Depot, Bell telephone, eBay online marketplace, Kodak camera). These products create new growth by making it easier for people to do something that historically required deep expertise or great wealth, and hence, they target non-consumers.

According to the disruptive innovation theory (Bower and Christensen 1995), organizations can use relatively simple, convenient, low-cost innovations to create growth and triumph over powerful competitors. That is, established incumbents almost always lose to attackers armed with disruptive innovations.

Christensen, Anthony, and Roth (2004) identify three customer groups that provoke different types of innovations: non-consumers, undershot consumers, and overshot consumers. Each customer group provides unique opportunities. Table 7.7 provides details. Companies can create "new-market disruptive innovations" to target non-consumers; they can launch "up-market sustaining innovations" to reach undershot consumers, and they can generate "low-end disruptive innovations" or modular displacements to reach overshot customers.

Strategic Innovations

[See Govindarajan and Trimble (2005)]

Strategic innovation involves testing new, unproven, and significantly different answers to at least one of the three fundamental questions of strategy: Who is your customer? What is the value you offer to the customer? How do you deliver this value? Strategic innovation proceeds with strategic experiments—high-growth, high-tech potential new businesses such as GM's OnStar, P&G's Tremor, Walt Dsiney's Moviebeam—that test the viability of unproven business models (Govindarajan and Trimble 2005: xvii).

Catalytic Innovations

Christensen et al. (2006: 96–97) describe a sub-category of disruptive innovation, called catalytic innovations. Catalytic innovators share five qualities:

1. They create systemic social change through scaling and replication.
2. They meet a need that is neither observed (because the existing solution is more complex than many people require) nor not served at all.
3. They offer products and services that are simpler, less costly than existing alternatives, and may be perceived as having a lower level of performance, but users consider them to be good enough.
4. They generate resources, such as donations, grants, volunteer labor, or intellectual capital, in ways that are initially unattractive to incumbent competitors.
5. They are often ignored, disparaged, or even encouraged by existing players for whom the business model is unprofitable.

Catalytic innovations take place under all structures, pro-profit and non-pro-profit, private or public, big or small. Examples of catalytic innovations abound.

Grameen Bank: Conventional banks are typically unwilling to lend to entrepreneurs or people without collateral, and the latter are forced to seek informal loans that could be exorbitantly expensive (with interest rates 300 to 3,000 percent). Grameen Bank is a micro-lending or micro-financing organization

TABLE 7.7   A Market Canvas for Generating Innovations

Customer group	Characteristics	Innovation	Signals	Examples
Non-consumers	They lack ability, buying power, or access to use existing products. They either don't use them, or hire professionals to do these jobs for them, e.g., traveling, house-improving, book-keeping, tax-filing, and word-processing, checking vital signs	New-market disruptive innovations	These innovations are user-friendly: they encourage and invite non-consumers to try these products	Model T cars for low-income homes, apartments or town houses as affordable housing, QuickBook for book-keeping, tax software for filing taxes, PCs for word-processing, mobile phones for expensive landline phones, e-mails or fax for transferring files, Home Depot for do-it-yourself home improvements, home medical kit for vital diagnostics
Undershot Consumers	Existing brand users who are frustrated with its current limitations. They are willing to pay premium prices for added conveniences and enhancements. Customers reward companies with premium prices for providing superior functionality, reliability, convenience, or customization	Sustaining up-market innovations	New features, attributes, and benefits added to existing products that are important to existing customers	Continuous improvements in Intel Pentium Series, Microsoft Windows, word-processing, mobile telephones, passenger cars with GPS, luxury trucks (Hummer I & II), home appliances, garden equipment, landscaping, snow removers, pain killers, health foods, health care products, beauty products, cosmetic surgery, financial products, and consumer and business privacy, security, safety products
Overshot Consumers	Existing brand users who have stopped paying high premium prices for product expansions, updates, and more sophisticated attributes. They have no use or diminishing utility for these additional frills. Companies innovate faster than customers' lifestyles can adapt them	Low-end disruptive innovations among most overshot customers	New business models to serve least-demanding customers	All deep discount stores such as TJ Maxx, Value World, Burlington Coat Factory, and Gibraltar Trading Centers, MCI in relation to AT&T, Southwest Airlines in relation mainline airlines
		Displacing innovations	Modular innovations that specialize on one or more functions. They cash in on modularity	Western Union in money transfers, specialty stores such as Dell, Jeans, Gap, Toys R'Us, Blockbuster, Whole Foods Market and health foods
		Downward migration of required skills	Emergence of rules allowing producers to generate simple products for lower skilled users	Credit Score companies rate buyers on simple rules such as length of stay in the last residence and in the last job, annual income, and history of bill-payments; all credit card companies

Source: Author's own.

Note: See also Christensen et al. (2004: 1–27).

that makes such loans possible with no collateral and with low interest rates. At the end of 2005, Grameen operated more than 1,250 branches, serving over 5.6 million borrowers in nearly 60,000 villages throughout Bangladesh. Since its inception in 1976, the bank has lent more than $5.2 billion with a recovery rate of more than 98 percent. The bank shares are owned 93 percent by its borrowers, 5 percent by the Bangladeshi government, and 2 percent by other private Bangladesh banks. The bank has been profitable almost every year since its inception.

Muhammad Yunus, a professor of Economics, founder of Grameen Bank, and Nobel Prize winner for Developmental Economics in 2006, believes that the poor have skills that remain under-utilized, mainly because existing institutions and policies fail to offer the support these people need. He founded the Grameen Bank in 1976 to supply credit to those who would not qualify as customers of established banks. Grameen Bank grants unsecured loans to the poor in rural Bangladesh. It differs from other lending institutions on three counts. First, priority is given to designing the system so that the loans can be repaid, and on time. Second, only the poorest villagers, the landless, are eligible. Third, the Bank makes efforts to lend primarily to women, who are not only economically but also socially impoverished.

The loan disbursal design is unique. To qualify for a loan, a villager must demonstrate that her family assets are below a certain threshold. She is not required to put up collateral; instead, she must join a five-member group and a 40-member center, and attend a weekly meeting. She must also share responsibility for the loans granted to the other members of her group; it is the group, not the Bank, which initially evaluates loan requests. Defaulters would spoil things for everybody, so group members must choose their partners wisely. The Grameen Bank has been profitable from the outset, and has inspired a global micro-credit movement that has spread to 65 developing countries, reaching over 17 million borrowers.

Low-cost Eye glasses.com: Over one billion people need glasses but do not own or cannot afford them. People who have correctable vision problems are often handicapped owing to lack of correction. Without glasses, simple tasks become more difficult or impossible, productivity slows down, and accidents occur more frequently. Based purely on the lack of productivity and enjoyment, the lack of eyeglasses is one of the largest solvable problems in the developing world. In fact, it is significantly more common than often-cited problems such as cataracts or glaucoma. Glasses could correct the majority of vision problems encountered in the developing world, reducing the impact of presbyopia, myopia, hyperopia, and astigmatism.

The surprisingly low penetration of glasses on a global basis is a result of the fundamental structure of the eye care industry. The current commercial eye care system is designed for the wealthy of the developed world, and espouses its customers' values. The system is characterized by extreme product diversity, customized product combinations, highly trained specialists, and a fashion focused product design and buying processes. As a result, prescription glasses are unaffordable by the majority of people in the world, and access is severely limited. In most developing nations, there are few optometrists, and those that are present live primarily in capital cities. A low-cost, scalable and wearable solution must be available. To be available, glasses should be easily purchased from a convenient local location. To be low cost, they should cost a few days' wages. In most situations, prices starting at US$5 are low cost. Cheap Eye Glasses project does exactly this.

Detroit Medical Center (DMC) extends its quality and comprehensive care to the inner city poor by training its nurses to begin offering care that doctors formerly had provided, but at a lower cost.

Minute-Clinic, MN: Minneapolis-based Minute-Clinic (MC) has 87 for-profit clinics located in 10 states in CVS stores and other retail locations, and provides fast, affordable walk-in diagnosis and treatment for common health problems, as well as vaccinations. MC employs quality nurse practitioners armed with software-based protocols, and applies strict rules of quality care. Patients that have complaints or problems outside the range of MC issues are referred to doctors or to a nearby emergency room. Underserved, uninsured, and underinsured patients find MC very convenient, adequate, and affordable. Recent surveys of MC's more than 350,000 patients indicate 99 percent satisfaction. MC was recently acquired by CVS because of its growth and profit possibilities. Other similar health care systems are RediClinics, Take Care Health Systems, and Wal Mart's in-store health clinics.

Freelancers Union, NY: Freelancers Union (FU) is a non-profit labor organization providing low-cost health insurance and other services to independently employed contractors, consultants, pro-temps, and other insurers in the New York area who could not otherwise afford insurance. FU offers comprehensive health group insurance at prices that are 30 to 40 percent lower than competing large insurance companies that often cater to large corporate clients, and would not serve the poor segments or small businesses. FU discovered this "blue ocean" and has enlarged its services and numbers to other parts of the state. The catalytic innovation model whereby FU acts as a marketer and broker while partnering with an established insurance carrier, is replicable, and FU is now expanding to other states.

Online Schools: For-profit Apex Learning and non-profit Virtual High School and Florida Virtual School, among others, provide specialized online classes (e.g., certain language courses, advanced placement courses that count for college credit) to thousands of students from public schools in poorer areas that do not or cannot afford to offer these courses. Online learning curricula offer such courses at a fraction of what landline courses would cost. According to the U.S. Department of Education, there were 40,000 to 50,000 secondary school students in 37 states participating in online curricula in 2005 offered by around 2,400 online charter schools and state and district virtual schools. However, students enrolled in online courses experience online learning as technically challenging and something which requires much higher levels of self-discipline and self-motivation than regular schools. Future catalytic innovations should try to make online education user-friendly and attractively self-motivating.

Community Colleges: These have dramatically changed the shape of higher education in the U.S. by expanding access to and redefining the goals of higher learning. Community colleges offer a lower cost alternative to four year over-priced universities, are more easily and locally accessible, and report higher placement rates. Community colleges now enroll around 44 percent of all undergraduates in the U.S. Most students pursue community college education for the first two years and then move to universities that allow the transfer arrangements.

Ashoka: A great catalytic innovation is the Ashoka model that purports to help the landless, home-less, and job-less people find space, shelter, and hope. Bill Drayton, the founder, was inspired by Vinoba Bhave, a Gandhian disciple, and joined him in the across-the-country pilgrimage to get a first-hand experience of destitution among the poorest of the poor in India. The result is a "Habitat for Humanity" in India.

Operational Innovation

Hammer (2004: 86) speaks of "operational innovation." It is the invention and employment of new ways of doing work. It is not the same as operational improvement or operational excellence. These terms refer to achieving high performance via existing modes of operation (e.g., reducing errors via total quality management [TQM] or Six Sigma; reducing costs via scale economies). Operational innovation invents entirely new ways of doing normal operations such as filling order, developing products, providing customer service, or doing any other activity that the entire firm performs. Thus, operational innovation is by nature disruptive, so it should be concentrated in those activities with the greatest impact on an enterprise's strategic goals (Hammer 2004: 88). Operational innovation has been central to some of the recent greatest success stories such as Wal-Mart, Toyota, and Dell.

Wal-Mart pioneered many operational innovations in relation to purchasing and distribution. One of the best known Wal-Mart's operational innovations is cross-docking from truck to truck, in which goods trucked to a distribution center from suppliers are immediately transferred to trucks bound for stores, without ever being placed in storage or warehouses. Cross-docking and supplementing operational innovations led to lower inventory levels, lower operating costs, and every day lower prices (EDLP). Between 1972 and 1992, Wal-Mart grew from $44 million in sales to $44 billion (an annual compound growth of 41.25 percent), powering past Sears and KMart with faster growth, higher profits, and lower prices. Currently (as of March 2009), Wal-Mart's gross sales are $405.607 billion (an annual 1992–2009 compound growth of 13.96 percent).

The Dell Business Model (also called the Dell's Triangle) is another excellent example of operational innovation. With online sales running over $20 million per day in 2004, Dell is pioneering many other operational innovations. Customers arrive at the online site, check out possibilities with a product "configurator," and order their computers. The business model has different levels of services for customers depending upon whether they are business or household, big or small accounts. But all get customized personal service. Dell's online approach is a powerful and flexible way of handling and retaining customers that create value for all. Dell also has an online information policy based on customer importance. Different classes of customers receive different amounts of information. The Dell's Triangle reflects the typical inverse relationship between the number and importance of customers in each class and the level of value they bring to all. At the top of the triangle is the "all customer class," the broadest category, and applies to anyone who visits the Dell website. Successive classes refer to more customer value and importance, and hence, more in-depth information sharing, personalization, and long-term relationships. Dell's market dominance in the PC market is phenomenal and lasting. Its operational innovations dominated or dislodged some of the biggest corporations in the PC world (Hammer 2004: 85).

Other companies have made enormous gains by similar operations innovations. For instance, in the late 1990s, IBM developed a new product development process that resulted in 75 percent reduction in new product development time cycle and 45 percent reduction in developmental expenses, and 26 percent increase in customer satisfaction with the new products. In 2002, Shell Lubricants reinvented its order fulfillment process by replacing a group of people who handled different parts of an order with one individual who does it all. Consequently, Shell reduced cash cycle time by 75 percent, operating expenses by 45 percent, and boosted customer satisfaction by 106 percent. Savings on time and increase in customer satisfaction are positively affected by operational innovations (Hammer 2004: 87).

Mergers, acquisitions, technology investments, and major marketing campaigns that stimulate growth, are more glamorous, are better understood by boards, shareholders, and the media, offer immediate gratification, and most often get the CEOs featured in business magazines, but are often unsuccessful and unproductive. On the other hand, operational innovations are less known and glamorous, but boost growth faster, with less risk and low cost. Redesigning procurement or transforming product development are in-house private operations that do not generate sensational news as do mergers and acquisition deals, and hence, are less pursued by managers. The only way to stay ahead of competition is by executing in a totally different way via operational innovations.

Platform versus Component versus Design Innovations

The innovation types described earlier (e.g., incremental versus radical innovation, sustaining versus disruptive innovation) define an innovation in terms of its effects rather than its attributes. Sood and Tellis (2005) instead define three innovation types based on the intrinsic characteristics of underlying technology:

- **Platform Innovation**: Emergence of a new technology based on scientific principles that are distinctly different from those of existing technologies. For instance, the compact disk (CD) that reads and writes data is based on a new platform, laser optics, while the prior technology was based on magnetism.
- **Component Innovation**: An innovation that uses new parts or components or materials within the same technological platform. For example, magnetic tape, floppy disk, and zip disk differ by use of components or materials, even though they are all based on the platform of magnetic recording.
- **Design Innovation**: A reconfiguration of the linkages and layout of components within the same technological platform. For example, floppy disks decreased in size from 14 to 8 inches in 1978, to 5.25 inches in 1980, to 3.5 inches in 1985, and to 2.5 inches in 1989, though each was based on magnetic recording.

Table 7.8 presents platform innovations of four categories of data management technology (desktop memory, desktop monitors, desktop printers, and data transfer) that went through a series of new technological evolutions. The performance (measured by its capacity to fulfill business and consumer needs) of each successor new technology starts below that of the old technology during its introductory phase, then, at some point (known as the inflection point), it enters its growth phase and improves rapidly (while the older technology improves at a much slower pace), crosses the old technology in performance, and then reaches its performance plateau, when the next technology emerges. Often, there could be multiple crossings in which two technologies may zigzag each other in performance, forming multiple S curves of step functions.

In general, new successor technologies exhibit the following phenomena (Sood and Tellis 2005):

1. The time interval between successive introductions of new technology or new platform decreases over time.
2. The time interval between successive improvements in performance of a given technology decreases over time.
3. The percentage increase in performance, calculated relative to the previous year, increases over time.
4. New platform innovations are introduced primarily by small market entrants.

TABLE 7.8 A Technological Evolution Canvas for Generating Innovations

Major technology category	Primary dimension	Technological performance metric	Technology platform	Technology principle
Desktop Memory	Storage Capacity	Bytes per square inch	Magnetic*	Records data by passing a frequency-modulated current through the magnetic head of the disk drive, thus generating a magnetic field that magnetizes the particles of the disk's recording surface.
			Optical*	Stores data using the laser modulation system; changes in reflectivity are used to store and retrieve data.
			Magnetic-optical*	Records data using the magnetic field modulation system, but it reads the data with a laser beam.
Display Monitors	Screen Resolution	Dots per square inch	Cathode ray tube (CRT)+	Forms an image when electrons, fired from the electron gun, converge to strike a screen coated with phosphors of different colors
			LCD+	Creates an image by passing light through molecular structures of liquid crystals.
			Plasma+	Generates images by passing a high voltage through a low-pressure, electrically neutral, highly ionized atmosphere using the polarizing properties of light.
			Organic light emitting device (OLED)#	Generates light by combining positive and negative excitrons (holes emitted by anodes) and electrons (emitted by cathodes) in a polymer dye using the principles of electroluminescence.
Desktop Printers	Print Resolution	Pixels per square inch	Dot Matrix+	Creates an image by striking pins against an ink ribbon to print closely spaced dots that form the desired image.
			Inkjet+	Forms images by spraying ionized ink at a sheet of paper through micro-nozzles.
			Laser+	Forms an image on a photosensitive surface using electrostatic charges. It then transfers the image into a paper using toners and heats the paper to make the image permanent.
			Thermal+	Forms images on paper by heating ink through sublimation or phase change processes.
Data Transfer	Speed of Data Transmission	Megabits per second	Copper/ Aluminum+	Transmits data in the form of electrical energy as analog or digital signals.
			Fiber Optics+	Transmits data in the form of light pulses through a thin strand of glass using the principles of total internal reflection.
			Wireless*	Encodes data in the form of a sine wave and transmits it with radio waves using a transmitter–receiver combination.

Source: Author's own.

Notes: See Sood and Tellis (2005: 152–68).

* The performance (measured by market utility for serving consumer needs) of these technologies follows an S curve: they have a slow start and then a sudden growth spurt via a single inflection point.

+ The performance of these technologies did not follow the traditional S curve, but was better approximated as a multiple step function or multiple S curves.

The performance curve could not be estimated owing to lack of data points.

5. New technologies come as much from new entrants as from large incumbents.
6. New technologies may enter above or below the performance of existing technologies.
7. The performance curves of a pair of competing technologies rarely have a single crossing.
8. The path of a technological evolution seems partially predictable.
9. Previous improvements in performance of the same technology, improvement of crossing by a rival technology, and especially, crossing by a rival firm, tend to signal immediate improvement of performance.
10. Since technological evolutions do not always follow a single point S curve, strategic technological planning and new product development programs based on S curves may be too risky.

Open Innovation

[See Huston and Sakkab (2006)]

The world's innovation landscape has changed. Important innovations rarely occur in big giant companies but in small and mid-size entrepreneurial companies. Some of these individuals were eager to license and sell their intellectual property. University and government labs were interested in forming industrial partnerships and they were seeking ways to monetize their research. The Internet has opened up access to talent markets throughout the world. A few companies like IBM and Eli Lilly were experimenting with a new concept of "open innovation," leveraging one another's (even competitors') innovation assets—products, intellectual property, and people.

P&G's new model for innovation and a new radical strategy is what they also call the "open innovation." Back in 2002, P&G's new product development team was brainstorming ways to make snacks more novel and fun, and someone suggested that we print pop culture images on potato Pringles. The technology to do it would be overwhelming, since P&G was not well versed with printing technologies. Instead of developing the technology from within, they circulated the idea as a problem throughout their global networks of individuals and institutions seeking ready-made solutions. They found one in a small bakery in Bologna, Italy, run by a university professor. He had invented an ink-jet method for printing edible images on cakes and cookies. P&G rapidly adopted this technology to solve its specific problem and by 2004 launched a new line of Pringles potato crisps with pictures and words—trivia questions, animal facts, jokes—printed on each crisp. The product was an immediate success, with double-digit growth during 2004–06.

Best innovations can come from connecting ideas across internal businesses. External connections can produce highly profitable innovations. P&G's recent model for innovation is to acquire 50 percent of their innovations outside the company. That is, half of P&G's new products will come from their own labs, and the other half would come from outside sources. This strategy does not replace the talent and work of its 7,500 researchers and support staff, but it certainly leverages it. Of course, to operationalize this open innovation model the company must create its own "connect and develop innovation model." By 2006, P&G had more than 35 percent of its new products in the markets come from elements that originated from outside P&G, up from about 15 percent in 2000. About 45 percent of the new initiatives of its product development have key elements that were discovered externally. Through connect and develop, and with improvements in other aspects of innovation related to product cost, design, and marketing, P&G's R&D productivity has increased by nearly 60 percent. P&G's innovation success rate has more than doubled, while the cost of innovation has fallen. Obviously, P&G's share price has risen from a low of $52 a share in 2000 to its double by 2005. P&G has currently a portfolio of 22 billion-dollar brands (Huston and Sakkab 2006: 61).

Management Innovation

[See Hamel (2006)]

Management innovation is a "marked departure from traditional management principles, processes, and practices or a departure from customary organizational forms that significantly alters the way the work of management is performed" (Hamel 2006: 75). Management innovation changes how managers do what they do. While operational innovation focuses on a company's business processes (e.g., procurement, supply chain management, transportation, logistics, costing, and customer support), management innovation targets a company's management processes (e.g., setting goals, motivating employees, coordinating and controlling activities, accumulating and acquiring resources, acquiring and applying knowledge, mergers and acquisitions, identifying and developing talent, building and nurturing relationships, and co-aligning company's strengths with market demand and needs). In large companies, the only way to change how managers work is to reinvent the processes that govern that work. Management processes such as corporate planning, capital budgeting, project management, product planning, human resources planning, and employee and executive talent development and retention are the gears that convert management principles into everyday practice and routines (Hamel 2006: 76).

Innovation is optimal value chain management. Innovation is company-pervasive and should positively affect all the producer–consumer value-chain stages of corporate planning, equity management, investment management, procurement, materials management, unfinished goods inventory management, process management, production operations management, human resource management, product management, and packaging, pricing, promoting, retailing, financing, and customer feedback management. Each stage in the value chain has its own innovation characteristics, strategies, and expected outcomes. Tables 7.9A and 7.9B sketch various types of innovation as a function of producer–consumer value-chain stages.

One can inculcate innovation into corporate culture—this is "intrapreneurial innovation"—and when this is accomplished, this can become a strategic weapon for product quality improvement new product development.

Often, "timing is an innovation." Introducing a product to the market at the right time, right place, and with a right marketing mix is a non-technological innovation that becomes a definite strategic and lucrative advantage. Over time innovations begin to migrate from their original market destination to various extended markets. Tables 7.9A and 7.9B illustrate this phenomenon.

Operational innovations are a subset of management innovations. Management innovations are ubiquitous in the company. They are relevant to R&D, to strategic planning, accounting, finance, and marketing departments.

Table 7.10 provides a snapshot of these management innovations that pervade the whole company. In fact, management innovations affect every stage of the producer and the consumer value chain, or end-to-end product processes that cross-departmental boundaries.

TABLE 7.9A   A Typology of Management Innovations as a Function of Producer Value Chain

Value chain	Innovation in	Characteristics	Management innovation (MI) strategies
Producer Value Chain	Corporate Planning	Mission management Vision management Setting goals and objectives Core business, core products, core competencies, and standards management Resource allocation management Mergers and acquisitions management Market environment management	Mission effectiveness Vision communication and diffusion Targeting/assessing goals and objectives Monitoring core business and products Developing core competencies and standards Resource allocation by MI success Mergers and acquisitions for MI success MI for capitalizing market environment
	Product Planning	Category planning Product line planning Brand management	MI for category planning MI for product line extensions MI for brand and community management
	Product Designing	Prototype designing Attributes designing Benefits designing Value designing	MI for prototype designing MI for product attributes designing MI for customer benefits designing MI for customer value enhancing
	HR Management	Talent identity management Recruiting management Employee development management Retention management Performance appraisal management Promotions management Bonus/commissions management	MI for talent identity management MI for recruiting skills and talent MI for personnel development MI for skills retention management MI for performance appraisal management MI for employee promotions management MI for bonus/commissions management
	Procurement	Centralized purchasing Decentralized purchasing Bargaining power management Supply chain management Transportation management Logistics management	MI for centralized purchasing MI for decentralized procurement MI for enhancing bargaining power MI for supply chain management MI for optimizing transportation management MI for logistics management
	Materials Management	Quality management Specifications management	MI for total quality management MI for OEM/ISO specifications management
	Unfinished Goods Inventory Management	JIT management Warehousing management Wastage management Theft management	MI for JIT inventory management MI for optimizing warehousing management MI for wastage reduction MI for theft elimination
	Process Management	Efficiency management Effectiveness management EPA management	MI for material and parts efficiency management MI for production process management MI for zero defects and emissions management
	Cash Flow Management	Payables management Receivable management Credit management	MI for optimal payables management MI for optimal receivables management MI for supplier/customer credit management
	Production Management	Production life-cycle management Economies of scale management Six Sigma quality management	MI for production life-cycle management MI for optimal scale economies management MI for Six Sigma product quality management

Source: Author's own.

TABLE 7.9B   A Typology of Management Innovations as a Function of Consumer Value Chain

Value chain	Innovation in	Characteristics	Management innovation (MI) strategies
Consumer Value Chain	Product Management	Product variety and assortment Brand quality and reputation	MI for product variety and assortment management MI for brand quality and reputation management
	Packaging Management	Sizing, labeling, package design Product bundling	MI for optimal sizing, labeling, and packaging MI for attractive product bundles
	Pricing Management	Premium, penetration pricing Product-price bundling	MI for pricing and market penetration MI for attractive product-price bundles
	Promoting Management	Promotional communications Promotional motivations	MI for clear and informative promotions MI for persuasive and compelling motives
	Retailing Mmanagement	Store name and reputation Store safety, security, and convenience	MI for store reputation management MI for store safety, security, and convenience
	Finished Goods Inventory Management	Store shelf place and space Inventory turnover Overstock inventory clearance	MI for attractive shelf-configuration management MI for faster inventory turnovers MI for clearing overstocked inventories
	Selling Management	Frontline sales representatives Customer problem-solving skills	MI for frontline ambassadorship MI for solving customer problems
	Customer Feedback Management	Customer complaints handling Soliciting customer feedback	MI for complaints handling and redress MI for ongoing customer feedback
	Customer Support Management	Product guarantees and warranties Product financing Product expansions and updates	MI for servicing guarantees and warranties MI for product financing and collection MI for product expansion/updates management

Source: Author's own.

THE INSTITUTIONALIZATION OF INNOVATION

The distinctive feature of the 20th century was that the inventive process became powerfully institutionalized and far more systematic than it had been in the 19th century. That is, inventions and innovations collaborated with organized research in universities, research centers, and corporations, and eventually generated a slew of products and services that enhanced (or occasionally, destroyed) civilizations. When in 1903 the Wright brothers crafted the first airplane, the clumsy contraption was held together with struts, baling wire, and glue, and the total distance traveled was a just a couple hundred yards. It required thousands of improvements and adaptation over a third of a century to manufacture the DC-3 in 1936 that could fly thousands of miles between cities with hundreds of passengers. Similarly, when in 1945 the first digital electronic computer, the Electronic Numerical Integrator and Computer (ENIAC), was put together, it was over 100 feet long, required thousands of cubic feet space, and necessitated the simultaneous functioning of over 18,000 vacuum tubes. Today, through 60 years of steady innovations, improvements, and miniaturizations, handheld PCs are million times more effective than ENIAC in storing, computing, and transmitting billions of bits of data. This is the power of institutionalized and organized innovation and commercialization (Mowery and Rosenberg 1998).

The institutionalization of innovation implies many complementary technologies and inventions in the industry where the innovation is primarily located, many ancillary technologies and inventions or

TABLE 7.10 Management Innovation (MI) Types: Domain, Roles, Constraints, and Results

MI Type	MI Domain	MI Role	MI	MI Results
Strategic Innovation	Executive leadership and charisma, strategic planning, capital budgeting, capital allocation, financial management, investments management, mergers and acquisitions, long-term debt management, equity decisions, debt-restructuring, and regulatory concerns	Business mission and vision statement; Business core values definition; Core customer identification; Addressing shareholder concerns; Supervision, direction, and annual results assessment	Poor executive leadership and charisma; Top-down approach upstream management; No exposure to real operations; Mid-stream operations are neglected as less glamorous	Precarious, uncertain, and often speculative expectations are unrealized. For instance, most mergers and acquisitions are unsuccessful. Only 15 percent success rate for strategic innovations. Hence, poorly managed.
Operational Innovations	Procurement, ordering, bargaining power via centralized versus decentralized purchasing, supply chain management, materials management, inventory management, process management, production management, quality management, new product development, sizing, packaging, and labeling management	Optimizing operations in terms of maximum meaningful outputs per unit of factor inputs; Optimal supply chain relations; Optimal order fulfillment cycle; Optimal time management; Total quality management; Zero defects and zero emissions management Optimizing new production and product life cycles	Supplier availability and credit; Materials quality and quantity; Levels of labor and personnel skills, dedication, and unions wage-salary administration; Working conditions (Occupational Safety and Health Adminstration [OSHA] compliance); Wastage, pilfering, hazard, and EPA rules	If done well, operational innovations can reap profits 85 percent of times via saving supply and production costs, increasing productivity, achieving high economies of scale, and high compliance with OSHA, EPA, ISO 9000 and other standards, and enhancing quality of products and services.
Accounting Innovations	Costing, First in and First Out (FIFO), Last in and First Out (LIFO), depreciation management, cost allocations, receivables management, payables management, operation cycle and cash cycle management, auditing, and pricing	Objective and transparent costing and cost allocations; Optimal cash flow management via receivables and payables management	Accounting irregularities; Doctoring accounts to suit managerial objectives; Cash flow crisis and insolvency	If done innovatively, accounting innovations can help management in cash flow optimization, cash budgeting, and forecasting.
Financial Innovations	Investments management, securities management, supply-credit management, short-term debt management, budget management, budget forecasting, cash flow management, cash flow forecasting, financial analysis reporting, and customer financing	Optimizing shareholder value; Optimizing financing decisions; Optimizing investment decisions; Optimizing cash flow management via debt, securities, and equity management	Insider-trading violations; Fudging and doctoring financial statements to suit managerial objectives or to please Securities Exchange Commission (SEC); Creditor and supplier opportunism	When financial management innovations are creative and productive, financial health (e.g., ROI, ROE, EPS) of the company can be managed, controlled, and predicted, with no financial crises.
Marketing Innovations	Market scanning, market intelligence, competitor intelligence, new product management, pricing, brand management, brand community management, product bundling, price-product bundling, discounts, rebates and coupons management, distribution, promotions, retailing, customer service, customer support, customer satisfaction, feedback, complaints handling and redress management	Optimizing sales in units and dollars, markets and target customers; Maximizing market share, profitability, ROS, ROM, ROQ, and customer satisfaction and loyalty; Optimal customer relations management (CRM) and total customer experience (TCE)	Industry and market stagnation; Consumer apathy and disloyalty; Competition dominance; Low demand elasticity; Changing consumer lifestyles; Forced product obsolescence	Creative marketing innovations can expand and sustain high levels of salespeople frontline ambassadorship, and hence, high customer awareness, interest, search, satisfaction, experience, advocacy, and lifetime loyalty.

Source: Author's own

improvements from other industries, many new products redesigned for greater safety and convenience, many cost-reducing scale economies so that products could be more affordable, many adaptations as consumers and producers discover new uses for these products, many capital investments and venture capitalists, and many regulatory interventions on the part of the government. According to Kuznets (1959: 33), a sustained high rate of economic growth depends upon a continuous emergence of new inventions and innovations, providing the bases for new industries and the decline of older industries. Often, the inter-sectoral flow of new technologies would revamp and resurrect older industries (e.g., synthetic-fiber radial tires, synthetic plastics for cosmetic surgery) that further contributed to the economic growth of nations. This inter-sectoral and international flow of goods (exports and imports) and technologies is a fundamental characteristic of 20th century innovation in the U.S. economy (Mowery and Rosenberg 1998: 5–6). For instance, innovations in the chemicals and electronic industries have spawned an enormous array of consumer and capital goods; the rise of the automotive and commercial aircraft industries have significantly increased the demand for advanced products in other industries (e.g., jet fuel, composite materials, synthetic products, and gasoline).

The role of science, universities, governments, culture, religion, economy, buying power, and consumer lifestyles in institutionalizing innovations must be recognized. While old and new technologies, old and new industries interact to generate new ideas and innovations, the process of commercialization is much conditioned upon market demand, which in turn, is a combined result of culture and religion, economics and consumer buying power, consumer habits and behaviors, consumer education and occupations, consumer communities and societies, cities and villages.

EMERGING TECHNOLOGIES AND EMERGING INNOVATIONS

[See *Technology Review* (2005), "Ten Emerging Technologies," *Technology Review*, May, 108(5): 53–53]

New technologies are emerging that could transform the Internet, computing, medicine, energy, and more. Some of these are:

- **Airborne Networks**: An Internet in the sky could let planes fly safely without ground controls or controllers. Air traffic control technology has not changed very much in the last 50 years. The system is based on elaborate ground-based radar systems, thousands of people watching blips on screens and who issue verbal instructions for landings, takeoffs, and course changes. The system is expensive, hard to scale up, and prone to delays when storms strike. Airborne networks offer an entirely different approach. Each plane in the sky could continually transmit its identity, precise location, speed, and direction-destiny to other planes in the neighborhood sky via an airborne network. Software would then take over, coordinating the system by issuing instructions to pilots on how to stay separated, optimize routes, avoid bad weather, and execute precise landings despite poor visibility. Short-term benefits for consumers: save time, reduce fuel consumption, and hence reduce prices. Long-term benefits: you could fit more planes in the sky, reduce landing or takeoff delays, additional safety, security, and privacy, and avoid accidents. Currently, the U.S. Air Force, NASA, and the Pentagon are working on defining the architecture of an airborne network and hope to launch this project between 2008 and 2012.

- **Quantum Wires**: Power transmission wires spun from carbon nanotubes could carry electricity farther and more efficiently. Richard Smalley, a Rice University chemist, has embarked on a four-year project to create a prototype of a nanotube based "quantum wire," a clear plastic tube that can hold thin, dark grey fibers comprising billions of carbon nanotubes. Cables made from quantum wires should conduct much better than copper. The lighter weight and higher strength of the wires would also allow existing towers to carry fatter cables with 10 times more capacity than the existing heavy and inefficient steel-reinforced aluminum cables used in today's aging power grids. Quantum wires would have less electrical resistance and would not dissipate electricity as heat. Smalley feels that quantum wires could perform even better than superconductors that need expensive cooling equipment. In fact, Jianping Lu, a physicist at the University of North Carolina at Chapel Hill has found that electrons could travel down a wire of perfectly aligned, overlapping carbon nanotubes with almost no loss of energy.
- **Silicon Photonics**: Optoelectronics which makes the material of computer chips emit light, could speed data flow. The Internet lives on beams of light. One hair-thin glass fiber can carry as much data as thousands of copper wires. But inside the computer, copper still rules, and we have reached the physical ability of copper to carry more information. Hence, switching to fiber optics would be necessary. Getting silicon to emit light could be the solution. A light signal's frequency is much more than that of an electrical signal, and so it can carry information thousands of times as much and faster. Light overcomes another major problem: as transistors get closed together, the electrical signals passing through them start to interfere with each other, like radio stations broadcasting at the same frequency. But currently turning silicon into a light emitter is very difficult: there is an energy-level mismatch between silicon's electrons and its positively charged "holes" (electron vacancies in its crystal structure). When an electron meets a hole, it is more likely to release its excess energy as vibration than as light. But in Fall 2004, a team of scientists at UCLA, became the first to make a laser out of silicon. In February 2005, Intel scientists reported a silicon laser that emitted a continuous beam instead of a pulsed one, a necessity for data communications. Intel has also created a silicon modulator, which allows them to encode data onto a light beam by making it stronger or weaker. Silicon photonics can be soon cost-effective in doubling computer speeds, possibly within five years.
- **Metabolomics**: A new medical diagnostic could spot diseases earlier and more easily. In their quest for developing more accurate and less invasive diagnostic tests, medical researchers are turning to metabolomics, the analysis of the thousands of small molecules such as of sugar or fat that are the products of metabolism. If metabolomic information can be translated into diagnostic tests, it could provide more accurate, faster, and earlier diagnoses of most diseases, such as autism, ALS (amyotrophic lateral sclerosis or Lou Gehrig's disease), Alzheimer's disease, bipolar disorder, Huntington's disease, and cancer. Metabolomics is an off-shoot of recent advances in genomics and proteomics, which have allowed researchers to begin to identify many of the genes and proteins involved in diseases. Computers and software can enable doctors and researchers to study metabolites in the same systematic fashion as genomic research so as to get a complete picture of the body's processes. Metabolites are best disease-markers, as well as give a comprehensive picture of complex changes underway in hundreds of molecules as a disease begins to develop.
- **Universal Memory**: Nanotubes make possible ultra-dense data storage. A circular wafer of silicon, about the size of a compact disk, sealed in an acrylic container, can store 10 billion bits of digital

information. Each bit is encoded not by an electric charge on a circuit element, as in conventional electronic memory, nor by the direction of a magnetic field, as in hard drives, but by the physical orientation of nanoscale structures. This technology could eventually allow vastly greater amounts of data to be stored on computers and mobile devices. No existing memory technologies can prove adequate in the long run. Static and dynamic random access memory (RAM), used in laptops and PCs, are fast but require too much space and power. Flash memory is dense but non-volatile—it does not need power to hold data, but is too slow for computers. Universal memory seeks to combine the advantages of both technologies. For this, we need a memory holding device whose cells are made of carbon nanotubes, each less than one-ten-thousandth the width of a human hair and suspended a few nanometers above an electrode. This default position, with no electric current flow between the nanotubes and the electrode, represents a digital 0. When a small voltage is applied to the cell, the nanotubes sag in the middle, touch the electrode, and complete a circuit—storing a digital 1. The technology can be refined where each nanotube encodes one bit, thus storing trillions of bits per square centimeter, thousands of times denser than flash memory. A typical DVD holds less than 50 billion bits total, and flash memory about 15–25 gigabits. If developed, the universal memory could outdate both DVDs and flash memory as storage devices. Nantero (partnering with Milpitas, CA-based LSI Logic) is experimenting on the universal memory by integrating its nanotube memory with silicon circuitry. Currently, its prototypes store only about 100 million bits per square centimeter. Suspending nanotubes is not the only way to build a universal memory. Other strategies include magnetic random access that Motorola and IBM are pursuing, and molecular memory where HP is the leader.

WHO INNOVATES?

An innovator is the firm that first invents and commercializes an innovation. From a radical incremental innovation perspective, a radical innovator invents and commercializes radical innovations; an incremental innovator invents and commercializes incremental innovations.

Apparently, originators of an innovation rarely innovate its successive stages. For example, in the typewriter industry, Remington started, Underwood followed, IBM broke the mold with "golf-ball" typewriters, Wang further modified it with the advent of word-processing, and now Microsoft seems to have taken over. Every change in the configuration in the computer disk drive industry (e.g., from 8.5 inch disks to 5.25 inch disks to 3.5 inch disks) was initiated by a non-incumbent (i.e., not an originator or market pioneer) and led to the downfall of the previously dominant firm. Thus, does the pioneer or originator have an advantage in generating innovations more than that of new entrants or entrepreneurs? We will take up this discussion in a later chapter in this book. For the present, we discuss which firms in general have a higher propensity to innovate.

Table 7.11 distinguishes between an innovator or a product pioneer, a market pioneer or one who bring innovations first to the market, and the current market leaders who are the most successful in terms of sales and profits regarding an innovation. As Table 7.11 indicates, often the three are not the same. Table 7.12, however, lists exceptions to this phenomenon.

One reason for this phenomenon is that innovations migrate quickly from industry to industry, and hence, stimulate different market pioneers and market leaders. Table 7.13 illustrates the phenomenon of innovation migrations.

TABLE 7.11   Pioneer versus Late Mover Advantage

Product category*	Product pioneer	Market pioneer	Current market leader
1. VCR	Ampex (1956)	Ampex (1963)	RCA/Matsushita (1977)
2. Microwave ovens	Raytheon (1946)	Amana (1966)	GE/Samsung (1979)
3. Dishwasher	Crescent (1900)	Crescent (1900)	GE (1935)
4. Laundry dryers	Canton (1925)	Canton (1925)	Whirlpool (1950)
5. Fax machines	Xerox (1964)	Xerox (1964)	Sharp (1982)
6. PC	MITS (1975)	MITS (1975), IBM (1984)	Dell (1995)
7. Camcorder	Sony, JVC (1982)	Kodak/Matsushita (1984)	RCA/Matsushita (1985)
8. Color TV	Bell Labs (1929)	RCA (1954)	Sony (1992)
9. Wine cooler	California Cooler (1979)	California Cooler (1981)	Seagram, Bartles & Jaymes (1984)
10. Liquid dishwashing detergent	Liquid Lux (1948)	Liquid Lux (1948)	Ivory Liquid (1957)
11. Laundry detergent	Reychler (1913)	Dreft (1933)	Tide (1946)
12. Disposable diapers	Chux (1950)	Chux (1950)	P&G/Pampers & Luvs (1961)
13. Frozen dinners	Swanson (1946)	Swanson (1946)	Stoufler (1956)
14. Light beer	Trommer's Red Letter (1961)	Trommer's Red Letter (1961)	Miller Lite (1975)
15. Diet Cola	Kirsch's No-cal Cola (1952)	Kirch's No-cal Cola (1952)	Diet Coke (1982)
16. Liquid laundry detergent	Wisk (1956)	Wisk (1956)	Liquid Tide (1984)
17. Dandruff shampoo	Fitch's (1919)	Fitch's (1919)	Head & Shoulders (1961)
18. Cereal	Granula (1863)	Granula (1863)	Kellogg (1906)
19. Cameras	Daguerrotype (1839)	Daguerrotype (1839)	Kodak (1888)?
20. Chocolate	Whitman's (1842)	Whitman's (1842)	Hershey (1903)
21. Canned milk	Borden (1856)	Borden (1860)	Carnation (1899)
22. Chewing gum	Black Jack (1871)	Black Jack (1871)	Wrigley (1892)
23. Flashlight battery	Bright Star (1909)	Bright Star (1909)	Eveready (1920)
24. Safety razors	Star (1876)	Star (1876)	Gillette (1903)
25. Sewing machine	Elias Howe (1842)	4 firms (1849)	Singer (1851)
26. Soft drinks	Vernors (1866)	Vernors (1866)	Coca-Cola (1886)
27. Tires	Hartford (1895)	Hartford (1895)	Goodyear (1898)
28. Copy machines	3M Thermofax (1950)	3M Thermofax (1950)	Xerox (1959)
29. Telephone	Ries (1865), Gray (1876), Bell (1876)	Bell (1877)	AT&T (Bell) 1877
30. Instant photography	Archer (1853)	Dubroni (1864)	Polaroid (1947), Digital Cameras (2000)
31. Video games	Magnavox Odyssey (1973)	Magnavox Odyssey (1973)	Nintendo (1985); Sony's PlayStations 1, 2 & Plus
32. Rubber	Goodrich (1869)	Goodrich (1869)	Goodyear (1898)
33. Personal stereo	Panasonic (1970)	Panasonic (1970)	Sony (1979); Bose (1985)
34. Canned fruit	Libby, McNeill, Libby (1868)	Libby, McNeill, Libby (1868)	Del Monte (1891)

Source: Golder and Tellis (1993: 164–65).

Notes: * A product category is a group of close substitutes distinct from other product categories.

An inventor is the firm that develops patents or important technologies in a new product category.

A product pioneer is the first firm to develop a working model or sample in a new product category.

A market pioneer is the first firm to sell in a new product category.

A market leader is the firm (brand) that has the dominant market share in a market.

TABLE 7.12   Pioneer Advantage: Long-lived Market Leaders

Product category	Long-lived market leader
Sewing Machine	Singer (1851)
Beer	Anheuser-Busch (1852)
Single Malt Liquor	Glenfidich (1850)
Blended Scotch	JW Black Label (1820), Chivas Regal (1825)
Shirts	Manhattan (1857)
Paint	Sherwin Williams (1870)
Soap	Ivory (1879)
Flour	Gold Medal (1880)
Soft Drinks	Coca-Cola (1886)
Bacon	Swift (1887)
Cameras	Kodak (1888)
Crackers	Nabisco (1990)
Toilet Tissue	Scott (1890)
Canned Fruit	Del Monte (1891)
Chewing Gum	Wrigley (1892)
Tea	Lipton (1893)
Soup	Campbell (1897)
Tires	Goodyear (1898)
Paper	Hammermill 1898
Canned Milk	Carnation (1899)
Chocolate	Hershey (1903)
Safety Razors	Gillette (1903)
Cereals	Kellogg (1906)
Pipe Tobacco	Prince Albert (1907)
Vegetable Shortening	Crisco (1911)
Mint Candy	Life Saver (1913)
Flashlight Batteries	Eveready (1920)
Dishwasher	GE (1935)
Laundry Dryers	Whirlpool (1950)
Laundry Detergent	Tide (1946)
Toothpaste	Crest (1955)

Source: Golder and Tellis (1993: 165).

TABLE 7.13   Extended Innovations as Migrations to New Markets

Product	Product extensions as migrations
Air conditioners	From businesses to home to car to portable?
Audio tape recorders	From sound studio to home to car to portable; now invaded by CDs
Calculators	From office to home to portable to PCs
Computers	From government to business or factory to home to portable
Microprocessors	From office desktop or factory floor to home to car to portable
Fax machines	From business to home to computer to mobile phones
VCRs	From TV recording studio to home to portable
Telephones	From business to home to portable to car to notebook PC to mobile phones
Satellite systems	From defense applications to business to home to car? To individuals?
Radios	From post office to home to portable to car
Movies	From theater to home to work to physical fitness centers
Movie cameras	From TV studio to home to portable to Internet clients
Still picture cameras	From studio to portable to notebook PC?
Electric generators	From utility companies to business to home to portable
Electric motors	From electric train to business to home to portable
Medical diagnostic equipment	From hospital to ambulatory units to home to portable to notebook PC? (e.g., blood pressure gages, blood sugar gages, kidney dialysis units).
Retailing	From streets to flea markets to malls to direct marketing to Internet marketing
Books	From libraries to business to home to computers to portable PCs to CDs to Internet
Music	From music studios to radio stations to home to portable CDs to notebook PCs
Home cooked meals	From homes to restaurant to fast foods to TV dinners to microwaves to?
Fitness equipment	From health clubs to home to portable?
Formal education	From schools/universities to homes to long-distance learning to notebook PC?
Vacationing	From homes to friends to hotels to resorts to overseas to Mars?
Sports	From homes to schools to colleges to minor leagues to major leagues to?
Religious services	From churches/synagogues to schools to homes to portable TV?
Weddings	From churches to courts to commercial wedding chapels to homes to parks
Birthing, delivery	From homes to hospitals to clinics to ambulatory medicine to?
Child care	From homes to baby sitters to professional day care to ambulatory centers?
Nursing the elderly	From homes to assisted living to nursing homes to hospice care to?
Funeral services	From homes to churches to funeral parlors to?
Burial services	From church cemeteries to public cemeteries to crematoria to homes?

Source: Expanded from Afuah (1998: 126).

In answering the question: who is most likely to innovate? Schumpeter (1934) maintained that entrepreneurs (and hence, small and new firms) are the most likely to innovate, but later (see Schumpeter 1949) changed his view to theorize that large firms with higher degrees of monopoly, larger capital bases and higher risk-absorption capacities, larger production and complementary assets that are necessary to commercialize an invention, are the most likely to innovate.

But the prevalent theory thereafter argues the opposite. Just because firms are too large, and therefore, too bureaucratic, they tend to be incompetent, suffer from technological inertia or kainotophobia (resistance to change brought about by a new technology), and hence tend to under-invest in new inventions and ventures, especially if they have made too many investments in existing products and markets (Henderson 1993; Henderson and Clark 1990).

Recently, Chandy and Tellis (2000), after extensive research in the consumer durables and office product categories, argued that incumbents or large firms have had significant role in radical innovations. They concluded:

- Over a 150-year period, small firms and non-incumbents have introduced slightly more radical innovations than large firms and incumbents.
- However, after World War II, large firms and incumbents have successfully introduced a majority of radical product innovations.
- Small firms and outsiders account for many more innovations in the U.S.A. than they do in other countries such as Western Europe or Japan.
- The U.S. accounts for almost two-thirds of radical product innovations in the consumer durables and office product categories, and Western Europe accounts for the most of the remaining.
- Japan has provided only a few radical innovations, and mostly in very recent years (e.g., Seiko's analog quartz watch in 1969, Konishiroku's auto focus color celluloid roll camera in 1977, Sony's Camcorder and digital camera in 1983 and mini-disk player in 1992, and Toshiba's digital video disk [DVD] player in 1997).

INNOVATION AS NEW INPUTS, NEW PROCESSES, AND NEW OUTPUTS

We may distinguish innovation as a new input, a new process, or a new output (that itself becomes input to another value-adding innovation).

- **Innovation as Inputs**: Incorporating new inputs in terms of new materials, components, and core products; new technologies, processes, and programs; new peoples, skills, and talents; new sites, spaces, and paces; new synergies, alliances, and collaborations.
- **Innovation as Process**: Basically, innovation is a process that converts inputs into outputs, is anything new in the industry, market, country, or the world in terms of purchasing materials, installing new processes, new production and inventory management, new packaging, customizing, and labeling, new distribution and delivery, new advertising and promotions, new retailing and shelving, new pricing and financing of products and services, new post-sales services and redress. Here, innovation is defined as a technology, strategy, or a management practice that a firm is using for the first time, or a significant restructuring or improvement in a process (Nord and Tucker 1987; O'Neill, Pouder, and Buchholtz 1998).
- **Innovation as Outputs**: As resulting from innovations as inputs and process, new market offerings such as core products and services, support products and services, updates and upgrades—these fulfill new needs, new wants, new desires, new ways of managing time, space, and pace, new ways of managing health, fitness, and looks; new ways of learning, growing, and developing, new ways of winning people, their trust and loyalty.

Innovation, thus, implies at least three knowledge sets: technological, market-, and business-related knowledge. All three are necessary for a successful product/service venture: the first, in producing it, the second in marketing it, and the third for both producing and marketing it (see Chapter 5). For adopter firms, the decision to adopt radically new technologies is difficult because of the associated uncertainties, the possibility that prior investments may be rendered obsolete, and high switching costs in adopting new technologies. Yet if a radically new technology is promising, it will create attractive market opportunities (Srinivasan, Lilien, and Rangaswamy 2002).

FACTORS AFFECTING CREATIVITY IN MARKETING PROGRAMS

[See Andrews and Smith (1996)]

- Research on factors affecting new product success has consistently found that the primary determinant of customer response is the degree to which the product provides meaningful benefits relative to competing alternatives (Andrews and Smith 1996; Cooper 1986).
- Innovations in general provide unique and meaningful benefits to products and services (Day 1994: 69; Rogers 1983: 134). Creativity or innovation is defined in terms of meaningful novelty of some output (e.g., a painting, a chemical compound) relative to conventional practice in the domain to which it belongs (e.g., abstract art, adhesives) (Hennessey and Amabile 1988).
- Thus, a creative product is that which evokes a meaningful difference from other competing products in the product category. A creative marketing program (e.g., advertising) represents a meaningful difference from marketing practices (e.g., media advertising) in a given product category (Haberland and Dacin 1992).
- In relation to marketing mature products, innovative initiatives emerge from a formal or informal marketing planning process undertaken by a product manager who works alone (often with informal input from others) or plays the central role in a small team of several assistant product managers (Lehmann and Winer 1994).
- Several factors affect creativity and innovation: (*a*) individual factors; (*b*) situational factors; and (*c*) motivational factors.

Individual Factors Affecting Creativity

- **Various problem-solving skills possessed by the product manager and his/her team**. Creative ideas often are the result of a process focused on solving a specific problem through combining existing concepts in new ways (Osborne 1963). However, before a new idea is conceived, the product manager should amass knowledge of the related and unrelated domains of interest (Amabile 1983). This knowledge serves as the raw material from which new ideas are synthesized.
- In marketing, such knowledge would include product and brand trends, competing and substitute products and brands, channel-knowledge, customer purchase and use knowledge (operating micro-environment), and market-demographic trends, political/legal trends, technological trends, and economic trends (macro-environment). Greater knowledge of the marketing environment increases a product manager's ability to analyze incoming data and extract useful information (Alba and Hutchinson 1987), ask the right type of questions (Miyake and Norman 1979), and will reduce the

time-cost of acquiring new information. Will too much knowledge blind and stifle creativity? It is not the quantity of information gathered that matters, but it is quality and the way it is organized; the latter trigger creativity.

- **Motivational Factors**: These relate to the product manager's level of intrinsic motivation (specific to a task; Amabile 1983) and willingness to take risk in expending the effort and energy necessary to create and innovate. For instance, any creative solution involves a large number of ideas or variations, and synthesizing them needs much effort, courage, focus, time, and talent. Risk of failure of a marketing program is related to its rejection by the top management or not being attractive to prospective consumers. One should take the risk of failure, or being rejected and opposed by peers or supervisors (Osborne 1963). Willingness to take risk is a key contributor to creativity, because it provides motivation to entertain ideas that deviate from the status quo (Amabile 1983) and to consider non-traditional ways to marketing.
- **Educational Factors**: The more diverse a product manager's education (arts, philosophy, economics, anthropology, psychology, and business) and experience (sales, advertising, packaging, promotion, pricing, and designing), greater the creativity of the marketing program (Andrews and Smith 1996).

Situational Factors Affecting Creativity

- **Problem-solving Style of the Product Manager**: Using a non-routine or heuristic process—one that departs from cookbook procedures—in solving problems facilitates creativity. A formal, programmed, or algorithmic process (i.e., following a specified set of steps) may yield output that is little different from the past. The creativity of a marketing program may be the best when planning formalization process is moderate.
- **Interaction Process Involved**: Much depends upon the level and quality of interaction set up by the product manager with people and other functional areas. The more a product manager interacts with members of other functional areas (e.g., sales personnel, R&D, new product designers), the greater the creativity of the marketing program.
- **The Time Pressure of Deadlines**: The greater the time pressure (measured by brevity, variety, fragmentation, fighting competitive fires) perceived by a product manager, the less the creativity of the marketing program.

ARCHITECTURAL INNOVATION AND MODULAR CORPORATE FORMS

[See Galunic and Eisenhardt (2001)]

Innovation as the creation of value within changing markets is emerging. Although efficiency and control in innovation management are important, dynamic capabilities within the organization that reflect flexibility, creativity, and timing are getting to be more important. Dynamic capabilities are "organizational and strategic processes by which managers manipulate resources into new productive assets in the context of changing markets" (Galunic and Eisenhardt 2001: 1229). Such dynamic capabilities could include knowledge transfer, integrative capabilities, product innovation processes, and other specific micro-processes and roles that form these capabilities. The corporate level processes by which multi-business firms reconfigure their resources for higher productivity and profitability are also called architectural innovations.

Galunic and Eisenhardt (2001) investigate how architectural innovations come about in firms: how the modern corporation, as a dynamic and social community, modulates its corporate resources as markets and other corporate players co-evolve. In particular, the authors view the corporation as a "social community," where dynamic capabilities are based on "communal imperatives" (such as encouraging the weak, rewarding the loyal, rescuing the distressed, and being fair while tolerating competition and conflict) rather than on purely economic reasoning (such as optimizing the technical fit between markets and resources to ensure rent maximization).

The authors report results from their 18-month field interviews with a large multi-business Fortune 100 company pseudo-named Omni Corporation that was basically an electronic company that had wide interests such as computer peripherals, computing-information technology (IT), and electronic instruments. The unit of analysis was a charter gain experience by a focal division of the firm. A "charter" is a product market domain in which a division actively participates and for which it is responsible within the firm. A typical charter in Omni included: the handheld computing charter, the high-end printing charter, and the video and wideband charter. Omni frequently revisited its corporate architecture as markets and divisions coevolved by reconfiguring divisional resources with old and new charters. A "charter gain" occurred, for instance, when a division obtained a product-market area of responsibility that was either new to the corporation or transferred from another division. Data were collected through interviews, questionnaires, observations, and company archives. Analysis began with detailed written accounts and schematic representations of each charter gain process and findings were grouped under various heads.

How did Omni gain new charters? The authors found three patterns:

- **New Charter Opportunities**: Industry changes to create new markets, and thus new charter opportunities. These are allocated to weak-to-modest divisions where there are many underutilized resources so that constrained charter positions get a boost.
- **Charter Wars**: Competition shifts within firm divisions and creates charter wars outside the organization: here aggressive and fittest divisions and loyal corporate citizens get to be the winners, leaving incentives for the weaker divisions to perform better. Charter wars also occur when rival divisions successfully attack and capture charters from other divisions. In other words, these charter wars gains are simply stories of "divisions becoming more fit in changing markets and so, winning new turf" (Galunic and Eisenhardt 2001: 1236).
- **Charter Foster Homes**: Orphaned charters arisen from industry, market, or competition changes, but hitherto unattractive and unexploited, are either abandoned or allocated to strong divisions as additional charters. Here, "corporate influence" of major executives was the key organization force at work. While "economic logic" (e.g., opportunity and profit maximization, optimal resource allocation for maximizing fit between divisional skills and track records and charter demands) was regularly used, "social logic" (e.g., encouraging under-privileged divisions, retraining obsolete skills, rescuing the distressed, rewards for cooperation and loyalty, recognizing steady performers) was also evidenced. Often economic logic reinforced social logic and vice versa. Economic reasoning alone was insufficient to predict how charter changes played out. The strong and opulent divisions were encouraged to "let some scraps fall from their plate" to fellow languishing divisions.

NEW CHARTER FOR OPPORTUNITIES WITHIN OMNI DIVISIONS

As industries and markets expand, emerge, converge, collide, and diverge, new charter opportunities spring within firms. For example:

- There occurred a gap between one Omni division that manufactured a high-end printing product that catered to a very specialized and sophisticated customer base, and another fellow Omni division that produced a low-end printing product to the small business segment. A niche emerged in the middle that could combine the base technology that was common to both products from middle-end printing products that served a less customized and specialized segment of small to middle businesses or demanding household customers. There was "horizontal relatedness" between these charters: that is, they represented complementary products within the same industry.
- One Omni division was closely involved in the developing of a new imaging technology. The new opportunity was to take this technology and merge it with a related technology, such as networking technology, so that a new business could be developed. There was a "vertical relatedness" between these charters: that is, they represented complementary products between divisions or industries.
- Another division was focused on a niche market: professional graphic design. Although initially this was a lucrative and high-growth market, it soon got saturated with new market entrants, and quickly became a large fish in a small pond. Combining this division with that of imaging technology within Omni opened new vistas, especially to "trapped and languishing performers" who were skilled but nevertheless desperately looked for growth.

Under all these and similar cases:

- A new charter was created, and subsequently allocated to another division based on both economic and social logic. New charters were often assigned not to the high-performer, visibly over-privileged divisions with their burgeoning empires, but to their smaller neighbors. This equalization opportunity creates its own corporate uplifting and cooperative morale and makes its own symbolic powerful statement of fairness and distributive justice.
- Corporate entrepreneurs (executives) managing several divisions were first to recognize these opportunities rather than divisional heads; obviously, the vision of the former was broad in "managerial bandwidth." Corporate entrepreneurs are not lost in divisional performance and venture details, but constantly look for new growth areas and new technologies to cope with changing markets and competitive pressure.

HOW OPERATIONAL INNOVATIONS TRANSFORMED PROGRESSIVE

[See Hammer (2004: 84–95)]

Progressive Insurance, an auto insurer based in Mayfield, Ohio grew from $1.3 billion sales in 1991 to $9.5 billion by 2002, a sevenfold increase in 11 years, or an annual compound growth rate of 19.8 percent during 1991–2002! What could explain this envious performance despite the fact that Progressive belonged to a 100-year-old, mature, low-growth industry of auto insurance? It did not diversify into new businesses, nor did it undertake mergers and acquisitions, nor did it go global. For years Progressive did little advertising, did not generate a slew of new products, nor did it grow at the expense of low margins, even when it set low prices. Yet the financial performance of Progressive (measured by the industry metric of [{expenses + claims payouts}/premiums] was around 96 percent, while the rest of the auto insurers scored 102 percent, running a 2 percent loss on their underwriting activities. Progressive grew dramatically since 1991, and is now the third largest auto insurer in the U.S.A. It outperformed its competitors also in profitability.

The secret of Progressive was its operational innovations. Progressive realized that the key to its profitability was customer retention because acquiring new customers through commission-based agents was twice as expensive. And the key to customer retention is making sure customers have rewarding interactions with the company. Hence, Progressive focused on streamlining claims; making them more pleasant and effective for customers, so that they could win their loyalty. Moreover, by offering better service at lower prices than its rivals, Progressive attracted competitors' customers, and what enabled Progressive to offer better service at lower prices was its operational innovation. The latter, as defined previously, is invention and deployment of new ways of doing work. Progressive invented new ways of filling orders, developing products, providing customer service, and the like. For instance, Progressive reinvented claims processing to lower its costs and boost customer satisfaction and retention.

For most of its history, Progressive focused on high-risk drivers, a market that it captured and served profitably with extremely precise pricing. Its operational innovation was called: Immediate Response Claims Handling. A claimant can reach a Progressive representative by phone 24 hours a day, and the representative then schedules a time when an adjuster will inspect the vehicle. The adjuster worked nine to five from a mobile claims van, which enabled to examine the vehicle at an average within nine hours, as also prepare an on-site estimate of the damages, and if possible, write a check on the spot, while the rest of the industry took almost seven to ten days for the job. The shortened cycle time dramatically reduced costs for Progressive in terms of:

- The cost of storing a damaged vehicle.
- Renting a replacement car for one day (around $28, roughly equal to the expected underwriting profit on a six-month policy).
- The company could handle more than 10,000 claims a day.
- Improved ability to detect fraud (because it is easier to investigate an accident before the skid marks wash away and witnesses leave the scene).
- Lower operating costs (as claimants often accept less money if it is given sooner than later with more hassle).

To supplement Immediate Response Claims Handling, Progressive allows customers to call an 800 number or visit its website where customers can compare premium rates and other prices with three local competitors. Progressive has also devised more scientific ways of assessing an applicants' risk by factoring in one's credit ratings, driving records, and other relevant variables. This enables accurate pricing which translates into increased underwriting profits. Apparently, customers who are joining Progressive by the droves are beginning to appreciate the company's fair and just policies and procedures.

INNOVATIONS AND MARKET ECOSYSTEMS

When a new innovation or new product's adoption by one segment depends on its adoption by several other segment participants, there has to be a system-wide switching of behaviors before change and market success can take place. The traditional levers that one company uses to launch its products, such as generating a new product and targeting unique customers with attractive promotions, cannot ensure market success. For instance, back in 1888, Kodak's tagline was "You press the button, we do the rest." By manufacturing cameras and film, as well as developing film rolls and making prints, and in 1891 by introducing cameras that users could reload themselves without using a dark room, and still later by developing inexpensive cameras and ensuring the widespread availability of film, Kodak single-handedly market-controlled the entire film camera industry and ensured its great success.

By contrast, many players were involved in the market success of digital photography. While Sony, Kodak, Nikon, and Minolta lead the digital camera market, many supporting networking systems were needed to supply complementary products such as:

- Emulsion film manufacturers like Kodak and Fuji.
- Printers like HP for printing photographs.
- PC manufacturers such as Dell and Apple for organizing digital pictures into albums and store them.
- Software manufacturers like Microsoft for digital imaging, editing, creating, organizing, and storing images online, and Adobe to broaden the reach of these digital technologies.
- Broadband communication companies that enabled transmission of digital images across continents.
- Internet companies, like Shutterfly, offered digital image-processing services that consumers would pay for.
- The manufacturers of cellular handsets, like Motorola and Sony Ericsson, differentiated their products nearing maturity by expanding them to use digital imaging and editing.
- Specialty retailers that sold cameras and accessories.
- Retail stores that sold film and developed prints.

Obviously, each of these supporting systems recognized its own market and profitability opportunities in joining the foray of the digital camera industry. But the very fact that these companies independently decided to support the digital cameras, collectively allowed the market to move swiftly from chemical film photography to its digital future (Chakravorti 2004).

As a contrast, see also the case of high definition television (HDTV). It should have been a great success by now, especially given that top electronics manufacturers such as Sony, Philips, and Thompson had invested billions of dollars in the development of TV sets with astonishingly high picture quality way back in the 1990s. But the technology success was not followed by market success. Critical HDTV complementary components were not ready for the market such as studio production equipment, signal compression technologies, and broadcasting standards were not developed or adopted in time. In 2005, more than a decade later, when the supporting infrastructure was finally market-ready, the pioneering HDTV console manufacturers are facing a new environment of new formats and new rivals. The lesson is: Innovation must be supported by innovation "ecosystems"—the collaborative arrangements through which the firms combine their individual offerings into a coherent market-ready customer-friendly solution (Adner 2006: 98). Similarly, offering Ferrari, an admirable engineering feat, in a world without gasoline or highways does not create value for customers.

Similarly, consider the case of Movielink—a joint venture between MGM, Paramount, Sony, Universal, and Warner Brothers Studios. Movielink offers consumers videos on demand from its large assembled movie library. But a mere Movielink technology is not enough for market success. For Movielink to get off ground, streaming media companies such as RealNetworks, Microsoft, and Apple have to develop technologies to ensure the security of the digital movie files. Other companies must have innovative technologies to compress video into digital files that can be transmitted easily and quickly. Further, cable TV operators, like Time Warner and Comcast, must grant Movielink access to their subscriber homes. Also, manufacturers of set-top boxes (e.g., Philips, Sony) must develop devices that will allow consumers to search, download, and watch movies. Rival companies (e.g., JVC, Panasonic) that are makers of VCR–DVD players and movie rental companies (e.g., Blockbuster) will resist the idea as eroding their market and market share. PC and video game console manufacturers will see Movielink as a threat to their product—because it is symbolic of home entertainment portals. Meanwhile, governments as regulators will be concerned about the anti-trust implications of the Movielink consortium. Internet-based upstarts will cut into the market enabling customers to exchange freely digital movie files, as Napster and others did with music files. Finally, consumers will have to change the ways in which they buy, rent, and watch movies (Chakravorti 2004). In short, for Movielink to succeed it would need an entire ecosystem of complementary technologies, products, markets, and networks to move forward in tandem.

By tapping the most powerful parties in the network, innovators can virtually reach everyone in the network: customers, suppliers of complementary products, local governments, international governments, supporting network communicating, computing, and storing systems, and the like. The consequences of the strategy an innovator chooses will depend upon the initial responses and counter-responses of other players. It is rather impossible for executives to identify their best strategies for bringing an innovation to the market without first anticipating and analyzing all the potential responses of complementary players (Chakravorti 2004: 63).

A network innovation's market success is conditioned on its network market equilibrium. The Nobel Prize winner, John Nash, defined market equilibrium as a situation in which every player in a market believes that he or she is making the best possible choices and that every other player is doing the same. Market equilibrium lends stability to the expectations of the players, validates their choices, and reinforces their behavior. Market disequilibrium, on the other hand, destabilizes expectations and choices of the players and introduces uncertainty and risk in decision-making. In this connection, Chakravorti (2004: 63) prescribes three tests for market equilibrium: (*a*) Is the innovation a "best choice" for consumers? If so, then the behavior of the consumers using the product will be stable; (*b*) Is the innovation a "best choice" for companies that supply complementary or competing products? If so, the behavior of the companies producing the product will be stable; (*c*) Can the innovator trust the behavior of the consumers and companies? If so, he or she can bank on the behavior and choices of consumers and supporting companies.

Adobe's Acrobat Portable Document Format software has emerged as the standard for the electronic creation and sharing of documents in their original form. By 2002, Adobe sold five million Acrobat "creator" programs, and users had downloaded 300 million Acrobat "reader" programs making Acrobat one of the world's most widely used software applications. How did Adobe gain and sustain this market leadership in an otherwise very competitive network market? Chakravorti (2004) has a three-part explanation for this success in relation to market equilibrium.

1. **It was the best choice for consumers**. John Warnock, co-founder of Adobe, created the Acrobat software in 1993 to ease its intra-office problems. Warnock and his team realized that computer users needed and created text, graphics, sound, color, and image-processing programs, but it was not easy to read them electronically. Each document needed a different software application that had to be, in turn, compatible with the user's computer system, before the user could read it. Adobe developed Acrobat software to reproduce the image of any document that any user could read with a related application. Consumers found it easy to download the Acrobat reader. They could now access a variety of documents produced in different formats that they could download frequently.

2. **It was the best choice for companies**. Content distribution channels preferred to offer content in a widely used standard format such as Acrobat. Small software developers created tools and capabilities around Acrobat as the latter was becoming the accepted standard. Large software developers did not feel compelled to develop substitutes for Acrobat; instead, they allowed it to be compatible with their own systems. Supporting a standardized format for electronic documents resulted in a greater overall usage of their word-processing applications and graphics software. Creators of content for mass audiences (e.g., online publishers, universities, and government agencies) found Acrobat useful for its cost-effectiveness and distribution, security, and accuracy. Specialized content creators (e.g., ad agencies, corporations) accepted Acrobat as the standard for electronic communications and would create their documents on multiple platforms.

3. **Adobe could trust its users and supporting companies**. Since Adobe did not charge consumers any money and publishers could not use the software to create content, Acrobat became complementary, not competitive, to the software giants. Adobe soon signed an agreement with Microsoft whereby the latter agreed to bundle Acrobat with its operating systems for the PCs. Adobe allied with AOL to distribute its Acrobat reader to its millions of subscribers, and AOL, in turn, was able to offer enhanced service. Google, the Internet's most popular search engine, agreed to "crawl" Acrobat documents during searches; this provided visibility for Acrobat while it enhanced Google's reputation for conducting comprehensive searches. Adobe offered the reader program for free, which improved the reader user network and the motivation to use it. That convinced content creators to use Acrobat, too. As more content became available in Acrobat format, more readers were motivated to download the program. Adobe soon enjoyed market equilibrium.

Wal-Mart and Microsoft have been great market successes in recent years. Their market dominance has been attributed to various factors such as mission and vision, aggressive marketing practices, and the like. But the success of these two very different companies derives from something larger than themselves: their respective business ecosystems (Iansiti and Levien 2004: 69). Their loose ecosystem networks are made of their suppliers, distributors, outsourcing firms, technology providers, makers of related products and services, and a host of other organizations they affect (and are affected) by their market offerings. Unlike other companies that focus on their internal resources and capabilities, both Wal-Mart and Microsoft have pursued strategies that not only aggressively further their own interests but also that of their business ecosystems. They have done this by creating "platforms" of services, tolls, and technologies that other members of the ecosystem can use to enhance their own performance.

For instance, Wal-Mart's procurement system offers its suppliers invaluable real-time information on customer demand and preferences, which provides the suppliers with significant cost advantages over their competitors. Such information can help the suppliers to match supply with demand across the entire ecosystem, increasing productivity and responsiveness for both Wal-Mart and its suppliers. More than half of Wal-Mart's cost advantage in the retail grocery business results from how the company manages its ecosystem of business partners (Iansiti and Levien 2004: 70). Microsoft's tools and technologies allow software companies to create programs easily for the widespread Windows operating system; these programs, in turn, provide Microsoft with a steady stream of new Windows applications. In both cases, these symbiotic relationships ultimately have benefited consumers—Wal-Mart gets quality goods at lower prices and Microsoft derives a wide array of new competing features. Although Wal-Mart and Microsoft are seemingly rough and tough on their supplier companies in the ecosystem, the complex interdependencies among these companies have made their business networks unusually productive, innovative, and enjoy sustainable competitive advantage. Each of their ecosystems today numbers thousands of firms and millions of people giving all decided advantage over others (Iansiti and Levien 2004).

CONCLUDING REMARKS

In summarizing our discussion, we may assess the creative potential of any proposed product, service, program, or solution by asking the following questions:

a. What is the compelling core vision and identity of this project that will enthuse all people involved?
b. What is the compelling core idea, product, or process that will energize all concerned?
c. Where is the shared vision—did it originate from the top, the bottom, or both? Best visions did not always start from the top.
d. Where are the design, creativity, and innovation in the product, brand, or service?
e. How do they stimulate and sustain high level of collaboration from all concerned stakeholders?
f. What are the assumptions (explicit or hidden) grounding the project? The validity of a project or a model is the validity of the assumptions that ground it.
g. What is the uniqueness of this project? Is it an off-the-rack solution? Off-the-rack solutions are insufficient in an age of perpetual change.
h. What is the core strategy behind this project that really differentiates it from alternatives?
i. Where does this strategic differentiation come from?
j. What is the decided leverage of this project, and where does it occur—the customers or producers, the supply-side or the demand-side?
k. If the Darwinian theory of the survival of the fittest is applied, will this project survive, why, and how long, and to what extent will it boost other company products, and company image?

Table 7.14 characterizes the old and the new world of innovation and opportunity. In today's competitive world, market superiority and position are fleeting at best. No company is immune to competitive technological advances and volatile customer preferences, and the consequent pressures of today's marketplace. Especially, in the digital world of connectivity and speed, technological edges are fleeting things, lasting four to six months, with product life spans or life cycles of less than 18 months. But many forms of innovations beyond those that are "technological" can achieve market dominance. These include:

TABLE 7.14   Creativity and Innovation in a Fast Changing World

Locus of change	The old world	The new world
Barriers to Competition	Ownership of factories	Renting or leasing of office spaces
	Sole access to local capital	Competitive access to globalized capital
	Technology patents	Cross-licensing/leasing technologies
	Regulatory protection	Deregulatory vulnerability
	Distribution chokeholds	Decentralized channels
	Advertising intensity	Local and focused advertising, shared advertising
	Dominant market share	Distributed market share
	Follow the industry leader	Change ahead of the curve
	Mergers, acquisitions, divestitures	Joint ventures, strategic alliances, joint investments
Core Values	Status quo, traditions, conventions	Radical innovation, market breakthroughs
	Rigidity, bureaucracy, verticality	Organizational resilience and agility, decentralization
	Goals and objectives	Vision, shared vision, mission, moving objectives
	Profitability, shareholder value	Growth, expansion, stakeholder value
	ROI, ROE, ROA	EPS, P/E, market valuations, Tobin's Q
Customers	Customer ignorance	Informed and perceptive customers
	Customer apathy	Customer enthusiasm and passion
	Customer product awareness	Customer product design involvement
		Customer supply chain involvement
	Customer product search	Customer materials purchasing involvement
		Customer manufacturing process control involvement
	Customer quality perceptions	Customer quality management involvement
	Customer constrained choices	Customer product packaging involvement
	Customer needs, wants, desires	Customer comparative pricing involvement
	Customer expectations	Customer bundling involvement
		Customer product financing/credit involvement
		Customer product/service feedback involvement
		Customer company control management
		Customer satisfaction management
		Customer loyalty control
		Customer delight management
Employees	Fixed repetitive jobs	Job rotation, enlargement, enrichment
	Piecemeal wage rate	Job benefits, perks, bonuses, pensions, legacy
		Job retraining
		Job learning and unlearning
		Job specialization
	Employee carrots/sticks management	Employee talents trumps obedience
	Jobs as only sources of income	Employee customized motivation
	Jobs outsourcing	Jobs as avenues of self-expression
	Employee firing	Severance packages
	Jobs displacement	Jobs replacement
Production Process	Assembly line	Job co-designing, co-creating, and co-appraisals
	Job routines	Perpetual innovation, competitor collaboration
	Job practices freeze	Best practices are obsolete at birth
	Production-work stability	Stability is fantasy
	Mass production, standardized products	Customized, personalized, individualized production
	Plant shutdowns	Plants redesign
	Plant relocations	Job relocations
	Work boredom	Work innovation
	Production inefficiencies	Production innovation
	Production alienation	Imagination beats knowledge
	Employee discipline	Production ownership
	Commoditizing quality, Six Sigma, TQM	Empathy trounces logic, production camaraderie
	Traditional technologies	Revolutionizing quality
		Green technologies

Source: Author's own.

(*a*) creating new product-delivery methods to meet market requirements; (*b*) creating customized solutions for each customer; (*c*) aggressive customer support and service; and (*d*) market-based cost and pricing that still maintains margins. (The Dell Computer Co. is a prime example of non-technological innovation that led to market dominance.)

What should America do to regain its leadership in world creativity and innovativeness? Innovation should be a non-partisan issue. Creative and innovative America should rise above any political bickering, culture wars, and short-term economic or political agendas. The U.S. is impeding its own progress when it makes scientific discovery (e.g., stem cell research) pass religious tests or when it tightens visa restrictions unnecessarily. Everyone has a stake in keeping the country open to foreign talent. While terrorism is a threat and homeland security is a priority, the arbitrary and sometimes brash methods the U.S. has adopted in screening foreign talent may not be in the long-term interests of the country. Over time, terrorism is less a threat to the U.S. than the possibility that creative and talented people will stop wanting to live within its borders (Florida 2004: 134).

Hurdles to Corporate Innovation

The biggest hurdle to innovation is the corporate longing for certainty about costs, market size, revenues, profits, and other quantities, none of which we can know when an idea is new. Ironically, CEOs are comfortable investing in dying businesses, decaying strategies, and shrinking markets, all of which they can see without a crystal ball. Oil entrepreneurs lacked certainty about which wells would produce black gold and which would fizzle, and yet they invested. Venture capitalists lack certainty about how ideas, markets, and business models would combine to produce profits, and yet they invest. Bravery and fortitude are indispensable virtues in creativity and innovation (Neumeier 2009: 129).

American universities and corporations have long been the educators and innovators of the world. If this engine stalls, it forebodes back for the America as well as for the rest of the world. America has a long history of resourcefulness and creativity to draw on, and it has transformed itself many times before, rebuilding itself many times before, especially after the Great Depression, and bouncing back after the Asian manufacturing boom of the 1970s and 1980s (when Japanese auto companies leaped to global prominence with manufacturing methods that made the worker make continuous improvements in quality and productivity). America should generously invest in R&D, in the same way it built the canals, railroads, and the expressway network to power industrial growth. According to the National Science Foundation (NSF), corporate R&D funding dropped by nearly eight billion in 2002—the largest single-year decline since the 1950s. Many state governments are slashing higher education funding for arts and culture while pumping millions into stadiums, convention centers, and other brick-and-mortar projects. These choices signal a profound failure to maintain an atmosphere of innovation in the U.S. The U.S. must generously invest in its creative infrastructure for the future. Education reform, at its core, must make schools into places that cultivate creativity.

Creativity is not a tangible asset like mineral deposits, something that can be hoarded or fought over, or even bought or sold. America must begin to think of creativity as a "common good," like liberty or security. It is something essential that belongs to everyone and must always be nourished, renewed, and maintained. Else, it will slip away (Florida 2004: 136).

To date, most of the efforts to design and develop new products for global markets focus on product development for the $10,000 gross national product per capita club of about 25 richest countries in the world that account for less than 15 percent of the world's population but who enjoy more than 78 percent of the world's buying power. It is time to focus on the development of new products and services for the neglected part of the world. The poor can be profitable (Prahalad 2004, 2006).

APPENDIX 7.1: MAJOR UNDERLYING PROCESSES RENOVATING THE WORLD OF HUMANITY AND HISTORY, CULTURES AND CIVILIZATIONS

New events	Starting point/input	Processes involved	Skills required	Terminal point/ output	Industry/ culture examples

Creation	Nothing
	Fancy/fantasy
	Idea/ideology
	Dream/vision
		Creativity drive
		Imagination/
		  aesthetics
		Ideation/praxis
		Realization/
		  communication
			Inspiration/genius
			Idiosyncrasy/craft
			Genius/charism
			Prophecy/charism/
			  daring
				Art (unique and
				  inimitable)
				Fabrications/design
				New paradigms/new
				  culture
				Revolution/new wave
					Fine arts/classic literature
					Collectors' items
					Industrial revolution
					M. L. King, Kennedy,
					  Gandhi

Invention	Ideas/concepts
	Basic
	  components
	Hypotheses
	Basic data
		Intuition/induction
		Experimentation
		Testing/
		  verification
		Data analysis/
		  testing
			Conceptualization
			Specialization
			Research skills
			Model building
				New concepts/
				  constructs
				New formulae/science
				New theories/
				  knowledge
				New models/new theses
					Unified energy/gravity
					$E = mc^2$
					New cures
					Freud, Einstein
					OR, MR, JIT, ..., models

Discovery	Problems
	Assumptions
	Presuppositions
	Hunch and luck
		Problem
		  formulation
		Deduction/
		  computation
		Adventure/
		  reasoning
		Serendipity/search
			Lateral thinking
			Logical thinking
			Risk absorption
			Search skills
				New solutions/new
				  cues
				New math/philosophy
				New land/mines
				New extensions
				New uses
					Congestion/overpopulation
					Topology
					Logical positivism
					Off-shore oil
					Alaska
					Getty
					Newton

Innovation	Inventions
	Art pieces
	Technologies
	Basic
	  ingredients
		Commercialization
		Mass duplication
		Transfers/
		  applications
		New combinations
			Engineering, R&D
			Cost efficiency
			Conversion skills
			Mass production
				Products/processes/
				  services
				Reproductions
				Applied technologies
				New formulations
					Radio, TV, X-ray, PCs
					Art markets, art galleries
					Plastics/optics/Laser
					New drugs, drinks

Venture	Investments
	New projects
	Old products
	Old services
		Deposits/shares/
		  stocks
		Implementation/
		  control
		Reformulations
		Differentiation
			Speculation/risk
			Management skills
			Re-merchandizing
			Franchising skills
				Capital gains
				Market value
				Enterprise management
				Product re-launch
				New service chains
					Stock/capital markets
					Mergers, alliances
					Amtrak, Hats, Casinos
					McDonald's, Walt Disney

BUSINESS TRANSFORMATION EXERCISES

7.1 Select at least 10 major inventions by industry. Under each invention, identify the specific invention, year of invention, author(s) of invention, when was it brought to the marketplace, under what brand, by whom, why the delay between invention and commercialization, what is and who is the leading brand currently. Specify reasons for current market leadership. Provide references by each invention item. Follow this example and its matrix form.

Industry	Basic invention/ year	Inventors	Innovation or commercialization/ year	Market pioneers	Reasons for the delay	Current leading brand	Current market leader company	Reasons for current market success
Aircraft	Powered flight/1903	Wright brothers	DC-3/1935	McDonnell Douglas	One of the component technologies missing	Boeing 765	Boeing/ Chicago, U.S.A.	Safety Capacity Comfort Speed Brand name
						Airbus 700	Airbus, Paris, France	Capacity Eco fuel

7.2 Classify the 10 or more inventions from BTE 7.1 into the technology–market newness 3x3 grid. Follow format of Tables 4.4 and 4.5. Explain your entries. Where do you expect this product to "migrate" in 5 years from now, and why?

7.3 Under each invention identified in BTE 7.1 and classified in BTE 7.2, distinguish the elements of design, creativity, and innovation. Identify elements of "form" versus "function" under each. See Figures 7.2A and 7.2B.

7.4 Distinguish between the following innovations by organizational origin, talent management, disruptive nature, global scope, economies of scale, and revolutionary potential:

a. Creativity versus innovation
b. Discovery versus innovation
c. Invention versus innovation
d. Venture versus innovation
e. Process innovation
f. Product innovation
g. Market innovation
h. Marketing innovation
i. Strategic innovation
j. Incremental innovation
k. Radical innovation
l. Disruptive innovation
m. Market breakthrough
n. Technological breakthrough
o. Catalytic innovation
p. Management innovation
q. Operational innovation

7.5 Using the categories of innovation and its related variables listed in BTE 7.4, explain the organizational origin, talent management, disruptive nature, global scope, economies of scale, and revolutionary potential of the following recent innovations:

a. Moon walk
b. Space walk
c. Airborn networks
d. Quantum wires
e. Silicon photonics
f. Metabolomics

g. Star Wars
h. Grameen Bank
i. Ashoka
j. World Eye Glass
k. Life-saving drugs

7.6 Define, distinguish, and explore the following innovations in reforming the schools systems that are reporting very high school dropout rates in the U.S.A.:

a. Sustaining innovation
b. Low-end disruptive innovation
c. New market disruptive innovation
d. Platform innovation
e. Component innovation
f. Design innovation

Chapter 8

The CEO as the Strategic Leader of Corporate-wide Innovation Management

Innovation is a messy process, hard to measure and hard to manage. Most people recognize it only when it generates a surge in corporate growth or when its absence forces corporate decline. Innovation, however, is both a vaccine against market slowdowns and an elixir that stimulates corporate growth. For instance, GM would have been far better off today if the company had matched the pace of innovation set by rivals Toyota and Honda. Apple would have been far worse off today had it not created the iPod, iTunes, and the iPhone. If innovation should succeed in any organization, then it must become a way of business life, not a marginal activity. Innovation should become integral to the structure, function, and fabric of an organization. The creativity that leads to game-changing ideas must continuously feed all the operations of the company (Rigby, Gruver, and Allen 2009).

While for most companies continuous innovation is a strategic imperative, the task of managing innovations seems to be narrowly defined. Most companies treat innovations as discrete objects or projects, whether they relate to a new or revamped process, new or retrofitted brand or service, or to a commercial innovation such as a new sales channel. Corporate executives fail to see innovations systemically as a part of the company's innovativeness—the capacity to ideate, conceive, develop, test, roll out, and improve new market offerings as a whole. Most executives look at just a part of the innovation process. Companies like Xerox, Intel, Gillette, and Sony fell behind for a while because of their systemic deficiency of viewing innovations as a vital process of the entire company at all times, where the whole is greater than the sum of its parts.

MANAGING CORPORATE INNOVATION

There is much literature on how to best manage innovation—empower employees, encourage initiatives, cultivate risk taking, overcome mindless status quo, and the like. However, managers need much more than such generic advice because there are many kinds of innovation (e.g., technological breakthrough, continuous process improvement, process revolutions, product/service innovation, disruptive innovation, radical innovation, market breakthrough, and strategic innovation), and each requires a profoundly different managerial approach (Govindarajan and Trimble 2005: xxi). Managing each type of innovation has to be itself innovative and creative (Florida 2004; Kanter 2003; Kaplan and Norton 2004, 2006).

When it comes to innovation, few modern corporate executives are more closely associated with revolutionary change than Steve Jobs, the iconic leader of Apple. During his tenure at Apple, the company's product introductions have altered not only how we talk but also how we live: the Mac, the iPod, iTunes, and the iPhone 3G. Now that Steve is ailing from but fighting pancreatic cancer, the Apple board has been seriously searching for a worthy successor. Innovation is critical for long-term success of Apple. Boardroom discussions on choosing a successor to Steve often center on two questions: How can we sustain innovation? Do we have a plan for developing future leaders who can facilitate this goal? Truly innovative executives are very rare. Perhaps five or ten percent of the high-potential managers within a company at any given time have the skills and attributes to become breakthrough innovators. Companies usually develop leaders who can replicate rather than innovate; that is, rising stars realize that to be promoted, they need to mirror incumbent leaders (Chon, Katzenbach, and Vlak 2008: 63–64).

Hamel and Getz (2004: 78) asked more than 500 senior and mid-level managers in large U.S. companies to identify the biggest barriers to innovation in their respective organizations. The number one response was "short-term focus" followed by "lack of time and resources." The first response indicates senior management's presumed obsession with near-term earnings, and the second response suggests that innovation is highly dependent on investment. Both factors limit a company's productivity and growth.

CENTRALIZATION AND DECENTRALIZATION FOR EFFECTIVE INNOVATION

Executives at conventional companies tend to hamper innovation by failing to distinguish between innovation units and capability platforms. Decentralized "innovation units" are profit centers (similar to strategic business units or SBUs), defined by product lines, brands, customer segments, geographic regions, and other boundaries. Their primary purpose is to choose which customers to serve, with what products, brands, and services to serve them, which competitors to challenge, and which capabilities to draw upon. The unit leaders must balance creative aspirations with commercial realities. What these units have in common is that the innovation buck stops here.

Centralized "capability platforms," on the other hand, are cost centers. They build competencies that innovation units can share. As shared platforms they create economies of scale, make investments that individual units cannot afford, and take risks that the smaller innovation units could not absorb. Both capability platforms and innovation units, however, must also be sources of sustainable competitive advantage. The innovation units own their final results, and hence, they must design, buy, and own as many capability-sourcing divisions as possible from the capability platforms.

At the Gucci Group with 10 business units, Robert Polet, who left Unilever to become the CEO of Gucci in 2004, believes in "freedom within the framework" in working together. The CEO and the creative director of each of the 10 business units' work together to construct a sentence that captures the essence of the brand. Then each brand's executive officer establishes the framework within which creative decisions will be made. Each brand's CEO maps out a three year plan showing the brand's strategic direction and projected financial performance. Brand and product development occurs within this context.

The ultimate judge of an innovation is the marketplace, not a higher ranking individual or committee within an organization. The innovation-brand should be the success, and not the star celebrity behind the brand. Centralization or decentralization, centralized capability platforms or decentralized innovation units in the final analysis—what really counts is the combining of creative art with the science of creative commerce, blending right brain creative directors with left-brain business analyzers, hiring, retaining, and developing competencies (cum personality traits) that foster team work, and protecting the creative team and safeguarding the artistic process. Creative people are comfortable with and thrive with ambiguity, fuzzy products, imaginative brands, where they accept the fact that they do not have control over the final product. They function well in an environment without detailed job descriptions, and work with people who have different styles of thinking and communicating, including their own.

HUMAN BRAIN HEMISPHERES AND INNOVATION

[See Rigby, Gruver, and Allen (2009: 79–86)]

Roger Sperry earned the Nobel Laureate for Medicine in 1981 for his work with epileptic patients whose *corpora callosa* (the bundles of nerves connecting their left and right brain hemispheres) had been severed. When the two hemispheres could not network with each other, their differences became more obvious. Since then, more work on the human brain has developed interesting propositions such as:

- For most people, the left-brain hemisphere is the seat of intelligence—it is better at processing language, logic, numbers, sequential ordering, and linear functions; it does well in math, reading and comprehension, scheduling and organizing.
- The right brain, on the other hand, specializes in non-verbal ideation, imagination, intuition, induction, and holistic synthesizing; it is more adept at handling images, graphics, music, colors, and patterns.
- In general, right-brain processing happens quickly, recursively, and in non-sequential patterns, while the left-brain processing is slow, deep, linear, analytical, analogical, and deductive.
- Almost nothing that we sense, feel, or understand is ever processed solely by one hemisphere; both contribute to nearly everything.
- However, they do so in different ways, and hence, our cognitive, volitive, and moral preferences exhibit significant differences.
- The right–left brain phenomenon may not explain some functions as writing and driving abilities; hence, some people are ambidextrous, and routinely switch between right-hand and left-hand functionalities.
- Despite these differences, however, we tend to use the best of what we have, from the right and the left brain, says Robert Omstein, director of the Institute for the Study of Human Knowledge, Stanford University. Much would depend upon how we use these two hemispheres.
- Most of us have strongly preferred approaches for drawing on our brains to solve simple and complex problems. Nevertheless, few people are extraordinarily skilled at drawing on all the regions of the brain.

If these propositions hold true, then a corporation is best run with a good combination of right- and left-brainer executives. For instance, the right–left brain partnership has been vital in the rapidly changing world of the fashion apparel industry. Every successful fashion company essentially reinvents its product lines and brands every season, thus cannibalizing on the previous year's brands and fashions. A fashion company that fails to innovate at this rapid pace faces certain death. Typically, in every fashion company, one partner, usually called the creative director, is the creative, imaginative, and intuitive right-brain individual who every day spins out new ideas and images to channel the wants and desires of its target customers. The other partner, the brand director, manager, or CEO, is invariably a left-brain, calculating, hard-nosed analytic, who works on the innovation margins and viability. Both talents combined, they successfully transit from ideas to invention to innovation to commercialization to market success. Table 8.1 summarizes distinguishing characteristics of the Left-Brain Business Director versus the Right-Brain Creative Innovation Director.

TABLE 8.1   The Left-brain Business Director versus the Right-brain Creative Director

Comparative dimensions	Left-brain business director	Right-brain creative innovation director
Personality Traits	Rational, logical, linear Literal, objective	Imaginative, intuitive, non-linear Whimsical, subjective
Input Traits	Language, grammar, verbal	Visualization, gestures, symbols, pictures Perceptual, metaphorical
Methodology	Quantitative, empirical Inductive, deductive reasoning	Qualitative Phenomenological Intuitive, experiential, analogical, and design thinking
Process Traits	Sequential analytical processing Long product life cycles Time-sensitive Objective metrics	Holistic framing Pattern synthesis Short product life cycles Time-free, leisured Customer metrics of ecstasy and delight
Innovation Culture	New product, brand, service oriented	New emotional brand experience Build passion for brands
Work Culture	Creative commercial partnership Factory assembly Control, prediction, and explanation as game-changer for the company Objective involvement in problem-solving	Strong design culture Innovation design studio Design as a game-changer for the company Immersion in creative problem-solving
Research Orientation	Market scanning before innovation	Customer research may be irrelevant for luxury goods
Competitor Focus	Block market entrants	Learn from successful competitors
Output Traits	Accuracy, speed, control Multiple rounds of improvements	Ambiguity, paradox "Eureka" moments of experimentation
Business Orientation	Cost-containment, revenue generation	Design perfection, delight generation
Business Performance	Maximizing sales revenues Maximizing market share Maximizing profitability	Total customer experience maximization Total customer loyalty development Customer perceived value maximization
Long-term Goals	Market leader Market success Profitable growth	Top design company in the market Innovation leader in the industry Increase creativity
Ethical Imperatives	Be legal, compliant, ecological	Be moral, ethical, trusting, caring, sharing, outreaching
Corporate Social Responsibility	Cause related giving as tax write-offs Local community development if profitable for the company	Life-enhancing, culture-refining, and art-developing contributions and market offerings

Source: Author's own.

Note: See also Rigby, Gruver, and Allen (2009).

The world's most innovative companies, argue Rigby, Gruver, and Allen (2009), operate with some form of right–left brain partnership. For instance:

- At Hewlett-Packard, the creative partner was the brilliant engineer Bill Hewlett while the business manager was the perceptive executive David Packard.
- At Microsoft, Paul Allen was the left-brain software engineer, while Bill Gates was the right-brain business and marketing wizard.
- At Apple, the CEO Steve Jobs, despite his current failing health, has held the brilliant creative designer torch, while his COO, Tim Cook has long handled the day-to-day business operations of the firm.
- At Proctor & Gamble (P&G), since June 2000 when A. G. Lafley became CEO, he was the left-brain director that managed innovation at the corporate level, while imaginative right-brain Claudia Kotchka directed the design thinking.
- At Chrysler of the early 1970s, Lee Iacocca was the business and marketing brain while the "car guy" Hal Sperlich (the creator of Ford Mustang) pioneered the Chrysler minivan.
- At Nike, a former track coach, Bill Bowerman developed Nike's running shoes, while his partner, Phil Knight, excelled in the financing, manufacturing, and the sales functions.
- At Starbucks, the right-brainer Howard Schultz conceived the iconic coffeehouse product format and its innovative support products, while CEO Orin Smith did the business management expanding Starbucks to over 16,000 retail and franchise outlets as of December 2008.
- At Calvin Klein, until 2003, Calvin Klein's alter ego was Barry Schwartz—the pair grew up together in the same New York City neighborhood and had been partners since the beginning of the Calvin Klein label.
- At Louis Vuitton and Marc Jacobs International, Marc Jacobs was the creative director, and his longtime partner, Robert Duffy, handled the business end.
- At Pixar, the right-brain creative director was Brad Bird while the left-brain rational, logical, and linear business mind was John Walker.

Most of these well-known teams worked together for years. The partners had agreements and disagreements, ups and downs, but they pulled together with a common purpose and a common framework. Marc Jacobs often infuriated Robert Duffy but they calmed down within a few days. At Pixar, John Walker and Brad Bird were known for their open fights. Some of the tension between partners is productive, while some of it is destructive, dooming the relationship. If a marriage between two corporate talents does not work, it must be terminated quickly, and one must be ready to order a divorce when required. For instance, at Apple, the legendary creative director Steve Jobs could not pull it together with John Sculley; the latter was replaced by Tim Cook. Often, when one of the duos moved on, partnership crumbled, and had to be reinstated with much difficulty.

A true both-brain individual (e.g., Leonardo da Vinci, the architect of St. Peter's Basilica in Rome and the Sistine Chapel) who is equally brilliant in artistic and analytic pursuits is exceedingly rare. Creative innovation and market success need teamwork. A creative duo that synergizes right-brain creative skills and left-brain management skills offers the best combination of ingraining innovation in business, making it a total customer experience delight. This right-brain duo synergy derives from a high level of the following characteristics (Rigby, Gruver, and Allen 2009: 81):

- **Awareness of Mutual Strengths and Weaknesses**: that includes a humorous acceptance of such differences, and a realistic assessment of what one can do well, where, how, and when.
- **Complementary Cognitive Skills**: Partners should seek those skills that balance their own working styles and decision-making approaches. They should learn to draw on each other's capabilities to the proper degree and at the right time.
- **Partners Trust Each Other**: They must believe in each one's competencies, accept mutual vulnerability, and should put one's own interests behind the corporate common good.
- **Raw Intelligence**: Partners should bring insightful observations and good judgment to the team's decisions.
- **Relevant Knowledge**: Partners pool experiences that apply directly to the challenge they face.
- **Strong Communication Channels**: Partners live and work in adjacent spaces, and speak to each other directly and frequently.
- **Motivation**: Partners are highly committed to the success of the business and each other.

WHY DO SOME FIRMS ENGAGE IN ONGOING TRANSFORMATION

The radical–incremental typology of innovation while useful does not fully explain why some firms go for radical and why others prefer incremental innovation as an intrapreneurial management policy. That is, this typology does not directly predict which firms will invest in radical and which in incremental innovations. For instance, why did the following happen?

- Intel and Mostek lost their leadership positions in DRAM memory chips during the transition from the 64K to the 256K chip—incremental innovations from an organizational perspective, despite being strong incumbents and investing heavily in the 256K DRAM. Currently, Intel is even eroding its semiconductor-microprocessor chip technology number one position relative to AMD, NEC, and others.
- Gillette led the men's and women's razor shaving technology and associated products for over 100 years until about 2003, when it slowed down its innovations, and was eventually bought by P&G in 2005.
- On the other hand, GE, an incumbent in the diagnostic medical industry, maintained its leadership and was successful in the transitions from X-rays to computerized axial tomography (CAT) scans to magnetic resonance imaging (MRI), both relatively radical innovations.
- Similarly, IBM maintained its dominant position in the computer industry during the radical transitions from vacuum tubes to transistors to integrated circuits in mainframe computers, and currently, to integrated IT business solutions—all radical innovations or innovativeness.

Several explanatory models for the foregoing situations have been proposed. We review some of them in the following paras.

Abernathy–Clark (1985) Model: There are two kinds of knowledge that underpin any innovation: technology and markets. A brand new innovation from a rival or from within may render a firm's technological capabilities obsolete while its marketing skills may remain intact, or vice versa. On the other hand, it may preserve both capabilities, or destroy both. Hence, focusing on the innovating firm, the model classifies innovations according to their preserving versus destroying impact on the manufacturer's existing technological and market capabilities as in Table 8.2A.

Thus, if a new innovation is "regular," that is, it preserves one's both technological and market capabilities, the firm may readily absorb it. If the innovation is "architectural" that destroys technological and market capabilities, the firm may be slow to adopt it. If the innovation is a "niche" that destroys market capabilities but preserves technological ones, then the firm may absorb the innovation and accordingly adopt correspondingly new market capabilities. (For another more constructive concept of "architectural innovation," see a later section.) Lastly, if the innovation is "revolutionary" that destroys ones technological but preserves marketing capabilities, then it may adopt the new innovation, assuming it is important for its market growth.

Thus, IBM readily adopted radical innovations while transiting from vacuum tube to transistor to integrated circuits in its mainframe computers, because neither of these innovations destroyed its market (distribution channel) capabilities. That is, these were "revolutionary" innovations. Similarly, GE speedily adopted radical innovations while transiting from X-rays to CAT scans to MRI, and currently to FMRI (functional MRI), relatively radical but revolutionary innovations, because neither of these innovations destroyed its distribution capabilities. On the other hand, Intel and Mostek were either afraid of cannibalism or of the total destruction of their market capabilities in transiting from 64K to 256K DRAM architecture, and hence were slow in adopting them, and lost their leadership to NEC and AMD.

Henderson–Clark Model (1990): The Abernathy-Clark model may explain innovation or innovation-adoption when (*a*) innovations are radical, and (*b*) when a firm focuses either on technological or marketing capabilities. However, it fails to explain adequately when innovations are incremental and when technological and marketing capabilities are equally important for a given firm. Henderson and Clark (1990) were still puzzled why some incumbents had so much difficulty in dealing with what appeared to be incremental innovations or minute changes in existing technologies, as in the Intel and Mostek cases. Similarly, Xerox stumbled for many years before finally developing a good small plain-paper copier, despite being a pioneer of the core technology of xerography. Seemingly, RCA was never able to lead the market for portable transistor radios despite its experience in the components of the portable radio (transistors, audio amplifiers, and loudspeakers).

Hence, Henderson and Clark (1990) suggested that since products are normally made up of components assembled together, building them must require two kinds of knowledge: knowledge of the components, and the knowledge of the linkages between them, which they called *architectural* knowledge. An innovation can impact (enhance or destroy) either component knowledge, or both, or neither. Thus, they came up with the grid as in Table 8.2B.

TABLE 8.2A The Abernathy–Clark Model of Innovation Adoption

	Technological capabilities	
Market capabilities	*Preserved*	*Destroyed*
Preserved	Regular Innovation	Revolutionary Innovation
Destroyed	Market Niche Innovation	Architectural Innovation

Source: Author's own.

TABLE 8.2B   The Henderson–Clark Model of Innovation

	Architectural knowledge	
Component knowledge	*Enhanced*	*Destroyed*
Enhanced	Incremental Innovation	Architectural Innovation
Destroyed	Modular Innovation	Radical Innovation

Source: Author's own.

Architectural knowledge is often tacit and embedded in the routines and procedures of an organization, making changes difficult to discern and respond to. Thus, Intel and Mostek had sound component knowledge but their lack of architectural knowledge might have slowed their transition from 64K to 256K architecture. Similarly, RCA possessed excellent component knowledge of transistors, audio amplifiers, and loudspeakers that went into a portable radio, but lacked architectural knowledge of linkages between them; hence they lead the market only for portable transistor radios. Similar would be the explanation in the case of Xerox in relation to the small plain-paper copier.

THE AFUAH–BAHRAM (1995) VALUE-ADDED CHAIN MODEL OF INNOVATION

The previous two models focused on the impact of innovation only on the firm's capabilities. One must also consider the impact of any innovation on other groups of the value chain such as competitors, suppliers, customers, and complementary innovators. That is, as discussed in the previous chapter, you must always match your innovation strategy to your innovation ecosystem (Adner 2006). Consider, for instance, Ford's electric car—it had a radical impact on the manufacturer (both technical and market knowledge), on the suppliers (from fuel injection system parts to electric car parts), on the complementary innovators (e.g., oil companies, gas station owners), but possibly just incremental impact on customers (from gas stations to home garage or workplace-based electric chargers) (see Table 8.3).

Similarly, Cray Computer's decision in 1988 to develop and market a supercomputer that would use gallium arsenide (GaAs) chips—a technology that yields 3.5 times faster chips and consumes half as much power as their silicon counterparts—that would have radical impact on suppliers, (but just incremental change to manufacturers, customers, and complementary customers) but has not succeeded yet owing to other problems.

In addition, the Dvorak simplified keyboard (DSK) arrangement, which by many estimates would perform 20 to 40 percent better than the traditional QWERTY keyboard, would radically affect users and customers, but would have an incremental effect on manufacturers, suppliers, and complementary innovators. Similarly, an electric car as an innovation would affect the customers less but have a more significant impact on the suppliers, the manufacturers, and the complementary innovators. Thus the incumbents (originators) or new entrants to an innovation will adopt an innovation depending upon:

- its (radical versus incremental) impact on all-important members of the value-added chain or innovation ecosystem: suppliers, manufacturers, customers, and complementary innovators; and
- the critical importance of the members of each value chain.

TABLE 8.3   The Afuah–Bahram Value-added Chain Hypercube of Innovation

Supply chain	Linkages between concepts and components	Core concepts	
		Reinforced	Overturned
Supplier	Changed	Incremental Innovation	Modular Innovation
Innovator	Unchanged	Architectural Innovation	Radical Innovation
	Changed	Incremental Innovation	Modular Innovation
Customer	Unchanged	Architectural Innovation	Radical Innovation
	Changed	Incremental Innovation	Modular Innovation
Complementary	Unchanged	Architectural Innovation	Radical Innovation
Innovator	Changed	Incremental Innovation	Modular Innovation
	Unchanged	Architectural Innovation	Radical Innovation

Source: Author's own.

For instance, the Internet and WWW significantly impact all members of the value-adding chain: suppliers, manufacturers, customers, and complementary innovators, and the impact is important to all these members (Afuah and Bharan 1995). Hence, this innovation is here to stay.

GATIGNON AND XUEREB'S (1997) MODEL OF DETERMINANTS OF RADICAL PRODUCT INNOVATION

Gatignon and Xuereb (1997) basically studied the organizational determinants of new product introductions and success. In this context, they explore the role of a firm's strategic orientation in new product success.

A firm's strategic orientation (SO) "reflects the strategic directions implemented by a firm to create the proper behaviors for the continuous superior performance of the business" (Gatignon and Xuereb 1997: 78; Narver and Slater 1990). Three major strategic orientations of the firm can be identified:

1. **Customer Orientation**: It is the firm's sufficient understanding of its target markets and buyers in order to create superior value for them (Narver and Slater 1990). It is the "set of beliefs that puts the customer interest first" (Deshpande, Farley, and Webster 1993). A customer-oriented firm has the ability and willingness to continuously identify, analyze, understand, and respond to customer and user-needs.
2. **Competitor Orientation**: It is the ability and willingness to identify, analyze, and respond to the competitor's actions (Narver and Slater 1990). Most successful innovative firms select certain types of new products as a function of market competitive characteristics (Cooper 1984). Hence, a competitor orientation is needed for the commercial performance of innovations.
3. **Technological Orientation**: Firms with strong technological orientation (TO) have strong R&D orientation; they are proactive in acquiring new technologies, and use sophisticated technologies in the development of new products (Cooper 1984, 1994). A technology-oriented firm can be defined as "a firm with the ability and will to acquire a substantial technological background and use it in the development of new products" (Gatignon and Xuereb 1997: 78). Such a firm uses its technical knowledge to build new technical solutions to answer and meet new user-needs.

Inter-functional coordination (IO) is needed to integrate these three strategic (customer, competitor, and technological) orientations; IO refers to specific aspects of the structure of an organization that facilitate communication between its functional units, and integrate resources to create superior value to customers. However, the role of the firm's strategic orientation and inter-functional coordination is contingent upon the market environment that is basically characterized as market growth, competitive intensity, and demand uncertainty.

Figure 8.1 connects all these constructs to hypothesize how a firm's strategic (customer, competitor, and technological) orientations with inter-functional coordination, contingent on market environment, can generate innovation characteristics (product radicalness/similarity, product advantage, and reduction of product costs).

The authors statistically derived and tested the following conclusions (Gatignon and Xuereb 1997: 85–86):

1. Innovative performances are directly related to innovation characteristics.
2. The greater the product radicalness ($\beta = 0.21, p < 0.01$), the smaller the product similarity with its competitors ($\beta = -0.12, p < 0.05$), the greater the product advantage ($\beta = 0.32, p < 0.01$), lower the product costs ($\beta = -0.28, p < 0.01$), and better the perceived innovation performance.
3. The greater the technological orientation, the greater the radicalness of the innovation being brought to the market ($\beta = 0.61, p < 0.01$), and lesser is the similarity of the innovation with that

FIGURE 8.1   The Role of a Firm's Strategic Orientation on Innovation Performance

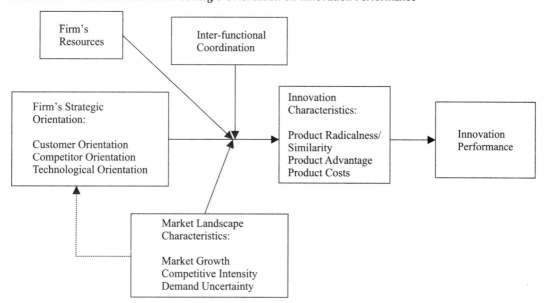

Source: Adapted from Gatignon and Xuereb (1997: 79).

Note: Bold lines indicate direct links to innovation characteristics and innovation performance. The dotted lines indicate that a firm's strategic orientation will affect innovation characteristics and innovation performance contingent upon market characteristics.

of its competitors ($\beta = -0.33$, $p < 0.01$), and greater the product advantage from the innovation ($\beta = 0.20$, $p < 0.01$).

4. The strategic orientation of the firm affected innovation only under market demand uncertainty conditions.

5. That is, in highly uncertain markets, the greater the customer orientation, the greater the performance of the innovation. (This assumes that in an uncertain market, customer orientation will generate critical information on market demand, and hence reduce uncertainty. Conversely, customer orientation may not positively affect innovation performance in markets that have low demand uncertainty.)

6. In highly uncertain markets, the greater the technological orientation, the greater is the performance of the innovation. (This assumes that in an uncertain market, technological orientation can generate critical information on innovation characteristics, which, in turn, can sharpen innovation performance. Conversely, technological orientation may not positively affect innovation performance in markets that have low demand uncertainty.)

7. In markets with low demand uncertainty, the greater the competitive orientation, the greater is the performance of the innovation. If demand uncertainty is high, higher levels of competitive orientation may hinder innovation performance. (This assumes that in an uncertain market, competitive orientation can generate critical information on market demand, and hence reduce uncertainty. Conversely, competitive orientation may not positively affect innovation performance in markets that have low demand uncertainty.)

8. Hence, under market uncertainty, a firm wanting to develop an innovation superior to the competition must have a strong technological orientation and a strong customer orientation.

9. A competitive orientation is recommended in high-growth markets but not under high market uncertainty.

Radical product innovation is linked intrinsically with a firm's product-market strategy and can set the tone for the rest of the marketing program (Gatignon and Xuereb 1997).

CHANDY AND TELLIS' (1998) MODEL OF DETERMINANTS OF RADICAL INNOVATIONS

Radical innovation is "the propensity of a firm to introduce new products that: (*a*) incorporate substantially different technology from existing products and (*b*) can fulfill key customer needs better than existing products" (Chandy and Tellis 1998: 475). Radical product innovation, thus, is essentially a function of two common dimensions: technology and markets. The first factor relates to what extent the technology involved in a new product is different from prior technologies. The second factor determines the extent to which the new product, on a per customer dollar basis, fulfills key customer needs better than existing products. If we consider two levels, high and low, for both these common dimensions, we can characterize four types of product innovations as sketched in Table 8.4. The four types of innovations in Table 8.4 are related by a series of S-curves of customer benefits as portrayed in Figure 8.2.

Benefits per customer dollar continue at first to increase increasingly or rapidly with an existing technology (T_1). However, they soon start to increase decreasingly or slowly as the technology matures—this

TABLE 8.4 Types of Product Innovations

	Customer need fulfillment per dollar on the product	
Newness of technology	Low	High
Low	**Incremental Innovation:** Involves relatively minor changes in technology and customer value: for example, railroad, bus transportation, basic air conditioners, refrigerators, washing and drying machines, iron boards, sewing machines, and barber's equipment	**Market Breakthrough:** The same core technology level now provides substantially higher customer benefits per dollar: for example, cable TV with signal compression systems that allow larger number of channels and programs
High	**Technological Breakthrough:** Substantially newer technology for the same customer benefits: for example, electronic imaging versus celluloid film in cameras, yet with no better resolution effects MRI versus ultrasound systems	**Radical Innovation:** New technology with new added benefits: for example, microwave ovens over regular ovens; PCs over mainframes; VCR over movies; cellular phones over regular phones; ethernet over modems, the Internet over previous communication channels; e-mail over EDI, Internet marketing over traditional sales media

Source: Author's own.

FIGURE 8.2 Dynamic View of Product Innovations

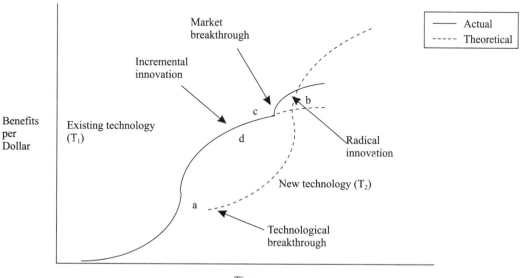

Source: Chandy and Tellis (1998: 47).

is incremental innovation S-curve.[1] If at some time thereafter in the history of that technology, a brand new technology (T_2) emerges, its product may be considered as a technological breakthrough. However, its commercial benefits may not be perceived immediately (or may be perceived as inferior to that of T_1). However, with research and advertisement, T_2 begins to improve rapidly in consumer benefits until it surpasses those of T_1, when it becomes a "radical product innovation." Faced with the threat of T_2, product champions of T_1 may make fresh efforts to improve the benefits of T_1, and this may become a "market breakthrough."

Determinants of radical innovation:

- Medium-sized firms (as opposed to very large or very small firms) are positioned best for radical product innovation because, unlike small firms, they have the critical mass and funds for research and do not suffer from the heavy bureaucracy of larger firms. However, larger firms have more capital or better access to financial resources, realize better economies of scale, and can spread risk widely. However, the fact is that most innovations in the U.S. come from medium- and small-size firms (Ettlie and Rubinstein 1987; Mitchell and Singh 1993, 1995; for a converse view, see Pavitt 1998).
- Other things being equal, size may not be a significant variable for radical product innovation (Chandy and Tellis 1998). Mere size is "neither necessary nor sufficient condition" for innovative performance (Schumpeter 1942: 101). The size effect on innovation may be weak. The Bell Telephone Company introduced the first telephone when it was small; the Buffalo Forge Company, a medium-sized firm, produced the first air conditioner; Raytheon, a large firm, introduced the first microwave oven.

WILLINGNESS TO CANNIBALIZE AND RADICALIZE PRODUCT INNOVATION

Traditionally cannibalization is related to sales—a loss in sales of a firm's current product due to its sales of its new product. Cannibalism is often dreaded as an after-effect of new product development within the same firm.

Cannibalization can be extended to include specialized or asset-specific investments such as tangible resources (e.g., specific manufacturing and processing equipment, specialized core products) and intangible assets (e.g., specialized organizational routines, specific knowledge, expertise or core competencies, and unique access to distribution channels). A new resource or technology can obsolesce both tangible and intangible assets.

---

[1] Technological life cycle models suggest that a technology usually evolves in a relatively predictable manner (Utterback 1994). One of these models is the S-curve. For instance, Foster (1986) argued that the rate of technological progress is a function of human effort. Given human effort, technological progress starts off slowly in the beginning, then increases very rapidly, and then diminishes as the physical limits of the technology are approached. For instance, supercomputers started as slow-speed single-processor architectures; then their speed of computing increased rapidly until their ability to compute started approaching a physical limit—the speed of light. The multiprocessor architectures emerged then and gave rise to a new S-curve, which also soon used their physical limits—the then communications bottlenecks. [For examples of other S-curves, see Afuah (1998: 121–25).]

When a new technology T_2 emerges but is in its embryonic stage, an incumbent firm with technology T_1 has two basic options: either choose to advance T_1 (possibly hoping for a market breakthrough) or switch to T_2, make fresh investments in it, and hence, potentially render current investments in T_1 obsolete. See Figure 8.2. The latter option cannibalizes on both investments in T_1 and sales in products related to T_1. However, the "willingness to cannibalize" may produce great returns in the form of radical product innovation.

Radical innovations do not always result in cannibalization or obsolescence of related products. For example, microwave ovens did not render conventional ovens useless (Chandy and Tellis 1998: 477).

Radical innovation is a "behavioral variable", while willingness to cannibalize is an "attitudinal trait" of the key decision makers in a firm whereby a firm is prepared to reduce the actual or potential value of its current investments in order to foster radical product innovation (Chandy and Tellis 1998: 475).

Firms that exhibit high willingness to cannibalize are more likely to be radical product innovators than other firms. Willingness to cannibalize implies readiness to change, to retrain, to sacrifice expertise on older products and assets, and accept risk of new technology and products.

Several factors may dampen willingness to cannibalize:

- **Cognitive Dissonance**: Strong perceived dissonance between the old and the new technologies, between the old and the new products.
- **Self-justification**: Excessive rationalization to maintain status quo or ego-based products.
- **External Justification**: Trying to "save face" in front of others.
- **Sunk Cost Fallacy**: Sunk costs must be realized before new investments are made.

Similarly, several factors may stimulate willingness to cannibalize:

- **Internal Markets**: Markets with high "internal autonomy" (high authority among strategic business unit [SBU] managers relative to corporate office) and "internal competition" (rivalry among SBUs of a firm). A combination of both spurs willingness to cannibalize.
- **Product Champion Influence**: This refers to the extent to which employees who advocate new product ideas affect the activities of the organization (Chandy and Tellis 1998: 478). Influential product champions with technical competence and high credibility can aggressively push new ideas to the top management with much political savviness and astuteness (Moorman 1995).
- **Focus on Future Markets**: This measures the extent to which a firm emphasizes future markets, customers, and competitors relative to the present ones. Current market orientation may inhibit organizations from developing truly breakthrough innovations (Kohli and Jaworski 1990: 13). Gatignon and Xuereb (1997) found that a strong current orientation led to less radical innovation among firms. Christensen (1997a) notes that dominant firms in the rigid disk-drive, copier, tire, minicomputer, and mainframe computer markets stayed too close to their customers and consequently lost their market position to the new generation of products. A future market focus broadens the horizons of managers and alerts them to new technologies, competitors, and customers (Moorman 1995).

Thus, in general:

- H_1: Firms that exhibit high willingness to cannibalize are more likely to be radical product innovators than others firms.

- H_2: The more specialized investments a firm has in current technology and its products, the lower will be its willingness to cannibalize those investments and products.
- H_3: Firms with active internal markets exhibit greater willingness to cannibalize than do other firms.
- H_4: The greater the influence of product champions in a firm, the greater is its willingness to cannibalize.
- H_5: The greater the future market focus of the firm, the higher is its willingness to cannibalize.

All five hypotheses were verified ($p < 0.01$) in an empirical study using key product managers in a large number of high-tech firms (Chandy and Tell is 1998).

INCUMBENT ROLE IN ADOPTING RADICAL INNOVATIONS

[See Chandy and Tellis (2000)]

Recently, Chandy and Tellis (2000), after extensive research in the consumer durables and office product categories, argued that incumbents or large firms have had significant role in radical innovations. They concluded:

- Over a 150-year period, small firms and non-incumbents have introduced slightly more radical innovations than large firms and incumbents.
- Small firms and outsiders account for many more innovations in the U.S.A. than they do in other countries such as Western Europe or Japan.
- However, after World War II, large firms and incumbents have successfully introduced a majority of radical product innovations.
- The U.S. accounts for almost two-thirds of radical product innovations in the consumer durables and office product categories, and Western Europe accounts for the most of the remaining.
- Japan has provided a few radical innovations, but mostly in very recent years (e.g., Seiko's analog quartz watch in 1969, Konishiroku's autofocus color celluloid roll camera in 1977, Sony's Camcorder and digital camera in 1983, mini-disk player in 1992, and Toshiba's digital video disk [DVD] player in 1997).

In this context, in further explaining new product successes or failures, one could examine the "organizational variables" of the innovators of the new products, such as size, history, reputation, country, duration of incumbency, and "product variables" such as consumer versus industrial products, and perishable versus durable products.

TECHNOLOGICAL OPPORTUNISM AND THE ADOPTION OF RADICAL INNOVATIONS

Why do firms proactively adopt radical technologies whereas others do not? Srinivasan, Lilien, and Rangaswamy (2002) respond to this question with a new construct—technological opportunism.

Opportunism in its positive form (as opposed to opportunistic behavior) implies that managers are proactive in responding to new opportunities in a way that does not violate principles of fairness (Hutt, Reingen, and Ronchetto 1988; Isenberg 1987).

Technology opportunism implies two components:

1. **Technology-sensing Capability**: is a firm's ability to acquire knowledge about and understand new technological developments. Such sensing can take place either "internally" (e.g., R&D, product innovations) or "externally" (e.g., universities, other industries, tech-markets, tech-tradeshows, tech-vendors, hightech conferences).
2. **Technology-response Capability**: is a firm's willingness and ability to respond to new technologies it senses. The firm is constantly in an "enactment mode" (Daft and Weick 1984) with respect to new technologies, exploring them as potential opportunities or threats. An organization may sense new technologies but not respond to it lest it should cannibalize its own products (Chandy and Tellis 1998). Others may forge ahead, be willing to cannibalize, and reengineer their business strategies to exploit the new technologies or at least stave off the threats posed by them.

After several field interviews with 18 senior managers of 15 organizations, Srinivasan, Lilien, and Rangaswamy (2002) operationalized technological opportunism (TO) ($\alpha = 0.89$) thus:

Technology-sensing capability: ($\alpha = 0.77$)

1. We are often one of the first in our industry to detect technological developments that may potentially affect our business.
2. We actively seek intelligence on technological changes in the environment that are likely to affect our business.
3. We are often slow to detect changes in technologies that might affect our business [R].
4. We periodically review the likely effect of changes in technology on our business.

Technology-response capability: ($\alpha = 0.83$)

5. We generally respond very quickly to technological changes in the environment.
6. This business unit lags behind the industry in responding to new technologies [R].
7. For one reason or another, we are slow to respond to new technologies [R].
8. We tend to resist new technologies that cause our current investments to lose value.

Technological opportunism differs from related concepts such as:

- **Organizational Innovativeness** (Deshpande, Farley, and Webster 1993): This is the degree to which a firm deviates from existing practices in creating new products and/or processes.
- **Technological Orientation** (Gatignon and Xuereb 1997: 78): This is the "ability and the will to acquire a substantial technological background and use it in the development of new products."

Technological opportunism differs from both as these refer to the capability of the firm to develop new technologies, products, and processes within the organization. In contrast, TO is the capability of the firm to sense and respond to new technologies, regardless of whether these technologies are developed internally or externally or are used in developing new products. For instance, Xerox's Palo Alto Research Center produced various revolutionary technologies in the 1970s, including the laser printer, the mouse, and graphical user interface. Xerox was both technologically innovative and technologically oriented, but not technologically opportunistic as it did not respond to its own technologies and never commercialized them into products. In fact, it was Hewlett-Packard (laser printer) and Apple (graphic user interface) who commercialized these technologies to products. In contrast, when IBM approached Microsoft in 1980 for an operating system for its forthcoming personal computer (PC), Microsoft was aware of another system Quick and Dirty Operating System (QDOS) developed by Seattle Computer Products that might work for this purpose, bought the rights to it, and developed MS-DOS based on QDOS. Microsoft was technologically opportunistic, innovative, and oriented.

An organization's capability to sense and respond to new products (technological opportunism) is distinct from its capability for creating new products (technology innovativeness) and may better explain radical technology adoption.

Strategy theorists emphasize how firms build competitive advantage by developing resources and capabilities (Wernerfelt 1984). Resources include difficult to imitate, firm-specific know-how (e.g., patents and licenses) or assets (e.g., plant and equipment, human capital). Capabilities include skills exercised through organizational processes (e.g., technology sensing, market sensing) that enable firms to use their resources (Day 1994; Teece, Pisano, and Shuen 1997b). TO, therefore, is an organizational process skill. Several strategy researchers (Bourgeois 1984; Child 1972) propose that organizations proactively manipulate their environments to achieve their objective. Consistent with this line of reasoning, "TO is a proactive manipulation of the environment for seeking and adopting new technologies."

Technological opportunism may not be enough for radical technology adoption; other concomitants may be necessary such as institutional pressures and complementary assets.

- **Institutional Pressures**: is the pressure to adopt new technology that can come from at least two sources: "stakeholders" (e.g., customers, employees, trading partners, investors, bankers, suppliers, media, and general public) whose social expectations the management must accept and incorporate; and from "competition," for seeking competitive advantage.
- **Complementary Assets**: The existence, knowledge, and use of related or complementary technology; for instance, computers in the case of adopting e-business technology. Prior research attests that complementary assets positively affect technology adoption (Cohen and Leventhal 1990; Rogers 1995; Tripsas 1998). The cost of learning and adopting new technologies will be affected by the extent to which the new technology is related to the pre-existing tech base or its absorptive capacity (Cohen and Levinthal 1990).

Accordingly, Srinivasan, Lilien, and Rangaswamy (2002), propose three hypotheses:

- H_1: The greater the firm's TO, the greater is the extent of technology adoption.
- H_2: The greater the institutional pressures on the firm to adopt the new technology, the greater is the extent of technology adoption.
- H_3: The greater the firm's ownership and use of complementary assets to a radical technology, the greater is the extent of technology adoption.

All three hypotheses were verified. [For measures and validation, processes of these constructs see Srinivasan, Lilien, and Rangaswamy (2002: 51–55).] Hence, radical technology adoption is not a random or chance phenomenon in firms; it is organized because of:

- TO (standardized parameter estimate [SPE] = 0.24, $p < 0.01$).
- Perceived usefulness of the technology (SPE = 0.19, $p < 0.01$).
- Complementary assets (SPE = 0.10, $p < 0.10$).
- Other institutional pressures (SPE = 0.29, $p < 0.01$).

The authors report a second study that examined the antecedents of TO, and found constructs like:

- Future focus (closer attention to future markets); (SPE = 0.36, $p < 0.01$).
- Top management's advocacy of new technologies; (SPE = 0.25, $p < 0.01$).
- Adhocracy culture (a culture that values flexibility, creativity, entrepreneurship, and adaptability); (SPE = 0.15, $p < 0.01$).

All three antecedents were positively related to TO.

MARKETING ORIENTATION AND PRODUCT INNOVATION

[See Lukas and Ferrell (2001: 239–47)]

Does market orientation promote or stifle new product innovation? Marketing orientation and innovation are currently viewed as stimuli to economic growth and major components of competitive advantage within the company. For instance:

- Several studies indicate that market-driven businesses create new products that transform market needs (e.g., Jaworski and Kohli 1993; Narver and Slater 1990).
- Some (e.g., Deshpande, Farley, and Webster 1993; Kohli and Jaworski 1990) suggest that market-oriented behavior yields superior innovation and greater new product success.
- Slater and Narver (1994) extend this view and conclude that businesses with a strong market orientation are best situated for new product success, no matter what the business environment.

On the other hand, others think differently:

- A market orientation is inherently biased against radically new products.
- A strong market orientation may lead to limitations and marginally new products (Bennett and Cooper 1979, 1981).
- Listening too closely to current markets can stifle commercialization of new technologies and lead to reduced competitiveness (Christensen and Bower 1996; Leonard-Barton and Doyle 1996).

In reconciling these conflicting views, and empirically verifying the link between market orientation and product innovation, Lukas and Ferrell (2001) match the two constructs (Han, Kim, and Srivastava 1998).

Market orientation is described as the process of generating and disseminating market intelligence for the purpose of creating superior buyer value (Kohli and Jaworski 1990; Narver and Slater 1990). There are three components to market orientation:

- **Customer Orientation**: Relative emphasis on collecting and processing information pertaining to customer preferences.
- **Competitor Orientation**: Relative emphasis on collecting and processing information pertaining to competitor capabilities.
- **Interfunctional Coordination**: Coordinated application of organizational resources to synthesize and disseminate market intelligence.

Similarly, product innovation defined as the process of bringing new technology into use has three basic categories (Booz, Allen, and Hamilton 1982; Olson et al. 1995):

- *Line Extensions*: Products still familiar to the business firm but new to the market.
- *Me-too-products*: Products new to the firm, but not the market.
- *New-to-the-world Products*: Products new to both the firm and the market.

Market orientation and product innovation are core strategic capabilities of market-driven businesses (Day 1990, 1994). By examining the individual links between the three components of market orientation and the three components of product innovation we can develop a finer grained understanding of relationships between these two constructs and capabilities. An empirical study based on information provided by key informants from 194 SBUs provided correlation coefficients between these two constructs as presented in Table 8.5A. As observed in Table 8.5A:

- Customer orientation is significantly correlated with new-to-the-world products ($r = 0.37$).
- Competitor orientation is significantly correlated with me-too-products ($r = 0.30$).
- Interfunctional coordination is significantly correlated with line extensions ($r = 0.43$).
- Customer orientation is significantly correlated with competitor orientation ($r = 0.32$).
- Interfunctional coordination is significantly correlated with competitor orientation ($r = 0.43$).
- Interfunctional coordination is significantly correlated with customer orientation ($r = 0.58$).

Table 8.5B presents the results of canonical correlation analysis in which the association between a set of predictor variables and a set of criterion variables is assessed by the canonical correlation coefficient. The latter estimates the strength of relationship between the linear composites of the predictor and criterion sets of variables. The canonical redundancy index summarizes and indicates how much variance in one set of predictor variables is shared by the other criterion set. The extracted "canonical weight" measures the simple linear correlation between an originally observed variable in the predictor or the criterion set and the set's linear composite and is interpreted like a factor loading. Both canonical weights and "canonical loadings" of each variable indicate the relative importance of that variable in each set of criterion or predictor variables: variables with larger loadings contribute more to the canonical function.

[A major concern in canonical correlation analysis (CCA) is the instability of the canonical weights that may vary with sample size or repeated samples from the same population. In which case, a statistically significant correlation may appear despite a weak relationship between criterion and predictor sets. Hence Sharma (1996) suggests a split sample analysis (i.e., run CCA on a randomly split sample). Accordingly, Table 8.5B presents CCA results from randomly half-split samples, and indicates stability of canonical coefficients.]

As seen in Table 8.5B, CCA yielded two significant canonical correlation coefficients for the split samples (0.62 and 0.61) and for the total sample (0.62), thus indicating a strong correlation between market orientation and product innovation constructs. The high value for the canonical weights and loadings suggest further analysis using regressions. Table 8.5C has the follow-up multiple regression results.

With line extensions as the first regression dependent variable, competitor orientation (CO) has a significant standardized coefficient ($b = -0.16$, $p < 0.05$), and so does inter-functional coordination (IC) ($b = 0.57$, $p < 0.001$). CO is negatively linked to line extensions—higher the CO, lesser the line extensions. IC is positively connected to line extensions—higher the IC, higher the line extensions.

With "me-too products" as the second regression dependent variable, all three predictor variables are significantly related to the dependent variable: customer orientation is negatively linked ($b = -0.18$, $p < 0.05$); hence, higher the customer orientation, lower the me-too products. CO has a significant positive standardized coefficient ($b = 0.48$, $p < 0.001$)—higher the CO, higher the me-too product. Thirdly, interfunctional coordination (IC) is negatively linked ($b = -0.25$, $p < 0.01$); that is, higher the IC, lesser the me-too products.

With new-to-the-world products as the third regression dependent variable, CO has a significant positive standardized coefficient ($b = 0.53$, $p < 0.001$)—higher the customer orientation, higher the new-to-the-world products. CO is negatively linked to new-to-the-world products ($b = -0.23$, $p < 0.01$)—higher the CO, lesser the new-to-the-world products.

Conclusions:

1. In general, businesses launch more line extensions with inter-functional coordination but less with competitor orientation.
2. Businesses launch more me-too-products with competitor orientation, but less with inter-functional coordination and customer orientation.
3. Businesses launch more new-to-the-world products with higher customer orientation, but less so with higher competitor orientation.
4. Combining 2 and 3: A greater emphasis on customer orientation increases introduction of new-to-the-world products but decreases me-too-products. This result goes counter to the traditional view that customer orientation generates only marginal innovation.
5. Two factors may support the result: (*a*) customers are more informed these days and can suggest innovative ideas than formerly; (*b*) customer orientation today is more focused, sophisticated, and uses advanced techniques of focus groups, group dynamics, and other advanced techniques, which can give clue on new-to-the-world products.
6. Combining 1, 2, and 3: A greater emphasis on competitor orientation should increase me-too-products but decrease new-to-the-world products and line extensions. This result matches earlier beliefs that competitor orientation generates product imitation (me-too-products).
7. Combining 1 and 2: A greater emphasis on inter-functional coordination should increase line extensions but decrease me-too-products. This finding also goes against the convention that inter-functional coordination is a source of "true" innovation.

TABLE 8.5A   The Effect of Market Orientation on Product Innovation: Correlation Matrix

Variable	2	3	4	5	6
1. Line Extensions	−0.03	0.01	0.16*	0.04	0.43***
2. Me-too-products		−.05	−0.18*	0.30***	−0.15*
3. New-to-the-world Products			0.37***	−0.11	0.07
4. Customer Orientation				0.32***	0.58***
5. Competitor Orientation					0.43***
6. Interfunctional Coordination					1.00

Source: Author's own.

Note: * $p < 0.05$; ** $p < 0.01$; *** $p < 0.001$

TABLE 8.5B   The Effect of Market Orientation on Product Innovation: Canonical Correlation Analysis

Variable	Canonical weights			Canonical loadings
	First split sample ($n_1 = 94$)	First split sample ($n_2 = 100$)	Total sample ($N = 194$)	
Criterion Set: Product Innovation				
1. Line Extensions	0.36	0.40	0.48	0.51
2. Me-too-products	−0.70	−0.71	−0.66	−0.71
3. New-to-the-world products	0.54	0.51	0.51	0.55
Predictor Set: Market Orientation	Redundancy Index = 0.14			
4. Customer orientation	0.63	0.60	0.54	0.62
5. Competitor orientation	−0.84	−0.84	−0.82	−0.38
6. Interfunctional coordination	0.51	0.56	0.60	0.56
	Redundancy Index = 0.11			
Canonical Correlation Coefficient:	0.62	0.60	0.62	
Canonical Root (eigenvalue)	0.61	0.61	0.64	

Source: Author's own.

TABLE 8.5C   The Effect of Market Orientation on Product Innovation: Results of Multiple Regression Analysis (Standardized Regression Estimates)

Variable	Line extensions	Me-too-products	New-to-the-world products
Customer Orientation	−0.11	−0.18*	0.53***
Competitor Orientation	−0.16*	0.48***	−0.23**
Interfunctional Coordination	0.57***	−0.25**	−0.14
R^2	0.22	0.22	0.20
N	194	194	194

Source: Author's own.

Note: * $p < 0.05$; ** $p < 0.01$; *** $p < 0.001$

8. Possible explanation for this inconsistency: higher level of inter-functional coordination may increase organizational stress, which in turn may settle with just line extensions (that extend current product offerings) and forego opportunities for breakthrough products.

Table 8.6 summarizes various arguments discussed thus far as to why some corporations are more innovative than others, or why some prefer radically transforming strategies to incremental transformations.

CORPORATE CULTURE FOR INNOVATION

Corporate culture refers to the core set of ideas and attitudes, policies, and practices shared by the members of a firm (Despandé and Webster 1989; Henard and Szymanski 2001; Tellis, Prabhu, and Chandy 2009). Obviously, such a corporate culture of attitudes and practices differs across various functions such as innovation management and new product development, human resources management, production management, financing management, and marketing management. While these attitudes and practices could be drivers of innovation, they can also be inhibitors of creativity and innovation. For instance, obsession with cash flows, profitability, shareholder value, accountability, structure, and processes can slow down, if not paralyze, corporate innovation. In this connection, Govindarajan and Trimble (2005: 5) speak of an organization code that enables or disables a company from pursuing innovation. Following Govindarajan and Trimble (2005: 5), Table 8.7 explores possible organizational codes of efficiency versus creativity in formulating corporate strategies.

Code A is about discipline and hierarchy while Code B is about creativity and democracy. Code A is risk averse and operational expertise, while Code B is risk-absorbing, creativity, innovation, and venturesome. In most companies, Code A is mainstream, and Code B is counter-culture. The Code A–Code B debate dominates today's corporate and political meetings and defines the agenda. The truth is, we need both. If we want new blood, new thinking, new innovations, new products and services, new and exponential growth, then we need more of Code B. *Creativity (Code B) should precede efficiency (Code A); business plan (Code B) should precede profitability (Code A).* You cannot expect long-term profitability without a new idea, without a new business plan, and without resultant corporate growth.

In relation to innovation management and new product development, Tellis, Prabhu, and Chandy (2009) identify three firm attitudes and firm practices that may drive innovation:

- **Willingness to Cannibalize**: This is an attitude that puts up for review and sacrifice current profit-generating assets, including current profitable and successful innovations, so that the firm can get ahead with the next generation of innovations (Chandy and Tellis 1998).
- **Future Orientation**: This attitude forces a firm to realize the limitations of the current technology and the emergence of a new generation of technology that may become dominant in the future (Yadav, Prabhu, and Chandy 2007).
- **Risk Tolerance**: This is an attitude that is ready to trade a current, sure stream of profit-generating assets for a future, uncertain stream of profits that can come from radical innovations (Tellis, Prabhu, and Chandy 2009).

Empowering innovation and product champions, establishing attractive incentives, and promoting internal markets and competition are three proven business practices that can engender and sustain

TABLE 8.6 A Synthetic Summary of Typologies, Antecedents, and Moderators of Radical Transformations in Corporations

| Model (year) | Determinants of radical technology adoption/diffusion | | |
	Typologies	Antecedents, moderators	Conclusions
Abernathy–Clark (1985)	Regular, revolutionary, niche, and architectural typologies	Regular innovations preserve, while architectural innovations destroy one's both technological and market capabilities. Niche innovation destroys market capabilities but preserves technological ones; revolutionary innovations destroy technological ones but preserves marketing capabilities.	The firm may readily absorb regular innovations, may be slow to adopt architectural innovations, and partly absorb niche and revolutionary innovations.
Henderson–Clark (1990)	Incremental, modular, architectural, and radical innovation typologies	Products that have components assembled together require two kinds of knowledge: knowledge of the components (component knowledge), and that of the linkages between them (architectural knowledge). An innovation that can enhance performance is one which has both component and architectural knowledge; else it may destroy innovation performance.	Develop both component and architectural knowledge to enhance performance of innovations that require both knowledge sets. Innovation performance is partial if only one set of knowledge is known.
Afuah–Bahram (1995)	Value-added chain model	Innovations are adopted to the extent these new products had incremental or radical impact on other groups of the value chain such as suppliers, competitors, retailers, and especially, customers.	Originators or new entrants to an innovation will adopt it if: (a) its radical or incremental impact on members of the value-added chain is desirable, and (b) if that member of the value chain is of critical importance to the firm.
Gatignon and Xuereb (1997)	Strategic orientation model	Strategic (customer, competitor, and technological) orientation of the firm positively helps adoption of radical innovations.	Strategic orientation of the firm determines innovation characteristics and performance success.
Chandy–Tellis (1998)	Incremental and radical innovations; market and technological breakthroughs	Radical innovations are those that provide substantially better technological and commercial (i.e., better performance per customer dollar) benefits compared to the previous levels of these products.	Focus on market breakthroughs and radical innovations for long-term profitability. A firm's "willingness to cannibalize" is a signifying unifying factor that spurs radical product innovation.
Chandy and Tellis (2000)	Incumbent innovation model	Long incumbents or large firms have significant role in radical innovations.	Long-time incumbency and firm size influence radical innovations.
Lukas and Ferrell (2001)	Market orientation	Market (customer, competitor, and technology) orientation is linked with product innovation (new-to-the-word products, me-too-products, and line extensions).	Customer and technology orientation enables new-to-the-world products; competitor orientation facilitates me-too-products and line extensions.
Srinivasan, Lilien, and Rangaswamy (2002)	Technological opportunism	Technological opportunism (sensing–responding to new technologies) positively enables radical technology adoption, given market demand uncertainty.	Promote technological opportunism among key employees for expediting radical technology adoptions and innovation performance.
McGahan (2004)	Industry change	External factors such as new technologies, innovations, energy sources, governmental regulations, and globalization can threaten your core activities or core products or both.	When both core assets and core activities are rendered obsolete by external factors, corporations must transform themselves by radical innovations.

Source: Author's own.

TABLE 8.7 Possible Organizational Codes of Efficiency versus Creativity

Domain	Code A: Maximize efficiency	Code B: Optimize creativity
Attitudes of exploration	Stick to your field of specialization Build on your skills and strengths	Think outside the box Expand your vision, mission, and identity
Domain of exploration	Exploit what you know Do what you know best Industry focus: convergent industries	Explore what you don't know Make happen things you don't know Cross-industry focus: divergent industries
Purpose of exploration	Cost containment	Revenue generation Exploring opportunities Capitalizing opportunities
Stimulus of exploration	Beat the competition Focus on core products and brands Explore and exploit red oceans	Ignore the competition Focus internally on skills, strengths, and core competences Explore "blue" oceans
Market-focus of exploration	You meet current customers needs	You anticipate future customer needs You explore current customer wants, desires, and dreams
Style of exploration	You organize, focus, and plan	You let things emerge You empower things to happen You enable unraveling and discovery
Process of exploration	You impose process and structure	You avoid process and encourage unstructured interaction You allow freedom and flexibility
Assessment of exploration	You demand accountability You impose outcome metrics	You expect shared vision and commitment You appreciate and acknowledge efforts, team spirit, and team learning
Outcomes of exploration	Efficiency, sales, cash flow, profitability, return on assets (ROA), return on investments (ROI), and return on equity (ROE)	Design, creativity, innovation, and long-term revenues, market share, brand renown, company reputation, ROI, return on invested capital (ROIC), earnings per share (EPS), P/E, Tobin's Q, and corporate social responsibility
Ecology of exploration	Minimal EPA compliance Exploit non-renewable resources	Optimizing eco-compliance Explore alternative energies, renewable energies, and fuels Contribute to clean air, land, water, and space
Future of exploration	Status quo Follow industry growth Industry follower, market follower Incremental innovations Incremental growth in sales Incremental growth of the company	Forging ahead, explore, discover, reinvent, redesign the future Industry leader, market leader, product pioneer Radical innovations, market breakthroughs, and technological breakthroughs Dynamic and exponential growth of sales, revenues, opportunities, investments, shareholders, and stakeholders Development of local communities

Source: Author's own.

Note: See also Govindarajan and Trimble (2005: 5).

the foregoing three pro-innovation attitudes. Related to these three pro-innovation attitudes are three strategies for innovation that Govindarajan and Trimble (2005: 17) investigate and demonstrate. They call existing business Core-Co and new emerging business NewCo.

- **Forgetting**: NewCo must forget some Core-Co's old success formulas, old and stable answers to what Core-Co's business is, and how it wins. Mere conversations and debates will not do this. NewCo must alter the organizational design in order to be distinct from Core-Co.
- **Borrowing**: NewCo can gain, however, critical competitive advantage from borrowing existing and successful expertise, skills, and resources of Core-Co such as manufacturing capacity, specialized skills, sales relationships, distribution channels, and supply chain management relationships.
- **Learning**: Whereas Core-Co's success formula is proven and stable, and NewCo is a guess, NewCo must learn, resolve critical unknowns in its new business plans, and zero in on a working business model as quickly as possible. If NewCo cannot forget Core-Co's old success formulas, it will struggle to learn its own.

The three attitudes and three strategies can help a firm to leapfrog from the stifling past into the creative future. A strategic experiment will be successful only to the extent it is willing to cannibalize, is future-oriented, is ready to take risk when necessary, is ready to forget the past, even the success formulas, is ready to borrow proven skills and resources from the past, and, above all, is ready to learn as it goes along its path to great success.

CEO'S CHALLENGES IN MANAGING INNOVATIONS

A common top management problem in managing innovations is that business goals are stated so broadly or vaguely that they do not help to identify the best opportunities and innovations to pursue from a cadre of available options. For instance, if the top-level goal is to "create growth," then is it best satisfied with a new technology that improves product performance by 20 percent and will empower you to take market share from your competitors? Instead, should you innovate new products or variants of existing brands that will enable you to tap into new markets that will ensure long-term corporate growth? Innovations are mere tools and skills, which by themselves do not ensure sustainable competitive advantage nor even steady profitability:

> As commercial processes commoditize in a developed economy, they are outsourced or transferred offshore or both, leaving onshore companies with unrelenting pressure to come up with the next wave of innovation. Failure to innovate equals failure to differentiate, which, in turn, equals failure to garner the profits and the revenues needed to attract capital investment. It behooves us all to use our brains to get out in front of this Darwinian process. (Moore 2004: 87)

Sony, for example, had an impressive new product record throughout the 1980s with market break-throughs such as the Walkman and the PlayStation. By the 1990s, however, Sony's engineers were becoming increasingly self-sufficient, complacent, and experienced insular suffering from a damaging "not invented here syndrome," while competitors were introducing next-generation products such as Microsoft's Xbox and Apple's iPod. Sony executives and engineers believed that outside sources of innovation were not so good compared to internal ones. Meanwhile, they missed great opportunities such as MP3 players, flat screen TVs, and instead developed unwanted products such as cameras that were incompatible with the worldwide standards of memory, storage, reproduction, and electronic transmission.

As observed in Chapter 7, creativity and innovation are not enough. There is a big difference between being a creative firm and an innovative enterprise: the former generates many ideas; the latter generates much cash (Levitt 1963). A failing company needs innovations that quickly turn into market-ready ideas to good products to good markets and good markets that turn into good cash and financial returns—this is the "innovation-to-cash chain" (Andrew and Sirkin 2003: 78). Motorola rose to prominence with the first generation of cell phones; Sony created instant wealth in fast spreading fads like the collector card game Pokémon.

Finding a great idea is not enough. You must find a great leader to endorse and sponsor it. Moreover, we need processes, techniques, and organizational designs that can conceptualize, prototype, design-test, and test-market and implement innovative ideas (Drucker 1985; Hamel 1999; Kim and Mauborgne 2000). Moreover, implementing innovations faces stiff internal resistance from accountants and finance people on grounds that they consume too many resources from marketing people that they cannibalize existing products, and from top executives that their financial performance results are not clearly predictable. Meanwhile, the competitors could go ahead and redefine the industry. Thus, Canon went ahead of Xerox; Wal-Mart forged ahead of KMart and Sears; Fuji bypassed Kodak; Toyota Prius outpaced Ford Escape, and in general, the foreign auto companies put U.S. auto companies behind.

Strategic innovators need more than a great idea. They need to move from idea to execution. With a great idea in hand, you move to a quest that would bring both great expectations and excruciating frustrations. Thus, leaders of any groundbreaking business idea: (*a*) need to attract funding, (*b*) learn quickly to predict success from failure, (*c*) rally people around a fuzzy view of the future, (*d*) reorganize to leverage the lessons learned, and (*e*) manage expectations of performance amid chaos.

Besides these five challenges and constraints, the leader must (Govindarajan and Trimble 2005: 2):

- Overcome tensions between the new idea and the old product that it may efface.
- Disengage core employees from existing products and deploy them to the new idea.
- Bring about changes in the existing power structure required to support the new idea.
- Siphon funds from the old products to new ideas.
- Recruit new talent, if necessary, to implement the new idea; this makes managerial task very challenging.

Strategic innovation and the strategic experiments that accompany it need the support of the organization. Both fail if the company relies solely on the heroism of a hyper-talented and hyper-passionate individual who has a great idea, and even has an executive champion to back it. For instance, Joline Godfrey, the leader of a great idea in Polaroid, created a business that focused on commercializing services that enhanced vacation experiences with photography. She had all the right stuff: boundless energy, ability to excite others enough to work long hours with her, and even had a dedicated senior executive champion. Nevertheless, she failed to obtain unflinching support from the top. Polaroid's old mentality of preserving the core business never gave her a fighting chance to succeed.

Gifford Pinchot (1985) in his book *Intrapreneuring* lays down "Ten Commandments" for intrapreneurs to succeed:

1. Come to work each day willing to be fired.
2. Circumvent any orders aimed at stopping your dream.
3. Do any job needed to make your project work, regardless of your job description.
4. Find people to help you.
5. Follow your intuition about the people you choose, and work only with the best.
6. Work underground as long as you can—publicity triggers the corporate immune mechanism.
7. Never bet on a race unless you are running with it.
8. Remember it is easier to ask for forgiveness than for permission.
9. Be true to your goals, but be realistic about the ways to achieve them.
10. Honor your sponsors.

Organizations are almost always more powerful than individuals. Hence, executive intrapreneurs with a strategic innovation idea will have to fight both the long odds facing any strategic experiment as also the organization fighting them at every turn.

INNOVATION MANAGEMENT AND NEW PRODUCT DEVELOPMENT VALUE CHAINS

Innovation is more than new product development. There is innovation in purchasing, in production processes, in product-price bundling, in employee motivation management, in marketing, in customer acquisition and retention, in business models, and everywhere in the corporation. The domain of innovation is very broad. Where a product is in its life cycle determines which kind of innovation will do the most good for the company (Moore 2004).

A company's innovation success is a function of many variables, market factors and execution stages. All these relate the entire new product development value-chain activities such as:

1. Generating new ideas—they could come from either the customer (market-push) or the company (technology-push); ideas could be unfulfilled customer needs, customer wants, or customer desires/dreams; this is the first level of possible customer involvement.
2. Converting new ideas into corresponding concepts—they are company's response to the new ideas.
3. Converting new concepts to corresponding prototypes—this demands design and creative thinking.
4. Pre-testing prototypes by target customers; this is the second level of customer involvement.
5. Designing by engineers of right materials and processes to convert pre-tested prototypes into products/services.
6. Design-testing by target customers; this is the third level of customer involvement.
7. Work-in-progress inventory management—JIT, inventory buffers, decoupling inventories.
8. Packaging and product bundling products/services into market-ready brands.
9. Package or price-product bundle-testing by target customers; this is the fourth level of customer involvement.
10. Test-marketing brands to choose an optimal mix of pricing, placing, and promoting new brands; this is the fifth level of customer involvement.

11. Finished products inventory management—JIT, inventory buffers, decoupling inventories.
12. Transportation, delivery, and distribution logistics management.
13. Advertising, promotions, press releases, new product arrival announcements, and aggressive marketing of the product/service bundles.
14. Financing brand purchases or organizing consumer credit; for example, GMAC, Ford Credit, GE Capital.
15. Service packaging—for example, warranties, guaranties, systems to honor warranties and guarantees; product return–refund–remedy policies and procedures.
16. Nationally launching brands with effective press release, PR, and attractive marketing programs.
17. Obtaining continuous customer feedback on brand delivery, brand distribution, brand user-friendliness, convenience (i.e., saving on money, energy, time, use-research, use, maintenance-research, maintenance, anxiety, risk, insurance, life-time, refund/return, salvage value or future value), brand quality, brand competitiveness, and customer satisfaction and delight. This is the last and continuous level of customer involvement.
18. Incorporating customer feedback, refine, and upgrade value-chain activities along Stages 1–17.

The organization's capacity for innovation is the product (not sum) of its skills (measured on a 0–10 scale) on each of these new product development phases. If the skill level at any stage is zero, the whole process of innovation may stall. An innovative company develops high skills at the "back end" (Stages 1–7, 18), "middle-stream" (Stages 8–12, 18), and "front end" (Stages 13–17, 18) of the entire value-chain development. A company needs high levels of design, creativity, and innovation skills at all stages, back end, middle end, and front end. Some manufacturing companies obsess over the back end (e.g., Toyota, GE, Microsoft), some focus on the middle chain values (e.g., Apple, Dell, Wal-Mart), and some concentrate on the front end (e.g., GM, Ford, Chrysler, Saks Fifth, Nordstrom, Morgan Stanley, Merrill Lynch).

In some companies (e.g., Corning, GE), the back-end innovation process may be split into a centralized hardcore research group that does the basic science for the invention of the prototype (Stages 1–4) and a single centralized development group to develop the new prototype to product-readiness (Stages 5–7). The innovation process involves the marked transfer of certain specific responsibilities from the research group to the development group. The marketing group steps to the plate next and takes the newly developed product to the market (Stages 8–18). In a typical company, different groups demand different set of underlying competencies, and hence, exert different type of power.

In general, power is centered in the group of people who have the core skill that creates a competitive advantage. For instance, in P&G, it may be the marketing group; in a logistic company such as the UPS, USPS, FedEx, it may be the operations groups, and in a hardcore science and engineering organization (e.g., Corning-CMT, GE), it may be the invention-prototype group (Govindarajan and Trimble 2005: 21–25). Accordingly, each group operates at a different level of risk, stress, uncertainty, anxiety, ambiguity, reliability, predictability, and, consequently, at a different level of creativity, innovativeness, exploration, experience, and strategic experimentation. Each group also bears different levels of contribution, performance, accountability, controllability, and profitability.

In general:

- Manufacturing companies focus on the back end (e.g., TPS of Toyota, TQM of Deming, and Six Sigma); here organizational memory of tried routines and proven procedures come into strong play.
- Electronic and entertainment goods companies concentrate on the middle chain of packaging industries (e.g., laptops, iPhones, iPods, cross-products, cross-licensing, cross-selling).

- Service-oriented companies naturally tend to surpass at the front end of being great ambassadors of the products and services to the target customers (e.g., front-desk management of hotels and investment banks, excellent store ambience and services of luxury retail outlets and restaurants, and hospitality of institutions like clinics, hospitals, and political campaign services).

Table 8.8 expands the value-chain of a new product development process into several more stages than the 18 considered earlier. At each stage there is different level of product risk (e.g., organizational stress, market uncertainty, and product ambiguity), organizational concerns (e.g., ecology, privacy, safety, security, corporate ethics and morality, and corporate social responsibility), and growth potential (e.g., via innovation, sustainable competitive advantage [SCA], profitability, market capitalization, and shareholder value).

Table 8.8 projects a high (H), medium (M), or a low (L) to describe the level of "stress," "concerns," and "potential" at each stage, depending upon the nature of the organizational task at that stage. Strategic experiments may be involved at each stage, and these place managers under great stress as they present a far more ambiguous environment at that stage. Under conditions of stress and ambiguity, managers naturally gravitate toward their familiar instincts (i.e., best planning templates, best and proven organizational routines, best organizational memory resources, or best inter-departmental relationships) without being aware of it. They naturally look first to customers they already know, create value propositions that have proved successful offerings in the past, or obviously seek to recreate existing processes.

Thus, in general, organizational memory defines what an organization will and will not do. Erasing memory is the crux of the "forgetting" challenge (Govindarajan and Trimble 2005: 26–27).

WHAT INNOVATORS LOOK LIKE

[See Chon, Katzenbach, and Vlak (2008: 64–65)]

The best innovators have very strong cognitive abilities, including excellent analytical skills. They zero in on the most important points and waste no time on peripheral issues. Once they isolate key factors, they can quickly see how all the pieces might fit together in an integrated whole. They have the ability to think strategically even in highly ambiguous situations.

Great innovators never rest on their laurels. Driven by a certain underlying insecurity, they do not necessarily rely on past success, but evaluate each new change with a clean slate. Just because something has worked in the past, they argue, it does not mean it will work in the future. They frame and reframe challenges from multiple vantage points and identify which solutions are very likely to be embraced by the influential people in their organization.

High potential innovators are socially aware of their surroundings at all times. They can walk into a conference room full of diverse constituents, including colleagues, customers, subordinates, bosses, vendors, and partners, and quickly discern the underlying motivation of each stakeholder. They leverage that information to craft and communicate a message that resonates with every constituent. This is the innovative art of bringing a diverse group into the same page, and it is absolutely essential to transforming an interesting idea into a company-wide innovation.

Successful innovators are persuasive and often charming. They know how to extract information from specific areas of an organization and then garner organizational support for potential projects. Innovation cannot thrive when new ideas simply die. Most successful innovators are able to persuade executives to share their interesting insights and ideas. They are extremely curious and are always shopping for new ideas without being intrusive. On the flip side, successful innovators use their skills and charm to push an unproven idea through the corporate machinery. It is a rare sales ability.

An innovator accesses resources and recombines ideas in ways that are unfamiliar to the organization. Doing so means moving beyond conventional boundaries and the safety of existing positions, which can be a lonely experience. Successful innovators bring the knowledge they have gained back to traditional hierarchies, which can be frustrating. They work equally well in large cross-functional teams and in extreme isolation. They exhibit a "unique psychological mix."

HOW DO YOU GROOM BREAKTHROUGH INNOVATORS

[Chon, Katzenbach, and Vlak (2008: 62–69)]

Finding and grooming the next generation of innovators is one key to corporate growth, but most companies smother their creative talent. The biggest challenge any growing company faces is to identify and foster the next generation of breakthrough innovators. Grooming innovators from within or from without, companies do a magnificent job of smothering creative spark; that is, they usually develop leaders who replicate than innovate. Nevertheless:

- Growth-oriented companies have intense talent-management processes in place and put identified innovators in the line of fire, where natural innovators thrive. Do not filter candidates for promotion to breakthrough innovations by competencies that are ingrained in the corporate culture. That is, do not judge your rising stars by how closely they resemble their peers and bosses. Conformity spells mediocrity. Breakthrough innovators are those who are willing to deviate from the norm, take real risks, and embrace different points of view. You should nurture and empower them. Empower them to choose their own innovation team from different parts of the organization, give them authority to set the tone, ground rules, strategy, and goals for it.
- Great companies scour for raw talent—they look among their high potentials to find people who are never content with the status quo or following yesterday's best practices but who display unusual skills. Good talent knows how to handle stress, manage complexity and ambiguity, and get others to believe in the ideas that he/she is pursuing. McDonald's provides would-be innovators to prove themselves in front of the top management. They are encouraged to work with senior executives in key line positions to identify innovations that have the potential to affect the entire organization. Some of these ideas are not necessarily product-related. They could relate, for instance, to how Wal-Mart and McDonald's collaborate or partner together and how could such partnership offer products/services that are scalable—an essential quality if an idea is to have any traction at McDonald's.
- Disengage future breakthrough innovators' prospects from ordinary duties. Do not let your great innovators be buried in their daily duties of line jobs and hidden from your top management. You need to know them and develop them. Your best innovators are not necessarily in HR departments; they are embedded in front line ambassadorial activities with your customers and suppliers. At McDonald's, executives comb through individual department plans semi-annually, hold talent

TABLE 8.8 Managing Innovation along Value Chains by Industries

Value chain	Value-chain components	Hardcore manufacturing industry			Software, electronic, and entertainment product industries			Banking, media, government, and other service industries		
		Risk: stress, uncertainty, ambiguity	*Concerns: ecology, privacy, safety, ethics, morals*	*Potential for: innovation, SCA, profitability*	*Risk: stress, uncertainty, ambiguity*	*Concerns: ecology, privacy, safety, ethics, morals*	*Potential for: innovation, SCA, profitability*	*Risk: stress, uncertainty, ambiguity*	*Concerns: ecology, privacy, safety, ethics, morals*	*Potential for: innovation, SCA, profitability*
Upstream Value Chain: Back-end Innovations (18 areas)	Innovation Idea	L	L	L–H	H	M	H	H	L	H
	Innovation Concept	M	M	L–H	H	M	H	H	L	H
	Creativity-Innovation	H	M	H	H	M	H	H	M	H
	Design	H	H	H	H	H	H	H	H	H
	Fabrication	H	M	M	L	L	L	L	L	L
	Materials	H	M	M	L	L	L	L	L	L
	Components	H	M	M	M	M	M	L	L	L
	Process Technology	H	H	H	M	H	M	L	L	L
	Prototype	H	M	H	H	H	H	L	L	L
	Patentability	M	L	H	H	H	H	L	L	M
	Assembly Line	M	L	L	L	L	L	L	L	L
	Supply Chain Management	M	L	L	L	L	L	L	L	L
	Purchasing	M	L	L	L	L	L	L	L	L
	Transportation Logistics	M	L	L	L	L	L	L	L	L
	Warehousing	L	L	L	L	L	L	L	L	L
	WIP Inventory Management	M	L	L	L	L	L	L	L	L
	Product Technology	H	M	H	M	M	M	M	M	M
	Quality Control	H	M	H	H	H	H	M	H	M
	FP Inventory Management	M	L	L	L	L	L	L	L	L

Midstream Value Chain: Mid-end Innovations (10 areas)	Product Sizing	M	L	H	H	M	L	L	L	M
	Product Packaging	H	H	H	H	H	H	H	H	H
	Product Labeling	M	L	L	H	L	L	H	L	L
	Instruction Manuals	M	L	L	H	L	L	M	L	L
	Order Processing	M	L	M	H	M	L	L	L	L
	Delivery Logistics	M	L	M	H	M	L	L	M	M
	Installation/Maintenance	M	L	L	H	L	L	M	L	L
	Inventory Replenishment	M	L	M	M	L	L	M	L	L
	Store Shelving	M	L	M	M	L	L	M	L	L
	Shelf Replenishment	M	L	M	M	L	L	M	L	L
Downstream Value Chain: Front-end Innovations (21 areas)	NPD Preannouncements	H	M	H	H	H	M	H	M	M
	Press Release	M	M	H	H	H	M	H	M	M
	Unit Costing	M	L	H	H	M	L	M	L	L
	Unit Pricing	H	M	H	H	H	M	H	M	M
	Price Bundling	H	M	H	H	H	H	H	H	H
	Product Bundling	H	M	H	H	H	H	H	L	L
	Rebate and Discounting	M	L	H	H	M	H	M	M	L
	Free Sampling and Testing	M	L	H	H	M	M	L	M	L
	Promotions and Advertising	H	L	H	H	M	M	L	M	M
	Credit/Financing	H	M	H	H	M	M	H	L	L
	Store Choice and Retailing	M	L	M	H	M	M	L	L	L
	Point of Purchase Display	M	L	M	H	M	M	L	L	L
	Salesperson service	H	M	H	H	M	M	H	M	M
	Servicing Warranties	M	M	H	H	H	H	H	H	H
	Customer Complaints	H	H	H	H	H	H	H	H	H
	Customer Redress	H	H	H	H	H	H	H	H	H
	Customer Loyalty	H	M	H	H	H	H	H	H	H
	Building Brand Community	M	M	H	H	H	H	M	M	M
	Customer Co-designing	M	M	H	H	H	L	H	L	L
	Customer Co-production	M	M	H	H	H	L	H	L	L
	Customer Co-partnering	M	M	H	H	H	L	H	L	L

Source: Author's own.

roundtables and succession planning discussions, perform talent calibration, and conduct systematic reviews in identifying and developing future breakthrough innovators. At Reuters (which merged with Thompson Corporation in April 2008 to form Thompson Reuters), the top executives use an initial mechanism called "predictive index" to identify potential innovators—this index surveys core drivers, core competencies, and core motivations of the subordinates as a basis for compiling a master list of rising stars.

- They test their innovators with live ammunition—they give them real projects and access to top management. Mentoring and peer network are crucial for providing support to future innovators. At Starwood, the parent company of hotel chains such as Westin, St. Regis, and Sheraton, rising innovators build and manage cross-functional teams to develop their projects and then present full-fledged marketing plans to the company's top executives.

- Great companies mentor and engage peer networks. Peer networks that meet regularly and have open channels of communication provide a sense of solidarity and a uniquely fertile environment to exchange ideas, share information, and inspire hope. Smart organizations pair innovators with carefully selected mentors who can continuously educate them about the people they are most likely to encounter and the interactions they are most likely to have. The mentors themselves need to be coached and supported by the CEO, thus strongly signaling the importance of the initiative. Mentoring should be a perfect supplement to the innovators' natural mix of intuition and curiosity. Mentors equip rising innovators with information about the people they are most likely to encounter and the interactions they are most likely to have. Innovators are encouraged to turn to peer networks for feedback. Peer networks also enable participants to answer more tangible questions, such as which parts of the organization are good sources of information, ideas, and insights available. In addition, where are the dead ends? Often a mentor who is often a senior member of the organization and who is also not an innovator cannot answer these questions. Peers will share information with one another that they might not reveal to a mentor. At Starwood, peer networks are called "collaboration circles," a group of cross-functional experts. The team typically includes specialists in marketing, operations, finance, accounting, and is composed of designers, developers, artists, photographers, and opera singers, depending upon the nature of entertainment innovation pursued. The group not only helps rising innovators navigate the grooming process, but also fuels the innovation process. The CEO of Starwood monitors the process to ensure it works.

- Actively manage investors' careers. Great companies carefully select and place prospective breakthrough innovators outside the regular structure, thereby, empowering them to create wholly new businesses. At JP Morgan Chase, the CEO and the head of HR spearhead "ascension plans" for breakthrough innovators, in concert with innovators themselves. The company creates new positions for rising stars if appropriate ones do not exist.

- Replant innovators in the middle. Once rising breakthrough innovators have been identified, developed, and established in the middle of the organization, the next question is where to place them so that they have the most impact in the organization. They must be placed where the nodes in the shadow organization are—those all-important hot spots that do not show up on formal organization charts, where innovations can be sparked. These nodes should make innovators become "innovation hubs," with easy access to influencers across the firm, more autonomy, and broader albeit ambiguous responsibilities—the hubs can better see how existing products, ideas, people, or even entire businesses can be recombined in new, value-adding ways.

Once you have spotted your high potentials, you must determine who among them has the real innovator's spark. Several companies, such as Thompson Reuters, Pitney Bowers, and Visa, do this in a series of one-on-one interviews, often conducted by outside assessment and leadership development experts. These experts present the candidates during interviews some complex but real-life scenarios from which the interviewer intentionally omits some key information in order to gauge whether they can weed through ambiguity, make realistic assumptions based on the data available, reach a decision, and articulate a clear compelling rationale for any trade-offs involved in it. The candidates are gradually given additional information.

Napoleon remarked that a general's most important asset is luck. Nevertheless, luck comes to people who are well prepared and manage to be in the right place at the right time. Napoleon's brilliance was in identifying future commanders early in their military careers and giving them access to resources, authority, and the opportunity to prove their mettle. He wanted his future leaders to be smart enough to recognize good ideas wherever they came from, and combine them with limited resources in a novel way to conquer seemingly invincible adversaries. The same is true of business innovation.

Given this graduated procedure, the interviewers should continually assess several qualifiers of breakthrough innovators such as:

- Can the candidates to breakthrough innovation recognize promising ideas, effectively lead cross-functional teams of experts to develop them, and sell them to top executives?
- Can the candidates evaluate what and why a given idea or model will have the best potential impact on performance and profitability and what does not and why?
- Can they tackle a complex issue, take it apart, and focus on the most salient issues? Can they make it viable, practical, and scalable?
- Can the team leaders, the future innovators, create, manage, and motivate a high-performance team, through excellent communication and persuasion skills, and develop a strong solution to a given customer or client problem?
- Can the rising stars work side-by-side with the company's experienced salespeople developing pitches, dissecting customer needs, accompany the team on client calls, discern what really make the key decision makers tick, and actually help close the sale?
- Can the rising stars, thus, teach experienced salespersons of the company a few new effective techniques in scanning, persuading, winning, and closing a significant sale?
- Can they critically reflect as to what evidence warrants changing existing positions, past beliefs, and mental models?
- Can they connect valuable new information additionally provided to them to revise their past proposed answers or solutions?
- Can they clearly and convincingly defend a decision or sell a point of view?
- Do they ask for feedback on the assessment process so that they can learn from their previous mistakes?

In a final series of interviews, the candidates should be able to explain without reservation what they do badly. If candidates do not do well in all these sequenced interviews and exercises, their level of talent and self-awareness is not sufficiently high for them to become successful innovators (Chon, Katzenbach, and Vlak 2008: 62–69).

TEN CHARACTERISTICS OF STRATEGIC EXPERIMENTS THAT GENERATE BREAKTHROUGH INNOVATIONS

[See Govinadarajan and Trimble (2005: xix–xi)]

1. They have very high potential for growth (e.g., 10 times over three to five years).
2. They focus on emerging or fuzzy (poorly defined) industries created by non-linear shifts in the industry environment.
3. They test an unknown business model that is launched before any competitor has proven itself and before any clear formula for making profits has emerged.
4. They are a radical departure from existing business or proven business definition and its assumptions about how businesses succeed: GM's OnStar and GMAC departed from selling autos to offering services. P&G's Tremor departed from consumer products to business services. Disney's Moviebeam augmented content production with new direct-to-consumer distribution.
5. They use existing assets and competencies: they leverage unused capital, assets, technologies, and skills.
6. They develop new knowledge and capabilities, by combining new and old, internal and external, within and outside the industry.
7. They are discontinuous rather than incremental value creations—they revolutionize the definition of a business rather than enhance performance within a proven business definition (via product line extensions, geographic expansions, or technological improvements).
8. They spell great multi-dimensional uncertainty across multiple functions: for example, who could be potential customers, with what value propositions, with what process and product technologies? For instance, which of the possible many services of OnStar would be beneficial to whom? How well could Tremor compete against traditional media-centered approaches to marketing? How would movie-distribution technologies evolve and affect Moviebeam's viability?
9. They could be unprofitable for several quarters or more (e.g., Toyota Prius, Ford Focus, Amazon. com), and hence, may be too expensive to repeat. You get only one chance.
10. No clear picture of performance early on—they are difficult to evaluate. Feedback is delayed and ambiguous, and executives may not know for several quarters whether they are succeeding or failing.

POPULAR TYPES OF INNOVATIONS

Geoffrey Moore (2004: 88) distinguishes several layers or types of innovations:

- **Disruptive Innovation**: This innovation appears from nowhere, creating a massive new source of wealth from certain technological discontinuities (e.g., Motorola's first generation cell phones; Sony's PlayStation One, Two, and Plus; Apple's iPod and iTunes; the collector card game Pokémon, and the like).
- **Application Innovation**: This innovation takes existing technology into new markets to serve new purposes (e.g., Tandem applied its fault-tolerant computers to the banking market to create ATMs; OnStar took Global Positioning Systems into the automobile market for roadside assistance).

- **Product Innovation**: This innovation takes established market offerings in established markets to the next level focusing on product performance increase (e.g., Intel releases its new microprocessor, Toyota releases its new hybrid Toyota Prius; Titleist Pro VI golf balls) or cost reduction (e.g., HP inkjet printers; Dell's PCs or laptops), usability improvement (e.g., Palm handhelds, Blackberry), or any other product enhancement (e.g., various cell phones; iPod to iTunes).

- **Process Innovation**: This innovation makes production processes of established products more efficient and effective (e.g., Wal-Mart's refinement of vendor-managed inventory process; Charles Schwab's migration to online trading; Dell's PC supply chain and order fulfillment systems; FedEx's package tracking).

- **Experiential Innovation**: This innovation makes surface or cosmetic modifications to improve customer experience of established products or processes (e.g., Disneyland, Avis Rental, American Place, Hard Rock Café, and MGM Casino).

- **Marketing Innovation**: This innovation significantly improves customer-interfacing processes by such things as marketing communications (e.g., Web-based marketing; viral marketing), consumer transactions (e.g., Amazon's e-commerce mechanisms; eBay's online auctions).

- **Business Model Innovation**: This innovation reframes an established value proposition to the customer or a company's established role in the value chain or both (Gillette's move from razors to razor blades; IBM's shift to on-demand computing, and Apple's expansion into consumer retailing).

- **Structural Innovation**: This innovation capitalizes on disruption to restructure industry relationships. For instance, Fidelity and Citigroup used the deregulation of financial services to offer broader arrays of products and services to consumers under one umbrella, thus becoming fierce competitors to traditional banks and insurance companies; Fannie May and Freddie Mac exploited credit deregulations to offer easy mortgage loans to homeowners who could scarcely afford them.

As an executive, what type of innovation would you focus on, when, and to what competitive advantage? Once we invoked the theory of core competencies to solve this problem, select the processes and products you are best at and focus your resources accordingly. However, "companies have discovered that being the best at something does not guarantee sustainable competitive advantage." A distinctive competence is valuable only if its drives or converts to purchase preferences. Customers ignore a company's core competencies in favor of products that are good enough and cheaper (Moore 2004: 88).

Each of these innovation types should respond to a given stage in the product or technology adoption life cycle as follows:

- **Early market** of enthusiastic adopters and innovators and lifestyle setters; the media comes with glowing reports about your sensational product. Capitalize on the "disruptive innovation" your product implies.

- **The Chasm:** The market stalls adoption; it needs more time to understand and prefer your product over existing brands; the media watches for further market reaction. The market-response chasm could deepen and widen but robust technologies withstand the chasm.

- **The Bowling Alley:** The market regains confidence in your product, and speaks well about your product; the late adopters or pragmatists now risk your product and embrace it; targeting one market influences and touches the other as in bowling when one pin hits the others. You should work on the "application innovation" to target multiple markets.

- **Tornado**: The technology has passed the test of usefulness, safety, and customer delight. It hits the market. Your product becomes the market format, standard, or benchmark. Customers of all stripes flood the market and do not wish to be left behind. You should then maximize and energize "product innovation" to meet this burst of market enthusiasm.
- **Early Main Street**: The era of hyper-growth has subsided, but the market is still growing nicely amidst early competition (oligopoly). Hit the market with exciting "process innovation" as customers are looking for systematic product improvements.
- **Mature Main Street**: Your product/service has been highly commoditized and there is strong competition; the growth flattens; your sales revenues are stagnant; your profits are still improving since fixed costs are recovered. It is an indefinite elastic market period. If you want to survive the tough competition, then you must heighten your "experiential innovation" to enrich customer experience and double up "marketing innovation" to increase differentiation.
- **Main Street Decline**: Your technology is obsolete; your product is not responding to current market needs; customers are bored and withdraw to better competing brands. At this juncture, you must pull your remaining levers to fight the declining market: "business model innovation" and "structural innovation."
- **The Fault Line**: Technology obsolescence has struck like an earthquake, exposing the gaping and slippery fault line between what you can sell and what the market desires. Your "survival innovation" strategies will be to buy your competitors (leveraged buy out) or merge with them. With the market nearing the fault line, reinventing the product or radical restructuring of your enterprise may be an option.
- **The End of Life**: Your market has vanished or is quickly vanishing. Hang to your old loyal customers for some solace. Spark fire by some "revival innovation" tactics; if none works, withdraw from the market and focus your resources on new opportunities.

Table 8.9 captures this interaction between the technology adoption line stages with corresponding types of innovation that can support it. The implication of Table 8.9 is that enterprises must mutate their core competencies and products over time to sustain attractive returns despite maturity or decline of the main street markets. At each stage, the management must introduce new types of innovation while deconstructing old processes and old organizational routines. The way to move forward is to aggressively extract resources from old legacy structures and processes and redirect them to serve the new innovation type.

As markets are commoditizing at one point in the value chain, they are, according to Christensen and Raynor (2003), de-commoditizing elsewhere. For instance, in the automobile industry today, normal vehicle maintenance is commoditizing while road side auto services are de-commoditizing. Hence, management must pursue a twofold path of concurrent construction and deconstruction. For construction, the goal is to create the next generation of competitive advantage through appropriate teams of executives, managers, and operators (see Table 8.9, last two columns). The concurrent deconstruction strategy is to withdraw resources stuck in unproductive assets, products, processes, and legacy structures, and redirect them to new technologies, processes, products, markets, and opportunities. Both construction and deconstruction processes should enhance differentiation and productivity. Both are necessary—a differentiation that does not drive customer preference is a liability.

TABLE 8.9   Mapping Types of Innovation with Technology Adoption Life Cycle Stages

Technology adoption cycle	Innovation life cycle	Market response cycle: revenue growth	Executive leader to manage the cycles	Team leader to manage the cycles
Early Market	Disruptive Innovation	The market adopts the new technology; a new tentative market category is created.	CEO: Emphasize technological breakthrough or discontinuity.	Marketing Entrepreneurs: Explore national launch; heavy PR.
The Chasm	Advocacy Innovation: Monitor adoption Forestall failure Welcome feedback Explain defects	The market hesitates, questions the new technology, and faces challenges in adoption.	General Manager: watch market response; withdraw product if chasm deepens and widens.	Marketing Managers: Foresee defects, solicit feedback, honor guarantees, apologize graciously, and repair damage.
Bowling Alley	Application Innovation	The initial uneasiness subsides; a new permanent market category emanates.	General Manager: Explore new market niches and related niches. Targeting one of them target the rest (as in bowling).	Engineering Manager: Take existing technologies to exploit new markets.
Tornado	Product Innovation	The product hits the market of innovators and early adopters; viral marketing sets in and the market blows up.	General Manager: Focus on performance improvement, cost-reduction, and more user-friendliness.	Engineering Manager: Focus on performance improvement, cost-reduction, and more user-friendliness.
Main Street (Early)	Process Innovation	The new category market moves to early main street.	VP for Operating: Make all processes more efficient and effective.	Operations Manager: Improve process performance at all levels.
Main Street (Mature)	Experiential Innovation	Competition is getting strong; consumers are bargain-hunting looking for the best experience.	VP Marketing: Focus on the total customer experience.	Customer Service Manager: Improve customer service at all levels.
	Marketing Innovation	Consumers are looking for differentiation in quality, price, and service.	VP Marketing: Focus on product and service differentiation.	Marketing Manager: Train and place skilled front line ambassadors for the product.
Main Street (Declining)	Business Model Innovation	Main street market is declining; customers are getting bored; they look for product newness.	CEO: Redesign the product or reframe the market.	General Marketing Manager: Enable redesigning the product or reframing the market.
	Structural Innovation	Customers are looking for a break before quitting your product.	CEO: Capitalize on deregulation or structural market changes to improve the product service.	General Manager: Cash cows fast; stem market decline; focus resources to improve product performance.
Fault Line	Survival Innovation	A sudden market withdrawal due to fierce competing products.	Marketing Manager: Save the decline; save the product; revamp the market.	Marketing Manager: Save the decline; save the product; revamp the market.
End of Life	Revival Innovation	Hard line customers may still patronize the product for nostalgic reasons.	VP Marketing: Phase out or withdraw the product if necessary.	Marketing Manager: Phase out the product quietly without hurting existing brands.

Source: Author's own.

Note: see also Geoffrey Moore (2004).

It is important to recognize that differentiation-creating innovation and productivity-creating deconstruction must be conducted in tandem. If you try the former without the latter, the inertia demon defeats you. If you try the latter without the former, you do nothing to overcome the forces of de-commoditization. (Moore 2004: 92)

Good CEOs do not back down from risk; they embrace it. Good and effective CEOs do not write policies; they write histories.

INNOVATION MARGINS

[See Hamel and Getz (2004: 76–84)]

A company should be able to raise the yield of its innovation investments substantially in order to justify such investments in an age of capital austerity. Achieving such a step function needs much more than just a bit of belt tightening of R&D budgets. It demands a fundamentally new way of thinking about innovation productivity, as well as a set of strategies that have the power to deliver more bang for every innovation buck (Hamel and Getz 2004: 78).

Both J. M. Juran and Edwards Deming argued that companies can reap big rewards by investing in the problem-solving skills of rank-and-file employees. That is, innovation belongs to every department and division of the firm, and not only to the R&D or new product development departments, and not restricted to the few imaginative geniuses in the company. Most executives not only fail to capitalize on the intellect of their employees, they waste a substantial share of their imagination. The cheapest way to tap innovation in your firm is to ask your employees for new ideas.

Cemex, the highly innovative Mexican cement maker, devotes nine days each year for harvesting employee ideas. Each of these innovation days focuses on a particular business or function. In preparation for this event, a sponsoring VP personally invites hundreds of employees to submit ideas around a chosen theme for developing novel customer solutions or for dramatically improving cost-efficiency. Cemex categorizes new ideas into four groups:

- **Stars** (big and valuable ideas that could be implemented immediately).
- **Balls** (valuable ideas that need to be bounced around for productivity or market readiness).
- **Apples** (good ideas for incremental improvement that could be put into practice right away).
- **Bones** (ideas that seem interesting but have little meat to them).

W. L. Gore, a $1.35 billion (2003) Newark, Delaware-based company that employs 6,000 people, has a flat organizational structure. There are no directors, no managers, no titles, and virtually no hierarchy. Employees are "associates" that do not have bosses; they have sponsors. Every associate can allocate 10 percent of one's time to innovate new ideas for the company. When a good idea emerges, it is up to the innovator to recruit colleagues to support its development. Gore refers to its organizational structure as a "lattice." Gore's "innovation democracy" has propelled the company into areas as diverse as fuel cells, medical devices, sealants, dental floss, and guitar strings. Thus, innovation can come from anyone and anywhere.

The company places a premium on serendipity. Gore's signature product, Gore-Tex, sprang from serendipity. Hoping to create a low-cost plumber's tape, Bob Gore, the founder's son and the company's current chairman, stretched a piece of polytetrafluoroethylene (PTFE) and discovered it had some amazing properties. When PTFE was laminated to fabric, the resulting material was waterproof and breathable—a boon to campers, hunters, athletes, and many others (Hamel and Getz 2004: 79).

A. G. Laffey, chairman of P&G, has challenged his company to source half its innovations from outside the company (e.g., buying technology, patents; outsourcing innovations, joint ventures; strategic alliances), up from roughly 20 percent. P&G's current success product, Swifter mop, used technology purchased from a Japanese competitor.

Not all radical innovations are risky. Risky investments are uncertain and expensive. Some radical ideas, like fusion power or nuclear power, are risky, but many are not. For instance, Starbucks debit card has an idea which is radical but not risky. Daily coffee drinkers were happy to pay their daily dose of caffeine weeks or months in advance, rather than wait longer at checking counters. Its technology (magnetic stripe debit card) was simple and well proven, and the idea could have been easily test marketed before rollout. The payoff was big. The card was launched in November 2001; within the first two months, Starbucks booked more than $60 million in prepayments. Since then, more than 30 million cards have been sold, and currently account for more than 15 percent of Starbucks sales.

Dramatic change always creates opportunities for radical innovation. Discontinuities in technology, demographics, lifestyle, regulation, and geo-politics can often be the launching pad for radical innovation. A recent major demographic trend in the U.S. is the steady increase in the number of single-person households. Apart from a microwave oven well-suited to such households, the household appliance industry has ignored this trend. The typical large dishwasher, for instance, is meant for large family households. At Whirlpool, a cross-company team studied the changing demographics and came up with Briva, a small in-sink dishwasher, convenient to use as a microwave oven. Briva can wash and dry a small load of dishes in less than five minutes. Incidentally, at Whirlpool, all 15,000 and more salaried employees are required to complete a two-hour online course on the basics of business innovation. They are also encouraged to contact the more than 500 innovation mentors across the company who have received extensive training in how to develop, test, and validate new ideas. It is a great way to equip your employees with skills to innovate.

TiVo is another example of radical innovations that responded to dramatic changes to busy single-person homes. You push a button, and you can record any show you like and then watch it any time you like. TiVo has made the experience of watching TV much like the experience of reading a magazine. You rarely read the magazine with all its contents and ads in one shot; you do it when you want. Briva and TiVo are good examples of a disciplined use of analogy. What if a dishwasher was more like a microwave oven? What if watching TV were more like reading a magazine? Analogical thinking can bring long ignored problems into sharp focus and point the way to radical solutions (see also, Gavetti and Rivkin 2005; Mascarenhas, Kesavan, and Bernacchi 2005a).

Consider Linux, the other operating system that Microsoft has been fighting against. In 2001, Linux had more than 30 million lines of source code, representing something like 8,000 person-years of development time. If these developers were highly skilled software engineers of a company, the development costs of Linux would have exceeded well over a billion dollars. Instead, it was created by volunteers on open standards—a development model even more efficient than outsourcing. Linux is a very strong competing operating system to Microsoft. IBM has adopted it—and it is now at the heart of its enterprise-computing strategy. Similarly, Epic Games, Digital Extremes, and NVIDIA, creators of the popular Unreal Tournament game, developed the game by enrolling thousands of their customers in a virtual development network. These game companies sponsored a $1 million competition that rewards individuals from around the world for innovative and enriching add-ons to the game.

Consider the race in the hybrid industry of energy-efficient cars. In the early 1990s, GM bet on big electric vehicles and chose to build the EV1, an egg-shaped, all-electric, zero-emissions vehicle. Launched with extravagant fanfare in 1996, EV1 was soon a commercial bust. After spending $1 billion on the project and producing only 700 units, the CEO pulled the plug by 1999. On the other hand, the Toyota Prius was a great success at Toyota because it pursued energy efficiency with a consistent strategy. After a multi-year development program, Toyota introduced the Prius in Japan in 1997, and later in the U.S.A, as an eco-friendly car. In 2003, Toyota sold more than 50,000 hybrid vehicles and planned to sell 300,000 annually during 2005–10. Consistency does not mean spending increasing amounts in innovation; it must mean specifying clearly your innovation goals, step up your investment if the innovation shows hope, and be sure your investments are profitable in the long run.

A careful analysis of hyper-efficient innovators reveals five indicators and imperatives (in the form of ratios) for boosting innovation margins:

1. **Raise the ratio of innovators to the total number of employees**: The higher the percentage of innovators in your company, whatever their formal job description, the higher the innovation yield. A good innovative company should have at least 30 percent innovators among its employees. You should achieve this ratio not necessarily from hiring innovators from outside, but from developing and training from among your employees in innovation processes or events. Ensure all employees are given the time, tools, and the space to be creative and innovative.

2. **Raise the ratio of radical innovations to incremental innovations**: The higher this ratio, the higher the innovation payoff. Incremental innovations such as retreads, updates, brand extensions, add-ons are good, but radical innovations (those that yield the biggest innovation payoffs and drive above average growth) drive a company's hotline growth. Radical innovations change customer expectations and behaviors (e.g., PayPal), change the basis of competitive advantage (e.g., what digital camera did to Sony and the photographic film industry; what iPod and iTunes did to Apple and the music industry), and changes industry economics (e.g., Southwest Airlines changed the airline industry economics).

3. **Raise the ratio of externally sourced innovations to internally sourced innovations**: The better a company is at harnessing ideas and energies from outsiders, the better its return on innovation investments. P&G does this routinely. This is how Linux was developed. This is how the very popular epic computer game, the Unreal Tournament, was developed. Regardless of how creative and innovative your innovators may be, there could be more innovation potential outside the company than within it. Currently, this is very evident in the outside online world of software hackers, music re-mixers, video producers, eBay auctions, and bloggers. Typical outside sources are licensing technology, polling lead users for new ideas, outsourcing R&D to universities, joining research consortia, and open standards.

4. **Raise the ratio of learning over investment in innovation projects**: The more efficient a company is at exploring new opportunities, learning much while risking little, the more effective will be its innovation efforts. Learning is achieved by successful experimentation. Unlike product testing that is product-focused, strategic experiments are business model-focused; they seek to explore the merits of a number of inter-related changes to a company's business model. Strategic

experiments are designed to create opportunities for iterative learning. Their basic principle is, "do not kill a great idea prematurely" (i.e., reduction of Type II or beta error). Product testing does the opposite: it typically winnows out unproductive ideas, with the basic principle, "do not invest on losers" (i.e., reduction of Type I or alpha errors).

5. **Raise the ratio of commitment over the number of key innovation priorities**: A firm that is deeply committed to a relatively small number of broad innovation goals and consistent in that commitment over time, will multiply its innovation resources. When it comes to innovation, consistency counts. Over time, small ideas compound, learning from experimentation accumulates, and competencies grow stronger. Teams develop a collective memory and avoid making the same mistakes twice. With this in mind, a company should commit itself to a relatively small number of medium-term innovation goals. The company should measure its commitment to these goals not by the level of its investment into these goals but by how persistently it pursues success.

In conclusion, competitive evolution has always favored companies that can do more with less, and this is true for innovation as it is for any other corporate functions or activities. To produce more growth per dollar of investment, you must produce more innovation per dollar of investment. That is, the company must parlay meager resources into radical, growth-generating innovation. It must learn to innovate boldly and consistently despite austerity (Hamel and Getz 2004: 84).

STUDY THE MARGINS OF THE FIRM

From the analysis thus far, we should be able to study and monitor the margins of the company. We should be able to determine which margins matter and are critical. That is, we should identify everything that has little to do with the margin-generating part of the business, regardless of effect on the revenues (Sutton 2002: 7). Thus one should:

- Identify key customers from cheap whining customers.
- Identify big accounts that generate most of your profits.
- Identify the major creditors, vendors, leaseholders, and mortgagers.
- Identify marginal performers (products, services, departments, people, and divisions) in the company.
- Identify and strengthen the winners.
- Identify where you can cut costs, especially on expensive administrative overheads.

We must be able to define and defend the margins, and specialize where the margin lives. Identify where we can cut costs by raising quality. Quality leads to money. Quality saves advertising dollars, returned products, warranty and guarantee service charges, bad feelings, and the cost of redoing the entire product (Sutton 2002: 228). The critical margins help to keep the most promising new development going, and stop spending on fuzzy ones. Manufacturing, marketing, and retailing divisions may have to be reshaped and redesigned in the process.

One should interview the CEO, and then the CFO, and all the VPs, asking each individual what the problem was and what their solution is. Meet them soon together, and feed them back with the problems and solutions of other leaders in the company.

EXTERNAL SOURCING OF INNOVATIONS

[See Nambisan and Sawhney (2007: 109–19)]

- P&G's recent new product development strategy includes "Connect + Develop" in which the company uses online R&D marketplaces and other innovation intermediaries to identify and acquire ideas and technologies from independent innovators.
- Intel's Intel Capital is the chip maker's new tool for investing in technology start-ups outside the company and for buying and developing them to enrich its core products.
- Nokia's Concept Lounge is an interactive forum to search and acquire innovative and futuristic product concepts directly from independent designers.

All three are great current examples of sourcing innovation from outside the company. Notwithstanding these success stories, most companies find it challenging to shop for innovation offerings that will develop their core business. There is no single best method yet for sourcing innovation externally. Based on interviews with senior managers of more than 30 major companies that in-source innovations from outside the organization, Nambisan and Sawhney (2007) offer some practical guidelines for optimizing the in-sourcing process.

First, the "innovation bazaar" can be characterized as a continuum with raw or patent-pending ideas on the one end, market-ready ideas in the middle, and market-ready products at the other end. You can shop for relatively raw and undeveloped ideas or new patents and then invest in their development and commercialization. At the other end of the spectrum, you could directly buy market-ready products, services, or process technologies and quickly market them. Right in the middle of the continuum, there are market-ready ideas that need further development and commercialization. In any case, the external sourcing innovation continuum involves four variables:

1. The **reach** the companies have as they search for innovations. Reach is the number of options the company is able to consider when buying an innovation.
2. The **cost** of acquiring and developing those ideas.
3. The **risk** involved in converting them into marketable products.
4. The **speed** with which the raw ideas can be brought to the marketplace.

Reach and risk are high for raw ideas, but they exponentially decrease as one seeks market-ready ideas or market-ready products. Similarly, speed and cost are high for market-ready products but they exponentially decrease as one is prepared to settle for market-ready ideas, just raw but patent-ready ideas or even unpatented but good ideas. Figure 8.3 portrays this market phenomenon.

Many companies rely on innovation intermediaries (see Figure 8.3) to find inventors for extending their reach and filtering process. These include:

- **Idea scouts** (e.g., Big Idea Group; Product Development Group) are those who seek and screen ideas in the inventor community on behalf of large firms who then review them for commercial potential. Idea scouts are paid up front and may share royalties paid to the inventor.
- **Patent brokers** are those who bring together inventors and firms that are interested in commercializing their patents, without representing either side.

FIGURE 8.3   The Continuum of External Sourced Innovations

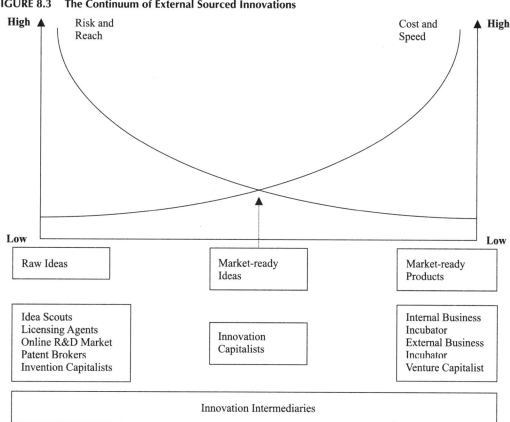

Source: Author's own.

Note: See Nambisan and Sawhney (2007: 109–19).

- **Licensing agents** are those who broker the licensing (rather than the sale) of patented technologies.
- **Invention capitalists** are those who buy patents from the inventors and then sell them to companies, often bundling related patents together.
- **Innovation capitalists (ICs)**: They trade in market-ready ideas. They seek promising ideas and concepts with high commercial potential, identify their inventors, assess the innovations and help the inventors to improve on the ideas and develop them further. Further interaction between ICs and inventors will develop and refine the product. The IC will bring deep industry knowledge and market focus to the product, while the inventor brings new ideas, tools, and techniques, until the marriage blend is a market-ready product. ICs attempt to optimize the four variables—cost, reach, risk, and speed (see Figure 8.3). Examples of ICs include Evergreen IP, Igniter IP.
- **Online R&D marketplaces** (e.g., InnoCentive, NineSigma, and yet2.com) can help match companies with promising ideas or patents. Eli Lilly, a pharmaceutical company, has spearheaded InnoCentive (www.innocentive.com), a solution-seeking website that Lilly, P&G, and other companies use to find answers to specific technical or scientific problems.

- **University-affiliated business incubators**: These invest in or nurture new products or ventures with the aim of readying them for acquisition by large firms (e.g., IDEO at Stanford University). Some venture capitalists also incubate market-ready products.

For instance, Staples, the office-supplies retailer, has been aggressively repositioning itself by seeking innovation intermediaries for developing its own private label products rather than merely sell branded or generic products.

Ever since A. G. Lafley took over P&G as CEO in early 2000, the company has also started sourcing innovation ideas from outside, developing them and taking then to the market as P&G branded products. Lafley argued that P&G could not and should not source all its innovations from within. After five years of investment, P&G now has a state-of-the-art process for sourcing innovation ideas externally, which includes a global network of resources and online knowledge-exchange sites. P&G acquired in 2001 from Nottingham-Spirk, its small product invention and development group, the SpinBrush Company, that made low-cost, battery-operated toothbrushes. The product was market ready, but the price tag was high, it being around $450 million, but it was a great success product line for P&G. The process of sourcing raw ideas externally complements P&G's core competency in executing ideas. P&G sales and profits have been up by 42 percent and 84 percent, respectively, over the past five years (Hansen and Birkinshaw 2007: 122).

Salesforce.com opened in January 2007 its first AppExchange incubator in San Mateo, CA, near its headquarters in San Francisco. Partner companies rent space there for about $20,000 a year, gaining access not only to communications and other infrastructure but also to technical, business, and market support. The primary purpose of this incubator is to enable the partner companies to develop applications that complement Salesforce.com's core technology platform. Meanwhile, Salesforce.com can also cherry-pick innovative applications for future acquisitions.

Intuit, the maker of the financial software programs Quicken and QuickBooks, is to import lot of raw ideas but had low skills for bringing those ideas to the market. When in January 2000 Stephen Bennett joined Intuit, he fixed this weakness. He demanded that clear business objectives be set for ideas in development, and he held people accountable for delivering on them. Intuit is now more market focused, equally imports and generates new ideas and bring them quickly to the market. Intuit's revenues and profits were up by 47 percent and 65 percent respectively from 2003, in part because of this effort (Hansen and Birkinshaw 2007: 122).

AGGRESSIVE MARKETING

If the company lacks internal innovation capabilities but its aim is to respond rapidly to market demand by introducing many new products and services, then as a CEO you could consider the following:

- Shopping for many raw ideas or patent-ready concepts implies your costs and reach of collecting these ideas is low, but it also implies that you must have a large capital and high new product developing skills to quickly and effectively develop these raw ideas, market test them, and roll them out. Not all raw ideas may reach the market.
- Shopping for a few market-ready ideas or concepts implies you have enough capital to buy and develop them and moderately high product developing skills to quickly and effectively commercialize these ideas, market test them, and launch them nationally or globally.

- Shopping for just one or two market-ready products implies you have large capital to acquire them and that you have a wide and effective distribution network to market them. Often, this strategy may imply buying not just the market-ready product but also the company that developed it. In which case, you may buy too much baggage of the company that you may have to discard at a cost (e.g., its sales force, commercialization infrastructure).

Table 8.10 suggests various strategy dimensions that one should consider in choosing among these three options. Under all three scenarios, one must address:

TABLE 8.10   Choosing your Innovation Sourcing Strategy

	Innovation sourcing		
Strategy dimensions	*Raw ideas patent-ready ideas*	*Market-ready ideas*	*Market-ready products and services*
Internal Innovation Capabilities	Low	Low	Low
Internal Innovation, Product Development Capabilities	High	Moderate	Low
Internal Marketing and Distribution Capabilities	High	High	High
Product Portfolio	Large number of diverse products	Products in a few key markets and industries	Products and services that expand, enhance, and update existing products
Core Objective	To connect as many companies with relevant raw ideas	To connect as many companies with relevant market-ready ideas	To connect as many companies with relevant market-ready products
Purpose of Innovation	Enhancement of existing products with raw ideas	Extension of brands and product lines with market-ready ideas	Exploring new product and service lines, new markets, and new product portfolios
Core Function	To create a brokering infrastructure in the ideas market	To create a networking infrastructure to find and develop market-ready ideas	To create a networking infrastructure to find and distribute market-ready products
Capital Investment	Low	Medium	High
Risk Assumed	High	Medium	Low
Intellectual Property Rights	Low unless patent-ready ideas	Moderate and shared between inventor and developer	High and bought or shared from the inventor
Market Potential	Around US$100 million	Around US$250 million	Around US$500 million
Cost of Evaluating Innovations	Low per raw idea; high across many ideas	Medium per market-ready idea; high across many such ideas	Low per market-ready product
Information Required to Develop Typical Innovation	Specific knowledge about each raw idea	Integrated knowledge from several involved business areas	If the product is acquired with the company, then information asymmetries of typical mergers and acquisitions
Innovation Portfolio	Weak, diffused, and long term given dependence on raw ideas from outside sources	Medium, complementary, supplementary, and with sustainable competitive advantage if market focused	Strong, focused, and immediate if product and company acquired match buyer's core business

Source: Author's own.

Note: See also Nambisan and Sawhney (2007: 114–16).

- **Complementary Issues**: When importing innovations externally, companies must consider their existing skills and processes for developing these innovations, pinpoint their unique challenges, and uniquely place and promote them in the marketplace.
- **Scaling Issues**: Whether a product can be manufactured cost-effectively in large quantities.
- **Incubation Issues**: Can you incubate these ideas or concepts within the company early before they are market-ready products? This in-house incubation will enable you to have close look at the innovative concepts or business before acquiring them.
- **Optimization Issues**: Wherever in the spectrum you are, try to optimize on reach, risk, cost, and speed.
- **Diffusion Issues**: What is your company strategy to diffuse the innovation through your company and its constituencies so that they all support and market your new product? Who is your "idea evangelist" to preach the good word about your new or emerging products or business concepts? Who will help launch this product in the nation and the globe?
- **Performance Issues**: Define and implement new key performance indicators focusing on specific deliverables from each link in the innovation value chain (see the following).

Salesforce.com, a leading producer of enterprise software applications for customer relationship management (CRM), has adopted both the marketplace and the incubation approach. In January 2006, Salesforce.com created the AppExchange, an online marketplace for software products from external developers that would complement the company's own product lines. It has been a great success. The AppExchange currently lists more than 500 on-demand applications ranging from finance to HRM to CRM. Salesforce.com's customers can browse these applications, try them out, and buy them from independent developers.

THE INNOVATION VALUE CHAIN

Innovation challenges differ from firm to firm. Do not assume that all organizations face the same obstacles to innovating and developing new products, services, or lines of business. The innovation value chain (IVC) is a sequential three-phase process that involves idea generation, idea development, and the diffusion of developed concepts. Across each phase, innovation managers must perform six critical tasks—internal sourcing, cross-unit sourcing, external sourcing, selection, development, and company-wide spread of the idea. Each is a link in the IVC. "The strength of your IVC is the strength of its weakest links." You must take an end-to-end view of your innovation efforts, and identify the strongest and the weakest links. Importing innovations from outside should reinforce your strongest links and strengthen your weakest links (Hansen and Birkinshaw 2007: 121–22).

Before importing innovative ideas from outside the organization, companies should consider their innovation value chain, its strongest links, its weakest links, and consider how they can exploit them for strengthening, complementing, or supplementing weakest links, and taking them to the marketplace. Any idea import should complement, supplement, strengthen, and reinforce all the links in your IVC, especially focusing on the weakest links. Michael Porter's value chain does exactly this—it supports the entire IVC. In Table 8.11, we feature the integrated flow of the IVC as described by Hansen and Birkinshaw (2007: 124). Identify the weakest links in your IVC. Often paucity of promising raw ideas can be your weakest link.

TABLE 8.11 The Innovation Value Chain: An Integrated Flow

Crucial questions	Raw innovation idea generation			Conversion to market-ready ideas and market-ready products		Diffusion
	Internal unit sourcing	Inter-departmental pollination	External sourcing	Screening, selection, and testing	Rapid development to enter the market	Company-wide support and promotion of the new fledgling product
Key Inquiry	Does the unit generate enough promising raw ideas?	Does the company create good innovative ideas by cross-unit collaboration?	Do we import enough good raw ideas from external sources?	Is the company good at screening, selecting, funding, testing, and funding good ideas?	Is the company good at converting ideas into good products, core businesses, and best practices?	Is the company good at diffusing new ideas and products across the company?
Key Strategy	What is our basic strategy to generate enough promising raw ideas internally?	What is our basic strategy (e.g., ongoing dialog; knowledge exchange) to create good innovative ideas by cross-business-unit collaboration?	What is our basic strategy to import enough good raw ideas from external sources? How do we network with sources suggested in Table 8.1C?	What are our basic tools and techniques to screen, select, fund, and test good new product ideas?	What is our basic strategy to convert ideas into good products, core businesses, and best practices?	What is our basic strategy to diffuse new ideas and products across the company?
Key Metric	The number of high-quality raw ideas, the unit generated in the last two years.	The number of high-quality raw ideas the cross-unit collaboration generated in the last two years.	The number of high-quality raw ideas you tapped from external sources.	Percentage of all ideas generated that were finally screened, selected, and funded.	Percentage of screened, selected, and funded ideas that lead to significant revenues and profits within the first year of product launch.	The rate of penetration into company departments, target markets, channels, and other promotional centers.
Key Corrective Mechanism	If our key metric is not fully realized, then what can the company strategize to rectify the weakness?	If our key metric is not fully realized, what then can the company strategize to rectify the weakness?	If our key metric is not fully realized, what then can the company strategize to rectify the weakness?	If our key metric is not fully realized, what can the company do to rectify the weakness?	If our key metric is not fully realized, what can the company strategize to rectify the weakness?	If our key metric is not fully realized, then what can the company strategize to rectify the weakness?
Key Control System	How can we continuously check that our corrective mechanism works in the desired direction?	How can we continuously check that our corrective mechanism works in the desired direction?	How can we continuously check that our corrective mechanism works in the desired direction?	How can we continuously check that our corrective tools and techniques work in the desired direction?	How can we continuously check that our corrective mechanism works in the desired direction?	How can we continuously check that our corrective mechanism works in the desired direction?

Source: Author's own.

Note: See also Hansen and Birkinshaw (2007: 124)

New raw ideas and concepts cannot succeed without proper screening and funding mechanisms. Improper screening skills and a shortage of seed money for high-risk projects can create bottlenecks, innovation silos, and paralyze innovativeness in the company. Further, no matter how well-screened and funded raw idea projects are, they must still be turned into revenue-generating processes, products, and services. Thirdly, concepts that have been sourced, screened, funded, and developed still need to be bought-in by the rest of the company, its suppliers, its creditors, its target customers, distributors, and retailers—in short, by its "innovation ecosystem" (Adner 2006; Afuah and Bahram 1995). An early universal buy-in from these constituencies can shorten and augment the new product development cycle.

Radical ideas do not start as surefire bets. A great idea becomes a commercial success through a recursive process of experimentation and learning. At the start, it is not always easy to discern if a new idea is smart or stupid. Hence, low-cost under-the-radar experimentation is important; it allows a company to fully explore the potential of a radical new idea by pre-checking market access and acceptance, technical feasibility, pricing, and cost economics. Experimentation helps avoiding the kind of expensive risk-taking that so often gives innovation a bad name (Hamel and Getz 2004: 82–83).

An excellent example of cross-unit collaboration is P&G's cross-functional new product unit. For instance, P&G developed Olay Daily Facials (a face cream that is an excellent cleanser and moisturizer) using a cross-functional team where experts from P&G's skin care, tissue and paper towel, and detergents and fabric softener groups joined. Their combined knowledge about surfactants, substrates, and fragrances generated the concept of Olay Daily Facials, a very successful product. P&G has over 30 such collaborative units.

A great example of an "idea evangelist" for diffusing new products is the European launch of Sara Lee's Sanex soap and shower products in the early 1990s. Sanex was first developed in Spain. It quickly penetrated the bath and shower segment market to assume leadership as a "healthy skin" concept. Sara Lee appointed Martin Muñoz, the president of the Southern European division of Sara Lee and a creator of Sanex, to be the product evangelist for Sanex in the rest of Europe. However, given the highly decentralized structure of Sara Lee in Western Europe made Muñoz's job very difficult. By sheer dint of perseverance and personal crusade, Muñoz visited Sara Lee's senior managers all over Europe and after two full years of evangelization managed to win them and their markets in four countries (the U.K., Denmark, Germany, and France). Thereafter, Sara Lee introduced Sanex in 29 other countries through similar evangelism and for several years was Sara Lee's best selling brand in the household and body care division.

Managers adopting the IVC will need to cultivate new roles for employees. For instance, team members at Siemen's Silicon Valley unit are external scouts, seeking and sourcing good ideas externally. At P&G, product developers and scientists assume the idea of internal idea brokers, dialoguing with colleagues across the company on devising new ways of combining technologies from different parts of the company to develop new products and businesses. At Shell, Leo Rodhart and the members of his GameChanger team act as internal value capitalists, funding and overseeing new ideas.

UNPACKING CREATIVITY

[See Unsworth (2001: 289–97)]

Two questions underlie engagement in the creative process: (*a*) Why do people engage in creative activity? (*b*) What is the initial state of the trigger? The first question involves the drivers for idea generation. These drivers could be "internal" or self-determined, or "external" or market-determined (e.g., job, R&D, customer need). The second question involves the degree of problem formulating needed at the starting point of the creative process. Some problems could be totally "open", unformulated, and unresolved whose solution needs to be invented or discovered, or the problems could be "closed" whose solutions or method to solutions are known. From the external–internal, open–closed categories, emerge four types (see the following) of creativity types illustrated in Table 8.12.

- **Response Creativity**: Externally driven and closely specified problem creativity. The individual has least control over problem-solving choices and individual autonomy is limited. The more external the drive, the more external are the constraints. In general, higher the constraints lesser the creativity. Creativity is focused on a closed problem and external constraint. Focus group creativity in organizational setting is responsive creativity. Routine occupational creativity whereby researchers, engineers, architects, scientists, and other professions solve day-to-day customer or client problems using given methods and procedures is also responsive creativity.
- **Expected Creativity**: Externally driven but open self-discovered problem creativity. The individual has some control over problem-solving choices. Individual autonomy is less limited. Creating artwork such as paintings, sculptures, poems, melodies, harmony, aesthetics, collages,

TABLE 8.12   Matrix of Creativity Types

Sources of creativity ⟶		Drivers for engagement	
		External	**Internal**
		Market determined, e.g., competition, technological obsolescence, new technologies, new customer lifestyles, new customer needs, new legal requirements, demands of globalization	Self-determined, e.g., cash flow problems, insolvency, lack of innovation, cost overruns, revenue decline, employee morale, slack, waste, apathy, corporate culture
Problem Type	**Open**	**Expected Creativity:**	**Proactive Creativity:**
	Unformulated and unresolved problems whose solution needs to be invented or discovered	(Required solutions to discovered problems.)	(Volunteered solutions to discovered problems, e.g., unprompted suggestions.)
		Examples: Creating artwork; ethanol, natural gas, solar systems, windmills, wave-power as alternative sources of energy.	Examples: Day-light saving, home generators, candle light, reduced consumption as alternative solutions to energy crisis.
	Closed	**Responsive Creativity:**	**Contributory Creativity:**
	Problems whose solutions or methods to solutions are known	(Required solutions to specified problems, e.g., responses produced by think tank.)	(Volunteered solutions to specified problems, e.g., contribution by non-project member.)
		Examples: Batteries, flashlights, sun-roofs, kerosene, diesel, … as alternative sources of light.	Examples: Go to bed early; family gathering under one light, candle-light dinners, reduced wattage, … as alternative sources of light.

Source: Author's own.

Note: See Unsworth (2001).

and the like belong to this realm of expected creativity. The artist is externally (e.g., demand, money, project) driven but has many avenues to seek solution.

- **Contributory Creativity**: Internally (self-determined) driven activity along clearly formulated problems is contributory, since most responses involve helping behaviors. Examples: an employee volunteering to solve another employee's problem; corporations volunteering to solve community problems; cause-related marketing; all volunteering. This is the zone of incremental innovation.
- **Proactive Creativity**: Internally (self-determined) driven activity along new, open, and freshly discovered problems. It is proactive in the sense problems are foreseen rather than reacted to. This is the most productive zone of creativity. Market and technological breakthroughs occur here, as do radical innovations. Taking personal initiatives are instances of proactive creativity. "Taking charge" is more innovative activity geared toward implementation. If the problem is only discovered, but not studied, then much problem (market and environment) scanning needs to be done in proactive creativity.

These are four types of creativity, and not levels of creativity. When focusing on levels, the dimensions (internal–external, closed–open) may not be "orthogonal" to each other; indeed, at a more abstract level any two dimensions may be driven by a third common factor. For example, an internally-driven closed problem could be sourced by a common external constraint. Further, no problem is entirely open or closed; no need is entirely internal or external. Hence, the four types of creativity are four *differential continua* rather than exclusive zones.

All four types can help new product design and development. New product development (NPD) is responsive if the designer was given explicit specifications and methodologies. NPD is expected if the specifications were not formulated. NPD is contributory if the problem was specified but not within the designer's role. Finally, NPD can be proactive if internally determined problem solutions are found for unformulated customer problems. Hence, the situational context in which creativity occurs must be considered (Amabile 1998).

Creativity is concerned with the generation of new ideas, whereas, innovation is also concerned with the implementation of new ideas. Creativity also looks into the process and behavior of creativity, while innovation is more outcome-focused. All four types of creativity need motivation (internal) and incentives (external); but proactive activity needs most motivation and internal dynamism (e.g., curiosity, invention, discovery, creation).

Constraints of time, cost, talent, energy, anxiety, dead lines, labor, and unions can constrain all four types of creativity, and mostly, these constraints can paralyze proactive creativity.

THE ROLE OF INFORMATION DIFFUSION ON INNOVATION

Innovation evolves over time and thus requires the use of knowledge in a dynamic setting. Market knowledge diffusion is a function of information acquisition, which is shaped over time by the dynamics of product diffusion and the firm's previous innovation activities. In this context, Marinova (2004) examines longitudinally (and cross-sectionally as previous literature did) the evolution of market knowledge, innovation, and performance over time. Market knowledge diffusion is conceptualized as a function of market knowledge level, change in market knowledge, and shared market knowledge among strategic decision makers. If markets are constantly changing (Hunt and Morgan 1995), and if innovation drives change and form success (Schumpeter 1942), then market knowledge, change in market knowledge, and shared market knowledge should enhance innovation effort.

- **Market Knowledge**: The two most salient features of a competitive market are customers and competitors. Hence, market knowledge must relate to customers and competitors. A decision maker who can correctly identify customer preferences and competitor moves has market knowledge. Market knowledge is necessary for determining the customer needs and wants of target markets and to satisfy them better than the competitors.
- **Market Knowledge Change**: Magnitude of knowledge change (absolute change, and not direction of change) in relation to customers and competitors between two points in time. Change in market knowledge may be viewed as adjustment to inaccuracies of current knowledge in relation to customers and competitors compared with "objective" reality in the market and brought about by new information or knowledge integration across different market aspects.
- **Shared Market Knowledge**: It is knowledge in terms of facts, concepts, and propositions simultaneously diffused, shared, and understood by multiple agents within the firm.

All three levels of knowledge impact innovation. Knowledge as accumulation of strategic information increases the capacity of organizations to interpret new information, especially if the latter is related to the accumulated knowledge. Hence, market knowledge has a positive effect on innovation effort.

The product is a variable tailored to changing needs of carefully selected customers. As the customer changes, so must the product, and the organization that provides the product must have built-in flexibility and adaptiveness (Webster 1997: 52). That is, enhancing innovation effort needs constant monitoring of market condition changes in relation to customer preferences or competitors' market strategies and offerings. Hence, both the level of market knowledge, and the absolute positive change from that knowledge are positively related to innovation effort.

Shared knowledge is organizational memory and organizational learning. Organizational interactions generate unique patterns of shared knowledge. A high degree of shared market knowledge among key decision makers intensifies the effect of knowledge on innovation effort. Inaccurate knowledge, however, can hinder innovation activities, delay new product development, and even introduce wrong products into the marketplace.

In conclusion, a firm that has a high level of accurate market knowledge of target customers and competitors, grows continuously in that knowledge, and actively diffuses that knowledge among all decision makers in the firm, is not only poised for great innovation effort, but also for innovations that improve sales, market share, and profitability performance (Marinova 2004).

MANAGEMENT INNOVATION FOR MARKETING INNOVATIONS

[Hamel (2006: 72–84)]

With the proper guidance of the CEO, management innovation can create long-lasting advantage under one or more of the following three conditions:

- **The innovation is based on a novel principle that challenges management orthodoxy**. The radical management principle at the heart of Toyota's capacity for relentless improvement is that its first line employees can be real problem solvers, innovators, and change agents and not merely cogs in a soul-less manufacturing system. While American auto companies relied on staff experts to generate process improvements, Toyota gave every employee the skills, the tools, and the permission to solve problems as they arose and to anticipate new problems before they occurred. Every year, consequently, Toyota has been able to get more out of its ordinary employees than its American competitors. Toyota's real competitive advantage was not the undervalued yen, its docile workforce, its lack of unions, its superior automation, or its Japanese culture as its American rivals have long argued, but "Toyota's ability to harness the intellect of its ordinary first line employees."

- **It is systemic, encompassing a range of processes and methods**. It is difficult for rivals to replicate a web of innovations spanning many management processes and practices. This was the advantage of Whole Foods Market that had grown to 161 stores since 1981 and to $3.8 billion in sales, with the highest profits per square foot in the retailing industry. John Mackey, the founder and CEO, has a unique management philosophy: a community working together to create value for other people. At the Whole Foods Market, the basic unit of analysis is not the store, but small teams that manage departments such as fresh produce, prepared foods, and seafood. Bonuses are paid to teams and not to individuals. Team members have access to comprehensive financial data, including the details of every co-worker's compensation. Executive salaries are capped: no corporate executive can draw a salary more than 14 times the company average. About 94 percent of the stock options are distributed among non-executives. Managers consult these teams on all store-level decisions and accord them a degree of autonomy that is nearly unprecedented in retailing. Each team decides what to stock and can veto new hires. What distinguishes Whole Foods Market is not one innovative management process but a unique system of processes that rivals can emulate but not easily copy.
- **It is part of an ongoing program of innovation, where progress compounds over time**. GE's leadership advantage is not individual product or market breakthrough but the result of a long-standing and unflagging commitment to improve the quality of its management stock—a commitment that regularly spawns new management innovations and methods. Not every management innovation creates competitive advantage. For every one that does, there could be dozens of other innovations that do not. Hence, unflagging innovation is a safe bet. In the long run, the more you innovate, the better are your chances of market success.

THE PROCESS OF MANAGEMENT INNOVATION

Hamel (2006: 80) considers the following 12 business processes as the 21st century's most important or noteworthy management innovations:

1. Scientific management (time and motion studies)
2. Cost accounting and variance analysis
3. The commercial research library: the industrialization of science
4. ROI analysis and capital budgeting
5. Brand management
6. Large-scale project management

7. Divisionalization
8. Leadership development
9. Industry consortia (multi-company collaborative structures)
10. Radical decentralization (self-organization)
11. Formalized strategic analysis
12. Employee-driven problem solving

Each of these management innovations verify three criteria: (*a*) it is a marked departure from previous management practice; (*b*) it confers a competitive advantage on the pioneering company or companies; and (*c*) it can be found in some form in organizations today. Important management innovations that just did not make this list include: business process reengineering, employee stock ownership plans, and accounting management. More recent innovations that appear quite promising are knowledge management, open source development, and internal markets. It may be too early to assess their lasting impact on management practice.

Recently, scientists eager to understand the sub-atomic world have virtually abandoned the certainties of Newtonian physics for the more ambiguous principles of quantum mechanics. It is no different with management innovation. *Novel problems demand novel principles.* Modern management practice is based on a set of century-old principles: specialization, standardization, planning and control, hierarchy, and the primacy of extrinsic rewards. The task of management innovation is to uncover unconventional principles that open up new possibilities for building new capabilities in one's organization and for crafting new leaders with enviable qualities.

This is what Dee Hock did in 1968, then a 38-year old banker in Seattle. The novel problem he faced related to Visa, America's fledgling credit card industry that had then splintered into a number of incompatible, bank-specific franchising systems. The unprecedented problem was how to build a system that would allow banks to cooperate in credit card branding and billing while still fiercely competing for customers. He and a small team brain-stormed for months and drummed up the following novel principles based on the principles of Jeffersonian democracy and biological systems:

1. Power and function in the system must be distributed to the maximum degree possible.
2. The system must be self-organizing.
3. Governance must be distributed.
4. The system must seamlessly blend both collaboration and competition.
5. The system must be infinitely malleable, yet extremely durable.
6. The system must be owned cooperatively and equitably.

After inventing designing, testing a business system based on the above six principles, Hock's team generated the Visa, the world's first nonstick, for-profit membership organization, whose basic product is coordination and service. Table 8.13 compares the old and the new management innovations principles, and their implications.

Whirlpool, the world's largest manufacturer of household appliances, was a good example of serial management innovation. In 1999, when Dave Whitwam was its CEO and chairman, he was frustrated by chronically low levels of brand loyalty for Whirlpool's appliance products. He instituted new management innovation principles with "innovation from everyone, everywhere" being his major slogan. He did not mind his company breaking rules for generating customer-pleasing innovations. He appointed

TABLE 8.13 Old versus New Management Innovation (MI) Principles

Old management innovation		New management innovation		Best industry examples of new MI principles application
Principles	Limitations	Principles	Implications	
Specialization	It limits cross-boundary learning that generates breakthrough ideas. May ignore industry convergence opportunities.	Cross-specialization across functions, competencies, and converging industries.	Integrated knowledge. Integrated management. Cross-functionality. Inter-industry symbiosis. Internal markets. Industry consortia.	Microsoft, GE, Intel, Sony, Kodak, Fuji, Toyota, BMW
Standardization	It leads to unhealthy affection for conformance. It sees the new and the whacky as dangerous deviations from the norm. Tendency to commoditize brands and services.	Customize, personalize, and individualize your products and services. Treat your market as one unique person. Mass customization for scale economies.	Modern technology (Internet, e-mail, broadband) makes customization and individualization easy and cost-effective. Open source development.	eBay, Adobe, Linux, Google, Yahoo!, Amazon.com, MSN.com, Travelocity.Com, Expedia.com, Priceline.com
Planning and Control	It believes that the environment is friendly, stable, and predictable. Past conditions the future. Too much investment in the past, and not in the future.	Transit from certain Newtonian physics to ambiguous quantum mechanics that better reflects today's volatile environment.	Turbulent, highly volatile, and tech-driven environment is very uncertain, risky, and unpredictable. Hence, the new business system must be infinitely malleable, yet extremely durable.	Visa, MasterCard, Discover, GMAC, Ford Credit, BCBS, Costco, Wal-Mart
Vertical Hierarchy	Deference to hierarchy and positional power breeds bureaucracy and reinforces outmoded power structures and belief systems. Bureaucracy can smother the flames of innovation.	Horizontal hierarchy or community empowerment. Power and function in the system must be distributed to the maximum degree possible. Governance must be distributed.	The system must seamlessly blend both collaboration and competition. Radical decentralization. Divisionalization. Customer co-option. Customer involvement.	McDonalds, Whole Foods Market, Home Depot, Best Buy, Circuit City, Whirlpool, Habitat for Humanity, Wikipedia
Fight Competition	Fire-fighting competition is a loss-loss or zero sum game. Fighting competition may impair you to identify and exploit new markets and new business opportunities.	Collaborate to compete. Disregard competition as irrelevant and explore new markets, new innovations, and "new blue oceans" (Kim and Mauborgne 2005).	Strategic collaborative alliances between competitors for core processes and core products, but competition for end products.	Southwest Airlines, Starbucks, FedEx, UPS, Cirque du Soleil, Apple's iPod and iTunes, Sony's PlayStations
Primacy of Extrinsic Rewards	A disproportionate emphasis on monetary rewards can discount the power of volunteerism and self-organization as mechanisms for aligning individual effort.	Primacy of intrinsic rewards. Job experience is great. The system must be self-organizing. The system must be owned cooperatively and equitably.	Employee stock ownership plans. Internal markets. Radical decentralization. Employee driven problem solving.	HP, Microsoft, Dell, Whole Foods Market, Saturn, Toyota, Credit Unions

Source: Author's own.

Note: See also Hamel (2006: 72–84).

Nancy Snyder, an innovation czar, as corporate VP, who rallied her colleagues around what would become a five year quest to reinvent the company's management processes. Key management innovations included (Hamel 2006: 76):

- Making innovations a central topic in Whirlpool's leadership development program.
- Substantial capital budgeting each year for very innovative projects.
- Every product development plan must include a sizable component of new-to-market innovation.
- Training more than 600 innovation mentors charged with encouraging innovation throughout the company.
- Enrolling every salaried employee in an online course on business innovation.
- Establishing innovation as a large part of top management's long-term bonus plan.
- Quarterly assessment of innovation outcomes of each business unit.
- Building an innovation portal that would give full access to all Whirlpool employees throughout the world.
- Developing a set of metrics to track and assess innovation inputs (e.g., number of engineering hours) to innovation throughputs (e.g., number of new ideas entering the company's innovation pipeline or portal) to innovation outputs (distinctive products, premium pricing, and customer loyalty).

It took some time for Whirlpool to internalize and implement this innovation program with its novel management innovation principles. The results were obvious. Jeff Fettig, current chairman of Whirlpool, estimates that by 2007, the innovation program will add more than $500 million a year to the company's top line. In a world of accelerated change, continuous management innovation and strategic renewal is the only insurance against irrelevance (Hamel 2006: 78). Change must also start at the top. It takes a strong leader to change a big company. To lead change, you need a very clear agenda. People are mostly against change, and with any change, there will always be winners and losers. A good leader makes change safe for all people concerned (Hamel 2006: 81). "No company can escape the fact that with each passing year, the present is becoming a less reliable guide to the future" (Hamel 2006: 84).

PRODUCT-CENTRIC VERSUS CONSUMER'S EXPERIENCE-CENTRIC INNOVATION

[This section is based on Prahalad and Ramaswamy (2003a, 2003b)]

The rapid spread of cell phones and other mobile devices, websites, and media channels are now enabling consumers to have access to more information and entertainment at greater speed and lower cost than ever before. However, the IT technology explosion has not necessarily resulted in better consumer experiences. However, globalization and ubiquitous connectivity are forcing companies to reexamine how they deliver value to customers. "The ability to reach out and touch customers anywhere, anytime, means that companies must deliver not just competitive products but also unique, real-time customer experiences shaped by the customer context of location, time, and event" (Prahalad and Ramaswamy 2003a).

"The next practices of innovation must shift the focus away from products and services and onto experience environments—supported by a network of companies and consumer communities—to co-create unique value for individual customers" (Prahalad and Ramaswamy 2003b: 12). Technology (e.g. digitization, bio-technology, smart materials) and major discontinuities in the competitive land-scape (e.g., deregulation, globalization, and ubiquitous connectivity) have developed to allow immediate access to an organization's entire value-chain activities, especially through the Internet.

Twenty years ago, a still camera was different from a video camera; a television was different from a computer; a telephone was different from postal mail. Today these different products and the different industries that created them are converging. Today a telephone is also an e-mail device, a text messenger, an electronic organizer, a handheld computer, and a camera. A portable laptop computer can be a television, a radio, an e-mail device, a text messenger, a faxing machine, an electronic organizer, a tele-phone, an electronic typewriter and word processor, an online shopping window, a computing device, a storage device, an entertainment console, and many other things. The distinctions between these pro-ducts, the industries they represent, and even the channels they are distributed by, are all blurring. Similar convergence is taking place in the health care and financial services industries. This development makes consumers informed, connected, active, and seek lasting experiences beyond mere customer satisfaction. Innovation must respond to this consumer change and demand.

How do we create customer value in this convergent digitized world? Product-centric companies believe that they can create value by product variety—this, in turn, leads to a product-centric innovation. While creating product variety is easier today, competing effectively for value through product variety is not. "Value will increasingly have to be co-created with consumers, and innovation must be focused on the co-creation experiences of consumers" (Prahalad and Ramaswamy 2000):

- Consider the OnStar in the field of telematics, widely launched by GMC in 2002—one aspect of which provides mobile information and services to auto drivers and passengers. Because the OnStar is integrated with the vehicle, it has access to all the internal sensors and can continuously monitor the vehicle functions and provide assistance when needed, guided by the satellite data. When a customer locks herself out of her car, OnStar can open the door remotely. When a car's airbag is deployed, OnStar can not only detect the accident but also can assess its severity; when a car is stolen, OnStar can help the police track it down; when a subscriber has an accident, the OnStar service representative contacts the local emergency service and dispatches a police car or ambulance to the scene. Currently, GMC is considering reconfiguring OnStar so that it can pro-vide services beyond those of safety and security to those of information, entertainment, and convenience. For instance, it can direct you to the nearest and best restaurant by nationality (e.g., Chinese, Italian), by status (5 versus 4 stars), by availability (e.g., short versus long waiting time) and, accordingly, make reservations for you. The driver merely has to press a button in the dashboard, and a call center operator will respond. This is a good case of "experience innovation" (Prahalad and Ramaswamy 2003b).

- Consider a cardiac patient who needs a pacemaker that monitors and manages heart rhythm and performance. While this is a great value to the patient, what is an added value is if the perform-ance of the heart was remotely monitored and any significant deviations altered both the doctor and the patient (including the spouse) simultaneously. If the patient was out of town, then his primary physician could suggest the doctor and the hospital he should immediately report to, and the primary physician would simultaneously send all the relevant digitized medical records to the out-of-town doctor so that diagnosis and treatment can be effectively coordinated. In this value-chain process, the value is not in the physical product (pacemaker), or in the communication and IT network that supports the value-chain process, or even in the skills network of doctors, nurses, ambulances, and the family. The value is in the co-creation experience that stems from the patient's interaction with all of these elements. "That is, value-creation is defined by the experience of a specific consumer, at a specific point in time and location, in the context of a specific event. The individual and his interactions define both the experience and the value derived from it" (Prahalad and Ramaswamy 2003b).

Based on these and other similar experience innovations, Table 8.14 distinguishes between traditional product- or company-centric innovations from consumer experience-centric innovations. "The ability to imagine and combine technological capabilities to facilitate experiences will be a key success factor in experience innovation, regardless of industry" (Prahalad and Ramaswamy 2003b: 18). For instance, generations ago the Sony Walkman broadened the consumer's ability to enjoy high-quality stereo music wherever the customer went. Now the digitization and compression of music files combined with the miniaturization of storage capabilities and microprocessors have made entire music collections easily portable.

Similarly, Apple's original iPod provided instant access to over 1,000 songs in a pocket-sized package; the newer version provides access to over 5,000 songs, as do similar competitive products. Both miniaturization and portability are product-specific innovations. Now the electronics entertainment companies must focus on experience-specific innovations. The number of songs, fast accessibility to the songs, and storage of songs is consumer-specific innovations. Further innovations should focus on consumer experience. "A new technology is important to consumers only when it increases

TABLE 8.14 Product-centric versus Consumer Experience-centric Innovations

Dimensions	Product-centric innovation	Consumer experience-centric innovation
Focus of Innovation	Company products and processes	Consumer experience environments
Basis of Value	Products and services	Co-creation experiences
Process of Value Creation	Firms create value through support systems such as suppliers, technology, and employees	Consumers co-create experience based on space, time, event, and communities in conjunction with firms, networking technologies, and social communities
Value-marketing Strategy	Supply-push and demand-pull strategies for firm's offerings	Experience-environment-pull co-creation strategies by the consumers with firms and networking communities
Purpose of Technology Innovation	Production and functionality of product-service features, attributes, and benefits	Co-production and co-functionality of consumer experiences
Mode of Value Production	Technology and systems integration	Consumer's individual and social experience integration
Focus of Supply Chain	Supports fulfillment of products and services	Individual and community experience network supports co-construction of personalized experiences.
Primary Source of Competitive Advantage	*Product space*: cost efficiency, quality and product differentiation and variety	*Solutions space*: Firms accumulated experience to resolve consumer problems.
		Experience space: The customers and their social communities are the locus and focus of innovation and advantage.
Typical Examples	All company- and supply chain-based products, brands, and services	New experience-based innovations such as OnStar, Pacemakers, LEGO Robots

Source: Based on Prahalad and Ramaswamy (2003c).

their personal freedom, makes life more convenient, or facilitates desires experiences" (Prahalad and Ramaswamy 2003b: 19). Accordingly, Sony is currently working to create the capacity for all its devices to be networked with one another so that user interactions are enabled, and simultaneous user sharing of music files is facilitated. The networking technology is central to experience innovation. In fact, interlinked music or text devices can be embedded anywhere—in cars, phones, PDAs, PCs, home stereos, game consoles, televisions, and Walkmans. Apple's new iMusic can network musicians, music libraries, devices, and music enthusiasts thus creating a rich experience environment for users in terms of personalized music, interaction, and information, anywhere, and in any mode.

Another more recent technological capability is "adaptive learning." For instance, Amazon.com computers follows its customer's purchases of books or CDs by content, themes, interests, purchase history, seriousness versus entertainment, and accordingly, suggest complimentary books or CDs as additional shopping cart items or as possible items at the next purchase. The computers use adaptive learning to counsel the customers. Similarly, TiVo's intelligent digital video recorder stores a consumer's personal viewing history, analyzes his tastes and interests, and uses the results to evaluate the programming available on the channels it can access. It then selects programs the consumer will probably like and records them digitally as they are being broadcast for the consumer when he returns to the device—all this without human intervention. This can progressively enrich consumer experience of a personalized video channel.

The intent of experience innovation is not per se to improve upon the product or service, but to enable the co-creation of an environment populated by companies, consumers, and their networks. Personalized experiences are the goal of experience innovation, and product-service innovations are means to that end. From this viewpoint, a new technological capability is meaningful to the extent it improves experiences desired by the consumer.

CONCLUDING REMARKS

Innovation is essential to organizational success. The problem is that it takes both halves of the brain to make it happen, the left-brain business manager as well as the right-brain creativity director. The right-brainers need high visioning and creative skills to foster a culture of curiosity and high risk-taking in the firm—primarily right-brain activities. The former business needs more analytics and metrics to weed non-promising ideas and prototypes, but also encourage and finance innovative market-ready ideas for market success. The right-brains of the firms may not be strong enough to transform intriguing ideas into market-ready products, projects and brands. The firm may also need right-brain marketers to build lasting and bonding relationships with target customers. Placing the correct brain type orientation in the right place and at the right time is a secret to market success.

In managing your "market-push" (and not "technology-push") innovation value chain or innovation portfolio, follow these guidelines:

1. **Be Market Focused**: See what are the market gaps, market niches, blue oceans, uncharted seas, untapped markets your company's core business can explore.
2. **Be Customer Focused**: Within each identified market identify your specific consumers, customers, clients, or market communities. Study their specific unmet needs, wants, desires, and dreams.

3. **Be Competition Vigilant**: See what your competitors are doing in this regard. Which blue oceans are they targeting? Do not assume they are ignorant of these blue ocean market opportunities.

4. **Be Innovation Value Chain Focused**: See Table 8.8. Identify your strongest links in the IVC as well the weakest links. For instance, are you good at generating raw innovative ideas both internally and externally, but poor in converting them to market-ready ideas or products and perhaps, even more weak in diffusing them to your relevant constituencies?

5. **Be End-to-end Innovation Focused**: View innovation as an end-to-end process rather than focusing on a part. This enables you to spot your stronger and weaker links simultaneously.

6. **Focus on Innovation Effectiveness**: Apart from incubating some ideas for some time, most of your innovation raw ideas should be market-ready ideas in less than 3–6 months, and these should be market-ready products within another 3–6 months. See Table 8.10.

7. **Focus on Business Effectiveness**: All along the new product life cycle chain focus on four critical areas: risk, reach, cost, and speed. See Figure 8.3.

8. **Focus on Profits and Growth**: High revenues with high CGS are no good. The bottom line is profits. Otherwise, the company has no retained earnings and cannot grow.

9. **Forecast Basic Financial Metrics**: From Guidelines 1–8, check on some financial fundamentals benchmarks such as return on development (ROD), Research & Development (R&D), return on quality (ROQ), return on marketing (ROM), return on sales (ROS), return on investment (ROI), return on assets (ROA) and its sub-derivatives, return on net assets (RONA), return on invested capital (ROIC), return on capital employed (ROCE), and return on business assets (ROBA), earnings per share (EPS) and price/earnings ratio (P/E).

On Innovating Innovation

[Thoughts from John Kao (2007)]

Innovate the innovation process. Weave innovation into the national fabric, purpose, and process of growth and expansion. Innovation should be a linchpin of public policy that influences national priorities, infrastructure investments, and the development of human capital (Kao 2007: 53):

- Think outside your specialties.
- Think outside the box. Thinking inside the box is to think within constraints and exploring alternatives or their combinations within a confined space. Hence, change constraints or set the right constraints, and ask the right kinds of questions.
- Innovation moves beyond old and established ways of thinking.
- Innovation is interdisciplinary and should cross boundaries.
- Innovation realizes value from ideas.
- Innovation is not just about intellectual property and patent law. It goes beyond it.
- It is not about high tech only; but transcends it.
- It is beyond the Silicon formula, "better, faster, and cheaper" products.
- Innovation entertains "impossible" possibilities, conducts meaningful experiments, consults outsiders with widely different backgrounds and divergent opinions, and takes daring intellectual and economic risks.

BUSINESS TRANSFORMATION EXERCISES

8.1 Using Table 8.11 assess your current developmental/global innovation. Is it a raw idea, market-ready idea, or a market-ready product, and why? Study its strategy dimensions that make it a promising raw idea. Alternatively, what makes it market-ready idea or a market-ready product?

8.2 Specifically, assess its cost, reach, risk, and speed. Using Figure 8.3, reassess the value of your innovation. What is the intellectual property (IP) involved? What are your IP rights? That is, is your innovation something that idea scouts or licensing agents, patent brokers, or invention capitalists will be interested in and why? Alternatively, will your innovation appeal to innovation capitalists and why? Alternatively, would you business-incubate it for further market development and how?

8.3 Assess the four innovation variables of your innovation from the customers' viewpoint. That is asses *risk* (user safety, privacy, security, benefit), *reach* (market, its size, its volatility and stability, its accessibility), *cost* (price, convenience, anxiety, savings on money, energy, space, pace), and *speed* (getting it market-ready, getting it home-ready, getting it use-ready, getting it service-ready, getting it expanded, updated, or redesigned). Hence, what is the value creation? What is the value added, to whom and why? Why should the customer buy your innovation and not that of your competitors?

8.4 Study your innovation value chain (IVC). Using Tables 8.8 and 8.15 identify and assess the strongest links in your IVC as well its weakest links. How will you reinforce your strongest links and revamp and strengthen your weakest links using strategies suggested in Table 8.15? Be specific. Based on the many examples cited in this handout, or from your experiences, how others have done in this regard, and how and what you will learn from them.

8.5 Based on your analysis from 8.1 to 8.4, (*a*) draw and defend your innovation value chain, and (*b*) based on (*a*), draw a corresponding business plan to execute your IVC. Your business plan should include costs at each stage of your value-added chain (e.g., costs per unit of invention [raw idea or market-ready idea or market-ready product], cost of prototype designing, cost of prototype testing, cost of pretest concept marketing, cost of product test marketing, cost of materials, cost of components, cost of parts, cost of assembling, cost of sizing, packaging, and labeling, costs of delivery and distribution logistics, cost of marketing, advertising, promotion, consumer credit, and PR, cost of commissions [or royalties] to innovation intermediaries, cost of financing, cost of government approval, cost of patenting, cost of warranty and service guarantees). Assess your revenues, cash flows, gross margins, contribution margin, net earnings and taxes. Hence, assess Earning before Interest and Taxes (EBIT), Earnings before Interest, Taxes, Depreciation and Amortization (EBITDA), and discounted cash flows. Will your innovation intermediary buy into it and why?

Chapter 9

The CEO as a Strategic Leader of Innovative Sustainable Competitive Advantage

Regardless of industry, almost all companies are operating on faster evolutionary tracks and at greater risks than ever before. In this context, a company's real core capability is its ability to continually redesign its value chain and to reshuffle its structural, technological, financial, and human assets in order to achieve maximum competitive advantage. Nevertheless, competitive advantage is at best a fleeting commodity that must be won again and again. That is, all players in the value chain—producers, suppliers, employees, retail channels, and customers—are also seeking their own competitive advantage. This competitiveness makes every value chain dynamic. Organizations today must continually disintegrate and reintegrate in order to quickly and continually assess which parts of their value chain are vulnerable, which parts are defensible, which corporate alliances make the most strategic sense, and which competitive threats are deadly (Fine et al. 2002). In this value-chain assessment process the value of the customer must be reinforced and recognized throughout the chain (Prahalad and Ramaswamy 2000, 2003b).

Conventional wisdom affirms that what a strategist should achieve is sustainable competitive advantage (SCA). Cynthia A. Montgomery (2008: 59–60), Professor of Strategy at the Harvard Business School (HBS), challenges this view. Although critically important, SCA is not the ultimate goal. SCA is a means to an end and not an end in itself. Strategizing only in terms of SCA, mistakes the means for the end and missions managers on an unachievable quest. SCA is essential to strategy but it is only a part of a bigger story, one frame in a motion picture. Strategic advantage changes from time to time, even as the world, both inside and outside the firm, changes not only in big, discontinuous leaps but also in frequent, smaller ones. Corporate identities are changed not only by cataclysmic restructurings and grand pronouncements but also by strategic decision after strategic decision, year after year, and CEO after CEO. An "organic" conception of strategy, therefore, recognizes that whatever constitutes strategic advantage will eventually change. Thus, the very notion that there is a strategic holy grail of SCA, that is, a strategy brilliantly conceived, carefully implemented, and valiantly defended through time, is dangerous.

THE THEORETICAL CONTEXT OF STRATEGIC RESOURCES

Traditional strategic tools such as portfolio planning, the experience curve, Profit Impact of Marketing Strategy (PIMS), Michael Porter's five strategy drivers, Edward Deming's TQM, core competencies (Prahalad and Hamel 1990), competing on capabilities, and the learning organization (Senge 1990, 2006), while they bring rigor and legitimacy to strategy at both the business unit and the corporate level, are challenged by the fast pace of global competition and technological change today. As markets move faster and faster and as technologies obsolesce quickly, managers complain that strategic planning is too static and too slow. Leading companies, such as General Electric (GE), build a large staffs that reflect growing confidence in the value of strategic planning. Threatened by smaller, a less hierarchical competitors, however, many corporate stalwarts such as IBM, Digital, GM, and Westinghouse, either have suffered devastating setbacks or undertaken dramatic transformation programs and internal reorganizations (e.g., GE, IBM, Sony). New questions corporate executives face today are:

- What gives a company a SCA?
- What are our strategically valuable resources that enable us to perform activities better and more cheaply than our rivals?
- Are these resources "physical assets" (e.g., a prime location), "intangible assets" (e.g., patents, skills, strong brands), or "capabilities" (e.g., a super-efficient manufacturing process), or combinations thereof?
- How do these resources drive corporate performance in a dynamic competitive environment?

No two companies are exactly alike because no two companies have had the same set of experiences, acquired the same assets and skills, or built the same organizational cultures. In the resource-based view (RBV), these assets and capabilities determine how efficiently and effectively a company performs its functional activities. Following this logic, a company is strategically positioned to succeed its rivals, if it has the best and most appropriate stocks of resources for its business and strategy (Collis and Rukstad 2008: 142). Whatever its source, we can attribute SCA to the ownership of a valuable resource that enables the company to perform activities better or more cheaply than its competitors. Our discussions on strategy are centered on identifying, investigating, and developing such valuable resources.

The resource-based theory of entrepreneurship is efficient and practical because it focuses on the strengths, assets, and capabilities of entrepreneurs and their ventures. It incorporates market opportunity and competition into the model while emphasizing resources (Dollinger 2003: 25). In the sections that follow, we review the theory of resources as proposed by Wernerfelt (1984) and Barney (1991, 2001a) in comparison with the theory of industrial organization (IO) of Michael Porter (1986a, 1991, 1996) and other market-based theories of SCA.

WHAT IS COMPETITIVE ADVANTAGE?

The theory of resources is anchored on the concepts of:

- Advantage (A)
- Competitive advantage (CA)
- Sustained competitive advantage (SCA)
- Sustained competitive resource advantage (SCRA)
- Sustained competitive marketing advantage (SCMA)
- Sustained competitive performance advantage (SCPA)

We discuss all these concepts in the following sections. All concepts are fundamental to successful entrepreneurship.

There are two major theories of SCA: The RBV derived from Resource Economics, and the market-based view (MBV), also called Industrial Organization (IO) theory, traditionally derived from Industrial Economics. We discuss both views, and supplement them with numerous later developments regarding sources of SCA.

According to the RBV view (sponsored by Barney 1990, 2001a, 2001b; Wernerfelt 1984):

- A firm gains "competitive advantage" (CA) "when its actions in an industry or market create economic value" and when a few competing firms are engaged in similar actions" (Barney 2001a: 9).
- Analogously, "competitive disadvantage" occurs "when a firm's actions in an industry or market fail to create economic value" (Barney 2001a: 10).
- A firm gains "competitive parity" "when its actions in an industry or market add value but several other firms are engaged in similar actions" (Barney 2001a: 22).

Major Substantive Assertions of RBV

Barney (1991: 106) defines resources as "valuable":

- "When they enable a firm to conceive or implement strategies that improve its efficiency and effectiveness"; and
- "When they exploit opportunities or neutralize threats in a firm's environment."

Table 9.1 summarizes this theory. According to this theory, the heterogeneity in the levels, value, inimitability, and non-substitutability of a company's resources and capabilities is the fundamental cause of interfirm performance variations (Barney 1991; Wernerfelt 1984).

However, what makes an asset valuable? Alternatively, which asset can sustain better value for customers and shareholders? How can we distinguish such assets from those that create less value to customers and shareholders? The RBV perspective of Barney (1991) (see also Hunt and Morgan 1995) suggests that such assets should be:

1. **Convertible**: The firm should be able to use that asset to convert an opportunity or neutralize a threat.
2. **Rare**: Possessed by very few rivals.
3. **Imperfectly Imitable**: Difficult to imitate for rivals.
4. **Non-substitutable**: The resource should not have perfect substitutes (i.e., rivals should not have strategically equivalent convertible assets or be able to develop them).

Of these four tests, the first is crucial: the assets must be convertible into use (i.e., customer value). Without the first test verified, the three remaining tests are irrelevant even if verified (Barney 1991). The value of such assets to any organization ultimately is not only their market or trade value, but also their value in use. Unless assets possess some value in use, they fail the critical test of potential contribution to competitive success; they are not convertible (Srivastava, Shervani, and Fahey 1998: 5).

TABLE 9.1 The Resource-based View (RBV) of Competitive Advantage (CA)

Authors	Major propositions	Critical comment
Wernerfelt (1984: 171)	Seminal founder of RBV: For the firm, resources and products are two sides of the same coin. Following Penrose (1959), Wernerfelt maintained that resources contribute to diversification, and diversification must match the "core competencies" of the firm.	Resources are important antecedents to products, and ultimately, to firm's performance. This notion emphasizes resources and diversification.
Barney (1991)	Second seminal founder of RBV: Organizational resources that are valuable, rare, difficult to imitate, and non-substitutable can yield SCA. Two assumptions: (*a*) resources are distributed heterogeneously across firms; (*b*) resources are "sticky," that is, cannot be transferred across firms without costs.	Emphasizes organizational framework of resources. Most RBV work is a development of Barney (1991).
Powell (1992: 552)	In order to generate SCA, a resource must provide economic value, must be presently scarce, difficult to imitate, non-substitutable, and not readily available in factor markets.	Repeats Barney (1991)
Bates and Flynn (1995: 235)	Resources are the determinants of firm performance; resources must be rare, valuable, difficult to imitate, and non-substitutable by other rare resources.	Repeats Barney (1991)
Michalisin, Smith, and Kline (1997: 360)	Such resources are "strategic assets; ownership or control of strategic assets determines which firms succeed and which do not."	Repeats Barney (1991) with no empirical support.
Bowen and Wiersema (1999: 628f)	Possession and utilization of unique, non-imitable, non-transferable, firm-specific resources generate SCA and better performance.	Repeats Barney (1991) with no empirical support.
Priem and Butler (2001a: 25)	Rarity and value are necessary conditions for CA, whereas non-imitability, non-transferability, and non-substitutability are each necessary condition for SCA but not sufficient conditions. That is, RBV may not help value creation for customers, but only value-capture for the corporation.	Barney (2001b: 42) replies: CA and SCA are a function of one's unique resources that must be *parameterized*; that is, contextualized. For instance, "firms operating in industries characterized by high rivalry, high threat of substitutes, high threat of entry, high buyer power, and high supplier power will perform at a lower level than firms operating in industries without these attributes" (2001b: 42).
Priem and Butler (2001a: 29)	Value of resources is determined by demand-side characteristics, which are exogenous to the RBV model. The firm's rare resources do not automatically create value greater than that of other firms in its industry if these rare resources do not generate added value to target customers.	If RBV must be useful, then all the five concepts of value, rarity, valuable (i.e., convertible to use), non-imitability, non-transferability, and non-substitutability must be properly parameterized with both supply-side and demand-side conditions of the market environment (Barney 2001b).

Source: Author's own.

Problems Regarding RBV of SCA

The fundamental RBV statement is "that valuable and rare organizational resources can be a source of CA" (Barney 1991: 107).

However, when do a firm's actions create market or economic value? The predominant answer to this question is the RBV of CA. Obviously, there is some circularity here. According to Priem and Butler (2001a: 25), Barney (1991) makes two fundamental arguments or assumptions:

- Rare (i.e., not widely held) and valuable (contributing to firm-efficiency or effectiveness) resources produce CA.
- When such resources are also non-imitable (i.e., they cannot be easily replicated by competitors) and non-substitutable (i.e., other resources cannot fulfill the same function), they produce SCA.

Barney's (1991) four criteria for resources to confer SCA, value, rarity, non-imitability, and non-substitutability, are "context insensitive" (i.e., they are non-contingent). Value of resources is determined by demand-side characteristics, which are exogenous to the RBV model (Priem and Butler 2001a: 29). That is, if the firm has rare resources, it does not automatically follow that it will create value greater than that of other firms in its industry. Rarity and value are necessary conditions for CA, whereas non-imitability, non-transferability, and non-substitutability are each a necessary condition for SCA but not the sufficient condition (Priem and Butler 2001a: 25).

Further, according to Priem and Butler (2001a: 25), the RBV theory of SCA:

- Does not explain why the firm exists as a form of organizing economic activity compared to other possible firms.
- Does not explain the scope and mission of the firm.
- Is a theory with generalized conditional statements that have some empirical content and some gnomic necessity.

Hence, Priem and Butler (2001b: 64) conclude: The RBV, as currently constituted, contains a theory of sustainability but not a theory of competitive advantage (i.e., value creation).

Barney (2001b) Responds to these Criticisms of RBV

Competitive advantage and SCA are a function of one's unique resources but the resources need to be parameterized (Barney 2001b); that is, contextualized. For instance, "firms operating in industries characterized by high rivalry, high threat of substitutes, high threat of entry, high buyer power, and high supplier power will perform at a lower level than firms operating in industries without these attributes" (Barney 2001b: 42). That is, if the RBV must be useful, then all the five concepts of value, rarity, valuable (i.e., convertible to use), non-imitability, non-transferability, and non-substitutability must be properly parameterized with both supply-side and demand-side conditions of the market environment (Barney 2001b).

Makadok (2001) also criticizes Priem and Butler (2001a) by invoking several RBV theorists such as Barney (1986a, 1986b) and Peteraf (1993) as genuine explanations of theories of value. Drawing on terminology recently coined by Bowman and Ambrosiani (2000), however, Priem (2001) counters

2001 (Makadok) by saying that RBV, at best, explains "value capture" but not "value creation." That is, according to Bowman and Ambrosiani (2000: 15):

- **Value capture** is profit—that is, the difference between the exchange value (i.e., revenue) that a firm received from customers for its product and its exchange value (i.e., cost) that the firm pays to the resource suppliers for producing the product.
- **Value creation** is the end-customer's use value or economic utility.

Thus, RBV explains value capture, but not value creation or end-users' use values or utility functions, and that such a theory must be imported from other bodies of literature.

Makadok (2002) responds to Priem (2001): RBV theory of value belongs to the strategic literature that primarily speaks of profits and firm profitability, and the latter is determined by the "value capture" of the firm. For the purpose of explaining profitability, customer utility or use value is relevant only insofar as it affects value captured by the firm, but it has no independent relevance of its own. For instance, Barney (1986a) focuses on explaining "above normal economic performance" as his primary dependent variable of interest. Hence, when Barney (1986a) speaks of estimating the "value" of a resource in strategic factor markets, his use of "value" necessarily means the value that a firm captures by acquiring the resource, and not the value created for end-customers.

However, what good is "captured value" if it does not translate into customer value? The real value of a firm's resources lies in the complex interplay between the firm and its competitive environment along three dimensions: (*a*) demand by customers; (*b*) scarcity: it cannot be replicated by competition, and (*c*) appropriation: the profits the resource generates are captured by the firm (Collis and Montgomery 1995). The intersection of all three dimensions creates value—both captured and created.

However, customer's (current or future) use value for a product/service which often may be a necessary condition but not a sufficient condition for the firm's use value for a resource. For instance, the captured value of a resource is dependent upon other sufficient market-factor conditions such as rarity, non-imitability, non-transferability, and non-substitutability. Other resources may be useful just for the company, and not for the end-customer. For example, better working conditions, less-wasteful production processes, and other cost-reduction methods—though their remote spillover effects would affect end-customers too.

Figure 9.1 is a synthetic solution of the RBV theory of SCA: it models and strategizes SCA. CA and SCA are defined at three levels: inputs (best employees, best suppliers, and best customers), processes (core competencies, core products, and core information), and outputs (strong brands and services, strong marketing SCMA, value creation for customers, and value capture for the firm). The immobility of input resources, the intangibility of process resources, and the non-imitability of output resources are all defined by the same two necessary conditions for CA (rarity, valuable to the customer and the firm) and three necessary conditions for SCA (non-imitable, non-transferable, and non-substitutable). The model implied in Figure 9.1 is dynamic with feedback loops—CA and SCA are each continual, interconnected, and dynamic value-creation processes.

WHAT MAKES A RESOURCE VALUABLE?

A resource is valuable primarily in relation to its competition. According to Collis and Montgomery (1995, 2008), a resource is strategically valuable if:

FIGURE 9.1   Modeling and Strategizing Sustainable Competitive Advantage

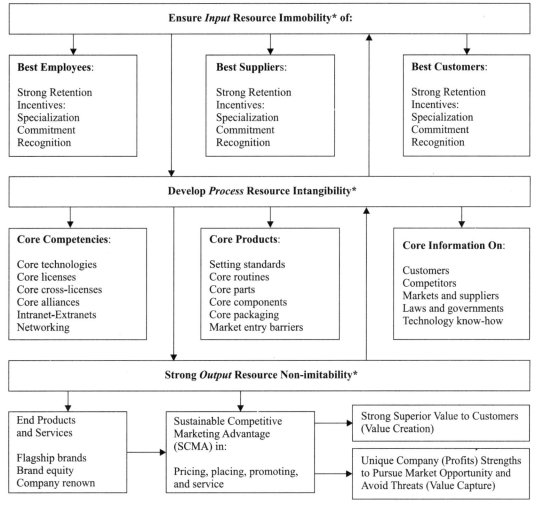

Source: Author's own.

Note: * Implies two necessary conditions for CA (rare, valuable) and three sufficient conditions for SCA (non-imitable, non-transferable, non-substitutable).

1. **It is hard to copy**: It is non-imitable, non-replicable, or non-duplicable. Inimitability does not last forever, as competitors are constantly vigilant of what you do, and strive to catch up. Rivals cannot copy these resources if they are characterized (this is unique added value test) by:

   • **physical uniqueness** (e.g., a highly prized real estate, a strategically placed business location, mineral rights, and patents); or if they involve what economists call;

   • **path dependency**, that is, they are built and accumulated on a very unique, non-imitable path; for example, company history and reputation, strong R&D division, organizational routines, high and convergent specializations, networking, brand loyalty, brand equity, deep customer relationship management (CRM) and supply chain management (SCM) relationships;

- **causal ambiguity**: the competitors cannot easily disentangle to determine what the scarce resource is or to recreate it; for instance, what is the nature and cause of Rubbermaid's success, GE's excellence, Southwest Airlines low-cost strategy, Wal-Mart's EDLP, Microsoft's genius, and Intel's market dominance? Most often causal ambiguity relates to a complex capability called organizational learning; and last.
- **economic deterrence**: the company preempts competitors by raising huge entry barriers; or the market is too small for a second entrant; the market is too capital-intensive or over-specialized for competitor market entry.

2. **It depreciates slowly**: This is a durability test. Coke is still a valuable brand after 125 years; P&G is still a highly prized consumer goods company since 1835; Disney's powerful brand name survived almost two decades of benign neglect between Walt Disney's death in 1966 and his successor, Michael D. Eisner, in 1984. Merck's pharmaceutical patents were long and non-duplicable. What accounts for durability? Many factors: complex technology (Intel), unique processes or formulations (Merck, Coke, Pepsi), unique product bundling (e.g., Garrison Keilor's *Lake Wobegon and A Prairie Home Companion* radio show since the late 1960s; Apple's iPod, iTune, and iPhone of 2000s), unique low-cost advantage (Wal-Mart; Southwest), or unique history and reputation (P&G, Mark & Spencer, Nordstrom, Saks Fifth Avenue).

3. **Your company controls the value**, and not necessarily its employees, suppliers, or customers. This is an appropriability test. That is, your company does not suffer terrible setbacks when you lose a key supplier, a major customer account, or a highly skilled employee. You are still leveraged and hold a value on your own. That is, the valuable resources that define a company are intrinsically and inextricably bound to the company. For instance, a critical resource of leveraged buyout (LBO) firms was the network of contacts and relationships in the investment banking community.

4. **The resource cannot be substituted**: This is the non-substitutability test. One of the reasons the railroad industry failed in the U.S. is because cars, airlines, trucks, and other modes of transportation became good and efficient substitutes. Similarly, the steel canning industry suffered when aluminum cans became cheap, cleaner, and lighter. The typewriter and carbon paper industries died when word processors substituted them.

5. **Your resources are superior to similar resources of your competitor**: This is the test of competitive superiority or distinctive competence. Examples are transformational leadership of the CEO, unique instrumentation of one's diagnostics, unique disaggregation of one's core competence (i.e., the way it breaks down to many unique skills and their synergies), and unique customization of one's products and services. For instance, Mark & Spencer's U.K. retailing resources had a decided advantage over those of its competitors—its retailing outlet occupancy costs were one percent compared to 3 to 9 percent industry average; customers recognized the M&S brand with minimal advertising; its employees were loyal—its turnover was low; its labor costs were 8.7 percent compared to 10 to 20 percent industry average; it had a bargaining power with its suppliers such that its goods sold cheaper but with higher quality than the competitors; lastly, its managerial hierarchy was more flat and lean than that of the competitors. The same argument can be made of industry champion Wal-Mart in relation to Dollar General, KMart, Sears, and Target.

Resources cannot be assessed in isolation, because their value is determined by these five market forces. Resources that are valuable in a given industry and in a given time period, may be non-valuable in another industry or in another time. Often, owing to strong competition, resources, otherwise valuable, become ineffective. Thus, for instance, there are hardly any dominating brands in the PC industry, in the lobster markets, in the auto market, in the micro-brewery industry, and the like. Hence, if you have SCA, then for maintaining your SCA, you must continually invest in your strategic valuable resources. Link your internal capabilities to the external industry environment of what the market demands and what competitors offer. This is what led to the success of Dell, Toyota, Apple, and Disney.

For instance, Eisner invested $50 million in "Who Framed Roger Rabbit" to create the company's first animation thus reviving Disney's commitment to animation. This was so successful, that Eisner has quadrupled the animation output since. Valuable resources might reside in a particular function (e.g., market scanning, animation, CRM, SCM, partner relationships management (PRM), and employee relationships management [ERM]) or in an asset, tangible or intangible. SCA is to develop a competitively distinct set of resources, upgrading them constantly, and deploying them in a well-conceived strategy (Collis and Rukstad 2008: 142–43).

For instance, in the 1970s, IBP was the first meat packing company in the U.S. to modernize; it realized SCA when it automated its plants located in cattle-rearing states and developed low-cost meat processing capabilities. Nevertheless, its SCA was temporary, and so too the high profits, for ConAgra and Gargill replicated these scarce resources and IBP lost its market edge and high profits.

THE INDUSTRIAL ORGANIZATION (IO) THEORY AND CA

The IO theory focuses on the external market to identify drivers of a firm's strategy and contends that the firm's performance is determined by this strategy. According to the IO framework, external market and industry structure determines a firm's strategy, which in turn determines its strategic and financial performance (Porter 1980, 1985; Scherer and Ross 1990).

The IO framework is best captured in the *Principle of Co-alignment* (Venkatraman and Prescott 1990): a fit or congruency between a firm's strategy and its environment has positive and significant implications for performance. Strategy is conceived as a firm's deliberate response to the external/industry market drivers and imperatives.

Thus, in the IO framework:

- The principal determinant of performance is a firm's strategy, and the primary drivers of the firm's strategy are external market forces or drivers.
- Competitive advantage is viewed as a position of superior performance that a firm attains through its co-aligned strategy whereby it can offer either undifferentiated (standardized) products at low prices or differentiated (customized) products at premium prices that customers are willing to pay (Day 1994; Porter 1990).
- The two most powerful CAs—customer captivity and economies of scale—are more achievable and sustainable in markets that are local or regional where barriers to competitive entry are strong. In this sense, it is perilous to chase growth across borders, since a global market's dimensions are wider and less defined than national or regional markets and face higher risks of eroding the advantages one has secured in smaller playing fields.

- The conduct of strategy, then, requires the competitive arena to be local, either in the literal and geographic sense or in the sense of being limited to one product or a handful of related ones (Greenwald and Kahn 2005: 95).

On the other hand, the RBV recognizes the importance of and uses the firm's internal organizational resources as determinants of the firm's strategy and performance (Barney 1991). That is, the differential endowment of the strategic resources among firms is the ultimate determinant of their performance (Barney 1991; Wernerfelt 1984). RBV theory uses the term "resources" in a broad sense. Barney (1991) defines resources as all assets, capabilities, organizational processes, firm attributes, information, knowledge, and the like that are controlled by a firm and that enable it to conceive and implement strategies that improve its efficiency and effectiveness. Porter (1991, 1996) argues that the most critical resources are those that are superior in use, hard to imitate, difficult to substitute for, and more valuable within the firm than outside. Prahalad and Hamel (1990) and Hamel and Prahalad (1994a) use the term "core competence" for this type of internal organizational resources.

Thus, according to RBV, a firm's CA reside in the inherent heterogeneity of the immobile strategic resources the firm controls (Barney 1991; Porter 1991). Strategy is firm's conscious move to leverage its idiosyncratic endowment of strategic resources (Hamel and Prahalad 1994a). Thus, the principal drivers of a firm's competitive strategy and performance may be internal to the firm. Although RBV recognizes that a firm's physical resources (land, capital, building) are important determinants of performance, it places primary emphasis on the intangible skills and resources of the firm (Barney 1991; Collins 1991; Hamel and Prahalad 1994a; Porter 1996) such as organizational culture and experience.

MARKET IMPLICATIONS OF A COMPETITIVE STRATEGY

Michael Porter (1996) derives the following implications of a good strategy:

- If there were only one ideal position, there would be no need for a strategy, other than win the race to discover it and preempt others from discovering it (Porter 1996: 68).
- Given competition, differentiating activities are the basic units of CA.
- One's overall advantage or disadvantage results from all (not just a few) activities of the firm (Porter 1996: 62).
- A company can outperform rivals only if it can establish a "difference that it can preserve."
- It must deliver greater value to customers or create comparable value at a lower cost, or do both.
- Superior financial performance then follows: delivering greater value allows a company to charge higher average unit (premium) prices and/or greater efficiency results in lower average unit costs (Porter 1996: 62).
- However, constant improvement in operational effectiveness (OE) is necessary to achieve superior profitability (Porter 1996: 63).
- While operational effectiveness is about achieving excellence in individual activities, or functions, strategy is about "combining" activities.
- Competitive advantage comes from the way the combined activities fit and reinforce one another. A good fit of activities can lock out competitors by creating a chain that is as strong as its weakest link (Porter 1996: 70). Fit is important because a company's discrete activities often affect one another.

- Strategic fit-based positioning should have a horizon of a decade or more, not a single planning cycle. Frequent shifts in positioning are very costly.

Thus, a "strategy is creating fit among a company's activities" (Porter 1996: 75). The success of a strategy depends upon many things or activities done well, not just a few, and in integrating the activities. Without a strategic fit, there is no CA or SCA.

Ultimately, all differences between companies in cost or price derive from its hundreds of supporting activities such as: generating new products and services, rolling them out faster than rivals, reducing defects, calling on customers, training employees, and negotiating with suppliers. These especially include:

- Establishing long-term relationships with one's retailer partners (PRM).
- Establishing long-term relationships with one's customers (CRM).
- Establishing long-term relationships with ones' suppliers (SCM).
- Establishing long-term relationships with one's employees (ERM).

Minimally, all four are required to create, produce, sell, and deliver one's products or services (Sawhney and Zabin 2002). Cost is incurred by performing these activities, and cost advantage derives from performing particular activities more efficiently than how competitors perform them. Product or service differentiation is also created by both the choice of activities and how they are performed.

All these considerations imply that a company benchmarks its resources, activities, and performance against its competitor (say, the industry champion). Nevertheless "great" (Collins 2001) companies ignore or transcend competitors to create their own uncontested "market spaces" (Kim and Mauborgne 2005), and thrive accordingly. Figure 1.1 (Chapter 1) can make provision for this "trans-competitive" strategy by omitting the third block ("Competitive Landscape") in column one.

The long-preserved trans-competitive advantage of Southwest Airlines is a set of its differentiating activities such as short haul, low-cost, no-frills, no meals, no first or business class, no seat assignments, no inter-airline baggage checking, friendly crew, and easy automated ticketing at the gate or by reservation. Thus, it bypasses travel agents passing on their commission to customers via low-cost tickets. Its target markets are "price-sensitive" business travelers, families, and students. Moreover, using a standardized fleet of Boeing 723 aircrafts that require uniform maintenance, Southwest offers point-to-point service between midsize cities, mostly using secondary airports where traffic is less intense and time-consuming. All these activities provide tremendous market (competitive) advantage, both individually and combined. Southwest executes fast turnarounds at the gate (less than 15 minutes) thus keeping planes in the air longer hours than rivals and offering frequent departures with fewer aircraft. It does all this so effectively that on the routes it serves a full-line service airline (e.g., American, Northwest) would never be efficient. A full-service airline is differently configured to get *convenience-sensitive* passengers from any point to any other point, thus reaching a large number of destinations, all major airports, short and long flights, bar and meals, coordination of schedules, and transfer baggage.

Exhibit 9.1 presents a five-stage schema for framing and developing your SCA.

OTHER SOURCES OF SUSTAINABLE COMPETITIVE ADVANTAGE

We review various conceptualizations regarding the source of SCA in the chronological order of their publication:

EXHIBIT 9.1   A Five-stage Schema for Building Sustaining Competitive Advantage

5. Focus on the Customer Group

Whom would you like to serve?
For example: the children's market? The youth? The singles?
The just married? Young families? The immigrants?
The Cubans? The Hispanics? The Latinos? The Asians?
The middle-aged? The senior citizens? The elderly?
The shut-ins? The nursing homes?

6. Focus on Specific Needs, Wants, and Desires

Of the customer group you want to serve.
Are there strong competitive rivals already serving there?
Do rivals serve these needs, wants, and desires better than you can?

7. If Not, Describe, Define, and Justify

Your *distinctive competence* in terms of man-power skills, technology, opportunity, retailing outlets, distribution
network, advertising and promotions, pricing and marketing mix strategiesthat can best serve these needs/wants/desires.
Re-assess your strengths/weaknesses vis-à-vis your competitors, domestic, and global.

8. Plan Action Immediately.

Be cost effective: Price advantages are best developed now.
Be quality conscious: Your best customers are quality bound.
Be service conscious: This sustains your best customers.
Organize an attractive package via best marketing mix strategies.

9. Monitor, Control, and Evaluate your Progress.

No competitive advantage lasts for ever.
What more should you do to sustain your competitive advantage?
What other product expansions, updates, substitutes, complements, new features, and benefits can you add to sustain
your competitive advantage?

Source: Author's own.

- A firm is not a collection of discrete businesses or strategic business units (this was the classical view in the 1970s and 1980s). A corporation is basically a portfolio of its core competencies. Core competencies are not component manufacturing skills (these can be outsourced if necessary). Core competencies produce core products (not mere components) that contribute to the competitiveness of a wide range of end products. The latter are physical embodiment of core competencies. See Table 9.2 for two contrasting views of the firm.
- "The real sources of advantage are to be found in the management's ability to consolidate corporate-wide technologies and production skills into competencies that empower individual businesses to adapt quickly to changing opportunities" (Prahalad and Hamel 1990: 81). "Core competencies are the collective learning in the organization, especially how to coordinate diverse production skills and integrate multiple streams of technologies" (Prahalad and Hamel 1990: 82). Unlike, physical assets, competencies do not deteriorate as they are applied and shared. They grow. However, competencies and knowledge fade if not used.
- It is only by integrating competencies across business units (SBUs) that one-time small companies like Canon, Honda, and NEC could compete with industrial giants like Xerox, Ford, and GTE respectively. Hybrid product opportunities like fax machines, handheld televisions, portable music

TABLE 9.2 Two Contrasting Concepts of the Firm

Corporate dimensions	Old concept: strategic business unit (SBU)	New concept: the firm as a set of competencies
Basis for Competition	Competitiveness of current products	Collaborate for developing core competencies in order to compete for products
Corporate Structure	Portfolio of businesses and product markets	Portfolio of core competencies, core products, and core markets
SBU Status	SBU owns all resources; autonomy is sacrosanct	SBU as a potential reservoir for core competencies; interdependence is vital
Resource Allocation	Capital allocated to discrete SBUs: SBU is the unit of analysis	Capital is allocated to build core competencies: the latter are units of analysis
Value Added to the Firm	Net earnings	Current and future core competencies

Source: Author's own.

keyboards, desktop computers, and camcorders will emerge only when core competencies across SBUs combine, coalesce, and cross-pollinate. Thus, Canon in the camera business proliferates in the copier business; Komatsu in the family bulldozer business succeeds in the giant earthmover and industrial farm equipment business. Table 9.3 outlines portfolio analysis of core competencies, core products, and end products of some modern successful companies. Figure 9.2 captures the new view of the firm as a portfolio of core competencies and core products.

- Rather than rarity of the resources used, it is the "relative difference" in the amount of value generated by firms that is elemental to CA (Schoemaker 1990: 1179).
- The organization that will truly excel in the future will be a "learning organization" that taps people's commitment and capacity to learn at all levels in an organization. The ability to learn faster than your competitors may be the only SCA in the future. As the globalized markets become more connected and businesses become more complex and dynamic, organizations have to learn and work together to make work more "learningful." It is no longer possible to have one person learning for the organization (e.g., like a Henry Ford for Ford, Alfred Sloan for GM, or Jack Welch for GE), and have everyone else follow the orders from the top strategist. The entire organization must have goals that are larger than individual goals. All people in the organization must learn together, complementing each other's strengths, compensating each other's weaknesses, trusting and supporting one another, and respecting one another. A learning organization can learn how to produce extraordinary results (Senge 1990: 4). The connections between personal and organizational learning, and the reciprocal commitment between individual and organization, can generate the special spirit of an enterprise made up of learners (Senge 1990: 8).
- Nelson (1991: 67–68) argues that SCA is based on a "hierarchy of practiced organizational routines, which define lower order organizational skills, how these are coordinated, and the higher order decision procedures for choosing what is to be done at lower levels."
- The firm is "a pool of physical facilities, learner skills and liquid capital" (Chandler 1992: 79). These become a firm's "organizational capabilities."
- Organization learning theory indicates that for market-based learning to form a source of SCA, a firm's market surveillance must be more alert, timely, and accurate than that of its rivals (Dickson 1992; Teece, Pisano, and Shuen 1997a).

TABLE 9.3   Portfolio Analysis of Core Competencies, Core Products, and End Products

Company	Portfolio of core competencies	Portfolio of core products	Portfolio of end products
Honda	Styling skills, design/development skills	Power trains, auto engines	Autos, trucks, motorcycles, lawn movers, generators
Canon	Fine optics, imaging, microelectronics, microprocessor skills, precision mechanics	Desktop laser printer engines (84 percent), semiconductors	Copier engines; Copiers: plain, battery, color, laser; Printers: laser, beam, color, bubble jet; Cameras: basic, fashion, electronic, digital; Image scanners; aligners (mask, stepper, excimer, laser); Fax: basic, laser
Sony	Miniaturization, microprocessor design, ultra thin precision Casing skills	Microprocessor controls Micro motors	VHS/Betamax; radios/stereos Cameras; 8 mm camcorders
3M	Substrates, coatings, adhesives	Pressure-sensitive tapes Coated abrasives	"Post it" notes; magnetic tapes; photo films; Overhead projectors
Apple	Digitization; Interactivity; File-sharing; Music patent network and copyrights	PCs, miniaturized PCs, seamless downloading, playback, search, instant access and retrieval devices; Internet-based storage and retrieval of music albums; texting devices; audio-resolution mechanisms	iMac; iPod; iTunes; iPhones
Philips	Optical (laser disk) media; Compact data storage/retrieval; Videotape recordings; Compactness in use	Semiconductor chips; Optical media devices; Videotape recorders	Razors; VCRs; Compact disks and cassettes; Radio/stereos

Source: Author's own.

- "Thus the firm-specific combination of physical facilities, learned skills, liquid capital, and learned organizational routines become the core competence or core capability of the organization" (Molz and Léveillé 1995: 314–15).
- Strategic marketing scholars identify a firm's "market orientation," that is, its ability to learn about its market environment and use this knowledge to guide its strategic responses to this environment, as the key driver of business performance (Hunt and Morgan 1995; Jaworski and Kohli 1993; Narver and Slater 1900).
- In highly competitive situations, however, it is misleading to explain SCA or even success by specifying individual strengths (Barney 1991, 2001), core competencies (Prahalad and Hamel 1990), or critical resources (Priem and Butler 2001a, 2001b). That is, the competitive values of individual

FIGURE 9.2   A New View of the Firm

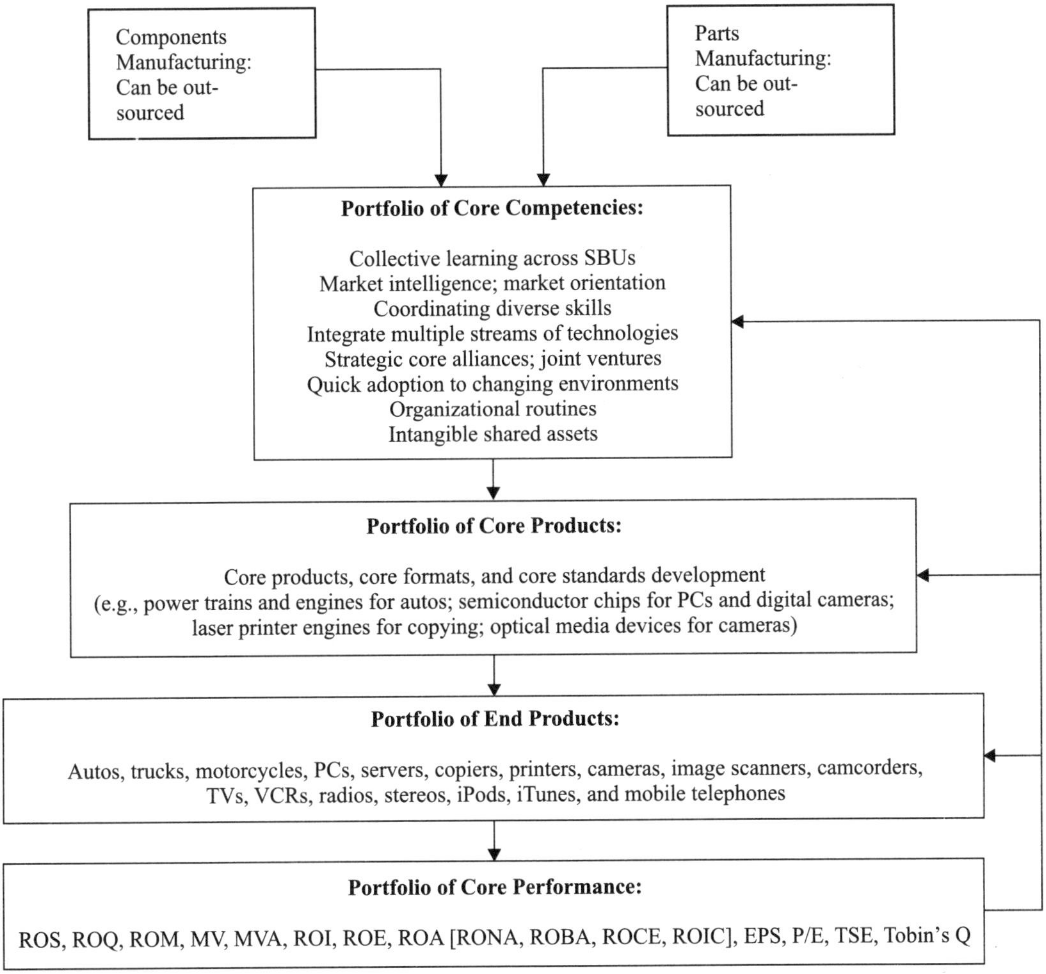

```
┌──────────────────┐                          ┌──────────────────┐
│ Components       │                          │ Parts            │
│ Manufacturing:   │                          │ Manufacturing:   │
│ Can be out-      │                          │ Can be out-      │
│ sourced          │                          │ sourced          │
└──────────────────┘                          └──────────────────┘
```

Portfolio of Core Competencies:

Collective learning across SBUs
Market intelligence; market orientation
Coordinating diverse skills
Integrate multiple streams of technologies
Strategic core alliances; joint ventures
Quick adoption to changing environments
Organizational routines
Intangible shared assets

Portfolio of Core Products:

Core products, core formats, and core standards development
(e.g., power trains and engines for autos; semiconductor chips for PCs and digital cameras;
laser printer engines for copying; optical media devices for cameras)

Portfolio of End Products:

Autos, trucks, motorcycles, PCs, servers, copiers, printers, cameras, image scanners, camcorders,
TVs, VCRs, radios, stereos, iPods, iTunes, and mobile telephones

Portfolio of Core Performance:

ROS, ROQ, ROM, MV, MVA, ROI, ROE, ROA [RONA, ROBA, ROCE, ROIC], EPS, P/E, TSE, Tobin's Q

Source: Author's own.

activities, individual skills and specializations are not enough; company competencies and resources must fit with the main corporate mission, vision, scope, and strategy; we cannot decouple them from the entire system or the strategy. The strategic fit constitutes a company's SCA: it is harder for a rival to match an array of tightly interlocked activities whose combined synergy systems generate the unique strength in which the company thrives (Porter 1996: 73).

- Dell Computers have signs around their Round Rock offices in Austin, TX, stating "customer experience—Own it?" Harley Davidson, Hilton Hotels, Starbucks, Rain Forest Café, Bubba Gumps, Planet Hollywood, and Hard Rock Café in promoting their products are not talking about their quality, design, price, or service as their main offering but "customer experience." In the wake of the increasing commoditizing of products and services, driven by the advent of the Internet, what the customers are desiring is not bargain-prices, excellent design, not even quality and service, but just an engaging, memorable total customer experience (TCE) of the product/service that companies offer. TCE is the new sustainable differentiator, a new source of CA (Shaw and Ivens 2002: 1–2).

- We are all familiar with arbitrage in its traditional form—the pure exploitation of differences. Many forms of arbitrage offer relatively sustainable sources of CA. As some opportunities for arbitrage disappear, others spring up to take their place. Arbitrage has been around for centuries. Many of the industries in which arbitrage have historically been applied, such as farming, mining, and textiles, are regarded as low-tech and mature industries. There is also a belief that well-run global enterprises have already reaped competitive advantage by arbitraging such generic factors of production such as capital and labor, both of which can be outsourced now. However, arbitrage is much more than cheap labor or capital, although these continue to be important. The scope of arbitrage, and hence of SCA, is as wide and deep as the differences that remain among countries. These differences could be cultural, administrative, geographical, and economic (CAGE), and each can generate SCA (Ghemawat 2003). Table 9.4 illustrates this CAGE framework for SCA.

- Research shows that executives must analyze three sets of factors before deciding on mergers, acquisitions, or collaboration (e.g., joint venture or strategic alliances): the resources and synergies they desire, the marketplace they compete in, and their competencies at collaborating. Companies must develop the ability to execute both acquisitions and alliances if they want to grow. Knowing when to use which strategy may be a greater source of CA, than knowing how to execute the strategies (Dyer, Kale, and Singh 2004: 110–11).

- All CAs is fleeting when competition is strong. Consider the luxury car market in the U.S. When Cadillac of GM and the Lincoln of Ford were the only significant competitors, their brands commanded higher prices, relative to costs, leading to high returns on invested resources. However, these high returns soon attracted competing brands: first the European models (e.g., Jaguar, Mercedes, BMW), and then the Japanese models (e.g., Acura, Lexus, Infiniti). The arrival of competing luxury cars did not lower the prices as it might have for a commodity such as copper or steel. The high differentiation of these competing luxury models prevented that possibility. However, profitability suffered and Cadillac and Lincoln lost sales to newcomers. As sales volumes fell, fixed costs (e.g., market scanning and intelligence, corporate planning, R&D, new product development, advertising, and special service support) per car sold increased, margins fell, and so the profits took the double hit of lower margins and reduced sales revenues. If market entry barriers were strong, this would not have happened. As long as barriers to entry are weak, and the market is attractive, there will be more entrants till all the excess profits are eliminated. Hence, SCA is primarily a function of your competition and the market entry barriers that you set up against competitive entry. Barriers to entry are easier to maintain in sharply circumcised local markets. Only within such confines can firms dominate their rivals and earn superior return on their invested capital. When competition is global in scope, the need to circumscribe the competitive arena is even greater. That is why Jack Welch, onetime CEO of GE, instead of setting revenue and growth targets, insisted that the only markets in which GE would do business, were ones it would be first or second in (Greenwald and Kahn 2005: 95–96).

- A few days before he died in November 2005, the management guru, Peter Drucker, wrote about the role of the CEO: The CEO is the link between the inside (i.e., the organization) and the outside

TABLE 9.4 Cultural, Administrative, Geographic, and Economic Arbitrage as a Source of SCA

Type of arbitrage	Domain of arbitrage	Illustrations of SCA via arbitrage
Cultural	Cultural arbitrage (CA) emphasizes inter-country cultural differences as a local SCA. CA is an increasing phenomenon. Its potential is being gradually realized. Both rich and poor nations are important platforms of CA. Tariffs or transport costs can also increase the viability of CA.	French culture has long determined the international success of French haute couture, cuisine, wines, and perfumes. International dominance of U.S.-based fast-food chains (27 of the world's 30 top fast-foods chains in 1990s and over 60 percent of world-wide fast-food sales). Persistent association of Brazil with football, carnival, sex, and other youth-oriented products. Molson's recent launch in Canada of A. Marca Bavaria, a super-premium beer from its Brazilian subsidiary. Haitian compass music and dance music from the Congo enjoy image advantages in their respective regions. European Union (E.U.) recently restricted labels such as Parma ham and Cognac brandy to countries of origin to reinforce natural advantages. Finland's excellence in wireless technology (e.g., Nokia) is getting to be tied to its culture.
Administrative	Administrative arbitrage (AA) deals with inter-country legal, institutional, and political differences as strategic opportunities. These are intangible assets that bear SCA. Some of AA strategies are illegal (e.g., smuggling, counterfeiting). AA can be used as leverage for tax abatements.	Tax differentials. For instance, Rupert Murdoch's News Corporation (NC) paid income taxes at an average 10 percent and less, compared to 30–36 percent it had to pay in the U.S., U.K., and Australia. These tax savings were critical to NC's expansion in the U.S. By placing its U.S. acquisitions into holding companies in the Cayman Islands, NC had good tax and interest (on debt) advantages. NC has incorporated around 100 subsidiaries in tax havens with low or no taxes, with limited financial disclosure laws. Many Chinese business people channel investment funds through foreign third parties and then back into China to secure better legal protection, tax concessions, and other favorable treatments. For similar reasons, Mauritius is one of top two sources of foreign direct investments (FDI) into India. In 1994, four big Swedish multinationals, ABB, Volvo, Ericsson, and Stora threatened to send $6.6 billion FDI abroad to bargain better domestic corporate tax rates.
Geographic	Geographic arbitrage (GA) is a function of shrinking inter-country distances owing to decreased communication (increased connectivity) and transportation costs.	Air transportation costs have declined more than 90 percent in real terms since 1930, more sharply than other modes of transportation. This boosts SCA via GA. In Netherlands, the Aalsmeer international flower market auctions more than 20 million flowers and 2 million plants every day, among them blooms flown in from India and sold to customers in the U.K. and U.S. the day they arrive. Lower transportation costs and greater connectivity have accelerated trade via World Trade Organization (WTO). Hong Kong-based L. & Fung uses GA in optimizing its supply-chain activities across more than 30 countries.
Economic	Economic arbitrage (EA) adds value via local factors such as labor, capital, technologies, and infrastructures. Labor arbitrage can be applied to R&D as well as to ongoing operations.	Labor-intensive and capital-light industries (e.g., clothing, toys) generate SCA via EA based on cheap labor. High-tech and capital-intensive companies can also use EA as SCA. Embraer, the Brazilian firm, uses cheap labor EA for its aircraft designs and regional jets. Its regional jets division assembly lines averaged $26,000 per employee in 2002 compared to $63,000 of its rival, Montreal-based Bombardier. The top Indian software services firms have used EA and posted returns of 50–75 percent and 30–40 percent growth a year over the past decade. Cemex, the international cement company, HQ in Mexico, has reduced its "Mexican risk" by trading its stock in NYSE, by extending operations in Spain where interest costs are lower and tax deductibles are great, and by seeking partnership with insurer American International Group (AIG) in Singapore.

Source: Author's own.

Note: See also Ghemawat (2003: 76–84).

(i.e., the society, economy, technology, markets, and customers). Inside is mostly costs; the outside is results. Without the outside, there is no inside. The SCA and growth of the company is the CEO's responsibility and legacy, and inward focus is the enemy of growth. Salespeople are outwardly focused, whereas, everyone else is inwardly focused.

- Climate change poses a serious problem for the world. Climate change poses business risks that are global, long-term, and irreversible in impact. The build-up of greenhouse gases in our atmosphere is changing our planet's climate at a rate unprecedented in human history. The year 2005 was the warmest over a century, and the 10 warmest years have all occurred since 1980. During 1950–2000, there has been a dramatic frequency and intensity of weather-related disasters (e.g., drought, epidemic, extreme temperature, famine, flood, tsunami, tornados, landslide, insect infestation, wave surge, wildfire, and wind-storm), most of them caused by climate change, even though the planet has warmed only by roughly 1 degree Fahrenheit during this period. Half of the fossil fuels ever burnt have been used since the end of World War II, and emissions continue to increase rapidly. Most climate models predict a 3 to 8 degree Fahrenheit increase in global temperatures by 2050, if current trends of greenhouse gas emissions continue. Informed consumers are increasingly patronizing companies that are seriously working at reducing greenhouse emissions. The U.S. governments (federal, state, and local), regardless of U.S.A's withdrawal from the Kyoto Protocol, are offering various tax shields and credits for investments in gas abatement projects. Thus, "companies that manage and mitigate their exposure to climate-change risks while seeking new opportunities for profit will generate a competitive advantage over rivals in a carbon-constrained future" (Lash and Wellington 2007: 96). A company can beat competition in two areas: (*a*) reducing exposure to climate-related risks, and (*b*) finding business opportunities without those risks.
- Most executives and management leaders now look to innovation as a principal source of differentiation and CA (Brown 2008: 86).
- Real training for learning is one that bridges the gap between university knowledge and industry knowledge, and between industry knowledge and company knowledge. Hence, institute training that teaches personal mastery and training that teaches collaboration, so that personal mastery can inform collaboration and vice versa. Training can explore how employees can build the value of the brand, and how they can help create customer delight, and how they can align individual actions and overall business strategy. This is known as "branded training." It is a type of education that is custom-fitted to the company's brand, culture, and mission. Without branded training, one company's skills and knowledge would look much like another's, and no company would gain a CA (Neumeier 2009: 139).

Table 9.5 summarizes the foregoing views of SCA from a chronological perspective of growth in understanding in SCA.

Currently most SCA is linked with creativity and innovation that generates SCA in the firms. Table 9.6 sketches a synthesis of the major divergent traditions and theories of SCA.

MORE PERSPECTIVES ON COMPETITIVE ADVANTAGE

SCA and Customer Interface: The new frontier of CA is the customer interface. Making your CA a winner will require the right people—and, increasingly, machines—on the frontlines (Rayport and

TABLE 9.5 A Chronological Growth in the Understanding of SCA

Authors (Year)	Defining SCA	Innovation mandate
Prahalad and Hamel (1990)	A corporation is a portfolio of its core competencies that produces core products better than your rivals do. Core competencies are the collective learning in an organization.	Innovate the consolidation of your core competencies that produces a portfolio of core products that is valued better than your rivals.
Senge (1990)	SCA is rooted in organizational learning that taps and empowers people's commitment and capabilities to learn at all levels of the firm.	Innovation is best sourced with organizational learning that enhances and empowers all capabilities within the organization at all levels.
Schoemaker (1990)	SCA is the relative difference in the amount of value generated by the firm's resources.	Innovation is the relative, positive, and significant difference in value from what is offered by the competing firms.
Barney (1991, 2001b)	Internal company resource that is rare, value-convertible, non-imitable, non-substitutable, non-transferable.	Innovation that results from the resource should also be rare, value-convertible, non-imitable, non-substitutable, non-transferable.
Nelson (1991)	Organizational capabilities are a hierarchy of lower order practiced organizational routines that result in higher order optimal decisions.	Innovate your organizational capabilities such that the lower order practiced organizational routines are geared to result in higher order optimal decisions, products, and profits.
Chandler (1992)	The firm is a pool of physical, financial, and human capabilities—combined well, these are organizational capabilities.	Innovate the optimal pooling of your human, financial, environmental, and physical resources and advantages.
Dickson (1992)	SCA is better when your market-based learning is more continuous, timely, alert, and accurate than your rivals.	Innovate the process that speeds your market-based learning as a continuous, timely, alert, and accurate process that outdoes your rivals.
Molz and Léveillé (1995)	SCA is the firm-specific combination of physical, financial, and learnt skills that become your core competence.	Innovate the optimal combination of your physical, financial, and learnt skills such that they become your core competence and SCA.
Hunt and Morgan (1995)	SCA is market orientation that learns the market environment and its needs and responds to them strategically.	Innovate your market orientation that learns the market environment and its needs in order to respond to them strategically.
Porter (1996)	A company's competencies and resources must fit with the main corporate mission, vision, scope, and strategy; we cannot decouple them from the entire system or the strategy. The strategic fit constitutes a company's SCA.	Hence, optimize the strategic fit between company recourses and competencies and market requirements.
Shaw and Ivens (2002)	Your SCA is the unique "enriching customer experience" your products/services generate in your target customers. The SCA of Dell, Harley Davidson, Starbucks, Hard Rock Café, Hilton Hotels, is just this.	Innovate your products/services such that they maximize the desirable and enhance customer experiences.
Ghemawat (2003)	Your SCA is your arbitrage—the pure exploitation of your differentiated products/services.	Innovate to maximize the arbitrage effect.
Dyer, Kale and Singh (2004)	Companies must develop the ability to execute mergers, acquisitions and alliances if they want to grow.	Knowing when to use which strategy may be a greater source of CA than knowing how to execute the strategies.
Greenwald and Kahn (2005)	SCA is fleeting when competition is strong. For example, Cadillac and Lincoln lost their SCA when competing brands (e.g., Lexus, Acura, Infiniti) flooded the markets.	SCA is primarily a function of your market barriers. Innovate your barriers.
Drucker (2005)	The CEO is the link between the inside and the outside of the firm. Inside is mostly costs; the outside is results. Without the outside, there is no inside.	The SCA and growth of the company is the CEO's responsibility and legacy. Inward focus is the enemy of growth.
Lash and Wellington (2007: 96)	"Companies that manage and mitigate their exposure to climate-charge risks while seeking new opportunities for profit will generate a competitive advantage over rivals in a carbon-constrained future."	Innovate greening products and services.
Brown (2008: 86)	Most leaders now look to innovation as a principal source of differentiation and CA.	Innovate your innovation process and strategy.
Neumeier (2009)	Real training for learning is one that bridges the gap between university knowledge and industry knowledge, and between industry knowledge and company knowledge. Without branded training, a company's skills and knowledge would look ordinary with no SCA.	Hence, institute training that teaches personal mastery and collaboration, so that personal mastery can inform collaboration and vice versa.

Source: Author's own.

TABLE 9.6 Synthesizing the Concept of SCA

Advantage	Necessary conditions	Sufficient conditions	Market determinants	Economic determinants
Competitive Advantage (CA)	Resources should be "rare" (i.e., not widely held).	Rare and valuable resources should produce core competencies, core processes, core products, and core marketing strategies.	Resources should be "convertible" into value for customers. There should be market need for these core products.	The economy should be bullish.
	Resources should be "valuable" (i.e., contribute to firm efficiency and effectiveness).		There should be buying power among consumers and businesses to purchase these core products.	Core supplies (capital, technology, manpower, materials, logistics) should be available.
Sustainable Competitive Advantage (SCA)	Resources should be "non-imitable" (i.e., non-replicable by competitor).	Non-replicable over at least the short term.	Less market rivalry; high cost of market entry	Patent protection of core technologies, core products, and core competencies
	Resources should be "non-substitutable" (i.e., other resources cannot fulfill the same function)	Non-substitutable over at least the short term.	High costs of substitution; less threat of substitution	High import costs and barriers for substitution
	Resources should be "non-transferable" (i.e., asset-specific)	Non-transferable over at least the short term; less opportunism in the firm.	High costs of transfer; less threat (e.g., buying power) of competition alluring your resources	High import costs and legal barriers for factor-transference
Sustainable Competitive Marketing Advantage (SMCA)	End products resulting from core products should be: *innovative*	Radical or market breakthroughs or at least incremental innovations	Innovation as improving quality of life	Controlled product obsolescence
	convenient (saving time, talent, search)	High brand equity and company renown	Least lifestyle discontinuity, unless enhancing	Value of saved time, search, money, cost, efforts, anxiety is high
	good value for the dollar	Easy availability; aggressive marketing	Perceived quality should be high	Perceived value of quality should be high

Source: Author's own.

Jaworski 2004: 47). Count the ways you serve your customers: retail stores, website, catalog, and customer service call centers. You serve them through touch points that are automated (e.g., vending machines, voice response units). Almost any large company has a broad collection of all these interfaces and keeps on investing more and more on them. However, what it requires most is an interface system that integrates all these disconnected activities to generate unique seamless capabilities to manage your customer relationships. A unique interface system is your CA, failing wherein your disconnected interfaces could be your greatest liabilities. "The truth is that interaction with customers, and the customer experiences that result from those interactions, are, for many businesses, the sole remaining frontier of competitive advantage" (Rayport and Jaworski 2004: 48).

SCA has Moved from Physical Assets to Intangible Assets: For over a century, companies competed on the basis of the assets they owned. For instance, AT&T, with its direct control of the American telephone network dominated the industry till 1983. Similarly, Bethlehem Steel with its large-scale manufacturing plants, and Exxon with its oil reserves, each dominated its respective industry with CA. However, in the 1980s, the basis of competition began to shift from hard assets to intangible capabilities. For example, Microsoft became the de facto standard in the computing industry through its skill in writing and marketing software. Wal-Mart transformed retailing through its proprietary approach to supply chain management and its information-rich, long-term customer and supplier relationships. In the late 1970s, the U.S. automakers began losing market share to Japanese companies, and they were forced to confront a growing gap in both cost and quality. Recognizing that upstream component quality was critical to their end product, the Big Three began to move design, engineering, and manufacturing work to specialized partners. To ensure the long-term success of such partnerships, both parties had to open their books, sharing detailed information that became the basis for continual quality and cost improvements over many years. Both parties shared in the savings generated from improved efficiency, which provided ongoing incentives to identify and eliminate unnecessary costs (Gottfredson, Puryear, and Phillips 2005). Thus, historically the locus and focus of CA has moved from physical assets to intangible service assets to long-term buyer–seller relationships (Srivastava, Shervani, and Fahey 1998; 1999). Moreover, it is no longer even ownership of capabilities that matters for SCA, but rather a company's ability to control and make the most of critical capabilities (Gottfredson, Puryear, and Phillips 2005: 134).

SCA is Moving from Qualitative to Quantitative Analysis: Because of global connectivity, massive database management and cheap computing costs, analytics are showing new sources of SCA. Organizations such as Amazon, Harrah's, Capital One, and the Boston Red Sox have dominated their fields by developing industrial strength analytics across a wide variety of activities, and data-crunching their way to victory (Davenport 2006: 99). At a time when firms are offering similar products and using comparable production, distribution, and marketing technologies, business processes are emerging to be one of the last points of differentiation or SCA. On a downstream perspective, these companies cashing on analytics know not only what their customers want, but also what prices they are willing to pay, how much they will buy at those prices, how much they will buy in their lifetime, and what will make them lifetime loyal. On an upstream viewpoint, these companies know their suppliers, the quality of their offerings, what prices they can bargain with them, how much and how often to order for them, and how they will cooperate to maintain JIT, optimal warehousing, delivery, and logistics. Companies fortified with analytics execute these business processes in an integrated and coordinated way, as part of an overarching strategy championed by top leadership and decentralized to decision-making at every level. They hire employees who have expertise in database management, data mining, and data analysis and business process applications.

Table 9.7 illustrates the booming industry of analytics with major successful champions in the field. As one would expect, this transformation requires a significant investment in technology, massive data silos, and the formulation of company-wide data management strategies (Davenport 2006). As Loveman, CEO of analytics at Harrah's frequently says, "Do we think this is true? Or do we know" for certain? These companies go beyond descriptive statistics (e.g., average revenue per employee, average order size) to predictive modeling that identifies the most profitable customers. They pool data generated in-house and from outside sources for a comprehensive understanding of their customers. They optimize supply chains, simulate alternatives, optimize shipments, and establish prices in real time to derive the highest yield from each customer transaction. Their complex models relate and predict operational costs to financial performance. Given top leadership with a passion for analytics, a company-wide embrace of analytics can bring about very desirable changes in organizational culture, processes, behavior, and skills for many employees.

Recent CEOs with a passion for analytics include Gary Loveman at Harrah's, Jeff Bezos at Amazon, Bill James at Boston Red Sox, and Rich Fairbank at Capital One. The New England Patriots, a team that devotes enormous amount of attention to stats, won three of the last four Super Bowls, and their payroll is currently ranked 24th in the league. Thanks to Michael Lewis' *Moneyball*, Oakland A's have demonstrated the power of stats in professional baseball. St. Louis Cardinals manager, Tony La Russa, brilliantly combines analytics with intuition to decide when to substitute a charged-up player in the batting lineup, or hire a spark-plug personality to improve team morale. Analytic HR strategies are engaging European soccer teams as well. Italy's A. C. Milan uses predictive models from its Milan lab research center to prevent soccer injuries by analyzing physiological, orthopedic, and psychological data from a variety of sources. Analytics must be combined with managerial intuition and judgment; one cannot replace the other. Good coaches, managers, and leaders, however, know when to run with the numbers and when to run with their guts (Davenport 2006: 103).

COMPETITIVE ADVANTAGE COMES FROM STRATEGY THAT IS LOCAL

[See Greenwald and Kahn (2005: 94–104)]

A CA is something a firm can do that rivals cannot match. CA either generates higher demand or leads to lower costs. CA based on demand gives a firm unequalled access to customers—known as "customer captivity." The more a firm can hold its target customers captive via brand equity, quality, lower costs, higher service, low searching costs, higher switching costs, and brand community strategies, the higher is demand-based CA. Cost-based CA, on the other hand, is supplier captivity, patented technological superiority that competitors cannot duplicate, and hence, strong economies of scale that significantly reduce costs. These three factors (customer captivity, tech superiority, and economies of scale) generate most CAs. The few other sources, such as government protection of subsidies, superior access to information, are specific to certain industries. All three factors of CA, however, are very vulnerable. Customer captivity can be weakened by demographic shifts, changing lifestyles, and competing brands. Technological superiority can erode by new innovations and when rival firms have access to that technology. Economies of scale are more stable if backed with supplier captivity, centralized purchasing,

TABLE 9.7 SCA via Analytics: Major Industry Champions [see also Davenport (2006: 98–107]]

Industry champions	Core business processes	Core analytics and key management software
Capital One has exceeded 20 percent growth in EPS every year since it became a public company.	Conducts more than 30,000 experiments a year, with different interest rates, incentives, direct-mail packaging, and other variables.	Its goal is to maximize the likelihood that potential customers will sign up for credit cards and will honor payment schedules. Uses "information-based strategy" to service and manage customers. Is currently hiring three times as many analysts as operations people, hardly a strategy for a bank!
UPS is a comprehensive analytics competitor. It has broadened its focus from logistics to customers for providing better service.	Tracks the movement of packages, identifies sources of problems, and assess customer retention and attrition. When data point to a potential defector, a salesperson contacts that customer to resolve the problem.	Uses most rigorous operations research and industrial engineering techniques with sophisticated statistics. The UPS Customer Intelligence Group accurately predicts customer defections by examining usage patterns and complaints.
P&G recently created an überanalytics group with more than 100 analysts.	The überanalytics group, centrally managed, undertakes supply chain management, sales, consumer research, and marketing.	Sales and marketing analysts supply data on opportunities for growth in existing markets to supply chain network analysts; the latter, in turn, use decision-analysis techniques to such new areas as competitive intelligence. P&G offer data and analysis to its retail customers, as part of programs called Joint Venture Creation, and to its suppliers to help improve responsiveness and reduce costs.
Harrah's	Aims much of its analytical activity at increasing customer loyalty, customer service, and related areas like pricing and promotions.	Promotions are no more based on paternalism and tenure, but on meticulously collected performance measurements as financial and customer service results.
Progressive regularly tests its process changes and implements as they are validated.	Uses thousands of experiments a year with insurance rates. The company defines narrow groups or cells of customers (e.g., motorcycle riders age 30 and above with college education, high credit scores, and no accidents).	For each cell, Progressive performs a regression analysis to identify factors that most closely correlate with the losses that cell group engenders. It then sets price for that cell that ensures maximum profit, uses simulation software to test the financial implications.
Marriott International has honed analytics to a science for the last 20 years	For establishing optimal price for guest rooms, conference facilities, catering, for frequent versus random customers, and even predicts hotel revenues at different hotel rates for 91 percent of its hotels.	"Revenue Management" and "Total Hotel Optimization" program. Customers notice the difference in every interaction; employees and vendors live the difference every day.
Wal-Mart	Supply chain management, JIT inventory management, cross-loading logistics, store replenishment, and predicting sales by products and brands.	Insists that its suppliers use its "Retail Link System" to monitor product movement by store, and to reduce stock-outs.
Amazon	Has dominated online retailing and turned profitable despite enormous investments in growth and infrastructure.	Customers can watch learning about them as its service gets more targeted with frequent purchases.
Dell	Supply chain management, JIT inventory management, packaging and delivery (via UPS), predicting sales, and budgeting and timing advertising and promotions.	Dell employed DDB Matrix, a unit of the advertising agency DDB Worldwide, to create a database over seven years that includes 1.5 million records on its print, radio, network TV, and cable TV ads, coupled with data on Dell sales before and after ads, thus enabling Dell to optimize its promotions.
Amazon hires Gang Yu, a software entrepreneur.	Gang Yu, one of the world' leading authority on optimization analytics, and his team study business processes at Amazon	Yu and his team study the constant flow of new products, suppliers, customers, and promotions, and design, build, and implement complex supply chain systems to optimize these business processes.

Source: Author's own.

price bargaining power, core competencies, standardizing and distribution logistics. Intel, Coca-Cola, GE, and IBM have long-standing economies of scale because of their upstream supplier captivity, core competencies, standards control and downstream customer captivity. Economies of scale, however, must be accompanied by customer captivity for CA to transit to SCA. Table 9.8 summarizes conditions for CA and SCA under local and global strategies.

Wal-Mart is a clear example of dominating the local market. Wal-Mart began in the south-central region of the U.S.A, expanding steadily at the periphery of its territory. Today, it dominates the world but its historical performance is local dominance. There are, however, competing explanations of Wal-Mart's success: enormous global spread versus local concentration, localized versus centralized purchasing power, and regional cross-loading logistics versus global labor exploitation. However, an enormous size per se does not deliver a CA. If the purchasing power that comes with size were solely responsible for Wal-Mart's success, then its profitability should have increased as the company grew. Yet its operating margins (EBIT) have not increased since hitting the high watermark in the mid-1980s, when it was one-third the size of KMart. Since 1985, Wal-Mart's operating margins (even when combined with those of Sam's Club) have been around five to seven percent of its sales. Whereas, its competitor Target, with its local geographical concentration, has done better than Wal-Mart on EBIT. Globalization beyond a certain point has diminishing marginal returns on sales, market share, margins, and control (Greenwald and Kahn 2005: 97).

Wal-Mart's purchasing power explanation defies economic logic. At least 90 percent of Wal-Mart's sales are from nationally branded products that are sold through a wide range of competing outlets. The producers of these brands, by their own testimony, are reluctant to favor one retailer over another, and thus, risk antagonizing a majority of their distributors. They offer discounts to Wal-Mart only to the extent that Wal-Mart's more efficient distribution systems lower their own costs. Looked at closely, purchasing power does not primarily account for Wal-Mart's success. The deterioration in the company's margins can be traced to its inability to replicate the same economies of scale advantages in the new regions it has entered. In fact, overseas returns for Wal-Mart, whether on sales or invested capital, are less than half its domestic margins (Greenwald and Kahn 2005: 99).

Globalization has eroded CA among the established drug companies, just as it did in the automobile industry. Their R&D and specialization, however, has always been focal and regional, thus retaining its SCA. Moreover, their marketing operations have been primarily local—selling new drugs to doctors, hospitals, and pharmacies via U.S.-based clinical trials, sales teams, and distribution systems. The efficient marketing of drugs has always required a full range of national marketing organizations. Comprehensive global networks of locally dominant entities are normally formed via licensing, cross-licensing, joint ventures, and cross-border mergers. The recent wave of transnational pharmaceutical mergers is easily explained by the presence of CA based on local economies of scale (Greenwald and Kahn 2005: 100).

Producers of non-durables such as Coca-Cola, Colgate-Palmolive, Nestlé, PepsiCo, and P&G have continued to be market leaders for several decades withstanding the challenges of globalization. The brands and products they sell have well-established global identities but most of their strategies are local and national. Local economies of scale in advertising and distribution are an important CA for all these companies, especially when combined with habit-based customer captivity.

The telecommunications and media industry is the most persuading example when local dominance followed local or regional strategies. The Internet, digitization, satellites, and other distribution technologies with their global reach and ubiquitous presence have been the great protagonists of global

TABLE 9.8 Competitive Advantage of Local versus Global Strategies

Source of CA	Local or regional strategy	Global strategy
Firms	GE, Microsoft, Intel, IBM, Cisco, Coca-Cola, Best Buy, Meijers, Target, Toyota, Honda, Renault, Citroën, Peugeot, Mercedes, BMW, Kroger, Walgreen, Wells Fargo	GM, Ford, Chrysler, Wal-Mart, Enron, Costco, Benetton, AT&T, WorldCom, Global Crossing
Upstream: Supplier Captivity	Local supplier-defined network Local/regional purchasing Local/regional bargaining power Local/regional supplier–buyer relationships Local/regional supplier credit and trust Local/regional supplier payment management Local/regional supplier–buyer commitment Local/regional supplier lifetime loyalty	Global supplier nebulous network Global centralized purchasing Global bargaining power Global supplier–buyer relationships Global supplier credit and trust Global supplier payment management Global supplier–buyer commitment Global supplier lifetime loyalty
Upstream: Patent Technological Superiority	Patents are enforceable primarily locally and regionally. Tech superiority is more sustainable locally.	Global patents are not institutionalized yet. Patent infringement is common globally than locally. Global tech superiority is less sustainable.
Midstream: Economies of Scale	Economies of 25–30 percent market share more likely in markets of restricted size. Local rivals will find harder to capture incumbent's 25–30 percent market share. Many fixed costs are fixed only within the region or product market in question. Mergers and acquisitions are primarily for better economies of scale (as in recent pharmaceutical mergers).	Economies more possible in larger markets, but their impact on local incumbents may be minimal. Expanding markets that cannot be served by existing (fixed cost) distribution systems will necessitate new investment. Globalization can undermine profits by undercutting existing economies of scale.
Midstream: Government Protection or Support	Government protection is mostly local and regional. Government subsidies are local.	Government protection across borders is problematic. Government subsidies beyond national boundaries may be suspect.
Downstream: Advertising and Promotions	Economies of scale in advertising are mostly local and regional based on language and culture. Regionally determined fixed costs for advertising, distribution, and store supervision provide local CA.	When markets are too big, diseconomies of coordination can prevail over economies of scale. Globally determined fixed costs for advertising, distribution, and store supervision have not yet provided local or global CA.
Downstream: Distribution Logistics	Distribution CA is primarily local and regional. Distribution has cultural and social elements that are local and national.	Global distribution systems erode operating margins owing to increasing fixed costs.
Downstream: Customer Captivity	Local/regional switching costs. Habit-based customer capture is local. Customer lifetime loyalty is a local phenomenon. Preferred customer groups are primarily local and national. Brand community formation is local.	Global consumer lifestyles are possible but locally satisfied. Global consumer communities are real but locally and nationally grouped and bonded together. Global consumer captivity is at best elusive.

Source: Author's own.

Note: See also Greenwald and Kahn (2005: 94–104).

interconnectedness and strategies. Yet the companies in this industry that have shown consistent superior performance are those that dominated local markets (e.g., eBay, Amazon.com, Google.com, Yahoo.com). Telecommunication companies that went purely national or global, such as Spring, Qwest, AT&T, are doing poorly. Telecommunication firms abroad, such as NTT in Japan, France Télécom, Deutsche Telekom, and Telefónica in Spain, are doing well because they have strong local franchises. Wireless communications in the U.S. are doing well for their strong localized presence, for example, Verizon in the Northeast (its base consists largely of the former wireless subsidiaries of NYNEX and Bell Atlantic), and Cingular customers came mostly from the wireless operations of Bell South and SBC, both regionally based organizations. The big media companies such as Time Warner, Viacom, Disney, and News Corporation have had enviably high annual revenue growth during 1991–2004 (21.3, 16.013.4, and 11.4 percent, respectively), possibly due to their global reach, but less than S&P 500 performance in terms of annual shareholder returns during 1991–2004 (1.4, 5.8, 8.3, and 7.8 percent, respectively). Global diffusion erodes their profitability (Greenwald and Kahn 2005: 101–02).

The more local, therefore, a company's strategies are, the better their long-term superior financial performance. Local strategies facilitate decentralization—and since Alfred Sloan established the superior efficacy and effectiveness of decentralized management—and decentralization matters for both product space and physical territory. GE's management talent is great but its effectiveness in being first or second in the markets it serves is because of its decentralized organizational structure (Greenwald and Kahn 2005: 103).

COMPETITIVE ADVANTAGE VIA MARKET-BASED INTANGIBLE ASSETS

An "asset" may be defined broadly as any physical, organizational or human attribute that enables the firm to generate and implement strategies that improve its efficiency and effectiveness in the marketplace (Barney 1991). The purpose of a business is to create and capture value and sustain it into the future (Sull 2005: 122).

Thus, assets can be tangible or intangible, on or off the balance sheet, and internal and external to the firm. However, regardless of the type of asset, the value of any asset ultimately is realized, directly or indirectly, in the external product marketplace (Srivastava, Shervani, and Fahey 1998). Hence, there are basically two types of market-based assets: relational and intellectual. Both are external to the firm; they do not appear on the firm's balance sheet, and are largely intangible. Yet "stocks" of these assets can be developed, augmented, leveraged, and valued. By their very nature these two market-based assets are convertible to use, rare, non-imitable, and non-substitutable:

- **Relational market-based assets** are outcomes of a firm's long-term relations with its various stakeholders: customers, suppliers, employees, distributors, retailers, strategic partners, community groups, and even governmental agencies (Srivastava, Shervani, and Fahey 1998).
- **Intellectual market-based assets** are the types of knowledge (e.g., facts, perceptions, beliefs, assumptions, market intelligence, market scanning, and market projections) a firm possesses about the market environment and its emerging conditions. This environment includes competitors, customers, channels, suppliers, employees, social and political interest groups, and international institutions.

Table 9.9 lists some of these relational and intellectual assets in relation to several stakeholder groups.

TABLE 9.9 Market-based Relational and Intellectual Assets and Shareholder Value

Type of market-based assets	Environment	Market-based asset	Market performance — Equity enhancement	Shareholder value influencer
Firm's long-term primarily *relational* market-based assets (ties, bonds, reciprocities) with:	Customers	Responsiveness Frontline service Commitment	Purchase patronage; purchase volume Brand loyalty Lifetime customer value	Market share Brand equity ROS Accelerated cash flows Enhanced cash flows
	Creditors, Investors, and Shareholders	Contract fulfillment Creditor and shareholder commitment	Creditor loyalty Investor loyalty Shareholder loyalty	Credit worthiness Investor trust Shareholder trust ROE Reduced volatility of cash flows
	Suppliers and Materials	Supplier commitment Supplier support and reciprocity	Supplier loyalty and trust Material quality assurance	Better product quality and performance Premium price ROQ
	Production and Employees	Development and retention of and commitment to employees and middle managers	Reduced production cycles; improved quality Employee dedication and loyalty	Faster market introductions Faster trials Faster adoption Prime mover advantage
	Channels and Retailers	Development and retention of and commitment to channel members and retailers	Channel member loyalty; retailer loyalty	Faster distributions in outlets Faster trials Faster adoption Fast mover advantage
	Strategic Partners	Seeking stable strategic alliance partners and projects	Reduced invention cycles; alliance partners' loyalty	Faster product/service innovations and commercialization
	Community Groups	Sensitivity to community group concerns and issues	Advocacy group loyalty; local community loyalty	Community group market share' local community market share

(Continued)

TABLE 9.9 *(Continued)*

Type of market-based assets	Environment	Market-based asset	Market performance	
			Equity enhancement	*Shareholder value influencer*
Firm's long-term primarily intellectual market-based assets (information, knowledge, technology, core competencies) in relation to:	Governmental Agencies	Compliance with all relevant laws and regulations	Government subsidy, loyalty, and tax havens; Government recognition	Government market share; Ecology-compliant share; pioneering in EPA compliance
	Customers	Market research and knowledge of customer needs, wants, and desires	Products/services that meet customers' needs, wants, and desires	Sales growth; Market share growth; Higher SCA; ROS; Accelerated and enhanced cash flows
	Creditors	Debt-risk spread and absorption; Planning cash flows and debt amortization	Enhanced capitalization and amortization; Better debt–equity ratio	Credit worthiness and trust; Investor trust; Shareholder trust; ROE
	Suppliers	Selecting, qualifying, and retaining desired suppliers; Better bargaining power and skills	Supply chain management to obtain the functionally best materials and supplies; JIT; Better inventory management	Better product input, process, and output quality control and performance; Premium value and price; Better ROQ, better logistics
	Employees	Selecting, qualifying, and retaining desired skills; Better training and specialization	Highly specialized non-transferable skills; Employee dedication; Employee loyalty	Better work flow in product/solution assembly; More effective manufacturing; State-of-the-art skills
	Channels	Selecting, qualifying, and retaining desired channels	Reduced distribution cycles; Channel dedication and commitment	Faster distributions and turnovers in outlets; Faster and steadier cash flows; more effective outlets
	Strategic Partners	Selecting, qualifying, and retaining desired strategic partners	Strategic partner loyalty and reduced risk	Faster product/service innovations and commercialization

Source: Author's own.

RELATIONAL EQUITY AS SCA

Relational equity (RE) relates to the wealth-creating potential of a company given its relationships with its stakeholders (Sawhney and Zabin 2002). RE is a key driver of growth and profitability. This is an intangible asset that is rare, valuable, human-asset specific, not easily imitable nor transferable, and hence, a source of SCA. RE has four key stakeholder groups: customers, channel partners, suppliers, or employees; firms cannot think about these four groups in isolation, but in a systemic whole that forms a value network or business ecosystem (Moore 1999) that arises from the relationships between all its vital parts. A company's relationships with each stakeholder group do not exist independent of each other, but mutually reinforce each other.

The four stakeholder groups are connected to four corporate dimensions that firms need to address, as indicated in Figure 9.3. These include:

- The **strategy** dimension primarily related to customers that defines the business and decides where the firm should go.

FIGURE 9.3   A Systems View of Relationships and Relational Equity

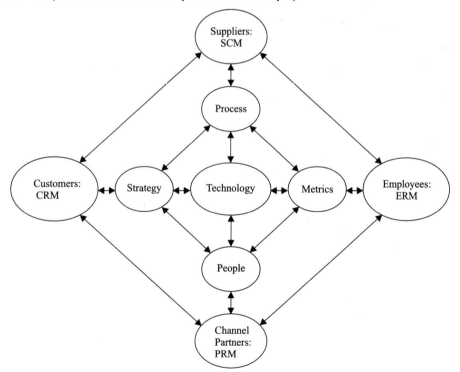

Source: Sawhney and Zabin (2002: 313–32).

Notes: *Legend:* CRM = Customer Relationships Management; PRM = Partner Relationships Management; ERM = Employee Relationships Management; SCM = Supply Chain Management.

- The **process** dimension primarily related to suppliers that defines and decides what the firm needs to do in order to get there.
- The **people** dimension primarily related to channel partners that defines who in the business organization will manage the process.
- The **metrics** dimension primarily relates to employees and tracks how well the people and the process are performing.

The innermost dimension, technology, links to all the others, and defines the role of the Internet in building relational equity (Sawhney and Zabin 2002). Table 9.10 describes the strategies for managing the relational life cycle.

SUSTAINABLE NEW PRODUCT ADVANTAGE AND STRATEGIC ARCHITECTURE

The concept of "strategic architecture" is "a road map of the future that identifies which core competencies to build and their constituent technologies" (Prahalad and Hamel 1990: 89). A company could build these core competencies within the company or with collaboration with others. Today competing companies collaborate to compete (Bleeke and Ernst 1991a, 1991b; Yoshimo and Rangan 1995); they typically collaborate to produce core competencies and core products but compete at the level of end products. Thus, Kodak and Philips collaborate in developing and manufacturing core products for both internal and external customers.

Questions to ask in identifying core competencies:

a. How long can we preserve our current SCA with our current core competence?
b. How central is our current core competence to perceived customer benefits?
c. What future opportunities would be foreclosed if we were to lose a new core competence?
d. Will the new competence to be built enable the firm to be a world player, a world leader in manufacturing, core product and end product market share?

Strategic architecture provides logic for product diversification (different product lines) and market diversification (different markets: North American Free Trade Agreement [NAFTA], EC, Pacific Rim, and Japan). Strategic architecture provides a template for resource allocation decisions; it provides a redefinition of the company and the markets it serves. Modern successful companies like 3M, Honda, Samsung, Canon, NEC, and Komatsu work along strategic architectures that build overarching core competencies across several core and end products. A company that redefines itself as a hierarchy of core competencies, core products, and market-focused business units and end products will be fit to fight in the global arena.

THE CONCEPT OF STRATEGIC INTENT AND SCA

[Hamel, Doz, and Prahalad (1989), *HBR*, January–February]

The concept of strategy has blossomed, and various layers of meaning have evolved such as:

TABLE 9.10   Strategies for Managing the Relational Life Cycle

Stakeholder group	Attract	Retain	Extend	Leverage	Relational capital assessment
Customers	Emphasize customer acquisition spending. Focus on promotions and outbound direct marketing; generate inbound referrals and reference ability.	Emphasize quality, selection, and convenience. Improve customer service; implement loyalty-marketing programs.	Expand into new product categories; offer complementary services; open up new channels and touch points.	Generate outbound referrals for partners. Resell third-party offerings to current customers; increase prices to improve profitability.	Customer satisfaction/churn rate. Customer lifetime value: share of customer spending. Customer integration and collaboration level. Customer referrals. Customer acquisition costs.
Suppliers	Identify suppliers that best match firm's needs and capabilities; focus on vendor development and training programs.	Improve supplier profitability by collaborative planning. Enter into risk- and reward-sharing contracts.	Consolidate supplier base; increase embeddedness with suppliers; broaden scope of supplier relationships.	Use supplier operations to create an end-to-end virtual manufacturing system. Extend connectivity to the supplier's suppliers.	Supplier satisfaction/commitment. Supplier responsiveness and reliability. Supplier cost productivity.
Channel Partners	Offer selling incentives. Invest in channel marketing and cooperative advertising.	Improve reseller profitability through collaborative marketing. Provide reseller training and support.	Manage reseller inventory and business processes. Invest in reseller reach extension.	Tap into the reseller's network partners. Offer third-party firms access to channel partners.	Channel partner satisfaction, stability and commitment. Level of partner's customer understanding. Channel partner's performance productivity.
Employees	Invest in employee recruitment and referrals. Offer sign-on bonuses and other incentives to join the firm.	Emphasize training and learning. Offer retention incentives such as stock options. Create opportunities for advancement.	Broaden skill and experience base; emphasize boundary-spanning roles.	Assist in training/ mentoring newer employees. Capture tacit knowledge to maximize organizational learning.	Employee satisfaction/turnover. Value added per employee. Employee tenure and seniority level. Employee skills and education level.

Source: Sawhney and Zabin (2002: 320, 328).

- **Strategic Planning**: The planning process typically acts as a "feasibility sieve." Strategies are accepted or rejected on standard questions such as: Do we have the necessary capital? Do we have the necessary skills and technologies? How will the competitor react? Has the market been thoroughly searched?
- **Strategic Fit**: Corporate match between company resources and market opportunities.
- **Generic Strategies**: Low cost versus differentiation versus focus.
- **Strategic Hierarchy**: Hierarchy in terms of ideals, ends, goals, and objectives.
- **Strategic Intent**: Seeking global leadership and sustained obsession for winning it at all organization levels of the corporation. Strategic intent envisions a desired global leadership position and establishes organizational criteria that the corporation will use to chart its progress. In general, global leadership is an objective that lies outside the range of strategic planning, strategic fit, generic strategies, and strategic hierarchy.

The following cases illustrate strategic intent:

- Komatsu in 1970 was 35 percent as large as Caterpillar International (measured by sales), scarcely represented outside Japan, and relied on only one product line (small bulldozers) for most of its revenue. It set out to "encircle Caterpillar" and by 1985 was a $2.8 billion company with product lines broad enough to include earth-moving equipment, industrial robots, and semi-conductors. In 1994, Komatsu's sales were $9.25 billion with Caterpillar at $14.34 billion.
- In 1970, Honda which was smaller than American Motors (AMC) and with no exported cars to the U.S.A., seriously intended to surpass AMC, Chrysler and even Ford. By 1987 it manufactured as many cars as Chrysler (then merged with AMC), and became a major contender to Ford in the U.S.A.
- Canon in 1970 was just struggling with its reprographics business and seemed pitifully small compared to the $4 billion giant Xerox, yet persistently went after Xerox, and by 1987 caught-up with Xerox in the global unit market share for copier engines.
- NEC in 1970 faced the turbulent information technology industry with big competitive giants, but its strategic intent exploited the then convergence of the computing and telecommunications industries, and became a major world leader in semi-conductors and microprocessors by 1987.
- Strategic intent (besides being an active unfettered ambitious intent) encompasses an active management process that includes corporate focus on winning, realized by: (*a*) motivating key people in the organization, (*b*) leaving room for individual and team contributions, (*c*) sustaining enthusiasm by providing new operational definitions of competence and success when circumstances change, and (*d*) using intent consistently to guide resource allocations.
- Strategic intent is stable over time in battling global leadership, provides consistency to short-term action, while leaving room for reinterpretation when new opportunities emerge. For example, Komatsu engaged in a succession of medium-term programs at exploiting specific weaknesses of Caterpillar or in building particular CAs. When Caterpillar threatened Komatsu in Japan, Komatsu responded by improving quality, drove down costs, cultivated export markets, and underwrote new product development.
- Strategic intent sets a target (e.g., to unseat the best or remain the best worldwide) that deserves personal effort and commitment. Traditional CEOs measure their success and contributions to

the company by augmented shareholder wealth. CEOs who believe in strategic intent measure success by global market share leadership (which typically yields shareholder wealth).

- Strategic intent implies a sizable stretch for an organization. Current capabilities and resources may not suffice and the firm may have to look for more. Traditional strategy works on a fit between existing resources and current opportunities.
- Strategic intent creates a sense of urgency, or quasi crisis by amplifying weak signals in the environment. For example, Komatsu budgeted on the basis of worst case exchange rates that overvalued the yen (180 yen per US$ when the actual rate then was 240).
- Strategic intent develops a competitor focus at every level through widespread use of competitive intelligence. Every employee should be able to benchmark one's efforts against the best rivals. For instance, Ford showed production line workers videotapes of operations of Mazda's most efficient plant.
- Strategic intent constantly retrains workers with necessary skills to compete and surpass competitor quality and low-cost. Managers should establish clear milestones and review mechanisms to track progress. They should foster reciprocal responsibility (shared pain means shared gain) between managers and workers.

Few CAs are long lasting. The essence of strategic intent is to create tomorrow's CAs faster than competitors can imitate those you have today.

SOME GLOBAL OPPORTUNITIES FOR BUILDING SCA AND CORE COMPETENCIES

- Identify trading blocs within which the firm wishes to compete, such as NAFTA, Borderless Europe, Japan, Pacific Rim, and Commonwealth of Independent States (CIS) and determine opportunities within each trading bloc.
- Determine the market entrance hurdles that must be conquered or circumvented such as: tariffs, duties, quotas, domestic content requirements, currency restrictions, profit expatriation clauses, and government stability.
- Identify comparative advantage of the nations or regions within each trading bloc such as: natural resources, low-cost energy, cheap labor, abundance of raw material, central geographic location, and high quality infrastructure.
- Identify activity clusters within the trading blocs. It is within them that most core competencies and core products develop. Typical examples are Silicon Valley for computer chip design, Northern Italy for shoes and boots, and Toronto's Bay Street and New York's Wall Street for financial institutions. These follow from comparative advantages listed above.
- Identify discrete activities of the value chain that must be in place to offer the product/service. A value chain represents the incremental steps necessary to offer a product, for example, raw material source development, R&D, market research, human resources development (HRD), capital management, manufacturing, warehousing, transporting, delivery, inventory management, and retail marketing.

SRCA VERSUS SMCA

The function of any corporate strategy is twofold. To generate:

- a sustainable resource-based competitive advantage (SRCA), and thus,
- a sustainable market-based competitive advantage (SMCA).

SRCA is not enough; higher order resources or core competencies are no good if they do not generate a marketplace position or SMCA. A resource is that entity that confers "enduring competitive advantages to a firm to the extent that it is rare or hard to imitate, has no direct substitutes, and enables companies to pursue opportunities or avoid threats" (Barney 1991). From a marketing perspective, "resources are the tangible and intangible entities available to the firm that enable it to produce efficiently and/or effectively a market offering that has value for some market segment or segments" (Hunt and Morgan 1995: 6).

A firm's basic resources are:

- **Financial**: for example, cash, cash equivalents, cash reserves, access to financial markets.
- **Physical**: for example, land, plant, equipment, buildings, warehouses, transportation logistics, retail outlets.
- **Legal**: for example, patents, logos, brand names, trademarks, licenses, cross licenses.
- **Human:** for example, competencies/skills/team skills, trust skills, knowledge of labor/management.
- **Organizational**: for example, codes of ethic, morale, controls, policies, organizational climate and culture.
- **Informational**: for example, consumer/market/competitor intelligence/knowledge.
- **Relational**: for example, consumer loyalties, supplier loyalties, creditor loyalties, shareholder loyalties.

Another characterization of resources is under the acronym PROFIT (Dollinger 2003: 38) that could be acid-tested given each sub-product of PROFIT a follows (Table 9.11).

Resources are "heterogeneous" across firms: that is, every firm has an assortment of resources that is at least in some ways unique. Resources may be also "immobile" across firms: that is, every firm has an assortment of resources that is, to varying degrees, not commonly or readily bought or sold in the marketplace; these resources are rather inimitable or non-tradable.

TABLE 9.11   RBV-based Characteristics of SCA

Resource	RBV-based criteria for SCA				
	Valuable	*Rare*	*Non-imitable*	*Non-substitutable*	*Immobile*
Physical	Yes	Sometimes	Not usually	Sometimes	Yes
Reputational	Yes	Yes	Yes	Yes	Yes
Organizational	Yes	Yes	Yes	Yes	Usually
Financial	Yes	Sometimes	No	No	No
Intellectual	Yes	Yes	Usually	Sometimes	Usually
Technological	Yes	Sometimes	Sometimes	Sometimes	Sometimes

Source: Dollinger (2003: 38).

SRCA works and builds along three main areas:

- **SRCA in Tangible Resources**: Tangible resources are the traditional fixed asset items such as land and location, building, office space and equipment, capital and cash flows, energy and machinery. These resources should generate comparative advantage (e.g., locational, financial, architectural advantages) only then can they be put to competitive use.
- **SRCA in Intangible Resources**: Some of these intangible resources are market information and intelligence (on customers, competitors, suppliers, laws and regulations, and latest domestic and international government policies) and technology (knowledge, know-how, state-of-the-art production capacities, patents, trademarks, and licenses, cross licenses, joint ventures and strategic alliances). Other SRCA-generating intangible resources include global scanning, niche detection, market intelligence, accurate forecasts, competitor surveillance, legal update and compliance, and patents as market entry deterrents. For SRCA, these resources must be competitively generated and competitively utilized.
- **SRCA in Human Resources**: These are both tangible and intangible resources, particularly in terms of committed personnel, their distinctive competencies, skills, and capabilities. These skills convert the tangible and intangible resources listed above to SMCA in all market offerings.

Because competition is a constant threat to firms in the free market system, each firm must generate and sustain its own SRCA that will yield a corresponding SMCA (Hunt and Morgan 1995).

External factors that can change resources to non-resources or even contra-resources include:

- A firm's SRCA can be easily neutralized or dissipated by the action of "consumers" (e.g., resources such as brand equity may change if consumer tastes, preferences, and lifestyles change). Your distribution resources may change if price conscious shoppers prefer buying from discount stores than from department stores or franchises you retail in.
- A firm's SRCA can be easily neutralized by the action of "governments" (e.g., changes in laws and regulations, patent and trademark policies, franchising laws, tariffs and duties, non-tariff trade barriers, can seriously affect resources).
- A firm's SRCA can also be easily neutralized by the action of "competitors" (e.g., re-innovating, imitating, or duplicating your flagship brands; acquiring, e.g., via LBOs, your best advantaged resources; alluring your personnel to their firms, and hostile takeover of your firm).

Hence, try to increase the lifespan of your SRCA by:

- **Ambiguity**: Why your customers prefer your products, which product attributes fascinate them and why, how and why they assess your quality as high should be company secrets that can delay imitation by competitors.
- **Immobility**: Make your resources immobile by developing strong commitment of skilled personnel, preferred suppliers, long-standing creditors, and loyal customers to your company. The more you know, respect, serve, and provide value-products to your customers, the longer their commitment to the company/brands.
- **Complexity and Interconnectedness**: Complex resources, complex combinations of resources, and their interconnectedness should render your resources non-imitable or non-duplicable.

- **Intangibility and Tacitness**: Long experiences, reputation, trustworthiness, long loyalties, and other hidden tacit talents of your skilled personnel should also render them inimitable; these are "time-compressed diseconomies", that is, resources hard to imitate in short spans of time.

SMCA should be developed along at least three areas:

- **SMCA in Cost Management**: It is "cost leadership" that is generated by mass production (standardization and globalization), experience curve and economies of scale, scope and time, purchase leadership (quasi monopsony), automation, robotics, and computerized inventory control.
- **SMCA in Quality Management**: This is "quality leadership" that is generated by state-of-the-art technology, quality control, automation, ISO 9000 and beyond, total quality management (TQM), zero defects, zero recalls, honored warranties, after-sales service, updating, upgrading, expandability, and salvage value.
- **SMCA in Marketing Management**: It is basically "price/brand leadership," company name, brand equity, flagship brands, brand loyalty, relational equity, distribution leadership, advertising leadership, promotional leadership, sales force leadership, retailing dynamics, and channel relationships.

Resource immobility generates "resource heterogeneity"; both generate SMCA for that firm (Barney 1991). SMCA exists when a firm's heterogeneous and rather immobile resources enable it to produce a market offering that, relative to competitive offerings, (*a*) is perceived by market segments to have superior value, and/or (*b*) can be produced at lower costs. However, note:

- To be simply different from one's competitors does not necessarily yield a position of competitive advantage (i.e., SMCA). One's product "differentiation" should produce an outcome that is perceived by one's target customers as superior value.
- A marketing strategy that generates both SRCA and SMCA, despite market turbulence (i.e., constantly changing demand, lifestyles, demographic shifts, psychographic departures, and new ergographic trends), technological turbulence, and competitive intensity, is a successful marketing strategy (Jaworski and Kohli 1993).
- SRCA should definitely lead to SMCA with no "causal ambiguity" between the two (Reed and Defilippi 1990).

As in the case of SRCA, even SMCA can degenerate if, among other things:

- Physical asset resources are not reinvested, adapted, renovated, not fully utilized, and not abandoned when dysfunctional.
- Informational and technological resources are not continuously updated or expanded, when they become obsolete and irrelevant, and not utilized for cost and quality and price/brand leadership.
- Personnel resources are underutilized or slacked, not updated and retrained, too labor intensive and cost-prohibitive, and constrained or restrained by bureaucratic procedures or union ordinances.

SRCA should have the following properties:

1. Relative resource uniqueness and immobility (this makes resource advantage more permanent).
2. Relative resource heterogeneity (i.e., different from your competitor firm).
3. Given resource immobility and heterogeneity, your relative resource, production, and marketing costs should be low compared to those of your competitors.
4. Your SRCA should produce a product of higher quality or value to the customers.
5. At least some major segments should perceive your product to be superior in quality to that of the competitors.

Conditions (3) and (5) are critical for CA and superior financial performance (SFP). Table 9.12 illustrates this.

SUSTAINABLE QUALITY-BASED COMPETITIVE ADVANTAGE (SQCA)

The traditional concept of "customer orientation" meant that a firm concentrates on providing products and services that fulfill customer needs. This strategy is necessary but not sufficient. Customer orientation means organizational commitment to customers such that customers and firms share interdependencies, values, and strategies over the long term (Schneider and Bowden 1999). To do this, firms must foster direct customer contact, collect information from customers about their needs, and use customer-supplied information to design and deliver products and services.

TABLE 9.12   The SRCA and SMCA Competitive Position Matrix

	Customer's value perception of market offering		
Resource, production, and marketing costs	*Lower*	*Parity*	*Superior*
Lower	Cell 1: SRCA High SMCA Low SFP?	Cell 2: SRCA High SMCA Better SFP High	Cell 3: SRCA High SMCA High SFP Best
Parity	Cell 4: SRCA Fair SMCA None SFP None	Cell 5: SRCA Fair SMCA Fair SFP?	Cell 6: SRCA Fair SMCA High SFP Fair
Higher	Cell 7: SRCA Low SMCA None SFP None	Cell 8: SRCA Low SMCA None SFP None	Cell 9: SRCA Low SMCA Fair SFP?

Source: Author's own.

Notes: Cell 3: Best represented by Japanese auto companies during 1970–2009.

Cells 7–8: Best represented by U.S. auto companies during 1980–89.

Cells 5–6: Best represented by U.S. auto companies during 1990–2009.

Cell 9: Best represented by German auto companies during 1990–96.

Cells 2–3: Best represented by GE, Sony, Microsoft, Dell, HP, and Wal-Mart.

Cells 4–5: Best represented by Enron, Tyco, World.Com, and most U.S. airlines.

Thus, today, "strategic competitive quality management" implies many things (see Lengnick-Hall 1996: 791–824):

- Deliberate choice among competing dimensions of quality (e.g., craftsmanship, proactive inspection, SQC, quality assurance, or excellence).
- The firm must consistently maintain sustainable competitive quality advantage.
- Customer is the focus of quality activities.
- Customer is the final arbiter of quality.
- Customer is actively involved in design and assessment of product/services.
- There should be emphasis of trust and development of effective loyalty relationships between firm and customers.
- There should be demonstrated commitment to customers through warranties and guarantees (e.g., Honda Accord).
- Increased sophisticated measures of customer satisfaction (e.g., JD Power & Associates and beyond).
- Increased measurement of customer expectations.
- Co-production concept in services.
- Customer as potential partner.

BENCHMARKING MARKETING CAPABILITIES FOR SUSTAINABLE COMPETITIVE ADVANTAGE

[See Vorhies and Morgan (2005: 80–94)]

Benchmarking is a market-based learning process by which an organization identifies and seeks to realize the best business standards and practices of top-performers in the industry. Over time, the target domain of benchmarking has shifted from the content of products and services offered, to strategies, to performance measures of industry captains, to the core competencies or organizational capabilities that produce superior performance outcomes (Anderson 1999; Ralston, Wright, and Kumar 2001).

Market-based organizational learning has been identified as an important source of SCA (Hult 1998; Slater and Narver 1995). A widely accepted market-based learning approach is benchmarking, a structured process by which firms seek to identify and replicate "best practices" in an industry to enhance their performance (Camp 1995). Yet despite the popularity of benchmarking and the theoretical importance of market-based learning, there is very little empirical support that benchmarking market-based learning capabilities can create SCA. Vorhies and Morgan (2005) sift through this empirical evidence.

Benchmarking organizational capabilities involves both content and process issues (Zairi 1998) and is a structured learning process that involves: (a) a search stage in which an organization identifies both standards of excellence and the industry captains that deliver them, (b) a gap-assessment stage in which the capability differences between the organization and the identified industry captain are assessed, and (c) a gap-reduction stage in which the organization plans improvement strategies to close the gap (Camp 1995).

Vorhies and Morgan (2005) identify three normative theories of SCA in supporting the main proposition that benchmarking organizational capabilities can generate SCA:

1. The RBV of SCA: The differentiation or heterogeneity in the level, value, inimitability, and non-substitutability of organizational resources and capabilities is the fundamental cause of inter-firm performance variations (Barney 1991; Wernerfelt 1984). To the extent that benchmarking against top-performers enables an organization to realize such heterogeneous resources, so that it can attain SCA (Teece, Pisano, and Shuen 1997a). Moreover, benchmarking itself as a higher-order organizational learning process can be rare, inimitable, and non-substitutable, and hence, induce SCA (Dickson 1992).

2. Strategic marketing scholars postulate that a firm's marketing orientation is a key driver of superior business performance (Hunt and Morgan 1995, 1996, 1997; Jaworski and Kohli 1993). Marketing orientation is an ongoing organizational capability of scanning, learning, and adapting to one's market environment. Benchmarking marketing orientation as an organizational capability can enhance and sharpen marketing orientation and hence, SCA (Day 1994; Slater and Narver 1995).

3. Organizational learning theory postulates that one's SCA is a function of market resources external to the firm such as changing preferences and lifestyles, changing incomes and buying power, shifting demographics and ergonomics, and changing regulations (e.g., EPA, OSHA) that an organization can continuously monitor, absorb, adopt, and be the first mover (Dickson 1992; Porter 1980, 1986a, 1986b, 1991, 1996). Benchmarking can enhance such environmental scanning and responding capabilities, and hence, generate SCA.

One must, however, first appreciate and validate the assumptions of the benchmarking theory itself since too much is at stake on benchmarking in this context. All the three stages of search, gap-assessment, and gap-reduction assessment in the benchmarking process are conditioned on the quality and process of benchmarking criteria and calibration:

1. First, one needs to identify and study the capabilities contributing to superior performance (Camp 1989). For instance, in marketing, such capabilities are yet to be identified (Menon et al. 1999; Moorman and Sloltegraaf 1999). In general, these capabilities should relate to transforming resources (e.g., marketing information, marketing mix) into valuable outputs in order to target consumers (Day 1994).

2. One could study individual capabilities separately and assess their "functional" value by benchmarking; or one could examine a set of related capabilities collectively for their "integrative" value by integrative benchmarking (Fawcett and Cooper 2001).

3. Theoretical literature indicates that in an organization interdependencies between individual capabilities often exist that can be a valuable source of SCA (Srivastava, Shervani, and Fahey 1999; Teece, Pisano, and Shuen 1997a). What is not established is whether these interdependencies should be functional or integrative or both for producing SCA (Vorhies and Morgan 2005).

4. How to calibrate the benchmarking function itself? Different benchmarking process design alternatives (e.g., searching for benchmarks within or across industries during the search stage, looking for a number of benchmark sites in growing gap-assessment) have differential impact and tradeoffs in benchmarking efficiency and effectiveness. Spendolini, Friedel, and Workman (1999) advocate limiting both the number of firms included in the benchmark search and focusing only on industries related to that of the benchmarking firm. Others, however, think otherwise.

5. Given the relatively small number of major firms in many industries (oligopoly) and the mimetic isomorphism among them (i.e., one copycatting the other) limiting benchmarking to one's own

industry may limit benchmarking effectiveness (Camp 1989). As a combination of several alternatives, scholars suggest "profile deviation analysis" that involves the following: (*a*) identify top-performing firms, (*b*) calibrate the characteristics of the firms that are considered important in determining their superior performance as an ideal profile, and (*c*) assess the relationship between deviation from this profile and the performance outcome of interest (Venkatraman and Prescott 1990).

In selecting benchmark sites, it is better to target firms that are superior in both market (e.g., sales, market share, customer satisfaction) and financial (current profitability, ROA, ROI, ROE) performance (Camp 1995; Spendolini 1992), and those that anticipate similar or better performance in the following year. Once the best-performers are identified, then the next step is to identify specific organizational capabilities that causally relate to market and financial performance. This done, subsequent gap-analysis can be measured by suitable measures, such as calculating the Euclidian distance from the benchmarking firm to the benchmarked firm on all the capabilities found relevant.

Vorhies and Morgan (2005) identified eight marketing capabilities associated with SCA as measured by inter-firm variance in performance and benchmarked against an industry top-performer on all eight capabilities. Table 9.13 summarizes their empirical results. Their significant results include: (*a*) organizational capabilities associated with superior business (e.g., market and financial) performance can be identified; (*b*) gap-assessment between the benchmarked firm and all other benchmarking firms in the study sample can be objectively measured by their significant departures from the top-performer; (*c*) the companies that significantly deviated from the top-performer on capabilities also significantly departed from performance outcomes (e.g., customer satisfaction, market effectiveness, profitability, ROA, and overall firm performance); thus (*d*) indicating that market and financial performance capabilities, if properly benchmarked can generate SCA. The study also reconfirms that market orientation if properly designed and implemented can be an ongoing source of SCA.

BENCHMARKING SCA USING STANDARD ACCOUNTING AND PROFITABILITY RATIOS

Appendix 9.1 lists standard accounting ratios that reflect CA and SCA. Other things being equal:

- **Profitability ratios** measure profits relative to firm size.
- **Liquidity ratios** measure a firm's ability to meet short-term financial obligations.
- **Leverage ratios** measure a firm's indebtedness.
- **Activity ratios** measure cost effectiveness of a firm's activities.

In general, all accounting ratios (see Appendix 9.1) have limitations. Chief among these are:

- They are a post-mortem analysis of the past and indicate nothing of the future.
- They are short-term annual figures; hence, for example, returns on R&D or assets invested over several years may not be seen in the balance sheets in the early years of investment.
- Balance sheets and profit and loss statements are often an accountant's opinions. Most accounting ratios can be manipulated by accounting methods such as FIFO (first in, first out) and LIFO

TABLE 9.13   Benchmarking Marketing Capabilities for SCA

Construct	Measured by number of items (Cronbach's α)	Measured on the top performer	Measured on top five performers	Profile of the entire sample (N = 230)	Significance of the sample deviation from the top performers
Product Development Capabilities	4 items (0.80)	6.00	6.25	4.72	$P < 0.01$
Pricing	4 items (0.83)	7.00	6.15	4.75	$P < 0.01$
Channel Management	4 items (0.90)	7.00	6.40	4.89	$P < 0.01$
Marketing Communications	4 items (0.84)	7.00	5.40	4.25	$P < 0.01$
Selling	4 items (0.80)	7.00	6.52	4.71	$P < 0.01$
Marketing Information Management	4 items (0.90)	6.00	5.84	4.47	$P < 0.01$
Marketing Planning	4 items (0.86)	7.00	6.45	4.56	$P < 0.01$
Marketing Implementation	4 items (0.91)	7.00	6.15	4.61	$P < 0.01$

Construct	Structural equations modeling (SEM) path modeled				SCA Rank significance based on the path coefficient and t-value
	Marketing capability interdependence		Overall firm performance		
	Coefficient	t-Value	Coefficient	t-value	
Product Development Capabilities	0.62	8.26	0.27	2.55	Six
Pricing	0.51	6.52	0.33	3.50	Three
Channel Management	0.50	7.13	0.23	2.76	Seven
Marketing Communications	0.72	9.37	0.34	3.18	Four
Selling	0.73	10.64	0.35	2.80	Five
Marketing Information Management	0.84	10.92	0.34	1.71	Eight
Marketing Planning	0.90	14.84	0.43	2.87	Two
Marketing Implementation	0.82	12.51	0.48	2.92	One
Outcome	Measured by Number of Items (Cronbach's α)				
Market Effectiveness	4 items (0.89)		0.78	8.33	One
Profitability	4 items (0.95)		0.68	7.93	Two
Customer Satisfaction	4 items (0.91)		0.67	7.34	Three
Marketing Capability Interdependence	NA		0.67	7.41	

Source: Author's own.

Note: See Vorhies and Morgan (2005: 80–94).

(last in, first out) of valuing inventories, straight-line versus accelerated depreciation methods, amortization, depletion, and so forth.

- They do not reflect intangible resources such as corporate history and renown, brand image, brand equity, accumulated organizational experiences, HRD, customer and supplier loyalties, employee skills and routines, corporate core competencies, corporate relational assets such as CRM, SCM, ERM, and channel PRM.

Other useful and more insightful financial performance measures include (see Barney 2001b: 38–66):

NOPLAT
(Net Operating Profit less Adjusted Taxes)

$$= \text{EBIT} - (\text{taxes on EBIT} + \text{charges on deferred income taxes})$$

IC
(Invested Capital)

$$= (\text{operating current assets} + \text{book value of fixed current assets})$$

$$- (\text{net other operating assets} + \text{non-interest bearing current liabilities})$$

WAATCD
(Weighted Average After Tax Cost of Debt)

$$= (\text{market value of debt}) (\text{after tax cost of debt})/\text{firm's market value}$$

$$= [D/(D + E)]C_d$$

Where D = market value of debt, E = market value of equity, and C_d = after tax cost of debt.

(Weighted Average Cost of Equity) WACE

$$= (\text{market value of equity})(\text{cost of equity})/\text{firm's market value}$$

$$= [E/(D + E)]C_e$$

Where C_e = cost of equity.

(Weighted Average Cost of Capital) WACC

$$= \text{WAATCD} + \text{WACE}$$

$$= [D/(D + E)]C_d + [E/(D + E)]C_e$$

ROIC (Return on Invested Capital)

$$= \text{NOPLAT/IC}$$

EP (Economic Profit) = IC(ROIC − WACC)

$$= \text{actual economic value created by the firm}$$

THE SIGNIFICANCE OF TOBIN'S Q

Two important ratios in assessing the value (that is, health or sickness) of the firm are market value added (MVA) and Tobin's Q defined as follows:

MVA = (market value of equity + market value of debt) − economic book value.
Tobin's Q = market value (MV) of the firm/replacement value of the firm's total assets.

Tobin's Q is MV of the firm divided by the replacement value of the firm's total assets. MV is the product of the number of outstanding shares (common + preferred) and the average value of the share price on a given day. Since the replacement value of a firm's total assets is difficult to estimate, Tobin's Q has been approximately estimated by:

- Market value (MV)/total assets = market value performance of the firm's assets.
- Market value/book value or "market-to-book" ratio of the firm.
- Value shareholders and other investors attach to the firm over and above its asset or book value.

By definition, the range of Tobin's Q is $0 \leq Q \leq \infty$. When Q is less than 1.0, it indicates poor investor confidence; that is, investors are not prepared to value the company more than the replacement value of its total assets. A value of 1.0 would mean market (investor) value matches book value. When Q exceeds 1.0, then, investors are appraising the company higher than its tangible assets. That is, they are prepared to pay special premium for the stock because of company's growing intangible assets, such as new core businesses, new core competencies, new core products, new core innovations, new core patents, new organizational procedures and routines, new strategic alliances, new joint ventures, and new market entries. The value the investors attach to these intangible assets can be very high. Hence, the upper bound of Tobin's Q is infinity.

For instance, Tobin's Q as market-to-book value of Fortune 500 companies has been approximately and consistently 3.5 over the recent years. A value of 3.5 is 2.5/3.5 = 71.43 percent over book value. That is, over 70 percent of the Fortune 500 companies' value lies in intangible (off the balance sheet) assets rather than in tangible book assets (Srivastava et al. 1997; Srivastava, Shervani, and Fahey 1997, 1998). There is a growing recognition that a significant proportion of the market value of firms today lies in intangible off-the-balance-sheet assets, rather than in tangible book assets (Srivastava, Shervani, and Fahey 1998).

On the other hand, a value of less than 1.0 for Tobin's Q would also imply that the assets of the firm:

- Have little or no intangible value.
- Market value of assets has depreciated.
- Investors and shareholders do not attach much value to the tangible and intangible assets of the firm.

For instance, most of the domestic auto companies (e.g., GM, Ford, Chrysler) have Tobin's Q less than 0.45, but they are not necessarily failing. Organizational performance is increasingly tied to intangible assets such as corporate culture, customer relationships, and brand equity. Yet controllers who monitor and track firm performance, traditionally concentrate on the tangible balance sheet assets of a firm such as cash, plants, equipment, and inventory. Little has been done in the last 20 years to project more accurately the "true" asset base of the corporation in the global marketplace (Srivastava, Shervani, and Fahey 1997).

Financial and economic analysts employ Tobin's Q to explain a number of diverse corporate phenomena such as (Chung and Pruitt 1994):

- Cross-sectional differences in investment and diversification decisions (Jose, Nichols, and Stevens 1986).
- The relationship between managerial equity ownership and firm value (McConnell and Servaes 1990).
- The relationship between managerial performance and tender offer gains (Lang, Stultz, and Walking 1989).

- Investment opportunities and tender offer responses (Lang, Stultz, and Walking 1989).
- Financing, dividend, and compensating policies.

Despite its influence over many aspects of corporate finance, however, Tobin's Q is not much used by corporate CEOs and financial CFOs, possibly because of their unfamiliarity with Q or because data for estimating Q are not readily available (Chung and Pruitt 1994). Most often, it is difficult to assess the "replacement" value of the total assets. Hence, researchers offer several alternatives to estimate the denominator in Tobin's Q. Existing formulae for Q (e.g., Lindenberg and Ross 1981) are extremely tough on data requirements. Current easier formulations of Tobin's Q (e.g., Chung and Pruitt 1994; Perfect and Wiles 1994) require more readily available data and less computational effort. Both formulations assume that the replacement value of the firm's plant, equipment, and inventories are equal to their book value. That is, approximate Tobin's Q is equivalent to market-to-book value of the firm.

YOUR INTERFACE SYSTEM AS A SOURCE OF SCA IN SERVICES

[See Rayport and Jaworski (2004: 47–58)]

Competitive differentiation along traditional dimensions of corporate performance is becoming largely unsustainable. Several reasons suggest this:

1. **Ours is an Era of Near Total Commoditization**: Competition-driven rapid technological advances, fast production cycles, and speeded-up technological obsolescence have provoked heightened customer expectations, faster consumer lifestyles, and hence, faster product life cycles. Several years ago consumer electronic Taiwanese businessmen adopted a "three-six-one" rule (three months to create a feature, function, and price configuration that differentiated a consumer offering, six months to harvest the market offered by that differentiation, and one month to liquidate the excess inventory when the offering became a commodity) or a ten-month production-product life cycle!
2. **Quality of Service Matters**: For many customers, the quality of service is more important than product price or performance. More and more customers switch vendors based on quality of service, and not on product features, functions, performance, and price.
3. **Quality Service Skilled Labor is Increasingly Scarce**: Given the greatly expanded scope of service work in the economy, getting qualified and appropriate service providers is difficult. In developed industrialized economies today, a vast majority of jobs (90 percent as per Bureau of Labor Statistics [BLS] studies) are service-oriented and involve interaction with customers. Hotels, airlines, and retailers of all stripes are experiencing hard time recruiting, developing, and retaining such qualified frontline ambassadors. Fast foods chains have traditionally recruited high school students for their frontline jobs, and there is a fast turnover rate of 138 percent. Well-honed interpersonal skills, emotional intelligence, and problem-solving capabilities that front-line office personnel need so much are in short supply. In other words, front office performance will condition back-office efficiency.
4. **New Forms of Interface Technology, however, are Emerging**: These can help frontline employees in customer-facing roles. Artificial intelligence machines are progressively becoming

user-friendly in managing customer interactions in sophisticated and unprecedented ways. For instance, interactive kiosks allow customers to order from a catalog of more than 78,000 items in an REI store. Kroger's four-lane self-checkout stations (costing about $100,000 for the full set-up) are becoming popular. Rite Aid is experimenting with similar sets of four-lane checkout stations for high traffic times.

A service human–machine interface system should have at least four human characteristics for SCA: (*a*) human physical presence and appearance, (*b*) cognition, (*c*) emotion or attitude, and (*d*) connectedness. Each of these human components needs to interface with appropriate electronic machine intelligence supplement systems so that the latter can reinforce the human component of the frontline operations.

Table 9.14 illustrates this fourfold reengineered human–machine interface systems with examples. The interface focuses on the strengths of emerging and evolving technologies to redesign radically business interactive processes. The focus now in services is "on such arrestingly human concerns as the personal, aesthetic, and emotional attributes of customer interactions, none of which was even contemplated by reengineering as it was originally conceived" (Rayport and Jaworski 2004: 49–50).

Customers in different situations want different things from an interface: information, advice, social exchange, affirmation, anonymity, discretion, and sometimes simply efficiency. The best starting point for front office re-engineering is an analytical understanding of the needs, wants, and desire patterns of your customers by segments, purchase occasion, as well as by competitive offerings.

For instance, drive-in customers in fast foods want speed, accuracy, and responsiveness. They do not expect anything other than simple human relations. Walk-in customers, however, want to relate to the real person behind the counter: face-to-face, pleasant, caring, helping, warm, and sensitive—a customer-fitting service. A good counter clerk should be able to discern by the age, gender, hunger, fatigue, and facial expression of the specific customer and the time of the day the customer arrives. Similarly, a frontline pharmacist should be able to dovetail his/her service to the customer by each one's wants and desires—some patients may need quick and efficient service while others may need sympathy and understanding.

Charles Schwab spent US$20 million creating Schwab Equity Ratings, an automated online service that provides buy and sell recommendations for roughly 3,000 equities. Its stock portfolio suggestions may not be necessarily better than those made by investment professionals, but they are of comparable quality.

One should match the interface type to the task. The job of a restaurant waiter is symbolic of a people-dominant service, even though waiters may use computers to place, track, and bill orders. A website or a vending machine is a machine-dominant service, even though the machines needed to be loaded and maintained. Call-centers with elaborate databases represent machine–people hybrids. Depending upon the nature of the interaction called, one could use machine-dominant, people-dominant, or hybrids to personalize services that have a SCA.

At the dawn of industrial automation more than a century ago, managers tried to train manual employees to work like machines. Assembly lines basically meant honing one's human skills to fit the technology of the assembly line. Time-and-motion studies became the driver and measure of industrial productivity. Today, the reverse is true. We are constructing and teaching machines to behave like real people with frontline roles. The human–machine interface is a virtuous blend of the two evolutions.

Utility meter readings are now commonly read over wireless networks. The meters report directly to utility companies on power usage, making the traditional door-to-door, worker-based meter-reading

TABLE 9.14   Reengineering the Human–Machine Interface System for SCA

Human component	Machine component to reinforce the human component	Interface examples
Physical: Frontline physical presence and appearance	Numerous ubiquitous, pervasive, intelligent devices such as mobile phones, BlackBerrys, palm devices, Pocket PC-based devices, MP3 players, high-tech wristwatches, IPods, and even smaller and smarter laptops	Front office personnel at five-star hotels—uniformed, clean-cut, courteous, authentic, business-like, and professionals—armed with intelligent devices instantly connect to back office or any other department of the hotel and its satellites. This is *physical differentiation* of service. It can orchestrate a seamless hospitality experience.
Cognitive: Understand customers, recognize patterns in their needs and wants, respond to them, and communicate articulately	According to Moore's Law, processing power doubles every two years through 2011. New transistor insulators, based on strontium titanate, may sustain this momentum even longer. Such processing speeds will enable front office people assess customers' current needs and patterns in relation to their past.	At Nordstrom, for instance, salespersons can offer graceful personalized solutions to customer's apparel problems by recognizing patterns in their needs, wants, and desires. Most major airlines with electronic tickets can jump long lines at the checking counter and check-in through ticketing kiosks. United allows this interaction in multiple languages.
Emotional: Attitude of respect, attention, listening, or emotionally calibrated with the customer	Artificial intelligence machines, mannequins, robots, and the like can read customers' facial expressions through visual sensors, listen to words, and respond with facial expressions of their own in socially appropriate ways.	The emotional interface is very useful in building long-term CRM and supplier relationship management (SCM), as well as ERM and channel PRM—the four vital areas of modern business management. Hertz allows Gold Card members to pick up their assigned cars without a service representative's assistance.
Synaptic: Well connected to other relevant resources important to the customer's experience	High speed broadband connectivity is getting to be ubiquitous in millions of households globally. Such power can connect to almost every intelligent device in the world in updating biodata, demographics, billing information, medical information, patient history, auto information, traffic violations, crimes, accidents, and almost any political, legal, and economic statistics.	Such synaptic interface can drum up recommendations and best buys on travel packages, entertainment, weekend hotspots, and the like. The hotel chain Club Quarters enables members to check in or out through an ATM-like machine in the lobby; it generates room keys and billing statements. Hilton, Marriott, and Sheraton have installed electronic kiosks to perform check-in and -out functions, upgrade rooms, leave messages for other guests, and through partnerships with airlines, even print boarding passes.

Source: Author's own.

Note: See also Rayport and Jaworski (2004: 46–58).

trips unnecessary. It is one of the better known examples of automation via machine-to-machine communication. Biolab, a supplier of swimming pool chemicals, has developed a system of remote sensors to monitor the water quality of its client's pools. The sensors send data across the cellular network to the company, and if the data reveals some chemical imbalance, the system pages the designated maintenance person or the next person in charge till the problem is resolved.

According to *World Robotics 2003*, a report by the International Federation of Robotics and the United Nations, if you index the price of robots and the cost of human labor with 1990 as the baseline, the robot price index has decreased from 100 to 36.9 (or to 18.5 if you factor in the higher performance quality of today's robots), while the index for human labor compensation has arisen from 100 to over 151. What this means is that people-dominant interfaces, which have long prevailed in traditional frontline services, are no longer the only or obvious choice at every point of connection between companies and their customers (Rayport and Jaworski 2004: 55).

A company's interface system has SCA when it combines the best of what peoples and machines can do. The task of managing the interface system the optimal way will be a major strategic imperative for most people-oriented companies. Those who crack the code of interface system optimization will own SCA.

CONCLUDING REMARKS

True CAs are harder to find and maintain than people realize. The odds are best in tightly drawn markets, not big, sprawling ones. That is, all strategy is local and all CA is primarily local (Greenwald and Kahn 2005: 95).

An entrepreneur with a good theory of how entrepreneurship works is practical and efficient. Entrepreneurship without any theory could be expensive. Real time failures cost money, time, and goodwill of customers and investors. There are thousands of opportunities for entrepreneurship, but one cannot try them all. Employing a good theory may help reduce the choices and select the best choice.

Is U.S.A Losing its Competitive Edge?

Competitive advantage is fleeting. For instance, in the 1960s the U.S. made almost all of the world's best automobiles, with the Detroit's Big Three—GM, Ford, and Chrysler—selling more than 80 percent of cars in the U.S.A. It was a shared monopoly, muscle-bound and mindless, increasingly locked into practices that their best people knew were destructive but unable to break out of so profitable a syndrome, wrote George Romney, the upstart president of American Motors. He warned half a century ago: "There is nothing more vulnerable than entrenched success." We know the rest of the story. The Big Three kept producing gas guzzlers while the Europeans and Japanese perfected smaller, fuel-efficient cars. After some time, some of the best auto talent from Detroit began to migrate; Ford's VP Marvin Runyon's team moved to Smyrna, Tennessee, to build Nissan's start-from-scratch plant. Nissan's managers and non-union employees operated the most efficient auto plant in North America. Today, while American taxpayers are bailing out GMC and Chrysler, foreign competitors (e.g., Mercedes, Toyota, Honda, Audi, Hyundai) are making most of the world's best cars, and the Big Three have less than 50 percent of the U.S. auto market share.

Even Toyota and Nissan are experiencing the recession. For the fiscal year that ended in March 2009, Toyota Motor lost US$4.9 billion and Nissan Motor lost US$2.6 billion, while Honda made a profit of US$1.5 billion. In 2010, Honda has predicted earnings around US$600 million, while Toyota is expected to lose US$5 billion and Nissan nearly US$2 billion. Thanks to the frugal, unhierarchical corporate culture nurtured by Takanobu Ito, 56, CEO of Honda since June 2009, Honda feels it has the right product and marketing mix for the times. Besides being the world's number one motorcycle maker, Honda has a line-up of gas-sippers (as opposed to the gas guzzlers of the Big Three) and seems to thrive in the North American market of compacts and economy cars. Honda's recent strength is owed to its culture—the company has long emphasized quick thinking, conservative investments, and a level-headed assessment of its own capabilities. Hence, Honda did not follow Toyota and Nissan a decade ago in building big pickups. Instead, Honda is realizing enormous economies of scale through its four key small and mid-size vehicles: the Fit compact, Civic and Accord sedans, and the CR-V small SUV; worldwide, each model sells more than 500,000 units annually, and together the four account for more than 75 percent of Honda's units sales (Rowley 2009: 57–59).

The U.S.A. still has almost all of the world's best universities. A recent Chinese survey ranked 35 American universities among the top 50 of the world, and eight were among the top ten. Our research universities (e.g., MIT, Stanford, Yale, UCLA, Harvard, Princeton, and University of Michigan) have been the key to developing the CA that attracted close to a million of the brightest students of the world in 2007. That year, the U.S.A. boasted over 6,000 public, private, non-profit, for-profit, or religious institutions of higher learning. The same year, the U.S. federal government competitively awarded over $32 billion for university research. The greatness and the autonomy of the American universities were unparalleled anywhere in the world. Yet, as with the case of the Big Three, there are signs of peril and stagnation within American higher education. Many colleges and universities are stuck in the glorious past. For instance, the fall-to-spring school year that was started during the American Revolution (when America was a nation of farmers and needed students to work in the fields during the summer) is still on and that long summer stretch underutilizes the universities and colleges by 40 percent, while the maintenance cost of running a university continues unabated throughout the year. Within academic departments, tenure, combined with age discrimination laws, is making faculty turnover problematic for a university to remain current, creative, innovative, and cutting edge in fast changing times. Aspiring young entrepreneurial and creative academic talent may not get easy approval for tenure and promotion from long established and entrenched professor colleagues steeped in mediocrity and status quo. Meanwhile tuition has soared exponentially, leaving graduating students with insurmountable loan debt. All these factors and others can cripple the fabled American university and erode its SCA within the next few decades (Alexander 2009).

Honing Your Competitive Strategy

According to Stalk and Lachenaur (2004a), the winners in business have always played "hardball"; that is, they used every legitimate resource and strategy available to them to gain advantage over their competitors. When they achieve CA, they attract more customers, increase revenues, gain market share, augment profits, weaken their competitors, and reward all stakeholders, including customers, employees, suppliers, and shareholders. They then reinvest their gains to invest into R&D, and thereby, improve processes, improve product quality, strengthen customer loyalty, expand business, explore new markets, and thus, further reinforce their CA. The more they continue in this virtuous cycle over a prolonged period, the better they can transform their advantage into decisive and sustainable CA.

Some people, however, are uncomfortable with the "hardball killer" concept, considering it to be mean and dirty. This is not true, argues Stalk (2006), even though competition in any form is about winning at the expense of one's rivals, and hardball practitioners do not apologize for it in the least. Nevertheless, refining the concept, Stalk (2006) now calls it a "strategic curveball" that will force the competitor to do two things:

- swing at a pitch that appears to be in the strike zone but in fact is not, and thus do something dumb that the competitor otherwise would not have done, or
- fail to swing at a pitch that appears not to be in the strike zone but in fact is; that is, fail to do something smart that the competitor otherwise would have done.

The second strategy forces alpha or Type I error (rejecting a right opportunity) on the competitor, while the first strategy induces beta or Type II error (accepting a wrong threat) on the competitor. That is, both curveball strategies are meant to fool or outfox the competitor. That is, curveball strategies enable you to gain an advantage that allows you to "strike out" your opponent. One achieves success in the marketplace, however, by ultimately winning customers, not by defeating competitors. Regardless of how one combats competitor, CA is to deliver products and services that customers value more than those of the competitor.

SCA and Corporate Social Responsibility

SCA is not everything. For instance, SCA should not compromise corporate social responsibility to all stakeholders, including the competitor. SCA should particularly include empowering the marginalized in one's community.

A productive way of innovating the corporation is to use Porter's drivers of economic growth. Table 9.15 uses Porter's (1985) model of primary activities and support activities and their intersection to chart out a "comprehensive innovation agenda" that is beneficial to both business and society. No business can solve all of society's problems or bear the cost of doing so. Instead, each company must select for its "innovation charter" those economic, market, and social issues that best intersect with its core business, core strategies, and "shared value" with the environment.

Table 9.16 uses the same Porter's (1985) framework to blueprint a comprehensive "innovative customer satisfaction" and "loyalty development agenda" that is beneficial to business and society, producers and consumers, buyers and sellers. No business can solve all of society's consumer problems or bear the cost of doing so. Instead, each company must select consumer issues that best intersect with its core business and "shared value" with the environment.

Table 9.17 once again uses Porter's (1985) model of primary activities and support activities to chart a comprehensive corporate social responsibility (CSR) agenda that is beneficial to both business and society. No business can or is expected to solve all of society's social and economic problems. Instead, each company must select social issues that best intersect with its core business and "shared value" with the environment. For instance, carbon emissions is a generic social issue for most companies, but critically important for the auto industry. Apparently, the primary drive of Toyota for hybrid cars was

TABLE 9.15 Innovation Value-chain Network for SCA as a Function of Company's Primary and Support Activities

Primary activities	Support activities			
	Procurement (e.g., components, machinery, advertising, and service)	Technology Development (e.g., product design, testing, process design, material research, market research)	Human Resource Management (e.g., recruiting, training, compensation system, firing, PR)	Firm Infrastructure (e.g., strategic planning, financing, investor relations)
Inbound Logistics (e.g., incoming materials, storage, data, collection, and customer access)	Innovative and transparent bidding (e.g., Dutch, reverse, interactive), proposals, and contracts. New SCM networks and dynamics for transactions and relational exchanges.	New technology collaboration and architecture for SCM, PRM, joint ventures, strategic alliances, CRM, and CSR.	Innovative, fair, and developmental recruiting practices, non-discrimination, minority recognition, equal employment opportunity, job advertising, and legal immigrant recruiting.	New and innovative management of stakeholders, especially shareholders and investors. New mission and identity visions for better financial planning, and equity leveraging.
Production Operations (e.g., assembly, component fabrication, branch operations)	Innovative involvement of suppliers and prospective customers as co-producers, co-owners, and co-partners in production. Establish innovative supplier and customer relations in production.	Innovative worker safety, OSHA compliance, conservation, energy use, recycling, alternative energy development, waste and emission controls, hazardous materials, and sustainability management.	Innovative worker development, retraining, education, safe working conditions, diversity and culture integration, worker morale, organization culture and climate.	Innovative production operations that maximize social transparency, ROQ, ROS, ROI, ROA, zero-emissions, environment-friendliness, and environment–organization fit.
Outbound Logistics (e.g., order processing, warehousing, report preparation)	Innovative inventory management. Innovative warehousing and transportation logistics (e.g., congestion, logging roads, emissions) and cross-docking logistics. Innovative payables and receivables management in relation to suppliers, distributors, channel members, and customers.	Innovative, state-of-the-art computerized technology to sizing, packaging so as to minimize waste, handling of consumables, biodegradable packaging, recycling, and disposal. Innovative track orders, shipment, and delivery systems.	Innovative corporate right-sizing, downsizing, and up-sizing policies and practices. Innovative layoff policies, retirement management, and pension funds management, employment buyouts, severance packages and golden parachutes. Innovative outsourcing policies and procedures.	Innovative and accurate financial reporting practices and Sarbanes-Oxley code compliance. Honest tax and payroll management. Innovative lobbying, government dealings, tax planning, and PR with affected local communities.
Marketing and Sales (e.g., sales force, promotion, proposal writing, Internet marketing, website design, and management)	Innovative market scanning, marketing intelligence, prospecting of customers, customer loyalty development, and brand community management. Innovative purchasing and pricing and affordable pricing for the poor.	Innovative, state-of-the-art Internet technology to mass-customize, customize, personalize, and individualize products and services via responsible sizing, packaging, labeling, and instruction manuals.	Innovative frontline sales force ambassadorship; information asymmetry reduction in pricing, bundling, and promotions. Innovative consumer credit and chronic indebtedness management, CRM and PRM	Innovative and effective corporate and consumer advertising. Innovative customer safety, privacy and security management, and total customer experience (TCE) management.
Customer Service (e.g., after-sales service, customer support, complaint resolution)	Innovative involvement of suppliers, partners, channel members, and customers to provide objective feedback and complaints handling and redress.	Innovative technology to honor and service warranties, guarantees, payment, complaints-redress and other support services.	Innovative involvement of sales force and all marketing personnel to deliver prompt and honest customer service, refunds, returns, rebates, and other support services	Innovative firm architecture for PR, CSR, social ecology, and community development.

Source: Author's own.

Note: See also Porter (1985) and Porter and Kramer (2006: 86).

TABLE 9.16 Customer Value Delivery (SCA) Network as a Function of Company's Primary and Support Activities

Primary activities	Support activities			
	Procurement	Technology development	Human resource management	Firm infrastructure
Inbound Logistics	Involve prospective customers as suppliers of ideas, designs, values, materials, components, and felt needs. Engage them in SCM.	Network with prospective customers before, during, and after purchase for ideas and feedback.	Involve personnel for customer acquisition, development, and retention.	The firm headquarters, factories, and channels should project value image to prospective customers.
Production Operations	Involve prospective customers as co-producers of ideas, designs, and customer value. Establish customer partnerships in production.	Deploy state-of-the-art computerized technology to mass customize and personalize products and services.	Involve personnel for focus groups, ad testing, pretest marketing, and test marketing products and services.	All production operations should be OSHA-compliant, employee-friendly, and open to public view and scrutiny. Maximize *customer–organization fit.*
Outbound Logistics	Involve prospective customers as channel members or advisors or managers.	Deploy state-of-the-art computerized technology to enable customers to track orders, shipment, and delivery.	Involve sales force personnel in promising and delivering orders in time, correct place, and as per order.	All outbound logistics infrastructure should project accurate information, motivation, and company image.
Marketing and Sales	Involve prospective customers in product and marketing mix decisions and activities, as also to ensure *attribute satisfaction.*	Deploy state-of-the-art Internet technology to customize products, sizing, packaging, prices, information, and promotions. Use technology for maximizing *information satisfaction.*	Involve sales force and all marketing personnel to provide precise and relevant information and motivation on products and services, as also to generate optimal *shopping satisfaction.*	All marketing and sales infrastructure should be dovetailed to deliver the high-quality CRM, best value for the customer dollar, and high *overall satisfaction.*
Customer Service	Involve and encourage customers to provide objective feedback, and in complaints handling and redress.	Deploy state-of-the-art computerized technology to mass customize warranties, guarantees, payment, complaints redress, and other support services.	Involve sales force and all marketing personnel to deliver prompt and proper customer service, refunds, returns, rebates, and other support services.	All customer service infrastructures should project fairness, integrity, and foster producer–customer mutual trust.

Source: Author's own.

TABLE 9.17 Corporate Social Responsibility Value-chain SCA Network as a Function of Company's Primary and Support Activities

Primary activities	Support activities			
	Procurement (e.g., components, machinery, advertising, and service)	Technology Development (e.g., product design, testing, process design, material research, market research)	Human Resource Management (e.g., recruiting, training, compensation system, firing, PR)	Firm Infrastructure (e.g., strategic planning, financing, investor relations)
Inbound Logistics (e.g., incoming materials, storage, data, collection, and customer access)	Open transparent bidding, ethical contracts, SCM, supplier well-being, supplier turnaround management, bribes, and kickbacks.	Relationships with universities; ethical research practices (e.g., animal testing, GMOs), product safety, scale economies, and cost containment.	Recruiting practices, discrimination, minority quota, equal employment opportunity, job advertising, and illegal immigrant recruiting.	Mission and identity, financial planning, leveraging, debt/equity management, cash flow management, equity building, debt conversion, equity financing.
Production Operations (e.g., assembly, component fabrication, branch operations)	Involve suppliers and prospective customers as co-producers, co-owners, co-partners in production. Establish healthy supplier and customer relations in production.	Worker safety, OSHA, conservations of materials, energy use, ecology impact, recycling, alternative energy development, emission controls, hazardous materials, waste management, and sustainability management.	Worker development, retraining, education, safe working conditions, diversity, child labor, discrimination, worker morale, organization culture and climate.	All production operations should be OSHA-compliant, environment-friendly, and open to public view and scrutiny. Maximize environment–organization fit.
Outbound Logistics (e.g., order processing, warehousing, report preparation)	Honest payables management in relation to suppliers, distributors, channel members and customers. Ethical operations and cash cycle management. Ethical and ecological warehousing and transportation logistics (e.g., congestion, logging roads, emissions).	Deploy state-of-the-art computerized technology to sizing, packaging to minimize waste, handling of consumables, bio-degradable packaging, recycling, and disposal. Ethical track orders, shipment, and delivery practices	Ethical layoff policies, retirement management, and pension funds management. Ethical employment buyouts and severance packages. Ethical golden parachutes. Ethical outsourcing policies.	Financial reporting practices and Sarbanes-Oxley code compliance. Honest tax and payroll management. Ethical use of lobbying. Transparency in dealing with governments, IRS, and affected local communities.
Marketing and Sales (e.g., sales force, promotion, advertising, proposal writing, Internet marketing, website design and management)	Ethical prospecting of customers, customer loyalty development, brand community management, customer lifetime loyalty management, ethical sales force management. Ethical purchasing management, pricing management, anticompetitive pricing, pricing policy for the poor.	Deploy state-of-the-art Internet technology to customize, personalize, and individualize products and services via responsible sizing, packaging, labeling, instruction manuals, and communications management.	Frontline sales force ambassadorship, information asymmetry reduction in pricing, bundling, and promotions, fair pricing, consumer credit and chronic indebtedness management, ethical CRM and PRM	Truthful corporate and consumer advertising, ethical target-advertising to vulnerable segments (e.g., children, teenagers, and the elderly), customer privacy and security management, honest value for the customer dollar, and total customer experience
Customer Service (e.g., after-sales service, customer support, complaint resolution, warranties and guaranties, repair, redress)	Involve and encourage suppliers, partners, channel members, and customers to provide objective feedback. Ethical complaints handling and redress.	Deploy state-of-the-art computerized technology to mass humanize and honor warranties, guarantees, payment, complaints-redress, and other support services.	Involve sales force and all marketing personnel to deliver prompt and honest customer service, refunds, returns, rebates, and other support services.	All customer service infrastructures should project fairness, integrity, and foster producer–customer mutual trust

Source: Author's own.

Note: See also Michael E. Porter (1985) and Porter and Kramer (2006: 86).

ecology driven. However, Volvo has chosen to make safety a central element of its CA. It is through strategic CSR that a company will make its most significant social impact and, at the same time, reap greatest business benefits.

Table 9.18 sketches typical corporate value-chain activities under strategic planning, operating and cash cycles, lists value-chain events under each, and raises strategic questions that have innovation–CSR potential and agenda. Each question properly framed and resolved can result in a strategic decision that has unique innovation and CSR opportunities. This is "strategic CSR" (Porter and Kramer 2006). Every value-chain event, decision, and activity should:

a. Mitigate harm to all stakeholders (this is the call of good corporate citizenship).
b. Prevent harm and protect people from harm (this is the call of preventive and protective forms of distributive justice).
c. Do well and promote good to society by correcting structured injustices (this is "responsive CSR," a clarion call of corrective distributive justice and beneficent distributive justice).

While performing (a), (b), and (c), a good company will also safeguard and leverage its capabilities for SCA—this is strategic CSR. Pioneering value-chain innovations and addressing social constraints to competitiveness are each powerful tools for creating economic and social value. When value-chain decisions and activities are fully integrated in a competitive and CSR context, it becomes strategic business and strategic CSR. Following are some examples of the same:

GE adopts underperforming public high schools near several of its major U.S. facilities and contributes between $250,000 and $1 million over a five year period to each school. GE managers and employees take an active role by working with school administrators to assess needs, mentor and tutor students. The results are excellent. Among other things, the graduation rate has doubled from 30 to 60 percent in four of the five worst performing schools during 1989–99, which has resulted in local communities being grateful to GE for their contribution. This has helped in improving relations with local communities, governments, and other important constituencies that GE needs. This also makes GE employees feel great pride in their participation.

Microsoft also does something similar. In partnership with the American Association of Community Colleges (AACC) Microsoft tries to build IT skills. AACC, with an enrollment of 11.6 million students, represents 45 percent of all U.S. undergraduates. Currently there are more than 450,000 unfulfilled IT positions in the U.S. alone. The shortage of IT workers is a significant constraint on Microsoft's growth. In AACC institutions, however, (*a*) IT curricula are not standardized, (*b*) classroom IT technology is outdated, and (*c*) there is no systematic professional development programs to keep the IT faculty up to date. Microsoft budgets annually $50 million for generating IT skills working around these three AACC constraints. The company sends employee volunteers to AACC to assess needs, contribute to curriculum development, and create faculty development institutes. The results are great. Microsoft recruits among successful IT undergraduates, thus reducing its searching and recruiting costs.

Nestlé (based in Switzerland) works directly with small farmers in developing countries to source its basic commodities (milk, coffee, and cocoa), on which much of its global business depends. The company's investment in local infrastructure and its transfer of world-class farming knowledge and technology over decades has produced enormous social benefits through improved health care, better education, and economic development—while giving Nestlé direct and reliable access to commodities it needs to maintain global competitiveness. For instance, Nestlé has been working in Moga, India,

TABLE 9.18   Corporate Value Chain and SCA Activities and Innovation–CSR Agenda

Strategic planning cycle	Operating cycle	Cash cycle	Value-chain events	Innovation–CSR strategic questions and decisions
			Business planning	What are our core business, mission, and vision?
				What are our core skills, patents, and competencies?
				What are our core markets, core customers, core demand?
				What are core products, core product lines, and core brands?
			Production planning	What is our product mix?
				What is our product design for each of our core products?
				What is our process design for each of our core products?
				What is our materials-component design for each product?
				From whom to buy? What is our innovative SCM?
			Buying raw materials	How much inventory to order?
				Just-in-time inventory?
				When to order?
				At what price? With what trade terms?
			Paying for the raw materials bought	Purchase on credit? Purchase on debit?
				Part payment? Prepayment?
				Borrow money for payment?
				Draw down cash balance to pay?
				Which specific product to produce?
				Which specific brand to produce?
				With what process technology? What patents do we need?
				With what production technology? What patents can we buy?
			Manufacturing the product	With which core competencies?
				Which employee skills to tap?
				How much to produce? When to produce?
				How to size and package the product?
				How to brand and label the product?
				How to manage the inventory?
				How to distribute the product? What is our innovative PRM?
				How to pre-announce the new product?
				How to promote and advertise the product?
			Selling the product	How to price the product?
				How to bundle the product?
				What price discounts? What rebates? What refund policies?
				What consumer credit and financing arrangements?
				What product/service guarantees and warranties?
				How do we build good customer relations?
				What is our innovative CRM?
				Selling exclusively through retailers?
				In which retail outlet types?
				Upscale? Middle-scale? Discount stores?
			Retailing the product	Urban versus rural stores?
				In big versus medium versus small cities or towns?
				Pay slotting allowances (i.e., buy selling space in the store)?
				Sell products on consignment (i.e., collect cash after sale)?
				Sell on credit to the retailers?
				Provide selling incentives to retailers?
				How to collect cash? When to invoice?
			Collecting cash from retailers or customers	Request payment within how many days from invoice?
				Request prepayment in full or in part?
				Request full payment on receiving the product?
				Request full payment within 30 days of invoicing?
				How to resolve chronic cash crisis among suppliers or consumers?
				What is our innovative CSR to customers and local communities?

Source: Author's own.

since 1962. Moga then had no electricity, transportation, telephones, or medical care. A farmer owned typically less than five acres of poorly irrigated land with infertile soil. Many owned a single buffalo that was just enough for their home needs. 60 percent of calves died newborn. With no electricity and refrigeration, milk could not be stored, or transported too far before getting contaminated. Nestlé built refrigerated dairies as milk collection points in each town and its trucks transported the milk. With the trucks came veterinarians, nutritionists, agronomists, and quality assurance experts. Medicine and nutritional supplements were provided for sick animals, and monthly training sessions were held for local farmers. Farmers quickly learnt that the milk quality depended upon the cows' diet, which in turn depended on adequate feed crop irrigation, which in turn, depended upon adequate supply of water from bore wells. Nestlé helped to build the farmer's value chain while building its own. In 1962, just about 180 farmers supplied milk to Nestlé. Today, Nestlé buys milk from more than 75,000 farmers in the region, collecting milk twice daily from more than 650 village dairies. Better and higher milk yield generates better income to farmers, better credit, better buying power, and higher standards of living. This is strategic CSR—Nestlé's distinctive strategy of working with farmers and sourcing reliable commodities cannot be separated from its CSR among involved local communities. While it makes shareholders happy, it first and foremost makes great social impact, which should be the first criteria of CSR success.

APPENDIX 9.1 Standard Accounting Measures of Competitive Corporate Performance

Ratio	Calculation	Interpretation
Profitability Ratios:		
Return on Sales (ROS)	Profits after taxes/Total sales	Measures efficiency of sales management
Return on Total Assets (ROA)	Profits after taxes/Total assets	Measures return on total investments in the firm
Return on Equity (ROE)	Profits after taxes/Total stockholders' equity	Measures return on total equity investments in the firm
Gross Profit Margin	(Sales – CGS)/Sales	Measures sales available to cover operating expenses other than CGS
Earnings per Share (EPS)	(Profits after taxes – Preferred stock dividends)/Number of common stock shares outstanding	Measures or common stock profitability
Price Earnings Ratio (P/E)	Current market price per share/After tax earnings per share	Measures anticipated firm performance; a high P/E ratio indicates that investors anticipate strong future firm performance
Cash Flow per Share	(Profits after taxes + Depreciation)/Number of common stock shares outstanding	Measures funds available to fund activities above current level costs
Liquidity Ratios:		
Current Ratio	Current assets/Current liabilities	Measures firm's ability to cover its current liabilities
Quick Ratio	(Current assets – Inventory)/ Current liabilities	Measures firm's ability to cover its short-term liabilities without selling its inventories
Leverage Ratios:		
Debt to Assets	Total debts/Total assets	Measures debt-financing of a firm's activities
Debt to Equity	Total debts/Total equity	Measures debt versus equity financing of a firm's activities
Times Interest Earned	Profits before interest and taxes/Total interest charges	Measures profitability over capital rent
Activity Ratios:		
Inventory Turnover	CGS/Average inventory	Measures inventory depletion or non-inventory costs of production
Accounts Receivable Turnover	Annual credit sales/Accounts receivable	Measures average time to collect on credit sales
Average Collection Period	Accounts receivable/Average daily sales	Measures average time to receive payment after a credit sale

Source: Author's own.

Chapter 10

The CEO as a Strategic Leader of Innovative Management of Corporate Growth

Wall Street analysts and investors demand annually double-digit growth rates from almost every publicly traded company. This is because without growth, stocks perform dismally and CEOs lose their jobs with or without executive compensations. Without growth, employees stagnate and executive careers stall. Without growth, organizations themselves grow stale, and lose their competitiveness (Govindarajan and Trimble 2005: xxiii). As a business ripens, however, growth inevitably becomes more difficult; that is, in general, aging may improve competencies in incremental innovation but damages competence in radical innovation (Sorenson and Stuart 2000). The cases of GM, Ford, and Chrysler in the domestic auto world, and those of Northwest, American, and Continental in the airlines industry illustrate this.

DIFFERENTIAL GROWTH AND DIFFERENTIATED LEADERSHIP

Different kinds of growth strategies require different kinds of leaders. Growth via turnaround is different from organic growth via homegrown products. Growth via new product development needs to harness innovation leadership. Growth via brand equity, brand extensions, and expanding product lines needs a strong marketing brand management leadership. Geographic expansion driving growth by penetrating new markets and customer accounts demands unique market expansion leadership. Expansionary growth via mergers and acquisitions requires due diligence skills and different assimilation and financial leadership talents for a successful acquisition-merger event (Gulati 2004: 127). Growth via bold acquisitions, however, rarely benefits investors, customers, and employees in the long run. This is called the mega-merger mouse trap (Harding and Rovit 2004). Organic growth that generates from within, on the other hand, is a more robust but difficult strategy that benefits all stakeholders alike. Organic growth needs strategic innovation—the latter delivers technological and market breakthrough growth. Through strategic innovation, corporations can not only stay ahead of change, they can create change. They can consistently create, grow, and profit from new business models (Govindarajan and Trimble 2005).

Table 10.1 captures most of the corporate growth strategies under two major categories: turnaround and transformation management. Even rescue, survival, and revival strategies under turnaround are basically growth strategies. Even termination strategies such as those presented in Chapter 7 or 11 are really growth strat-egies, from a state of crisis and insolvency to move on to found new corporations. In this chapter, we will primarily discuss mergers, acquisitions, and alliance growth strategies.

TABLE 10.1 Classifying Corporate Growth Strategies

Major growth domain	Types of growth	Context of growth	Growth sub-strategy
Turnaround	Rescue and Revival	Failing Company	Cash Flow Crisis Management Inventory Management Receivables Management Payables Management Operating Cycle Management Cash Cycle Management Employee Motivation Management Bank Workout Management Supplier Chain Rescue Management Distributor Chain Rescue Management Customer Satisfaction Management Organizational Downsizing and Outsourcing Plant Shutdowns and Labor Retrenchment Domestic or Offshore Outsourcing
	Survival or Death	Insolvent Company	Debt Restructuring Equity Restructuring Private Equity Fund-raising Divestitures Rescue Mergers or Joint Ventures Hostile Takeovers Chapter 11: Reorganization Chapter 7: Liquidation
Transformation	Organic (Growth from Within)	New Product Development	Plant Redesign, Relocation, Renovation Creativity and Innovation, Invention and Patents Importing and New Materials Management New Product Launches New Product Promotions Management New Product Support Services Management
		Brand Development	Brand Equity and Reputation Management Brand Community Management Celebrity Endorsement Management
		Product Lines Extension	Deepening Product Assortment Widening Product Lines Complementary Product Lines
		Geographic Expansion	Exporting and Export Branch Management Foreign Direct Investments Capturing New Domestic Markets Capturing New Trade Regions Capturing Continental Markets Pure Licensing Agreements Domestic and Global Franchising
	Growth from Organic and Outside Sources	Collaboration	Cross Licensing Foreign Technical Collaboration Non-equity Strategic Alliances Equity Strategic Alliances
	Growth from Outside Sources	Joint Ventures	Minority Joint Ventures Fifty-fifty Joint Ventures Majority Joint Ventures Wholly Owned Subsidiaries
		Diversification	Vertical Integration and Horizontal Integration Divestitures to Finance Market Concentration Mergers and Acquisitions Spin-offs and Equity Carve Outs Tracking Stock

Source: Author's own.

ORGANIC GROWTH: GROOMING THE NEXT GENERATION

Finding and grooming the next generation of innovators is one key to corporate growth, but most companies smother their creative talent. The biggest challenge any growing company faces is to identify and foster the next generation of breakthrough innovators. Grooming innovators from within or from without, companies do a magnificent job of smothering creative spark; that is, they usually develop leaders who replicate than innovate. Successful growth companies, however, have intense talent-management processes in place and put identified innovators in the line of fire, where natural innovators thrive. Mentoring and peer network are crucial for providing support to future innovators. Once rising breakthrough innovators have been developed and established in the middle of the organization—where they become "innovation hubs"—they can better see how existing products, ideas, people, or even entire businesses can be recombined in new, value-adding ways (Chon, Katzenbach, and Vlak 2008: 64–5):

> Every major industry was once a growth industry. However, some that are now riding a wave of growth are very much in the shadow of decline. Others that are thought of as seasoned growth industries have actually stopped growing. In every case, the reason growth is threatened, slowed or stopped, is not because the market is saturated. It is because there has been a failure of management. (Levitt 1960/2004)

Every CEO wants to find ways for the company to grow, but real power lies in doing so profitably, and that takes serious work. Some 10 years ago, everybody talked about corporate top line growth; then the focus was cost containment and tightening the belt; in essence, before you could grow, you had to shrink. Five years ago sometime around 2003, the topic of top line growth re-emerged, but then the focus was on profitability. Currently, all CEOs are re-focusing on top line growth, but now the emphasis is on translating top line growth to shareholder value (Stewart 2004). Executives are raising the bar on themselves, which is a good thing. To meet their top line growth goals, however, they must find ways to distinguish their market offerings by continuous innovation, deepening customers and supplier relationships, and creative bundling of products and services, thus providing personalized "solutions" to concrete customer needs (Gulati 2004).

MAJOR CORPORATE GROWTH OPTIONS

Corporate growth is basically both "internal" and organic from homegrown products or "external" and from outside. The latter can be "expansionary" via mergers, acquisitions, and joint ventures or "intensive" via divestitures, franchises, corporate spin-offs, and equity carve outs. The capital realized from franchises, divestitures, spin-offs, and equity carve outs is pumped back into organic growth or into specialized products.

Organic growth can occur either through proven, established businesses and industries, and this can occur either via maintaining or expanding one's market share. The more promising organic growth is in new and untested business definitions (e.g., globalization, outsourcing, plant relocation and redesign) and new industries (e.g., digital technologies, demographic shifts, regulatory change). The latter growth is non-linear, explosive via radical innovations, market breakthroughs, and technological breakthroughs. Accordingly, Table 10.2 provides another taxonomy of corporate growth strategies.

TABLE 10.2   A Taxonomy of Corporate Growth Strategies

Phenomenon	Type of growth	Growth strategies	Strategic means	Typical industry examples
Corporate Growth	External	Expansionary	Mergers Acquisitions Joint ventures Collaborations	AOL, eBay, K Mart Enron, Tyco, Global.com
			Strategic alliances	Xerox-Canon, Kodak-Fuji, NUMMI
			Franchises	McDonald's, Wendy, Seven-Eleven
		Intensive	Divestitures	GMAC, Jaguar, Hummer, Saturn, Land Rover
			Corporate spin-offs Equity carve outs	Visteon, Delphi, Mopar
	Internal or Organic	Within established or proven businesses or industries	Maintaining or expanding market share in growing or emerging markets	Northwest-Delta, Ann-Hauser Bush, Sears-K Mart, Wal-Mart, Macy's
			Capturing larger share of mature markets often through product innovations	Southwest Airlines, Amtrak, McDonald's, Cirque du Soleil, Fed-Ex-Kinko
		Into new and untested business definitions and industries (e.g., globalization, digital technologies, demographic shifts, regulatory change)	Innovating new business models	Dell, eBay, Amazon.com, GE, P&G Google
			Strategic innovation that leads to technological and market breakthroughs	Apple's iPod, iTunes, and iPhones Blackberry, Sony, GE, Toyota Prius, Honda Insight OnStar, Disney's Moviebeam

Source: Author's own.

Note: See also Govindarajan and Trimble (2005: xxiv).

TABLE 10.3   A Framework for Organic Growth

Internal or Organic Growth	Within existing or proven businesses or industries ("Red Oceans")	Maintaining or expanding the profitability of these entities so that it trains and motivates the employees
		Capturing larger share of markets through newer product and service offerings
	Establishing new and untested business definitions and industries ("Blue Oceans")	Establishing new business models/entities
		Strategic innovation in establishing new markets and offerings as the destination of particular market or product

Source: Kim and Mauborgne (2004).

Within the domain of organic growth, one could visualize several promising options for corporate growth (Table 10.3).

Incremental growth through incremental innovations is no longer enough. To continue to grow, the company must do new things, break all rules, redefine the industry, or get into new and untested industries.

SOME CRITICAL OBSERVATIONS ON CORPORATE GROWTH STRATEGIES

Virtually all corporations stall and stagnate at some point in their lifetime, and their stalling typically follows the period of their highest growth. Few large companies avoid stalling in revenue growth. The average Fortune 500 Company loses 74 percent of its market capitalization in the decade surrounding the growth stall, and the CEO and senior teams' turnover is more than half the time (Olson and Bever 2008).

Growth, real growth, depends on innovation. Surely, a big acquisition can inflate a company's top line but it is hardly fair to call this growth; "agglomeration" would be a better word. Acquisition deals (e.g., Tyco, Vivendi, HealthSouth, and Daimler-Chrysler) rarely produced above average growth for more than a few years at a time. Nevertheless, you will hardly find a company that has shown strong growth for over a decade without demonstrating world-class innovation. Whether the company invented a new industry structure (e.g., Microsoft when it de-verticalized the computer industry), pioneered a new business model (e.g., Dell, Costco), or launched a bountiful brood of sleek new products (e.g., Nokia, Apple), innovation is the fuel for growth. When a company runs out of innovation, it runs out of growth. A company cannot outgrow its competitors unless it can out-innovate them (Hamel and Getz 2004: 76–77).

Numerous studies confirm that mature companies attempting to grow by entering new businesses (e.g., acquisitions, mergers, joint ventures, or entering disconnected new markets) fail more often than not; the failure rate could be as much as 90 percent (Christensen 2002; Christensen et al. 2004). The usual explanation is that companies mismanage the venturing process. That is, the executives are too risk-averse, their expansion cultures are inappropriate, they fail to provide sufficient incentives, and they involve the wrong managers. Nevertheless, the real problem may be elsewhere—a shortage of suitable opportunities rather than a shortage of courage or venturing skills, and hence, they do not develop any significant new business. Often, the total costs of expansions exceeded even optimistic forecasts of the potential value of the few successes. Corporate venturing units are still useful, but they do not solve the growth problems of mature companies (Campbell 2004: 27–28).

No organization can achieve greatness without a vigoros leader who is driven by a passion to succeed. A leader has to have a vision of grandeur, a vision that can produce eager followers in vast numbers. In business, the followers are customers. In order to nurture these customers, the entire corporation must view itself as a customer-creating and customer-satisfying organism. "Management must think of itself not as producing products but as providing customer-creating value satisfactions." The organization must learn to think of itself not as producing goods or services but as buying, developing, and retaining customers, and as doing the things that will make people want to do business with it. The chief executive has the inescapable responsibility for creating this environment, this viewpoint, this attitude, this aspiration (Levitt 1960/2004: 149).

Stable, healthy growth is built on the profitability of customers, and not on their raw numbers or their loyalty. In making direct-marketing decisions, too many executives overemphasize short-term cost over long-term gain, favoring the pursuit of customers who are cheap to acquire and cheap to retain without necessarily being profitable. Clearly, companies that focus only on customers who are easy to acquire and retain are not allocating their resources, as efficiently as they should. Maximizing the likelihood of acquiring or retaining an individual customer is not the same as maximizing overall customer profitability. Maximizing customer acquisition and customer retention separately does not maximize profits; they must make direct marketing a single system of acquisition, retention, and profitability (Thomas, Reinartz, and Kumar 2004).

A company is poised to grow if it has an inherent cost advantage (e.g., Dell, Microsoft, Southwest, Wal-Mart). But most companies do not have such advantage and still must grow. Meanwhile, most companies across a wide range of industries have increasingly begun to identify "maturation" and "commoditization" as emerging challenges to corporate growth. Because of globalization, maturing technologies, ease of imitation, decreasing barriers to market entry, open standards in technology markets, or pressures from customers who are themselves being squeezed, more and more companies are feeling the intensity of price competition, leading many to describe their business as commodity markets (Gulati 2004: 125). "Commoditization is a deadly game—it destroys your sustainable competitive advantage (SCA) of unique differentiation of product, brand, market, and customer." Under such a situation, you are constantly scrambling to make your margins, and cannot think of top line growth.

INTERNATIONAL CHAMPIONS OF PROFITABLE GROWTH

Many companies have posted significant top-line growth over the past two decades in their economic regions (e.g., Wal-Mart in North America, BP in Europe, Toyota in Asia, and News Corporation in Australia), but the question is, which of these corporations were best in converting all of that growth into shareholder value? At the request of *Harvard Business Review* (for their July–August 2004 Special Issue on Top Line Growth), G. Bennett Stewart III (2004), Senior Partner, Stern Stewart & Co, a New York-based management consulting firm, researched this question. He and his colleagues began by identifying the companies with the highest absolute annual revenue growth during 1983–2003, and ranked the companies according to revenue growth. They next calculated the market value added (MVA) to the shareholders of each company (= total market value – total capital invested) since its inception. They eliminated companies that posted negative MVA at the end of the 20-year period, and ranked the remaining companies according to their MVA scores. They then divided the MVA of each company for 2003, by its 2003 revenues, to generate a ratio that indicates efficiency of translating revenues into added shareholder value. They again ranked the companies by the MVA 2003/Revenues 2003 ratio scores. They next added to the ranks (revenue growth rank in 2003, and MVA/revenue rank) to form a (un-weighted) composite rank to form an overall rank of these companies. We present their results of the highest 20 top line growth companies in North America (Table 10.4), Europe (Table 10.5), Asia (Table 10.6), and Southern Hemisphere (Table 10.7).

The top line growth companies listed in Tables 10.4 to 10.7 show considerable diversity in terms of countries, industries, revenue growth, revenue size, and MVA size. Table 10.8 captures this diversity phenomenon in top line corporate growth.

As is clear from Table 10.8, among the 20 top line growth companies of each economic region, there is a decisive "country concentration." That is:

- All 20 top line growth companies hail from the U.S.A. in the North American region.
- Seventeen are from Japan in the Asian region.
- Thirteen are from Australia and seven from South Africa in the Southern Hemisphere region.

TABLE 10.4   North American High-growth Value Adders

Overall rank	Company (Location, Industry)	Revenue 2003 (US$ billion)	Revenue growth	Revenue growth rank	MVA 2003 (US$ billion)	MVA/ Revenue 2003	Rank: MVA/ Revenue 2003
1	General Electric Fairfield, CT; Diversified	134.2	107.4	3	251.6	1.88	7
2	Wal-Mart Bentonville, AK; Retail	244.5	239.8	1	185.8	0.76	13
3	Altria Group NY, NY; Tobacco/food	81.8	72.4	4	62.6	0.77	12
3	Home Depot Atlanta, GA; Retail	58.0	58.0	6	56.4	0.97	10
3	Microsoft Redmond, WA; Software	32.2	32.1	15	227.7	7.07	1
6	Exxon Mobil Irving, TX; Energy	246.7	158.2	2	114.1	0.46	15
6	IBM Armonk, NY; Computer services	89.1	49.0	8	96.5	1.08	9
6	Johnson & Johnson New Brunswick, NJ; Health care products	41.9	35.9	13	101.1	2.41	4
9	Pfizer NY, Pharmaceuticals	45.2	41.4	10	77.1	1.71	8
10	Dell Round Rock, TX; Computers	35.4	35.4	14	80.4	2.27	5
10	P&G Cincinnati, OH; Consumer products	43.4	30.9	16	105.3	2.43	3
12	Intel Santa Clara, CA; Semiconductors	30.1	29.0	18	168.4	5.59	2
13	Hewlett Packard Palo Alto, CA; Computers	73.1	68.4	5	25.3	0.35	16
14	Target Minneapolis, MN; Retail	48.2	41.2	11	22.9	0.48	14
14	UPS Atlanta, GA; Transport/delivery	33.5	27.5	19	68.7	2.05	6
16	Costco Issaquah, WA; Retail	42.5	42.5	9	9.8	0.23	17
17	Cardinal Health Dublin, OH; Health care products	50.5	50.3	7	7.4	0.15	2.0
18	Walgreen Deerfield, IL; Retail	32.5	30.1	17	29.5	0.91	11
19	Boeing Chicago, IL; Aerospace	50.5	39.4	12	10.3	0.20	19
20	Viacom NY, Media	26.6	26.3	20	6.1	0.22	18

Source: Stewart (2004: 60).

TABLE 10.5   European High-growth Value Adders

Overall rank	Company (Location, Industry)	Revenue 2003 (US$)	Revenue growth	Revenue growth rank	MVA 2003 (US$)	MVA/ Revenue 2003	Rank: MVA/ Revenue 2003
1	Nestlé Vevey, Switzerland; Food	71.2	59.2	5	65.6	0.92	5
2	Total Courbevoie, France; Energy	132.0	92.4	3	83.5	0.63	8
3	GlaxoSmithKline London; Pharmaceuticals	38.3	36.9	11	122.2	3.19	1
4	Eni Rome, Italy; Energy	64.9	50.7	7	46.2	0.71	6
5	BP London, U.K.; Energy	232.6	185.5	1	102.3	0.43	13
5	Royal Dutch/Shell Group The Hague, Netherland; Energy	201.9	124.8	2	89.5	0.44	12
7	Nokia Espoo, Finland; Telecom equipment	37.1	34.5	13	61.6	1.66	2
8	France Telecom Paris; Telecom	58.1	57.4	6	26.5	0.46	11
9	Deutsche Telecom Bonn, Germany; Telecom	70.3	42.2	9	38.0	0.54	10
9	Telefónica Madrid, Spain; Telecom	35.8	30.8	16	46.6	1.30	3
9	Tesco Hertfordshire, U.K.; Retail	41.6	38.3	10	23.0	0.55	9
12	Carrefour Paris; Retail	88.9	79.0	4	29.1	0.33	16
13	Olivetti Ivrea, Italy; Tech + Office products	29.6	27.4	18	27.9	0.95	4
14	BT London, U.K.; Telecom	31.9	22.1	20	22.6	0.70	7
15	Suez Paris; Utilities	49.9	49.1	8	9.9	0.20	20
16	Statoil Stavanger, Norway; Energy	37.3	33.3	14	14.0	0.38	15
17	BMW Munich, Germany; Automotive	41.5	35.7	12	9.1	0.22	18
18	EADS Paris; Aerospace	38.0	27.6	17	15.7	0.41	14
19	METRO Dusseldorf, Germany; Retail	67.5	32.1	15	14.8	0.21	19
20	Deutsche Post Bonn, Germany; Transport/ delivery	49.6	25.8	19	14.0	0.28	17

Source: Stewart (2004: 61).

TABLE 10.6   Asian High-growth Value Adders

Overall rank	Company (location, industry)	Revenue 2003 (US$)	Revenue growth	Revenue growth rank	MVA 2003 (US$)	MVA/ Revenue 2003	Rank: MVA/ Revenue 2003
1	Toyota Aichi, Japan; Automotive	136.0	109.0	1	43.6	0.32	5
2	Nippon Telegraph & Telephone Tokyo; Telecom	92.5	63.8	2	24.3	0.26	7
3	Samsung Electronics Seoul, S. Korea; Consumer electronics	47.6	41.3	8	20	0.42	3
4	Sony Tokyo, Japan; Consumer electronics	63.3	57.6	3	10.6	0.16	10
5	Honda Tokyo; Automotive	67.5	41.2	9	18.2	0.27	6
6	Canon Tokyo; Camera, office equipment	29.8	25.1	15	23.6	0.79	1
7	Mitsubishi Tokyo; Diversified	112.9	44.4	5	7.9	0.07	14
8	Hitachi Tokyo; Diversified	69.4	49.4	4	3.0	0.04	16
8	NEC Tokyo; Computers	39.8	30.8	12	8.8	0.22	8
8	Nissan Tokyo; Automotive	57.8	23.6	18	30.7	0.53	2
11	Matsushita Electric Osaka; Consumer electronics	62.7	42.6	6	3.0	0.05	15
11	Toshiba Tokyo; Computers	47.9	34.6	10	6.9	0.14	11
13	Fujitsu Tokyo; Diversified	39.1	32.9	11	5.2	0.13	12
14	Indian Oil New Delhi; Energy	22.6	21.4	20	7.4	0.33	4
14	Mitsui and Company Tokyo; Diversified	112.1	42.1	7	4.7	0.04	17
16	Mitsubishi Electric Tokyo; Electronics	30.8	22.7	19	5.2	0.17	9
17	Ito-Yokado Tokyo; Retail	28.3	24.2	17	3.1	0.11	13
18	Itochu Tokyo; General trading retail	88.6	30.7	13	1.2	0.01	19
18	Sumitomo Tokyo; General trading consumer goods	78.2	25.2	14	2.1	0.03	18
20	China Petroleum & Chemical Beijing; Energy	51.3	24.5	16	0.2	0.00	20

Source: Stewart (2004: 62).

TABLE 10.7   Southern Hemisphere High-growth Value Adders

Overall rank	Company (location, industry)	Revenue 2003 (US$)	Revenue growth	Revenue growth rank	MVA 2003 (US$)	MVA/ Revenue 2003	Rank: MVA/ Revenue 2003
1	BHP Billiton Melbourne, Australia; Energy/ natural resources	17.5	13.5	4	35.8	2.04	2
2	Telstra Melbourne, Australia; Telecom	15.4	12.1	5	30.8	2.00	3
3	News Corporation Sydney, Australia; Media	22.4	21.1	1	9.4	0.42	8
4	Woolworths Sydney, Australia; Retail	19.7	17.0	2	8.2	0.41	9
5	Rio Tinto Group Melbourne, Australia; Mining	8.2	5.3	12	20.8	2.54	1
6	SABMiller Group Johannesburg, S. Africa; Beverages	10.0	6.8	9	6.8	0.68	5
7	Coles Myer Tooranga, Australia; Retail	20.3	16.0	3	4.5	0.22	13
8	Brambles Group Sydney, Australia; Mfg/transport	5.9	5.5	11	3.0	0.51	6
8	Wesfarmers Perth, Australia; Energy/chemicals	5.6	5.0	13	4.5	0.82	4
10	Amcor Abbotsford, Australia; Packaging	8.0	7.1	6	1.8	0.23	12
11	Sasol Johannesburg, S. Africa; Energy	8.7	7.0	7	1.9	0.21	14
12	Leighton Holdings Sydney, Australia; Construction, project management	3.6	3.3	15	1.8	0.50	7
13	Australian Gas Light Co. North Sydney, Australia; Energy	2.9	2.5	16	1.1	0.38	10
14	Lend Lease New South Wales, Australia; Real estate services	7.4	6.9	8	0.4	0.05	19
15	Tiger Brands Sandton, S. Africa; Food	3.3	2.1	18	1.1	0.34	11
16	Metro Cash and Carry Johannesburg, S. Africa; Wholesale food distribution	7.3	6.2	10	0.1	0.01	20
17	CSR New South Wales, Australia; Construction, building materials	5.5	3.7	14	0.6	0.11	17
18	Pick'n Pay Stores Cape Town, S. Africa; Retail	3.2	2.2	17	0.6	0.20	15
19	Nampak Sandton, S. Africa; Packaging	2.6	1.8	20	0.4	0.14	16
20	Anglo American Platinum Johannesburg, S. Africa; Metals	2.5	1.9	19	0.1	0.06	18

Source: Stewart (2004: 63).

TABLE 10.8   The Diversity Phenomenon of Top Line Corporate Growth

Economic region	Country diversity	Industry diversity	Revenue growth rate diversity	Growth size diversity	
				Revenues	MVA
North America	U.S.A. (20 companies)	Retail (5)	>100% (3)	>$B100 (3)	>$B100 (7)
		Computers (3)	50–100% (4)	$B50–100 (6)	$B50–100 (6)
		Health care products (2)	25–50% (13)	$B25–50 (11)	$B25–50 (2)
		Aerospace (1)	<25% (0)	<$B25 (0)	<$B25 (5)
		Consumer products (1)			
		Diversified (1)			
		Energy (1)			
		Media (1)			
		Pharmaceuticals (1)			
		Semiconductors (1)			
		Software (1)			
		Tobacco/food (1)			
		Transport/delivery (1)			
Europe	France (5)	Energy (5)	>100% (2)	>$B100 (3)	>$B100 (2)
	U.K. (4)	Telecommunications (4)	50–100% (5)	$B50–100 (6)	$B50–100 (4)
	Germany (4)	Retail (3)	25–50% (12)	$B25–50 (11)	$B25–50 (6)
	Italy (2)	Aerospace (1)	<25% (1)	<$B25 (0)	<$B25 (8)
	Switzerland (1)	Food (1)			
	Spain (1)	Pharmaceuticals (1)			
	Netherlands (1)	Tech/office products (1)			
	Norway (1)	Automotive (1)			
		Telecom equipment (1)			
		Transport/delivery (1)			
		Utilitics (1)			
Asia	Japan (17)	Diversified (4)	>100% (1)	>$B100 (3)	>$B100 (0)
	S. Korea (1)	Consumer electronics (3)	50–100% (2)	$B50–100 (9)	$B50–100 (0)
	China (1)	General trading/retail (3)	25–50% (12)	$B25–50 (7)	$B25–50 (2)
	India (1)	Automotive (3)	<25% (5)	<$B25 (1)	<$B25 (18)
		Energy (2)			
		Camera, office product (1)			
		Consumer goods (1)			
		Computers (1)			
		Electronics (1)			
		Telecom (1)			
Southern Hemisphere	Australia (13)	Energy (2)	>100% (0)	>$B100 (0)	>$B100 (0)
	South Africa (7)	Retail (3)	50–100% (0)	$B50–100 (0)	$B50–100 (0)
		Packaging (2)	25–50% (0)	$B25–50 (0)	$B25–50 (2)
		Wholesale (1)	<25% (20)	<$B25 (20)	<$B25 (18)
		Beverages (1)			
		Construction (1)			
		Food (1)			
		Mfg/transport (1)			
		Media (1)			
		Metals (1)			
		Mining (1)			
		Project management (1)			
		Real estate (1)			
		Telecom (1)			

Source: Author's own.

Note: Based on Tables 10.4 to 10.7.

- Five come from France.
- Four each from Germany and U.K. in the European region.

Among top growth companies, the "industry concentration" is varied:

- In U.S.A, it is mostly retail (5), computers (3), and health care products (2).
- In Europe, energy (5) and telecommunications (4) dominate, with three retail companies.
- In Asia, "diversified" (4) dominate, with three each from consumer electronics, general retail, and automotive.
- In Australia–South Africa, there is a large spread of top line growth among industries, with energy, retail, and packaging showing some form of concentration.

Revenue growth rates of 2003 differ considerably across regions:

- In U.S.A, three companies reported over 100 percent growth, and 17 between 25 and 100 percent.
- In Europe, only two companies posted over 100 percent growth, while 17 swung between 25 and 100 percent.
- In Asia, only one company recorded over 100 percent growth, while 14 were between 25 and 100 percent.
- In the Southern Hemisphere, all 20 companies showed growth rates below 25 percent.

Lastly, there is a significant "size concentration" in relation to 2003 revenues and 2003 MVA:

- In U.S.A, three companies recorded over $100 billion in revenues and seven companies over $100 billion in MVA.
- In Europe, three firms reported over $100 billion in revenues and only two firms over $100 billion in MVA.
- In Asia, three companies recorded over $100 billion in revenues but zero companies in over $100 billion in MVA.
- In the Southern Hemisphere, almost all companies registered revenues and MVA of less than $25 billion.

In general, judged by 2003 revenues and MVA data, we may conclude the following:

- Countries within an economic region played a significant role in recording top line corporate growth rates.
- Energy (10 companies) and retail (13 companies) industries recorded top line growth in all four regions.
- Four European companies recorded top line growth in the telecom industry, one in Asia and one in Australia.
- The automotive industry (three companies) and consumer electronics industry (three companies) were doing extremely well in Asia, but hardly anywhere else.
- Thirty-five (44 percent) of the 80 top line corporate growth companies of 2003 in the world mostly came from energy (10), retail (13), telecom (6), and diversified (5) industries.

- Top line corporate growth opportunity in the world seems to be in the services industry (retail [13], telecom [6], consumer electronics and office products [7], diversified [5], computer and software services [5], food and beverages [4], health care and pharmaceutics [4], transport/delivery [3], media [2], packaging [2], and other services [5] = 56 services companies or 70 percent) than in the manufacturing sector.

Table 10.9 lists top line corporate growth destroyers of the world.
We observe the following trends of the 15 low-growth companies listed:

- Five (33 percent) are from the energy industry, two from U.S.A (Chevron-Texaco, ConocoPhillips), one from Europe (Repsol YPF, Madrid, Spain), one from Asia (Nippon Oil, Japan) and one from the Southern Hemisphere (Caltex Australia, Sydney).

TABLE 10.9 World's High-growth Value Laggards or Destroyers

Economic region	Companies, (city, industry)	Revenue 2003 (US$)	Revenue growth (%)	MVA 2003 (US$)	MVA/ Revenue 2003
North America	Ford Motors Dearborn, MI; Automotive	164.2	119.7	17.2	0.10
	General Motors Corporation (GMC) Detroit, MI; Automotive	185.5	110.9	0.9	0.01
	ChevronTexaco San Ramon, CA; Energy	120.0	92.7	14.3	0.12
	ConocoPhillips Houston, TX; Energy	105.1	89.8	5.4	0.05
	McKesson San Francisco, CA; Health care	57.1	53.9	(7.4)	(0.13)
Europe	Daimler-Chrysler Stuttgart, Germany; Automotive	136.4	97.7	4.6	0.03
	Volkswagen Wolfsburg, Germany; Automotive	87.2	66.7	(20.3)	(0.23)
	Ahold Zaandam, Netherlands; Retail	70.7	62.9	9.0	0.13
	Repsol YPF Madrid, Spain; Energy	46.9	46.9	5.9	0.13
	Vodafone Newbury, U.K.; Telecom	45.2	45.2	(79.1)	(1.75)
Asia	Nippon Oil Tokyo, Japan; Energy	35.3	22.4	(1.0)	(0.03)
Southern Hemisphere	Quantas Airways New South Wales, Australia; Airline	8.5	7.3	(0.2)	(0.02)
	Caltex Australia Sydney, Australia; Energy	7.8	5.9	(0.3)	(0.03)
	Sappi Johannesburg, S. Africa; Pulp-paper	4.4	3.9	(0.2)	(0.05)
	Mayne Nickless North Sydney, Australia; Telecom	3.9	3.3	(0.9)	(0.22)

Source: Stewart (2004: 60–63).

- Hence, the energy debacle affected all the economic regions in 2003.
- Four are automotive (Ford, GM, Daimler-Chrysler, and Volkswagen).
- Two are telecom companies (Vodafone, U.K.; Mayne Nickless, Australia).
- The remaining four are each from the health care (McKesson, CA), retail (Zaandam, Netherlands), airline (Quantas, Australia), and pulp-paper (Sappi, Johannesburg) industries.

If we consider all the data in Tables 10.4 to 10.9, then within the same year (2003) and within the same industry, and under more or less similar economic conditions, some companies are winners, and some losers—as is illustrated in Table 10.10. Other things being equal, top-line growth, therefore, is primarily an internal variable relating to planning, resources, top management leadership, managerial and employee skills, innovation and new product launches, and the like. Table 10.11 represents an inter-regional comparison of 2003 growth performance.

TABLE 10.10   Global Top Line Corporate Growth: Winners and Destroyers of 2003

Industry	Top line growth winners	Top line growth destroyers	Percentage winners
Automotive	BMW (Germany) Toyota (Japan) Honda (Japan) Nissan (Japan)	Ford (U.S.A.) GM (U.S.A.) Daimler-Chrysler (Germany) Volkswagen (Germany)	4 vs 4: 50%
Energy	Exxon Mobil (U.S.A.) Total (France) Eni (Italy) BP (U.K.) Royal Dutch/Shell (Netherlands) Statoil (Norway) Indian Oil (India) China Petroleum (China) Sasol (S. Africa) Australian Gas (Australia)	Chevron Texaco (U.S.A.) ConocoPhillips (U.S.A.) Repsol YPF (Spain) Nippon Oil (Japan) Caltex (Australia)	10 vs 5: 67%
Telecom	France Telecom (France) Deutsche Telecom (Germany) Telefónica (Spain) BT (U.K.) Nippon (Japan) Telstra (Australia)	Vodafone (U.K.) Mayne Nickless (Australia)	6 vs 2: 75%
Retail	Wal-Mart (U.S.A.) Home Depot (U.S.A.) Target (U.S.A.) Costco (U.S.A.) Walgreen (U.S.A.) Tesco (U.K.) Carrefour (France) METRO (Germany) Ito-Yokado (Japan) Itochu (Japan) Woolworths (Australia) Coles Myer (Australia) Pick'n Pay Stores (S. Africa)	Ahold (Netherlands)	13 vs 1: 93%
All four industries	23 companies	12 companies	23 vs 12: 66%

Source: Author's own.

TABLE 10.11 Inter-regional Comparison of 2003 Growth Performance ($ Billions)

Stats	North America Revenues	North America MVA	Europe Revenues	Europe MVA	Asia Revenues	Asia MVA	Southern Hemisphere Revenues	Southern Hemisphere MVA	All four regions Revenues	All four regions MVA
Number of Companies	20	20	20	20	20	20	20	20	80	80
Sum	1,439.9	1,707.0	1,418.0	862.1	1,278.2	229.7	180.0	133.7	4,316.1	2,932.5
Mean	71.995	85.35	70.90	43.105	63.91	11.485	9.0	6.685	53.951	36.656
SD	64.611	73.461	55.758	33.618	31.41	11.58	6.457	10.340	51.873	51.247
Median	46.7	72.9	49.75	29.1	60.25	7.15	7.35	1.85	41.012	27.750
Max	246.7	251.6	232.6	122.2	136.0	43.6	22.4	35.8	246.7	251.6
Min	26.6	6.1	29.6	9.1	27.6	0.2	2.5	0.1	2.5	0.1
Range	220.1	244.6	203	113.1	113.4	43.4	19.9	35.7	244.2	251.5
Pearson's Correlation	$P=0.406$ ($p<0.001$)		$P=0.591$ ($p<0.001$)		$P=0.321$ ($p<0.010$)		$P=0.549$ ($p<0.001$)		$P=0.941$ ($p<0.000$)	

Stats	North America Revenue growth	North America MVA/2003 revenues	Europe Revenue growth	Europe MVA/2003 revenues	Asia Revenue growth	Asia MVA/2003 revenues	Southern Hemisphere Revenue growth	Southern Hemisphere MVA/2003 revenues	All four regions Revenue growth	All four regions MVA/2003 revenues
Sum	1,215.2	31.99	1,084.8	14.51	787.1	4.09	147	11.87	3,234.1	62.46
Mean	60.76	1.60	54.24	0.72	39.36	0.20	7.35	0.59	40.43	0.78
SD	52.78	6.92	40.09	0.69	20.32	0.199	5.62	11.58	39.92	1.14
Median	41.3	0.94	37.6	0.5	33.75	0.15	5.85	29.1	32.1	0.41
Max	239.8	7.07	185.5	3.19	109	0.79	21.1	2.54	239.8	7.07
Min	26.3	0.15	22.1	0.2	21.4	0	1.8	0.01	1.8	0
Range	213.5	6.92	163.4	2.99	87.6	0.79	19.3	2.53	238	7.07
Pearson's Correlation	$P=-0.256$ ($p<0.001$)		$P=-0.181$ ($p<0.011$)		$P=-0.0003$ ($p<0.980$)		$P=0.214$ ($p<0.010$)		$P=0.021$ ($p<0.781$)	

Source: Author's own.

RECENT CHAMPIONS OF CORPORATE GROWTH

Regardless of the economic cycle, irrespective of the overall publishing trends in the business book market, the management and professional literature on corporate growth is growing, but lacks in novelty, validity, and utility (Ghemavat 2004). Knowledge about best growth strategies and practices is scarce, especially in relation to growth that stems from strategic innovations. Every strategic experiment is a unique approach to growth management. Growth via erecting entry barriers, once common, now is getting obsolete; instead, great companies seek organic growth through radical innovation and organizational change, new markets and new sources of competitive advantage (Prahalad and Hamel 1990; Prahalad and Lieberthal 2003). We review some case studies of recent champions of corporate growth.

Kevin Sharer, CEO Amgen

[See Hemp (2004: 66–74)]

An Annapolis, Maryland graduate, Kevin Sharer was an officer in the U.S. Navy's nuclear submarine program, and then a consultant at McKinsey. He joined GE in 1984 as a staff assistant to Jack Welch, and later, was a general manager of two divisions (first software, then satellites), both in fast-growing and rapidly changing industries. He joined MCI, a long-distance provider, in 1989 as head of sales and marketing, rising to be president of the business markets division during a period of its spiraling growth. In 1992, he came to Amgen, the world's largest biotech company, as president, COO, and heir apparent to CEO Gordon Binder. Sharer became CEO in May 2000 and chairman in January 2001.

Amgen had two main products, both developed in the late 1980s: Epogen (an anti-anemia drug for kidney dialysis patients) and Neupogen (an anti-infection drug for cancer chemotherapy patients), both "large molecule" products as proteins that must be injected into the patients. As CEO, Sharer sought to broaden Amgen's offerings into the "small molecule" product market of pills. The company soon launched Aranesp (a second-generation anti-anemia drug that lasts longer between injections than Epogen) and Neulasta (a second-generation anti-infection drug with similar benefits over Neupogen). Both were great successes.

As part of his growth strategy, Sharer sought acquisitions of rival biotech firms. His most significant acquisition was Immunex for $11 billion in 2002, the third largest biotech company and the maker of Enbrel, a drug that treats inflammation in arthritis patients. These acquisitions have spurred Amgen's growth—2004 revenues and earnings were expected to reach $10 billion and $3 billion, up from $3 billion and $1 billion in 2000, respectively. Amgen, however, is facing fierce competition from rival Johnson & Johnson, which sells competing drugs.

Paul Hemp, a senior editor at *Harvard Business Review*, interviewed Kevin Sharer in 2004. Here are some interesting points on growth-oriented strategies that resulted from the discussion:

- In 1989, when Sharer quit GE to become the youngest VP of Sales & Marketing at MCI, within three months he met with CEO, Bert Roberts, and argued that MCI must change its business model from a geography-driven to markets-oriented business, and reorganize, accordingly. In selling and implementing this change, Sharer met with tremendous opposition from the divisional VPs since their jobs were getting reorganized and this change was not in their best interests. Sharer was soon isolated, ignored, resisted, and complained about. The CEO warned Sharer. Kevin soon realized that even though he was doing the right thing (working for the best interests of the company), he was doing it the wrong way. Sharer learnt the hard way that one needs to become credible and enlist support inside the company before one would start trying to be a change agent.

- When Sharer joined Amgen in 1992, the company was doing very well, but mostly from two products, Epogen and Neupogen. There were about 2,000 people with sales a little over $1 billion and the company was the leader in the biotech industry. Sharer, however, knew nothing about the industry—his last brush with health care was ninth grade biology. Therefore, Kevin began to learn the business from the ground up—with a series of biology and bio-tech classes and lab sessions from his own internal scientists. By the time he became CEO in 2000, he was well acquainted with the industry and the business. "If I hadn't that chastening experience at MCI, I could have easily blown up early on at Amgen," reflected Sharer (Hemp 2004: 69).
- Sharer as CEO wanted to take Amgen to the next stage of growth. He had to initially fight some ingrained perceptions. One of them was: if you have great and successful products like Epogen and Neupogen, then you need no marketing; the products sell by themselves. However, Sharer had to convince them that no matter how great are the products you have, you may have to convince the doctors to prescribe them and the insurers to pay for them. Moreover, your de facto two-product monopoly could end as soon as the competition enters, and Johnson & Johnson and Abbott Labs were already threatening to enter. You cannot grow without innovation and marketing.
- Since Sharer took over in 1992, Amgen went through three or four stages of growth. The first involved restructuring the management team and changing the culture so that Amgen could launch new products. The next was when the company acquired Immunex in 2002 with its popular drug Enbrel, followed by Aranesp and Neulasta. With this acquisition, Amgen went through a period of hyper-growth, as it ramped up the production and marketing of all drugs, hired many scientists, and expanded geographically. "We were barely in control as we tried to keep up with the growth," said Sharer (Hemp 2004: 69). Amgen wants to grow by 20 percent each year.
- It is crucial that the board is thinking with you, particularly when you are growing fast. If you do not have the board with you, you cannot seize opportunities (e.g., acquisitions, divestitures, mergers) as they come up. With the board, however, you should not allow the preferences of a few members to keep you from building a structure that will allow you to grow.
- Sharer carefully and painstakingly built a ten-person top management executive team at Amgen. His rationality: A top management team is the most revealing window into a CEO's style, values, and aspirations. You cannot overestimate the value of this team, particularly when you are growing fast. When you go from being a $3 billion company to a $10 billion company in four years, you would better have a top management team with $20 billion worth capability in them. At this rate of growth, you want to over man the challenges, rather than play catch-up, because otherwise things will implode.
- The key of our success is that I trust my executive team, and they trust me. We work together as a leadership team rather than as a rubber stamp operation for me. My CEO model is that of "prime minister"—if you do not have the support of independent, strong, and knowledgeable cabinet members, you do not have a job at the next elections, if not earlier. This is different from a "presidential" model, where you have a bunch of "yes" people in your cabinet, and you fire the dissenters.

- This view of the CEO follows the way Sharer is evaluated. Each year, the nine people who report to Sharer present to the board a collective review of the CEO's performance without the CEO being present. The board calls the CEO later for a talk. This may not always be a comfortable exercise, but it is healthy for everybody. Even the CEO can stand some coaching. "In fact, one of the best ways to grow as a CEO is to listen to your executive team, which has a near perfect understanding of your leadership balance sheet" (Hemp 2004: 73).

Kenneth W. Freeman, Chairman: Quest Diagnostics

[See Gulati (2004: 126–28)]

Quest Diagnostics belongs to the medical testing industry. The industry is highly fragmented with over 4,500 independent lab companies, each reaping around $5 million in revenues, who must also compete with thousands of labs in the hospitals and physicians' offices. Ken Freeman became CEO of Quest in May 1995. Ken's education in corporate growth grew from two mistakes:

1. More than 30 years ago, around 1975, Ken worked as a financial analyst in Corning that made glass for color TV—the richest division in the company at that time. Ken used a tried-and-tested strategy for boosting revenue: raising prices every year. The division's largest customer was RCA, and they threatened every year to build their own glass factory. Eventually, RCA did it, and Corning was forced to adopt a variable pricing policy that quickly eroded profitability.
2. Around 20 years later, May 1995, Ken–was CEO of Corning Clinical Laboratories (which, incidentally, along with Corning Nichols Institute, was spun off in 1996 as Quest Diagnostics) and was expected to turn around the organization that had grown rapidly through acquisitions. It had devoured close to 300 independent testing labs over a 13-year period. At this time, the industry had major compliance problems with Medicare. Businesses fled as the service and reputation of Corning Clinical Laboratories suffered. The company was soon unprofitable.

Ken felt that the company had to earn the right to grow. He froze acquisitions for three years during 1995–98, while concentrating on building discipline in the business. Ken engaged every employee in the turnaround process, first establishing a set of core values and clear and consistent goals for everyone. Ken created ground rules and best practices for integrating acquisitions that included rigorous metrics for customer retention, employee satisfaction, and other ambitious financial targets. It was only after 1998 when it became barely profitable that Quest began looking for new acquisition opportunities. Now Ken was firmly determined to do much due diligence such that full integration of an acquired company was possible. A good acquisition target was SmithKline Beecham Chemical Laboratories (SBCL) with $1.6 billion in revenues. Acquiring SBCL, even though the largest acquisition in the medical testing industry, would change the industry with Quest Diagnostics as the clear industry leader. Quest acquired SBCL in August 1999, and immediately focused on integration of technologies, skills, information systems, and employees for the next two years. During this assimilation process, Quest's revenues grew steadily each year at four to five percent, keeping pace with the industry.

In order to grow better and faster, Quest targeted hospitals and not so much physician clinics. Hospitals have different needs from those of the physicians—the patients are numerous and much sicker, and the hospitals require a more specialized menu of tests, a higher degree of responsiveness, and answers to more technical questions, and hence, much quicker turnaround times in all testing services. Quest soon created a separate sales force for hospitals and began dedicating labs to that segment. The revenues began to swell. During 1998–2003, Quest more than tripled its revenues, from $1.5 billion to $4.7 billion. More than half of that, around $2.6 billion, came from mergers and acquisitions (M&A); organic growth accounted only for $0.6 billion. Ken, accordingly, worked on accelerating organic growth in areas like genomics and other sophisticated tests. Meanwhile, Quest continues to seek growth by expanding its product offerings via joint ventures and long-term relationships with outside companies, large and small.

Today, Quest Diagnostics is a health care company prepared to grow organically through new product offerings in medical science and technology. Hence, in order to best capitalize on this new rapidly evolving business model, Ken continues to be chairman of Quest but passed on the CEO baton to Surya Mohapatra, COO of Quest for five years, a Ph.D. in medical physics, and who has more than 25 years of experience in the health care industry, including diagnostic imaging.

Starbucks Inc.

The Starbucks Coffee Company was founded in 1971 and opened its first location in Seattle's Pike Place Market. By 2007, the company became the world's leading coffee retailer, roaster, and brand of specialty coffee house in North America, Europe, Middle East, Latin America, and the Pacific Rim. No one else was offering what customers were seeking—a high-quality coffee, individualized service, and a comfortable coffeehouse atmosphere. From a few dozens of stores in 1992 when Starbucks went public, the coffee bar giant has grown exponentially. Actually, by the end of 2008, Starbucks had 16,875 locations worldwide, with 11,537 locations in the U.S. alone. The company began opening its stores following new housing developments into the suburbs and exurbs, where its outlets became pit stops for real estate brokers and their clients. It also "carpet-bombed" the business districts of large cities, especially the financial centers, with nearly 200 outlets in Manhattan alone. Fueled by the capital markets, during 2007–08, it opened an average of six stores a day! Starbucks appeared determined to have as many locations as McDonald's in half the amount of time! Since its initial public offering (IPO) in 1992, its stock price appreciated close to 6,000 percent by 2007!

The company was long renowned for its expertise at selecting prime locations for its ubiquitous stores. For much of the last 15 years, the commercial real estate executives at Starbucks were known for their rigor in selecting locations for their stores. Besides studying demographics, Starbucks evaluated its potential locations by other specific factors such as the education level in various neighborhoods, the traffic flow on both sides of a given street, the ease with which drivers could make a right turn for their java fix on their way to the office.

Google.com

Google, the most successful and most talked about company today, has grown by increasing its powerful presence on the Internet. As of January 2008, Google controlled 68.6 percent of the total market share and volume of all search engines. Their stocks peaked at $724.80. Currently, its market share has dropped down to 63 percent and its stock price is around $311.5, off 57 percent from its peak value.

Google has a huge innovation surplus and its "design factory" keeps expanding, and hence, it can very cannily expand into new areas with a wide array of innovations, all of which fit into the great mosaic of its master business plan. Google has a lofty vision and soul-stirring goal—it asks its employees to help "organize the world's information and make it universally accessible and useful." Google uses an "idea management system" that allows employees to e-mail innovative ideas for products, processes, and even businesses to a company-wide suggestion box. Once ideas are collected, all employees can comment on them, and rate their chances of success. This type of "open organizational brainstorming" is an inexpensive yet very effective tool to stimulate and build a culture of creativity and innovation. There is little wonder that Fortune's "100 Best Companies to Work For" recently named Google number one.

Leaders must lead. Managers must manage. Both do, but this does not mean, however, that creative and innovative ideas have to come from the top. Good leaders and managers know how to generate new ideas from the ranks and files too. They enable and empower their employees to think big, to think far into the future, to redesign the company, and to reinvent and innovate the company. Richard Teerlink attributed his remarkable success of turning around Harley-Davidson to just this: "You get power by releasing power." Sheryl Sandberg asked her people to give frank feedback on whatever they see is or is not working. She learnt this lesson early at Google before moving into the company's Facebook unit as its COO: "I thank every person who ever raised a problem publicly." In this sense, a leader becomes a steward of organizational energy.

INTERNATIONAL CHAMPIONS OF BAD GROWTH

Royal Ahold, the Dutch supermarket food retailer, began its international expansion in the 1970s and accelerated it in the 1990s, eventually acquiring businesses throughout Europe, U.S.A., Asia, and Latin America, to become the fourth largest retailer of the world. Royal Ahold, however, is yet to harvest net benefits from this globalization. Its global economies of scale are not yet realized, especially given it is a food retailing industry where global suppliers control the price and distributions. Moreover, Ahold has not benefited from its cross-border synergies as its common information systems and management processes are far from being standardized and coordinated. Worse, in order to report its forecasted earnings, Ahold indulged in financial irregularities and accounting shenanigans. In 2007, Ahold sold most of its U.S. operations to private equity firms. Its rapid globalization failed (Alexander and Korine 2008: 76).

ABN Amro, a Dutch financial-services firm, acquired banks in numerous countries but did not achieve the integration needed to generate value from its international network. Some of the ostensible and expected benefits of its globalization strategy were questionable and failed to realize. By the time ABN Amro entered regional markets such as Brazil and Italy, its rivals were already well established there. Moreover, ABN Amro lacked the will or the skills to set up common information systems and management processes that would yield economies of scale across national and international markets. These and other considerations lead to its ultimate dismantling. ABN Amro was dismembered in 2007 by the Royal Bank of Scotland, Fortis, and Banco Santander, largely along geographic lines (Alexander and Korine 2008).

Starbucks, despite its great growth success from 1971 to 2008, currently, has been straying from the exacting real estate science that it had perfected and that which guided it through its first expansion-wave of 1992–2008. Early July 2008, Starbucks announced it would shutter 600 of its underperforming stores and lay off some 14,000 employees in the process. It has significantly scaled back plans to open new outlets. The current recession in the U.S. is hurting countless retailers and restaurant chains (Bradstone 2008). Though a flagging recessionary economy and soaring gas prices could account for at least some of Starbuck's woes, there seem to be other major in-company problems triggering this sudden decline. Some of these internal inherent problems include:

- Starbucks was so determined to meet the growth promises it had made to Wall Street that it relaxed its standards for selecting new store locations. The potential rewards of rapid growth led Starbucks astray.
- Its recent overexpansion in some regions and putting its stores or franchises too close together in the same market area has backfired. Starbucks misjudged the risks of planting stores close to each other, leading to decline in store sales. The company agreed that 70 percent of the stores marked for closing in July 2008, were opened after 2006.
- It also overextended itself in certain regions (e.g., Florida and the South and in Southern California which are among the hardest hit by the housing crisis) where the older demographics and hot weather are not generally conducive to creating long lines of customers eager to cough up $4 for foam-top lattes.
- In 2004, Starbucks announced it would double its pace of expansion with a goal of reaching 15,000 stores in the U.S.A. by 2010. That ambitious target led to a frenzy of getting locations opened, disregarding cannibalization and location demographics, psychographics, and ergographics.
- Many of the newer stores were located in areas of potential but unrealized population growth. The housing crisis and real estate chaos derailed much of that planned potential for development—the projected traffic patterns never materialized. Some of these areas did not pan out as expected.
- Starbucks has too many licensed stores in bookstores and supermarkets which can siphon traffic from more profitable company-owned stores. Some stores were licensed to locate within hundred yards from an existing licensed or company-owned store.
- Starbucks pursued international growth at a breakneck pace, even though margins abroad have been only about half of its domestic operations.

Wachovia Corporation

Wachovia Corporation, based in Charlotte, NC, is one of the largest commercial lending, retail banking and leasing services in the U.S., and operated under four divisions: General Bank, Wealth Management, Capital Management, and Corporate and Investment Banking. General Bank services retail, small business and commercial customers, and is number two by national deposit market share. Wealth Management serves high net worth, personal trust, and insurance business, and is the fourth largest wealth manager in the U.S. Capital Management provides asset management, retirement, and retail brokerage services, and is the third largest full service retail brokerage house in the U.S. Lastly, Corporate and Investment Banks are fully-integrated capital raising, market making, and financial advisory services banks. In 2007, Wachovia ranked 46 among Fortune 500 with US$46.8 billion in revenue. It was the fourth largest bank holding company in the U.S. with banking and financial centers in 21 states and Washington D.C. Wachovia provided brokerage services through its subsidiary, Wachovia Securities. (In 2005, Wachovia was among 53 other companies that contributed the maximum $250,000 to the second inauguration of President George W. Bush.)

Wachovia was considered a well-run conservative bank. Wall Street, however, wanted Wachovia to grow and expand in order to be among the top 10 of the globe. Expanding means, taking more risks. Wachovia looked for easy expansions via mergers and acquisitions than via organic growth by bettering internal operations.

Wachovia also began lowering underwriting standards in order to expand operations. The company's poor credit decisions soon resulted in big bad loans, which was followed by job cuts, major charge-offs, missed earnings forecasts, and increasing pressure on its share price. In 2000–01, Wachovia got involved in bad syndicated loans (these are loans offered by a group of lenders to provide financing for a single borrower) to dot.com companies that eventually got busted. The first hostile takeover bid came from Sun Trust Banks Inc. in 2000. To avoid this, Bud Baker (CEO and Chairman) sought merger with the First Union Corp. in April 16, 2001. Ken Thompson, CEO of First Union agreed, as he found the need for Wachovia's expertise in customer service and wealth management. The merger would make Charlotte a major banking center. Wachovia's shareholders got short-changed—they received very small premiums for their stock and were asked to trade their shares for those of First Union. Baker did very well—the merger doubled his severance package; he would also receive $1.5 million annual retirement package for life. The merger cut down on 1,300 local jobs and the merged bank changed its name to Wachovia Corporation in September 2001.

The merged bank pursued bigger and riskier deals in an attempt to make a one-stop financial franchise, and thus be able to rank among the three big giants, Bank of America, JP Morgan Chase, and Citigroup. Wachovia bought Prudential Securities in February 2003 and South Trust Corp. in June 2004 for $14.3 billion, making Wachovia one of largest Southeast banks. June 2007, Wachovia bought AG Edwards for $6.8 billion. Wachovia posted record earnings, quarter after quarter, primarily coming from acquisitions. Meanwhile, for cutting costs further, Wachovia cut 10,750 jobs and did their jobs through offshore outsourcing.

In May 2006, CEO Kenneth Thompson announced that Wachovia would acquire Golden West Financial Corporation, a giant in the California mortgage business, in a cash-and-stock deal valued at $25.5 billion. At this time, Golden WFC was the nation's second biggest Savings & Loan bank after Washington Mutual. Golden WFC was big on the option of adjustable-rate-mortgage (ARM) that lets borrowers effectively choose how much they want to pay each month. (About 99 percent of Golden WFC's $122 billion loan portfolio was made up of option ARMs—a single-product-focused company since the 1980s.) By the time of acquisition, more borrowers were choosing to pay the minimum or interest only on loans, ignoring the principal altogether. Golden WFC aggressively marketed such loans by lowering underwriting standards—their apparent rationale was to make home buying more affordable for lower income customers or make the American dream home come true. Wachovia soon got into option ARMs. People overbought and soon began to default on payments. Wachovia posted a quarterly loss of $8.9 billion in July 2008, the second largest quarterly loss in U.S. banking history. Kenneth Thompson was fired as chairman in May 2008 and as CEO in July 2008. In the third quarter of 2008, Wachovia lost $23.9 billion or $11.18 per share, and took an $18.8 billion write-down to reflect its lower market evaluation. On September 26, 2008, Wachovia's stock plunged by another 27 percent due to the seizure of Washington Mutual the previous night. On the same day, several businesses and institutional depositors quickly withdrew money from Wachovia to drop their balances to below $100,000 insured by the Federal Deposit Insurance Corporation (FDIC)—an event called a "silent run" in banking circles. FDIC is an independent agency created by the US Congress to maintain stability and public confidence in the public banking system. The exact amount of money withdrawn is not yet known, but the amount was large enough that on the morning of Monday, September 29, 2008, the FDIC board pressured Wachovia to put up itself for sale over the weekend to Citigroup, acting under a 1991 law empowering the FDIC to deal with large bank failures on short notice.

Wachovia's new CEO, Bob Steel, had little choice but to agree with the FDIC order. The same morning of September 29, 2008, 45 minutes before the markets opened, Bob Steel announced the company's intention to sell its banking operations to Citigroup for US$2.2 billion in an open bank transaction facilitated by the FDIC. Wachovia also negotiated with Wells Fargo but Wachovia's subsidiaries, however, were not placed into receivership. Wachovia is expected to continue as a publicly traded company and would retain its retail brokerage and Evergreen asset management subsidiaries. The brokerage unit has 14,600 financial advisors and manages more than $1 trillion in trade, third in the U.S. after Merrill Lynch and Citigroup's Smith Barney. The Citigroup sale offer fell through, and Wells Fargo of San Francisco has bought Wachovia in a deal initially worth $15 billion.

ASKING THE RIGHT GROWTH-RELATED QUESTIONS

New businesses grow through three main stages, and in each, the top management should ask the right questions as follows (Garvin 2004: 20):

1. **Experimentation Stage**:
   a. What is our market niche?
   b. Who are our customers?
   c. What products/services should we offer them?
   d. Do we have the technology/skills/passion to offer them?
   e. Are they profitable?
2. **Expansion Stage**:
   a. How rapidly should we expand our business?
   b. How should we grow?
   c. Where do we want to grow?
   d. How do we expand?
      i. By new product/service offerings?
      ii. By exploring new markets?
      iii. By tapping new customers?
      iv. By reaching out to new geographic regions?
      v. By buying our competitors?
   e. What functional and human resources do we need for these expansions?
   f. How can we obtain them?
      i. By acquisitions?
      ii. By mergers?
      iii. By joint ventures?
      iv. By strategic alliances?
      v. By cross-licensing?
      vi. By freeing capital from divestitures?
   g. How can we organize the new resources for short-term and long-term profitability?

3. **Integration Stage**:
   a. How do we link the new businesses to the old ones?
   b. How should we manage, reorganize, restructure, and refocus such that we ensure long-term consistency and success?
   c. How do we ensure continued growth and profitability?

Asking the right questions at the right time with the right people helps us to answer the right questions with right answers. Otherwise we indulge in answering the wrong questions, or solving the wrong problems (Tukey's Type III errors). This is where we can waste precious resources of mind, money, and materials. Table 10.12 presents a canvas for business creation and corporate growth based on the three stages of experimentation, expansion, and integration.

Focusing on corporate growth requires an attitude adjustment. When you think of forces that contribute to the long-term growth and prosperity of your company, you do not think of the budgeting process. Quite the opposite. Note the following points:

- Typical bottom-up budgeting, with its focus on earnings, its emphasis on making short-term numbers and performance ratios, is one of the forces arrayed against you.
- Instead, use budgeting as a tool to introduce and reinforce growth. Focus on investments in people, R&D, technology, core products, and market development; these live on to drive long-term revenue growth, cash flows, and shareholder value creation.
- Budgets are annual or semi-annual; hence time-restrictive.
- Instead, adopt two to three year rolling plans (that you can update, extend, or revise regularly) that follow not annual fiscal year dates but your company's normal business cycle.
- Toyota and several Japanese firms do this (Howell 2004: 21–22).

TABLE 10.12 Stages of Business Creation and Growth

Stage	Basic questions	Basic inputs	Basic processes	Basic outputs
Experimentation	What is our market niche? Who are our customers?	Leadership Imagination Intuition Creation Exploration Discovery Invention	Market scanning Market intelligence Markets identification Market segmentation Market assessment Customer assessment	New market spaces New market ventures New market entries New markets New regions New customers
	What products/services should we offer them? Do we have the technology/skills/passion to offer them? Are they profitable?	Innovation Technology Patents Collaboration Alliances Human skills	New product ideation New product concept New product prototype New product testing New product packaging New product bundling New product promotion	New core products New products New services New brands New extensions New bundles New experiences New delight

(Continued)

TABLE 10.12 *(Continued)*

Stage	*Basic questions*	*Basic inputs*	*Basic processes*	*Basic outputs*
Expansion	How rapidly should we expand our business? How should we grow? Where do we want to grow?	Planning Forecasting Strategizing Analytics	Vertical integration Horizontal integration Forward integration Backward integration Regional integration Globalization	Organic growth External growth Internal growth Business growth Industry convergence Product convergence Product divergence
	How do we expand?	Scouting Scanning Exploring	By new product/service offerings? By exploring new markets? By tapping new customers? By reaching out to new geographic regions? By buying our competitors?	New markets New regions New customers New products New services New brands New extensions New bindles
	What functional and human resources do we need for these expansions? How can we organize the new resources for short-term and long-term profitability?	Scouting Scanning Exploring Budgeting Organizing Planning	Human skill scouting Skills development Skills retention Skills retraining Patenting Licensing technologies Cross-licensing Centralized purchasing Supply chain management	New skilled competencies New trained routines Best practices Best technologies Best processes Best licenses Best cross-licenses Best suppliers Best relationships
	How can we obtain them?	Scouting Scanning Exploring Due diligence Negotiations	By acquisitions? By mergers? By joint ventures? By strategic alliances? By cross-licensing? By freeing capital from divestitures?	New innovations New products New markets New skills New brands/models New brand communities New line extensions
Integration	How do we link the new businesses to the old ones? How should we manage, reorganize, restructure, and refocus such that we ensure long-term consistency and success? How do we ensure continued growth and profitability?	Strategic planning Reorganizing Creativity Leadership Analysis Synthesis	Systems thinking Design thinking Creative problem-solving Customer refocus Market refocus New financing focus Corporate restructuring Corporate reengineering Lean enterprise management Debt restructuring Equity restructuring Equity spin-offs Equity carve-outs	Integrated business Expanded business Corporate growth New market regions New market development New trade partners Global control Consistent business Increasing revenues Increased net cash flows Increasing market share Increasing profitability Increasing ROI, ROE, ROIC, EPS, P/E, Tobin's Q

Source: Author's own.

Note: See also Garvin (2004).

Given the rolling plan format, budgets should be called "profit plans," or even better, "future net cash flow plans." When Warren Buffett assesses a company for its growth potential, he does not look into budgets and financial statements, but on its "intrinsic value," on cash flows rather than on accounting profits. "The intrinsic value of any firm is the net present value of the future stream of cash flows it will generate." Most executives do "due diligence" based on intrinsic value when considering acquisitions or mergers. If projected cash flows are insufficient to justify the proposed price, they reject the deal.

Thus, managers should reformat their planning and budgeting templates to highlight cash rather than accounting net income. If you have to use budgets, then the budget should focus on growth drivers such as R&D investments, process improvement technologies, new markets and customers, intellectual and social capital—these drive long-term growth, cash flows, and value creation (Howell 2004: 22).

SHOULD WE GO GLOBAL IN ORDER TO GROW?

[See Alexander and Korine (2008: 70–77)]

Currently, forces driving globalization are powerful. Apparently, business benefits of growing global can be tremendous. Accelerated removal of political and regulatory barriers to cross-border trading and investment over the past 15 years, along with advanced technologies that empower to conduct business around the world 24 hours a day, have made global presence easy, attractive, and mandatory. Both big and small companies feel the strategic imperative to go global in one form or another in order to grow. Much of this pressure comes from financial markets, investment bankers and consultants, the media, and the global moves of their rivals.

Some globalization growth strategies have been successful. In 2000, the Royal Bank of Scotland was very successful acquiring Natwest, a much larger U.K. rival, and for the subsequent overhaul of its target's culture. Telefónica, Spain's former telephone monopoly, has successfully expanded throughout much of the Hispanic world. During 2003–08, GE's Commercial Finance business has moved rapidly and effectively into dozens of non-U.S. markets. Renault's path-breaking alliance with Nissan has proved, to this point, beneficial for the French and Japanese automakers. Nevertheless, focusing on these success stories, corporate executives must not conclude that a globalization strategy is a blanket requirement for doing and growing business. This in turn leads many companies to scrutinize insufficiently their proposed globalization strategies (Alexander and Korine 2008: 77).

Thus, many have stumbled in their globalization strategies—mis-steps that have benefited their rivals. For instance, the Royal Bank of Scotland (RBS) was not very successful with disparate banking acquisitions from ABN Amro spread across more than 50 countries. These acquisitions stretched RBS's balance sheets making the companies more vulnerable to financial crisis. So many companies seem to share unquestioned assumptions about the need to go global, and are lulled by apparent safety in numbers, as they move toward potential disaster. Businesses with ill-conceived and ill-considered global-ization growth strategies are often poised to become the next targets for breakup or corporate overhaul by activist shareholders, just as companies with poorly planned diversification strategies were targets in the past. Today's activists include private-equity firms, hedge funds, and traditional pension funds who wield tremendous influence singly or in collaboration. However, "today's predators could be tomorrow's prey!"

Alexander and Korine (2008) expect this trend to continue, as firms in many industries recklessly pursue global strategies. For instance, in the emerging renewable-energy industry (e.g., bio-fuel, solar, wind, compost energy), so many companies are racing to establish a global position in Africa, Asia, and Latin America. They are completely underestimating the managerial, political, and cultural challenges involved along the way.

Consider the following cases:

- AES, a U.S.-based energy firm that operates 124 power generation plants in 29 countries in five continents has yet to benefit from globalization. AES's share price has tumbled since investors' initial enthusiasm for globalization, and some investment advisers are calling for the firm to split into three or more parts.
- In 1998, Jürgen Schrempp, CEO Daimler-Benz, the architect of the deal that sought merger with Chrysler in order to create a world corporation, never attained the power over suppliers and markets that this global corporation was supposed to deliver. Yielding to shareowner pressure, he resigned, freeing up his successor to sell Chrysler to the private-equity giant Cerberus in 2007.

All these enterprises failed because their global growth strategies were deeply misguided, or because international execution was more difficult than anticipated. Before launching a global move, senior executives should conduct a simple but rigorous self-assessment to gauge the likelihood of success. Doing this can ensure that their international efforts make strategic sense and avoid potentially disastrous consequences.

Many businesses in formerly state-owned industries, such as telecommunications, postal services, and utilities, have responded to deregulation with aggressive globalization. Faced with limited growth opportunities and increasing competition in the domestic markets, companies went global in order to grow. They hoped to use their domestically honed competencies for providing voice and data, communication, delivering letters and packages, or distributing water or electricity, in foreign markets with easy transfer. Most of these companies were disappointed when they could not standardize these services globally owing to increasing regulation of such industries abroad, varying local conditions, environmental regulations, and markedly different infrastructures (e.g., uncoordinated electricity grids, waterways, and distribution channels). Faced with challenges several companies have reversed their global strategies.

For instance, Kelda, a U.K. water utility service, sold its U.S. business six years after acquiring it. Deutsche Telecom has made its U.S. Unit, T-Mobile U.S.A., a completely independent business that could be sold off at any time. Both found global standardizing of services and realization of global economies of scale difficult owing to tough local regulations and labor unions, insurmountable local competition, and unrelenting government bureaucracies. For similar reasons, rival telecom operator Vodaphone was forced by its shareholders to sell off its Japanese subsidiary, J-Phone. Wal-Mart has struggled to get its partner firms and local employees abroad (especially in India, China, and Brazil) to adopt its work routines. ABN Amro's global empire was dismantled by predators because their international business was a collection of mostly unrelated operations in countries ranging from Brazil to Monaco. The company achieved few economies of scale. For instance, it could not capitalize on its global brand name because local country banks mostly kept their original names.

Alexander and Korine (2008: 72–73) suggest three sets of questions for senior executives to reflect on before going global:

- **Are there potential benefits for the company?** Where and when would the benefits of globalization show up in the financial statements? What is the expected economic value of each benefit? How detailed and solid is our understanding of each benefit? What is the hard evidence that other companies in similar circumstances have been able to realize these benefits?
- **Do we have the necessary management skills?** What skills do we need in order to realize the expected economic benefits? The theoretical advantages of achieving economies of scale at home are very difficult to realize abroad on a global scale. Thus, do we have coordinated supply and support across borders despite diverse cultures and political constraints? Do we have a clear track record of exhibiting or realizing such coordinating skills in the past? Do we know how further to develop them?
- **Will the costs of globalizing outweigh the benefits?** Companies frequently pay far too much to enter foreign markets. What will it cost the company in terms of management time and business process investment, to realize the benefits of the globalization strategy? Even if we have the required skills stated earlier, are there unanticipated collateral damages to our business that may make our entire international endeavor counter-productive? What do critics from our other business units have to say about the cost of globalization and its potential impact on their business unit performance? What would be the most productive alternative use of all the resources that we plan to earmark to our globalization strategy?

In the context of these three sets of self-assessment questions, it is good to question the generally unquestioned assumptions such as:

- That a company must go global in order to grow.
- That globalization is the in thing that one must do to survive corporately.
- Going global to grow is the management trend (if not a fad).

Globalization, together with other buzz words or labels such as "reengineering," "corporate reorganization," "corporate related diversification," "going online," and the like are so broad in context as to become meaningless, and executives mindlessly embrace and pursue them for keeping up with economic and corporate trends and fads, but at a huge expense. Often enough, stock market guru analysts, business media, management consultants, investment bankers, financial markets, and the Wall Street proclaim from housetops that going global is the best "new paradigm" there is, and the best strategy a senior executive can pursue for corporate growth and competitive advantage. Soon senior corporate executives begin to believe this fad/trend and feel pressurized to follow it. Globalizing is not necessarily bad; nor is it necessarily good. It plays out because rushing to embrace the globalization rubric or trend often precludes careful examination of the benefits and costs of globalization that a company chooses in a given country, context, and period (Alexander and Korine 2008: 74). A typical case in point is Starbucks discussed earlier.

GROWTH STRATEGY PRINCIPLES

First, define your value proposition. Your growth strategy should be determined by your value proposition. For instance, is your value proposition low-price leadership? If you are a low-price leader like

Wal-Mart, Dell, or Medco, then you must extend low-cost value relative to adjacent competitive markets. If your value proposition is innovation leadership (e.g., P&G, GE, 3M), then the growth strategy must be continuous innovation that builds your SCA. If your value proposition is relational and building lasting relationships (e.g., IBM, Fidelity Investments, GE Aircraft), then you must create value to your long-term customers by offering integrated solutions. Table 10.13 expands this discussion.

Executives should enunciate clear principles of good growth strategy early on in their business pursuit. Each principle should be based on honest chances of succeeding. We could state some of these principles as critical questions as follows:

- Will the proposed venture offer attractive market potential in terms of revenues?
- Is this a proposal where the company has sufficient skills, learning, and expertise?
- Or, is this proposal in a domain where the company has sufficient advantage to cover the learning costs?
- Will the proposal enable the company to pursue vertical integration with its suppliers?
- Will the proposal enable the company to pursue horizontal integration with its competitors?
- Will the proposal enable the company to strengthen its major flagship brands?

TABLE 10.13 Analyzing and Establishing Growth Strategies

The core value proposition of the company	Growth strategy in line with the core value proposition	Current examples of this core value proposition
Low-price Leadership	Every day low pricing (EDLP), lower prices than competitors, extend low cost value than adjacent markets	Wal-Mart, Dell, Best Buy, Medco, Walgreen
Innovation Leadership	Be a first mover, be a market leader with this innovation; innovate continuously to ensure SCA	P&G, GE, 3M, Sony, Apple
Total Customer Experience	Your product/service should maximize and memorialize engaging experience of customers	American Place, Hard Rock Café, Avis Rental, Disney World
Total Business Solutions	Offer comprehensive and competitive solutions to your client's business problems	IBM, SAP, Oracle, Unisys, Dell
Relational Value Leadership	Cultivate genuine, lasting, trusting, and honest relationships with your key customers or clients	Fidelity Investments, IBM, GE Aircraft
Performance Value Leadership	Engage in continuous innovations for exploiting converging and emerging technologies to shape and build new markets	Intel, Microsoft, Nokia, Gennentech
Low-cost Travel Leadership	Offer cheap, safe, reliable, and efficient travel value to your customers with no frills	South West, EasyJet, Travelocity.com
Great Customer Convenience	Offer products and services that save on time, money, talent, search, energy, anxiety, and convenience	One-stop shopping, Meijers, Home Depot, BCBS
Great Buyer–seller Networking	Bring all major buyers and sellers together, online or offline, and facilitate effective trading	Ariba.com, Covisnt, eBay, Amazon.com
Comprehensive and Reliable Information Updates	Offer comprehensive and extensive information sources and updates	Google.com, Yahoo!, all other major search engines
Customized and Personalized Market Information Leadership	Offer critical and constantly updated market/stock/financial information to specific clients	Bloomberg.com, Edmunds, Evenbetter.com; Campare.frictionless.com

Source: Author's own.

- Will the proposal enable the company to broaden its core product lines?
- Would the proposed venture support the core business, and not undercut it?
- Will the company support the proposed venture with an effective leadership team?
- Will the proposed venture offer attractive market potential in terms of net earnings?

In essence, long-term winners sustain their growth by "edging out" from their core, by "natural extensions" of their resources, or by "reaching out" with those resources into new markets (Day 2004: 26).

CORPORATE GROWTH THROUGH INCREMENTAL INNOVATIONS

The purpose of innovation is growth. One can grow, however, without innovations. Simply retaining customers and improving the targeting and coverage of new ones can yield significant revenue growth, especially in inefficient markets, where innovation is not required to retain customers. Moreover, one could get the maximum advantage out of one's minimal innovations. Incremental product innovations can be particularly good at locking in current customers. "At every point of reduced customer churn is an additional point of revenue growth" (Treacy 2004: 30).

For instance, Nextel, the mobile phone provider, is a leader in its industry at reducing turnover or churn (22 percent versus 31 percent for the industry). The company's target in 2004 for reduced churn was 19 percent, and in 2005, was 16 percent. Nextel did not plan reaching those goals through big breakthrough products or processes. It provided simple incremental innovations such as a one-button-to-talk service or workaday enhancements for its highly trained call center reps bent on generating happier customers.

Similarly, Paychex was launched in 1971, with a capital of $3,000 and one employee, to serve a market of small businesses that ADP and other payroll processors had missed. Paychex had no fancy technology, no radically different and risky businesses processes. By 2003, Paychex's revenues rose to $1.1 billion and the company garnered 27 percent after-tax profit margins.

As a contrast, consider companies that went broke after pursuing breakthrough innovations. Webvan went for its novel and massive distribution infrastructure, but failed to bring in enough revenues from its online grocery customers. AutoNation had grandiose plans to build used-car superstores, but quickly withdrew from this expensive novel idea and reversed back to new-car dealerships, an older and more reliable business model.

The time to launch radical or breakthrough innovations, is not when they are necessary for your business but when they are necessary to your marketplace. If they are foisted on a market that is not ready for them, big innovations can take years to catch on. Videophone providers have learnt that lesson for more than 25 years. GM learnt in 1999 when it withdrew its glamorous 100 percent electric car IV1 after spending more than a billon on its development since 1991. Similarly, often radical business model innovations are too radical for their markets—that is, customers will not pay for that invention.

Breakthrough innovations are important, no doubt, in creating enormous wealth, but they need to be implemented at the right time and the right place. Grand slams and home runs can certainly win baseball games. Constantly swinging for the fences, however, does not make good sense, not when many bunts and singles can generate robust growth. Going after breakthrough innovations may be glamorous, but mounting evidence suggests that they should be the last growth strategy you should try (Treacy 2004: 29–30).

COMPANY GROWTH THROUGH MERGERS AND ACQUISITIONS

Mergers and acquisitions (M&A) have become increasingly popular in current business practice, especially horizontal M&A (i.e., M&A that take place in the same industry, often between direct competitors) (Homburg and Bucerius 2005). Technological changes often trigger corporate restructuring through M&A (Sudarsanam 2003). In which case, firms seek to alter the competitive structure of their resources through exploitation of resources and capabilities they have built internally or acquired through M&A (Resource-based View [RBV] Theory of SCA).

On the other hand, firms could alter the competitive structure of their markets through exploitation of resources and capabilities they have built internally or acquired through M&A (Industrial/Organization [I/O] theory of SCA). Table 10.14 characterizes this phenomenon. Firms merge in order to gain sustainable competitive edge (SCA) over their rivals through cost-reduction, or augmenting market power and revenues, or through both cost-reduction and market augmentation strategies. The RBV has been used frequently as a theoretical explanation for why M&A occur (Anand and Singh 1997; Karim and Mitchell 2000). Acquiring products and technologies are more useful for improving growth than are merging with or acquiring companies. This makes the pursuit of core competencies and SCA focused.

TABLE 10.14 Mergers and Acquisitions as Functions of Competitive Resource and Market Corporate Restructurings

Seeking competitive restructure of resources?	Seeking competitive restructure of markets?	
	Yes	*No*
Yes	Vertical Acquisitions Vertical Mergers Horizontal Acquisitions Horizontal Mergers (Both cost-reduction and market-power strategies) RBV Theory of SCA I/O Theory of SCA	Vertical Acquisitions Vertical Mergers (Primarily cost-reduction strategies) RBV Theory of SCA
No	Horizontal Acquisitions Horizontal Mergers (Primarily market-expansion strategies) I/O Theory of SCA	Organic Development Core Business Development Core Competencies Development Core Markets Development Pure Licensing Agreements Technical Collaboration Joint Ventures Strategic Alliances (Primarily re-investment strategies) RBV Theory of SCA I/O Theory of SCA Status Quo (In which case, the company may face underperformance, decline crisis, insolvency, bankruptcy, and death.)

Source: Author's own.

Acquisitions for the sake of acquisitions do not make sense—this was the problem with Enron, America Online (AOL), and Yahoo.com.

Acquisitions remain the quickest route companies have to new markets and to new capabilities. As markets globalize, and the pace at which technologies change continues to accelerate, more and more companies are finding M&A to be a compelling strategy for growth (Rappaport and Sirower 2001: 74).

In recent decades, especially 1998–2003, growth through M&A has been a critical part of the success of many companies (Gilson 2001; Sudarsanam 2003). Horizontal mergers in particular, that is, mergers which take place in the same industry and often between direct competitors, are becoming even more commonplace (Homburg and Bucerius 2005; Krishnan and Park 2002). Technological changes often trigger corporate restructuring through M&A (Sudarsanam 2003). Cisco and GE Capital are two excellent examples of established companies that have successfully used acquisitions to grow the top line of brands and products (Di Georgio 2002a). Daimler-Chrysler merger and the Disney-Pixar alliance, on the other hand, have been failures. Mergers, however, also take place in the context of their firm's political structure, culture, and social processes, and these impact the merger decision as well as its effectiveness.

Companies try various survival and growth strategies before declaring insolvency:

- **Right-sizing**: Most companies engage in "right-sizing," a decision to deliberately and immediately expand (upsize) or contract (downsize) a company and the scale of its operations.
- **Upsizing**: Generally, there is only one way of "upsizing" a company "internally": by selling right types of products and services at the right time, in the right place, and to the right type of customers.

There are two ways a company can upsize "externally": mergers and acquisitions.

- A "merger" combines two or more companies to produce a new corporate entity. The original companies lose their identities, and their outstanding shares of common stock are exchanged for shares in the new company.
- Even though different, M&A are frequently studied as a single phenomenon.
- In "acquisitions," the majority ownership of a firm changes, with acquiring firm obtaining control and authority over the acquired firm. Acquisitions work best when the main rationale for acquiring is cost-reduction and not revenue-generation. You can easily define and measure cost-reduction, visibly see it and control it. However, there is more risk with revenue enhancements; they are more difficult to implement.
- In "consolidations," a dominant player folds smaller companies into its already finely tuned machinery.

TYPES OF MERGERS

Various types of mergers occur in the business world:

- **Horizontal mergers** occur within the same industry, and often with direct competitors.
- **Vertical mergers** occur across supplier industries, and often with one's direct materials or finished goods suppliers.

- **Pioneering mergers** are those in which two or more companies unite to enter a market when neither was equipped to enter alone. For instance, in 1989, SmithKline Beckman and Beecham PLC, each strong in some markets but unable to penetrate others, by merger became the world's fourth largest pharmaceutical company with tentacles in every continent.
- **Talent-scout mergers** are those in which one company buys another to access its skilled people, patents, or processes. Microsoft has grown mostly using this approach.
- **Diversification mergers** are mostly revenue hunters. These are companies who want to spread investment risk across related or unrelated industries, grow big as well, and increase their market share and dominance. Typical examples are Quaker Oats that bought Gatorade and Snapple, and KMart that purchased Builders Square, Borders, and Office Max.

In the 1960s, many mergers involved conglomerates like Textron or ITT buying up unrelated companies in order to hedge against economic cycles. Many acquirers financed their deals through debt and were subsequently unable to manage their debts without slashing staff and operating budgets, or selling assets at rock-bottom prices. Most of these companies have since sold off their disparate divisions (e.g., KMart sold Borders, Office Max, and Pace).

Co-founded by Steve Case in 1985, AOL entered the new millennium as the world's leading online service firm, with more than 25 million paying subscribers and a phenomenal revenue growth rate. AOL grew mainly by acquiring smaller firms, which like itself provided Internet connection (or IPS, Internet provider service) to subscribers in various regions and continents of the world. In 2001, AOL merged with the world's leading media company, Time Warner Inc., and became successfully transformed into an Internet colossus. The acquisition price of Time Warner for AOL was $106 billion, the largest ever in corporate America. With combined revenues of $36 billion, the new giant, AOL Time Warner Inc., was touted as "the world's first media and communications company of the Internet Age." By the Fall of 2003, however, the failure to realize revenue from the $106 billion acquisition of Time Warner Inc. resulted in the dramatic fall of AOL stock in excess of 60 percent in 2003–04. This led to the resignation of Steve Case as chairman, a transfer of control to the Time Warner side of management, and the dropping of AOL from the corporate name. The AOL bubble had burst.

On March 5, 2006, AT&T announced its plans to acquire South Bell for $60 billion. In 1993, AT&T had bought McCaw for its cellular telephony, a critical asset for the telecommunication business, as it would have been very difficult for AT&T to build that asset from the scratch. In 2001, SBC merged with AT&T. With all these M&A, AT&T may once again be the industrial telecommunication giant it always was (until MCI won antitrust suit against AT&T in 1983).

WHY DO COMPANIES SEEK MERGERS, ACQUISITIONS, OR ALLIANCES?

Firms merge in order to gain sustainable competitive edge (SCA) over their rivals through cost-reduction, or augmenting market power and revenues, or through both cost-reduction and market augmentation strategies. The RBV has been used frequently as a theoretical explanation for why M&A occur (Anand and Singh 1997; Karim and Mitchell 2000). Acquiring products and technologies are more useful for improving growth than are mergers. This makes the pursuit of core competencies and SCA focused. Acquisitions for the sake of acquisitions do not make sense—this was the problem with Enron.

Other major reasons for M&A are:

- Acquisitions remain the quickest route companies have to new markets and to new capabilities. As markets globalize, and the pace at which technologies change continues to accelerate, more and more companies are finding M&A to be a compelling strategy for growth (Rappaport and Sirower 2001: 74).
- In every M&A, one company plans to bring to the other company what the latter lacks (e.g., aggressive management skills, technology), hoping to benefit from the other what it lacks (e.g., access to the other company's markets, money, flagship brands). Both hope the marriage is made in heaven (Cliffe 2001: 106–07).
- "Acquiring is much faster than building ground up, and speed (speed to market, speed to positioning, speed to becoming a visible company) is absolutely essential in the new economy" (Alex Mandl, Chairman and CEO of Teligent, cited in *Harvard Business Review* 2000).
- "An acquisition becomes attractive if it offers us a new consumer segment or geographic market to sell our products to or if it adds new products to one of our core categories" (Mackey McDonald, Chairman of VF Corporation, cited in *Harvard Business Review* 2000).
- In fact, M&A have been the single most important factor in building up market capitalization (Alex Mandl cited in Carey 2000: 3). For some Internet companies, M&A are certainly the fastest way to expand and solidify their businesses. For instance, in 1999, Yahoo! bought GeoCities to build competitive mass and expand user base. The recent HP–Compaq merger is an interesting case to study (Datta 1991).
- This does not mean that internal growth and alliances are irrelevant today. It is better to build internally when you have the state-of-the-art process and product technology to capitalize quickly on a market opportunity. If you do not have it, however, then you would buy from a company that has it, as long as there is a "strategic fit" between the buying and the merging company (Seth 1990a, 1990b; Shrivastava 1986).
- The RBV has been often used as a theoretical explanation why M&A occur (Anand and Singh 1997; Karim and Mitchell 2000). According to RBV, superior business performance is primarily sourced by its resources that meet four requirements—value, rarity, imperfect imitability, and non-substitutability (Barney 1991). Since some of these resources cannot be internally generated, as many firms engage in M&A in building rare and valuable resources to improve their SCA.

As companies find it increasingly tougher to achieve and sustain growth, they place their faith in M&A, strategic alliances and joint ventures in order to boost sales, market share, profits, and, importantly, stock prices. For instance, American companies announced 74,000 acquisitions (i.e., an average 14,800 each year) and 57,000 alliances (an average of 11,400 each year) during 1996–2001, their combined dollar amount exceeding well over $12 trillion. During those six years, CEOs signed an acquisition and partnership almost every hour each business day. The pace has slowed down since—only 7,795 acquisitions and 5,048 alliances in 2002, and 8,385 acquisition deals and 5,789 alliance agreements in 2003.

WHY DO SOME MERGERS AND ACQUISITIONS SUCCEED

- Porter (1987) suggests that good acquisitions should start with a good strategy. For instance, John Chambers, CEO of Cisco Systems, combined key strategies from HP (that is, to break markets into segments) with GE's philosophy of being the first or second in every segment Cisco wanted to compete. Cisco, accordingly, developed a matrix of market segments, identified where they were dominant, where they were not, and if within 6 months they could not dominate a given market segment, they acquired a company that did.

- According to Porter (1987), successful acquisitions rely on sharing activities. Mike Volpi, manager of acquisitions for Cisco, looked for privately held start-ups that have just tested their product, and are flexible and need a lot of leverage that a big company like Cisco can bring. Such companies can also leverage Cisco's manufacturing, distribution, IT systems, accounting systems, HR, while Cisco can help the start-ups to reach more quickly into the marketplace and push larger volumes. In general, Cisco wants to manufacture, package, and ship the new products under the Cisco label within 3–6 months from the closing of the M&A deal.

- M&A activity must be a strategic macro-process critical to the bottom line. For instance, a company that undertakes $1 billion M&A a year, must show at least 10 percent improvement each year that would drive $100 million to the bottom line. Successful M&A activities, such as those of Cisco and GE Capital, obtained this result with consistency (Di Georgio 2002a, 2002b). A 20 percent improvement each year could pay off the acquisition in less than 5 years. One needs scale and scope to compete in the new and global economy, and M&A provides just that.

- M&A offers new channels of distribution for existing products. For instance, Cisco Systems has successfully grown through its acquisitions—between 1993 and 2001 it acquired over 70 companies (Fortune 2001) and since going public in 1990, Cisco's revenues have grown 31 to 40 percent each year.

WHY DO MOST MERGERS AND ACQUISITIONS FAIL?

One could use many criteria for judging M&A failure:

- Many mergers do not create the shareholder value expected of them (Light 2001: 138).
- When there is no 20 percent improvement each year that could pay off the acquisition in less than five years.
- Most M&A resulted in higher than expected costs and lower than acceptable returns.
- In most M&A talented individuals leave, and it is time-consuming, risky, and expensive to replace them later. Hence, if key players chose to leave, the M&A may be a failure.
- In a great majority of M&A combinations, one plus one yielded less than two.
- A vast majority of M&A fail to deliver the synergies, competitive advantages, and shareholder value they promised.

Given these criteria, reasons for M&A failures are many. We investigate some major perspectives of such failures.

Cross-cultural Perspectives

- Failure to select and negotiate the right deal and effectively implementing the merger or acquisition. If the right M&A deal is not struck, effective implementation is not going to matter.

- Mergers are rarely between equal partners. The word "merge" itself can actually mislead staff expectations and lead to disaffection and key people leaving, thus destroying shareholder value (Grundy 2003: 11).
- The combination of cultural differences between the merging firms and an ill-conceived HR integration strategy is one of the most common reasons for an M&A failure (Light 2001: 138).

Marketing Perspectives

Effects of M&A on marketing activities and outcomes have been mixed and not much attention has been devoted to post-merger impact (PMI) issues in marketing (Homburg and Bucerius 2005). Some post-merger effects studied include:

- There is considerable risk of losing customers in M&A (Becker and Shelton 2002). This is because, during the integration phase that every M&A calls for, managerial energy is often absorbed to internal integration issues and, accordingly, diverted from customer issues (Hitt, Hoskisson, and Ireland 1990) and service quality (Urban and Pratt 2000). This can cause customer retention problems.
- Following M&A, some customers may anticipate uncertainties about their future relationship with the merging firms, specifically related to pricing, quality of products and services, sales representatives, and distributors. Such anticipations may encourage restraint or defection (Chakrabarti 1990; Reichheld and Henske 1991). Moreover, the competition may exploit this situation and try to alienate customers.
- In several M&A talented crew jumped ship, seriously eroding product and service quality and frustrated customers complain or exit.

Structural Perspectives

- Structure influences behavior. People with different skills and attitudes can produce marvelous results of structure-disciplined behaviors that generate common good. If there are no systematic structures, benchmarks, control systems, and accountability systems, most M&A deals will fail.
- All systems have natural boundaries, and most M&A activities run across many departments and organizational boundaries. Too many boundaries and bureaucracies can involve long delays between cause (e.g., M&A activity) and effect (e.g., improving bottom line). Hence, improving reaction time via cross-functional and cross-departmental boundaries is a key to M&A success.
- People learn best from experience. In large bureaucratic organizations, people are often prevented from experiencing the consequences of many of their important decisions. Such a situation can make outcome accountability difficult (Di Georgio 2002a, 2002b).

Implementation Perspectives

- Ineffective implementation also wreck a number of promising M&A deals. Corporations are not taking a systems approach to the process of acquiring and integrating acquisitions (Di Georgio 2002a: 137).

- When two merging companies are of equal size, then cultural wars ensue when both refuse to understand the unique strengths or weaknesses of the other. Consider what happened between AT&T and NCR, Quaker Oats and Snapple. Cultural wars between them disintegrated and disabled them from achieving their financial goals.
- Every uncontrolled M&A activity that diverts executive time and operating capital from internal growth, negatively affects worker productivity and morale.
- A vast majority of M&A, however, fail to deliver the synergies, competitive advantages, and shareholder value they promised. Such was the case when PC maker, Compaq, merged with mainframe vendor, Digital Equipment Corporation, when retail broker Charles Schwab merged with institutional banker U.S. Trust and when entertainment giant Time Warner merged with Internet marketer AOL. In all three cases, the problem was not a lack of opportunity; in fact, there were too many, but a consistent failure to exploit those opportunities. Much of the competitive advantage of each business partner was blunted when it was fused with an opposing business model (Moore 2005).

There is considerable evidence that many M&A activities have been unsuccessful. Mark and Mirvis (1998) report that more than 75 percent of the corporate M&A deals failed to attain projected business results. LaJoux (1998) studied 15 M&A cases of which a majority reported failure rates ranging between 40 and 80 percent. A survey of 600 top HR executives and CEOs engaged in M&A activities (see Rubis 2001; Schmidt 2002) reveals several reasons for M&A failure: inability to sustain financial performance (65 percent), loss of productivity (60 percent), incompatible M&A partner cultures (55 percent) and clash of management styles (53 percent), slow decision-making (51 percent), and wrong people selected for key jobs (50 percent).

Dyer, Kale, and Singh (2004) have studied acquisitions and alliances for over 25 years, tracking several over time from announcement to amalgamation or annulment. They affirm that most acquisitions and alliances fail, while a few succeed. On an average, failed acquisitions destroy shareholder value more than failed alliances. In general, acquired firms gain value around 30 percent while acquiring firms experience a wealth loss of 10 percent and more over five years after the merger completion. Research also suggests that 40 to 55 percent of alliances breakdown prematurely and inflict financial damage on both partners (Dyer, Kale, and Singh 2004: 109).

According to Dyer, Kale, and Singh (2004), acquisitions and alliances fail because very few executives compare or distinguish between acquisitions and alliances before choosing one over the other growth strategy. Hence, often they acquire firms they should have collaborated with, or ally with firms they should have long acquired. The two growth strategies differ in many ways. Acquisition deals are competitive, based on market prices, and risky. Alliances are cooperative, negotiated, and not so risky. Companies habitually deploy acquisitions to cut costs or improve scale economies, but use partnerships to enter new markets. Knowing when to use which strategy may be a greater source of SCA than knowing how to execute them.

Coca-Cola and Proctor & Gamble (P&G) announced in February 2001, that they would create a $4 billion joint venture that would control about 40 brands and employ more than 10,000 people. Coca-Cola would transfer Minute Maid, Five Alive, Fruitopia, Cappy, Kapo, Sonfil, and Qoo brands, among others to the new company, while P&G would contribute two of its beverage brands, Sunny Delight and Punica, and a snack brand, Pringle Chips. Coca-Cola would benefit from P&G's expertise in nutrition to develop new drinks, and P&G's flagging beverage and snack brands would get a boost from Coca-Cola's global distribution system. The new company hoped to slash costs by $50 million. The deal soured. Coke's stock fell by six percent the day the alliance was announced, while P&G's shares rose by two percent. Investors wondered why Coke would agree to share 50 percent of the profits from a fast-growing segment with a weak rival in its core business. If Coke really needed P&G's soft drinks technology and brands, then why did it not buy these brands outright, rather than risk on a joint venture? The partner companies wondered the same thing: they terminated the alliance in July 2001 (Dyer, Kale, and Singh 2004: 110).

In October 1999, Intel paid $1.6 billion in cash to buy the $131 million DSP Communications that manufactured chips for wireless handsets. Intel hoped to break into the wireless communications market. The acquisition, however, was a failure. Intel's stock price fell by 11 percent over three days after the deal was made. Investors were concerned about the 40 percent premium that Intel paid for DSP's shares. Moreover, people tend to leave high-tech firms when bigger companies absorb them, and technologies get obsolete quickly. These factors trigger post-acquisition trauma. Sure enough, Intel lost most of DSP's key people and its biggest wireless customer, Kyocera, when Intel absorbed the start-up DSP. Intel had to write off $600 million of goodwill by 2003. Intel would have done better seeking alliance with DSP rather than buy it outright (Dyer, Kale, and Singh 2004: 110).

HOW CAN YOU SAVE MERGERS AND ACQUISITIONS?

- Learn from reasons why M&A activities failed (see the previous section). The VPs should head teams that have honed the ability to assess whether a target company's technology when combined with the acquirer's abilities will provide solutions that customers demand; that is, the VPs should head teams that have mastered the ability to execute acquisitions and alliances (Dyer, Kale, and Singh 2004: 115).
- Execute "due diligence" before the M&A deal, and objectively assess each one's assets and liabilities, strengths and weaknesses, threats and opportunities, successes and failures. Write reports on these due diligence processes and results. After the deal is over, integration activities should use these reports for best insights into each merging company.
- Thus, assess whether a target company has a technology that is critical to your core products. The target company's technology when combined with yours must provide integral solutions that customers demand immediately and in the future. If so, acquire the technology or business right away. If not, seek equity or non-equity alliance as a stepping stone to acquisition. For instance, Cisco has about 25 percent of its acquisitions as small equity alliances that seek accelerated development of products. If product development succeeds, Cisco has options built into alliances to proceed to acquisitions. It takes between 12 and 18 months for Cisco to build trust with alliance partners and to decide if both companies could work together (Dyer, Kale, and Singh 2004: 115).

Organizational Factors

- Putting two companies together requires disconnecting and reconnecting hundreds of processes and procedures as quickly as possible. This needs team work, team members with project management skills, a structure within which the teams can operate effectively, and well-organized teams do better than uncoordinated teams (Ashkenas, Lawrence and Francis 2001: 189).

- The people involved in M&A are often strangers, thrown together in a joint enterprise, often against their will. Besides keeping the day-to-day business going, these people at both companies need to build new relationships which often involve bridging language and culture gaps. This can be a daunting task, but it must be done by facilitating social connections among people on both sides.
- The success of any M&A starts with an understanding of power on both sides—who has it and how to use it (Light 2001: 141).
- Despite the differential power base in a merger situation, what is crucial to the success of any merger is to bring top people together as quickly as possible, decide on performance goals, identify key people on both sides who could do it, and thus ensure effective ways to run the organization better.
- If you are the top key players in the new entity-to-be, do not waste your time on getting regulatory approval of the merger. Leave that task to good lawyers. Instead, focus on the integration plan of redefining new mission and goals of the new company, establish selection criteria for people who can realize those goals, and conduct an objective performance appraisal of the people whom you consider to select and retain as the top executives in the new company (Light 2001: 146).
- As a top key player, your major priority is to deliver the benefits of the merger that were promised to the shareholders and the public.

Operational Factors

- Porter (1987) examines four diversification strategies: (*a*) portfolio management, (*b*) restructuring, (*c*) transferring skills, and (*d*) sharing activities. He concludes that his study of 33 Fortune 500 companies during 1950–86 revealed that acquisitions that rely on transferring skills and sharing activities offer the best avenues for value creation. Successful diversifiers and acquisitions in his study made a disproportionately low percentage of unrelated acquisitions, minimizing exchanges where there were no clear opportunities for transferring skills and sharing activities.
- If acquisitions are of failing companies, then you may use a playbook approach to acquisitions that have proved successful in the past. However, when you are acquiring or merging good and successful companies, you need very creative and imaginative plans to retain and develop what is best in each company.
- All M&A activities expect perfect assimilation of each other's resources, talents, technologies and processes, organizational cultures and climates. Either mere assimilation, however, does not work, or it does not happen with perfect integration. The real work begins after the deal of M&A. The goal is to create a wholly new third company or to maintain two separate identities while sharing strengths.

Knowledge-based Innovation Factors

- The effects of M&A on a company's knowledge development and innovations are not very straightforward. Some scholars believe that M&A, in general, tend to hurt innovative capacities in firms. They act as a "poison pill" for innovations (Ernst and Vitt 2000; Hitt et al. 1991a, 1991b).

- Ahuja and Katila (2001), however, think otherwise. Prabhu, Chandy, and Ellis (2005) argue and empirically demonstrate that firms that first engage in internal knowledge development can learn and profit from M&A that helped to deepen the firm's internal knowledge. M&A serve as a "tonic" for innovation.
- That is, a firm's ability to create knowledge is a key factor of its ability to innovate and engage in successful M&A. New knowledge does not arise in a vacuum. Rather, it is a "path-dependent" outcome of building on prior knowledge, innovations, and M&A (Prabhu, Chandy, and Ellis 2005).
- Thus, a firm's internal knowledge can be a key predictor of its ability to use external knowledge via M&A to create innovations. The theory of knowledge-based view (KBV) helps to explain the role of knowledge in post-merger and post-acquisition innovations.
- Successful innovations from M&A involve: (*a*) the ability to choose the M&A target with the most promising knowledge, (*b*) the capacity to absorb knowledge made available by M&A, and (*c*) a need to exploit that knowledge to create new knowledge and innovations.

Technical Knowledge and M&A Success

- A special type of knowledge or "know-how" is "technical knowledge," which is defined as "scientific knowledge applied to useful purposes" (Prabhu, Chandy, and Ellis 2005: 115). Technical knowledge is not easily transferable but combinable across fields.
- Technical knowledge can be internal or external to the acquiring firm. "Internal technical knowledge" is based on learning core businesses, core competencies, and core products by employees within the firm via creation, distribution, and diffusion of knowledge within the boundaries of the firm. On the other hand, "external technical knowledge" originates outside the firm in relation to new technical advances, innovations, new ways of ecological conservation, new products and services, and new markets and trading areas. Acquisitions can be a great source of internal and external knowledge for the acquiring firm, thus serving the firm from being locked out of areas of future technological, environmental, and commercial markets.

Depth, Breadth, and Similarity of Knowledge

- Technical knowledge can be developed in "depth" within a field and in "breadth" across fields through acquisitions. Development of knowledge across fields assumes that the domain of knowledge has some "similarity" (or overlap) across the fields. All three aspects of technical knowledge, namely, depth, breadth, and similarity are important in relation to M&A.
- Firms that have very low or no internal knowledge of what M&A can offer fail to absorb and integrate M&A into the firm (Cohen and Levinthal 1989). Firms with deep internal knowledge are best positioned to leverage mergers and acquisitions to create innovations.
- M&A provide an important means to deepen internal knowledge in the firm and/or bring external knowledge into the firm (Bierly and Chakrabarti 1996). Internal knowledge enables firms to develop core competencies, especially in domain that are complex and deeply integrated within other domains of knowledge (Chesbrough and Teece 1996). In contrast, external knowledge enables firms to keep abreast of new technical developments, thus increasing the flexibility of the firm in dynamic environments (Grant 1996).

- By deepening and replenishing their stock of internal and external knowledge via R&D and M&A, firms can avoid "technological lockouts" from new developments and technologies in the competitive arena (Cohen and Levinthal 1989).
- M&A succeed to the extent they help firms to innovate. Firms with high depth of relevant knowledge produce more innovations from M&A, than do firms with low depth of that knowledge (Prabhu, Chandy, and Ellis 2005).
- The breadth of technical knowledge can also help absorb M&A and innovate. Integrating knowledge from across different fields, especially in technically complex industries, is a key to absorb M&A and innovate (Bierly and Chakrabarti 1996). Breadth of knowledge that cuts across several related fields have spurred innovations via serendipity.
- Firms with a broad base of knowledge are less likely to develop core rigidities and thus be locked out of emerging technical domains (Leonard-Barton 1992, 1995).
- Broader knowledge gives firms greater flexibility and adaptability in responding to dynamic environmental changes (Volberda 1996).
- The similarity of knowledge between the acquirers and the target M&A is crucial to the ability of the acquirer to innovate (Mowery, Oxley, and Silverman 1996). A firm's capacity to absorb new knowledge from M&A is conditioned on how its prior knowledge is related to the new knowledge it seeks via M&A (Cohen and Levinthal 1990).
- Thus, firms with moderate similarity of knowledge with that of the M&A can absorb better and produce more innovations from the M&A (Prabhu, Chandy, and Ellis 2005).
- However, one should clarify also the differences (e.g., competitive advantages, organizational routines and processes, innovations and new product development strategies, and aggressive marketing approaches of each firm) between merging firms that exist, why they exist, and how they made each firm successful.

Integration Factors

- In any case, assimilation is not absorption. It is not forcing your culture on the other. Integration is difficult unless both parties are ready to change, sacrifice, compromise, and forget their egos. One should appoint an ad hoc "integration manager" to bring about integration (Cliffe 2001: 113).
- The integration manager should shepherd everyone through the often rocky and uncharted territory that the two organizations must cross before they can function as one. The integration manager should be able to assess complex situations quickly, relate to many levels of authority smoothly, and bridge gaps in culture and perception between the two companies. This manager must thoroughly understand the culture, strengths, and weaknesses of both parent companies, and must possess enough clout to be effective (Ashkenas, Lawrence and Francis 2001: 183).
- Avoid cultural wars between merging or acquired companies. As soon as the M&A deal is over, encourage a good retreat of key people from both firms to a third party resort. During the retreat work on three Cs of integration: clarity of goals, conflict resolution, and consensus building. Enable in-depth discussions and dialogue that clarify goals and build consensus.
- In the integration process, speed is critical. Most M&As fail because the integration process is not fast enough (Light 2001: 141).

- One should work on the mechanics of good integration. Appreciate each one's understanding of its core business, core products, core markets, and core financial goals, and devise ways for integrating them.
- Conflicts between merging companies cannot be resolved by power or politics—you win the battle by doing so but lose the war. You destroy the very reason why you got into the M&A deal. Back off the bureaucracy.
- A company's "best assets wear shoes." Your best assets are people and their intangible goodwill and skills. Build strengths by bonding people from both firms. Good and long-standing relations between people from both firms, and at all levels, will never fail a merger. Devise good incentives and development plans for retaining your top talent on either side.
- Once this is done, explore cost-reduction strategies. Even well-managed firms offer opportunities for cost reduction. Passing the saved costs to the customers can strengthen and expand markets. Financial accountants can do the cost-reduction job well. However, closely monitor cost-containment performance.
- Make the numbers. Agree on strategic and budgetary goals. Set up a two, three, or five year business plan and sweat all the details, mental models, nuts and bolts, assumptions, and constraints of the plan. If you have set some financial goals for the M&A, then formulate strategies to achieve them within the time period planned. Once cost reduction is underway, then focus should be on revenue expansion via new technologies and innovations, new products and new markets.
- The acquisition or merger is about adding strategic value to all the entities. Hence, go beyond cost reductions to creating value for your customers and shareholders. Marshall joint vision, flexible architecture, and empowering leadership in planning and implementing the value creation program.
- Bring shared visions, common values, and strong mutually strengthening beliefs to the table. Cross-sell your resources and talents, synergize your divisions and departments, and build excitement about the merged entity's future.
- Identify key people from both firms to generate and implement the integration plan, and monitor closely that they achieve its goals and objectives.

Porter (1987) studied diversification records of 33 large and prestigious companies operating during 1965–86 and found that most of them had divested many more acquisitions than they had kept. That is, the companies had divested more than half of their acquisitions in new industries, more than 60 percent in new fields, and 74 percent in unrelated businesses. Little wonder, the corporate strategies of most of these companies had dissipated instead of creating shareholder value.

Porter (1987) observes that only lawyers, investment bankers, and original sellers prospered in most of the acquisitions he studied, and not the shareholders. Obviously, lawyers and investment bankers who negotiate and push M&A deals may not care about strategic fit or successful implementation. If part of the commissions that lawyers and investment bankers were entitled for were conditioned on the final outcomes of the M&A deal, all parties to such deals would be seriously responsible. BP follows this model in some of its most innovative deals in the North Sea (Di Georgio 2002a: 141).

Moore (2005) argues that the best strategic merger or acquisition moves for a company are ones that supplement rather than complement one's dominant business model. For instance, consider companies such as IBM, Cisco, and SAP; Goldman Sachs, Swiss Re, and the World Bank; Boeing, Tektronix, and Honeywell; Bechtel, Accenture, and IDEO; and Apache, Halliburton, and Burlington Northern—these

B2B corporations target a small number of large enterprises as their primary customers. As a contrast, consider corporations like Nestle, P&G, and Nike; Dell, Apple, and Sony; Hertz, Hilton, and United Airlines; and eBay, Google, and Amazon—these are B2C companies that are consumer-oriented and target large volumes of small customers. The economic formulae between these two sets of companies are different. In the first category of complex-systems model, vendors seek to grow a customer base of a few thousands, with no more than a handful of transactions per customer per year with average revenue per transaction from six to seven figures.

Contrastingly, in the second category of volume-operations model, vendors seek to build a customer base of a few millions, with tens and hundreds of transactions per customer per year but with average revenue per transaction of relatively few dollars. The two categories of companies represent two different organizational models, different organizational and operational structures, different focus of relationships in systematizing transactions and retaining customers. Mergers or acquisitions between these two category companies could be difficult, if not disastrous.

As a complementary source of corporate growth, Table 10.15 presents Michael Porter's model of five forces as explanation of mergers, acquisitions, and divestitures.

Culled from interviews with chairpersons and CEOs that acquired, merged or bought-out firms (see Carey 2000), Table 10.16 outlines some general observations on acquisitions, mergers, or takeovers.

CHOOSING AN ACQUISITION VERSUS ALLIANCE GROWTH STRATEGY

Dyer, Kale, and Singh (2004) argue that the choice between acquisitions and alliances should be based upon resources and synergies both partners bring to the venture. They distinguish three types of resource synergies:

- **Modular Synergies**: The partnering companies manage resources independently and pool only the results for greater profits. For instance, if an airline and a hotel chain seek to collaborate, then allowing hotel guests to earn frequent flyer miles, or clubbing airline and hotel choice, are pooling results via modular synergies. Hewlett-Packard and Microsoft have created a non-equity alliance that pools their system integration and enterprise software skills, respectively, to create technology solutions for small and big customers.
- **Sequential Synergies**: One completes its tasks and passes on the results to the partner who does the rest. For instance, a bio-tech firm that specializes in discovering new drugs, like Abgenix, planning to work with a pharmaceutical giant that is more familiar with Food and Drug Administration (FDA) approvals process, such as AstraZeneca, is seeking sequential synergies. Both partners need to customize their resources to some extent if the sequences must be seamless.
- **Reciprocal Synergies**: Both partners work closely together and execute tasks through an iterative and interactive knowledge-sharing process. Partnering firms need to combine and customize resources to make them reciprocally interdependent. In the mid-1990s, Exxon and Mobil combined and customized their resources along the entire value chain and thus became very competitive. M&A become more useful here than strategic alliances. Exxon and Mobil merged in 1999.

Much would also depend upon the "nature of the resources." If resources are hard (e.g., buildings, plants, real estate), acquisitions are better, whereas if resources are primarily soft (e.g., intellectual

TABLE 10.15 Porter's Model of Five Forces as Explanation of Mergers, Acquisitions, and Divestitures

Competitive forces	Strengthening factors	Weakening factors
Threat of New Entrants	Low level of entry barriers Low scale economies Low scales of learning Low capital requirements Low cost advantage Easy access to distribution channels	Increase the level of entry barriers by M&A that promote: High economies of scale High scale of organizational learning Capital-intensive technologies Absolute cost advantage Nationwide distribution structure
Threat of Product Substitutes	Low relative price of substitutes Buyer propensity to substitute Low product switching costs Superior performance of substitutes	Combat the threat of product or service substitutes by: Acquiring substitutes Merging with high performing substitutes Make switching difficult for buyers by bundling your product with substitutes
Threat of Supplier Concentration	Supplier concentration Quasi monopoly Supplier network of contracts Supplier bargaining power Non-availability of substitutes High supplier switching costs to buyers	Fight supplier power by: Acquiring suppliers (vertical or backward integration) Buying suppliers that have high bargaining power Centralized purchasing that increases your bargaining power
Threat of Buyer Concentration	Buyer concentration Quasi monopsony Buyer global networks Buyer bargaining power Buyer information Low cost of switching to other sellers	Fight buyer power by mergers, acquisitions, and divestitures that gives privileged access to: Major buyers and/or larger markets Major suppliers and distributors that reinforce product quality Highly specialized skills, competencies, and technologies that ensure high SCA Major supermarkets to enhance bargaining power
Threat of Current Competitive Rivals	Low industry growth High fixed operating costs Excess capacity Low product differentiation Seller concentration	Combat competition by: Acquiring smaller rivals to improve the scale economies of production, learning, and scope High product differentiation via innovations in product and marketing Focus on core products and core competencies via corporate strategic alliances with major rivals Merge to reduce excess capacity, thereby reducing price competition

Source: Author's own.

TABLE 10.16   Some General Observations on Acquisitions, Mergers, or Takeovers

Dimensions	Acquisitions	Mergers	Buyouts
What?	Primarily acquire process and product technologies, and products or services from other companies.	Companies merge with other companies, both retaining some form of identity.	An acquiring company buys the target company, and the latter loses its identity.
Why?	For improving growth: to create larger platforms for growth. They add value in many ways. You can also cut costs through acquisitions. But acquisitions work out best when geared for growth.	Merging is no good if you have a very good brand name and image. That's why Merrill Lynch did not merge with e-brokerage firms when going into e-business. They used their name as leverage away from price and technology.	Buy out firms with technologies or products/services you cannot build from the scratch. Thus, eBay bought out PayPal, Yahoo! bought GeoCities.
When?	When you have good venture capital to finance your acquisitions. When acquisitions provide entry into new consumer market segments or new geographic markets to sell existing products. Have the management and tech talent for the new process/products you buy.	Merge to strengthen your core business and competencies. The risk of venturing too far from your core business is not worth it. Diversifying outside your core business can be dangerous. The pharmaceuticals that diversified into cosmetics or services are refocusing on health business. Diversification caused failures during 1960–90 (e.g. ITT, SCM, Enron).	Need for speed forces companies to acquire rather than to build. The smart Internet companies (e.g., AOL, Yahoo! eBay, WorldCom) are using high market caps as currency to buy companies and quickly solidify their positions in the new net economy.
With Whom?	Gear acquisitions to the needs of your company and the realities of the industry. In the steel and chemical industries most M&A was driven by industry need to consolidate. Focus on the business portfolio, people, and processes. Settle the uncertainty of who is going to report to whom, who is responsible for what.	There should be a cultural fit between companies: U.S. companies rarely merge with Japanese companies with much success. They have a different mindset, a different pace and space. Often, the best solution is to forge partnerships with independent companies. Do not merge with companies too big for you—AOL–Time–Warner marriage did not last long!	Better, buy companies within your business space, than outside it. Thus, define your core business first, and then buy companies that enhance it. Buy small companies where the entrepreneurs know much about their business.
How?	All acquisitions should be well integrated with the core business. Allstate acquired many companies but integrated them with their core business.	Have your management structure completely laid out before merging. Establish good and open communications with merging parties. Explain what will happen to whom and why.	Buy out companies that reinforce your core business. Specify clearly, what happens to the first and second tier of management of the firm you buy out.
Necessary Conditions?	Good rationale for integrating the business. What is the logic of this acquisition? Is it a cost-takeout?	Be open on globalization and all that it implies. When merging foreign companies, know to localize your management styles. That's the reason Goldman Sachs, Morgan Stanley, and Merrill Lynch succeeded.	In buyouts, people immediately start thinking about themselves. What plans do you have for the future and the family of the employees bought out?
Sufficient Conditions?	Look for cross-cultural blend in international acquisitions. The U.S.–U.K. philosophies and management styles are very different still. For example, European firms are less aggressive than U.S. firms in cutting costs.	Organizational cultures need to blend. Price Waterhouse and Cooper merged but battled with each for long years before their different cultures began to blend. Make it a merger of equals. Equal board members from merged companies.	Some severance packages make millionaires. How do you retain them after a buyout? This was a major problem when Pfizer, Warner-Lambert, and American Home Products were buying each other out.

Source: Carey (2000).

capital, brand equity, skills, software), then strategic alliances work better than acquisitions. Hard assets are easy to value, and companies can generate synergies from them relatively quickly. For instance, Masco Corporation grew its home improvement products business by acquiring 150 companies during 1974–2004, 20 of which were during 2000–02. After every acquisition, Masco quickly scaled up the acquired firm's manufacturing capacity to generate economies of scale.

When companies must generate synergies by combining HR (soft), they are best done via alliances than through acquisitions. Research suggests that employees of acquired companies become soon unproductive because they are disinclined to work in the predator's interests and believe they have lost freedom. This is what happened when NationsBank (now BankAmerica) acquired Montgomery Securities in 1997—the culture was too different between commercial and investment banks. Key employees left and BankAmerica never benefited from the acquisition.

Another factor to consider in choosing between acquisitions and alliances is "resource redundancy." Acquisitions work better when resource redundancy is very high, but alliances functions better when resource redundancy is low. The acquiring company can use the surplus resources to generate economies of scale, or they can cut costs by eliminating these resources. One of the key driver for the HP–Compaq merger was resource redundancy.

Dyer, Kale, and Singh (2004) next consider "external market factors" in choosing between acquisitions and alliances. Two major exogenous market factors in this connection are market uncertainty and competition. Risks exist when companies can only assess the probability distribution of future payoffs; the wider the distribution, the higher the risk. Uncertainty exists when it is not possible to assess future payoffs. Uncertainty may relate to the technology or the product. Relevant questions in this regard are: Is the technology better than existing or potential rivals? Will the product work? Will the consumers use the technology, the product, or the service arising from both? How long will it take for the entire nation to use the service? Higher the uncertainty, more useful are equity or non-equity alliances rather than acquisitions. An alliance, typically, implies less money, less time, less exposure; if the results of that alliance are good, then the partners could go for a merger. Hoffman-La Roche acquired Genentech in June 1999 for $2.1 billion. The latter had developed a clot-busting drug, TPA, but had not completed effectiveness studies or sought FDA approval. Six months later, comparative studies found that Roche that had priced TPA at $2,200 per dose, was only as effective as Streptokinase of Hoechst who priced it at $200 a dose. Given the high uncertainty in drug development, Roche should have refrained from acquisition.

In relation to competition, if the resources you are desperately looking for are very much in demand, then you should buy them right away to defeat competition. If not, plan on equity or non-equity alliances that afford you better flexibility.

Table 10.17 summarizes the arguments of Dyer, Kale, and Singh (2004) in relation to choosing between alliances and acquisitions under different market conditions. All things being equal, when a company estimates the outcome of a collaboration to be highly or moderately uncertain, it should enter into a non-equity or equity alliance rather than acquire the company. An alliance will limit the firm's exposure since it has to invest less money and time than it would in an acquisition. If the results of the collaboration, however, are good and robust, then the company could move towards acquisition. Conversely, if the results of collaboration are not good, then the company can easily withdraw from the alliance.

Cisco led an acquisition-led growth strategy for years—it absorbed 36 firms during 1993–2003. During the same period, however, Cisco also entered into more than 100 alliances and managed them well. Because of this well-balanced dual growth strategy, Cisco's sales and market capitalization grew by an average of 36 percent and 44 percent, respectively, every year during this period.

TABLE 10.17   How to Choose between Acquisitions and Alliances as Growth Strategies

Factor	Sub-factors	Growth Strategy	Reasons
Type of Synergies	Modular	Non-equity alliances	Allows greater independence between partners
	Sequential	Equity alliances	Enables interdependency and flexibility between partners
	Reciprocal	Acquisitions	Expects much iterative and interactive dependencies between partners and resources
Nature of Resources	Mostly soft	Non-equity alliances	Allows for complementarity and enhancement of mutual resources
	Soft and hard	Acquisitions	Enables best exploitation of mutual resources for economies of scale
	Mostly hard	Equity alliances	Enables sharing of hard and soft resources independently
Resource Redundancy	Low	Non-equity alliances	Allows for complementarity and enhancement of mutual resources
	Medium	Equity alliances	Enables more efficient capacity utilization
	High	Acquisitions	Enables best exploitation of mutual resources for economies of scale, or cost reductions via divestitures of surplus resources
Market Uncertainty	Low	Non-equity alliances	Enables better flexibility and contract reversibility in low-risk sharing
	Medium	Acquisitions	Enables better taming and spread of market uncertainty and risk
	High	Equity alliances	Enables better spread of uncertainty and risk
Level of Competition	Low	Non-equity alliances	Enable better function under low competition
	Medium	Equity alliances	Enable better commitment and efficiency under medium competition
	High	Acquisitions	Acquisitions seal and protect resources from the high competitive rivals

Source: Dyer, Kale, and Singh (2004: 109–15).

A PERMANENT OPPORTUNITY TO GROW: PRODUCT TO CUSTOMER ORIENTATION

Back in 1960, Theodore Levitt, then a lecturer in business administration at the Harvard Business School, wrote an article titled "Marketing Myopia," which has since been a classic for all executives focused on growth. We paraphrase some growth-related ideas and strategies that might be still valid and valuable, after almost half a century:

- There is no such thing as a growth industry. There are only companies that are organized and operated to create and capitalize on growth opportunities.
- Executive focusing on growth should remember four principles: (*a*) do not believe that growth is not assured by an expanding and more affluent population; (*b*) do not believe that there is no competitive substitute for your industry's major product; (*c*) do not believe too much in mass production and its assumed price-scale economies; and (*d*) do not be preoccupied in experimentation and innovation that reduces manufacturing costs.
- The railroads did not stop growing because the need for passenger and freight transportation declined. That need grew. Moreover, the railroads stagnated not because that need was filled by competitive substitutes (e.g., cars, trucks, passenger, and cargo planes) but because it was not filled by railroads themselves. They lost customers to others because they continued to focus on railroad business (product focus) rather than on the transportation business (customer focus). The railroad industry can still grow if it focuses on the transportation business.
- Hollywood barely escaped a total annihilation by television. As with railroads, Hollywood defined its business incorrectly—it focused on the movie business (product focus) and not on the entertainment business (customer focus).

- A thoroughly customer-oriented management can keep the industry growing even after the obvious opportunities for growth have been exhausted. For instance, DuPont and Corning succeeded not because of their unquestioned product and technical competence but because of their customer focus. Both companies constantly looked for opportunities to apply their technical expertise to the creation of customer-satisfying uses, which accounted for their prodigious growth.
- The electricity industry, presumably a "natural monopoly," is still surviving despite the countless electricity lines that vulgarize our cities and backyards and despite the frustrating street and service interruptions during storms. Instead of focusing on electricity (product focus), had they focused on the energy business (customer focus), it would have sustained much larger growth via other energy sources such as solar, wind, chemical fuel cells, and the like.
- If thinking is an intellectual response to a problem, then the absence of a problem leads to the absence of thinking. For instance, if you mistakenly believe your product has an automatically expanding market, then you will not give much thought to how to expand it. This is what led to the episodic decline of the petroleum and automobile industries. Top executives of both industries believed that an expanding and affluent population will ensure permanent demand for their products and lack of effective competitive substitutes will keep demand for their indispensable generic product strong. Both focused on their generic products (gasoline, vehicles) and not on energy or transportation (customer focus). Complacency and wrong-headedness can stubbornly convert opportunities into near disaster.
- The history of every dead and dying "growth" industry shows a self-deceiving cycle of bountiful expansion and undetected decay. There is no guarantee against product obsolescence. If a company's research does not make a product obsolete, another's will.
- The difference between marketing and selling is more than semantic. Selling focuses on the needs of the seller to convert product into cash; marketing centers on the needs and satisfaction of the buyer. Mass production fuels selling; personalized product fuels marketing. *One of the greatest enemies of growth is mass production.*
- In the motor city of Detroit mass production was the most famous, most honored, and had the greatest impact on the then society. The industry is now failing. Detroit never really researched on customers' wants; it only researched their preferences between annual car models it had already decided to offer. Detroit is mainly product-oriented and not customer-oriented. The domestic auto manufacturers have left customer needs pretty much to the auto dealers and to the servicing agencies.
- *Marketing effort is still viewed as a necessary consequence of the product. In reality, the converse is true—the product should become the consequence of marketing.* This is the legacy of mass production, with its parochial view that profit resides essentially in low-cost full production.
- Henry Ford was the most brilliant and the most senseless marketer in American history. He was senseless because he refused to give the customer anything but a black car. He was brilliant because he fashioned a production system designed to fit the markets—that everybody could afford a car. He invented the assembly line because he had concluded that at $500 he could sell millions of cars. Mass production was the result, not the cause, of his low prices. This was a price-driven costing marketing strategy, and not the conventional cost-driven pricing (selling) strategy.
- The tantalizing profit possibilities of low unit mass production costs may be the most seriously self-deceiving attitude that can afflict a company, particularly a "growth" company, where an apparently assured expansion of demand already tends to undermine a proper concern for the importance

of marketing and the customer. The usual result of this narrow preoccupation is that instead of growing, the industry declines. It usually means that the product fails to adopt to the constantly changing patterns of consumer needs and tastes, to new and modified marketing institutions and practices, or to product developments in the competing or complementary industries. The industry has its eyes so firmly on its own specific product that it does not see how it is being made obsolete. This is "product provincialism" at its worst. *The historic fate of one growth industry after another has been its suicidal product provincialism.*

• It is not surprising that having created a successful company by making a superior product, management continues to be oriented towards the product rather than the people who consume it. It develops the philosophy that continued growth is a matter of continued product innovation and improvement. This is marketing myopia at its worst.

GROWTH BY CREATING NEW BUSINESSES

"Some problems are so complex that you have to be highly intelligent and well-informed just to be undecided about them," wrote Laurence J. Peter, the business humorist (cited in Garvin 2004: 18). Top line corporate growth is one of those complex problems, especially when it comes to creating new businesses within large complex companies. Such new business creations have various names in the literature: corporate venturing, corporate entrepreneurship, corporate intrapreneuring, and corporate innovation.

Garvin (2004: 18–21) summarizes 10 things CEOs should know in regard to creating new businesses:

1. **Ultimately, Growth Means Starting New Businesses**: Technology creates new products and services, but it can quickly obsolesce them as well. The digital camera destroyed the Polaroid instant photography business. Markets can saturate. After establishing over 1,000 stores, Home Depot realized it could not grow anymore in the U.S. Wal-Mart is also in that same quandary.

2. **Most New Businesses Fail**: In the 1970s and 1980s, 60 percent of the small business start-ups failed in their first six years. During the same period, several big businesses (e.g., DuPont, Exxon, IBM, P&G, Sara Lee, 3M, and Xerox) either divested or closed 44 percent of their internally operated start-ups and 50 percent of the joint ventures in the first six years.

3. **Corporate Culture is the Biggest Deterrent to Business Creation**: New ventures flourish best in open, exploratory environments, but most large corporations are geared toward mature, predictable, and efficient businesses. A growing business is one which encourages mavericks with diverse perspectives tolerates well-reasoned mistakes, and provides resources for exploratory ventures that empower its employees to be entrepreneurs. CEOs that reward conformists and rule followers, demand error-free performance, and insist on party line will destroy corporate venturism.

4. **Separate Organizations do not Work, at Least not for Long**: Believing in freedom and independence, big corporations in the 1960–80s (e.g., Boeing, Exxon, GE, Gillette, Levi Strauss, and Monsanto) set up separate internal venture divisions. Not all were successful. In the 1990s, companies like Bertelsmann, Chase, Intel, and UPS favored corporate venture funds to nurture nascent businesses by offering managerial oversight, funding in stages, and technical advice. These did not last more than five years. Triggered by abundant resources and freedom, separation

from the mainstream organization results in brief surges of enthusiasm, but in the long run it generates power struggles, culture clashes, and wastefulness.

5. **Starting a New Business is Essentially an Experiment**: New ventures can go wrong in many ways. Custom failure (insufficient demand, overpriced products), technology failure (inability to provide the promised functionality), operational failures (inability to deliver at the required cost or quality level), organizational failure (institutional barriers to doing what is desired), and competitive failures (new market entrants) can paralyze new businesses. They need to experiment. You cannot always figure out product designs or business models fully in advance. They should design experiments with high "discriminating power" (i.e., ability to distinguish between two or more competing hypotheses). Good experiments begin with clear objectives; they are designed to produce targeted insights and rapid feedback, and they should generate measurable and actionable results.

6. **New Businesses Proceed through Distinct Stages, Each Requiring a Different Management Approach**: Three stages are conceivable: experimentation, expansion, and integration; each stage poses a different set of questions and hence, different solutions (see the section before this). Each stage, accordingly, demands different talents and perspectives, and hence, new leaders. The first stage of experimentation needs an adventurous, visionary-missionary leader known for bold thinking and creativity, and the usual performance measures are the number of new customers, new patents, new technologies, new prototypes, and new products generated. The second stage of expansion needed a venture-task leader with organizational and selling skills and the typical metrics of performance are sales, market share, penetration rates, new customers, new markets, new trade regions, and new geographic regions. The third stage of integration needs great operations managers who can do the integration between the old and new businesses, customer bases and markets, and the long-term performance metrics are financial in nature such as return on investments (ROI), return on equity (ROE), return on assets (ROA), earnings per share (EPS), and P/E.

7. **New Business Creation Takes Time**: A lot of time, at an average seven to nine years. All three stages of new business creation, experimentation, expansion, and integration, especially, the first, are time-consuming, need to be tested and validated, and, thus, take time to unfold. Customers' first reactions are not always good predictors of long-term sustainability. Home Depot that started in 1991 did not stabilize until late 1998.

8. **New Businesses Need Help Fitting in with Established Systems and Structures**: The greatest concern of new business leaders is that they and their ventures will become organizational orphans. Especially when they combine offerings from several divisions or target markets that fall into the white space of the organizational chart, new ventures find it very difficult to find an organizational home. The problem, and the tension, is to achieve the right balance between identity and integration. If you insist on too much independence, then it will be orphaned; if you seek too tight a link to old structures, you will not differentiate your offering. Top executives should expect deviation from predictions. Sales predictions, financial performance predictions are tricky because of high levels of uncertainty. Large forecast errors in the first-year sales and profits make new businesses targets of critics. Go/no decisions should seldom be based on large initial returns of realized target budgets.

9. **The Best Predictors of Success are Market Knowledge and Demand-driven Products and Services**: Success in new businesses increases when your target market is a group of old

familiar customers and when you staff your business by people who know the target market very well. Both ensure that your product offerings are right solutions to right customer problems.

10. **An Open Mind is Hard to Find**: Every large company has a mental model or an implicit theory—a largely unstated view of how the business works and money is made. The biggest hurdle for new businesses is mental—the way senior managers think about business, technologies, products and services, customers and competitors. Many executives view all new businesses through the filter or lens of their mental models, and judge or assess success by how well they conform to their mental models. Few new businesses are not able to clear this test, however, nor should they. When they do, every new business looks like the old.

THE WAY INDUSTRIES EVOLVE

[This section is derived from McGahan (2004: 86–94)]

You cannot make intelligent investments within your organization unless you understand how your whole industry is changing. If the industry is in the midst of a radical change, you will eventually have to dismantle obsolete businesses. If the industry is experiencing incremental change, you will probably need to reinvest in your core (McGahan 2004: 87). How can you understand industry change and how does industry structure affect your business—are two good questions to think about.

McGahan (2004) argues that industries evolve along four trajectories—radical, progressive, creative, and intermediary. The four trajectories set boundaries on what will generate profits in a business. Many companies have incurred losses because they tried to innovate outside of those boundaries. A firm's strategy or plan for achieving a good return on invested capital cannot succeed unless it is aligned with the industry's change trajectory.

There are two types of threats of obsolescence:

1. **Threat to Industry's Core Activities**: The activities that have historically generated profits for the industry are threatened when they become less relevant to suppliers and customers because some new alternatives have emerged outside the industry. Some of these core activities include processing technologies, production technologies, purchase bargaining power, inventory management, packaging and labeling, branding and sizing, distribution and delivery, marketing and customer feedback, warranty and guarantee services, supplier and customer relations. For example, in the auto industry many auto dealerships are becoming obsolete because the Internet can provide far better services 24/7 to customers.

2. **Threat to Industry's Core Assets**: The resources, knowledge, patents, specialized equipment, core products, and brand capital are those that have historically made the organization unique. These are threatened to the extent that they fail to generate value they once did. In the pharmaceutical industry, for instance, blockbuster national brand drugs are constantly threatened as patents expire and new drugs are developed.

When an industry's core activities and core assets are threatened with obsolescence, then radical innovation strategy is needed to fight both threats. When an industry's core activities are threatened but not its core assets, then intermediating change is needed. When an industry's core assets are threatened but not its activities, then creative change is needed. Finally, when an industry's both core activities and core assets are not threatened, then progressive innovation or change is needed. Table 10.18 captures these four trajectories of change.

Radical Change: When an industry's core activities and core assets are threatened with obsolescence, then "radical" innovation or disruptive change is needed. This phenomenon normally occurs following radical innovations in the industry (e.g., Boeing, the personal computer [PC], word processing, the Internet, computerized axial tomography [CAT], magnetic resonance imaging [MRI], arthroscopy surgery, wireless phones) or radical regulatory changes (deregulation of the trucking, airline, and advertising industry; imposition of higher EPA standards) or radical changes in consumer lifestyles (e.g., decreased preference for cigarettes during the last 20 years in the U.S.) During the 1980s and 1990s about 20 percent of the U.S. industries experienced radical change.

A typical example in this zone is the travel agency industry. Both core assets and core activities were threatened when the airlines implemented the Semi-automatic Business Research System (SABRE) and other reservation systems to enhance direct price competition, and when Web-enabled systems

TABLE 10.18   Trajectories of Industry Change

Threatening Factors

Mostly external: Radical changes in technology, digitization and the Internet, competition, government regulation, energy sources, communication equipment, trade, and globalization

Core Assets	Core Activities	
Examples: Strategic location, buildings, infrastructure, IT architecture, technologies, patents, specialized equipment, core products, flagship brands, and market knowledge	Examples: Processing, production, purchasing, inventory management, distribution, supply chain management (SCM), customer relationship management (CRM), employee relationship management (ERM), and channel partner relationship management (PRM)	
Threatened	**Threatened**	**Not threatened**
	Radical Change	**Creative Change**
	Corporations must constantly change both core assets and core activities	Corporations must renovate core resources and assets
	Typical industries include: Travel agency, landline telephone, and overnight letter-delivery carriers	Typical industries include: Filming industry, music industry, oil and gas exploration, health foods, pharmaceuticals, sports team ownership, and investment banking
Not Threatened	**Intermediating Change**	**Progressive Change**
	Corporations must constantly renew and strengthen core activities	Corporations must incrementally change and adapt both core assets and core activities
	Typical industries include: Management consultancy, automotive dealerships, auctioning, and investment brokerage	Typical industries include: Commercial airlines, long-haul trucking, online marketing, education, health care, insurance, and banking

Source: McGahan (2004: 90).

(e.g., Travelocity, Orbitz, Expedia) offered new value through online monitoring of available airline flights and fares, hotel accommodations and fares, car rentals and fares, and diner and theater reservations.

Another example is the postal and overnight letter delivery industry. Radical innovations like the fax machines, rapidly increasing usage of the Internet and the e-mail (especially securely encrypted e-mail) threatened the postal industry. However, it has not destroyed it completely; this is primarily because people's preference for post mail has not changed. Overnight delivery of packages and letters is still increasing and the business is still thriving.

Industries that are on a radical change trajectory often remain profitable for a long time, especially if companies in these industries scale back their commitments accordingly, and innovatively respond to the new radical changes. The best strategy in the midst of radical change is not exiting (as some companies do), or merging, or acquiring, but on building up your core assets and core activities. For instance, Federal Express acquired Kinko's to create deeper relationships with small and mid-size businesses that need documentation, document storage, and dissemination services. Similarly, the computer mainframe business has not been blanked out by the proliferation of PCs and workstation manufacturers. The encyclopedia companies quickly responded to the threat of online search engines by experimenting with new products such as online encyclopedia, e-books, new and aggressive distribution channels, and rapidly updating their products.

Intermediate Change: When an industry's core activities are threatened but not its core assets, then "intermediating" change strategy is needed. It typically occurs when customers and suppliers, employees and channel partners have new or better options. That is, business activities for dealing in both downstream (channel partners and customers) and upstream (suppliers, top managers, and skilled employees) markets are simultaneously threatened. This change is hardest to manage among the four changes described earlier. It is the most challenging because corporations must simultaneously preserve their valuable assets and restructure their key long-term relationships with major stakeholders such as customers and suppliers.

Typical industry examples in this category of intermediating change include auto dealerships, management consultancy firms, investment brokerages, and auction houses. Consider gigantic management consultancy firms like Arthur Anderson, PriceWaterhouseCoopers, and other large brokerage firms. They had long confronted criticism about conflict of interest in their analyst and management consultancy organizations. But what most threatened their core activities was the recent market downturn and corporate frauds—both of which were tied to fundamental changes in the information available to investors and companies seeking investment capital. In the music industry recording companies are beginning to sell their services *à la carte* to aspiring musicians rather than make huge investments upfront in the development of the artists, their art (e.g., production, choreography, sound management), and in the marketing (radio promotions, image management) of their programs. Similarly, for instance, eBay and other online auctioning companies have seriously affected the core activities of the auctioning industry. Some of these companies have, however, capitalized on their appraisal expertise online and are selling it for a fee on the Internet when valuables are auctioned.

Creative Change: When an industry's core assets are threatened but not its activities, then "creative" change is needed. In this trajectory, relationships with customers and suppliers are generally stable, but core assets are obsolesced. The film industry is a typical example. Large production companies enjoy ongoing relationships with actors, agents, theater owners, and cable television executives. Within this framework they produce and distribute films all the time and command superior performance over the long term. But radical changes in the photography industry (e.g., digital camera, digitization of text, graphics, sound, color, 3D, and animation) and in the IT sector (e.g., the Internet, Web television, cable television) have rendered their old assets obsolete.

Other industries in this trajectory of creative change are oil and gas exploration, pharmaceuticals, and pre-packaged software. In the pharmaceutical industry, companies must research, develop, and test new drugs constantly when flagship drug brands get obsolete. In oil and gas explorations, new EPA standards and the Organization of the Petroleum Exporting Countries (OPEC) constraints can seriously affect exploring, drilling, pipelining, mining, and refining assets. In the pre-packaged software industry, developers must constantly change, update, expand, and install new software packages that get quickly get obsolete. In the organic health and diet food industry, producers must constantly generate organically safe and cholesterol-free produce and packaged foods. Innovations in the creative trajectory occur in fits and starts depending upon change in external forces like people's lifestyles, health consciousness, or changes in environmental regulations.

Progressive Change: When an industry's core activities and core assets are not threatened, that is, buyers and suppliers have incentives enough to preserve the status quo, managers must respond to retain customers and suppliers by "progressive" incremental innovations or changes. Hence, industries in this trajectory are basically more stable than in other trajectories. Typical industries in this trajectory currently are discount retailing, commercial airlines, long-haul trucking, online marketing, education, health care, insurance, and banking. These industries are relatively stable, but corporations must constantly carve out distinct positions on geographic, technical, or marketing expertise. This is how Wal-Mart sustains its industry leadership and dominance in discount retailing. Southwest Airlines is not into radical innovations, but the few incremental changes it does such as finding new flight routes or making its basic services attractive is enabling it to be the most profitable airline.

WHICH TRAJECTORY ARE YOU ON?

Several steps of self-analysis may be necessary to answer this question:

1. Determine which industry you belong to and who your direct competitors are. Your direct competitors are: (*a*) those companies who your customers and suppliers switch to by about 5 percent change in your prices, (*b*) those that target the same buyers or suppliers as you do, and (*c*) those companies that use similar technologies to create value as you do.
2. Define your industry's core assets and activities by using certain tests such as: if these core assets or activities were eliminated would your profits be significantly lower a year from now? For instance, in the auctioneering industry appraising works of art is a core activity; in the beverage industry, Coca-Cola is a core asset. The disappearance of these core assets or activities will damage your profits.
3. Determine if your assets or activities are getting obsolete. They are obsolete if they are potentially irrelevant to your business, customers, and profitability.
4. Finally, given your analysis under (1) through (3), determine in which trajectory your corporation is.

See also Table 10.18 for determining your trajectory.

CONCLUDING REMARKS

Table 10.19 raises several contextual questions regarding organizational growth and suggests some prospects. Strategic leaders need to ask these and other related questions before strategizing corporate growth.

Are limits to corporate growth real? Are some corporations too big to fail? Conversely, are some corporations too big not to fail? After the collapse of Lehman Brothers, Bear Stearns, American International Group (AIG), Washington Mutual, Merrill Lynch, Wachovia, and other financial giants, no organization, howsoever big or small, is immune from collapse. The most damaging ones are very hard to anticipate with any confidence. In 1996, a single power-line failure in Oregon led to a massive cascade of power outages that spread across all the states west of the Rocky Mountains, leaving tens of millions of people without electricity. Engineers can reliably assess the risk that any single power generator in a given network will fail under some conditions or constraints. But once a cascade starts, they can no longer know what these conditions and constraints will be for each generator—because in a dynamic and complex system conditions could change dramatically depending upon what else happens in the network. The result is that systemic risk that can cause the system as a whole to fail may not be related in a simple way to the risk profiles of the system's parts (Watts 2009: 16). In short, it is difficult to detect and contain systemic risk of oversized corporations.

TABLE 10.19   Contextual Problems of Organizational Growth: Questions and Prospects

Problem context	Critical questions	Prospects and opportunities	Industry examples
The organization is too big	Is it too big to fail? Is it too big to grow? Is it too big to control? Is antitrust kicking in?	Economies of scale Economies of scope Economies of power Centralized purchasing Centralized recruiting High bargaining power	Wal-Mart, Exxon GMC, Ford, Toyota GE, IBM, HP, Dell City-Group, Chase, Lehman Brothers, Wachovia Catholic Church
The organization is too small	Is it too small to fail? Is it too small to grow? Is it too small to survive? Is it too small to worry?	Check breakeven points. Check breakeven prices. Check dumping opportunities. Explore selling opportunities. Explore closing prospects.	Inner city branches Inner city churches Inner city schools Old village farms
The organization is too old and aging fast	Too old to rejuvenate? Too old to innovate? Too old to compete? Too old to survive? Is growth difficult?	If yes, phase it out. Try incremental innovations. Reposition your SCA. Divest what is good. Liquidate or close.	Old chemical plants Old oil refineries Railroad and cruising companies Old steel companies Some retail companies
The industry is stagnating	Can you revive the industry? Is it worth reviving? Can you explore new markets? Can you transfer it to Less Developed Countries (LDCs)?	If yes, phase it out. If yes, innovate radically. Explore foreign markets. Transfer it to LDCs if they can use it to advantage.	Most paper and printing mills, for example, Cirque de Soleil Cigarette industry Dow Chemical plants to China

(Continued)

TABLE 10.19 *(Continued)*

Problem context	Critical questions	Prospects and opportunities	Industry examples
There is tough competition	Too many new market entrants? Too easy entry barriers? Can you buy competition? Can you merge with competitors?	Ignore competition and explore new market spaces. Scout for good acquisitions. Plan carefully mergers or joint ventures.	All "blue oceans" Southwest, NYPD IPod, iTunes, and iPhones PayPal by eBay, Hotmail by Microsoft KMart and Sears
There is very low market demand	Can you create demand? Open new markets? Expand existing markets? Extend existing brands? Innovate new products? Innovate new delivery systems? Innovate new services?	Technological breakthroughs Market breakthroughs Augment markets Extend brands by size, color, … Radical new products Radically new logistics New financing/mortgaging services	Ultrasound, MRI, FMRI, stents iPod, Itunes, iPhones, PlayStations Cell phones, Internet, WWW Cell phones, Blackberry Microwave ovens, Arthroscopy Wal-Mart's cross-docking systems GMAC, Ford Credit, Fannie May, Freddie Mac, Countrywide
Market is saturated	Is domestic market saturated? Is the global market saturated? Are all domestic market segments saturated? If yes to all above, can you stop producing for a while?	Penetrate foreign markets Reposition/re-innovate product Try market augmentation and segmentation.	Cigarettes, beer, Internet, cell phones Hybrid cars, electric cars, solar cars Jeans for all ages, genders, and races; cars for the handicapped, Attention Deficit Trait (ADT); U.S. autos are stalling production
Stagnant growth	Are you growing organically? Seeking external growth? Technology growth stagnant?	Improve homegrown products. Innovate homegrown products. Innovate within. Strategize suitable M&A. Seek strategic alliances.	P&G, Dell, Apple, IBM, GE P&G, Dell, HP, Apple, IBM, GE P&G, Dell, GE, Apple, Sony, Toyota Bank mergers, hospital mergers, auto mergers (Chrysler and Fiat), NUMMI, Xerox–Canon, Kodak–Fuji
Ecological demands are mounting	Are you meeting greening standards? Are you polluting the environment? Are you depleting non-renewable resources?	Reduce carbon emissions, meet Corporate Average Fuel Economy (CAFÉ) standards Reduce harm to water, air, land, forests, rivers, fish, animals, … Conserve non-renewable resources; expand them, instead	Cap and carbon emission markets Alternate energies Global climate change mandates, UNO greening standards and goals Global sustainability organizations Social entrepreneurship

Source: Author's own.

Financial systems are far more complex than power grids, but the fundamental problem of the systemic risk is the same. In 2008, we experienced an unequalled financial crisis that has precipitated a global blackout. Risk managers may assess the risk of their own institution on the assumption that conditions in the rest of the financial world would remain predictably stable. But in a crisis situation, these conditions change unpredictably. No one suspected that financial banks the size of Lehman Brothers and Wachovia would collapse suddenly as they did, and so risk managers did not build such contingencies into their risk assessment models.

How then can we reduce the risk of cascades in the financial systems? The solution may be to make the system less complex to start with, and thus reduce the chance that any one part can trigger a catastrophic chain of events and domino effects. The risk was invisible because it was systemic—it resulted from the unpredictable interplay of the myriad parts in the system. Hence, one should reduce the system complexity by size and variability. This implies, therefore, that we limit how big companies are allowed to become big. There must be limits to growth (see related archetypes under systems thinking in Chapter 4). Regulators should routinely review firms and ask, "Is this company too big to fail?" If yes, the company could be required to downsize or right-size, divest business lines, stall mergers and acquisitions, until regulators decide that size and complexity would no longer pose a risk to the whole system.

It also means that we refrain from excess leverage, lax oversight, and faulty executive compensation structures. The idea that you need to give executives a stake in company profits in order to give them the right incentives has currently caused too much damage. Even though Harvard economist Michael Jensen strongly advocated that the managers' interests need to be aligned with those of shareholders, yet this proposition has escalated into exorbitant executive compensation packages that have been self-destructive, observes Nobel Laureate Paul Krugman of Princeton (Cliffe 2009: 17).

Even though we all hate too much government interventions, yet anti-trust law already permits regulators to prevent firms from growing too big to stifle competition. Moreover, recent history has demonstrated that free markets left to themselves do not automatically control systemic risk, any more than they can automatically create competition. Thus, pragmatically speaking, government interventions are required to prevent free markets from destroying themselves. The efficient markets theory of the economists still naively believes that the private sector knows what it is doing—and this has led to our near-total failure, argues Paul Krugman, to regulate the financial markets (Cliffe 2009: 17).

It also means more transparency and a systemic reduction of buyer–seller information asymmetry (Mascarenhas, Kesavan, and Bernacchi 2008). Investment banks, hedge funds, private equity funds, index funds, and in general, derivatives, have morphed into complex, non-transparent, ubiquitous commodities that are vulnerable to trouble and failure. Firms should not be allowed to grow too big, too complex, and too opaque to fail in the first place (Watts 2009: 16).

Chapter 11

The CEO as a Person of Self-mastery through Executive Spiritual Development

I believe that if one man gains spiritually the whole world gains with him, and if one man falls, the whole world falls to that extent.... You just raise your own consciousness and you will raise the consciousness of the entire world. (Mahatma Gandhi)

(Easwaran 1995)

No one gives unless one has it. The executive or corporate strategy cannot excel the executive, the ultimate strategist. Unless the chief executive and the top management are transformed spiritual people, they will not be able to transform and spiritualize the company in a lasting way. One's self-mastery, one's mental models, one's shared learning, one's team spirit, and the "Fifth Discipline"—systems thinking—are integral components of what values we have, what we are, what we become, and our ultimate being. This chapter focuses on the CEO as a strategist for self-mastery through executive spiritual development. Corporate executives are leaders, not mere managers of people. In order to lead, direct, guide, and steer people and organizations, corporate executives must be authentic leaders, honest men and women with integrity, ethics, and morality, executives with vision and mission, passion and compassion, spiritual maturity and humanity.

One's religion and its scriptural, congregational, and worship resources may help one's self-mastery and spiritual development. However, it is not always necessary. Even atheists, agnostics, and downright secular people can achieve self-mastery and spiritual maturity through the development of their spirit, soul, conscience, vision, mission, values and goals, virtues and discipline. Executives must redefine their job. They must give up the "the old dogma of planning, organizing and controlling," and realize "the almost sacredness of their responsibility for the lives of so many people." The fundamental task of leaders, argues Bill O'Brien, former president of Hanover Insurance, is "providing the enabling conditions for people to lead the most enriching lives they can" (O'Brien 1989). This task cannot be fulfilled unless and until the corporate leaders themselves experience enriched lives of self-mastery and spiritual development.

In the higher levels of critical thinking such as responsive, creative, and generative (see Chapter 4, Table 4.1, bottom three rows), the critical thinker needs spiritual mastery and development. In systems thinking, Peter Senge (1990, 2006) and Senge and his associates (1994, 1999, 2000) postulate four disciplines for spiritual development: self-mastery, shared vision, mental models, and team-learning. One requires an enhanced experience of all four disciplines for a full development of one's humanity and humanization, executive and servant leadership. Chapter 4 dealt with the CEO as a system thinker. This chapter focuses on self-mastery as a gateway to executive spiritual development, which essentially implies the perfecting of one's critical thinking through the five disciplines.[1] The next and the last chapter (Chapter 12) will incorporate the remaining three disciplines of shared vision, mental models, and team learning into a CEO's spiritual repertoire.

THE CRITICAL IMPORTANCE OF EXECUTIVE SPIRITUAL DEVELOPMENT

Since his first edition in 1990, and working on his revised edition of *The Fifth Discipline*, Peter Senge (2006) met with countless number of practitioners of organizational learning (e.g., managers, business and social entrepreneurs, teachers and school principals, military leaders, police chiefs, and community organizers) who found an infinite array of imaginative ways to work with and utilize the five disciplines. In their own ways, each created an alternative system of management based on love rather than fear, curiosity rather than an insistence on "right" answers, and learning rather than controlling. These interviews revealed fresh insights into how master practitioners initiate change and deal creatively with the challenges of sustaining momentum. Most found that building enterprises capable of adapting to changing realities clearly demands new ways of thinking, operating, and organizational learning.

Organizations are becoming more and more horizontally networked, weakening thereby the traditional vertical hierarchies, thus, potentially opening up new capacity for continual learning, innovation, and adaptation. Our economies and markets are more global than ever; consequently, so is business. In global business, cost and performance pressures are relentless. The time available for people to think and reflect is becoming scarce. The globalization of business and industrial development are raising material standards of living for some, while lowering for many. All too often, the production of financial capital seems to occur at the expense of social and natural capital. At the same time, the interconnected world creates a greater awareness of others than has ever before existed. It is an unprecedented time of cultures colliding, ideologies clashing, and violence erupting. This is the time we need to learn from one another (Senge 2006: xv–xvi). Corporate, technological, and religious-cultural enclaves are things of the past. The promise of a truly generative dialogue among civilizations holds great hope for the future. Not all this is possible without self-mastery, team-learning, shared visions, revised and shared mental models—the essence of executive spiritual development.

In addition to business successes, we need a host of new possibilities in applying organizational learning tools and principles in areas that are becoming more urgent and relevant today than ever before: from growing more environmentally sound businesses and industries to addressing social problems like global income inequality, global poverty and disease, improving global food production, increasing terrorism and gang violence, transforming school systems, and promoting economic and ecological development. In all these settings, openness, reflection, deeper dialogue and conversations, personal mastery and shared vision, team learning, and shared mental models uniquely energize change, and understanding the systemic causes of problems is crucial (Senge 2006: xvii).

Donald Rothberg battled all his adult life from his years at Yale and thereafter with two vocations— to dedicate himself to justice and social change (external transformation) and explore the depths of

---

[1] The concept of organizational learning flourished in the 1990s, triggered by Peter M. Senge's (1990) *The Fifth Discipline*, and countless other publications, workshops, and field books (e.g., Senge et al. 1994, 1999, 2000). This chapter and the next are heavily dependent upon this vast material, on the revised edition of *The Fifth Discipline* (Senge 2006), and other related material on executive spiritual development.

human consciousness to an awakening of his deeper spiritual nature (inner transformation). After more than 30 years of such a struggle, he writes his experiences in his *The Engaged Spiritual Life: A Buddhist Approach to Transforming Ourselves and the World* as follows:

> Without spiritual development, well-meaning attempts to change the world will probably unconsciously replicate the very problems we believe we were solving. Unfortunately, we can see this all too clearly in the history of the revolutions, where so often after an oppressor was stopped, the purported liberator was soon revealed as a new oppressor. Violent solutions all too frequently only beget further violence. Without transforming ourselves and coming to know ourselves deeply through sustained spiritual inquiry and practice, we may only make things worse. We also run the risk of not having the kind of resources of wisdom, compassion, equanimity and perseverance necessary to respond to the great needs of our times without being quickly burnt out by anger and frustration. Outer transformation thus entails inner transformation. (Rothberg 2006: 5)

The prevailing system of management, Edward Deming believed, is, at its core, "dedicated to mediocrity." It forces people to work harder and harder to compensate for failing to tap the spirit and collective intelligence that characterize working together at their best. Thus, the "five disciplines" affirm new principles of management (Senge 2006):

- There are ways of working together that are vastly more satisfying and more productive than the prevailing system of management. Just getting people to talk to one another as a way to rethink how their organization was structured can create a sustainable competitive advantage.
- Organizations work the way they do because of the way its people work, think, and interact. The changes required ahead are not only in the organizations we work but in ourselves as well. Organizational learning is about each one of us where personal mastery is at the core. All these changes fall into place if they are accompanied by personal mastery.
- In building learning organizations there is no ultimate destiny or end state, only a lifelong journey. This journey requires enormous reservoirs of patience, and the results we achieve are more sustainable because the people involved have really grown. [See *Business Transformation Exercise 11.1.*]

UNDERSTANDING EXECUTIVE SPIRITUAL DEVELOPMENT

According to Bill O'Brien, spiritual development is "advanced maturity." Truly mature people build and hold deep values, make commitments to goals larger than themselves, are open, exercise free will, and continually strive for an accurate picture of reality. O'Brien points to a deficiency in modern society's commitment to human development: "Whatever the reasons, we do not pursue emotional development with the same intensity with which we pursue physical and intellectual development. This is all the more unfortunate because full emotional development offers the greatest degree of leverage in attaining our full potential" (O'Brien 1989). In this chapter, we will explore a wholesome approach to executive development—physical, intellectual, emotional, and spiritual:

> If there aren't fundamental shifts in how people think and react, as well as in how they explore new ideas, then all the reorganizing, fads and strategies in the world won't add up to much. Changing the way we think means continually shifting our point of orientation. We must make time to look inward: to become aware of, and

study, the "tacit" truths we take for granted, the ways we create knowledge and make meaning in our lives, and the aspirations and expectations that govern what we choose from life. But we must also look outward: exploring new ideas, and different ways of thinking and interacting, connecting to multiple processes and relationships outside ourselves, and clarifying our shared visions for the organization and the largest community. Changing the way we interact means redesigning not just the formal structures of the organization, but the hard-to-see patterns of relationships among people and other aspects of the system, including the systems of knowledge. [Sarason (1990) cited in Senge et al. (2000: 20)]

The essence of spiritual development is this continuous fundamental paradigm shift in how we think, look inward, look outward, explore, reorient, act, react, interact, proact, and live values that humanize humanity.

Spiritual development is the real development of one's inner spirit. A small number of organizational leaders are recognizing the radical thinking of corporate philosophy that a commitment to individual and organizational learning requires. Bill O'Brien believes that "the total development of our people is essential to achieving our goal of corporate excellence." Full personal development impacts individual happiness. To seek personal fulfillment only outside of work and to ignore the significant portion of lives that we spend working, would be to limit our opportunities to be happy and complete human beings (O'Brien 2006). Real leaders who have experienced spiritual development know how to balance their duties to the family, company, industry, and society, one's country and the planet earth.

Leadership is about motivating others to achieve superior results. It demands that individuals rise above the five inherent human temptations to CEOs that Patrick Lencioni explores (1998) : (*a*) choosing one's corporate status over corporate results; (*b*) choosing one's popularity over accountability; (*c*) choosing certainty over clarity; (*d*) choosing harmony over productive conflict; and (*e*) choosing vulnerability over trust. Fighting all these executive temptations needs deep executive spirituality that is grounded on honesty, integrity, vulnerability, and authenticity.

Kazuo Inamori, founder and president (retired in 1995) of Kyocera, a world leader in fine ceramics technology (used in electronic components, medical materials, office automation, and communication equipment), has as his corporate motto: Respect Heaven and Love People. According to Inamori, spiritual development occurs through the sub-conscious mind, willpower, and the action of the heart. He teaches his employees to look inward as they continually strive for "perfection" guided by the Kyocera motto. Inamori believes that his duty as a manager starts with "providing for both the material good and spiritual welfare of my employees." Tapping the potential of people, Inamori affirms, will require new understanding of the "subconscious mind," "will power," and "action of the heart" (Inamori 1985):

> When the industrial age began, people worked 6 days a week to earn enough for food and shelter. Today, most of us have these handled by Tuesday afternoon. Our traditional hierarchical organizations are not designed to provide for people's higher order needs, self-respect and self-actualization. The ferment in management will continue until organizations begin to address these needs, for all employees. (Inamori 1985)

According to O'Brien, the morals of the marketplace do not have to be lower than in other activities. He believes there is no fundamental tradeoff between the higher virtues in life and economic success. He believes we can have both. In fact, he believes that over the long term, "the more we practice the higher virtues of life, the more economic success we will have" (O'Brien 1989). Traditionally, corporate organizations have supported people's development instrumentally—you develop people in order to develop the organization. To view human development as an instrument of organizational development is devaluating humans and human relationships. In the type of organizations we seek to build, says O'Brien, the fullest development of people is on an equal plane with financial success. Practicing the virtues of life and business success is not only compatible but enriches one another. This is, however, a far cry from the traditional marketplace morality.

Max de Pree, retired CEO of Herman Miller, views human relationships beyond contracts to covenants. In contrast to the traditional written "contract" between the employee and the employer, what we need is a "covenant between the organization and the individual. Contracts are just a small part of human relationships. A complete relationship needs a covenant of shared meanings and values, shared commitment to ideas, to issues, to values and goals, and to management processes. Covenantal relationships reflect unity, grace, and poise. They are expressions of the sacred nature of relationships" (De Pree 1989).

Henry Ford, founder of Ford Motor Corporation, wrote a century ago:

> The smallest indivisible reality is, to my mind, intelligent and is waiting there to be used by human spirits if we reach out and call them in. We rush too much with nervous hands and worried minds. We are impatient for results. What we need ... is reinforcement of the soul by the invisible power waiting to be used. ... I know there are reservoirs of spiritual strength from which we human beings thoughtlessly cut ourselves off. ... I believe we shall some day be able to know enough about the source of power, and the realm of the spirits to create something for ourselves. ... I firmly believe that humankind was once wiser about spiritual things than we are today. What we now only believe, they knew. (Ford 1926)

Ekanath Easwaran, a professor, a pilgrim to the U.S.A since 1959, the founder of the Blue Mountain Center of Meditation in Berkeley, CA in 1961, a spiritual guru to tens of thousands all over the world, and a prolific author of over 25 books on spirituality of daily life, writes as follows in his *Your Life is Your Message* (Easwaran 1995: 10–11):

> Without a spiritual foundation, I don't think any political or economic policy, however new, however brilliant, can fill the crying needs of humanity or protect the earth from the pressure those unfulfilled needs exert on it.... The only way to influence people for the better—your family, your friends, your club, your class, your clinic, your society, even your enemies—is through your personal example. Harmony with the environment—the alleviation of our environmental crisis, and harmony with others—the easing of our social, political and economic difficulties, both begin with a third harmony: harmony with ourselves.... We need a way of life which gives back more than it takes, enhancing the world around us rather than exploiting and polluting it.

Richard Wolman, author of *Thinking with your Soul*, writes of the "spiritual" this way (Wolman 2001: 26):

> By spiritual I mean the ancient and abiding human quest for connectedness with something larger and more trustworthy than our egos—with our own souls, with one another, with the worlds of history and nature, with the indivisible winds of the spirit, with the mystery of being alive.

William Bloom (2001: 12) writes:

> In the moments of powerful beauty, emotions move that can melt even the thickest and most cynical of skins. Endorphins flow. There is a release of tension. Energies, internal and external, connect.... To create

and to work consciously with these moments of connections is to exercise what we might call spiritual muscles and our spiritual intelligence. What do I mean by spiritual? I simply mean that whole reality and dimension which is bigger, more creative, more loving, more powerful, more visionary, more wise, and more mysterious—than materialistic daily human existence. There is no theology or belief system that relates to this meaning of spiritual.

Scientific evidence—mostly from the field of neuroscience, which concerns our basic biology and how our brains develop—shows that the human child is "hardwired to connect." We are hardwired to connect to other people, to moral and spiritual meaning, and to openness to the transcendent. Meeting these basic needs for connections is essential to health and human flourishing. [From *A Report to the Nation from the Commission on Children at Risk*, YMCA of the U.S.A., Dartmouth Medical School, Institute for American Values; cited in Covey (2004: 59).]

When we look around and see today's companies and brands beset by distrustful customers, disengaged employees, and suspicious communities, we can link these problems to a legacy of management style that lacks any real humanity. The model for 20-th century management was not the warm humanism of the Renaissance, but the cold mechanics of the assembly line, the laser-like focus of Newtonian science applied to the manufacture of wealth. The assembly line was intentionally blind to morality, emotions and human aspiration—all the better to make your competitors and customers to lose so you can win. Yet business, at bottom, is not mechanical but human. *Today we are finding that innovation without emotion is uninteresting. Products without aesthetics are un-compelling. Moreover, a business without ethics is unsustainable.* The management model that got us here is underpowered to move us forward. To succeed, the new model must replace the win-lose nature of the assembly line with the win-win nature of the network. (Neumeier 2009: 4–5)

This is precisely the challenge of executive spiritual development. [See *Business Transformation Exercise 11.2.*]

EXECUTIVE LEARNING AND SPIRITUAL DEVELOPMENT

In an age of accelerated change, how we learn is vastly more important than what we learn. The ability to acquire new knowledge quickly is the fundamental skill that underpins a culture of innovation. "Every enterprise is learning and teaching institution. Training and development must be built into it at all levels—training and development that never stop" (Drucker 1991). If you want a culture of non-stop innovation, you need a system of non-stop training (cited in Neumeier 2009: 138).

As observed in earlier chapters, real training for learning is one that bridges the gap between university knowledge and industry knowledge, and between industry knowledge and company knowledge. Training that teaches personal mastery is training that teaches collaboration, so that personal mastery can inform collaboration and vice versa. Training should explore how the frontline employees can build the value of the brand, and how they can help create customer delight, and how they can align individual actions and overall business strategy. This is known as "branded training." It is the type of education that is custom-fitted to the company's brand, culture, and mission. Without branded training, one company's skills and knowledge would look much like another's, and no company would gain a competitive advantage (Neumeier 2009: 139).

For many years, the common definition of learning within the Society for Organizational Learning (SOL) network has been—"learning is a process of enhancing learners' capacities, individually and collectively, to produce results they truly want to produce." This definition emphasizes two crucial features of learning: (*a*) the building of capacity for effective action, as opposed to intellectual understanding only; and (*b*) this capacity builds over time, often over considerable time (Senge 2006: 364). This definition, however, has some limiting constraints in relation to the objective of learning:

- The objective of learning thus defined is "enhancing learners' capacities." Capacities imply limits—limits of past or present skills, tools, methods, metrics, and benchmarks of learning.
- The outcomes of learning are assessed by the production of "results" the learners truly want to produce. This is also limiting—limits of intended, estimated, and projected results all of which are conditioned on the learners' aspirations and the experiences of past or present learning.
- What happens when what you "truly want to produce" is mediocre, conditioned by past and present, determined by your competitor, or at the expense of the competitor, or just unfair, unjust, or wrong?

ORGANIZATIONAL LEARNING AS SPIRITUAL DEVELOPMENT

To broaden the scope of learning and to free it from any arbitrary limits, we define learning as "internalizing the world around you to expand your possibilities for others—to create a better world." In this sense, learning implies inputs (the world around you), process (internalizing), and outputs (expanding your possibilities to create a better world). All three constituents of learning are important and controllable, especially, the process, one you can control most. "Learning in this sense is all you are (inputs), all you become (process), and all you can be for others (outputs)." All learning should be continuous, dynamic, linear, non-linear, and circular. When circular, the outcomes of learning continuously become your inputs and feedback at each subsequent stage of learning.

Our definition of learning removes the unnecessary limiting constraints implied by the SOL definition of learning:

- The objective of learning thus defined is "expanding your possibilities." "Possibilities" do not necessarily imply any limits—limits of skills, tools, methods, metrics, and benchmarks of past, present, or the future. The horizons of learning are infinite. Possibilities could include, however, but not restricted to, capacities in terms of skills, aptitudes, attitudes, endowments, and cultural legacies. Possibilities can also transcend them.
- The domain (inputs) of one's learning is one's "world around." Of course, one could restrict this world to oneself—this is learning in solitude, or at its worst, in loneliness or solipsistic learning. One could confine one's world to one's nuclear family of immediate blood relatives—this is familial learning. On the other hand, one could open and redefine one's world, thus expanding one's possibilities of learning.
- From a corporate perspective, one's "world" does not have to be restricted to or defined by hitherto served target niches, known markets, traditional industries, and even, historically served countries, trade regions, and continents. The whole world is the domain, scope, scale, and challenge of learning.
- The basic process of learning is "internalizing." One could internalize individually, or in groups, teams, and organizations. Internalizing can be personal, customized, collective, or organizational.

In short, one could expand the domain, process, and content of internalizing by interactions with multiple stakeholders.

- This definition assesses outcomes of learning in terms of "expanding" one's possibilities. There is no limit to one's expanding possibilities, neither in terms of the past, present, or the future. One could totally transcend and surpass one's past or present experiences, aspirations, expectations, and desires, and even defy the future. This makes room for radical, creative, innovative, adventurous, and inventive learning—both individually and collectively. That is, one's learning could transcend or surpass industry norms and standards.

- Further, the outcomes of learning is "expanding one's possibilities"; one could contract (negative expansion) one's possibilities—this is negative learning. This happens when corporate ego, myopic vision, greed, avarice, and selfishness rule the process of internalization and make it tragically self-centered, symptomatic, quick fix, and short term. A current example of negative learning is corporate fraud in all its deviant forms and its escalation today.

- On the contrary, positive learning expands one's possibilities to limitless expansions and opportunities. For instance, one could include possibilities to avoid evil (malfeasant justice), to prevent evil (preventive justice), to protect people from evil (protective justice), to set up procedures to avoid, prevent, and protect people from evil (procedural justice), and even to do good (beneficent justice). There is no limit to one's expanding one's possibilities other than one's imagination and goodwill.

- Finally, one can expand one's possibilities despite or regardless of competition. Using competition or an industry champion as a benchmark limits one's learning, confining it to "red oceans." Real learning can and should include "blue oceans" that defy or disregard competition or benchmarking, and capitalize unexplored markets (Kim and Mauborgne 2004).

In the process of removing unnecessary limiting constraints, however, our definition of learning could easily suffer from being too abstract, too comprehensive, an ivory tower, and an aspiration to a better world without concrete prescriptions. It may seem that this definition overemphasizes the forests and pays little attention to the trees. As a result, learning may be difficult to implement. Moreover, lack of standards and tools for assessment of learning may make learning unproductive and untested.

On the contrary, our definition of learning is practical and readily applies to all ages and stages of one's life: child learning, adolescent learning, teenage learning, dating learning, courtship learning, romance learning, adult learning, marriage learning, divorce learning, remarriage learning, senior learning, and old-age learning. As an illustration of how our definition of learning is practical, Table 11.1 describes some of these stages and age groups of learning. Learning thus defined can be applied to individuals (personal learning, customized learning), groups (e.g., group learning, team learning, social leaning), organizations and corporations (organizational learning), and institutions, churches, schools, colleges, universities, and other associations (institutional learning).

Organizational learning can generate or lead to both strategic and operational leadership. In *strategic leadership*, the leader learns to position the organization into the future, takes a long view and has bigger perspective, seeks ways to grow the business and expand its capabilities, questions the status quo, and encourages new thinking. In *operational leadership*, the leader learns to focus the organization on short-term results, manages day-to-day details of implementation, conserves resources by cutting costs and being selective about priorities, and gets things done using procedures and process discipline (Kaplan and Kaiser 2009: 103). Learning as we understand it can be both strategic and operational.

TABLE 11.1   Characterizing Learning at Different Life Stages

Life stages	Constituents of learning		
	Inputs *(The world around you)*	*Process* *(Internalizing the world)*	*Outputs* *(Expanding your possibilities for others)*
Baby (0–1 years)	Mom, dad, food, feeding, toys	Eating, crying, sleeping—the "oral–anal" stages of learning	Seeking attention Seeking 24/7 service
Children (1–6 years)	Mom, dad, grandparents, siblings, cousins, food, toys, clothes, kindergarten	Eating, sleeping, observing, listening, tearing toys, assembling them back, active, cuddling and bonding	Toddling/walking skills Speaking/communicating Drawing/painting skills Memorizing skills Reacting/bonding skills; recognizing, growing skills
Adolescents (6–12 years)	Parents, grandparents, siblings, peers in school, teachers, sports, food, TV, TV games, Internet, Internet games, books, …	Homework assignments Reading, memorizing Writing, counting, computing Questioning, searching, googling Electronic gaming, athletics, sports Fun-engagement and entertaining	Math, soft sciences, language skills, reading and writing skills, grammar skills, athletic skills, rudimentary creativity skills
Teenagers (13–19 years)	Parents, grandparents, siblings, peers in school, teachers, friends, neighbors, sports, food, pajama parties, TV, TV games, Internet, Internet games, textbooks, novels, movies, news, teenage magazines, laptops, stereo, CDs, cell phones, iPods, iTunes, WiFi, twitters, flickers, …, part-time job	Homework projects Computing, memorizing Creative writing and reading Inquisitive, exploring, googling, mining Describing, analyzing Experimenting, adventurous Dating, bonding, blossoming Minor league sports Being alone; entertaining and partying	Accumulating data, info Retrieving data skills Seeking meaning skills Seeking knowledge Exploring skills Analytical skills Experimentation skills Fun/excitement skills Athletic and sports skills Growing/blossoming skills Solitude coping skills
Early Adulthood (20–25 years)	Parents, grandparents, siblings, College–university professors, buddies, serious books, journal articles, non-fiction novels, newspapers, national magazines, serious movies, Blackberry, organizers, laptops, You Tubes, podcasts, full time jobs, …	Seeking meaningful job/ careers Training on the job, retraining Understanding, arguing Analyzing, synthesizing Conceptualizing, theorizing Creating, discovering, inventing, innovating, venturing Competing, daring, risk-taking Loving, going steady	Credentials, degrees Job/career skills Understanding skills Analytical skills Theory-building skills Creativity/innovation skills Entrepreneurship skills Competitive skills Romance skills

(Continued)

TABLE 11.1   *(Continued)*

| Life stages | Constituents of learning | | |
	Inputs (The world around you)	Process (Internalizing the world)	Outputs (Expanding your possibilities for others)
Family Life (26–50 years)	Spouse, dream home, parenting, children, parents, grandparents, siblings, relatives, friends, neighbors, hospitality, entertaining, informal parties Income, credit, borrowing Groceries, buying, bargains Boss, work, responsibility Debt and investments Health, home, and life insurance	Getting engaged, married Family planning, parenting Nursing, nurturing children Budgeting, earning, saving Buying, storing, bargain-hunting Planning your first home Educating children, re-educating oneself Cooking, groceries, entertainment Job-training, retraining Moonlighting Job mobility and flexibility Debt-equity planning Insurances planning	Marriage preparation skills Family planning skills Parenting/nurturing skills Budgeting, saving skills Shopping and storing skills Home-building skills Educating/education skills Cooking/entertaining skills Career development skills Job mobility skills Investing skills Risk reduction skills
Empty Nesters (51–75 years)	Spouse, children, grand children, home, health, meals, job, extended family, money, wealth, properties, second home, vacations, cruises, TV, Internet	Mid-career seeking and planning Changing careers, retraining Retiring, volunteering, post-retirement jobs Wealth management, legacy planning Vacationing/energizing/recreating	Mid-career planning skills Retraining skills Retiring, volunteering skills Wealth management/legacy skills Reenergizing skills
Seniors (75+ years)	Health care, food, bingo, cards, TV, medicine, doctors, nurses, hospices	Aging, senior living, health maintenance Keeping engaged and active	Aging and health skills Senior-living/engaging skills

Source: Author's own.

Learning thus conceived gives one a broader, more grounded view of how well a company learns from internalizing its defined and undefined world and how adeptly it refines its strategies and processes for expanding its possibilities and market opportunities. Moreover, one cannot be too specific about the inputs, process, and outputs of learning especially in the face of intensifying competition, advances in technology, market and business turbulence, information explosion, and constant shifts in customer lifestyles. That is, organizational learning is not only a matter of articulating a clear vision, giving the employees the right incentives, and providing lots of training. This assumption is flawed and risky, especially in the face of intensifying and changing competition, rapid advances in technology, and constant shifts in customer demand preferences and everyday lifestyles. Each company can develop a profile of its distinctive approach to learning and then compare its progress of learning against a benchmark within the industry or a related industry (Garvin, Edmondson, and Gino 2008: 110).

Teaching, training, counseling, mentoring, coaching, administering learning assurance tests, exams, and assignments, reading book projects, and classroom and laboratory work do not necessarily ensure learning until "each method or module empowers the inputs, process, and outcomes of learning to expand one's possibilities for meaning and contribution." Similarly, course syllabi, course materials, required readings, classroom lectures, discussions, dialog, and experience-sharing, homework, individualized or group projects and assignments, and so on, do not necessarily induce and ensure student or subordinate learning—until and unless each of these traditional pedagogical methods empower the inputs, process, and outcomes of learning to expand one's possibilities for meaning, efforts, and contribution to the common good. In this sense, individual, social, and organizational learning transcend data, information, textbooks and journal articles, lab work and library research, workshops and seminars, field and experimental work, internships and fellowships, and even concepts, theories, and models of knowledge. In other words, mere sophisticated inputs or elaborate processes of learning do not necessarily ensure desired learning outcomes. In this sense, organizational learning is organizational spiritual development, and individual learning in the organization is executive spiritual development.

WHAT IS GOOD ORGANIZATIONAL LEARNING?

Consider, General Motors (GM), the largest, most profitable company in the world in the early 1970s. GM presumably defined organizational learning as "a process of enhancing learners' capacities, individually and collectively, to produce results they truly want to produce." GM believed that relentless execution—the efficient, timely, and consistent production and delivery of goods and services—was the surefire path to customer satisfaction and financial results. The manufacturing-based economy, however, has transitioned to information-based economy. Even flawless execution-efficiency based on the manufacturing-based economy cannot guarantee enduring success in the knowledge-based auto economy. The influx of new knowledge in most fields makes it easy to fall behind. Confident of the wisdom of its approach, GM was wedded to a well-developed competency in centralized control and high volume execution. It was trying to produce results it truly wanted—for example, "X" number of millions of vehicles produced and sold in a given year regardless of increasing competition and market saturation. Despite this strategy of learning and execution, GM steadily fell behind, lost ground in subsequent decades, and posted a record $38.7 billion loss in 2007. GM's managerial mind-set that enabled efficient executive execution inhibited employees' ability to learn, innovate, and expand possibilities for GM.

On the other hand, consider GE. Since the 1980s, the company has constantly evaluated its activities, found ways to expand and improve, and built the expectation that learning will be an ongoing exercise in expanding one's possibilities. GE did not focus on execution, making sure that a given process (or capacity) is carried out; instead, it continued to reinvent itself with possibilities and operations in every field from wind energy to medical diagnostics. It posted a $22.5 billion profit in 2007 (Edmondson 2008). [See *Business Transformation Exercise 11.3.*]

EXECUTIVE SPIRITUAL DEVELOPMENT AS CRITICAL HIERARCHICAL LEARNING

Thinking fuels learning by type, mode, and level, and vice versa. Thinking and, consequently, learning can be hierarchical, starting from low-level inactive and passive learning to high-level creative and generative learning. The hierarchical process, if properly channeled, could constitute the ladder of executive spiritual learning and development. In Chapter 4, Table 4.1, we discussed hierarchical learning from the viewpoint of explanation as a process. Now we revisit hierarchical learning from the viewpoint of skills as outputs. Following Senge (1990, 2006), Table 11.2 distinguishes various levels of individual and organizational learning thus:

- When we *think inactively* or passively, our learning is inactive that mostly leads to ignorance, makes it primitive or status quo, memory-laden, or it is just a refusal to learn.
- When we *think reactively*, reacting to everyday facts, episodes, events, and crises, then our corresponding learning is event or crisis learning, and which is mostly descriptive and narrative.
- When our *thinking is proactive*, we anticipate events, problems, constraints, and market reactions; we use our anticipation, speculation, prediction, and forecasting skills on past, current, and future events and execute what we might call prospective learning, predictive learning, extrapolative learning, futuristic learning, or proactive learning.
- When our *thinking is interactive* in groups or teams, we learn to dialogue, discuss, listen, empathize, and discern about past, current, and future events, and our learning modes, accordingly, are dialogical, consensual, discursive, and discerning, and this leads to empathetic learning.
- When we undertake *interpretive thinking* on texts, scripts, event-narratives, literature, and religious scriptures, our focus is primarily on the way we speak and communicate, our language and syntax, our vocabularies and voices, our idioms and metaphors, our figures of speech, and our expressions and gestures. The process generates hermeneutic (interpretive) learning, linguistic learning (analysis), patterns learning (archetypes and templates), and values/morals learning.
- When our *thinking is responsive*, and we investigate patterns and trends in current and past data and events, we engage in statistical analysis-synthesis. This process generates trends learning, patterns discovery, associative learning that explores the associations between data and trends and patterns, experiential learning that analyzes experiences of people, significance learning that unravels the meaning of people's experiences, causal learning that explores causes of various trends and patterns, and cultural learning that examines cultures that are formed from trends and patterns of behavior.
- When we are engaged in *creative thinking*, we study trends in market and industry needs, wants, desires, gaps, and niches, and engage in creative, inventive, innovative, discovery, and adventurous modes of learning that create, invent, discover, innovate, and commercialize various products and services that respond to those needs, wants, desires, dreams, gaps, and underserved niches.
- Finally, when we rise to *generative thinking* that seeks to explore, unravel, and understand the latent structures, processes, antecedents, determinants, and concomitants underlying human, organizational, and market behavior and events, local, national, or global, then we engage in structures learning, mental models learning, multi-cultures learning, multi-disciplinary and interdisciplinary learning, inductive and deductive learning, and metaphysical and theological learning.

Table 11.2 summarizes various types and progressive levels of learning in terms of inputs, processes, and levels of thinking and the corresponding modes and outcomes of learning. The levels and categories of thinking and learning depicted in Table 11.2 are not mutually exclusive and collectively exhaustive. They are overlapping, complementary, and mutually supportive and reinforcing, as should be in all human, organizational, and corporate learning. There is, however, a progression, depth, and meaning in learning as you ascend from mere inactive or passive learning to creative and generative learning.

TABLE 11.2 Hierarchical Ways of Thinking and Learning in Complex Business Environments

Hierarchical level of learning	Domain of learning [Inputs]	Frequently asked questions [Process]	Type of learning [Process]	Outcomes of learning [expanding one's possibilities for others] [Outputs]
Inactive	Some past events Everyday events	Mostly past runs of questions	Passive learning Learning by memory	Inaction, ignorance Memory, status quo
Reactive	Everyday events Everyday crisis	Who did, what, to whom, and when?	Event learning Crisis learning	Description capacity Narrative capacities
Proactive	Past events Current events Future events	Who will do? Will do what? When? Will do to whom? With what results?	Prospective learning Futuristic learning Predictive learning Extrapolative learning Proactive learning	Anticipation skills Speculation skills Prediction skills Forecasting skills Proactive experiments
Interactive	Past events Current events Future events	Who did, what, to whom, and when? Who does what, to whom, and when? Who will do what, to whom, and when?	Dialogal learning Consensual learning Discursive learning Discernment learning Empathetic learning	Dialogue–discussion Team learning Shared meaning Shared discernment Shared sensitivities
Interpretive	Language of events Meaning of events History of events History of values	Who are these people? How do they think? How and why and with whom do they communicate?	Linguistic learning Hermeneutic learning Archetypal learning Communicative learning Values/morals learning	Linguistic analysis Interpretation Human archetypes Social archetypes Value/moral archetypes
Responsive	Patterns of behavior Long-term trends Past experiences	What happened? How did it happen? How long did it happen? With whom did it happen? Why did it happen? With what consequences? Who bore consequences?	Trend learning Pattern learning Associative learning Experiential learning Significance learning Cultural learning Causal learning	Analysis-synthesis Patterns, trends History, meaning waves Shared experiences Shared meaning Shared culture Civilization
Creative	All or none of the above	What are market trends? What are market needs? What are market wants? What are market desires? What are market gaps? What are market niches? What are industry needs? What are industry wants? What are industry dreams?	Market intelligence Analyzing market needs Analyzing market wants Analyzing market dreams Creative learning Inventive learning Discovery learning Innovative learning Adventurous learning	Entrepreneurship Undertaking risk Incremental innovation Radical innovations Market breakthroughs Tech breakthroughs Industry breakthroughs Venture creation Founding corporations
Generative	Structures and processes of behaviors and events Our mental models Our paradigms	What are the underlying structures, determinants, antecedents, and causes of current and past events? What causes patterns of human or social, national or global behavior? What are your mental models that underlie your current explanations of events and patterns of behavior?	Structural learning Mental model learning Multidisciplinary learning Interdisciplinary learning Inductive learning Deductive learning Causal learning Spiritual learning Metaphysical learning Theological learning Transcendental learning Eschatological learning	Unraveling structures Mental models Framing hypotheses Verifying theory Designing experiments Generating knowledge Explaining change/growth Internalizing spirit/values Truth, wisdom, philosophy Theology, salvation Immortality, eternity, heaven, hell, destiny

Source: Author's own.

The higher the level executives are engaged in learning, the better are the turnaround and transformation prospects and desired outcomes. Known and tested "processes" of learning are self-mastery, shared vision, mental models, team learning, and systems thinking (Senge 1990, 2006; Senge et al. 1994, 1999, 2000). [See *Business Transformation Exercise 11.4.*]

THE WHOLE-PERSON PARADIGM OF LEARNING

According to Covey (2004), learning is a function of the human body, mind, heart, and spirit. Accordingly, we assume that all human learning is an integral and interactive function of the body, mind, heart, and spirit. That is, we learn through and with all that defines us:

- *Body* (brain, organs, instincts, drives, appetites, and physical discipline).
- *Mind* (brain, faculties, upbringing, education, intellectual discipline, nurture, and culture).
- *Heart* (brain, emotions, traits, love, empathy, compassion and kindness, zeal, and passion).
- *Spirit* (brain, willpower, vision, mission, direction, moral courage, conscience, and commitment).

Properly disciplined, all four can be inputs, processes, and outcomes of learning. All four components and dimensions are integral part of individual, social, and organizational learning. Thus:

- Neglecting the body makes all learning disembodied, unmotivated, and irrelevant (abstract and ethereal).
- Disengaging the mind makes learning irrational, illogical, unretentive, inconsistent, and non-defensible.
- Undercutting the heart makes learning dispassionate, unenthusiastic, apathetic, disenfranchised, and dehumanized.
- Undermining the spirit makes learning unanchored, undirected, disempowered, chaotic, dis-integrated, and without a destiny.

According to Stephen Covey (2004: 20–24), most human, social, organizational, economic, and political problems arise from an incomplete paradigm of who we are—our fundamental view of human nature. The fundamental view of human nature tells us that we as objects, or even subjects, are not things that need to be taught, trained, motivated, and controlled. We are fundamentally a human, complex but a sacred system of four-dimensional drives—the body, mind, heart, and the spirit representing the physical/economic (body, needs), the mental (mind, wants), the social/emotional (heart, desires), and the spiritual (spirit, dreams) dimensions of our life, biography, geography, and history. Given these four dimensions, we have duties to live (survival), to love (relationships), to learn (growth and development), and to leave a legacy (of meaning, significance, and contribution). These are the four basic needs, wants, and motivations of all people, regardless of race, color, religion, nationality, gender, age, geography, and time. In this whole-person paradigm of human beings, learning can and should occur in all four domains and along all four dimensions—learning to live (body), learning to love (heart), learning to learn (mind), and learning to leave a legacy (spirit).

Managers, teachers, parents, and supervisors should use the whole-person paradigm in their training, motivating, directing, retraining, and empowering their subordinates. Else, you force to make the wrong choices, to live selfishly, to love self-centeredly, to learn and grow wrongly, and to leave a legacy of hate and destruction. Table 11.3 outlines the domain and direction of learning in the whole-person paradigm of human development in the context of learning on the job. Employee learning is predicated as a function of one's choices in the corporate environment and the way the boss treats you in relation to your body, mind, heart, and spirit needs and aspirations. Thus, when all four dimensions of the worker are totally denied, the only choice and learning mode for the worker is to "quit or rebel." On the other hand, when workers are paid fairly (body), listened to carefully (mind), treated kindly (heart), and duly recognized for their meaningful (spirit) efforts and contributions, then learning on the job is progressively empowered and enhanced. That is, as the employees get each of their body, mind, heart, and spirit expectations and needs progressively met and fulfilled, the learning attitudes move from learning to obey, to compliant learning, to cooperative learning, to committed learning, to creative learning, and finally, to innovative ownership learning. [See *Business Transformation Exercise 11.5.*]

ORGANIZATIONAL LEARNING AND A SUPPORTIVE ENVIRONMENT

According to Senge (1990, 2006), learning is creating, acquiring, and transferring knowledge, and a learning organization is a place where employees excel at creating, acquiring, and transferring knowledge. Organizational research over the past two decades has revealed three broad factors or building blocks that are essential for organizational learning and adaptability: (*a*) supportive learning environment, (*b*) concrete learning processes and practices, and (*c*) leadership behavior that reinforce learning. It is presumed that employees skilled at creating, acquiring, and transferring knowledge could help their firms cultivate tolerance, foster open discussion, and think holistically and systemically. Such a learning organization is supposed to adapt to the unpredictable more quickly than their competitors can.

Organizational learning needs a supportive environment. According to Garvin, Edmondson, and Gino (2008: 111–16), a supporting learning environment has four distinguishing characteristics:

- **Psychological Safety**: In order to learn, employees must feel comfortable and welcome to express their thoughts about work at hand, and not fear being belittled or marginalized when they disagree with peers or supervisors, ask naive questions, own up mistakes, or present a minority viewpoint.
- **Appreciation of Differences**: "Learning occurs when people become aware of opposing ideas." Recognizing different and opposing perspectives on the same problem increases energy and motivation, sparkles fresh thinking, and prevents lethargy and drift.
- **Openness to New Ideas**: Learning should not be confined just to correcting mistakes or solving problems. It should invite new ideas, novel approaches, and untested and unknown solutions. Employees should be encouraged to take the risk of exploring new ways of resolving problems.
- **Time for Reflection**: Supportive learning environments should free supervisors and employees from the pressures of too many deadlines and overscheduled days and weeks. Such pressures compromise their ability to think analytically and creatively, diagnostically and proactively. Give them time for reflection.

These are the four levers of change and learning. Managers need to deploy different levers or combinations thereof in bringing about specific forms and levels of organizational learning. The behavior

TABLE 11.3   The Domain and Direction of Learning in the Whole-person Paradigm of Human Development

Your work choices	Type of learning	The role of the superior in responding to your:			
		Body (Needs)	*Mind (Wants)*	*Heart (Desires)*	*Spirit (Dreams)*
Rebel or Quit	Learn to rebel or quit: better quit than be enslaved	You are not paid fairly	Your opinions are not welcome	You are treated unfairly and unjustly	Your spirit is crushed; you do not belong here
Malicious Obedience	Learn to obey: you need the job	You are paid adequately	You and your opinions are not respected	You are treated just as a number—a factor of production!	Your presence is hardly recognized or missed
Willing Compliance	Compliant learning: I need the experience	You are paid deservedly	Your opinions are welcome	You are not treated kindly as you deserve	Your efforts and contributions are not recognized
Cheerful Cooperation	Cooperative *learning*: I like the job and the experience	You are paid deservedly	Your opinions are welcome and considered	You are treated kindly and with respect	Your meanings and contributions are getting to be acknowledged
Heartfelt Commitment	Committed learning: The job brings out the best in me	You are paid more than adequately	Your opinions are welcome and considered seriously	You are treated kindly, respectfully, and with dignity	Your meanings and contributions are recognized and rewarded
Creative Excitement	Creative learning: I learn to be creative, innovative, and venturesome	You are paid more than deservedly	Your opinions are welcome, and considered seriously in the strategic stages of decision making and implementation	You are treated with reverence; you are excited being here; you would not trade this place for anything in the world	Your meanings and contributions are recognized, rewarded, and creatively incorporated into corporate strategy and decisions
Passionate Ownership	Passionate and dedicated learning to be creative, innovative, dynamic, and expansive	You are an owner; you pay yourself from profits, dividends, and stock options	Your opinions are crucial, expected, and valued seriously in the strategic stages of decisions making and implementation	You are treated as an owner, partner and co-producer; you enjoy being here; the organization is part of your mission and identity	Your meanings and contributions are expected, crucially important, recognized, awarded, and creatively incorporated into corporate strategic planning and decisions

Source: Author's own.

Note: See also Covey (2004: 22–24).

of mangers and leaders can strongly influence organizational learning. When leaders demonstrate a willingness to entertain alternative points of view, employees feel emboldened to offer new ideas. When leaders actively question and listen to employees, they prompt dialog and debate. Managers need to be specially sensitive to local cultures of learning, which can vary widely across units. The goal of organizational learning is to promote dialog, not critique. [See *Business Transformation Exercise 11.6.*]

EXECUTION AS LEARNING VERSUS EXECUTION AS EFFICIENCY

The best organizations have figured out how to learn quickly while maintaining high quality standards. Edmondson (2008: 62) calls this "execution as learning" as opposed to "execution as efficiency." Most management systems in use today were designed and conditioned by the manufacturing-dominated era in which firms were organized to execute as efficiently as possible. For instance, in an auto-related factory management, pioneering thinkers like Henry Ford and Frederick Taylor sought to parcel out simple, repetitive tasks to workers strapped to long assembly lines, in order to reduce the likelihood of human error while producing as many cars as possible. Later, manufacturing managers used statistical methods such as statistical quality control (SQC) to spot-check errors or defects in the production systems. Underlying the notion of "execution as efficiency" of a simple, controllable production system was the notion of a simple, controllable employee. They assumed that workers are best motivated by incentives (e.g., more money, more pay for tasks completed) and disincentives (e.g., reprimands, less pay, job loss). While this system worked well for the manufacturing industry, it left behind a legacy of worker fear and dehumanized labor.

In contrast, with the rise of knowledge-based industries in the information age, it is very inadequate to measure employee productivity by hours worked, number of repetitive tasks done, or number of pieces or units produced. Performance in the information and knowledge-based economy is increasingly based on non-quantitative factors such as innovation, ingenuity, imagination, experimentation, team-learning, interpersonal skills, and resilience in the face of adversity.

Organizations that focus on "execution as learning":

- Use the best knowledge obtainable (which is understood to be a moving target) to inform the design of specific process guidelines.
- They enable and empower their employees to collaborate by making information available when and where it is needed.
- They routinely capture process data to discover how work is really being done.
- They study these data in an effort to find ways to improve.

Table 11.4 contrasts execution as efficiency with execution as learning. Edmondson (2008) argues that a critical prerequisite for execution as learning is the need to foster psychological safety. The latter means several things: do not penalize your employees if they ask for help or admit a mistake; no one can perform perfectly in every situation when knowledge and best practices are both moving targets. Psychological safety does not operate at the expense of employee accountability. Most effective organizations achieve high levels of both.

Given that psychological safety can be high or low, and worker accountability for meeting demanding goals can be high or low, Edmondson (2008: 64) distinguishes the following zones of performance:

- **Apathy Zone**: low psychological safety and low accountability. Employees are apathetic and spend much time jockeying for position; examples: typical large and top-heavy bureaucracies (e.g., governments, government organizations) where people may perform functions, but the preferred modus operandi is to curry favor than share ideas.
- **Anxiety Zone**: low psychological safety but high accountability. Employees are anxiety-prone, and fear to offer tentative ideas, try new things, or ask colleagues for help. Typical examples: some investment banks and high-powered consultancies.

TABLE 11.4 Contrasting Execution as Efficiency with Execution as Learning

Critical dimensions	Execution as efficiency	Execution as learning
Nature of Industry	Primarily manufacturing; factory management environment that is routine, stagnant, and rigid.	Knowledge- and information-based economy that is networked, dynamic, and emergent and where knowledge is continuously changing and challenging
Problem Identification	Managers detect and formulate problems; managers may be slow to detect market opportunities, and hence, could delay, discourage and under-staff investments in areas where learning is critically needed.	Employees in conjunction with managers continuously scan markets to discern, identify, and specify the problems and their market opportunities.
Problem-solving Process	Problem-solving is rarely required; employee judgment or solution is not expected; they are supposed to ask managers when they are not sure.	Problem-solving is horizontal, continuous, and dynamic, with new problems and new solutions sought constantly through worker teams.
Problem Resolution	Leaders provide answers and solutions; the leaders think they can do no wrong; they believe their solutions are the best and most effective	Leaders set direction and articulate the mission for problem-solving; employees collaborate and initiate wise decisions without management intervention; they keep exploring for better resolutions.
Solution Implementation	Employees follow directions; speed, efficiency and results are all that matter; managers that overemphasize results can discourage new technologies and methods where results are delayed but more sure than current results.	Employees (usually in teams) discover answers or tentative solutions and set implementation strategies; no solution can be permanent or perfect in every situation when knowledge and best practice are moving targets.
Production Schedules	Optimal work processes are designed and set up in advance; they may not plan on learning on the job.	Tentative work processes are set up as a starting point; worker teams decide best schedules based on maximum productivity.
Production Changes	Network processes are developed infrequently; implementing change is a huge undertaking.	Work processes keep developing; small changes (experiments and improvements) are a way of life.
Feedback Processes	Feedback is typically one-way and top-down; employees are fearful of expressing concerns or volunteering ideas, suggestions or corrections lest they be marginalized or penalized; critical ideas and information fail to rise to the top.	Feedback is always two-way and multiple-way and horizontal—among peers and team members; the leaders may provide feedback via coaching and mentoring.
Employee Motivation	More pay, more benefits, bonuses, commissions and promotions motivate work; reprimands motivate worker compliance.	Respect, recognition, interaction, team-work, dialogue, and discussion make work humanizing, meaningful, and enriched, and productivity and creativity follow.
Employee Psychology Safety	Fear of the boss or of consequences of non-compliance is the work-environment; worker psychological safety could be minimal.	Team spirit, collegiality, transparency, freedom to express oneself, mutual respect, generosity, compassion, and empathy constitute the work environment, morale and camaraderie; worker psychological safety is enhanced amidst tough feedback and difficult dialog.
Organizational Learning and Accountability	Worker fear and anxiety cripple the learning process; employees do not have enough time to learn; unhealthy internal competition could stifle learning; accountability may be low.	Worker freedom, comfort, recognition, and satisfaction generate and enhance continual learning, experimentation, and innovation; accountability is high.
Creativity and Innovation	Low creativity; incremental innovations if ever; creativity-innovation are discouraged unless they come from the top.	High creativity, discovery, invention, innovation, exploration, experimentation, risk-taking, and adventure—all tasks are opportunities for learning.
Long-term Performance Goals	Mostly short-term and symptomatic solutions; long-term goals and realizations are dubious, unpredictable, unclear, unshared, and rarely realized.	Long-term strategic planning is continuous, shared, collaborative, prospective, and assured; long-term strategies and solutions determine short-term tactics.
Hence, Nature of Execution	Execution is to demonstrate decisiveness, efficiency, and competence; hence, managers may tend to choose easier tasks, and lose out when it comes to learning.	Execution is inquiry, reflection, humility, collaboration, experimentation, undertaking risk, and learning in the service of high performance. Leaders are willing to fail and, in the process, learn.

Source: Author's own.

Note: See also Edmondson (2008: 60–67).

- **Comfort Zone**: high psychological safety but low accountability: Employees really enjoy working with one another but are not challenged enough; they do not work very hard. Typical examples: some family businesses, religious organizations, and small consultancies.
- **Learning Zone**: high psychological safety and high accountability. The focus here is on collaboration and learning in the service of high performance. Typical examples: great hospitals, high tech research centers, and radical innovation project teams.

Organizations that adopt the execution-as-learning model do not focus on getting things done more efficiently than competitors do, but on learning faster. They find out quickly what works and what does not work; they absorb new knowledge while executing, and often, sacrificing short-term efficiency and goals. In the process, they are ready to learn from the industry or even from the competitor's best practices as long as they facilitate learning. Such organizations, however, know that today's best practices may not be the best tomorrow, or would not work in every situation. While execution-as-efficiency focuses on performance (outcome) data, execution-as-learning pays attention to process data that describes how work and performance unfold. The goal of collecting process data is to understand what goes right and what goes wrong, and why, so as to prevent failures from recurring. In general, organizations where trust and respect thrive, and flexibility and innovation flourish, execution-as-learning is easy to adopt. Such organizations empower, rather than control, ask the right questions, rather than provide the right answers, they focus on flexibility, rather than insist on adherence, and they automatically move to a higher level of execution. [See *Business Transformation Exercise 11.7.*]

EXECUTIVE SPIRITUAL DEVELOPMENT AS REACHING YOUR POTENTIAL[2]

If learning implies expanding your possibilities by internalizing the world around you, a practical question for a leader or a senior executive is, "Am I reaching my potential?" This question is not the same as asking, "How do I rise to the top?" or "How can I be successful in my career?" Rather, it is about taking a very personal look at yourself, how you define or redefine success in your heart of hearts, and then, finding a path to get there. The conventional wisdom about the attractiveness of various careers changes constantly in the U.S. Some 25 years ago, one sought the medical and the legal professions as financially most rewarding and socially desirable. Currently, hedge funds, private equity, or working for investment banks are hot fields, though this seems to be changing with the 2008 global financial market collapse.

Step back and reassess your career. Recognize that managing your career is your responsibility. Too many executives feel victimized in their careers, when, in fact, they may have substantial degree of control. For seizing control, writes Robert Kaplan (2008: 45–49), you must take a fresh look at your behavior in three main areas: knowing yourself, excelling at critical tasks, and demonstrating character and leadership.

---

[2] This section is based on Robert Kaplan (2008: 45–49). Even though Kaplan does not speak directly about executive spiritual development in his article, yet in the light of our discussions thus far, we can discern essential elements of executive spiritual development in the "reaching your potential" discussion his article initiates.

- **Knowing Yourself**: Assess your current skills and performance. Identify two or three of your greatest strengths and greatest weaknesses. Identifying key strengths is easy, but identifying and facing your worst weaknesses is difficult. Do some serious reflection. Consult your friends or enemies who will tell you the brutal truth. Seeking coaching, and asking for, and being receptive to, very specific feedback from a wide variety of people at various levels (superiors, colleagues, and subordinates) within your organization should be an ongoing process. This feedback of strengths and weaknesses, especially from your subordinates, is not easy; it takes much humility, and willingness to confront your weaknesses. You can best do this on a one-on-one basis and in conversations, and you must give potential coaches time to learn that you are sincere. Typical strengths are high skills, extensive knowledge, detail-orientation, decisiveness, and hardworking. Typical weaknesses or flaws are micromanagement, dictatorial styles, arrogance, failing to listen, and not respecting one's colleagues or subordinates. Obviously, as your career progresses, this feedback will make you face new challenges and demands. When your coaches see you value their inputs and actually act on their feedback, they are likely to become more proactive and comfortable in providing feedback. Moreover, being in the same unit or division, they will perceive a stake in this—your happiness and self-fulfillment, your success and progress will ultimately be their success and strength. Next, having more or less assessed your strengths and weaknesses, reassess what you are doing and your current career. Are you doing the right thing? Do you love and enjoy what you do? Does your job reinforce your strengths and challenge your weaknesses? Whatever the career, "loving what you do gives you the strength to weather personal setbacks, overcome adversity, face and address your weaknesses, and work the long hours typically needed to reach your full potential" (Kaplan 2008: 47).
- **Excelling at Critical Tasks**: It is very difficult to succeed if you do not excel at the tasks that are central to your chosen enterprise. Hence, identify three or four most important activities that lead to success in your business division. For instance, if you are managing a large sales force, the crucial tasks may be attracting, retaining, and developing outstanding salespeople, customer or market segmentation, and client-relationship management. If you are looking for a new career, you need to know what will drive success in the new position, whether you have the skills to drive this success, whether you will enjoy these tasks, and do accordingly what it takes.
- **Demonstrating Character and Leadership**: Both make the difference between good performance and great performance. Great executives with character and leadership love to coach and mentor. They inspire and empower employees. They have the mindset of an owner—they figure what they would do if they were the ultimate decision maker. One measure of character is the degree to which you put the interests of your company and colleagues ahead of your own. Excellent leaders are willing to do things for others without regard to what is in it for them. They sacrifice the short-term benefits to their own division, to the long-term goals that benefit the entire organization. They have the courage to trust that the company will eventually reward them, even if their current actions may not be in their own short-term interest. Good leaders speak up and do not play it safe or stay silent, even when they must express unpopular views. Good leaders do not appreciate a nodding audience but encourage a dissenting crowd, because it is only through dissenting opinions that you can make better decisions and choices. You can stall your career by playing it safe. On the contrary, most leaders are better appreciated for their well thought-out opposing views than for their agreement.

In conclusion, reaching your potential requires introspection (know yourself) and certain proactive behaviors (excelling at critical tasks, demonstrating character and leadership). Managing your career is 100 percent your responsibility and you need to act accordingly. Every rewarding career has its bad days, bad weeks, and even bad months. Great leaders with great character face setbacks and discouraging situations; they do not abandon their plans when they hit these bumps. There is nothing anyone can do to prevent you from reaching your potential. The challenge is yours to identify your dream, and develop the skills to get there, and exhibit character and leadership as you get there. They have the courage to periodically reassess, make adjustments, and pursue a course that reflects who you truly are (Kaplan 2008: 48–49).

If currently you believe you do not know what you want, or you believe you do not have a personal vision, then do not take yourself seriously:

> A vision exists within each of us, even if we have not made it explicit or put into words. Our reluctance to articulate our vision is a measure of our despair and a reluctance to take responsibility for our own lives, our own unit, and our own organization. A vision statement is an expression of hope, and if we have no hope, it is hard to create a vision. (Block 1991: 113)

Hence, know yourself, empower yourself, build hope, and then formulate your personal vision. [See *Business Transformation Exercise 11.8.*]

EXECUTIVE SPIRITUAL DEVELOPMENT AS HIGH COMMITMENT–HIGH PERFORMANCE[3]

Managing the tension between performance and people is at the heart of a CEO's job. Firms are both *economic organizations* whose survival and prosperity depend on the delivery of superior value in an unforgiving global marketplace and *social institutions* that profoundly shape the lives of the employees. Too many executives view their organization primarily through one lens or the other. For many CEOs under fierce pressure from the Wall Street and the capital markets, the focus is entirely on the shareholder, with a single-mindedness that can lead to employee disenchantment and loss of capacity to deliver long-term superior value. For other CEOs, who perhaps have a commanding market share or operate in protected markets, concern for employees' motivation, culture, and heritage can too easily slide into complacency, inwards focus, and loss of competitive vitality (Eisenstat et al. 2008: 51). Resolving the tension between performance and people without sacrificing either is an executive calling that needs executive spiritual development. Spiritually developed CEOs succeed in harnessing the energy and commitment of their people to implement change that may be wrenching and dramatic but, which creates a platform for future success. "Finding and holding a firm's moral and strategic center in a competitive market is a calling and an art, not an engineering problem" (Eisenstat et al. 2008: 57).

---

[3] I am carving this material primarily from Eisenstat et al. (2008: 50–57). Even though the five authors do not speak directly about executive spiritual development, yet in the light of our discussions thus far, we can discern essential elements of executive spiritual development in the high-commitment–high-performance (HCPC) leadership paradigm they describe in their article.

When in 2000 Tim Solso took over as CEO of Cummins (Columbus, IN) that manufactures diesel engines and related technologies, one of his first moves was to launch a global program to rearticulate the mission of Cummins and to reaffirm its values. Six months into his tenure, Cummins that was highly leveraged hit a recession that lasted through the first half of 2003. Demand in its core markets dropped almost by 70 percent and more. To ensure the company's survival, Solso and his team took some radical steps. They closed the original manufacturing plant of Cummins in Columbus, IN, restructured its truck engine business, and laid off a significant portion of its workforce. Very conscious of the pain that accepting layoffs of long-term colleagues causes among those that are retained, Solso created energy around the company's mission and values, whereby, employees were prepared to invest in learning new skills leading to the development of new products and services even as the layoffs took place. Solso and his team mobilized the remaining workforce to support the company's strategic shift to focus on the less cyclical areas of distribution and service, making future layoffs less likely. Solso also capitalized on the long-standing commitment of Cummins to the environment and its resulting expertise in pollution control devices to build a distinctive source of sustainable competitive advantage. By the end of 2007, Cummins more than doubled its sales, its total employment increased by more than 33 percent, and its net earnings and stock price increased more than fivefold. Such remarkable achievement in a relatively short time in a tough competitive global marketplace came about from strong mission and values that are ultimately sourced by a high level of spiritual development among the top leaders.

Spiritually, high-commitment–high-performance (HCHP) leaders are motivated by far more than financial success. They feel personal responsibility as stewards of the future of their firms. Pushing for superior performance is very challenging, and in many cases, it required CEOs to make extraordinarily bold and unconventional moves. They did not take the commitment of their employees for granted, lest that strategy should destroy the social fabric of their organizations. They were focused, intense, and involved day-to-day with their people and operations, personally creating the link between the people who do the work and the performance they must deliver. According to the extensive research of Eisenstat et al. (2008: 53–54), HCPC leaders combined four strategies:

- **Earning Trust**: They earned the trust of their organizations through their openness to the unvarnished truth and brutal facts about their organization. They shared information with, and received feedback from all stakeholders. This openness led to a sense of shared reality and trust.
- **Engaging with the Organization**: The central part of any CEO's job is communication, and HCPC leaders go to extraordinary lengths to ensure that their communications with people were direct and unmediated. They were deeply engaged with their people, and their exchanges were direct and personal. Employees had a deep connection with the CEO and were seldom surprised to meet the CEO. HCPC leaders displayed an authentic concern for their employees.
- **Maintaining Focus of Consistency and Purpose**: Given trust and engagement, these CEOs were able to mobilize their people around a focused agenda. Establishing relationships of high trust and direct connection is a necessary precondition, but not a sufficient condition for transforming an organization into HCHP status. Shifting the behavior of thousands of people to align with new competitive requirements demands extraordinary focus and consistency of purpose. HCPC leaders do not implement all feasible strategies all the time; they must focus on the two best and most promisingly effective strategies, and work on them for four to five years, before going for the next best. The reinforcement and continuity of direction are also the real jobs of the CEO.

- **Creating Collective Leadership Capability**: They were all strong individuals that believed that they succeeded only as part of a committed leadership team. They devoted considerable efforts in building their firm's collective leadership capabilities. Collective leadership is more common and effective among non-American and non-U.K. CEOs. The American–U.K. model is still a top-down leadership approach.

We can infer instances of executive spiritual development from the following CEO testimonies:

- Leif Johnson, CEO of Volvo in Gothenburg, Sweden (that manufactures trucks, buses, construction vehicles, and industrial engines), made the extraordinary bold move of selling one of the jewels in the crown of Swedish industry, the Volvo car division, to Ford. He explains: "For me, the work in the organization has a soul and values and a purpose that transcends only making money. That soul does not end with me; it will be passed on to the next generation."
- Ed Ludwig, CEO of Becton, Dickinson of Franklin Lakes, NJ (that manufactures medical supplies, devices, and diagnostics), expresses his more personal motivation that drove him to build a great firm: "Being a CEO is like answering a call to bring the organization to a better place than where you found it." When he took over as CEO, he commissioned a taskforce of trusted managers to conduct open-ended interviews with key executives about the challenges the firm faced. Among the top brutal facts he confronted and admitted was a major SAP project that he had launched in a previous position as CFO and spent over $100 million on it. Ludwig publicly acknowledged that the program was broken and bore significant responsibility for it. He and his team shut the program down for nine months to fix the identified problems. They re-launched the program, which is now the foundation of the company's success.
- Doug Conant, CEO of Campbell Soup, Camden, NJ (manufactures food products), told the authors: "You can't talk your way out of something you behaved your way into. You have to behave your way out of it." You cannot "shift the burden" of your bad decisions; face them, and all your people will be enriched by it (Eisenstat et al. 2008).
- Jorma Ollila, former CEO of Nokia, Espoo Finland (that manufactures cell phones and related technologies), placed all his bets on the mobile phones while selling off the other businesses of the firm. He says: "My job was twofold: to make sure that people had an opportunity to realize the potential of what there was in this business, number one. And number two, we needed to get rid of the no-growth business—the cable, the television etc."
- Allan Leighton, chairman of Royal Mail Group, London (postal and distribution services), when asked how he built trust in his workforce at Britain's Royal Mail Group (RMG), answered simply: "Tell the truth. I never mislead people. If I say 'it's rubbish,' then they know it's bad. If I say '30,000 jobs are going,' they know 30,000 jobs are going. If I say 'it's working,' they know its working." Allan personally visited more than half of RMG's 1,600 delivery offices. Every time he saw a mail carrier on his rounds, he stopped to talk. Leighton and his staff maintain an e-mail account called "Ask Allan," which gets about 200 messages a day, each of which receives an acknowledgment within 15 minutes of receipt and a full response within seven days. Every 12 weeks, Allan sets aside three days with all the delivery office managers (about 350 in each group) for open exchange, communications, with no agenda. Leighton said: "If you believe, as I do, that the operators know best, then, spend your time with the operators. Don't spend time with all the treacle in the middle."

- Russ Fradin, CEO of Hewitt Associates of Lincolnshire, IL (that specializes in HR services), was particularly insistent that managers share in any personnel reductions inflicted on the workforce. If he trimmed frontline employees by five percent, then he did the same along all the ranks from the ground up to the executive suite. Having the officers share the pain made it clear that everyone was in the same boat. That is, he demonstrated a real respect for all employees as people with important lives and rights. Said Fradin: "The people in the call center are just as important as people in the executive suite."

- One CEO, while reflecting on the wrenching offshore outsourcing task that exported thousands of jobs from Europe and U.S.A. to India, China, and other cost-effective labor zones, struggled with this decision, but came to believe it was consistent with his own core values and that of his firm. He said, "The people who we're hiring today in India have the same value in God's eyes as the people who work in our hometown."

Leaders of HCPC organizations refuse to choose between people and profits. They share the mission and purpose of the organization across the entire organization in order to realize a collective vision that is better aligned to face the unforgiving global marketplace. A collective vision that is built on the old formula of commitment, community, and common purpose is no longer sufficient in the hypercompetitive global marketplace of today. Most of the HCPC leader organizations Eisenstat et al. (2008) studied (e.g., Cummins, Herman Miller, Ikea, Nokia, and Timken) had a small rural geographic base, a homogenous workforce, and were highly committed to their employees and local communities. However, the same companies are now almost global, and their HCPC leaders go far more than the old formula for success. They invested considerable effort in forging an emotionally resonant shared purpose for their people. At the heart of this resonant shared purpose is a three-part hope or promise:

- **Building a Better World**: This goes beyond building a great brand and reputation that promotes corporate citizenship. It must include global citizenship responsibilities such as drilling bore wells for fresh water to millions of African and Asian rural homes, building and promoting basic education to the marginalized. Peter Sands, CEO of Standard Chartered Bank, based in London, U.K., that provides international banking services, mobilized the whole bank around a blindness prevention project that helped more than a million people recover sight—this greatly helped to build the bank's world reputation as well as make the shared vision of the employees resonant, focused, and mission-directed. At Herman Miller, Zeeland, MI (that designs and produces artistic office furniture), the CEO Brian Walker commended and supported world-enhancing projects, such as 20 Herman Miller employees building a school in India with vacation time that had been donated by others.

- **Delivering a Performance to be Proud Of**: Brian Walker of Herman Miller said: "People won't get fulfillment from an organization that isn't recognized as being high performance." Best employees want to work with other stellar employees. High performance means performance accountability up and down the production/service value adding chain. Best efforts are not good enough—you must actually deliver on your performance commitments.

- **Providing Opportunities for Growth**: At the heart of the HCHP value proposition is the opportunity for employees to realize their personal and professional potential. Employees are not excited by cost-reduction or capital-efficiency or share-buyback strategies; they want to go to a job that is self-fulfilling and they are excited about because of the right self-growth initiatives.

- **Keeping Perspectives**: Great HCPC CEOs know how to balance and respond to the relentless demands of the markets with their role of stewarding, mentoring, and shepherding their employees. They know how to devote quality time to their family and yet work long hours in the office. They know how to be actively concerned about and address local community problems and little league sports, while being immersed in their business operations.

In short, HCPC CEOs know what to do, how to do it well, when to do it best, and with whom to do it when it comes to energizing their employees or enhancing their local communities, and at the same time driving superior corporate performance. For the HCHP CEOs, finding and holding a firm's moral and strategic center in a competitive market is a spiritual calling and an inspired art, and not a mechanistic engineering problem. Because of their passionate commitment to corporate superior performance, employee self-fulfillment, and local community development, they do not make trade-offs between people and profits—they enhance both and build great firms that last and contribute. [See *Business Transformation Exercise 11.9.*]

THE DISCIPLINE OF SELF-MASTERY AS EXECUTIVE SPIRITUALITY

They who would govern others, first must be masters of themselves. For Peter Senge, executive spirituality is *personal mastery*. Mastery does not mean gaining dominance over people or things. It means a special level of proficiency (as in a master craftsperson, master chef, and master bridge player).[4] "Personal mastery goes beyond competence and skills, though it is grounded in competences and skills. It goes beyond spiritual unfolding or opening, although it requires spiritual growth. It means approaching one's life as a creative work, living life from a creative as opposed to reactive viewpoint" (Senge 1990: 141). Personal mastery is not something you possess or dominate. It is a proficiency, it is a process. It is a lifelong discipline. People with high level of personal mastery are acutely aware of their ignorance, their incompetence, and their growth areas. In mastery there is a sense of effortlessness and joy; it stems from your ability and willingness to understand and work with the forces around you.

Characteristic Features of Self-mastery

A striking number of business people agree that among all the learning disciplines, they are most drawn to personal mastery—they are surprisingly generous; they want not only to improve their own capabilities, but also improve the capabilities of the other people around them. They recognize that an organization develops and grows along with its people. They also believe in the central tenet of this discipline of

---

[4] The term "mastery" can be traced to the Sanskrit root "*mah*" (meaning greater, as in the word *maharaja*, greater king). Through the centuries, the Latin equivalent (*magister*) and the Old English word "master" have degraded mastery to domination—as in "I am your master; you are my slave." A variation of the word, however, evolved in medieval French "*maitre*" that meant someone who was exceptionally skilled and proficient, as in "master of a craft." Mastery as used here reflects self-proficiency—a capacity not only to produce results, but also to "master" the principles underlying the way you produce the results (Senge et al. 1994: 194).

self-mastery: *no one can increase someone else's personal mastery. We can only set up conditions that encourage and support people in their quest of personal mastery.* It is increasingly clear that learning does not occur in any enduring fashion unless it is sparked by people's own ardent interest and curiosity. That is, learning must be related to one's own vision (Senge et al. 1994: 193).

When personal mastery becomes a discipline—an activity we integrate into our lives—it embodies two underlying movements. The first is continually clarifying what is important to us. The second is continually learning how to see current reality more clearly. The juxtaposition of vision (what we want) and a clear picture of current reality (where we are relative to what we want) generates what Senge calls "creative tension," a force to bring them together, caused by the natural tendency of tension to seek resolution. The essence of personal mastery is learning how to generate and sustain creative tension in our lives. "Learning" in this context does not mean acquiring more information, but expanding one's ability to produce the results we truly want in life. It is lifelong generative learning (see Table 4.1 and Table 11.2). In addition, learning organizations are not possible unless they have people at every level who practice it (Senge 1990: 141–42).

People with high levels of personal mastery are more committed. They take more initiative. They have a broader and deeper sense of responsibility in their work. They learn faster. For all these reasons, great many organizations espouse a commitment to fostering personal growth among their employees because they believe it will make the organization stronger (Senge 1990: 143).

According to Peter Senge (1990, 2006), the discipline of personal mastery involves a series of practices and principles that must be applied to be useful. These practices and principles lay the groundwork for continually realizing and expanding personal mastery in us. Self-mastery is exploration. As T. S. Eliot puts it: "We must never cease from exploring. At the end of all our exploring will be to arrive where we began and know the place for the first time" (cited in Covey 2004: 60).

Values are deeply held views of what we find worthwhile. They come from many sources such as parents, teachers, siblings, peers, religion, people we admire, books and culture. Some of these are "espoused values" that we profess we believe in, while others are "values in action" that guide our actual behavior. In this regard, Table 11.5 attempts taxonomy of executive values for spiritual development. According to Bill O'Brien, former president of Hanover Insurance, truly mature people build and hold deep values, making commitments to goals larger than themselves, being open, exercising free will, and continually striving for an accurate picture of reality. Personal mastery is a function of both espoused values and values in action. Identifying and nurturing one's most important values is an effective process of personal mastery. [see *Business Transformation Exercise 11.10.*]

Leadership is about motivating others to achieve superior results. It demands that we rise above five inherent executive temptations CEOs face every day:

1. Choosing one's corporate status over corporate results.
2. Choosing one's popularity over accountability.
3. Choosing certainty over clarity.
4. Choosing harmony over productive conflict.
5. Choosing invulnerability over trust.

Fighting all these executive temptations needs deep executive spirituality that is grounded on honesty, integrity, vulnerability, and authenticity (Lencioni 1998).

TABLE 11.5 A Taxonomy of Executive Values for Spiritual Development

Context of values	Values	Context of values	Values
Family	Affection: loving and caring Family harmony and peace Grandchildren and great-grandchildren Pets Extended family: relatives and friends	Environment	Ecological awareness Location Nature Public service Reducing pollution
Skills	Competence Creativity Decisiveness Ethical practice Excellence Expertise Freedom Helping other people Helping society Influencing others Leadership Sophistication	Virtues	Accountability Fortitude, courage, bravery Honesty, integrity Loyalty, dedication Order (tranquility, stability) Prudence Purity, spousal fidelity Responsibility, commitment Self-care Serenity Simplicity of life Temperance, frugality Truth Wisdom
Life	Adventure Being around people, open and honest Community Country Democracy Economic security Ethicality Excitement Fast living Friendships Fun Independence Involvement Morality Pleasure Privacy Security Spirituality	Accomplishments	Achievement Advancement and promotion Fame Financial gain Freedom Growth Inner harmony Intellectual status Market position Merit Money Personal development Power and authority Quality relationships Recognition Reputation Self-respect Wealth
Work	Challenging problem Change and variety Close relationships Competition Effectiveness Efficiency Fast-paced work Job tranquility Knowledge Meaningful work Physical challenge Quality of what I take part in Supervising others Work under pressure Work with others Working alone	Culture	Antiques Arts Athletics Composing Dancing Debating Music Poetry Possessions Publishing Reading Singing Speaking Sports Religion Theater Writing

Source: Author's own.

Self-mastery as a Function of PQ, IQ, EQ, and SQ

Once, during a sabbatical in Hawaii, while on work on his book *The 7 Habits of High Effectiveness*, Stephen Covey was meditatively pacing through the library stacks, when he pulled down a book to read the following:

- Between stimulus and response there is space.
- In that space lies our freedom and power to choose our response.
- In those choices lie our growth and happiness.

That is, there is a space between whatever happens to us and our response to it. The size of this space may be largely determined by our genetic, biological, and social inheritance as well our present circumstances. With many who grow up with unconditional love in supportive circumstances, the space may be quite large, and so are the corresponding responsibilities. For those born in poverty, racial suppression, oppressive injustice, poor schooling, dysfunctional parents, and addictive compulsions, the space is narrow. This may force them to be a victim of their circumstances more than to be the author of their decisions and choices. Regardless of the circumstances, however, real spirituality is to discover, expand, and utilize the space between our stimuli and our corresponding responses. The more we use this space to make informed, ethical, and moral decisions, the more spiritually developed we are. Figure 11.1 characterizes this stimulus–response space.

The maverick psychiatrist R. D. Laing captured the challenge of stimulus–response space as follows (cited in Covey 2004: 43):

FIGURE 11.1   The Inputs, Process, and Outputs of Self-mastery

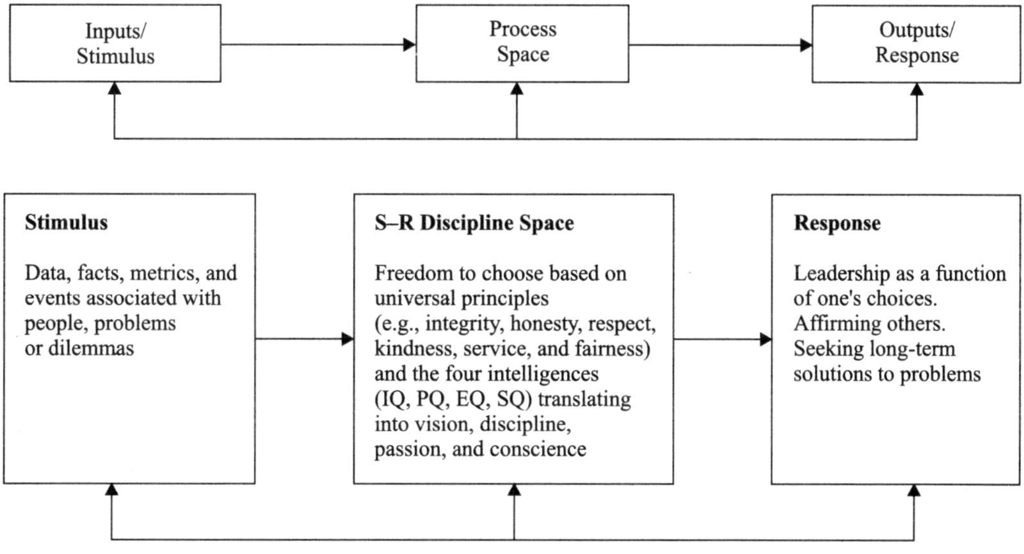

Source: Author's own.

- The range of what we think and do is limited by what we fail to notice.
- Moreover, because we fail to notice that we fail to notice, there is little we can do to change.
- Until we notice how failing to notice shapes our thoughts and deeds.

No matter our genetic, biological, or sociological preconditioning, we have the power to choose how we respond to the stimuli despite these constraints. Moreover, parents, teachers, siblings, or even peers can be the "transition persons" helping us to fight our conditionings. They can help people from their "yesterday holding them hostage today or tomorrow." We literally can create the world in which we live. As William James, the American philosopher–psychologist–pragmatist used to say, "when we change our thinking, we change our lives."

Covey (2004: 40) affirms that all human beings have latent and mostly undeveloped or "unopened" gifts along three layers of human greatness:

- **Freedom and Power to Choose**: This is our birth gift. Next to life, the power or freedom to choose is our greatest gift as opposed to suppression, oppression, victimization, terrorism, and blame and guilt so prevalent in our society today. We are a product more of choice than our nature (genes) or nurture (upbringing, environment). *Genes and culture do influence us, but do not determine us as our choices do.* Humans act, while animals, robots, and computers react. The essence of being human is to direct our own life, to reinvent our potential, to change our future, and to reinvest in it and ourselves. Endangered species survive only by our consent; they do not have freedom or power to choose. They lack self-awareness. They cannot reinvent themselves. Our power and freedom to choose empowers all our other gifts; it enables us to elevate our life to higher and higher levels. We are not merely a product of our past or of our genes, or of how other people treat us—all these may influence us but not determine us. We are self-determining through our choices.[5]
- **Natural Laws or Universal Principles**: In order to use our stimulus–response space wisely we need good principles or natural laws to live by rather than today's culture and its quick-fix solutions. Principles (such as fairness, kindness, respect, honesty, integrity, service, generosity) are timeless, self-evident, and universal; they transcend time, culture, geography, race, and religion. For example, we can never have enduring trust without trustworthiness—this is a natural law. *Natural authority* is the dominion of natural laws. We have power to choose, to reinvent ourselves, and to redirect our destiny. This is natural authority. *Moral authority* is the principled use of our freedom and power to choose. Natural laws (e.g., laws of gravity, thermodynamics, and global climate change) and moral universal principles (e.g., trust, truthfulness, honesty, integrity, kindness, and compassion) should control the origin (inputs), process, and consequences of our

---

[5] Students of behaviorism as proposed by founder John B. Watson and follower B. F. Skinner may recall that there are two major versions of learning theory: (*a*) classical conditioning (identified with Pavlov's dogs) and (*b*) operant or instrumental conditioning (identified with Skinner's rats). The former believes that stimuli that precede or accompany behavior condition behavior, while the latter affirms that stimuli (e.g., rewards) that come after behavior, condition behavior. While both theories state that learning takes place via environmental stimuli, they also deny human freedom, free will or "self" whereby we own our behavior. Human beings, Skinner observed, are mere "repertoires of behaviors" and these behaviors are fully explained by outside factors that Skinner called "environmental contingencies." A person is not an originating agent, but a point at which many genetic and environmental conditions intersect to form a joint effect. Thorndike called this the Law of Effect (Skinner 1971, 1974; Thorndike 1911; Watson 1930).

choices. "Back of every noble life there are principles that have fashioned it" (Lorimer 1936). For instance, when trust, the glue of human and societal relationships, is destroyed, we tend to be unkind, violent, mistrustful, and dishonest to people.

- **The Four Intelligences**: This is our third birth gift, much unexplored, and possibly, still unopened. According to Stephen Covey (2004), human spirituality is grounded on four magnificent parts of our nature: body, mind, heart, and spirit that have corresponding four capacities or intelligences: physical or body intelligence (PQ), mental intelligence (IQ), emotional intelligence (EQ), and spiritual intelligence (SQ). EQ, in the long run, is a more accurate determinant of successful communications, relationships, and leadership than IQ. Persons with very high IQ but low on EQ may not know how to relate with people, and worse, they may intellectually rationalize their ineffective behavior with people. With great team-artists, major league sports celebrities, great CEOs, and world-famous political charismatic leaders, EQ has been the primary determinant of star performance than PQ and IQ. The body, with its complements of mind, instinctual drives, and spirit, balances and harmonizes the functioning of all four intelligences. Our body with its mind and spirit components is a brilliant piece of machinery that outperforms even the most advanced computer. Our capacity to act on our thoughts, feelings, memories, and emotions, and to make things happen, is unmatched by any other species in the world (Covey 2004: 51–52).

Table 11.6 summarizes the challenges of PQ, IQ, EQ, and SQ for self-mastery and executive spirituality. SQ relates to the whole reality and dimension that is bigger, more creative, more loving, more powerful, more visionary, wiser, and more mysterious than the materialistic daily human existence. While IQ relates to becoming more knowledgeable, PQ relates to becoming more healthy and strong, EQ relates to becoming more relational and sensitive, and SQ relates to becoming a person (Rogers 1961). Unlike PQ that all living being possess in various degrees, IQ that computers and robots have, and EQ that higher mammals possess, SQ is uniquely human and most fundamental. It defines our quest and longing for meaning, vision, and value; it allows us to dream and to strive; it underlies the things we believe in and hope for; it makes us human (Zohar and Marshall 2000).

We must develop all four capacities or intelligences. We may not be able to develop any one of them to its mature, sustainable level without working on all four.

> This is what integrity means. It means the *whole* of our life is integrated around principles. Our capacity for production and enjoyment is a function, in the last analysis, of our character, our integrity. This takes constant effort to develop the physical muscle fiber, the emotional/social muscle fiber, the mental muscle fiber and the spiritual muscle fiber by getting us out of our comfort zones and doing those exercises that cause the fiber to break (pain); then it is repaired and enlarged and strengthened after a proper period of time of rest and relaxation. (Covey 2004: 63; see also Loehr and Schwartz 2003).

If great achievement is measured by lives of great achievers—those whose lives, writings, or deeds had the greatest influence on us, those who have made significant contributions to history and humankind, and those who have simply made great things or institutions happen—then great achievement has had a pattern. Through their persistent efforts and inner struggles, they have greatly expanded their four native intelligences or capacities. These were people with a *vision* (function of high IQ), *discipline* (function of high PQ), *passion* (high EQ), and a sensitive *conscience* (high SQ) that respected the dignity of all human beings, rich and poor, young and old, white and non-white alike.

TABLE 11.6 Self-mastery as a Function of PQ, IQ, EQ, and SQ

Intelligences	Domain and definition	Major functions	Self-mastery challenges
PQ: Physical Intelligence (Discipline)	Body (physical well-being): health and strength	*To Live:* Something unconscious that happens within our body controlling the respiratory, circulatory, metabolic, nervous, and other vital systems. PQ constantly scans our environment, adjusts to it, destroys diseased cells, and fights for survival.	PQ controls and coordinates bio-chemical and bio-physical coordination that controls our reflexes, instincts, drives, passions, habits, manual skills and, body routines. PQ manages the entire human body system, much of it unconscious. High PQ is not enough: athletes, boxers and heavy weight fighters have it and it did not necessarily humanize them.
IQ: Mental Intelligence (Vision)	Mind (Mental well-being): becoming more knowledgeable, capable, and experienced	*To Learn:* It is our ability to reason, analyze our reasons and reasoning, think abstractly, use language, visualize, conceptualize, theorize, and comprehend.	High IQ is not enough: brilliance is not necessarily humanizing. Adolph Hitler and Bernard Madoff had high IQ.
EQ: Emotional Intelligence (Passion)	Heart (**Emotional well-being**): more loving, relational, and giving	*To Love:* It is our self-knowledge, self-awareness, social sensitivity, empathy, and ability to communicate successfully with others. It is a sense of timing and social appropriateness, having the courage to acknowledge weaknesses, and express and respect differences.	Abilities such as leadership, successful communications and relationships are primarily a function of EQ than IQ. High EQ is good but not sufficient: it provides passion but not humanity.
SQ: Spiritual Intelligence (Conscience)	**Spirit and Will** (**Spiritual well-being**): becoming a person, free, fulfilled, and fulfilling	*To Leave a Legacy:* SQ represents our search and drive for meaning, vision, and value and connection with the infinite. SQ is "thinking with your soul" (Wolman 2001: 26) and represents the ancient and abiding human quest for connectedness with something larger and trust-worthier than our world and us. SQ underlies the things we believe in and role our beliefs and values play in the actions we take Unlike PQ that all living beings have, IQ that computers and robots have, and EQ that higher mammals possess, SQ is uniquely human and most fundamental. SQ is the essence of what makes us human	SQ is the central and the most fundamental of all four intelligences because it becomes the source of guidance of the other three. It stands for our quest for our longing for meaning, vision and value; it allows us to dream and to strive; it underlies the things we believe in and hope for; it makes us human.
PQ + IQ + EQ + SQ: Human Intelligence (Integral Humanism)	The Person: Integrated spirituality	*To Liberate:* This intelligence is the best combination of high levels of all four basic intelligences—PQ, IQ, EQ, and SQ. Such people have and generate total freedom to choose, to become, and to be what humans should be. They are governed by certain principles such as honesty, integrity, kindness, respect, fairness, and service. This is what heroic saints and sages are made of. This state represents the perfection of human dignity, spirituality, and fulfillment. The normal outcomes of such intelligence are principled and directed life, total emancipation and transcendence, self-actualization and freedom, health and happiness, peace and harmony.	High IQ, EQ, and SQ is a great combination: Nelson Mandela, Martin Luther King, Jr., Mohandas Gandhi, and a few others had them. High IQ, PQ, EQ, and SQ is a perfect combination. The prophets and patriarchs of the Old and New Testaments are good examples. Contemporary examples are Mother Teresa, Dorothy Day, and potentially, President Barack H. Obama, and you

Source: Author's own.

- **Vision** is seeing with the mind's eye what is possible in people, in projects, in causes, and in enterprises. "Vision results when our mind joins need with possibility."
- **Discipline** is paying the price to bring that vision into reality. It is to deal objectively with the hard and brutal facts and events of reality and doing what it takes things to happen. "Discipline arises when vision joins with commitment."
- **Passion** is the fire, the desire, the strength of conviction, and the drive that sustains the discipline to achieve the vision. "Passion arises when human need overlaps unique human talent." In relationship and organizational settings, passion includes compassion.
- **Conscience** is the inward moral sense of what is right and what is wrong, the drive toward meaning and contribution. "It is the guiding force to vision, discipline, and passion."

Table 11.7 lists equivalent concepts, virtues, or strategies that capture vision, discipline, passion, and conscience of great leaders and achievers and under the dominant zones of mind, body, heart, and the spirit. The best leaders operate in four dimensions: vision, discipline, passion, and conscience. These are the four basic intelligences, the four forms of perceiving, communicating, doing, and achieving that define great achievers. The visionary leader thinks big, thinks new, thinks ahead, and most importantly, is in touch with the deep structure of human consciousness and creative potential. When a duly-informed conscience governs vision, discipline, and passion, leadership endures and changes the world for good. In other words, *moral authority makes formal authority work.* When vision, discipline, and passion are governed by formal authority and not moral authority (conscience), it can also change the world, but mostly by weakening and destroying it (Covey 2004: 64–93). Corporate greed and corporate fraud are not driven by the moral authority of one's informed conscience but merely by formal authority (e.g., law, legalism, and circumventing law). The 2008 financial market crisis and the antecedent home mortgage and foreclosure debacles were not driven by moral authority. [See *Business Transformation Exercise 11.11 and 11.12.*]

CONCLUDING REMARKS: SELF-MASTERY VIA GANDHIAN PRINCIPLES

Mahatma Gandhi, one who founded and liberated India in 1947 from British colonialism and subjugation, and without any political office, spoke of seven things that can destroy us:

1. Wealth without work
2. Pleasure without conscience
3. Knowledge without character
4. Commerce without morality
5. Science without humanity
6. Worship without sacrifice
7. Politics without principle

Each represents an end being accomplished through an unprincipled or unworthy means. Each one of these seven ends can be falsely attained, but ultimately they will destroy us and our civilization. Table 11.8 elaborates this dynamic. [See *Business Transformation Exercise 11.13.*]

TABLE 11.7   Self-mastery via Vision, Discipline, Passion, and Conscience

Great achievement attributes	Dominant zone of achievement			
	Mind	Body	Heart	Spirit
Vision (Great IQ)	Long-term perspective	Strategic thinker	People believer	Idealistic
	Anticipates future	Strategic skills	Sets expectations	Dreamer
	Thinks outside the box	Strategic choices	Hopeful	Visionary
	Philosophical	Strategic doer	Audacious	Path-breaking
	Theological	Strategic achiever	Adventurous	Pioneering
	Thinks destiny	Feels destiny	Shares destiny	Breathes destiny
Discipline (Great PQ)	Competent	Execution	Focused	Autonomous
	Consistent	Hard-working	Committed	Self-disciplined
	Logical	Enduring	Constant	Decisive
	Learning	Takes initiative	Tenacious	Willing to sacrifice
	Unlearning	Realistic	Daring	High willpower
	Retraining			
Passion (Great EQ)	Affirming	Driving	Optimistic	Courageous
	Influential	Forging	Hope	Fearless
	Motivating	Gathering	Humor	Emphatic
	Inclusive	Forceful	Fun	Synergistic
	Creative	Leading	People oriented	Connected
	Discovering	Stewarding	Sensitive	Charismatic
	Innovative	Challenging	Shepherding	Energizing
	Imaginative	Dynamic	Embracing	Radical
Conscience (Great SQ)	Intuitive	Servant	Respectful	Inspired
	Wise	Caring	Compassionate	Ethical
	Integrity	Abundant	Cause oriented	Moral
	Wholesome	Generous	Responsible	Equitable
	Truthful	Outreaching	Accountable	Enthusiastic
	Seeking counsel	Humble	Principles-led	Zealous
	Just	Justice-seeking	Inequality-reducing	Fair
Vision + Discipline + Passion + Conscience = Saint	Prudent	Yoga	Calmness	Peace
	Seeking silence	Tranquility	Detachment	Graceful
	Seeking solitude	Frugality	Conserving	Harmony
	Meditation	Simplicity	Ecological	Union with nature
	Contemplation	Renunciation	Trusting	Union with mankind
	Seeking wisdom	Self-effacing	Trustworthy	Union with God

Source: Author's own.

Note: See also Covey (2004: 67).

On the contrary, great executive and corporate spirituality is premised on the opposite principles:

- Wealth with work
- Pleasure with conscience
- Knowledge with character
- Commerce with morality
- Science with humanity

TABLE 11.8   Self-mastery: Gandhian Principles of Self-preservation and Self-destruction

Principles that can destroy civilizations	Seeking ends via unprincipled and unworthy means	Industry bad practices	Seeking ends via principled and worthy means	Industry best practices
Wealth without Work	Corporate fraud Creative accounting Insider trading Accounting irregularities Financial irregularities Ponzi scheming	Gambling, casinos, playing lottery, stealing, usurping, confiscating, misappropriating	Wealth with work Hard and honest work Job skills retraining Creation, discovery Invention, innovation Venture, partnership Entrepreneurship	GE, P&G, Apple Microsoft Blackberry iPods, iTunes, iPhones Kodak, Sony, Xerox Dell, eBay, Amazon.com
Pleasure without Conscience	Teenage sex, safe sex Same-sex live-ins Premarital live-ins Fraudulent wealth Marital infidelity Insider trading Padding expenses	Destroying competition Price gouging Excessive dumping Predatory pricing Market-entry barriers Market dominance Golden parachutes	Pleasure with conscience Legal/religious marriage Procreative sex Responsible pleasure Rest and relaxation Earned holidays Happy retirement	Ethical market success Moral entertainment Planned productivity Deserved profitability Corporate Rest and Relaxation (R&R) Legitimate perks Just severance packages
Knowledge without Character	Doctoring data Massaging data to suit bias Rejecting unpleasant data Deceptive data Under-disclosure Information overload Competitor espionage	False income statements Understating debt Overstating incomes Tampering test markets Misrepresentation Hiding product defects Competitor blackmail	Knowledge with character Transparency Openness in all dealings External auditing Truth in reporting Truth in advertising Truth in product quality	Patents, trademarks Open standards Open scrutiny Open accounting Open costing and margins Substantiating ads Product excellence
Commerce without Morality	Deception Opportunism Undue price wars Artificial shortages Market gluts Market dumping	Deceptive promotions Opportunistic behavior Annihilating competition Underserved markets Over production Over-dumping	Commerce with morality Blue ocean strategies Resist opportunism Serving ghettos JIT and optimal inventory Honest market offerings	Executive morality Open competition Executive integrity No market underserved No product shortages Healthy products
Science without Humanity	Animal torture Human experimentation Stem cell research Water-boarding Narcotic medicine Euthanasia, culture of death	Guinea pigs Prisoners as lab objects Abortions, infanticide Prisoner extortion Over-drugging the elderly Mercy-killing	Science with humanity: Responsible research Adult stem cell research Respecting prisoners Humanizing geriatrics Respect for life	Ethical genetic research Ethical experimentation Ethical stem cell labs Human dignity to all Respecting the elderly Sanctity of life
Worship without Sacrifice	Over-religiosity Fundamentalism Exclusivism Religious bigotry	Religious fanatics Bible belts Religious segregation Religious wars	Responsible worship Responsible exegesis Accepting diversity Avoiding wars	Responsible cults Unbiased hermeneutics Open churches Non-violent religions
Politics without Principle	Exaggerated nationalism Ethnocentrism Racial discrimination Unjust wars Preventive wars Prisoners of war Unilateral military combat Nuclear arms-building Negative political campaign	Holocausts Ethnic cleansing Tribal genocide Collateral damage Unilateral aggression Terrorist detainees Unprovoked aggression Excess nuclear stockpiles Candidate bashing	Genuine nationalism Polycentricism Anti-discrimination No-wars policy No wars, negotiate Prisoner human dignity Bilateral treaties Nuclear disarmament Positive political campaign	Responsible citizenship Multiracial cultures Multitribal diversities Peaceful truces Open dialog Compassion to all Multilateral harmony Denuclearize countries Open and honest contest

- Worship with sacrifice
- Politics with principle

In concluding our discussion on executive spirituality, we summarize the words of Carl Rogers (1961) on "good life," which is another equivalent to spiritual life. Rogers is recognized by the world as the founder of Person Centered Philosophy. Writing about "goof life," he observes:

I have gradually come to one negative conclusion about the good life. It seems to me that the good life is not any fixed state. It is not, in my estimation, a state of virtue, or contentment, or nirvana, or happiness. It is not a condition in which the individual is adjusted or fulfilled or actualized. To use psychological terms, it is not a state of drive-reduction, or tension-reduction, or homeostasis.

The good life is a *process,* not a state of being. It is a direction not a destination. The direction which constitutes the good life is that which is selected by the total organism, when there is psychological freedom to move in any direction. This organismically selected direction seems to have certain discernible qualities which appear to be the same in a wide variety of unique individuals. The good life, from the point of view of my experience, is the process of movement in a direction which the human organism selects when it is inwardly free to move in any direction, and the general qualities of this selected direction appear to have a certain universality.

BUSINESS TRANSFORMATION EXERCISES

1. Edward Deming affirmed that there are ways of working together that are vastly more satisfying and more productive than the prevailing system of management. Explore the following alternative ways of infusing and guiding spiritual development in your organization.

   a. Effective leaders create an alternative system of management based on love rather than fear, curiosity rather than an insistence on "right" answers, and learning rather than controlling.
   b. Master practitioners initiate change and deal creatively with the challenges of sustaining momentum.
   c. "Changing the way we interact means redesigning not just the formal structures of the organization, but the hard-to-see patterns of relationships among people and other aspects of the system, including the systems of knowledge" (Sarason 1990).
   d. Just getting people to talk to one another as a way to rethink how their organization was structured can create a sustainable competitive advantage.
   e. Organizations work the way they do because of how its people work, think, and interact. The changes required ahead are not only in the organizations we work, but in ourselves as well.
   f. Organizational learning is about each one of us—personal mastery is core. All these changes fall into place if they are accompanied by personal mastery.
   g. In building learning organizations there is no ultimate destiny or end state, only a lifelong journey. This journey requires enormous reservoirs of patience, and the results we achieve are more sustainable because the people involved have really grown.

2. Spiritual development is the real development of one's inner spirit. Bill O'Brien, former president of Hanover Insurance, believes that "the total development of our people is essential to achieving our goal of corporate excellence." Full personal development impacts individual happiness. Inamori, former president of Kyocera, believes that his duty as a manager starts with "providing for both the material good and spiritual welfare of my employees." Following O'Brien and Inamori, how will you assure the spiritual development of the people in your organization using the following challenges expressed by great CEOs?

a. To seek personal fulfillment only outside of work and to ignore the significant portion of our lives that we spend working, would be to limit our opportunities to be happy and complete human beings (O'Brien 2006). Real leaders who have experienced spiritual development know how to balance their duties to the family, company, industry, and society.

b. Our traditional hierarchical organizations are not designed to provide for people's higher order needs, self-respect, and self-actualization. The ferment in management will continue until organizations begin to address these needs, for all employees" (Inamori 1985).

c. The morals of the marketplace do not have to be lower than in other activities. There is no fundamental trade-off between the higher virtues in life and economic success. Over the long term, the more we practice the higher virtues of life, the more economic success we will have (O'Brien 1989).

d. Max de Pree, retired CEO of Herman Miller, views human relationships beyond contracts to covenants. In contrast to the traditional "contract" between the employee and the employer, what we need is a "covenant "between the organization and the individual. Contracts are just a small part of human relationships. A complete relationship needs a covenant of shared meanings and values, shared commitment to ideas, to issues, to values and goals, and to management processes.

e. Traditionally, corporate organizations have supported people's development *instrumentally*—you develop people in order to develop the organization. To view human development as an instrument of organizational development is devaluating humans and human relationships (O'Brien 1989).

3. The Society for Organizational Learning (SOL) defines *learning as a process of enhancing learners' capacities, individually and collectively, to produce results they truly want to produce*. This definition emphasizes two crucial features of learning: (*a*) the building of capacity for effective action, as opposed to intellectual understanding only; and (*b*) this capacity builds over time, often over considerable time (Senge 2006: 364). In contrast, our definition of learning is: *internalizing the world around you to expand your possibilities*. In this sense, learning implies inputs (the world around you), process (internalizing), and outputs (expanding your possibilities). All three constituents of learning are important and controllable, especially, the process, one you can control most. Learning in this sense is all you are (inputs), all you become (process), and all you can be (outputs). All learning should be continuous, dynamic, linear, non-linear, and circular. When circular, the outcomes of learning continuously become your inputs and feedback at each subsequent stage of learning. Argue how the latter definition of learning improving on that of SOL on the following parameters:

   a. The objectives and scope of personal learning.
   b. The domain, scale, and destiny of personal learning.
   c. The passion and motivation of personal learning.
   d. The dynamic inputs of personal learning.
   e. The dynamic process of personal learning.
   f. The expanding outcomes of personal learning.
   g. The objectives and scope of organizational learning.
   h. The domain, scale, and destiny of organizational learning.
   i. The passion and motivation of organizational learning.
   j. The dynamic inputs of organizational learning.
   k. The dynamic process of organizational learning.
   l. The expanding outcomes of organizational learning.

4. Thinking fuels learning by type, mode, and level, and vice versa. Thinking, and consequently, learning can be hierarchical, starting from low-level inactive and passive learning to high-level creative and generative learning. Following Table 11.2, distinguish, analyze, and illustrate the following forms of organizational learning in your firm:

    a. Inactive or passive learning
    b. Unlearning
    c. Reactive learning
    d. Proactive learning
    e. Interactive learning
    f. Empathetic learning
    g. Discernment learning
    h. Interpretive or hermeneutic learning
    i. Responsive learning
    j. Experiential learning
    k. Adventurous learning
    l. Creative learning
    m. Innovative learning
    n. Generative learning
    o. Spiritual learning
    p. Transcendental learning

5. According to Covey (2004: 20–24), learning is a function of the human body, mind, heart, and spirit. Accordingly, in this whole-person paradigm of human beings we assume that all human learning is an integral and interactive function of the body, mind, heart, and spirit. Covey contends that most human, social, organizational, economic, and political problems arise from an incomplete paradigm of who we are— our fundamental view of human nature. How will you incorporate the following factors in generating organizational learning in your corporation?

    a. The fundamental view of human nature tells us that we not things or objects or even subjects that need to be taught, trained, motivated, and controlled.

    b. We are fundamentally a human, complex but sacred system of four-dimensional drives—the body, mind, heart, and the spirit representing the physical/economic (body: needs), the mental (mind: wants), the social/emotional (heart: desires), and the spiritual (spirit: dreams) dimensions of our life, biography, geography, and history.

    c. Neglecting the body makes all learning disembodied, unmotivated, and irrelevant (abstract and ethereal).

    d. Disengaging the mind makes learning irrational, illogical, unretentive, inconsistent, and non-defensible.

    e. Undercutting the heart makes learning dispassionate, unenthusiastic, apathetic, disenfranchised, and dehumanized.

    f. Undermining the spirit makes learning unanchored, undirected, disempowered, chaotic, disintegrated, and without a destiny.

    g. Given these four dimensions, we have duties to live (survival), to love (relationships), to learn (growth and development), and to leave a legacy (of meaning, significance, and contribution).

    h. There are four basic needs, wants, and motivations that all people experience, regardless of race, color, religion, nationality, gender, age, geography, and time. Thus, learning can and should occur in all four domains and along all four dimensions—learning to live (body), learning to love (heart), learning to learn (mind), and learning to leave a legacy (spirit).

6. Organizational learning needs a supportive environment. Following Garvin, Edmondson, and Gino (2008: 111–16), how would you nurture a supporting learning environment in your corporation based on the following four distinguishing characteristics?

    a. *Psychological Safety*: In order to learn, employees must feel comfortable and welcome to express their thoughts about work at hand, and not fear being belittled or marginalized when they disagree with peers or supervisors, ask naive questions, own up mistakes, or present a minority viewpoint.

    b. *Appreciation of Differences*: Learning occurs when people become aware of opposing ideas. Recognizing different and opposing perspectives on the same problem increases energy and motivation, sparkles fresh thinking, and prevents lethargy and drift.

    c. *Openness to New Ideas*: Learning should not be confined just to correcting mistakes or solving problems. It should invite new ideas, novel approaches, untested and unknown solutions. Employees should be encouraged to take the risk of exploring new ways of resolving problems.

    d. *Time for Reflection*: Supportive learning environments should free supervisors and employees from the pressures of too many deadlines and overscheduled days and weeks. Such pressures compromise their ability to think analytically and creatively, diagnostically and proactively. Give them time for reflection.

7. The best organizations have figured out how to learn quickly while maintaining high quality standards. Edmondson (2008: 62) calls this "execution as learning" as opposed to "execution as efficiency." Most effective organizations achieve high levels of both. Both are functions of two underlying factors: psychological safety, and worker accountability. Given that psychological safety can be high or low, and worker accountability for meeting demanding goals can be high or low, Edmondson (2008: 64) distinguishes the following zones of performance. How would you design organizational learning in your corporations mindful of the following four zones?

    a. *Apathy Zone* (low psychological safety and low accountability): Employees are apathetic and spend much time jockeying for position; examples: typical large and top-heavy bureaucracies (e.g., governments, government organizations) where people may perform functions, but the preferred modus operandi is to curry favor than share ideas.

    b. *Anxiety Zone* (low psychological safety but high accountability): Employees are anxiety-prone, and fear to offer tentative ideas, try new things, or ask colleagues for help; typical examples: some investment banks and high-powered consultancies.

    c. *Comfort Zone* (high psychological safety but low accountability): Employees really enjoy working with one another but are not challenged; they do not work very hard; typical examples: some family businesses, religious organizations, and small consultancies.

    d. *Learning Zone* (high psychological safety and high accountability): The focus here is on collaboration and learning in the service of high performance; typical examples: great hospitals, high tech research centers, and radical innovation project teams.

8. If learning implies expanding your possibilities by internalizing the world around you, a practical question as an executive leader is, *Am I reaching my potential?* This question is not the same as asking, "How do I rise to the top?" or "How can I be successful in my career?" Rather, it is about taking a very personal look at yourself, how you define or redefine success in your heart, body, mind, and spirit, and then, finding a path to get there. For seizing control, Kaplan (2008: 45–49) suggests that you look at your behavior in three main areas: knowing yourself, excelling at critical tasks, and demonstrating character and leadership. Keeping this in mind, how would you plan to reach your potential mindful of the following factors?

    a. Recognize that managing your career is your responsibility. Too many executives feel victimized in their careers, when, in fact, they may have substantial degree of control.

    b. Know yourself.

    c. In assessing yourself, typical strengths are high skills, extensive knowledge, detail-orientation, decisiveness, and hardworking.

    d. In assessing yourself, typical weaknesses or flaws are micromanagement, dictatorial styles, arrogance, failing to listen, and not respecting one's colleagues or subordinates.

    e. Obviously, as your career progresses, this feedback will make you face new challenges and demands. Hence, having more or less assessed your strengths and weaknesses, reassess what you are doing and reassess your current career.

    f. Are you doing the right thing?

    g. Do you love and enjoy what you do?

    h. Does your job reinforce your strengths and challenge your weaknesses?

    i. Whatever the career, "loving what you do gives you the strength to weather personal setbacks, overcome adversity, face and address your weaknesses, and work the long hours typically needed to reach your full potential" (Kaplan 2008: 47).

    j. Identify critical tasks in your job and career, and excel in them. It is very difficult to succeed if you do not excel at the tasks that are central to your chosen enterprise.

    k. Demonstrate character and leadership in all that you think, decide, and do. Both make the difference between good performance and great performance.

9. Resolving the tension between performance and people without sacrificing either is an executive calling that needs executive spiritual development. Spiritually developed CEOs succeed in harnessing the energy and commitment of their people to implement change that may be wrenching and dramatic but, which creates a platform for future success. "Finding and holding a firm's moral and strategic center in a competitive market is a calling and an art, not an engineering problem" (Eisenstat et al. 2008: 57). According to the extensive research of Eisenstat et al. (2008), spiritually, high-commitment–high-performance (HCHP) leaders have the following virtues: How would you inculcate them in your spiritual development for HCPC?

    a. HCPC leaders are motivated by far more than financial success. They feel personal responsibility as stewards of the future of their firms. Pushing for superior performance is very challenging, and in many cases, it required CEOs to make extraordinarily bold and unconventional moves.

    b. They did not take the commitment of their employees for granted, lest that strategy should destroy the social fabric of their organizations.

    c. They were focused, intense, and involved day-to-day with their people and operations, personally creating the link between the people who do the work and the performance they must deliver.

    d. They earned the trust of their organizations through their openness to the unvarnished truth and brutal facts about their organization. They shared information with, and received feedback from, all stakeholders. This openness led to a sense of shared reality and trust.

    e. The central part of any CEO's job is communication, and HCPC leaders go to extraordinary lengths to ensure that their communications with people were direct and unmediated.

    f. They were deeply engaged with their people, and their exchanges were direct and personal. Employees had a deep connection with the CEO and were seldom surprised to meet the CEO. HCPC leaders displayed an authentic concern for their employees.

    g. Given trust and engagement, HCPC CEOs were able to mobilize their people around a focused agenda. Establishing relationships of high trust and direct connection is a necessary precondition, but not a sufficient condition for transforming an organization into HCHP status. Shifting the behavior of thousands of people to align with new competitive requirements demands extraordinary focus and consistency of purpose.

    h. HCPC leaders do not implement all feasible strategies all the time; they must focus on the two best and most promisingly effective, and work on them for 4 to 5 years, before going for the next best. The reinforcement and continuity of direction is also the real job of the CEO.

    i. They were all strong individuals that believed they succeeded only as part of a committed leadership team. They devoted considerable efforts in building their firm's collective leadership capabilities.

      j. Collective leadership is more common and effective among non-American and non-U.K. CEOs. The American–U.K. model is still a top-down leadership approach.

10. Values are deeply held views of what we find worthwhile. They come from many sources such as parents, teachers, siblings, peers, religion, people we admire, books, and culture. Some of these are "espoused values" that we profess we believe in, while others are "values in action" that guide our actual behavior. Following Table 11.5 which is a taxonomy of commonly held values that you can control and aspire under various life-contexts, do the exercises that follow (Senge et al. 1994: 209–11):

      a. Classify the foregoing values into your "espoused values" and "values in action" and explain. Allow overlaps.

      b. Given (a), choose 10 values among the *espoused values* and 10 *values in action* that are most important to you now. Explain.

      c. From among (b) choose five espoused values and five values in action that are still more important to you. Explain.

      d. From among (c), short-list three espoused values and three values in action that are even more important to you. Explain.

      e. Finally, from (d), select just one espoused value and one value in action that is the most important to you. Explain.

      f. What would your life be without the two values under (e), and why?

      g. Does your personal vision include these values, why or why not?

      h. Do these values contribute to your personal mastery, why or why not?

      i. What would your organization be without the two values under (e), and why?

      j. Does your shared vision with superiors, colleagues, and subordinates at work include these values, why or why not?

      k. Do these values contribute to your personal mastery in relation to your organization? Explain.

11. No matter our genetic, biological, or sociological preconditioning, we have the power to choose how we respond to the stimuli despite these constraints. Covey (2004: 40) affirms that all human beings have latent and mostly undeveloped or "unopened" gifts along three layers of human greatness:

      a. *Freedom and Power to Choose*: The power or freedom to choose is our greatest gift as opposed to suppression, oppression, victimization, terrorism, blame, and guilt so prevalent in our society today. The essence of being human is to direct our own life, to reinvent ourselves and our potential, to change our future, and to reinvest in it. Our power and freedom to choose empowers all our other gifts; it enables us to elevate our life to higher and higher levels.

      b. *Natural Laws or Universal Principles*: In order to use our stimulus–response space wisely we need good principles or natural laws to live by rather than the culture of today and its quick-fix solutions. Principles (such as fairness, kindness, respect, honesty, integrity, service, generosity) are timeless, self-evident, and universal; they transcend time, culture, geography, race, and religion. *Moral authority* is the principled use of our freedom and power to choose.

      c. *The Four Intelligences*: Human spirituality is grounded on four magnificent parts of our nature: body, mind, heart, and spirit that have corresponding four capacities or intelligences: physical or body intelligence (PQ), mental intelligence (IQ), emotional intelligence (EQ), and spiritual intelligence (SQ). In the long run, EQ is a more accurate determinant of successful communications, relationships, and leadership than is IQ. Our capacity to act on our thoughts, feelings, memories, and emotions, and to make things happen, is unmatched by any other species in the world (Covey 2004: 51–52).

12. We must develop all four capacities or intelligences (PQ, IQ, EQ, and SQ). We may not be able to develop any one of them to its mature, sustainable level without working on all four. "This is what integrity means.

It means the *whole* of our life is integrated around principles. Our capacity for production and enjoyment is a function, in the last analysis, of our character, our integrity. This takes constant effort to develop the physical muscle fiber, the emotional/social muscle fiber, the mental muscle fiber, and the spiritual muscle fiber by getting us out of our comfort zones and doing those exercises. In designing and developing your executive spirituality how will you coordinate these four intelligences with the four functions that follow (see Table 11.6 and Table 11.7)?

a. *Vision* is seeing with the mind's eye what is possible in people, in projects, in causes, and in enterprises. Vision results when our mind joins need with possibility.
b. *Discipline* is paying the price to bring that vision into reality. It is to deal objectively with the hard and brutal facts and events of reality and doing what it takes things to happen. Discipline arises when vision joins with commitment.
c. *Passion* is the fire, the desire, the strength of conviction, and the drive that sustains the discipline to achieve the vision. Passion arises when human need overlaps unique human talent. In relationship and organizational settings, passion includes compassion.
d. *Conscience* is the inward moral sense of what is right and what is wrong, the drive toward meaning and contribution. It is the guiding force to vision, discipline, and passion.

13. Mahatma Gandhi spoke of seven things that can destroy us. Each represents an end being accomplished through an unprincipled or unworthy means. Gandhi claimed that each one of these seven ends can be falsely attained, but ultimately they will destroy us and our civilization. These unprincipled means can be applied to individuals, groups, and organizations. Using Table 11.8, how would you enhance the spiritual development of your organization and its employees by inculcating the opposite of the following propensities?

a. Wealth without work
b. Pleasure without conscience
c. Knowledge without character
d. Commerce without morality
e. Science without humanity
f. Worship without sacrifice
g. Politics without principle

Chapter 12

The CEO as a Strategic Leader with a Shared Personal and Corporate Vision

I believe if one man gains spiritually, the whole world gains with him and, if one man falls, the whole world falls to that extent. (Mahatma Gandhi)

(Easwaran 2009)

Personal mastery needs a personal vision that comes from within us. Vision is applied imagination. Albert Einstein said "Imagination is more important than knowledge" (Senge 1990)). Most of us do not envision or realize our own potential. "Most people live in a very restricted circle of their potential being. We all have reservoirs of energy and genius to draw upon of which we do not dream" (William James cited in Covey 2004: 70). Memory is past, it is finite; but vision is future, it is infinite. "Without vision we all suffer from an insufficiency of data. We look at life myopically, that is, through our own lens, our own world. Vision enables us to transcend our own autobiography, our past, to rise above our memory," said Sir Laurens van der Post, an author, filmmaker, and world-renowned storyteller (Covey 2004).

Personal mastery is to raise our level of consciousness. You just raise your own consciousness and you will raise the consciousness of the world. This is what the above quote of Gandhi means:

All of us can give a great gift to the world by looking at our life and gradually removing from it the things that are not simple and beautiful…. As you dive deeper and deeper into your consciousness, you will make the discovery that your needs are not just for your own personal satisfaction and prestige, but for enriching the lives of all those around you. You will begin to think as urgently about the needs of others as you've been thinking about your own. With this expansion of consciousness comes a flood of loving energy that transforms your life and the world around you. The idea of buying or doing something for yourself at the expense of others or of the forests or rivers or air becomes unthinkable. (Easwaran 1992: 23–24)

VISION, MISSION, GOALS, AND OBJECTIVES

Vision is different from mission or purpose. Purpose is a direction; vision is the destiny. Vision is intrinsic, that is, we pursue a vision for its intrinsic value; purpose may be relative to an end we desire. Purpose may be abstract; but a vision is concrete. Purpose without vision has no sense of appropriate scale. Relative visions may be appropriate for a while, but they never lead you to greatness. The end is not of an instrumental but an absolute value, but purpose may have an instrumental value—that is, the purpose becomes the means to an end. The end is the reason why we exist, live, and operate—a personal vision. The end is why an organization exists, lives, and operates—a corporate vision. Visions are ends that we really want to do, and what we really must do. The ends (and not purposes or means) make our work, family, society, and industry worthwhile. Personal mastery is a discipline and a process by which we continually focus and refocus on what we truly want—on our visions.

Visions are multifaceted. Some are *material facets* as where we want to live, how we want to live, what wealth we need to accumulate, and so on. We may change these relative visions as we grow. There are *personal facets* to our visions such as health, freedom, honesty, integrity, and accountability. There are *social facets* to our visions such as compassion, hospitality, kindness, forgiveness, charity, generosity, volunteering, and self-sacrifice. Some of these personal or social facets are relative visions, and some are absolute visions. Some *corporate facets* to our visions are growth, corporate success, generating jobs, generating new green products, creating wealth, supporting neighboring communities, contributing to national growth, and the like.

There is great power in viewing people separately from their behavior; when we do this, we affirm their fundamental and unconditional worth. This affirming vision not only frees them to become their best but, in the process, we too are freed from reacting to undesirable behavior. Cultivating the habit of affirming people (that is, frequently and sincerely communicating your belief in them and their potential), especially teenagers who are going through identity crisis, is an important mission of our vision (Covey 2004: 71–73).

Most adults have little sense of real vision. They may have goals and objectives, but these are not visions. Seeking increases in sales revenues, market share, margins and profits, employee satisfaction, wealth and shareholder value, are all good goals and objectives, but they are not visions. They are *means* to an *end* that is greater than all of them—the end is the vision. The end is a goal by itself; it has intrinsic, ultimate, and permanent value. [See *Business Transformation Exercise 12.1.*]

VISION AND LEADERSHIP

The distinction between management and leadership has long been recognized. Most agree that mangers manage for continuous improvement to the status quo, while leaders are a force for change that compels a group to innovate and depart from the routine. Leadership is essentially about realizing change. Hence, a prerequisite of a leader is the ability to create and articulate a better future for the company. That is, if there is no vision, there is no leadership.

Just as leadership is not so much who one is as what one does, so too is vision. Vision encompasses the abilities to frame the current practices as inadequate, to generate new ideas for new strategies, and to communicate possibilities in inspiring ways to others. Thus, being visionary is not the same as being charismatic; the latter visions alone. Great leadership visions rarely emerge from solitary analysis. As great leaders search for new paths, they engage in vigorous exchange with an array of people inside and outside the organization to figure out that they understand and know how to realize the desired future.

Great leaders play a key role in managing stakeholders above, across, and outside their units. Vision is a must-have for enterprise leadership, regardless of gender. Luckily, vision is a capability that can be learned, mostly at the elbow of a master leader (Ibarra and Obodaru 2009: 64–65). Find role models and study how they develop and communicate strategic ideas. As your vision develops, find opportunities to articulate it. Do not wait until your vision is perfect. Try out draft versions of your vision as it matures and even after it matures. Nobody will perceive your vision if you do not share it. Great visions also come from inside—from your self-confidence, competence, conscience, imagination, intuition, and instincts.

CRITICAL COMPONENTS OF LEADERSHIP

The Global Executive Leadership Inventory (GELI) is a 360-degree feedback instrument developed (by Manfred Kets de Vries, Pierre Vrignaud, and Elizabeth Florent-Treacy) at the Global Leadership Center of the famous business school, Insead, in Fontainebleau, France. In order to identify significant dimensions of exemplary leadership, the authors interviewed more than 300 senior executives, male and female, over a course of three years. The emerging questionnaire was subsequently validated on an international sample of senior executives and MBA students, male and female. The resultant instrument, GELI, identifies and measures degrees of competency in the following critical components of leadership:

1. **Envisioning**: This is articulating a compelling vision, mission, and strategy that incorporate a multicultural and diverse perspective and connect employees, shareholders, suppliers, and customers on a global scale. Great leaders inspire others.
2. **Empowering**: This follows envisioning at all levels of the organization by delegating and sharing information.
3. **Energizing**: Energizing and motivating employees to achieve the organization's goals.
4. **Designing and Aligning**: Creating world-class organizational design and control systems and using them to align the behavior of employees with the values and goals of the organization.
5. **Rewarding and Feedback**: Setting up appropriate reward structures and giving constructive feedback.
6. **Team Building**: Creating team players and focusing on team effectiveness by instilling a cooperative atmosphere, promoting collaboration, and encouraging constructive conflict.
7. **Outside Orientation**: Making employees aware of outside constituencies such as customers, suppliers, shareholders, and other interest groups, including local communities affected by the organization.
8. **Global Mindset**: Inculcating a global mentality, instilling values that act as a glue between the regional or national cultures represented in the organization.
9. **Tenacity**: Encouraging tenacity and courage in employees by setting a personal example in taking reasonable risks.
10. **Emotional Intelligence**: Fostering trust in the organization by creating (primarily by example) an emotionally intelligent workforce whose members are self-aware and treat others with respect and understanding.

Male respondents rated women higher on components 3 to 7, 9, and 10, and rated themselves higher on component 1. Female respondents rated themselves higher on components 1, 3 to 7, 9, and 10. There was no appreciable difference along components 2 and 8 in both groups (Ibarra and Obodaru 2009: 62–70). Vision is not just a matter of style; it implies substance. It is not a bunch of meaningless mission statements pinned on your bulletin board. Vision is all about strategic acumen, change, and positioning know-how. Strategic analysis demands a solid grasp of what is happening outside your group and your company. Great leaders build a solid external network as a first line of defense against insular thinking, and leverage their vision using the network. You may have a great vision, but without a network of inside and outside stakeholders to leverage it, you are doomed to fail.

According to GELI, great visionary behavior entails doing three things well (Ibarra and Obodaru 2009: 69):

- **Sensing Opportunities and Threats in the Environment**: You can do this by simplifying complex situations, and by foreseeing events that will affect your organization.
- **Setting Strategic Direction**: Encourage and explore new businesses; define new strategies; make decisions keeping the big picture (long term, big scale, large scope) in mind.
- **Inspiring Constituents**: Challenge the status quo; be open to new ways of doing things; inspire others to look beyond limitations. [See *Business Transformation Exercise 12.2*]

CREATIVE TENSION

Often, there are gaps between our visions and reality, between our dream homes and the houses we live in, between our dream university and our actual education institutions, between our professional dream job and our present job, and in general, the gap between where we want to be and where we are now. Often, these gaps make our visions fanciful and unrealistic, our efforts desperate and we tend to give up our visions—these are emotional tensions. On the other hand, these gaps can also energize us to action, to improvement, and to invest our best talent and efforts. When the gap between vision and reality is a creative energy, Senge (2006: 140) calls it a "creative tension" while Robert Fritz (1989) would call it a "structural tension." Tension, by its nature, seeks resolution, and the most natural resolution of this tension is for our reality to move closer to what we want (Senge et al. 1994: 195).

Creative tension is like a rubber band that you stretch between the two poles of your vision and current reality, with one hand representing current reality and the other representing vision. You may choose to pull toward current reality (i.e., you lower your vision), or you may choose to pull toward your vision (i.e., you hold or heighten your vision). Lowering visions is easy; it lowers our emotional tension; it erodes our moral and industry standards; but the price is that we abandon what we really want: our vision. This is a symptomatic solution—a reinforcing mechanism. Lowering visions is similar to eroding goals or lowering standards, or "shifting the burdens"—archetype problems and structures we discussed in Chapter 4 under the case of *WonderTech*. The problems may recur, and you may lower standards further to reduce the gap between vision and reality, and soon you encounter the recursive spiral of failure.

Lowering goals is the dynamics of compromise, the path of mediocrity, and the refuge of the pusillanimous. You may deny the gap and flee from it, and this is cowardice. You may ignore the gap; pretend there is no bad news or there is no gap; you declare victory; and this is self-deception. Alternatively, you redefine the gap or the bad news as not so bad by lowering the standard against which it is judged—and this is fraud or deliberate misrepresentation. Either way, we keep on eroding our goals, and eventually, surrender our dreams. Hence, an accurate and insightful view of current reality is as important as a clear vision.

On the other hand, holding to the visions or even enhancing them is the balancing process that represents the "fundamental solution"—that is, you take actions to bring reality to align with your vision. Changing reality, however, takes time; there is a delay between the cause and the effect. Great leaders do not lower visions; they hold on to them. Truly creative people use the gap between vision and current reality to generate creative energy for change. The discipline of personal mastery entails at least three imperatives:

- Personal mastery teaches us not to shrink back from seeing the world as it is, even if it makes us uncomfortable. Looking closely and objectively at current reality is one of the most difficult tasks of personal mastery.
- On the other hand, personal mastery mandates that we do not lower our vision, even if it seems that it is an impossible vision. Paradoxically, the content of the vision is not important in itself. As Robert Fritz (1989) wrote: "It is not what the vision is; it is what the vision does."
- Personal mastery teaches us to choose. Choosing is a courageous act—you are electing the choices, actions, and results that will make into your destiny.

Each imperative is like a "voice" within us—the voice of vision, the voice of current reality as we perceive it, and the voice of conscience that mandates critical choice. In the discipline of personal mastery, we listen to, and hold a conversation with all three voices, knowing that the power that pulls us toward our vision emerges from the relationship between these voices (Senge et al. 1994: 196). Best leaders keep on striving for the vision or standard they set to themselves. People achieve extraordinary results with extraordinary visions—even if the final results happen to be different from their original level and intent.

Mastery of creative tension transforms the way we view failure. Failure is simply a shortfall, an evidence of the gap between our vision and our current reality. Failure, then, becomes an opportunity for learning—about the current reality that we fail to assess, about the strategies that did not work, about the mistakes we made but did not learn from, or about the clarity of vision that we need. Ed Land, founder of Polaroid and inventor of instant photography, had one plaque on his wall that read: *Mistake is an event, the full benefit of which has not yet been turned to your advantage.* Mastery of creative tension brings out our capacity for perseverance and patience. It leads to a fundamental shift in our whole posture toward reality. Current reality becomes the ally and not the enemy. An accurate and insightful view of current reality is as important as a clear vision.

Thus, the principle of creative tension is the central principle of personal mastery, integrating all elements of the discipline. Most of us impose biases on our perceptions of current reality. That is, "we learn to rely on our concepts of reality more than on our observations of reality" (Fritz 1989). It is easier to assume reality which is similar to our preconceived ideas than to freshly observe what we have before our eyes. If the first choice in pursuing self-mastery is to be true to your own vision, the second fundamental choice is to your commitment to truth. The two are equally vital in generating your creative tension.

Those who are convinced that a vision or result is important, work for it; they commit themselves to that result and are ready to change their life and lifestyle in order to reach it. They assimilate the vision not just consciously, but even unconsciously, at a deep level where it changes even their behavior. They have a sense of deliberate patience—with themselves and the world—and more attentive to what is going on around them. All of this produces a sustained sense of energy, passion, and enthusiasm that (often after a delay) produce substantial tangible results, which, in turn, make the energy and passion stronger and more focused. We may not snap instantly into this frame of mind, but with the discipline of personal mastery, we can progressively cultivate a way of thinking that makes us more competent and confident to realize the vision (Senge et al. 1994: 195).

An executive VP introduced himself at an Innovation Associates course saying, "I've lost five good people. I am here to find out what's been going on in my organization." At the end of the course (that included much personal mastery material), he confessed that his employees felt they were not independent enough to pursue their own visions at his company. "I want to rework the structures that made these people feel blocked" (cited in Senge et al. 1994: 220). One of the most intriguing aspects of personal mastery is the changes it induces in an organization's design. When corporations embrace the discipline of personal mastery among all its people they are compelled to rethink their investment of money, time, energy, intelligence and attention in designing new element of infrastructure that ensure development of employee capabilities. [See *Business Transformation Exercise 12.3.*]

STRUCTURAL CONFLICT AND CREATIVE TENSION

Most of us grow to experience two opposite beliefs about systemic forces that limit us:

- Our basic *powerlessness* or inability to bring into being all the things that we really care about.
- Our basic *unworthiness*—we do not truly deserve to have what we truly desire.

We believe in both these opposites. We fight our powerlessness by achievement, and we concede to our unworthiness by slowing our achievement. Robert Fritz (1989) calls this aspect of our creative tension a "structural conflict," because it reflects a structure of conflicting forces pulling us toward and simultaneously away from what we really want. We may be unaware of this structural conflict in all that we think, aspire, do, and undo—nevertheless, our unawareness contributes to the power of the conflict.

Structural conflict complements or explains creative tension. One systemic force stretches us between our vision and our current perception of reality (this is creative tension), and the other systemic force stresses us in the opposite direction and lies between our perception of current reality and our perception of the powerless/unworthiness dyad (this is structural conflict). Fritz identifies three coping strategies by which we manage our structural conflict:

- **Vision erosion**—we erode or compromise our vision.
- **Conflict manipulation** or negative vision—we focus on getting away from what we do not want (e.g., anti-smoking, anti-war, anti-drugs, anti-nuclear war policies and efforts) rather than moving toward what we do want.
- **Willpower**—we psyche ourselves up to overpower all forms of resistance to achieving our goals. That is, we motivate ourselves through heightened volition. Success-conscious leaders do this—they marshal tremendous willpower to do the things they want to do despite the price and risk they entail, to fight any obstacle or defeat any opposition that comes in the way.

These coping strategies are unavoidable. Moreover, it is difficult to recognize them while we are playing them out, especially because of tensions and pressures that often accompany them. In relation to willpower, however, we often may act without leverage; that is, there may be little economies of scale and means. We do attain our goals, but at a tremendous cost, enormous efforts, and overwhelming exhaustion. We become victims of our ambitions. Often, we might wonder whether the success was worth all the trouble. Ironically, people hooked on success and the willpower that goes with it, may look for obstacles to overcome, dragons to slay, and enemies to vanquish. Secondly, willpower success may result in many unintended consequences (e.g., breakdowns in health and/or marriage, terrible relationships with teenager children, little time for people). Much would depend upon the personal mastery we achieve through these conflicts, tensions, and coping strategies.

COMMITMENT TO TRUTH AND STRUCTURAL CONFLICT

Commitment to truth is a disarmingly simple yet a profound strategy for dealing with structural conflict. Commitment to truth does not necessarily mean the absolute moral standard of being committed to Truth who is God or the final ultimate cause of this universe. It means a relentless willingness to root out the ways we limit or deceive ourselves from seeing what is, and continually to challenge our theories of why things are the way they are. It means continually broadening our vision and awareness (like an athlete on the field), and deepening our understanding of the structures underlying current events and our current behavior.

Thus, the first critical task when dealing with structural conflicts is to recognize them and their consequences on human and organizational behavior. Structures of which we are unaware often hold us prisoners. Once we see them, name them, and confront them they will no longer have the same hold on us. This is equally true for individuals as it is for organizations. Individual and organizational psychological difficulties can be understood and changed only by understanding the structures of interdependencies and close relationships (e.g., within families, within corporations) that exist. Each leader focuses on one or the other coping strategy. Once we understand these structures, we may be able to alter them so that we could free people and organizations controlled by them. Once an operating structure is recognized, the structure itself becomes part of the "current reality." In the context of creative tension and structural conflicts, our commitment to truth becomes a liberating and generative force.

Life always avails the option of seeing the truth, no matter how blind and prejudiced we may be. If we have the courage to respond to that option, we have the power to change ourselves profoundly. The power of truth is to see reality more and more as it is, to cleanse the lens of our perception, and to awaken ourselves from self-imposed distortions of reality—this is a common search across all major religions of the world (Senge 2006: 150). The truth shall set you free.

The goal of all spiritual disciplines, writes Ekanath Easwaran (1995: 37) is gradually to bring the mind to a perfect stillness. In automotive terms, you are downshifting from overdrive to top gear, then to second, and finally to neutral. When you develop the capacity to put your mind into neutral, you will have acquired inexhaustible patience. You will be able to listen to another person's point of view with much concentration and detachment. The attitude of open-mindedness, of listening to opposing points of view and being prepared to learn from them, is the beginning of kindness, and kindness is the foundation of a harmonious world. Hurry is unkindness.

USING THE SUBCONSCIOUS

People with high levels of self-mastery perform extraordinarily complex tasks with grace and ease. For example, Michael Phelps was the sportsman of the year 2008, a title he very well deserves for his swimming super ordeals at the 2008 Summer Olympics that won him eight gold medals. Similarly, consider great sculptors (e.g., Michael Angelo), architects and painters (e.g., Leonardo Da Vinci), musicians (e.g., Bach, Beethoven, and Mozart), pop musicians (the Beatles, Elvis Presley, Michael Jackson), and major league players (e.g., Joe DiMaggio, Babe Ruth, Nolan Ryan, Roger Clemens, Michael Jordan, Larry Bird, Gordie Howe, and Wayne Gretzky). These heroes developed their skills through years of diligent and drilling training. They performed with marvelous effortlessness and grace. How did they do it? A good theory is that of the subconscious. They performed these extraordinarily complex tasks not because of their conscious mind (which is very limited in its domain and potential), but because of the subconscious or "zoning" that took over (and which can deal with complexity 10 times more efficiently). Their persistent self-mastery with its accumulation of drills, skills, and habits got engraved into their subconscious.

It is said that human beings possess both a conscious and the sub-conscious mind, the latter perhaps ten times more potent than the former. The subconscious operates below or behind our conscious mind and awareness. Sigmund Freud and Carl Jung called it the *unconscious*, which in their theory has implications far beyond the cognitive and skills aspects of human achievement. In Freud and Jung, the unconscious is a given that is inherited and deterministic. In the theory of the subconscious, it is freely and subconsciously cultivated. Most of the nascent and everyday skills that we learnt slowly and consciously (e.g., eating, walking, talking, singing, reading, writing, playing music, driving, and the like) slowly enter into our subconscious and get archived ready for retrieval and use. Because of its high potentiality, the subconscious can be trained to deal effectively with extraordinary levels of skill and complexity, even as the great artists of human history, men and women, did and left behind as a great legacy. Without the subconscious, we could not explain how human beings could attain such wondrous heights of perfection, skill, and grace.

Once the repertoire of their subconscious has been built and established, the great skilled artists do not so much focus on the process as much on the outcome while performing. They focus on the desired intrinsic result, and not on the process details; and this is a skill too. Great leaders and artists know how to separate the process from the outcome, the means from the end, the interim goals and values from the intrinsic and permanent goals and values, and the desired outcome from the process that can achieve it (Senge 2006).

Patanjali was a teacher of meditation in ancient India called Raja Yoga. *Raja* means "king," and so *raja yoga* is those disciplines that have come down in all the great religions through which men and women born commoners become royalty. Their kingdom is not money, power, fortune, or any material possession. If you ask them, "What is your kingdom?" they will answer with quiet, unshakable confidence, "We rule the country of our mind and the kingdom of our life." Unless and until we have some measure of sovereignty over our thinking process, lasting fulfillment will be beyond our reach (Easwaran 1992: 17–18).

For all the foregoing reasons, self-mastery is best nurtured and empowered by silence and meditation, by heart and intuition, by imagination and commitment—these help to quiet the conscious mind and focus on and nurture the subconscious. Making choices is important in our life, but only when the choices are made through the subconscious—the choices, then, are more objective and realistic. Experienced managers have rich intuition about complex systems, even though they may not explain them. Their intuition tells them that cause and effect are not close in time and space, that obvious solutions produce more harm than good, and that short-term fixes produce long-term problems. The integration of reason and intuition enables us to see things interconnected and interdependencies between actions and the reality that underlies them. Integrating intuition and reason may prove to be one of the primary contributions of systems thinking (Senge 2006: 158). [See *Business Transformation Exercise 12.4*]

MANAGING OUR MENTAL MODELS

"Mental models are the images, assumptions, and stories that we carry in our minds of ourselves, other people, institutions, and every aspect of the world" (Senge et al. 1994: 235).[1] We particularly have mental models of our institutions such as corporations, work departments, families, governments, churches, political parties, and social associations. Philosophers, starting from Plato and Aristotle, have discussed mental models for millennia. We are bound by them; they are active; they shape how we act. We make sense of the world around us and take action through our mental models.

Some basic properties of our mental models include (Senge 2006: 163–90; Senge et al. 1994: 235–37):

- **We are our mental models**. We do not carry our family, our work, our organizations, and our corporations in our minds. What we carry in our heads, however, are their images, representations, assumptions, and stories.
- **Mental models determine what we see**. Mental models select what we see, and condition how we see. Our mental models affect us as to what we see and how we see reality. They determine our selective observations. They shape our perceptions. We navigate through the complex environment of our world with cognitive "mental maps."
- **Mental models shape how we act**. For example, if we believe that people are basically trustworthy, we will talk to new acquaintances much more freely than if we believed that people are not trustworthy.
- **Mental models are usually "tacit"**—existing below the level of awareness, they are often untested and unexamined; and hence, could be flawed. Therefore, the core task of the discipline of personal mastery is to bring our mental models to the surface and critically examine them, and talk about them with minimal defensiveness.
- **All mental models are simplifications of reality around us**; hence, they cannot be good or bad, right or wrong. We are often unaware of our mental models, and the models remain unexamined; hence, they remain unchanged, when the rest of the world keeps on changing. As the world keeps on changing, the gap between our mental models and reality widens, leading to increasingly counter-productive decisions and actions. Unquestioned models can be disastrous.
- **We do not have any anointed or authorized mental models**; we have a philosophy of mental modeling (O'Brien 1989). The goal in practicing the discipline of mental models is not necessarily

---

[1] The concept of mental models is ancient going back to the Greek philosophers. The phrase, "mental model," however, is modern, possibly coined for the first time by Kenneth Craik, a Scottish psychologist in the 1940s. Several disciplines and scholars now use the phrase such as cognitive psychologists (e.g., Philip Johnson-Laird of Princeton University), cognitive scientists (e.g., Marvin Minsky and Seymour Papert of MIT), and management scientists (Senge et al. 1994: 237).

agreement or convergence. Many divergent and disagreeing mental models can co-exist. We need to examine them, however, and periodically test them against situations that come up. This requires an organizational commitment to "truth"—an outgrowth of personal mastery.

Albert Einstein once wrote, "Our theories determine what we measure" (Senge 1990). Howard Gardner (1984) writes, "To my mind, the major accomplishments of cognitive science has been the clear demonstration of ... a level of mental representation" active in diverse aspects of human behavior. Gardner believes that *our mental models determine not only how we make sense of the world, but also how we take action*. (Gardner 1984) Chris Argyris (1991, 1993), who worked on mental models and organizational learning for over 40 years at Harvard, observed, "Although people do not always behave congruently with their espoused theories (what they say), they do behave congruently with theories-in-use (their mental models)." [See *Business Transformation Exercise 12.5*]

This seemed to be the problem with the Detroit auto industry. According to the management consultant Ian Mitroff (1988), the domestic auto executives, especially those of GM, entertained the following long-standing and unquestioned assumptions about the car world as necessary conditions for success:

- The auto companies are in the business of making money, not cars.
- American car buyers and users mostly care about styling.
- Cars are primarily status symbols; styling therefore is more important than quality.
- Hence, American consumers need many models with different styles.
- The American car market is isolated from the rest of the world.
- Auto workers do not have an important impact on productivity or product quality.
- Everyone working in the auto system has no need for more than a specific, fragmented, compartmentalized understanding of the business.

This mental model was unexamined, unchallenged, and got all three into trouble (Senge 2006: 165–66, footnote 5). It is interesting, in the recent Congressional hearings (December 4–5, 2008), after which all three promised to cut down on models, emphasize quality, and focus on fuel-efficient hybrid models. Their cash crisis and desperate need for a federal bailout forced them finally to change their long-standing mental model.

Mental models at a corporate level involve two types of skills: skill of reflection and skills of inquiry. Skills of reflection concern the slowing down our own thinking processes so that we can become more aware of how we form our mental models and the ways they influence our actions. Skills of inquiry concern how we operate in face-to-face interactions with others, especially in dealing with complex and conflicting issues.

The most crucial mental models in any organization are those shared by key decision makers. Corporate executives need continually to examine these mental models so that they can consider a range of decisions, projects, and actions in consonance with the vision and goals of the organization.

The core discipline of mental models, according to Senge (2006: 178–87), includes four skill levels:

- **Reflective Theoretic Skills**: We must make a distinction between espoused theories (what we view or profess—e.g., people are basically trustworthy; our clients are best assets) and theory-in-use (what we do—e.g., we delegate responsibility to trusted people; we are totally client-focused). Learning is eventually all about action. One basic reflective skill involves using gaps between what we say and what we do as a vehicle for becoming more aware. If we do not recognize the gap between our espoused theories and theories-in-use, no learning can take place. It is often difficult to recognize our theory-in-use (the eye cannot see the eye!); but an outsider can act as a "ruthlessly compassionate partner" to help us with our reflective skills and detect our underlying theories-in-use.

- **Recognizing Leaps of Abstraction**: Our minds move at lightening speed, and ironically, this often slows our learning. For instance, we immediately jump from observations to generalizations without testing the latter. We often make generalizing judgments about people based on a few facts, and worse, we treat them as axiomatic facts and act on them.[2]

- **Left-hand Column**: This method comes from a type of case presentation used by Chris Argyris and his colleagues at MIT. It is a powerful technique for beginning to "see" how our mental models operate in particular contexts and situations. The technique reveals how using our mental models we might manipulate data, facts, arguments, and logic to prove the validity of our predetermined outcomes. The left-hand column starts with selecting a specific situation where we confront diverging differences such that we have stopped from interacting, learning, and moving ahead. On the right-hand side, we write the narrative of engagement (e.g., a decision, strategy, project, presentation, or solution implementation). On the left-hand side, we write the corresponding but hidden or underlying assumptions or generalizations, and show how they influence our behavior. If we are honest and transparent, the left-hand column should quickly tell us how our assumptions and generalizations hinder and undermine learning, and how our reasoning and actions contribute to make matters worse.

- **Balancing Inquiry and Advocacy**: Most managers are trained to be advocates—to be problem solvers, to figure out what needs to be done, and enlist whatever support is needed to get things done. Successful managers, presumably, debate forcefully and influence others. Inquiry skills, meanwhile, may go unrecognized and unrewarded. As managers rise to senior positions, however, they confront very complex and diverse issues that they may not be able to resolve merely by their advocacy skills. They begin to feel the need of other expert insights, they need the skills to inquire, and they feel the need to learn. At this stage, managers need to blend their advocacy and inquiry skills to promote collaborative learning.

When we are in a pure advocacy mode, our goal may be to win an argument or a predetermined outcome, and, hence, we tend to use data selectively, presenting only the data that confirms our position. On the other hand, when we are in a pure inquiry mode, the goal may be a hypothesis or theory, and the tendency might be to conduct selective research, explanation, inferencing, and prediction to ground our pet theory. Both methods are flawed, biased, and result in win–lose situations. Instead, when we balance

---

[2] Senge (2006: 178–80) illustrate this theory by an example. Laura was recently hired as a new HR director. All watch Laura and observe some of her specific behaviors or "habits" such as staring off into space when people talk to her, cutting people off when they speak, never attending office parties, muttering a few words during performance appraisal, and then dismissing them, and so on, and we generalize—"Laura does not care about people." This is a leap of abstraction. We do not question such generalizations; in which case, leaps of abstraction impede learning. Moreover, untested generalizations can easily become a basis for further generalizations (e.g., Laura does not care about people; she must be a loner; she is a very unhappy woman; …). [In fact, Laura had a hearing impediment that she did not tell anyone, but made her painfully self-conscious during conversations.]

inquiry and advocacy, the goal is no more to win an argument, but to find the best argument or solution in true partnership, even at the expense of rejecting our pet theory and vested arguments. When there is inquiry and advocacy, creative win-win outcomes are more likely to emerge. Balancing inquiry and advocacy is a "learning discipline" that takes time to master; it implies that we are prepared to change our veteran mental models, pet theories, vested arguments, and predetermined outcomes. It may also mean willingness to expose the limitations in our own thinking, and our willingness to be wrong (Senge 2006: 183–87). Table 12.1 contrasts pure advocacy, pure inquiry, and balancing inquiry–advocacy approaches. [See *Business Transformation Exercise 12.6*]

Our conscious mind is ill-equipped to deal with large numbers of concrete details. If, for example, we thumb through a hundred photographs of strange individuals, most of us will have trouble remembering each face, but we will remember categories such as tall men, mostly women, mostly elderly men, and so on. As the psychologist George Miller noted, we have a tendency to focus on a limited number of separate variables (say, 7 ± 2) at any one time. Our rational minds are adept in abstracting from the concrete—substituting simple concepts for many details, and then reasoning them in terms of these concepts. We must learn to separate facts from our generalizations, and where possible, test the latter. We must be aware of our leaps of abstraction. Dealing with our assumptions is critical to inquiry. Our assumptions and generalizations influence our behavior, our conversations and actions.

Often, entire industries can develop chronic misfits between mental models and reality. This could be true of all stagnant industries in the U.S., such as railroad, shipping, steel, rubber, paper, and airlines. Most often, mental models are deeply embedded in the firm's management tradition. In general, close-knit industries can be very vulnerable because all the member companies look to each other for the same standards of best practice.

In this context, Royal Dutch/Shell's mental model is worth considering. It was founded in 1907 from a gentleman's agreement between Royal Dutch Petroleum and the London-based Shell Transport and Trading Company. The company grew to more than a hundred operating companies around the world, and was led by managers from as many different cultures. Royal Dutch/Shell tried to build a consensus mental model. In 1972, one year before the Organization of the Petroleum Exporting Countries (OPEC) oil crisis, Royal Dutch/Shell found out that Europe, Japan, and the U.S. were becoming increasingly dependent upon oil imports, which mostly came from a small number of oil-exporting countries (e.g., Iraq, Iran, Libya, Saudi Arabia, and Venezuela). These oil-exporting countries, on the other hand, were deeply concerned about their falling oil reserves. As large oil producers, these countries were gaining economic power and all were planning to limit production—in other words, there would be a sellers' market controlled by the oil-exporting nations.

When OPEC launched oil embargo suddenly in the winter of 1973–74, Shell with its centralized planning staff responded differently from the other major oil companies. Shell slowed their investments in refineries, and designed refineries that could adapt to whatever type of crude oil was available. It also forecasted energy demand at a consistently lower level than their competitors did, and consistently more accurately. Shell also quickly accelerated development of oilfield outside OPEC. Shell discovered the power of managing mental models. In 1970, the company was considered the weakest of the seven largest oil companies. By 1979, it was perhaps the strongest, and directly competing with Exxon.

Learning how to work with new mental models led to the success of British Petroleum (BP). Unlike Shell's model of centralized planning staff model, BP adopted a distributed or decentralized planning model. During the last two decades or so, it has risen rapidly to rank number two among global oil companies in sales and volume, second only to Exxon. By late 1990s, BP operated 150 local profit centers,

TABLE 12.1 Contrasting Three Methods of Discourse: Pure Advocacy, Pure Inquiry, and Balancing Inquiry and Advocacy

Methodology	Mental model processes	Pure advocacy (A)	Pure inquiry (B)	Balancing inquiry and advocacy (A&B)
Problem-solving	Starting input bias	This is my position	This is my hypothesis and theory	Can we consider alternative positions, hypotheses, and theories?
	Process bias	These are my reasons	This is the data collection	Can we consider alternative reasons, and look at other relevant data sets?
	Outcome bias	This is the way I argue my position based on these reasons	This is the way I analyzed the data to draw this conclusion	Can we consider competing ways of reasoned-arguments and data analysis?
Chris Argyris' "Left-hand Column" Thinking	Untested generalizations	This is the way things are	This is what the truth is	This is the way we see things are
	Unexamined assumptions	This is my presumed view of things	This is my basic theory and paradigm in thinking	Let us consider views different from those of A. Let us examine theories rival to those of B
	Uncollaborative impasse behavior	I am determined to do this; these are the facts that corroborate my position	I am totally convinced about this theory and the explanation. This is the only way we can think	Let us engage in conversation, reciprocally reviewing our work, efforts, methods, and outcomes A to B, and B to A: "Here is my view and this is how I arrived at it. How does it sound to you?" What data or logic might change our views? Could some of A's "facts" be mere assumptions? Could B learn skills of inquiry to refine his thinking?
Solution Assessment	Gaps between espoused theory and theory-in-use	Thus, this is the way to go—reinforcing advocacy	Thus, this is the way I plan to go—reinforcing theory	Let us consider reciprocal inquiry and reciprocal advocacy
	Leaps of abstraction: jumps from observations to generalizations	This is the way I reason, explain, and establish my position	This is the way my research, data collection, and data analysis lead to these conclusions	Let us examine the assumptions and generalizations underlying positions of both A and B Let us look for gaps in A's reasoning Let us examine B's conclusions and the data they are based upon
Solution Implementation	Final alternative selection	I will do it my way	I will do it my way	Let us talk and we will know what to do. We need to dialog; we need team learning. We will review together our divergent positions and do it our combined way

Source: Author's own.

and local business unit managers had much greater authority. John Browne, BP's CEO since 1995, was passionate about building a performance culture with a flatter organization where more people would think issues for themselves and assume bottom-line business accountability. Even though Browne recognized the danger of distributing power lay in possible fragmentation that made organizational learning across various business units difficult, yet he maintained variety of networks to keep people connected and transparent, and open to learn from or challenge each other's mental models.

Shell and BP's successful mental models suggest three important facets of developing and testing corporate mental models:

- Develop tools that promote personal awareness and reflective skills.
- Develop a culture that promotes inquiry and challenges our thinking.
- Develop infrastructures that try to institutionalize regular practice with mental models.

All three facets are important, in whatever order, as long as they thrive in commitment, connectedness, openness, merit, and flexibility to change. Openness discourages games-playing; and merit (i.e., making decisions based on the best interests of the organizations) is an antidote to the disease of hierarchies and bureaucratic politics. In the traditional authoritarian top-down organization, the dogma was managing, organizing, and controlling, says Bill O'Brien, ex-CEO of Hanover; but in the learning organization, the new dogma is vision, values, and mental models. The healthy corporations systematize ways to bring people together to develop the best possible mental models for facing any crisis or economic turbulence. According to Chris Argyris (1986), teams and organizations trap themselves in "defensive routines" that insulate their mental models from examination. Hence, they develop a "skilled incompetence" (i.e., highly skillful in protecting themselves from the pain and threat of the learning organization) that fails to learn and remain incompetent at producing the results they really want (Argyris 1986).

There are subtle patterns of reasoning that affects and underlies our behavior. Such patterns lead us to make generalizations and assumptions about people, corporations, society, and even about ourselves. We never communicate these assumptions and generalizations directly, but anyhow, think, speak, decide, and behave based on them. These are our mental models in action. Argyris (1993) called this our "action science" of games-playing that we have come to accept. We need to challenge our mental models continually and consistently, especially if we choose to engage ourselves in difficult issues and learn from everyone involved. It is by maintaining incredibly high standards of openness, transparency, merit, cooperation, and commitment that we can live our core values and vision to the full.

WESTERN VERSUS ORIENTAL ETHICAL PARADIGMS AND MENTAL MODELS

Mental models differ across nations, races, and continents. The typical Western mental models that reflect Western European and North American thinking considerably differ from the Oriental mental models that reflect the thinking of Eastern nations such as China, Japan, and India.

Table 12.2 presents Western versus Eastern mental paradigms on fundamental concepts such as rights, duties, claims, entitlements, primacy, work, society, and the like. Table 12.3 contrasts Western versus Oriental ethical thinking criteria. In general, the Western mind thinks in individualist terms of the primacy of the individual before that of the social. The Oriental mind is the opposite, placing the social before the individual, respecting social and community rights and claims before those of the individuals.

TABLE 12.2 Western versus Oriental Ethical Thinking Paradigms

Ethical domains and dimensions	The western (occidental) conceptual-individualistic paradigm		The eastern (oriental) experiential-social-community paradigm	
	Concept	Individualism	Experience	Community
Claims	Rights versus duties; every right implies a corresponding duty.	Rights and duties are primarily individual and personal.	Claims are experiences of our social obligations versus social privileges.	Rights and duties are primarily communal and social privileges to serve society and country.
Primacy	Individual primacy over social primacy.	Primary loyalty and allegiance to self and then, to society.	Social primacy over individual primacy; the country and society come first, we follow.	We owe primary loyalty and allegiance to the country and society; the latter will protect us.
Rights	Rights are my entitlements; I have deserved them.	The country and its constitution should endow, bestow, and protect my entitlements.	Rights are shared privileges at best; we must collectively work and seek them.	Collective and responsible sharing of rights as social privileges generates peace and harmony.
Work	Work is the impression of my personality on matter.	Work is an entitlement; family wages are legitimate claims.	Work is our collective impression of our personalities and talents on matter.	Work is a social privilege and duty; we work for society and our country.
Change	Change is a threat; when an opportunity, we welcome it as long as it does not force us to change; we fear as well as seek change.	If change is to create something new, then let me appropriate it; but not necessarily share it; we may change nature to improve it; change is revolution.	Change is natural, eternal, cyclic, and recursive; it is always for the better, unless we distort it.	We change as nature changes and evolves; we change with nature; change is evolution and harmony. "The world has changed; we must change with it" (President Barack H. Obama).
Current Reality	Current reality is an enemy; fight against it; we perceive it with a bias or prejudice.	I fight against what is, what we are; we reject it if it is not what we want to be.	Current reality is an ally, an opportunity, and a gift; we co-created it; let us fathom and make most of it.	If current reality is not what we want to be, let us not lower or erode our standards, but strive for them.
Nature	Nature is a competitive resource; we need to master and exploit it.	The part of nature I appropriate is my personal property.	Nature is sacred; it is a sacred space; it is a shared and sharing opportunity.	Nature must be revered and respected; it is best shared together and for posterity.
Time	Time is linear, irreversible and limited; a threat; an enemy, fight against it.	Time is for me, for us; it is a property; my time is not yours.	Time is cyclic, recursive, and repetitive; it is free and unlimited; time is an ally, work with it.	Time is a social resource; time spent for society is time spent for us.
Privacy	Privacy is personal and individual; it is my right to be alone, and not to be interfered with.	Forced disclosures violate my privacy rights.	Privacy is social and collective; it is society's gift to me for the growth of society.	Shared disclosures strengthen privacy; mutual transparency or open society build communities.
Culture	Shared and market-created lifestyles, fashions, fads, and festivities	We share values and meanings that reinforce our individualism, wealth, privacy, and primacy.	Shared and inherited social meanings and values, grand historical narratives, and hyper-norms	We share, celebrate, and leave for posterity social values and meanings that reinforce our collective lives, vision, and destiny.

Source: Author's own.

TABLE 12.3 Western versus Oriental Ethical Systems

Ethical domains and dimensions	The western (occidental) ethical system		The eastern (oriental) ethical system	
	Concept	Individualism	Social concept	Community
Deontology	That act is moral that safeguards more rights and duties than any other alternative competing act.	Rights and duties are primarily individual and personal.	That act of ours is moral that safeguards maximum number of social rights and obligations.	Rights and duties are primarily communal and social privileges to serve society and country. Deontologism should be social.
Utilitarianism	That act is moral that has the highest benefits over costs accruing to the greatest number.	Costs and benefits are as perceived by the individual who acts.	That act of ours is moral that has the highest social benefits over social costs accruing to the greatest number.	Collective and responsible sharing of costs and benefits generates peace and social harmony. Utilitarianism should be social.
Justice	That act is moral that equitably distributes rights and duties, costs and benefits across the greatest number of stakeholders.	The scope, domain, and efficiency of the distribution of costs and benefits, rights, and duties is as one perceives it.	That act of ours is moral that equitably distributes social rights and duties, social costs and benefits across the greatest number of stakeholders.	Social justice is founded on social primacy of the society and our country over individual primacy. Justice is to give to all their due.
Responsibility	That act is moral that best fulfills my responsibility to people affected by my decisions and actions.	Responsibility is being accountable to the consequences of my actions.	That act of ours is moral that best fulfills our responsibility to people affected by our decisions and actions.	Real responsibility is social accountability of all the stakeholders in a society or country.
Trusting Relationship	That act is moral that generates the best mutual trust.	Trust is an individual trait and reflects one's confidence in the other's positive intentions and promises.	That act of ours is moral that generates the best reciprocal trust among all in a group or society.	The strength and quality of a society is the strength and quality of its bonding and trusting relationships with one another.
Compassion	That act is moral that promotes compassion unto the marginalized.	I will be compassionate to you if you are to me. Compassion is reciprocal.	That act of ours is moral that promotes maximum compassion unto all marginalized.	Compassion is absolute and unconditional service to the one who needs it from us.
Generosity	That act is moral that indicates self-less generosity to the other.	I will be generous to you if you are to me. Generosity is reciprocal.	That act of ours is moral that empowers our self-less generosity to one another.	I will be generous to you regardless of your generosity to me.
Commitment	That act is moral that spells the highest commitment to the other cause or person.	I will be committed to you if you are committed to me. Commitment is mutual and reciprocal.	That act of ours is moral that ensures the highest commitment to the other cause or person.	I will be committed to you regardless of your commitment to me.
Loyalty	That act is moral that best reflects my loyalty to the other.	I will be loyal to you if you are loyal to me. Loyalty must be mutual and reciprocal.	That act of ours is moral that best reflects our unconditional loyalty to one another.	I will be loyal to all of you regardless of your loyalty to me.
Culture	That act is moral that safeguards the best values of our culture.	We share values and meanings that reinforce our individualism, privacy, and primacy.	That act of ours is moral that best reflects and reinforces our positive cultural values.	Shared and inherited social meanings and values celebrate and perpetuate great cultures.

Source: Author's own.

Both tables express different approaches to basic moral, ethical, and managerial issues; they are products of different cultures. Both make sense in their own domain, culture, and social paradigm. The two can lead, however, to opposite conclusions. This leads us to discover that there is more than one way to look at complex issues. It helps us to break down the walls of cultural, national, and continental boundaries, and of millennia of divisive history and thinking. The two approaches combined can have a profound impact on revising, refining, and expanding our mental models. Most of the time, all we have is our mental models of assumptions, generalizations, and never "truths," and we always see the world through our mental models. Our mental models are very incomplete, and often chronically non-systemic (Senge 2006: 174).

We need, however, mental models that combine the best of both approaches, the Occidental and the Oriental, the individual and the social, the pragmatic and the spiritual, the utilitarian and the deontological, individual justice and social distributive justice, and the active and the contemplative. [See *Business Transformation Exercises 12.7 and 12.8*]

CREATING OR REVISING OUR MENTAL MODELS

Working with our mental models is a discipline that offers the highest leverage for change. It is not a mere intellectual exercise. It empowers us to navigate through changing times. "Most of our mental models are flawed, untested, and unexamined; they represent our automatic and incomplete thinking, our automatic and unconscious responses to reality." Often, our mental models are based on incomplete or erroneous data and equally incomplete assumptions and have created the chronic business problems of today. Using the skills of inquiry and reflection will help us to revise, change, or enhance our mental models. We need courage, patience, and spirituality to surface, confront, and question our mental models on a regular basis, especially with others in trusted teams.

In speaking about mental models, Chris Argyris points out our basic flaw, what he calls a "ladder of inference"—a common mental pathway of increasing abstraction, often leading to misguided beliefs. A typical "ladder of inference" may look like one in Figure 12.1. There is a reflexive loop in our thinking: our beliefs affect what data we select next time (Senge et al. 1994: 243–46). All this flawed thinking can tale place rapidly, that I am not even aware I did it. All the rungs of the ladder take place in my head— they are the "leaps of abstraction." *Each rung represents an uncontested assumption or generalization or beliefs. The only thing that is common for all of us is the bottom most rung: Observable Data and Experiences.* This could be seen by all, for instance, from a videotape or a tape recorder, a DVD or YouTube. A repetitive experience of the ladder of inference causes deep-seated attitudes. If we did such ladder-thinking regarding people in our team, making quick negatives judgments and generalizations about them, the team could be divisive, and even threatened with bitter enemies.

We can correct our flawed ladder of thinking using various corrective mechanisms (Senge et al. 1994: 245–65):

- Becoming more aware of our thinking and reasoning (reflection).
- Making our thinking and reasoning more visible to others (transparency, advocacy).
- Inquiring into the thinking and beliefs of others (inquiry).
- Re-looking at the observable data behind my statements (objectivity).
- Stating our assumptions, and describing the data that led to them (discussion).

FIGURE 12.1   The Ladder of Inference

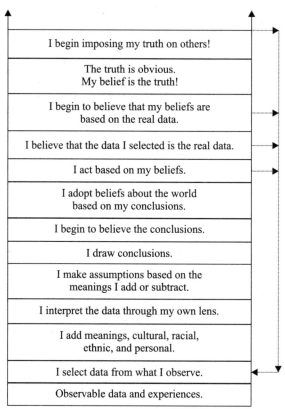

I begin imposing my truth on others!

The truth is obvious.
My belief is the truth!

I begin to believe that my beliefs are
based on the real data.

I believe that the data I selected is the real data.

I act based on my beliefs.

I adopt beliefs about the world
based on my conclusions.

I begin to believe the conclusions.

I draw conclusions.

I make assumptions based on the
meanings I add or subtract.

I interpret the data through my own lens.

I add meanings, cultural, racial,
ethnic, and personal.

I select data from what I observe.

Observable data and experiences.

Source: Author's own.

- Explaining our assumptions and our reasoning explicitly (explanation).
- Making sure we truly understand the views of others (dialog).
- Exploring, listening, and offering our own views in an open way (shared vision).
- Seeing that everyone agrees on what the real data is (data consensus).
- When confused with other views, we ask, can you run me through your reasoning and interpretation of the data? (shared inquiry).
- How did we get from this data to that abstract assumption of yours? (search).
- Is your conclusion your interpretation of mine? Or, vice versa? (dialog).
- I am sorry, what is self-evident to you is not so to me (concession).
- Can we also obtain independent observations of this data and their conclusions? (objective inquiry).
- In case of an impasse, seek ways for designing experiments or inquiry for obtaining new information on the issue at hand (re-search, re-inquiry).
- Avoid building your "case" when someone else is speaking from a different point of view (listening).

Asking such questions or doing this exercise is not easy, cautions Argyris. Nevertheless, this is the essence of team building and team-learning. There is something exhilarating about showing other people the links of your reasoning. They may or may not agree with you, but they can see how you got there. You may often be surprised yourself to see how you got there, once you trace out the links (Senge et al. 1994: 246). Refrain from being defensive when your ideas are questioned. If you are advocating something worthwhile, then it only gets stronger by being tested. Reveal where you are least clear in your thinking and reasoning. Rather than making you vulnerable, it diffuses the force of advocates who are opposed to you, and invites improvement (Senge et al. 1994: 256–57).

"Skilled incompetence" is a premise that most skilled people in day-to-day communication cannot unearth their mental models until they "unlearn" how to protect themselves from feeling threatened. Argyris (1986, 1991), who coined this phrase, strongly believed that most of us could cultivate the intellectual and emotional vulnerability, without having actually to fail. Argyris and Schön (1978) introduce action maps—charts showing how dysfunctional mental models, held by different people in the same organization, reinforce, and influence each other. For instance, two experts in the same department could not agree on resolving a problem in their department. They did not recognize or discuss this lack of disagreement. Instead, they engaged in fancy footwork to avoid facing it, which only heightened the severity of their dilemmas. As more people get involved, these interpersonal dynamics escalate into "secondary inhibiting loops"—coalitions, vested group-thinking, and committees that spend their time second-guessing and outmaneuvering each other. Such futile group dynamics can camouflage errors and destroy open behavior transparency.

One thing is to be open to revise and refine our mental models, and another thing is to practice and live them, and even institutionalize their practice in corporations. Institutionalizing mental models is a practice to think and rethink about our assumptions and generalizations, and thereby, accelerate learning as a whole. Long-term success of our strategic planning and our corporations depends upon the process whereby management teams change their shared mental models of their company, their markets, and their competitors. Planning is learning; corporate planning is organizational learning and both should include sharing and questioning our mental models. We need, what Rich Teerlink, former CEO of Harley-Davidson, calls "circle coaches" (people who possess acute communication, listening, and influencing skills, and are highly regarded by all the circle members) to facilitate getting our mental models into the open, and thereby expedite organizational learning.

Systems thinking, without the discipline of shared mental models, is ineffective. The two disciplines go together. The discipline of mental models focuses on exposing hidden assumptions; the discipline of systems thinking focuses on how to restructure assumptions to reveal causes of significant problems. Entrenched mental models can thwart changes that come from systems thinking. Hence, managers must learn to reflect on their current mental models—until prevailing assumptions are brought into the open, there is no reason to expect mental models to change, and there is little purpose in systems thinking. (Senge 2006: 189). Ultimately, the payoff from integrating systems thinking and mental models will be not only improving our mental models (i.e., what we think) but altering our ways of thinking (i.e., how we think)—shifting from mental models dominated by events to mental models that recognize long-term patterns of change and the underlying structures producing these patterns (Senge 2006: 190).

SHARED VISION

[See Senge (2006: 191–215); Senge et al. (1994: 295–347)]

A vision (from the Latin word *videre*) is a picture of the future you seek to create for yourself (personal vision; e.g., spousal vision, parent vision, career vision), for your group (group vision; e.g., family vision, team vision), or for your organization (organizational vision; e.g., corporate vision, church vision, club vision). It is a statement of where you are, where you want to go, why you want to go there, how to get there, and what you will be like when you get there. The more richly detailed and visual your image of the future is, the better and more compelling is your vision. The vision gives shape and direction to the organization's future (Senge et al. 1994: 302). Values are a central part of an organization and its shared vision.[3] A mission or purpose drives the organization to its desired vision.[4] We may never realize the ultimate mission or purpose of an organization, but you could achieve many visions along the way.

You cannot have a learning organization without a shared vision. A shared vision is not an idea, howsoever noble it might be, such as freedom, honesty, and integrity. It is, rather, a force in people's hearts, a force of impressive power. It may be inspired by an idea, but once it is compelling enough to get support from people, then it is no longer an abstraction. It is palpable and powerful; people are moved by it. It is an overarching goal—the loftiness of the target compels new ways of thinking and acting. In the midst of greatness, pettiness and mediocrity disappear. In the absence of a great vision or a dream, pettiness and mediocrity prevail. A shared vision is also like a rudder to keep the learning process on course when stresses develop. Few forces in human affairs are as powerful as a shared vision.

A vision does not have to come from the top leader. An individual leader's vision may succeed in carrying an organization through a crisis. A shared vision implies a deeper challenge—it creates a sense of purpose that binds people together and propels them to fulfill their deepest aspirations. Catalyzing people's aspirations does not happen by accident; it requires time, care, and strategy. The discipline of building a shared vision is a never-ending process whereby people in an organization articulate their common beliefs, stories, tensions, and anxiety around a vision, purpose, and values, why their work matters, and how it fits in a larger world (Senge et al. 1994: 298).

In its simplest form, a shared vision is an answer to the question: "What do we want to create?" At the organizational level, a shared vision is something that the stakeholders throughout the organization carry in their hearts and heads. The shared vision creates a sense of community that permeates the entire organization and gives unity and coherence to its diverse activities. When people share a common vision,

---

[3] Distinguish a value from a vision. Value (from the French verb *valoir* = to be worth) describes how we intend to operate on a day-to-day basis, and how we intend to pursue and realize our vision. A great vision without good values is terrible. As Bill O'Brien points out, Adolph Hitler's Germany was based on a clear shared vision, but its values were monstrous. Values are best expressed in terms of behavior—for instance, how we want to behave with each other (honesty, forbearance), with our customer (respect, friendliness, honesty), our community (compassion, generosity, cooperation), and our corporation (loyalty, dedication, openness) (Senge et al. 1994: 302).

[4] Vision is not the same as mission or purpose. The word "mission" (from the Latin verb *mittere* = to throw, to let go, to send, to mission) expresses the reason why we are here, the reason of our existence as a person, as a group, as an organization, or as a corporation. The word "purpose" (from the Latin verb *proponere* = to declare, to state) is equivalent to mission, except that the latter has military connotations (Iraq mission; mission accomplished) or religious overtones (missions to the Far East; missionary work).

they are connected and committed to one another having it; they are bound together by a common aspiration. People seek shared vision in order to be anchored and connected. Shared visions derive their power from a common caring. The more lofty the target, the better the shared vision, and vice versa.

Shared vision, accordingly, can be both intrinsic as well as extrinsic; the former focuses on realizing something relative to an insider (e.g., internal standards of excellence, top management's vision, or goals of an innovative charismatic leader), while the latter focuses on achieving relative to an outsider (e.g. competitor, industry champion). An extrinsic shared vision (e.g., defeating a competitor) is something transitory; once that is achieved, the company may move on to something higher, such as being number one in the industry. Both extrinsic and intrinsic visions can co-exist in the same company. But extrinsic visions are limited in scope; such defensive goals rarely call forth creativity, innovation, and passion of building something new. Intrinsic visions, on the other hand, are exhilarating; they lift collective aspirations; they create the spark and excitement, passion and dedication to what we do, just because what we do really matters.

It is impossible to imagine the great accomplishments of some of the following founders and corporations without a shared vision:

- Theodore Vail had a vision of universal telephone service that took 50 years to bring about—the AT&T.
- Henry Ford envisioned common people, not just the wealthy, owning their own automobiles—the Model T.
- Sam Walton's discount store grew from nothing to defeat the giant KMart in 1990, and to grow eight times its size by 2008 to over $350 billion in annual sales—the Wal-Mart.
- Steven Jobs, Steve Wozniak, and their Apple co-founders saw the power of the computer to empower people—the Apple Macintosh platform was born that eventually shaped the look and feel of all operating systems.
- Bill Gates with Paul Allen created the industry leader Microsoft from an under-the-staircase computer den to an empire in less than three decades.
- Michael Dell was a college dropout but a computer repair wiz; his vision makes him the second largest computer retailer in the U.S. today.
- Cannon started from nothing and matched Xerox in less than two decades.
- Komatsu came from behind and matched giant Caterpillar in less than two decades.

These visions of the founders and cofounders were opted shared visions of the thousands who were inspired by them, at all levels of the organization, focusing their energies and creating a common identity among enormously diverse people.

Other things being equal, a shared vision:

- Sets a long-term goal that is worthy of lifetime commitment.
- Establishes an overarching goal; the loftiness of the target compels new ways of thinking and acting.
- Compels courage so naturally that people do not even realize the extent of their coverage; courage is simply doing whatever is needed in pursuit of the vision. All trouble is trivial compared with the importance of what we are trying to create.
- Exposes our ways of thinking with all its flaws and biases, helps us to give up deeply held views, and recognizes personal and organizational shortcomings.

- Forces us to take long-term view of the great things we do, and not short-term fixes; shared vision fosters a long-term view. The Japanese believe that building a great organization is like growing a tree; it takes 25 to 50 years. The creators of classic art, Middle Ages cathedrals, priceless sculptures, and fine arts in music engaged in a lifetime persistent and consistent pursuit.
- Fosters risk-taking and experimentation. When you are immersed in a vision, you may not know how to do it; hence, you run an experiment. You change direction and run another experiment. Everything is an experiment; but there is no ambiguity, because shared vision provides the right direction. But there is no guarantee either; but you are committed nonetheless.

A SUCCESSFUL STRATEGY FOR BUILDING SHARED VISION

In building a shared vision and meaning, we must keep in mind the following precepts (Senge et al. 1994: 298–300):

- Every organization has a destiny: a deep purpose for which the organization exists. It is an emerging purpose that may never fully be spelt out or realized. Choosing to listen continually for that sense of emerging purpose from all stakeholders is shared vision in process.
- One can often find clues to understanding an organization's deeper purpose in the founder's aspirations, and in the reasons why its industry came into being. Organizational vision and mission statements often lack depth because they fail to connect to the industry's overarching reason for existence. For instance, the overarching purpose of the telecommunications industry is to set up a medium for universal communication; that of the medical and pharmaceutical industries is to improve human health; that of the insurance industry is to manage risk by spreading it across populations. When your organization connects to the overarching purpose of its industry, there is a deeper sense of purpose, and there is shared vision.
- Not all visions are equal; those that tap into an organization's deeper sense of purpose, and articulate specific goals that represent making that purpose real, have unique power to engender aspiration and commitment, and to generate a shared vision.
- Many members of an organization who are deeply committed to the organization have a collective sense of its underlying purpose—listening to their sense of purpose generates shared vision. Like mental models, however, this shared sense of purpose may be often *tacit*—obscured by conventional day-to-day practices, the prevailing organizational culture, and the barriers of the organization's structure.
- The art and heart of building a shared vision is to set up open, transparent, and ongoing processes where people at all levels and roles in the organization can speak from the heart about what really matters to them about the organization and be heard by the senior management. A shared vision emerges from a coherent process of reflection and conversation.

All of these precepts suggest that a shared vision should focus around building shared meanings— a collective horizontal (and not vertical) sense of what is important and why. As multiple teams from different departments of the organization meet together and share their meanings and purpose about the organization, the whole organization is engaged and enriched, and multiple strands of shared meaning begin to bind the organization together.

If we treat organizations as communities, and leaders would treat members as those who have chosen to work for the organization, then *the ultimate glue that binds people is not what they get from the organization, but what they contribute to the community.* Top management would not assume formal authority over the members, but see itself as serving the community and its larger vision. Every employee, every team, every department should be encouraged to forge its own shared sense of meaning and its own unique sense of contribution to the whole. Each one should be able to say what he or she has to say about one's vision, purpose, and meaning with perfect freedom, with no limits, encumbrances, or reprisals—this could be a rich database for an emergent shared vision.

Shared visions are spread through personal contact. An organization should set up informal communication networks (e.g., email, e-conferencing, e-bulletins, blogs, Facebook, Twitter, LinkedIn, and YouTube) so that personal contact between all members is facilitated. But nothing can substitute personal interactions in groups.

TEAM LEARNING

[Senge 1990: 233–69, 2006: 216–52; Senge et al. 1994: 349–441]

Team learning is the process of aligning and developing the capacity of a team to create the results its members truly desire. It builds on the discipline of developing shared vision. It also builds on personal mastery, for talented teams are made of talented individuals (Senge 2006: 218).

A successful aligned team has a shared vision, commonality of purpose, goal, and direction; there is an understanding of how to complement one another's skills and efforts, and the energies of team members begin to harmonize. There is less wasted energy. On the contrary, a resonance or synergy emerges and dynamizes the entire team. Individuals do not necessarily sacrifice themselves or their personal interests to the larger team vision—rather, the shared vision and aligned efforts become an extension of their personal vision. Alignment is a necessary condition for team learning and success. Given alignment, individuals get empowered to work together as a team. The teams that need one another to act are the best teams; they form the key unit in the learning organization. The championship sports teams and great jazz ensembles provide metaphors for acting in spontaneous yet coordinated ways that make great teams.

On the other hand, the fundamental characteristic of an unaligned team is wasted energy. Individuals may work extraordinarily hard, but their efforts are not coordinated and do not translate into team effort. There is considerable dissensus, dissipation, and dysfunction among team members. It could be an all-star team with tremendous individual specialized talent, but the talents do not blend; instead, they go in different, and at times, divergent, and destructive directions. In dysfunctional teams there could be powerful forces at work that tend to make the intelligence of the team less than, not greater than, the sum of the intelligence of individual team members. Many of these forces are often within the direct control of the team members.

Individual learning or talent may often be irrelevant for organizational or team learning. Individuals learn at all times, and yet there may not be organizational learning. If teams learn, however, they become a microcosm for learning throughout the organization. Insights gained can translate into action. Skills developed can propagate to other individuals and to other teams. The team's accomplishments can be a benchmark or set the standard for learning together for the larger organization (Senge 2006: 219).

TEAM LEARNING AS A COLLECTIVE DISCIPLINE OF DIALOG AND DISCUSSION

Team learning is a collective discipline. Discipline is execution, making things happen, the sacrifice entailed in doing whatever it takes to realize that vision. Discipline is the embodiment of one's will-power. Discipline defines reality and accepts it; it is the willingness to get totally immersed in it, rather than deny it. It acknowledges the stubborn, brute facts of things as they are, and not as what we want them to be. Happiness is defined as the ability to subordinate what you want now for what you want eventually. Discipline does this—it denies immediate short-term gratification to delayed long-term fulfillment; it sacrifices the present for a future good. Discipline calls for subordination and sacrifice of the current fleeting moment to the lasting joy of a worthy future. Discipline is a trait common to all successful people. Generally, people who spend their time making excuses are those who lack focus and discipline (Covey 2004: 73–75).

The discipline of team learning involves mastering the practices of dialog and discussion, the two distinct ways that teams converse in. In dialog, there is the free and creative exploration of complex and subtle issues, a deep listening to one another and suspending of one's own views. By contrast, in a discussion, different views are presented and defended and there is a search for the best view to sup-port decisions that must be made. Dialog and discussion are potentially complementary, but most teams lack the ability to distinguish between the two and to move consciously between them. Team learning also involves learning how to deal creatively with the powerful forces opposing productive dialog and discussion in working teams. Chief among these are what Chris Argyris called "defensive routines"— these are habitual ways of interacting (e.g., "smoothing over" differences, "winner-take-all" attitudes, "speak out" with no bars, and the like) that protect us and others from threat or embarrassment, but which also prevent us from learning. Yet the very defensive routines that thwart learning also hold great potential for fostering learning, if we can learn how to unlock the energy they contain. The inquiry and reflection skills treated under "mental models" can help in releasing this energy, which can then be focused on dialog and discussion (Senge 2006: 220). Obviously, the discipline of team learning, like in championship sports, orchestra, jazz, and theater, need practice.

Collaborative learning takes place through conversations that involve two primary types of human discourse: dialog and discussion. Both dialog and discussion are important to a team capable of continuous generative learning. Their power, however, lies in their synergy, which may not be present when the distinction between them is not appreciated. "Collaborative learning can be more insightful, more intelligent than we can possible be individually. The IQ of the team can, potentially, be much greater than the IQ of the individuals" (Senge 2006: 221–22).

TEAM LEARNING AND DIALOG

David Bohm, a leading quantum physicist, also developed a theory and method of dialog. Dialog occurs, he said, when a group becomes open to the flow of a larger intelligence. The word "dialog" comes from the Greek root *dia* (= through) and *logos* (= word, or more broadly, meaning). Bohm sug-gested that the original meaning of dialog was the "meaning passing or moving through … a free flow of meaning between people, in the sense of a stream that flows between two banks."

"Quantum theory," argues Bohm, "implies that the universe is basically an indivisible whole, even though on the larger scale level it may be represented approximately as divisible into separate existing parts. In particular, this means that, at a quantum theoretical level of accuracy, the observing instrument and the observed object participate in each other in an irreducible way. At this level, perception and action therefore cannot be separated." The purpose of science is not the "accumulation of knowledge" (since most scientific theories are eventually proven false) but rather the creation of "mental maps" that guide and shape our perceptions and action, bringing about a constant "mutual participation between nature and consciousness" (cited in Senge 2006: 222). In systems thinking, it means that what is happening is often the consequence of our own actions as guided by our perceptions.

Early in his career, Bohm drew an analogy between the collective properties of electronic particles and the way human thought works. Later, he conceded that, unlike the system-wide movements of electronic seas, human thought is basically incoherent, and hence, counter-productive. In order to make human thought coherent, "we must look on thought as a systemic phenomenon arising from how we interact and discourse with one another" (cited in Senge 2006: 223).

The purpose of a dialog, argues Bohm, is to reveal the incoherence of our thought. The contradictions and confusion in our thinking are an indication of our thought-incoherence—that is, our thinking is producing consequences that we do not really want. Bohm identifies three types of thought-incoherence:

1. **Our thought denies that it is participative**. For instance, consider prejudice. Once we stereotype a person or a group, our prejudicial thought becomes an active agent, participating in shaping our conversations, discourse, and dialog, and how we see and how we act.
2. **Thought stops tackling reality** and "just goes, like a program." We are much programmed and conditioned in our thinking, given our upbringing, schools and colleges, and later, workplaces. We are actors playing a role, trapped in the theater of our own thoughts, prejudices, assumptions, and generalizations. Reality may change, but our theater continues. We operate in the theater defining problems and identifying solutions and actions forgetting the larger reality from which the theater is generated.
3. **Thought establishes its own standard of reference** for fixing problems, problems it created in the first place.

The main point of this theory is not to strive for some abstract ideal of coherence. It is rather for all participants to work together to become sensitive to all the possible forms of incoherence. Dialog helps us to see the participatory and representative nature of our thought, to become more sensitive to and acknowledge the incoherence in our thought. In dialog, people become observers of their own thinking. We must distinguish between "thinking" as an ongoing process as distinct from "thoughts" that are results of the process of thinking. Bohm says that this distinction is very important in correcting the incoherence of our thinking. Our thinking may be individual, but our thoughts are mostly collective. For one thing, our language is entirely collective. Our culture is a collective sharing of meanings. Most of our assumptions stem from the pool of culturally accepted assumptions.

Bohm identifies three basic conditions necessary for a dialog (Senge 2006: 226):

a. All participants must suspend their assumptions; suspending assumptions does not mean that you suppress or give them up, but that you hang them in front of you, constantly available for questioning and examination. We cannot do this if we are unaware of our assumptions, or unaware that our views are based on our assumptions. Hence, we cannot suspend assumptions if we over-defend our own rigid or non-negotiable views and opinions.

b. All participants must regard one another as colleagues; this is important, because thought is "participative." The conscious act of thinking of one another as colleagues contributes toward interacting as colleagues; it enables mutual quest for deeper insight and clarity.

c. There must be a "facilitator" who "holds the context" of dialog; otherwise, each participant may force one's views to the discussion, thus pulling away from dialog. Given conditions (a) and (b) the facilitator must keep the process of dialog moving.

These three conditions enable the "free flow of meaning" to pass through a group, by diminishing resistance to the flow. In dialog, suspending assumptions must be done collectively. That is, all participants must suspend their assumptions, even though this is a difficult task. Further, dialog can occur only when a group of people see each other as colleagues. All dialog involves some risk and vulnerability; suspending our assumptions (in as much as they are our mental models and define our identity) also implies some risk and vulnerability; willing to treat each other as friends or colleagues spreads this risk and makes our vulnerability bearable. Choosing to view your adversaries as "colleagues with different view" has the greatest benefits.

Hierarchy is antithetical to dialog. Hierarchy based on power, authority, seniority, past record, leadership, and the like comes with most organizations. But if hierarchy or privilege of rank brings with it dominant views and opinions and top-town strategies, then there is no genuine dialog. Privileges of rank and authority must be surrendered to dialog. Even fears of junior colleagues to speak out must be surrendered to dialog. The artistry of dialog lies in experiencing the flow of meaning and seeing the one thing that needs to be said now (Senge 2006: 229).

Given the foregoing discussion on dialog, Bohm describes several properties of a good dialog:

- In a dialog, a group accesses a larger "pool of common meaning" that we cannot access individually. The whole organizes the parts, rather than the parts trying to pull into a whole. The purpose of a dialog is to go beyond any one individual's understanding.

- In a dialog, we think not in opposition or interaction, but in collaborative participation; we win not individually but collectively, and we gain insights that we could not achieve individually.

- In a dialog, a new kind of mind begins to come into being based on the development of a common meaning, and people participate in this pool of common meaning that is capable of constant development and change.

- In dialog, a group explores complex problems from many viewpoints. Individuals suspend their own assumptions and judgments but communicate them freely. The result is a free exploration that brings to the surface the full depths of people's experience and thought, and yet can move beyond their individual views.

- Hence, when we are engaged in a genuine dialog, the conversations begin to have a "life of their own," taking us in directions we could never have imagined or planned in advance.

- In dialog, people begin to see the stream that flows between the banks. They begin to participate in this pool of common meaning.

- In dialog, a kind of sensitivity develops that goes beyond what is familiar, what we normally recognize as thinking. This sensitivity is a like a "fine net" that gathers the subtle meanings in the flow of thinking. This sensitivity, Bohm believes, lies at the root of real intelligence (Senge 2006: 225).
- For Bohm, dialog is a team discipline; it cannot be achieved individually.

Based on the discussions, Table 12.4 distinguishes the processes of dialog and discussion in resolving complex problems.

LACK OF SHARED VISION AND THE CURRENT COLLAPSE OF FINANCIAL INSTITUTIONS

The financial markets have grown very complicated of late; speculative instruments like credit default swaps, derivatives, and hedge funds have made financial institutions very unstable. In the midst of this financial market turmoil, our contention is that the problem of saving the financial markets is a "wicked" problem, and its resolution must be crafted very carefully, and if possible, without any government intervention. The problem statement and resolution-search should both be within the framework of free market systems, where the free enterprise should be able to design its own correcting mechanisms without governmental control or dependence. Moreover, the unnecessary complexity of most modern speculative financial instruments makes them non-transparent, and the companies that trade these instruments fail to provide a shared corporate vision.

In this context, is federal bailing out a real solution to failing financial institutions? The Federal Reserve Bank bailed out Bear Stearns and AIG, while the U.S. Treasury bailed out both Fannie Mae and Freddie Mac. But the same federal agencies refused to bail out very similar companies like Washington Mutual, Lehman Brothers, Merrill Lynch, Goldman Sachs, and Morgan Stanley when they were in trouble. If Fannie Mae and Freddie Mac were both quasi-government companies and the government was justified in bailing them out, how do we justify the bailout of totally private companies such as Bear Stearns and AIG? Moreover, was federal bailout a good solution to these ailing companies?

Way back in 1973, the government bailed out Chrysler and guaranteed when banks loaned US$8 billion to the failing company. Lee Iacocca, the Chrysler CEO who negotiated the loan, returned the loan within 1978, five years before it was due. But the loan did not cure the problem. Chrysler failed thereafter.

President George Bush Sr. bailed out Savings and Loan Associations using $167 billion of taxpayers' monies in 1987. The S&L Banks have never recovered fully yet. A giant S&L, Washington Mutual, failed recently and is looking for a buyer.

FANNIE MAE AND FREDDIE MAC

Fannie Mae and Freddie Mac hold or guarantee US$5.4 trillion in mortgages and hold or guarantee 42 percent of all home loans. Between the two companies, they lost over $105 billion in market capitalization, a combined loss of 98.7 percent in less than a year (see Table 6.1). Both companies borrowed much too much, almost 50 to 100 times their net worth, and just a drop of one percent in the value of

TABLE 12.4   Distinguishing the Processes of Dialog and Discussion in Resolving Complex Problems

Dimensions	Dialog	Discussion
Definition	A free flow of meanings between people on a complex problem.	A free presentation and defense of one's views on a complex situation.
The Role of Assumptions	All assumptions are suspended or held for scrutiny.	Assumptions underlying individual views are discussed.
Vision	Dialog articulates a unique vision of team learning.	Discussion builds a common view of the problem.
Skills Needed	Skills of reflection and inquiry primarily as mental models hone the team vision.	Skills of reflection and inquiry primarily as carefully weighed viewpoints.
Skills Used	Transparent reasoning that is open to risk and vulnerability.	Defensive reasoning and defensive routines that are less open to risk and vulnerability.
Process and Purpose	You share from a larger pool of meanings that freely flow in a dialog. You explore complex issues and present different views on the complex problem for discovering a new view.	Different views are presented and defended to provide a useful convergent analysis of the complex problem situation.
Process Outcomes	You develop deep trust and respect in order to enable full flow of meanings. You present your view gracefully, while carefully listening to alternative viewpoints. You develop a richer understanding of the uniqueness of each one's view.	You present your view, and discuss it. If time permits, you listen to competing views, and allow controlled discussion. You try to develop a better understanding of the uniqueness of each one's view.
Relationships	Deep trust and respect between team members as colleagues.	Careful analysis of views expressed without prejudice to any team member.
Outcomes	You do not necessarily seek agreement but divergence so that a richer grasp of the complex issues evolves.	You need to reach some convergence, agreement, and decision. You arrive at a final alternative choice and decision.
Focus	The focus of dialog is sharing from a larger pool of meanings.	The focus of discussion is action.
By-products	New actions emerge as by-products of dialog.	The final optimal alternative selected for action.
Consensus	*Open and up*: each participant has a vision and view, a way of looking at reality; each person's view is a unique perspective of a larger reality; I look out through your view and you through mine, so that we each see something new we have not seen alone. Consensus by divergence and enriched disagreement. Consensus by commitment and committed vision.	*Focus and down* to seek a common denominator in multiple individual views. Consensus is built from the content of individual views. Consensus is arrived by convergence and agreement. Consensus by compliance.
Conflicting Issues	Conflicting issues can be a productive fodder for dialog and divergence.	Conflicting issues can be a destructive fodder for discussion and convergence.
Best Use	Best suited for deeply and personally affecting issues such as faith, reciprocal trust, religion, commitment, and passionate dedication to a cause.	Best suited for serious but impersonal issues, problems, and dilemmas such as nature of one's work, markets, products, customers, suppliers, and creditors, competitors, and the like.

Source: Author's own.

Note: See also Senge (2006: 183–90).

their assets landed them in big trouble. The Treasury Department rescued each by US$100 billion on September 15, 2008. However, both CEOs were fired. The federal rescue of these companies, however, puts the U.S. government at least temporarily in charge of providing financing to America's troubled housing market. This deal is at an ultimate cost to taxpayers whose ramifications no one can predict (Gunther 2008: 70).

The problem of Fannie Mae and Freddie Mac can partly be due the Federal Reserve Board's cutting short-term rates to ridiculously low levels over the years. The Fed can cut only short-term rates and not long-term rates. Today the rate is two percent; it was as low as one percent during June 2003–June 2004. Alan Greenspan, Fed Chairman for 18 years, cut short-term rates sharply in reaction to the bubble-pop of the stock market in 2001 and to fears of non-existent deflation in 2003. When the Fed cuts short-term rates to help troubled financial companies, it can cause several unintended consequences, such as big borrowers' bingeing on cheap money. Freddie Mac and Fannie Mae did just that. Even people got carried away by the low short-term teaser mortgage rates. They not only bought houses much bigger than they could afford to pay, they even bought multiple houses on speculation, hoping to flip them at a profit. That drove the housing prices sky high. People kept buying them. The borrowers assumed that when the short-term teaser rates became due, they would be able to refinance with new teasers.

But the Fed started raising short-term rates gradually in June 2004. The lending banks, foreseeing this, discontinued teaser rates and people could not refinance their homes. Meanwhile, the overpriced housing market began tumbling down, and this hurt them. They were paying ridiculously higher premiums based on inflated housing prices but which, by now, had lost over 25 percent of their value at an average. As house prices fell, more loans went into foreclosure. The housing market decline began feeding on itself, and, in turn, threatened U.S. and world financial markets. Ben Bernanke took over as Fed Chairman in 2006 and, as his predecessor, has been bailing out sick financial companies that were basically imprudent (Sloan 2008). "This is welfare for the rich," declared maverick investor Jim Rogers (cited in Gunther 2008: 72). Wall Street claimed federal welfare.

September 16, 2008, the Federal Housing Financing Agency named non-executive chairmen for Freddie Mac (John A. Roskin, a corporate reorganization expert) and Fannie May (Philip A. Laskawy, former head of Ernst & Young), and chief executives for Fannie May (Herbert M. Allison Jr.) and Freddie Mac (David M. Moffert) (*New York Times*, Wednesday, September 17, 2008, A18).

LEHMAN BROTHERS

This storied investment-banking firm sought bankruptcy protection, Monday, September 15, 2008. That was a warning lesson for all of Wall Street. Lehman played, and ultimately lost, a dangerous game involving high stakes bets and huge borrowings. Its reported profits grew attractively through 2007. But to keep its profits growing, Lehman was taking more and more risks. Lehman borrowed too much money, invested it into deals of dubious quality, and then insisted that all was well with the company, when in fact not all was going that well. In August 2007, it announced shutdown of one of its home-lending units.

Lehman Brothers is a 158-year old name but not a firm that old. For decades, Lehman was torn in internal feud between its trader division (led by Dick Fuld) and the banking division (led by Steve Schwarzman and Pete Peterson). The bankers wanted the firm to use its own capital to do deals, and the traders opposed it. The trader–banker war so weakened Lehman that it was sold to American

Express in 1984. Fuld stayed on, while Schwarzman and Peterson founded the Blackstone Group and became billionaires. In 1994, AmEx gave up its financial supermarket strategy, and spun off a small under-capitalized firm called Lehman Brothers, with Dick Fuld as CEO. Fuld, who decades ago had opposed the firm do big and aggressive deals with its own capital, was now indulging in the same.

In October 2007, with the real-estate collapse well underway, Lehman, in partnership with the Tishman Speyer real estate firm, paid US$22.2 billion for a leveraged buyout of a big apartment developer, Archstone. Losses on this deal surfaced almost immediately and Fuld ignored them or refused to talk about them. In February/March 2008, Lehman raised US$5.9 billion by raising stock. In May/June 2008, Lehman tried to find foreign investors as well as domestic investors. In June 2008, Lehman raised US$6 billion in new capital. On September 10, 2008, Lehman announced plans to spin off majority of remaining real estate assets into a new public company, sell majority of its investment-management division, and cut its dividend.

In March 2008, the Fed had bailed out Bear Stearns, and also announced that it would make huge loans available to eligible investment banks. Lehman failed the test of eligibility—it never could regain the confidence and support of the market, the Fed or the Treasury. On September 15, 2008, Lehman Brothers, staggered by losses on its toxic commercial and residential real estate assets, and failing to get federal guarantees to support the company's troubled real estate portfolio, filed for bankruptcy protection of its holding company. In its filing, Lehman listed liabilities of US$613 billion and assets of US$639 billion.

On September 17, 2008, an ex-Morgan Stanley Banker, Robert E. Diamond Jr., president of Barclay's, the British bank, struck a tentative deal to buy Lehman's core capital markets businesses and trading operations for US$1.75 billion. The deal also includes Lehman's Midtown Manhattan headquarters building and two data centers valued at US$1.5 billion. The judge overseeing Lehman's bankruptcy proceedings must approve this deal. Barclay's was interested in Lehman's investment banking and trading platform as part of its strategy to penetrate the American market and to compete with American-based giant investment banks such as Citigroup, JP Morgan Chase, and Bank of America. Mr. Diamond discussed with Lehman's president, Herbert H. McDade III, the benefits of combining Barclay's leading position in Europe with Lehman's strength in the U.S. (White and Dash 2008: C1).

AMERICAN INTERNATIONAL GROUP (AIG)

AIG, the giant insurance company, has an assortment of businesses ranging from aircraft leasing to life insurance for Indians to retirement plans for elementary schoolteachers. The company provided US$440 billion of insurance to investors who bought securities backed by mortgages.

Though the name is American, AIG is rooted in Asia. Its founder, Cornelius Vander Starr, was a World War I veteran, who traveled to Asia with only 300 Japanese Yen (les than US$3 by current exchange rates) and started the company in Shanghai in 1919. With a partner, he sold marine and fire insurance, and expanded rapidly in Philippines, Indonesia, and China by hiring local agents as managers, a business strategy AIG uses even today. Nearly half of AIG's 116,000 direct employees, that is, about 62,000 are in Asia (Glater 2008: C1).

Maurice R. Greenberg, the current CEO of AIG, joined the company in 1960 and has built AIG to create a global empire operating in complementary businesses. Mr. Greenberg focused on making giant commercial deals, increasing its share of the life insurance business, auto insurance, environmental liability insurance, insurance against kidnapping, and protection from suits against the company's officers and directors. AIG claims that its companies are the largest underwriters of commercial and industrial insurance in the U.S.A. Its aircraft leasing business owns more than 900 planes and is part of the company's financial services group. AIG was planning to buy 73 new aircraft in 2008.

Mr. Greenberg had indeed expanded AIG by acquiring hundreds of businesses all over the world. Nevertheless, he was ousted from AIG because of an accounting scandal in 2005. After Greenberg's departure, AIG restated its books over a five year period and instituted conservative new accounting policies. But before the company could rebuild itself, it became embroiled in the home mortgage crisis. The complicated multi-transactional business that led AIG to the brink of bankruptcy is as follows (Andrews 2008: A1):

- Banks write mortgages to home owners and sell them to investment banks.
- The investment banks package the mortgages into securities and sell them to investors.
- To protect investors against defaults, AIG sells insurance on those securities.
- AIG puts up collateral to guarantee it could repay investors, if needed.
- The contracts said that if AIG's credit ratings were cut, it would have to provide additional collateral.
- Concerned about the declining value of AIG's own investment portfolio, the credit rating agencies cut AIG's ratings on Monday, September 15, 2008, forcing the company to put up more collateral.
- If AIG had failed to put up collateral, investors' holdings would have been at risk, perhaps leading to losses around the world.

Moody's planned to lower AIG's credit ratings unless it raised billions of dollars in capital. AIG was desperately seeking capital to avoid a collapse. Despite government's pressure, AIG failed to get a bank loan from JP Morgan Chase or Goldman Sachs to avoid bankruptcy. AIG was a day away from insolvency.

Sunday evening, September 14, 2008, AIG's executives desperately pleaded the government to provide a US$40 billion bridge loan to stave off a crippling downgrade of its credit ratings. Its shares fell by 61 percent on Monday, September 15, 2008, and another 21 percent the next day, Tuesday, to close at US$3.75 per share. With time running out, the same Tuesday, September 16, 2008, acting to avert a possible financial crisis worldwide, the Federal Reserve Bank agreed to an US$85 billion bailout of AIG that would give the government an ownership stake in the troubled insurance giant. Anticipating the deal, the New York Stock Exchange (NYSE) stock market was up by 1 percent on Tuesday and up by 2 percent in early trading in Asian markets on Wednesday morning.

If AIG had collapsed and was unable to pay all of its insurance claims, institutional investors around the world would have been instantly forced to reappraise the value of billions of dollars in debt securities, which in turn would have reduced their own capital and the value of their own debt. Moreover, if AIG was forced to raise the money by liquidating its real estate and other assets at fire sale prices, the move could drive property prices even lower thus forcing countless other companies to mark down the values of their own holdings.

This decision came just two weeks after the Treasury took over the quasi-government mortgage finance companies Fannie May and Freddie Mac. This bailout, however, was the most radical intervention in private business in the history of central banking. The bailout effectively put taxpayer money at risk while protecting bad investments made by AIG (Andrews 2008: A1). Paradoxically, the previous weekend, the Bush administration and Treasury Secretary Mr. Paulson had flatly refused to use taxpayers' money to bail out Lehman Brothers and to avoid the distress sale of Merrill Lynch to Bank of America. In March 2008, the government had bailed out another investment bank, Bear Stearns, by engineering a fire sale to JP Morgan Chase for US$29 billion.

WASHINGTON MUTUAL

Washington Mutual, the nation's largest thrift or savings association based in Seattle, was in a terrible plight. If the government bailed it out, it could half in size its Federal Deposit Insurance Corporation's funds (FDIC, an agency that Congress created during the Great Depression to regulate banks and protect customer accounts), which protect bank depositors at thousands of banks and savings and loan associations. Washington Mutual's stock tumbled as fears spread about financial institutions, and after Standard & Poor's cut its credit to a junk bond rating on Monday, September 15, 2008. The bank has a strong deposit base, but the uncertainty of the financial markets and the declines in housing values have clouded its outlook. Its stock closed at US$2.01 a share on Wednesday, September 17, 2008. With roughly 1.6 billion shares, the thrift has a market value of US$3.4 billion. Given the recent fate of other companies, however, the thrift may be forced to sell for a lesser amount. The bank was up for sale on Wednesday, September 17, 2008, and Morgan Stanley and Wachovia entered merger talks (Fabrikant 2008).

LACK OF SHARED VISION AND TRANSPARENCY

There is much fear about the destructive potential of the complex financial instruments, like credit default swaps, that brought AIG to its knees. The market for such dubious instruments has exploded in recent years, and it is almost entirely unregulated. While bailing out AIG would always stir controversy, the government should crack down regulation on the use of credit default swaps. The swaps are not securities and are not regulated by the SEC. While they perform the same function as an insurance policy they are not insurance in the conventional sense, and so insurance regulators do not monitor them either. AIG's crisis grew primarily out of its financial products unit, which dealt in complex debt securities and credit default swaps. AIG's complex debt securities had already lost billions of dollars in value in the months before the AIG crisis began, primarily because their value depends upon home values. But in two days, September 11–12, 2008, the swaps AIG's financial products unit had sold began eating up billions of dollars of AIG's cash and liquid assets. This ultimately paralyzed AIG as it could not find a way to keep up with increasing cash requirements under the terms of its swap contracts (Andrews 2008: A 18).

Thus, in most of the foregoing cases of collapsed financial institutions, one could make a strong case for lack of buyer–seller information asymmetry, lack of transparency, and lack of corporate shared vision. Moreover, there was hardly any team learning, discussion, and its necessary counterpart, dialog, among stakeholders concerned. In a discussion, we present and defend different views to provide a useful analysis of a given situation. In a dialog, different views are presented as a means toward discovering a new view. In a discussion, we make decisions; in a dialog, we explore complex issues. We need discussion in a team when we must reach some agreement before making decisions; on the basis of a commonly-agreed-upon analysis, we weigh alternative views, and given a productive convergent discussion, we select the best alternative for implementation. In contrast, in a dialog, divergence is expected, and we do not necessarily seek agreement, but a richer grasp of complex issues. Both dialog and discussion can lead to a new course of action; but actions are often the focus of discussion, whereas, new actions emerge as a by-product of dialog.

Imagine if the top executives of Fannie Mae, Freddie Mac, Lehman Brothers, AIG, or Washington Mutual had engaged in serious discussion and dialog with other major stakeholders, their respective disasters would never have happened. Open dialog and discussion foster transparency, information asymmetry reduction and dispel oppressive secrecy—they are the only gateway we know to corporate integrity and executive spiritual development.

CONCLUDING REMARKS

Cultivating creative tension in personal mastery, that is, building a shared vision, and helping people see the systems and mental models of current reality, can move a whole organization forward, because organizations are as propelled by creative tension as individuals are. The first step in organizational learning is learning to generate and manage creative tension within you. The leader has the responsibility to pursue personal mastery, not just for one's own sake, but for everyone else in the organization. Unless the leader has a high degree of self-knowledge and self-understanding, there is the risk that he or she may use the organization for oneself (Senge et al. 1994: 196). This was the origin of corporate fraud.

A dynamic CEO's shared vision is vital for the learning organization because it provides the focus and energy for generative learning. It creates a common mission and identity for all. The work or task is no longer separate from the self. People identify themselves with their company so strongly that they could not define their real self without including their company and their task. Generative learning is expanding your ability to create, and it is abstract and meaningless until people become excited about a vision they truly want to accomplish. A shared vision is not a top management vision imposed top-down. Such a vision, at best, commands compliance, not commitment. A shared vision, in contrast, is one that many people are truly committed to, because it reflects their own personal vision. Generative learning occurs only when people are striving to accomplish something that matters deeply to them. Generative organizational learning is the quintessence of executive spiritual development that this book advocates. Table 12.5 summarizes what corporate leaders and employees with personal mastery can bring to an organization.

In coaching your subordinates in having a personal vision, avoid the temptation to lead them to a vision you prefer. Do not cut them short by saying, "No, that vision is not right for you. Pick another one." Your task is to support people in their personal choices, whether you agree with them or not. Similarly, do not analyze or over-dissect their vision. Help them bring their deep desires to the surface. If people express their personal vision by things they dream or desire (e.g., dream parents, dream education, dream home, dream job, dream wealth, dream spouse, dream family, dream vacation, dream sports vehicle), ask them, "If you could have it now, would you take it?" People are often imprecise about their desires, even to themselves. Probe further: "[W]hat would you do if you had it?" "Assume you have it, what does that bring you?" (Senge et al. 1994: 201–07). People do not want these things as *ends* in themselves but as a *means* for something beyond them. May be you could probe the ultimate ends of their personal vision.

TABLE 12.5   What Corporate Leaders and Employees with Personal Mastery Can Bring to the Organization

Corporate domains	Contributions to energize and empower the organization from:	
	Executive leaders with personal mastery	*Corporate employees with personal mastery*
Assessing Current Reality	They are constantly looking for new ways of doing business in the best way. They are weary of traditional forms and models of employee motivation (e.g., carrots and sticks; doom and gloom speeches). They know that people are not motivated primarily by money, recognition, and fear. They assume that people will commit and contribute because they want to learn, to do good work for its own sake, and to be recognized as people.	Do not belittle yourself. Suspend your doubts, worries, fears, and concerns about the limits of your future. Create a new sense of what you want. If you have doubts about whether you deserve rewards, imagine the rewards you would want if you *did* deserve them. If you are feeling uneasy about something you desire, it can be a clue to potential learning. A year or two from now, it may be yours! Organizations tend to be far more accepting of our goals and interests for ourselves than our fears lead us to expect.
Shared Vision	Leaders develop a vision tapping into the depth of their own heart, mind, aspiration, and spirit. They build aspiration and inspiration by promoting personal mastery. They have a longing to serve something greater than themselves. They will define their personal vision: what they want to create of themselves, the organization, and the world around them. They empower employees to tell you exactly what personal mastery means to them and to the organization as a whole. They desire to have a joyful life for the corporation, its employees, and themselves.	A personal vision is not a done deal, already existing and waiting for you. It is something you create, re-create, throughout your life. Since it is your vision, it cannot run away with you; it can only increase your awareness. Your life has a unique purpose; fulfill it through what you do, your interrelationships, and the way you live. Describe that purpose, as another reflection of your aspirations. Do not denigrate your personal vision and aspirations, your dream university and dream home, your dream spouse and dream vacation. Instead, ask yourself why do you desire these things more than others? Is there a sense of self-fulfillment that is driving your desires?
Investing in Personal Mastery	Leaders develop a personal mastery before they work it on others. Leaders provide conditions for people to develop their capacity to create in the organization what they most care about. They invest time, energy, and money far beyond most managers today consider appropriate to create an environment that helps employees become high-quality contributors. They focus on improving the personal development of their charges.	Employees develop a personal mastery before they work it on other colleagues. Employees provide conditions for peers to develop their capacity to create in the organization what they most care about. They invest quality time, combined energy, and supplementing skills to create an environment that helps fellow employees become high-quality contributors. They focus on improving the personal development of their co-workers.
Passionate Culture	Leaders come to work with enthusiasm and passion, clear vision and commitment, caring and focus. There is an ease, grace, and effortlessness about the way things get done. They coach and guide to enable work to flow seamlessly among teams and across functions. They inject a healthy pride and pleasure in every aspect of the enterprise. They enjoy their leadership roles and want subordinates to enjoy their work too.	Employees come to work with enthusiasm and passion trying to understand the shared vision and commitment of the leader. There is an ease, grace, and effortlessness about the way they do things and get them done. Work flows seamlessly among teams and functions. They take pleasure and pride in every aspect of the enterprise. They enjoy the work they do and relish their collective accomplishments.

Source: Author's own.

Each of them has immeasurable power and capacity to reinvent our lives. Our vision should enable to tap into our own mind and heart, our own voice and energy, and our own unique talent and dream. Our vision should give each of us a sense of unique "calling"—a sense of self, a sense of our own destiny, a sense of our own unique mission and identity, a sense of our unique role in life, a sense of unique purpose and meaning. My vision should guide me to a cause beyond me and bigger than me that is worthy of my commitment.

Our vision does not necessarily stop with our own vision. Our vision should include those of others, especially their unseen potential. Seeing people through the lens of their potential and their best actions, rather than through the lens of their current behavior or weaknesses, generates positive energy that reaches out to embrace others. Vision is more than just getting things done, accomplishing some task, achieving something; it is about discovering and expanding our view of others, affirming them, believing in them, and helping them discover and realize the potential within them—helping them find their own voice; helping them to "learn." This affirming action is also one of the keys to rebuilding broken relationships and to successful parenting. This affirming shared personal vision is the only hope of a broken world on the brink of a World War III. Our revised mental models, our creative tensions, our global team learning capacities are our only peaceful weapons to heal and mend our shattered relationships and our myopic fragmented visions.

A concluding thought. The corporate world, despite its current brokenness and vulnerabilities, can be the savior of a failing world, and not governments and bureaucracies. CEOs of the world arise, unite, and be that beacon of hope through your self-mastery and executive spiritual development, through your revised mental models and your shared personal sacred vision!

BUSINESS TRANSFORMATION EXERCISES

1. Personal mastery needs a personal vision that comes from within us. Vision is applied imagination. Each of them has immeasurable power and capacity to reinvent our lives. Our vision should enable to tap into our own mind and heart, our own voice and energy, and our own unique talent and dream. As a potential CEO, how would you develop a personal vision for your corporation, keeping in mind the following characteristics of a personal vision?

   a. Vision is different from purpose. Purpose is a direction; vision is the destiny. Vision is intrinsic that we pursue for its intrinsic value; purpose may be relative to an end we desire. Purpose may be abstract; vision is concrete. Purpose without vision has no sense of appropriate scale.

   b. Visions are multifaceted. Some are *material facets* as where we want to live, how we want to live, what wealth we need to accumulate, and so on. We may change these relative visions as we grow.

   c. There are *personal facets* to our visions such as health, freedom, honesty, integrity, and accountability.

   d. There are *social facets* to our visions such as compassion, hospitality, kindness, forgiveness, charity, generosity, volunteering, and self-sacrifice. Some of these personal or social facets are relative visions, and some are absolute visions.

   e. Some *corporate facets* to our visions are growth, corporate success, generating jobs, generating new green products, creating wealth, supporting neighboring communities, contributing to national growth, and the like.

   f. Our vision does not necessarily stop with our own vision. Our vision should include those of others, especially their unseen potential.

g. Seeing people through the lens of their potential and their best actions, rather than through the lens of their current behavior or weaknesses, generates positive energy that reaches out to embrace others.

h. Vision is more than just getting things done, accomplishing some task, achieving something; it is about discovering and expanding our view of others, affirming them, believing in them, and helping them discover and realize the potential within them—helping them find their own voice; helping them to "learn."

i. There is great power in viewing people separately from their behavior; when we do this, we affirm their fundamental and unconditional worth. This affirming vision not only frees them to become their best but, in the process, we too are freed from reacting to undesirable behavior.

j. Cultivating the habit of affirming people (that is, frequently and sincerely communicating your belief in them and their potential), especially teenagers who are going through identity crisis, is an important mission of our vision (Covey 2004: 71–73).

k. Most of us do not envision or realize our own potential. "Most people live in a very restricted circle of their potential being. We all have reservoirs of energy and genius to draw upon of which we do not dream" (William James; cited in Covey 2004: 70).

l. Memory is past; it is finite; but vision is future, it is infinite. "Without vision we all suffer from an insufficiency of data. We look at life myopically, that is, through our own lens, our own world. Vision enables us to transcend our own autobiography, our past to rise above our memory" (Covey 2004).

2. Leadership is essentially about realizing change. A prerequisite of a leader is the ability to design and articulate a better future for the company. If there is no vision, there is no leadership. Vision is a capability that can be learned, mostly at the elbow of a master leader (Ibarra and Obodaru 2009: 64–65). In assessing your leadership, the Global Leadership Center, Insead, in Fontainebleau, France, has developed the Global Executive Leadership Inventory (GELI), a 360-degree feedback instrument that identifies critical components of effective leadership. How would you assess your leadership on the following components?

a. **Envisioning**: Articulating a compelling vision, mission, and strategy that incorporate a multicultural and diverse perspective and connect employees, shareholders, suppliers, and customers on a global scale; great leaders inspire others.

b. **Empowering**: This follows envisioning and at all levels of the organization by delegating and sharing information.

c. **Energizing:** Energizing and motivating employees to achieve the organization's goals.

d. **Designing and Aligning**: Creating world-class organizational design and control systems and using them to align the behavior of employees with the values and goals of the organization.

e. **Rewarding and Feedback**: Setting up appropriate reward structures and giving constructive feedback.

f. **Team Building**: Creating team players and focusing on team effectiveness by instilling a cooperative atmosphere, promoting collaboration, and encouraging constructive conflict.

g. **Outside Orientation**: Making employees aware of outside constituencies such as customers, suppliers, shareholders, and other interest groups, including local communities affected by the organization.

h. **Global Mind-set**: Inculcating a global mentality, instilling values that act as a glue between the regional or national cultures represented in the organization.

i. **Tenacity:** Encouraging tenacity and courage in employees by setting a personal example in taking reasonable risks.

j. **Emotional Intelligence**: Fostering trust in the organization by creating (primarily by example) an emotionally intelligent workforce whose members are self-aware and treat others with respect and understanding.

3. As a senior HR manager, you are coaching your struggling subordinates to personal mastery, shared vision, shared mental models, and team learning. Keeping this in mind, how will you handle the following responses, all in relation to the corporation the person works? (Senge et al. 1994: 202–04).

   a. I cannot have what I want.
   b. I want what you want.
   c. It does not matter what I want.
   d. I do not care what I want. I want what is good for the organization.
   e. I already know what I want.
   f. I am afraid of what I want.
   g. I have lost hope. I do not want anything anymore.
   h. I do not know what I want.
   i. I know what I want, but I cannot have it in this organization.
   j. I will do whatever it takes to get what I want.

4. Most of us grow to experience two opposite beliefs about systemic forces that limit us: (*a*) Our basic *powerlessness* or inability to bring into being all the things that we really care about; (*b*) Our basic *unworthiness*—we do not truly deserve to have what we truly desire. We believe in both these opposites, and fight our powerlessness by achievement. Or, we concede to our unworthiness by slowing our achievement. Robert Fritz (1989) calls this aspect of our creative tension a "structural conflict," because it reflects a structure of conflicting forces pulling us toward and simultaneously away from what we really want. Structural conflict complements or explains creative tension. In dealing with structural conflict and creative tension in your present job, how will you resolve them by using the following coping mechanisms?

   a. One systemic force stretches us between our vision and our current perception of reality (this is *creative tension*).
   b. The other systemic force stresses us in the opposite direction and lies between our perception of current reality and our perception of the powerless/unworthiness dyad (this is *structural conflict*).
   c. *Vision erosion*—we erode or compromise our vision.
   d. *Conflict manipulation* or negative vision—we focus on getting away from what we do not want (e.g., anti-smoking, anti-war, anti-drugs, anti-nuclear war policies and efforts) rather than moving toward what we do want.
   e. *Willpower*—we psyche ourselves up to overpower all forms of resistance to achieving our goals. That is, we motivate ourselves through heightened volition.
   f. *Commitment to the truth*: It means a relentless willingness to root out the ways we limit or deceive ourselves from seeing what is, and continually to challenge our theories of why things are the way they are.
   g. *Deploying your sub-conscious*: It is said that human beings possess both a conscious and the subconscious mind, the latter perhaps ten times more potent than the former. The subconscious operates below or behind our conscious mind and awareness.

5. Mental models are the images, assumptions, and stories that we carry in our minds of ourselves, other people, institutions, and every aspect of the world. We are bound by our mental models; they are active; they shape how we act. We make sense of the world around us and take action through our mental models. Examine your mental models in relation to your job and the company against the following basic properties of mental models:

   a. *We are our mental models*. We do not carry our family, our work, our organizations, and our corporations in our minds, but do in our heads, heart, and spirit.

b. *Mental models determine what we see.* Our mental models affect us as to what we see and how we see reality. They determine our selective observations. They shape our perceptions.

c. *Mental models shape how we act.* For example, if we believe that people are basically trustworthy, we will talk to new acquaintances much more freely than if we believed that people are not trustworthy.

d. *Mental models are usually "tacit."* Existing below the level of awareness, they are often untested and unexamined; hence, could be flawed.

e. *All mental models are simplifications of reality around us;* hence, they cannot be good or bad, right or wrong.

f. *All mental models resist changing.* As the world keeps on changing, the gap between our mental models and reality widens, leading to increasingly counter-productive decisions and actions. Unquestioned models can be disastrous.

g. *We do not have any anointed or authorized mental models.* The goal in practicing the discipline of mental models is not necessarily agreement or convergence. Many divergent and disagreeing mental models can co-exist.

h. *All mental models need to be tested.* We need to examine them and periodically test them against situations that come up. This requires an organizational commitment to "truth"—an outgrowth of personal mastery.

6. According to the management consultant Ian Mitroff (1988), the domestic auto executives entertained several long-standing and unquestioned assumptions about the car world as necessary conditions for success. How will you question, examine, and contest the validity of the following:

   a. The auto companies are in the business of making money, not cars.
   b. American car buyers and users mostly care about styling.
   c. Cars are primarily status symbols; styling therefore is more important than quality.
   d. Hence, American consumers need many models with different styles.
   e. Our customers do not buy cars on price; they only care about prompt delivery.
   f. The American car market is isolated from the rest of the world.
   g. Workers do not have an important impact on auto productivity or product quality.
   h. Everyone working in the auto system has no need for more than a specific, fragmented, compartmentalized understanding of the auto business.
   i. Which of these are "espoused theories" or "theory in use," and why?
   j. Which of these are "leaps of abstraction," and why?
   k. Which of these represent "left-hand column thinking," and why?
   l. Which of these represent "pure inquiry," "pure advocacy," or "balancing of inquiry and advocacy," and why? (See Table 12.1)

7. Tables 12.2 and 12.3 indicate there are alternatives to ways to think, to look at complex issues, judge ethically and morally, and, accordingly, execute actions. The Western versus the oriental approaches help us to break down the walls of cultural, national, and continental boundaries. The two approaches combined can have a profound impact on revising, refining, and expanding our mental models. Most of the time, all we have is our mental models of assumptions and generalizations, never "truths," and we always see the world through our mental models. Our mental models are very incomplete, and often chronically non-systemic. How would you use the following oriental insights from Table 12.2 to revise your Western mental models?

   a. *Claims:* Our claims are experiences of our social obligations versus social privileges; they are primarily communal and social privileges to serve society and country.

b. *Primacy*: Social primacy is over individual primacy; the country and society come first, we follow. We owe primary loyalty and allegiance to the country and society; the latter will protect us.

c. *Rights*: Rights are shared privileges at best; we must collectively work and seek them.

d. *Work*: Work is our collective impression of our personalities and talents on matter; work is a social privilege and duty; we work for society and our country.

e. *Change*: Change is natural, eternal, cyclic, and recursive; it is always for the better, unless we distort it; we change as nature changes and evolves; we change with nature; change is evolution and harmony.

f. *Current Reality:* Current reality is an ally, an opportunity and a gift; we created it; let us fathom and make most of it.

g. *Nature:* Nature is sacred; it is sacred space; it is a shared and sharing opportunity; nature must be revered and respected; it is best shared together and for posterity.

h. *Time:* Time is cyclic, recursive, and repetitive; it is free and unlimited; time is an ally, work with it. Time is a social resource; time spent for society is time spent for us.

i. *Privacy:* Privacy is social and collective; it is society's gift to me for the growth of society. Shared disclosures strengthen privacy; mutual transparency or open society build communities.

j. *Culture:* Shared and inherited social meanings and values, grand historical narratives and hyper-norms. We share, celebrate, and leave for posterity social values and meanings that reinforce our collective lives, vision, and destiny.

8. Table 12.3 indicates there are alternatives to ways to think and judge the morality of executive acts as opposed to the Western ethical systems of morality and virtue. The two approaches combined can have a profound impact on revising, refining, and expanding our mental models. How would you deploy the oriental ethical systems of thought and judgment as described in Table 12.3 to revise your Western mental ethical models?

a. *Deontology*: That act of ours is moral that safeguards maximum number of social rights and obligations.

b. *Utilitarianism*: That act of ours is moral that has the highest social benefits over social costs accruing to the greatest number.

c. *Justice*: That act of ours is moral that equitably distributes social rights and duties, social costs and benefits across the greatest number of stakeholders.

d. *Responsibility*: That act of ours is moral that best fulfills our responsibility to people affected by our decisions and actions.

e. *Trusting Relationship*: That act of ours is moral that generates the best reciprocal trust among all individuals in a group or society.

f. *Compassion*: That act of ours is moral that promotes maximum compassion unto all the marginalized.

g. *Generosity*: That act of ours is moral that empowers our self-less generosity to one another.

h. *Commitment*: That act of ours is moral that ensures the highest commitment to the other cause or person.

i. *Loyalty*: That act of ours is moral that best reflects our unconditional loyalty to one another.

j. *Culture*: That act of ours is moral that best reflects and reinforces our positive cultural values.

Bibliography

Abbott, A. (1990) "Conceptions of Time and Events in Social Science Methods," *Historical Methods*, 23: 140–50.

Abernathy, W. and K. B. Clark (1985) "Mapping the Wings of Creative Destruction," *Research Policy*, 14: 3–22.

Achrol, Ravi S. (1991) "Evolution of the Marketing Organization: New Forms of Turbulent Environments," *Journal of Marketing*, 55(October): 77–93.

Achrol, Ravi S. and Philip Kotler (1999) "Marketing in the Network Economy," *Journal of Marketing*, 63(Special Issue): 146–63.

Achrol, Ravi S., Torger Reve, and Louis W. Stern (1983) "The Environment of Marketing Channel Dyads: A Framework for Comparative Analysis," *Journal of Marketing*, 47(Fall): 55–67.

Ackerman, R. W. (1975) *The Social Challenge to Business*. Cambridge, MA: Harvard University Press.

Ackerman, R. W. and R. A. Bauer (1976) *Corporate Social Responsiveness*. Reston, VA: Reston Publishing.

Ackoff, Russell L. (1974a) "Beyond Problem Solving," *Decision Sciences*, 5(2): 10–15.

——— (1974b) *Re-designing the Future: A Systems Approach to Societal Problems*. New York: John Wiley & Sons.

——— (1978) *The Art of Problem Solving*. New York: Wiley.

——— (1979) "The Future of Operational Research is Past," *Journal of Operational Research Society*, 30(2): 94–104.

——— (1981) "The Art and Science of Mess Management," *Interfaces*, 11(1): 20–26.

——— (1981a) *Creating the Corporate Future: Plan or be Planned For*. New York: John Wiley & Sons.

——— (1981b) "The Art and Science of Mess Management," *Interfaces*, 11(1): 20–26.

Ackoff, Rusell L. and Daniel Greenberg (2008) *Turning Learning Right Side Up: Putting Education Back on Track*. Philadelphia, PA: Wharton School Press.

Ackoff, Rusell L. and Fred E. Emery (1972) *On Purposeful Systems*. Chicago, IL: Aldine Atherton.

Adner, Ron (2006) "Match your Innovation Strategy to your Innovation Ecosystem," *Harvard Business Review*, 84(4, April): 98–106.

Afuah, Allan N. (1998) *Innovation Management*. Oxford: Oxford University Press.

Afuah, Allan N. and N. Bahram (1995) "The Hypercube of Innovation," *Research Policy*, 24: 51–76.

Agnew, Jean-Christopher (1986) *Worlds Apart*. Cambridge: Cambridge University Press.

Ahuja, Gautam and Riitta Katila (2001) "Technological Acquisitions and the Innovation Performance of Acquiring Firms: A Longitudinal Study," *Strategic Management Journal*, 22(3): 197–220.

Aiello, Robert J. and Michael D. Watkins (2001), "The Fine Art of Friendly Acquisition," in *Harvard Business Review on Mergers and Acquisitions*, pp. 23–44. Harvard Business School Press.

Ajami, Riad and Dara Khambata (1991) "Global Strategic Alliances: The New Transnational," *Journal of Global Marketing*, 5(1/2): 55–69.

Akaah, Ishmael P. (1989) "Differences in Research Ethics Judgments between Male and Female Marketing Professionals," *Journal of Business Ethics*, 8(May): 375–82.

Alba, J. W. and J. W. Hutchinson (1987) "Dimensions of Consumer Expertise," *Journal of Consumer Research*, 13: 411–54.

Alderson, Wroe (1957) *Marketing Behavior and Executive Action*. Homewood, IL: Irwin.

——— (1964) "Ethics, Ideologies and Sanctions," in *Report of the Committee on Ethical Standards and Professional Practices*. Chicago: American Marketing Association.

Alexander, Lamar (2009) "The Three Year Solution: How the Reinvention of Higher Education Benefits Parents, Students, and Schools," *Newsweek*, October 26: 26–33.

Alexander, Marcus and Harry Korine (2008) "When you Shouldn't Go Global," *Harvard Business Review*, 86(12): 70–77.

Allmendinger, Glen and Ralph Lombreglia (2005) "Four Strategies for the Age of Smart Services," *Harvard Business Review*, 83(10): 131–45.

Althusser, L. (1970) *For Marx*, translated by Ben Brewster. New York: Vintage Books.

Althusser, L. and E. Balibar (1970) *Reading Capital*, translated by Ben Brewster. New York: Vintage Books.

Amabile, Teresa M. (1983) *The Social Psychology of Creativity*. New York: Springer–Verlag.

——— (1998) "How to Kill Creativity," *Harvard Business Review*, 76(5, September–October): 77–88.

Amit, Raphael and Paul J. H. Schoemaker (1993) "Strategic Assets and Organizational Rent," *Strategic Management Journal*, 14(1): 33–36.

Anand, Jaideep and Harbir Singh (1997) "Asset Redeployment, Acquisitions and Corporate Strategy in Declining Industries," *Strategic Management Journal*, 18(Summer Special Issue): 99–118.

Anderson, B. (1999) "Industrial Benchmarking for Competitive Advantage," *Human Systems Management*, 18(3/4): 287–96.

Anderson, Erin (1988) "Transaction Costs as Determinants of Opportunism in Integrated and Independent Sales Forces," *Journal of Economic Behavior and Organization*, 9 (May): 247–64.

Anderson, Erin, Håkan Håkansson, and Jan Johansson (1994) "Dyadic Business Relationships within a Business Network Context," *Journal of Marketing*, 58(October): 1–15.

Anderson, James C. and James A. Narus (1990) "A Model of Distributor Firm and Manufacturer Firm Working Partnerships," *Journal of Marketing*, 54(January): 42–58.

Anderson, Philip and Michael L. Tushman (1991) "Managing through Cycles of Technological Change," *Research Technology Management*, 34(3): 26–31.

——— (1990) "Technological Discontinuities and Dominant Design: A Cyclical Model of Technological Change," *Administrative Science Quarterly*, 35(4): 604–33.

Andreasen, Alan R. (1975) *The Disadvantaged Consumer*. New York, NY: The Free Press.

——— (1982) "Disadvantaged Hispanic Consumers: Research Perspectives and Agenda," *Journal of Consumer Affairs*, 16(Summer): 46–61.

——— (1993) "Revisiting the Disadvantaged: Old Lessons and New Problems," *Journal of Public Policy and Marketing*, 12(Fall): 270–75.

——— (1995) *Marketing Social Change: Changing Behavior to Promote Health, Social Development and the Environment*. San Francisco: Jossey Bass.

——— (1997) "From Ghetto Marketing to Social Marketing: Bringing Social Relevance to Mainstream Marketing," *Journal of Public Policy and Marketing*, 16(Spring): 129–31.

——— (2002) "Marketing Social Marketing in the Social Change Marketplace," *Journal of Public Policy and Marketing*, 21(1): 3–14.

Andreasen, Alan R. and Jean Manning (1990) "The Satisfaction/Dissatisfaction and Complaining of Vulnerable Consumers," *Journal of Consumer Satisfaction/Dissatisfaction and Complaining Behavior*, 3: 12–20.

Andrew, James P. and Harold L. Sirkin (2003) "Innovating for Cash," *Harvard Business Review*, 81(9): 76–85.

Andrews, Edmund L. (2008) "Fed in $85 Billion Bailout Plan of Faltering Insurance Giant," *The New York Times*, Wednesday, September 17 pp. A1, A18.

Andrews, Jonlee and Daniel C. Smith (1996) "In Search of the Marketing Imagination: Factors Affecting the Creativity of Marketing Programs for Mature Products," *Journal of Marketing Research*, 33(May): 174–87.

Andrews, Kenneth R. (1971) *The Concept of Corporate Strategy*. Homewood, IL: Dow Jones Irwin.

Andrews, Lori B. (2005) "Patents on Human Genes: An Analysis of Scope and Claims," *Science*, 307: 1566–67.

Ansari, Asim and Carl Mela (2003) "E-Customization," *Journal of Marketing Research*, 40(May): 131–45.

Anscombe, Elizabeth G. (1958) "Modern Moral Philosophy," *Philosophy*, 33(January): 1–19.

Ansoff, Igor H. (1965) *Corporate Strategy*. New York: McGraw-Hill.

Anthony, Scott D., Matt Eyring, and Lib Gibson (2006) "Mapping your Innovation Strategy," *Harvard Business Review*, 84(5): 104–13.

Argyris, Chris (1986) "Skilled Incompetence," *Harvard Business Review*, 64(4): 74–79.

———— (1991), "Teaching Smart People how to Learn," *Harvard Business Review*, 69(3): 99–109.

———— (1993) *Knowledge for Action*. San Francisco, CA: Jossey-Bass.

———— (1996) *Organizational Learning II: Theory, Method, and Practice*. Reading, MA: Addison-Wesley Longman.

Argyris, Chris and Donald A. Schön (1978) *Organizational Learning: A Theory of Action Perspective*. Reading, MA: Addison-Wesley.

Aristotle (1985) *Nicomachean Ethics*, translated by Terrence Irwin. Indianapolis: Hacket Publishing Company.

Armstrong, Arthur and John Hagel III (1996) "The Real Value of On-Line Communities," *Harvard Business Review*, 74(May/June): 134–41.

Arndt, Johan (1979) "Toward a Concept of Domesticated Markets," *Journal of Marketing*, 43(Fall): 69–75.

———— (1983) "The Political Economy Paradigm: Foundation for Theory Building in Marketing," *Journal of Marketing*, 47(Fall): 44–54.

Arrow, K. J. (1974) *The Limits of Organizations*. New York: Norton.

Arrow, Kenneth J. (1993) "Social Responsibility and Economic Efficiency," in Thomas Donaldson and Patricia H. Werhane (eds), *Ethical Issues in Business* (4th edition), pp. 255–66. Englewood Cliffs, NJ: Prentice Hall.

Arun, Ravi and Jitendra V. Singh (2005) "Getting Offshoring Right," *Harvard Business Review*, 83(11):135–43.

Ashforth, B. E. and B. W. Gibbs (1990) "The Double-edge of Organizational Legitimation," *Organization Science*, 1(2): 177–94.

Ashkenas, Ronald, Demonaco Lawrence, and Suzanne Francis (2001) "Making the Deal Real: How GE Capital Integrates Acquisitions," *Harvard Business Review on Mergers and Acquisitions*, pp. 185–199.

Ashworth, Jon (2008) "B of A's Bid for Countrywide is a Canny Move," *The Business*, London, January 19, p. 1.

Associated Press (2008) "Big Cities Battle Dismal Graduation Rates: Less than 50 Percent of High School Students Graduate in 17 of U.S.'s Largest Cities," Washington, April 1, p. A1.

Astley, W. Graham (1984) "Toward an Appreciation of Collective Strategy," *Academy of Management Review*, 9(3): 526–35.

Astley, W. Graham and Charles J. Fombrun (1983) "Collective Strategy: Social Ecology of Organizational Environments," *Academy of Management Review*, 8(4): 576–87.

Austin, John (2006) *The Vital Center: A Federal-State Compact to Renew the Great Lakes Region*. The Brookings Institution Metropolitan Policy Program.

Azevedo, Marcello De Carvalho (1982) *Inculturation and the Challenge of Modernity*. Rome: Pontifical Gregorian University.

Bahm, Archie J. (1975) "Planners' Failures Generate a Scapegoat," *Policy Sciences*, 6: 103–05.

Bajaj, Vikas (2008) "New Phase in Finance Crisis as Investors Run to Safety," *The New York Times*, Thursday, September 18, pp. A1, A 28.

Baker, Stephen and Manjeet Kripalani (2004) "Software: Will Outsourcing Hurt America's Supremacy?" *Business Week*, NY (Special Report), March 1, pp. 84–95.

Balachander, Subramanian and Sanjoy Ghose (2003) "Reciprocal Spillover Effects: A Strategic Benefit of Brand Extensions," *Journal of Marketing*, 67(1, January): 4–13.

Barbaro, Michael (2008) "Retailing Chains Caught in a Wave of Bankruptcies," *The New York Times*, Tuesday, April 15, pp. A1, A16.

Barney, Jay B. (1986a) "Strategic Factor Markets: Expectations, Luck, and Business Strategy," *Management Science*, 32: 1231–41.

———— (1986b) "Organizational Culture: Can it be a Source of Sustained Competitive Advantage?" *Management Review*, 11(July): 656–65.

———— (1991) "Firm Resources and Sustained Competitive Advantage," *Journal of Management*, 17(March): 99–120.

———— (1991) *Gaining and Sustaining Competitive Advantage*. Prentice-Hall.

———— (2001a) *Gaining and Sustaining Competitive Advantage*. New York: Prentice-Hall.

———— (2001b) "Is the Resource-based 'View' a Useful Perspective for Strategic Management Research? Yes," *The Academy of Management Review*, 26(1, January): 41–57.

Barthes, Roland (1972) *Mythologies*, translated by Annette Lavers. London: Cape.

Basadur, M. (1989) *Creative Problem Solving*. Ancaster, Ontario, Canada: Center for Research in Applied Creativity.

Bassi, Laurie and Daniel McMurrer (2007) "Maximizing your Return on People," *Harvard Business Review*, 85(3): 115–24.

Bates, K. and J. Flynn (1995), "Innovation History and Competitive Advantage," *Academy of Management Journal*, Best Paper Proceedings, pp. 235–39.

Bateson, G. (1971) *Steps to an Ecology of Mind*. New York: Balentine.

Baumhart, Raymond C. (1961) "How Ethical are Businessmen?" *Harvard Business Review*, 39(6–19, July–August): 156–76.

Bear, John C. (2004) "What's my DNA Worth, Anyway? A Response to the Commercialization of Individuals' DNA Information," *Perspectives of Biology and Medicine*, 47(2): 271–85.

Becker, Katrin (2007) "Conceptual Framework for Considering Instructional Design as a Wicked Problem," *Canadian Journal of Learning and Technology*, 33(1): 85–108.

Becker, Mathias M. and Michael J. Shelton (2002) "Keeping your Sales Force after the Merger," *The McKinsey Quarterly*, 4: 106–15.

Belk, Russell W. (1985) "Materialism: Trait Aspects of Living in the Material World," *Journal of Consumer Research*, 12(4): 265–80.

——— (1988) "Possessions and the Extended Self," *Journal of Consumer Research*, 15(September): 136–69.

Bell, Daniel (1973) *The Coming of the Post-Industrial Society*. New York: Basic Books.

——— (1976) *The Cultural Contradictions of Capitalism*. New York: Basic Books.

Bellah, Robert N., Richard Madsen, William M. Sullivan, Ann Swidler, and Steven M. Tipton (1985) *Habits of the Heart: Individualism and Commitment in American Life*. New York, NY: Harper and Row.

——— (1991) *The Good Society*. New York: Alfred A. Knopf.

——— (1992) *The Good Society*. New York: Vintage Books.

Belo, Fernando (1981) *A Materialist Reading of the Gospel of Mark*. Maryknoll, NY: Orbis Books

Bennett, Roger. C. and Robert G. Cooper (1979) "Beyond the Marketing Concept," *Business Horizons*, (June): 76–83.

——— (1981) "The Misuse of Marketing: An American Tragedy," *Business Horizons*, 24(November–December): 51–61.

Bennis, Warren G., and Robert J. Thomas (2002) *Geeks and Geezers: How Era, Values, and Defining Moments Shape Leaders*. Boston: Harvard Business School Publishing.

Benson, Peter (1992) "The Basis of Corrective Justice and its Relation to Distributive Justice," *Iowa Law Review*, 77: 515–28.

Bernstein, R. (1983) *Beyond Objectivism and Relativism*. Philadelphia: University of Pennsylvania Press.

Berry, Leonard L., Lewis P. Carbone, and Stefan H. Haeckel (2002) "Managing the Total Customer Experience," *Sloan Management Review*, MIT, 43(3, Spring): 85–90.

Bierly, Paul and Alok Chakrabarti (1996) "General Knowledge Strategies in the U. S. Pharmaceutical Industry," *Strategic Management Journal*, 17(Winter Special Issue): 123–35.

Birkinshaw, Julian, Henrik Bresman, and Lars Hakanson (2000) "Managing the Post-Acquisition Integration Process: How the Human Integration and Task Integration Processes Interact to Foster Value Creation," *Journal of Management Studies*, 37(3): 395–425.

Black, M. (1955/1981) "Metaphor," *Proceedings of the Aristotelian Society*, 55: 273–94.

Blair, Elizabeth and Eva Hyatt (1995) "The Marketing of Guns to Women," *Journal of Public Policy & Marketing*, (Spring): 117–27.

Bleeke, Joel and David Ernst (1991a) *Collaborating to Compete*. Somerset, NJ: John Wiley and Sons.

——— (1991b) "The Way to Win in Cross-Border Alliances," *Harvard Business Review*, 69(6, November–December): 127–35.

Block, Peter (1993) *Stewardship: Choosing Service over Self-Interest*. San Francisco, CA: Berrett-Koehler Publishers.

——— (1991) *The Empowered Manager: Positive Political Skills at Work*. San Francisco, CA: Jossey-Bass.

Bloom, William (2001) *The Endorphin Effect*. London, U.K.: Judy Piatkus Publishers.

Blythe, Stuart, Jeffrey T. Grabill, and Kirk Riley (2008) "Action Research and Wicked Environmental Problems," *Journal of Business and Technical Communication*, 22(3, July): 272–98.

Boland, Richard and Fred Collopy (2004) *Managing as Designing*. Stanford, CA: Stanford University Press.

Bollier, David (1997) *Aiming Higher*. Chicago: Amacom.

Booz, E., J. Allen, and C. Hamilton (1982) *New Products Management for the 1980s*. Chicago, IL: Booz, Allen, Hamilton Ltd.

Borgmann, Albert (2000) "The Moral Complexion of Consumption," *Journal of Consumer Research*, 26(4): 418–22.

Bossidy, Larry and Ram Charan (2002) *Execution: The Discipline of Getting Things Done*. New York: Crown Business.

Bourdieu, Pierre (1984) *Distinction: A Social Critique of the Judgment of Taste*. Cambridge, MA: Harvard University Press.

Bourgeois, Leonard Jay III (1984) "Strategic Management and Determinism," *Academy of Management Review*, 9(4): 586–96.

Bowen, H. and Margaret Wiersema (1999) "Matching Method to Paradigm in Strategy Research: Limitations of Cross-Sectional Analysis and Some Methodological Alternatives," *Strategic Management Journal*, 20: 625–36.

Bower, J. L., and C. M. Christensen (1995) "Disruptive Technologies: Catching the Wave," *Harvard Business Review* 73(1, January–February): 43–53.

Bowman, C. and V. Ambrosiani (2000) "Value Creation versus Value Capture: Towards a Coherent Definition of Values in Strategy," *British Journal of Management*, 11(1): 1–15.

Bradach, Jeffery L., Thomas J. Tierney, and Nan Stone (2008) "Delivering on the Promise of Non-profits," *Harvard Business Review*, 86(11): 88–97.

Bradstone (2008) "The Empire of Excess: Lax Real Estate Decisions Hurt Starbucks," *The New York Times*, Friday, July 4, 2008, C1 and C2.

Brandt, Steve and Chris Havens (2008) "Cities Consider going after Lenders," *McClatchy-Tribune Business News*, Washington, February 2.

Breen, Timothy H. (1993) "The Meaning of Things: Interpreting the Consumer Economy in the Eighteenth Century," in John Brewer and Roy Porter (eds), *Consumption and the World of Goods*, pp. 249–60. London: Routledge.

Brenkert, George (2002) "Social Products Liability: The Case of Firearms Manufacturers," *Journal of Public Policy and Marketing*, 21(1): 14–25.

Breyer, Ralph (1934) *The Marketing Institution*. New York: McGraw Hill.

Brightman, H. J. (1988) *Group Problem Solving: An Improved Managerial Approach*. Atlanta: Business Publishing Division, Georgia State University.

Brinkley, Peg (2003a) "Pharmacogenomics Fire Sale," TheScientist.com, April 4. Available online at http://www.the-scientist.com/news/20030404/02/

———— (2003b) "Sobriety amid Celebration," TheScientist.com, April 14. Available online at http://www.the-scientist.com/article/display/21260

Brown, S. L. and K. M. Eisenhardt (1995) "Product Development: Past Research, Present Findings, and Future Directions," *Academy of Management Journal Review*, 20: 343–78.

Brown, Stephen, Robert V. Kozinets, and John F. Sherry, Jr. (2003) "Teaching Old Brands New Tricks: Retro Branding and the Revival of Brand Meaning," *Journal of Marketing*, July, 67(3): 19–33.

Brown, Tim (2008) "Design Thinking," *Harvard Business Review*, 86(6): 84–92.

Brown, Tom J. and Peter A. Dacin (1997) "The Company and the Product: Corporate Associations and Consumer Product Responses," *Journal of Marketing*, 61(January): 68–84.

Brownie, Douglas (2000) "Benchmarking Your Marketing Process," *Long Range Planning*, 32(1): 88–95.

Buchholz, Rogene A. (1993) *Principles of Environmental Management: The Greening of Business*. Englewood Cliffs, NJ: Prentice-Hall Inc.

Buckingham, Marcus and Donald O. Clifton (2001) *Now, Discover Your Strengths*. New York: The Free Press.

Bucklin, Louis P. and Sanjit Sengupta (1993) "Organizing Successful Co-Marketing Alliances," *Journal of Marketing*, 57(April): 32–46.

Buehler, Kevin, Andrew Freeman, and Ron Hulme (2008) "Owning the Right Risks," *Harvard Business Review*, 86(8): 102–10.

Burke, K. (1962) *A Grammar of Motives and a Rhetoric of Motives*. New York: The World Publishing Co.

Business Week (2008) "Ken Lewis on why B of A is Buying Countrywide," January 28, New York, p. 19.

Büyükdamgacr, Güldal (2003) "Process of Organizational Problem Definition: How to Evaluate and How to Improve," *Omega*, 31(4, August): 327–38.

Calhoun, John (2001) "Driving Loyalty: By Managing the Total Customer Experience," *Ivey Business Journal*, 65(6): 69–79.

Calmes, Jackie (2009) "House Approves $819 Billion Plan for Economic Aid," *New York Times*, Thursday, January 29, pp. A1, A15.

Camillus, John C. (1996) "Reinventing Strategic Planning," *Strategy & Leadership*, 24(3, May–June): 6–7.

——— (2008) "Strategy as a Wicked Problem," *Harvard Business Review*, 86(5): 98–106.

Camp, Robert C. (1989) *Benchmarking: The Search for Best Practices that Lead to Superior Performance*. Milwaukee, WI: ASQC Quality Process.

——— (1995) *Business Process Benchmarking: Finding and Implementing Best Practices*. Milwaukee, WI: ASQC Quality Process.

Campbell, Andrew (2004) "Stop Kissing Frogs," *Harvard Business Review*, (July–August): 27–28.

Campbell, Andrew, Jo Whitehead, and Sydney Finkelstein (2009) "Why do Good Leaders Make Bad Decisions," *Harvard Business Review*, 87(2): 60–67.

Capon, Noel and Rashi Glazer (1987) "Marketing and Technology: A Strategic Co-Alignment," *Journal of Marketing*, 51(July): 1–14.

Capraro, Anthony J. and Rajendra K. Srivastava (1997) "Has the Influence of Financial Performance on Reputation Measures been Overstated?" *Corporation Reputation Review*, 1(1): 86–93.

Carbone, Lewis P. and Stephan H. Haeckel (1994) "Engineering Customer Experiences," *Marketing Management*, 3(Winter): 8–19.

Carey, Dennis (2000) "A CEO Roundtable on Making Mergers Succeed," *Harvard Business Review*, 78(3): 145–54.

——— (2001) "Lessons from Master Acquirers: A CEO Roundtable on Making Mergers Succeed," in *Harvard Business Review on Mergers and Acquisitions*, pp. 1–22. Cambridge, U.K.: Oxford University Press.

Carroll, Paul B. and Chunka Mui (2008) *Billion-Dollar Lesson: What you can Learn from the most Inexcusable Business Failures of the Last 25 Years*. New York: Penguin Group.

Cavanagh, Gerald F. (2006) *American Business Values: A Global Perspective* (5th edition). Englewoods Cliffs, New Jersey: Prentice-Hall.

Chaffee, John (1988) *Thinking Critically* (2nd edition). Boston, MA: Houghton Mifflin Co.

Chakrabarti, Alok K. (1990) "Organizational Factors in Post Acquisition Performance," *IEEE Transactions and Engineering Management*, 37(4): 259–68.

Chakravorti, Bhaskar (2004) "The New Rules for Bringing Innovations to Market," *Harvard Business Review*, 82(3): 58–67.

Chandler, A. (1992) "Organizational Capabilities and the Economic History of the Industrial Enterprise," *Journal of Economic Perspectives*, 6: 79–100.

Chandler, G. N. and S. H. Hanks (1994) "Market Attractiveness, Resource-based Capabilities, Venture Strategies, and Venture Performance," *Journal of Business Venturing*, 9: 331–49.

Chandy, Rajesh K. and Gerard J. Tellis (1998) "Organizing for Radical Product Innovation: The Overlooked Role of Willingness to Cannibalize," *Journal of Marketing Research*, 35(November): 474–87.

——— (2000) "The Incumbent's Curse? Incumbency, Size, and Radical Product Innovation," *Journal of Marketing*, 64(July): 1–17.

Chandy, Rajesh K., Jaideep C. Prabhu, and Kersi D. Anita (2003) "What will the Future Bring? Dominance, Technology Expectations, and Radical Innovation," *Journal of Marketing*, July, 67(3): 1–18.

Chatterjee, Sayan (1986) "Types of Synergy and Economic Value: The Impact of Acquisitions on Merging and Rival Firms," *Strategic Management Journal*, 7(2): 119–39.

Chatterjee, Sayan and M. Lubatkin (1990) "Corporate Mergers, Stockholder Diversification, and Changes in Systematic Risk," *Strategic Management Journal*, 11: 255–68.

Chaudhuri, Saiket and Benham Tabrizi (1999) "Capturing the Real Value in High-Tech Acquisitions," *Harvard Business Review*, (September/October): 123–30.

Cheese, Peter, Robert J. Thomas, and Elizabeth Craig (2008) *The Talent Powered Organization: Strategies for Globalization, Talent Management, and High Performance.* London and Philadelphia: Kogan Page (www.accenture.com).

Chesbrough, H. W. and David Teece (1996) "When is Virtual Virtuous? Organizing for Innovation," *Harvard Business Review*, 73(3): 65–73.

Child, John (1972) "Organizational Structure, Environment, and Performance: The Role of Strategic Choice," *Sociology*, 6: 1–2.

Childre, Doc and Bruce Cryer (1999) *From Chaos to Coherence.* Boston: Butterworth-Heinemann.

Chon, Jeffrey, Jon Katzenbach, and Gus Vlak (2008) "Finding and Grooming Breakthrough Innovators," *Harvard Business Review*, 86(11): 62–69.

Christensen, Clayton M. (1997a) *The Innovator's Dilemma: When New Technologies Cause Great Firms to Fail.* Boston: Harvard Business School.

——— (1997b) "How to Identify and Build Disruptive New Businesses" *MIT Sloan Management Review*, Spring.

——— (2009) *The Innovator's Prescription: A Disruptive Solution for Health Care.* Boston, MA: Harvard Business School.

Christensen, C.M. and J. L. Bower (1996) "Customer Power, Strategic Investment, and the Failure of Leading Firms," *Strategic Management Journal*, 17: 197–218.

Christensen, C.M., Heiner Baumann, Rudy Ruggles, and Thomas M. Sadtler (2006) "Disruptive Innovation for Social Change?" *Harvard Business Review*, December: 94–103.

Christensen, C.M., Jerome H. Grossman, and Jason Hwang (2009), *The Innovator's Prescription: A Disruptive Solution for Health Care.* New York: McGraw-Hill.

Christensen, C.M., and M. Overdorf (2000) "Meeting the Challenge of Disruptive Change," *Harvard Business Review*, (March–April): 66–76.

Christensen, C.M., Mark W. Johnson, and Darrell K. Rigby (2002) "Foundations for Growth: How to Identify and Build Disruptive New Businesses," *Sloan Management Review*, MIT, Spring, 43(3): 22–31.

Christensen, C.M., and Michael E. Raynor (2003) *The Innovator's Solution: Using Good Theory to Solve the Dilemmas of Growth.* Boston: Harvard Business School Press.

Christensen, C.M., Scott D. Anthony, and Erik A. Roth (2004) *Seeing What's Next: Using the Theories of Innovation to Predict Industry Change.* Boston: Harvard Business School Press.

Chung, Kee H. and Stephen W. Pruitt (1994) "A Simple Approximation of Tobin's Q," *Financial Management*, Autumn, 23(3, Autumn): 70–74.

Churchman, C. West (1974) "Wicked Problems," Guest Editorial, *Management Science*, 14(4, December): 1M7.

Cliffe, Sarah (2001) "Can this Merger be Saved?" in *Harvard Business Review on Mergers and Acquisitions*, pp. 103–28. Harvard Business School Press.

——— (2009) "Economist Paul Krugman on being Surprised by the Spread of the Downturn," *Harvard Business Review*, June 17.

Cohen, Wesley M. and Daniel A. Levinthal (1989) "Innovation and Learning: The Two Faces of R&D," *Economic Journal*, 99(397): 569–96.

——— (1990) "Absorptive Capacity: A New Perspective on Learning and Innovation," *Administrative Science Quarterly*, 35(March): 128–52.

Collins, D. J. (1991) *Corporate Advantage: Identifying and Exploiting Resources.* Boston: Harvard Business School Press.

——— (1999) "Turning Goals into Results: The Power of Catalytic Mechanisms," *Harvard Business Review*, July–August, 77(4): 71–80.

——— (2001) *Good to Great.* New York: Harper Business.

Collins, D. J. and Jerry I. Porras (2002) *Built to Last: Successful Habits of Visionary Companies*. New York: Harper Business.

Collis, David J. (1991) "A Resource-based Analysis of Global Competition: The Case of the Bearings Industry," *Strategic Management Journal*, 12(Summer): 49–68.

Collis, David J. and Cynthia A. Montgomery (1995) "Competing on Resources: Strategy in the 1990s," *Harvard Business Review*, 73(4): 118–28; reprinted as "Best of HBR" in *Harvard Business Review* (July–August 2008), pp. 140–50.

———— and Michael G. Rukstad (2008) "Can You Say What Your Strategy Is?" *Harvard Business Review*, (April): 82–90.

Conklin, Jeffrey E. (2003) *Dialog Mapping: An Approach for Wicked Problems*. London, UK: CogNexus Institute.

———— (2006) "Wicked Problems and Social Complexity," in *Dialogue Mapping: Building Shared Understanding of Wicked Problems*. New York: Wiley & Sons.

Conner, Kathleen R. (1991) "A Historical Comparison of Resource-based Theory and Five Schools of thought within Industrial Organization Economics: Do we have a New Theory of the Firm?" *Journal of Management*, 17(March): 121–54.

Cook, Karen S. and Richard M. Emerson (1978) "Power, Equity, Commitment in Exchange Networks," *American Sociological Review*, 43(October): 721–38.

Cooper, Cary L. (ed.) (2000) *Theories of Organizational Stress*. New York: Oxford University Press.

Cooper, James C. (2008) "Putting Inflation on the Back Burner," *Business Week*, January 28, p. 12.

Cooper, John M. (1986) *Reason and Human Good in Aristotle*. Indianapolis, IN: Hecket Publishing Company.

Cooper, R. G. (1979) "The Dimensions of Industrial New Product Success and Failure," *Journal of Marketing*, 43: 93–103.

Cooper, Robert G. (1984) "New Product Strategies: What Distinguishes the Top Performers?" *Journal of Product Innovation Management*, 2(2): 151–64.

———— (1993) *Winning at New Products*. Reading, MA: Addison-Wesley.

———— (1994) "New Products: The Factors that Drive Success," *International Marketing Review*, 11(1): 60–76.

Corsten, Daniel and Nirmalya Kumar (2005) "Do Suppliers Benefit from Collaborative Relationships with. Large Retailers? An Empirical Investigation of ECR Adoption," *Journal of Marketing*, 69(July): 80–94.

Couger, Daniel J. (1995) *Creative Problem Solving and Opportunity Finding*. Danvers, MA: Boyd & Fraser Publishing Co.

Covey, Stephen R. (1989) *The 7 Habits of Highly Effective People*. New York: Free Press.

———— (2004) *The 8th Habit: From Effectiveness to Greatness*. New York: Free Press.

Coyne, Kevin P., Patricia Gorman Clifford, and Renee Dye (2007) "Breakthrough Thinking from Inside the Box," *Harvard Business Review*, 85(11): 71–78.

Cyert, Richard M. and Garrel Pottinger (1979) "Towards a better Microeconomic Theory," *Philosophy of Science*, 46: 204–22.

Dacey, J. S. (1989) *Fundamentals of Creative Thinking*. New York: Lexington Books.

Daft, Richard L. and Karl E. Weick (1984) "Toward a Model of Organizations as Interpretation Systems," *Academy of Management Review*, 9(2): 284–95.

Datta, Deepak K. (1991) "Organizational Fit and Acquisition Performance: Effects of Post-Acquisition Integration," *Strategic Management Journal*, 12(4): 281–97.

Davenport, Thomas H. (2006) "Competing on Analytics," *Harvard Business Review*, 86(1): 98–107.

Davis, G. (1986) *Creativity is Forever*. Dubuque, IA: Rendall/Hunt Publishing Co.

Davis, James H., David F. Schoorman, and Lex Donaldson (1997) "Toward a Stewardship Theory of Management," *The Academy of Management Review*, 22(January): 20–48.

Davis, Keith (1973) "The Case for and against Business Assumption of Social Responsibilities," *Academy of Management Journal*, 16: 312–22.

———— (1975) "Five Propositions for Social Responsibility," *Business Horizons*, 18(2): 17–23.

Davis, Keith and R. L. Blomstrom (1975) *Business and Society: Environment and Responsibility* (3rd edition). New York: McGraw-Hill.

Day, George S. (1990) *Market-Driven Strategy: Process for Creating Value*. New York: The Free Press.

——— (1994) "The Capabilities of Market-Driven Organizations," *Journal of Marketing*, 58(October): 37–52.

——— (1997) "Strategies for Surviving a Shakeout," *Harvard Business Review*, 75(2, March–April): 92–102.

——— (2004) "Which Way Should you Grow?" *Harvard Business Review*, (July–August): 24–26.

Day, George S. and David B. Montgomery (1999) "Charting New Directions for Marketing," *Journal of Marketing*, 63(Special Issue): 3–13.

——— and David B. Montgomery (1999) "Charting New Directions for Marketing," *Journal of Marketing*, 63(Special Issue): 146–63.

Day, George S. and Prakash Nedungadi (1994) "Managerial Representations of Competitive Advantage," *Journal of Marketing*, 58(April): 31–44.

Day, George S. and Robin Wensley (1988) "Assessing Advantage: A Framework for Diagnosing Competitive Superiority," *Journal of Marketing*, 52(April): 1–20.

De Bono, E. (1970), *Lateral Thinking: Creativity Step by Step*. New York: Harper & Row.

——— (1976) *Teaching Thinking*. Middlesex, U.K.: Penguin Books.

——— (1992) *Serious Creativity: Using the Power of Lateral Thinking to Create New Ideas*. New York: Harper Business.

De George, Richard T. (1990) *Business Ethics* (3rd edition). New York, NY: MacMillan.

——— (1995) *Business Ethics* (4th edition). Englewood-Cliffs, NJ: Prentice Hall Inc.

——— (1999) *Business Ethics* (5th edition). Englewood-Cliffs, NJ: Prentice Hall Inc.

De Grace, Peter and Leslie Hulet Stahl (1990) *Wicked Problems, Righteous Solutions: A Catalogue of Modern Software Engineering Paradigms*. Englewood Cliffs, New Jersey: Yourdon Press.

Deming, W. E. (1982) *Quality, Productivity and Competitive Position*. Cambridge: MIT, Center for Advanced Engineering Study.

De Pree, Max (1989) *Leadership is an Art*. New York: Doubleday.

Derrida, J. (1976) *Of Grammatology*, translated by G. C. Spivak. Baltimore and London: Johns Hopkins University Press.

Deshpande, Rohith, John U. Farley, and Frederick Webster, Jr. (1993) "Corporate Culture, Customer Orientation, and Innovativeness in Japanese Firms: A Quadrad Analysis," *Journal of Marketing*, 57(January): 23–37.

Despandé, Rohit and Frederick E. Webster (1989) "Organizational Culture and Marketing: Defining the Research Agenda," *Journal of Marketing*, 53(January): 3–15.

Deutsch, M. (1960) "The Effect of Motivational Orientation upon Trust and Suspicion," *Human Relations*, 13: 123–39.

Dewar, Robert and Jane Dutton (1986) "The Adoption of Radical and Incremental Innovations: An Empirical Analysis," Management Science, 32(11): 1422–33.

Dewey, John (1910) *How to Think*. Washington D.C. Health & Co.: Philosophical Books Library.

Dickson, Peter R. (1992) "Toward a General Theory of Competitive Rationality," *Journal of Marketing*, 56(January): 69–83.

Dierickx, Ingemar and Karel Cool (1989) "Asset Stock Accumulation and Sustainability of Competitive Advantage," *Management Science*, 35(12): 1504–13.

Dietz, Mary, Sheridan Barker, and Nancy Giberson (2005) "Solving a Wicked Problem: Knowledge Management Systems can Create New Educational Environments where Resources are Expended on Proactive Activities, such as Closing the Achievement Gap," *Leadership*, 34(3, January–February): 20–23.

Di Georgio, Richard M. (2002a) "Making Mergers and Acquisitions Work: What we Know and Don't Know—Part I," *Journal of Change Management*, 3(2): 134–48.

——— (2002b) "Making Mergers and Acquisitions Work: What we Know and Don't Know—Part II," *Journal of Change Management*, 3(3): 259–74.

DNA Science (2001) "DNA Sciences Registers 10,000 Gene Trust Participants in Less than One Year," *Press Release, DNA Sciences, Inc.*, July 19, Freemont, California, USA.

Dobbs, Kevin and Berry Kate (2008) "B of A CEO: Countrywide Deal Value 'Very Attractive'," *American Banker*, 173(9): 22.

Dollinger, Marc J. (2003) *Entrepreneurship: Strategies and Resources* (3rd edition). New Jersey: Pearson Education, Inc.

Donaldson, John (1992) *Business Ethics: A European Casebook*. London: Academic Press.

Donaldson, Lex and James H. Davis (1991) "Stewardship Theory or Agency Theory: CEO Governance and Shareholder Returns," *Australian Journal of Management*, 16: 49–64.

———— (1994) "Boards and Company Performance: Research Challenges the Conventional Wisdom," *Corporate Governance: An International Review*, 2: 151–60.

Donaldson, Thomas (1982) *Corporations and Morality*. Englewood Cliffs, NJ: Prentice-Hall Inc.

———— (1999) "Making Stakeholder Theory Whole," *The Academy of Management Review*, 24: 237–42.

Donaldson, T. and Dunfee T. (1994) "Toward a Unified Conception of Business Ethics: Integrative Social Contracts Theory," *Academy of Management Review*, 19(2): 252–84.

———— (1995) "Integrative Social Contracts Theory: A Communitarian Conception of Economic Ethics," *Economics and Philosophy*, 11(April): 85–112.

———— (1999) *Ties that Bind: A Social Contracts Approach to Business Ethics*. Cambridge, MA: Harvard University Business School Press.

Donaldson, T. and L. E. Preston (1995) "The Stakeholder Theory of the Corporation: Concepts, Evidence, and Implications," *Academy of Management Review*, 20: 65–91.

Donaldson, T. and Patricia H. Werhane (1993), *Ethical Issues in Business: A Philosophical Approach* (4th edition). Englewood-Cliffs, NJ: Prentice-Hall Inc.

Doney, Patricia M. and Joseph P. Cannon (1997) "An Examination of the Nature of Trust in Buyer-Seller Relationships," *Journal of Marketing*, 61(April): 35–51.

Donnelly, J. H. and J. M. Ivancevich (1975) "Role Clarity and the Salesman," *Journal of Marketing*, 39(January): 71–74.

Doorley, Thomas L. and John M. Donovan (1999), *Value-Creating Growth: How to Lift your Company to the Next Level of Performance*. San Francisco: Jossey-Bass.

Dornoff, R. J. and C. B. Tankersley (1975–76) "Do Retailers Practice Corporate Responsibility?" *Journal of Retailing*, 51(Winter): 33–42.

Douglas, Mary and Baron Isherwood (1979) *The World of Goods*. New York: Norton.

Dowling, J. and J. Pfeffer (1975) "Organizational Legitimacy: Social Values and Organizational Behavior," *Pacific Sociological Review*, 18: 122–36.

Drucker, Peter F. (1954) *The Practice of Management*. New York: Harper & Row.

———— (1980) *Managing in Turbulent Times*. New York: Harper and Row.

———— (1985) "The Discipline of Innovation," *Harvard Business Review*, (May–June): 67–72.

———— (1989) *The New Realities*. New York: Harper and Row.

———— (1991) *The Essential Drucker*. Harper Collins.

———— (1999) *Management Challenges for the 21st Century*. New York: Harper Business.

———— (2005) "Managing Yourself," *Harvard Business Review*, (January): 100–09.

———— (2006) "What Executives Should Remember," *Harvard Business Review*, (February): 144–52.

Drumwright, Minette E. (1994) "Socially Responsible Organizational Buying: Environmental Concern as a Noneconomic Buying Criterion," *Journal of Marketing*, 58(July): 1–20.

———— (1996) "Company Advertising with a Social Dimension: The Role of Noneconomic Criteria," *Journal of Marketing*, 60(October): 71–87.

Duhigg, Charles (2008a) "At Freddie Mac, Chief Discarded Warnings Signs," *The New York Times*, Tuesday, August 5, pp. A1, A16.

———— (2008b) "Freddie Mac's Biog Loss dims Hopes of Turnaround," *The New York Times*, Thursday, August 7, pp. C1, C4.

Duncan, R. B. (1972) "Characteristics of Organizational Environments and Perceived Environmental Uncertainty," *Administrative Science Quarterly*, 17: 313–27.

Duncker, K. (1945) "On Problem Solving," *Psychological Monographs*, 58(5): 270.

Dunfee, Thomas W. (1991) "Business Ethics and Extant Social Contracts," *Business Ethics Quarterly*, 1: 23–51.

———, N. Craig Smith, and William T. Ross, Jr. (1999) "Social Contracts and Marketing Ethics," *Journal of Marketing*, 63(July): 14–32.

Dyer, Jeffrey H., Prashant Kale, and Harbir Singh (2004) "When to Ally and When to Acquire," *Harvard Business Review*, (July–August): 109–15.

Easwaran, Ekanath (1992) *Your Life is Your Message*. The Blue Mountain Center of Meditation, Berkeley, CA: Nilgiri Press.

——— (1995) *Your Life is your Message*. Tomales, CA: Nilgiri Press.

Eccles, Robert G., Kersten L. Lanes, and Thomas C. Wilson (2001) "Are you Sure you have a Strategy?" *Academy of Management Executive*, 15(4): 48–59.

Edmondson, Amy C. (2008) "The Competitive Imperative of Learning," *Harvard Business Review*, (July–August): 60–67.

Eiseman, Elisa and Susanne B. Haga (1999) *Handbook of Human Tissue Resources: A National Resource of Human Tissue Samples*. Cambridge, MA: Cambridge University Press.

Eisenstat, Russell A., Michael Beer, Nathaniel Foote, Tobias Fredberg, and Flemming Norrgren (2008) "The Uncompromising Leader," *Harvard Business Review*, (July–August): 50–57.

Emerson, R. M. (1962) "Power-Dependence Relationships," *American Sociological Review*, 27: 31–41.

——— (1981) "Social Exchange Theory," in M. Rosenberg and R. H. Turner (eds), *Social Psychology: Sociological Perspectives*, pp. 30–65. New York: Basic Books.

Emery, Fred E. and Eric Trist (1973) *Towards a Social Ecology*. New York and London: Plenum Press.

Epstein, D. Jonathan (2008) "Salvaging Foreclosed Houses: Subprime Lending Crisis," *McClatchy-Tribune Business News*, Washington, February 3.

Ernst, David and James Bamford (2005) "Your Alliances are too Stable," *Harvard Business Review*, (June): 133–46.

Ernst, Holger and Jan Vitt (2000) "The Influence of Corporate Acquisitions on the Behavior of Key Inventors," *R&D Management*, 30(2): 105–19.

Ettlie, John E. and A. H. Rubinstein (1987) "Firm Size and Product Innovation," *Journal of Product Innovation Management*, 4: 89–108.

Evan, W. M. and R. E. Freeman (1988) "A Stakeholder Theory of the Modern Corporation: Kantian Capitalism," in T. Beauchamp and N. Bowie (eds), *Ethical Theory in Business*, pp. 75–93. Englewood Cliffs, NJ: Prentice Hall.

Evans, Philip and Bob Wolf (2005) "Collaboration Rules," *Harvard Business Review*, (July–August): 96–104.

Evans, Robert (2004) "Diverse Views of Outsourcing," *Information Week*, Manhasset, February 2, p. 60.

Fabian, John (1990) *Creative Thinking and Problem Solving*. Chelsea, MI: Lewis Publishers, Inc.

Fabrikant, Geraldine (2008) "Washington Mutual is Said to Consider Sale," *The New York Times*, Thursday, September 18, p. A29.

Falkenberg, A. W. (1996) "Marketing and the Wealth of Firms," *Journal of Macromarketing*, 15(1): 4–24.

Farrell, Diana (2004) "Beyond Offshoring: Assess your Company's Global Potential," *Harvard Business Review*, (December): 82–91.

——— (2006) "Smarter Off shoring," *Harvard Business Review*, June: 84–92.

Favaro, Ken, Tim Romberger, and David Meer (2009) "Five Riles for Retailing in a Recession," *Harvard Business Review*, (April): 99–104.

Fawcett, Stanley E. and M. Bixby Cooper (2001) "Process Integration for Competitive Success: Benchmarking Barriers and Bridges," *Benchmarking: An International Journal*, 8(5): 396–412.

Ferrell, O. C. and John Fraedrich (1991) *Business Ethics*. Boston: Houghton Mifflin Co.

Ferrell, O. C. and Larry Gresham (1985) "A Contingency Framework for Understanding Ethical Decision Making," *Journal of Marketing*, 49(Summer): 87–95.

Ferrell, O. C. and Steven J. Skinner (1988) "Ethical Behavior and Bureaucratic Structure in Marketing Research Organizations," *Journal of Marketing Research*, 25(February): 103–10.

Ferrell, O. C., Steven J. Skinner and John Fraedrich (1989) "A Synthesis of Ethical Decision Models for Marketing," *Journal of Macromarketing*, 9(Fall): 55–64.

Fine, Charles H., Roger Vardan, Robert Pethick, and Jamal El-Hout (2002) "Rapid Response Capability in Value-Chain Design," *MIT Sloan Management Review*, 43(2): 23–30.

Firat, A. Fuat and Alladi Venkatesh (1995) "Liberatory Postmodernism and the Reenchantment of Consumption," *Journal of Consumer Research*, 22(3, December): 1239–67.

Fisk, George (1974) *Marketing and the Ecological Crisis*. New York: Harper and Row.

Fisk, Raymond P. (1982) "Towards a Theoretical Framework for Marketing Ethics," *Southern Marketing Association Proceedings*, pp. 255–59.

Fleckenstein, William A. (2008) *Greenspan's Bubbles: The Age of Ignorance at the Federal Reserve*. New York: McGraw-Hill Books.

Fletcher, George P. (1972) "Fairness and Utility in Tort Theory," *Harvard Law Review*, January, 85(3): 537–73.

Florida, Richard (2004) "America's Looming Creativity Crisis," *Harvard Business Review*, (October): 122–38.

Ford, Henry (1926), "Why I Favor Five Days' Work With Six Days' Pay," *World's Work*, (October): 613–16.

Ford, Jeffrey D. and Laurie W. Ford (2009) "Decoding Resistance to Change," *Harvard Business Review*, (April): 99–104.

Foster, R. (1986) *Innovation: The Attacker's Advantage*. New York: Summit Books.

Fox, Pimm (2004) "Open-Source Model for Outsourcing," *Computerworld*, 38(4, January 26): 18.

Fox, Richard W. and T. J. Jackson Lears (1983) *The Culture of Consumption*. New York, NY: Pantheon.

Foxman, Ellen R. and Paula Kilcoyne (1993) "Information Technology, Marketing Practice, and Consumer Privacy: Ethical Issues," *Journal of Public Policy and Marketing*, 12(Spring): 106–19.

Frankena, William (1973a) "The Ethics of Love Conceived as an Ethics of Virtue," *Journal of Religious Ethics*, 1: 21–31.

——— (1973b) *Ethics* (2nd edition). Englewood-Cliffs, NJ: Prentice-Hall.

——— (1975) "Conversations with Carney and Hauerwas," *Journal of Religious Ethics*, 3: 7–26.

——— (1980) *Thinking About Morality*. Ann Arbor, MI: University of Michigan Press.

Freeman, R. Edward (1984) *Strategic Management: A Stakeholder Approach*. Boston, MA: Harper Collins.

——— (1999) "Divergent Stakeholder Theory," *The Academy of Management Review*, 24: 233–36.

Freeman, R. E. and D. R. Gilbert, Jr. (1988) *Corporate Strategy and the Search for Ethics*. Englewood Cliffs, NJ: Prentice Hall.

French, Peter A. (1979) "The Corporation as a Moral Person," *American Philosophical Quarterly*, 3: 207.

Friedman, M. (1970) "The Social Responsibility of Business is to Increase its Profits," *New York Times*, 32 (September 13): 122–26.

Fritz, Robert (1989) *The Path of Lease Resistance*. New York: Fawcett-Columbine.

Frooman, J. (1999) "Stakeholder Influence Strategies," *The Academy Management Review*, 24: 191–205.

Furman, Frida Kerner (1990) "Teaching Business Ethics: Questioning the Assumptions, Seeking New Directions," *Journal of Business Ethics*, 9(January): 31–38.

Gabarro, John J. (2007) "When a New Manager Takes Charge," *Harvard Business Review*, (January): 104–03.

Gable, Myron and Martin T. Topol (1988) "Machiavellianism and the Department Store Executive," *Journal of Retailing*, 64(1, Spring): 68–84.

Galbraith, Jay R. (1974) "Organization Design: An Information Process View," *Interfaces*, 4(May): 28–36.

——— (1982) "Designing the Innovative Organization," *Organizational Dynamics*, (Winter): 5–25.

Galbraith, John Kenneth (1956) *American Capitalism*. Boston, MA: Houghton Mifflin.

——— (1958) *The Affluent Society*. Boston, MA: Houghton Mifflin.

——— (1967) *The New Industrial State*. Boston, MA: Houghton Mifflin.

——— (1973) *Economics and the Public Purpose*. Boston, MA: Houghton Mifflin.

——— (1976/1982) "The Dependence Effect," in *The Affluent Society* (3rd edition), pp. 127–39. New York: Houghton Mifflin.

Galpin, Timothy J. and Mark Herndon (2000) *The Complete Guide to Mergers and Acquisitions: Process Tools to Support M&A Integration at Every Level*. San Francisco: Jossey-Bass.

Galunic, Charles D. and Kathleen M. Eisenhardt (2001) "Architectural Innovation and Modular Corporate Forms," *The Academy of Management Journal*, 44(6, December): 1229–50.

Ganesan, Shankar (1994) "Determinants of Long Term Orientation in Buyer-Seller Relationships," *Journal of Marketing*, 58(April): 1–19.

Gardner, Howard (1984) *Frames of Mind: The Theory of Multiple Intelligences*. NewYork: Basic Books.

Garrett, Laurie and Scott Rosenstein (2005) "Missed Opportunities," *Harvard International Review*, 27(1, Spring): 64–70.

Garvin, David A. (2004) "What Every New CEO Should Know about Creating New Businesses," *Harvard Business Review*, (July–August): 18–21.

———, Amy C. Edmondson, and Francesca Gino (2008) "Is yours a Learning Organization?" *Harvard Business Review*, (March): 109–16.

Gatignon, Hubert and Thomas S. Robertson (1985) "A Propositional Inventory for New Product Diffusion Research," *Journal of Consumer Research*, 11(March): 849–67.

——— (1989) "Technology Diffusion: An Empirical Test of Competitive Effect," *Journal of Marketing*, 53(January): 35–49.

——— (1993) "The Impact of Risk and Competition on Choice of Innovations," *Marketing Letters*, 4(July): 191–204.

Gatignon, Hubert and Jean-Marc Xuereb (1997) "Strategic Orientation of the Firm and New Product Performance," *Journal of Marketing Research*, 34(Special Issue, February): 77–90.

Gavetti, Giovanni and Jan W. Rivkin (2005) "How Strategists Really Think: Tapping the Power of Analogy," *Harvard Business Review*, 85(4): 54–65.

George Horace Lorimer (1867–1937) "Back of every noble life there are principles that have fashioned it," *Saturday Evening Post*. It is accessible in "In "The Speaker's Electronic Reference Collection," Apex Software, 1994."

Geertz, Clifford (1973) "Thick Description: Towards an Interpretive Theory of Culture," in *The Interpretation of Cultures* (Selected Essays by Clifford Geertz), pp. 3–30. New York, NY: Basic Books.

Geroski, Paul, Steve Machin, and John Van Reenen (1993) "The Profitability of Innovating Firms," *Rand Journal of Economics*, 24(2, Summer): 198.

Gerstner, Louis V. (2002) *Who Says Elephants Cannot Dance?* (Inside IBM's Historic Turnaround). New York: Harper Collins Publishers.

Getzels, J. W. and M. Csikszentmihalyi (1975) "From Problem Solving to Problem Finding," in J. W. Getzels and I. A. Taylor (eds), *Perspectives in Creativity*, pp. 1–36. Chicago: Aldine Publishing Co.

Ghemavat, Pankaj (2004) "Growth Boosters," *Harvard Business Review*, 82(7): 35–40.

——— (2007) "Managing Differences: The Central Challenge of Global Strategy," *Harvard Business Review*, 85(3): 58–68.

Ghemawat, Pankaj (2003) "The Forgotten Strategy," *Harvard Business Review*, 86(10): 76–87.

Ghoshal, Sumantra (2005) "Bad Management Theories are Destroying Good Management Practices," *Academy of Management Learning and Education*, 4(1): 75–91.

Gilbert, S. M., Y. S. Xia, and G. Yu (2006) "Strategic Outsourcing for Competing OEM's that face Cost Reduction Opportunities," *IIE Transactions*, 38: 903–15.

Gilmore, James H. and Joseph B. Pine II (1997) "The Four Faces of Mass Customization," *Harvard Business Review*, 75(1): 91–101.

——— (2002) "Customer Experience Places: The New Offering Frontier," *Strategy and Leadership*, 30(4): 4–11.

Gilson, Stuart C. (2001) *Creating Value through Corporate Restructuring: Studies in Bankruptcy, Buyouts, and Breakups*. New York: John Wiley & Sons.

Glater, Jonathan D. (2008) "A.I.G. is still Profitable, with a wide Array of Enterprises," *The New York Times*, Wednesday, September 17, pp. C1, C 9.

Glazer, Rashi (1991) "Marketing in an Information-Intensive Environment: Strategic Implications of Knowledge as an Asset," *Journal of Marketing*, 55(October): 1–19.

Glazer, Rashi and Allen M. Weiss (1993) "Marketing in Turbulent Environments: Decision Process and Time-Sensitivity of Information," *Journal of Marketing Research*, 30(November): 509–21.

Goffee, Rob and Gareth Jones (2007) "Leading Clever People," *Harvard Business Review*, 85(3): 72–79.

Goldenberg, Mazursky J. and Sorin Solomon (1999) "Toward Identifying the Inward Templates of New Products: A Channeled Ideation Approach," *Journal of Marketing Research*, 36(May): 200–10.

Golder, George and Gerard Tellis (1993) "Pioneer Advantage: Marketing Logic or Marketing Legend," *Journal of Marketing Research*, 30(May): 164–65.

Goldfield, Michael (2005) *The Decline of Organized Labor in the United States and the Impact of Globalization*. Detroit: Wayne State University.

Goodpaster, Kenneth E. and John B. Matthews, Jr. (1982) "Can a Corporation Have a Conscience?" *Harvard Business Review*, 60(January–February): 132–41.

Goodwin, Cathy (1991) "Privacy: Recognition of a Consumer Right," *Journal of Public Policy and Marketing*, 10(Spring): 149–66.

Goodwin, Doris Kearns (2009) "Leadership Lessons from Abraham Lincoln," *Harvard Business Review*, 87(4): 43–47.

Goolsby, Jerry R. and Shelby D. Hunt (1992) "Cognitive Moral Development and Marketing," *Journal of Marketing*, 56(1, January): 55–68.

Gottfredson, Mark and Keith Aspinall (2005) "Innovation versus Complexity: What is too much of a Good Thing?" *Harvard Business Review*, 83(10): 62–73.

Gottfredson, Mark, Rudy Puryear, and Stephen Phillips (2005) "Strategic Sourcing: From Periphery to the Core," *Harvard Business Review*, 83(2): 132–39.

Govindarajan, Vijay and Chris Trimble (2005) "Building Breakthrough Businesses within Established Organizations," *Harvard Business Review*, 85(5): 58–70.

Gowans, Christopher W. (ed.) (1987) *Moral Dilemmas*. New York, NY: Oxford University.

Graham, G. (1990) *Living the Good Life: An Introduction to Moral Philosophy*. New York, NY: Paragon.

Granovetter, Mark S. (1985) "Economic Action and Social Structure: The Problem of Embeddedness," *American Journal of Sociology*, 91(November): 481–510.

Grant, Robert M. (1996) "Toward a Knowledge-based Theory of the Firm," *Strategic Management Journal*, 17(Winter): 109–32.

Greely, Henry T. (2001) "Human Genomic Research: New Challenges for Research Ethics," *Perspectives of Biology and Medicine*, 44(2): 220–30.

Greenwald, Bruce and Judd Kahn (2005) "All Strategy is Local," *Harvard Business Review*, 83(8): 94–107.

Grönroos, Christian (1990) "Relationship Approach to Marketing in Service Contexts: The Marketing and Organizational Behavior Interface," *Journal of Business Research*, 20(1): 3–11.

Grossman, Sanford J. and Oliver D. Hart (1986) "The Costs and Benefits of Ownership: A Theory of Vertical and Lateral Integration," *Journal of Political Economy*, 94(4): 691–719.

Grundy, Tony (2003) *Smart Things to Know about: Mergers and Acquisitions*. Oxford, U.K.: The Capstone Publishing Ltd. (A John Wiley & Sons Co.).

Guilford, J. P. (1957) "A Revised Structure of Intellect," *Report of Psychology*. Los Angeles: University of Southern California, 19: 1–63.

——— (1967) *Fundamentals of Creative Thinking*. New York: Lexington Books.

Gulati, Sanjay (2004) "How CEOs Manage Growth Agendas," *Harvard Business Review*, 82(7): 124–32.

——— and James B. Oldroyd (2005), "The Quest for Customer Focus," *Harvard Business Review*, 83(4), 92–101.

Gundlach, Gregory T. and Patrick E. Murphy (1993) "Ethical and Legal Foundations of Relational Marketing Exchanges," *Journal of Marketing*, 55(October): 25–46.

———, Ravi S. Achrol, and John T. Mentzer (1995) "The Structure of Commitment in Exchange," *Journal of Marketing*, 59(January): 78–92.

Gunther, Marc (2008) "Paulson to the Rescue," *Fortune*, September 29, pp. 68–78.

Gunther, Rita McGrath and Ian MacMillan (2005) "Market Busting: Strategies for Exceptional Business Growth," *Harvard Business Review*, 83(3): 80–91.

Gustafsson, C. (2002) "From Concept to Norm—An Explorative Study of Office Design Management from an Organizational Perspective," *Facilities*, 20(13/14): 423–31.

Haberland, Gabriele S. and Peter A. Dacin (1992) "The Development of a Measure to Assess Viewers' Judgments of The Creativity of An Advertisement: A Preliminary Study," in John F. Sherry, Jr. and Brian Sternthal (eds) *Advances in Consumer Research* Volume 19, pp. 817–825. Provo, UT : Association for Consumer Research.

Håkansson, Hakan and Ivan Snehota (1993) "No Business in an Island: The Network Concept of Business Strategy," *Scandinavian Journal of Management*, 5(3): 187–200.

———— (1989) "No Business is an Island," *Scandinavian Journal of Management Studies*, 4(3/89):187–200

Hamel, Gary (1999) "Bringing Silicon Valley Inside," *Harvard Business Review*, 77(5): 70–84.

———— (2000) "Waking up IBM: How a Gang of Unlikely Rebels Transformed Big Blue," *Harvard Business Review*, July–August.

———— (2002) *Leading the Revolution*. Boston, MA: Harvard Business School Press.

———— (2006) "The Why, What and How of Management Innovation," *Harvard Business Review*, 84(2): 72–84.

———— (2007) *The Future of Management*. Boston, MA: Harvard Business School Press.

———— (2009) "Moon Shots for Management," *Harvard Business Review*, (February): 91–99.

Hamel, Gary and C. K. Prahalad (1985) "Do you Really Have a Global Strategy?" *Harvard Business Review*, 63(July–August): 139–48.

Hamel, Gary and C. K. Prahalad (1994a) "Competing for the Future," *Harvard Business Review*, 72(4, November–December): 122–28.

———— (1994b) *Competing for the Future: Breaking through Strategies for Seizing Control of your Industry and Creating the Markets of Tomorrow*. Boston, MA: Harvard Business School Press.

Hamel, Gary and Gary Getz (2004) "Funding Growth in an Age of Austerity," *Harvard Business Review*, 82(4): 76–84.

Hamel, Gary and Liisa Välikangas (2003) "The Quest for Resilience," *Harvard Business Review*, September, 52–65.

Hamel, Gary, Yves L. Doz, and C. K. Prahalad (1989) "Collaborate with your Competitors—and Win," *Harvard Business Review*, 67(1, January–February): 133–39.

Hammarskjöld, Dag (2001) *Markings*. New York: Alfred A. Knopf.

Hammer, Michael (2004) "Deep Change: How Operational Innovation can Transform your Company," *Harvard Business Review*, 82(4): 84–95.

Hammond, John S., Ralph L. Keeney, and Howard Raiffa (2006) "The Hidden Traps in Decision Making," *Harvard Business Review*, 84(1): 118–26.

Han, Jin K., Namwoon Kim, and Rajendra K. Srivastava (1998) "Market Orientation and Organizational Performance: Is Innovation a Missing Link," *Journal of Marketing*, 62(4, October): 30–45.

Hansen, Morten T. and Julian Birkinshaw (2007) "The Innovation Value Chain," *Harvard Business Review*, 85(6): 121–30.

Harding David and Sam Rovit (2004) "The Mega-Merger Mouse Trap," *Wall Street Journal*, February 17, p. B2.

Hare, Richard M. (1978) "Justice and Equality," in John Arthur and William Shaw (eds), *Justice and Economic Distribution*, pp. 207–21. Englewoods Cliffs, NJ: Prentice Hall.

Hart, S. (1986) "Steering the Path between Ambiguity and Overload: Planning as Strategic Process," in M. Dluthy and K. Chen (eds), *Interdisciplinary Planning: Perspectives for the Future*, pp.36–53. Rutgers, NJ: Center for Urban Policy.

Harvard Business Review (2000) "A CEO Roundtable on Making Mergers Succeed," (May–June): 145–54.

Hays, Constance L. (2003) "2 Ex-officials at Kmart Face Fraud Charges," *New York Times*, October 30.

Hemp, Paul (2004) "Amgen CEO, Kevin Sharer: A Time for Growth," *Harvard Business Review*, 82(7): 66–74.

Henard, David and David Szymanski (2001) "Why Some New Products are More Successful than Others," *Journal of Marketing Research*, 28(August): 362–79.

Henderson R. (1993) "Underinvestment and Incompetence as Responses to Radical Innovation: Evidence from the Photolytic Alignment Equipment Industry," *Rand Journal of Economics*, 24: 248–70.

Henderson, Rebecca and K. B. Clark (1990) "Architectural Innovation: The Reconfiguration of Existing Technologies and the Failure of Established Firms," *Administrative Science Quarterly*, 35(1): 9–30.

Hennessey, B.A. and T.M. Amabile (1988) "The Conditions of Creativity," in R. J. Sternberg (Ed.) *The Nature of Creativity*, pp.11–38. New York: Cambridge University Press.

Henry Kaufman (2008) "Transparency and the Fed," *Wall Street Journal* (Eastern edition), p. A.13.

Herzenhorn, David M. (2009) "Following the Money," *New York Times*, Thursday, January 29, pp. A1, A15.

Hill, Charles W. and Thomas M. Jones (1992) "Stakeholder-Agency Theory," *Journal of Management Studies*, 29(2, March): 131–54.

Hill, Charles W. Jeffrey S. Harrison, and Duane R. Ireland (2001) *Mergers and Acquisitions: A Guide to Creating Value for Stake Holders*. New York: Oxford University Press.

Hitt, Michael A., Robert E. Hoskisson, and Duane R. Ireland (1990) "Mergers and Acquisitions and Managerial Commitment to Innovation in M-Form Firms," *Strategic Management Journal*, 11(4): 29–48.

Hitt, Michael A., Robert E. Hoskisson, Duane R. Ireland and Jeffrey S. Harrison (1991a) "Effects of Acquisitions on R&D Inputs and Outputs," *Academy of Management Journal*, 34(3): 693–706.

——— (1991b) "Are Acquisitions a Poison Pill for Innovation?" *Academy of Management Executive*, 5(4): 22–34.

Hochstein, Marc (2007) "Countrywide Works with Illinois Attorney General," *American Banker*, 172(240, December 14): 9.

Hofstadler, R. D. (1979) *Godel, Escher, Bach: An Eternal Golden Braid*. New York, NY: Vintage Books.

Hogarth, R. M. (1987) *Judgment and Choice: The Psychology of Decision* (2nd edition). New York: Wiley.

Homburg, Christian and Matthias Bucerius (2005) "A Marketing Perspective on Mergers and Acquisitions: How Marketing Integration Affects Postmerger Performance," *Journal of Marketing*, January, 69(1): 95–113.

Horn, R. (2001) "Knowledge Mapping for Complex Social Messes." Available online at http://www.stanford.edu/-rhrn/a/recent/spchKnowldgPACKARD.pdf

Howell, Robert A. (2004) "Turn your Budgeting Process Upside Down," *Harvard Business Review*, 82(7): 21–22.

Hubbard, Ruth and Giles Paquet (2007) *Gomery's Blinders and Canadian Federalism*. Canada: University of Ottawa Press.

Hult, G. T. M. (1998) "Managing the International Sourcing Process as a Market-Driven Organizational Learning System," *Decision Sciences*, 29(1): 193–216.

Hunt, Shelby D. (1991) *Modern Marketing Theory: Critical Issues in the Philosophy of Marketing Science*. Cincinnati, OH: South-Western Publishing Co.

——— (1995) "The Resource-Advantage Theory of Competition: Toward Explaining Productivity and Economic Growth," *Journal of Management Inquiry*, 4(December): 317–32.

——— (1997a) "Competing through Relationships: Grounding Relationship Marketing in Resource-Advantage Theory," *Journal of Marketing Management*, 13(4): 431–45.

——— (1997b) "Resource-Advantage Theory: An Evolutionary Theory of Competitive Firm Behavior," *Eastern Economic Journal*, 23(4): 425–39.

——— (1999) "The Strategic Imperative and Sustainable Competitive Advantage: Public Policy and Resource-Advantage Theory," *Journal of the Academy of Marketing Science*, 27(2): 144–59.

——— (2000) *A General Theory of Competition: Resources, Competences, Productivity, Economic Growth*. Thousand Oaks, CA: SAGE Publications.

——— (2002) *Foundations of Marketing Theory: Toward a General Theory of Marketing*. New York: ME Sharpe.

Hunt, Shelby D. and Arturo Z. Vasquez-Parraga (1993) "Organizational Consequences, Marketing Ethics and Salesforce Supervision," *Journal of Marketing Research*, 30(February): 78–90.

Hunt, Shelby D. and Robert M. Morgan (1995) "The Comparative Advantage Theory of Competition," *Journal of Marketing*, 59(April): 1–15.

——— (1996) "The Resource-Advantage Theory of Competition: Dynamics, Path Dependencies, and Evolutionary Dimensions," *Journal of Marketing*, 60(October): 107–14.

——— (1997) "Resource-Advantage Theory: Snake Swallowing its Tail or a General Theory of Competition," *Journal of Marketing*, 60(October): 74–82.

Hunt, Shelby D., Robert M. Morgan and Scott J. Vitell (1986) "A General Theory of Marketing Ethics," *Journal of Macromarketing*, 6(Spring): 5–16.

———— (1991) "The General Theory of Marketing Ethics: A Retrospective and Revision," in N. Craig Smith and John A. Smith (eds), *Ethics in Marketing*, pp. 775–84. Chicago, IL: Richard D. Irwin.

Hunter, James D. (1991) *Culture Wars: The Struggle to Define America*. New York: Basic Books.

Huston, Larry and Nabil Sakkab (2006) "Connect and Develop: Inside Proctor & Gamble's New Model for Innovation," *Harvard Business Review*, 84(3): 58–67.

Hutt, Michel D., Peter H. Reingen, and John R. Ronchetto Jr. (1988) "Tracing Emergent Processes in Marketing Strategy Formation," *The Journal of Marketing*, 52(January): 4–19.

Iansiti, Marco and Roy Levien (2004) "Strategy as Ecology," *Harvard Business Review*, 82(3): 69–78.

Ibarra, Herminia and Mark Hunter (2007) "Managing Yourself: How Leaders Create and Use Networks," *Harvard Business Review*, 85(1): 40–49.

Ibarra, Herminia and Otilia Obodaru (2009) "Women and the Vision Thing," *Harvard Business Review*, 87(1): 62–70.

Inamori, Kazuo (1985) "The Perfect Company: Goal for Productivity," Speech given at Case Western Reserve University, June 5.

Isaksen, S. G. and D. J. Treffinger (1985) *Creative Problem Solving: The Basic Course*. Buffalo, NY: Bearley Ltd.

Isenberg, Daniel (1987) "The Tactics of Strategic Opportunism," *Harvard Business Review*, 65(March/April): 92–97.

Janger, Edward J. (2005) "Genetic Information, Privacy and Insolvency," *Journal of Medicine and Ethics*, 33: 75–84.

Janis, I. I. and L. Mann (1977) *Decision Making*. New York: Free Press.

Jaworski, Bernard J. and Ajay K. Kohli (1993) "Market Orientation: Antecedents and Consequences," *The Journal of Marketing*, 57(3, July): 53–71.

Johnson, David (2006) "Important Cities in Black History," Pearson Education. Available online at www.Factmonster.com/spot/bhmcities.1

Johnson, Jean L., Ravipreet S. Sohi, and Rajdeep Grewal (2004) "The Role of Relational Knowledge Stores in Interfirm Partnering," *Journal of Marketing*, 68(3, July): 21–36.

Johnson, M. (ed.) (1981) *Philosophical Perspectives on Metaphor*. Minneapolis: University of Minnesota Press.

Johnson, Mark W., Clayton M. Christensen, and Henning Kagermann (2008) "Reinventing your Business Model," *Harvard Business Review*, 86(12): 50–59.

Jones, Mary Gardiner (1991) "Privacy: A Significant Marketing Issue for the 1990s," *Journal of Public Policy and Marketing*, 10(Spring): 133–48.

Jones, Thomas M. (1979) "Corporate Governance: Who Controls the Large Corporation?" *Hastings Law Journal*, 30: 1261–86.

———— (1980) "Corporate Social Responsibility Revisited, Redefined," *California Management Review*, 22(3): 9–67.

———— (1991) "Ethical Decision Making by Individuals in Organizations: An Issue-Contingent Model," *Academy of Management Review*, 16(2): 365–95.

———— (1994) "Essay on the Toronto Conference," *Business and Society*, 33: 98–101.

———— (1995) "Instrumental Stakeholder Theory: A Synthesis of Ethics and Economics," *The Academy of Management Review*, 20(2): 404–37.

Jones, Thomas M. and A. C. Wicks (1999) "Convergent Stakeholder Theory," *The Academy of Management Review*, 24: 206–21.

Jong, Ad de, Ko de Ruyter and Jos Lemmik (2004) "Antecedents and Consequences of the Service Climate in Boundary-spanning Self-managing Service Teams," *Journal of Marketing*, 68(2): 18–35.

Jonsen, Albert R. (1968) *Responsibility in Modern Religious Ethics*. Cleveland: Corpus Books.

Jose, M. L., L. M. Nichols, and J. L. Stevens (1986) "Contributions of Diversification, Promotion, and R&D to the Value of Multiproduct Firms: A Tobin's Q Approach," *Financial Management*, (Winter): 33–42.

Jung, Carl G. (1971) *Psychological Types*. Princeton, NJ: Princeton University Press.

Jung, L. S. (1983) "Commercialization of the Professions," *Business and Professional Ethics Journal*, 2: 57–81.

Juran, J. M. (1991) "Strategies for World-Class Quality," *Quality Progress*, 24(3): 81–85.

Kabanoff, B. (1991) "Equity, Equality, Power, and Conflict," *The Academy of Management Review*, 16(April): 416–41.

Kahl, Jack and Tom Donelan (2004) *Leading from the Heart: Choosing to be a Servant Leader*. Westlake, OH: Sage Publications.

Kahneman D. and A. Tversky (eds) (2000) *Choices, Values and Frames*. Cambridge, U.K.: Cambridge University Press.

Kalwani, Manohar U. and Narakesari Narayandas (1995) "Long-term Manufacturer-Supplier Relationships: Do they Pay Off Supplier Firms?" *Journal of Marketing*, 59(January): 1–16.

Kamta, Prasad (2006) "Potential of Gandhian Economic Ideas for Eradication of Poverty in India," *IASSI Quarterly*, 25: 1.

Kanter, Rosabeth Moss (2003) "Leadership and the Psychology of the Turnarounds," *Harvard Business Review*, 81(6): 58–69.

———— (2006) "Innovation: The Classic Traps," *Harvard Business Review*, 84(10): 72–82.

Kao, John (2007) *Innovation Nation: How America is Losing its Innovation Edge, Why it Matters, and What we can do to Get it Back*. New York: The Free Press.

Kaplan, Jack M. (2003) "Buying Existing and Turnaround Businesses and Opening Franchises," in *Patterns of Entrepreneurship*, Chapter 12, pp. 355–80. New York: John Wiley & Sons, Inc.

Kaplan, Robert E. (2008) "Reaching your Potential," *Harvard Business Review*, 86(7): 45–49.

Kaplan, Robert S. and David P. Norton (2004) "Measuring the Strategic Readiness of Intangible Assets," *Harvard Business Review*, 82(2): 52–63.

———— (2005) "The Office of Strategy Management," *Harvard Business Review*, 83(9): 72–81.

———— (2006): "How to Implement a New Strategy without Disrupting your Organization," *Harvard Business Review*, 84(3): 100–09.

Kaplan, Robert S. and Robert B. Kaiser (2009) "Stop Overdoing your Strengths," *Harvard Business Review*, 87(2): 100–03.

Karim, Samina and Will Mitchell (2000) "Path-Dependent and Path-Breaking Change: Reconfiguring Business Resources following Acquisitions in the U. S. Medical Sector 1978–1995," *Strategic Management Journal*, 21(10–11): 1061–81.

Kaufman, Stephen P. (2008) "Evaluating the CEO," *Harvard Business Review*, 86(9): 53–57.

Kerley, Richard (2007) "Controlling Urban Car Parking—An Exemplar of Public Management?" *International Journal of Public Sector Management*, 20(6): 519–30.

Khanna, Tarun, Krishna G. Palepu, and Jayant Sinha (2005) "Strategies that Fit Emerging Markets," *Harvard Business Review*, 83(9): 63–76.

Khurana, Rakesh (2007) *From Higher Aims to Hired Hands: The Social Transformation of Business Schools and the Unfulfilled Promise of Management as a Profession*. Princeton and London: Princeton University Press.

Kim, W. Chan and Renée Mauborgne (1997) "Value Innovation: The Strategic of High Growth," *Harvard Business Review*, 75(1, January–February): 102–12.

———— (1999) "Creating New Market Space," *Harvard Business Review*, January–February, 77(1): 83–93.

———— (2000) "Knowing a Winning Business Idea when you See it," *Harvard Business Review*, 78(5):129–38.

———— (2003) "Tipping Point Leadership," *Harvard Business Review*, 83(4): 60–69.

———— (2004) "Blue Ocean Strategy," *Harvard Business Review*, 84(9): 76–85.

———— (2005) *Blue Ocean Strategy: How to Create Uncontested Market Space and make the Competition Irrelevant*. Boston, MA: Harvard Business School Press.

———— (2009) "How Strategy Shapes Structure," *Harvard Business Review*, 87(8): 73–80.

King, Jonathan B. (1993) "Learning to Solve the Right Problems: The Case of Nuclear Power in America," *Journal of Business Ethics*, 12: 105–16.

King, Jonathan B. and David Acklin (1995) "Creating Common Ground: A Lesson from the Past," *Journal of Business Ethics*, 14(1): 105–16.

Kingsley, H. L. and R. Garry (1957) *The Nature and Conditions of Learning*. Englewood Cliffs, NJ: Prentice-Hall.

Kohlberg, Lawrence (1981) *The Philosophy of Moral Development*. New York: Harper & Row.

Kohli, Ajay K. and Bernard J. Jaworski (1990) "Market Orientation: The Construct, Research, Propositions and Managerial Implications," *Journal of Marketing*, 54(2): 1–18.

———— (1995) "MARKOR: A Measure of Market Orientation," *Journal of Marketing, Research*, 30(4): 467–78.

Kotler, Philip (2004) *Marketing Management: The Millennium Edition* (11th edition) (International). London: Prentice-Hall.

Kotler, Philip and Gerald Zaltman (1971) "Social Marketing: An Approach to Planned Social Change," *Journal of Marketing*, 35(July): 3–12.

Kotler, Philip and Mantrala Murali K. (1985) "Flawed Products: Consumer Responses and Marketer Strategies," *Journal of Consumer Marketing*, 2(3, Summer): 27–36.

—— and Sidney J. Levy (1967) "Broadening the Concept of Marketing," *Journal of Marketing*, 33(January): 10–15.

—— (1971) "Demarketing, Yes, Demarketing," *Harvard Business Review*, 49(6): 74–80.

Kotter, John P. (2007) "Leading for Change: Why Transformation Efforts Fail," *Harvard Business Review*, 85(1): 96–103.

Krishnan, Hema A. and Daewoo Park (2002) "The Impact of Work Force Reduction on Subsequent Performance in Major Mergers and Acquisitions—An Exploratory Study," *Journal of Business Research*, 55(4): 285–92.

Kuhn, T. A. (1970) *The Structure of Scientific Revolutions*. Chicago: University of Chicago Press.

Kumcu, Erdogan and Hohn W. Vann (1991) "Public Empowerment in Managing Local Economic Development: Achieving a Desired Quality of Life Profile," *Journal of Business Research*, 23(1): 51–65.

Kuznets, Simon (1959) *Six Lectures on Economics Growth*. Glencoe, IL: Free Press.

Kwak, Hyokjin, Zinkhan George M., and Warren A. French (2001) "Moral Orientation: Its Relation to Product Involvement and Consumption," *Advances in Consumer Research*, 28: 431–36.

Lacayo, Richard (1991) "Nowhere to Hide," *Time*, November 11, pp. 34–40.

Laczniak, Gene R. (1983) "Framework for Analyzing Marketing Ethics," *Journal of Macromarketing*, 3(1): 7–18.

—— (1999) "Distributive Justice, Catholic Social Teaching, and the Moral Responsibility of Marketers," *Journal of Public Policy and Marketing*, Spring, 18(1): 125–29.

Laczniak, Gene R. and Patrick E. Murphy (eds) (1993) *Ethical Marketing Decisions: The Higher Road*. Boston, MA: Allyn and Bacon.

Lafley, A. G. (2009) "What Only the CEO Can Do" *Harvard Business Review*, 87(5): 54–62.

Lajoux, Alexandra Reed (1998) *The Art of M&A Integration: A Guide to Merging Resources, Processes, and Responsibilities*. New York: McGraw-Hill.

Lakoff, G. and M. Johnson (1980) *Metaphors we Live By*. Chicago: University of Chicago Press.

Lamb, D. (1991) *Discovery, Creativity and Problem-Solving*. Brookfield, VT: Gower Publishing Co.

Lang, L. H. P., R. M. Stultz, and R. A. Walkling (1989) "Managerial Performance, Tobin's Q, and the Gains from Successful Tender Offers," *Journal of Financial Economics*, (September): 137–54.

Lansiti, Marco and Roy Levien (2004) "Strategy as Ecology," *Harvard Business Review*, 82(3): 68–81.

Larry, Huston and Nabil Sakaab (2006) "Connect and Develop: Procter and Gamble's New Model for Innovation," *Harvard Business Review*, 84(3): 58–67.

Larson, Rikard and Sydney Finkelstein (1999) "Integrating Strategic, Organizational and Human Resources Perspectives on Mergers and Acquisitions: A Case Survey of Synergy Realization," *Organization Science*, 10(1): 1–26.

Lash, Jonathan and Fred Wellington (2007) "Competitive Advantage on a Warming Planet," *Harvard Business Review*, 85(3): 94–103.

Laurie, Donald L., Yves L. Doz, and Claude P. Sheer (2006) "Creating New Growth Platforms," *Harvard Business Review*, 84(5): 80–90.

Lehmann, Donald R. and Russell S.Winer (1994a) *Product Management*. New Jersey: Prentice Hall.

—— (1994b) *Analysis for Market Planning*. Richard Irwin.

Leigh, James H., Patrick E. Murphy, and Ben M. Enis (1989) "Perceived Societal Benefits of Selected Product Classes: A Test of Product Differentiation Framework," *Journal of Macromarketing*, 9(2): 44–54.

Lencioni, Patrick (1998) *The Five Temptations of a CEO: A Leadership Fable*. San Francisco, CA: Jossey-Bass Inc.

Lengnick-Hall, Cynthia A. (1996) "Customer Contributions to Quality: A different View of the Customer-Oriented Firm," *The Academy of Management Review*, July, 21(3): 791–824.

Leonard-Barton, Dorothy (1992) "Core Capabilities and Core Rigidities and Organizational Learning," *Strategic Management Journal*, 13(Special Issue): 111–25.

—— (1995) *Wellsprings of Knowledge*. Boston: Harvard Business School Press.

Leonard-Barton, D. A. and J. Doyle (1996) *Commercial Technology: Imaginative Understanding of Users*. Boston, MA.: Harvard Business School Press.

Levitt, Theodore (1958) "The Dangers of Social Responsibility," *Harvard Business Review*, 36(September–October): 45–51.

——— (1960/2004) "Marketing Myopia," *Harvard Business Review*, 38(3): 138–49.

——— (1963) "Creativity is not Enough," *Harvard Business Review*, pp. 137–44.

——— (1983) "The Globalization of Markets," *Harvard Business Review*, 61(3): 90–98.

Levy, Michael and Alan J. Dubinsky (1983) "Identifying and Addressing Retail Salespeople's Ethical Problems: A Method and Application," *Journal of Retailing*, 59(Spring): 46–66.

Levy, Sidney J. (1959) "Symbols for Sale," *Harvard Business Review*, 37(4): 117–24.

Lewis, Sharon (2008) "The Tissue Issue: A Wicked Problem," *Jurimetrics*, 48(Winter): 193–215.

Li, Haiyang and Kwaku Atuahene-Gima (2001) "Product Innovation Strategy and the Performance of New Technology Ventures in China," *The Academy of Management Journal*, 44(6, December): 1123–35.

Light, David A. (2001) "Who Goes, Who Stays?" in *Harvard Business Review on Mergers and Acquisitions*, pp. 129–48. Boston, MA: Harvard Business School Press.

Likierman, Andrew (2009) "Successful Leadership–How would you Know?" *Business Strategy Review*, 20(1): 44–49.

Lindenberg, E. B. and S. A. Ross (1981) "Tobin's Q Ratio and Industrial Organization," *Journal of Business*, 54(1): 137–54.

Lindler, Mark (2008) "Dollar Shift: Chinese Pockets filled as Americans Emptied theirs," *New York Times*, Friday, December 26, pp. A1, A14.

Loehr, Jim and Tony Schwartz (2003) *The Power of Engagement*. New York: Simon & Schuster.

Luchins, A. S. (1946) "Classroom Experiments on Mental Set," *American Journal of Psychology*, 59.

Lukas, Bryan A. and O. C. Ferrell (2001) "The Effect of Market Orientation on Product Innovation," *Journal of the Academy of Marketing Science*, 28(2, Spring): 248–62.

Lukas, Bryan A. and James R. Brown (1996) "Interdependency, Contracting, and Relational Behavior in Marketing Channels," *Journal of Marketing*, 60(October): 19–38.

Lusch, Robert F. and Michael G. Harvey (1994) "Opinion: The Case of Ran Off-Balance Sheet Controller," *Sloan Management Review*, 35(Winter): 101–05.

Lutz, Robert (2005) *Detroit Free Press*, January 18, p. A1.

Lysonski, S. (1985) "A Boundary Theory Investigation of the Product Manager's Role," *Journal of Marketing*, 54(January): 85–101.

Lysonski, S., Alan Singer, and D. Wilemon (1989) "Coping with Uncertainty and Boundary Spanning in the Product Manager's Role," *Journal of Consumer Marketing*, 6(Spring): 33–44.

MacIntyre, Alasdair (1981) *After Virtue: A Study in Moral Theory*. Indiana: Notre Dame University Press.

——— (1984) *After Virtue: A Study in Moral Theory* (2nd edition). Indiana: Notre Dame University Press.

——— (1999) *Dependent Rational Animals: Why Human Beings Need the Virtues*. Chicago, IL: Open Court.

MacMillan, Ian C., Alexander B. van Putten, and Rita Gunther McGrath (2003) "Global Gamesmanship," *Harvard Business Review*, 81(5): 62–73.

Macneil, Ian R. (1980) *The New Social Contract: An Inquiry into Modern Contractual Relations*. New Haven, CT: Yale University Press.

Maher, Kris (2004) "Next on the Outsourcing List," *Wall Street Journal*, March 23, p. B1.

Makadok, R. (2001) "A Pointed Commentary on Priem and Butler," *Academy of Management Review*, 26: 498–99.

——— (2002) "The Theory of Value and the Value of Theory," *Academy of Management Review*, 27(1): 10–13.

Mandel, Michael (2007) "The Real Cost of Off-shoring," *Business Week* (Cover Story: June 18), pp. 28–34.

Mandela, Nelson (1994) *Long Walk to Freedom*. Boston: Little, Brown and Company.

Mangurian, Glenn E. (2007) "Realizing What You're Made Of," *Harvard Business Review*, 85(3): 125–34.

Marchionne, Sergio (2008) "Fiat's Extreme Makeover," *Harvard Business Review*, 86(11): 45–48.

Marinova, Detelina (2004) "Actualizing Innovation Effort: The Impact of Market Knowledge Diffusion in a Dynamic System of Competition," *Journal of Marketing*, 68(3, July): 1–20.

Marks, Mitchell L. and Philip H. Mirvis (1998) *Joining Forces: Making One Plus One Equal Three in Mergers, Acquisitions, and Alliances*. San Francisco: Jossey-Bass Publishers.

——— (2001) "Making Mergers and Acquisitions Work: Strategic and Psychological Preparation," *Academy of Management Executive*, 15(2): 80–92.

Martin, Roger (2007a) "How Successful Leaders Think," *Harvard Business Review*, 85(6): 60–67.

——— (2007b) *Opposable Mind*. Boston, MA: Harvard Business School Press.

Martin, J. (1995) "Ignore your Customer," *Fortune*, pp.121–26.

Marx, Karl (1930/1967) *Capital*, translated by Eden and Cedar Paul. London: Dent & Son.

Mascarenhas, Oswald A. J. (1976/1980) *Towards Measuring the Technological Impact of Multinational Corporations in Less Developed Countries* (Ph.D. Thesis, Wharton School, University of Pennsylvania, 1976). New York: Arno.

——— (1980) "Productivity as a Function of Social Structure," *Management and Labor Studies*, June, 6(1): 10–20.

——— (1981) "Marx, and Corporate Social Responsibility," *Management and Labor Studies*, December, 7(2): 265–81.

——— (1982) "Corporate Social Responsibility Revisited," *Management and Labor Studies*, June, 8(1): 16–25.

——— (1987) "Towards a Theology of Consumption," in *AMA Winter Theory Conference: Proceedings*. TX, San Antonio.

——— (1988a) "Can we Humanize Consumption? Tasks and Models," in *1988 AMA Winter Theory Conference: Proceedings*. CA, San Diego.

——— (1988b) "Towards a Meta-Satisfaction Macro Consumer Behavior Model," in *1988 AMA Winter Theory Conference: Proceedings*. CA, San Diego.

——— (1995) "Exonerating Unethical Marketing Executive Behaviors: A Diagnostic Approach," *Journal of Marketing*, April, 59(2): 43–57.

——— (2002), "Virtue Ethics in Marketing: Characterizing the Virtuous Marketing Executive and the Profession," *Working Paper*, College of Business Administration, University of Detroit Mercy.

——— (2008) *Responsible Marketing: Concepts, Theories, Models, Strategies and Cases*. North Richland Hills, TX: Roval Publishing Co.

Mascarenhas, Oswald A., Ram Kesavan, and Michael D. Bernacchi (2003) "Co-Managing Online Privacy—A Call for Joint Ownership," *The Journal of Consumer Marketing*, 20(7): 686–702.

——— (2004) "Customer Value-Chain Involvement for Co-Creating Customer Delight," *The Journal of Consumer Marketing*, 21(7, Special Issue): 486–96.

——— (2005a) "Global Marketing of Lifesaving Drugs: An Analogical Model," *The Journal of Consumer Marketing*, 22(7): 404–11.

——— (2005b) "Governmental and Corporate Roles in Diffusing Development Technologies: Ethical Macromarketing Imperatives," *The Journal of Nonprofit and Public Sector Marketing*, 13(1&2): 271–92.

——— (2005c) "Progressive Reduction of Economic Inequality as a Macromarketing Task: A Rejoinder," *The Journal of Nonprofit and Public Sector Marketing*, 13(1&2): 313–18.

——— (2005d) "Passive Consumption of Harmful Products: Theoretical Considerations and Managerial Implications," in *Exploring New Frontiers in Marketing*, M. B. Kunz, D. A. Larson, and J. Wiles (eds), *2005 Midwest Marketing Conference*. pp. 153–58, Chicago.

——— (2006a) "Lasting Customer Loyalty: A Total Customer Experience Approach," *The Journal of Consumer Marketing*, 23(7): 397–405.

——— (2006b) "Global Marketing of Lifesaving Drugs: An Analogical Model," *The Journal of Consumer Marketing*, 22(7): 98–114.

——— (2008) "Buyer-Seller Information Asymmetry: Challenges to Distributive and Corrective Justice," *Journal of Macromarketing*, 28(3, January): 68–84.

Maschke, Karn J. (2005) "Navigating the Ethical Patchwork: Human Gene Banks," *Nature Biotechnology*, 23: 530–44.

Matsuno, Ken, John T. Mentzer, and Aysegul Ozsomer (2002) "The Effects of Entrepreneurial Proclivity and Market Orientation on Business Performance," *Journal of Marketing*, 66(July): 18–32.

Maurer, J. G. (1971) *Readings in Organizational Theory: Open Systems Approaches*. New York: Random House.

Mayer, Roger C., James H. Davis, and David F. Schoorman (1995) "An Integrated Model of Organizational Trust," *Academy of Management Review*, 20(July): 709–34.

Mayo, Michael A. and Lawrence J. Marks (1990) "An Empirical Investigation of a General Theory of Marketing Ethics," *Journal of the Academy of Marketing Science*, 18(Spring): 163–71.

McCloskey, D.N. (1983) "The Rhetoric of Economics," *Journal of Economic Literature*, 21(2): 481–517.

McConnell, J. J. and H. Servaes (1990) "Additional Evidence on Equity Ownership and Corporate Value," *Journal of Financial Economics*, 27(October): 595–612.

McCullough, David (2008) "Timeless Leadership: A Conversation with David McCullough," *Harvard Business Review* (March).

McDougal, P. P., J. G. Covin, R. B. Robinson, and L. Hernon (1994) "The Effects of Industry Growth and Strategic Breadth on New Venture Performance and Strategy Content," *Strategic Management Journal*, 15: 537–54.

McGahan, Anita M. (2004) "How Industries Change," *Harvard Business Review*, 82(9): 86–94.

McGrath, R. G. and I. MacMillan (1995) "Discovery-Driven Planning," *Harvard Business Review*, 73(4): 44–54.

——— (2005) "Market Busting: Strategies for Exceptional; Business Growth," *Harvard Business Review*, 83(3): 80–91.

McKee, D. O., P. R. Varadarajan, and W. M. Pride (1989) "Strategic Adaptability and Firm Performance: A Marketing-Contingent Perspective," *Journal of Marketing*, 53(July): 21–35.

Menon, Anil, P. Rajan Varadarajan, Phani Tej Adidam, and Steven W. Edison (1999) "Antecedents and Consequences of Marketing Strategy Making: A Model and Test," *Journal of Marketing*, 63(April): 18–40.

Merton, Robert (1968) *Social Theory and Social Structure*. New York: The Free Press.

——— (2009) "Making the Financial Markets Safe," *Harvard Business Review*, (October): 84–85.

Meyer, J. W. and W. R. Scott (1983) "Centralization and the Legitimacy Problems of Local Government," in J. W. Meyer and W. R. Scott (eds), *Organizational Environments: Ritual and Rationality*, pp. 199–215. Beverly Hills, CA: SAGE Publications.

Michalisin, M.D., R.D. Smith and D.M. Kline (1997) "In Search of Strategic Assets," *International Journal of Organizational Analysis*, 5: 360–87.

Michael, D. N. (1985) "With Both Feet Planted Firmly in Mid-Air: Reflections on Thinking about the Future," *Futures*, 17(2): 94–103.

Michaels, Ronald E., Ralph L. Day, and Erich A. Joachimsthaler (1987) "Role Stress among Industrial Buyers: An Integrative Model," *Journal of Marketing*, 51(April): 28–45.

Milgrom, P. R. and J. Roberts (1992) *Economics, Organization and Management*. Englewood Cliffs, NJ: Prentice Hall.

Miles, Raymond E. and Charles C. Snow (1978) *Organizational Strategy, Structure, and Process*. New York: McGraw Hill.

Miner, Anne S., Christine Moorman, and Paula Bassoff (1997) "Organizational Improvisation and New Product Development," *Marketing Science Institute Report Number 97–110*. Cambridge, MA: Marketing Science Institute.

Mintzberg, H., D. Raisinghari, and A. Theoret (1976) "The Structure of 'Unstructured' Decision Processes," *Administrative Science Quarterly*, 21(2): 246–75.

Mitchell, Will and Kulwant Singh (1993) "Death of the Lethargic: Effects of Expansion into New Technological Subfields of an Industry on Performance in a firm's Base Business," *Organizational Science*, 2(5): 152–80.

——— (1995) "Spillback Effects of Expansion when Product-Types and Firm-Types Differ," *Journal of Management*, 21(1): 81–100.

Mitroff, Ian (1988) *Break-Away Thinking*. New York, NY: John Wiley.

Mitroff, Ian I. and Murat C. Alpaslan (2003) "Preparing for Evil," *Harvard Business Review*, 81(4): 109–15.

Miyake, N. and D.A.Norman (1979) "To Ask a Question, One Must Know Enough to Know What is Not Know," *Journal of Verbal Learning and Verbal Behavior,* 18(3): 357–364.

Mizik, Natalie and Robert Jacobson (2003) "Trading Off between Value Creation and Value Appropriation: The Financial Implications of Shifts in Strategic Emphasis," *Journal of Marketing*, 67(1, January): 63–76.

Mohammed, Rafi A., Robert J. Fisher, Bernard J. Jaworski, and Gordon J. Paddison (2004) *Internet Marketing: Building Advantage in the Network Economy* (2nd edition). New York: McGraw-Hill.

Molz, Rick and Jacinte Léveillé (1995) "A Reconceptualization of Competitive Advantage in the Transnational Environment," *Canadian Journal of Administrative Sciences*, 12(4): 314–24.

Montgomery, Cynthia A. (2008) "Putting Leadership Back into Strategy," *Harvard Business Review*, 86(1): 54–60.

Montoya-Weiss, Mitzi M. and Roger Calantone (1994) "Determinants of New Product Performance: A Review and Metaanalysis," *Journal of Product Innovation Management*, 11(5): 397–417.

Moon, Youngme (2005) "Break Free from the Product Life Cycle," *Harvard Business Review*, 83(5): 86–94.

Moore, Geoffrey A. (2004) "Darwin and the Demon: Innovating within Established Enterprises," *Harvard Business Review*, 82(4): 86–92.

———— (2005) "Strategy and your Stronger Hand," *Harvard Business Review*, (December): 62–72.

Moore, James (1999) *The Death of Competition: Leadership & Strategy in the Age of Business Ecosystems*. New York: John Wiley.

Moorman, Christine (1995) "Organizational Market Information Processes: Cultural Antecedents and New Product Outcomes," *Journal of Marketing Research*, 32(August): 318–35.

Moorman, Christine and Anne S. Miner (1995) "Walking the Tightrope: Organizational Improvisation and Information Use in New Product Development and Introduction," *Marketing Science Institute Report Number 95–101*. Cambridge, MA: Marketing Science Institute.

Moorman, Christine and Jon R. Austin (1995) "The Paradox of Low Quality and High Use: Researchers' Influence on the Nature and Utilization of Market Information," *Marketing Science Institute Report Number 95–116*. Cambridge, MA: Marketing Science Institute.

Moorman, Christine, Rohit Deshpandé, and Gerald Zaltman (1993) "Relationships between Providers and Users of Market Research: The Role of Personal Trust," *Marketing Science Institute Report Number 93–111*. Cambridge, MA: Marketing Science Institute.

Moorman, Christine and Rebecca J. Slotegraaf (1999) "The Contingency Value of Complementary Capabilities in Product Development," *Journal of Marketing Research*, 36(May): 239–57.

Morgan, Fred W. (1982) "Marketing and Product Liability: A Review and Update," *Journal of Marketing*, 46(Summer): 69–78.

———— (1999) "Product Liability Obligations of Component Parts Suppliers," *Journal of Public Policy and Marketing*, Fall, 18(2): 189–96.

Morgan, Robert M. and Shelby D. Hunt (1994) "The Commitment Trust Theory of Relationship Marketing," *Journal of Marketing*, 58(July): 20–39.

Morath, Eric (2008) "Chrysler's Challenge: A Year after Cerberus' Takeover, Automaker Struggles to Drive Forward," *The Detroit News*, Tuesday, August 5, pp. 1A, 7A.

Morgan, Rose (2008) "Predatory Lending Practices and Subprime Foreclosures, Distinguishing Impacts by Loan Category," *Journal of Economics and Business*, 60(1, January/February): 1–13.

Morris, Joe (2001) "Innovation as a Strategic Advantage: The Art of the Intangibles." Available online at http://www.dell.com/us/en/gen/corporate/press/presoffice_us_2001-03-07-aus-001.htm

Morrison, Mike (2007) "The Very Model of a Senior Manager," *Harvard Business Review*, 85(1): 27–38.

Mowery, David C., Joanne E. Oxley, and Brian S. Silverman (1996) "Strategic Alliances and Interfirm Knowledge Transfer," *Strategic Management Journal*, 17(Winter): 77–91.

Mowery, David and Nathan Rosenberg (1998) *Paths of Change: Technological Innovation in 20th Century America*. Cambridge, MA: Cambridge University Press.

Nadler, David A. (2007) "The CEO's Second Act," *Harvard Business Review*, 85(1): 66–76.

Nambisan, Satish and Mohanbir Sawhney (2007) "A Buyer's Guide to the Innovation Bazaar," *Harvard Business Review*, 85(6): 109–19.

Narver, J. C. and S. F. Slater (1990) "The Effect of a Market Orientation on Profitability," *Journal of Marketing*, 54(4, October,): 20–35.

Nason, Robert W. (1989) "The Social Consequences of Marketing: Macromarketing and Public Policy," *Journal of Public Policy and Marketing*, 8: 242–51.

Navarro, Jesus, Peter Hayward, and Joseph Voros (2007) "How to Solve a Wicked Problem? Furniture Foresight Case Study," *Foresight*, 10(2): 11–29.

Naumann, Earl (1995) *Creating the Path to Sustainable Customer Competitive Advantage Value.* Idaho: Thomson Executive Press.

Neilson, Gary L., Karl L. Martin, and Elizabeth Powers (2008) "The Secrets to Successful Strategy Execution," *Harvard Business Review*, 86(6): 60–70.

Nelson, R. (1991) "Diffusion of Development: Post-World War II Convergence among Advanced Industrial Nations," *Strategic Management Journal*, 12: 61–74.

Neumeier, Marty (2009) *The Designful Company: How to Build a Culture of Nonstop Innovation.* Berkeley, CA: New Riders.

New York Department of Consumer Affairs (1991) "Invisible People: The Depiction of Minorities in Magazine Ads and Catalogs," The City of New York, Consumer Department Affairs.

——— (1992) *The Poor Pay More for Less: Part 2: Automobile Liability Insurance.* The City of New York, Consumer Department Affairs.

Newell, A. and H. A. Simon (1972) *Human Problem Solving.* Englewood Cliffs, NJ: Prentice-Hall.

Newstrom, John W. and William A. Ruch (1975) "The Ethics of Management and the Management of Ethics," *MSU Business Topics*, 23(Winter): 29–37.

Newton, Lisa H. and Maureen M. Ford (1990) *Taking Sides: Clashing Views on Controversial Issues in Business Ethics and Society.* Guilford, CT: The Dushkin Publishing Group, Inc.

Niebuhr, Richard H. (1963) *The Responsible Self.* New York, NY: Harper and Row.

Nielsen, K. (1978) "Class and Justice," in John Arthur and William Shaw (eds), *Justice and Economic Distribution*, pp. 225–45. Englewood Cliffs, NJ: Prentice Hall.

——— (1979) "Radical Egalitarian Justice: Justice as Equality," *Social Theory and Practice*, 5: 2.

Nielsen, K. (1985) *Equality and Liberty: A Defense of Radical Egalitarianism.* Totowa, NJ: Rowman and Allanheld.

Nord, W. R. and S.Tucker (1987) *Implementing Routine and Radical Innovations.*

Norman, Richard and Rafael Ramírez (1993) "From Value-Chain to Value Constellation: Designing Interactive Strategy," *Harvard Business Review*, 71(July–August): 65–77.

Nunes, Paul F., Brian A. Johnson, and R. Timothy S. Breene (2004) "Selling to the Moneyed Masses," *Harvard Business Review*, 82(4): 94–104.

——— (2006) *Character and the Corporation.* Cambridge, MA: The MIT Press.

O'Brien, Bill (2006) *Character and the Corporation.* Cambridge, MA.

——— (1989) "Advanced Maturity," Hanover Insurance, 100 North Parkway, Worcester, MA 01605.

O'Connor, Gina Colarelli, Mark P. Rice, Lois Peters, and Robert W. Veryzer (2003) "Managing Interdisciplinary, Longitudinal Research on Radical Innovation: Methods for the Study of Complex Phenomena," *Organization Science* 14(4, July–August): 1–21.

Olson, Eric M., Orville C. Walker, and Robert W. Ruekert (1995) "Organizing for Effective New Product Development: The Moderating Role of Product Innovativeness," *Journal of Marketing*, 59(January): 48–62.

Olson, Matthew S. and Derek van Bever (2008) *Stall Points: Most Companies Stop Growing—Yours Doesn't Have To.* New Haven, CT: Yale University Press.

Olson, Matthew S., Derek van Bever and Seth Verry (2008) "When Growth Stalls," *Harvard Business Review*, 86(3): 50–60.

O'Neill, H. M., R. W. Pouder, and A. K. Buchholtz (1998) "Patterns of Diffusion of Strategies across Organizations: Insights from the Innovation Diffusion Literature," *Academy of Management Review*, 23: 98–114.

Osborne, A. F. (1963) *Applied Imagination: Principles and Procedures of Creative Problem Solving.* New York: Charles Scribner's Sons.

Pacanowsky, Michael (1995) "Team Tools for Wicked Problems," *Organizational Dynamics*, 23(3): 36–52.

Palmisano, Sam J. (2004) "Leading Change when Business is Good," *Harvard Business Review*, 82(11): 60–70.

Palvia, Shailendra C. Jain (2003) "Global Outsourcing of IT and IT Enabled Services: Impact on US and Global Economy," *Journal of Information Technology Cases and Applications*, 5(3): 1–11.

Parasuraman, A. (1998) "Customer Service in Business-to-Business Markets: An Agenda for Research," *Journal of Business and Industrial Marketing*, 13(4/5): 309–21.

Parasuraman, A. and George M. Zinkham (2002) "Marketing to and Serving Customers through the Internet: An Overview and Research Agenda," *Journal of the Academy of Marketing Science*, 30(4): 286–95.

Parasuraman, A. and Dhruv Grewal (2000) "Serving Customers and Consumers Effectively in the Twenty-First Century: A Conceptual Framework and Overview," *Journal of the Academy of Marketing Science*, 28(Winter): 9–16.

Parnes, S. J. (1967) *Creative Behavior Guidebook*. New York: Charles Scribner's Sons.

———— (1981) *The Magic of Your Mind*. Buffalo, NY: CEA and Bearley Ltd.

———— (1988) *Visioning*. East Aurora, NY: D. O. K. Publishers.

Parker, Philip M. and Miklos Sarvary (1994) "An Integrated and Cross-cultural Study of Diffusion Theory," Working Paper, INSEAD, France.

Parsons, Talcott (1960) *Structure and Process in Modern Societies*. Glencoe, NY: The Free Press.

Pascale, Richard, Mark Millemann and Linda Gioja (1999) "Changing the Way we Change," in *Harvard Business Review on Turnarounds*, pp. 55–88. Boston, MA: Harvard Business School Press.

Paul, Richard W. and Linda Elder (2002) *Critical Thinking: Tools for Taking Charge of your Professional and Personal Life*. Englewood Cliffs, New Jersey: Prentice-Hall.

Pavitt, K. Patel (1998) "Technologies, Products and Organization in the Innovating Firm: What Adam Smith Tells us and Joseph Schumpeter Doesn't," *Industrial and Corporate Change*, 7: 433–52.

Penley, Larry Edward (2009) "It's Time to Shape the Future of Education," *BizEd*, 7(3): 32–39.

Penrose, E. T. (1959) *The Theory of the Growth of the Firm*. New York: John Wiley.

Perfect, S. B. and K. W. Wiles (1994) "Alternative Constructions of Tobin's Q: An Empirical Comparison," *Journal of Empirical Finance*, 1(3): 313–41.

Perlmutter, Howard V. and David A. Heenan (1986) "Cooperate to Compete Globally," *Harvard Business Review*, March–April, 64(2): 136–52.

Perrow, Charles (1984) *Normal Accidents: Living with High-Risk Technologies*. New York: Basic Books.

Peter, Paul J. (1981) "Construct Validity: A Review of Basic Issues and Marketing Practices," *Journal of Marketing Research*, 18(May): 133–45.

Peteraf, M. A. (1993) "The Cornerstones of Competitive Advantage: A Resource-based View," *Strategic Management Journal*, 14: 179–91.

Peters, Thomas J. and Robert H. Waterman, Jr. (1982) *In Search of Excellence*. New York, NY: Harper and Row.

———— and Nancy Austin (1985) *A Passion for Excellence*. New York, NY: Random House.

Peterson, Robert A. (1995) "Relationship Marketing and the Consumer," *Journal of the Academy of Marketing Science*, 23(Fall): 278–81.

———— (1997) "Electronic Marketing: Visions, Definitions, and Implications," in R. A. Peterson (ed.), *Electronic Marketing and the Consumer*, pp. 1–16. Thousand Oaks, CA: SAGE Publications.

Pfeffer, J. (1981) *Power in Organizations*. Marshfield, MA: Pitman Publishing.

———— (1982) *Organizations and Organization Theory*. Marshfield, MA: Pitman Publishing.

———— (1992) *Managing with Power: Politics and Influence in Organizations*. Boston: Harvard University Press.

———— (1994) *Competitive Advantage through People: Unleashing the Power of the Work force*. Boston, MA: Harvard Business School Press.

Pfeffer, J. and G. R. Salancik (1978) *The External Control of Organizations*. New York: Harper and Row.

Pine, Joseph B. II and James H. Gilmore (1998) "Welcome to the Experience Economy," *Harvard Business Review*, 76(4, July–August): 97–106.

Pinchot, Gifford (1985) *Intrapreneuring: Why you don't have to leave the Corporation to become an Entrepreneur*. New York, NY: Harper & Row.

Pitman, Brian (2003) "Leading for Value," *Harvard Business Review*, 81(4): 41–48.

Podolny, Joel M. (2009) "The Buck Stops (and Starts) at Business School," *Harvard Business Review*, 87(6): 62–67.

Porter, Michael E. (1979) "How Competitive Forces Shape Strategy," *Harvard Business Review*, 57(2): 137–45.

—— (1980) *Competitive Strategy*. New York: The Free Press.

—— (1985/1998) *Competitive Advantage*. New York: Free Press.

—— (1986a) *Competitive Advantage*. New York: The Free Press.

—— (1986b) "Changing Patterns of International Competition," *California Management Review*, 28(Winter): 9–40.

Porter, M. E. (1987) "From Competitive Advantage to Corporate Strategy." *Harvard Business Review* 65(3), May–June.

—— (1990) *The Competitive Advantage of Nations*. New York: Free Press.

—— (1991) "Toward a Dynamic Theory of Strategy," *Strategic Management Journal*, 12(Winter): 95–117.

—— (1996) "What is Strategy?" *Harvard Business Review*, 74(6): 6, 61–78.

—— (2008) "Why America Needs an Economic Strategy," *Business Week*, November 10, pp. 39–42.

Porter, Michael E. and Mark R. Kramer (2002) "The Competitive Advantage of Corporate Philanthropy," *Harvard Business Review*, 80(11): 57–78.

—— (2006) "Strategy and Society: The Link between Competitive Advantage and Corporate Social Responsibility," *Harvard Business Review*, 84(12): 78–92.

Porter, Michael E. Jay W. Lorsch, and Nitin Nohria (2004) "Seven Surprises for New CEOs," *Harvard Business Review*, 82(10): 114–21.

Postman, Joel (2009) *SocialCorp: Social Media Goes Corporate*. Berkeley, CA: New Riders.

Powell, T C. (1992) "Strategic Planning as Competitive Advantage," *Strategic Management Journal*, 13(7): 551–58.

Prabhu, Jaideep C., Rajesh K. Chandy, and Mark E. Ellis (2005) "The Impact of Acquisitions on Innovation: Poison Pill, Placebo, or Tonic?" *Journal of Marketing*, January, 69(1): 114–30.

Prahalad, C. K. (1995) "Weak Signals versus Strong Paradigms," *Journal of Marketing Research*, 32(3): 3–8.

—— (2004) "The Poor can be Profitable," *Fortune*, November 17, pp. 70–72.

—— (2006) *The Fortune at the Bottom of the Pyramid: Eradicating Poverty trough Profits*. Pearson Education Inc: Wharton School Publishing.

Prahalad, C. K. and Gary Hamel (1990) "The Core Competence of the Corporation," *Harvard Business Review*, 68(3): 79–91.

—— (1990) "The Core Competence of the Corporation," *Harvard Business Review*, 68(May/June): 79–91.

Prahalad, C. K. and M. S. Krishnan (2008) *The New Age of Innovation: Driving Co-Created Value through Global Networks*. New Delhi: Tata McGraw-Hill.

Prahalad, C. K. and Kenneth Lieberthal (2003) "The End of Corporate Imperialism," *Harvard Business Review*, 81(7): 109–18.

Prahalad, C. K. and Venkatram Ramaswamy (2000) "Co-opting Customer Experience," *Harvard Business Review*, 78(January–February): 79–87.

—— (2003) "The New Frontier of Experience Innovation," *MIT Sloan Management Review*, 44(4): 12–19.

—— (2003a) *The Future of Competition: Co-Creating Unique Value with Customers*. Boston, MA: Harvard Business School Press.

—— (2003b) "The New Frontier of Experience Innovation," *MIT Sloan Management Review*, Summer, 44(4): 12–19.

Priem, Richard L. (2001) "The Business-Level RBV: Great Wall or Berlin Wall?" *Academy of Management Review*, 26: 499–501.

Priem, Richard L. and John E. Butler (2001a) "Is the Resource-Based 'View' a Useful Perspective for Strategic Management Research?" *The Academy of Management Review*, 26(1, January): 22–41.

—— (2001b) "Tautology in the Resource-based View and the Implications of Externally Determined Resource Value: Further Comments?" *The Academy of Management Review*, 26(1, January): 57–66.

Quelch, John A. and Katherine E. Jocz (2009) "How to Market in a Downturn," *Harvard Business Review*, 87(4): 52–53.

Radas, Sonja and Steven M. Shugan (1998) "Seasonal Marketing and Timing New Product Introductions," *Journal of Marketing Research*, 35(August): 296–97.

Ralston, Deborah, April Wright, and Jayendra Kumar (2001) "Process Benchmarking as a Market Research Tool for Strategic Planning," *Marketing Intelligence and Planning*, 19(4): 273–81.

Rangaswamy, Aravind and Gary L. Lilien (1997) "Software Tools for New Product Development," *Journal of Marketing Research*, 54(February): 177–84.

Rappaport, Alfred (2006) "Ten Ways to Create Shareholder Value," *Harvard Business Review*, 84(8): 66–76.

Rappaport, Alfred and Mark L. Sirower (2001) "Stock of Cash? The Trade-Offs for Buyers and Sellers in Mergers and Acquisitions," in *Harvard Business Review on Mergers and Acquisitions*, pp. 73–102. Harvard Business School Press.

Rawls, John (1958) "Justice as Fairness," *The Philosophical Review*, 67: 164–94.

——— (1971) *A Theory of Justice*. Cambridge, MA: Harvard University Press.

——— (2001) *Justice as Fairness: A Restatement*. Cambridge, Massachusetts: Belknap Press.

Rayport, Jeffrey F. and Bernard J. Jaworski (2004) *Best Face Forward: Why Companies Must Improve their Service Interfaces with Customers*. New York: Perseus Distribution Services.

Reardon, Kathleen K. (2007) "Courage as a Skill," *Harvard Business Review*, 85(1): 58–65.

Reason, J. (1990) "The Contribution of Latent Human Failures to the Breakdown of Complex Systems," *Philosophical Transactions of the Royal Society of London*, Series B, 327: 475–84.

Reed, R. and R. J. Defilippi (1990) "Causal Ambiguity, Barriers to Imitation, and Sustainable Competitive Advantage," *Academy of Management Review*, 15: 88–102.

Reichheld, Frederick F. (1994) "Loyalty and the Renaissance of Marketing," *Marketing Management*, 2(4): 10–21.

Reichheld, Frederick F. and Brad Henske (1991) "The Only Sure Method of Recouping Merger Premiums," *Journal of Retail Banking*, 8(2): 9–17.

Reilly, David and Peter Eavis (2008) "Beware, Investors, of Search for Countrywide-Like Deals," *Wall Street Journal* (Eastern Edition), January 12, p. B1.

Rhodes, David and Daniel Stelter (2009) "Seize Advantage in a Downturn," *Harvard Business Review*, 89(2): 50–59.

Rieker, Matthias (2008) "Does Countrywide Deal Signify a Bottom," *American Banker*, 173(9): 20–20.

Rigby, Darrell K., Kara Gruver, and James Allen (2009) "Innovation in Turbulent Times," *Harvard Business Review*, 87(6): 79–86.

Rifkin, Glenn (1997) "Growth by Acquisition: The Case of Cisco Systems," *Strategy and Business*, (April).

Rindfleisch, Aric and Christine Moorman (2001) "The Acquisition and Utilization of Information in New Product Alliances: A Strength-of-ties Perspective," *Journal of Marketing*, 65(2, April): 1–18.

Ring, Peter S. and Andrew H. Van De Ven (1992) "Structuring Cooperative Relationships between Organizations," *Academy of Management Review*, 19(January): 90–118.

Ring, Peter Smith and Andrew H. Van de Ven (1994) "Developmental Process of Cooperative Interorganizational Relationships," *Academy of Management Review*, 19(1):90–118

Ritchey, Tom (2002) "Modeling Complex Socio-technical Systems using Morphological Analysis," adapted from a paper presented at the Swedish Parliamentary IT Commission, Stockholm, December 2002, and available online at www.swemorph.com/pdf/it-webart.pdf

——— (2005) "Wicked Problems: Structuring Social Messes with Morphological Analysis," Swedish Morphological Society. Available online at www.swemorph.com

——— (2006) "Problem Structuring using Computer-Aided Morphological Analysis," *Journal of the Operational Research Society*, 57(7): 792–801.

Rittel, H. W. J. and M. M. Webber (1973) "Dilemmas in a General Theory of Planning," *Policy Science*, 4(2): 155–69.

Roberts, Nancy C. (1997) "Public Deliberation: An Alternative Approach to Crafting Policy and Setting Direction," *Public Administration Review*, 57(2): 124–32.

——— (2000) "Wicked Problems and Network Approaches to Resolution," *The International Public Management Review*, 1(1): 1–19.

——— (2001) "Coping with Wicked Problems," in L. Jones, J. Guthrie and P. Steane (eds) *International Public Management Reform: Lessons from Experience*. London: Elsevier.

Robin, Donald P. and Eric R. Reidenbach (1993) "Searching for a Place to Stand: Toward a Workable Ethical Philosophy for Marketing," *Journal of Public Policy and Marketing*, 12(Spring): 97–105.

Robin, Donald P. and Eric R. Reidenbach (1987) "Social Responsibility, Ethics, and Marketing Strategy: Closing the Gap between Concept and Application," *Journal of Marketing*, 51(January): 44–58.

——— (1988) "A Framework for Analyzing Ethical Issues in Marketing," *Business and Professional Ethics Journal*, 5(2): 3–22.

Rogers, Carl R. (1961) *On Becoming a Person*. Boston: Houghton Mifflin.

Rogers, Everet M. (1983) *Diffusion of Innovation*. New York: The Free Press.

——— (1995) *Diffusion of Innovations*. New York: The Free Press.

Romer, Paul (1994) "New Goods, Old Theory, and the Welfare Costs of Trade Restrictions," *Journal of Development Economics*, 43(1): 5–38.

Rooke, David and William R. Torbert (2005) "Transformations of Leadership," *Harvard Business Review*, 83(4): 66–76.

Rosenhead, Jonathan (1996) "What's the Problem? An Introduction to Problem Structuring Methods," *Interfaces*, 26(6): 117–31.

Ross, J. E. (1993) *Total Quality Management: Text, Cases and Readings, Delray Beach*. FL: St. Lucie Press.

Ross, W. D. (1930) *The Right and the Good*. Oxford: Clarendon Press.

Rothberg, Donald (2006) *The Engaged Spiritual Life: A Buddhist Approach to Transforming Ourselves and the World*. Boston, MA: Bacon Press.

Rothman, K. J. (1986) *Modern Epidemiology*. Boston, MA: Little Brown & Co.

Rothschild, M. L. (1999) "Carrots, Sticks and Promises: A Conceptual Framework for the Behavior Management of Public Health and Social Issues," *Journal of Marketing*, (October): 63.

Rotter, Julian B. (1967) "A New Scale for the Measurement of Interpersonal Trust," *Journal of Personality*, 35: 651–65.

——— (1971) "Generalized Expectancies for Interpersonal Trust," *American Psychologist*, 26: 443–52.

——— (1980) "Interpersonal Trust, Trustworthiness, and Gullibility," *American Psychologist*, 35: 1–7.

Rotzoll, Kim B., James E. Haefner, and Charles H. Sandage (1986) *Advertising in Contemporary Society: Perspectives toward Understanding*. Cincinnati, OH: South-Western Publishing Co.

Rowley, Ian (2009) "What Put Honda in the Passing Lane," *Business Week*, October 19, pp. 57–59.

Rubis, L. (2001) "Merger Mania Means. Much More Work for HR," *SHRM News*, January 21.

Ruggiero, V. R. (1990) *Beyond Feelings*. Mountainview, CA: Mayfield.

——— (1991) *The Art of Creative Thinking*. New York: Harper Collins Publishers.

Rumelt, Richard P. (1987) "Theory, Strategy, and Entrepreneurship," in David J. Teece (ed.), *The Competitive Challenge: Strategies for Industrial Innovation and Renewal*. Cambridge, MA: Ballinger.

Rust, Rowland T., Anthony J. Zahorik, and Timothy L. Keiningham (1995) "Return on Quality (ROQ): Making Service Quality Financially Accountable," *Journal of Marketing*, 59(2, April): 58–70.

Rust, Roland T., Christine Moorman, and Peter R. Dickson (2002) "Getting Return on Quality: Revenue Expansion, Cost Reduction, or Both," *Journal of Marketing*, 66(4, October): 7–25.

Rust, Roland T., Valerie Zeithaml, and Katherine N. Lemon (2004) "Customer-Centered Brand Management," *Harvard Business Review*, 82(8): 110–20.

Rust, Roland T., Katherine N. Lemon, and Valerie A. Zeithaml (2003) "Return on Marketing: Using Customer Equity Focus Marketing Strategy," *Journal of Marketing*, 68(1, January): 109–27.

Rust, Roland T., Tim Ambler, Gregory S. Carpenter, V. Kumar, and Rajendra K. Srivastava (2004) "Measuring Marketing Productivity: Current Knowledge and Future Directions," *Journal of Marketing*, 69(4, October): 76–90.

Saimee, Saeed and Kendall Roth (1992) "The Influence of Global Marketing Standardization on Performance," *Journal of Marketing*, 56(2): 1–17.

Sandour, Richard L. (2008) "Our Global Warming and the use of Markets to Solve Environmental Problems," *The Robert P. Maxon Lecture Series, April 2008*, The George Washington University, School of Business, Washington DC.

Sarason, Seymour B. (1990) *The Predictable Failure of School Reform*. San Francisco: Jossey-Bass.

Sawhney, Mohanbir and Jeff Zabin (2002) "Managing and Measuring Relational Equity in the Network Economy," *Journal of the Academy of Marketing Science*, 30(Fall): 320–328.

Scherer, F. M. and David Ross (1990) *Industrial Market Structure and Economic Performance.* Chicago: Rand McNally.

——— (1993) *Industrial Market Structure and Economic Performance* (3rd edition). Boston: Houghton Mifflin.

Schmidt, J. A. (2002) "Business Perspective on Mergers and Acquisitions," in J. A. Schmidt (ed.), *Making Mergers Work.* Alexandria, VA: Society for Human Resource.

Schneider, Benjamin and David E. Bowden (1999) "Understanding Customer Delight and Outrage," *MIT Sloan Management Review*, 41(1, Fall): 35–45.

Schoemaker, P. J. H. (1990) "Strategy, Complexity and Economic Rent," *Management Science*, 36: 1178–92.

Schoemaker, Paul J. H. and Robert E. Gunther (2006) "The Wisdom of Deliberate Mistakes," *Harvard Business Review*, 84(6): 108–16.

Schumacher, E.F. (1973) *Small is Beautiful: Economics as if People Mattered.* London, U.K: Biond & Briggs.

Schumpeter, John A. (1942) *Capitalism, Socialism and Democracy.* New York: Harper & Row.

Schumpeter, Joseph A. (1934) *The Theory of Economic Development: An Inquiry into Profits, Capital, Credit, Interest, and the Business Cycle.* Cambridge, MA: Harvard University Press.

——— (1949) "Economic Theory and Entrepreneurial History," in *Change and the Entrepreneur.* Cambridge, MA: Harvard University Press.

Schwartz, Norman (1997) "The Concepts of Necessary and Sufficient Conditions," Department of Philosophy, Simon Fraser University, Vancouver.

Schwaber, Ken and Mike Beedle (2001) *Agile Software Development with Scrum.* Englewood Cliffs, NJ: Prentice Hall.

Schwartz, Sharon and Kenneth M. Carpenter (1999) "The Right Answer for the Wrong Question: Consequences of Type III Error for Public Health Research," *American Journal of Public Health*, 89(8, August): 1175–80.

Selden, Larry and Ian C. MacMillan (2006) "Manage Customer-Centric Innovation—Systematically," *Harvard Business Review*, 84(4): 108–16.

Sen, Sankar and C. B. Bhattacharya (2001) "Does Doing Good Always Lead to Doing Better? Consumer Reactions to Corporate Social Responsibility," *Journal of Marketing Research*, 38(May): 225–43.

Senge, Peter M. (1990) *The Fifth Discipline: The Art and Practice of Learning Organizations.* New York: Doubleday.

——— (2006) *The Fifth Discipline: The Art and Practice of the Learning Organization* (revised edition). New York: Currency Doubleday.

Senge, Peter M., Art Kleiner, Charlotte Roberts, Richard Ross, and Bryan Smith (1994) *The Fifth Discipline Fieldbook: Strategies and Tools for Building a Learning Organization.* New York: The Crown Business Publishers.

Senge, Peter M., George Roth, and Bryan Smith (1999) *The Dance of Change: The Challenge of Sustaining Momentum in Learning Organizations.* New York: The Crown Business Publishers.

Senge, Peter M., Nelda Cambron-McCabe, Timothy Lucas, Bryan Smith, Janis Dutton, and Art Kleiner (2000) *Schools that Learn: A Fifth Discipline Fieldbook for Educators, Parents, and Everyone who cares about Education.* New York: Random House.

Seth, Anju (1990a) "Value Creation in Acquisitions: An Empirical Investigation," *Strategic Management Journal*, 11(2): 99–115.

——— (1990b) "Sources of Value Creation in Acquisitions: An Empirical Investigation," *Strategic Management Journal*, 11(6): 431–46.

Sethi, Rajesh (2000) "New Product Quality and Product Development Teams," *Journal of Marketing*, 64(April): 1–14.

Shankar, Venkatesh (1998) "New Product Introduction and Incumbent Response Strategies: Their Interrelationship and the Role of Multimarket Contact," *Journal of Marketing Research*, 36(August): 327–44.

Shankar, Venkatesh, Gregory S. Carpenter, and Lakshman Krishnamurthi (1998) "Late Mover Advantage: How Innovative Late Entrants Outsell Pioneers," *Journal of Marketing Research*, 35(February): 54–70.

Sharma, Sattish (1996) *Applied Multivariate Techniques.* New York: John Wiley & Sons.

Shaw, Colin and John Ivens (2002) *Building Great Customer Experiences.* Palgrave: Macmillan.

Sherer, F. M. (1970) *Market Structure and Economic Performance.* Chicago: Rand McNally.

Sherman, Nancy (1989) *The Fabric of Character: Aristotle's Theory of Virtue.* London: Clarendon Press.

Sherry, John F. Jr. (1983) "Gift Giving in Anthropological Perspective," *Journal of Consumer Research*, 10 (September): 157–68.

Sheth, Jagdish N., Bruce I. Newman, and Barbara L. Gross (1991) *Consumption Values and Market Choices: Theory and Applications*. Cincinnati, OH: South-Western Publishing Co.

Sheth, Jagdish N. and Atul Parvatiyar (1995) "Relationship Marketing in Consumer Markets: Antecedents and Consequences," *Journal of the Academy of Marketing Science*, 23(Fall): 255–71.

Shortell, Stephen M. and Edward J. Zajac (1990) *Innovations in Health Care Delivery*. San Francisco, CA: Jossey–Bass Publishers.

Shrivastava, Paul (1986) "Post-Merger Integration," *Journal of Business Strategy*, 7(1): 65–76.

Simon, Herbert A. (1960) *The New Science of Management*. New York: Harper & Row.

——— (1969) *The Sciences of the Artificial*. Cambridge, MA: MIT Press.

——— (1977) *Models of Discovery*. Dordrecht, Netherlands: D. Reidel Publishing Co.

Singh, Jitendra V., Robert J. House and David J. Tucker (1986) "Organizational Change and Organizational Mortality," *Administrative Science Quarterly*, 31: 587–611.

Skinner, B. F. (1971) *Beyond Freedom and Dignity*. New York: Bantam Vintage.

——— (1974) *About Behaviorism*. New York: Knopf.

Slater, Stanley F. and John C. Narver (1994), "Does Competitive Environment Moderate the Market-Orientation Performance Relationship?" *Journal of Marketing*, 58(January): 46–55.

——— (1995) "Market Orientation and the Learning Organization," *Journal of Marketing*, 59(3, July): 63–74.

——— (1998) "Customer-led and Market-oriented—Let's not Confuse the Two," *Strategic Management Journal*, 19(10): 1001–06.

Sloan, Allan (2008) "Fannie, Freddie, Ben and Alan: How Keeping Short Rates Low Created the Biggest Taxpayer Bailout in History," *Fortune*, September 29, p. 32.

Sloan, Allan and Roddy Boyd (2008) "The Lehman Lesson: What Went Wrong with the Storied-investment Banking Firm is a Warning for all of Wall Street," *Fortune*, September 29, p. 84.

Smith, Adam (1776/1961) *An Inquiry into the Nature and Causes of the Wealth of Nations*, C. J. Bullock (ed.), Volume 10, Harvard Classic Series. New York: Collier.

Smith, Craig N. (1990) *Morality and the Market: Consumer Pressure for Corporate Accountability*. London: Routledge.

——— (1994) "The New Corporate Philanthropy," *Harvard Business review*, 72(May–June): 105–19.

——— (1995) "Marketing Ethics for the Ethics Era," *Sloan Management Review*, 36(4): 85–97.

Smith, Craig N. and John A. Quelch (1993) *Ethics in Marketing*. Boston, NA: Irwin.

Smith, Craig N. and Elizabeth Cooper-Martin (1997) "Ethics and Target Marketing: The Role of Product Harm and Consumer Vulnerability," *Journal of Marketing*, 61(July): 1–20.

Smith, David K. Jr. (1988) "Ethics for Marketers in the 80's: Framework, Applications, and Observations," in Alan J. Shapiro (ed.), *AMA 1988 Winter Theory Conference Proceedings*. CA, San Diego.

Smith, G. F. (1987) "Managerial Problem Identification," *OMEGA International Journal of Management*, 17(1): 27–36.

Sonnenfeld, Jeffrey A. and Andrew J. Ward (2007) "Firing Back: How Great Leaders Rebound after Career Disasters," *Harvard Business Review*, 85(1): 76–86.

Sood, Ashish and Gerard J. Tellis (2005) "Technological Evolution and Radical Innovation," *Journal of Marketing*, 69(3, July): 152–68.

Sorenson, Jesper B. and Toby E. Stuart (2000) "Aging, Obsolescence, and Organizational Innovation," *Administrative Science Quarterly*, 45: 81–112.

Sorescu, Alina B., Rajesh K. Chandy, and Jaideep C. Prabhu (2003) "Sources and Financial Consequences of Radical Innovation: Insights from Pharmaceuticals," *Journal of Marketing*, October, 67(4): 82–102.

Spendolini, Michael J. (1992) *The Benchmarking Book*. New York: American Management Association.

Spendolini, Michael J., Donald C. Friedel, and James Workman (1999) "Benchmarking: Devising Best Practices from Others," *Graphic Arts Monthly*, 71(10): 58–62.

Spreng, Richard A., Scott B. MacKenzie, and Richard W. Olshavsky (1996) "A Reexamination of the Determinants of Consumer Satisfaction," *Journal of Marketing*, 60(3, July): 15–32.

Srinivasan, Raji, Gary L. Lilien, and Aravind Rangaswamy (2002) "Technological Opportunism and Radical Technology Adoption: An Application to E-Business," *Journal of Marketing*, 66(July): 47–60.

Srivastava, Rajendra, T. H. McInish, R. Wood, and A. J. Capraro (1997) "The Value of Corporate Reputation: Evidence from the Equity Markets," *Corporate Reputation Review*, 1(1): 62–68.

Srivastava, Rajendra, Tasadduq A. Shervani, and Liam Fahey (1997) "Driving Shareholder Value: The Role of Marketing in Reducing Vulnerability and Volatility of Cash Flows," *Journal of Market-focused Management*, 2(1): 49–64.

——— (1998) "Market-based Assets and Share-Holder Value: A Framework for Analysis," *Journal of Marketing*, 62(January): 2–18.

——— (1999) "Marketing, Business Processes, and Shareholder Value: An Organizationally Embedded View of Marketing Activities and the Discipline of Marketing," *Journal of Marketing*, 63(Special Issue): 168–79.

Stalk, George Jr. (2006) "Curveball: Strategies to Fool the Competition," *Harvard Business Review*, 84(8): 114–23.

Stalk, George Jr. and Ron Lachenauer (2004a) "Hardball: Five Killer Strategies for Trouncing the Competition," *Harvard Business Review*, 82(4): 62–73.

——— (2004b) *Hardball: Are you Playing to Play or Playing to Win?* Boston, MA: Harvard Business School Press.

Steiner, George A. and John F. Steiner (1991) *Business, Government, and Society: A Managerial Perspective* (6th edition). New York, NY: McGraw-Hill, Inc.

Stern, Louis W. and Thomas L. Eovaldi (1984) *Legal Aspects of Marketing Strategy: Antitrust and Consumer Protection Issues*. Englewood Cliffs, NJ: Prentice-Hall Inc.

Stewart, G. Bennett, III (2004) "Champions of Profitable Growth," *Harvard Business Review*, 82(7): 60–63.

Stiglitz, Joseph (2007), "Interview with Joseph Stiglitz by John Authors," FT.com site. Available online at http://docs.Google.com

Stremersch, Stefan and Gerard J. Tellis (2002) "Strategic Bundling of Products and Prices: A New Synthesis for Marketing," *Journal of Marketing*, 66(January): 55–72.

Stone, Brad (2008) "The Empire of Excess: Lax Real Estate Decisions hurt Starbucks," *The New York Times*, Friday, July 4, pp. C1, C2.

Sturdivant, Fredrick D. (1969) *The Ghetto Marketplace*. New York: The Free Press.

Sturdivant, Fredrick D. and A. Benton Cocanougher (1973) "What are Ethical Marketing Practices?" *Harvard Business Review*, 51(6):10–12.

Suchman, M. C. (1995) "Managing Legitimacy: Strategic and Institutional Approaches," *The Academy of Management Review*, 20: 571–610.

Sudarsanam, Sudi (2003) *Value Creation from Mergers and Acquisitions*. Pearson Education.

Sull, Donald N. (2005) "Strategy as Active Waiting," *Harvard Business Review*, 83(8): 120–30.

Suppe, F. (1977) *The Structure of Scientific Theories* (2nd edition). Chicago: University of Illinois Press.

Sutton, Gary (2002) *The Six-Month Fix: Adventures in Rescuing Failing Companies*. New York: John Wiley & Sons.

Sutton, R. I. and B. M. Staw (1995) "What Theory is Not," *Administrative Science Quarterly*, 40: 371–84.

Takeuchi, H. and I. Nonaka (1986) "The New Product Development Game," *Harvard Business Review*, 64(1): 137–46.

Taleb, Nassim N., Daniel G. Goldstein, and Mark W. Spitznagel (2009) "The Six Mistakes Executives Make in Risk Management," *Harvard Business Review*, 87(9): 78–81.

Teece, David J. (1980) "Economies of Scope and the Scope of the Enterprise," *Journal of Economic Behavior and Organization*, 1: 223–47.

——— (1986) "Profiting from Technological Innovation: Implications for Integration, Collaboration, Licensing, and Public Policy," *Research Policy*, 15: 285–305.

Teece, David J., Gary Pisano, and Amy Shuen (1997a) "Dynamic Capabilities and Strategic Management," *Strategic Management Journal*, 21(Special Issue): 1147–61.

——— (1997b) "Dynamic Capabilities and Strategic Management," *Strategic Management Journal*, 18(7): 509–33.

Tellis, Gerard J., Jaideep C. Prabhu, and Rajesh K. Chandy (2009) "Radical Innovation Across Nations: The Preeminence of Corporate Culture," *Journal of Marketing*, 73(1, January): 3–23.

Terray, E. (1972) *Marxism and Primitive Society: Two Studies*, translated by M. Klopper. New York: NY Monthly Review Press.

Terris, Harry (2008) "Countrywide Slams Bankruptcy Rumor," *American Banker*, 173(6, January 9): 20.

The Detroit News (2008) "Detroit Ranks Lowest in Graduation Rates," April 2.

The Standish Group (1994) *Charting the Sea of Information Technology—Chaos*. Dennis, MA, USA: The Standish Group International.

Thomas, David A. (2004) "Diversity as Strategy," *Harvard Business Review*, 82(8): 98–109.

Thomas, Jacquelyn, S. Thomas, Werner Reinartz, and V. Kumar (2004) "Getting the Most out of all your Customers," *Harvard Business Review*, 82(7): 116–23.

Thompson, Arthur A., Jr., A. J. Strickland III, and John E. Gamble (2008) *Crafting and Executing Strategy: The Quest for Competitive Advantage* (16th edition). Irwin: McGraw-Hill and Irwin.

Thorndike, Edward L. (1911) *Animal Intelligence: Experimental Studies*. New York: Macmillan.

Timmons, Jeffrey A. (1999) *A New Venture Creation*. New York: McGraw-Hill.

Treacy, Michael (2004) "Innovation as a Last Resort," *Harvard Business Review*, 82(7): 29–30.

Tripsas, Mary (1998) "Unraveling the Process of Creative Destruction: Complementary Assets and Incumbent Survival in the Typesetter Industry," *Strategic Management Journal*, 18(Special Summer Issue): 119–42.

Trout, D. D. (1993) *The Thin Red Line*. San Francisco: West Coast Regional Office, Consumers Union of U.S., Inc.

Trout, Jack (2004) *Trout on Strategy: Capturing Mindshare, Conquering Markets*. McGraw-Hill.

Tsalikis, John and David J. Fritzsche (1989) "Business Ethics: A Literature Review with a Focus on Marketing Ethics," *Journal of Business Ethics*, 8: 695–743.

Tukey, J.W. (1972) "Data Analysis, Computation and Mathematics," *Quarterly of Applied Mathematics*, 30: 51–65.

Turner (1945) "The Mental Element in Crimes at Common Law," in *The Modern Approach to Criminal Law*, pp. 205–32. London: Macmillan.

Tushman, M. L. and P. Anderson (1986) "Technological Discontinuities and Organizational Environments," *Administrative Science Quarterly*, 31: 439–65.

Tversky, A. and Kahneman, D. (1982) "Judgments of and by Representativeness" in D. Kahneman, P. Slovic, and A. Tversky (eds) *Judgment under Uncertainty: Heuristics and Biases*. New York: Cambridge University Press.

Tversky, A. and D. Kahneman (2000) "Judgment under Uncertainty: Heuristics and Biases," in D. Kahneman, P. Slovic and A. Tversky (eds), *Judgment and Uncertainty: Heuristics and Biases*, pp. 1–17. Cambridge, U.K.: Cambridge University Press.

Tybout, Alice M. and Gerald Zaltman (1974) "Ethics in Marketing Research: Their Practical Relevance," *Journal of Marketing Research*, 11(November): 357–68.

Unsworth, Kerrie (2001) "Unpacking Creativity," *The Academy of Management Review*, 26(2, April): 289–98.

Urban, David J. and Michael D. Pratt (2000) "Perceptions of Banking Services in the Wake of Bank Mergers: An Empirical Study," *Journal of Services Marketing*, 14(2): 118–31.

Utterback, J. M. (1994) *Mastering the Dynamics of Innovation*. Cambridge, MA: Harvard Business School Press.

Vaile, R., E. Grether, and R. Cox (1952) *Marketing in the American Economy*. New York: Ronald Press Co.

VanGundy, A. B., Jr. (1988) *Techniques of Structural Problem Solving* (2nd edition). New York: Van Nostrand Co.

Vann, J. W. and E. Kumcu (1995) "Achieving Efficiency and Distributive Justice in Marketing Programs for Economic Development," *Journal of Macromarketing*, 15(Fall): 5–22.

Varadarajan, Rajan P. and Daniel Rajaratnam (1986) "Symbiotic Marketing Revisited," *Journal of Marketing*, 50(January): 7–17.

Varble, D. L. (1972) "Social and Environmental Considerations in New Product Development," *Journal of Marketing*, 36(October): 11–15.

Vargo, Stephen L. and Robert F. Lusch (2004) "Evolving a New Dominant Logic in Marketing," *Journal of Marketing*, 68(1, January): 1–17.

Velasquez, Manuel G. (1983) "Why Corporations are not Morally Responsible for Anything they Do," *Business and Professional Ethics Journal*, 2: 1–18.

—— (1988) *Business Ethics: Concepts and Cases* (2nd edition). Englewood-Cliffs, NJ: Prentice Hall Inc.

—— (1992) *Business Ethics: Concepts and Cases* (3rd edition). Englewood-Cliffs, NJ: Prentice Hall.

—— (2002) *Business Ethics: Concepts and Cases* (5th edition). Englewood Cliffs, NJ: Prentice Hall.

Venkatraman, N. and John E. Prescott (1990) "Environment-Strategy Coalignment: An Empirical Test of its Performance Implications," *Strategic Management Journal*, 5(2): 171–80.

Verganti, Roberto (2006) "Innovating through Design," *Harvard Business Review*, 84(11): 114–22.

Vlastos, Gregory (1962) "Justice and Equality," in Richard Brandt (ed.), *Social Justice*, pp. 31–72. Englewood Cliffs, NJ: Prentice Hall.

Volberda, Henk W. (1996) "Toward the Flexible Form: How to Remain Vital in Hypercompetitive Environments," *Organization Science*, 7(July/August): 359–74.

Vorhies, Douglas W. and Neil M. Morgan (2003) "A Configuration Theory Assessment of Marketing Organization Fit with Business Strategy and its Relationship with Marketing Performance," *Journal of Marketing*, 67(1, January): 100–15.

—— (2005) "Benchmarking Marketing Capabilities for Sustainable Competitive Advantage," *Journal of Marketing*, 69(1, January): 80–94.

Watson, John B. (1930) *Behaviorism* (revised edition). Chicago: University of Chicago Press.

Wathne, Kenneth H. and Jan B. Heide (2004) "Relationship Governance in a Supply Chain Network," *Journal of Marketing*, 68(January): 73–89.

Watts, Duncan (2009) "Too Big to Fail? How about too Big to Exist?" *Harvard Business Review*, 87(6):16.

Weaver, G. R. and L. K. Trevino (1994) "Normative and Empirical Business Ethics," *Business Ethics Quarterly*, 4: 129–44.

—— (1904/1958) *The Protestant Ethic and the Spirit of Capitalism*. New York: Charles Scribner's Sons.

Weber, Max (1947) *The Theory of Social and Economic Organization*. New York: Free Press.

—— (1978) "Economy and Society: An Outline of Interpretive Sociology," in G. Roth and C. Wittick (eds) *Economy and Society*, Vol. 1. Los Angeles, CA: UCLA Press.

Webster, Frederick E. (1997) "Can Marketing Regain a Seat at the Table?" Management Science Institute (MSI) Working Paper No. 03–113.

Webster, Frederick E., Jr. (1988) "The Rediscovery of the Marketing Concept," *Business Horizons*, 31(May–June): 29–39.

—— (1992) "The Changing Role of Marketing in the Corporation," *Journal of Marketing*, 56(October): 1–17.

—— (1994) "Defining the New Marketing Concept," *Marketing Management*, 2(4): 22–31.

—— (1997) "The Future Role of Marketing in the Organization," in D. R. Lehmann and K. E. Jocz (eds), *Reflections on the Futures of Marketing*. Cambridge, MA: Marketing Science Institute.

—— (2000) "Understanding the Relationships among Brands, Consumers, and Resellers," *Journal of the Academy of Marketing Science*, 28(1, Winter): 17–23.

—— (2002a) "Marketing Management in Changing Times," *Marketing Management*, 10(January/February): 18–23.

—— (2002b) "The Role of Marketing and the Firm," Chapter 3 in Barton A. Weitz and Robin Wensley (eds), *The Handbook of Marketing*, pp. 66–84. London: SAGE Publications.

—— (2005) "A Perspective on the Evolution of Marketing Management," *Journal of Public Policy & Marketing*, 24(1, Spring): 121–26.

Weick, K. (1979) *The Social Psychology of Organizing*. New York: Random House.

Weinrib, Ernest J. (1995) *The Idea of Private Law*. Boston, MA: Harvard University Press.

—— (2001) "Correlativity, Personality, and the Emerging Consensus on Corrective Justice," *Theoretical Inquiries in Law*, 2: 105–24.

—— (2002) "Corrective Justice in a Nutshell," *University of Toronto Law Journal*, 52(4, Autumn): 349–56.

Weiser, Benjamin (1995) "Judge Imposes a Rare Sanction on GM in Upcoming Pickup Truck Trial," *The Washington Post*, September 10, p. A1.

Weiss, Allen M. and Jan B. Heide (1993) "The Nature of Organizational Search in High-Technology Markets," *Journal of Marketing Research*, 30(May): 220–33.

Wernerfelt, Birger (1984) "A Resource-Based View of the Firm," *Strategic Management Journal*, 5(2, April–June): 171–80.

Wertheim, Edward G., Cathy Spatz Widom, and Lawrence H. Wortzel (1978) "Multivariate Analysis of Male and Female Professional Career Choice Correlates," *Journal of Applied Psychology*, 63(April): 234–42.

Wertheimer, M. (1982) *Productive Thinking*. Chicago: The University of Chicago Press.

White, Ben and Eric Dash (2008) "Barclays Reaches $1.75 Billion Deal for Lehman Unit," *The New York Times*, Wednesday, September 17, pp. C1, C10.

Whitehead, Alfred North (1925) *Science and the Modern World*. New York: Macmillan.

Williamson, Oliver E. (1975) *Markets and Hierarchies: Analysis and Antitrust Implications*. New York: Free Press.

——— (1985) *Economic Institutions of Capitalism*. New York: Free Press.

——— (1991) "Introduction," in O. E. Williamson and S. G. Winter (eds), *The Nature of the Firm: Origins, Evolution, and Development*, pp. 3–17. New York: Oxford University Press.

——— (1993) "Opportunism and its Critics," *Managerial and Decision Economics*, 14: 97–107.

Williamson, Peter J. and Ming Zeng (2009) "Value-for-Money Strategies for Recessionary Times," *Harvard Business Review*, 87(3): 66–75.

Wilson, Eric (2008) "Retail Chain said to Face Bankruptcy," *The New York Times*, Wednesday, July 9, pp. C1, C4.

Wind, Jerry and Vijay Mahajan (1997) "Issues and Opportunities in New Product Development: An Introduction to the Special Issue," *Journal of Marketing Research*, *Special Issue on Innovation and New Products*, 34(February): 1–12.

Wolman, Richard (2001) *Thinking with your Soul*. New York: Harmony Books.

Wood, Donna J. (1990) *Business and Society*. Glenview, IL: Harper Collins.

——— (1991) "Corporate Social Performance Revisited," *The Academy of Management Review*, 16(4): 691–718.

Wootton, Barbara (1963) "Eliminating Responsibility," in Barbara Wootton (ed.), *Crime and the Criminal Law*, pp. 40–57, 58–84. London: Sweet & Maxell Ltd. Reprinted in Joel Feinberg and Hyman Gross (eds) (1975), *Philosophy of Law*, pp. 439–54. Belmont, CA: The Dickenson Publishing Co.

Yadav, M., Jaideep, C. Prabhu, and Rajesh K. Chandy (2007) "Managing the Future: CEO Attention and Innovation Outcomes," *Journal of Marketing*, 71(October): 84–101.

Yaziji, Michael (2004) "Turning Gadflies into Allies," *Harvard Business Review*, 82(2):110–19.

Yoshimo, M. Y. and S. Rangan (1995) *Strategic Alliances*. Cambridge, MA: Harvard Business School Press.

Yourdon, Edward (1997) *Death March Projects: The Complete Software Developer's Guide to Surviving "Mission Impossible" Projects*. New Jersey: Prentice Hall.

Zairi, Mohammed (1998) *Benchmarking for Best Practice*. Oxford, U.K.: Butterworth-Heinemann.

Zaltman, Gerald, Christian R. A. Pinson, and Reinhard Angelmar (1973) *Metatheory and Consumer Research*. New York: Holt.

Zaltman, Gerald, Karen LeMasters, and Michael Heffring (1982) *Theory Construction in Marketing*. New York: Wiley.

Ziamou, Paschalina and S. Ratneshwar (2003) "Innovations in Product Functionality: When and Why Explicit Comparisons are Effective?" *Journal of Marketing*, 67(2, April): 49–61.

Zohar, Danah and Ian Marshall (2000) *SQ: Connecting with our Spiritual Intelligence*. New York: Bloomsbury.

Company Index

Author Index

Subject Index

About the Author

Oswald A. J. Mascarenhas is the Chairman of the MBA Programs, St Aloysius Institute of Management and Information Technology (AIMIT), St. Aloysius College, Mangalore. He recently finished his term in the prestigious position of *Charles H. Kellstadt Chair Professor of Marketing and Ethics* in the College of Business and Administration, University of Detroit Mercy, Detroit, Michigan—a position he held for 27 years until June 28, 2010.

Dr. Mascarenhas completed his MBA and PhD from Wharton Business School, University of Pennsylvania, USA. He served XLRI, the Jesuit Premier School of Management in Jamshedpur, India, as Professor of Marketing and Director of Public Systems Research during 1977–1983. He was honored with the Best Teacher Award in 1992, and the prestigious Distinguished Faculty Scholar Award in November 2008; both at the University of Detroit Mercy, Detroit, Michigan.

He has more than four decades of teaching experience. He has been teaching Internet Marketing, E-Business and Entrepreneurship, Global Marketing, New Product Management, and is currently into teaching Business Turnaround Management, Ethical Imperatives of Business Turnarounds, and Business Transformation Management.

His research deals with ethics of domestic and global, offline and online marketing strategic, innovation management, internet marketing and consumer privacy, and currently, business turnaround and transformation management, creativity and innovation management. He has also authored many books like *Towards Measuring the Technological Impact of Multinational Companies in India, New Product Development: Marketing Research and Management* and *Responsibile Marketing: Concepts, Theories, Models, Strategies and Cases.*